IFIP Conference on
Human-Computer Interaction – INTERACT '84
London, U.K., 4-7 September, 1984

Organisers

The conference was organised by the Task Group on Human-Computer Interaction
– formerly IFIP WG 6.3

in association with the

ACM	Association for Computing Machinery (SIGCHI)
BCS	British Computer Society
ES	Ergonomics Society
HFS	Human Factors Society
IEEE	Institute of Electrical and Electronics Engineers Inc
	(United Kingdom and Republic of Ireland Section)
IEE	Institution of Electrical Engineers
IERE	Institution of Electronic and Radio Engineers
IEA	International Ergonomics Association
IFAC	International Federation of Automatic Control (SECOM)
IFIP	International Federation for Information Processing (WG 8.2)

Organising Committee

Professor B. Shackel, UK *(Chairman)*
Ms L. Borman, USA
Dr D. W. Davies, UK
H. L. Davis, USA
Professor G. Johannsen, Federal Republic of Germany
D. J. Pullinger, UK
Dr M. L. Schneider, USA
T. F. M. Stewart, UK

International Programme Committee

Professor B. Shackel, UK *(Chairman)*
R. C. Anderson, UK
Dr P. Barnard, UK
Dr I. D. Benest, UK
J. L. Bennett, USA
Dr H. Bergman, Canada
Professor R. K. Bernotat, Federal Republic
of Germany
Dr A. Bisseret, France
Professor H-J. Bullinger, Federal Republic
of Germany
Professor C. R. Cavonius, Federal Republic
of Germany
Professor A. Chapanis, USA
Dr W. Dzida, Federal Republic of Germany
Professor E..A. Edmonds, UK
Dr M. Eisenstadt, UK
Professor J. J. Florentin, UK
Professor J. D. Foley, USA
Professor B. R. Gaines, Canada
Professor E. Grandjean, France
Dr T. R. Green, UK
Professor J. Griese, Switzerland
Dr J-M. Hoc, France
J. R. Hughes, UK

Dr W. Jensen, Norway
Professor P. T. Kirstein, UK
Professor F. Land, UK
Dr J. B. Long, UK
Dr E. D. Megaw, UK
R. B. Michaelson, UK
Dr T. P. Moran, USA
Professor A. F. Newell, UK
Dr J. Palme, Sweden
M. Peltu, UK
D. Perry, UK
Dr R. W. Pew, USA
Dr H. R. Ramsey, USA
Dr D. L. Scapin, USA
N. R. Schroder, UK
Professor B. Shneiderman, USA
Dr R. Spence, UK
Professor W. Strasser, Federal
Republic of Germany
Dr J. C. Thomas, USA
Dr M. J. Underwood, UK
Professor R. C. Williges, USA
Dr K. Wimmer, Federal Republic
of Germany
R. F. Yates, UK

HUMAN-COMPUTER INTERACTION – INTERACT '84

Proceedings of the IFIP Conference organised by
the Task Group on Human-Computer Interaction – formerly IFIP WG 6.3
London, U.K., 4-7 September, 1984

edited by

B. SHACKEL

HUSAT Research Centre
Department of Human Sciences
University of Technology
Loughborough, U.K.

1985

NORTH-HOLLAND – AMSTERDAM · NEW YORK · OXFORD

ISBN: 0 444 87773 8

Published by:

ELSEVIER SCIENCE PUBLISHERS B.V.
P.O. Box 1991
1000 BZ Amsterdam
The Netherlands

Sole distributors for the U.S.A. and Canada:

ELSEVIER SCIENCE PUBLISHING COMPANY, INC.
52 Vanderbilt Avenue
New York, N.Y. 10017
U.S.A.

Library of Congress Cataloging in Publication Data

IFIP Conference on Human-Computer Interaction
    (1984 ; London, England)
    Human-Computer interaction.

    "Proceedings of the IFIP Conference organised by
the Task Group on Human-Computer Interaction,
formerly IFIP WG 6.3, London, U.K., 4-7 September,
1984."
    Includes indexes.
    1. Interactive computer systems--Congresses.
2. Human engineering--Congresses. I. Shackel,
B. (Brian), 1927-   . II. International Federation
for Information Processing. Task Group on Human-
Computer Interaction. III. Title.
QA76.9.I58I35 1984   001.64   85-10239
ISBN 0 444 87773 8

PRINTED IN THE NETHERLANDS

PREFACE

The importance of this subject — Human-Computer Interaction — has gained widespread recognition in the computing and information technology industry during the last few years. The number of professional human factors specialists working in the US industry is estimated to have increased between two and three times since 1980. The Japanese 5th Generation programme, and the European ESPRIT and British Alvey programmes, have all placed a special emphasis upon the "man-machine interface". This focussing of attention upon human-computer interaction (HCI) has only served to show how meagre is our knowledge of this subject, compared with the sophistication of the computing technology, and how much research is needed to advance the technology of human interaction with computers.

From this background, the IFIP Task Group on Human-Computer Interaction (formally IFIP Working Group WG 6.3) proposed and organised the first major international conference, designated INTERACT '84. This first IFIP Conference on Human-Computer Interaction provided a unique opportunity for researchers and practitioners in the relevant human sciences, ergonomics, psychology and human factors, to come together with researchers and designers in computing and information technology and to share their expertise in this rapidly expanding multi-disciplinary area.

This book contains the texts of all the papers presented at the conference; because of its length a note of the background may be relevant. To the surprise of the Programme Committee, a total of 282 synopses were received for consideration. These were reviewed critically, but even so the Committee felt that it could not eliminate many because the quality was so promising; so it was recognised that the Conference could become a useful medium for reviewing the current state-of-the-art. Therefore, 180 authors were invited to write their papers, but were informed that the full papers also would be refereed. Finally, 152 papers were accepted for the Conference and are published here.

This volume certainly contains the largest collection of research papers in human-computer interaction to date and gives a fair view of the current position and the range of topics being studied. This book therefore provides a good overview for the many colleagues in the human sciences and in the computer and information technology industry who were unable to join the 568 attendees from 20 countries at the Conference.

The arrangement of the papers has been thoroughly revised so as to provide a meaningful structure for the book, to group together related papers, and to facilitate both skimming and also searching for specific topics of relevance to the reader's current concerns. However, the problem of what sequence to use, both for the various topic sections and within those sections, raised many questions. Finally it was decided to follow two broad sequences, one for between sections and one within.

The first, for the sequence of topic sections, is based upon a categorisation scheme for the Domains of IT Ergonomics, developed from suggestions in the IFIP INTERACT Newsletter, and presented in a report for the Commission of the European Communities (Ergonomics in Information Technology in Europe — a Review; HUSAT Memo No 309, Shackel 1984, to be published). This scheme starts with aspects of the human user, and proceeds through hardware interface, software interface, cognitive aspects, work, environment and methods and techniques to the ergonomic aspects of specific IT applications.

So, the book starts with two keynote addresses, which review the past, present and possible future of human-computer interaction, and proceeds through the following broad subject areas.

1. Keynote Addresses
2. User Aspects
3. Hardware Interface
    (Displays, Workstations, Input and Output)
4. Software Interface
    (Dialogue Interaction, Software Tools)
5. Cognitive Aspects
    (Language, Knowledge Based Techniques, Modelling Users)
6. Design and Implementation
    (Methods, Guidelines, Evaluation, Training)
7. Wider Issues and Applications
    (Organisation and Social Aspects, Aids for the Disabled)
8. Two Theme Sessions with Application Emphasis
    (Behavioural Issues in the System Development Cycle, Usage Aspects of Electronic Mail,
    Conferencing and Journals)

The contents follow the above sequence and broad areas, and the papers are divided into named sections which provide meaningful groupings within the broad areas.

Within various sections, particularly those on design and evaluation, the papers have been ordered so as to move from the more concrete and specific aspects to the more abstract and theoretical issues, and from case study examples to more formalised methods and rules.

It is interesting that the scope and balance of the range of papers presented at the conference appear to support some conclusions about the progress of HCI research presented in the review mentioned above. Four general aspects can be noted. First, it is evident that on balance there has been sufficient attention to hardware ergonomics, and that while such work should continue, because there are still problems, the present scale of work does not need to be enlarged. Second, it is evident from the growing attention to these aspects, that software human factors and cognitive ergonomics are rightly regarded as one of the important areas needing considerable growth; it is particularly noticeable, in the INTERACT conference papers, that there is much attention to dialogue design but still relatively little attention to many other important issues in this wide topic. Third, related to the last, is the basic issue of human cognitive characteristics and performance when interacting with computing and IT systems, about which we know far too little and for which we have few theoretical bases. Although there is, rightly, more attention to design issues, there is still far too little sound theoretical background for design recommendations. Fourth, the inter-relation of computing and IT systems with job and organisation structure and functioning comprises a gap equally as large and complex; again there is still relatively little attention to this important aspect.

Thus, while the extent of work exemplified by this book is encouraging, and the range of studies is considerable, the only correct conclusion from a review of our present state of knowledge is that at last we are beginning to recognise and understand just how much we do not know and how much needs to be studied. The funds which have been allocated to HCI studies within the various national programmes have thus revealed the extent of our ignorance; it is to be dearly hoped that funds devoted to HCI in the future will be large enough to reduce significantly the extent to which our knowledge about computer technology exceeds our knowledge about human usage of that technology.

In the final editing of papers for this book, changes have only been made in cases where this was felt to be essential to clarify the meaning. However, no concern has been felt where the syntax has strayed from the contemporary English idiom. On the contrary, it is felt that the international flavour of the contributions is enhanced by allowing authors a wide degree of licence in this respect.

Finally, sincere thanks must be recorded to those whose contributions have been essential to create this book. IFIP owes a great debt to the members of the Programme Committee who laboured long and hard in reviewing the full text of papers and advising on revisions so as to ensure a good standard. Similarly the staff of the IEE Conference Services deserve much appreciation for their tireless administrative help with all aspects of the conference and handling of the papers. The final thanks must go to the authors, who actually did the work.

BRIAN SHACKEL

University of Technology
Loughborough, UK

March 1985

CONTENTS

WORKSTATIONS AND WORKPLACE ISSUES

INPUT AND OUTPUT — SOME NEW APPROACHES

INPUT METHODS AND COMPARISONS

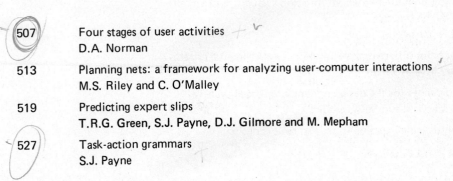

EVALUATION — APPROACHES AND METHODS

LEARNING AND TRAINING

USAGE ISSUES IN ELECTRONIC MAIL, CONFERENCING AND JOURNAL SYSTEMS

Contents

KEYNOTE ADDRESSES

FROM ERGONOMICS TO THE FIFTH GENERATION: 30 YEARS OF HUMAN-COMPUTER INTERACTION STUDIES

Brian R. Gaines

Department of Industrial Engineering
University of Toronto, Ontario, Canada M5S 1A4

From the earliest days of computer systems it was realized that computers were essentially tools to be used by people and that good human factors were an essential part of system design. In the early years the struggle to generate reliable, low-cost hardware and software dominated the industry and human factors played a minor role in computer science and technology. In the past decade, however, advances in vlsi and software engineering have made advanced computer systems increasingly widely available and manufacturers have turned to human factors for product differentiation. In particular, human-computer interface requirements have a dominant role in fifth generation computer specifications. This paper surveys the development of human-computer interaction research from the 1940's through to the present day. The goals and expectations of the research, trends in the literature, the status of the results, and the directions of future development, are discussed.

1. IN THE BEGINNING

At this first IFIP conference on human-computer interaction (HCI) it is appropriate to review computer history and the growth of human factors studies concerned with all aspects of computing. It is tempting to commence in 1879 with the Merrifield committee's concern that Babbage's analytical engine might be abused by people who used it for **Sisyphean** tasks. They take logarithms as a comparison and note:

"Much work has been done with them which could more easily have been done without them ...more work has been spent on making tables than has been saved by their use." [17]

Any computer manager who has spent six years laboriously rolling the stone of a new installation of one generation to a peak of cost-effective service and is then faced with starting all over again with an incompatible next generation machine knows the meaning of a Sisyphean task. We have been guilty of that abuse and have learned to pay for emulation, compatibility, portability, enhancibility, modularity, integratibility and the like.

Probably, a proper starting point for concern with human factors lies with Mauchly who, in discussing EDVAC programming in 1947 notes the importance of ease of use of subroutine facilities, remarking:

"Any machine coding system should be judged quite largely from the point of view of how easy it is for the operator to obtain results." [16]

Replace "machine" by "virtual machine" and you have an aphorism which lies at the heart of HCI design today. However, in the early years the problems of making any form of operational computer far outweighed such ease of use considerations, and we have to move on some 20 years to see the beginnings of human factors studies of HCI as we know them today.

2. INTERACTIVE SYSTEMS

Shackel's 1959 paper [24] on the ergonomics of a computer console is an isolate. Ten years later, in surveying work on man-computer interaction, Nickerson [21] remarks on its paucity and quotes Turoff to the effect that psychology should be able to contribute greatly to the design of interactive systems:

"when one looks at some of the current systems of this nature, it becomes quite evident that the evolution of these systems has not been influenced by this field."

It is salutary to note that Nickerson wrote a paper 24 years later entitled **Why interactive computers are sometimes not used by people who might benefit from them** [22], and I expect that he, and many at this meeting, will be prepared to echo Turoff's remarks today.

The first time-shared interactive systems, MAC, JOSS and BASIC, came on the air from 1963 onwards and stimulated interest in the human factors problems of non-specialist users. In 1967 Mills remarked:

"the future is rapidly approaching when 'professional' programmers will be among the least numerous and least significant system users." [18]

Hansen [13] at the 1971 FJCC seems to have made the first attempt to tabulate some user engineering principles for the design of interactive systems.

3. THE EARLY LITERATURE

The landmark year was 1969: **Ergonomics** had a special issue based on papers to be given at an **International Symposium on Man-Machine Systems**; the **IEEE Transactions on Man-Machine Systems** reprinted the same papers to give them wider circulation; and the **International Journal of Man-Machine Studies** commenced publication.

As editor of **IJMMS** I can attest to the
difficulty of obtaining true human factors
material for publication in those days. As a
scientific discipline the field did not yet
exist, but what we could pass on was a wide
variety of user experience of interactive
systems applied to many tasks. The 1969 issues
contain papers on teaching systems, learning
machines, natural language processing, speech
recognition, radiological reporting, automated
psychological testing, and air traffic control.
Conputers are stimulating and the world was
alive with imaginative computer applications
from the earliest days onwards. It just took a
long time for our scientific knowledge and
professional skills as psychologists to begin
to catch up with our creative imaginations as
computer users.

Sackman's **Man-Computer Problem Solving** [23] in
1970 and Weinberg's **Psychology of Computer
Programming** [36] in 1971 did much to stimulate
interest in the possible applications of human
factors principles in computing science. I
would date the beginnings of experimental
psychological interest in HCI as 1973 with the
publication of Sime, Green and Guest's paper
[31] on the **Psychological evaluation of two
conditional constructions used in computer
languages**. The same year saw the publication
of Martin's **Design of Man-Computer Dialogues**
[15] and Wasserman's paper at the NCC on **The
design of 'idiot-proof' interactive programs**
[34]. The choice of a less insulting term for
naive, non-professional, or **casual** users has
been a continuing problem.

4. GROWTH IN THE LITERATURE

The mid-1970's was the beginning of the era of
the personal computer and the availability of
low-cost computers with graphic displays led to
their increasing use in psychological studies,
and a boom in the associated literature. The
decline in computer costs and the decreasing
differences in computer facilities led to
increasing commercial interest in good human
factors as a marketing feature. **Ease-of-use**
and **user-friendliness** began to be seen as
saleable aspects of computer systems, and human
engineers as product generators. Labor
organizations intensified commercial interest
as they promoted legislation relating to human
factors of computer systems in the workplace,
particularly the ergonomics of displays [10].
The papers from commercial sources further
expanded an already swelling literature.

Conferences on almost any computing topic felt
is timely to have a session on the human
factors associated with it. More and more
sessions at human factors meetings were devoted
to HCI topics. The 1980's saw many books on
HCI [1,2,3,11,12,25,26,29,30,33] the monthly
publication of **IJMMS** and two new journals on
human factors in computing, **Behaviour and
Information Technology** and **Human-Computer
Interaction**.

5. FIFTH GENERATION COMPUTING

The culmination of this interest may be seen in
the Japanese announcement in 1981 of a program
of development for a **Fifth Generation** of
computing systems, and the funding of the ICOT
research center in Tokyo. As Mota-oka,
Chairman of the Managing Committee, notes:

"In these systems, intelligence will be
greatly improved to match that of a human
being, and, when compared with conventional
systems, man-machine interface will become
closer to the human system." [19]

and Karatsu, Chairman of the Social Needs
Committee, reiterates the HCI theme:

"Until today, man had to walk toward the
machine with effort to fit precisely. On the
contrary, tomorrow, the machine itself will
come to follow the order issued by man." [19]

Fig. 1 shows the "conceptual diagram" of fifth
generation computers, and it is notable that
the user interface is one of "speech, natural
language, pictures and images" to a system
processing "knowledge" rather than information.
Fuchi, the Director of the ICOT Research
Center, writes of **The Culture of the Fifth
Generation Computer** [14], and we can see it as
being **user natural** in its human factors. The
next generation of computers will operate
comfortably within the culture of person-person
interaction; HCI will no longer be different.

We may see the Japanese proposal as a natural
response to advances in computer technology
that have given us massive power in hardware
and software at low cost [7]. The technology
which limited us for so long has now
outstripped our demands and we can expect a
shift from technology-push economics in
computer systems to those of market-pull. The
HCI is what the customer sees as a computer and
is where the market requirements are being
expressed. We will increasingly build systems
top-down from user needs rather than bottom-up
from technology availability.

However, my remarks above about our creative
imaginations being well in advance of our
scientific knowledge and skills applies with
force to the fifth generation conceptual
diagram. The hardware and software rings are
full of structure which is expanded in detail
in the accompanying text. The human ring is
empty and the Japanese program has no
activities designed to fill it. Logic tells us
that the third ring should contain the
psychological structure of the user but it does
not yet tell us what this is.

Thus, this conference takes place at a historic
time when the human-centred strategy of fifth
generation computing has captured imaginations
around the world. Hopefully, it may provide
the focus for activities that will fill the
third ring and give us foundations for the
human role in next generation computer systems.

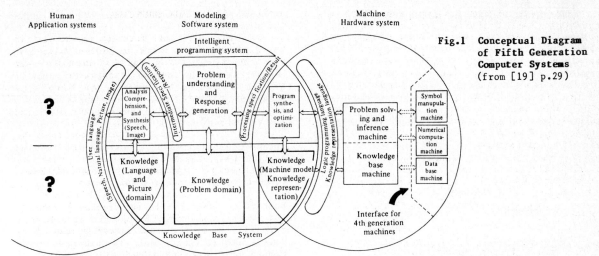

Fig.1 Conceptual Diagram of Fifth Generation Computer Systems (from [19] p.29)

6. ARTIFICIAL INTELLIGENCE, PSYCHOLOGY AND HCI

There has long been a close, but ambivalent, relationship between studies of **artificial intelligence** (AI) and those of HCI. Their key joint roles in the fifth generation program makes it important to examine this relation and those to other areas such as cognitive science and software engineering. Abstract definitions are probably of less value than a simple example that exaggerates the differences in approach. Consider a problem of overcoming the barriers to database access by casual users:

the AI approach to this problem might be to build a better database system with understanding of the user, his requirements, and natural language communication, i.e. to put all the load on the computer and make it clever enough to deal with the casual user;

the applied psychology approach might be to develop a training program for casual users that gave them as rapidly and effectively as possible the skills to use the database, i.e. to put all the load on the person and make him clever enough to cope with the computer;

the HCI approach might be to determine where the problems lie in the interface between user and computer and design a communication package that helps him formulate his requests in a way natural to him but which can be translated easily into a form natural to the database, i.e. to remove as much of the load as possible from both systems and share what is left between them.

In practice, a pragmatic system designer will take what he can get from all three areas and put together a working system. However, the example shows, in very simplistic terms, both the close relationships between the disciplines and their differing orientations. Fig. 2 incorporates related disciplines into an influence diagram indicating the rich structure now underpinning person-computer applications.

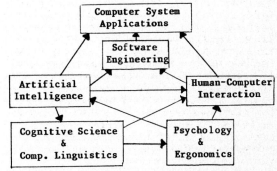

Fig. 2 Influences Between Disciplines

AI and HCI are now major influences on computer applications and both have influenced software engineering: AI by the development of symbolic languages for knowledge processing and HCI by developments for dialog engineering. AI has also had a direct influence on HCI by the introduction of intelligent interfaces and natural language processing. It has also had an indirect influence through its promotion of interest in cogntive science and computational linguistics which provide tools for HCI. These areas have also become influential in psychology and ergonomics providing foundations for HCI. Completing the loop, psychology in its turn has influenced thinking in AI where the goal has been to emulate human intelligence rather create truly **artificial** intelligence.

The diagram is over-simplified and cases can be made for counter-influences to those shown but it serves to show the rich environment for HCI studies, theory and applications that now exists. We are already at a stage where some of the wilder speculations of a few years ago [5] are becoming reality. Fifth generation systems, incorporating advances in all these areas, will provide us with a new **medium** for communication that subsumes those now available and expands our modes of existence [27].

7. THE VIRTUAL MACHINE HIERARCHY AND HCI

The concept of **virtuality** has proved an extremely useful one in computer science [35]; we can view any computer system as either a programmable machine with certain features together with a program, or as a (programmable) virtual machine (VM) with extended features. VM's form a natural hierarchy, for example the natural language interface of SHRDLU [37] is a program in PLANNER which is written in LISP which is written in...:

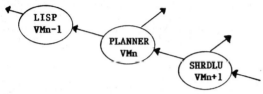

Fig. 3 Virtual Machine Hierarchy

The extra arrows indicate that PLANNER could have been written in some language other than LISP and SHRDLU could have been in something other than PLANNER. The de-coupling between levels of the VM hierarchy is important to a user who need be aware only of the level which he accesses. Nelson [20] has emphasized that the user sees the virtual machine not the underlying one, and Smith has noted this as a design principle of the Xerox Star:
  "if everything in a computer system is visible on a display screen, **the display becomes reality.**" [32]

If the VM hierarchy is extended to show the people involved in its design, implementation and use, a surprisingly large number of HCI studies may be set in an integrated framework [6]:

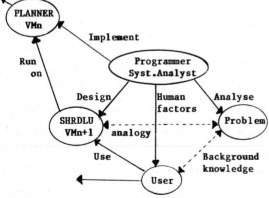

Fig. 4 Extended Virtual Machine Hierarchy

The **user** is now seen to be part of the VM hierarchy, perhaps a secretary creating a VM for an executive who wishes to send mail but cannot use a word processing VM.

The **systems analyst & programmer** team is seen as mediating between the **problem** and the two levels of the VM hierarchy, at one of which the

solution is designed and at the other of which it is implemented.

The remaining lines indicate other relations: that the systems analyst has to take into account the human factors of the user; that he generally assumes the user to have some background in the problem; and that there is a relationship of analogy between the problem and the VM solving it [4].

In the context of expert systems the problem becomes that of mimicing the expert, analysis is knowledge engineering [28], and human factors are embedded in a dialog shell [9].

Most HCI studies can be set in this framework. The user may use other VM's and import expectations of these to his understanding of VMn. An analyst/programmer team can be examined taking into account the four relationships shown, and the expansion of these when the task requires design and implementation of multiple levels of the VM hierarchy. We can see that the technical problem of whether a VM is matched to a problem, e.g. whether Pascal or LISP is better for natural language processing, is confounded by many human variables: the programmer may know Pascal better than LISP; or he may know LISP well yet not understand the problem; or he may understand both but not take into account the user interface; and so on.

The concepts in this diagram can be formalized to any required degree within a category-theoretic framework [8], although our knowledge of the human components is only just beginning to justify such formality [28].

8. CONCLUSIONS

The past thirty years has seen a swing in human factors in HCI from lip-service and regrets that they are neglected to a wide range of in-depth studies both academic and commercial. It has also seen a swing from human factors based primarily on **introspection** to those based on experimental studies [6]: **ethological** where programmers and users are studied in their natural habitats; **experimental** where they are boxed in a laboratory micro-world and their behavior monitored; and **statistical** where the dynamics of user populations are analysed.

The growth in the literature, new journals and specialist conferences in the 1980's shows that these studies are beginning to bear fruit. The empty third ring in the Fifth Generation diagram indicates that we still have much to do and discover. Only when we know as much about the natural phenomena of people as we do about the artificial phenomena of hardware and software will human factors achieve its desired maturity. Perhaps the natural/artificial distinction will be then have disappeared as we merge with our artefacts into true man-machine symbiosis. There is a Chinese curse, "May you live in exciting times" -- we surely do.

9. REFERENCES

[1] Badre, A. and Shneiderman, B. (eds.),
Directions in Human Computer Interaction
(Ablex, New Jersey, 1982).

[2] Coombs, M.J. and Alty, J.L. (eds.),
Computing Skills and the User Interface
(Academic Press, London, 1981).

[3] Degano, P. and Sandewall, E. (eds.),
Integrated Interactive Computing Systems
(North-Holland, Amsterdam, 1983).

[4] Gaines, B.R., Analogy categories, virtual
machines and structured programming, in
Goos, G. and Hartmanis, J. (eds.), GI -
5.Jahrestagung Lect. Notes in Comp. Sci.,
34 (Springer, Berlin, 1975) 691-699.

[5] Gaines, B.R., Man-computer communication -
what next ?, International Journal of
Man-Machine Studies, 10(3) (1978) 225-232.

[6] Gaines, B.R., The role of the behavioural
sciences in programming, in Structured
Software Development Vol.2 (Infotech
International, Maidenhead, UK, 1979) 57-68.

[7] Gaines, B.R., A framework for the fifth
generation, Proceedings of National
Computer Conference, 53 (AFIPS Press,
Arlington, Virginia, 1984).

[8] Gaines, B.R. and Shaw, M.L.G., Analysing
analogy, in Trappl, R., Ricciardi, L. and
Pask, G. (eds.), Progress in Cybernetics
and Systems Research Vol.IX (Hemisphere,
Washington, 1982) 379-386.

[9] Gaines, B.R. and Shaw, M.L.G., Dialog
shell design, Proceedings of INTERACT'84:
(North-Holland, Amsterdam, 1984).

[10] Grandjean, E. and Vigliani, E. (eds.),
**Ergonomic Aspects of Visual Display
Terminals** (Taylor & Francis, London, 1980).

[11] Green, T.R., Payne, S.J. and van der
Veer, G.C. (eds.), The Psychology of
Computer Use (Academic Press, London, 1983).

[12] Guedj, R.A., tenHagen, P.J.W., Hopgood,
F.R.A., Tucker, H.A. and Duce, D.A. (eds.),
Methodology of Interaction (North-Holland,
Amsterdam, 1980).

[13] Hansen, W.J., User engineering principles
for interactive systems, Proceedings of
the Fall Joint Computer Conference, 39
(AFIPS Press, New Jersey, 1971) 523-532.

[14] Hirose, K. and Fuchi, K., The Culture of
the Fifth Generation Computer (Kaimeisha,
Tokyo, 1984).

[15] Martin, J., Design of Man-Computer
Dialogues (Prentice-Hall, New Jersey, 1973).

[16] Mauchly, J.W., Preparation of problems
for EDVAC-type machines, in Randell, B.
(ed.), The Origins of Digital Computers:
Selected Papers (Springer-Verlag, Berlin,
1973) 365-369.

[17] Merrifield, C.W., Report of a committee
appointed to consider the advisability and
to estimate the expense of constructing
Mr.Babbage's Analytical Machine, in
Randell, B. (ed.), The Origins of Digital
Computers: Selected Papers (Springer,
Berlin, 1973) 53-63.

[18] Mills, R.G., Man-machine communication
and problem solving, in Cuadra, C.A. (ed.),
**Annual Reviews of Information Science and
Technology,** 2 (Interscience, NY, 1967).

[19] Moto-oka, T. (ed.), **Fifth Generation
Computer Systems** (North-Holland, Amsterdam,
1982).

[20] Nelson, T., Interactive systems and the
design of virtuality, **Creative Computing,**
6(11) (1980) 56-62.

[21] Nickerson, R.S., Man-computer
interaction: a challenge for human factors
research, **IEEE Transactions on Man-Machine
Systems,** MMS-10(4) (1969) 164-180.

[22] Nickerson, R.S., Why interactive computer
systems are sometimes not used by people
who might benefit by them, **International
Journal of Man-Machine Studies,** 15(4)
(1981) 469-483.

[23] Sackman, H., **Man-Computer Problem Solving**
(Auerbach, Princeton, 1970).

[24] Shackel, B., Ergonomics for a computer,
Design, 120 (1959) 36-39.

[25] Shackel, B. (ed.), **Man/Computer
Communication** (Infotech International,
Maidenhead, UK, 1979).

[26] Shackel, B. (ed.), **Man-Computer
Interaction: Human Factors Aspects of
Computers and People** (Sijthoff &
Noordhoff, The Netherlands, 1981).

[27] Shaw, M.L.G. and Gaines, B.R., Fifth
generation computing as the next stage of
a new medium, **Proceedings of National
Computer Conference, 53** (AFIPS Press,
Arlington, Virginia, 1984).

[28] Shaw, M.L.G., Knowledge engineering for
expert systems, **Proceedings of INTERACT'84**
(North-Holland, Amsterdam, 1984).

[29] Shneiderman, B., **Softare Psychology**
(Winthrop, Cambridge, Massachusetts, 1980).

[30] Sime, M.E. and Coombs, M.J. (eds.),
Designing for Human-Computer Interaction
(Academic Press, London, 1983).

[31] Sime, M.E., Green, T.R.G. and Guest, D.J.,
Psychological evaluation of two
conditional constructions used in computer
languages, **International Journal of
Man-Machine Studies,** 5(1) (1973) 105-113.

[32] Smith, D.C., Visibility in the Star user
interface, **Proceedings of Graphics
Interface '83** (National Research Council
of Canada, Ottawa, 1983) 181.

[33] Smith, H.T. and Green, T.R. (eds.), **Human
Interaction with Computers** (Academic Press,
London, 1980).

[34] Wasserman, T., The design of idiot-proof
interactive systems, **Proceedings of the
National Computer Conference, 42** (AFIPS
Press, New Jersey, 1973) M34-M38.

[35] Weegenaar, H.J., Virtuality and other
things like that, **Proceedings of IEEE
COMCON, CH1388-8/78** (1978) 287-293.

[36] Weinberg, G.M., **The Psychology of Computer
Programming** (Van Nostrand Reinhold, New
York, 1971).

[37] Winograd, T., **Understanding Natural
Language** (Edinburgh University Press, 1972).

Human-Computer Interaction — INTERACT '84 / B. Shackel (ed.)
Elsevier Science Publishers B.V. (North-Holland)
© IFIP, 1985

Designing for People in the Age of Information

B Shackel

Department of Human Sciences, Loughborough University, UK

Some characteristics of the Information Age and the importance of
human factors issues are outlined. Immediate questions for the next 7
years or so are discussed, including 9 substantive areas needing research
(from a recent survey) and the development and better implementation of
design procedures. Longer term questions discussed are - the passing of
paper, the reduction of writing, the victory of voice, the wired society
and the expert in the system. Finally, some of the important broader
issues are mentioned and the need for synergy by human and information
engineers is emphasised.

1. INTRODUCTION

1.1 Aims

In this paper I aim to present a view of
some of the problems and research needs in
Human-Computer Interaction as we move into
this new age. After illustrating the
importance of the human factors issues, I
shall review some immediate questions which
are evident over the next seven years to
1990; and then in the following decade.
Finally I shall mention some broader issues
which should not be overlooked, and I shall
emphasise my belief that the information age
will prove to be a beneficial revolution, or
rather evolution. Any such discussion of
future possibilities must, of course, assume
that there is no war or major nuclear
perturbation, that there are no revolutionary
social disruptions, and that any changes
needed in social structures and institutions
occur fast enough to ensure appropriate
distribution of the economic wealth which
could be produced in the Information Age.

1.2 Growth of the technology

The speed of growth has surprised
everyone, even those directly involved. It
was caused by the reduction in size of the
switching unit fundamental to all electronic
computers. The first three generations of
basic components, the valve, transistor and
large scale integration, are already passing,
and the fourth generation of Very Large Scale
Integration is already well advanced.

Evans (1979) nicely illustrated the
change of scale by comparing it with the
improvements in cars with advances in
automobile engineering. "But suppose for a
moment", he says, "that the automobile
industry had developed at the same rate as
computers and over the same period: how much

cheaper and more efficient would the current
models be? If you have not already heard
the analogy, the answer is shattering.
Today you would be able to buy a Rolls Royce
for £1.35, it would do 3 million miles to the
gallon, and it would deliver enough power to
drive the Queen Elizabeth II. And if you
were interested in miniaturisation, you could
place half a dozen of them on a pinhead.".

This growth in power and speed, and
reduction in size and cost, has led to
enormous growth in the usage of the resulting
equipment. The growth in usage rapidly led
to the coining of the name ´Information Age´.

2. THE INFORMATION AGE

2.1 Introduction

But is this title merely newspaper
hyperbole? Probably not, there is little
doubt that the Information Age will be and
indeed already is radically different from
the other ages which have been identified as
historical references. Essentially, the
other ages involved an increase in the
physical powers of mankind over material
objects and forces, and the machines all
enhanced or replaced human physical muscular
capabilities. Whereas information is
concerned with mental and logical powers in
relation to human decisions and behaviour,
and Information Age machines will enhance or
replace mankind´s intellectual powers and
capabilities.

Further, there have only been three
major changes so far in the basic method of
transferring information, since the oral
tradition (the tribal memory transmitted by
voice) of primitive times. These changes
were successively the development of writing,
and then much later printing, and now the

changes just beginning with the technology of information. Although voice and text are still each a principal medium, information technology already facilitates many new and faster ways of preparing, transmitting, recording, indexing and retrieving such information. Further, the new facilities such as film and colour video recording provide cheap new ways of transferring information never hitherto available for most people. As Marshall McCluan succinctly said "it is the frame itself which changes with a new technology, not merely the picture within the frame".

The many ways in which the Information Age will be different from the others have been discussed by many writers (of whom perhaps the first and best was Toffler 1970 & 1980, but see also for example Evans 1979, Forester 1980 and Stonier 1983). The latter summarises some important features at the end of his second chapter on the profile of the post-industrial economy.

"The technologically advanced sector of global society has moved into a post-industrial economy whose characteristics may be listed as follows:
1. It is primarily a service economy rather than a manufacturing one, with the knowledge industry predominating.
2. As a reflection of no.1, the labour force is no longer dominated by people who work with machines (machine operatives), but by information opeatives.
...
6. The post-industrial economy is characterised by unprecedented affluence both at the private level and in the public sector.
7. Changes are taking place at an exponential rate rather than linearly."

2.2 What is Information Technology (IT)

It is very obvious that hitherto much more attention has been given to information technology than to issues concerned with information science or the Information Age. Although interest and work already existed, the strong focus of attention upon the coordinated concept of information technology, including major emphasis upon ergonomics/human factors, was stimulated by the conference upon Fifth Generation Computer Systems in October 1981 in Japan (Moto-Aka, 1982).

Following the Japanese stimulus, there have been developed two major schemes in Europe. The first is the European Strategic Programme for R & D in Information Technologies (ESPRIT); the second is the Alvey Programme in Britain (Alvey 1982).

Both these programmes place considerable emphasis upon human factors and the "man-machine interface" (under which term the organisers now recognise that all aspects of human-system interaction need to be considered). However, neither of these programmes offer a formal definition of information technology, so perhaps the following may be useful –

"Information technology is the coordinated application of knowledge about computers, communications and people, so as to research, design, install, operate and maintain integrated interactive systems which serve and satisfy human information needs".

That definition aims to counteract the pre-existing tendency for ´technology push´, which permeates the field of information technology, by placing emphasis upon the purpose in terms of human needs. The importance of the meaning and quality of the information, rather than the speed and cheapness of the transport mechanism, was nicely illustrated by Dr. Murray Laver in the 1982 British Library Research Lecture. He drew the analogy of the system technologists really being, as it were, removal contractors for the bits of information, which are handled very fast but without much interest in the quality or the meaning – rather like a removal man who might list the Venus de Milo as "one statue, weight 70 kg, arms damaged"!

2.3 The Importance of the Human Factors Issues

There is now no doubt about the importance of human factors in the eyes of the computer industry in the USA, where there is much greater development of human factors in industry than in Europe. This was particularly evident in the large numbers of human factors professionals from industry amid the more than 1,000 audience attending the CHI´83 Conference (Boston, December 1983) on Human Factors in Computer Systems. Ironically, this rapid growth in attention to human factors in the US industry is attributable, at least in part, to an ´ergonomic standard´ which has been questioned by ergonomists in Europe, namely the German DIN standard for keyboard height to be not more than 30 mm. The recognition that an ergonomic standard could override all other considerations in the marketplace came as a big surprise and had a powerful effect on quite a number of US companies.

To illustrate this changed situation one merely has to note the marked change of emphasis upon human factors in IBM which was handed down from the very top. As a result, special conferences were held (e.g. see Chapanis 1981, Shackel 1981b, Smith 1981,

Wright 1981), a worldwide programme of short courses for IBM engineers was instituted, and usability now became of equal importance with functionality in the IBM development and marketing philosophy.

The following excerpt is typical of the writings of quite a number of the ergonomists ´crying in the wilderness´ in this field some years ago, but it is taken directly from a lecture by the IBM Vice President and Chief Scientist (Branscomb 1983).

> "All that has changed. No longer the exclusive tool of specialists, computers have become both commonplace and indispensible. Yet they remain harder to use than they should be. It should be no more necessary to read a 300 page book of instructions before using a computer than before driving an unfamiliar automobile. But much more research in both cognitive and computer science will be required to learn how to build computers that are that easy to use. That is why our industry is paying increasing attention to the field of applied psychology called human factors, or ergonomics.......Equally neglected has been human factors at the level of systems design. We know that system architecture has significant and widespread implications for user friendliness, but we know next to nothing about how to make fundamental architectural decisions differently, in the interest of good human factors....
> ...Thus the effort to design for ease of use could benefit enormously from basic research, not only in adaptive systems and computational linguistics, but above all in terms of controlled experiments involving actual use by representative end users – for you can´t evaluate ease of use without use."

Again, the US Department of Defence has recently established the STARS program (see Computer 1983) to achieve major improvements in software development. Within that program there is also a major commitment to human factors, so as to improve the usability of software tools, not merely for the end users but also for the software developers (Kruesi 1983). Finally, in Britain the case has been presented in an authoritative and well-illustrated report by the National Electronics Council (1983). Several case studies are described to emphasise the need to design for people, and wide-ranging policy recommendations are made to stimulate action by the appropriate bodies (ie Government, manufacturers, user organisations, standards bodies, educators, users and human factors practitioners).

3. SOME IMMEDIATE QUESTIONS

For convenience the main discussion is divided into two parts.
For the next six or seven years to 1990, the immediate questions are seen to be the need for much more research and the need to develop, test and improve the design procedures for ergonomics in information systems. For the subsequent decade the pace of change is such that one can only be tentative, but a number of more general questions seem to need the attention.

Incidentally, throughout this discourse adequate attention cannot be given to many areas of information technology. Therefore, I shall not mention such large fields as process control and factory automation and robots, but shall be referring primarily to the relevance of the Information Age for some aspects of business, commercial, and professional life and home and leisure activities.

3.1 Research Gaps and Needs

In the last two years several surveys have been made from which the conclusions indicate various major gaps in knowledge and needs for research (Committee on Human Factors 1983, van Apeldoorn 1983, Shackel 1984a). I shall presume here only to summarise the results from my survey, for the Commission of the European Communities, on Information Technology Ergonomics in Europe.

My first approach was to gather and appraise a wide range of recently published and unpublished reports from as many relevant research groups as possible. A classification scheme for the domains of IT Ergonomics was devised, and then revised while analysing the contents of both the research reports and the information gathered during subsequent visits.

Then most of the principal research groups in Europe were visited, and the scope of their current work was recorded and similarly classified against the list of domains of IT Ergonomics. This analysis has shown that there are many gaps in the coverage. Out of 46 sub domains in the classification scheme, there appears to be too little attention being given to 25.

During the visits made to the principal research groups, the experts visited were invited to give their suggestions about future research needs. From the many research needs suggested by the experts, some were suggested independently by at least one third to one half and so are seen as principal issues.

Combining these data gives a list of nine substantive areas needing attention.

(1) Theory Especially in Cognitive Ergonomics
The need for major developments in theory, especially in cognitive ergonomics, was emphasised widely.   The work of Card, Moran and Newell (1983) is a first step in this direction, which also shows how much is yet to be done.

(2) Cognitive/Software Interface
The recognition of the importance of the cognitive and software interface is shown by the recent attention to this subject by most research groups, and by the recent rapid growth of published work.

(3) User Variables and Models of Users
Much basic work is needed, both empirical and theoretical, to develop our scientific understanding of the characteristics and performance of humans as IT users.   It is generally agreed that models of user behaviour will be valuable, but the problem is to ensure that the research does not become too theoretical. Good solutions need a concrete task and situation for valid modelling; associating the research with designers may help to ensure that the models have practical relevance.   A useful review has recently been presented by Laughery (1984).

(4) Measurement Methods
Various shortcomings in measurement methods were emphasised.   For example, Bernotat said "measuring methods have to be improved, especially concerning mental workload and influences from the social environment.   Some agreement or even standardisation of basic measuring procedures would help to make data comparable".   For example, the Mosso Ergograph established a ´classic´ procedure for measuring muscular fatigue.   We have no equivalent reliable and accurate method to measure mental load and mental ´fatigue´ (cf. Moray, 1982, 1984).

(5) Knowledge for Usability Design
Views were expressed strongly about how much we have yet to learn about usability, so as to be able to produce valid guidelines. As Sanders said "we need, but do not have, rules for how to design software to be easy to use; also we need rules of when and where to provide ´short cuts´ for skilled users, e.g. when using menus.   But the real problem here is to understand, to have full knowledge of, the development of skill by the user in such situations".   We need extensive research studies of different types of users, doing different types of task, with different hardware and software tools, so as to establish a comprehensive understanding of

the parameters of usability.

(6) Procedures and Tools for Designers
Given that appropriate knowledge is available, the next and equally important issue is the methods, procedures or tools by which that knowledge is applied during the design process.   Faehnrich gave an example of a new method which needs to be developed much further to "produce rapid prototyping tools; the idea is to make trial versions or prototypes of human-computer interfaces as ´real products´ in the market sense, so that one can talk about ´price´ and ´quality´ and then ask users for an evaluation of the prototype against these and other factors". However, Eason pointed out that "designers may need some help from us (and perhaps we need to develop and test appropriate procedures) so that the potential learning from prototypes and pilot schemes is actually obtained and used iteratively to produce a better final design".

(7) Work, Workplace and System Operation
Very little work was found in the literature on aspects related to system installation and usage, and to the work and workplace - especially user support, social issues and the influence of IT upon work, job and organisation structure and functioning.

(8) Standardisation Issues
Standardisation is seen by many experts as of almost equal importance with improving knowledge and improving design methods. Several pointed out a tendency to move rapidly and perhaps prematurely into draft standards.   Again, several emphasised that much testing work is needed on proposals for standards, to check them for many different types of user and usage so as to make them truly application independent.   This is particularly important for the software interface.

(9) Organisational and Social Issues
The organisational and social aspects range very widely from, for example, the organisational consequences of word processor applications (cf. Simpson et al 1980) to the potential for alienation and loss of identity implicit in the isolated monitoring jobs which may become typical of the automated factory.   There are even fewer simple answers to these organisational and social questions than to the other research areas identified above.

Although these are suggested to be some of the principal research issues to be addressed during the next seven years to 1990, of course not all will be finished and many may well overlap into the following decade.

3.2   Design Procedures

There is widespread recognition of the need to develop better design procedures (including evaluation), so as to design better information systems for people to use. It is also acknowledged that much more needs to be done to ensure widespread application of existing knowledge and methods; this leads to the question of how best to organise the design process to include human factors.

Regarding design methods, there is no comprehensive and generally accepted manual on how to design good human factors into computer systems.   However the guidebook by Damodaran et al (1980) is a very promising first attempt; with feedback from evaluation during regular use it could be developed into a useful manual.   A good text on design methods in general is that by Jones (1970). An approach to workstation design has been simply described in chapter two of Shackel (1974), and Galitz (1981) has produced a useful guide to the design of screen formats. The design of documentation by successive evaluation has been reported by Sullivan & Chapanis (1983).   Finally, a comprehensive catalogue of ergonomic design methods reported in North America has been presented by Meister (1984).

Evaluation is an important design procedures;   indeed some would say that design is nothing but ´test and try again´. Certainly the complexity of information systems and the speed of technological change is such that design must be a very flexible and iterative process, with evaluation at each stage.   Good discussions and reviews of evaluation methods have been presented by Margulies (1976), Chapanis (1981) and Williges (1984).

The question of how best to organise within a commercial company, so as to ensure attention to human factors issues, has seldom been addressed in the literature.   The general policies which companies might adopt were discussed briefly by Shackel (1966); however these were not specific to computers or information system design.   Hirsch (1981) provides an excellent review of the facilities of a human factors laboratory and the way that these facilities can be used during product design and development. Finally Thomas (1984) has discussed exactly the issue in question and has presented his views on how to achieve good human factors in computer systems.

4.   SOME LONGER TERM QUESTIONS

In relating our research on human aspects to the growth of technology in the information age, one especially important factor is timescale.   There is little value in applied research if it is overtaken before completion by basic changes in the related occupation, equipment or environment. Therefore, we need to look ahead and consider what may be the general trends.   The pace of change is such that one can only be rather tentative, but a number of more general questions will be considered which are already being raised and which to need considerable research if we are to produce good designs for human use.

4.1   The Passing of Paper ?

The first of these is the possibility of the passing of paper.   One of the misnomers in current talk about the information age is the phrase ´the paperless office´.   It is true that Lancaster´s (1978) excellent book was entitled Towards Paperless Information Systems, but his timescale was probably realistic, with the relevant chapter title being ´Scenario for an Electronic Information System for the Year 2000´.

However, from another point of view it is certainly true that we need to move rapidly to use less paper;   there is already some concern about the speed of net reduction in the world´s total forest coverage.   The technology is advancing rapidly to help, and the passing of the printed book is at least a possibility by the year 2000.

Already portable computers are nearly as small as books and can contain the storage for at least a full length novel.   It will not be long before the Dynabook concept of Kay and Goldberg (1977) and Goldberg (1979) becomes a reality.   The technology already exists to do this, but the best design for human use is not known.   As just one example of the ergonomics issues which need to be investigated is the procedures involved to skim through the text and find various places.   The present standard scrolling procedures on terminal screens are unsatisfactory and a best method has not yet been proved.

Related to this is the important question of browsing.   It is right to ask, all the time, about various developments into the information age ´What will the human user lose and what gain?´.   Clearly we should never lose worthwhile facilities, except if they are overtaken by a much greater gain. With the electronic book, we are in danger of losing the capability to browse unless

appropriate methods are studied by
ergonomists and implemented.   Browsing is
rightly regarded by many scientists, when
asked, as an important feature - vital for
serendipity. And serendipity is certainly
important in science - Sir Fred Dainton
illustrated this nicely if naughtily by
saying that "Serendipity is going to look for
a needle in a haystack and finding the
farmer's daughter instead".

4.2   The Reduction of Writing ?

The psyho-motor skill of handwriting is
complex and slow.   Children have
considerable difficulty in learning it and
have already been shown to produce written
output much faster if they learn via a
keyboard instead of by handwriting (Martin,
1981).   Moreover, the potential for keying
speed is much higher.   Even inexperienced
typists can produce output nearly as fast as
handwriting, and skilled typists produce
output three to four times faster than
handwriting.   Moreover, stenotyping which
uses a chord   keyboard and includes short
forms of words can be eight to ten times
faster than handwriting.

As a result, perhaps in time keying will
become widespread and handwriting may
gradually fade away.   First, of course,
there would need to be available widely and
cheaply a suitable device to grip
conveniently with one or both hands, and with
touch pads or keys for operation by relevant
fingers and thumbs.   Research by Martin
(1981) has shown the best allocation of
characters to keys and an appropriate form of
training.   Users would need to have access
readily to printers or word processors in
almost any location;   alternatively, the
device would need to have built in word
processing capability as does the Microwriter
machine.   However, the Microwriter is not
optimised in its ergonomic design;   neither
the key positions nor the assignment of keys
to letters and fingers is optimum.

The ultimate form of such a device would
need to be produced to good aesthetic
standards to gain acceptability.   Having
achieved a good prototype with the basic key
layouts established ergonomically, industrial
designers would produce a range of pleasing
forms which could be held in one hand or both
hands, kept in pockets and handbags etc.

Of course at the same time there would
need to be an appropriate replacement for the
handwritten signature.   However this aspect
is already covered;   both fingerprint and
voiceprint automatic detection and analysis
systems are understood to be in development.
Again, we have little experience relevant to
the consequences of the reduction of
handwriting.   There are many interesting
issues to be explored.

4.3   The Victory of Voice ?

It is rather generally assumed in
technology circles that many problems of
human-computer interaction will be solved
when speech input and output have been
perfected.   It is only a matter of time, so
the thought goes, that this will solve all
problems.   The technological position is as
follows.   Speech output devices are fairly
well advanced, and by five years should be in
good shape.   However, the current position
with speech recognition is not so far
advanced;   the best devices give recognition
at 92-98% success rate, with vocabularies of
about 250 words (some claim 500-1000 words),
but for separate utterance only.   The
general view is that it will be at least five
to ten years before efficient, reliable
recognition of continuous speech is
available.

However even more important questions
are whether in fact people will find this
interaction medium better, and what are its
characteristic constraints, advantages and
disadvantages, in relation to human
interaction with information systems?
Chapanis (1976) ran an elegant series of
experiments which showed that problem solving
tasks involving two persons collaborating are
significantly impeded if the voice medium is
removed from the available communication
channels.   Van Nes (1978) and Moore & Ruth
(1984) have shown the potential advantages
for certain types of task even with existing
limited speech recognition devices.
However, Braunstein and Anderson (1961) ran
an experiment on data entry and found their
subjects preferred keyboard data entry and
did not like voice data entry.   Again, Crane
(1984) compared voice and touch screen for
data entry on a C^3 display and found no
advantage for voice.   Recently Lambert (1984)
has written a useful review of the general
advantages and limitations of voice data
entry and of the issues to be studied before
adopting the method.

Clearly there is ample scope for
valuable research.   For which tasks and
situations is speech input to an information
system appropriate, and for which not?
Under what conditions can this method best be
used, and what are significant contra-
indications?   Again, are there fundamental
differences in speaking with machines
compared with any other type and mode of
interaction?   The point is that with all
other machines and tools used by humans, the
control or the interaction is mediated
mechanically.   Only live objects respond to
the human voice.   Is this difference

fundamental, and if so what are its
implications?

4.4 The Wired Society ?

The development towards what Martin
(1978) called ´The Wired Society´ has been
growing for some time (eg. see Hiltz and
Turoff, 1978, Johannsen, Vallee and Spangler,
1979; Vallee, 1982). In this very wide
subject area only a few aspects will be
mentioned, and for example the whole field of
public service broadcasting will not be
considered.

With names like electronic mail,
electronic conferencing, electronic journals,
etc., it is hardly surprising that people are
sometimes confused. In fact the electronic
versions are not dissimilar from the
traditional forms, but there is at least one
fundamental difference; the mail, the
conference reports and the journals are not
delivered to you in your absence - you have
to call up and ´log in´ to a network or
computer somewhere and identify yourself,
usually with a password, so as collect your
material (rather like calling at a post
office to collect mail from a P.O. box
number).

The BLEND programme (Shackel 1982) is an
example of ergonomic research related to
information systems. An electronic
conferencing system is used as the basis for
exploratory experiments upon the electronic
journal concept. During the three years to
date, the BLEND team and the 50 scientists
participating have developed a monthly
newsletter, a Refereed Papers Journal Compuer
Human Factors, a Poster Papers Journal, a
References   Abstracts & Annotations
Journal, and have participated in a number of
teleconferences (Shackel et al 1983).

Many other kinds of network activity are
developing. The Prestel activity is well
known in Britain, as is ´Compuserve´ and ´The
Source´ in the USA. However the computer
hobbiest and news network operating within
Prestel, called Micronet 800, is perhaps not
so well known. Among the many future uses
for networks, the provision of home teleshopping
and home banking have been proposed. There
is already an exploratory service for these,
again via Prestel, called Homelink and being
operated by the Nottingham Building Society.

However, these exploratory developments
are somewhat overshadowed by whole community
experiments. Lee (1983) describes the ´Hi-
OVIS´ experiment in Japan, in which a
township near Nara was built as an
experimental ´wired society´, comprising a
two-way interactive communication system

complete with a TV set, a camera, a
microphone, and a keyboard at each home
terminal.

Again, as an example of larger issues,
the problems of structuring and organising
the information in the various systems for
clarity, easier retrieval by users etc. is
easy to state but will undoubtedly need
plentiful research. Many issues of wider
societal and political consequence are raised
in an interesting and amusing way by Vallee
(1982). Ultimate issues, such as the
potential for alienation - with the
loneliness of the self epitomised in the
isolation at the end of a communication
cable - is explored by Michael Frayn in his
novel ´A Very Private Life´.

4.5 The Expert in the System ?

An expert system, as defined by Michie,
is a machine embodiment of some branch of
human expertise, not only by the criterion
that it can answer questions reliably in the
relevant problem solving area ("What is wrong
with this patient?", "Are there precedents
for this application of patent law?" etc.)
but also by the criterion that the system
represents the problem domain in something
like the conceptual terms used by the human
expert. The key consequence of adopting a
human style of knowledge representation is
that it is then capable also of answering, in
ways which make sense to the human user,
questions of the quite different form "How
did you work that out?".

There are at present relatively few
examples of successful expert systems. Much
research is being stimulated by the Japanese
Fifth Generation programme and by the British
Alvey programme. Nevertheless, the work is
complex and abstruse, and the number of
researchers available is low. Even fewer
are the number of researchers in ergonomics
with sufficient understanding to collaborate
directly with expert system design groups.
Attention needs to be given to this
developing situation of human and computer as
interacting knowledge systems, which at last
will come closer to Licklider´s (1960) vision
of symbiosis, so as to develop research and
expertise amongst ergonomists about this
subject.

Another aspect is the potential use of
expert systems to convey human factors
information. We can certainly envisage
considerable advantages if guidelines for
designers and if system documentation can be
developed in the form of expert systems.
Incidentally, a final thought comes to mind
about the expert in the system. Given the
cost of developing such systems it is likely
that only one will be developed for each

major area of usage, but given one expert system for medical diagnosis - where does one go for and how does one obtain a genuine medical second opinion?

5.   CONCLUSION

This paper and this conference deals principally with technical matters, as it should.   But design does not operate in a vacuum, and designing for people must include recognition of many broader issues not considered here.   Among these the questions of control (who is in control, the human or the computer), work and leisure are discussed briefly elsewhere (Shackel 1984b).

The fundamental reason why I, as an ergonomist, welcome the information age is that at last we can foresee machines doing the tedious work which no-one wants, with people able to concentrate on what they prefer and only they can do well for each other.   What that means basically is all the activities where person-to-person interaction is the principal feature, for example:- teaching (all levels of education, for computer aided instruction will only be a useful tool, however sophisticated, and not a replacement); nursing (and medical services generally, but nursing above all); caring for others, for example for the young and for the old, for example hotels, restaurants and holiday services etc.; and also managing - because, despite the uses of computers to aid management, studies widely have shown that about 70% of a manager's work is interacting with people.   But to achieve this we must break the equation 'work = job' or 'work = employment'.   Until we can move on from the traditional work ethic, we shall not even start to address the many other changes in attitude, in societal and economic organisation, and in industrial and even personal relationships, which are needed if we are to enter the information age with success and enjoy it.

Finally, we must develop a true synergy and symbiosis between workers in human engineering and in information engineering. I believe that the potential will exist to allocate many boring, dangerous, undignified or meaningless functions and tasks to the machine, and thus to enable people to be released and to grow.   But I am convinced that this will not be achieved successfully by the computer and information scientists and technologists alone - the human sciences and ergonomics have a fundamental part to play.   This is well summarised by the Duke of Edinburgh (1984) at the end of 'Men, Machines and Sacred Cows' - "The real truth is that, whatever our material achievements, we are still human, and that it is the facts

of human nature and not the binary system which must govern human affairs".

References

Alvey 1982   A Programme for Advanced Information Technology; Report of the Alvey Committee.   London, HMSO.

Branscomb L M 1983   The computer's debt to science.   Perspectives in Computing, 3.3, 4-19 (published by IBM).

Braunstein M & Anderson N W 1961   A comparison of the speed and accuracy of reading aloud and key-punching digits. IEEE Trans. on Human Factors in Electronics, HFE-2, 56-57.

Card S K, Moran T P & Newell A 1983 The Psychology of Human-Computer Interaction.   Hillsdale NJ, Erlbaum.

Chapanis A 1976   Interactive human communication: some lessons learned from laboratory experiments.   Paper to NATO ASI on Man-Computer Interaction, pp 65-114 in Shackel (1981a).

Chapanis A 1981   Evaluating Ease of Use. Proc. IBM Software & Information Usability Symposium, Poughkeepsie NY, 15-18 September, pp 105-120.

Committee on Human Factors 1983   Research Needs for Human Factors.   National Research Council Report.   Washington DC, National Academy Press.

Computer 1983   Special issue on the DoD STARS Program (Software Technology for Adaptable Reliable Systems. Computer, 16.11, 9-104.

Crane P M 1984   Human factors comparison of touch screen and voice command data entry on a C^3 display.   Digest of Technical Papers SID International Symposium, vol 15, 231-4.

Damodaran L, Simpson A & Wilson P 1980 Designing Systems for People.   ISBN 0-85012-242-2.   NCC Publications, National Computing Centre, Oxford Road, Manchester.

Edinburgh HRH Duke of 1984 Men, Machines and Sacred Cows. London, Hamish Hamilton.

Evans C 1979   The Mighty Micro. London, Gollanez.

Forester T 1980   The Microelectronics Revolution.   Oxford, Blackwell.

Frayn M 1968   A Very Private Life.
London, Fontana/Collins.

Galitz W O 1981   Handbook of Screen Format
Design.   Wellesley Mass, QED Information
Science

Goldberg A 1979   Educational uses of Dyna
book.   Computing & Education, 3, 247-266.

Hiltz S R & Turoff M 1978   The Network
Nation.   Reading, Mass., Addison-Wesley.

Hirsch R S 1981   Procedures of the human
factors center at San Jose.
IBM Systems Journal, 20.2, 123-171.

Johannsen R, Vallee J & Spangler K 1979
Electronic Meetings.   Reading, Mass.,
Addison-Wesley.

Jones J C 1970   Design Methods.
New York, Wiley.

Kay A & Goldberg A 1977   Personal dynamic
media.   Computer, March 10.3, 31-41.

Kruesi E 1983   The human engineering task
area.   Computer, 16.11, 86-96.

Lambert D R 1984   Voice control of displays.
Digest of Technical Papers SID International
Symposium, vol 15, 224-226.

Lancaster F W 1978   Towards Paperless
Information Systems.
New York, Academic Press.

Laughery K R Jnr 1984   Computer modelling of
human operators in systems.   Proc. 1984
International Conference on Occupational
Ergonomics   Vol 2 Reviews;   pp 26-34.
Human Factors Association of Canada, PO Box
1085 B, Rexdale, Ontario M9V 2B3.

Lee A M 1983   A Tale of Two Countries.
Journal of the Operational
Research Society, 34.8, 253-263.

Licklider J C R 1960   Man-computer
symbiosis.   IRE Trans. Human Factors in
Electronics, March, HFE1, 4-11.

Margulies F 1976   Evaluating man-computer
systems.   Paper to NATO ASI on Man-Computer
Interaction, pp 521-536 in Shackel (1981a).

Martin J 1978   The Wired Society.
Englewood Cliffs NJ, Prentice-Hall.

Martin J M 1981   A Study of Keying Skills
and Various Alphanumeric Keyboards.
Doctoral Thesis, Loughborough University.

Meister D 1984   A catalogue of ergonomic
design methods.   Proc. 1984
International Conference on Occupational
Ergonomics Vol 2 Reviews;   pp 17-25.
Human Factors Association of Canada,
PO Box 1085 B, Rexdale, Ontario M9V 2B3.

Moore C A & Ruth J O 1984   Use of voice
integrated with aircraft cockpit displays.
Digest of Technical Papers SID International
Symposium, vol 15, 227-230.

Moray N 1982   Subjective mental workload.
Human Factors, 24.1, 25-40.

Moray N 1983   Mental workload.   Proc. 1984
International Conference on Occupational
Ergonomics Vol 2 Reviews;   pp 41-46.
Human Factors Association of Canada,
PO Box 1085 B, Rexdale, Ontario M9V 2B3.

Moto-Aka T 1982   Fifth Generation Computer
Systems - Conference Proceedings.
North Holland Publishing Co.

National Electronics Council 1983
Human Factors in Information Technology.
Published by the NEC (National Electronics
Council, UK);   distributed by Wiley, London.

Shackel B 1966   Ergonomics and design.
In S A Gregory (Ed) The Design Method.
London, Butterworths.

Shackel B 1974   Applied Ergonomics Handbook.
London, Butterworths.

Shackel B 1981a   Man-Computer Interaction.
Alphen-aan-den Rijn, Netherlands,
Sijthoff & Noordhoff.

Shackel B 1981b   The Concept of Usability.
Proc. IBM Software & Information Usability
Symposium, Poughkeepsie NY,
15-18 September, pp 1-29.

Shackel B 1982   The BLEND system - programme
for the study of some ´Electronic Journals´.
The Computer Journal, 25.2, 161-168;
Ergonomics, 25.4, 269-284.

Shackel B, Pullinger D J, Maude T I &
Dodd W P 1983   The BLEND-LINC project on
´Electronic Journals´ after two years.
The Computer Journal, 26.3, 247-254.

Shackel B 1984a   Ergonomics in Information
Technology in Europe - A Review.
HUSAT Report no. 309 (for the Commission of
the European Communities);   Loughborough
University, HUSAT Research Centre.

Shackel B 1984b   Ergonomics in the
Information Age.   The Ergonomics
Society - The Society Lecture 1984;
Ergonomics, to be published.

Simpson A, Eason K D and Damodaran L 1980
Job design and training in word processor
applications.   HUSAT Subscription Research
Report no. 2.   Loughborough University,
HUSAT Research Centre.

Smith S L 1981   The Usability of Software -
Design Guidelines for the User-System
Interface.   Proc. IBM Software & Information
Usability Symposium, Poughkeepsie NY,
15-18 September, pp 31-52.

Sullivan M A & Chapanis A 1983   Human
factoring a text editor manual.   Behaviour
& Information Technology, 2.2, 113-125.

Stonier T 1983   The Wealth of Information.
London, Methuan.

Thomas J C 1984   Organising for human
factors.   Personal communication
from IBM Research Centre, Yorktown Heights;
to be published.

Toffler A 1970   Future Shock.
London, Pan Books.

Toffler A 1980   The Third Wave.
London, Collins.

Vallee J 1982   The Network Revolution.
Berkeley California, The And/Or Press.

van Apeldoorn J H F 1983   Man and
Information Technology: Towards Friendlier
Systems.   Delft University Press.

van Nes F L & van der Heijden J 1978
The use of computers by ordinary people.
IPO Annual Progress Report 13, 102-107.

Williges R C 1984   Evaluating human-computer
software interfaces. Proc. 1984 International
Conference on Occupational Ergonomics
Vol 2 Reviews;   pp 81-87.
Human Factors Association of Canada,
PO Box 1085 B, Rexdale, Ontario M9V 2B3.

Wright P 1981   Problems to be Solved When
Creating Usable Documents.   Proc. IBM
Software & Information Usability Symposium,
Poughkeepsie NY, 15-18 September, pp 53-103.

Wright P 1983   Manual dexterity : a user-
oriented approach to creating computer
documentation.   Proc. Conference Human
Factors in Computer Systems CHI´83; New York,
Assoc. for Computing Machinery; pp 11-18.

USER ASPECTS

Human-Computer Interaction — INTERACT '84 / B. Shackel (ed.)
Elsevier Science Publishers B.V. (North-Holland)
© IFIP, 1985

USERS IN THE REAL WORLD

David Owen

Institute for Cognitive Science, C-015
University of California, San Diego,
La Jolla, California 92093

Based on the premise that people demonstrate a considerable degree of competence at formulating and achieving goals in the world, this paper seeks to identify and examine the relationship between the crucial characteristics of the real world and inherent or acquired human skills that support this competence, in order to improve the human computer interface. Aspects examined include a "naive physics" of computing and the reconstruction of propositionally held information.

Introduction

Much of the current work on human-machine interface design starts with an analysis of difficulties users experience with specific existing software systems, e.g., operating systems and editors. This paper explores a complementary approach based on the premise that we demonstrate a considerable degree of competence at formulating and achieving goals in the world which does not readily transfer to a computing environment. The task is to identify and examine the relationship between the crucial characteristics of the real world and inherent or acquired human skills and motivations that support this apparent competence, with the aim of providing the same kind of support in a computing environment.

Two aspects are examined here. The first is concerned with the formulation and achievement of explicit goals, the kind which are generally inferable from people's actions and the second seeks to emphasise the importance of non-explicit meta goals, evidence of which is less apparent. An inherent danger in this kind of approach is that of limiting the exploitation of a new tool/medium to existing concepts, without exploring new ones. The intent here is to identify and acquire an understanding of issues at a level which does not evaporate in the face of new ways of structuring activities and is not bound to existing or anticipated hardware.

Formulating and Achieving Goals in the Real World

People somehow become acquainted with a range of tools/agents, how to mobilise them, and how to formulate goals in a way which relates to the means of achieving them. This sometimes involves perceiving existing situations, deciding on desirable changes, setting up preconditions for the changes, and then uttering the appropriate incantation to invoke the tool/agent (Norman, 1984). Alternatively and less precisely, partially understood current and desired states may motivate the heuristic choice of some strategy, which is believed to lead in roughly the right direction. In doing this people draw on a whole range of skills, memory aids, and in particular, input to the total range of senses. Furthermore the skills seem well adapted to the cues and representational modes of the real world.

So what is it about these skills and the real world that facilitates this apparent competence, and to what extent can they be exploited equally well in an interface?

The 'Naive Physics' of Computing

People acquire a degree of knowledge of the 'naive physics' of the world (Hayes, 1978); approximately how physical cause and effect mechanisms work, and there is a growing field of research concerned with establishing the primitives of this physics. DiSessa for example (diSessa, 1983) uses protocols to probe a naive subject's understanding of 'sponginess', exposing the degree to which it is sufficient to explain some everyday phenomena and its limitations on confronting less common situations. Naive physics provides a basic understanding of what may or may not be possible, which is exploited in many situations.

- It is powerful in determining the plausibility of proposed combinations of tool-object-outcome. For example, it allows the user to infer the relative appropriateness of a sponge and a hammer for a task.

- It supports the innovative use of tools: a screwdriver can be used to open a tin of paint.

- It supports short cuts: having understood the essential procedures laid out in a recipe, many people will follow it only as is necessary to get the main effect.

- It is particularly important in being able to cope when things go wrong: when water does not emerge from the end of a hose pipe, most people are capable of generating some debugging strategies.

Similar situations are to be found in the computing domain but require a very different naive physics.

- In which contexts, for example, is it appropriate to use "rm" to remove something, and is it like removing a spot from a window or removing a chair from a room? Is "rm" or "mv" or mouse movement plus three clicks the appropriate way of changing the location of a word in a file and can it also be used, say, to delay the execution of some command for ten seconds?

- Some computing systems, like UNIX, [1] positively encourage the innovative combination of their facilities.

- When lengthy, perhaps menu-based, interactive interfaces become irritating rather than supportive, it is desirable to short cut the prescribed procedure and issue just those commands which are relevant to the immediate task. To do this one must have an understanding of what is relevant.

- It is also the case that things occasionally go wrong, and one then needs some capacity to analyse why.

The question then arises as to what might be the important notions in a naive physics of computing. One reason for addressing this question for the real world is to be able to present new information in a way which facilitates the transition from novice to expert (diSessa, 1983). But in the computing domain there is the opportunity, at least to some extent, to tackle the problem the other way round, that is to induce in the user a naive physics which will be more easily extendible. So an equally relevant question might be how best to help people acquire that knowledge.

The physics of computing. This deserves a longer examination than is possible here, but lets us consider one important aspect. The computing domain is one of symbols and so it seems the essential 'physics' is at least in part that of symbols and their manipulation rather than of the objects which are represented. People appear to be familiar with symbolic representations and their limitations in the world. Only in cartoons do people knock nails in with a photograph of a hammer but it is accepted that a photograph gives a reasonably reliable idea of shape and colour. Similarly, the fact that one can do things to symbolic forms which are not possible on the real thing is not unknown. It is reasonable to cut out the picture of the hammer and put it in a collage positioned over a picture of a nail, or declare that the saltcellar is Paris! What is not familiar is the degree to which the use of symbols can be exploited in new domains. It is possible for example to represent and manipulate tiny patches of a single letter in a font editor. Even the means of seeing the symbols is indirect; there is no absolute guarantee that what is evident on the screen is in any other sense there. [2] This substantial difference between everyday use of symbols and their use on a computer makes it hard to infer the similarity.

Hand in hand with the symbols explosion goes the capacity to break down hitherto elemental operations on symbols and, with almost limitless flexibility, combine them into new compound actions. A simple example apparent in studies of editors is the difficulty some people have with the process of inserting text in a line where there is apparently no space (Riley and O'Malley, 1984). It exposes the limitations of appealing to real world analogies without revealing the essential differences in the 'physics' of the domains. Not only is it necessary for the user to grasp the possibility of decomposition and understand the new range of elemental operations but also to comprehend and accept a program designer's decision as to what constitutes an improved combination. [3] On the one hand this flexibility exceeds people's experience in that it is available in new domains. To return to the collage example, it is not normally possible to devise a tool which will, in one action, both make space for and position a picture of a thumb between the hammer and the nail. On the other hand, it falls short of people's experience of a domain in which they do make heavy use of symbol manipulation, namely that of natural language. In this domain one can convey the same information in many different ways and to a large extent rely on the hearer's shared access to the world. [4]

Inferring a naive physics. Two related conditions which seem to be important may be inferred from analyses of naive physics by diSessa (diSessa, 1983) and McCloskey (McCloskey et. al., 1983). The latter describes and analyses the commonly held misconception that an object that is carried by another moving object (a person running with a ball) will, if dropped, fall to the ground in a vertical straight line. Their hypothesis is that the misconception results from a misperception of events in the world caused by an inappropriate use of reference frames. However, it is clear that people can straighten out similar misconceptions without formal physics training if there is sufficient motivation. Spear fishermen for centuries have been able to cope with position distortions caused by the different refractive indices of air and water. For most people, the straight line misconception does not interfere with any common goal. But in the case of the fisherman, the absence of a fish on the end of the spear is unambiguously a failure of some understood and explicit intermediate goal towards eating. This would indicate that in the computing domain it is necessary to expose to the user the implicit subgoals of a compound command, at least in one form of that command. For example in the UNIX operating system there is no command which will simply create an empty file. Invoking an editor on a non-existent file will usually succeed in creating it and, amongst other things, will assign to it some protection status. However, the editor gives no indication that this is happening and in general there is little evidence that a complicated protection structure is being automatically developed until one attempts to transgress it. The intent here is not to reiterate the "more meaningful error messages" chestnut, but to suggest that the user be allowed to absorb the notion of (in this case) protection by making its presence as a sub-task apparent in non-error situations. [5]

In diSessa's (diSessa,1983) probing of a subject's comprehension of elasticity, it was apparent that a major stumbling block to extending the understanding of how a tennis ball could bounce, to how a steel ball-bearing could bounce, was the fact that the elastic properties of a tennis ball are visible,

whilst normally those of a ball-bearing are not. In fact the interviewer, in attempting to convince the subject of the similarity, points out that with strobe photography the squishiness of a ball-bearing could also be seen. The argument is again one for visibility. To fully exploit a person's capacity to infer a useful naive physics, as much as possible should be made apparent of both the nature of a procedure and the properties of the objects involved. [6]

None of the above is intended as an argument for making computing systems mimic their real world physical counterparts. On the contrary, the use of icons that look like filing cabinets is of questionable value if associated concepts are not supported.

Representational Modes

There is a range of ways in which people can sense and subsequently represent the world: sight, sound, touch. Much of the state of the world is permanently apparent in different, often analogical, representational forms which people trade on heavily to distribute the load of comparing, remembering and understanding. In the computing domain we are essentially reduced to one perceptual channel to sense the nature of, and interact with, the encapsulated world. One is not subjectively conscious of having to translate the softness of a sponge and the hardness of a nail to a different representational form to perceive the mismatch. For an equivalent operation on a machine one has to know or be given a quantised textual description of the relevant properties of an object and an agent in order to assess the appropriateness of their combination.

It can be seen as an inevitable consequence of the compression of the world into a limited space to be viewed propositionally through a small window. It is a powerful property of the computing medium that a large amount of information can be held in a small space, but that is incompatible with the space-taking analogical forms of representation which it is possible to make use of in the real world. In this respect computers and the world stand at different extremes in the tradeoff between compactness and multi-dimensional accessibility.

There is a challenge therefore to make a shift in this tradeoff, to relieve the user of the overwhelming emphasis on propositional forms of representation and reconstruct the information so held into

more immediately accessible forms. Mice and larger
bit-mapped terminals are undoubtedly useful, but
they still represent a preoccupation with improving
ways of interacting with a window on the encapsulated world rather than providing qualitatively
different access mechanisms. An example is the
notion of location in, and movement around, a
directory structure. The power of analogical
representations of these notions is only minimally
exploited, but imagine a device attached to your
workstation which had drawn out on it a plan of
your directory structure, and that on that plan you
could physically place and move a counter. The
position of the counter indicates your current working directory, and moving the counter would be
equivalent to issuing a change directory command
via the keyboard. The user would not have to
remember the commands or mouse clicks necessary
to change directory, or the exact name of the directory. Recognising the position of the counter in
relation to the physical characteristics of the pad
might make it unnecessary to read the label.
Current screen-based solutions require either a temporary change of screen to see your relative position
in a graphic representation or force you to read and
parse the directory name if it is permanently
displayed. Even the direct action of moving the
counter significantly changes the nature of the interface. It replaces moving a mouse, in order to move a
pointer, to indicate the object on which some subsequently and similarly indicated action is to be performed. Of course advances in touch sensitive 'flat'
screens may allow a more sophisticated implementation than the one suggested above. The argument
here is that there is a particular property of the
world which people exploit, that future developments might explore.

Knowledge Acquisition

Having constructed an environment full of wonder-
ful facilities, how are users going to find out about
them? There are many sources of information for
the motivated seeker both for a computer interface
and in the rest of the world. However much of the
information about tools/agents in the world seems
to be acquired at times when it is not being directly
sought and may not be relevant to any immediate
goal: billboards, T.V. advertising or watching other
people without necessarily being in an accepted
student/teacher situation. One becomes aware of
the facilities with almost no special effort, but
knowledge of their existence may influence how
some future goal is achieved or to the extent that

goal generation is 'tool availability' driven, whether
they are even generated. Even if a facility is
known and used, seeing it used or described by
someone else can increase one's own understanding
of it. There is little exploitation of this kind of dissemination of information in most computing systems and although many possibilities may spring to
mind the exact nature of this kind of knowledge
acquisition, and the conditions under which it is
acceptable, rather than irritating, are not obvious.

A pilot study addressing this issue has recently
begun at UCSD. It currently takes the form of a
program which users may call as a displacement
activity, which will display on the screen a small
piece of information about the local computing
environment. It may also be called with an argument which serves to confine the information to a
particular subject (e.g., vi, an editor and C, a programming language). To try and establish the kind
of information it is useful to present, users are
asked to indicate whether they find each instance of
interest. [7] A simple editor is being developed which
will allow people to contribute their own database
entries, and it is intended to make the system self
maintaining by allowing user responses to censor the
contributions. [8] Evaluation of the facilities will be
based on a log of its use, comparison of the usage of
several existing commands before and after its introduction, and user comments.

Hidden Goals and Explicit Goals

This section is an attempt to push the same examination of the real world for a contribution to a
more amorphous aspect of what makes one interface
better than another. There are several established
ways of assessing the effectiveness of different interfaces, e.g., ease of learning, frequency of mistakes,
effective throughput. But these may miss a range of
important characteristics which contribute to a
user's subjective feeling on using the interface. We
appear to have a range of non-explicit emotional
and aesthetic requirements whose satisfaction is
rarely the main objective, but which influence the
route taken to achieving a more concrete goal.
These 'hidden' goals are difficult to identify but
their influence can be seen in some kinds of
behaviour. For example, the motives behind travelling to work by the scenic route one day and the
highway another are hardly explained by 'needing a
change of view.'

Two extremes in the degree to which explicit goals
or 'hidden' goals are being satisfied occur in the

use of tools and toys respectively. The description of something as a tool (work) implies that one is most interested in the explicit outcome of its application, and in general less interested in the means by which it is achieved. For a toy or game although there is often an ostensibly desired outcome, like amassing gold pieces or scoring points, the main object of the exercise is to satisfy ill-defined hidden goals almost as a side effect of how the overt goal is achieved. This sweeping generalisation serves to convey a sense of the distinction being used. From this I want to argue that the subjective degree of satisfaction afforded by two different ways of doing the same job, or using two functionally equivalent interfaces, reflects the degree to which they satisfy by side effects, the user's hidden goals.

There is little future in attempting a detailed analysis of the concept of "pleasure," and that is not what is being suggested here. The best that can be hoped for is some approximate classification of behavior patterns that the satisfaction of 'hidden' goals apparently precipitates, and attempt to provide the opportunity for similar behaviour in constructing an interface.

As an example consider the behaviour exemplified by the use of alternate routes to work. It would indicate that in spite of the fact that one input device may be optimal for speed and efficiency for a particular application, it is important to provide functionally equivalent, sub-optimal alternatives merely for variety. For example, a system which relied heavily on a 'mouse' or speech input without the provision for performing the same tasks via a keyboard or a data-pad would not facilitate what appears to be an important aspect of human behaviour.

But what lies behind a craftsman's attachment to a particular tool, a golfer's loyalty to a particular driver, or a traveller's preference for a particular travel agent?

Is it that the qualities, capacities and limitations of these extensions are thoroughly understood and trusted, that they will not spring surprises? If so then the argument made in an earlier section for making explicit the consequences of using a computing facility is reinforced.

Is it that the tool in the hand of the user acts as a procedural memory? In other words, the user no longer has to remember a detailed specification of what he wants to achieve, only that whatever it is, it can be achieved by his use of that tool. It allows the specification of a desired outcome, and the selection of the means for achieving it, to be collapsed into a single mental step. If so, then perhaps one program designer's way of carving up the space of possible activities and providing tools accordingly may be adequate.

Is it that the the tool and its implications for the organisation of the domain are a function of the personality of the user and that every time they are used, the user's own identity or image is gratifyingly reinforced? (Although this may seem somewhat esoteric, it is a phenomenon which is exploited everyday in the advertising world.) If this is the case then there is little satisfaction in being forced to absorb the identity of the program designer, however objectively efficient it may prove to be. Users should be given every opportunity to modify tools to reflect their own conceptual framework.

Concluding Remarks

I have attempted to draw attention to some aspects of the way we interact with the world, and how they might be exploited to improve interaction with a computer. One direction indicated by some of these aspects is towards making the user more aware of how things are done and why they are done that way. A different view holds that the machine should be developed as an intelligent agent, which will infer a lot about the user's intentions and not trouble them with any details. These views are not mutually exclusive, but they do represent a difference in emphasis which there has not been space to discuss.

References

[1]   diSessa, A.A., Phenomenology and the evolution of intuition, in Gentner, D.and Stevens, A.L., (eds.), Mental Models (Erlbaum, London, 1983).

[2]   Hayes, P.J., The naive physics manifesto, in Michie, D. (ed), Expert Systems in the Microelectronic Age (Edinburgh Univ. Press, 1978).

[3]   McCloskey, M., Washburn, A. and Felch, L., Intuitive Physics: The straight-down belief and its origin, Jrnl of Experimental Psychology: Learning, Memory and Cognition Vol. 9, No. 4, (1983) 636-649

[4]   Norman, D.A., Four stages of user activities, Proceedings of the First IFIP Conference on Human-Computer Interaction (London, September 1984).

[5]   Riley, M.S. and O'Malley, C., Planning nets: a frame-
        work for studying user-computer interaction, Proceed-
        ings of the First IFIP Conference on Human-
        Computer Interaction (London, September 1984).

Footnotes

The ideas result from interactions with the UCSD Human-
Machine Interaction project, including Liam Bannon, Allen
Cypher, Steve Draper, Donald Norman, Mary Riley, and Paul
Smolensky, and with Brenda Laurel of Atari. Sondra Buffett
helped in improving the presentation.

This research was conducted under Contract N00014-79-C-
0323, NR 667-437 with the Personnel and Training Research
Programs of the Office of Naval Research and by a grant from
the System Development Foundation. Requests for reprints
should be sent to David Owen, Cognitive Science C-015;
University of California, San Diego; La Jolla, California,
92093, USA.

1. UNIX is a trademark of Bell Laboratories.

2. In 'insert' mode in the vi editor one can delete characters just entered without leaving that mode. The cursor moves
back over them and they are 'lost' to the editor but they are
not removed from the screen.

3. Even a model requires some understanding of the nature of the objects involved which might limit the value of its
use in isolation. It could be regarded as part of a bootstrapping
process.

4. Witness the difficulty people have with understanding
how blindness or deafness affects the shared access assumptions. Blind people are often shouted at, and deaf people
guided round obstacles.

5. An approach being tried at UCSD (Draper, unpublished) is an interactive version of a general file creation program which makes explicit the attributes associated with a file
including its protection by requesting them explicitly and reporting impossible combinations of options with reasons for
the inappropriateness.

6. The problem here is that few of the physical properties
that distinguish objects in the world are inherent in computer
objects (eg. different file types). To arbitrarily assign them may
lead to confusing inconsistency. More relevant properties are
implied by the operations it is sensible to perform on them (eg.
print,execute). At the very least this difference could be made
clearer. Some ways of doing this, short of operating system re-
writes, are being explored at UCSD in a simple editor and a
"notepad" system (Cypher unpublished).

7. So far, surprisingly few people specify a subject,
although those who do predictably have a higher "interest hit
rate", (60% versus 40% overall). Also whether people stop using the facility does not seem closely related to the success of
their first few uses.

8. Although some pieces of information have been very
popular, others not at all, it is not yet clear what the crucial
differences are, and so some kind of self censoring seems important.

Human-Computer Interaction — INTERACT '84 / B. Shackel (ed.)
Elsevier Science Publishers B.V. (North-Holland)
© IFIP, 1985

Choice of Interface Modes by Empirical Groupings of Computer Users

K. M. Potosnak

Institute for Perception Research (IPO)
Technische Hogeschool Eindhoven
5600 MB Eindhoven
The Netherlands

A method for classifying computer users on a large number of variables was developed and tested. The method was based on cluster analysis and yielded seven groups of users and non-users. Volunteers from each group used a computer program which allowed them to choose among three modes of interaction: prompts, commands and form-filling.

Overall, people preferred the prompts and the form, but used the prompts the most. People with the most use and knowledge of computers used the commands more than the other groups. Discussion focuses on the hypothesis that naive users prefer a system-driven mode of interaction, while experienced users prefer a user-driven mode.

INTRODUCTION

Recent approaches to increasing the usability of computers tend to fall into two categories. The first approach is based on the assumption that judicious application of certain principles or guidelines (both general and specific) will make all systems easier to use. Indeed, designing for population stereotypes is a well-known basis of human factors engineering. This approach is illustrated by the work of Hayes, Ball and Reddy [9], [10]. These authors "have established a set of abilities a computer system should have if it is to interact gracefully with its users."

The other approach that has been taken in making computers more usable is to design them specifically for the types of people who will use them. Investigating the effects of user characteristics on performance with and attitudes toward different system interfaces has been used to develop user-specific guidelines. An example is presented by Rich [15], who argues that "A much better system would be one in which the interface presented to each person was tailored to his own characteristics rather than to those of some abstract 'typical' person." It has also been suggested that alternative modes of interaction be included within one interface so that users may select the methods that suit them [8], [11], [13].

Results of previous research support both of these approaches. That is, there are some important similarities among groups of people in their use of computers [3], [12], and there are some important differences [4], [6], [16]. The methodology used in these and other, similar studies has been to divide people into different groups and then measure their performance and attitudes with various system designs. Unfortunately, most methods of grouping people in these studies have been based on only one or two variables; the variables themselves seem to

have been selected rather arbitrarily; and no single classification has been used consistently across studies.

Because of these problems, it is nearly impossible to come to any definite conclusions concerning which aspects of computers need to be tailored for different users and which do not.

The aim of the present research was to test an empirical method of dividing people into groups of computer users. If a more comprehensive and less arbitrary method of classifying people can be developed, then more reliable and consistent tests of similarities and differences among these people can be performed.

The study differs from previous work in several ways:

1. The classification of computer users was conducted for a large sample of people.

2. The classification was based on a large number of variables.

3. Correlations among the variables were taken into account statistically.

4. Quantitative variables were not arbitrarily dichotomized or partitioned.

5. A relatively large number of groups was obtained.

6. Some people from each group were tested in an experiment in which they were allowed to choose from a selection of three interfaces, rather than being exposed to only one interface design.

The focus of this paper is on the experimental test of the classification rather than on the grouping method itself, which is reported in detail elsewhere [14]. Therefore, only a brief summary of the classification method and the obtained groups is presented. The remainder of the paper describes the procedure and major results of the experiment.

CLASSIFICATION OF USERS

A 45-item questionnaire was sent to 481 randomly selected employees of Sinai Hospital of Baltimore, Maryland. Distribution was not restricted to only those people who had used a computer before. Hospital employees were chosen because there are many types of people who work in hospitals and computers are used in a large variety of ways in hospitals.

Most of the items on the questionnaire had been used in previous research with different types of computer users. Other items were included as potentially important with regard to computer use. The items covered the following topics:

a. age, sex and education
b. the respondent's job
c. locus of control[1]
d. perceptions of skills and abilities
e. attitudes toward computers
f. availability of computers
g. computer courses taken or taught
h. uses of computers
i. amount of use of computers
j. quality of use of computers
k. current use of computers

Completed questionnaires were received from 263 employees (return rate = 54.7%). To determine the factor structure of the items, a principal components analysis of the correlations among the 45 items was conducted. Nine factors were revealed and were named:

I   amount of computer use
II   age
III   amount of computer knowledge
IV   job status
V   interpersonal skills
VI   male-female roles
VII   attitudes
VIII creativity
IX   locus of control

To control for correlations among the questionnaire items, the results of the principal components analysis were used to weight each person's responses. These standardized factor scores were the inputs to a cluster analysis which used a variation of MacQueen's k-Means method with coarsening and refining parameters [2]. This method allowed for a variable number of clusters and was repeated until convergence (i.e., until there was no change in cluster membership from one run to the next).

Seven clusters were obtained. Descriptions of the clusters were based on the original 45 variables. Because of the complexity of the differences among the clusters, they are desig-

nated by letters of the alphabet, rather than by a short name which might tend to overemphasize only one of many traits. The outstanding characteristics of each group are summarized in Table 1.

One questionnaire item that was not included in the cluster analysis was the respondent's job title. After the clusters were obtained, a list was constructed of the job titles of people in each group. It was expected that such a list would be helpful in naming the groups. In fact, some current classifications rely heavily on this variable (see [7] for example). However, the list showed that there was more variability than consistency in the distribution of job titles among clusters. For example, there were managers and secretaries in every cluster and nurses and technicians in most of the clusters.

EXPERIMENTAL TEST OF CLASSIFICATION

The experimental application was a computerized mail order facility with which subjects could order merchandise selected from mail order catalogs. A program called the Mail Order Merchandise (MOM) program was implemented so that the user could choose from three interface modes: prompting, commands and form-filling.

The prompt mode was accessed via a set of programmed function (PF) keys. Once a PF key was pressed, the program launched into a series of questions or prompts to obtain the necessary ordering information.

The command mode was invoked whenever anything was typed in the command input field in the lower part of the screen. Subjects could enter all or part of the information with commands. Some abbreviation was allowed, but a strict adherence to syntax rules was required. Either of these two modes could be accessed at any time during the task regardless of the mode of previous inputs.

The form mode could be accessed via either of the other two modes. Subjects could use the order form on the screen for a subset of the available actions and these could be used at any time.

Subjects. For the experiment a small number of volunteers from each cluster were available. There were 3, 3, 2, 3, 4, 4, and 2 subjects from groups A through G, respectively.

Procedure. The experimental procedure involved the following steps:

1. tutorial on the IBM 3277 terminal and keyboard [see 1] (30 min.)
2. practice using terminal (15 min.)
3. familiarization with MOM program and documentation (20 min.)
4. practice using MOM program (40 min.)

Table 1
Characteristics of Seven Groups of Computer Users Obtained by Cluster Analysis

	G r o u p						
characteristic	A	B	C	D	E	F	G
size of group	50	74	25	17	36	31	30
age	youngest						oldest
% female	54	58	8	29	31	74	73
education	college		college		highest		lowest
locus of control			most external				most internal
jobs			most technical	most pressure	most variable, supervise most		least technical most routine
skills				high in sales & teaching	high in science low in clerical	high in manual & artistic	low in all except clerical
amount of computer use	low	low	high	low	low	high	low
amount of computer knowledge	low	low	high	low	low	low	low
attitude toward computers		poor	good		poor		poor
currently use computers	no	no	yes	yes	yes	yes	no
number years computer use	4-6	0	8-10	3	3	4	3-4

5. mail order task
6. attitude questionnaire
7. debriefing

The entire experimental procedure took about three hours. The purpose of the experiment was not to determine whether subjects could learn to use the MOM program, but rather to see how they used it once they were somewhat familiar with it. Therefore, subjects were allowed to ask the experimenter for help, but only if they could not solve a problem themselves. During the ordering task, subjects were required to record their questions on paper before asking for help.

During the sessions a large number of dependent variables were measured, including: task times, errors, amount of use of each mode, amount of switching between modes, and attitudes.

RESULTS

Attitudes. With regard to attitudes, there were two results of interest. First, subjects in group B rated the tutorial as more difficult than did subjects in groups C, D or G. Secondly, Table 2 shows the average ratings for subjects in each group of how much they liked the prompts, the form and the commands. As can be seen in

Table 2, there were no significant differences among the groups in their ratings of the modes. However, across all groups, subjects reported that they liked using the prompt and the form modes significantly more than they liked using the commands.

Table 2
Average Ratings of Liking of Modes by Groups

	Group						
Mode	A	B	C	D	E	F	G
prompt	5.3	5.0	5.0	5.0	6.2	5.0	5.0
form	6.3	5.3	6.5	5.3	5.2	6.0	6.5
command	3.0	3.0	3.0	5.3	4.0	4.5	3.5

Note: 7= liked extremely; 1=disliked extremely

Performance. The remainder of the results concerned subjects' performance with the MOM program. The most outstanding finding was that the prompt mode was used more than the other two modes by all of the groups. Figure 1 shows the average number of times each mode was accessed by each group during the ordering task. Similar graphs were obtained for the number of actions performed in each mode and the amount of time spent in each mode. It was also found that subjects used the prompt mode significantly more during the second half of the task than the first half of the task.

In using the MOM program, subjects were allowed to change modes as often as they liked. A mode "run" consisted of all the actions performed in either the prompt of the command mode before switching to the alternate mode (since the form was accessed only from within one of the other modes, it was not included in this measure). The average number of mode runs for groups A through G, respectively, was: 4.0, 3.0, 15.5, 3.7, 3.0, 3.5 and 12.0. Analyses showed that group C had significantly more mode runs than groups A, B, D, E and F (but not more than group G). Also, the people in group C performed more actions in the command mode than people in groups A, B, E and F.

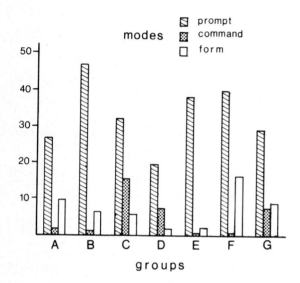

Figure 1 : Mean number of times each mode was used by each group during the MOM task

DISCUSSION

The three modes included in the MOM program were chosen to represent the distinction between user-guided and system-guided interaction. Prompting is an interactive mode that is controlled or paced by the computer. With the commands the user controls the dialogue. The form-filling mode involves little dialogue between the user and the computer. However, with the form the user can control the rate and sequence of inputs. Is has been hypothesized that some users, particularly naive ones, benefit from having the computer guide the interaction, while other users, for instance experienced ones, will prefer to control the interaction themselves [4], [8], [11].

The results of this experiment can be interpreted in terms of this hypothesis. For example, people in group C used the command mode more and switched modes more often than most of the other groups. One of the major characteristics of group C was that these people scored very highly on measures of both computer use and computer knowledge. In contrast, people in group F, who scored highly on computer use, but not on computer knowledge, did not use the commands. The people in group C may have used the commands more than the other groups because they had a higher amount of computer knowledge, not just a higher amount of computer use.

From these results it might be concluded that computer knowledge was the major variable to distinguish among the groups in this task. However, because of the limited time period involved in this study, group differences in performance over time could not be observed. Even though subjects were given an hour to practice with the MOM program before any dependent variables were measured, they all might still have been relatively inexperienced with it. The overwhelming result was that subjects in all groups used the prompt (system-guided) mode the most (see Figure 1). If the hypothesis concerning user-guided versus system-guided interaction is correct, then experience with a specific program was of most importance in this study. Results obtained by Gilfoil [8] and by Hiltz and Turoff [11] show that it takes much longer than two of three hours before users can be considered experienced with a particular system. Although it was not a factor in this study, the pattern of results might have been different if performance had been measured over a longer period of time.

So far the discussion has focused on the prompts and the commands. But what about the form mode? Comparison of the subjects' ratings with their performance shows that there is little correspondence between their attitudes toward the form and their use of it (as there is for the prompt mode). The format of the order form was developed directly from the actual order blanks included in the mail order catalogs. Therefore this was probably the most natural and appropriate mode for the task. Perhaps that is why subjects liked it so much. However, the form could not be used for some actions such as "mail the completed order to the company." Also, the form mode was subordinate to the other two modes because it could only be accessed from within one of the other modes. These reasons alone may have been sufficient to discourage subjects from using the form.

CONCLUSIONS

The aim of this study was to classify computer users (and non-users) with an empirical method and to determine whether there were any differences among the obtained groups in their use of three interface modes. It was found that it is possible to develop a classification scheme based in cluster analysis. The advantages of this method are that: many variables and their interactions can be taken into account; artificial dichotomies for quantitative variables can be avoided; and all types of people can be classified, not just those at the extremes.

A subsequent test of the classification with only a small number of subjects showed a few differences among the groups. However, there was also a great deal of consistency in the choices people made during their first interaction with the MOM program.

An important point throughout this project has been that computer experience is not a unitary concept. The principal components analysis yielded two separate factors for computer use and computer knowledge. The cluster analysis resulted in groups that could be distinguished on the basis of these two types of variables. In addition to use and knowledge, the experiment showed the importance of a third aspect of computer experience: program-specific experience. All of these variables (and probably others, such as task expertise) can affect the ways in which people use computers.

ACKNOWLEDGEMENTS

The work summarized here was conducted while I was at the Communications Research Laboratory of the Johns Hopkins University, Baltimore, Maryland and was funded by a research agreement with the IBM Corporation System Products Division under the direction of Professor Alphonse Chapanis. The preparation of this paper was done at the Institute for Perception Research (IPO) where I was the recipient of a research fellowship from the University of Technology, Eindhoven, The Netherlands.

FOOTNOTE 1 : Locus of control refers to people's perceptions of how much control they have over the events in their lives. The actual items were from the "Internal" sub-scale used by Coovert & Goldstein [5].

REFERENCES

[1] Al-Awar, J., Chapanis, A., and Ford, W.R., Tutorials for the first-time computer user, IEEE Transactions on Professional Communication PC-24(1) (1981), 30-37.

[2] Anderberg, M.R., Cluster Analysis for Applications (Academic Press, New York, 1973).

[3] Barnard, P.J., Hammond, N.V., Morton, J., Long, J.B., and Clark, I.A., Consistency and compatibility in human-computer dialogue, Int. J. Man-Machine Studies 15 (1981) 87-134.

[4] Benbasat, I., Dexter, A.S., and Masulis, P.S., An experimental study of the human/computer interface, Communications of the ACM 24 (1981) 752-762.

[5] Coovert, M.D. and Goldstein, M., Locus of control as a predictor of users attitudes toward computers, Psych.Reports 47 (1980) PT2 1167.

[6] Dzida, W., Herda, S., and Itzfeldt, W.D., User-perceived quality of interactive systems, IEEE Transactions on Software Engineering SE-4, No. 4 (1978) 270-276.

[7] Eason, K.D., Damodaran, L., and Stewart, T.F.M., Interface problems in man-computer interaction, in Mumford, E. and Sackman, H. (eds.), Human Choice and Computers (North-Holland, Amsterdam, 1975).

[8] Gilfoil, D.M., Warming up to computers: A study of cognitive and affective interaction over time, in Proceedings of the Human Factors in Computer Systems Conference (Gaithersburg, Maryland, 15-17 March 1982) 245-250.

[9] Hayes, P.J., Ball, J.E. and Reddy, D.R., Breaking the man-machine communication barrier, Computer 14 (1981) 19-30.

[10] Hayes, P.J. and Reddy, D.R., Steps toward graceful interaction in spoken and written man-machine communication, Int. J. Man-Machine Studies 19 (1983) 231-284.

[11] Hiltz, S.R. and Turoff, M., Human diversity and the choice of interface: A design challenge, ACM SIGSOC Bull. 13 (1982) 125-130.

[12] Ledgard, H., Singer, A., and Whiteside, J., Directions in Human Factors for Interactive Systems (Springer-Verlag, New York, 1981).

[13] Nievergelt, J., Errors in dialog design and how to avoid them, in International Zurich Seminar on Digital Communications: Man-Machine Interaction (Swiss Federal Institute of Technology, Zurich, 9-11 March 1982) 199-205.

[14] Potosnak, K.M., Choice of Computer Interface Modes by Empirically Derived Categories of Users, doctoral dissertation, The Johns Hopkins University, 1983. (Can be obtained from University Microfilms International; 300 North Zeeb Road; Ann Arbor, Michigan 48106; U.S.A.)

[15] Rich, E., Users are individuals: individualizing user models, Int. J. Man-Machine Studies 18 (1983) 199-214.

[16] Walther, G.H. and O'Neil, H.F., On-line
     user computer interface--The effects of
     interface flexibility, terminal type, and
     experience on performance, in Proceedings
     of the National Computer Conference,
     AFIPS 43 (1974) 379-384.

Human-Computer Interaction — INTERACT '84 / B. Shackel (ed.)
Elsevier Science Publishers B.V. (North-Holland)
IFIP, 1985

THE SOCIAL PSYCHOLOGY OF COMPUTER CONVERSATIONS

Dianne Murray and Nigel Bevan[*]

National Physical Laboratory
Teddington, Middx, England.

Human conversations are complex interactions motivated by both task-related and social goals. It is proposed that the optimal form of conversational interaction with a computer is a computer conversation which closely emulates the nature of a human conversation in similar circumstances. The cultural differences between computer conversations and human conversations are identified, and it is suggested how the crucial social factors in human conversation could be integrated into a conversational model of computer interaction, structured by the need to achieve mutual goals.

INTRODUCTION

Among the many possible forms of human-computer interaction (HCI), an important category is "conversational interaction", that is dialogues between a human and a machine which are similar to conversations between humans. Such conversational interaction occurs when users question or instruct the computer in a "conversational language" [1], while the computer responds with information, some or all of which has a natural language type syntax.

The underlying need in HCI is for straightforward communication:
> "the ability of the man to communicate his needs to the machine in the most concise way consistent with his conversational fluency, and with the ability of the machine to express itself clearly in response" [2].

This paper is concerned with an aspect of conversational interaction which is often overlooked: namely that the machine presents a subset of the behaviour of a human communicator, and that the user naturally applies to the situation the habits, skills and reactions appropriate to conversation with another human.

Given that humans often impart personality to inanimate objects, and tend to project their own expectations onto computer dialogues [3], it is hardly surprising that a computer system should be perceived as having human-like characteristics. This is particularly so for computer-naive users. For example, when a computer was used for medical interviewing many patients stated that they found the computer friendly, and preferred being interviewed by a computer rather than by a doctor [4].

[*] The order of authors, which will alternate, has no significance.

There is currently conflicting advice for the systems designer as to whether this intrinsic inclination of the user to respond to human characteristics in a computer conversation should be encouraged or discouraged. For instance Shneiderman [5] states: "Build computer systems that behave like tools... Don't attribute human names or attributes to programs and systems." In contrast Cuff [6] believes that "a courteous, coherent rational dialogue flow is important, using terms the user can understand, and maintaining a conversational content"; and Spiliotopolous [7] found that introducing random encouragement and chattiness into a computer interview significantly increased its acceptability.

COMPUTER CONVERSATIONS

Human conversations are complex interactions motivated by both task-related and social goals. It is contended here that the optimal form of interaction between human and computer is a "computer conversation" which should closely emulate the nature of a conversation between human and human in similar circumstances. This applies not only at the task level, but also at the social and non-verbal level which is so important in motivating and facilitating human conversation. In the case of the medical interview, it is important that the computer should have a good "bedside manner" [8].

To determine the appropriate social content of computer conversations, it is first necessary to understand the social psychology of human conversations. This is considered in detail with reference to the cultural setting of conversations. An analogy is then made between human-human conversations and human-computer conversations, with particular attention to human interaction through reduced communication channels, such as in a telephone conversation.

What makes communication with computers so difficult at present is that they have neither an internal representation which can model the user's needs and behaviour, nor the capability to make "metacomments" about the dialogue itself [9]. The fundamental requirement is for the machine to model and thus interpret the user's task-related and psychological behaviour when communicating, and to dynamically model the conversational interaction itself.

The paper ends with a discussion of how such models could be incorporated into interactive systems and how the important social factors in human conversation could be integrated into computer dialogues to provide a framework for a social psychology of computer conversations.

CONVERSATION AS A GOAL-ORIENTED DIALOGUE

Conversational interaction with a computer involves two participants working towards a common goal in a "cooperative dyadic dialogue". For a computer to successfully support this interaction requires implementation of a model based on an understanding of an equivalent human conversation.

One simple model of communication is provided by information theory: a sender encodes information, transmits it via a channel, and a receiver then decodes the information.

Effective communication requires that the two dialogue partners have a shared world perspective. This should include an acknowledgement of mutual goals and an ability to direct the conversation towards the achievement of these goals. Such a shared model will facilitate the ability of a participant to identify the intended purpose of the dialogue on a task level, and also provide a context for recognizing the other participant's desire to communicate and willingness to continue participating on a psychological level.

Thomas [9] has emphasised that an Encoding-Decoding model is a gross oversimplification of the normal complex process of human communication. He proposes instead a Design-Interpreter model which asserts that one participant designs a message as a means of achieving certain goals, while the partner interprets this message in a context of world knowledge which includes the perceived goals of the other.

Although messages are objectively sent from sender to receiver, the sender requires an internal model of the state of the receiver in order to design a message, and the receiver can only interpret the message in the context of a model of the state of the sender. Thus the design criteria for messages are determined by the sender's model of the receiver. In the context of HCI this emphasises how important it is for the user to have an accurate model of the computer, and for the computer to respond not directly to the user input, but to an interpre-

tation of that input based on global knowledge including a model of the individual user.

Although this implies that the computer requires an accurate model of the user, Thomas [9] suggests that provided the user's intentions are correctly identified, it may be possible to give a "satisfying" response, which will fulfill conversational goals, rather than a literally correct answer. Rich [10] proposes that instead of identifying each user individually, the system could classify users into one of a number of "user stereotypes" which model a canonical user.

A sophisticated model of goal-oriented conversation has been developed by Levin and Moore [11] based on what they call "dialogue games". This model extends Newell and Simon's [12] goal-oriented approach in human problem solving to human language. It suggests that the goals held by two parties in a dialogue are closely related and mutual understanding of the goals is essential for language comprehension. Knowledge of goal structures is used to achieve implicit communication. Thus a statement such as 'I can't make it work' triggers the "Helping" dialogue game and is interpreted not as a statement of fact, but as a request for help. A dialogue game specifies the goals and knowledge state of the participants, and a set of mutually complementary sub-goals which provide a means for achieving the main goal.

However, the dialogue games model only takes account of task-related goals. Social psychological research has shown that people enter into a conversation with more than one type of goal. Three categories have been identified [13] over a variety of social situations:

a) achieving a specific task;

b) social acceptance and developing relationships;

c) one's own physical well being.

Since physical well being is not normally a determining factor in a conversation, this suggests that the two important goal categories are task-related and social.

In computer conversations, the main goal will usually be a task involving giving or receiving information, while any human conversation will also seek to achieve a number of social goals. These social goals often conflict with the task goals, and may include the desire to make a good impression, to increase one's status, to be praised, to influence the other, or to increase or decrease the likelihood of subsequent conversations. An important factor in achieving these goals will be the perception of the other person's personality which will in part be determined by the style of the verbal content of the message, and the associated non-verbal behaviour.

SOCIAL DETERMINANTS OF CONVERSATION

An important factor influencing the nature of a
conversation will be the initial attitudes
towards the conversational event, and towards the
person to be communicated with. There is
evidence that people's expectations of conversational events are primarily based on their
attitudes towards these events [14].

Poyatos [15] has suggested that human cultural
activity can be systematically analysed to define
the determining elements of social behaviour.
This analysis includes consideration of either
the social environment or individual behaviour;
the type of sign (oral, visual, tactile, etc) or
influence (conventions, social roles, etc); and
the location (home, school, office etc). These
define a cultural setting, eg visual environment
in the office. This form of analysis enables one
to identify a number of cultural settings in
which different forms of conversational behaviour
are appropriate.

Each social situation contains a constellation of
cues which help determine initial attitudes, even
before the participants are present. The expectations and subsequent content of a conversation
are conditioned by the social context of the
physical surroundings. Thus a conversation
initiated by "Tell me about your work" would
assume a different significance if started over
lunch, when summoned for an interview, or in a
working environment.

Bennett and Bennett [16] have defined six
important components of the physical environment
in a cultural setting which influence social
behaviour. The first three broadly describe the
the setting: the physical characteristics of the
location; the appearance of the people and any
objects involved; and the spatial relationship of
the individuals. The interaction will also be
crucially influenced by three types of modifiers
to this setting: physical modifiers such as
light, sound or colour which affect the emotional
tone or mood of the interaction; the duration of
the interaction compared with conventional or
subjective expectations; and the order of events
prior to the interaction, and expected after it.
The attitudes generated by these components will
influence the expectations and potential social
goals of the interaction.

The conversation will also be influenced by the
the relative social roles and the perception of
the personality of the other participant. For
example conversation in an interview is initially
constrained by roles, and further determined by
an interviewer who appears friendly, formal, or
hostile. There is also evidence to suggest that
people are more likely to communicate with others
whom they believe are similar to themselves [17].
The social roles will heavily influence both the
social and task goals of the conversation. At
the social level there may be a desire to either

modify or strengthen an existing role or
relationship. At the task level the roles may
determine who controls the conversation, what
topics are acceptable, and the duration of the
conversation.

LEVELS OF COMMUNICATION

During a conversation communication takes place
at three distinct levels:

a) the information content of statements
   made;

b) the verbal style used in selecting the
   particular form of words to express the
   meaning;

c) the non-verbal behaviour, including
   paralanguage (such as grunts), facial
   expressions, and gestures and posture.

Information content combined with complementary
non-verbal signals furthers the task goals.
Attitudinal information about the social goals
can be communicated at any level. However
attitudes are least influenced by explicit
statements. The emotional content of a conversation is rarely expressed explicitly in verbal
terms, and non-verbal behaviour has much greater
emotional impact [17].

When communicating a simple factual statement,
there is an active design process to select
syntax and semantics and express these in an
appropriate verbal style. Since the same facts
can be communicated in many different ways, the
exact choice of words and style can express the
sender's feelings and attitudes. In particular
the "immediacy" of a statement [18] indicates how
close the sender feels himself to the topic of
conversation. To the question "Was it a good
party?", answers with decreasing immediacy would
be: "I enjoyed the party", "I enjoyed the food",
and "They enjoyed the party". It is thus
apparent that a statement made during conversation communicates information beyond the bare
facts in order to support the sender's social
goals.

The process of normal human conversation includes
a wide repertoire of non-verbal signals. It is
often assumed that it is possible to deduce what
has been communicated from a verbal transcript of
a conversation. In fact the meaning of any
utterance is subtly modified by paralanguage
(such as pauses, umms and errs), and kinesic
elements including facial expressions, gestures,
and posture. The linguistic, paralinguistic and
kinesic components combine to give complete
meaning to an utterance [15], so that for
instance, tone of voice and facial expression can
totally change the "literal" meaning of a verbal
statement. Other non-verbal signals can be used
to further social goals quite independently of
the meaning of the verbal communication.

COMPUTER CONVERSATION AS A FOREIGN CULTURE

To what extent are the processes involved in
normal human conversation applicable to computer
conversations? A naive user's experience of
interacting with a computer is comparable to
conversing with a person from a foreign culture
which has quite different social conventions.
Computer conversations involve communication in
order to obtain information or give instructions,
but take place in a strange "culture". While
actual words and meaning to be conveyed may be
clear, there are uncertain conventions for
appropriate social and non-verbal behaviour (for
example to initiate, control, or change the
direction of communication). This makes it
difficult to fulfill task goals efficiently, and
severely limits the range of social goals.

The conventions of interactive computing define a
different culture with its own rules of
behaviour. Deciding how to identify oneself to a
computer (eg by typing HELLO or an ID code) can
be as mystifying as deciding how to greet a
chieftain on a Polynesian island. Within the
computer culture, sub-cultures have become
established with common language and conventions:
behaviour in a CP/M sub-culture can be totally
misunderstood in a UNIX sub-culture.

The computer culture can itself be analysed in
the same way as a human culture. The physical
situation in which a computer conversation takes
place both defines a cultural setting and
modifies expectations about the dialogue by
influencing the surrounding social environment.

In any computer interaction the physical
environment in which the computer is located
feeds initial expectations of the forthcoming
dialogue and sets a cognitive framework for
entering into the conversation. Expectations
based on prior experience mean that different
types of dialogue would be expected of computers
located in a games arcade, on an office desk-
top, or in the rigid functional setting of a
data-entry room. For example, one would be very
surprised in the latter case to be presented with
a colourful screen full of Pac-men!

Just as first impressions are important in human
conversations, so the computer conversation will
be influenced by the appearance of the computer
terminal. A pleasant, welcoming, familiar
appearance will engender positive attitudes.
Other cues such as a manufacturer's name, or
message on the screen, may enable identification
with a particular sub-culture. At the social
level this will influence attitudes, while at the
task level it will give expectations of a
particular dialogue structure.

HOW DO HUMAN AND COMPUTER CONVERSATIONS DIFFER?

Quite apart from the initial social setting,
computer conversations currently differ from
human conversation in some quite fundamental
ways. Only certain types of human conversation
can be emulated, and the computer normally has a
narrowly defined topic of conversation and a
predetermined social style and role so that it is
not seen to respond dynamically as a human would.
There is little scope for metalinguistic commentary and the computer uses a restricted set of
communication channels. This limits the social
responsiveness of the computer, and the relevance
of social goals. Although well learnt social
skills make people responsive to the immediate
social behaviour of the computer, they are aware
that the results of their interaction will not
have the same social consequences in terms of
subsequent attitudes, roles and opinions that
would apply in a human conversation.

Computer conversations tend to emulate certain
limited types of human conversation. Wish,
Deutsch, and Kaplan [19] identified four fundamental dimensions underlying people's perceptions
of interpersonal relations. These were cooper-
ative/competitive, equal/unequal, intense/super-
ficial, and formal-task/informal. Most computer
conversations are intended to be cooperative,
equal, intense, and task-oriented, which puts
them in the same category as business partners.
Care should be taken to ensure that dialogues do
not emulate an inappropriate relationship. For
instance a competitive rather than cooperative
interaction might be associated with business
rivals, while an unequal relationship could be
likened to a computer in the role of parent
treating the user as a child. It is very easy
for the user to feel treated like a child by some
long-winded prompting interfaces, and the
unsympathetic wording in some error messages.

Most existing interactive systems are designed to
support a specific task in a rigid formal manner,
and they incorporate a pre-determined social and
conversational style. Even if the system can
support more than one type of task, each topic is
usually compartmentalised within a specific
operating mode which must be explicitly entered
and exited. Conversation is only possible within
the subject-matter and style of the particular
mode. This can engender a sense of single-minded
purposefulness which limits the flexibility of
the conversation at both a task and social level.
The system may be difficult to use at a purely
functional level, and practical suggestions to
overcome these difficulties include direct
manipulation [20], shortcuts, and mixed-
initiative dialogues [21].

One important feature of human conversation is
the capability for metalinguistic commentary
which enables the dialogue itself to be discussed. At the task level this includes topics

such as the content, speed, and direction of the conversation. Most computer systems provide limited support for metacomments through selecting a different system mode, but this often loses the context of the current conversation. Thomas [9] has emphasised the importance of recognising and acting on metacomments which are embedded in a conversation.

Metacomments are widely used in human conversations to further social goals, such as encouraging the other participant or indicating approval or disapproval of a particular course of action. It is difficult to design computer systems which are responsive to this type of comment from the user, thus limiting the the type of social goals which can be achieved.

It is much easier to incorporate social metacomments in the computer's conversation. Examples include the addition of chatty or encouraging phrases [7], and variations in immediacy [18]. Social goals and rewards which can be obtained from a computer conversation include praise from the computer for answering questions correctly, a feeling of achievement from successful interaction without mistakes, and an increase in status associated with taking control in a mixed initiative dialogue. Well designed computer systems should provide opportunities for the user to achieve all these goals.

The potential advantages of incorporating speech recognition and synthesis in future interaction is indicated by the results of experiments [22] comparing a variety of human communication channels, which showed that interaction was most effective when speech was present.

Existing computer conversations use a limited range of modes of communication. Conventional computer presentation on a VDU means that very little non-verbal behaviour in the form of paralinguistic or kinesic signals is possible. There are comparable circumstances where human conversation takes place with reduced cues, the most common being telephone conversations. The lack of visual cues influences the nature of the conversation by increasing the number of verbal expressions of agreement or disagreement [23] and making interruption of the other participant more difficult [24]. Computer conversations thus require specific provisions to confirm the continuing attention of both participants [23], and to enable dialogue in either direction to be interrupted if necessary.

Some forms of non-verbal communication are possible using a VDU [25]. The changing moods of the communicator can be represented by the form of the material on the screen, which may be confusing, clearly laid out, or highlighted in colour. One of the most important functions of a colour display is to motivate the user through the pleasing appearance and interest of a well designed screen. Another factor is the length of pauses. At a task level guidelines exist for maximum acceptable response times [26]. At a

social level it may be important to introduce pauses where they would be appropriate in human conversation, for instance between the display of self-contained units of information on the screen. In some circumstances an unnaturally short response time can be disrupting [5].

CONCLUSIONS

Humans have complex communicating behaviour encompassing both task and social goals. Social goals as evidenced by attitudinal and cultural factors are important determinants of human conversations. Computer conversations retain sufficient human-like characteristics to be judged by many of the same criteria as human conversations, and people will naturally tend to apply their existing habits, skills and reactions, to computer conversations. The computer will thus be most effective when it accurately emulates the user's implicit model of conversational behaviour.

The principles of human-human conversation can be adapted to human-computer conversation, identifying the problems common to both, and the crucial differences. This process will clarify how computer conversations can be enhanced to more closely emulate human conversations.

For a human and computer to communicate effectively a shared world perspective is required, implying that the user has an accurate model of the computer, and that the computer has an accurate model of the user. In open-ended interaction, the computer's model should include the ability to identify the user's overall goals, and support the use of dialogue games to achieve them. Conventional computer interaction only enables the user to achieve a series of short term goals in an unstructured way.

Existing models of human-computer interaction [9,11,27] emphasise the need to keep track of the user's implicit goals as the focus of attention changes. A true conversational model will extend the goal structure to provide a broader context for the interaction, taking account of the overall purpose of the conversation in both task and social terms. To achieve this requires a clear understanding of the social psychological principles of conversation which have been explored in this paper.

A goal-oriented model of computer conversation based on these principles is being developed by the authors [28] to provide an overall framework for interpretation of the dialogue. The system will include user models based on stereotypes [10], and could be implemented following the principles of general net theory [29]. It is intended to incorporate this model in the design of an adaptive computer interface meeting the requirement that "the machine's image of the user be a genuine psychological image" [30]. We believe it is important that this psychological image is able to respond to the user's complex conversational behaviour.

REFERENCES

[1] Kupka I. & Wilsing N. Conversational Languages, (Wiley, Chichester, 1980).

[2] Kennedy T.C.S. The design of interactive procedures for man-machine communication. Int. J. Man-Machine Studies, 6 (1974) 309-334.

[3] Thimbleby H. Dialogue determination. Int. J. Man-Machine Studies, 13 (1980) 395-404.

[4] Evans C.R. Improving the communication between people and computers, in Shackel B. (ed): Man-Computer Interaction, (Sijthoff & Noordhoff, Netherlands, 1981).

[5] Shneiderman B. Software Psychology, (Winthrop, Cambridge, Mass, 1980).

[6] Cuff R.N. On casual users. Int. J. Man-Machine Studies, 12 (1980) 163-187.

[7] Spiliotopoulos V. & Shackel B. Towards a computer interview acceptable to the naive user. Int. J. Man-Machine Studies, 14 (1981) 77-90.

[8] Bevan N. Meet Mickie, the well mannered micro, in Whitbread M.(ed): Microprocessor Applications in Business and Industry, (Castle House, 1979).

[9] Thomas J.C. A design interpretation analysis of natural English with applications to man-computer interaction. Int. J. Man-Machine Studies, 10 (1978) 651-668.

[10] Rich E. Users are individuals: individualizing user models. Int. J. Man-Machine Studies, 18 (1983) 199-214.

[11] Levin J.A. & Moore J.A. Dialogue games: metacommunication structures for natural language understanding. Cognitive Science, 1 (1977) 395-420.

[12] Newell A, & Simon H.A. Human problem solving, (Prentice Hall, Englewood Cliffs, N.J., 1972).

[13] Graham J., Argyle M. & Furnham A. The goal structure of situations. European J. of Social Psychol., 10 (1980) 345-366.

[14] Pervin L.A. A free-response description approach to the analysis of person-situation interaction. J. Personality and Social Psychol., 34 (1976) 465-474.

[15] Poyatos F. New Perspectives in Non-Verbal Communication, (Pergamon Press, Oxford, 1983).

[16] Bennett D.J. & Bennett J.D. Making the scene, in Stone G. & Farberman H.: Social Psychology through Symbolic Interactionalism, (Ginn-Blaisdell, Waltham Mass., 1970).

[17] Argyle M. Social Interaction, (Tavistock Publications, London, 1969).

[18] Wiener M. & Mehrabian A. Language within Language: Immediacy, a channel in verbal communication, (Appleton, New York, 1968).

[19] Wish M., Deutsch M. & Kaplan S.J. Perceived dimensions of interpersonal relations. J. Personality and Social Psychol., 33 (1976) 409-420.

[20] Shneiderman B. The future of interactive systems and the emergence of direct manipulation. Behaviour and Information Technology, 1 (1982) 237-256.

[21] Nickerson R.S. On conversational interaction with computers, in: Treu S. (ed), User oriented design of Interactive graphics systems, (ACM, New York, 1976).

[22] Chapanis A. Interactive human communication: some lessons learned from laboratory experiments, in Shackel B. (ed): Man-Computer Interaction, (Sijthoff & Noordhoff, Netherlands, 1981).

[23] Wilson C. & Williams E. Watergate words: a naturalistic study of media and communication, (Communications Studies Group, University College, London, 1975).

[24] Cook M. & Lalljee M.G. Verbal substitutes for visual signals in interaction. Semiotica, 6 (1972) 212-221.

[25] Jones P.F. Four principles of man-computer dialogue. Computer Aided Design, 10 (1978) 197-202.

[26] Miller R.B. Response time in man-computer conversational transactions. Proceedings Spring Joint Computer Conference, 33 (1968) 267-277.

[27] Hayes P., Ball E. & Reddy R. Breaking the man-machine barrier. Computer, 14 (1981) 19-30.

[28] Bevan N. & Murray D. Conversational models of computer interaction. In preparation. (1984).

[29] Oberquelle H., Kupka I. & Maass S. A view of human-machine communication and co-operation. Int. J. Man-Machine Studies, 19 (1983) 309-333.

[30] Hollnagel E. What we do not know about man-machine systems. Int. J. Man-Machine Studies, 18 (1983) 135-143.

Human-Computer Interaction — INTERACT '84 / B. Shackel (ed.)
Elsevier Science Publishers B.V. (North-Holland)
© IFIP, 1985

MINIMALIST DESIGN FOR ACTIVE USERS*

John M. Carroll

Computer Science Department
IBM Thomas J. Watson Research Center
Yorktown Heights, NY 10598 USA

Recent studies in computer human factors indicate that novice learners of office systems are "active", preferring self-initiated problem solving to rote drill and practice as a learning strategy. But in high-function systems users may need help in exploring basic functions without being distracted by advanced material. Two experimental approaches to this problem are outlined: The MINIMAL MANUAL attempts to support active learning by providing concise instruction focussed on easy-to-understand goals. The TRAINING WHEELS WORD PROCESSOR encourages exploration of basic functions by disabling the more advanced functions that can distract and confuse novices.

Over the last two years, we have been studying the plight of the first time user of computer word processing equipment ([5], [6], [11] [12]). In our studies, participants were asked to learn basic text entry and revision skills, including the use of menus for formatting and printing, and the interpretation of system messages. We asked participants to "think aloud" as they progressed; that is, to verbalize their thoughts, plans, and concerns regarding the learning task. Learning in this situation appears to be very frustrating. System interfaces are inscrutable to the novice and the accompanying training materials provide little help in penetrating these mysteries.

0.1 Troubles with manuals. Contemporary self-study manuals tend to consist of rather extensive exposition augmented by narrowly focussed exercises and practice drills. However, even though our learners desperately needed this training, they could not use it very successfully in this form. We believe that one reason for this is that people prefer to be active learners. New users we have observed tend to "jump the gun" when introduced to new word processing topics -- including signing on the system. They plunged right into the topic without reading the manual fully or in some cases at all. A second reason, we believe, is that people *cannot* be passive in this learning situation. Learners who tried attentively to follow out the instructions step by step frequently committed small errors that totally side-tracked them. Manuals cannot anticipate the variety of potential learner errors, and accordingly cannot support error recognition, diagnosis, and recovery processes adequately. Even small errors can seriously derail learners, forcing them to resort to active, self-initiated, learning strategies in order to recover. Third, even when learners both attentively followed the manual and avoided the pitfalls of small errors, they often did not know what they had done or why, exclaiming "What did we do?".

Rote descriptions and practice are resisted, and even when complied with, prove difficult to follow and assimilate. But perhaps more important, they are not adequate for communicating the detailed procedural and declarative knowledge needed for understanding and solving problems in a complex task domain like text editing. Learners resort to more heuristic reasoning processes like abduction (generating hypotheses on basis of very limited information) and adduction (verifying hypotheses within these same limitations of information) rather than through more principled reasoning processes (like deduction or induction). These processes produce conclusions that are less constrained, but which open up the possibility of discovering knowledge on the basis of impoverished information.

0.2 Troubles with systems. Analogous problems can be cited with respect to the interface itself. Contemporary systems require new users to master novel and complex design elements that are not always obvious or intuitive. When learners try to find information relevant to their current situation, or to interpret their current situation at all, they frequently focus on considerations that are non sequiturs from the perspective of the system. Conversely, they quite often fail to respect the seemingly arbitrary distinctions that, from the system's perspective, are crucial. One participant, who finally succeeded in executing an operation after more than one try, wondered whether her earlier failures were somehow due to her having hit the ENTER key "in the wrong way". To an experienced user this is a nonsensical possibility, but new users do not know enough to rule out interpretations which seem obviously wrong to an experienced user.

Mistaken interpretations like this create confused concepts -- the user ends up making distinctions that have no real consequence. The cases in which users fail to respect the system's actual fine distinctions are worse, for in these cases there *are* very frustrating consequences. One system we studied has multiple ways of deleting material and of moving the cursor. But the key that moves the cursor on the typing page display, causes an error condition when employed on a menu display. Conversely, the key that cancels menus is invalid if used on the typing page display. Participants in our studies tended, at least at first, not to see these distinctions.

The problems occasioned by users drawing unwarranted distinctions and of failing to recognize actual distinctions also interact to produce tangled -- and very nearly undiagnosable -- hybrids. And this does not by any means exhaust the inventory of problems we have identified. From all this, one might be moved to recommend that learners be discouraged from *any* thinking at all. For it is their reluctance (and inability) to passively accept the system *as it is* that causes most of the learning difficulty we have observed. Nevertheless, the novices we have studied are active learners. They do not passively read or follow along rote exercises. They try things out according to self-generated agendas of needs and goals. They construct theories on the fly to explain what the system does. And they spontaneously anchor much of this active reasoning in their prior knowledge (e.g., of typewriters). (See [2], [7] and [10]).

0.3 The minimalist design program. In sum, the problem seems to be that novices try to learn systems by exploration, although this strategy is perhaps not advisable -- that is, from a more expert perspective -- and, as our studies make painfully clear, is not supported by either the interface design or the manual design of current systems. One can take a hard line here about novice explorers getting what they "deserve" or paying their "dues", but one can also face the facts: we can design systems and training to be pretty much any way we want, but human preferences and propensities are fixed constraints. With this sentiment in mind, I want to outline two projects currently underway: one attempts to provide a manual design that could better support our novice explorers, the second attempts to provide a "training" interface design that might also afford better support for the active learning strategies we have documented.

In both cases, I will be describing designs that were developed iteratively in conjunction with human factors testing with real users (office temporaries). Moreover, as will become clearer below, both the training manual and the training interface were also originally conceived of and then designed in direct response to our empirical studies of people trying to learn to use commercial word processors. Hence, both should be regarded as codified *results* of human factors research, generally and in their particulars. Finally, both projects have involved extensive empirical testing. (See also [9]).

1. The Minimal Manual.

Impressed by the frustration and failure we observed when novices attempted to learn to use commercial word processing systems by means of the commercial self-study books that accompany them, Bob Mack, Clayton Lewis and I embarked on a series of studies of "minimalist" training instruments. At the very beginning of this stream of work, we observed a learner who was given essentially *no* training material whatsoever. Her learning was quite chaotic, but she noticed far more information on the display than her typical self-study counterpart. However, she made only halting and non-convergent progress in learning to use the system [1].

We retreated from this extreme "training" procedure in our subsequent work. In one effort, we have trained operators to use the word processing function of office systems using Guided Exploration "cards" [8]. We ended up with a set of about 20 cards (drastically less than the 150 or so pages of self-study manual). In all of this work, a guiding principle has been that learners simply will not read, and that in particular they will not read purely expository materials or be led through purely rote practice exercises (as opposed to *doing* task-oriented

things). Guided exploration via the cards was a mixed success. Learning by guided exploration is sometimes quite chaotic -- and in their own statements, our learners have often expressed a desire for more structure.

Where can we go next? One possibility is to move toward a manual that incorporates elements of the Guided Exploration approach. That is, we might re-introduce the structure of a manual, but in doing so try also to codify some of the principles we have concluded were helpful to our guided exploration learners. The Minimal Manual was constructed for the core function of a commercial word processor. (For details, see [3]). However, while it addresses the same topics as the commercially developed self-study manual that accompanies the system, its design differs in several key ways:

1.1 Less to read. First, the Minimal Manual is less than a quarter as massive as other primers, 45 pages in all. We achieved this by eliminating all repetition, all summaries, reviews, and practice exercises, the index and the troubleshooting appendix. All material not related to doing things was eliminated or radically cut down (the welcome to word processing overview, descriptions of the system status line, details on the system components, the chapter entitled "Using the display information while viewing a document.", etc.). Novice learners do not read manuals effectively or reliably, hence it may be better to spare them the details and include only critical specifics.

As is now well-known, real operators must schedule their training around a host of other work activities. Designers of self-study primers have responded to this by organizing small, independent modules. The problem is -- as we learned in our prior work -- these modules are in fact not nearly small enough. Learners get lost within them. In the Minimal Manual, topics average less than 3 pages (a fifth the typical length).

1.2 Greater task orientation. Manuals often include chapters like "Using the display information while viewing a document", which no word processing tyro would ever really *decide* to undertake. The creation of a real document is often delayed until halfway through the manual. Yet the creation of a real document is the overriding goal that novices bring to this learning situation.

The Minimal Manual seeks to be more task oriented in that its topics (modules) are directed at real work activities instead of merely rote exercise. Chapter headings are task oriented, the Table of Contents serves as a simple index that even a computer naive person can understand as being meaningful: "What is this thing all about?", "Typing something", "Printing something on paper", "Revising something you have typed", etc. Realistic and open ended work exercises are included, under the heading "On Your Own" (see 1.3 immediately below). One reason to include such exercises is to maintain and foster the connection between training and real work. After all, operators must try to learn to use office application systems in the midst of also trying to do their actual work.

1.3 More learner initiative. The learner is cast in a more active role by the Minimal Manual. Its step-by-step exercises give only abbreviated specifications of procedures, leaving some of the detail for the learner to discover or infer. For example, when the arrow cursor keys are introduced in Chapter 4, explicit practice with the down arrow key is followed by the general statement that the other keys work analogously, and by the invitation to "Try them and see." Or again, when the coded Cancel key is first introduced, as a general error recovery, it is explicitly stressed that the user must "use Cancel by holding down the Alternate Shift key while pressing the Cancel key" (Chapter 1). Our earlier work showed that failing to code such keys is a common error. Later in the Minimal Manual, Cancel is still suggested as a general error recovery, but in a more abbreviated form: "If you make a mistake, press Alternate + Cancel and start again." (Chapter 7).

The learner must fill in the steps -- by referring back in the Minimal Manual, by remembering, or by experimenting. In addition, explicitly *non*-step-by-step exercises, labeled "On Your Own," have been incorporated into the manual at the end of most of the topic modules (e.g., Chapter 4): "As you can see on page 4:3, more deletions, insertions, and replacements are suggested for the Smith Letter document. Practice your revision skills by trying some of these. When you have practiced enough, print out Smith Letter (refer to Chapter 3 for help with printing)."

In our prior work, we have found that self-study books are sometimes so complete that learners spend all of their time with their noses in the book. They may not coordinate what they are supposedly learning with what is actually happening on the display. The Minimal Manual attempts to encourage the learner to attend to the display by posing questions to learners regarding prompts. Thus, instead of merely saying that the system will prompt for a document name, and to type the name and press Enter, the Minimal Manual asks the learner "Can you find this prompt on the display?: "Type document name; press Enter." or gives a contingent instruction "Make sure that the word processor is prompting you: "Type document name; press Enter".

1.4 More error recovery information. Despite these reductions in massiveness, there is one category of information that has been greatly increased in the Minimal Manual. This is error recovery information. Most self-study primers do not provide learners with suggestions as to what they can to do if the step-by-step procedure doesn't seem to work out as it should. If novices are going to explore on their own (willingly or in response to prior errors) they are going to make mistakes and get lost. When this happens, they need help in getting back on course. Error recovery information is a distinct category of information in the Minimal Manual.

Specific error recovery information addressed the chief errors we had inventoried. For example, we had found that learners had trouble with the diskette name concept and often typed an incorrect diskette name when prompted, which had the effect of leaving the system hung up. The system in fact had a specific recovery procedure for this problem, but the commercially developed training manual failed to mention it, and learners did not manage to find it in the ancillary documentation. The Minimal Manual included the specific error recovery information for this error. Another error that was typical for learners was pressing the Cancel key without holding

down the Alternate Shift. Cancel is perhaps the best general error remedy the system offers, but has an entirely different meaning when used without the Alternate Shift, and one which leads to complex side effects. We referred to the key as "Alternate + Cancel" throughout the Minimal Manual, to stress the correct key combination -- and we referred to it frequently (to remind learners of its use in error recovery).

1.5 Reference use after training. People using training manuals also use them for reference. This makes sense since part of the learning that goes on when someone works through a training manual is the learning of the book itself. Nevertheless, learners are frustrated in trying to extend training manuals to a new use as reference manuals because all of the explanations, side-tracks, and drills of the manual become camouflage for the kernel information being sought. Learners we have observed often cannot successfully use their self-study materials as reference aids when they try to cross the bridge from "training" to "using". The Minimal Manual should be more extensible for use as a reference both because it is briefer overall and because it is pitched more explicitly at real components of real work (see 1.2 above).

Finally, the "On Your Own" sections of the Minimal Manual often suggest open ended exercises that refer back to other topic modules, thereby encouraging learners to make use of the training manual for reference. This strategy is based on accepting the fact that learners are going to try to use their training books for reference in any case. Our response is to design the books, therefore, to *train* learners in using them for reference.

1.6 Empirical verification. We have tested the Minimal Manual in two large studies. The first study (designed by Jim Ford, Penny-Smith Kerker, and Georgia Gibson) involved 49 learners who used one of five training methods (including two variations of the Minimal Manual) for up to seven full working days. In this study, the Minimal Manual proved to be 40% faster than the other manuals for the basic topic areas it covered -- and to produce learning achievement at least as good as the other methods. The Minimal Manual only covered basic topics, where the commercial manuals covered advanced topics as well. In a later phase of the experiment, Minimal Manual learners were transferred to the advanced topics sections of a commercial manual. Notably, they still were 40% faster, but in this comparison their performance on learning achievement tests was better by a factor of ten. In sum, this experiment provides evidence that the Minimal Manual design is substantially more effective than comparable state-of-the-art commercial manual designs.

A second experiment is being completed now (with Sandra Mazur) in which 32 learners used either the Minimal Manual or a commercially developed alternative. This study is focussing on each learner in detail for 6 hour sessions. Our goal is to analyze the advantages of the approach more finely than mere time and performance studies afford. We know the approach works, but we still have much to learn about why it works and how it can be optimized.

2. The Training Wheels Word Processor.

The minimalist training materials we have designed face a paradox in the fact that the system function they attempt train against is often rather "maximal". That is, contemporary office application systems are capable of many advanced functions. But advanced functions can create problems for the learner who is not ready for them. How can these problems be avoided? Our approach is to limit the learner to only simple functions, and to make advanced functions unavailable.

2.1 Learning simple things first. Why would anyone want to do this? Put directly, learning something that is simple is easier and less frustrating than learning something that is complicated. This should not sound either trivial or paradoxical. Reading Dick and Jane books facilitates reading Russell and Wittgenstein, even though the former is simple and the latter complicated. Indeed, even in the domain of word processing the general training strategy has been to first address simple function and only then more complicated function. It is merely an extension of this strategy to suggest that we first *provide* simple function and only then provide more complicated function.

How can this be done? This question is not simple. There are possibly as many ways to limit function as there are to provide it in the first place. But one simple and direct method suggests itself immediately. One can "close off", or disable, the function of a full system, providing a message like "X is not available in the Training Wheels System.", with X being whatever advanced function a novice ought not to get into at first. This was the approach taken in the design of the Training Wheels Word Processor (as implemented by David Boor). (For details, see [2], [3] and [4]).

Most basically, one wants a word processor to type in documents, to edit documents already typed in, and to print. From this bare bones perspective, functions like Spelling Aids, Format Changing, Menu Skipping, Save-keys, Pagination, and Merging Data, are extras. In a word, this is the design of the Training Wheels System. One loads the system in the same way as one would the full system. One sees the same Home Menu, the first menu that comes up. But then the limitations begin to emerge. From the Home Menu, one can *only* select "a", for Document Tasks. The other choices merely elicit the system response "X is not available on the Training Wheels System"., with X being choices like Program Diskette Tasks, Data Diskette tasks, Merge Tasks, etc.

2.2 Positive transfer of learning. Notice how this addresses three problems of the novice explorer. First, the need for a training manual has been vastly reduced. (We developed a single Guided Exploration-type card as basic instructional material for the Training Wheels System.) Second, the sometimes reckless novice can safely explore. Menu choices can be tried and tested without fear of inadvertently getting into things like Program Diskette Tasks -- which will be confusing to the first time user, but which are a choice on the Home Menu (and an important set of functions for more skilled users).

Third, the novice -- while "protected" from the consequences of reckless exploration -- *has* seen the choices,

seen the full menus, and even tested the operations involved in making the choices. And all at no cost in terms of side-tracks and the frustration of getting lost. In psychological jargon, these common interface elements provide a basis for "high positive transfer" between the Training Wheels System and the full system interface. For when this novice graduates to the full system, the same displays will appear and the same keys can be pressed. However, instead of the disabled function messages, the full function will be engaged.

To make this point, let us briefly tour the Training Wheels System. After loading the system, the Home Menu appears. The only route open at this point is choice "a", Document Tasks. Having arrived at the Document Tasks Menu, the user can select "a" to create a document, "b" to edit a document, "d" to print a document, or "f" to return to the Home Menu. Printing can only be selected if the user has immediately before selected create or edit. Otherwise, a disablement message comes up: *"Print Document" is only available after a "Create" or a "Edit" document.* We return to this specific disablement below.

All three of Create, Edit, and Print evoke a prompting sequence to elicit from the user a document name and then a work diskette name (just as they do on the full system). When these have been specified, either the Create or Edit Document Menu or the Print Menu appears, depending on what was originally requested by the user. However, none of the menu options on either of these two menus is active in the Training Wheels System. Indeed, the only productive thing the user can do on these menus is to press Enter. In the case of the Create or Edit Document Menu, this brings up the Typing Area, and allows the user to enter data. In the case of the Print Document menu, this causes the specified document to be sent to the printer for printing on paper, and returns the Document Tasks Menu to the display.

Typing Area function can also be complex. Its complexity derives not from a diversity of menu selections and branching, but from a diversity of special function keys, Word Underscore, Required Backspace, Center, etc. These function keys are very useful, indeed necessary, to the skilled user of word processing equipment, but they can confuse the novice. They sometimes perform a powerful function without apparently altering the displayed document (e.g., Required Backspace). None of these function keys are active in the Training Wheels System. The user can type regular alpha-numeric characters and line returns, and can delete by backspacing. But nothing else works.

So far, a stripped down word processing system has been sketched in which nearly everything is disabled and labelled as such by messages of the type "X is not available in the Training Wheels System". It has been argued that the sheer reduction of complexity is a plus for novices, and further that there should be a positive transfer of learning due to the fact that the menus, messages, and prompts that *can* be reached are identical to those of the full system -- and the fact that the disablement messages themselves, by specifically saying "not available in the Training Wheels System", invite the new user to understand that these disabled keys *will* be available in another version of the system, the non-Training Wheels version. These points can be sharpened by examining the specific error states that the Training Wheels System "saves" its novice users from.

2.3 Common error states are unreachable. The Training Wheels System also blocks several error states which seem to be characteristic problems for novices, based on our observational studies. We have already referred to the pervasive tendency of new users to recklessly try menu choices like Program Diskette Tasks (from the Home Menu) only to encounter trouble in returning to where they started their exploratory excursion. We might call this the Exotic Menu Choice error. As noted, the Training Wheels System eliminates this sort of error by responding: *(Program Diskette Task) is not available on the Training Wheels System.* A second typical error is the Print First error. Users really want to achieve something real with system, and fast. It is typical that a new user requests a print on Document Tasks *before* creating any documents to print. The system prompts for a document name and then for a diskette name -- but of course the user has no document name to give, because there is no document to print. As noted earlier, this error cannot be committed on the Training Wheels System because it is impossible to request a print before creating or revising. One gets the disablement message: *"Print Document" is available only after a "Create" or a "Edit" document.*

Perhaps a more frustrating case is the Parameter Loop error. On menus like Create or Edit Document and Print Document, there is a highlighted prompt: "Type id letter; press Enter". From these menus, a user need not choose any menu parameter at all, and indeed there is another message on the display "When finished with this menu, press Enter". However, the latter message is not highlighted and new users never seem to see it. They do see the former message however, and they invariably type a letter to specify a parameter. Having done so, they are now prompted "Type Your Choice; press Enter". Two problems now occur. First, people type "Your Choice" -- which is taking things too literally and leads to a tangle of errors. Second, they correctly enter a choice -- only to again be presented with the highlighted prompt "Type id letter; press Enter". Very frequently, new users *again* go through the your-choice business, redundantly respecifying the original menu parameter, or altering another parameter. This can go on and on, hence the name Parameter Loop. This error state is unreachable in the Training Wheels System because *all* of the parameters on the Print Document and the Create or Edit Document menus are disabled. On these menus, users either press Enter to go on, or Cancel to go back. Nothing else works.

Another troubling problem for novices is the Alternate Shift Error. The full system has a dangerous Utility key. "Dangerous" because it brings up the Utility Menu when pressed, anywhere. Novice users have particular difficulty with understanding the concept of transfer of control [13], and the Utility key abruptly transfers control to the Utility Menu. Thus, a user who presses Utility in the Typing Area is whisked away from the document he or she was working on to a menu offering seemingly inscrutable choices. The problem is further complicated

when the Utility Menu is dismissed (by making a choice and pressing Enter), since control is returned to the state from which Utility was originally called. However, the user has quite typically forgotten all about this state and is as confused by its return as by its original disappearance. This error is relatively easy to make because Utility is the nonalternated variant of Cancel, and users trying to Cancel often get Utility by failing to hold down the Alternate Shift key. The Alternate Shift Error state is unreachable in the Training Wheels System because the Utility key is disabled.

A fifth error is the Print Queue error. Sensibly enough, the full system allows multiple print jobs to be queued. Novices of course lack the concept of a "queue" (they lack the term as well). Moreover, because they often fail to operate the Message key -- either at all or at the appropriate times, novices get inconsistent feedback from the system regarding the success their print jobs. We have found that it is extremely typical that new users issue multiple print requests, not even realizing that multiple prints have been requested. When they (finally) get paper output, they conclude that the print was a success, and they go on to other things. However, the queued prints -- the ones they have not yet put on paper -- remain in the print queue. This leads to several further problems. For example, if the user now requests another print of an entirely new document, and then goes on to put it on paper, the output will be what was queued and not what was just requested. Or, if the user now attempts to edit the document that is in fact queued to print, an inscrutable error message comes up: "(document name) in use." Novice users just don't know what is happening in these cases. The Print Queue error state is unreachable in the Training Wheels System because its print queue can hold only one document. A user who requests a second print gets a message: *Only one document at a time can be printed on the Training Wheels System.*

Another inaccessible error state is the Diskette Name error. In the course of creating, revising, and printing a document, the user is prompted by the system to specify a document name and a diskette name, in that order. The typical case is that the user has one data diskette which is named WORK. Hence, to the prompt "Type diskette name; press Enter", the user should type in the name WORK. New users have trouble with these prompt sequences. They often type the document names incorrectly, and have to retype. However if they mistype the diskette name, say WROK instead of WORK, the system now prompts "Insert diskette WROK". Of course, the user has no diskette WROK to insert. The Diskette Name error state is unreachable in the Training Wheels System because it only accepts the name WORK as a response to the diskette name prompt. Entering any other name evokes the message: *Diskette "WROK" is not available on the Training Wheels System.*

2.4 Conclusion and working plans. The Training Wheels System (1) makes many error states unreachable for novice users, (2) encourages positive transfer of learning to the full function system by maintaining common interface elements, and (3) provides a new sort of solution to the problem of learning by exploration, namely the solution of encouraging -- not penalizing -- such learning effort. The Training Wheels System can be a real "exploratory environment" [1] for learning -- responsive to users (in virtue of its many disablement messages), forgiving of errors (by blocking them), and encouraging active learning strategies. And it can as well be a real step toward mastering the full function of an office application system.

Beyond these considerations, the Training Wheels System might be useful on other grounds as well. First, it could be a very convenient level of word processing function for temporary office personnel. Imagine the situation in which an office temp is required for a single day in an office which is equipped with several word processors. The permanent secretarial staff are advanced well beyond the Training Wheels level of function, but the one-day temp is starting from scratch. This person can be assigned a Training Wheels System with which no very serious errors can be made, and with which something useful can be accomplished, even if not the more skilled jobs involving tables and format changes. Another possible case is the office principle, that recalcitrant discretionary user. These people -- conventional wisdom suggests -- have no taste for manuals or start-up time of any kind. Perhaps a system that is so simple that errors are virtually all blocked, that can reduce its training manual to a single card -- even at the cost of more limited function, is just the environment this class of new user might need to break into the regular use of word processing -- and other electronic office -- equipment. (These possibilities were suggested by David Boor.)

Finally, the Training Wheels System can be part of a new approach to to training. Instead of following through a single manual with a single system, we might imagine the Training Wheels System, with rather spare training materials, as the first module of a training program that could involve several "staged" manual-system interfaces. As a specific case, the Training Wheels System affords all of the function necessary to complete Chapters 1-3 of the Minimal Manual discussed in Section 1 above. The two could be conjoined into a single training program in which the first stage consisted of the Training Wheels System, with its Guided Exploration card or with Chapters 1-3 of the Minimal Manual, followed by the full system, with Chapters 4-15 of the Minimal Manual. Indeed, one could imagine breaking the training into many more stages -- with the possibility of reducing the overall volume of printed material much further than even the Minimal Manual.

We have carried out several experimental evaluations of the Training Wheels System. In the first two studies we asked 24 learners to use either the Training Wheels System or the complete commercial system to learn to type and print out a simple document. In one study we asked learners to learn by the book, to follow the manual in learning, and in the other study we asked them to learn by doing, that is to focus on getting the job done. The results of these studies were quite encouraging: learners using the Training Wheels System got started faster, produced better work, and spent less time not only on the errors that our design blocked, but on the errors we did not block -- indicating a generalized facilitation of

learning. Moreover, the magnitude of these advantages increase over the course of the experiment. Lastly, the Training Wheels learners performed better on a system concepts test we administered after the experiment [4].

Minimalist design gambles on the expectation that if you give the learner *less* (less to read, less overhead, less to get tangled in), the learner will achieve *more*. The early results on Minimalist design are in, and they are encouraging. Furthermore, these early results were not costly in terms of development time: the Minimal Manual and the Training Wheels Word Processor, were designed and implemented at a cost of less than a man-month [3]. It is surprising when both users and developers can get more for less, but it makes for a happy ending.

Note. I am grateful to Clayton Lewis for his comments.

References.
[1] Carroll, J.M. The adventure of getting to know a computer. *Computer,* 15 (1982) 49-58.
[2] Carroll, J.M. Presentation and form in user interface architecture. *Byte,* 8 (1983) 113-122.
[3] Carroll, J.M. Designing MINIMALIST training materials. IBM Watson Research Center (February 1984).
[4] Carroll, J.M. and Carrithers, C. Training wheels in a user interface. *Communications of the ACM,* (1984).
[5] Carroll, J.M. and Mack, R.L. Actively learning to use a word processor. In W.E. Cooper (ed.) *Cognitive aspects of skilled typewriting,* (Springer-Verlag, New York, 1983).
[6] Carroll, J.M. and Mack, R.L. Learning to use a word processor: By doing, by thinking, and by knowing. In J.C. Thomas and M. Schneider (eds.), *Human factors in computing systems.* (Ablex, Norwood, NJ, 1984).
[7] Carroll, J.M. and Mack, R.L. Metaphor, computing systems, and active learning, IBM Watson Research Center (October 1982).
[8] Carroll, J.M., Mack, R.L., Lewis, C.H., Grischkowsky, N.L., and Robertson, S.R. Learning to use a word processor by Guided Exploration, IBM Watson Research Center (January 1984).
[9] Carroll, J.M. and Rosson, M.B. Usability specifications as a tool in iterative development. In H.R. Hartson (ed.), *Advances in Human-Computer Interaction,* (Ablex, Norwood, NJ, 1984).
[10] Carroll, J.M. and Thomas, J.C. Metaphor and the cognitive representation of computing systems. *IEEE Transactions on Systems, Man, and Cybernetics,* 12 (1982) 107-116.
[11] Lewis, C.H. and Mack, R.L. The role of abduction in learning to use text-processing systems. American Educational Research Association, Annual Meeting (March 1982).
[12] Mack, R.L., Lewis, C.H., and Carroll, J.M. Learning to use word processors: Problems and prospects. *ACM Transactions on Office Information Systems,* 1 (1983) 254-271.
[13] Miller, L.A. Programming by non-programmers. *International Journal of Man-Machine Studies,* 6 (1974) 237-260.

Human-Computer Interaction — INTERACT '84 / B. Shackel (ed.)
Elsevier Science Publishers B.V. (North-Holland)
© IFIP, 1985

THE ROLE OF EXPERIENCE IN EDITING

Mary Beth Rosson

Computer Science Department
IBM Thomas J. Watson Research Center
Yorktown Heights, NY 10598 USA

An important question for designers of text-editing systems is the use to which the systems are put by experienced users. Most systems provide a range of function from basic to very advanced, yet their designers typically do not know whether users ultimately make use of the full range of function, or indeed whether they develop effective use of even the most basic function. In the present work, survey and automatic monitoring methodologies were combined to study experienced editor users. The two methods provided converging evidence that not all users learn to exploit a system's facilities simply through continued experience with the system. Many time-saving strategies (e.g., assignment and use of program function keys) were associated with job type and with prior experience on other editing systems. The implications of the results for the design of editors are discussed.

The study of experienced users of text-editing systems is becoming increasingly important, as more and more individuals begin to use these systems routinely. In the past, a good deal of interest and research has focused on the problems of novices learning to use editors, and the implications of these problems for the design of better systems are beginning to be understood [1], [2], [3]. However, it is critical that this understanding be complemented with a similar analysis and interpretation of experienced users' behavior, so that this information too can be fed into system design.

One question of particular interest concerns the extent to which users come to exploit a system's function as they gain experience. In the best of all possible worlds, users acquire new function naturally, as their needs of a system increase, so that experienced users have not only logged many hours of system use, but in so doing, have also developed the most effective methods for fulfilling their needs. But while this description paints quite a rosy picture, we simply have no good reason to think that it is accurate. This is especially distressing, given the current vogue of supplying "fast paths" for the experienced user: we have no real evidence that experienced users use even the most basic function in a system effectively, much less that they also have picked up on available shortcuts!

Initially, the literature appears to support an experience-expertise relationship. Card, Moran, and Newell [4] deduced selection rules that accounted for 80% of the editing behavior of a small group of experienced users, suggesting that these users had fairly well-defined heuristics for carrying out their work. Tyler and Roth [5] added the finding that novices were less likely to demonstrate selection rules than experienced users, preferring instead to rely on a single, sometimes inefficient, strategy. Finally, Folley and Williges [6] demonstrated that when confronted with the description of a novel editor, users experienced on other systems took advantage of more commands in solving paper-and-pencil editing problems than did users with no previous experience.

These experiments provide general support for the notion that with practice, users do increase their knowledge of both general editing concepts and editor-specific heuristics. But Card et al. also report behavior not entirely consistent with this notion: in their first experiment, they observed a strong tendency for users to rely on a dominant method unless it is "obviously inefficient"; in their second experiment, one of the four users showed no selection at all among the methods available. Although it may be the case that users develop *predictable* methods, the *optimality* of these methods remains to be established.

The findings of these experiments must be evaluated in light of another factor as well-- they describe behavior on experimenter-designed tasks performed in a laboratory environment. As a result, it is not certain that the behavior patterns observed would parallel those found in natural editing environments. Particularly in cases where the user is being filmed and timed, he or she is likely to feel an implicit demand for his or her "best" editing behavior. It is important to confirm that behavior observed in these more artificial settings is isomorphic to that of users carrying out everyday editing tasks.

Little research has examined the natural editing behavior of experienced users. The studies that do exist have provided useful information on the general usage patterns of experienced users ([7], [8], [9]), but they have not looked for variation in these patterns across levels of experience. Further, because the focus has been on general descriptions, no attempt has been made to understand what variables -- either in addition to or in place of experience with system itself -- influence editing behavior. Yet an understanding of such variables is key to the design of systems intended for effective longterm use.

This paper reports selected results from two related studies of routine users of a text-editor. In the first, a large number of users answered questions about their prior experience, current use and evaluation of the system; in the second, a smaller group of users selected from the survey population were studied more intensively via computer monitoring. In both cases, the approach was to examine the relationships between editor experience and a variety of usage variables.

METHOD

The Editor.

Xedit is a powerful text-editor combining screen-oriented editing with an extensive repertoire of commands. That is, users can opt to revise text in *fullscreen* fashion, viewing it on a screen, moving a cursor to words to be changed, and typing over, deleting, or inserting characters as necessary. Another option is to execute commands from a command line that refer to particular lines or groups of lines. Xedit also provides a method for easy execution of some commands that operate on lines of text (e.g., copying, moving or deleting blocks of text) from a *prefix area* that is contiguous to the displayed text. Finally, the system allows for extensive user customization through the creation of *profiles* that allow one to set up a particular environment (e.g., controlling various display characteristics, defining command synonyms, setting up definitions of program function keys), as well as through a *macro* facility used for writing procedures to extend the function of the base system.

Data Collection.

Xedit survey. The survey included 18 questions. Some were directed toward general background information (e.g., job, education), some toward editing experience (e.g., length and frequency of Xedit use, types of documents edited, familiarity with other editors), some toward use of particular Xedit facilities (e.g., macro writing, assignment of program function keys), and some toward evaluation of the system (likes, dislikes, suggested changes).

Respondents were 121 employees at the Watson Research Center; all participated voluntarily. Analysis of responses to the background and experience questions indicated that they varied along three major dimensions. First, they reported differing amounts of Xedit experience, with estimates ranging from 1 to 57 months, for 12 minutes to 8 hours per day. These length and frequency estimates were combined to yield an *hours of use* index, ranging from 11 to 5720 hours, with an average of 901 across the 121 users. The users also varied considerably in their experience with other editors, ranging from no prior experience at all, to experience with 15 other systems; the average was 2.8. Finally, the respondents came from three major job categories: there were 32 secretaries, 40 non-programming researchers, and 49 programmers.

Xedit monitoring. The user population for the monitoring work consisted of 38 individuals selected from the pool of employees responding to the survey. The population reflected variations along the three major user dimensions identified in the survey: The Xedit hours of use estimate ranged from 90 to 2640 hours for these users, with an average of 909; their experience with other editors ranged from 0 to 7, with an average of 2.3; and there were 17 secretarial users, 11 non-programmer researchers, and 8 programmers.

Each user was unobtrusively monitored for five days. Although users knew they were participating in a monitoring study, the monitoring itself was invisible to the users -- many claimed to have forgotten that the program was running. The program collected a variety of information about the editing that took place. Information about each command was stored: the string entered, the command executed by Xedit (including an indication of whether it was a macro or not), and whether the command had been entered via a PF key. Also collected were data about the file the command was applied to-- the identity and size of the file, as well as any effects the command had on the file. These effects included changes in position within the file, lines inserted, deleted or modified by command application, and lines changed via full-screen editing activity. Finally, the program collected timing information-- at what time a command was entered, and when its execution had been completed.

RESULTS

The survey and monitoring work provided a great deal of information about the general use of Xedit, as well as the effects of experience on use. Many of these results will not be reported here; for more detailed information, see Rosson [10], [11], [12]. The following discussion will combine the survey and monitoring results to examine several usage patterns --the use of the Xedit macro facility, of programmable function keys, and the fullscreen editing facilities -- that seem particularly relevant to the issue of increased system exploitation with experience.

Xedit Macros.

Survey data. One expectation was that the number of macros written by individuals would be a function of their experience with Xedit. The survey results indicated that on the average, users had written 11.5 macros. However, the variable was highly skewed, with less than half of the users (58) having written any macros at all. Among users who had written macros, the average was 23.4.

Prior to examining the effects of experience on macro writing, the effect of job type were partialled out; because writing a macro is much like writing a program, it is expected that general computer sophistication will strongly influence macro-writing (This was in fact true, with $r = .39$, $p < .0001$). The resulting partial correlation coefficients indicated that macro-writing was strongly associated with the hours of use index ($r = .55$, $p < .0001$ for the effect of Xedit experience). However, it also demonstrated a strong relationship with users' prior experience with other editing systems ($r = .49$, $p < .0001$): users who had used a large number of other systems had written a greater number of macros.

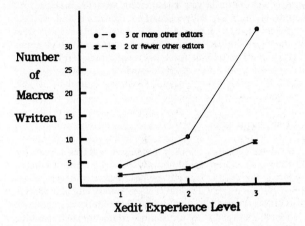

Figure 1. *Macros written as a function of Xedit experience and experience with other editors. The three experience levels represent average indices of 151, 566 and 1915 hours of use.*

As can be seen in Figure 1 (users have been separated into three levels of Xedit experience and two of experience with other editors), interpretation of these findings must be tempered by the presence of an interaction. When all three terms (with the effect of work type partialled out of each) were entered into a simultaneous multiple regression, all predicted independent portions of the variance ($F(1,110) = 11.16$, $p < .002$ for Xedit experience; $F(1,110) = 6.20$, $p < .02$ for prior editor experience; and $F(1,110) = 7.29$, $p < .008$ for the interaction). Users experienced on a number of other systems are much more likely to write macros as they gain experience with Xedit than those experienced on few of them. An important point to note is that the effects of editing history *increase* as users gain experience. That is, it is not simply that knowing about other editors gives one an "edge" early in use of a new one; as users gain experience with a given editor, experience with other editors becomes even more important in customization efforts.

Because these findings are correlational in nature, it is difficult to interpret them with certainty. But one account of the interaction between Xedit experience and experience with other editors is that increased experience with a single system may not be sufficient to induce full exploitation of its capacities. Familiarity with other editors probably gives users a more informed perspective on the potential of such systems, so that they will search out, and if necessary, create for themselves, a richer

system. The challenge for designers of such systems will be to induce learning of advanced function such as this by users unfamiliar with other systems.

Monitor data. In the monitoring work, it was possible to determine how many different macros were used by an individual over the five day period -- their macro repertoire. This measure ranged from zero to 21 macros, with an average of 3.8 across the 38 users. It was also associated with the Xedit experience index ($r = .39$, $p < .02$); a user's macro repertoire increased with experience with the system. However, even though the *use* of macros requires no prerequisite programming skill, and though a number of general-purpose macros are available in public storage, macro repertoire was also strongly associated with job type, in that researchers are much more likely to use macros than secretaries ($r = .41$, $p < .02$). In fact, multiple regression indicated that neither Xedit experience nor job type had an independent effect on macro usage; only the interaction of the two variables predicted an independent portion of the variance ($F(1,34) = 12.91$, $p < .001$). With experience, researchers added a number of macros to their command repertoire, but this was much less likely for the secretarial users.

One possible explanation for these findings revolves around the editing needs of researchers vs. those of secretaries; the editing work done by secretaries may not have any need of extensions to the system. However, examination of the macros used by researchers argues against this, as many of the macros represent very general-purpose extensions of the basic fullscreen editing facilities, extensions likely to be useful to anyone needing even the most basic function in Xedit. A more likely explanation lies in the steps necessary to take advantage of the public macros: discovering and accessing the stored procedures may require more expertise with the operating system than secretaries are likely to have.

Programmable Function Keys.

Survey data. Survey respondents were asked to report their program function (PF) key settings, and the number of key assignments that differed from the defaults was tabulated for each subject. On the average, users had reassigned 5.2 of the 12 keys, and this number demonstrated the expected increase with Xedit experience ($r = .31$, $p < .01$). With increased use of the editor, users appear to discover the PF key settings most appropriate to their needs. However, as Figure 2 illustrates, the work type variable has an even stronger effect on customization of PF keys: the programmers averaged 7.7 key reassignments, non-programmer researchers 4.7, and secretaries 1.1 (the simultaneous multiple regression revealed independent effects of both Xedit experience, $F(1,97) = 6.00$, $p < .02$ and work type, $F(1,97) = 15.60$, $p < .0001$). Note that the two user characteristics do not interact; the difference in key assignment across work types is present even for the most experienced users, whose Xedit experience estimates average close to 2000 hours. This is an important point, as it suggests the difference is not attributable simply to an initial delay in taking advantage of this customization feature-- whatever is producing the differences affects even quite experienced users.

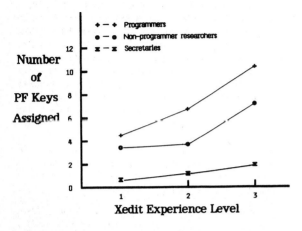

Figure 2. *Number of PF keys re-assigned as a function of Xedit experience and job type. The three Xedit experience levels represent average indices of 151, 566 and 1915 hours of use.*

Two possibilities come to mind in trying to account for the effect of work type on key customization. The first is the usefulness of the default settings. These defaults were prepared with text-editing in mind, and it may be that users who spend most of their time editing text (e.g., secretaries and non-programmer researchers) would find the defaults satisfactory. In contrast, users who edit different kinds of files (e.g., programs, directory files) might need different kinds of functions, inducing them to re-assign their keys. An informal survey of PF key re-assignments, however, weakens the case for this account, as many of the changes made reflect simple refinements of the default settings, or extensions of very general-purpose functions. A more critical factor may be the manner in which PF keys are customized, by making changes to the Xedit profile. This is essentially the same thing as writing a macro (albeit a very simple one in this case), and it seems inevitable that amount of programming experience would affect users' ability to understand and make the necessary changes.

Monitor data. Also of interest was the *use* of PF keys. Thus, a measure of PF key repertoire -- the number of different PF keys, with a maximum of 12, used across the 5-day monitoring period -- was calculated for each user. The measure ranged from 1 to 12, with an average of 7.9 keys. Close to 50% of all commands were issued via PF keys. Surprisingly, though, the measure demonstrated no tendency to increase with Xedit experience. Instead, PF key repertoire was related to users' prior experience with other editing systems. Specif-

ically, increased experience with other *fullscreen* editors was associated with larger PF key repertoires ($r = .50$, $p < .01$).

It may be that the influence of prior experience on the use of PF keys reflects a recognition of possibilities similar to that proposed for the effect of prior experience on macro-writing. That is, perhaps users familiar with systems driven largely by function keys (as many screen editors are) are more likely to recognize and use the potential offered by the 12 PF keys. This suggests that the opportunities provided by the current PF key interface (i.e., its default assignments and their application to editing) must be made more obvious, so that even users without prior experience to generalize from will be able to take advantage of them.

Fullscreen Editing.

Survey data. Survey responses indicated that the fullscreen editing facilities of Xedit (e.g., the ability to move the cursor to text on the screen and type over, delete, or insert characters) were a very popular feature of the system. Reference to these facilities was the most common response to a question asking users to describe "the three things you like most about Xedit", accounting for 23% of the comments offered. However, the questions in the survey provided little information about users' actual use of these facilities.

Monitor data. The monitor study confirmed the popularity of the fullscreen editing option in Xedit, as analysis showed that 93% of the modification transactions (distinct from the insertion or deletion of lines or groups of lines) were of this type. Almost a third of the 38 users relied entirely on fullscreen editing for text modification. Of interest, though, was not simply the frequency with which this function was used, but the effectiveness with which it is used. One component of effective fullscreen editing involves the extent to which users have integrated the use of PF key function with the built-in character modification functions. The use of PF keys while engaged in fullscreen editing can increase efficiency in two ways: First, it allows execution of a command without first moving the cursor to the command line; if PF key assignments are made appropriately, the cursor will also remain in the text area after the command is executed, facilitating additional fullscreen revisions. Second, users can combine the function of the PF keys with the "entering" of fullscreen changes, as the interrupt provided by a PF key causes current screen changes to be saved prior to execution of the function assigned to the key.

Based on this reasoning, a measure of the integration of PF key use into fullscreen editing was devised, representing the proportion of fullscreen transactions that were combined with the PF key execution of some other function. This integrative strategy was relatively common; on the average, users ended 41% of their fullscreen transactions in this manner. However, as for the more general PF key repertoire measure, the variable showed no tendency to increase with experience. Rather, it was again related only to users' prior experience with fullscreen editors ($r = .52$, $p < .002$), suggesting that the development of this specific type of strategy may not occur naturally with experience, but depend instead on other sources of knowledge.

DISCUSSION

The combination of the survey and monitor results indicate that users do not come to exploit an editor's features simply as a function of increased experience with the system. This appears to be true even for very basic features such as the integration of PF keys into simple editing procedures. Rather, variables such as prior experience with other editing systems and job type, seem to have important consequences for the acquisition of effective editing methods.

The findings imply that designers should not assume that users will take advantage of the "efficient" methods provided for them as they gain experience. Part of the problem is undoubtedly motivational -- in some cases, users may well suspect that some better way of accomplishing a goal exists, but simply wish to spend the time to learn about it. This type of problem is a hard one to design away, as it is difficult to provide motivation that doesn't exist. However, designers can certainly attempt to reduce the motivational prerequisite for extending knowledge, by making the new skills as easy and safe to learn as possible. Alternatively, the design might attempt to increase a user's general motivational level, perhaps by incorporating game-like features into the interface (cf. [13]). Still other options involve modifications of social and organizational structures so that they provide greater reinforcement for acquiring expertise.

The implications of the prior experience and job type variables seem more readily amenable to design solutions. So, for example, designers can certainly work to make better methods more obvious, reducing the need for users to have had prior experience on related, but different, systems. One possibility focuses on the design of training and reference materials, in which information might be included not only about how to perform certain procedures, but also about *when* the procedures are likely to be useful. A more extreme approach might be to provide facilities for automatic monitoring and evaluation of users' editing procedures (with their permission, of course), so that suggestions for improved methods can be made.

Much of the effect of job type seems attributable to variations in computer sophistication, and an obvious solution is the elimination of general computing experience prerequisites for the development of more efficient methods. For instance, the designer of an editor might work to develop an interactive, "watch me, now do this" macro facility, one that even users unsophisticated about computers in general would be able to use. Other aspects of customization might be simplified in the same fashion: PF key settings, as well as other environmental variables, could be set interactively, while the user was using the editor, instead of indirectly in a user profile.

In sum, these data provide an important lesson about experienced users of powerful computing systems: not all will learn to use the system as imagined by the designer. The problems accompanying longterm learning -- lack of relevant background knowledge, the desire to "get something done", rather than to learn more about the sytem, difficulty in understanding and executing complicated procedures -- are strikingly similar to those observed for brand-new users [14], suggesting that the design of function intended for experienced users must be undertaken with the same care as that devoted to the design of function encountered by brand-new users.

ACKNOWLEDGMENTS

I thank David N. Smith for his invaluable assistance in developing the program to monitor use of Xedit. Without his help, it would have been impossible to collect information about editing in a natural environment. Pieces of the work reported here also appear in Rosson [10] and [11].

REFERENCES

[1] Bott, R. *A study of complex learning: Theory and methodology*, CHIP Report 82 (University of California at San Diego, La Jolla, CA, 1979).

[2] Carroll, J. M., and Carrithers, C. *Blocking user error states in a training system*, IBM Research Report RC 10100 (IBM Watson Research Center, Yorktown Heights, NY, 1983).

[3] Mack, R. *Understanding text-editing: Evidence from predictions and descriptions given by computer-naive people*, IBM Research Report RC 10333 (IBM Watson Research Center, Yorktown Heights, NY, 1984).

[4] Card, S. K., Moran, T. P., and Newell, A. Computer text editing: An information-processing analysis of a routine cognitive skill, *Cognitive Psychology* 12 (1980), 32-74.

[5] Tyler, S. W., Roth, S., and Post, T. The acquisition of text-editing skills, in *Proceedings - Human Factors in Computer Systems* (Gaithersburg, MD, March, 1982).

[6] Folley, L. and Williges, R. User models of text editing command languages. In *Proceedings - Human Factors in Computer Systems* (Gaithersburg, MD, March, 1982).

[7] Boies, S. J. User behavior on an interactive computer system, *IBM Systems Journal* 13 (1974) 2-18.

[8] Hammer, J. M., and Rouse, W. S. Analysis and modeling of freeform text editing behavior, in *Proceedings - 1979 International Conference on Cybernetics and Society* (Denver, CO, 1979).

[9] Whiteside, J., Archer, N., Wixon, D., and Good, M. *How people really use text editors*, DEC Human Engineering Research Report (DEC, Maynard, MA, 1982).

[10] Rosson, M. B. Patterns of experience in text editing, in *Human Factors in Computing Systems Proceedings* (Boston, MA, 1983).

[11] Rosson, M. B. *Effects of experience on learning, using and evaluating a text-editor*, IBM Research Report RC 10322 (IBM Watson Research Center, Yorktown Heights, NY, 1984).

[12] Rosson, M. B. *Characterizing freeform editing behavior*, Unpublished manuscript (IBM Watson Research Center, Yorktown Heights, NY, 1984).

[13] Carroll, J. M. The adventure of getting to know a computer, *Computer*, November (1982), 49-58.

[14] Carroll, J. M., and Mack, R. Learning to use a word processor: By doing, by thinking, and by knowing, in Thomas, J. C. and Schneider, M. (Eds.), *Human factors in computing systems* (Ablex, Norwood, NJ, 1983).

Human-Computer Interaction — INTERACT '84 / B. Shackel (ed.)
Elsevier Science Publishers B.V. (North-Holland)
© IFIP, 1985

ON-LINE COMPOSITION OF TEXT

S. K. Card
Xerox Palo Alto Research Center
Palo Alto, California

J. M. Robert
NASA Ames Research Center
Moffett Field, California

L. N. Keenan
Xerox Palo Alto Research Center
Palo Alto, California

The use of text-editors for writing original text has been little studied despite the importance of the task. A study conducted by Gould found that the composition rate of writers using a text editor was more than 50% slower than the same writers writing by hand. We show that the source of the slowness is the design of the text editor and that using a display-oriented editor writers can write as fast and good typists faster than by hand. Like Gould, there was no quality difference based on the source of the letters and users of the text editor made many more modifications. Fewer than half of the modifications users made actually improved the text.

The use of computer-based text-editors for the composition of letters, reports, and other documents is now becoming widespread. Business offices, university faculty, and private individuals are purchasing personal computing equipment in hopes that the time-consuming process of writing can be made to consume less time and that the quality of the final product can be improved.

In the history of literacy, many instruments have been used to record written prose. Whether or not these instruments had a detectable effect on the final result, each certainly gave its own color to the process. The slowness of the quill pen must have provided the seventeenth century writer ample time to plan the elaborate conceits popular in the writing of the day. The modern dictation machine, which allows a rapid production of words but preserves no visible memory of what has already been said, must require a rather different mental discipline of composition. Computer-based text-editors can be expected to add their own characteristics to the writing process.

Several studies have examined the writing process itself and the role of cognitive processes in writing (see [1][2][3]). Gould[4] has studied the writing process when different methods of composition (handwriting, dictating, speaking) are used. On the other hand, text editors have been studied for the task when the alterations are already specified (see [5][6]).

Not much is known, however, specifically about the use of text editors for original composition. In one of the few investigations on this topic, Gould[4] conducted a study on the time required to compose short business letters, comparing writing them by hand or with a text-editor. In his study, principals composed eight letters, four by hand and four using the line-oriented text-editor they commonly employed. Handwritten letters were composed at an average of 13.9 words/min, but letters composed with the text-editor were composed at only 8.4 words/min, that is, the text editor required on average 65% more time than by hand. Writers using the text-editor also made many more changes to the letters while composing them (41.3 changes when using the text-editor compared to 8.5 changes when handwriting).

Of course, handwritten letters, with their crossouts and marginalia, are only approximately equivalent to the printed letter of a text-editor. By the time they were typed by a secretary in Gould's experiment, the handwritten letters had consumed more manhours and required more elapsed time than the letters of writers who used text-editors. The letters written in Gould's study were typical business letters of a page or two whereas the advantage of text-editors probably increases as the composition lengthens. There is no question that text-editors are useful for longer documents. Still, it is interesting to understand better what Gould's results have to say about the effect of the text editor on the composition time, on modifications, and on quality of letters. Does a text-editor actually make the composition go more slowly without affecting quality and are the results peculiar to a particular class of editors or to editors in general? To find out, we ran Gould's experiment again but this time with a display-oriented editor rather than the line-oriented editor of his experiment. To insure comparability of results, we used the same set of letters and instructions as had been used in the original experiment.

METHOD

Writers

Eights subjects available at the Xerox Palo Alto Research Center participated as writers in the experiment. All but one (who was beginning a B.A.) had advanced academic degrees and all had used the Bravo text-editor daily for several years to compose memos and papers. Their ages ranged from 20 to 32 years old (average 27 years). These writers typed a mean of 47 words/min (range 32 to 70 words/min) on a five-minute typing test (This includes time to correct their own typing errors and time added to their scores to estimate the time they would have required to correct the errors they left). Gould's subjects ranged from 27 to 50 years old and were research professionals in the IBM Watson Research Laboratory. They typed a mean of 41 words/min. While our subjects had similar occupations and place of employment, they were on the average slightly faster typists, younger, and occupied less senior positions.

Text-Editor

Writers used the display-oriented editor Bravo (designed by Charles Simonyi and Butler Lampson at The Xerox Palo Alto Research Center in about 1975). This editor displays a page of text in black characters on a white screen in an assortment of proportional typographic fonts. During insertions the screen is adjusted after each keystroke to maintain appropriate line breaks and right-margin justification. Users do not type carriage returns at the end of lines. Relative to Gould's analysis of why his line-oriented text-editor took longer than handwriting in his experiment, Bravo should represent a substantial improvement: (1) It uses a mouse for positioning the cursor. Except for the time required going back and forth from the mouse to the keyboard, this should enable the cursor to be positioned nearly as fast as by hand.[7] (2) Formatting is controlled by two-keystroke codes as the user composes the text. The results of formatting commands occur automatically and visibly, with changes updated after each input keystroke. (3) There is no lockout for typing ahead (although users cannot point ahead). The system runs on a personal computer (a Xerox Alto) with reasonably good response time.

Letters

Gould generously supplied the instructions and letter materials provided to his subjects, and these were used with no important changes. There were four letters, each of which had two versions:

Messages Letters. Both of these were short, informal messages about personal data. Subjects were told that the only criteria used to evaluate their performance would be composition time.

Routine Letters. These were replies to inquiries about (Version 1) the locations and model numbers of audio-visual equipment and (Version 2) the schedules and experience of some teachers. The relevant information was available in the documents given to the subjects. Writers were told that their performance would be evaluated on the basis of composition time and accuracy of information.

Map Letters. Here writers had to give road directions to five towns (Version 1) in the north and (Version 2) in the south of California. This task differs somewhat from Gould's comparable task since we used towns in California instead of those in New York and Pennsylvania. The writers were told that their letters would be evaluated primarily upon the accuracy and clarity of their instructions, and secondarily upon the time to compose them. One of the writers mistakenly handwrote the Map Letter he should have composed with the text-editor. His data and the data of the other writer paired with him in the counterbalancing were therefore excluded from the analysis.

Competitive Letters. In these letters, the writers were to attempt to win a contest in which (Version 1) they nominated their favorite teacher for an award, or (Version 2) they tried to convince a customer to order paper supplies from their company. The writers were told that after the experiment judges would select the winner in each contest. Two criteria would be used to evaluate their performance: primarily how well they did in the contest and secondarily the composition time.

Procedure

Each participant wrote two letters of each of four types for a total of eight letters. A letter of each type was written by pen on a pad of paper and the other was written with the Bravo text-editor. The order in which each method was used, the order in which the letters were written, and the particular version of a type of letter associated with a method were counterbalanced across the subjects following a latin square design. The two versions of a type of letter were always written one immediately after the other. The subjects worked three sessions about 1.5 hours each to compose the eight letters. Each session was scheduled on a different day.

At the beginning of the first session, writers were given some general directions followed by a typing test. Then they had to write a very short letter with each method as a warmup to get used to the general procedure. Following this a folder containing instructions for a specific letter was handed to the writer. He opened the folder to read the first instructions about the type of letter that he would have to write and about the criteria that would be used to evaluate his letter. Then he

hit the <DEL> key on the keyboard, read the second instructions about the specific letter to write, composed the letter and hit the <DEL> key again when the task was done. The entire session was videotaped; a separate video-camera recorded the developing prose for the handwriting condition. Beginning and ending times for writing a letter were determined from analysis of the videotape.

RESULTS

Composition speed

There was no substantial difference between the rate at which writers could compose with the display editor (12.2 words/min) and the rate at which writers could compose by hand (12.0 words/min) (see Table 1). The ratios between composition rates using the editor or writing by hand were:

	Display editor/ Hand (This study)	Line-editor/ Hand (Gould)
Message Letter	1.09	0.69
Routine Letter	0.95	0.39
Map Letter	1.00	0.66
Competitive Letter	0.97	0.65
Mean	*1.00*	*0.60*

The ratios for the display editor used in this study are close to one, indicating that text-editing and handwriting rates are nearly the same. The ratios for the line-oriented text editor used in Gould are 0.69 and below (mean 0.60), indicating that handwriting was substantially faster. Our writers were slightly slower than Gould's when handwriting letters, reflecting probably the greater experience in letter writing of his subjects.

Quality of Letters

Like Gould, we could detect no quality difference between letters composed by hand or with a text-editor. Gould assessed the quality of his letters by having a panel of judges rate the letters on various dimensions. He found no differences between the quality of handwritten and text-edited letters. This could have been because there were no quality differences, but it could also be because of the interjudge variability in judgments. As Gould says, "As was the case with the other types of letters, there was much variability in which ones were selected by each of the six judges" ([4], p. 598). Although Gould's judges presumably would have been members of the relevant audience for these letters, they were not necessarily skilled judges of composition per se. Therefore we had an expert judge rate (without knowing which were composed on an editor and which were composed by hand) each of the letters on style, mechanics, and content.

The expert judge had had twenty years of experience as a professional editor and is the author of a widely used handbook on grammar and style. She had no difficulty whatever making swift and confident judgments about specific shortcomings in each of the letters. Each of the letters was presented in an identical printed form (the handwritten letters were first typed) and randomized so she was unable to tell which letters had been text-edited and which handwritten. She was informed of the evaluation criteria given the subjects. Specific shortcomings were noted in each letter and a rating A, B, C, D, or F was given on each of style, mechanics, and

TABLE 1
COMPOSITION RATE

	This study[a]		Gould (1981)[b]	
	Display-editor	Hand-writing	Line-editor	Hand-writing
Composition time (min)				
Message Letter	2.6	2.2	1.9	1.3
Routine Letter	10.3	8.1	16.1	8.2
Map Letter[c]	47.7	46.8	69.4	47.5
Competitive Letter	30.5	29.7	30.6	19.7
Mean	*22.8*	*21.7*	*29.5*	*19.2*
Letter length (words)				
Message Letter	36	34	21	24
Routine Letter	100	88	80	103
Map Letter	483	463	472	510
Competitive Letter	304	280	251	242
Mean	*231*	*216*	*206*	*220*
Net composition rate (words/min)[d]				
Message Letter	17.3	15.9	12.5	18.2
Routine Letter	10.3	10.8	5.2	13.4
Map Letter	10.6	10.6	7.3	11.1
Competitive Letter	10.4	10.7	8.5	13.0
Mean	*12.2*	*12.0*	*8.4*	*13.9*

[a]Each number, unless noted, is the mean of 8 writers.
[b]Each number is the mean of 10 writers.
[c]Based 6 subjects instead of 8.
[d]Computed by averaging rates for each subject.

content. In addition, the letters were rank-ordered according to their perceived overall quality.

Letters written using the text-editor and those written by hand both received about the same overall rating of between a C and a D (in numbers, 3.3 for the text-editor and 3.5 for the handwriting, see Table 2). Both sorts of letters did not differ significantly from each other on mechanics, style, or content.

The mean ranks of the letters are given in Table 3. One of the Competitive Letters appears to receive a lower ranking when written with the text-editor, but the lower ranking was not significant (Kolmogorov-Smirnov $D = 0.125$, $p > .20$).

Modifications

Modifications or revisions can be considered an inevitable part of the writing process. As Murray[8] asserts: "Writing is rewriting . . . And yet rewriting is one of the writing skills the least researched, least examined, least understood, and—usually—least taught." (p. 85) Even in short letters, like the ones in this experiment, modifications are numerous and turn out to be intriguing in a study about the influence of the medium on the writing process. Most of the modifications were made during the course of the composition itself, not at the end of the process. Few subjects waited to begin making modifications until completing the letter.

Writers made many more modifications to their letters when they used the text-editor than when they wrote by hand (see Table 4). They made an average of 23.3 modifications to each letter using the display editor, but only 5.0 when composing by hand, a factor of 4.6. The number of modifications when using the display-oriented editor was about half that used by Gould's writers with the line-oriented editor. This difference reflects the economy in commands that can be achieved in a display editor and was undoubtedly a major contributor in the faster composition rates achieved with the display-oriented compared to the line-oriented editor. This is confirmed by noting that the difference in the number of commands used for the two editors is greatest in those letters requiring more formatting (the Routine and Map Letters).

Gould's writers also made more modifications than ours when handwriting the letters (8.5 for his compared to 5.0 for ours), but these are entirely due to the Map Letter and probably means that our writers found it somewhat easier to find their way in California than his in New York and Massachusetts, a fact well known among Californians.

Reasons for Modifications

Why do writers make so many more modifications when they use a text editor than when handwriting? One possibility is that they make more typing errors than handwriting errors, so the numbers reflect the extra time spent correcting these. Another possibility is that writers make more modifications because the editor provides more features for the user as well as more distinctions he must manipulate. For example, the text-editor used in this experiment allowed users to set tabs, change the margins, or set the typefonts (or even color) of individual words. A writer composing by hand would not make a separate modification to set tabs, he would simply place his pen at a certain place; he would not reset the left and

TABLE 2
MEAN QUALITY OF LETTERS
(1 = Best, 5 = Worst)

	Display Editor	Handwriting
Mechanics	3.2	3.5
Style	3.7	3.8
Content	3.1	3.3
Mean	*3.3*	*3.5*

NOTE: Message Letters are excluded from the analysis. Results are based on 8 subjects for the Routine and Competitive Letters and on 6 subjects for the Map Letters.

TABLE 3
MEAN RANK OF LETTERS FOR QUALITY[a]
(1 = Best, 8 = Worst)

	Display Editor	Handwriting
Routine Letter	4.5	4.5
Map Letter[b]	4.8	4.8
Competitive Letter	5.1	3.8
Mean	*4.8*	*4.4*

[a]Message letters excluded.
[b]Based on 6 instead of 8 subjects.

TABLE 4
NUMBER OF MODIFICATIONS
(Based on four subjects)

	This study		Gould [4]	
	Display-editor	Hand-writing	Line-editor	Hand-writing
Message Letter	2.8	0.5	2.3	0.7
Routine Letter	15.8	4.0	30.8	3.7
Map Letter	37.8	5.5	86.9	20.3
Competitive Letter	36.8	9.8	45.0	9.3
Mean	*23.3*	*5.0*	*41.2*	*8.5*

right margins after typing the letter–only by recopying the letter could he achieve this effect; he would not think of expressing himself through creative typography. A final possibility, of course, is that writers make more modifications because they spend more time refining the text, since the text-editor makes this easier to do.

As Table 5 shows, this last hypothesis appears to be the correct one. Each of the modifications for the Competitive Letters (the only letters in which any real compositional skills were utilized) was examined to ascertain the probable reason why the modification was made. The table shows increases in the number of modifications made within almost every category, but the bulk of the modifications (74%) are to refine the text. This is lower than the 80% devoted to refining the text when for handwriting, a reflection of the extra burdens and opportunities of using the editor. Still 73% of the *increase* in the number of modifications comes from increases in the number of modifications devoted to refining the text:

	Modifications			
	Display Editor	Hand-writing	Dif.	%Dif.
Extra work	17	1.5	15.5	+ 16%
Extra distinctions	13.3	3	10.3	+ 11%
Refining Text	103	32	71	+ 73%

Effectiveness of Individual Modifications

If so much of the increase goes into refining the text, one would think that the text-editor produced text would receive higher quality judgments than the handwritten text. Yet neither we nor Gould were able to detect substantial, reliable quality differences among the two sources of text. We therefore had our expert judge rate the individual modifications to the Competitive Letters to determine whether they improved the letter, did not matter, or made it worse.

Only about half (45%~49%) of the modifications did improve the letters, 37%~45% seemed not to make any difference, and 10%~14% actually made the letters worse (Fig. 1). Interestingly, the text-editor had slightly more modifications that improved the letter than for the hand written letters (49% vs. 45%), but it also had more modifications than handwriting that made it worse (14% vs. 10%).

DISCUSSION

Our main conclusion is that letters can be composed at least as fast on a well-designed text-editor as by hand. It has never been in doubt that this is true when the total time-cost of composition is in question. In Gould's study[4], the mean number of words written divided by the mean letter preparation time, over all his letters and including secretarial and proofing time was 7.3 words/min for the line-oriented text-editor and 6.2 words/min for writing by hand (computed from Gould's Table 1). It has furthermore never been in doubt that text editors speed the process of preparing even

TABLE 5
REASONS FOR MODIFICATIONS
(Competitive Letter, Based on 4 subjects)

REASON FOR MODIFICATION	NUMBER	
	Editor	Hand
EXTRA EDITOR-INDUCED WORK		
TYPOGRAFICAL ERRORS	13	1.5
Example: *careingly --> caringly*		
EDITOR SPECIFIC ERRORS OR METHODS	4	0
Example: *[Undo time insertion]*		
TOTAL	17 (12%)	1.5 (4%)
EXTRA EDITOR FEATURES OR DISTINCTIONS		
FORMATTING	13.3	1
Example: *[Insert blank lines between paragraphs]*		
PAGINATION	0	2
Example: *[Number the page]*		
TOTAL	13.3 (10%)	3 (8%)
REFINING OF THE TEXT		
REWORDING	39.8	17.5
Example: *several different --> a variety of*		
RESTART	27	5
Example: *Another important part of our --> An important policy of ours*		
DEVELOPMENT	17	5
Example: *to- buy 1000 reams of white bond paper --> to buy 1000 reams of 8-1/2 x 11 white bond paper*		
CONTENT	12	2
Example: *[Add several sentences between two existing sentences.]*		
PUNCTUATION	7.2	2.5
Example: *, --> and*		
TOTAL	103 (74%)	32 (80%)
GRAND TOTAL	139 (100%)	40 (100%)

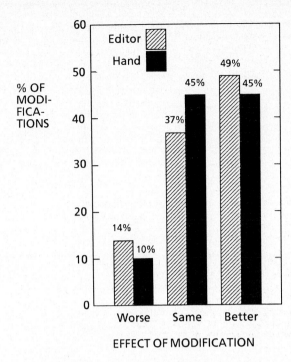

Fig. 1. Effect of individual modifications on the text.

TABLE 6
COMPOSITION RATES (words/min)
(Each number based on 4 writers)

	Slow Typists (Ave 34 wpm)		Fast Typists (Ave 59 wpm)	
	Display-editor	Hand-writing	Display-editor	Hand-writing
Message Letter	11.5	13.7	23.1	18.1
Routine Letter	9.2	10.4	11.5	11.1
Map Letter[a]	9.3	9.6	11.8	11.6
Competitive Letter	7.2	10.2	13.5	11.2
Mean	*9.3*	*11.0*	*15.0*	*13.0*

[a]Each number based on 3 writers.

moderate-sized documents to which relatively small amounts of new text or corrections are being added (almost all reports and similar documents quickly reach this state) since the unaltered text need not be typed or otherwise reproduced. But Gould's results suggested that the raw composition rate with text-editors is slower, that "text-edited letters required 50% more time to compose than did written letters" ([4], quoted from abstract). Our results show that the slower composition times are not a property of text-editors in general, but are a function of text-editor design.

What opportunities are there for a text-editor to speed raw composing speed beyond what can be accomplished by hand? There would seem to be at least the following:

Faster input. One way in which text-editors enable faster composition is simply by allowing writers who type well to increase the rate at which they can physically get down the words of their composition. This factor is well-known in our laboratory where several computer scientists type at rates in excess of 100 words/min and make full use of this rate to generate their papers and books. We purposefully chose writers for our experiment who varied in typing speed so as to be able to assess the effect on their composition speed. As we can see from Table 6, the four fastest typists were much faster writers (15.0 words/min) than the slowest four typists (9.3 words/min). This was not only true for a trivial writing task (the Message Letter) in which we would expect typing skills to be a great advantage but also in the most composition intensive task (the Competitive Letter). In both of these the fast typists composed their letters about twice as fast as the slow typists. The exception to this rule was one writer who was both the slowest typist and one of the faster writers. In general, though, typing speed was directly related to composing

speed with about 3 additional words/min of typing speed translating into 1 additional word/min in composing speed (based on the Competitive Letter).

Interestingly, the fast typists were also a bit faster at handwritten composition.

Help with difficult text. Another opportunity for the text-editor to speed writing is with difficult text. With difficult text, the writer churns through heavy revisions of restarts, recastings, and rewordings as he is writing. When this is done on paper, the resource of the white space on the paper quickly becomes consumed and the crossouts and marginalia become difficult to decipher. By contrast, in a display editor such as the one used in this experiment, the text is neat and easily readable after every keystroke. Alternative wordings can be temporarily stored in the text to disappear as the way becomes clear. Indeed it is common for users of these systems to complain that they find it very taxing to compose difficult text without the editor.

Enabling of new writing strategies. Studies of writing have identified a number of strategies writers employ to produce text. Text-editors enable a new set of strategies, such as quickly laying down headings and notes, then gradually expanding them; or leaving elipses in the text where the writing is routine so as quickly to be able to sketch out a series of ideas before they are forgotten.

An interface to document processing. A final opportunity for aiding the composition derives from the fact that once a partial composition is in a computer processable form, the power of the machine can be brought to bear as an aid. Spelling checkers are one example. Devices for the detection of writing lapses (split infinitives, which hunts, etc) are another example. The use of computer based specifications for bibliography formats, heading style, footnote numbering, etc. is an obvious way to make substantial improvements in composition rates. Finally, the use of artificial intelligence and linguistics based tools that take into account the structure and content of the document could be of aid.

Handwritten composition is not a bad benchmark against which to measure the performance of computer-based text-editors for writing. Paper and pen comprise a simple, rapid, and supple system for writing. Good computer-based writing tools should not fall below this simple standard, nor, our results suggest need they.

REFERENCES

[1] Cooper, C. R. and Oddell, L. (eds.), Research on Composing: Points of Departure (National Council of Teachers of English, Urbana, Illinois, 1978).

[2] Gregg, L. W. and Steinberg, E. R. (eds.), Cognitive Processes in Writing (Lawrence Erlbaum Associates, Hillsdale, New Jersey, 1980).

[3] Rosenberg, S. (eds.), Sentence Production: Developments in Research and Theory. (Lawrence Erlbaum Associates, Hillsdale, New Jersey, 1978).

[4] Gould, J. D. Experiments on composing letters: Some facts, some myths, and some observations, in L. W. Gregg and E. R. Steinberg (eds.), Cognitive Processes in Writing (Lawrence Erlbaum Associates, Hillsdale, New Jersey, 1980), 97–128.

[5] Card, S. K.; Moran, T. M.; and Newell, A., The Psychology of Human-Computer Interaction, (Lawrence Erlbaum Associates, Hillsdale, New Jersey, 1983).

[6] Embley, D. W. and Nagy, G., Behavioral aspects of text editors, Computing Survery 13 (1981), 33–70.

[7] Card, S. K.; English, W. K.; and Burr, B. J., Evaluation of mouse, rate-controlled isometric joystick, step keys, and text keys for text selection on a CRT, Ergonomics 21 (1978), 601–613.

[8] Murray, D. M. Internal revision: a process of discovery, in C. R. Cooper and L. Oddell (eds.), Research on Composing: Points of Departure, (National Council of Teachers of English, Urbana, Illinois, 1978), 85–103.

VISUAL AND DISPLAY CHARACTERISTICS

Human-Computer Interaction — INTERACT '84 / B. Shackel (ed.)
Elsevier Science Publishers B.V. (North-Holland)

LEGIBILITY OF THE VDT REQUIRED FOR HIGH PERFORMANCE TASK

Hiroshi TAMURA
Noboru TAKEMATSU

Faculty of Engineering Sciences
Osaka University
TOYONAKA, OSAKA, JAPAN 560

This paper proposes an experimental method to evaluate legibility of the display and efficacy of the pointing device, to be applied to compare human performance both at VDT and paper-pencil system. The result confirmed the performance is still considerably low compared to the paper-pencil system. The difference is larger for the task of the higher work load. The measure of performance defined in this paper may be used as the objective of improving devices.

1. INTRODUCTION

One aim of developing a modern work station is to realize the paperless office. Computer assisted offices have great merits in processing data, copying and editing documents. These data and documents are usually monitored and corrected on the video display terminal. However, error detection and correcting behaviour on the video display terminals furnished with the CRT and the pointing device is not so efficient as in paper-pencil systems.

In view of the human productivity, there is an urgent need to improve legibility of video display and manupilation of the pointing device. What seems crucial in improving the legibility, is choice of the appropriate measure of legibility, as well as the task adopted to the evaluation.

First in this paper, the requirements to be fulfilled by the task to be applied to the legibilty evaluation are discussed. With regards to these requirement, a set of tasks to be applied to the legibility evaluation is proposed. These tasks may have different work load and can be applied to the evaluation of both paper and CRT legibility.

Performance loss due to the use of the key input and the video display are measured using these tasks. The loss increases with the increase of the task level. Only the performance evaluation is reported in this paper. Psychological and physiological strain of the operator are also measured in the experiment to be reported elsewhere.

2. TASK REQUIREMENT

Integration of various elemental functions are necessary even to perform a very simple task. Among them are visual, perception, short and long term memory, comparision, linguistic and social knowledge, logical decision, response and response check functions.

In view of legibility evaluation, the task should have the higher weight on the visual function and the less on knowledge, memory and decision logic. The response method should be so simple and clear that ordinary operators can perform it at the minimum endeavour without special exercise.

In some cases, reading of sentences is used for the task. In this case, transformation of the visual stimuli to the oral motor behaviour would be the greater effort than the perception of characters. In reading exact perception of the individual character is not required.

In other cases, simple arithmetic operation, like adding numbers of one digit, is used. Here the perception of digits is necessary for the correct response, but his main effort may be concentrated in the arithmetic operation instead of perception of digits. Correcting mis-spelling in sentenses or differetiating animal name from plant are other types tasks. The task which require specific knowledge to the operator is not appropriate. But on the contrally, any task requires certain knowledge to some extent. Use of the ramdom dot patterns will be a possible way of eliminating knowledge effect of individual subjects. But the rarely experienced pattern will require long time of adaptation to the task. Thus the use is knowledge should be limited to those which have already well established in the operator. Perception of character would be done by such knowledge. Legibility of the letter face is also a matter of subject in those countries in which complex characters are used in the sentences.

Operator's capability to the key board operation is also effecting the performance of video display terminals. In case of legibility evaluation, effect of key board operation should be minimized as much as possible. For this purpose, the number of keys to be used for the responses should be so much as that of ten-keys.

In addition to the above requirements, the following items are considered in the design of the tasks used for the legibility evaluation:

1) The task can be applied either to paper or video display work,

2) without modification to the hard and software of the systems, commercially used.

3) Not only the performance of the system as total, but also its component devices together with their envirnment can be evaluated.

4) The task may have vast variety and the work load can be adjustable.

5) The response method of task is so simple that anyone who can read letters may easily participate.

3. LEGIBILITY EVALUATION

The following is the outline of the task designed for the legibility evaluation of the video display terminal.

1) On the screen of the video display are shown several lines of characters. Suppose 40 characters are in a line.

2) The operator is asked to find out a target sequence inplanted in the lines. The target is a sequence of the same characters in case of level 1 task.

3) When the target is found, the operator moves the cursor to the location of the target using step keys or other pointing device.

4) Then the operator moves his eye sight to the timer which is located near the display and read the time of detection. He is required to inserts the reading of the timer to the space erea under the target. The number of the digits required for the reading is preferrably 2.

5) The operation may continue from several to ten pages. Scolling may be avoided within a page. When a new page is opened, the reading of the timer is also inserted at beginning on the top of the page.

In case of paper work, the same text is printed on the paper, and the reading of the timer is written down by the pencil to the text.

In Japan at least four kinds of characters are in use: hirakana, katakana, kanji and Arabic numerals. Usually they are used intermixed in a sentences. In many computer terminals only katakana and alfa-numeric were available. These katakana terminals have been evaluated to have low legibility by most users.

Some pages of the text are made up of the lines consisting only of katakana, hirakana, kanji or numeral for the comparision of usual Japanese writing in which kana and kanji are intermixed together.

The specific characteristics of the CRT used in the video display terminals are listed in Table 1.

There are some reasons to postulate that phospher light with a narrow spectral band will impose strain to the lens accommodation systems of the human eyes. For this reason the phospher ingredients are carefully adjusted so that the phospher light may have a broad spectral width.

Level of Visual Work Load

Four levels of task are defined depending on the visual work load. Japanese and English version of the text for each level are shown in Fig.1.

Level 0

Text whose targets are clearly marked so that the subject can identify them at a glance. Thus the visual search is not required in this level. The subject has to read the timer, and insert it to the location where a target is identified. This level of task is introduced to evaluate subject's adaptation to keyboard operation.

Level 1

The target is the sequence of the same two characters in a line. The number of the targets in a line is fixed to 2, and this was informed to the operator in advance. Thus the operator may move to the next line as soon as he find the second target in a line.

Level 2

The target is the sequence of three letters with the same letter in the head and the tail. For the successful detection of this target, the subject has to use extended visual search field or frequent eye movement. The work load increases considerable at this level. The number of the targets in a line is fixed to two and this is informed to the operator.

level 3

The target is same as in level 2, but the number of target is not fixed. Thus the operator has to inspect every part of the line thoroughly and inspect it again lest he may not fail to find remaining targets. When number of targets is not fixed, the search time increases. The actual number of targets in a line is from one to three with the average of two.

4. ANALYSIS OF PERFORMANCE

The performance is evaluated by average search time and number of failures, mis-detections and long searches. The failure is the target not detected in the trial. Mis-detection is the operator's reporting non-target. In the level 1 and 2 tasks, a mis-detection is normally accompanied with a falure. In the level 1 and 2 tasks, the failure is seldom, since the operator may search for the target until they may count up to the fixed number. So it sometimes take long time for the operator to detect a rest of the target in a line. In the analysis of the search time, the search time which is extremely long compared with most others has been found. It might in some cases due to ill operations of the step keys, and in other cases due to temporal failure of visual functions.

In calculation of the average search time, such long search time had better be excluded. Thus we adopted following procedure to differentiate the long search time from the normal. And the number of errors is defined as the sum of the number of failure and the long search.

From the differece of the recorded time of detection, a sequence of search time corresponding to a target is determined for each page. Then the sequence is arranged in the ascending order. Here it is denoted by

$$x_1,\ldots,x_i,\ldots,x_n$$

$$0 =< x_i =< x_{i+1}$$

Now the average of the x's excluding upper and lower 2k elements is to be obtained. The average and the standard deviation of the x's may be denoted by A_k and S_k. They are determined by

$$A_k = \frac{1}{n-2k} \sum_{i=k+1}^{n-k} x_i$$

$$S_k = \sqrt{\frac{\sum x_i^2}{n-2k} - \frac{(\sum x_i)^2}{(n-2k)^2}}$$

$$k = 0,1,2,\ldots$$

If the inequality:

$$A_k - A_{k+1} < max(0.5, 0.2S_k)$$

is satisfied, A_k is the average search time

of the page. Otherwise, X_{n-k} is regarded as a long search, and excluded from the averaging. Then increment k by 1, and repeat the above procedure again.

5. AVERAGE SEARCH TIME

The search time averaged over a page is dependent on the character type and task level. In Fig.2 the average search time for the different character types are plotted to the paper work of the three levels, and the VDT work of level 3.
From these plots, considerable difference in average search time is observed between level 1 and 2, but the difference is small between level 2 and 3. This may be due to the fact that the target itself is essentially same in these levels. Another difference is marked between paper and VDT of the level 3. This may be due to insufficient legibility of the CRT and other input devices.

When character types are compared, kana-kanji sentence is shortest in search time at all levels. Katakana or hirakana sentences were sometimes supposed to be easier to read, but actually they were not. The search time of number(r) of level 3 is not shown due to some artifact included.
As shown in Fig.1c, a trial was composed of 10 pages of operation. After the search time is averaged over a page, it is averaged again to derive that of a trial. Hereafter the average search time denotes that of a trail.

6. TASK ADAPTATION

In Fig.3 is shown records of 4 operators who are all young and well accustomed to use keyboard and VDT. The experiments were done in two days. At the beginning and at the end of the each day work, level 0 task was applied in order to estimate adaptation to the key board operation of the work station used for the experiment. Every operator showed certain improvement in performance during the day, but the improvement in the second day is less apperant than in the first.

The two (KT & IW) among the four showed more apperant improvement in level 0 tasks and improvement of level 1 performance is associated to that of level 0. Thus the task adaptation is made mainly in key board operation for these operators and the visual search function was alreay well adapted to the task.

For the rest of the operators ,the improvement in the level 0 task is less dominant, while their average search time is considerably large for the level 1 task. Thus for them the visual search was more strain than the key operation. They showed apperant improvement in performance of the level 1 task. This result is suggesting a possibility of applying the tasks to the evaluation of adaptation process individual operator.

Since the visual work load of the level 1 task is not so high, the final performance of the level 1 task is not very different from that of the level 0.
It seems very interesting that although the operators felt considerable fatigue at the end of each day's work, their performance was still on the way of improvement.Thus the performance itself cannot be used as the measure of fatigue or the stain.

7. PAPER AND VDT WORK

Now the performance of the paper and VDT work is compared. For this experiment, VDT-II was specially prepared to have better legibility and less eye strain. The raster frequency was highered to 66Hz and long persistance phospher was adopted. The phospher components were carefully chosen , so that the phospher light may have wide spectral band width.
In this experiment, two operators who are well accustomed to VDT operation and aged around 20 have participated. They showed steady performance during four day experiments, except the one KW on the first day, whose performance was too low. So his result of the first day was rejected from the data.

The abscissa of the Fig.4 is taken to the level of the task, and the ordinate is taken to the average seach time. For the paper work, the level 0 task was not tested, since the work load of level 1 task is not so high and the performance of the level 0 and 1 task are almost equal, as it can be seen from the case of VDT work.
Now the performance of paper and VDT are compared at the level 1 task. The difference can be understood to be due to insufficient specifics of the step key and insertion operation compared to the paper and pencil input. It may be the target of the developing an more efficient input sytems.

When performance of level 1, 2 and 3 are compared, the average search time increases more in VDT than in paper work. In Table 2 is shown the error rate of the operators. For the level 0 and 1 task, the failure is almost 0. But for the level 2 task some difference in the long seach is noticed, denoted by *, between paper and VDT work.
In the level 3 task, the sum of the long search and failure is almost at a level both

in paper and VDT task.

8. Conclusion

The computer assisted office can achieve high performance successfully in many aspects, but when viewed from the human performance, the efficiency of display and input device has not reached to the level of paper-pencil system. It seems necessary to obtain some more basic data on the human performance, in order to achieve essential improvement in interface between man and computer.

Level 0
まずここで示す新手法の特特は母休ガラス組成に産科モリブ
　　X　　　　　　　　　　X

Level 1
差周波光と和周周光を発生させることとより、成功したので
　　　　　　　12　　　　　　　　14

Level 2
東北東に駐車場、1階に展示場、商茶喫茶室が設けられら、

Level 3
新会社はしかし優秀な技術を背暴に、ますますこの分野で先

a) Japanese version

Level 0
Error detection and correction behaviour
　x　　　　　　　　　　　X
Level 1
on the good video display temminal is

Level 2
not so efficient as in paper pencil

Level 3
systems. Hirakana   sentences are more

b) English version

```
kana-kanji    2 pages
hirakana      1
kanji         2
kanji phrase  1
katakana      1
number        1
kana-kanji    2
            -------
total         10
```

c) page structure of the trial

Fig.1 Text Samples of the level 0-3 task

Table 1 Specific characteristics of the
         Video display

VDT	I	II
frame rate(Hz)	50	66
interlace	non-	with
persistence	medium	long
spectral band	wide	wide
peaks	2	3
color	white	white
dot/character	24*24	24*24
character/line	40	40
line/page	14	42

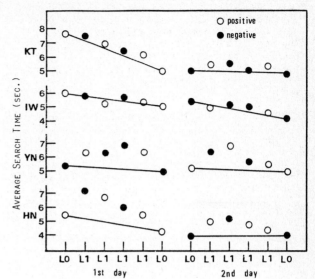

Fig.3 Task Adaptation of the four
        Operators

Table 2 Error Rate of VDT and paper work
         (in %)

level	operator work	K VDT	K Paper	M VDT	M Paper	
1	LS	1.4	1.1	.6	.5	
	F	0	.7	0	.1	
	SUM	1.4	1.8	.6	.6	
2	LS	4.6	2.9	4.3	2.7	*
	F	.3	.5	1.2	.0	
	SUM	4.9	3.4	5.5	2.7	
3	LS	1.9	2.3	.5	2.8	
	F	9.3	8.6	7.7	6.7	
	SUM	11.2	10.9	8.2	9.5	

SUM = LS + F
LS: long search
F : failure

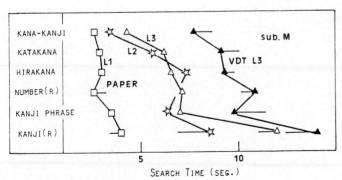

Fig.2 Search Time for the various text
       Characters and Task Levels
       (r) : random sequence

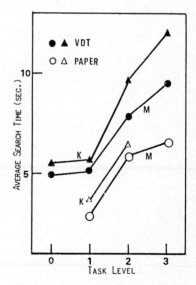

Fig.4 Average search Time of the Paper
      and VDT work of the various Task Levels

Human-Computer Interaction — INTERACT '84 / B. Shackel (ed.)
Elsevier Science Publishers B.V. (North-Holland)
IFIP, 1985

65

AN INVESTIGATION OF VISUAL DISCOMFORT AMONGST CLERICAL WORKERS WITH SPECIFIC REFERENCE
TO THE VDU AS A POTENTIAL CAUSAL FACTOR

Howell Istance and Peter Howarth[1]

Institute for Consumer Ergonomics
University of Technology, Loughborough, UK

This paper reports the results of a field survey of visual discomfort amongst 192
subjects divided into 4 occupational groups. Each subject was studied over the 5
consecutive days of a working week. Pre-work and post-work recordings of subjective
symptoms were made on each day and of objective measures of visual function on 2
days. It was intended that the four groups comprise two matched pairs of 'VDU-users'
and 'non-VDU users'. Post hoc analysis showed that one of the two pair of groups
could be considered thus. No significant differences were found between the
'VDU user' group and the 'non-VDU user' group in terms of subjectively reported
visual discomfort or objective measures of visual function.

1. INTRODUCTION

As the number of Visual Display Units (VDUs)
used at workplaces in industry and commerce has
increased, so has public concern over the
possibility of adverse effects to the health and
well being of those individuals who use them.

Studies in the early seventies discussed
possible relationships between different forms of
visual asthenopia/eye strain/visual fatigue and
work involving the use of VDUs (e.g. Boisson,
Baure and Couvillon, (1), Hultgren and Knave,
(8). Concern has also been expressed about
the relationship between VDU use and postural
problems (Cakir, Reuter, von Schmude, and
Armbruster, (3), occupational stress (McKay)
and Cox, (11), Smith, Stammerjohn, Cohen and
Lalich, (18), facial rashes (Ryecroft and
Calnan, (16), Tjonn, (20), and cataracts (Zarat
(21).

A comprehensive review of investigations up till
1981 of possible relationships between
occupational stress factors and the use of VDUs
is provided by Dainoff (6). A number of large
field surveys conducted over the last decade have
suggested that the incidence of symptoms of
astheropia and complaints concerning visual
discomfort are higher amongst VDU operators than
amongst other groups of clerical workers. It is
doubtful that general statements which associate
increased incidences of symptoms of visual
discomfort to VDU use are justified in view of a
number of shortcomings in the previous studies.
These shortcomings have been discussed in (9),
(2) and (19).

Such shortcomings include:-

- inadequate definition of target populations
  when selecting groups of 'VDU-users'

- failure to include suitable control groups
  of 'non-VDU users'

- inadequacies in matching groups of 'VDU
  users' and 'non-VDU users' where control
  groups have been incorporated in studies

- emphasis on the VDU as the object of study
  where pre-conceived notions about
  detrimental health effects may have
  influenced outcomes.

- inadequate attention to the validation of
  data gathering instruments. For example,
  checking general estimates of the frequency
  of occurrence of single symptoms of
  occupational stress obtained by
  questionnaire or interview with
  day-by-day recording or reporting of the
  presence of respective symptoms.

A discussion of the ergonomics problems associated
with VDU's must maintain a clear perspective over
whether the VDU itself is the primary cause of the
problem or whether the cause lies elsewhere and it's
association with the VDU is either indirect or
incidental.

Examples of the latter are groups of factors
primarily associated with the introduction of
administrative computer systems to organisations
leading possibly to detrimental changes in task
organisation and job demands and which may be
quite independent of the VDU itself (18).

Another group of factors may be those which have
always been present in the office working
environment, such as discomfort glare, but have
only received widespread attention in relation to
possible detrimental occupational stress aspects
of work involving VDU's.

This paper reports the main findings of a two
year study (9). This work was carried out under
contract No. 7206-00-802 between the European
Coal and Steel Community and the Institute for
Consumer Ergonomics. The study took the form of
a field survey of 192 subjects performing similar
tasks either with or without a VDU, and was
conducted over the period 1980-1982.

The intention of the survey was to examine levels
of visual discomfort and objective measures of
visual functions amongst the sample of 'VDU
users' and the respective matched control groups
of 'non VDU-users'.

The working null hypothesis was formulated that no difference exists between the treatment and control group within each job type, in terms of measures of visual discomfort or of visual function. No predictions were made about the effect of working with a VDU, and no alternative hypothesis was formulated which predicted the direction of any difference found between the control and treatment groups.

Four groups of clerical workers were studied in the main survey. At the outset of the project, it was intended that the four groups should represent two pairs of matched samples of VDU-users and non-VDU users, each pair representing a different type of job.

The job types were:-

        Job Type 1 - Word Processor Operators
                      (VDU users)
                      Typists (non VDU users)

        Job Type 2 - Data Preparation Operators
                      (VDU users)
                      General Clerical Workers
                      (non VDU users)

The survey included 35 word processor operators, 59 typists, 44 data preparation operators and 54 general clerical workers, who worked in a total of 21 offices within 10 different organisations or companies.

The organisations from which the samples were drawn were predominantly local government organisations but also included a central government department, a nationalised industry and two private industries.

Word Processor Operators (WP):

All subjects worked in a bureau or pool which provided a centralised service to the organisation or a department within the organisation. Each office was led by a supervisor who distributed work amongst the operators. All operators undertook the input of text material, mostly from both audio and visual sources. All operators were also responsible to some extent for checking, correcting/amending and printing. Supervisors who did not undertake text material input and other staff who predominantly carried out one of the three latter tasks, such as printer operation, were not included.

Typists (TY):

These were organised in a similar way to the WP group, and formed the corresponding group of non-users. All subjects in this group worked in pools or bureaus led by a supervisor, and again provided a centralised service to the organisation or to departments within the organisation. The source materials consisted of both audio and written copy, and non-typing workers such as supervisors were not

included in the sample.

Data Preparation (DP):

These formed the second group of VDU user. These operators worked in pools or bureaus under supervision of a supervisor, and provided a centralised data punching or data entry service for the organisation. The work involved punching or verify-punching numeric or alpha-numeric data at high speed from batches of paper documents.

General Clerical Workers (GC)

It was intended at the outset that this group should include people whose work predominantly consisted of routine manual processing of large volumes of documents such as invoices. There was however considerable variation in the tasks, and in levels of responsibility and autonomy inherent in the jobs of the subjects within this group.

All subjects were full-time employees, whose main task activities during the day were associated with one of the task categories described above (i.e. there were no intermittent or part time users of VDUs included). Each subject had their own workplace within an office at which the majority of the day's activities were carried out. All participation in the survey was voluntary on the part of the individual.

2. DATA COLLECTED DURING THE SURVEY

Subjects in each office were studied over the five consecutive days of a working week. On each day subjects completed a pre-work questionnaire, normally within 15 minutes of arriving at the office and a corresponding similar post work questionnaire, normally within 15 minutes before leaving the office. These asked for ratings of single symptoms of visual discomfort, an overall rating of visual discomfort, ratings of other symptoms of occupational stress including headaches, postural discomfort or pain and general tiredness.

At lunchtimes on each day one or more questionnaires were completed by subjects. These obtained subjective ratings or responses regarding the workplace and working environment, perceptions of job design factors, outcomes relating to job satisfaction and motivation, and perceived health.

On two of the days of the week, a series of pre-work and corresponding post-work measures of visual function were made on each subject at their workplace. The days on which these measures were taken were either Monday and Thursday or Tuesday and Friday.

The tests performed were:-

- Near heterophoria, horizontal and vertical (Maddox Wing)

- Near heterophoria (horizontal) through +3.00 D lenses (Maddox Wing)

- Stimulus accommodative-convergence/ accommodation (AC/A) ratio determined by combining the results of the two previously mentioned factors.

- Near point of convergence (RAF rule)

- Near point of accommodation (RAF rule)

- Accommodative state (Mallett Unit duochrome test) (12)

- Fixation disparity, horizontal and vertical (Mallett unit) (12).

This battery of tests took less than four minutes to administer to each subject, the tests all being done at the person's workplace.

Furthermore, a series of measurements of the physical working environment were carried out during the week in each office and for each subject's workplace. These included measurements of illuminance and luminance of task relevant objects or areas, assessment of glare and aspects of the thermal and acoustic environments of the office. Where appropriate measures were recorded to obtain a maximum and a minimum value for the variation in the parameter over the survey week.

Prior to the week of the survey each subject underwent a series of vision screening tests and completed a general questionnaire about their vision. These were administered by an ophthalmic optician who also administered or supervised the vision measures listed above made during the survey week.

3. POST HOC EXAMINATION OF THE DEGREE OF MATCHING ACHIEVED BETWEEN THE GROUPS.

The following factors were examined for each of the above groups to determine to what extent the two pairs could be considered matched.

- age
- sex
- length of time in present job
- variations with respect to the task contents of the jobs of subjects within each group
- job design factors as perceived by subjects
- visual characteristics of the groups
- general health status
- some aspects of the physical environment

Group	WP	TY	DP	GC
n	35	59	44	54
mean age s.d	36.3 14.8	30.2 11.7	22.3 7.0	32.3 12.4
% female	100	100	100	67
Years in Mean present s.d job	3.30 2.49	4.50 3.49	2.62 2.87	4.06 3.46

Table 1 : Demographic data from Groups

Post hoc examination of the characteristics of the four groups of subjects led to the conclusion that only one pair of samples of VDU users and non-VDU users stipulated in the original design, could be considered to represent a matched pair of samples of VDU users and non-VDU users, namely the Word Processor Group and Typist Group respectively. Differences between the Data Preparation Group and the General Clerical worker group principally with respect to the nature of the work and age distributions of the two groups, dictated that these groups could not be considered as matched samples. Some reservations are also made, however, about the degree of matching obtained between the Word Processor Group and the Typist Group, in terms of age, assessment of some job design factors and job satisfaction. These differences were, however, consistent with the general feature that the Word Processor subjects had all previously been typists who had at some stage been retrained as word processor operators.

Thus, the data was analysed at two levels.

Level 1 -
Between all four groups of clerical workers, with no predictions being made about any influence of job type or VDU use on the ouctomes.

Level 2   -
Between 'VDU-users' (Word Processor Operators) and 'non-VDU users' (Typists) with no predictions being made about any influence of VDU use on the outcomes.

4. ANALYSIS OF THE SUBJECTIVE RATINGS OF VISUAL DISCOMFORT OBTAINED DURING THE SURVEY WEEK.

The questionnaire developed for use in this survey was structured so that each individual should firstly rate the degree of each of a number given symptoms on each of the pre-work assessments and post work assessments made during the week of the survey. These were:

i)   tiredness of the eyes
ii) soreness of aching of the eyes
iii) soreness or irritation of the eyelids
iv) watering of the eyes

iv) dryness of the eyes
vi) a sensation of hot or "burning" eyes
vii) a feeling of "sand in the eyes"
and viii) overall visual discomfort.

The intention of this was to prepare the subjects to make an overall rating of general visual discomfort by firstly considering each of a number of possible symptoms in turn, (i-vii). The subject's overall rating (viii) was then taken as the primary numeric index of visual disomfort for the comparison between groups. Examination of correlation coefficients between the responses to items i - iii on separate occasions showed this approach to be justified.

Comparisons were subsequently made regarding tiredness of eyes (i), other single symptoms of visual discomfort (ii-vii), and subjective ratings of impaired visual function.

For each of these questions a five point rating scale was used, the scales for both the pre-work and the corresponding post-work questions going from 1 (no discomfort) to 5 (very bad discomfort). The difference between these two ratings on any one day, the change over the day data was therefore on a nine-point scale, from -4 to +4. One cannot assume any of the data to be at a higher measurement level than ordinal, as one can neither assume equality of scale intervals nor that a given scale interval will mean the same thing to different people.

Initial analysis of the data was conducted assuming nominal status of the data, this being dichotomised into presence/absence or increase/no increase. For a number of the analyses statistical significance was approached, and they were then repeated assuming ordinal level data (i.e.assuming significance of the individual scale rating values), Meddis' system of unified analysis of variance by ranks being used. (13) This uses the rank mean of a frequency distribution of the scale rating values obtained from a sample. Subjects across all samples who give the same scale rating value are assigned the same shared-rank, summing the ranks within each sample and dividing by the number in the sample gives the rank mean of the sample. Under the null hypothesis these will be the same for each group and this is tested for by the statistic H, which has a similar distribution to chi-square.

4.1   Variations in responses by day of the week.

Analysis of the data pertaining to change over the day' of ratings of overall visual discomfort (i.e. the post-work rating minus the pre-work rating) on each day of the week for all subjects irrespective of group, showed a greater proportion of subjects who recorded an increase in rating on Mondays compared with the other days of the week. A lesser proportion recorded an increase in their ratings of visual discomfort on Fridays than on other days of the week.

Meddis' version of Friedmans two-way analysis of variance by ranks (14) was used to examine whether the difference in the distributions of scale values for the different days were

likely to have occurred by chance. This showed the differences between the days of the week to be highly statistically significant (Table 2).

Rank Means	(143 subjects)	
Monday	3.52	
Tuesday	2.98	H = 37.338
Wednesday	2.93	(probability of
Thursday	2.97	occurrence under
Friday	2.63	Ho = .001.

Table 2. Ranks Means of 'change over day' in rating of visual discomfort.

Only subjects who made all five pre-work assessments and all five post-work assessments were included in this particular analysis.

On further examination of whether the above effect was equally apparent in each of the four groups it was found that it was mainly the DP and GC Groups (i.e. the groups of job type 2) which exhibited this effect.
The presence of the day-of-the-week effect meant that the data collected on the different days were not independent of each other. Consequently all the data relating to subjective symptoms were analysed separately for each day.

4.2   Comparisons of changes in ratings of overall discomfort over the different days of the week.

Level 1 analysis -all four groups of clerical workers
A comparison between the four groups studied showed that there was no difference between the groups with respect to increases in ratings of visual discomfort on four of the five days of the week. Analysis assuming ordinal satus of the data (Figure 1b) shows that there is a significant difference between the groups on Mondays, with the Data Preparation showing the greatest amount of increase. Analysis assuming nominal level of measurement (figure 1a) which only takes account of the proportion of subjects in each group who show an increase over the day in their rating of overall visual discomfort, shows a similar pattern but the level of statistical significance is approached but not reached.

It is considered that this difference is primarily due to the 'beginning of the week' effect and not to work or task related differences which occurred on Mondays and not on the other days of the week.

Level 2 analysis - 'VDU users' (WP) and 'non-VDU users' (TY).
In figure 1a values of ^{2} were recalculated using data from these two groups only and and with a correction for continuity applied. (17). In figure 1b; Meddis' equivalent of the Mann-Whitney test has been applied to the data from the WP and TY groups only. In neither case are there significant differences between the two groups on any of the five days of the week. There are no consistency in the ordering of the groups which would imply the presence of an underlying effect which is not large enough to attain statistical significance.

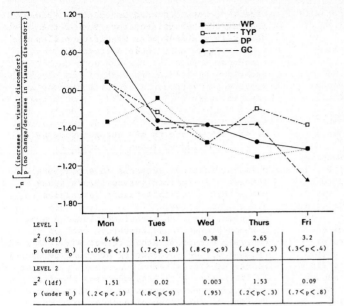

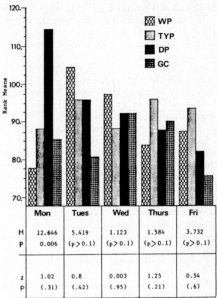

LEVEL 1	Mon	Tues	Wed	Thurs	Fri
x^2 (3df)	6.46	1.21	0.38	2.65	3.2
p (under H_o)	(.05<p<.1)	(.7<p<.8)	(.8<p<.9)	(.4<p<.5)	(.3<p<.4)
LEVEL 2					
x^2 (1df)	1.51	0.02	0.003	1.53	0.09
p (under H_o)	(.2<p<.3)	(.8<p<9)	(.95)	(.2<p<.3)	(.7<p<.8)

	Mon	Tues	Wed	Thurs	Fri
H	12.646	5.419	1.123	1.584	3.732
P	0.006	(p>0.1)	(p>0.1)	(p>0.1)	(p>0.1)
z	1.02	0.8	0.003	1.25	0.54
P	(.31)	(.42)	(.95)	(.21)	(.6)

Figures 1a and 1b: Analysis of Changes in Ratings of Overall Visual Discomfort

Figure 1a: Nominal Measurement   Level 1: All 4 groups
Figure 1b: Ordinal Measurement   Level 2: WP and TYP groups only

Note: The probabilities shown in brackets indicate non-achievement of statistical significance at 5% level

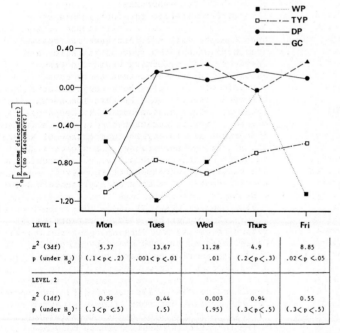

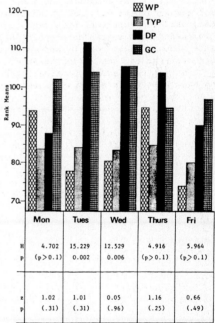

LEVEL 1	Mon	Tues	Wed	Thurs	Fri
x^2 (3df)	5.37	13.67	11.28	4.9	8.85
p (under H_o)	(.1<p<.2)	.001<p<.01	.01	(.2<p<.3)	.02<p<.05
LEVEL 2					
x^2 (1df)	0.99	0.44	0.003	0.94	0.55
p (under H_o)	(.3<p<.5)	(.5)	(.95)	(.3<p<.5)	(.3<p<.5)

	Mon	Tues	Wed	Thurs	Fri
H	4.702	15.229	12.529	4.916	5.964
P	(p>0.1)	0.002	0.006	(p>0.1)	(p>0.1)
z	1.02	1.01	0.05	1.16	0.66
P	(.31)	(.31)	(.96)	(.25)	(.49)

Figures 2a and 2b: Analysis of Pre-Work Ratings of Overall Visual Discomfort

Figure 2a: Nominal Measurement   Level 1: All 4 groups
Figure 2b: Ordinal Measurement   Level 2: WP and TYP groups only

Note: The probabilities shown in brackets indicate non-achievement of statistical significance at 5% level

Comparisons of changes of ratings of tiredness of the eyes were performed in a similar way. The results of the analysis were in complete accordance with those described above for both levels of analyses.

4.3 Comparison of changes of ratings of other single symptoms of visual discomfort over the different days of the week.

Level 1 analysis - all four groups of clerical workers

No significant differences were found between the groups for each single symptom of asthenopia. In most cases the numbers of subjects who recorded an increase in their ratings of a symptom from pre-work to post-work assessment were so small in relation to the group size as to preclude meaningful statistical analysis. This applied to the following single symptoms: eyelids sore or irritated; eyes watering/running; eyes dry; eyes hot/burning; a feeling of sand in the eyes. In some cases the proportion of subjects who showed a decrease in the rating of the symptom at the end of the day approached the proportion who showed an increase. In these cases there is little justification for considering the causes of changes in levels of the single symptom to be work-related. In the case of the symptom 'eyes-sore/aching' a statistical analysis was applied to the data. No significant differences between the groups were found on any of the days. However, the observed differences on Mondays were consistent with those found in analyses of overall visual discomfort. Where analysis was not considered appropriate, observation of the data indicated that a greater proportion of subjects who showed increases and decreases in ratings over the day came from the Data Preparation and the General Clerical worker groups than from the other two groups.

Level 2 analysis. VDU users (WP) and non-VDU users (TY).

Group Change over day	WP			TY		
	-ve	0	+ve	-ve	0	+ve
eyes sore or aching	1	26	8	3	40	12
eyelids sore or irritated	5	25	5	2	46	6
eyes watering or running	0	33	2	5	45	5
eyes dry	2	31	2	3	48	3
eyes hot or burning	1	29	5	0	48	5
feeling of sand in eyes	1	33	1	2	48	4

(-ve = decrease in rating over day)
(0 = no change in rating over day)
(+ve = increase in rating over day)

Table 3 : Frequency data - Wednesdays only for single symptoms of asthenopia

With the exception of symptom (ii), it was not considered appropriate to perform any statistical comparisons between the WP and TY groups for similar reasons to those described above. Wednesday's data for responses to each of questions pertaining to each of the other single symptoms of asthenopia are presented as an example. (Table 3).

4.4 Comparisons of responses to questions pertaining to subject symptoms of impaired vision.

No significant differences between groups for symptoms of impaired vision (blurring of characters at distance close to the new point, and double vision). In the first case (blurring of characters), only the difference scores between pre-work and post-work ratings were considered appropriate for analysis. This was because of lack of control over the reference points used by subjects when making judgements. Unlike Laubli et al(10) who reported finding differences between the groups they studied with respect to 'blurring of near sight', no significant differences were found in this survey. With regard to the symptom of double vision the numbers of subjects whose post-work rating of the symptom was greater than their pre-work ratings were so small as to preclude any meaningful statistical analysis.

4.5 Separate Analysis of Pre-Work Ratings and Post-Work Ratings respectively over the different days of the week.

When the pre-work and post-work ratings were considered separately then significant and consistent differences between the groups emerged. In terms of pre-work levels of visual discomfort on the different mornings of the week, the Data Preparation group had a somewhat higher level of visual discomfort than the general clerical group. Both of these groups had visual discomfort levels higher than those of the Typist and Word Processor Groups, which were similar to each other (Figures 2a and 2b). Over the week the ranges of percentages for those in each group showing some degree of visual discomfort before work began were as follows: Data preparation 27% - 53%; General Clerical 44% - 55%; Word Processor 22% - 47%; Typist 25% - 35%. Dainoff (5) in reporting pre-work levels of 'eyestrain' from a 5-day study of twenty-three library workers using VDUs in a centralised cataloguing service, quoted a level of 30%. It would seem that this is some sort of mean score, but it is of a similar magnitude to the levels recorded in this survey for the Typists and Word Processor operators.

A similar pattern of differences between groups was found when the post-work ratings of visual discomfort were analysed. The Data Preparation group had higher levels of visual discomfort than the other three groups. The Word Processor and Typist groups have similar levels to each other but were lower than the other two groups. The General Clerical Worker group was intermediate between the Data Preparation and the Word Processor/Typist groups but was more similar to the latter two groups in the post-work results than was the case with the pre-work results. The ranges of percentages of each group reporting some degree of overall post-work visual discomfort over the days of the week were as follows: Data Preparation 63% - 74%; General Clerical Workers 48% - 81%; Word Processor Operators 49% - 60% and Typist 43% - 62%. In accordance with the findings of other studies there are substantial proportions in all of the groups who reported some degree of visual discomfort at the end of the day. The figure reported by Dainoff for post work levels of 'eyestrain' in the study previously referred to, was 62.2%. This is of a similar magnitude to the upper end of the ranges for the Typists and Word Processor Operators.

If comparisons between the four groups were made solely on the basis of the post-work data on visual discomfort, it is possible to draw erroneous conclusions. Considering the ordering between the groups found in terms of post-work levels of visual discomfort and the fact that the Data Preparation Groups had higher levels of post-work visual discomfort than the other groups, one might be tempted to conclude that the differences between the groups were entirely due to differences in work-related factors in the preceding eight hour work period. Differences between groups in their pre-work levels of visual discomfort show this to be an incorrect assumption.

The findings from separate and similar analyses of pre-work and post-work ratings of tiredness of the eyes are very similar to those described above.

Level 2 analysis - VDU users (WP) and non-VDU users (TY).
When comparisons were made between the data obtained only from these two groups, again using χ^2 with a correction for continuity (nominal data) and the Mann Whitney test (ordinal data) then no significant differences were found (Figures 2a and 2b).

There was no consistency in the ordering between the groups over the days of the weeks which might have suggested an underlying effect. Again these findings are mirrored in the analysis of ratings of tiredness of the eyes.

Considering these data on the levels of pre-work and post-work visual discomfort and tiredness of the eyes then it can be inferred, and it is hardly surprising, that people doing different types of jobs experience different degrees of visual discomfort, irrespective of whether they use VDUs or not. Furthermore, as these differences appear in the pre-work ratings as well as the post-work ratings, the differences cannot solely be attributed directly to factors which the different groups are exposed during their working day. It is too simplistic and naive a view to attribute the pre-work

differences totally to residual effects of the previous days work. It is likely that a series of factors contribute to the recorded levels of pre-work discomfort in the different groups, which are related to the group of subjects in a broader sense and not only to the work they do. Such factors could include evening activities, length and quality of sleep, length of journey to work, general attitudes and motivation at the beginning of the day, health status and vision status and possible residual effects from the previous day's work. It was shown that there was a high degree of association between pre-work ratings of visual discomfort and pre-work ratings of general tiredness. A similar association was reported in (7). Furthermore, it was shown that there was an inverse relationship between pre-work ratings of general tiredness and the age of the subject. Younger subjects reported higher levels of pre-work tiredness than older subjects, which is the opposite to what one might expect if pre-work tiredness was solely determined by residual effects of the previous day's work.

5.0   SUMMARY OF CONCLUSIONS FROM EXAMINATION OF THE PRE-WORK AND POST-WORK MEASURES OF VISUAL FUNCTION.

Three measures were used for making comparisons between groups: namely changes over the first day (either Monday or Tuesday from pre-work to post-work measurements; changes over the second day (either Thursday or Friday) from pre-work to post-work measurement; changes over the week from pre-work measurement, first day to post-work measurement, second day.

Level 1 analyses - all four groups.
The analyses performed on the objective data will not be reported in detail here. All but one of the statistical tests performed failed to reach significance at the 0.05 level. The one that did was the change in the near point of convergence over the week, the analysis of variance F ratio being 3.34, which was significant at the 0.02 level. Over the first and over the last days, however, the F ratios for this test were 0.84 and 0.39 respectively, and it was concluded that this was a spuriously significant result which occurred because of the number of statistical tests performed rather than because of any true difference between the groups.
The variance ratios for the AC/A measures on three of the four occasions (2.50, 2.49, 2.28) were significant at the 0.1 level, although not at the 0.05 level. The fourth (1.52) was not significant. It was noted the rank order of the magnitude of the AC/A ratio on these three occasions was the same as that of the mean age of the groups (DP, TY, GC, WP). Morgan and Peters (15) have shown that the stimulus AC/A ratio does not change with age; when the data for all subjects was grouped by age no trend was apparent, which concurs with their results. Examination of the change in the AC/A ratio over the day and over the week showed no difference between the groups.

The factor of age was again noted when the near point of accommodation data was examined; analysis of covariance was performed on the results, age being the covariate, and no significant difference was found between the groups.

Level 2 analysis - VDU users (WP) and non-VDU
                          users (TY).
The age profiles of the WP and TY groups were similar (Table 1), and there was therefore less concern about age-related changes such as amplitude of accommodation. Where appropriate, however, age was still taken into account. The conclusion from the level 2 analysis was the same as that from the level 1 analysis, namely that no significant differences could be found which might indicate any differential change in visual function between the groups.

6.0   DISCUSSION OF FINDINGS

The results from the survey show that there is no justification for general statements to the effect that VDU operators or users suffer greater visual discomfort than groups of clerical workers who do not have occasion to use VDU's in their work. Recently Campbell and Durden (4) have reviewed the physiological visual factors associated with the use of VDU's, and conclude that there are no obvious reasons why clerical work using VDU's should produce any effects which are different from any other sedentary clerical work. Certainly there are work situations in which intensive use of VDU's for prolonged periods will result in high levels of visual fatigue and discomfort. However, similar outcomes may be expected from analogous situations involving sedentary clerical workers where VDU's are not used.

The findings of this survey do not diminish the importance of current recommendations regarding workplace and environmental design, job design or task organisation, hardware and software design. The high levels of visual discomfort recorded for both VDU users and non-VDU users alike testify to this. No attempts were made to compare 'good' and 'bad' situations with respect to these recommendations.

The survey indicates a need for action to lower levels of visual discomfort and fatigue amongst clerical workers in general rather than allowing complacency about the role of the VDU itself as a causal factor. However over emphasis on the VDU itself as potential source of occupational stress may well detract from a series of broader issues associated with the working environment which may have a far greater bearing on both visual and general occupational stress in the office.

7.0   FOOTNOTES

[1] Peter Howarth is now at the School of Optometry, University of California, Berkeley.

8.0   REFERENCES

1   Boissin, Baure, and Couvillon, Mise au point et résultats d'utilisation d'un appareil équipe d'un tulse cathodique, Congress de la Société d'Ergonomie de Langue Francais, Lyon (1971).

2   Brown, B.S., Dismukes, K., and Rinalducci, E., Video display terminals and vision of workers. Summary and overview of a symposium, Behaviour and Information Technology 1, (2), (1982), 121-140.

3   Cakir, A., Reuter, H.J., von Schmude, L., and Armbruster, A., Untershungen zur Anpassung von Bildschirmarbeitsplatzen an die physiche und psychische Funkshionsweise des Mensche, Forschungsbericht Humanisierung des Arbeitslegens (Bonn: Der Bunderminister fur Arbeit und Socialordnung) (1978).

4   Campbell, F.W., and Durden, K., The visual display terminal issue: a consideration of its physiological, psychological and clinical background, Ophthalmic and Physiological Optics 3 (2), (1983), 167-174.

5   Dainhoff, M.J., Visual fatigue in VDU operators, in Ergonomics Aspects of Visual Display Terminals, ed. Grandjean. E, and Vigliani, E., Taylor and Francis, London (1980).

6   Dainhoff, M.J., Occupational Stress Factors in VDT operation, Behaviour and Information Technology, 1, (2), (1982), 141-176.

7   Happ, A.J. and Beaver, C.W., Effects of work at a VDT-intensive laboratory task on performance, mood and fatigue symptoms, Proc. Human Factors Soc. 25th Annual Meeting (1981).

8   Hultgren, G. and Knave, B., Discomfort glare and disturbances from light reflections in an office landscape with CRT display terminals, Applied Ergonomics, 5, (1), (1974).

9   Istance, H.O., and Howarth, P.A., Ergonomic problems in the use of Visual Display Units, Report to the European Coal Steel Community Research contract 7206-00-802. Institute for Consumer Ergonomics, University of Technology, Loughborough, (1983).

10   Laubli, T., Hunting, W., and Grandjean,E., Postural and Visual Loads at VDT workplaces. II Lighting Conditions and Visual Impairements, Ergonomics, 24, (12), (1981), 933-944.

11 MacKay, C. and Cox, T., Ocupational stress
    associated with visual display unit
    operation in Health Hazards of VDUs? 2,
    H.U.S.A.T., University of Technology,
    Loughborough, (1981).

12 Mallett, R.J.F., The investigation of
    heterophoria at near and a new fixation
    disparity technique, The Optician,
    December 1964,

13 Meddis, R., Unified analysis of variance by
    ranks, British Journal of Mathematical and
    Statistical Pschology, 33, (1980), 84-98.

14 Meddis, R., OMNIBUS. Analysis of variance
    by ranks, Department of Human Sciences;
    publication No. 347, University of
    Technology, Loughborough, (1980).

15 Morgan, M.W. and Peters, H.B.,
    Accommodation convergence in presbyopia,
    American Journal of Optometry, 28, (1951)
    3-10.

16 Ryecroft, R. and Calnan, C., (1980),
    Facial rashes among visual display
    operators, in Health Hazards of VDUs? 1,
    H.U.S.A.T., University of Technology,
    Loughborough.

17 Siegal, S., Non-Parametric Statistics
    for the Behavioural Sciences, McGraw-Hill
    Book Company, New York, 1956.

18 Smith, M.J., Stammerjohn, W.E., Cohen, B.
    and Lalich, N.R., Job stress in video
    display operations, in Ergonomic aspects
    of visual display terminals, ed. Grandjean,
    E., and Vigliani, E., Taylor and Francis,
    London, (1980).

19 Starr, S.J., Thompson, C.R., and Shute,
    S.J., Effects of Video Display Terminals
    on Telephone Operators, Human Factors,
    24, (6), (1982), 699-711.

20 Tjonn, H., Report on facial rashes among
    VDU operators in Norway, in Health Hazards
    of VDUs? 1, H.U.S.A.T., University of
    Technology, Loughborough, (1980).

21 Zarat, M., Cataracts and visual display
    units, in Health Hazards of VDUs? 1,
    H.U.S.A.T., University of Technology,
    Loughborough, (1980),

Human-Computer Interaction — INTERACT '84 / B. Shackel (ed.)
Elsevier Science Publishers B.V. (North-Holland)
© IFIP, 1985

VISUAL DISCOMFORT AND CATHODE RAY TUBE DISPLAYS

Arnold Wilkins

Medical Research Council Applied Psychology Unit
15 Chaucer Road, Cambridge CB2 2EF, England

Visual stimuli can induce a variety of noxious effects, including unpleasant
illusions, tired eyes, headaches and seizures.   The stimulation responsible for
these effects is quite specific and includes that from televisions and text.
According to a general theory of visual discomfort reviewed here, the effects have
a common physiological basis.

1. INTRODUCTION

Certain visual stimuli (such as the pattern shown in Figure 1) are capable of inducing a variety of unpleasant effects, including eye-strain, headaches and even seizures.   This review will begin by describing the temporal and spatial parameters of the stimuli that induce seizures.   It will then be shown that precisely the same stimuli evoke unpleasant visual effects in persons without epilepsy, and that these visual effects are associated with the headaches that certain people suffer.   Televisions and printed text can provide stimulation that has parameters within the range appropriate for the provocation of seizures and other unpleasant effects.   The relevance for the design of visual display units is discussed.

2. TEMPORAL PARAMETERS

One in 20 patients with epilepsy is photosensitive and liable to suffer seizures that are visually-induced.(1)   In patients with a history of such seizures, and in some others besides, flickering light induces epileptiform EEG activity (consisting of spikes or spikes and slow waves).(1,2,3)   The frequency of diffuse flicker at which these paroxysmal abnormalities are most likely to occur is 15-20Hz, although some patients are sensitive at frequencies as high as 50Hz and as low as 4Hz.(2,3)   The studies on which these statistics are based have used the conventional "photostimulator" - a high-power gas discharge lamp.   Little is known about the effects of varying the modulation depth of the light, although modulation of 10% or so can be quite sufficient to induce seizure activity.(4)   Even less is known about the effects of the area of the visual field stimulated, although it has been shown that a stimulus of

a given size is more provocative when presented in the centre of the visual field than at the periphery.(2)

3. SPATIAL PARAMETERS

A flickering light is less epileptogenic when it is diffuse than when it is patterned (2), although patterns do not have to be intermittent in order to be epileptogenic. Continuously-illuminated stationary patterns of striped lines will induce epileptiform abnormalities in about one third of photosensitive patients.(3)   The epileptiform activity is more likely in response to patterns of stripes than patterns of checks or plaids. The spatial frequency of the stripes at which the activity is most likely to occur is about 3 cycles/degree, depending somewhat on the area of the visual field receiving stimulation.(3)   The ratio of the width of the bars to their separation is important.   The probability of paroxysmal activity is maximal when the stripes have equal width and spacing; that is, when the duty cycle is 50%.(5)   The contrast of the stripes is also important. The probability of seizure activity increases precipitously with Michelson contrast in the range 10-30%, but further increase in contrast has relatively little effect.(3)   The luminance of the pattern is relatively unimportant.   Provided the luminance is within the photopic range, a decrease in luminance by a factor of about ten is generally required in order to reduce appreciably the probability of paroxysmal activity.(3)

The probability of paroxysmal activity is also dependent on the size of the pattern and its position in the visual field.   If the stimulation is confined to the periphery, paroxysmal activity will occur only when the pattern is very large.   The increase in

Figure 1: An epileptogenic pattern

threshold size over and above that for central vision depends on the cortical magnification.(3) The probability is greatest when both eyes see the same stimulus and is reduced by binocular rivalry or monocular viewing.(3)

3. INTERACTION BETWEEN SPACE AND TIME

The spatial and temporal frequency tuning of the paroxysmal response appear to be independent. If a pattern of stripes is vibrated in a direction orthogonal to the stripes the frequency of vibration at which paroxysmal activity is most likely to occur is 10-20 Hz, regardless of the spatial frequency of the pattern.(6) The spatial frequency at which paroxysmal activity is most likely remains the same as for a stationary pattern - about 3 cycles/degree - regardless of vibration frequency. Over a wide range of velocities of motion, patterns that drift continuously toward fixation are very much less epileptogenic than those whose motion is vibratory (through one or one half cycle of the pattern). Patterns which are static (and therefore whose only retinal motion is the result of the movements of the eye that occur during fixation) are more epileptogenic than those that drift. They are less epileptogenic than patterns that vibrate or oscillate in phase.(7) The eye is continually in motion, and this motion, whether normal or abnormal, would therefore appear to play a role in the induction of paroxysmal abnormalities. Although little is known about the eye movements of patients with photosensitive epilepsy, they are not obviously abnormal. Recordings using a limbus tracker with a resolution of about 1/10 deg., made in collaboration with colleagues John Findlay and Colin Binnie, have not consistently revealed abnormalities.

4. ORIGIN OF THE SEIZURES

There is now considerable converging evidence that the paroxysmal activity arises in the visual cortex and can remain localised within it. The neurons in the visual cortex generally respond more to contours that drift than to those that are stationary on the retina, and sometimes they respond only to one direction of movement. As a result, vibratory pattern movement, whether imposed by the movements of the eyes or superimposed on them, can play a role in synchronising the activity of visual neurons, thereby facilitating the epileptic process.(8)

In summary, both diffuse flicker and certain patterns can induce seizures as the result of the synchronised excitation of cortical neurons. The relationship between the temporal and spatial selectivity is not well understood although the eye movements that occur during fixation may play a role.

5. RELATION BETWEEN SEIZURES AND DISCOMFORT

People without epilepsy find the patterns that induce seizure activity unpleasant to look at. When asked to judge the pleasantness of patterns of stripes using techniques that control for range effects (9) samples of normal volunteers report "pleasantness" to vary with parameters of spatial frequency, duty cycle and contrast in the same way as the probability of paroxysmal activity.(5) They report illusions of various kinds: colours, blurring and bending of the stripes, shimmering, flickering and shadowy shapes. These illusions were first reported in the scientific literature in the last century and they have received intermittent investigation ever since. Many of the illusions have defied explanations in terms of ocular factors and recently interpretations of some of the illusions in terms of cortical inhibition have been proposed.(10) The frequency with which the illusions are reported is determined by all the parameters that influence the probability of paroxysmal EEG activity in epileptic patients, in almost precisely the same way. The illusions do not appear to dissociate from one another but can be considered as different features of the same visual response (at least to a first approximation). It has been argued that the illusions are produced by processes similar to those that induce seizures, namely by a spread of cortical excitation that involves the stimulation of cells inappropriate to the visual stimulus. This spread of excitation is assumed to be more localised than that which occurs during seizure activity.(5)

There are differences from one person to another as regards susceptibility to the illusions, and these differences are statistically related to the incidence and nature of the headaches they suffer. There is a weak correlation (which accounts for about 20 % of the variance) such that persons who suffer frequent headaches tend to report more illusions. This correlation only obtains when the pattern has a maximally epileptogenic spatial frequency. Persons who suffer unilateral headache consistently on the same side tend to report illusions predominantly in one visual hemifield. The illusions are more commonly reported by persons who suffer migraine headache.(5)

6. TELEVISIONS AND TEXT

The above description of the stimulus parameters of visual discomfort is not as divorced from the subject of man-machine interaction as it might at first appear. In the everyday environment there are two common sources of epileptogenic stimulation. The first is television and the second printed

text.   Television can present one of the most
epileptogenic forms of environmental
stimulation, particularly when it is viewed at
close quarters.   A substantial proportion of
photosensitive patients suffer seizures only
when watching television.   The sensitivity to
television-induced effects depends on the frame
frequency and on the line interlace.   Patients
who are sensitive to diffuse intermittent light
at frequencies as high as 50Hz are sensitive to
television at conventional viewing distances.
Their sensitivity depends somewhat on the
retinal subtense of the screen (which is
determined by the viewing distance and the size
of the screen).   The interlacing lines
approximate a pattern of stripes vibrating at
frequencies close to those that are maximally
epileptogenic.   When viewed at close quarters
the lines on the television screen have a
sufficiently low spatial frequency to be
epileptogenic.   For this reason most patients
suffer attacks only when they are close to the
screen.(11)

Television not only provokes seizures.
It is commonly reported to precipitate headache
as well.(12)

The successive lines of printed text
comprise a pattern of stripes with a
fundamental spatial frequency that averages 1.4
cycles/degree, and is therefore within the
epileptogenic range.   The duty-cycle of this
"grating" varies considerably from one text to
another, in the range 45%-75%.   Much of this
range is epileptogenic.   The average contrast
of lines of text (as distinct from the contrast
of the ink on the page) is difficult to
measure, depending as it does on the width and
spacing of the component letter strokes as well
as the contrast of the ink on the paper.   We
have obtained estimates of the mean contrast of
a line using fibre optics to measure the
average reflectance of a linear segment.   The
contrast varies slightly with typeface (fount),
but is comparatively unaffected by the size of
the text (point) or the spacing between the
lines (leading).   The estimates of contrast
(which for technical reasons are conservative)
range from 14% to 22% and are therefore within
the epileptogenic range.   Following upon these
measurements we have observed the incidence of
epileptiform discharges in two photosensitive
patients while they read.   Both were highly
sensitive to patterns of stripes.   The
incidence of discharges was significantly
increased by reading and reduced when the
patients read using a mask that covered the
lines of text above and below those being read,
allowing only three lines of text to be
seen.(4)

The reading mask is not only effective in
reducing seizures.   In placebo-controlled
studies it has been shown to reduce "eyestrain" and headaches in people who suffer
these disorders when they read.(13)

7. VISUAL DISPLAY UNITS

Most visual display units use cathode ray
tube displays and combine some of the properties
of television with those of printed text; they
potentially compound the epileptogenic
properties of one with the other.   Although
many displays suppress the line interlace that
is characteristic of television, the rate at
which the screen is refreshed is usually
similar.   The modulation of the intermittent
light is also similar because short-persistence
phosphors are typically used.   Very often the
spatial characteristics of the display are more
epileptogenic than those of printed text
because insufficient space is left between the
lines of letters.   As a result, the duty cycle
is closer to the 50% maximum at which
paroxysmal activity is most likely to appear.
From viewing distances at which the text is
usually read it has a spatial frequency within
the epileptogenic range.   Grandjean (14) has
shown that as the modulation depth of the light
emitted by the phosphor increases so do
complaints of discomfort.   His findings tie in
well with the general theory of discomfort
outlined in this paper.   It is also of
interest how similar to the visual effects
induced by epileptogenic pattern stimulation
are the complaints of visual discomfort
outlined in the Health and Safety Executive's
report on visual display units (faint colours
surrounding objects, temporary blurring of
vision, and spots in front of the eyes).(15)
Persons who complain of these effects tend
to report more illusions in epileptogenic
patterns.(5,13)

At the time of writing there are
indications that persons who see more illusions
tend to have unstable fixation.   Moreover, the
observation of such patterns decreases the
stability of fixation.(16)   It would therefore
appear likely that epileptogenic stimulation
can effect oculomotor control in a way that
depends on the individual's sensitivity to such
stimulation.   The intermittent illumination of
the phosphor on a visual display unit may
interfere with oculomotor control, and
experiments are currently underway to test this
hypothesis.

The findings outlined in this paper are
many and disparate.   Where the findings are
physiologically robust they relate to a
relative small proportion of the population.
Where more generally relevant they deal with
phenomena as ill-defined as pain and visual
illusions.   Nevertheless the evidence, diverse
as it is, combines to form a coherent picture,
one that describes a physiological stress of
the visual system.   There is increasing
implication of temporal intermittency and
spatial repetitiveness in the induction of this
stress, and the discomfort that ensues.   This
evidence comes not only from the
photoconvulsive effects of light, and the

psychophysics of illusions and discomfort outlined above. There is recent evidence that cells in the visual system of the cat respond to the intermittent light output of conventional fluorescent tubes at frequencies as high as 120Hz.(17) The human occipital EEG shows synchronous activation at frequencies that approach 100Hz (18) and human performance is improved if the depth of modulation from fluorescent tubes is decreased and the frequency raised (19). Taking all these strands of evidence together, one is led to the conclusion that if cathode ray tubes are to be used to display text, not only should the lines of text be adequately spaced, but either the modulation of the light emitted should be reduced by the use of a long persistence phosphor, or the refresh rate should be increased above 50Hz. How much higher than 50Hz the refresh rate should be in order to prevent discomfort has yet to be determined.

ACKNOWLEDGEMENTS

Thanks are due to the Medical Research Council for support, the Electricity Council Research Centre for the loan of equipment, and to IBM UK Ltd for the use of a Personal Computer.

REFERENCES

[1] Newmark, M.E. and Penry, J.K., Photosensitive epilepsy: a review (Raven Press, New York, 1979).

[2] Jeavons, P.M. and Harding, G.F.A., Photosensitive epilepsy (Heinemann, London, 1975).

[3] Wilkins, A.J., Binnie, C.D. and Darby, C.E., Visually-induced seizures, Progress in Neurobiology, 15 (1980) 85-117.

[4] Wilkins, A.J. and Lindsay, J., Common forms of reflex epilepsy: physiological mechanisms and techniques for treatment, in Pedley, T.A. and Meldrum, B.S. (eds.), Recent Advances in Epilepsy II (Churchill Livingstone, London, in press).

[5] Wilkins, A.J., Nimmo-Smith, I., Tait, A., et al., A neurological basis for visual discomfort, Brain (in press).

[6] Binnie, C.D., Darby, C.E. and Wilkins, A.J., Pattern sensitivity: the role of movement, in Lechner, H. and Aranibar, A. (eds.), Proceedings of the Second European Congress of Electroencephalography and Clinical Neurophysiology (North Holland, Amsterdam, 1979).

[7] Binnie, C.D. and Wilkins, A.J., Sensitivity to moving patterns: implications for the role of synchronisation in epileptogenesis, in preparation.

[8] Meldrum, B.S. and Wilkins, A.J., Photosensitive epilepsy: integration of pharmacological and psychophysical evidence, in Schwartzkroin, P. and Wheal, H.V. (eds.), Electrophysiology of epilepsy (Academic Press, London, in press).

[9] Poulton, E.C., Models for biases in judging sensory magnitude, Psychological Bulletin, 86 (1979), 777-803.

[10] Georgeson, M.A., Psychophysical hallucinations of orientation and spatial frequency, Perception, 5 (1976), 99-111.

[11] Wilkins, A.J. Darby, C.E., Binnie, C.D. et al., Television epilepsy - the role of pattern, Electroencephalography and clinical Neurophysiology, 47 (1979), 163-171.

[12] Debne, L.M., Visual stimuli as migraine trigger factors, in Rose, C.F. (ed.) Progress in Migraine Research 2 (Pitman, London, in press)

[13] Wilkins, A.J. and Nimmo-Smith, I., On the reduction of eye-strain when reading, Ophthalmic and Physiological Optics, 4 (1984) 53-59.

[14] Grandjean, E., Ergonomics of VDU's: review of present knowledge, in Grandjean, E. and Vigliani, E. (eds.) Ergonomic aspects of visual display terminals, Proceedings of the international workshop, Milan, March 1980 (Taylor and Francis, London, 1980).

[15] Mackay, C., Human factors aspects of visual display unit operation (H.M.S.O., London, 1980).

[16] Findlay J.M. and Wilkins, A.J., Ocular stability and the perception of illusions, paper read to the Experimental Psychology Society, Manchester, April 1982.

[17] Eysel, U.T. and Burandt, U., Fluorescent tube light evokes flicker responses in visual neurons, Vision Research, in press.

[18] Brundrett, G.W., Human sensitivity to flicker, Lighting Research and Technology, 6 (1974), 127-143.

[19] Rey, P. and Rey, J.P., Les effets compares de deux eclairages fluorescents sur une tache visuelle et des tests de "fatigue", Ergonomics 6 (1963), 393-401.

Human-Computer Interaction — INTERACT '84 / B. Shackel (ed.)
Elsevier Science Publishers B.V. (North-Holland)
© IFIP, 1985

QUANTITATIVE MEASURES OF THE
SPATIAL PROPERTIES OF SCREEN DESIGNS

Dennis J. Streveler
Anthony I. Wasserman

Section on Medical Information Science
University of California, San Francisco
San Francisco, California 94143 USA

This paper proposes certain quantitative measures for analyzing the spatial properties of screen designs and for designing experiments aimed at determining optimal values for the measures. The measures result from the application of three analytic techniques termed boxing analysis, hot-spot analysis, and alignment analysis.

1.   INTRODUCTION

Screen designs can suffer from overcrowding, can lack any recognizable organizing principle, and can be aesthetically displeasing. It has been long been recognized that poor screen design can have a detrimental effect on the human performance of its user by decreasing search speed, provoking errors, and complicating machine operations. [GALI p.1] Good design, on the other hand, can aid visual decoding and improve human performance.

1.1 DOMAIN OF DISCUSSION

For our purposes it is useful to make a distinction between the syntax (format, shape, layout, spatial properties) and the semantics (content, meaning) of screen design. This distinction is artificial, but it is made for similar, pragmatic reasons for its application in other areas of computer science: it is clearly much easier to analyze syntax objectively than to implement a representational form which could be used to manipulate semantics.

In this paper we address the syntax of screen designs. The discussion is restricted to an examination of single screens, presented on monochromatic alphanumeric display terminals. It is not that color, windows, graphics, and the like are not interesting topics of discussion. The restrictions are a result of growing awareness that little is yet known about the fundamental nature of screen design. It is necessary to understand its basic concepts and only then to generalize them to more complicated devices.

1.2 EXISTING GUIDELINES

For more than a decade there has been an awareness that there was a need to develop effective methods for the design of human/computer interfaces rather than to continue with ad hoc methods. In particular screen design of screen layouts has been relegated little attention.

In the previous decade, guidelines for designing interfaces, and included among them guidelines for designing screens, began to emerge. [ENGE MART WASS GALI WILL SMIT BAI SHNE and others]   These guidelines were almost entirely subjective, offering little information about their applicability to different user classes or about how to evaluate alternative interfaces objectively. Their major contribution has been to heighten awareness concerning the importance of interface design.

Some guidelines are broad and vague:

> "a. Display a small amount of information at one time
> b. Have one idea per display ...
> e. Use formats designed for clarity
> f. Strive for similarity"   [MART p.316-7]

While this type of pedagogy has intuitive appeal, it is difficult to know how one applies such guidelines or how one measures their degree of application. And one is left to philosophically muse over the meaning of "one idea" and "clarity" and "simplicity". How is the designer persuaded to know whether his presentation is clear, similar, or restricted to one idea? How is he/she to be guided to improve the design?

Other guidelines are, on the other extreme, very narrow:

> "In presenting text collections on a small screen, there should be a maximum of 50-55 characters on each line. On larger screens, break up text into two (or more) columns of 30-35 characters per line. Separate columns by at least 5 spaces if the text is not right justified and by 3-4 if the text is right and left justified." [ENGE p.10]

Other guidelines exhort the practitioner to high standards of screen design seemingly without providing any suggestions about how it is to be accomplished:

> "Simply, simplify, simplify!"
> [MORA p.486]

"Project a 'natural', uncomplicated 'virtual image of the system" [SHNE p.251 attributed to Cheriton]

It is not that these guidelines are wrong, but rather that one must know how to apply them in a specific context.

What is needed is a set of measures which can be explicitly stated, validated through experimentation, and then used to objectively evaluate a screen design or compare the relative merits of alternative designs.

2. ANALYTIC TECHNIQUES

Toward the goal of seeking objective measures, we have explored three analytic techniques: boxing analysis, hot-spot analysis and alignment analysis. We describe these measures and then illustrate them, using three screen designs from existing computer systems. (No claims are made about the merits of the designs; the reader may form his/her own opinions.)

Most of the quantitative measures which appear in this paper are byproducts of these three analytic techniques.

2.1 BOXING ANALYSIS TECHNIQUE

The first technique, called boxing, identifies spatially proximate groups of items appearing in a screen design. Boxing involves finding groups of items which are completely surrounded by white-space[1], and then drawing the smallest possible rectangular box around them.[2]

This technique was motivated by many existing guidelines which refer to "grouping" or "chunking" or "visual association".

Chunking is a fundamental principle of human memory. Although it is usually associated with human short-term memory, it is often also associated with visual sensory memory. [SPOE]

In early stages of the visual decoding of a screen, an attempt is made to impose structure on the visual field. Cohesive groupings of screen elements allow viewers to perceive the large screen as having identifiable pieces. [GALI p.14]

Several gestalt principles of visual organization may also be applicable: the principle of proximity states that visual objects grouped together and separated from other groups tend to be perceived together. The principle of closure may be applicable since a group of items, bounded by sufficient white-space may, in a sense, be closed. [SPOE]

There is also a purely mechanical reason to suspect that proper "boxing" may aid screen design: if one can visually search a screen hierarchically, then the number of required searches (eye fixations) can be minimized. (This is an analogous argument to the one advanced in support of a computer binary search vs. a linear search of a database.)

"In viewing a display screen, the eye will have to fixate several times in making a search. The task can be facilitated by structuring the format with this searching procedure in mind by dividing the data into discrete blocks." [CROP p.96]

Existing guidelines contain many references to the concept of boxing:

"On a large ... screen, areas ... may be separated by blank spaces in sufficient quantity to state unequivocally that each area is confined within those blank areas." [ENGE p.8]

2.2 HOT-SPOT ANALYSIS TECHNIQUE

Intensity is a common physical property. Hot-spot analysis is a means of representing relative intensities across a visual field, as an alternative to physically measuring them with an optical device.

Relative intensity is computed by calculating a moving average of intensity at each character position on the screen. [3] The results are presented as a topography of intensity.

The peaks provide useful information about the attention centers of the design. Areas of higher intensity can be considered areas of higher information richness. Lacking any heuristics to the contrary, it seems reasonable to expect that the eye would be drawn to these areas when searching for data items.

The valleys provide information regarding the relative scarcity of the "voids" in the visual field. The location and relative scarcity of these voids is important when assessing the difficulty of eye movement across them. Frequently a user is asked to traverse "voids" in the visual field when moving, for example, between prompt and datum. [See Fig 1C]

2.3 ALIGNMENT ANALYSIS TECHNIQUE

Alignment analysis is useful in judging the tabular structure of a screen design.

An alignment point is said to be left or right, depending on where strings of characters begin and end. The number of alignment points is calculated for each column of the display. The number of consecutively repeated alignment points in a column is called the strength of alignment in that column.

There are at least two independent reasons why alignment is important. First, it evokes our notion of list processing (defeating our impulse to read). Second, it provides a sort of visual straightedge along which our eyes can accurately travel.

Many existing guidelines mention alignment.

"The use of structuring techniques for alpha-

```
GOLDBERG,CHARLES W  100000343  26 M  INP 127 1 W

1221:0001R  COLL: 12/21/77 4:20 PM  LOG: 12/21/77 2:46 PM
   ORDERED: CBC & DIFF
    CBC
=>     WBC                          23*   TH/MM3       (5-10)
=>     RBC                         4.9    MIL/MM3      (4.6-5.8)
=>     HGB                          15    GM/DL        (14.0-17.0)
=>     HCT                          45    VOL %        (42-51)
=>     MCV                          92    CUMICRON     (84-103)
=>     MCH                          31    UUGM         (27-32)
=>     MCHC                         32    %            (31-37)
    DIFFERENTIAL
=>     POLYS                        80*   %            (40-75)
=>     BANDS                         6    %            (0-10)
=>     LYMPHS                        9*   %            (20-45)
=>     MONOS                         1    %            (0-14)
=>     METAMYELO                     3*   %            (0-0)
=>     MYELOCYTE                     1*   %            (0-0)
=>     TOT CELL CT                 100    WBC CNTD
=>     RBC MORPH                NORMAL
=>     PLATELETS                NORMAL
```

<--- Fig 1a.(to left) The screen design being analyzed. Notice that the design has a visual deadspot between the laboratory test names and their values. Notice also the highly regimented way in which <--- columnar alignment is used in this design.

Fig 1b.(to right) A result of boxing analysis. ---> The disturbing gap between the test names and their values is clearly visible (box#5 and #9&12). Notice the left-side extension to box#5 which results from the use of the unneeded pseudo-graphic character combination "=>", and results in some unrelated fields being trapped in box#5 (at top). --->

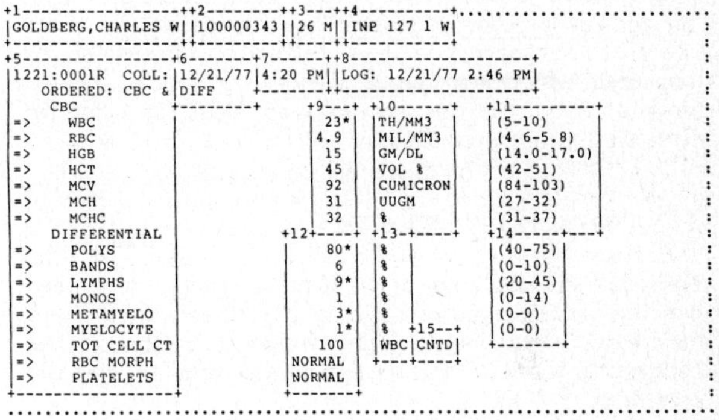

Character set used to show increasing intensity is: .`-:=\X@#

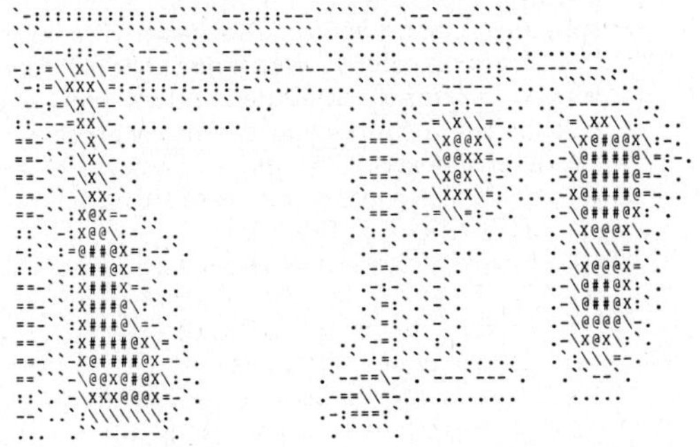

<--- Fig 1c.(to left) A result from hot-spot analysis. From this analysis, one can clearly see the gap mentioned above. Notice also the "hot" area on the far right of the display which includes the relatively unimportant test normal values. Notice that the design is somewhat compressed to the left as evidenced by the void in the far right of the <--- design.

Fig 1d.(to right) A result from alignment analysis. ---> The markers "/" and "{" indicate the begin and end of each field. Alignment "runs" are calculated and appear at the bottom of the figure. Notice the very heavy alignment score, the highest appearing anywhere in the design, present at columns 1&2 which result from repetition of the attention-grabbing, but meaningless pseudo-graphic character combination "=>". --->

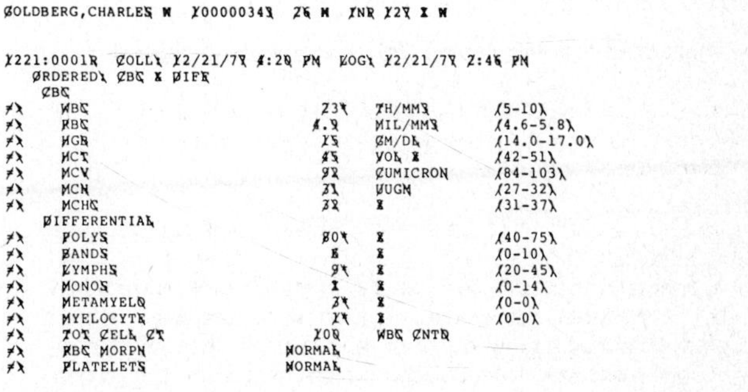

```
ALIGNMENTS
1....1..............................1............1..................... LEFT
4...1.4...1.1.....1...........1..164....31...........2.................... LEFT

.1...................................................................... RIGHT
.5......6.1...3.2....................74..16...1..1.........1.3............... RIGHT
```

Fig 1. A SAMPLE SCREEN, an example from a clinical laboratory reporting system, is shown at top. Partial results from three descriptive computer analyses -- boxing analysis, hot-spot analysis and alignment analysis -- follow.

numeric displays (include the notion that) information should be presented in a fixed, tabular formation so that users can develop spatial expectancies." [TULL p.549]

"When presented in tabular form, data should be aligned vertically and left-justified." [DAVI p.126]

3. QUANTITATIVE MEASURES

Quantitative measures of screen design can be categorized as physical, associative, or aesthetic. We restrict ourselves in the following discussion to measures which can be expressed as single values. Most of the measures are derived from the analytic techniques presented above.

3.1 PHYSICAL MEASURES

The most obvious physical measure is loading or screen density. Investigators have long realized that there may exist some optimal screen density, although the optimum seems to vary somewhat according to personal preference [VITZ].

It is our as yet unproven hypothesis that optimal loading is also a function of the experience level of the user and the degree to which the display design matches the underlying conceptual data model. [TSIC]

Proper loading in most circumstances seems to be no more than about 40% [WILL GALI] -- a design exceeding this by any significant amount tends to be 'too busy', 'too crowded' or 'too cluttered'.

"As the information density becomes higher the human perceptual channels become overloaded and errors occur." [CROP p.96]

Interestingly enough a screen which is not overcrowded according to this guideline may still appear overcrowded. [See Fig 3A]

Character loading scores for the sample displays:

SCREEN	LOADING
1	.22
2	.13
3	.32

A sparsely loaded screen design may also be a problem. It may under-stimulate a user and actually impair performance, since there is a trade-off between providing too much information, which overloads the human visual processor, and too little, which provides too narrow a context and thus relies too heavily on human short-term memory.

Loading as a measure is, however, problematic. In the discussion above, and indeed throughout the model presented in this paper, occupied character positions are the atomic unit of analysis. Several variants to

character loading suggest themselves:

(a) Pixel loading

Is it 'fair' that a period and a capital 'M' should be considered to contribute equally to the loading score? If we are measuring 'loading' of the visual sense, then computing pixel loading may be more meaningful.

(b) Field loading

Given the human's faculty to chunk and group, perhaps the number of fields which appear in a design is a more accurate measure of cognitive loading.

SCREEN	SCORE
1	104
2	51
3	128

(c) Box loading

At yet a higher cognitive level, it may be appropriate to consider the number of separately inscribed groups of information (called 'boxes' in the discussion above) as a loading measure. This is particularly appealing in analyzing the task of searching the screen, since heuristics might suggest which region(s) of the screen to search first. Thus the number of boxes present may be of interest.

SCREEN	SCORE
1	15
2	6
3	11

3.2 ASSOCIATIVE MEASURES

A format which is lightly loaded but 'misgrouped' is indeed still difficult to visually decode. The boxing analysis technique described above is a useful descriptive tool for demonstrating possible visual association of fields. From it certain quantitative measures can be derived:

(a) Average distance between boxes

For readability purposes, one would like white-space to well serve the task of separating 'ideas' or dissimilar groups of data. This measure can then be thought of as measuring the effectiveness of the use of white-space as a separator.

(b) Average distance between boxes/total number of boxes

A normalized measure of the equitable use of white-space as a visual separator.

```
CUSTOMER NUMBER 758-003-49326
LEGAL NAME   FLANAGAN CHEMICAL COMPANY

  INVOICE TO:          SHIP TO:
HADEN FLATS PLANT    HADEN FLATS PLANT
P.O. BOX 783         94 NEW ROCHELLE RD.
ENGLEWOOD CLIFFS     NEW ROCHELLE
NJ 07632             NY 10636


SALESMAN #53730 B.L. JONES



IS THE ABOVE INFORMATION CORRECT?
* * * * *   ANSWER YES OR NO
```

<--- Fig 2a.(to left) The screen design being analyzed.
Notice the strong symmetry in this design. Notice
<--- also the frugality of the design.

Fig 2b.(to right) A result of boxing analysis.   --->
Few boxes appear (only 6), and their obvious similarity in shape and size provide an interesting
contrast to the demonstration in Fig 1. Notice the
design's poor balance and its nearly complete
avoidance of the right hemiscreen.   --->

```
:............................................................:
: +1-------------------+                                      :
: |CUSTOMER NUMBER 758-003-49326 +2------+                    :
: |LEGAL NAME   FLANAGAN CHEMICAL|COMPANY|                    :
: +-------------------+----------+-------+                    :
: +3-----------------+  +4--------------------+               :
: | INVOICE TO:      |  | SHIP TO:            |               :
: |HADEN FLATS PLANT |  |HADEN FLATS PLANT    |               :
: |P.O. BOX 783      |  |94 NEW ROCHELLE RD.  |               :
: |ENGLEWOOD CLIFFS  |  |NEW ROCHELLE         |               :
: |NJ 07632          |  |NY 10636             |               :
: +------------------+  +---------------------+               :
: +5------------------------+                                 :
: |SALESMAN #53730 B.L. JONES|                                :
: +--------------------------+                                :
:                                                             :
: +6-----------------------------------+                      :
: |IS THE ABOVE INFORMATION CORRECT?    |                     :
: |* * * *   ANSWER YES OR NO           |                     :
: +-------------------------------------+                     :
:                                                             :
:                                                             :
:............................................................:
```

Character set used to show increasing "heat" is: .`-:=\X@#

<--- Fig 2c.(to left) A result from hot-spot analysis.
The important information appears in areas of high
visual intensity. Notice also the pleasing
<--- symmetry of the hot spots.

```
CUSTOMER NUMBER 758-003-4932%
LEGAL NAME   FLANAGAN CHEMICAL COMPANY

INVOICE TO%           SHIP TO%
HADEN FLATS PLANT     HADEN FLATS PLANT
P.O% BOX 783          9% NEW ROCHELLE RD%
ENGLEWOOD CLIFFS      NEW ROCHELLE
N% 07632              N% 10636


SALESMAN #53730 B.L% JONES
```

Fig 2d.(to right) A result from alignment analysis.   --->
Both important areas coincide with alignment
"edges". Perhaps increased use of alignment could
have improved however the readability of the top-
most area of the display.   --->

```
IS THE ABOVE INFORMATION CORRECT%
* * * * *   ANSWER YES OR NO
```

```
ALIGNMENTS                                          ...... LEFT
..8.........1.............3..1.............................. LEFT
                                                    ...... RIGHT
.........1..1.................1..1.......................... RIGHT
```

Fig 2. A SAMPLE SCREEN, an example from an <u>accounts payable system</u>, is shown at top.
Partial results from three descriptive computer analyses -- boxing analysis, hot-
spot analysis and alignment analysis -- follow.

(c) Average size of box

Small boxes in general may be granular and not serve as useful in providing a strong grouping pattern. Its unit of measure is area, expressed in character positions squared, and can be calculated as height times width.

From hot-spot analysis, several quantitative measures are proposed:

(d) Number of foci

Topographically one can count the number of foci where local maxima of intensity occur. A display with too many such foci may indicate a poorly organized display; a display with too few may indicate one which is too bland and uninteresting.

(e) Normality of intensity distribution

A probability distribution can be constructed from the values of intensity computed across the visual field. It would appear that a Gaussian distribution might indicate a 'natural' distribution of intensity. A measure can be suggested which reflects the degree of fit of the empirical distribution to the Normal.

There are many visual cues which can be used to persuade the eye into perceiving items as being related. Columnar alignment almost certainly is the most powerful of these visual cues. It promotes visual association by pointing out lists of items. [4]

Possible measures of the likely effect of an alignment strategy are:

(a) Total number of repeated alignments

This is a measure of the list-orientation of the display.

SCREEN	SCORE
1	121
2	17
3	54

(b) Total number of repeated alignments/number of fields

This is a normalized measure of (a).

SCREEN	SCORE
1	1.16
2	.33
3	.42

(c) Maximum number of repeated alignments in any one column

SCREEN	SCORE
1	15
2	8
3	5

(d) Avg number of repeated alignments (over columns)

SCREEN	SCORE
1	1.51
2	.21
3	.67

3.3   AESTHETIC MEASURES

There exists a design aesthetic. Certain designs naturally appeal to the eye while others are displeasing.

The notion of what is artistic has evolved throughout man's history. Many of the notions systematized by the disciplines of of art and the graphic arts can be applied to contrived, computer-generated scenes in much the same way as they can be applied to natural scenes.

(a) Balance

Man's disdain for the unbalanced is a common experience. (How many times have you adjusted the painting over the mantle?) The exact reason for this disdain is not well understood.

Balance is easy to measure. It can be computed as simply the absolute cartesian difference between the actual center-of-mass (computed in the classical way) and the physical center of the screen.

Thus a perfectly balanced scene would yield a score of zero. A large score, i.e. an improperly balanced scene, may indicate a design whose content is densely packed into one quadrant of the screen.

Balance scores for the sample displays:

SCREEN	BALANCE SCORE
1	11.20
2	20.91
3	9.30

(b) Symmetry

The eye's appreciation of the symmetric is demonstrated the longstanding appeal of the kaleidoscope. This factor is more difficult to specify quantitatively. The following measures are computable:

```
                 S U R G E R Y   S C H E D U L I N G
         DATE   O/R  START/STOP  ROOM/BED SURGEON NUMBER/NAME      CALL-INIT
WED  08-01  5     1200  1400          16025 BROWN J C               CGH
PATIENT ID   PATIENT NAME           ADDL NAME   TITLE AGE SEX ADM-DT OUTPT?
         MYERS MARTH R              GRAYSON        MRS  24Y  F  07-28
DIAGNOSIS                           SPECIAL INSTRUMENT
  CHOLECYSTOLITHIASIS
INFO:
OPER ONE   COLECYSTECTOMY
OPER TWO
ANESTHESIA STAND-BY ANESTHESIOLOGIST         POST DATE  FS XRAY-EQP FILM
  GENERAL       N    56789 BAKER C B         JRC  07-31
SP INSTRUCTION
BLOOD PRODUCTS

STANDARD PREPS

ADDRESS
  1901 SOUTH BOULEVARD           APT 3 A      CHARLOTTE,N C    28205
HOME PHONE     ADDL PHONE    ADM DOCTOR NUMBER/NAME    ACCOM   BIRTH-DATE
  704-535-4163  704-523-1641   16025 BROWN J C         PRVT    08-31-53
RESPONSIBLE PARTY        TELEPHONE    REL INFO
  MYERS MARTHA R              704-535-4163
REMRKS CALL DR BROWN WHEN PATIENT ARRIVES
```

<--- Fig 3a.(to left) The screen design being analyzed. Notice the chaotic nature of the design, its nearly complete lack of symmetry, and its poor balance. This design suffers from many semantic problems as well.

<---

Fig 3b.(to right)

A result of boxing analysis.   --->
Notice that only few, large boxes appear. These boxes enclose unrelated data, and demonstrate little or no symmetry. Poor balance is also readily apparent. Notice that the title gets divided between three boxes (box#1,2,3) which dilutes its effectiveness substantially. Notice the strange little box (box#9) which is tucked inconspicuously between its two amorphous neighbors (box #5&10).   --->

```
+--------+1---------------+2-------+3------------------------------+
+4--------+   S U R G E R Y |C H E D U L I N G                    :
:    DATE | O/R  START/STOP| ROOM/BED|SURGEON NUMBER/NAME  CALL-INIT:
WED 08-01 |5    1200 1400  |         : 16025  BROWN J C     CGH    :
PATIENT ID| PATIENT NAME   |         :ADDL NAME  TITLE AGE SEX ADM-DT OUTPT?:
+5--------+                |         :GRAYSON      MRS  24Y  F  07-28:
DIAGNOSIS                  :         +-----------------------------:
  CHOLECYSTOLITHIASIS      :         :SPECIAL INSTRUMENT           :
INFO:                      +---------+-----------------------------:
OPER ONE  COLECYSTECTOMY   :
OPER TWO                          +6---+7----+8--------------+
ANESTHESIA STAND-BY ANESTHESIOLOGIST :POST|DATE|FS XRAY-EQP FILM|
  GENERAL      N    56789 BAKER C B  :JRC |07-31+--------------+
SP INSTRUCTION                       +----+----+
BLOOD PRODUCTS
+9------------------------------:
|STANDARD PREPS|
+10-----------+                               +11---------+
ADDRESS                                       :           :
  1901 SOUTH BOULEVARD     APT 3 A   CHARLOTTE,N C  : 28209 :
HOME PHONE    ADDL PHONE  ADM DOCTOR NUMBER/NAME  ACCOM:BIRTH-DATE:
  704-535-4163 704-523-1641  16025 BROWN J C  PRVT : 08-31-53 :
RESPONSIBLE PARTY       TELEPHONE    REL INFO       +---------+
  MYERS MARTHA R            704-535-4163
REMRKS CALL DR BROWN WHEN PATIENT ARRIVES         :.............:
```

Character set used to show increasing "heat" is: .`-:=\X@#

<--- Fig 3c.(to left) A result from hot-spot analysis. Many small local peaks of intensity appear, but none which would clearly draw the viewer's attention. Except for a rather strangely shaped deadspot, no areas of visual distinction are present. Instead one gets the impression of bland sameness across most of the visual field.

<---

```
               S U R G E R Y   S C H E D U L I N G
        DATE   O/R  START/STOP  ROOM/BED SURGEON NUMBER/NAME    CALL-INIT
WED  08-01  5    1200  1400          16025 BROWN J C             CGH
PATIENT ID   PATIENT NAME          ADDL NAME   TITLE AGE SEX ADM-DT OUTPT?
         MYERS MARTH R             GRAYSON       MRS  24Y  F  07-28
DIAGNOSIS                          SPECIAL INSTRUMENT
  CHOLECYSTOLITHIASIS
INFO:
OPER ONE   COLECYSTECTOMY
OPER TWO
ANESTHESIA STAND-BY ANESTHESIOLOGIST        POST DATE  FS XRAY-EQP FILM
  GENERAL       N    56789 BAKER C B        JRC  07-31
SP INSTRUCTION
BLOOD PRODUCTS

STANDARD PREPS

ADDRESS
  1901 SOUTH BOULEVARD          APT 3 A     CHARLOTTE,N C    28209
HOME PHONE    ADDL PHONE    ADM DOCTOR NUMBER/NAME    ACCOM   BIRTH-DATE
  704-535-4163  704-523-1641   16025 BROWN J C        PRVT    08-31-53
RESPONSIBLE PARTY       TELEPHONE    REL INFO
  MYERS MARTHA R             704-535-4163
REMRKS CALL DR BROWN WHEN PATIENT ARRIVES

  ALIGNMENTS
                                                                     LEFT
5.....1.1.....2.1.1...........2..1...2.11.....1.2....2....21...1.1...1..1.  LEFT

                                                                     RIGHT
...1.1.1.2...2...............1.2....1.1.1.......2........11.............1. RIGHT
```

Fig 3d.(to right)

A result from alignment analysis.   --->
Little, if any, alignment is present. No strong alignment edges appear. One is left with the impression that the viewer's eyes would be left to rove aimlessly around this design when attempting to search for data of interest.   --->

Fig 3. A SAMPLE SCREEN, an example from a <u>hospital information</u> <u>system</u>, is shown at top. Partial results from three descriptive computer analyses -- boxing analysis, hotspot analysis and alignment analysis -- follow.

(1) Number of prominent axes
of symmetry

This is the classical notion of symmetry.

(2) Similarity of boxes

Rather than be concerned with axes, this
approach measures the similarity of the
size of boxes used in the layout.

4.   USEFULNESS OF MEASURES

There are two ways in which such a set of measures
could be immediately useful:

4.1   AS AN EXPERIMENTAL TOOL

Experiments could be devised which correlate quantitative measures of screen syntax with measures
of human performance. Four measures of human
performance are of particular interest:

(a) Learning -- who long does it take a human to
accommodate a new screen design? A human
employs several faculties of human memory in
that process including locational and episodic memory.

(b) Retention -- how well/long does a human retain the ability to efficiently use a screen
design? This is a particularly important
issue when dealing with discretionary and
casual users.

(c) Search speed -- how long does it take a human
to search for a particular datum of interest
from the visual field. Searching seems a
much more common computer-related task than,
say, reading.

(d) Error rate -- at what rate are errors committed by a user while searching the visual
field?

With an appropriate experimental tool, optimum
ranges of values for the screen measures could be
assessed by observing correlations between the
screen measures and the human performance measures. Experiments can be focused to gather
results concerning different classes of users,
different classes of user function, and different
visual devices.

4.2   AS A SOFTWARE DESIGN TOOL

Using the 'gold standards' developed through
experimentation, designers could receive a
computer-generated, objective analysis of their
proposed screen designs. It would be especially
useful to receive comparative data concerning two
or more design alternatives, since it is much
easier to decide that one alternative is 'better'
than another, as opposed to having to render an

opinion as to the 'absolute goodness' of a
particular design.

5.   CONCLUSIONS AND FUTURE DIRECTIONS

This paper has introduced certain quantitative
measures of screen design. Many more questions
suggest themselves:

(a) More and different measures of merit could be proposed. We need measures which are natural, are
intuitively simple, are relatively easy to compute.

(b) One or more overall measures, which are combinations of the individual measures, need to be
devised. Such overall 'goodness' measures would
be especially useful in choosing between design
alternatives.

(c) We have restricted our domain to simple video
terminals. An understanding of what makes for
'good' designs using these devices may provide
insights into how to tackle many remaining problems -- e.g. how best to deal with color, enhanced
video attributes, higher-resolution devices, win-
dowed presentations and the like.

(d) Assuming these measures can be validated and shown
to be sensitive to human performance, acceptable
values for the measures need to be compiled and
presented in the form of a design handbook and
software tools.

(e) A challenge remains regarding how best to devise
software tools which provide an acceptable
interface to the designer, presenting the design
critique in a context he/she can understand, and
in a way which suggests improvement in the screen
design being created.

FOOTNOTES

[1] Other video attributes might also serve as visual separators -- different video intensities (reverse video, half-video), different colors.

[2] There is one exception to that rule. It involves two adjacent 'words' (defined as two boxes with height of one line which are separated by one column). This exception is made so as not to artificially separate two English words which would otherwise result in two separate boxes.

[3] The computation is does as follows. Each character position is either occupied or not (0 or 1). In calculating the intensity at a particular position of the screen, the character residing there, and its neighbors contribute to the 'moving average' of intensity at that point. Contributions from neighboring characters are dampened by a factor of $1/2^d$, where d is the distance (in character positions) of the contributing character to the position of interest. Thus a character which is 4 positions away will contribute only as $1/2^4$ to the the total intensity at the point.

[4] Other possible visual cues include pseudo-graphic characters, lines of '-', bullets, columns of vertical bars or of some other 'special' character.

REFERENCES

Bailey, Robert W., Human Performance Engineering: A Guide to System Designers, Prentice-Hall, 1982.

Card, Stuart K. et al, The Psychology of Human-Computer Interaction, Erlbaum, 1983.

Cropper, Ann G. and S.J.W. Evans, "Ergonomics and Computer Display Design", The Computer Bulletin, July 1968.

Danchak, M.M., "CRT Displays for Power Plants", Instrumentation Technology, vol. 23, no. 10, 1976, pp. 29-36.

Davis, Elaine G. and R.W. Swezey, "Human Factors Guidelines in Computer Graphics: A Case Study", Int'l J. Man-Machine Studies, vol. 18, 1983, pp.113-133.

Engel, Stephen E. and Richard E. Granda, Guidelines of Man/Display Interfaces, IBM Technical Report TR 00.2720, December 1975.

Galitz, Wilbert O., Handbook of Screen Format Design, Q.E.D. Information Sciences, Inc., Wellesley, Mass., 1981.

Human Factors in Screen Design, Human Performance Associates, Mendham NJ, 1984.

Martin, James, Design of Man-Computer Dialogues, Prentice-Hall, 1973.

Monty, R. and Sanders, J. (eds.), Eye Movements and Psychological Processes, Erlbaum, 1976.

Morland, D. Verne, Human Factors Guidelines for Terminal Interface Design, Communications of the ACM, vol. 26, no.7, July 1983, p.486-489.

Peterson, David E., "Screen Design Guidelines", Small Systems World, Feb 1979, p.19-37.

Ramsey, H. Rudy and Michael E. Atwood, Human Factors in Computer Systems: A Review of the Literature, Science Applications, Englewood CO, Technical Report SAI-79-111-DEN, September 1979.

Shneiderman, Ben, Software Psychology: Human Factors in Computer and Information Systems, Winthrop, 1980.

Smith, S.L. and A.F. Aucella, Design Guidelines for the User Interface to Computer-Based Information Systems, MITRE Corporation, Report Number ESD-TR-83-122.

Siegel, Arthur I. and M.A. Fischl, "Dimensions of Visual Information Displays", J. of Applied Psychology, vol.55, no.5, 1971, p.470-476.

Spoehr, K.T. and S.W. Lehmkuhle, Visual Information Processing, Freeman, 1982.

Stewart, Thomas F.M., "Displays and the Software Interface", Applied Ergonomics, vol.7, no.3, 1976, p.137-146.

Streveler, Dennis J. and Peter B. Harrison MD, "Measuring the 'Goodness' of Screen Designs", Proceedings of the Seventeenth Annual Hawaii International Conference on System Sciences, January 1984, vol. 1., pp.423-430.

Teitelbaum, Richard C. and Richard E. Granda, "The Effects of Positional Constancy on Searching Menus for Information", CHI'83 Conference Proceedings, Human Factors in Computing Systems, Boston, December 1983, p.150.

Tsichritzis, D.C. and F.H. Lochovsky, Data Models, Prentice-Hall, 1981.

Tullis, Thomas S., "An Evaluation of Alphanumeric, Graphic and Color Information Displays", Human Factors (Special Issues: CRT Viewing), vol.23, no.5, October 1981, p.541.

Tullis, T., "The Formatting of Alphanumeric Displays: A Review", Human Factors, December 1983, pp.657-682.

Vitz, P.C., "Preference for Different Amount of Visual Complexity", Behavioral Science, vol. 11, 1966, p.105-114.

Wasserman, Anthony I., "The Design of Idiot-proof Interactive Systems", Proceedings of the National Computer Conference, vol. 42, AFIPS Press, Montvale NJ, 1973.

Human-Computer Interaction — INTERACT '84 / B. Shackel (ed.)
Elsevier Science Publishers B.V. (North-Holland)
© IFIP, 1985

VDT SCREEN RESOLUTION AND
OPERATOR PERFORMANCE

Jeffrey L. Harpster and Andris Freivalds

Department of Industrial and Management Systems Engineering
The Pennsylvania State University
University Park, PA, USA.

The study compared operator performance on a visual search task with the resolution of the display used. The four displays consisted of low, high, high resolution simulating low resolution and hard copy print as a control. Performance was significantly worst on the low resolution, better for the high resolution modes displays and was best for hard copy print. An explanation based on the spatial frequency characteristics of the display stimulating the accommodative system is given.

1. INTRODUCTION

In the past 20 to 30 years the United States has undergone, for practical purposes a computer revolution. Computer usage has multiplied by a factor of ten in the past decade and is estimated to double every two to four years [1]. Consequently, the major input/output device, the visual display terminal (VDT), will be increasing in numbers to approximately 30 million, or about one VDT for every three white-collar workers [2]. Along with this increased profusion and usage of VDTs, there has arisen an increased number of complaints from workers of general eye discomfort, eye strain, difficulty in focusing, double vision, etc. as compared to hard copy print users. These complaints have been substantiated by many surveys of large numbers of VDT workers in various occupations [3-14]. Several laboratory studies have attempted to identify causes for these complaints by examining screen color [15], various screen conditions [16], contrast reversal [17], fatigue [10], and ophthalmological measures [18,19]. However none of the studies closely correlated changes in physical characteristics of VDT's with operator performance while actually working on VDT tasks.

There exist several distinct physical differences between VDT's and hard copy print which might account for the complaints and decreased performance. First of all, VDT's and hard copy print differ in image quality. VDT's tend to be blurred in comparison to hard copy print. The transition from dark to light is more gradual for the VDT's than for the hard copy print. It can be seen from figure 1 that VDT characters have a gaussian variation of luminance within each dot or pixel. Since the printed material contains sharp edges it will also contain high spatial frequencies. On the other hand, VDT's do not have the sharp edges, and the presence of high spatial frequencies is doubtful.

The extent to which the higher spatial frequencies are missing is undoubtedly related to the resolution of the screen. Since the pixels are smaller on the higher resolution screen it is hypothesized that the luminous profile of a high resolution pixel will also be different than that of a low resolution pixel.

Other differences include a form of temporal instability of the VDT known as flicker. As soon as an image is presented on a VDT it begins to fade at a rate that is dependent on the phosphor of the screen and must be continually regenerated by the frequency of line current. Another form of temporal instability is due to the lateral movement of the characters on the screen referred to as jitter and most commonly is due to faulty synchronization of the line scanning or instability of the power supply. A fourth problem, found also in hard copy print but typically worse for VDT's is glare which can act to reduce the contrast between the characters and the screen.

It was decided to limit the scope the study to only one of the four major physical differences between hard copy print and VDT screens - the spatial frequency characteristics as determined by the resolution of the VDT or hard copy display. Thus, the main objective was to correlate operator performance on a visual search task with the resolution of the display for both VDT and hard copy displays.

2. METHODS

Five college age students with normal, or corrected to normal, near and far visual acuity (20/20) were tested. Corrections, if necessary were worn during all experiments.

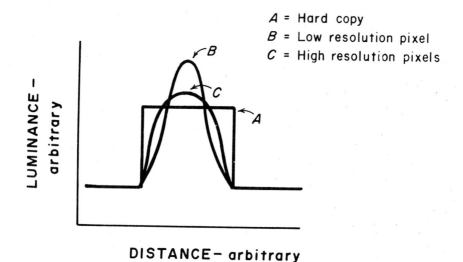

A = Hard copy
B = Low resolution pixel
C = High resolution pixels

Fig. 1 Luminance Distribution for Various Pixels and Hard Copy Print

A Princeton Graphics Terminal (PGS HX-12) driven by an IBM personal computer, (PC) was used for the displays. Three different types of displays were generated. The first type contained 640X 200 pixels, corresponded to the normal IBM-PC high resolution mode and was termed the high resolution narrow (HRN) mode. The second contained 320 x 200 pixels, corresponded to the normal IBM-PC low resolution mode and was termed low resolution wide (LRW), because the characters were the same height but twice as wide in width and stroke width as in HRN. The third utilized the high resolution mode but was programmed such that the characters were identical in size to the low resolution wide mode. Therefore it was termed the high resolution wide (HRW) mode. A fourth display of hard copy print acted as a control. The pages of characters printed by the IBM-PC printer were displayed on the front of the screen of a uniform luminance of 39 cd/m². The illumination in the room was less than 10 lux and the contrast of all displays was over 90%. The spatial frequency characteristics of each of the displays was determined in a seperate study [20].

The subjects were tested in two sessions of two hours each on a visual search task similar to Mourant et al. [21]. The subjects were to find four numbers from a large pattern of numbers on the display. The time to find all four numbers was recorded as the response time for that trial. The order of presentation was as follows.

1) 10 LRW patterns
2) 10 HRN patterns
3) 10 HRW patterns
4) 10 hard copy patterns
5) 10 hard copy patterns
6) 10 HRW patterns
7) 10 HRN patterns
8) 10 LRW patterns

Ten practice trials were given before each of the two sessions. (A pilot study had indicated that little improvement in performance was to be gained after ten trials).

3. RESULTS

Analysis of variance of the mean response times indicated that there was a main effect for screen type (f = 8.83, P<.001) with no main effect for sessions (f = .05, p>.5). Since there was no significant difference in the two sessions, the assumption that there was no learning - after ten trials - appears to be valid and the values from the two sessions could be averaged. Further analysis of the mean response times (plotted in Fig. 2) by Duncan's Multiple Range Test indicated that the significantly slowest mean response time was for the low resolution wide screen. The hard copy print had the fastest mean response time. However, it was not significantly different from the two high resolution screens at the .05 level of significance.

4. DISCUSSION

The hypothesized relationship of screen resolu-

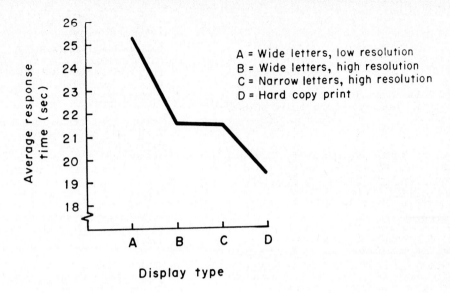

Fig. 2 Plot of Average Response Times for Search Task on Various Displays

tion and operator performance on a visual search task was shown to be significant. The low resolution screen with lowest spatial frequencies gave the worst response times, hard copy print with highest spatial frequencies yielded the best response times and both high resolution screens with intermediate spatial frequencies gave similar response times. A plausible explanation for such results lies in the functioning of the human visual system.

The main visual mechanisms in VDT viewing are accommodation, adaptation and convergence, of which the former is most important in the present study. Accommodation is the change in the curvature of the lens of the eye to bring into sharp focus, stimuli - at varying distances. Nervous mechanisms control accommodation through the action of the intraocular ciliary muscles [22]. While at rest for most people, the eyes accommodate to an intermediate position of 1.5 diopters [23]. An important feature of this resting position is that this is the only distance for which the eye is accurately focused . At any other distance, the accommodation will be a compromise between the pull of the stimulus and the tendency of the eye to regress towards the resting position. Furthermore it was found in the late 60's that the visual system has different sensitivities for different spatial frequencies. The first measurement of the spatial bandwidth of the human visual system was made by an electrical engineer trying to decide how much spatial information to provide viewers of television [24]. Campbell and Robson [25,26] were then able to

develop and improve techniques for measuring the human contrast sensitivity function. Using this function Charman and Tucker [27] found that accommodation was more accurate for the higher spatial frequencies than for low or middle frequencies. Owens [28] found similar results, though, at slightly lower frequencies. Thus low resolution VDT displays with low spatial frequencies would not prove to be a sufficiently strong stimulus for the accommodative system and decreased performance should result as a consequence of the inadequate accommodation.

Thus one would argue for the use of high resolution VDT's rather than low resolution ones. However, more work will have to be done to determine how many pixels are necessary for improved performance since neither high resolution display (HRN, HRW) was significantly worse than hard copy print. Perhaps a larger number of subjects would have produced a significant difference. Also, studies over extended time periods need to be conducted in order to identify effects of spatial frequency in screen resolution on subjective feelings of visual fatigue eye strain and other complaints voiced by VDT operators. In any case, the results of the present study demonstrate the need for the accounting of screen resolution into the design of VDT's.

REFERENCES

[1]   Gantz, F. and Peacock, J.   Computer systems and services for business and industry.   Fortune 108(8), (1981) 39-94.

[2]   United States Bureau of the Census, Statistical Abstracts of the United States, (Washington D. C. 1979) Table No. 685, p.415.

[3]   Holler, H., Kundi, M., Schmid, H.,Stidl,H., Thaler, A. and Winter, N.   Stress and Strain on the Eyes Produced by Work with Display Screens (Vienna, Austria, Austrian Trade Union Association, 1975).

[4]   Haider, M., Slezak, H., Holler, H., Kundi, M., Schmid, H., Stidl, H.G., Thaler, A., and Winter, N.   Arbeitsbeanspruchung und Augenbelastung an Bildschirmgeraten (Wien: Vlg. des O.G.B. Automationsausschuss de Gewerkschaftsbundes der Privatengestellen. 1975).

[5]   Gunarsson, E. and Östberg, O.   The physical and psychological working environment at a terminal-based computer storage and retrieval system (Stockholm: Swedish National Board of Occupational Safety and Health, Department of Occupational Medicine, Report 35, 1977).

[6]   Cakir, A., Reuter, H.J., Schmude, L., and Armbruster, A.   Untersuchungen zur Anpassung von Bildschirmarbeitsplatzen an die physische und psychische Funtionsweise des Menschen (Bonn. West Germany: Ed. Der Bundesminister for Arbeit und Sozialordnung.   P.O.B. D-5300, 1978).

[7]   Coe, J.B., Cuttle, K., McClellan, W.C., Warden, N.J., and Turner, P.J.   Visual display units.   (Wellington, New Zealand Department of Health, Report M/1/80, 1980).

[8]   Gunnarsson, E., and Soderberg, I.   Eyestrain Resulting from VDT Work at the Swedish Telecommunications Administration. Eye Changes and Visual Strain During Various Working Procedures.   Stockholm: National Board of Occupational Safety and Health, 1980.

[9]   Sauter, S.L., Arndt, R., and Gottlieb, M. A Controlled Survey of Working Conditions and Health Problems of VDT Operators at the New York Times.   (Unpublished report prepared for The Newspaper Guild. Department of Preventive Medicine, University of Wisconsin. 1981).

[10] Dainoff, M.J., Happ, A., and Crane, P., Visual Fatigue and Occupational Stress in VDT Operators, Human Factors, 23 (1981) 39-94.

[11] Smith, M.J., Cohen, B.G.F., Stammerjohn, L.W., and Happ, A.   An investigation of health complaints and job stress in video display operations.   Human Factors, 23 (1981) 387-400.

[12] Smith, A.B., Tanaka, S., and Halperin, W. A Preliminary Report on a Cross-Sectional Survey of VDT Users at the Baltimore Sun. (Cincinnati: National Institute for Occupational Safety and Health; 1982.)

[13] Dainoff, M.J.   Occupational stress factors in visual display terminal (VDT) operation: a review of empirical research.   Behaviour and Information Technology (1982) 141-176.

[14] National Research Council Video Display, Work, and Vision (National Academy Press, Washington D.C., 1983.)

[15] Haider, M., Kundi, M., and Weissenbock, M.   Worker strain related to VDUs with differently coloured characters.   In E. Grandjean and E. Vigliani (Eds.) Ergonomic Aspects of Visual Display Terminals. (London: Taylor and Francis, Ltd., 1980). 53-64.

[16] Laubli, T., Hunting, W., and Grandjean,E., Visual Impairments in VDU Operators related to environmental conditions, in E. Grandjean and E.Vigliani (Eds.), Ergonomic Aspects of Visual Display Terminals, (London, Taylor and Francis, Ltd. 1980) 85-94.

[17] Bauer, D., and Cavonius, C.R.   Improving the legibility of visual display units through contrast reversal, in E-Grandjean and E. Vigliani (Eds.)   Ergonomic Aspects of Visual Display Terminals (London, Taylor and Francis, 1980) 137-142.

[18] Krueger, H.   Ophthalmological aspects of work with display workstations.   in E. Grandjean and E. Vigliani, eds., Ergonomic Aspects of Visual Display Terminals (London: Taylor & Francis, 1980) 31-40.

[19] Östberg, O.   Accommodation and visual fatigue in display work. in E. Grandjean and E. Vigliani, eds., Ergonomic Aspects of Visual Display Terminals.   (London: Taylor and Francis, 1980) 41-52.

[20] Harpster,J. and Freivalds,A. Effects of Image Quality on Visual and Task Performance on VDT and Hard Copy Tasks submitted to Human Factors (1984).

[21] Mourant,R.R.,Lakshmanan,R.,Chantadisai R., Visual fatigue and cathode tube display terminals.   Human Factors,23(1981)529-540.

[22] Guyton, A.C. Textbook of Medical Physiology, 4th Ed. (W.B. Sanders Co., Philadelphia, PA. 1971).

[23] Leibowitz, H.W., and Owens, D.A., Anomalous myopias and the intermediate dark focus of accommodation, Science, 189 (1975) 646-648.

[24] Schade, O.H., Optical and Photoelectric analog of the eye. J. Opt.Soc.Am., 46 (1956) 721-739.

[25] Campbell, F.W. and Robson, J.G., Application of Fourier analysis to the modulation response of the eye. J.Opt.Soc.Am. 54 (1964) 635-652.

[26] Campbell, F.W. and Robson, J.G., Application of Fourier analysis to the visibility of gratings, J. Physiol. 197 (1968) 551-566.

[27] Charman, W.N. and Tucker, J., Dependence of accommodation response on the spatial frequency spectrum of the observed object. Vision Research, 17 (1977) 129-139.

[28] Owens, D.A., A comparison of accommodation responsiveness and contrast sensitivity for sinusoidal gratings. Vision Research 20 (1980) 159-167.

WORKSTATIONS AND WORKPLACE ISSUES

Human-Computer Interaction — INTERACT '84 / B. Shackel (ed.)
Elsevier Science Publishers B.V. (North-Holland)
© IFIP, 1985

'ENVIRONMENT' PROBLEMS IN INTRODUCING OFFICE INFORMATION SYSTEMS

J. J. Florentin

Department of Computer Science,
Birkbeck College, Malet Street,
London WC1E 7HX, England

At the present time many organisations are changing from centralised time-sharing computing to distributed office information workstations. There are technological advantages, but there is also felt to be a very significant advantage in placing computers under local and personal control. Experience with three such situations unfortunately shows that in organisations with shared information there is a need for central data control which can make such local autonomy infeasible. The difficulties, and a possible future resolution, are discussed.

INTRODUCTION

Many organisations considering the introduction of distributed office information systems (OIS) do not start from a manual paperwork system. Often their staff already use VDU terminals connected to a central time-shared computer system. The working procedures for users of 'office of the future' (OIS) workstations and for users of traditional time-sharing terminals are different. An OIS workstation is a computer in its own right, subject to local user control, whilst a terminal relies entirely on a central computer which is under central control. One prime difference in procedures is that an OIS workstation user has to take far greater responsibility for correct computer operations than a time-sharing terminal user. On the other hand the OIS workstation is more private, personal and felt to be under close individual control, whilst a time-sharing terminal is shared, and under the control of central staff sometimes not personally known to the user. Call this mixture of user responsibility, privacy and personal control the computing environment.

The author has been involved as a technical computer consultant in three organisations where individual workstations are being introduced to supplement existing time-sharing terminals. Initially it was thought that staff could readily change over to workstations, or could freely switch from terminal to workstation according to the work in hand. These assumptions proved to be false, and it became evident that the computer environment had to be considered much more carefully. After one to two years' experience a number of issues have not been fully resolved, and the author now believes that 'office of the future' scenarios ignore important issues which arise from the differences between personal, private paperwork, and company 'public' shared paperwork. The difference between a private notebook and a company form can be vital to staff, but computers do not inherently recognise any

distinctions in the nature of documents they manipulate. Computer systems designers have to impose such distinctions, often with clumsy security mechanisms.

This paper gives a computer systems designer's view of the nature of the environment problem. First a situation which has developed in many organisations is described, then salient features of the time-sharing and OIS environments are described.

For the purpose of discussion assume an organisation having a head office with a central computer, and several geographically dispersed branches under local management.

MOVING AWAY FROM TIME-SHARING

An important complication has arisen in most organisations with time-sharing. Local managers have bought stand-alone word-processors and local micro-computers, sometimes clashing with the central data processing department over the purchase. This uncoordinated collection of machines does not constitute an OIS because the different machines cannot sensibly communicate data to each other (although the salesmen often claim that they can!). However, this situation is a precursor of an OIS and influences people's views on how an OIS should work.

Almost always local managers buy stand-alone machines to gain local control over computing. There seem to be two main reasons for wanting local control:

- bad relationships readily develop between local management and the central data processing department, and local management is tempted to 'go it alone'

- local managers are suspicious that data kept centrally can be inspected surreptitiously by head office accountants, and so wish to keep their data locally.

MOTIVE FOR GOING TO OIS

When main management considers moving to an OIS
there are two main issues:

- the advent of cheap micro-electronics has made
  it technologically more efficient to provide
  many small computers rather than to share out
  a single large computer

- the burgeoning collection of local stand-alone
  machines (as above) fragments organisational
  data and documents into isolated caches which
  are not accessible to other parts of the
  organisation. This is seen as a bar to
  effective central management.

In this situation higher management are tempted
to hope that an OIS will provide local technical
computing power, while allowing access to data
and documents from anywhere in the company.

THE ENVIRONMENT OF TIME-SHARING

Some characteristics of the time-sharing
environment are:

- a user can log on at a terminal anywhere and
  still receive exactly the same computing
  services. Facilities thus move with the
  individual.

- users have to negotiate the use of facilities
  with a central data processing department.
  The central data processing department deals
  with the technicalities of computing, while
  a branch deals with the technicalities of the
  business. Misunderstandings thus readily
  arise.

- the central data processing department takes
  full responsibility for the correct functioning of computing equipment, and for safeguarding data and documents. In the present state
  of technical development considerable training
  is required to take on these responsibilites.

- data and computing services are shared by
  several users.

THE ENVIRONMENT OF STAND-ALONE MACHINES

As noted above the main characteristics of
stand-alone machines are: local control,
local responsibility and locally restricted
access to data and documents, hence privacy.
Local responsibility for safeguarding data and
documents ought to imply some special training.

THE ENVIRONMENT OF THE 'STANDARD' OIS

The typical 'office of the future' is said to
comprise a communications network connecting
two kinds of devices. One device is the office
workstation and the other is a 'server'. An
office workstation provides a single individual
with the totality of information facilities
required, ranging from word-processing, electronic mail, keeping a work diary up to
accessing company databases. Server devices

provide communal facilities such as storing
large quantities of data and sending it to workstations on demand.

The environment of such an OIS is complex and
reflects the way that responsiblity is carried
for:

- regularly entering data into servers so that
  the information retrieved by workstation users
  is fully up-to-date

- safeguarding data against machine and human
  errors

- securing data against unauthorised access

- providing a succession of new program and data
  facilities, and validating standards for new
  facilities; for example, ensuring that the
  user interface is 'friendly'

- informing all users of new facilities on the
  network, giving training in their use, and
  creating channels so that users can influence
  new developments on the network.

Office of the future literature often casually
assumes that an entire office staff can cooperate to carry the above responsibilities, an
assumption which the author doubts.

DESIGN OF AN OIS ENVIRONMENT

The first issues to be settled when designing an
OIS are:

- the exact facilities to be provided by the OIS
  system

- who is going to be responsible for various
  aspects of running the system.

The next issue is to select a general pattern of
system. There are two radical patterns: either

1. the OIS network closely mimics the existing
   time-sharing system. All responsibilities are
   kept by the central data processing department.
   Actual computing processing is dispersed to
   workstations for technological efficiency, but
   is not truly under local control. This
   approach is technically attractive, but will
   seriously disappoint branch managers who seek
   greater local autonomy;   or

2. there is true autonomy at branch or even
   individual user level by carrying out all
   processing on local workstations without any
   central coordination. Individual users have
   to be trained to carry responsibility for data
   and machinery used in common. In the author's
   judgment this is quite infeasible in any
   organisation having common data, although it
   might work in, say, a university where
   different departments have quite separate
   activities.

ILLUSTRATIONS OF ENVIRONMENT DESIGN

Organisation 1 used a time-sharing system for
large-scale word processing, information storage

and financial analysis. Word processing put a
heavy load on the central system. A change to
an OIS was first suggested by a senior manager
who had a personal computer that could convert
financial results to graphical form while the
time-sharing terminals could not display
graphics.

In this installation a change to OIS was made
mainly to spread the computing load of word
processing; however, entirely new graphics
facilities would continue to work (from the
users' viewpoint) as before, but the new
graphical display and printing would be under
local user control. It happens that display and
printing can be put under local control without
special precautions, since there are no reper-
cussions on a network community if a print-out
goes wrong at one location. After a year there
have been no changes in user habits, and little
comment from users. The OIS installation has
replaced some of the time-sharing terminals with
workstations, but the effect has been wholly
technological.

Organisation 2 had acquired a large number of
stand-alone machines although it had a powerful
time-sharing system. The isolation of data into
local caches was perceived as a serious problem
for central management. The manager of the
central data processing service had initially
taken an 'enlightened' and 'liberal' view of
local computing facilities, and had tried to
cooperate by offering advice to local managers.
Local managers had welcomed this advisory
service. However, the central data processing
department had not properly understood that
local managers wanted to put their computing
facilities outside central control. On
realising the situation central higher management decided to set up a new group in management services to rationalise facilities so that
data in branches would be generally accessible.

A complex situation has developed here. The way
forward was seen to be the introduction of new
equipment which would harmonise local and central
needs by having local workstations which would
be technically compatible with the central
computer. Unfortunately, available equipment
does not match the demands which would be made
on it, and new equipment has actually produced
further complications.

Organisation 3 had information retrieval, word
processing and financial analysis on a time-
sharing system. The system was overloaded, and
it was decided to introduce workstations
connected to the central computer in place of
some of the terminals. Initially it was
envisaged that some of the processing would be
offloaded to workstations without changing the
nature of the system. After six months certain
office staff have contrived to shift a great
deal of their work to the workstations, and
there is clearly a desire for greater self-
autonomy. At first it seemed that only certain

individuals wanted this autonomy, but it now
seems that these individuals were those with a
natural flair for coping with operating the
equipment. Others might want the autonomy, but
lack the technical competence to achieve it with
present equipment. The shifting of work to
workstations is not now taking place under a
plan where responsibilities are clearly
allocated, and the intention of keeping the
original computing pattern is not being achieved.
A new pattern of the allocation of specific work
between the central computer and workstations is
emerging.

CONCLUSIONS

Many commercial office organisations are moving
from central time-shared computers to collections of individual office workstations. There
are technological advantages in this, but it is
also often felt within organisations that
greater local and personal control over computing is very desirable. Unfortunately, computer
systems designers can find it impossible to
produce reliable systems which allow substantial
local autonomy because of the sharing of information amongst many independent users. To
prevent corruption of shared data it is necessary to give skilled central staff control over
(nearly all) data.

Office of the future predictions have raised
hopes of a more personalised computing atmosphere. Immediately current technology cannot
enable this, so that, for example, in the
author's personal experience British managers
simply refuse to put their diaries on to workstations. On the other hand the emergence of
truly portable computers could make a great
change. A portable computer would be operated
most of the time quite outside the company
information system. On occasions determined
entirely by the owner the portable computer
could be connected to the company system and
information exchanged. A portable computer
which was easy to use, and yet which was
compatible with the company information system,
might yield the improvement in atmosphere
which, alas, distributed workstations are not
likely to give.

Human-Computer Interaction — INTERACT '84 / B. Shackel (ed.)
Elsevier Science Publishers B.V. (North-Holland)
© IFIP, 1985

A Universal Workstation Concept for Air Command & Control Application

K. Camm

Command, Control and Sensors Division
S.H.A.P.E. Technical Centre, The Netherlands

The shortcomings of air defence and management information system terminals and workstations in an integrated air command and control system are discussed and the requirements for a universal workstation "kit" based on "off-the-shelf" commercial products are introduced. A design outline for such a workstation is presented with several examples of its capabilities in a tactical air system to support the concept, based on work in SHAPE Technical Centre's ACCS Test Bed.

1. Introduction

The NATO strategy of flexible response requires the air force commander to consider and direct the use of his air power for all forms and levels of conventional warfare to combat a threat, not only in the air, but also on the ground or at sea. He may have to use his resources for counter-air operations against airfields, the interdiction of a second echelon advance, close air support of ground forces, and reconnaissance operations, as well as for air combat in air defense situations.

In the past, the command and control for air defence, with its associated ground environment system, has been considered as a largely autonomous task. The support of offensive missions and other types of operations has been conducted by other organisations with their associated systems, and coordination between them has been minimal and ad-hoc.

The speed of modern warfare and the flexibility of today's multi-role aircraft, combined with the need for close coordination in a common airspace, requires a single unified air command and control organisation, and this inevitably requires a re-appraisal of the way that air force commanders and their staffs perform their function, especially with regard to their interaction with computers. The design of the workstation becomes all-important.

Two generic classes of data processing have emerged in air command and control applications: air defence (AD) systems and management information (MI) systems. The former deal with the threat from the air, and are necessarily highly reactive and time-constrained in operation; the latter have not been so time-constrained, being used for pre-planned operations, resource management, and administration - usually at higher level headquarters.

The type of workstation used in each of these systems has been traditionally very different.

AD sites have to rely heavily on the use of computer graphics as the fastest means of appreciating a situation that is changing rapidly. Intersite data are transmitted by bit-packed messages on special-purpose data links that are almost exclusively used for the transmission of radar-derived data. An operator in this type of environment has usually no time to appreciate collateral data which have a geographical significance, unless these data are presented geographically and superimposed on his radar-derived data. Little use has been made of the character-oriented communications interfaces that have become standard commercial practice for the transmission of text.

As a result, AD systems have developed as special-purpose graphics systems with little capability for handling collateral information from sources other than AD sites. They typically employ arrays of pushbuttons, alert lights, and controls for the graphics display, specifically designed for fast response in a task as it was known at system definition time. These workstations are expensive, staff require considerable training and although the computer programs can be changed to keep pace with evolving tactics and tasks, the workstation often can not.

Unlike the AD systems, the MI systems have been heavily influenced by commercial ADP bureau practice. Originally introduced as "batch-process computer-shops" for status reports and trend analysis work, they have become increasingly interactive, but they have remained essentially monolithic, text-oriented systems with little or no capability for using interactive graphics, or dealing with bit-packed messages on special-purpose data links, so there have been fundamental data-exchange difficulties between the MI and AD sites.

As ground support, interdiction, and reconnaissance operations have become increasingly complex and reactive, the tactical headquarters supported by MI systems have had an increasing need to use the system as responsively as their AD counterparts. Although improvements in transaction-processing and data base structures have led to systems that can be used directly by the operational staff as well as the programmer/analyst, division of responsibilities between these two groups of user is often fuzzy, and the classic keyboard/tabular data terminal, common to both, is designed for the programmer and not for the military decision maker.

Much of this decision-making relies on the use of maps, for intelligence on the ground situation and for tactical planning. These same headquarters also have to be appraised of the air situation confronting their subordinate AD sites. Interactive graphics could be used to considerable effect for all of these purposes, but this has been difficult to support with the type of MI system architecture in use.

Stand-alone systems have been tried which allow symbols and lines to be "sketched" on computer-drawn maps for circulation by closed-circuit TV, but this has not allowed the MI data-base and the graphics to be used in an integral sense for interactive planning, and the amount of detail that can be drawn on a TV-resolution display is inadequate for the interactive planning envisaged.

As neither the classic MI terminal nor the AD workstation is particularly well-suited to its evolving tasks, what can be done to improve them and the efficacy of an integrated air C^2 system at the same time?

2.   The STC Air Command & Control System Test Bed

To support SHAPE and the NATO nations (and more recently the ACCS Team in Brussels) in the writing of system specifications for their unified air C^2 system, STC maintains a small collection of netted computers and workstations referred to as the "ACCS Test Bed". This covers operations at the tactical planning and tasking (MI) levels, AD sites, and the airbases, and among other things has been used to investigate the feasibility of a universal workstation for handling the spectrum of activities, tasks, and data encountered across an air C^2 system.

A primary constraint in the current economic climate is that such an improved workstation should not cost more than a typical AD work-station of today, e.g. a UKADGE or a GEADGE workstation. This focusses attention on exploiting the civilian video and microprocessor market to the maximum extent possible, (within the constraints of TEMPEST and EMP protection requirements where these are necessary), rather than resorting to special-purpose military displays.

The major problems with these workstations can be overcome by a suitable re-appraisal of the man-machine interface (MMI); the remaining problems will require a change in system architectural design. A "hybrid" architecture is required that embodies design principles from both the AD and MI type systems. This paper deals only with the workstations in such an enhanced hybrid environment.

The MMI re-appraisal can be summarised as:
- providing the capability for displaying a wider class of collateral graphics and tabular data classes at AD sites, and replacing the hardware pushbuttons and

other controls with a device which has the same inherent flexibility and growth capability for new tasks as the computer software, and which requires less training;
- providing an improved MI terminal that replaces the typewriter keyboard with an operational-task-oriented "panel" offering task options and data base querying capabilities for decision-making purposes by means of easy-to-use sets of "push-button" sequences; and,
- providing an interactive graphics work-station at tactical headquarters for situation display and tactical planning.

If all three sets of improvements for AD sites and tactical headquarters can be implemented with one "universal" workstation kit, there would be additional logistic advantages which reduce the life-cycle costs and improve the overall flexibility of the air C^2 system; tasks can be transferred from one organisation to the other when this is seen to be more efficient; workstations can be temporarily used for other tasks when the operational load peaks; and overall, the system becomes more resilient to battle damage and equipment outages.

Work with the Test Bed has shown that commercially available technology can produce a "universal" workstation for performing the expected graphical tasks at both an AD site and a tactical headquarters in an integrated air C^2 system at reasonable cost. Also, by keeping the design modular, a subset of the workstation elements can be used to produce an improved tabular data MI terminal.

As a result of this work, one NATO operational command is already exploiting this concept.

3.   The Range of Technology Investigated

For the provision of an operational-task-oriented "panel" on an MI terminal (and also the replacement of the hardware pushbuttons on an AD workstation), a "touch-display" method is an obvious choice.

This technique involves a computer-derived "menu" displayed on a VDU, covered by a transparent overlay incorporating a touch-position sensing mechanism. Touching an item on the list can trigger any desired software action; a mathematical calculation, a change of picture on the graphics display, the formatting of a new tabular data display, the display of the next menu – or all of these actions together.

There is virtually no limit to the number and flexibility of the action sequences that can be built up, and with careful design the next step in a complex sequence is always clear without extensive user training.

A fast response in the user/touch panel/ computer/display loop is important if the user is to consider the panel as a set of pushbuttons.

The application of touch displays to AD systems

is not new, but the application to an integrated force management/airspace management system is a new departure, and the depth of application software developed to check the applicability has been relatively extensive.

Since this work began STC has produced a range of workstations, all using this method but employing different technologies for the display of the menu and the detection of the touch position. These technologies include plasma panels, monochrome CRTs, and colour CRTs, with various overlays using capacitative, infra-red, conductive, or ultrasonic wave techniques.

Operational requirements for the graphics can be divided into three categories of activity:
- sketching-in data on a map background for broad tactical overview purposes. These data have no dynamic movement; they are only erased or modified over relatively long intervals of time.
- automatically displaying dynamic situation data. Typically, this involves large numbers of symbols, each with individual dynamic movement and all displayed in relation to a map background.
- sketching-in data as part of an inter-active planning process. Such data have arithmetic or geometrical significance as well as visual significance. Graphical precision, resolution, and quality are key parameters, and a precision map background can be a requirement for some applications. Dynamic movement of the sketched-in data is involved, but usually only in response to "push button" actions.

Technologies investigated have included:
- high resolution (4096x4096) displays using rear-port-projected maps in combination with computer-derived vector graphics;
- high resolution (4096x4096) displays using medium-persistence, monochrome phosphors, or 4-colour penetration layer phosphors (Penetrons), with vector-writing speeds fast enough to generate detailed map outlines with dynamic data overlays;
- high resolution (1024x1024) and medium-to-low (512x512 or lower), bit-mapped, multi-colour displays.

For pointing/drawing on the graphics surface, the range of technologies covered has included:
- touch overlays (using a higher resolution than for the menu selection, with a continuous sampling rate of 20 Hz);
- sketching pads, using a "mouse", and,
- joystick and rolling ball cursor controls.

In the Test Bed, these workstations are currently operating with live (real time) air tracks transmitted from the NATO Air Defence Ground Environment (NADGE) system, and in applications in route planning, ground situation display, and complex force management/airspace management.

4. A Candidate Universal Workstation

The design which has attracted most attention from operational staffs and visitors from the defence industry uses high resolution colour technology (Fig. 1).

The exploded view (Fig. 2) shows the main elements of the workstation. The 5 items comprising the man-machine interface are:
- a medium resolution (625 lines) CRT, driven by an STC-modified Teletext chip offering 8 colours for the foreground and background, used for displaying tabular/text data, with a menu (maximum of 16 touch labels) underneath;
- a touch-sensitive overlay using a matrix of collimated infra-red beams;
- a high resolution (1024x1024), multi-colour CRT, used for all graphics displays;
- a rolling ball, used to control a cursor symbol on the graphics display, for selection or drawing, in conjunction with the touch menu; and,
- an optional alphanumeric keyboard.

Note that these items are only inter-connected through the medium of a stored-programme device directly accessible to the user's application task software (Fig. 3). This device can be a dedicated microprocessor in the workstation or a larger, external processor, depending on the number of workstations and the economic constraints. However, a certain amount of dedicated hardware is necessary, whatever the configuration, to provide constant refresh of the two displays, the continuous sampling and integration of counts from the rolling ball control, and the interpretation of touches on the touch-sensitive overlay.

The modular construction of the workstation allows a tabular-data-only workstation (with or without a keyboard) to be assembled by only using the components inside the dotted outline on Fig. 3 (with an attendant gain in system software simplification through the use of common components).

The graphics microprocessor currently being used contains eight (1024x1024 pixel) planes, a video latch and a video look-up table. Instructions (and data) for drawing lines, circles, characters, etc. are transferred to the graphics microprocessor via a direct-memory-access interface. This processor converts them to a pixel image and loads them into the pixel planes delineated by the application.

All eight planes can be used to provide one composite picture, but they can also be divided into groups by means of the video latch to let them be considered as a "background" group, one (or two) "foreground" groups, and/or a "middle-ground" group, for superimposing three independent pictures. The graphics requirements for the applications vary so much that the memory plane grouping, video latch, and video look-up table cannot be permanently "fixed"; each task down-loads its own program for setting-up the microprocessor.

Once every frame (1/30th of a second), the entire image memory is scanned in synchronism

with the graphics CRT electron beam movement.
Any pixel containing data, offers the data to
the video latch, a device which acts like eight
gates; each controlled independently.

Data passing through the video latch activates
the video look-up table. This has 256 locations
each of which can contain 12 bits of information, preset by instructions from the application program. The 12-bit output word is used
in three groups of four bits to obtain 16
different intensities of red, green, and blue,
so that 4096 different colours are (theoretically) displayable, and 256 may be selected
for any one setting of the video look-up table.

5. Typical Use of the Workstation in Air C^2

The applicability of the MMI has been verified
by developing a number of task sequences and
menu trees appropriate to the level of automation being considered for the tactical application tasks in the Test Bed. Map facilities are
considered as common to all workstations; any
user can call up any map from a set of digitised
maps on disc.

Map retrieval uses a quantised "zoom" capability, based on a "tree-structure" retrieval
mechanism. At the apex of this tree is a basic
map covering the overall operational area. To
use this facility, the user calls for a grid
overlay that divides the picture into nine
equal sub-areas. By selecting one of these
sub-areas (by touch), a smaller scale map of
it is retrieved from the disc and displayed. By
superimposing the grid again, the sub area can
be divided into a further nine sub-areas, etc.

Each map is separately compiled "off-line" from
a digitised data base referred to as the "CIA
World Data Base No. 2", using an appropriate
detail filter in terms of distance resolution
and topographical feature.

Each time the map is changed, any line, circle,
oval, or polygon constituting a tactical overlay
or a flight plan, etc., is automatically re-
scaled, shifted, and "scissored" at the edges,
to retain conformity with the map. Names,
symbols, and speed vectors (for air tracks)
need not change their size.

The foreground picture superimposed on the map
depends on the activity and task of the user at
the workstation. Examples are:

a)   *In a tactical decision-aid role*.   The
rolling ball is used in conjunction with an
associated menu to define an area on the displayed map. Its coordinates are used automatically in the search of a large, ground installation data base, for targets with a menu-selected
criterion.   (Bridges are a classic example).

The individual targets found in the search are
retained in a list, marked on the map, and
offered for target assignment. As each target
is considered, the tabular CRT displays a matrix
of airbases (squadrons that can be considered
for a ground attack) versus the various types of
ordnance appropriate to the squadron aircraft,

Fig. 1:   General Appearance

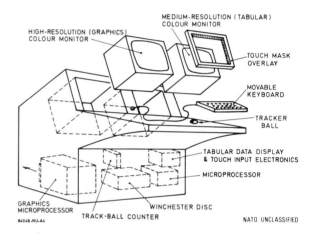

Fig. 2:   Exploded View

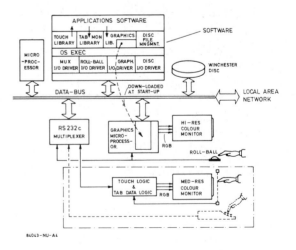

Fig. 3:   Block Schematic

showing the distance involved, the number of aircraft needed with each type of ordnance to achieve a given probability of success, the combat radius when carrying each type of ordnance, and the expected availability: Fig. 4.

The associated menus (one is shown in Fig. 4) allow the user to execute a number of trial "what if" type operations to determine the probabilistic outcome: trial assignments with different numbers of aircraft in the mission; missions with mixed types of ordnance; multiple missions from several squadrons; or missions run at different times for a more favourable availability. The user can use menu-actions to display alternative items in the matrix, such as the number of remaining stocks at the airbase (of the particular ordnance type being considered).

As decisions are made, their impact on missions already considered, and those still to be considered, is continuously shown to the planner, to allow for an iterative form of planning.

b)   In a computer-assisted graphics role.   By selecting an appropriate task, a user can generate, modify, or selectively filter: the ground situation picture (Fig. 5 & 6); or an airspace coordination plan (Fig. 7 & 8).

The Ground Situation entails Intelligence staff drawing up a picture of the most likely position of own and enemy ground forces, missile sites, air defence locations, and any other area which might be hazardous to overfly.

The Airspace Coordination Plan entails Air Coordination staff drawing up a picture of flight refuelling zones, patrol lanes, vertical dispersion orbits, restricted operating zones, and flight corridors, taking account of the Ground Situation.

Both "pictures" are generated by using the rolling ball or specifying latitude/longitude coordinates via tailored menus (Fig. 6 & 8) to place data for circles, polygons, lines, and symbols in an appropriate data base with an associated tactical name.

These data are used to automatically generate tactical overlays on request (Fig. 5 & 7), superimposed on the map on the requester's workstation, in accordance with the area offset or scale factor in use there. The tactical names are used to identify the various items on the display, but they are also used as a "sort-key" to enable the user to selectively filter the picture to his own needs.

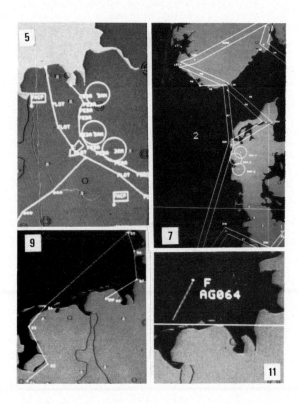

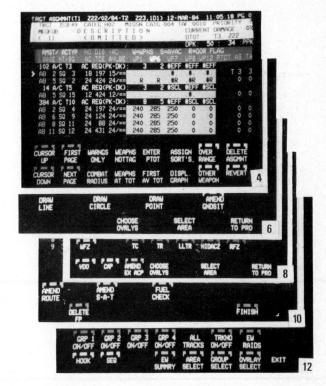

Only selected users are allowed to modify these two generic forms of graphics overlay, which are then made available via the data base for other users at other workstations.

By using the map plus overlays, a mission planner can check the feasibility of a projected mission by "drawing" in the route (Fig. 9) to conform to the airspace coordination plan, avoiding hazardous areas to the maximum extent possible. Menus (Fig. 10) are provided to "sketch" the flight legs from airbase to targets via pre-surveyed navigation points stored in the data base. The speed, height, initial fuel, and times over selected way points may all be modified. The flight performance envelopes of the aircraft concerned are used to calculate the expected fuel margins. The planner may also use the ground situation to estimate the risk probability for any particular mission.

A Flight Coordinator may use the same background overlays for determining mission-to-mission or mission-to-coordination-plan conflicts.

c)   In a "passive" monitoring role.   The user selects Air Situation Monitoring and a particular geographical area via appropriate menus. The data in a central track store at the site (continuously updated from data links or filed route plans) are automatically sampled for the area selected, and transferred every few seconds to his graphics microprocessor. Alternate memory plane "foreground" groups, switched between each sample are used to move tracks with a once-per-second update rate, providing an impression of continuous movement at expanded scales.

The map can contain a considerable amount of detail and can take as long as 8-10 seconds to re-draw, but as it is static until the user calls for a change, it is beneficial to treat the map separately by drawing it in a set of background planes that are unaffected by the air track foreground switching process.

However this incurs a penalty: as the number of planes determines the range of simultaneous colours obtainable, any division of the planes into groups reduces this range, e.g., eight planes will offer 256 colours but four groups of two planes (a background, middle ground and two alternative foregrounds) will only offer ten colours in total.

The graphics processor displays each track with a velocity vector and either a track number or an identification symbol (Fig. 11); the choice is made by touch menu (Fig. 12).

Other menus allow categories of air tracks to be displayed by establishing a pre-selection matrix. Any particular track can be interrogated for further tabular information display, by pointing via the rolling ball. The displayed data will update automatically at the following sampling intervals without any further selective action by the user.

6.   Final Comments and Further Work

In summary, a universal workstation for air C^2 application, must provide:

-   the real-time air picture;
-   detailed map backgrounds (rivers, roads, railways, terrain, national boundaries);
-   tactical data overlays (air corridors, ground defence positions, danger areas, flight plans);
-   a wide range of tabular data derived from a local data base or incoming messages;
-   an application-tailored, easy-to-use, MMI (clear symbology, displayed operating instructions, pushbutton operation);
-   rapid response in the man-machine loop (e.g. the display of selected data within a few seconds of demand; and,
-   a clear indication to the user that his action is being responded to (e.g. an audible tone accompanied by a visual signal such as blinking of the action label).

The investigative work in the STC ACCS Test Bed has shown that a universal workstation providing these facilities is feasible for the range of applications encountered in a tactical air C^2 system, using civil-market components, with an aggregate cost no higher than current AD workstations but with a considerably higher capability. Furthermore, the current trend indicates that they will become progressively cheaper.

Future work will be directed towards the investigation of alternative methods of providing equivalent capabilities at lower cost; e.g., investigating the use of a flat electroluminescent panel for the touch control, and the retrieval of maps stored by laser on video discs.

Human-Computer Interaction — INTERACT '84 / B. Shackel (ed.)
Elsevier Science Publishers B.V. (North-Holland)
© IFIP, 1985

HUMAN FACTORS ASPECTS OF TERMINALS FOR NON-EXPERT USERS

W. Noê

Siemens Munich, F.R.G.

Continuing advances in office automation are putting computer power on the desks of more and more non-expert users. An example of this is interactive videotex, which is intended to give every white-collar worker low-cost access to databases in the office. This calls for a new class of terminals, which should be easy to operate and suit the non-expert users' needs.

1. INTRODUCTION

It is characteristic of many white-collar jobs that they use computer power in a variety of ways, but usually only as a casual support for office work. Many of these users are not particularly familiar with or properly trained in operating computer terminals. If an office terminal is to find widespread use right up to the manager's desk, it must cater to the special needs of these non-expert users.

This paper will explain what is to be understood by a casual or non-expert user and the situations in which non-experts use computer terminals. The human factors of these users as well as their applications affect the technical and ergonomic design of non-expert terminals, as represented here by the BITEL videotex telephone.

2. THE NON-EXPERT USER

The non-expert user is characterized not only by his job profile, but also by his attitude to office equipment, his knowledge of it and his habits in using it. The latter characteristics include the human factors typical of the non-expert user.

2.1 The non-expert user and his job

Whatever the line of business, office work involves the collection, recording, manipulation, reproduction and distribution of information. Such activities constitute the principal function of certain white-collar specialists or experts (e.g. text processing by an "expert" typist or software generation by an "expert" programmer). In other jobs, these information-handling activities are merely a supporting component, e.g. as part of a planning or management function, and exercised in a non-expert manner (such as text processing without special training or practice); in this context the user is to be seen as a layman. It can be observed that the higher the qualifications of staff using office automation, the greater is the proportion of non-expert users among

them (cf. Fig. 1). This means that planning experts or managers, for example, need more and more technical support for their jobs, but use them in a (non-expert) manner quite different to that of seasoned specialists.

Analysis of typical non-expert users' jobs shows that their tasks can be broken down into activities which can be translated into terminal requirements; technical functions meeting these requirements can then be defined (cf. Fig. 2).

It is striking here that certain activities are recurrent in the most widely varying jobs. Typical recurrent activities are telephoning with many different people, sending brief messages (instead of telephoning), retrieving information and answering inquiries (including those of a personal nature) and telephoning when one is away from or not available at one's normal work place.

2.2 The human factors

The following distinctions can be made between expert and non-expert users:

The expert user realizes the need for proper training, has had plenty of practice, willingly adapts to the "machine" and accepts complicated operating procedures as the price of advanced user options.

The non-expert user, on the other hand, expects operating procedures to follow his "natural" behavior and allow for his habits. He does not accept training, exercises little self-discipline and is rather impatient. He usually has little interest in technical issues, does not read any long manuals and expects the terminal to follow "his" way of thinking (and not that of the programmer). His reactions are subjective and emotional.

The expert user accepts the terminal as an integral part of his job. The way in which the non-expert users' place of work is arranged (i.e. his desk), however, is arbitrary and follows no set pattern. The non-expert user expects a terminal used only casually to be as unobtrusive as possible, taking up little more desk space than a telephone.

3. REQUIREMENTS FOR NON-EXPERT TERMINALS

3.1 Service feature requirements

Analysis of applications shows that a versatile office terminal should have the following basic functions:

- support functions for telephoning, e.g. a personal register and a notepad for important calls or those that fail to get through;
- an electronic pass for identification;
- an electronic appointments diary;
- a portable or pocket electronic personal register;
- a facility for access to data services providing both specialized information (e.g. R&D report archives) and general information (e.g. timetables);
- an electronic mailbox in which brief messages can be deposited for telephone users who cannot be reached or do not wish to be disturbed.

These requirements show that the subscriber terminal in question has to be multifunctional, i.e. a terminal integrating several communication services in a single unit. This has considerable impact on the user interface design.

3.2 User interface design requirements

The user interface design is determined by both the human factors typical of the user base and the service features needed. The non-export user expects easy and obvious operating procedures according to his way of thinking. The service features require certain keys, controls and displays: a screen, a keyboard for entering letters and numbers, function keys, visual displays of equipment status and a card reader.

In the design stage, it must be realized that there will be only one user interface (made up of the various keys and controls) and that this will be used for different services.

All these requirements can be translated into certain basic rules of user interface design:

- There should be as few keys and controls as possible, i.e. only essential functions should be visible at the user interface. These are the keys common to all services, such as keys for letters and digits and function keys for the "first step", e.g. a key for access to a data service. Further operating procedures should be handled via soft keys (with variable functions) or

screen menus.

- Easy-to-begin operation by means of self-explanatory function keys and on-screen prompts and user helps. This is particularly important for gaining access to a service and changing from one service to another; here experience shows that for non-expert users needing few services, function keys with LED displays are preferable to menu selection. Ideally, function keys should be provided with symbols and self-explanatory texts. The text helps the beginner and the symbol facilitates the location of a key once its function is known.

  Standard operating procedures for all services. The screen, for example, will be used in more or less the same way for all services (e.g. uniform menu presentation with selection by digits), or information for all services (whether telephone numbers, appointments or texts) will be stored with the same operating procedure.

- Use of soft, dynamically labeled keys and menus. Functions concerning the displayed information on the screen (e.g. editing functions such as insertion or deletion) are typical soft-key applications. Menus should preferably be used for entry functions, i.e. to select a service or a larger block of functions. These are generally the functions initiating a procedure in which other information has not yet displayed on the screen. The same or similar functions should be located on the same soft keys or in the same menu positions for all services.

4. BITEL - A NON-EXPERT USERS' TERMINAL

The BITEL videotex telephone is a multifunctional, integrated communication terminal for telephoning, interactive videotex and local support functions. Occupying little desk space, the compact BITEL has a 7" monochrome screen, integrated keyboard, telephone set and chip card reader (Fig. 3).

4.1 Service features

The service features of BITEL satisfy all the requirements of non-expert users:

- Its personal registers and notepad can store names, telephone numbers, addresses and more. A special-purpose register is particularly useful for storing operating procedures associated with the central service features of SPC telephone exchanges (e.g. call diversion).

- The videotex register can be used to set up an index of keywords for frequently needed videotex pages. Not only the number under which the page is to be found, but also more complex commands, such as log-on procedures etc., can be stored.

- Programmable keys for direct access (repertory dialing), telephone services (operating procedures) or passwords.

- An appointments diary supports personal scheduling. The notepad register also reminds the user of important calls.

- A small text memory allows short texts, e.g. messages, to be generated off-line and sent to the public videotex center (to the recipient's videotex mailbox) and printed out locally. The user has simple correction aids at his disposal (via the soft keys).

- The text memory can also store information retrieved from the videotex computer for later use.

- Information from personal registers and passwords for access to the videotex center can be stored on a chip card. If the card is inserted into someone else's BITEL, the terminal works with the data stored on that card.

4.2 Operation

Keyboard

The BITEL console comprises a keyboard for letters, a keyboard for numbers, several hard-coded function keys and five soft keys with variable functions.

The compact alpha keyboard for letters is designed for two-finger operation, as most non-expert users are not used to bothhands-tenfinger typing. This keyboard is also used to call up pages from the telephone register, make videotex entries and edit short texts and register entries.

Three hard-coded function keys give access to the telephone and videotex services and to local functions. LED displays indicate which service has been activated and, if two services are used concurrently (e.g. videotex and telephony), the service to which the keyboard is assigned, i.e. the service being momentarily used.

Each soft key is assigned three groups of functions, corresponding to the three services (Fig. 4). Experience shows that if the soft function keys are located close to the screen, up to five of them, arranged in a row, can be easily operated. If the keyboard and screen are separate or a larger number of soft function keys is required, they must be split up into blocks (e.g. two blocks of three keys). As the soft keys are for optional functions only (basic functions can be performed without them), they are activated by the user as required. If the soft function keys are not thus activated, they can be used as programmable keys, e.g. as repertory dialers or to store a password.

Screen

All registers have the same structure, new entries being numbered by single digits in ascending order (Fig. 5). When an entry number is selected, the telephone number, page number or operating procedure denoted is automatically dialed, called up or initiated respectively by the terminal. Information is entered in the registers, the appointments and text memories using the same operating procedure with the same functions. Here screen prompts give the user step-by-step support.

4.3 Practical experience

Laboratory experiments and field trials have supplied a lot of findings on user interface design. Two design features deserve special mention here: the menu selection method for the registers and the procedures for changing from one function to another.

Menu selection

Selection from a menu, i.e. from a register, by means of single-digit numbers is a straight-forward procedure, even for the layman. Separate keys for the various menu lines are unlikely to be anymore reliable or faster to operate and have the disadvantage that they would have to be located outside the keyboard area (i.e. on or beside the screen) in an unfamiliar manupulation plane (almost vertical). Menu selection by means of a cursor is in any case far more difficult and unfamiliar to the layman.

Changing functions

It is obvious that the user has to rely heavily on the screen for the various operating procedures: the screen is his main visual link with the terminal and he becomes irritated if the display changes or disappears unexpected, i.e. before he has finished the previous operation. Switching from register selection to storage operation is a typical example: the user has selected a telephone number from the register and notes that some other item of information is no longer correct. Now, without changing anything on the screen (as the desired line has already been selected), he wishes to switch to storage and enter new information. This means that the user interface design may have to provide "short cuts" for such spontaneous wishes in the operating procedures. The best solution here is to integrate such changes into the standard procedure so that they meet the "natural" behaviour of the user.

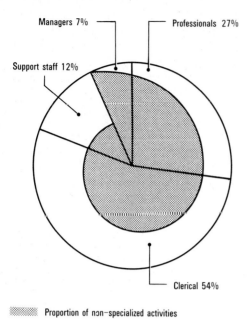

Managers 7%   Professionals 27%
Support staff 12%
Clerical 54%

▒▒▒▒ Proportion of non-specialized activities

Fig. 1 White-collar workers by occupational groups

FUNCTIONS	ACTIVITIES	REQUIREMENTS
Organizing conferences		
–Preparation	Telephoning with various partners	Telephone features, telephone register
	Coordination	Written messages
	Retrieving relevant information	Database access
	Travel preparations	Timetable inquiries
	Production and distribution of conference literature	Word processing, text communication
–Execution	Retrieving personal information	Electronic pass
	Telephoning with staff	Pocket telephone register
	Thelephoning when not available at normal work place	Message service Electronic mailbox
–Follow-up	Production and distribution of the minutes	Word processing, text communication
Writing drafts	Retrieving information	Database access
	Research	Access to archives
	Text entry	Word processing
Updating knowledge	Research on specialized topics	Access to archives

Fig. 2 Typical job profile of a non-expert user, e.g. a planner

Soft keys
Hard-coded keys
Alphanumeric keyboard
Cursor controls
Card reader
Service selection
Number keyboard

Fig. 3 BITEL multifunctional terminal for interactive videotex and telephony   (BITEL = Bildschirmtelefon)

	K		1. BLATT
1	Kaufmann	K ZL Syst KE 21	«44150»
2	Kleinke	K ZL Syst KE 2	«48678»
3	Knobloch	PN VS 111	«61210»
4	Keiner	ZVW 141	«26573»
5	Klein	K ZL Syst KE 3	«25226»
6	Koch, Dr.	K ZL P PK 2	«25175»
7	König, Prof., Wien		«7-0043 222 4712»
8	Kümpel	K ZL Syst KE 21	«44810»
9	Kay Andrew, Sir, London		«135-48539»

Gebuhr TelUhr Druck BtSeit ----

Fig. 5 Screen display of a page from the telephone register

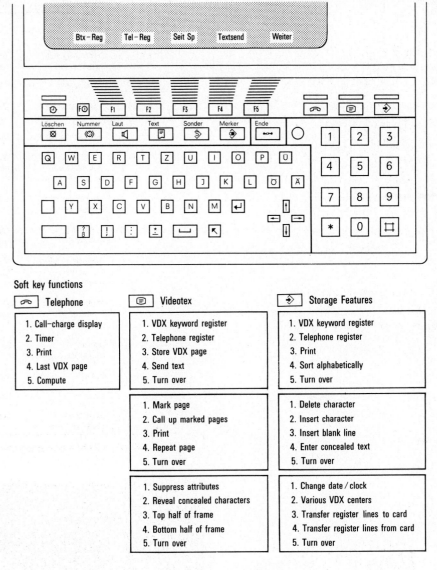

Fig. 4 Keyboard and soft keys of BITEL multifunctional terminal

Soft key functions

Telephone
1. Call-charge display
2. Timer
3. Print
4. Last VDX page
5. Compute

Videotex
1. VDX keyword register
2. Telephone register
3. Store VDX page
4. Send text
5. Turn over

1. Mark page
2. Call up marked pages
3. Print
4. Repeat page
5. Turn over

1. Suppress attributes
2. Reveal concealed characters
3. Top half of frame
4. Bottom half of frame
5. Turn over

Storage Features
1. VDX keyword register
2. Telephone register
3. Print
4. Sort alphabetically
5. Turn over

1. Delete character
2. Insert character
3. Insert blank line
4. Enter concealed text
5. Turn over

1. Change date / clock
2. Various VDX centers
3. Transfer register lines to card
4. Transfer register lines from card
5. Turn over

REFERENCES:

/¯1_7 Teger, S.,L., Factors impacting the
        evolution of office automation,
        Proceedings of the IEEE, Vol. 71,
        No. 4, April 1983, p. 503-511

/¯2_7 Carne, E.B., Ciano, J.M., Human Factors
        in business telecommunications,
        Proceedings of the World Telecommuni-
        cation Forum 83, Oct. 83,
        p. 2.9.4.1-2.9.4.5

/¯3_7 Helmrich, H., Dr., Novel terminals for
        attractive ISDN services, Proceedings
        of the World Telecommunication Forum 83
        Geneva Oct. 1983, p. 2.9.3.1-2.9.3.4

/¯4_7 Gilch, G., Dr., BITEL - A new communi-
        cation instrument, telcom report 6
        (1983) No. 5, p. 288-292

Human-Computer Interaction — INTERACT '84 / B. Shackel (ed.)
Elsevier Science Publishers B.V. (North-Holland)
IFIP, 1985

COMPREHENSIVE DEVELOPMENT FOR PEOPLE IN STA; EFFORTS AND RESULTS

Per Abrahamsson

Swedish Telecommunications Administration (STA)
Stockholm, Sweden

Abstract:

The coming and growing use of video display terminals (VDT's) in Operators' Workstations in STA has been accompanied by rising worries for
negative health effects from the operators and their Trade Unions.

This paper reports efforts made within STA in order to eliminate possible problems, such as physical discomfort of various kind, reduced job
satisfaction etc.

Also reached and expected results are reported.

Keywords:

Ergonomics, human factors, operators, operator services, telematics,
video display terminals (VDT's), workstations and environment.

1. INDRODUCTION

The use of VDT's grows very rapidly during the present Information Age in almost every industrial activity; also in
Telephone Operator Centres. The reason
is of course that the VDT has proved to
be a valuable new tool in this technology.

However, since some years also rising
concern about negative factors, e.g.
visual fatigue, neck and back pains,
and - lately - dangerous radiation, and
reduced job satisfaction etc., has been
apparent among operators and their Trade
Unions.

Lately, also National Health Authorities have - to a certain extent - supported such claims.

It's of utmost importance to seek for
solutions to eliminate those problems,
which - if verified - might reduce or
even eliminate the expected productivity gains when VDT's are used.

A program for this has been established
and it's utilized as one of the activities in all design work with VDT

workplaces. This paper reports some of
the results of that work.

2. BACKGROUND

During the 1970's STA has run detailed
studies of the Operator Service Systems.

The studies cover performance of present
systems and operators' support material;
directories, tickets etc., efficiency,
job satisfaction, service of quality, analysis of new and/or altered services.

Mechanization of the support material(s)
also increased during that period. Early
examples were D.A. Workstations with me-
chanized files (DAS-M and DAS-C; according to U.S.' vocabulary) presented at
the 1972 HFT' Symposium in Stockholm,
Sweden, and to introduce systems with computerized time and charge facilities etc.,
e.g. the AT&T' TSPS (Traffic Service
Position System).

Hence, a decision was taken to design a
Telematics System, covering all kinds of
Operator Services, i.e. D.A. and Intercept
Service, Absent Subscribers Service, Toll,
Mobile, and Conference Services etc.

3. METHODOLOGY

We started to form a number
of Working Parties, one for each problem area. They were first of all such
concrete things as the various existing
services (toll traffic, directory assistance, intercept service, absent subscribers'service, wake up service etc.)
provided, but also more abstract subjects as service levels, operator manuals and other "paper aids" etc.

In all these W.P.'s the operators were
represented both with persons appointed
by their Unions and by the employer,
OTA. Our experience of this co-operation
work-wich, especially at that time,
were rather unique, I believe - is very
good. As far as I know the operators
also liked this methodology, which at
that time was not mandatory from the
STA side. Today there are special laws
in Sweden to ensure the users' influence
on new systems and methods, <u>before</u> they
are implemented.

Therefore, we claim that we have "entered human adaptability in the system
engineer's calculations", as somebody
has put it, and we started with that
policy comparably long time ago.

Another important part of the work has
been to study and analyse modern systems
and equipment in other Administrations,
in operation and/or in the design phase.

Hence, studies have taken place in North
American and European countries, mainly
U.S.A. and U.K.

As a result the W.P.'s came out with
a number of suggestions to start various
projects with live tests. Those were
to be run in a step by step mode, in order to find out what to do - or not to
do - next, i.e. to avoid most of the
pitfalls which might arise.

The main objectives for the tests - and
the permanent systems to follow - were:

1. Improved working conditions for the
   operators, i.e. ergonomically designed workstations and a matched environment in the operating room with
   all known good human factors' elements considered.

2. Efficient and operator-friendly systems and equipment enabling an increased traffic load at lower total
   costs (systems, equipment, maintenance, operation, administration).

3. Provide better and/or new (or altered) services (such as secretary/
   translation services, message storage and forwarding etc.) and service
   levels (such as time to answer, time
   for searching, call set up time etc,)
   to the customers.

To achieve this we have worked according
to the following "ten commands":

1. Task analysis,
2. Modelling and prediction,
3. Simulation and test,
4. Functional specification,
5. Technical specification (fulfilling
   the functional one),
6. Design and/or purchase,
7. Installation and field test,
8. Evaluation, which might lead to,
9. Changes and Final evaluation, and
10. Verification of calculated investment
    and profit.

Before the functional and technical specifications for a certain service were
written we started with <u>three basic spe-
cifications</u>.

One for the <u>localities</u> (operator and system rooms) <u>design</u> from an ergonomic
viewpoint, one for the <u>workplaces</u> with
its <u>environment</u>, and one for <u>systems
design</u>, including the computer systems
for files, timing, charging, notes etc.
Both the basic and the detailed specifications have been achieved in close
and constructive co-operation with the
operators' representatives.

4. FIELD TESTS(FULL SIZE)

Up to now we have - by following the
above rules - initiated two field tests
which are in permanent operation since
the beginning of 1979.

Intercept and Number-to-name- Information Services. The first one is a system for combined <u>Intercept</u> and <u>Number-
to-name Information Services</u>.The <u>latter</u>
which in STA is considered as a "luxory
service" is to be charged to the customer.

The system includes an Automatic Call
Distributor (A.C.D.) for individual
queueing of the calls and a fare as
possible distribution of calls to idle
operators.

The computer holds files for all subscribers, both vacant and operational
numbers. It also holds information for
secret numbers and chargable numbers,
i.e. numbers published in the latest

issue of the phone book.

The operators' room, workplaces, and systems are designed to the rules given in the three basic specifications mentioned.

The VDT in the workplace is not of the CRT type but it is of a flickerfree plasma type with red characters on a black background. It hangs on a mechanism which allows the operator to tilt, to angle, to rise or to lower, and to adjust the distance to it easily.

The keyboard of a low profile type, is common for <u>both</u> the telephone and the computer systems, and with a minimum of keys (approx. 30 keys), LED's etc. In fact it can be considered as an early example of applied telematics. In operational service maybe even before the French created the "motherword", Télématique for telematics. All operator equipment exept the VDT screen is designed by STA.

The system is used in Stockholm and I'd like to take this opportunity to invite those who might have a deeper interest in it to come and study it. Just make a contact with me (see the end of this paper).There are also posters exhibited here at this conference from the operators' room.

Toll Traffic

The other system we started field tests with in 1979 is a typical hook on system to test "computer aids".

We were well aware of - as mentioned above - the T.S.P.S. and other similar systems for toll traffic,and we felt that they had good qualities from various aspects. The only drawback - as we saw it - was that they all were an integrated part of a certain SPC System, and non of these systems were in operation in Sweden. Consequently, to implement an Operator System of e.g. the T.S.P.S. type would also require the purchase and implementation of the appropriate SPC System, and hence very high costs. Therefore we looked for a stand alone Operator System or - even better-an add on system, which could be connected to our existing Operator System for combined Toll and Mobile Traffic. Although that system (cordless) was designed and implemented already in the late 1950's it still had full A.C.D. facilities, automatic start and stop of timing, and automatic release of the lines at the end of a call. So what

we really needed was such facilities as storing of telephone numbers, automatic billing, a number of look up files, watching of booked calls etc.

At a study visit to British Post Office (today named B.T.) in 1974, I first heard of their development of the ACRE (Automatic Call Recording Equipment) System. That system was designed after the same philosophy we were looking for, so we decided to investigate the possibilities to make use of the B.T. work in this area.

The discussions led to a joint venture between (at that time) a British ITT Co. (S.T.C.), B.T., and S.T.A. with the objectives to develop a similar system for STA. This system is named OPAS (Operator Position Assistance System), which is the S.T.C. trade name for it, and it is connected to our Toll Traffic System, model 57 in a location some 120 miles West of Stockholm. A variety of the system (OPAS II) is in operation in Oslo, Norway.Our objectives with this field test was to find out the operators' reactions when working whith this new technique, possible rationalization effects, and impact on maintenance routines. Our, and our operators', experiences are very good regarding all those aspects.

Also in this system a non CRT type of VDT is used. In this case it is of the electroluminiscent type, manufactured by two British companies. It can display up to 80 characters at the same time, which is enough for this application. The characters are completely flickerfree (refrech frequency approximately 1,000 Hz),easy to read without eye fatigue (yellow-green on a dark background), and non-reflective (VDT lowered into a space with black walls).

One of the posters at our exhibition shows pictures from the installation, and a rather detailed article on the project is available at the conference (1).

5. LIMITED TESTS

Simultaneously with the full scale field tests we also have run a number of smaller, limited tests for various purposes. Examples of such purposes are what effect(s) intensive VDT work might have on the operators, ergonomical aspects on workplaces,including equipment and environment, and work organisation when utilizing the new techniques.

Directory Assistance

During 1981-82 (part of the time) we
have run a comprehensive field test for
the Directory Assistance Services with
ten Operator Positions in the South of
Sweden (Malmoe).

Objectives for that have been e.g.
file organization, searching techniques, workplace and locality arrangements, layout and design of VDT forms
and keyboard(s) medical tests (eyestrain
etc.), VDT eyeglasses tests etc. When
found necessary operators were then
provided special VDT eyeglasses.

The workstation, which is of STA design
and manufacture, had already been under
development for a couple of years when
the D.A. test begun. It can be equipped with suitable keyboard(s), VDT
screen(s) etc. depending on the applica-
tion.It has such features as i.a. motor
driven height adjustment. The height
set is displayed in a small "window" on
top of the workplace shelf. A brochure
(with an English translation) is available at the conference.

After the original tests were closed in
1982, a local project has followed with
the purpose to study various organisation forms, various workplace types and
their grouping, arrangements for mixing
paper files (for the Nordic Countries)
and computer files in the same workstation etc.

There are a number of reports from the
test available - most of them in Swedish, of course - and the one about
the medical findings,written in English,is listed at the end of this
paper(2).

The Operator System (ES101), to be combined with the computer system, will
be described in the STA Technical paper
Tele, no. 2/1984 (English edition) (3).
Also this system - including the above
mentioned workplace - might be studied
in Sweden, preferably in Stockholm,
where we have a number of installations
for various applications.

Operator Centres for Text Telephones

In order to allow telephone traffic
between hearing impaired persons and the
normally hearing, we provide Intermediate Centres for such traffic. At
these centres the operators "relay"
the content of the written information
on the VDT screen by reading it to the
hearing person, and vice versa typing

the verbal information to the hearing
impaired person.

Special Workstations for this purpose
also have been developed, and they are
displayed on a poster in this conference.

6. FUTURE WORK

Built on the experiences from the above
mentioned field tests and surveys we
are now in the process of finalizing
the development work, and the first
centre for terminating traffic, i.e.
Directory Assistance Services, Intercept Service, Absent Subscribers Service
etc. went into Service earlier this
year. During the period of 1984-87 the
system will be implemented country-
wide. At some of the centres also non-
terminating traffic, i.e. Toll and Mobile
Traffic, Conference Call Traffic etc.
will be handled.

To achieve good traffic handling efficiency the centres will be grouped to a
limited number of regions, i.e. a number of Operator Centres are remotely
connected to and controlled from a
common system, ES101.

One important thing in the design work
is to find a good as possible - and
with large enough screen - VDT. We
therefore have written a specification -
bearing in mind all the good human factors - and sent it to a number of manufacturers for tender. This VDT, which we
call "Terminal 85", is now on the market from at least one of the manufacturers (The Finnish Co. Nokia). It still
is a VDT of CRT type.

We use the "split screen" concept for
this VDT in order to use only one VDT
for both the telephone and the computer
systems (idea of telematics).

As everyone knows work is going on in
the industry to come up with VDT's
utilizing other techniques, and we look
forward to successful results of this
R&D work all around the world.

7. SUMMARY AND CONCLUSIONS

The surveys, specification work, and
tests reported in this paper have shown
that Operator Centres utilizing contemporary switching and computer techniques can be designed, not only efficiently and economically but also in an
Operator-friendly and "Human" way. To
achieve these objectives it's - in our
opinion - of utmost importance that
the following rules apply:

1. Carefully <u>survey</u> the present situation in terms of type of traffic(s), systems and equipment, job elements, job satisfaction or job discomfort.

2. Write <u>functional specifications</u> bearing <u>in mind</u> not only efficiency and money, but also pay careful attention to the new job design, ergonomically good workstations with high quality VDT's, together with the surrounding environment (such as materials and colours in furniture, walls, curtains, carpets etc., lighting arrangements, climate control equipment, functional chairs etc.), and other human factors of importance for the specific job (e.g. provide properly tested eyeglasses, aimed for the specific task, and provide good conditions to the operators/end users).

3. Co-operate with the Operators (End Users) <u>well before</u> developing work is initiated, <u>in fact</u> during a whole project, including evaluation and verification.

REFERENCES:

(1) Abrahamsson, P., Persson, E. and Jacobson, B., Implementation of OPAS-I in the Swedish Telephone Network, Electrical Communications, Volume 55, Number 3 (1980) 177-183.

(2) Hedman, L. and Briem, E, Changes in Focusing Accuracy of VDU-operators as a Function of Age, Hours worked, and Task, Tenth International Symposium on Human Factors in Telecomminucations (HFT) (Helsinki, Finland, 1983).

(3) Abrahamsson, P., Joelson, A. and Nilsson, E-Ch., ES101-STA's First Microcomputerbased Telephone Operator System, Tele (English Edition), Number 2 (1984) 9 pages.

CONTACT INFORMATION:

<u>Adress:</u> Mr. Per Abrahamsson, STA Headquarters, Dept. Nfm, Room N1:26, <u>S-12386 Farsta.</u> Sweden

<u>Phone no:</u> +4687131546 or +4687131000, extn. 1546.

<u>Telex no:</u> 14970, gentel s.

<u>Telefax no:</u> +4687133358 (group 2).

Human-Computer Interaction — INTERACT '84 / B. Shackel (ed.)
Elsevier Science Publishers B.V. (North-Holland)
© IFIP, 1985

THE IMPAIRMENT OF CONCENTRATION AS A CONSEQUENCE OF COMPUTER WORK

Kazuo Saito, Toshiyuki Hosokawa and Kunihiko Nakai

Department of Hygiene and Preventive Medicine,
Hokkaido University School of Medicine,
Sapporo, Japan

In this presentation, we set out to describe the impact of working a computer and the impairment of computer-workers from the work physiological view point. Attentional phenomena will be classified and discussed from the standpoint of higher nervous functions. We analyse the physiological basis of visual attention required for the operation of computers by the electrophysiological methods of brain waves, and the auditory evoked response of the electroencephalogram.
The VDT work-load as an example of computer-work will be made clear by an analysis of a physiological performance test and of the neurochemical substances in the urine of the workers.

1. Introduction

Now that we have entered the information age, many kinds of computer seems to have spread rapidly throughout workplaces such as offices, industries and institutes. It is therefore very important to understand the peculiarities of a computer system and the human physiological characteristics evoked during the operation of a computer. Of course, the computer is nothing but one of the many tools that have been devised by human beings, but until now most of these tools help or substitute for human physical work; the computer,however, is different in that it helps or substitutes for human mental work. The fact that this difference exists, though, leads to confusion: for instance, some people seem to believe that a computer is absolute, while others reject it in terror because it robs them of a job. As overconfidence in the computer can lead to many baneful consequence, as, for instance thoughtlessness, it is very important to recognize that a computer is nothing but a tool. Rapidity of calculation speed, a large memory capacity with no lapses of memory are characterized as peculiarities of a computer system, but it cannot think comprehensively: it can only put given instructions into practice. As to the human aspects of a human-computer system, the following characteristics can be noted: (1) a man generally makes about 2% mistakes; (2) a man gets tired easily, particularly in simple repeated tasks , and (3) when a man habituates himself to a computer, he can insert information into the computer by hand without thinking visually at all.
Fig. 1 shows one of the relationships in the human-computer system. Developers, producers, operators and maintenance men all play important roles in this system. Visual attention to the CRT display is required of the operator of a computer dealing with information. A failure to consider the above mentioned human characteristics in the human-computer system results in a number of errors, wastes time, and

developer of hardware

producer of software | computer | maintenance man

operator

Fig.1. Human-Computer Relationship

causes frustration,. di_satisfaction and fatigue of the persons concerned in operating the system.

2. The physiological basis of visual attention required for the operation of a computer.

Visual attention is necessary for the operation of a computer. Attention is a complex function of the brain, and continuous concentration of attention for a long time causes stress brought about by excess of work. Attention phenomena themselves are classified into (1) the intensive phenomena of attention itself, which is to say attentiveness, arousal, the orientation of reaction and the concentration of attention, (2) selective phenomena of attention, which is to say the selection by property, selection by location and receptor adjusting responses and attention[1]. On the other hand, attention of function consists of (1) selective attention, (2) responses to stimuli in short time memory such as recognition, learning, memory, comparison, judgement and their relationships with each other, and, (3) the capacity and the degree of these relationships, as well as the regulating function of both selective attention and other functions. These attentional phenomena depend upon the level of consciousness, which signifies arousal, wakefulness, drowsiness, sleep, alertness and excitement. All of these conditions are higher nervous functions. Excess of concentrated attention for a long time causes a lowering of the higher nervous activities and mental fatigue. This abnormal weakening of central nervous functions will lead to the condition of thoughtlessness.

3. The relationship between attention and brain waves.[2~5]

3.1 Visual attention level and alpha wave of EEG.

Twenty-three healthy male subjects between the ages of 18 and 31 were engaged in this experiment. Brain waves from occipital area (Oz) were recorded with monopolar lead for three kinds of attentional condition: a 10-minute period with eyes opened in a dark room; a 10-minute period watching a green light, and a 10 minute period maintaining concentration while taking a TAF-test. An alpha wave (8-13 Hz) taken by a band pass analyzer from the brain waves was used to compared the three conditions. The results revealed that the stronger the level of visual attention the greater the decrease in alpha wave appearance. The mean voltages and standard errors of the alpha wave for 5 seconds when put into the analyser were 22.33 ± 2.12 µV for the state of eyes open in darkness, 13.46 ± 1.08 µV for the state of watching a green light, and 10.61 ± 0.83 µV while maintaining concentration. That is, the appearance of the alpha wave decreased in the following order: eyes open in darkness, simple watching of a

Table 1. Distribution of brain waves from vertex (Oz) during eyes closed at rest, eyes opened at rest and maintaining concentration

frequency in Hz	eyes closed at rest	maintaining concentration	significance
3.5	5.1± 0.6	6.3± 0.7	N S
4.0	8.2± 0.7	9.4± 0.7	N S
4.5	12.9± 0.9	13.4± 0.6	N S
5.0	15.4± 1.1	18.8± 0.9	$P<0.02$
5.4	17.3± 1.6	22.6± 0.8	$P<0.01$
5.9	20.4± 1.8	26.9± 0.9	$P<0.01$
6.5	28.2± 2.0	36.1± 1.4	$P<0.01$
6.9	36.3± 2.5	41.2± 1.8	N S
7.4	56.3± 6.1	51.4± 2.5	N S
8.0	81.9±10.0	59.8± 3.2	$P<0.05$
8.3	96.6±12.2	65.3± 3.8	$P<0.05$
8.7	117.6±13.5	73.9± 4.3	$P<0.01$
9.1	125.5±13.3	77.4± 4.5	$P<0.01$
9.5	129.9±12.0	83.7± 5.1	$P<0.01$
10.0	129.9±11.5	87.6± 5.6	$P<0.01$
10.5	131.6±10.6	97.4± 6.3	$P<0.01$
11.1	116.8± 9.0	98.2± 6.7	N S
11.8	108.6± 8.5	102.1± 7.5	N S
12.5	100.1± 7.6	104.2± 7.6	N S
13.3	99.0± 8.5	114.6± 9.4	N S
14.3	88.7± 8.0	113.5± 9.7	$P<0.10$
15.4	87.6± 9.5	115.9±10.8	$P<0.10$
16.7	83.9± 9.5	118.1±11.5	$P<0.05$
18.2	89.6±11.9	128.2±13.4	$P<0.05$
20.0	82.9±11.0	126.3±14.0	$P<0.05$
22.2	77.9±11.8	124.7±16.1	$P<0.05$
25.0	62.6± 9.7	104.1±14.3	$P<0.05$

Values show average and standard error of 14 examinees.

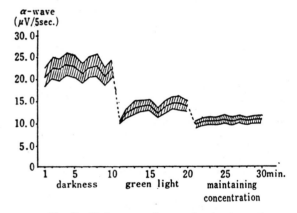

Fig.2. Alpha wave for each minute under three states: eyes opened in darkness, simple watching of a green light and maintaining concentration.

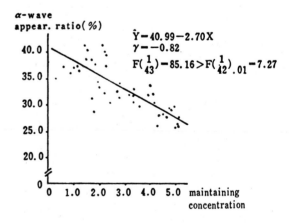

Fig.3. Correlation between alpha wave appearance ratio and maintaining concentration

green light and the maintaining of concentration. The appearance of the alpha wave significantly varied with the lapse of time in the
state of eye-open in darkness, but it did not
vary during the simple watching in a green
light nor while maintaining concentration (Fig.
2). It was also observed that the lower the
level of the maintenance of concentration, the
stronger the alpha attenuation (Fig. 3). These
results indicate that there is a significant
relation between the maintenance of concentration and the grade of alpha attenuation.

3.2 Frequency distribution and its autocorrelogram of EEG during visual attention.

The brain waves of fourteen healthy male
students between the ages of 19 and 21 were
recorded by monopolar lead from the occipital
area (Oz) during the state with eyes closed and
during the maintenance of concentration while
taking a TAF test. The original waves of EEG
were analysed by a micro computer (Nihon Kohden
ATAC 1200) and were computed into an interval
histogram of 3.5-25 Hz.
Table 1 shows the frequency distribution of the
brain waves by means of computer-analysis.
Theta-waves of 5-6.5 Hz in EEG frequency
increased significantly during the state of
maintaining concentration in comparison with the
eyes closed state as a control condition. A
significant decrease in alpha-waves of 8-10.5 Hz
and a significant increase in beta-waves of
14.3-25 Hz were recognized during the state of
maintained concentration. The distribution of
the number of brain waves per 5 seconds for each
of the three states for a period of 5 minutes is
shown in Fig. 4. The mean numbers of brain
waves and the standard errors for this 5 minute
period were 2401.6 ±99.2 during the eyes-closed
state, 1963.3 ±140.5 during the eyes-open
state, and 2467.3 ±141.3 in the state of maintained concentration. This shows a significant
difference between the three states. The
frequency distribution by interval histogram and
the autocorrelogram of these three states can be
seen in Fig. 5.

3.3 Auditory evoked response and the lowering of
visual attention level.

The auditory evoked responses (AER) of seven
healthy male students between the ages of 19 and
27 were recorded by monopolar lead from the
vertex (Cz) before and after a thirty-minute
period of maintained concentration while taking
a TAF-test. Auditory stimuli for AER were of
1000 Hz pure tone, 70 dB(C), and 50 msec in
duration. Stimuli were given one hundred times
every two seconds. Peak latencies and the peak
to peak amplitudes of AER were compared between
the normal level and the lowered level of
attention, before and after the 30 min mental
load of maintaining concentration while taking
the TAF-test.
The results showed no significant changes in any
of the peak latencies of AER but significant
decreases in peak to peak amplitudes of N_1-P_2
and P_2-N_2 were recognized in the lowered state
of maintaining concentration level. These
results suggest that the lowering of brain
activities caused by a mental work-load
requiring concentration of attention results in
a decrease in amplitude of the EEG evoked
response.

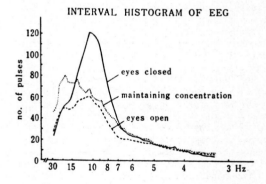

INTERVAL HISTOGRAM OF EEG

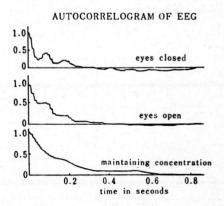

AUTOCORRELOGRAM OF EEG

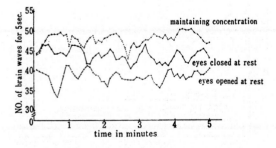

Fig.4. Distribution of brain waves from vertex
(Cz) during eyes closed at rest, eyes
opened at rest and maintaining
concentration

Fig.5. Interval histogram and autocorrelogram
of EEG from vertex (Cz) during eyes
closed at rest, eyes opened at rest and
maintaining concentration

4. The impact of computer work.

4.1 The impairment of computer-workers.

Computer work causes mental fatigue, neck and
upper limb disorder, low back pain, etc., among
the operators. Keyboard operations of computer
terminals and computer-aided work require
intease attention upon the CRT and the keyboard.
In VDT work, such complaints as neck, upper limb
and low back pains include postural discomfort
due to constrained work postures, neck,
shoulder, and upper limb fatigue and pains due
to repetitive upper limb motions, persistent
eyes strain brought about by a high visual load,
irritating work procedures, and the feeling of
being driven to work by controlled work methods.
The unfavourable environmental conditions such
as limited work space, disturbance by glare and
reflections, low display contrast, and uncomfortable microclimate easily enhance these
complaints. Working a computer for a long time
while suffering from these complaints causes the
lowering of the higher nervous activities, particularly the concentration of attention: the
result is a lowering of the ability to think,
causing thoughtlessness and a large number of
errors, decrease in work efficiency, and a
diminution in the amount of work.

4.2 Changes in physiological performance and neurochemical metabolism brought about by VDT work.

The healthy male VDT-workers between the ages of
30 and 41 were engaged in VDT work and clerical
work for a comparison of both types of work.
These subjects worked for two hours in the
morning and two hours in the afternoon. VDT
adopted in this work was a kind of visual
display terminal completing the layout of drafts
which had been input into the VDT and designated
on a newspaper.
Critical flicker fusion frequencies (CFF) near
point distance, dopamine (DA), norepinephrine
(NE), epinephrine (E), 3,4 dihydroxy phenyl
acetic acid (DOPAC), homovanillic acid (HVA),
vanil mandelic acid (VMA), and 3,methoxy-4-

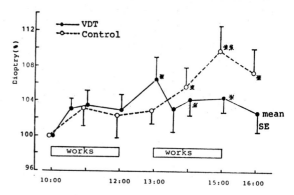

Fig.7. Changes in near point of accommodation due to VDT and clerical works
* p<0.05, ** p<0.01

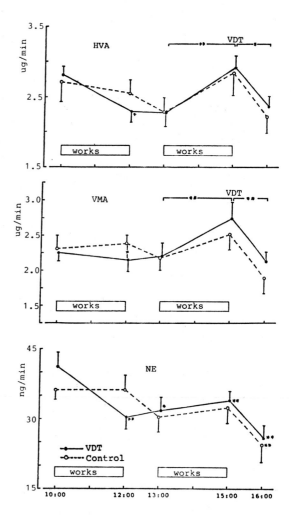

Fig.8. Changes in free-norepinephrine,
VMA, and HVA in urine of VDT and
clerical works
* p<0.05, ** p<0.01

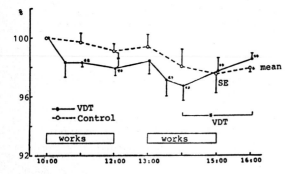

Fig.6. Changes in CFF value due to VDT
and clerical works
* p<0.05, ** p<0.01

hydroxy phenyl ethylene glycol (MHPG) in the urine of the subjects were measured for both VDT work and for clerical work used as a control. Significant lowerings of CFF values during VDT work in comparison with clerical work were also recognized (Fig. 6). The results of behavioral observation of the VDT workers showed that the items of "to see VDT", "to see keyboard", "to see draft", and "to see outside" were 51.3 %, 25.9 %, 12.8 %, and 10.0 % of total operation time for two hours respectively. VDT workers complained of more subjective symptoms concerning to visual fatigue which are eye strain, eyes ached, blurred vision, change in color perception, redness of eyes, and tearing than clerical workers as a control. These complaints of visual fatigue more remarkable for the work in the afternoon than that in the morning. Percentages of the behavior to see out side during VDT work was 7.6 % in the morning and 12.8 % in the afternoon. Different changes between VDT work and clerical work were observed at the distance of the near point (Fig. 7). Significant changes in the neuro-transmitting substances of urine were observed in NE, HVA, and VMA, but it was not observed in DA, E, DOPAC, and MHPG for either type of work (Fig. 8). These results show that the qualitative and quantitative evaluation of computer-work is possible if these physiological and neurochemical indicators are employed.

5. Conclusion

We have therefore shown that working a computer causes dysfunction of accommodation, visual fatigue, and the lowering of brain activities. These mental and visual impairments among computer workers can be analysed by objective methods such as physiological performance tests, brain waves, the evoked potential of EEG, and the analysis of neurochemical substances in urine and blood.

References:

1) Berlyne, D.E., The development of the concept of attention in psychology. Attention in Neurophysiology, edited by Evans, C.R. and Mulholland, T.B. (Butterworths, London, 1969).

2) Saito, K. and Takakuwa, E., Auditory and visual evoked responses in concentration of attention, Japanese Jrnl. 28 (1973), 340-346.

3) Saito, K. Relationship of concentration of attention to EEG, and visual and auditory evoked responses, Clinical Brain Wave, 19 (1977) 167-176.

4) Kamita, N. Saito, K. and Takakuwa, E., Relationship between visual attention and EEG, Hokkaido Jrnl. Med. 52 (1977) 467-473.

5) Kamita, N. Saito, K. and Takakuwa, E., EEG and VEP during visual attention with eye movement, Hokkaido Jrnl. Med. 52 (1977) 475-486.

Human-Computer Interaction — INTERACT '84 / B. Shackel (ed.)
Elsevier Science Publishers B.V. (North-Holland)
© IFIP, 1985

DIALOGUE HANDLING WITH USER WORKSTATIONS

Tom Carey

Department of Computing and Information Science
University of Guelph
Guelph, Ontario, Canada, N1G 2W1

This paper discusses the requirements for a user workstation in an open network environment. The workstation implements the dialogue component of an interactive application, while the functional or computational component may be implemented on a network host machine. Distributing processing in this way is influenced by ideas from three areas: software ergonomics, software engineering, and computer networks. An initial prototype workstation is reviewed, and research issues shaping a new implementation are described.

1. PROBLEM: THE ELUSIVE ALL-PURPOSE INTERFACE

The research described in this paper focusses on the needs of people accessing a variety of computer application services in a network environment. Typical target users would be office workers in large organizations, who would interact with information systems having differing organizational scopes.

The kinds of applications projected for this group would include

- personal tools, chosen by the user based on professional needs and tasks

- services local to a department or group, like text formatting, project control or local filing and retrieval

- central systems which are controlled on an organizational level: these systems would include corporate-wide messaging and data processing to maintain a corporate information infrastructure

- external services, like conferences or data bases, accessed through public networks.

These services will be controlled at organizational levels appropriate to their scope.

To interact with such a variety of application services with varying frequencies, users need common dialogue styles and a coherent set of common operations. This need is well-documented elsewhere [1].

The common operations should include at least information management facilities: creating, destroying and transferring information objects.

For the common dialogue styles, we include at least three elements:

- display style, the way a display screen or other medium is used for communication (windows, spatial cues, etc.)

- conversational style, including menus, command languages, macro extensions and direct manipulations

- assistance and orientation style, the way a user obtains help with individual problems or navigates and browses around the system (the "excursion task" [2]).

How can we provide a consistent interaction when there are various levels of application scope? We could try to close off the service network, so that all software must fit a prescribed standard interface. But the failure of large corporations to inhibit the spread of personal hardware suggests this is not productive. Tools for personal and professional task management need to be chosen personally, and the most we can hope is that some small set of interaction standards may emerge. Even these are likely to have enough annoying differences to require some local integration, and there will always be old applications which don't meet any known standard.

Our research is investigating dialogue style integration via dialogue distribution through a user workstation. Central to our approach is the view of dialogue style as a personal issue, which naturally belongs in the personal scope of the network, within the workstation.

We emphasize that there will need to be several dialogue styles because

- a user needs to have a progression of styles as exposure to an application grows [3].

- therefore users may need different styles for applications used with different frequency [4].

2.   SEPARATING DIALOGUE AND FUNCTION

Recent work on separating dialogue components
and functional components in interactive systems
has influenced our view of solutions to the
problem of consistent interfaces [5,6,7].

Such a separation removes the following from
functional processes to distinct interaction
processes

- the format of various types of information
  on a display or other output device

- the physical symbols and their properties

- the syntax of command grammars and display
  of menus

- provision of syntactic error messages and
  helps

This separation makes it easier to offer
alternate interaction styles (a dialogue style
plus other details like syntax and interaction
device techniques). Applications can be written
to be independent of a particular user-oriented
interaction style. The interactive components
form a dialogue manager shared by all functional
applications. Distinct roles are then available
to dialogue authors building parts of the
dialogue manager and to functional programmers
writing computational modules for applications.

Commercial implementations of some portions of a
dialogue manager are becoming available in
products like the Visicorp Operating Environment
(VisiOn) and the Lisa dialogue toolkit. (These
are based on a single dialogue style.)

J. D. Foley has used as an analogy a data base
management system, which provides an abstract
data model as a back-end functional model. A
user interface management system [8] provides an
abstract interaction model as a front-end.

These ideas interact with the multi-functional
office network to yield

- the concept of a user workstation as a
  separate interaction processor implementing
  the dialogue manager, analagous to

special-purpose data base processors now
available. This is illustrated in Figure
1.

- the need for support of different
  interfaces between the dialogue component
  and the functional component, because the
  open network environment outlined in the
  previous section will involve applications
  written for different dialogue managers.
  This includes applications which currently
  contain their own interaction components
  and have their own particular dialogue
  style.

3.   RELATED WORK

Since we are not addressing the problem of
common operations in applications, our
workstation research follows different
directions than that of dialogue gateways like
the NBS Network Access Machine [9]. That user
workstation provides integrated semantics for a
set of functionally similar services--different
bibliographic retrieval systems. The
workstation translates between the common user
language and the specific host retrieval
language, including transforming system
responses. Similar gateways can be developed
for other services, like electronic mail, which
are alike in concept but differ in details.

We have been influenced by the abstract
interaction handler at George Washington
University [7], which our first software
architecture followed closely. The interaction
handler uses an application representative in an
intermediate language to drive the interaction.
Various interaction styles are available as
separate modules, giving style-independent
applications and application-independent styles.
The interaction handler communicates with the
functional components via procedure calls.
Another somewhat similar development which has
also been helpful to us is the Dialogue
Management System [6].

Our more recent software design generalizes
common style information into an abstract data
type, rather than having it repeated in each
application representation. We are also using a
message passing protocol rather than procedural
calls. Both changes reflect the open network
requirements.

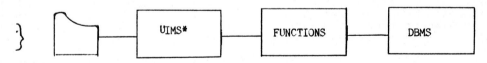

Figure 1

Front-ends / Back-ends for Functional Components

* UIMS: User Interface Management System

Network aspects have been explicitly considered in RIG [10], a distributed operating system with a common command language interpreter which interacts with a tool interface process for each network tool. All these processes are intended to interact through message passing. Our proposal has the conversational style, including the command interpreter, and the tool interface process both in the workstation. We also would like to offer a more diverse set of dialogue styles.

The Augment User Interface Service [11], also has elements of a dialogue manager, although it is not workstation-based. The manager has a command language grammar to represent each application written to use the dialogue interface. There are two style choices for a 'foreign' application. They can be accessed through the consistent command language style, through an extended application representation to map between the application interface and the UIS standard style. Alternately, the user can access the external application in its native style via a reach-through interface.

The semantic-level assistance we would like to provide in the future is similar to that of the Rand Intelligent Terminal Agent (RITA) [12]. RITA consists of a number of agents aiding file transfers on the ARPA network; the semantics of this application service were represented using production rules and a context of information about the current status of objects. With the rules expressed in limited natural language, an explanation mechanism was provided: the agent showed the user on request what rules were being applied. Since we envision common rules for various applications, we currently plan to use frames to represent application semantics.

4. PREVIOUS PROTOTYPE WORKSTATION

We previously implemented a skeleton dialogue workstation, using IBM Personal Computers as workstation processors [13]. The PC was chosen as a typical state of the art processor configuration for a majority of office workers. The workstation software is insulated from the particular hardware choice through use of a portable operating system.

The skeleton implementation was in PORT [14], a system/language developed at the University of Waterloo specifically for portability. The operating system runs on several other processors as well as the IBM PC; it is designed to be easily moved to a new processor, but is compiled directly to native machine code to increase efficiency. PORT is a single user, real-time system with concurrent processes communicating by message passing.

The implementation was restricted to user choices for integrated display styles. Users select an application service and a display style; the workstation establishes the network session, provides a screen window and creates a dialogue style handler. These are three concurrent processes communicating by message passing, as shown in Figure 2. The dialogue handler organizes the contents of a virtual display which the screen handler uses to drive a physical screen window (the user can dynamically alter the physical window size or scroll physical window contents within the virtual display contents).

The user will choose from the following illustrative dialogue style options:

- a reach-through to the existing application display style, in which case the dialogue handler is minimal

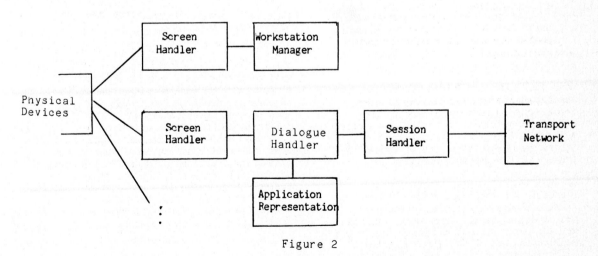

Figure 2

Workstation Software Architecture

- a change in spatial cues, for example
command line appearing at the top rather
than the bottom of the physical screen.
This is performed within the screen handler
by treating each such movable unit as a
subwindow of the application window.

- organization of the application screen into
subwindows of different types. In an
application written for a low-level
dialogue protocol, eg. scroll-mode or
page-mode terminals, this involves
interpreting system responses like error
messages, prompts and status reports and
sending them to different subwindows. In
an application written for a high-level
protocol, the dialogue handler redirects
these system responses according to a
user-specified screen map. The
presentation handler performs this
translation process, and also translates
user entries into the form expected by the
application.

One of the subwindows of the application window
is a data window, whose semantics we do not
consider. The others are control windows for
commands, status, error messages and helps. The
protocols which interest us are concerned only
with these dialogue control aspects. A separate
protocol could be applied to the data window.

5.   CURRENT IMPLEMENTATION ISSUES

The initial implementation left several issues
to be addressed later:

- the dialogue styles were incorporated in
procedural code. A nonprocedural
representation was planned for future
designs, to enable users and systems
professionals to customize a style.

- application-dependent syntax was stored in
a grammar form. A stronger representation
of these rules was also needed to enable
user assistance to be local to the
workstation for managing user input.

- when user input and bursts of traffic from
the network coincided, display of user
input could be noticeably delayed (and
occasionally lost). We might have avoided
this by altering the design away from
strict message-passing, but we wanted to
preserve our low module coupling.

- we chose not to design an appropriate
structure for the application software to
take full advantage of the dialogue
distribution, partly since other efforts
were directed to that end [6]. The future
network context of our work suggested
different approaches to the interface
between application and dialogue.

Representation issues: our current design
effort is developing abstract data types for
dialogue styles, as suggested by Shaw [15]. The
application designer can specify application
rules using a style abstraction, so that a set
of style instances can be chosen by a user.

The application representation in the
workstation is also based on a data type, the
interaction node. Instances of this type are
commands or modes. The type will have elements
to record the data objects accessible, the
language syntax (using an extended LL(1) grammar
as in [16]), preconditions and postconditions,
and a script of usual action sequences.

We need a type mechanism extensive enough to
allow inheritance of attributes from nodes to
commands, but we do not appear to need the
dynamism of Smalltalk-like objects or the
open-endedness of a frame-based representation.

Processor design: We expect future workstations
with sufficient processing resources to dedicate
processors to both user and network
communications. Planning has begun for a target
workstation which has a multiprocessor hardware
architecture (a Convergent Technology
Megaframe). In addition to the communication
processors, one processor will be running an
assistance program which monitors activity
continuously in order to provide help.

One might naturally expect the dialogue protocol
to serve as an interface for applications whose
functional processing is also based in the
workstation. We are reluctant to make
predictions about how compatible the dialogue
interfaces will be, since the timing of
responses to the user will affect the processing
done by the dialogue manager and the messages it
passes to the functional components. This
impact of distributed processing on dialogue
management is one of the aspects we hope to be
able to explore.

Application links: In our current design, the
dialogue workstation simulates a Unix Shell for
an application.

The future applications we expect to include
will be written to interface with network
protocols. The most prominent scheme for
network protocols is the 'reference model for
open systems interconnection' of the
International Standards Organization [17]. This
separates network operations into seven layers,
from low-level basic physical control to
high-level, application specific information.
Within that framework, the distribution of
dialogue processing to a workstation suggests
virtual dialogue protocols. Like proposed
virtual terminal protocols, they would be common
applications service elements.

The interesting question in the network framework is the definition of the classes of virtual dialogue protocols. It appears certain that the application processor must have some information about the class of dialogue seen by the user. At the same time we want to keep that information as minimal as possible, to facilitate change by the user and preserve the low coupling of dialogue and application.

6. CONCLUSION

We have proposed a distribution of processing for network applications, in which interaction is based in a user workstation and functional components run on network hosts. The advantages of this arrangement include

- separation of dialogue from application writers

- ability to offer personalized dialogue styles

- potential to integrate external applications

- localized processing overheads

Broadly put, the personal workstation becomes the focus of personal aspects of application use.

7. ACKNOWLEDGEMENTS

This work was supported by the Office Communications System Group of Canada's Department of Communications and the Natural Sciences and Engineering Research Council. Dick Foster and Blair Nonnecke implemented the initial prototype. Current design contributors include Laverne Douglas, Dick Foster, Sigrid Grimm, and Karl Langton. Terry Dehaan and Dick Foster assisted in production of this paper.

8. REFERENCES

[1] Norman, D., Steps Toward a Cognitive Engineering, Proc. Conf. on Human Factors in Computer Systems, 1982, p. 378-382.

[2] Dzida, W., S. Herda and W.D. Itzfeldt, A Paradigm for Task-Oriented Man-Computer Interaction, in Methodology of Interaction ed. R. Guedj et. al., North-Holland, 1980, p. 189-193.

[3] Schneider, M.L. et. al., Designing Control Languages from the User's Perspective, in Command Language Directions ed. D. Beech, North-Holland, 1980, p. 181-198.

[4] Carey, T.T., User Differences in Interface Design, IEEE Computer, November, 1982, p. 14-20.

[5] Chevance, R.J., Principles of a Dialogue Processor, in Teleinformatics 79, ed. Boutmy and Danthive, North-Holland, 1980.

[6] Roach, J., H.R. Hartson, R. Ehrich, T. Yunten and D. Johnson, DMS: A Comprehensive System for Managing Human-Computer Dialogue, Proc. Conf. on Human Factors in Computer Systems, 1982, p. 102-105.

[7] Feldman, M.B. and G.T. Rogers, Toward the Design and Development of Style-Independent Interactive Systems, Proc. Conf. on Human Factors in Computer Systems, 1982, p. 111-116.

[8] Foley, J.D., User Interface Managment Systems, seminar at University of Toronto, April 1983.

[9] Treu, S., Uniformity in user-computer interaction languages: a compromise solution, Intl. J. of Man-Machine Studies, Vol. 16 (1982), p. 183-210.

[10] Lantz, K., Command Interactions in Distributed Systems, Proc. IEEE Compcon Fall 1980, p. 25-32.

[11] Engelbart, D.C., Toward High-Performance Knowledge Workers, AFIPS Office Automation Conference '82 Digest, p. 279-290.

[12] Anderson, R.H. and J. Gillogly, The Rand intelligent terminal agent as a network access aid, Proc. NCC, 1976, p. 501-509.

[13] Carey, T.T., A Workstation For Interaction Styles, Proc. IEEE Compsac, 1982, p. 303-308.

[14] Malcolm, M.A., Waterloo Port User's Guide, Institute for Computer Research, University of Waterloo, January 1983.

[15] Shaw, M. et. al., Descartes: A Programming Language Approach to Interactive Display Interfaces, Proc. ACM Sigplan Conference, June 1983, p. 100-111.

[16] Olsen, D.R., Automatic Generation of Interactive Systems, Computer Graphics, January 1983, p. 53-57.

[17] Zimmerman, H., OSI Reference Model--The ISO Model of Architecture for Open Systems Interconnection, IEEE Trans. Comm., Vol. Com-28 (1980), p. 425-432.

INPUT AND OUTPUT – SOME NEW APPROACHES

Human-Computer Interaction – INTERACT '84 / B. Shackel (ed.)
Elsevier Science Publishers B.V. (North-Holland)
IFIP, 1985

135

NEW TECHNIQUES FOR GESTURE-BASED DIALOGUE

Martin Lamb and Veronica Buckley

Computer Systems Research Group
University of Toronto, Toronto
Ontario M5S 1A4, Canada

A music editor is described which requires no typing and which has been used
successfully by children as young as three years of age. No syntax errors are possible, and all input methods are intuitive - stroking, pointing, dragging and circling,
for example. Commands (such as move, delete or copy) are not specified by words, but
are conveyed by gesture; (for instance, in order to delete an item, the user merely
circles it and pushes it off the screen).

Throughout the programs, the auditory, visual and kinesthetic modalities are employed
either simultaneously or in immediate proximity, thereby reinforcing the intuitive
nature of the interface. Alternative user-models of interaction are supported. The
techniques presented form the basis of a computerised Learning Environment for music
and a User-Interface Management System.

The music editor which I would like to describe
was developed originally for use with young
children. Although it may appear somewhat irregular to place children in a central position
in the development of sophisticated software
techniques, we felt that with children we could
at least be sure of the efficacy of our user
interface. If instructions are not clear to a
small child, one is likely to know about it.
We realised that any user interface comprehensible to children would almost certainly be
comprehensible to adults, whether experienced
in computing or not. Moreover, we felt that if
our interface techniques could be made succinct
enough to convey the abstract, they would
probably be successful in conveying more readily
grasped concrete matters.

Once the scope of our project had been determined, there remained the task of selecting the
most suitable area of computing for testing our
user interface. Although our first thoughts on
this were in the direction of computer-aided
design and then simulation, it soon became
clear that it would be virtually impossible to
measure the efficacy of an interface used in
either of these areas with any degree of accuracy.
For this reason we decided to concentrate our
work in the field of computer-aided learning.
Here, we felt, reasonably precise testing would
at least be possible; a specific set of concepts
could be laid down for use, and specific tests
be later carried out to determine the children's
understanding of those concepts. Such testing
obviously goes beyond the limits of subjective
appraisals, so often detrimentally affected by
"bells and whistles" with no real purpose,
distracting optional extras full of sound and
fury, as it were, and signifying nothing in
particular. The current widespread use of
unnecessary colour and visual effects is a case
in point.

One last decision remained to be made — the
selection of a subject area within the field of
computer-aided learning. Through our previous
research, we had come to realise the richness
of music as a field of learning for children,
and the suitability of the computer as a medium
of music instruction (Lamb, 1978, 1982; Lamb and
Bates, 1979). The decision to work on computer-
aided music instruction was consequently made.
As we had anticipated, it bore fine fruits;
not only did we produce an effective interface
for music instruction, but the interface techniques developed in this way proved to be
immediately applicable in CAD/CAM (Lamb, 1984).

Probably the most important aspect of the user
interface which I am about to describe to you
is that it is completely intuitive. Intuition,
of course, is a matter of some variation between
one person and the next — a fact which must be
taken into account if everyone approaching an
interface is to have an equal chance of reacting
intuitively to it. We decided to provide for
three different but apparently equally intuitive
modes of communication — auditory, visual and
kinesthetic. Throughout the program, these
modalities are employed either simultaneously
or in immediate proximity, thereby reinforcing
the already intuitive nature of the interface.
By this, I mean that the computer's response
is entirely appropriate to the user's gestural
input.

A further very important aspect of the interface
is that it has been designed to preclude the
possibility of any inadvertent error on the
user's part. Gone forever the message: SYNTAX
ERROR. The only interactions available to the
user at any time are those which are syntactically correct. During editing, for example,
the selected musical fragment in fact becomes
the cursor, and follows the movements of the

user's hands, forcing the user to complete the command sequence underway, so ensuring correct syntax. The command menu, too, has of course been carefully designed as part of this unassailably correct syntax; nothing is displayed on the screen unless it is immediately usable. The user, the child, may explore the program in whatever way she chooses; only those instructions which make sense to the program will be affected, and in every case it will undertake the closest possible approximation to the user's instruction, if the instruction itself is impossible to carry out. In this way the system has been made supremely robust.

I would like to give an example of this. One section of the program deals with acoustics, the physics of sound, in a combination of pictorial and auditory terms. In one part of this section, the user is given, on-screen, a rectangle containing a graphed representation of the amplitude envelope of a particular wave, while the corresponding sound of the wave is heard at a given pitch. By 'picking up' a corner of the graphed envelope, via a mouse or graphics tablet, the user can alter the envelope, with the sound altering correspondingly. Now, it is a matter of mathematical fact that the amplitude envelope of a specific sound can be graphed only in a limited number of ways. It cannot, for instance, at any stage become a multi-valued function. The user of our program will realise this at once, should she attempt to reshape the graph in such a way as to contravene mathematical principles. In this case, the program will accommodate her gestures, producing the nearest mathematically correct value for the function.

It will readily be appreciated that even this small corner of one interactive screen functions as an "intelligent" picture.

Having outlined the principles on which our system is based, I would now like to describe some of the specific gestures involved in this interaction.

With her finger, the child draws a shape on the graphics pad. Simultaneously, the corresponding shape appears on the screen, superimposed on musical staves. This shape crystallises into musical notation with the same shape, which the child then hears played by the computer. After adding more shapes in the manner just described, the child may select parts of this music by circling it, again using one finger on the graphics pad. The selected fragment is then tracked as the cursor, following the child's finger movements. The fragment can be moved about on the staves and heard played at the corresponding pitches. The child is in this way introduced to the concept of transposition.

With her other hand, the child strokes one of two sliding strips connected to the computer. One of these strips controls the horizontal expansion and contraction of the musical fragment, corresponding to the musical concepts of augmentation and diminution. Once diminished to the point of nothing, the fragment then emerges out the other side of nothing, as it were, to appear backwards — in musical terms, in retrogression. The second sliding strip exercises similar control in a vertical direction. Stroking it upwards proportionately increases the relative intervals between the notes of the fragment, while stroking it downwards decreases them gradually to nothing; from this point they emerge upside-down, corresponding to the musical concept of inversion. As always, the child can hear the transformed fragment played at the touch of a button on the graphics pad.

Once the desired transformations of the fragment have been carried out, it may be anchored to the stave at a position of the child's choosing.

The music is at this point displayed as white-on-black. Dipping her finger into on-screen paint pots, the child can orchestrate the music by finger painting it with the available colours, each of which corresponds to a particular instrumental timbre. Red, for example, represents a trumpet; blue, a clarinet, and so on. The music can then be replayed, with each note voicing the timbre appropriate to its colour.

In this intuitive way, even very young children can explore concepts usually taught only at an advanced level of musical training.

The musical learning environment known as MUSICLAND in fact comprises four educational computer games. Each of the games focuses on a different aspect of musical creativity. The first two, whereby the child draws a musical shape and orchestrates it with colour, have to some extent been already described (see Figures 1 and 2). The third and fourth games represent, as it were, a musical perspective in wide-angle and zoom respectively (see Figures 3 and 4). One allows the separate musical fragments of the child's own design to be pieced together to form a compositional whole. The other allows an instrumental timbre corresponding to one of the coloured paint pots to be modified or completely redesigned. This is achieved by manipulating a small "intelligent picture" corresponding to the sound's amplitude envelope (as has been already described) and by increasing or decreasing the relative strengths of the sound's overtones by modifying a bar graph. A bar's height represents the loudness of the overtone whose overtone-number is displayed beneath the bar. When a child points to a bar, using her finger on the graphics pad, and slides it up or down, the sound and picture change instantaneously so she can see and hear the change in loudness of that overtone. In

Figure 1: Shapes drawn by the child crystallise into musical notation which the computer then plays. Shapes can be transformed by stretching, squeezing, turning them over or inside out.

Figure 2: The child learns to orchestrate by finger painting the notes with colours, each of which represents a different instrumental timbre. To move to another of the MUSICLAND games, the child points to one of the arrows at the bottom of the screen.

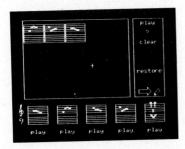

Figure 3: The separate musical fragments of the child's own design (shown at the bottom of the screen) are pieced together to form a compositional whole.

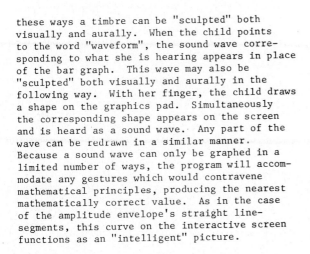

Figure 4: By manipulating parts of the picture, a child experiments with overtones, waveforms and amplitude envelopes, thereby creating new timbres for use in the game shown in Figure 2.

these ways a timbre can be "sculpted" both visually and aurally. When the child points to the word "waveform", the sound wave corresponding to what she is hearing appears in place of the bar graph. This wave may also be "sculpted" both visually and aurally in the following way. With her finger, the child draws a shape on the graphics pad. Simultaneously the corresponding shape appears on the screen and is heard as a sound wave. Any part of the wave can be redrawn in a similar manner. Because a sound wave can only be graphed in a limited number of ways, the program will accommodate any gestures which would contravene mathematical principles, producing the nearest mathematically correct value. As in the case of the amplitude envelope's straight line-segments, this curve on the interactive screen functions as an "intelligent" picture.

In this intuitive way, children and professional musicians can explore complex concepts which are usually incomprehensible when taught in the traditional manner, that is, by a teacher presenting facts from a textbook.

Next, I would like to describe the gestures involved in editing a piece of music. In these examples, a cursor and puck are used.

The child begins by pointing to "transform" whereupon the cursor turns into a quill with which she selects part of the music by circling it. If, after two seconds, nothing further is circled, a copy of the selected notes is then tracked as if it were the cursor, following the child's hand movements. Wherever the child

points on the music, hey presto! a copy of the
tracked notes is anchored there. This can be
repeated as often as she fancies since the notes
continue to be tracked until either they are
pushed off the screen or the child picks up the
cursor puck and shakes it in mid air to make
the originally circled notes vanish. In either
case, the cursor then resumes its usual cross-
hairs shape.

It will readily be appreciated that by circling
and then pointing and/or shaking the puck in
mid air, a child can easily and intuitively
copy, move or delete notes. Using an appropriate picture as the cursor not only ensures that
the user will complete the command which she
has begun — it also eliminates syntax errors.

When testing a user interface with children,
we reply to questions like "How do I do
such-and-such?" with the suggestion "Do what
you think is obvious". Whatever the child does
next we watch carefully, and if she is unsuccessful we try to modify the interface to
accommodate her expectations. On one occasion
an interesting dilemma arose when two different
"obvious" ways were found for moving a rectangular box containing music to another location
on the screen. Some children pointed to the box,
whereupon it became the cursor, and then pointed
to the destination to anchor it there. The
others tried to drag the box to the desired
location by holding the cursor button down
throughout the entire manoeuvre. Fortunately,
we can support both user-models: (1) picking
up the box, carrying it to the destination, and
putting it down; and (2) dragging the box all
the way there. Once the child has selected the
box (by pressing the cursor button when the
cursor is inside the box) it is tracked when
either the cursor button is released when still
inside it, or the cursor crosses the boundary
of the box with the button still pressed. A
change in button state then anchors the box.

In the many different ways which I have described,
the user interface has been made transparent to
children — the severest of critics. The use
of gesture intimately coupled with sound and
colour graphics has exciting implications for
computer-aided learning in many fields, as well
as for the design of future user-interfaces
in general.

REFERENCES:

Lamb, M.R., André Tchaikovsky meets the
computer: a concert pianist's impromptu
encounter with a musicianship teaching aid.
International Journal of Man-Machine Studies,
Vol. 10 (1978) 593-602.

Lamb, M.R. and Bates, R.H.T., Computerised
Aural Training, Journal of Computer Based
Instruction, Vol. 5 (1974) 30-37.

Lamb, M.R., An Interactive graphical modelling
game for teaching musical concepts, Journal
of Computer Based Instruction, Vol. 9, No.2
(1982) 59-63.

Lamb, M.R., A Versatile and Accessible User
Interface Management System, Proceedings of
the International Computer-Aided Design
Conference, Brighton, U.K. (1984) 8pp.

Human-Computer Interaction — INTERACT '84 / B. Shackel (ed.)
Elsevier Science Publishers B.V. (North-Holland)
© IFIP, 1985

ON-LINE CURSIVE SCRIPT RECOGNITION

C A Higgins and R Whitrow

Department of Computing and Cybernetics, Brighton Polytechnic, England
Department of Computing and Microprocessor Applications, Trent Polytechnic, England

A method is proposed for the automatic recognition of handwritten words using a
hierarchical description. Possible letters and segmentation shapes are suggested
by matching the script to stored templates. Ambiguities are resolved using higher
level context in the form of letter quadgrams and a dictionary lookup.

1. INTRODUCTION

Early application to the cursive script recognition (CSR) problem started around 1960 and
many became active in this field at this time
[3-5,7]. Most researchers were, however, using
CSR as a simpler medium for studying the problems of segmenting continuous speech, and
turned their attention to this problem from
about 1965 leaving CSR relatively unsolved.
1973 saw the revival of interest in CSR with
Sayre's static system [10] and the number of
people involved in CSR increased steadily from
then on [1,2,6,8,9]. A large proportion of
recent work has been sponsored by commerce and
industry and due to pecuniary interests not all
activities and results are reported in the
current literature. Much of this involvement
now stems from the desire for improved man-
machine communication and interfaces. The
cheaper, faster, more powerful microprocessor
systems now available make CSR a viable proposition, especially in the area of office automation. As well as an interactive terminal/
editor for converting cursive to typewritten
script, other uses include aids for the handicapped (eg conversion from cursive script to
speech or braille for the blind to "read", or
to speech to allow a dumb person to communicate
audibly).

In all script recognition systems the input
data is either in the form of a binary image or,
as in our case, a sequential list of coordinate
pairs. The latter is an easier problem to
solve as more imformation is present, but the
former has wider applications in its ability to
read off-line, already written script. From
the crude data a set of features is extracted
which is then used in the recognition attempt.
Cursive script, unlike handprinted characters,
is not naturally segmented into discrete characters that can be studied individually. This
leads to two basically different approaches to
the CSR problem.

One method is to try to recognise the entire
word as a single entity. Here a global vector
of features extracted from the script is matched
to a stored dictionary and some form of nearest

neighbour method used to choose the best candidate [1,2]. This word recognition method has
the advantage of speed, and avoids problems
associated with segmentation. It has the disadvantage of a limited vocabulary and the need
to train the machine with samples of each word
in the vocabulary. Training can be reduced or
avoided but this involves selecting author
independent features, a difficult task.

The second method which we use - CSR by segmentation and character recognition - is slower
and more difficult, but can have the advantage
of a much wider vocabulary. User specific training can also be achieved where only a subset of
all possible words needs to be trained. The
major problem with this method is that first a
character must be extracted from the script
before an attempt can be made to recognise it.
Acknowledgement as a possible character not
necessarily identification of which character
has been detected is all that is required to
obtain segmentation. To achieve optimum results
segmentation shapes rather than points are considered, and segmentation shape recognition
proceeds in parallel with character recognition.
The types and feature vectors associated with
each segmenting shape as well as each character
are considered to form a description of an
individual author's style of writing.

2. THE METHOD

The goal of our work is to produce a practical
CSR system with a higher recognition rate for a
majority of authors. Since humans find some
handwriting illegible, it seems unlikely that
machine recognition of totally unconstrained
script is possible in the near future. Thus to
achieve our aim some restrictions are placed on
the size, orientation and style of writing.
Initially a good clear script, readily recognis-
able by a human reader is required, although
later it is hoped to relax this restriction.
The minimum size of script is dictated by data
pad resolution and is about two millimetres for
the centre region height of a word. Horizontal
orientation (base line slant) must be close to
zero. The time sequential nature of the data
inherent in an on-line system is preserved and

used, although acceleration and velocity information is not (ie it is a static rather than
dynamic system). Long letters (eg l, h, f, g)
should be significantly longer than short letters (eg a, c, e) and unusual letter formation
is forbidden. Diacritical marks (ie the dot in
i and j and the bar in t) are required. Only
the 26 lower case letters of the English alphabet are allowed.

The recognition system builds an ambiguous hierarchical description of the word [8]. At each
level of the description, related primitive
objects are matched to known templates to create
an object on the next level. Uncertainties as
to object identities on one level are passed to
a higher level where contextual information can
be applied to resolve these ambiguities. An
object will only be created if its initial
weight (goodness of fit to a template) lies
below some threshold value. The weight (d) is
obtained in the following manner. Each template
contains a list of which features are relevant
and their mean value and standard deviation from
a training set. The weight is the Euclidean
distance in n-dimensional vector space of the
object from its template (where n is the number
of feature tests to be applied) - zero weight is
a perfect fit. Binary decisions are used to
resolve ambiguities of objects at higher levels
rather than the relaxation methods of Hayes and
Peleg [9]. The speed performance of the system
has been a major consideration and so integer
arithmetic has been used wherever possible.
This leads to the use of approximate rather than
mathematically strict functions for feature calculations. Also turning points rather than dips
(counter clockwise turns of at least 110° [10])
are used for initial segmentation. Finally, the
major speed consideration has been in template
matching. The straight forward method of finding the intersection of two lists (one of templates, the other of primitives) to generate a
new object is slow, and methods of avoiding this
process will be described in later sections.

3. PREPROCESSING

The raw data for the recognition system consists
of a time ordered, sequential list of positive
coordinate pairs (level 0 description) obtained
from a pressure sensitive data pad. Pen lifts
are preserved and represented by the coordinate
(0, 1). Although the input script, by the very
nature of being 'cursive', is in general a
smooth continuous curve with few discontinuities
it is converted to a discrete description by the
data pad. Unlike many CSR systems we do not
attempt to smooth this data as this is time consuming and leads to some loss of detail.
Instead, any noise is removed during the detection of turning points, and further processing
of the data is performed with this discrete
nature in mind.

The slope of the script from the vertical is
calculated, and if this exceeds a threshold

value, a shearing movement is applied in the x
direction to skew the word into a vertical position. A list of turning points is formed by
detecting a change in direction of more than
two resolution units. This eliminates noise
due to erroneous single unit 'wobbles'. Ten
types of turning point are defined: start, stop,
X max, X min, Y max, Y min, and pairwise combinations of these last four. The turning point
list along with features associated with each
turning point (described below) constitutes the
level 1 description of the script.

The final preprocessing stage is the calculation
of the base line (BL), upper half line (UH) and
upper centre line (UC) positions (figure 1).
These lines define four horizontal regions. The
lower region contains only deep letters (eg g,
y). The centre region only small letters (eg a,
e, n) and the upper region only tall letters
(eg t, h, l). The upper centre region is an
ambiguous zone into which both small and tall
letters may transgress. The BL is obtained by
calculating the mean and standard deviation of
the Y coordinates for all minima. This calculation is repeated with extreme turning points
removed until the standard deviation is less
than a threshold value obtained from a table

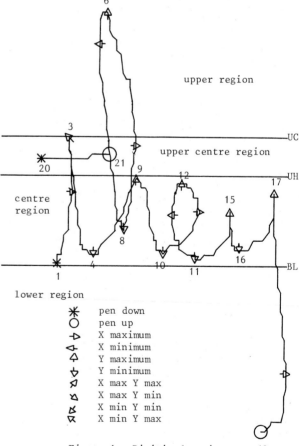

	pen down
	pen up
	X maximum
	X minimum
	Y maximum
	Y minimum
	X max Y max
	X max Y min
	X min Y min
	X min Y max

Figure 1 : Digitised script   19

(of standard deviation against number of turning points). The BL is considered to be just below all the remaining Y minima. A similar calculation for maxima gives the UH line and UC line. The tables for these calculations were obtained from a training set of 340 words (170 by each of two authors) which also indicated the need for an ambiguous upper centre region.

4. FEATURE GENERATION

The features must be of sufficient detail and wide enough variety to describe the script adequately, but should not require excessive time to calculate and apply. In an adaptive system they must also be capable of changing as training proceeds.

Seven features are used to describe the script at and around each turning point, and these fall into two categories. These are the type of turning point (one of ten) and the region in which it lies (one of four). The five continuous features used where the range of values is (theoretically) infinite are: change in X and Y over the five points preceding, and five points succeeding the turning point (four features), and the angle between points 3 before and 3 after the turning point. Additionally one feature describing the curvature of the arc between two successive turning points is used. Only one feature is required here since the possible behaviour of the script in each of these regions is limited due to the absence of turning points.

Tests for several extra features may also be applied, although these are optional and depend on whether the shape being tested for requires them. These features are associated with the position of one turning point relative to another and the distance separating them. They are applied discriminately since they require relatively large amounts of calculation time.

The application of features to give a distance measurement (d) of the 'goodness of fit' of an object to its template is as follows. Firstly, a value (x_i) for a feature (F_i) is determined from the script sample. A distance (d_i) relative to the standard deviation (σ_i) of test samples from the mean $(\bar{x}_i)$ for F_i is calculated by

$$d_i = \frac{(\bar{x}_i - x_i)}{\sigma_i}$$

The Euclidean distance of the object from its template is then calculated using

$$d = \left(\frac{\sum_{i=1}^{n} (d_i)^2}{n} \right)^{\frac{1}{2}}$$

where n is the number of dimensions and the numerator is applied to enable the distances of objects of differing dimensionalities to be compared.

5. PRIMARY SHAPE FORMATION

Groups of turning point records are matched to primary shape templates (PSTs) to produce the level 2 description of a word - a multi-threaded structure of possible shapes. To speed template matching the two discrete features (type and region) of the first two turning points in a shape template are used to index into a four dimensional array. This array contains a pointer to a list of all PSTs that begin with these four features. An attempt is then made to match subsequent features to the remaining vectors for each PST in turn. If the weight obtained from this matching lies below a threshold value, a shape record is created. This record contains the shape type, the weight, the index of its start and end turning points and a pointer to the PST that spawned it. This pointer is used later during training to alter the feature vectors of the PST. The shape record is linked into the level 2 structure in two ways. Firstly, it is linked to a list of all shapes that start at a particular turning point. There is one list for each turning point in the level 1 description. Secondly, the shape record is linked to a list of all shapes of the same type. The head of each list for each type of shape is an array of pointers and this enables rapid matching of shapes to templates at the next stage of the recognition attempt.

6. HIGHER SHAPE FORMATION

The level 2 structure is now expanded by combining physically adjacent pairs of shapes together to create new shapes. These are included in the structure by adding them to the two types of list described above. Higher shape templates (HSTs) describe which two shapes may be combined to create which new shape. The weights of the two initial shapes, plus the vector matching process applied to the intervening turning point are used to calculate a weight for the new shape. To increase the speed of template matching the two types of shape list are used in the following manner. For each HST the first of the two necessary shapes is used to select the list of all shapes of this type. The end point of each element in this list is used to obtain the list of shapes that starts at this turning point. If any shapes in this second list are the same as the second required shape from the template, a match has occurred and the weight calculation is then performed. To overcome the problems associated with pen lifts and to create connecting shapes that span pen lifts and diacritical marks, the HST matching is a recursive process.

The final shapes created in this process are in fact the letters and segmentation shapes which describe the author's style. These letters and segmentation shapes are used to form the next level in the hierarchy - the completed letter graph.

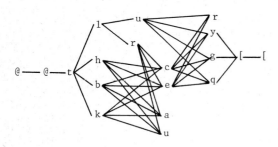

Figure 2 : The letter graph

7. THE LETTER GRAPH

The level 3 description is a graph (or trellis)
representing the entire word. Nodes on the
graph represent possible letters, and the links
(or arcs) of the graph represent segmentation
shapes. The graph is formed by creating a node
for each letter that exists in the level 2 description. These nodes are linked together
whenever a connection (segmentation) shape can
be found in the level 2 description which separates and is physically contiguous with both
letters. Two start nodes (@) and stop nodes ([)
are included to assist processing (figure 2).
Pathways through the trellis represent the different possibilities for the word and must be
traced from left to right (ie no backtracking)
to ensure a sequence of non-overlapping but
touching words.

To trace each pathway and look up the resulting
word in a dictionary is not feasible since the

time taken to do this would be excessive due to
the large number of possible routes. An attempt
is first made to reduce the size of the graph
using letter quadgrams. Any sequence of four
letters (a quadgram) is either allowed or dis-
allowed in English. A boolean array of this
information was prepared using the letter
sequences found in a dictionary. A link in the
level 3 description is deleted if there are no
quadgrams that span it. A level 3 node (ie a
letter) is deleted if there are no forward or
backward links from it. Deletions of nodes
often lead to deletions of links and vice versa.
Repeated attempts are made to delete links until
all remaining links (and nodes) are permissable.
When no further deletions are possible, a stable
reduced graph has been formed, and this is
usually much smaller (about an order of magnitude) than the original graph.

All the remaining paths in the graph are now
traced from left to right and each word generated is looked up in a dictionary. If the word
is found in the dictionary, then it is one of
the possibilities that the script may represent.
A ranked list is made of all possibilities, and
each word in the list has a weight associated
with it calculated from the weights of all the
constituent letters and segmentation shapes.
Three types of successful recognition can occur
and in decreasing desirability these are:

1. One correct word in the list.
2. A (short) list of words with the correct
    word having the highest weight.
3. A list of words containing the correct word
    somewhere.

Figure 3 shows how the various levels of the
hierarchy are constructed from preceding levels.

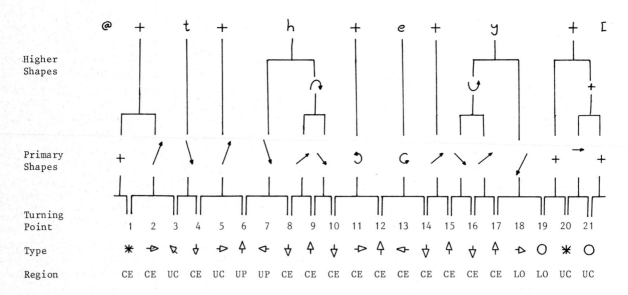

Figure 3 : A hierarchical description

For clarity only the shapes, letters and segmentation shapes actually used to form the correct word are shown, a large number of incorrect objects would also be created during the recognition attempt.

8. CONCLUSION

Initial tests of the CSR system used a sample of 100 cursive words, and a dictionary of 26k words. The number of possible quadgrams is $27^4 = 531441$ (if 'start' is included as a character in the first two positions and 'stop' in the last two) of which approximately 5% are allowable. This is a small enough percentage to disambiguate the letter graph to a high degree. The correct word was contained in the list of possible words in a large majority of cases. Failure to include the correct word was due to the lack of a correct template for a slightly unusual letter or connection shape, and can be rectified by including new templates. Training of the system is presently applied manually and until automatic training is implemented, this leads to inaccurate feature values for the templates. This in turn gives incorrect weighting to some shapes and letters and hence the correct word does not always have the best weight. Problems are always likely to occur, however, with words having no diacritical marks or easily distinguished features such as long letters (eg even, common). Groups of words that differ only in one or two places also pose problems (eg far-for, baud-band).

The varying dimensionality of features for different shapes can favour long (high dimensionality) or short (low dimensionality) shapes, depending on which functions are used to determine weights. After the implementation of automatic training, experiments will be carried out to find which functions give the best compromise. Diacritical marks will also be used to fuller advantage. At present if a dot appears above two 'spikes' in the script, the letter i is created in two positions in the letter graph. These two letter i's should, however, be mutually exclusive as only one dot is present.

Work is also required on what to do with the list of possible words. It should be possible to use phrase, sentence or subject level context as well as word weight to select the correct word. Finally, it should be possible to cope with any (consistent) style of handwriting no matter how non-standard, if the CSR system is designed to build its own templates by selecting which primitives to combine together, and which features are relevant.

REFERENCES

[1] Brown M K and Ganapathy S, Cursive script recognition, Proc 1980 Int Conf on Cybernetics and Society (1980) 47-51.

[2] Brown M K and Granapathy S, Preprocessing techniques for cursive script word recognition, Pattern Recognition 16 (1983) 447-458

[3] Earnest L D, Machine recognition of cursive writing, Proc IFIP Congr (1962) 462-465

[4] Eden M, Handwriting and pattern recognition, IRE Transactions on Information Theory (1964) 160-166

[5] Eden M and Halle M, The characterisation of cursive writing, 4th London Symp Info Theory (1961) 287-299

[6] Ehrich R W and Koehler K J, Experiments in the contextual recognition of cursive script, IEEE Trans Comp 24 (1975) 182-194

[7] Frishkopf L S and Harmon L D, Machine reading of cursive script, 4th London Symp Info Theory (1961) 300-316

[8] Hayes K C, Reading handwritten words using hierarchical relaxation, Computer Graphics and Image Processing 14 (1980) 344-364

[9] Peleg S, Ambiguity reduction in handwriting with ambiguous segmentation and uncertain interpretation, Computer Graphics and Image Processing 10 (1979) 235-245

[10] Sayre K M, Machine recognition of handwritten words: a project report, Pattern Recognition 5 (1973) 213-228

Human-Computer Interaction — INTERACT '84 / B. Shackel (ed.)
Elsevier Science Publishers B.V. (North-Holland)
© IFIP, 1985

ON-LINE ACQUISITION OF PITMAN'S HANDWRITTEN SHORTHAND AS A MEANS OF RAPID DATA ENTRY

C.G.Leedham[*], A.C.Downton[*], C.P.Brooks[+] and A.F.Newell[#]

*   Department of Electronics and Information Engineering, University of Southampton, UK
+   Possum Controls Ltd., Slough, UK
#   Department of Electrical Engineering and Electronics, University of Dundee, UK

In this paper we discuss the use of Pitmans shorthand as a means of converting dictation speed speech (up to 120 wpm) directly into readable text for computer entry or direct output. The Pitman shorthand notation is compared to a machinography or machine compatible script and the recognition problems associated with handwritten shorthand are discussed. The requirements of a writing tablet and instrumented pen for on-line acquisition of Pitman shorthand are described and the preprocessing techniques which have been usefully applied to the raw data are outlined.

1. INTRODUCTION

In applications such as verbatim reporting and office dictation, the ability to produce a simultaneous printed transcript or computer compatible text file of spoken language is often desirable. Unfortunately, typists using the conventional QWERTY keyboard cannot achieve even dictation speeds of 120 wpm, while typical verbatim speeds (180 wpm) are 2-3 times faster than normal typing. Automatic simultaneous recognition and transcription of speech offers an obvious solution to this problem but the recognition of unlimited vocabulary connected speech requires many more years of directed research [1].

An alternative means of obtaining real-time verbatim data entry is to use one of the shorthand systems which have been developed specifically for verbatim recording. These systems record speech phonetically and can be divided into two groups, machine shorthand (e.g. Palantype, Stenograph and Grandjean) and handwritten shorthand (e.g. Pitman and Gregg). Machine shorthand potentially offers the most reliable solution because of the consistency of keyboard data and ease of interfacing to a computer. Automatic transcription of machine shorthand is reported in a companion paper [2]. The use of machine shorthand however is at present confined almost exclusively to the verbatim reporting profession, and is thus not widespread. Handwritten shorthand on the other hand is extensively used both for verbatim reporting and in the office. Based upon examination results provided by the Pitmans Examination Institute it is estimated that Pitman shorthand (the most popular shorthand system in the United Kingdom) has over one million practising users worldwide capable of recording at speeds of 120 wpm. Approximately half of this number work in the United Kingdom.

Because of its widespread availability, written shorthand would form an attractive medium for fast text entry to computers and word processors if the initial data acquisition and recognition problems could be overcome. A research project at Southampton University has therefore investigated on-line acquisition, recognition and transcription of written shorthand as a possible man-machine interface. In this paper we discuss the suitability of Pitman shorthand for automatic recognition and transcription, the data acquisition equipment required for on-line entry and the recognition problems caused by the variability of the shorthand script from writer to writer and from the same writer from time to time are discussed. Details of the recognition strategy used in our work are described elsewhere ([7]-[9]).

2. SHORTHAND AS A MACHINOGRAPHY

2.1 The structure of Pitman shorthand.

The Pitman shorthand notation [3],[4] records speech phonetically, dividing the English language into 40 phonemes comprising 24 consonants, 12 vowels and 4 diphthongs. Each phoneme is assigned a simple geometric penstroke as shown in Fig.1 and each word is written as a physically separate phonetic outline. To abbreviate the script a number of compound consonant sounds (eg. /BR/ and /PL/) are represented by circles, hooks or loops attached to a consonant stroke. The consonant sounds are represented as a connected string of strokes, hooks, loops and circles as illustrated in Fig.1(d) and the vowel and diphthong sounds are added as dots, dashes and small angular symbols in one of three positions separated from, but in close proximity to, appropriate consonant strokes in the consonant kernel. The consonant strokes may be written at three different lengths and with two different thicknesses or pressures to convey further phonetic information. The hooks, loops and circles may also be written in two different sizes. In addition commonly occurring words and phrases are written as single simple penstrokes (called shortforms) to increase speed.

Fig.1 (a) Consonant strokes.

Written stroke	Associated Phoneme (Pen pressure) :light:	:heavy:
＼	P (aPe)	B (oBoe)
⌐	T (ouT)	D (Day)
‒	K (oaK)	G (Go)
‿	N (No)	NG (thiNG)
＼	F (Face)	V (Vote)
⫫	TH (moTH)	DH (THey)
⁄	CH (CHum)	J (aGe)
⌐	S (Sew)	Z (Zero)
∪	SH (SHow)	ZH (uSHual)
⌒	M (May)	*
⌢	L (Load)	*
⌒	W (Way)	*
⁄	Y (Yes)	*
⁄	R (Ray)	*
⌐	R (eRode)	*
⁄	H (Hot)	*

(b) Vowel symbols.

Feature and position	Associated Phoneme (Pen pressure) :light:	:heavy:
• 1st	Ă (bAg)	AH (cAr)
• 2nd	Ĕ (bEt)	Ā (pAy)
• 3rd	Ĭ (If)	Ē (plEAse)
⹁ 1st	Ŏ (tOp)	AW (jAW)
⹁ 2nd	Ŭ (Up)	Ō (ObOe)
⹁ 3rd	OO (bOOk)	OO (blUE)

(c) Diphthong symbols.

Feature	Associated Phoneme Position 1st	2nd	3rd
⌄	I (bY) *	*	
＞	OI (bOY) *	*	
⌐			OW (OUt) *
⌐			U (dUty) *

* Phoneme not assigned to this position.

(d) Example outlines.

⌒	transistor	⌐	standard
⌐	weave	⌐	broke

Fig.1   The basic penstrokes of Pitman shorthand.

2.2 The characteristics of a machinography.

To ease the difficulty in machine recognition of handwritten script it is possible to design a script which is specially adapted to automatic recognition. Such a script is termed a machinography and it has been suggested [6] that it should exhibit the following features—
1. The script should possess the same linguistic structure as the local dominant script.
2. The script should be composed of a small number of simple shapes (pattern primitives) which are both easily written and recognised.
3. The symbols of the alphabet should correspond directly to individual pattern primitives.
4. The script should possess structure on numerous levels and there should be parallels between the linguistic and physical significance of pattern primitives.
5. The script should possess a simple well-defined physical and linguistic syntax.
6. The boundaries between individual primitives should be clearly marked for automatic detection by machine.

2.3 Pitman shorthand as a machinography.

In many ways Pitman shorthand exhibits these characteristics. The shorthand structure is fully defined in that phonetic components can only be formed in one way and consequently it is not necessary to make allowance for different formations of the same phonetic component or pattern primitive. The shorthand is constructed from a fairly small number of simple shapes which are often (but not always) easily isolated by physical separation, or if they are connected, by closure, angularity or high rate of curvature. In addition the shorthand is structured at two levels: each word is formed as a separate outline as in normal orthographic script, and the consonant sounds, which convey the most meaning in a word, are physically isolated from the less informative vowel sounds.

The major difference between a machinography and Pitman shorthand is the phonetic nature of the shorthand. There is no direct correspondence between letters and pattern primitives; instead each pattern primitive corresponds to a phoneme of speech: it is this which permits shorthand to be recorded at high speed. To produce an orthographic script it is therefore necessary to perform phoneme-to-grapheme conversion. The idiosyncrasies of English spelling make this a non-trivial task and consequently some words will be incorrectly spelt unless a large number of spelling rules or virtually unlimited dictionary are used.

In comparison with Pitman shorthand, Gregg, the other major handwritten shorthand system intended for the English language is much further from being a machinography. Gregg shorthand also records speech phonetically but is more cursive in style, making it more difficult to isolate the boundaries between the phonetic symbols. Furthermore, the vowel sounds are incorporated in the cursive line thus compounding the recognition and transcription problem.

3. ACQUISITION OF HANDWRITTEN SHORTHAND

3.1 Data collection.

Most shorthand writers prefer to use a ring bound notepad of roughly A5 size (210mm x 149mm) which is lined at approximately 8mm intervals. The short line length minimises the lateral hand movement whilst writing and the ring binding allows rapid page turning: both are necessary to maintain a high recording speed. Shorthand writers mostly use either a pencil or ballpoint pen: a pencil is preferred since it produces a visible distinction between thick and thin strokes which encourages the writer to distinguish voiced sounds.

In order to acquire Pitman shorthand in real-time a digitising writing tablet is required to monitor the pen position and since commercial writing tablets only monitor pen movement, some means must be provided to measure line thickness. Line thickness is associated with writing pressure and consequently an instrumented pen which detects the pressure exerted by the pen tip on the paper can be used to obtain this information. Alternative input devices which do not require a specialised pen such as pressure sensitive writing surfaces were considered but the engineering and ergonomic problems associated with this form of input are considerable. The writing surface must be as natural and easy to use as a notebook and pen on a desk. A pressure sensitive writing tablet surface of about A5 size and sensitive enough to detect variation in handwriting pressure is prone to accidental activation from many extraneous objects and thus requires a handrest. Alternatively a small writing area of one line height and width could be used with a step paper feed each time a new line is required. This solution may be practical but requires further development and trials.

On-line acquisition of shorthand data allows not only the shape and pressure of the outline to be recorded but also dynamic information about the writing sequence and pen velocity. This dynamic information is invaluable in the automatic recognition process since knowledge of the direction in which a particular stroke was written or the rotational direction of a circle, hook or loop avoids many possible confusions in the outline classification.

An early study [7],[8] successfully investigated the feasibility of both recognising and transcribing Pitmans handwritten shorthand. This study used a Datapad writing tablet to record pen movement and a ballpoint pen fitted with a click-action switch to record writing pressure. The recognition procedure used in this prototype system isolated each shorthand outline from any neighboring outline and attempted to recognise each outline using a two stage structural recognition strategy. Evaluation of this prototype system showed that a considerable improvement in performance would be obtained if the data acquisition equipment and data preprocessing were improved.

3.2 Writing tablet.

During the feasibility study it was concluded that a writing tablet with a static resolution of better than 0.2mm in both axes was required to represent accurately the smaller features of the Pitman notation. At that time the only writing tablet which had the required static resolution was the Datapad tablet which was later improved and renamed the Micropad [5]. This tablet operates by a pen causing a point contact between two parallel resistive sheets separated by a small air gap. The tablet surface does not require a specialised pen and can be activated by hand contact alone. Therefore a handrest has to be provided to ensure that this does not happen. Micropad samples the pen position approximately 220 times per second and a new sample is only sent if it differs from the previous sample. This feature of the tablet enables some indication of the pen velocity at any point on the outline to be recorded since the time duration between transmitted samples

will, on average, be greater when the pen is moving with low velocity as occurs at sudden changes in pen direction.

3.3 Instrumented pen.

Evaluation during the initial feasibility study showed that the original click action ballpoint pen was neither ergonomically satisfactory nor did it provide accurate pressure information. A novel instrumented stylus was therefore developed for use with the Micropad tablet. The stylus design is based on a clutch pencil and a small displacement transducer. The clutch of the pencil is sprung relative to the pen body over the 0.5mm working range of the displacement transducer as shown in Fig. 2(a). The principle of operation of the displacement transducer is shown in Fig. 2(b). The transformer primary winding is driven by an alternating voltage which induces varying voltages in the two secondary windings depending upon the position of the moveable core. The secondary windings are wound and connected such that the output voltage varies proportionally to the core position. This pen design has the following advantages

1. The displacement transducer is inexpensive in comparison to other load transducers (strain gauges and piezoresistive cells) and there is no need for overload protection. The majority of people who write cursive script (including shorthand) typically use a writing pressure of 200g. However, pressure peaks of several kilograms are frequently encountered at dots and full stops.

2. The small displacement of the transducer provides a cushioned feel as if writing on a wad of paper (as in the case of a ring bound notebook). This is preferred by most writers.

3. With variation in writing pressure soft graphite (2B) provides some visible feedback between thick and thin strokes.

4. The increased friction between graphite and paper helps to reduce 'skate' on the writing tablet surface and consequently improves the data quality.

The prototype pen shown in Fig. 2(c) is slightly more bulky than a consumer clutch pencil but need not be if the pen body were used as the former for the LVDT windings.

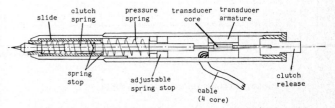

Fig.2(a) Construction of the instrumented pencil.

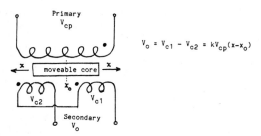

Fig. 2(b) The LVDT principle.

Fig. 2(c) The prototype instrumented pencil.

The pen position, pen pressure and inter-sample time for a typical shorthand outline obtained from the Micropad tablet and this instrumented clutch pencil are shown in Fig. 3.

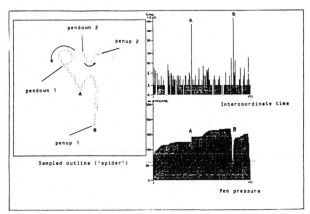

Fig. 3. The raw real-time data.

4. PREPROCESSING OF RAW DATA

4.1 Imperfections of the input data.

From a detailed study of shorthand collected using the Micropad writing tablet a number of imperfections were observed in the digitised data. Recognition of shorthand outlines is

considerably more successful if these imperfections are removed before attempting the recognition process. Some of these imperfections are specific to the Micropad writing tablet but most will be encountered on any writing tablet. One problem is the occurrence of accidental penlifts during the formation of each outline. These are found mainly at the start and end of shorthand outlines and at thick to thin stroke transitions in the consonant kernel, and occur when the writing pressure is less than the minimum required to activate the tablet surface. It is not possible to correct for lost data at the beginning and end of shorthand outlines but accidental penlifts which occur between stroke endpoints can often be identified.

At points of low pen velocity the sampling frequency of the writing tablet interacts with the quantisation levels of the tablet surface to cause the samples to oscillate between adjacent coordinates. In addition there is a small amount of noise present in the digitised outline caused partly by the thickness of the pen tip providing an imprecise point contact and partly by imperfections in the tablet surface. The outline must be smoothed to reduce the effect of this noise.

4.2 Preprocessing.

Accidental penlifts are detected by measuring the absolute distance between the pen-up and pen-down point and the time duration of the penlift at all occurrences of a pen-up/pen-down in each shorthand outline. Practical trials using the Micropad and instrumented pencil showed that if the absolute distance between the pen-up and pen-down point is less than 1mm and the time duration of the penlift is less than 150mS then the penlift was not intended and should be deleted.

Repetitive oscillatory samples, which occur when the pen is moving slowly, are detected by searching for two identical samples which have only one other sample between them. When this occurrence is detected the central sample and the second repetitive sample are deleted. The inter-coordinate time for each of the deleted samples is added to the following sample to ensure the pen velocity information is maintained. The pen pressure information of the deleted sample is averaged with the following samples value of pen pressure. Typically this technique removes approximately 10% of all samples in the shorthand outline. The sampled outline is then smoothed by reducing the rate of change in either axis by a constant amount if it exceeds a maximum value.

During recognition of shortforms [9] the full resolution of the writing tablet is not required and a filtering technique is employed to reduce the amount of later processing. This filtering algorithm ignores all subsequent samples which come within a fixed distance of the current sample. A new sample is only accepted when the minimum distance from the current sample is exceeded. For shorthand outlines a minimum distance of two samples was used which typically reduces the number of samples by 50% (effectively halving the resolution of the tablet).

The effect of these smoothing and filtering algorithms on two typical shorthand outlines is shown in Fig. 4.

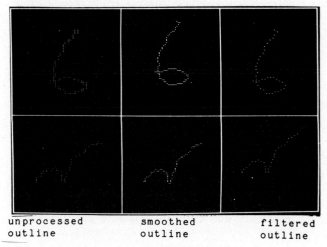

unprocessed outline   smoothed outline   filtered outline

Fig. 4. Preprocessing of the raw data.

5. VARIABILITY OF PITMAN SHORTHAND

5.1 Measurements of variability.

As with any handwritten data there is considerable variation in handwritten Pitman shorthand from writer to writer and from the same writer from time to time. It is this variation which makes the automatic recognition process so difficult compared with machine shorthand. In particular the length, inclination and curvature of consonant strokes vary as do the size and formation of hooks, loops and circles. The variation in stroke length is such that a considerable amount of confusion can occur between halved and normal length strokes and between normal and doubled length strokes. Based on an analysis of 1700 consonant strokes selected at random from the scripts of four writers the variation in stroke length is shown in Fig. 5. Normal length strokes are approximately ten times more frequent than halved length strokes and over fifty times more frequent than doubled length strokes. Since there were insufficient numbers of halved and doubled strokes in the shorthand scripts to determine their exact distribution estimated distributions are shown which assume their respective mean lengths are half and double the mean of the normal length strokes and have the same proportional standard deviation found for the normal length strokes. The mean stroke lengths for the four writers varied from 5.8mm to 8.3mm and the standard deviation from 1.09 to 1.58.

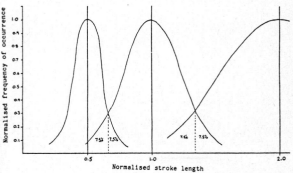

Fig. 5 Length variation of Pitman strokes.

The variation in angle of inclination of consonant strokes to their ideal inclination was also analysed for these four writers. The results of measuring the angle of inclination to the horizontal for 500 strokes and assigning each to its intended terminating sector is shown in Fig. 6. The distribution in each case was normal but with varying standard deviations. The horizontal strokes (sector 0) are consistently written close to the horizontal producing a narrow distribution. The vertical strokes (sector 6) on the other hand have a wider distribution. The major reason for the narrow distribution of horizontal strokes is thought to be the presence of the horizontal writing line which the writer is able to write on or parallel to. This is borne out by the other four sectors where no line indication is provided (including the vertical) having wider normal distributions. Designating sector boundaries by the line $y=4x$ and its transpositions, sectors 0 and 6 (horizontal and vertical) are the narrowest. Therefore in an attempt to constrain the distribution of vertical strokes nearer to the vertical special shorthand writing paper has been designed containing feint vertical lines at 1mm spacing. These provide a visible but not distracting vertical indication.

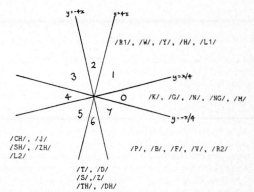

Fig. 6(a). Definition of Pitman stroke terminating sector.

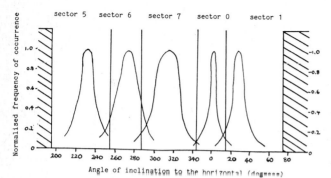

Fig. 6(b) Variation in angle of inclination to
the writing line for Pitman strokes.

5.2 Estimation of potential performance.

The readability of Pitman shorthand by a person
who is unfamiliar with the writers style is an
interesting measure of how well we might expect
a high quality automatic recognition system to
perform. To this end two secretaries were each
asked to transcribe two passages of unfamiliar
shorthand. One passage was written during a
100wpm examination at one of the Pitman training
colleges and the other was written by a
professional verbatim reporter of some years
experience. Neither of the secretaries were
given any indication of the subject content of
either passage. The results showed that in the
examination script 97.5% of the outlines were
correctly transcribed and in the professional
script only 48% of the outlines correctly
recognised and transcribed. The majority of the
outlines correctly transcribed in the
professional writer's script were the shortforms
and phrases which are simpler in structure than
vocalised outlines and consequently more easily
recognised. Generally it has been observed that
the professional writers script rapidly becomes
extremely personalised with use and eventually
becomes little more than a memory jogger rather
than a complete phonetic record. It has also
been observed that a shorthand passage written
by one writer is not always perfectly
transcribed by the same writer if sufficient
time has passed for the original dictation
session to be forgotten.

From the examination of variability and
readability of handwritten shorthand it is
apparent that the recognition and transcription
performance of an automated recognition process
is unlikely to produce an acceptable quality
transcript unless the shorthand is written to as
near 'text book' quality as possible. That is,
the writer must maintain the style they had as a
student taking care to write consonant strokes
consistently and ensure total or near closure of
circles and loops. Hooks must also be well
formed and preferably all vowels and diphthongs
included. The reason for shorthand style

deteriorating from 'text book' quality is the
lack of feedback encountered in its everyday
use. It is very unusual for anyone other than
the original shorthand writer to read her
shorthand notes and consequently personal styles
are allowed unconstrained development. If
suitable feedback were provided from an
automatic transcription device personal
shorthand styles would not be allowed to develop
to such a large extent. Indeed it is likely that
if recognition and transcription feedback were
taken into account the overall recognition
accuracy would increase slightly as the user
became more familiar with the machine.

7.   CONCLUSIONS

The popularity and well defined structure of
Pitmans handwritten shorthand make it suitable
for on-line transcription of speech at up to 120
words per minute. An A5 size writing tablet with
rapid paper change facilities and an
instrumented pencil based on an LVDT could form
the basis of the human interface for on-line
acquisition of shorthand.

If the shorthand style is constrained to that
which is produced by the successful student of
shorthand improved recognition and transcription
techniques will enable a readable simultaneous
transcript to be produced automatically.

REFERENCES

[1] Lea Wayne.A.(ed.), Trends in Speech
     Recognition. Prentice-Hall Inc., Englewood
     Cliffs, New Jersey. 1980.
[2] Downton A.C., Brooks C.P. Automated Machine
     Shorthand Transcription in Commercial
     Applications. 1984. (this volume).
[3] Pitman shorthand, New Course. New Era
     Edition. Pitman Publishing.
[4] Pitman 2000 shorthand. First course. Pitman
     Publishing. 1975.
[5] Micropad Maintenance Manual. MPD 4000 Quest
     Micropad Ltd. 1980.
[6] Wellisch H.H., The Conversion of Scripts,
     Its Nature, History and Utilization. John
     Wiley and Sons. 1978.
[7] Brooks C.P., Newell A.F. Simultaneous
     Transcription of Pitman's New Era
     Shorthand. 2nd Int.Conf.Microprocessors in
     Automation and Communications. London UK,
     27-29 Jan. 1981. pp.171-179.
[8] Brooks   C.P.,   Newell A.F. Computer
     Transcription of Handwritten Shorthand as
     an Aid for the Deaf - A Feasibility Study.
     submitted to Int. J. Man-Machine Studies.
     1984.
[9] Leedham C.G., Downton A.C. On-line
     recognition of shortforms in Pitmans
     handwritten shorthand. Proc. 7th Int. Conf.
     Patt. Rec. Montreal, Canada 30th July -
     4th Aug. 1984.

Human-Computer Interaction — INTERACT '84 / B. Shackel (ed.)
Elsevier Science Publishers B.V. (North-Holland)
© IFIP, 1985

AUTOMATED MACHINE SHORTHAND TRANSCRIPTION IN COMMERCIAL APPLICATIONS

A.C.Downton and C.P.Brooks*

Department of Electronics, University of Southampton, UK.
*Possum Controls Ltd., Slough, UK.

This paper describes the development and evaluation of a Palantype machine shorthand transcription system for court reporting and commercial applications. The system is based upon a transcription computer which provides special purpose software for transcription from Palantype to English, for efficient editing of transcripts, and for maintaining and optimising the Palantype to English dictionary. The design of the user interface to the system and the dictionary structure are described in detail, to illustrate how these aspects influence the overall efficiency and commercial viability of the system.

1. INTRODUCTION

A long-standing goal of human-computer interaction has been direct computer input by voice. As well as being a natural medium of communication for man, voice input is attractive because speech communication typically takes place at two or three times the rate which can be achieved with computer input devices such as the QWERTY keyboard. Unfortunately, unrestricted speech input to the computer of the type required in the electronic office or for verbatim reporting remains a long-term objective of research. Rapid text acquisition is however possible using written or machine shorthand. Machine shorthand (Palantype in the UK, Stenograph in North America) is widely used for verbatim reporting and provides the potential of a very simple physical interface to the computer via a chord keyboard (Figs. 1 and 2). Speech is coded using a phonetic and syllabic coding system which must be transcribed to English to recover the original text (1).

An earlier project at Southampton University developed a portable aid for the deaf based upon Palantype machine shorthand (Downton and Newell (2), Downton et al. (3)). The microprocessor aided speech transcription system used a fixed dictionary of about 1500 common words to produce a verbatim textual output from speech comprising about 75% perfect orthography. Words not matched in the dictionary were transliterated using phonetic to orthographic rules which produced pseudo-orthographic spellings. These were found to be readable in most cases.

Such a system clearly has important commercial applications if the quality of output can be increased sufficiently to make it worthwhile to edit the transcript to perfection rather than to retype it (as would normally be done by the Palantypist). Transcription from Palantype to English forms only one part of a commercial machine shorthand transcription system however. Other requirements are:

* a special purpose editor, for efficient proofing of transcripts,
* a method of initially recording transcripts in computer compatible form,
* facilities for generating and modifying Palantype to English dictionaries,

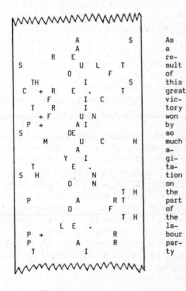

Fig. 2. Sample Palantype band output.

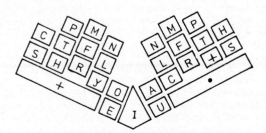

Fig. 1. Palantype keyboard layout

* utilities for printing transcripts, manipulating transcript files, and accounting.

Though any computer can in principle provide these facilities, research in North America (Delaplain (4)) has shown that small locally based mini- or microcomputers must be used as the basis of the system if operational problems are to be successfully overcome. Furthermore, since the facilities required are comparable in complexity to those required in a general purpose computing environment, but the users of the system are unlikely to have any computer expertise, the user interface design is of vital importance.

This paper describes the design and development of a commercial transcription system which fulfils these requirements, and shows how the various tasks involved in verbatim reporting can best be divided between the Palantypist and the computer. Two aspects of the system, the operating system user interface and the dictionary structure, are discussed in detail, while a third aspect, the Palantype editor, is the subject of a companion paper (Dye et al. (5)).

2. THE VERBATIM REPORTING PROCESS

The traditional approach to pen and machine shorthand verbatim recording involves two phases, recording and transcription. During the recording phase, the shorthand reporter takes down a verbatim note of proceedings on paper or a machine shorthand band (Fig. 2). Subsequently, (s)he will transcribe the shorthand note to produce a verbatim transcript. This transcription process typically takes 4 or 5 times as long as the original reporting task, and during this time the reporter is not available for further recording work, the task in which (s)he is very highly trained. A major objective in developing a computer-aided transcription (CAT) system was therefore to reduce the time which must be spent by a reporter on transcription, and hence to improve productivity and turnaround time.

The CAT equivalent of the traditional reporting process uses an electronic replacement for the mechanical Palantype machine. This equipment duplicates the function of the original machine using a small thermal printer to provide a paper recording, but also contains a cassette data recorder which records an image of the keys pressed for subsequent computer transcription. In addition, provision is made for a direct connection from the machine to the transcription computer to enable simultaneous transcription to be performed if required. This has application as an aid for the deaf, or where very fast turnaround is required, and means that transcription must be performed at verbatim speed or faster.

When transcription is required, the cassette record is read into the transcription computer, and the transcription program translates the Palantype codes into a draft transcript which can be viewed on a computer terminal and edited to perfection by the Palantypist. The transcript can then be printed out in its final form. It is unlikely that computer transcription will ever be able to produce a perfect transcript, thus eliminating the editing stage, because even if every word in the English language (including every proper noun) is included within the transcription dictionary, the Palantypist is still bound to make keying errors from time to time, and these will result in mistranslations or failure to match the relevant Palantype code.

3. THE PALANYPE OPERATING SYSTEM (PALOPS) AND USER INTERFACE

The Palantype transcription system makes use of the industry-standard CP/M microcomputer operating system. Palantype, text, and system software files, but not the transcription dictionary, conform to the CP/M file structure. Because the CP/M console processor is not suitable for naive users, a new user interface (PALOPS) based upon a hierarchical menu structure of commands is superimposed on CP/M. The menu hierarchy is chosen to reflect the Palantypists model of the verbatim reporting process, based upon extensive trials and evaluation during development.

To the user, PALOPS appears as a multi-level tree-structured command processor in which commands are invoked by typing the first letter of a mnemonic displayed on the bottom (menu) line of the screen. The menu line is maintained consistently throughout all functions provided by the system, and at any time summarises the level within the command hierarchy and the range of commands currently accessible. If the user fails to select a command within a few seconds of invoking a new menu, additional help information on each of the possible commands accessible is displayed, on the assumption that the delay in selection is due to lack of familiarity with the system.

The provision of a new console processor superimposed upon the operating system also enables a number of other valuable facilities to be incorporated without the need to write a complete operating system. Since the normal sequence of use of the system is to read a cassette tape onto disk, and then transcribe, edit and print the disk file, the concept of a workfile is introduced and all disk operations automatically reference this file unless a different file is explicitly named. This relieves the user from having to specify a filename as an argument for every command.

Rather than generating separate files for the untranslated Palantype, transcribed Palantype and edited transcript files, a single file is used for each transcript. Initially this file contains only the original Palantype codes, but, when transcription takes place, the transcribed text is interleaved with the raw Palantype within the same file and delimited using non-displayed control codes. Thus a single workfile will ultimately contain all of the information relating to a transcript. This is of particular importance during the editing phase of the transcription task since it enables the editor normally to display only the transcribed text, but to refer immediately to the Palantype codes associated with a particular piece of text if necessary.

4. THE PALANTYPE TRANSCRIPTION PROGRAM

4.1 Specification of requirements

The design of the Palantype transcription program presents a number of novel problems. Palantype transcription is essentially a dictionary translation process, but with a number of additional constraints. Firstly, the dictionary translation must cope with the fact that the input Palantype codes, which are a pseudo-phonetic representation of speech, are split into syllables of speech (called chords) rather than words. The transcription process must therefore attempt to reconstruct the correct word boundaries during translation.

Secondly, the dictionary contents must be readily modifiable by the Palantypists themselves and this facility must be integrated into the transcription system as a whole. Although in principle all Palantypists use the same codes for representing the same English words, trials of our previous transcription aid for the deaf showed that there are invariably small differences and personal idiosyncracies in each Palantypist's recording style. If the same dictionary were to be used for every Palantypist, the dictionary would inevitably have to represent a compromise between different Palantypists' styles, and thus would produce a lower quality transcript than a dictionary capable of being optimised individually for each Palantypist. Since the overall cost-effectiveness of the Palantype CAT system is strongly dependent on the time spent editing the draft transcript to perfection, it is essential to obtain the highest possible draft transcript quality.

A further justification for providing a user-defined dictionary is to cater for subject dependent vocabularies. Our earlier work on the Palantype aid for the deaf showed that a dictionary of about 1000 most common words was the maximum which could be defined independent of subject matter, and this conclusion is supported by Schwartz (6). For larger dictionaries, the required dictionary contents become increasingly subject dependent, and, since verbatim recording of quite specialised subject material is often required, increasingly difficult to predict.

A third constraint imposed on the dictionary translation process is that the dictionary must

be stored in a two level memory system. This can be deduced by extrapolation from our earlier work, where a 1000 word dictionary was stored in about 30 kbytes of memory. Since a full dictionary system requires a dictionary of typically 20000 words, about 1 Mbyte of storage is needed to encode this dictionary (including Palantype chords, English transcriptions and pointers). (A generous estimate of memory is made to allow for the fact that the most common thousand words in English are typically rather short.) Though it is quite possible to configure a microcomputer system with this amount of memory, the cost is rather excessive; perfectly adequate transcription performance can be achieved using a two level memory system (i.e. a combination of semiconductor memory and a floppy or hard disk backing storage medium) as is shown below. In any case, a floppy disk is required for archiving the dictionary so that different dictionaries generated by different operators can be used on the same transcription system.

A fourth constraint on the transcription process is that it must be capable of translation at verbatim speed or faster, to accomodate the requirement for simultaneous transcription under some circumstances. Such a requirement is easy to achieve if the full dictionary is stored in memory, but much more critical if the dictionary is stored on a secondary storage medium such as floppy disk.

Finally, the problem arises of how to deal with Palantype codes for which no dictionary match can be found. Since there is often a requirement to produce an immediate draft quality transcript, it may not be acceptable simply to print out the pseudo-phonetic Palantype code directly if there is no match. This is a particularly important point in applications where the system may be used to provide a service for the deaf.

4.2 The Palantype dictionary structure

The initial problem of determining where word

/A	P+/AUT		about
/A	P+/UF		above
/A	P+RO/*T+		abroad
/A	T+/I	SH/N	addition
/A	T+/I	SH/NL	additional
/A	T+RE/S		address
/A	C+R/I*	P+L/	agreeable
/A	C+R/I*	M/NT	agreement
/A	C+R/I*		agree
/A	C+R/I*T+		agreed
/A	HE/T+		ahead
/A	P/A	R/NT	L/I	apparently
/A	P/A	R/NT		apparent
/A	SC/		ask
/A			a
/ACT			act
/AS			as

Fig. 3. Sample dictionary entries ordered to achieve a sequential longest match.

boundaries exist within the transcript can be overcome by adopting a longest-match strategy within the dictionary translation process. The objective is then to look for the maximum length sequence of Palantype codes for which a valid entry exists within the dictionary. One way to do this is simply to order the dictionary search so that long words are always tested before short words containing the same initial Palantype code sequence (e.g. McCoy and Shumway, (7))(Fig. 3). Unfortunately, this approach is particularly inefficient since the most commonly used words are generally short and hence tend to be encountered at the end rather than the beginning of the dictionary. Thus, for example, in matching the word "a" every other word with the initial syllable "a-" would have to be checked first.

A much more efficient approach is to use a trie search (Knuth, (8)) in which the dictionary is arranged in a tree-like structure according to the number of Palantype syllables (or chords) in each word (Fig. 4). At the first chord level a sequential list of every possible initial chord is stored together with a set of pointers which point either to valid successor chords of a particular chord, or to the required English word if no valid successor exists. At second and subsequent chord levels are stored lists of possible successor chords to each first level

chord. During translation, the first chord in the incoming data stream is matched against the first chord list, and if a match is found, the second chord is matched against the set of possible second chords which follow the matched first chord. This process continues until no further matching is possible at which point the longest match has been obtained and the current chord becomes the first chord of the next word to be matched.

This structure is quite efficient since only one representation of each chord is required at each level, and it also minimises the chord-lag between input chord and output text. For this reason it was used as the basis of the dictionary organisation within our aid for the deaf, where the dictionary was permanently programmed into ROM. The major disadvantage of the structure is the difficulty of making changes to the dictionary since dictionary insertions require a large number of existing entries to be moved. Furthermore the structure cannot easily be extended efficiently to a two-level memory system because of the very slow translation which would result from a sequential search carried out on the disk.

These problems can be resolved by modifying the trie structure so that at each trie level chords are matched using a binary tree, in which the implicit pointers provided by the original list structure are replaced by explicit pointers (Fig. 5). Thus the dictionary search may be speeded up and changes made much more easily at the expense of a slight increase in the storage requirement for each dictionary entry. To ensure the fastest possible transcription, words are entered into the dictionary during the initial

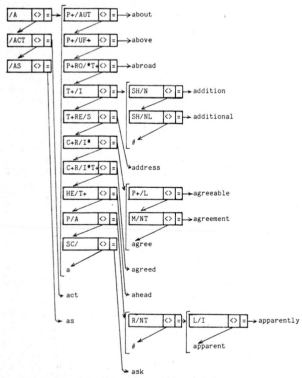

Fig. 4. Example trie-structured dictionary using the same data as Fig. 3.

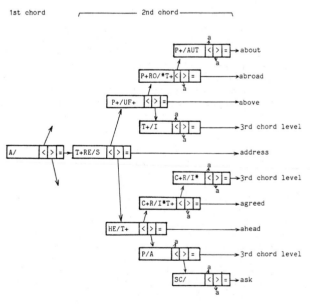

Fig. 5. Second chord list of Fig. 4 structured according to a binary search.

dictionary compilation phase in rank frequency of occurence in English; thus the most common words are nearest to the root of the tree/trie and are found first when the dictionary is searched. Roughly 1000 most common words representing about 75% of normal English speech are stored in memory; during translation these words can be matched without needing to access the backing storage medium at all, giving high translation speed. The binary tree dictionary structure used within the trie means that not only are words matched within about 15 comparisons, but also that there are a large number (about 2000) of pointers from memory extending the dictionary structure onto disk. Most branches of the tree emanating from these pointers are quite small and can thus be contained within a single disk sector. Hence, during translation, many words will be matched without requiring any access to the backing storage medium at all, while those which do access backing storage will normally be found by a single disk seek and sector read operation.

Palantype chords which cannot be matched by the dictionary are transliterated to a suitable phonetically based spelling in a fashion analogous to the previous aid for the deaf. This improves the readability of the draft text significantly, and in many cases speeds up subsequent editing operations since the transliterated word can often be edited to perfection very simply.

Fig. 6 shows an example of the unedited draft transcript of the system using a 12000 word dictionary. In trials, typical transcription speeds of about 350 w.p.m. have been measured, but this includes overheads associated with reading the input Palantype chord file and writing the output transcript file as well as accessing the dictionary on 8" double-sided double-density floppy disk. Because the dictionary is structured in a rank-ordered fashion, the current dictionary covers about 95% of normal English. Thus, further words added to it are likely to be accessed infrequently, and the transcription speed should therefore be almost independent of dictionary size.

4.3 Dictionary modification

The system is initially supplied with a base dictionary of several thousand most common words already entered in rank order. This is necessary to ensure that the dictionary structure is organised to optimise translation speed. Subsequently, the dictionary may be enlarged, and entries may be modified, though it is not envisaged that many dictionary entries will be deleted. Although the Palantypist may not add additional dictionary entries in rank order, this has little effect upon the transcription speed since new entries in general represent uncommon words constituting less than 10% of the total text.

Although software is provided to add words to the dictionary explicitly, the main mechanism for dictionary enlargement is via the text editor used to correct the draft transcript. Corrections to text which has not been transcribed by the dictionary are optionally stored within a logging file which subsequently updates the main dictionary. Thus the dictionary can automatically be enlarged as a by-product of the editing task, significantly reducing the workload of the Palantypist. This aspect of the system is described in detail by Dye et al. (5).

5. EVALUATION

The design described above is based upon extensive trials of equipment in courts and elsewhere. A three month trial of the prototype electronic Palantype machine was organised in conjunction with Possum Controls Ltd., BTG and the Lord Chancellors Department, and identified many of the operational problems associated with the introduction of CAT into court reporting (9). The trial showed that a high quality verbatim speech to text transcription system can significantly increase the efficiency of verbatim reporting, but that training and support are essential if user acceptance of new technology and working methods is to be obtained.

Several applications for the system as an aid for the deaf have also been investigated. These include the provision of a deaf telephone system via PRESTEL (Grossfield et al. (10)), and use of the system for live subtitling of television (Baker et al. (11)).

6. CONCLUSIONS

This paper has described the specification, design and development of a computer-aided machine shorthand transcription system for verbatim reporting. The system is compatible with present reporting practice and presents a simple and straightforward model of the transcription process to the Palantypist. It has been designed to maximise the efficiency of the Palantype transcription process and minimise the time spent by the Palantypist editing the draft transcript and developing the Palantype/English dictionary. The system has recently been launched commercially both for verbatim reporting and as a communication aid for the deaf.

REFERENCES

1. "The Palantype method of machine shorthand", Palantype Organisation, 1978.

2. Downton, A.C. and Newell, A.F., 1979, Int. Jnl. Man-Machine Studies, 11, 667-680.

3. Downton, A.C., Arnott, J.L. and Newell, A.F., 1980, "Palantype machine shorthand in the Electronic Office", IERE Conf. Proceedings, 45, 193-202.

4. Delaplain, R., 1980, "Computer aided transcription – state of the art", report of the CAT analysis project, National Centre for State Courts, Williamsburg, Virginia.

5. Dye, R., Newell, A.F. and Arnott, J.L., 1984, "An adaptive editor for shorthand transcription systems", Interact '84.

6. Schwartz, E.S. (1963), Jnl. Ass. Computing Machinery, 10, 413–439, p415.

7. McCoy, E.B. and Shumway, R., (1979), American Annals of the Deaf, 124, No. 5, Chapter 24.

8. Knuth, D.E., (1973) "The Art of Computer Programming – v.3, Sorting and Searching", Addison-Wesley.

9. "Computer assisted transcription of Palantype machine shorthand", Lord Chancellor's Department, July 1982.

10. Grossfield, K., King, R.W., Martin, M.C. and Tolcher, D.J. (1982) British Jnl. Audiology, 16, 27–38.

11. Baker, R.G., Downton, A.C., and Newell, A.F., (1980), "Processing of visible language 2", Plenum Press, 445–457.

ACKNOWLEDGEMENTS

The work reported in this paper was funded via SERC research grants GR/A 87609 and GR/B 12636. Additional funding for the development of prototype equipment was provided by BTG, Possum Controls Ltd., and the Lord Chancellor's Department. The authors are also grateful for help provided by British Telecom, RNID, IBA and ORACLE Teletext Ltd.

```
PALANTYPE TRANSCRIPTION SYSTEM by Possum Controls Ltd.          Page - 01
File name: L15.PAL
```

```
          If  you  look  at  his  personal  account  for  the        10:36

     year  end  seventy  six  seven  seven  you  will  find

     it  at  page  fourteen,  pages  thirteen  and  fourteen,

     you  will  see  that  on  page  thirteen  his  personal

05   account  stand  in  credit  for  about  three  and  a  half

     thousand  in  June  seventy  six,  no  ac  tivdty  on  it.

     That  figure  remains  until  December,  as  we  see

     at  page  fourteen,  and  then  on  thirty  one  December   10:37

     there  is  a  de  bit  yf  ul  of  two  thousand,  on  five

10   January  a  transfer,  they  are  both  transfers,

     two  thousand  an  fun  thousand.  If  you  look  at  page

     seventy  one,  keep  your  finger  in  page  fourteen

     an  look  at  seventy  one  and  see  what  happened.  Those

     two  sumts  of  two  thousand  an  one  thousand  were

15   credited  to  the  limited  companies  account  on  thotes

     two  dates.  You  see  the  two  credit  entries  on  that

     page,  that  then  puts  it  in  credit  to  the  some

     of  two  hundred  and  sixty  two  poungs  odd.

          QUESTION:  Who  wjos  it  too  insity  ga  tdh

20   transfer  of  those  funds  from  the  pfi  vat  account

     to  the  limited  companies  account.

          ANSWER:  Mr.  ████████? He  is  the  only              10:38

     person.

          QUESTION:  I  said  who  was  the  author  of  the

25   eye  tea  that  the  sums  should  be  transferred  fromf

     the  private  count  to  the  limited  company  account.

          ANSWER:  It  may  have  been  are  suggestion.

          QUESTION:  Can  you  tell  us  whether  it  Watts

     or  was  not.

30        ANSWER:  It  was  a  mutual  agreement  to  cover
```

Fig. 6. Sample unedited transcript using a 12000 word dictionary Palantype transcription system.

Human-Computer Interaction — INTERACT '84 / B. Shackel (ed.)
Elsevier Science Publishers B.V. (North-Holland)
© IFIP, 1985

An Adaptive Editor for shorthand transcription systems

R.Dye, A.F.Newell & J.L.Arnott.
University of Dundee
Scotland

An automatic transcription system for machine shorthand takes the output from a shorthand machine, and converts it into a Draft Transcipt. This draft transcript needs to be edited to perfection using word processing techniques. A suite of programmes has been written which takes advantage of the particular characteristics of Palantype transcripts to provide a very efficient editing environment. The editor adapts to the user in a way which improves his efficiency without an overhead of the necessity to learn complex control structures. Some of these facilities are also appropriate to a standard word processing environment.

INTRODUCTION - Editors for machine shorthand

A large number of Text Editors are now commercially available which offer substantially similar facilities, the major difference between the various kinds being the user-interface and certain specialised commands. Essentially, however, they are all designed to manipulate text and only use information specifically contained in that text. "Paledit", however has been specially designed as an adaptive editor for Palantype Shorthand Transcription Systems. It uses information over and above that contained in the original text to provide an efficient and effective editing enviroment for machine shorthand. In addition the Editor is able to adapt to the characteristics of the user and in this way further reduce the amount of keyboarding necessary. Although "Paledit" is intended for shorthand transcription, a number of the ideas contained in this Editor are applicable to standard editing situations.

Traditionally, a verbatim reporter personally transcribes his/her shorthand note to produce a record or minute of a meeting or court appearance. Transcribing these notes is a long and expensive procedure, typically taking four or five times longer than the original meeting. Recently, however, automatic transcription systems have been developed for machine shorthand ;in particular, a system has been developed for Palantype machine shorthand, and is described in an accompanying paper by Downton & Brooks.(1) It has proved successful both as a simultaneous translation aid for the deaf and also as an aid for shorthand reporters in their normal commercial activities.

THE NEED FOR A SPECIALISED EDITOR

In general an automatic palantype transcription system will not produce an absolutely perfect transcription on a single pass. Operator errors will inevitably occur and also the system dictionary is unlikely to contain all the words typed [apart from obscure English or foreign words, proper names frequently cause incorrect output]. If a perfect transcript is required, the output from the automatic transcription system will need to be edited. The cost or time necessary to produce a perfect report of a meeting is a combination of the cost of producing the automatic transcription and the cost of editing this initial draft transcription to perfection. These two factors are interelated in that the more accurate the draft transcript is the less editing needs to be done on it.

The accuracy of the automatically produced Draft Transcript depends on the skill of the Palantypist, the size of the dictionary employed and the algorithms used to spell non-dictionary matched chords. With competent operators and a 20,000 word dictionary somewhere between two and five percent of words are incorrectly spelled but this figure rises if the listening conditions are poor or if the speaker is not fluent. The amount of editing required is thus likely to be significant. An important feature of any Palantype Transcription System is therefore the editor program, its ease of use and its efficiency.

Draft Transcripts could be edited using a standard word processing program such as wordstar. This would be less than ideal, however, because the task of editing Draft Transcripts from a Palantype Transcription System is significantly different from normal editing in a number of ways. In addition there are advantages, particularly for naive users, if the suite of programs within a system has a unity of structure and style. For these reasons it was decided that a special purpose editor should be designed. This would run under "PALOPS", the operating system which has been developed for the Transcription System and would be tailored specifically for editing Draft Transcripts from an Automatic Palantype Transcription system.

THE CHARACTERISTICS OF A DRAFT TRANSCRIPT.

"Paledit" was thus designed to contain the normal features found in word processors but a powerful additional set of special commands was added. These commands were based on the extra information which is available from a Draft Transcript plus knowledge of previous editing strategies used by the palantypist/editor. The command structure was carefully designed to be compatible with the command structure of the Transcription System's Operating System.

An example of a Draft Transcript is shown in figure 1. This contains rather more errors than would be normally expected in order to illustrate more clearly the types of errors which can occur.

Figure 1 also shows an example of the format of the display during the editing task. The command structure which was adopted for the editor was compatible with the "PALOPS" operating system and was based on a system of menus which were displayed along the bottom of the screen. A command is selected, from a menu displayed, by typing the initial letter of the command name on the keyboard. In common with other

standard editors, "Paledit" has the following facilities: Full cursor controls, Insert, Replace, Delete, Move. Find and Substitute commands. As a final document is normally intended to be a verbatim report based on the shorthand note, little large-scale editing, such as moving paragraphs, will be needed.

The editing of Draft Transcripts differs from that of normal typed text in a number of important ways:

(a) It is potentially easier to predict where editing is required because, where a transcription algorithm is weak, spelling errors are likely to occur.

(b) Due to the syllabic nature of palantype coding there are a large number of false word boundaries.

(c) A significant proportion of the mis-spelled words are unrecognisable without reference to context. These are generally uncommon words which have been mis-keyed by the palantypist.

(d) There is substantially more repetition of particular errors than would be expected in normal text.

(e) Correctly spelled but wrong words occur fairly frequently, for example homophones which are palantyped in exactly the same way.

On the basis of these characteristics of palantype Draft Transcripts, specialised editing commands were added to the standard commands. It was decided that a substantially more efficient system could be designed if some of these commands could

```
[02:15] writing about dart Moore Mr. James mill dren the
environment correspondent at the western more ningm news which
circumstance lates widely in the west country said , oh dart
Moore , thigh name is controversy . [02:15] rarely has a
journalist so ken a troere word . there are competing not to
say conflicting interests of all kinds , for example , there
are the farmers who live by the soil of dart Moore , there is
the [02:15] army which depends to a great extent on the use of
dart Moore for exercises since it is a remote area . there are
China clay companies fich pro tuse China clay whic is of great
importance to exports and to thotes [02:16] employed in the
industry . there are the ram blrs anth nature lovers who see
dart Moore as a marvellous place to get away from the ma ding
crowd . there are the con Sir va shni sts generally who want to
--------------------------------------------------------------
Edit: Exit Cue Linkup Replace Unprocessed Insert Delete Other
```

Figure 1. The editor displaying part of a transcript
        (Time codes are normally displayed, but the underlining has
        been added to demonstrate the effect of the Cue command).

make use of information which is not normally available in conventional editing systems. Thus the file from the transcription software was designed to contain the translated draft transcript interleaved with semi-phonetic data (Palanforms) and processing information. Although normally only the draft transcript is displayed, this interleaved data is always available for use by the editor software.

SPECIALISED EDITOR COMMANDS

Three basic commands were developed, Cue, Link, Unprocessed plus a very powerful Try command.(2)

CUE COMMAND

The Cue command allows the user quickly to locate likely editing points. When this command is used (by typing C) the cursor rapidly scans from its current position to the next most likely editing point. For example transliterated chords are seldom correctly spelled and would be some of the words which the cue command would locate. In Figure 1 the places where the cursor would stop on an example of text are underlined.

LINK COMMAND

Due to the syllabic nature of the palantype code Draft Transcripts contain a number of false word boundaries and these can be removed by the Link command. This feature takes the form of a word joining command. The effect of using this on a fragmented word is shown below.
(The link command must be issued four times to link the five fragments together)

> con Sir va shni sts
> conSir va shni sts
> conSirva shni sts
> conSirvashni sts
> conSirvashnists

UNPROCESSED COMMAND

It may be the case that weaknesses in the transcription algorithm obscure the correct wording of a sentence and the palantypist may wish to refer back to the original palanforms. The Unprocessed command gives the user the ablity to display the original palanforms from which a piece of text originated. Figure 2. shows the effect of this command. A single line of text is shown in its unprocessed form but, as can be seen, the unprocessed text is generally slightly longer than the processed version and spills over on to the next line. When in this mode cursor commands can be used to change the line which is being displayed in its unprocessed form.

AUTOMATIC EDITING USING THE TRY COMMAND

In order to reduce the amount of mental and physical processes required to perform a given editing task, a number of semi-automatic editing features are being examined. These are based on the concept of a TRY command. If an incorrect word is noted the operator presses the T key to initiate a TRY. The software will then attempt to correct the word automatically using the information available to it and will display this new attempt on the screen.

Four techniques have been used
1) More sophisticated transliteration
2) Spelling correctors
3) Adaptive techniques, and
4) Dictionary updating.

1. Transliteration technique

As editing progresses and syllables are linked using the LINK command more accurate word boundary information becomes available. Transliteration rules using this extra information have a higher probability of producing the correct

```
[02:15] writing about dart Moore Mr. James mill dren the
environment correspondent at the western more ningm news which
circumstance lates widely in the west country said , oh dart
Moore , thigh name is controversy . [02:15] rarely has a
+Y/UR NL/I ST/ SOE/ C/N /A TRO/U^R+ +F/URT+ /^ THE/R /AR CO/M P/
I^ T/IN+ NO/T TO/nterests of all kinds , for example , there
are the farmers who live by the soil of dart Moore , there is
```

Figure 2. The editor displaying the original palantype chords

spelling of a word, than the transliteration rules used during the original transcription.

The transliteration technique was implemented and proved quite successful in coping with words which had been correctly palantyped. Figure 3 shows some examples of transliteration applied within an actual draft transcript.

```
-------- Correctly palantyped --------

dart Moore               --> dartmoor
ram blrs                 --> ramblers
vis tours                --> vistors
me dee val               --> medeval
Anna national            --> anational
eye wrong cal            --> ironcal
were vent ly             --> furvently
circumstances lates      --> surclates
in ec sour sity ble      --> inecsaustible
con Sir va shni sts      --> consurvationists

------- Incorrectly palantyped -------

to you ring              --> turing
num blr                  --> numbler
O bly ga hns             --> obligahns
```

Figure 3. Transliterations

Although as can be seen transliteration does not always yield the correct spelling of a word, it will often significantly reduce the amount of editing that the user is required to perform.

2. Spelling correctors

Using a dictionary of approximately 200 common words the Try command attempts to find a word which closely resembles the mis-spelled word. It was expected that the spelling correction techniques would be most successful when employed to correct minor spelling mistakes on common words such as;
(a) One letter incorrect
(b) One letter missing
(c) An extra letter inserted
(d) Two adjacent characters transposed,
but was likely to fail, or indicate an incorrect word, if the word is uncommon or badly spelled.

A program was developed to demonstrate the possiblities of spelling correctors, and this confirmed earlier expectations. The spelling corrector performed well under the condition mentioned above. Examples of its performance are:

```
turing   ---> during
whic     ---> which
thits    ---> this
numbler  ---> number
rom      ---> from
```

The problems of automatically correcting uncommon words which have been mis-keyed and common words which have been badly mis-keyed are very large and can only be satisfactorily resolved by resorting to analysis of sentence structure and making use of context. It is thus unlikely that a significant proportion of these edits can be performed fully automatically. However information about previous similar edits may be used to reduce the editing task in these cases. The two methods of implementing this technique have been investigated are; a dictionary update and an "adaptive" editor.

3. An adaptive editor - An Editing System which learns from past editing operations.

The editor's function is to correct errors in the draft transcript caused by a combination of palantypist's errors and short-comings in the transcription algorithms. The user provides the information necessary to correct these errors, in the form of editor commands. In a conventional editor this information is discarded and cannot be used again. The information provided by the user however reveals details about the individual palantypist and the subject matter of the transcript.

The details revealed about the palantypist are:
(a) Common strokes mis-keyed by the palantypist.
(b) Individual preference when selecting a palanform to represent a word, when several different palanforms can be used, and
(c) Subject matter details in the form of unusual words which have occurred in the conversation but were not found in the dictionary.

In "Paledit" information about previous edits is retained and this information can be used to repeat editing operations. Thus when the Try command is initiated the editor sifts through its memory and trys to find out if the information required to correct a particular word is available. If this information is found, the editor performs the edits automatically. The volume of information gathered during the editing of a large draft transcript may become too large to manage efficiently, and some of it may prove to be of only limited value. If all of this information were to be retained within the system the available memory would soon become exhausted. Thus a memory system which can estimate the value of an item of information and be able to discard information if necessary has been developed.

4. Dictionary update information

In order to provide an adaptive mechanism the editor software automatically stores the information that it has acquired during the editing process on a file. This information is written to the file in a form which is compatible with the source file used to create the transcription dictionary. This file can thus be used to update the transcription dictionary and thus provide better draft transcripts in the future.

In the overall speech transcription system this information can thus be used to increase system efficiency. If the information is made available to, and made use of by, the transcription process, the system will not only adapt to the characteristics of the individual user but also to the type of job the user is performing. Such a system is able gradually to improve the quality of its original Draft Transcript and therefore reduce the amount of time required to edit the draft to produce a final copy.

PRELIMINARY RESULTS

"Paledit" forms an integral part of a working commercial Palantype Speech Transcript system.(3) The Special features of the editor have significantly improved the efficiency of the editing task although the amount of usage of any facilities of an editor is obviously crucially dependent on the quality of the Draft Transcript. No formal tests have yet been performed, but a preliminary study has shown that a saving in time of the order of 30% can be obtained when using "Paledit" rather than a conventional wordprocessing package such as Word-Star to edit the transcript files.

The CUE command provides a very useful highlighting of possible editing points, and it and the TRY command have been found to be particularly popular with users: it is very tedious to have to perform an identical task a number of times, and "TRY" has provided a much more usable technique than traditional 'global' editing.

CONCLUSIONS

An editor has an important role to perform in any machine shorthand speech transcription system, not only in the correction of the errors that occur in the Draft Transcript but also in provision of information about these errors to the overall system. This information can be used to allow the transcription system to evolve and improve with use.

In order to increase the efficiency of the editing process "Paledit" makes use of the following sources of information: Information about the transcription process, data concerning previous edits, phoneme to grapheme translation rules, and a dictionary of common words.

The use of this information has produced a a significant reduction in the keying effort needed to edit Draft Transcripts. In addition, however, the adaptive nature of the editor is particularly beneficial as it reduces the tedious tasks of having to repeat certain edits a large number of times during an editing session. There is great psychological benefit in finding that the computer has learned to correct a particular type of error, or that it can suggest re-spellings of incorrect words. Equally the user knows that unambiguous corrections can be incorporated into the transcription part of the system and thus they will not appear again on Draft Transcript offered for editing.

Although "Paledit" was designed specifically for editing Draft Transcripts from a Palantype shorthand transcription system, many of the ideas which have been developed and incorporated into this editor have more general applicability and point to some ways in which editor design could progress in the future.

BIBLIOGRAPHY

[1] Downton A.C. & Brooks C.P. "Automated machine shorthand transcription for court reporting and in commercial applications", Proc. Interact conference.

[2] Patent Application No. 8331871

[3] Palantype Speech Transcription System. Possum Controls Ltd.

****

Human-Computer Interaction — INTERACT '84 / B. Shackel (ed.)
Elsevier Science Publishers B.V. (North-Holland)
© IFIP, 1985

INTERACTIVE STEREOSCOPIC COMPUTER GRAPHIC DISPLAY SYSTEMS

Neil Storey, J. Ffynlo Craine

Department of Engineering,
University of Warwick,
Coventry, U.K. CV4 7AL

Conventional CRT displays give only a two dimensional representation of three dimensional objects which means that depth information can be presented only indirectly, using such techniques as hidden line removal, shading and object rotation. Improved perception of 3D images is possible by presenting to the viewer a stereoscopic pair of two-dimensional images. To be truly effective, the image presented by a stereoscopic display should change as the viewing point moves. Such a system requires a knowledge of the user's head position and orientation in order to compute the view to be presented to each eye. The paper describes an approach to a system of this type.

1. INTRODUCTION

The explosive growth in the use of computer aided design during recent years has brought with it the need to be able to display many kinds of three dimensional objects as realistically as possible. Unfortunately, no satisfactory technique exists yet for presenting truly three dimensional images of objects, but a wide range of optical and psychological phenomena have been exploited to give the illusion of three dimensions using currently available technology. For two dimensional displays these include such depth cueing techniques as hidden line removal, shading and object rotation. However, these techniques ultimately present only an illusion of depth.

In time true 3D displays based upon holographic techniques may overcome these problems [2] [18]. However, the generation of holograms from computer-generated data in real time presents considerable technical problems [17], and holographic displays seem likely to remain prohibitively expensive for the majority of engineering applications for some time.

2. DEPTH PERCEPTION

When considering the design of a display system for three dimensional objects, various factors associated with vision and the perception of depth must be considered. There are many "visual depth cues", and in analysing any scene it is likely that a number of cues would be used. However, the more important visual depth cues probably include the following:

(1) Motion parallax. When an observer moves his or her head, objects which are closer appear to move more rapidly than those more distant. Similarly, if two objects are moving with the same speed, the object closer to the viewer will appear to move faster than the one further away. Thus rotating an object on a conventional display provides the viewer with more information about the three dimensional shape of the object.

(2) Kinetic and static interposition. The way in which one object may partially obscure a view of a more distant object provides information as to the relative distances of the two objects, which is why hidden line removal is important for the realistic display of three dimensional objects. This effect is enhanced when one or both objects are moving.

(3) Kinetic vector effect. When the viewer and scene move steadily with respect to one another, the continuous manner in which the view changes provides information about the scene.

(4) Linear Perspective. Parallel lines appear to converge at some distant point, providing another important clue as to distance.

(5) Stereopsis. When observing a real object, each eye is presented with a slightly different view, because of their physical separation. As the line of sight of each eye converges at the observed object, its range may be determined by triangulation.

(6) Size constancy. The brain has prior knowledge of the size of many objects, and it can use this knowledge to estimate the range of an object from its apparent size.

(7) Accommodation. The degree of focussing necessary in the eye to produce a clear retinal image provides a cue to an object's distance.

(8) Texture gradation and shading. There is a gradation of texture from rough in the foreground to smooth in the distance.

Similarly, shading depends upon the intensity of illumination. This provides information about the angle presented by a surface to the light falling upon it, and may also provide more direct information about distance if the intensity of illumination varies with position.

(9) <u>Aerial perspective</u>. The clarity of more distant objects may be reduced by environmental effects such as haze and mist.

The relative importance of each effect depends upon the particular scene and possibly upon the individual observer.

3. EXPLOITING DEPTH CUES IN COMPUTER DISPLAYS

Some of these depth cues are used by artists, who have long been faced with the problem of portraying three dimensional views in two dimensions [3] [4]. We are accustomed to interpreting two dimensional illustrations of three dimensional objects. In doing this we make use of size constancy, perspective, texture gradation, shading and aerial perspective.

The generation of an image by a computer may require a large amount of computation. Simple display systems make use of only the most elementary depth cueing methods such as perspective and hidden line removal. More sophisticated systems add to these the use of shading and aerial perspective to improve the illusion of depth, but at the expense of a considerable increase in computational complexity, especially if curved edges are to be reproduced. In practice the limited computational power available often means that only static images can be drawn. Even the very best static image could be compared only with a painting or photograph, in that many potentially valuable depth cues are missing.

When motion can be displayed, kinetic effects such as motion parallax and kinetic interposition can be exploited to give a more realistic illusion of three dimensionality. However, kinetic effects should arise not only from the motion of the object being viewed, but from the motion of the observer, and only the former is under the control of the display system. Thus, with a conventional display, if the viewer moves his or her head, he or she will simply have a different view of the same two-dimensional image. This is comparable with the use of film and television to portray three dimensional scenes, and the very best dynamic computer graphic techniques could be expected to give a display comparable to a high quality television picture. However, depth cues such as those of stereopsis, accommodation and motion parallax due to head motion, are still not exploited.

In order to produce depth cues due to accommodation, a display must produce an image in which rays of light appear to come from the surface of the three-dimensional object being displayed, rather than from a flat surface. This can be achieved using holographic techniques, but these currently present considerable technical difficulties. Some existing methods for producing three dimensional images do provide depth cues due to accommodation. These include the use of moving mirrors [5] [19] [20] [21] [22]. However these systems generally create only a limited perception of depth and cannot produce correct hidden-line removal.

Binocular vision provides us with important information about an object, and yet this information is completely lost with a two-dimensional display. A stereoscopic pair of images can be generated relatively easily by extension of existing two-dimensional techniques without recourse to more exotic technology. In most cases, stereopsis provides a more important cue than accommodation.

Depth cues due to motion of the head are important when viewing real objects. As the viewpoint changes, different parts of the object can be seen and the perspective changes. This effect is particularly important when the object is close to the observer. However, although this effect is obtainable with holographic techniques, it is not produced by conventional computer display systems.

4. STEREOSCOPIC DISPLAYS

It has been known for over a century that perception of 3D images is possible by presenting to the viewer a stereoscopic pair of two-dimensional images. This technique is both simpler and cheaper to implement than a holographic system, and the use of stereoscopic displays can greatly enhance the interpretation and assimilation of three dimensional material. Stereoscopic computer graphics are potentially of immense value in adding realism to images of three dimensional objects and allowing rapid and accurate visualisation of workpieces when using computer aided design.

Many techniques have been developed for the presentation of stereoscopic images for photographic and television applications [3] [13] [16]. This work has generally attempted to produce non-localised images that can be seen from a range of positions and hence simultaneously by a number of viewers. Such systems have usually employed head mounted apparatus to provide the two eyes with different views of the scene being displayed. The techniques used include the use of filters to separate images of different colours (typically red and green) [10]; cross polarised filters to separate images of different planes of polarisation; and "eye-switching" spectacles which blank out the view from each eye in turn to separate images which are multiplexed in time [7] [8] [14].

Stereoscopic displays have been produced which do not require any head mounted apparatus. Some such systems work by generating two or more localised images using an optical arrangement and restricting head position so that the eyes are positioned to see an appropriate pair of images [9]. Other systems simply present both images to both eyes and rely on the "pattern recognition" abilities of the viewer to interpret the information correctly. These approaches both have associated problems: the first restricts the viewing position to correspond with that of the images, and the second is difficult to interpret for non-experienced users. It is for these reasons that the majority of applications of stereoscopic displays have used non-localised images and some form of head mounted spectacles.

Most stereoscopic displays are specifically designed so that the same view is seen from any position. However, when a person moves their head they expect, subconsciously, that their field of view will change accordingly. The fact that the stereoscopic image does not change as the viewing point is changed results in a very disturbing effect. Because "distant" parts of the image show the same angular motion as those "closer" to the viewer, the image appears to rotate as the head moves. This effect is most pronounced with those parts of the stereoscopic image which are "closest to" and "furthest from" the viewer.

A second effect is that a stereoscopic image appears to have the correct orientation and perspective only when viewed from the point for which the stereoscopic pair was calculated. When seen from any other point it appears to have the wrong orientation and to be distorted. This is a serious shortcoming when the display is being used for applications such as computer aided design where a correct perspective may be vital. Either the image must be adjusted as the viewing point changes or the viewer's head must be constrained from moving. The latter alternative would not appear to be particularly attractive.

To be truly effective a stereoscopic display should be position dependent since the image should change as the viewing point moves. This is difficult to achieve if the image is to be viewed by more than one person at the same time and applications such as stereoscopic film and broadcast television must generally be content with a position-independent display. However, when the image is part of a man-machine interface this restriction to a single viewer is not a serious shortcoming. Moreover, because the material to be displayed is computer generated, it is possible to calculate the appropriate views for each eye, provided that their position is known. This produces an image which appears to be stable in space, and in which distances and perspectives are correct. It also allows the viewer to move his or her head to obtain different views of an object within the

limitation of the field of view of the display [6]. Clearly, such a system requires a knowledge of the user's head position and orientation in order to compute the appropriate view to be presented to each eye.

5. HEAD POSITION DETERMINATION

Over the years many techniques for measuring head position have been used in a number of applications. These range from rather inelegant mechanical arrangements using apparatus connected to the head by levers or wires, to highly sophisticated non-contact methods.

Most techniques have used some active or passive apparatus mounted on the head. Typical of the passive approach is the use of a stationary optical transmitter and receiver with reflectors mounted on the head, often on some form of spectacles. This technique has two main variants: either an omni-directional transmitter is used with a receiver which scans its field of view to locate the reflected signal, or the receiver is omni-directional and a scanning transmitter is used.

Examples of the use of active head-mounted apparatus are the use of light emitting diodes (LEDs) mounted on spectacles with a fixed detector or camera which can locate their position; and the complementary arrangement of head-mounted photodetectors and one or more fixed scanning light sources. These techniques have been successfully incorporated into many systems, including military applications such as the use of head position for targetting of both airborne and groundbased weapons and navigational equipment. These applications have also led to the development of the "space synchro" which uses a nutating magnetic field and a head-mounted detector [23]. The phase and direction of the magnetic field can be used to calculate the position and orientation of the detector, and hence the head. However, this technique is expensive.

Ideally, a head-position measuring system for use with a stereoscopic display should require no head-mounted equipment. This is a practical possibility using, for example, a television camera to observe the operator, and a pattern recognition system to identify the position of the eyes. Two cameras, or a single camera with a split field of view, would allow range to be measured in addition to angular position, or this could be measured directly by optical or other means.

6. AN INTERACTIVE STEREOSCOPIC SYSTEM

A knowledge of head position is also useful in the display of images [6] [15]. Since the location of the eyes is known the stereoscopic images need only be local, and they can be made to "follow" the eyes using a "steerable" display which generates the calculated view for each eye in the appropriate position. This produces a stereoscopic display system which allows the user to move his head to obtain kinetic depth cues without creating distortions of the object being viewed.

An interactive stereoscopic display system would present the viewer with virtually all the visual cues listed in section 2 with the exception of accommodation. An interactive stereoscopic image of this type would offer the computer aided designer a three dimensional "drawing board". The system used for head position determination could be developed to allow the simultaneous determination of the position of a pointer which could be used as a 3D "light pen". In this way the viewer could interact with the image to make modifications or to move it within the field of view.

7. ARCHITECTURES

Hitherto, vector scan displays have been used for computer graphic display systems, but nowadays they are losing favour to raster scan devices [1]. This is largely because the vector scan display is suited only to drawing lines (hence its name) and cannot perform functions such as polygon filling which can be done with raster displays. Consequently the vector scan technique is not particularly suited to displaying solid objects realistically. However, the vector scan display is generally superior to its raster scan counterpart in terms of resolution. A line drawn on a raster scan display is formed from points in a fixed matrix, unlike a line drawn on a vector scan display in which only the end-points are constrained in such a way. The effects of finite resolution within any display will limit the degree of realism which is attainable. In the case of a stereoscopic display this is complicated by the fact that depth perception is achieved by comparing the positions of edges, so that quantisation of edges will affect the apparent position of the object.

A very large amount of computation is required to convert information from a description of a scene into a form suitable for connection to a television monitor [12]. Simple systems cope with this problem by means of a bit plane in which each pixel of the image is represented by a memory word. However, the amount of computation required means that a relatively long time - seconds or even minutes - is required to build up the image in memory. This time can be greatly reduced by using special LSI display controller chips, but the amount of time taken to form an image of any but the simplest kind often precludes the generation of moving pictures.

Even if a circuit were capable of calculating the state of all the pixels in the time between successive frames of a TV picture, the bandwidth of the bit plane presents a "bottleneck". Currently available dynamic RAMs have access times in the order of 150ns, to which must be added the execution time of the circuit modifying the state of each pixel. This might be expected to raise the time per pixel to the order of 200ns or more. The time available to calculate a new frame is 16.7 or 20 ms, depending upon the frame refresh rate (60 or 50Hz) of the display, which means that the maximum number of pixels which can be handled by a single process is at most about 100000. This corresponds to a resulution in the display of approximately 300 pixels in both the X and Y directions. Modern graphic displays require appreciable higher resolution, but the total number of pixels in the display rises as the square of its linear resolution, and as the image positions must be updated during each frame as the head moves, no more time is allowable for each head frame. Thus a 4096x4096 pixel display would require more than 16 million words of memory with an access time in the order of one nanosecond.

The high processing speed required to produce a steerable display precludes the use of conventional bit-plane techniques in the video generator and therefore the video signals must be produced directly using very high speed logic circuitry. The simple analysis of the last paragraph is, of course, very approximate. For example, it excludes the time taken to transform the image from its descriptive form within the display computer to the display output, which requires a considerable amount of arithmetic in order to "project" a three dimensional object to a stereoscopic pair of two-dimensional images. Clearly the task is too great for a single processor using the technology available. However, the low cost of microprocessor technology allows several processors to be included within a system at reasonable cost. There are many ways in which a number of processors could be combined to handle the computation required in this application. A set of special purpose processors could operate in parallel, each of them being responsible for a separate part of the displayed image. This method is quite attractive for high resolution displays, because if each processor has independent access to its own memory it is not limited by the bandwidth "bottleneck" already referred to.

Another way to divide the computation involved is to construct a "pipeline" of processors, in which the output from one process is connected to the input of the next. In this way data flows through the pipeline on its way to the screen. Different types of processor can be used, the choice depending upon the function which it is to perform. Mathematically intensive operations such as transformation can be carried out by a 16-bit general purpose processor or by a high speed signal processing circuit. Some of the signal processors currently available are capable of performing a multiplication in well under one microsecond so that a large number of points can be transformed in the time available.

The later stages in the pipeline require a large amount of information to be processed within the time taken to display one line of the picture, that is, about 64 microseconds. In this case, because of the high speeds required, special purpose state machines designed using logic circuits are necessary. Operating speeds of some tens of megahertz are needed for this section, a daunting but by no means impossible task.

It is not difficult to identify the main processes which must be performed in this pipeline architecture.

(1) The three dimensional scene must be projected to give the two views as seen by the two eyes. This requires input from the head position sensor and from the internal scene description. The result is a set of "patches" with attributes such as colour, shape, position in the display, and distance from the observer. This last attribute is important because it allows the effects of interposition to be displayed.

(2) Next, the points at which this patch overlaps each line of the display are calculated. These points appear in the order in which they are calculated.

(3) The points are sorted into the order in which they will appear on the line. This requires the use of special hardware; ideally a content-addressable memory would provide a fast parallel method of sorting, but very high speed serial methods can give sufficiently rapid operation.

(4) The attribute of the surface closest to the viewer is then determined for each pixel along the line, making use of the distance attribute referred to in (1) above.

(5) This attribute must then be converted into a colour, and perhaps an antialiasing filter used to minimise the visual impact of the quantisation caused by the display raster.

All except the first process must be carried out in two separate channels, one for each eye. Thus in addition to having a pipelined architecture, the design must also have a limited degree of parallelism. The resulting system will have about ten processors, which not long ago would have represented a complicated design. However, the availability of LSI logic circuits makes such a system feasible even for displaying quite complicated scenes [11]. The use of special purpose logic circuits and high speed logic such as ECL would allow a considerable increase in the complexity of scene available with this technique.

8. CONCLUSIONS

A system for the display of animated stereoscopic images has been proposed in which the imformation presented to the viewer is changed as the viewpoint is altered. Work on such a system is currently under way, funded by a grant from the Science and Engineering Research Council. While the implementation of a system of this type presents considerable technical problems, it is believed that the improved visual depth cueing achievable with such a system will justify the effort required to overcome these problems.

9. ACKNOWLEDGEMENT

The authors wish to thank Dr. E.L. Hines and Mr. I. Sexton for their assistance in the preparation of this paper.

10. REFERENCES

[1] Blinn J.F., "Raster Graphics", Computer Graphics, ed Booth K.S. IEEE 1979

[2] Bexton S.A., "Survey of Holographic Stereograms", SPIE Vol. 367 1982

[3] Nakayama K., "Geometric & physiological aspects of depth perception", SPIE Vol. 120 1977

[4] Tyler C.W., "Spatial limitations of human stereoscopic vision", SPIE Vol. 120 1977

[5] Fuchs H., "Design of Image editing with a space filling three dimensional display based on a standard raster graphics system", SPIE Vol. 367 1982

[6] Sutherland I.E., "A head mounted three dimensional display", AFIPS FJCC 1968

[7] Roese J.A. & Khalafalla A.S., "Stereoscopic viewing with PLZT ceramics", Ferroelectrics 1976

[8] Roese J.A. & McCleary L., "Stereoscopic computer graphics for simulation & modelling", proc. Siggraph 1979

[9] Butterfield J.F., "Autostereoscopic displays using a stereo-pair of images", SPIE Vol 162 Visual simulation and image realism, 1978

[10] Smith C., "The secrets of television in depth", New scientist, 21 Jan. 1982

[11] Fussel D. and Rathbone B.D. "A VLSI oriented architecture for real time raster display of shaded polygons", Graphics Interface 1982

[12] Black S.R., "Digital processing of 3-D data to generate interactive real-time dynamic pictures", SPIE Vol 120 Three-Dimensional imaging, 1977

[13] Lane B., "Stereoscopic displays", SPIE Vol 367 Processing and display of Three-Dimensional data, 1982

[14] Robinson M. and Sood S.C., "Real-time depth measurement in a stereoscopic television display", SPIE Vol 367 Processing and display of Three-Dimensional data, 1982

[15] Fisher S., "Viewpoint dependent imaging: an interactive stereoscopic display", SPIE Vol 367 Processing and display of Three-Dimensional data, 1982

[16] Butterfield J.F., "Very high resolution stereoscopic television", SPIE Vol 120 Three-Dimensional imaging, 1977

[17] Perimutter R.J., Goodman J.W. and Macovski A., "Digital holographic display of medical CT images", SPIE Vol 367 Processing and display of Three-Dimensional data, 1982

[18] Huff L. and Fusek R.J., "Application of holographic stereograms to three-dimensional data display", SPIE Vol 367 Processing and display of Three-Dimensional data, 1982

[19] Sher L.D., "3-D or not 3-D", Proc. 15th Int. Conf. on systems sciences, Vol 2, 1982

[20] Mark H. and Hull F., "Three-Dimensional viewing of tomographic data-The Tomax system", SPIE Vol 120 Three-Dimensional imaging, 1977

[21] Rhodes M.L., Stover H.S. and Glenn W.V., jr., "True three-dimensional (3-D) display of computer data", Medical applications, SPIE Vol 120 Three-Dimensional imaging, 1977

[22] Simon W.and Walters T., "A spinning Mirror auto-stereoscopic display", SPIE Vol 120 Three-Dimensional imaging, 1977

[23] "Helmet Mounted Systems," Electronic Engineering, p 17, Vol. 52, No. 644. Oct. 1980

INPUT METHODS AND COMPARISONS

Human-Computer Interaction — INTERACT '84 / B. Shackel (ed.)
Elsevier Science Publishers B.V. (North-Holland)
© IFIP, 1985

INPUT DEVICES FOR PUBLIC VIDEOTEX SERVICES

M. Francas
Microtel Pacific Research Limited
Burnaby, B.C., Canada

D. Goodman and J. Dickinson
Simon Fraser University
Burnaby, B.C., Canada

ABSTRACT

A number of experiments aimed at developing effective key-press input devices for public videotex services are reported. Results generally indicated that performance differences were minimal across a variety of devices for different types of users (novice and experienced). There were, however, some distinct preference differences exhibited by the two user groups. Novices strongly favoured a simple minimal-function keypad, whereas subjects trained to a high level of Telidon proficiency preferred the perceived functionality of a full-sized keyboard, even though it did not lead to improved performance.

INTRODUCTION

A major thrust of the videotex industry has been, and continues to be, the provision of public information retrieval services. Videotex technology allows users to retrieve information from remote databases and display the information in colour graphics and text format on a self-contained terminal. Numerous videotex terminals currently exist in locations such as shopping malls, hotel lobbies, airport lounges and public libraries, and their numbers are increasing. Public-access use is often regarded as a logical gateway to the penetration of videotex into the home, as well as being a potentially profitable market in its own right.

At present, most public videotex systems use a keyboard or keypad input device. While a mouse or touch-sensitive screen, or even limited voice recognition, are potentially appropriate input mechanisms for public information systems, it seems likely that key-press devices will retain their prevalence, at least for the next few years. Recent research on Telidon (Canada's videotex system) has indicated that many of the problems encountered by new users are at least partially due to design deficiencies of the input devices provided with most public-access terminals (see Dillon & Tombaugh, 1982).

The users of public-access videotex can be defined as "casual users" - i.e. they generally access the system on an infrequent basis. This user group is very diverse and consists of people with varying amounts of previous videotex and computer experience, and differential expectations and requirements of the system. The majority are "novice" videotex users who are accessing the system for the first or second time (Wescom, 1982, Reference Note 3). On the other hand, the number of "sophisticated" users -, i.e. those with previous experience and some proficiency in using videotex - can be expected to grow as the technology becomes more pervasive. It was felt that a major factor contributing to difficulties, at least for novice users, was the perceived complexity of many of the available keypads.

Unfortunately, previous research on keyboards and keypads provides minimal guidance for the design of effective key entry devices for an application such as public videotex. While considerable research has been done on keyboard design (see Alden, Daniels and Kanarick, 1972 and Noyes, 1983, for reviews), most of it has been concerned with lengthy typing tasks by skilled users. The available research on keypads has examined either a hand-held device for residential use (Hearty, 1982) or specific keypad applications with trained users (Butterbaugh, 1982). This work is not particularly relevant to the task domain and user group under consideration in the present study.

Norman and Fisher (1982) evaluated several keyboard layouts with naive and expert typists. They found that merely changing the arrangement of the keys had minimal effect on users' performance or preference, and suggested that perhaps a redesign of the overall configuration was required to significantly impact performance. The present research was aimed at developing and examining an alternative key configuration, based on the notion of simplicity for novice users. At the same time, a major concern was the tradeoff between simplicity or ease of use for the novice and flexibility for the sophisticated user.

The research proceeded in three phases. Phase One consisted of a series of "user trials", which employed a cost-effective, iterative research methodology to provide design specifications for the construction of keypad prototypes. Phase Two was concerned with evaluating simple, minimal-function keypads whereas in Phase Three the minimal-function keypads were contrasted with a multifunction alphanumeric keypad and a full-sized Telidon keyboard.

PHASE ONE: USER TRIALS

User Trials were conducted in order to provide input for the construction of keypad prototypes and reduce the number of variables to be manipulated in the formal experiments. Three sets of user trials were conducted (Experiments 1A, 1B and 1C), each one progressively more focused than the last.

Data from the User Trials provided design recommendations for a number of parameters, such as key arrangement, key size and shape, colour combination and the locations and labels for specific keys. From the point of view of the present research, the most salient design parameter was the overall configuration of the keypads. Experiments 1A and 1B indicated that the two most popular configurations were a linear arrangement, with the function keys and numerics arranged in horizontal rows, and a square arrangement with the function keys clustered around a touch-telephone numeric layout. These two keypad configurations were compared in Experiment 1C.

The preference rankings in Experiment 1C showed that 60% of subjects preferred the square arrangement and 40% favoured the linear. The average rating on a ten-point user satisfaction scale (where 1=poor and 10=excellent) was 6.8 for the square and 6.1 for the linear, with variability greater for the latter. This was not an overwhelming preference and it was felt that further data were required. Consequently, two prototype keypads that conformed exactly to the specifications of the models used in Experiment 1C were constructed, and were evaluated in a formal experiment utilizing actual Telidon interaction (see Fig-

ure 1 for the two prototype designs).

Figure 1

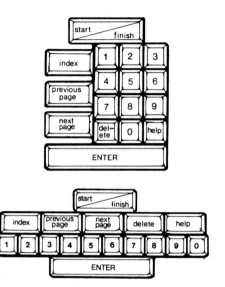

Figure 1.   The design of the keypads.

PHASE TWO: MINIMAL - FUNCTION KEYPADS

In this phase, the keypad prototypes were interfaced to a Telidon terminal. The minimum number of keys required to interact with the Telidon database depends on the method employed to search for information. If keyword-search techniques are not considered, then only the numeric keys and a small set of special functions are required for effective interaction. Our initial assumption, supported by subsequent results, was that new users did not use keywords but relied primarily on menus to traverse the database. Consequently, only the ten numeric keys and seven special function keys were considered in the attempt to develop an optimal minimal-function configuration for Telidon use. The keypads were identical in terms of colour combination, key type, size and labels of specific keys but differed in overall configuration. Several field experiments were conducted at a local shopping mall, comparing performance and preference for the square and the linear pads. Only one of the experiments is discussed in the present paper; a more comprehensive presentation of research results is included in Goodman, Dickinson and Francas, Reference Note 1.

Method

Thirty four Telidon-naive subjects were required to find specific information via Telidon (e.g. last night's baseball scores). An Apple II microcomputer recorded measures of the speed and accuracy of subjects' performance on these typical information retrieval tasks. After the test session, a post-test questionnaire was administered which elicited preference rankings and user satisfaction ratings (on the same ten point scale as was used in Experiment 1C). The questionnaire also identified previous computer, calculator and/or typing experience. Similar data collection procedures were invoked in all subsequent experiments.

Results

The data indicated that speed and accuracy of performance were similar with both keypads. The questionnaire results, however, showed a preference for the square pad, with 68% of subjects preferring this design, and 32% choosing the linear arrangement. On the user-satisfaction scale, the mean values were 7.0 for the square design and 6.0 for the linear. These scores suggest a fairly high degree of acceptance for both arrangements. Furthermore, the preference results are very similar to those obtained in Experiment 1C which verifies the replicability of the simulation technique employed in the User Trials . (See also Francas, Goodman and Dickinson, Reference Note 1.) As expected, the interaction between preference and previous experience with calculators showed that a stronger preference for the square arrangement was shown by those with more calculator experience. There were no such trends between previous calculator, computer or typewriter experience and preference for the linear keypad.

PHASE THREE: COMPARATIVE ANALYSIS OF KEYPADS AND KEYBOARDS

Experiment 3A: Naive Users

Method

Sixty subjects were randomly assigned to one of four input device conditions (i.e. square keypad, linear keypad, small alphanumeric keypad and full-sized Telidon keyboard) and required to perform typical Telidon tasks. The alphanumeric keypad had some obvious deficiencies (e.g. small keys, labels in between rather than on keys), but was included because at the time this research was conducted, it was one of the common input devices on public Telidon terminals. On completion of the test session, which took approximately 20 minutes, subjects were shown the three input devices that they had <u>not</u> used and were asked to rank order the four devices in terms of preference. Finally, a questionnaire was administered which elicited satisfaction ratings and open-ended comment on several aspects of the input device that the subject had used.

Results

Figure 2 contrasts the number of task completions with the minimal devices versus the full-sized keyboard for each of the four tasks.

Figure 2

NUMBER OF NAIVE SUBJECTS SUCCESSFULLY COMPLETING TASKS

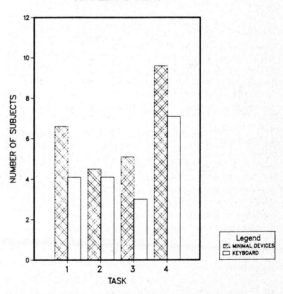

It is evident from Figure 2 that across the four tasks subjects using the minimal devices consistently performed as well as or better than those using the keyboard. It should be noted that these differences were not statistically reliable. In addition, 40% of the keyboard group failed to complete a single problem while the corresponding mean for the minimal keypad groups was only 23%.

User preference results clearly favoured the minimal-function keypads over the alphanumeric devices. Table 1 presents results of the preference ranking question that was asked of subjects immediately following the experimental session.

Table 1

	Mean Pref. Rank	% of 1st or 2nd Pref.
Square Pad	1.92	78%
Linear Pad	2.15	67%
Alphanumeric Pad	3.47	17%
Keyboard	2.48	36%

The devices were ranked from 1 to 4 with 1 being most preferred and 4 being least preferred.

Table 1 shows that the alphanumeric keypad is clearly the least preferred of the four devices. Secondly, the two minimal pads are preferred over the keyboard by novice users. Almost 73% of users selected the minimal pads as their first or second preference; the corresponding figure for the keyboard was only 36%. This indicates a positive correlation between preference and performance for these novice users.

Experiment 3B: Experienced Users

This experiment examined the effectiveness of the four input devices for experienced Telidon users. It is reasonable to assume that a growing number of people interacting with public-access terminals have had some previous experience with Telidon and their requirements, which may well be different to those of the novice user, need to be reflected in the choice of an input device.

Method

Twelve naive Telidon users were selected from the Simon Fraser University community and were trained to a criterion level of Telidon proficiency. Because the keyword-search technique was an important component of the training protocol, subjects used the full-sized keyboard (with its full set of alphanumeric and function keys) in the training session. Subjects were required to perform four Telidon problems (similar to those used in Experiment 3A) with each of three input devices - i.e. a minimal function pad (either the square or the linear), the existing keypad and the full-sized keyboard. The order of presentation of input devices was counterbalanced.

Results

As expected, there were no significant differences in performance between those who used the square pad and those who used the linear design as their minimal-function device. Therefore, performance data have been collapsed across the two designs and presented as a single score for a minimal-function input device.

Table 2 shows that experienced subjects performed equally as well with each of the input devices. In particular, their performance was no better with the full-sized keyboard than with a minimal function device. This result supports the view proposed by Moran (1981) that changing user interface parameters often has minimal effect on the performance of expert users.

Table 2

	Mean Tasks Comp.	Time to Completion
Minimal Pads	3.4	275.5
Alphanumeric Pad	3.3	289.5
Keyboard	3.2	278.3

None of these differences are statistically significant.

However, questionnaire data indicated that experienced users did have a strong preference for the full-sized keyboard. Table 3 shows the mean preference rankings for the various input devices and also the percentage of respondents who ranked each device first.

Table 3

	Mean Pref. Rank	% of 1st Pref.
Minimal Pads	1.8	9%
Alphanumeric Pad	2.8	0
Keyboard	1.1	91%

As for the novice users in Experiment 3A, the alphanumeric keypad was the least preferred device. In fact, 82% of subjects ranked it last. This was no doubt due to the deficiencies of the particular alphanumeric keypad used. As stated earlier, it was included in the study primarily as a control condition.

Summary of Phase Three

The experienced users, who had been trained on the full-sized keyboard, showed no advantage in performance with this device over a minimal pad or the alphanumeric keypad. They did, however, indicate a marked preference for the keyboard and felt limited by the lack of keyword capability with the minimal-function device, even though a breakdown of Experiment 3b results on the basis of search strategy showed that the use of keywords did not allow them to retrieve the information any faster.
The novice users in Experiment 3A performed best with the minimal pads, though differences in performance between the devices were minimal. They clearly preferred the minimal-function pads over the existing pad and the keyboard. These results suggest that there is a tradeoff of some sort between the simple keypads preferred by the new user, and a full alphanumeric device which is perhaps more functional for the experienced user.

CONCLUSION

The results of Experiments 3A and 3B demonstrate that performance differences between four distinct key-press input devices were minimal for both novice and experienced users. On the other hand, clear preference differences were exhibited and, for a discretionary application such as public videotex use, it is perhaps these preference results which should guide design decisions. User preferences indicate that differential requirements exist for different types of users. These requirements should be appropriately weighted by videotex system designers according to the relative importance of the respective user groups. The Wescom (1982) report states that, of all people who accessed Telidon terminals during a recent public field trial, 84% were novice users. On this basis, it appears that, at least for the immediate future, the specific needs of the novice user should be given prime consideration.

The concept of touch screen entry for public-access videotex has raised considerable interest and some preliminary research is planned to examine touch screen entry for novice computer users. Published human factors research on the use of a touch screen or a mouse for item selection is very scarce. Both of these devices appear to be viable contenders for public videotex systems, particularly if menu selection remains the dominant information search strategy, and formal evaluations in field settings should be carried out.

Acknowledgement

The research reported here was made possible by a grant from the Science Council of British Columbia.

REFERENCE NOTES

1. Goodman, D., Dickinson, J. and Francas, M, Human Factors Design Considerations for Public Videotex Input Devices, Submitted.

2. Francas, M., Goodman, D. and Dickinson, J., Evaluation Techniques for Product Development in the Computer Communications Industry, Submitted.

3. Wescom Communications Studies and Research Ltd., Report 2A; Diary Evaluation, B. C. Telephone Co. Telidon Field Trial Evaluation. September, 1982.

REFERENCES

Alden, D.G., Daniels, R.W. and Kanarick, A.F., Keyboard Design and Operation; A Review of the Major Issues. Human Factors, 1972, 14(4) 275-293.

Butterbaugh, L.C., Evaluation of Alternative Alphanumeric Keying Logics, Human Factors, 1982, 24(5); 520-533.

Dillon, R.F. and Tombaugh, J.W. Psychological Research on Videotex. Behaviour Research Methods and Instrumentation, 1982, 14, 191-197.

Hearty, P.J., Human Factors and Telidon Keypads: A New Design and an Examination of the Current Models. Ottawa: Department of Communications, 1982.

Moran, T., An Applied Psychology of User-Computing Surveys, Vol. 13, No. 1, March 1981.

Norman, D.A., and Fisher, S. Why Alphabetic Keyboards Are Not Easy to Use: Keyboard Layout Doesn't Matter Much., Human Factors, 1982, 24(5); 509-519.

Noyes, J., The Qwerty Keyboard: a review. Int. J. Man-Machine Studies (1983), 18, 265-281.

Human-Computer Interaction — INTERACT '84 / B. Shackel (ed.)
Elsevier Science Publishers B.V. (North-Holland)
© IFIP, 1985

COMPARISON OF INPUT DEVICES FOR CORRECTION
OF TYPING ERRORS IN OFFICE SYSTEMS

R. Haller, H. Mutschler, M. Voss

Fraunhofer-Institut für Informations- und
Datenverarbeitung, Karlsruhe, F.R. of Germany

In an experiment several devices for correction of typing errors in office systems were compared. They were chosen with regard to an increasing degree of compatibility between input operation and system's response. The task was the correction of typing errors in a letter already prepared on a word processor. After positioning the cursor on the erroneous character with one of the six locators light pen, graphic tablet, mouse, tracking ball, cursor keys, and speech recognizer, it had to be replaced by the right character with one of the two correctors α-keyboard and speech recognizer. Concerning the locators the results corresponded roughly to the degree of compatibility with voice input as the slowest and light pen as the fastest device. There were no essential differences between correctors.

1. INTRODUCTION

The growth of interactive computing facilities over the last years, e.g. for office systems, has led generally to a bigger interest in their ease of use. Common office terminals include an alphanumerical (α-) keyboard with additional function and cursor keys for information input. There is a fixed assignment of textual information to the α-keyboard, of control information to α-keyboard or function keys, and of graphic information to cursor keys. For better userfriendliness various new input devices are being developed, e.g. touch screen, light pen, mouse, graphic tablet, joystick, tracking ball, speech recognizer.

The evaluation of an input device depends on the task of the user, e.g. the cursor positioning for typing error correction in office systems. Experimental comparisons of several input devices for the positioning task are found in the literature (see Fig. 1). Evaluation criteria were completion time or error rate. But as can be seen from Fig. 1 different and incomplete sets of input devices were compared. They often do not include conventional keyboard or cursor keys as reference. Furthermore the differences measured between the input devices are rather low, and different evaluation criteria were used. From the references cited in Fig. 1 it can be concluded:

o Direct eye-hand coordination (touch input devices, light pen) speeds up positioning time and is therefore well suited (and well accepted) for the positioning task.

o Input devices with high positioning accuracy (e.g. tracking ball) are not very fast, and vice versa, i.e. positioning accuracy and positioning time are not independent from each other.

Reference	/1/	/2/	/3/	/4/	/5/	/6/
Touch input			⊗			⊗
Light pen (or gun)	x	⊗	⊗			x
Graphic tablet					⊗	x
Mouse	⊗			⊗		
Joystick	x		x	x	⊗	x
Tracking ball			x		⊗	⊗
Keybord, Cursor keys		x		x		x

Figure 1: Experimental comparisons of different input devices for the positioning task (x compared devices, ⊗ best devices).

The results are not complete enough for the practical application in office systems. Therefore, a comparison of systematically chosen input devices for office systems was conducted based on theoretical considerations of compatibility. Instead of an isolated input procedure we have chosen the correction of typing errors, which is a task sequence consisting of a cursor positioning task with a "locator" (with limited accuracy given by the discrete structu-

re of textual information) and a character replacing task with a "corrector".

2. SYSTEMATIC CHOICE OF INPUT DEVICES TO BE COMPARED

For a given task input devices can be
classified with regard to the compatibility between input operation and system's answer. At a given time the user
sends an input signal to a technical
system with a given input device. By
doing this he is making some experiences while receiving information through
different sensory information channels
and while processing them as connected
ones. The complete set of this feedback
information can be divided into two
structured subsets:

First there is the immediate on-line
Feedback F connected directly with the
input operation I, e.g. the tactual,
auditive and/or visual feedback while
pressing a key. Secondly there is the
subset of system's Responses R after
some time delay, i.e. system's general
behaviour (e.g. a status change) and
information given by a display.

From this point of view the compatibility between input operation like activating an input device and system's
answer like a cursor movement is partly
represented in the similarity/overlapp-
ing of the spatial, temporal, and functional structures of the informational
subsets F and R. So a "good compatibility" can be seen as user's "well-organ-
ized" experience during and after an
input operation.

The display of the desired system's
response for the cursor positioning
task consists of a cursor movement from
a starting point to a destination
point, visually received from a screen.
The different input devices available
for cursor positioning are differently
compatible related to this task, considering first the number and kind of
sensory channels involved into the on-
line feedback F and secondly the degree
of similarity between e.g. the spatial
structures of F and the cursor movement
on the screen R. (The compatibilities
I-F and I-R are not considered for this
task because they are partly represented in F-R.)

Derived from this consideration input
devices available for cursor positioning are listed in Fig. 2 with decreasing "overall" compatibility, grouped
into subsets with roughly the same compatibility. The brackets characterize a

less good similarity between the on-
line feedback structure and the corresponding cursor movement behaviour. Concerning the sensory channels the different F-R compatibilities are defined
as observation ("visual"), cutaneous
sensing ("tactual"), subcutaneous sensing ("proprioceptive"), and hearing
("auditive") of the effector/input device being coincident to the cursor
movement. For the present study this
classification is sufficient for a systematic choice of input devices, which
have to be compared, e.g. for investigating the hypothesis "the more compatible input device is a better one" (by
a given criterion like positioning time
or subjective rating). Beside compatibility there are more features to be
included in an overall ergonomic evaluation, such as physiological adaptation
(e.g. static muscle work) and embedding
in a task sequence (e.g. effects of
frequent changing between different
input devices). Thus, the hypothesized
rank order in Fig.2 was established
only due to the compatibility criterion
considered as an important one by the
authors.

Input device	Spatial compatibility
Touch input, Light pen	(visual), (tactual), (proprioceptive)
Graphic tablet, Mouse	tactual, proprioceptive
Joystick, Tracking ball	tactual, (proprioceptive)
Cursor keys	(tactual), (proprioceptive)
Speech input	(auditive)

Figure 2: Different input devices with
different compatibility (decreasing from
top to bottom, see text) related to the
cursor positioning task.

3. EXPERIMENT

3.1 Apparatus

Figure 3 shows the experimental set up.
All input devices but the cursor keys
were typical commercially available
devices. A Bosch M50BB monitor with
50 cm diagonal was used linked to the
α-keyboard of a VT 100 terminal.

Locator devices: The light pen LG 81
(IITB) is activated by the electronical
beam of the Crt-screen passing its

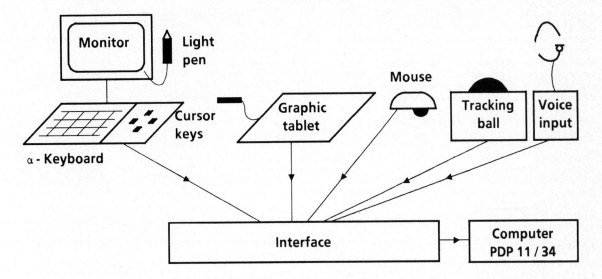

Figure 3: Experimental apparatus with different locator devices (light pen, cursor keys, graphic tablet, mouse, tracking ball, voice input) and corrector devices (α-keybord, voice input).

nearby sensor tip. The calculated position is transferred to the computer by activating the push switch at the light pen's tip against the terminal's glass plate. The <u>graphic tablet</u> Bit Pad One (Summagraphics Corporation) operates according to the magnetostrictive principle with a mouse-like activator. By reducing the active tablet area with masking cardboards an alternative gain of 1:1 or 1.4:1 was achieved. The <u>mouse</u> P4 (ibs) needs a rough base plate to keep the metallic ball at its bottom side from slipping. Its resolution is 15 counts/mm. The <u>tracking ball</u> TB 200 (Penny & Giles) (51 mm diameter) with a resolution of 200 counts/ball revolution has a minimal rotatory shift of 1.8°. By downsampling, the minimal shift of the tracking ball as well as the mouse can be increased and a lower gain can be attained. The <u>cursor keys</u> of the VT 100 keyboard were discarded because of the low compatibility between their linear arrangement and the two-dimensional cursor movements. Instead, four additional cross-shaped cursor keys each with two sequentially activated switching contacts are used. By closing the first contact the cursor moves one character position in the respective direction. Switching over to the second contact results in a continuous cursor movement with predefinable speed. The speaker-dependent <u>voice recognizer</u> CSE 1060 (Computer Gesellschaft Konstanz) compares isolated words spoken into a head-set microphone with previously tenfold trained reference patterns. In a pilot experiment an optimal compound method for cursor positioning was found: First, an absolute

positioning by vocal indicating the character coordinates in a 5 character-spaced-grid, e.g. "0-2-1-5" line 2/row 15. Then, if the erroneous character was missed, a relative positioning by vocal indicating the direction of the character position from the cursor and the number of cursor steps between, e.g. "rechts-2" for two steps to the right.

Corrector devices: The above mentioned voice recognizer was used for voice input of the correct character by means of the German phonetic alphabet "Anton, Ärger, Berta, ..., Zacharias". The α-keyboard of the voice recognizer was used for alternative typing of the character.

The input devices sent their data to a PDP 11/34 computer. The computer simulated a text system by displaying a previously typed letter with typing errors and controlled the experiment.

3.2 Subjects

Three male and three female Subjects (Ss), 21 to 28 years old students, participated in the experiment. They had experience in handling conventional computer keyboards and some contact to voice input. They were highly motivated because of their interest in this technology. They were paid for the sessions.

3.3 Experimental Procedure

The Ss had to correct an already prepared faulty one-page-letter which was automatically displayed black on grey on the monitor. There were 18 one-cha-racter-replacement-errors ("erroneous characters") on the top, in the middle, and at the bottom of the letter. They were identified automatically one by one by an underlying white area for eliminating irrelevant search times. First, the Ss marked the identified character with one of the locators by absolutely positioning the black cursor from the home position at the top left corner of the monitor to the character locus; corrections after a faulty po-sitioning were possible. Then, the Ss corrected the erroneous character by replacing it by the correct character with one of the correctors. Subsequent-ly, the next erroneous character was identified, marked, and replaced etc. Therefore, "positioning time" means the time between the beginning of the cha-racter identification and the last mo-vement of the cursor before correction. "Replacing time" means the subsequent time up to the moment of the typing or recognizing the correct character.

At the beginning of each session the Ss were trained for the input procedure with the actual locator device. The test trial was started when an asymp-totical training level was reached. During training a convenient gain (speed) was chosen by Ss for graphic tablet, mouse, and tracking ball (cur-sor keys). The voice recognizer was "trained" with digits and the phonetic alphabet at the beginning of the first session and these reference patterns were checked at the beginning of the following sessions. Times and errors of positioning and replacing, respective-ly, were measured as dependent variab-les.

3.4 Experimental Design

A 6 locators x 2 correctors x 3 error loci x 6 typing errors per locus x 6 Ss repeated measure design was used, i.e. each factor level was assigned to each S. The locator, corrector, and error loci levels were balanced across Ss. There were up to 6 sessions for all Ss with one or two locator trials each. A partial disruption of the experimental design was necessary: Adding up the pulses from mouse and tracking ball per FORTRAN software was not in real-time first and resulted in a buffer pipeline mechanism with an delayed cursor cont-rol. Therefore, these two locator trials were repeated after the complet-ion of the experimental series and were scored instead of the previous ones.

3.5 Results

Fig. 4 shows the resulting positioning times as a function of locator (bar groups) and locus of the character to be corrected (bar hatchings). They are averaged across correctors, characters per locus, and Ss. (Exception: The gra-phic tablet data of one S were removed because of untypical long positioning times).

If character loci are considered, the positioning times of the cursor keys are increasing significantly with lar-ger distance between cursor home posi-tion and error locus (Wilcoxon test (middle-top, bottom-middle): $T=0$, T_{krit} $(n=6; \alpha=1\%)=0$, $\mu_T=10.5$). The positioning times of the light pen show a similar but not significant tendency while those of voice input don't dif-

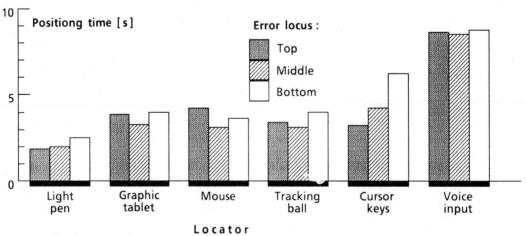

Figure 4: Time for cursor positioning as a function of locator and error locus averaged across correctors, typing errors, and Ss

fer. The positioning times of graphic tablet, mouse, and tracking ball tend to be minimal at medium distances (not significant).

If, additionally, averaged across error loci, the positioning time of light pen (2.1 s) is the least, that of voice input (8.6 s) is the longest; they differ from all others significantly according to Wilcoxon tests (All: $T=0$, $T_{krit}(n=6; \alpha=1\%)=0$, $\mu_T=10.5$, to graphic tablet : $\mu_T=7.5$). The averaged positioning times of graphic tablet, mouse, tracking ball, and cursor keys (3.7s, 3.6s, 3.5s and 4.5s) do not differ significantly from each other (All: $T>0$, T_{krit} $(n=6; \alpha=1\%)=0$, $\mu_T=10.5/7.5$). But the cursor keys clearly tend to be slower than the other three devices.

The second part of the task sequence was to replace the erroneous character. The totally averaged replacing times were 1.5 s ± 0.1 s for the α-keyboard and 1.8 s ± 0.2 s for voice input. The difference was not significant (Wilcoxon test : $T=3$, $T_{krit}(n=6; \alpha=1\%)=0$ $\mu_T=10.5$). Thus, both correctors were equivalent.

Replacing after positioning with mouse was generally faster, after positioning with graphic tablet generally slower than other combinations. There were no interactions of replacing times between locators and correctors with the exception of voice/voice resulting in larger replacing times than voice/α-keyboard.

The averaged positioning errors, i.e. positioning the cursor not correctly on the erroneous character, were 0% (light pen, cursor keys), 0.9% (voice input), 1.4% (graphic tablet), 4.2% (mouse), and 5.6% (tracking ball). The "touch sensitivity" of the ball-based devices resulted in a relatively high positioning error rate. Thereby, those Ss with a high gain tended to make the most errors.

The averaged correcting errors, i.e. typing or saying another wrong character, were 0.5 % (α-keyboard) and 1.8 % (voice input). Most of the voice input errors were recognition errors of the voice recognizer.

The input devices were subjectively evaluated by means of questionnaires. A paired comparison of the locators ("better", "equal", "worse") resulted in the ranking order

light pen (0.9),
mouse (0.7),
tracking ball (0.6), cursor keys (0.6),
graphic tablet (0.3), voice input (0.3),

with the portion of "better"-answers in brackets. The given reasons for the high ranking order of the light pen were the "fast, convenient, exact" way of cursor positioning. The space required for graphic tablet was specified as disadvantage of this device. The rigid syntax and the necessary stops between successive words of voice input was criticized to be "cumbersome" and "troublesome".

A repeated paired comparison of the correctors resulted in the ranking order α-keyboard (0.5), voice input (0.4).

3.6 Discussion

The average positioning times and - to some extent - the subjective ratings of the different locators confirm the hypothesized rank order of the locators which were established on the basis of on-line feedback/system answer compatibility: The positioning times in Fig. 4 increase from light pen with high compatibility to voice input with low compatibility. An exception is the tracking ball which does not differ from graphic tablet and mouse. The difference of the proprioceptive information feedback does not seem to be essential.

The positioning times as a function of character locus represent the nature of the different locators relating to coarse and fine positioning. Time for coarse positioning with cursor keys increases linearly with distance of error locus because of a constant cursor speed at the second contact; fine positioning with the first contact was felt to be convenient. The positioning times with voice input are identical for all character loci, because of distance independence of the voice syntax. At the beginning of the hand motion for coarse positioning with graphic tablet, mouse, and tracking ball one gets a sensation of the respective locator dynamics. Then a fast fine positioning is possible if the distance has been long enough. At longer distances the time portion of coarse positioning is becoming dominant. Thus, for these locators a minimal positioning time is at medium error distances.

There were no interactions of correcting times between locators and correctors with the exception of voice input. The combination of voice locator/

voice corrector is worse than voice locator/α-keyboard corrector according to the stricter serial information processing of the verbal system.

Reconsidering the literature of Fig. 1 the input devices with a higher compatibility at the left are mostly one of the best ones. The least agreeing result to that is [6] where the tracking ball is the most precise device (but one of the slowest ones!). A grouping of the seven input devices to four device types plus voice input as fifth would have been possible.

The following recommendations can be formulated:

o If considered in isolation light pen is best suited for the cursor positioning task in office systems with regard to input times. Its problems are grasping and the "putting away" and the static work in long-term tasks.

o Mouse and tracking ball are suited, too, if their "touch sensivity" is reduced by a sufficiently low gain. The advantage of the mouse is its space for control keys. The tracking ball is advantageous because of its low space demand thus allowing its integration in a keyboard.

o Cursor keys and graphic tablet are less suited. Cursor keys are too slow if no speed change for coarse positioning, e.g. by force control, is made available. Graphic tablet needs too much space on the table.

o Voice input is not suited for cursor positioning but for alphanumerical input. Its potential advantage is its use in integrated tasks with manual co-devices.

This investigation was part of a research supported by the Federal Ministry of Research and Technology (BMFT).

REFERENCES

[1]   English, W.K.; Engelbert, D.C.; Berman, M.L.: Display-selection techniques for text manipulation. IEEE Trans. Hum. Fact. Electron. HFE-8 (1976),S.5-15.

[2]   Goodwin, N.C.:Cursor positioning on an electronic display using light-pen, lightgun, or keyboard for three basic tasks. Human Factors 17 (1975), 289-295.

[3]   Gärtner, K.-P.; Holzhausen, K.-P.: Human Engineering Evaluation of a Cockpit Display/Input Device Using a Touch Sensitive Screen. AGARD Conference Proceedings No. 240: Guidance and Control Design Considerations for Low-Altitude and Terminal-Area Flight, 1978, 7.1-7.13.

[4]   Card,S.K.; English,W.R.;Burr,B.J.: Evaluation of Mouse, Rate-Controlled Isometric Joystick, Step Keys, and Text Keys for Text Selection on a CRT. Ergonomics 21 (1978), 601-613.

[5]   Pitrella, F.D.; Holzhausen, K.-P.: Selection and Experimental Comparison of Computer Input Devices. Forschungsinstitut für Anthropotechnik, Wachtberg-Werthhoven, FAT-Bericht Nr.57, 1982.

[6]   Albert, A.E.:The effect of graphic input devices on performance in a cursor positioning task. Proc. Hum.Fact.Soc.26thAnn.Meeting, Washington/USA, Oct.25-29, 1982, 54-58.

Human-Computer Interaction — INTERACT '84 / B. Shackel (ed.)
Elsevier Science Publishers B.V. (North-Holland)
© IFIP, 1985

A Cerebral View of Task Optimality
in Japanese Text Typing

Takeshi Okadome and Yamada-Hisao

Department of Information Science
Faculty of Science, University of Tokyo

Hiroshi Watanabe

Department of Control Engineering
Faculty of Engineering,
Tokyo Institute of Technology

Kenji Ikeda and Masao Saito

Institute for Medical Electronics
Faculty of Medicine, University of Tokyo

ABSTRACT

We discuss an activity of typists' brains during touch typing, based on knowledge of experimental psychology and cerebral physiology, especially in connection with the functional lateralization of cerebral hemispheres. Our hypothesis is that a skilled copy typist depends heavily on the cortical reflex in response to direct visual information from a manuscript, but depends less on the linguistic facility of the left hemisphere. As an indication of the validity of the hypothesis, we report our results of the measurements of typists' electroencephalograms (EEG) during Japanese touch typing. Our findings are preliminary but they are compatible with the hypothesis.

1. Introduction: The Japanese writing system and some Japanese input methods

By far the most common Japanese writing system is based on the mixed use of kanzis (Chinese characters), kanas (about 80 characters), the Roman alphabet, Arabic numerals, and other alphabets and symbols. The largest kanzi dictionary today lists more than 50,000 distinct kanzis. In general, however, a typist working in a given subject area only uses about 1,000 kanzis on a daily basis.

In Japanese there is no orthography in the Western sense, and a sentence may be "spelled out" entirely with syllabic kanas. However, almost all normal writing is a mixture of kanzis and kanas (and some others).

Japanese is an agglutinate language, in which the grammatical components are affixed to the ends of words one after another rather inseparably. So syntactic and semantic analysis of sentences by computer used in kana-to-kanzi conversion is extremely difficult with the present state of art.

Other basic information concerning kanzis that is essential in order to appreciate the difficulty of Japanese text handling is that (a) a single kanzi may be read in several different ways (*kun* sounds) depending on its meaning, and that (b) to a given *on* sound, many different kanzis correspond, having different meanings (i.e., the homophone problem).

In order to cope with such problems, a variety of typing systems have been devised in the past. However, none is considered satisfactory for all purposes.

These Japanese typing systems may be classified into three types; full display systems, coded input systems and kana-to-kanzi conversion systems [22].

With some intermediate exceptions, these three roughly correspond to three categories of typing methods; sight (hunt-and-peck) typing, blind (touch) typing, and pseudotouch typing, respectively.

Because of the large size of the character set needed for Japanese text, by far the majority of the input work in Japan is still performed by some sight methods. Although we expected "two-stroke code" typing to be the best input method for Japanese touch typing by specialists in information processing [22], it is generally considered difficult to learn since it is necessary to memorize from 1,000 to 2,000 kanzi codes.

But, as noted in Figure 1, learning curves for three "two-stroke kanzi code" typing methods and for two English typing methods go through a fairly narrow band, even though kanzi code typing is thought to be much more difficult than English typing. Among these systems, DSK is the rationalized Dvorak keyboard for English. With the exception of such highly optimized DSK the difficulty of Japanese touch typing is comparable to that of English.

2. Possible Hemispheric Lateralization of Cerebral Functions in Typing

2.1. Cerebral Hemisphericity

Since the research of Roger W. Sperry and his group [15], the lateralization of functions between the left and the right hemispheres of the cerebrum has been extensively studied, and a fair number of facts about it have been accumulated [1, 2, 3, 4, 9].

The most distinguished function of the left hemisphere is its linguistic facility. The functions of the right hemisphere are not as distinctly definable as those of the left [4]. For example, the right hemi-

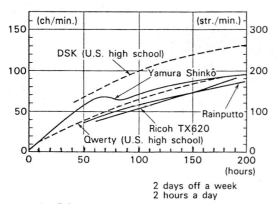

3:   Two-Stroke Kanzi Code Typing.
2:   English Typing (U. S. High School).

Fig. 1 Schematic Comparison of Learning Curves.

sphere is known to control "manipulo-spatial tasks", in which a spatial context is mapped onto the perceptual and motor activities of the hands [14].

2.2. Typing Tasks and Hemisphericity

There are some indications that an experienced (English-language) copy typist types more under the control of the right hemisphere than the left.

The first indication is the observation that an experienced typist is often capable of carrying out a matter of fact conversation while copy typing a text of normal complexity on a familiar subject.

Our second observation is that when experienced copy typists are at work, the great majority of them place their manuscripts to the left of their typewriter. We have asked several people who are knowledgeable about typing both in Japan and in the United States for possible explanations, but have not received any which are convincing.

Here, we need to recall some facts about visual lateralization and lateral eye and head turning, both of which have bearing on the functional lateralization of the cerebral hemispheres. First, the anatomical structure of the eyes is such that the nerves from the left half of the retina (upon which the image of the right visual field, RVF, impinges) of both eyes are connected to the left cerebral hemisphere (LH), and the right half of the retina for the left visual field (LVF) to the right cerebral hemisphere (RH).

Next, we note a well-known phenomenon. When the LH is more actively used (e.g., by a verbal task), the eyes (and even the head) generally tend to turn to the right, even when active use of the eyes is not involved [10, 12, 13]. Turning to the opposite direction is generally less conspicuous when people are engaged in manipulo-spatial tasks. The phenomenon is reciprocal in that when the eyes are turned to the right, the LH is more activated, and vice versa.

Based on these neuropsychological facts and the typists' behavior, we conjectured that an accomplished copy typist relies less on the left (language) hemisphere than on the right (manipulo-spatial) hemisphere. If copy typing involves activity of the LH rather than the RH, then it should be advantageous to place a manuscript at the left. That is, an experienced typist may be typing directly through a cortical reflex of the manipulo-spatial RH in response to information from the left visual field.

2.3. Mental Fatigue and Hemisphericity

In the case of typing, the problem of mental fatigue may be more serious than that of physical fatigue because the former appears to have a higher correlation with occupationally related disorders than the latter. The former is also more difficult to measure or estimate. Fortunately, recent research in cognitive psychology offers some fruitful suggestions in this area.

Tucker et al. [19] showed experimentally that, when people are under stress conditions, there is increased frequency of eye movements toward the left direction. This suggests, in conjunction with the correlation between the direction of eye turning and the more actively used (i.e., dominant) hemisphere as we discussed above, that there is greater activation of the right cerebral hemisphere than of the left under a stressed condition, indicating that the right hemisphere is more robust.

Therefore, if our interpretation is correct, then for the design of a Japanese typing system (and perhaps similar man-machine interfaces in general) it may be advantageous to take the robustness of the RH into account.

The reporting of various subjective symptoms of typists was also studied by the Ricoh research team. Operators are asked to answer yes or no to questions about the presence of standard fatigue symptoms after 90-minutes sessions performing some specific tasks in the morning and again in the afternoon. Results of the research indicate that two-stroke code touch typing is by far the best of the three input-related tasks because of less fatigue.

The results of these experiments may be attributable to the dominancy of different cerebral hemispheres. Two-stroke code touch typing is similar in character to simple pattern matching, while vocal transmission requires apparent left hemisphere dominance. Thus we see another indication that a task which requires less left hemisphere activity causes less fatigue.

3. Bipole EEG Measurement

We speculated that, if our hypothesized mechanism adequately explains the observations of English typing, then the same mechanism may be in effect for Japanese touch typing with a proper choice of typing method.

It has been claimed that electroencephalograph (EEG) asymmetry reflects the lateral specialization of cerebral hemispheres for both verbal and spatial tasks [5, 6, 7, 8]. The existence of strong beta waves indicates the active use of an alert hemisphere, whereas the existence of certain strong bipole alpha waves indicates the idling of an awake hemisphere (Figure 2). With this knowledge, we have tried to experimentally test our hypothesis by comparing EEGs taken during Japanese touch typing with ones taken during performances of other standard verbal and spatial tasks [21].

Since Japanese touch typing methods have not been well established, there were no Japanese touch

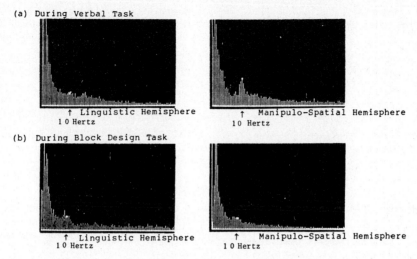

(a) During Verbal Task

↑ Linguistic Hemisphere
1 0 Hertz

↑ Manipulo-Spatial Hemisphere
1 0 Hertz

(b) During Block Design Task

↑ Linguistic Hemisphere
1 0 Hertz

↑ Manipulo-Spatial Hemisphere
1 0 Hertz

Fig. 2 Brain Wave Power Spectra.

typists we could turn to for our test. Therefore, we took two typists who were under training with the Japanese touch typing system "T-code" we have developed [11].

3.1. Methods and Procedures

The experiment was conducted in three sessions with a significant amount of time between sessions. Each session consisted of two sets of four tasks each (see Table 1). Three of these tasks (i.e., reading, writing, and block design) are of ordinary varieties and are discussed in [21]. Here we discuss only the Japanese typing task.

The Japanese typing task was to use T-code, consisting of two-stroke codes for characters. In the first two sessions subjects typed sentences which were selected from their training texts, and in the third session they typed first-sight material. Subjects typed the given texts without checking or pausing.

3.2. Subjects, Measurement and Analysis

The subjects were two female university graduates of ages 23 and 24, and began T-code training for 2 hours a day, 5 days a week, in April, 1982. For both subjects, the total training time was about 120 hours by the first session, 300 hours by the second session, and 330 hours by the third session.

During each of the tasks, we measured the subjects' EEG at points T3-P3, T4-P4 (in the ten/twenty electrode system, see Figure 3) on their scalps [16, 17]. Quiescent state EEGs were also measured for reference with the eyes open and closed, before and after each set of tasks.

Measurement data were recorded by a data recorder via FM radio transmission. The data were then transformed into a power spectrum using a fast Fourier transform (FFT). Each sample was for 6 sec. We chose a reasonable band width and defined the intensity of the right and the left alpha power by integrating the spectrum for this interval. Then we calculated the ratio of the right and the left alpha power (i.e., R/L ratio) using a microcomputer. We

eliminated obvious artifacts in the data by checking them against the EEG curves drawn by a pen recorder. Although our tasks (especially the typing) involved a considerable amount of muscular movements, artifacts from them were less than we had initially feared.

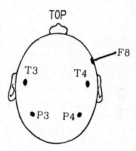

Fig. 3 Electrode Locations in the Ten/Twenty Electrode System.

3.3. Results and Discussion

Table 1 shows the R/L ratios of alpha power centered at 10 Hz, and Table 2 shows the ratios of each task's R/L ratio to that of the block design task. There is no special reason in choosing the block design as a standard. Since we had only two subjects, our results do not give a measure of statistical significance. However, they suggest several possibilities. In an experiment such as this, an interpretation of individual differences is one of the major difficulties. The EEG patterns taken from subject B during the verbal and block design tasks showed significant deviations from the norm. The EEG patterns taken from subject A were fairly standard. In spite of the differences between the subjects, we see some similarities. In both subjects the R/L ratio for the typing task is closer to that of the block design task than to that of the verbal task. In other words, it seems that typing is more of a manipulo-spatial task than a verbal task.

Subject A

session	Session I		Session II		Session III	
task	1	2	1	2	1	2
eyes open	1.27		0.65	1.15	1.98	1.59
eyes closed	1.42	1.25	1.09	1.03	1.26	1.31
typing	1.56	1.51	1.17	1.31	1.60	1.43
reading	1.44	1.52	0.85	0.89	1.37	1.29
writing	1.52	1.94	1.45	1.39	1.89	1.74
block design	1.67	1.59	1.32	1.31	1.63	1.58

Subject B

session	Session I		Session II		Session III	
task	1	2	1	2	1	2
eyes open	0.59	0.54	0.58	0.61	0.43	0.53
eyes closed	0.44	0.44	0.96	0.93	0.48	0.45
typing	0.62	0.67	0.94	0.90	0.42	0.41
reading	0.86	1.13	0.99	1.11	0.52	0.53
writing	0.85	0.97	0.85	0.95	0.44	0.45
block design	0.57	0.64	0.78	0.71	0.44	0.41

Table 1. The R/L ratios of alpha power centered at 10 Hz.

Subject A

session	Session I		Session II		Session III	
task	1	2	1	2	1	2
eyes open	0.76		0.49	0.87	1.21	1.00
eyes closed	0.85	0.79	0.83	0.79	0.77	0.83
typing	0.93	0.95	0.88	1.00	0.98	0.90
reading	0.86	0.95	0.64	0.68	0.84	0.82
writing	0.91	1.22	1.10	1.06	1.16	1.10
block design	1.00	1.00	1.00	1.00	1.00	1.00

Subject B

session	Session I		Session II		Session III	
task	1	2	1	2	1	2
eyes open	1.04	0.84	0.74	0.86	0.97	1.29
eyes closed	0.78	0.69	1.23	1.30	1.09	1.06
typing	1.10	1.03	1.20	1.27	0.95	1.00
reading	1.51	1.75	1.26	1.56	1.17	1.30
writing	1.50	1.52	1.08	1.33	0.99	1.11
block design	1.00	1.00	1.00	1.00	1.00	1.00

Table 2. The ratios of each task's R/L ratio to that of the block design task.

4. Monopole EEG Measurement and Topography

4.1. Topography System

Here we briefly describe the topography system. For the details, see reference [20] or some others.

The topography system consists of two parts. One derives the equivalent EEG potential (EP) defined as the square root of the average EEG power within a desired frequency band of the EEG power spectrum for a 40 sec duration. The EEG data are of the monopolar type. We placed 12 electrodes on the scalp according to the international ten/twenty electrode system with the base lead affixed at both earlobes.

The other function of the system is computation (spatial interpolation and quantization) and mapping. This map is made in a circular form, and is the (EEG) topograph.

4.2. Subjects and Measurement

Our subjects were the same as in the experiments of Section 3. They had about 500 hours of total (training and production work) typing experience at the time of the experiment and they were able to type 100 - 120 Japanese characters per minute for first-sight material. The types of tasks were almost the same as in the previous experiments except that there were two different typing tasks, typing task 1 (on a well practiced text), and typing task 2 (on first-sight text).

During the measurements in each task, we drew the EEG curves of 12 channels with a pen recorder and when we recognized obvious artifacts, we excluded them from the data. Some measuring instruments are susceptible to the interference from the external electromagnetic field, and our experiment was conducted in an electrically shielded room.

4.3. Results and Discussion

Here we mainly discuss topographs of beta waves and the results from the typing tasks. The voltage scale for each is indicated at the side of Figure 4. The top of each topograph corresponds to the frontal lobe, the right to the right hemisphere, and the left to the left hemisphere. (The frequency bandwidth of the beta 1 wave is 13.0 - 19.8 Hz and that of the beta 2 wave is 20.0 - 29.8 Hz.) Other results and their discussions are given in [18].

The EEG topographs of the quiescent state with the eyes closed (See examples in Figure 4) show right and left near symmetries.

Beta 2   Beta 1
Subject A   Subject B

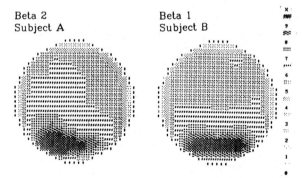

Fig. 4 Topographs in Quiescent State with Eyes Closed.

Figure 5 shows example topographs of typing task 1 (using the well practiced text) and Figure 6 shows some of typing task 2 (using the first-sight text). They show remarkable right and left equivalent EEG potential (EP) *asymmetries*. The topographs here show that EPs of the right hemisphere are overall much higher than those of the left. Specifically, in the topographs for subject A, the EP around point F8 (in the ten/twenty electrode system, see Figure 3) at the right side of the frontal lobe is much higher. This is area 44 or 45 (of the Brodmann Atlas) in the right hemisphere. In the cerebral physiology it is not yet well known what functions are performed in areas 44 and 45 in the right hemisphere. Some conditions in measurements might cause the tentative excess of the EP around point F8 for subject A.

The topographic patterns taken during typing task 1 (using the well practiced text) appear almost the same as those taken during typing task 2 (using the first-sight text).

Beta 2
Subject A

Beta 1
Subject B

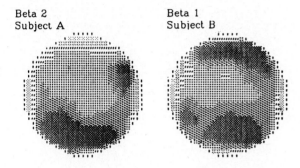

Fig. 5 Topographs in Typing Tasks on a Well Practiced Text.

Beta 2
Subject A

Beta 1
Subject B

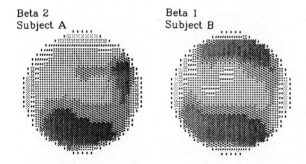

Fig. 6 Topographs in Typing Tasks on First-Sight Text.

5. Concluding Remarks

The characteristics of brain waves widely vary from individual to individual, and it appears that what we know about the nature of brain waves is still limited and the accurate interpretation of EEG measurements is yet to be perfected. In particular, the topography system itself was devised for clinical diagnosis, and there are several problems with using it for measurements during task performances by normal people.

Nevertheless, our findings have some interesting implications. For example it appears that linguistic facilities may not play a significant role in reflex touch typing of Japanese.

In addition, we have plotted brain wave topographs of native American touch typists and have obtained similar EP patterns.

At present, the most popular Japanese input method is the kana-to-kanzi conversion system because of the shorter initial start-up time required. However, with this method a typist would not be able to take advantage of a well developed cortical reflex and would always be slowed down by the need to make conscious decisions. It aspires to use purely phonetic input, but the sound of a kanzi varies depending on its intended meaning in the context, and the involvement of the linguistic facility is inevitable. In addition, the typist always has to be consciously concerned about catching possible wrong homophone selections by the conversion system. Although the decisions and selections involved in each instance are minor, the constant succession of such conscious decisions is irritating and fatiguing.

If our hypothesis is correct, touch typing by unique coding should be better for a professional (copy) typist than kana-to-kanzi conversion because it would allow faster typing with less fatigue.

We think our work provides important insights having physiological foundations into the design of an ergonomically sound input method and accompanying training procedure of typists for it.

Acknowledgement

We gratefully acknowledge the generous assistance rendered by Messrs. Atsushi Shirasawa and Kenzo Yamamoto of Nippondenki (NEC) San-ei Co., Ltd., during our experiments. We also thank Mr. Rand Waltzman of Teknowledge, Inc., of Palo Alto for suggesting improvements to the organization of the text and for polishing our English.

References

1. Bogen, J. E., "The other side of the brain, I: Dysgraphia and dyscopia following cerebral commissurotomy; II: An appositional mind.," *Bulletin of the Los Angeles Neurological Society* 34 pp. 73-105; 135-162 (1969).

2. Bogen, J. E. and Bogen, G. M., "The other side of the brain, III: The corpus callosum and creativity," *Bulletin of the Los Angeles Neurological Society* 34 pp. 191-220 (1969).

3. Bogen, J. E., Tennouten, W. D., and Marsh, J. F., "The other side of the brain, IV: The A/P ratio," *Bulletin of the Los Angeles Neurological Society* 37 pp. 49-61 (1972).

4. Bradshaw, J. L. and Nettleton, N. C., "The nature of hemispheric specialization in man," *Behavioral and Brain Sciences* 4 pp. 51-91 (1981).

5. Doyle, J. C., Orstein, R., and Galin, D., "Lateral specialization of cognitive mode, II: EEG frequency analysis," *Psychophysiology* 11 pp. 567-578 (1974).

6. Galin, D. and Orstein, R., "Lateral specialization of cognitive mode, I: An EEG study," *Psychophysiology* 9 pp. 412-418 (1972).

7. Galin, D. and Ellis, R., "Asymmetry in evoked potentials as an index of lateralized cognitive processes: Relation to EEG alpha asymmetry," *Neuropsychologia* 13 pp. 45-50 (1975).

8. Galin, D., Johnstone, J., and Herron, J., 'Effects of task difficulty on EEG measures of

cerebral engagement,'' *Neuropsychologia* **16** pp. 461-472 (1978).

9. Gazzaniga, M. S. and LeDoux, J. E., *The Integrated Mind,* Plenum Press, New York (1978).

10. Gur, R. E. and Gur, R. C., ''Correlates of conjugate lateral eye movements in man,'' in *Lateralization in the nervous system,* ed. S. Harnad,Academic Press, New York (1977).

11. Hiraga, Y., Ono, Y., and Yamada, H., ''An assignment of key-codes for a Japanese character keyboard,'' *Proceedings of 8-th International Conference on Computational Linguistics,* pp. 249-256 (1980).

12. Kinsbourne, M., ''Eye and hand turning indicates cerebral lateralization,'' *Science* **176** pp. 539-540 (1972).

13. Kinsbourne, M., ''The control of attention by interaction between the cerebral hemispheres,'' in *Attention and performance IV,* ed. S. Kornblum,Academic Press, New York (1973).

14. LeDoux, J. E., Wilson, D. H., and Gazzaniga, M. S., ''Manipulo-spatial aspects of cerebral lateralization: Clues to the origin of lateralization,'' *Neuropsychologia* **15** pp. 743-750 (1977).

15. Myers, R. E. and Sperry, R. W., ''Interocular transfer of a visual form discrimination habit in cats after section of the optic chiasm and corpus callosum,'' *Anatomical Record* **115** pp. 351-352 (1953).

16. N.A.N., ''Report of the Committee on methods of clinical examination in electroencephalography,'' *Electroencephalography and Clinical Neurophysiology* **10** pp. 370-375 (1958).

17. N.A.N., ''Report of the Committee on the status, recruitment and training of students in electroencephalography and clinical neurophysiology,'' *Electroencephalography and Clinical Neurophysiology* **10** pp. 376-378 (1958).

18. Okadome, T., Yamada, H., Ikeda, K., and Saito, M., ''Another brain wave study of cerebral hemisphericity in Japanese touch typing,'' Technical Report 83-13, Department of Information Science, Faculty of Science, University of Tokyo, Tokyo (1983).

19. Tucker, D. M., Roth, R. S., Arneson, B. S., and Buckingham, V., ''Right hemisphere activation during stress,'' *Neuropsychologia* **15** pp. 697-700 (1977).

20. Ueno, S. and Matsuoka, S., ''Topographic display of slow wave types of EEG abnormality in patients with brain lesions,'' *Medical Electronics and Biological Engineering* **14** pp. 24-30 (1976). (In Japanese)

21. Watanabe, H., Yamada, H., Ikeda, K., and Saito, M., ''Cognitive aspects of reflex-code typing for Japanese text,'' *Procedings of International Conference on Chinese Information Processing,* (1983).

22. Yamada, H., ''Certain problems associated with the design of input keyboards for Japanese writing,'' pp. 305-407 in *Cognitive Aspects of Skilled Typewriting,* ed. W. E. Cooper,Springer-Verlag, New York (1983).

Human-Computer Interaction — INTERACT '84 / B. Shackel (ed.)
Elsevier Science Publishers B.V. (North-Holland)
© IFIP, 1985

A COMPARISON OF SELECTION TECHNIQUES: TOUCH PANEL, MOUSE AND KEYBOARD

John Karat, James E. McDonald and Matt Anderson

International Business Machines Corporation
Austin, Texas 78758

A study was conducted testing user performance and attitudes for three types of
selection devices. The subjects were tested on target selection practice tasks, and
in typical computer applications using menu selection and keyboard typing. The study
showed an advantage for on-screen touch panel over keyboard selection, and for
keyboard selection over mouse entry. Differences between this result and those
reporting an advantage of mouse selection are discussed.

1. INTRODUCTION

The process of doing work using a computer
system can be broken down into three steps. The
user must understand the goal of the work to be
accomplished, formulate a task solution (a
series of steps to accomplish a work goal), and
carry out the plan. Whether the user is solving
old problems with a new system, or is experienced with the computer as a problem solving tool,
the final stages require relating the steps of
the solution to the system in a "language" that
the system will understand.

Given that humans have only limited information
processing resources, one goal for system designers is to make the process of relating the
user's goal to the system as easy and natural as
possible. One technique has been the development of interfaces using menus from which an
alternative is selected, rather than typed from
memory. While menu selection on a computer has
generally involved typing on a keyboard, several
recent workstations have designed interfaces
utilizing "more natural" selection mechanisms
(e.g., pointing and voice recognition).

If we examine the process of making selections
from everyday lists, we would find several common selection mechanisms. These include verbal-
izing the selection ("I would like a cheese-
burger and fries."), pointing with the hand to a
selection on a list ("Give me this one.") or
possibly marking a selection with a pencil. It
is interesting to note that selection in a
restaurant reverts to pointing under many
circumstances (e.g., unpronounceable entrees).
One argument for utilizing devices such as touch
panels or joysticks in a computer system is that
they provide a mechanism which allows the user
to point in a relatively natural fashion (i.e.
with a mechanism that tracks hand movement).

The purpose of the current study was to examine
three ways of selecting items in a menu driven
computer system. The methods considered were
selection by pointing and touching an on-screen
item with the hand, selection by moving an

on-screen pointer with an off-screen device, and
selection by typing an identifier associated
with a given display item. These methods can be
thought of as representing different degrees of
"naturalness" of selection.

There are likely to be tradeoffs in the
consideration of selection mechanisms. Though
the mechanics of typing have been studied
extensively (e.g., [3]), relatively little is
known about the limitations of other selection
mechanisms in general computer dialogue use. It
seems intuitive that some pointing devices are
more natural than keyboards for some applications (e.g., graphics), but little is known
about the merits of these devices in applications which currently require the use of a
keyboard for input (e.g., text tasks).
Selection by pointing has been evaluated in a
number of recent studies which carry out
movement of an on-screen pointer through manipulation of off-screen devices, such as keyboard
cursor keys, joysticks, tracker balls and mice
[1]. These studies generally find the mouse to
be the best off-screen pointer manipulation
device, and the mouse was used in this study.

The current experiment was designed to address
some points not considered in reported work.
First, the tasks commonly used in pointer studies were target selection tasks (tasks in which
a subject points to a target randomly positioned
by the system on a VDT). The work reported here
uses a menu system where users were asked to
solve problems using the system. We would like
to verify the conclusions of target experiments
in a more realistic computer dialogue. Next,
most previous studies have not included touch
panels. While there is some recent work which
has included evaluations of touch screens [7],
this work is confined to target selection tasks.
Additionally, previous studies have failed to
evaluate the most common form of menu selection,
the typing of an identifier associated with an
item. Finally, we included a situation in which
menu selection was only part of the dialogue.
Some of our experimental tasks involved typing
information on the system keyboard.

1.1 A Simplified Theory of Selection

While the structure, the terminology used, and a host of other factors undoubtedly affect the use of a menu system, the current work focuses on the selection process. This is done to provide a manageable problem domain for applied cognitive psychology. We treat the selection process as an event consisting of several components. This technique has been found useful in modeling human cognitive behavior [4, 2].

There are many well learned "natural" selection procedures. If someone makes a menu selection in normal human interaction, it is not generally necessary to instruct them in how to do it (although someone did at one time). For human-computer interactions, a menu can help the user to decide <u>what</u> to do, and <u>how</u> to do it. The user may have to be instructed in a "new" selection method (i.e. telling them that the machine can't hear them or doesn't know where their finger is pointing). For a new user there may be cognitive costs associated with learning the new method. If the selection method is not a simple extension of well learned procedures, the user must devote attention to figuring out how to convey the selection to the system. On the other hand, studies have shown that well learned methods tend to be performed very rapidly and with little cognitive requirements (e.g., [5]).

With a "natural" menu selection the user:

> Carries out the decision process, then indicates the choice.

For a "new" selection process, the user must:

> Carry out the decision process, figure out how to indicate the choice, then indicate the choice.

With experience, the additional steps required to figure out how to indicate the choice become well learned themselves. That is, the procedure for indicating a choice becomes automatic, and the individual does not have to devote additional resources to it. The exact mechanisms for procedure automation are not considered here (see [6], for a more detailed discussion), only the distinction between new and relatively well known procedures is needed. Even though people do learn new procedures, a desirable system design goal is to limit device-specific knowledge (knowledge required to operate specific system components). This makes learning through the integration of system procedures into existing knowledge easier by making computer dialogue consistent with "natural" dialogues.

This might suggest an advantage for direct pointing, but the issue is still complex. Card, Moran and Newell [2] have shown that formal task analysis can be used to aid in making design decisions. This task analysis breaks behavior down into a number of cognitive cycles and motor components, and can be used to predict operator performance. If we assume users are familiar with all three methods, it is possible to carry out such an analysis and reduce selection for each to a single thought cycle and a single physical movement. Though the distances moved by the hand may vary for the three methods, the difference would be slight, and the analysis would suggest little difference between the methods. However, it does not seem that this analysis captures all elements needed to insure "ease of use" for a range of users.

While a keystroke-level analysis might work for well learned tasks, it is not clear that it can be extended to more complex tasks. One problem with using such a model in a cognitively complex domain is estimating with any certainty the number of cognitive cycles required for an activity. The thought cycles are viewed by Card et al. [2] as corresponding to a processing cycle of about 100 msec. duration. While it might be possible to agree on the number of cognitive steps of this time order required for fairly simple well learned tasks, cognitive science has not developed sufficiently to provide detailed models for much of normal cognitive behavior. It is not clear that pointing with a mouse requires the same amount of cognitive processing as finger pointing, or if switching input devices increases processing. We could provide estimates of cognitive load for switching between input devices, but we would certainly want to verify empirically such estimates before accepting them as valid. Since a large percentage of task time might be spent in simply making selections, it is important to carefully consider the tradeoffs involved.

2. METHOD

2.1 Subjects

Twenty-six subjects (25 females and one male) were paid to participate in the study. Subjects were obtained from a temporary employment agency and ranged in age from 18 to 57 years with self reported typing rates ranging from 30 to over 100 words per minute. Forty-two percent of the subjects had obtained college degrees, fifty percent had some college but no degree, and the remaining eight percent had completed high school. Most of the subjects (83%) reported some word processing experience, but only four had any programming experience. Two subjects failed to complete the experimental tasks and were excluded from the analyses. All reported analyses are based on data obtained from the 24 subjects who successfully completed the experiment.

2.2 Apparatus and Task Environments

An IBM Personal Computer (PC) served as the experimental controller. Three independent input devices were attached to the PC (a touch panel, a mouse, and a keyboard) such that each could be used to select options from menus presented on the "task display" (a 13 inch IBM Color

Monitor). The input devices were an Elographics analog-membrane touch panel, a Mouse Systems optical mouse, and a standard IBM PC keyboard. The "instruction display" (a 12 inch IBM Monochrome Monitor) was used to present instructions, application descriptions, and individual menu tasks to the subjects. Subjects sat facing the two displays with the keyboard located between the subject and the displays throughout the experiment. The touch panel was attached to the front of the task display during all input device conditions. The mouse was located on a metal pad next to the subject's preferred-hand side of the keyboard during the mouse-device conditions, and was moved away for keyboard and touch panel conditions. The keyboard was used as a menu selection device for the keyboard-device condition, and for entering text into "fields" during all three conditions.

Two computer-based systems were developed for the experiment and simulated on the PC. The two menu task environments (applications) simulated a computer telephone aid and a personal appointment calendar. Both of the applications appeared to the subject as hierarchically organized menus from which the subjects selected options. Additionally, half of the tasks that the subjects were asked to perform required the entry of typed information into the system (such as names, comments or telephone numbers). Thus subjects performed tasks (e.g., calling someone from a directory or changing an appointment) which required selecting options with a device and typing into selected fields from the keyboard. The system responded to subject input by appearing to perform the specified actions (actual telephone connections were not made nor did an appointment data base exist).

The two applications differed in structure and complexity. The depth (number of selections needed to reach a given action) and breadth (number of options available from a given state) of the two systems' menu hierarchies were different. The number of menu selections for the required tasks ranged from one to eight for the telephone system tasks, and from three to eleven for the calendar tasks. The calendar tasks included: reviewing daily schedules, checking past and future appointments, scheduling new appointments, and modifying existing appointments. The telephone tasks involved calling persons listed in various directories and modifying those directories by changing the contents of entries, deleting entries, or creating new entries.

2.3 Experimental Design

All subjects used all three input devices to perform tasks within both applications. This resulted in a 3 (device) by 2 (application) within-subjects design. The order in which the subjects used the input devices was based on a Latin-Square, with three device orderings used (keyboard/touch panel/mouse, touch panel/mouse/keyboard, and mouse/keyboard/touch panel). Application order (telephone/calendar or calendar/telephone) was counterbalanced across subjects. This resulted in a total of six groups to which the subjects were assigned in a pseudo-random fashion. Within each condition, the order of presentation of individual tasks and applications remained constant across devices. A set of practice trials preceeded each set of tasks. During an experimental session, subjects used the first input device to perform 25 practice trials, 10 tasks in the first application, 25 additional practice trials, and then performed 10 tasks in the second application. This procedure was repeated for the two remaining input devices. In total, subjects completed two sets of practice trials (one set before each application) and two sets of application tasks (10 tasks in each task environment) for each of three devices.

2.4 Procedure

Subjects received practice with the appropriate input device prior to performing tasks within an application. Practice consisted of selecting a target "button" which appeared in random locations on the task display. Subjects were instructed to select the target as rapidly as possible while keeping selection errors to a minimum. Targets were outlined boxes (14x13 mm) with a single letter inside. On each practice trial the screen would go blank and then the target box would appear. The position of the target box and the box label ("a" through "z") were randomly selected on each trial.

Selection with the touch panel involved touching anywhere inside the target with the subject's finger. Selection with the keyboard involved typing the letter which appeared inside the target box. Selection with the mouse involved positioning the screen pointer inside the target and pressing any button on the mouse. Movements of the mouse resulted in equal movements (1:1) of the pointer on the task display. Target selection time was measured from the appearance of the target on the display to the selection of the target with the input device.

Following the 25 practice trials subjects read general task instructions along with a brief description of the upcoming application (no attempt was made to develop a complete instruction manual for the applications). The first menu panel of the appropriate application appeared on the task display and the task descriptions were presented sequentially on the instruction screen. The successful completion of one task (detected by the simulation system) initiated the presentation of the next task description and returned the application to the first menu panel. Subjects learned the telephone and calendar systems by attempting to complete the assigned tasks. No additional assistance was provided.

Subjects performed the same 20 tasks using each of the three input devices. Visually, the menus were identical for each input device condition.

A single prompt line at the bottom of the screen displayed "Select your choice." (since the tasks followed practice with the current selection method, we did not expect or observe confusion with how selections were to be made). All tasks required menu selections, and half of the tasks also required text entry into "fields". In order to enter text into fields, subjects first selected the target field on the task display. After selection the field was "activated" by the system, and visually identified by a prompt line. Subjects then typed the required information into the selected field, using backspace correction if necessary, and deactivated the field when finished by pressing the RETURN key. Task completion time was measured from the presentation of the problem on the instruction screen to completion of the entries to satisfy the goal stated in the problem.

3.   RESULTS

3.1   Preference Data

Subjects were asked to indicate preferences between the input devices for the experimental tasks. After all tasks were completed, subjects were asked to answer a series of questions comparing all pairs of input devices for different task types (practice, selection only, and selection with typing), and applications. There was no significant difference between the preference ratings for the two applications (calendar and telephone), or between the practice and selection only tasks. Table 1 summarizes the results for the 24 subjects.

	Selection Only			Selection with Typing		
	Touch	Key	Mouse	Touch	Key	Mouse
First	12	11	1	7	17	0
Second	11	10	3	14	6	4
Third	1	3	20	3	1	20

Table 1. Preference order for input devices.

For all tasks the subjects preferred the keyboard or touch panel to the mouse. The keyboard and touch panel were given similar preference ratings for selection only tasks. For tasks with both selection and typing, subjects preferred the keyboard over the touch panel. The difference between stated preference based on task type indicates some desire by subjects not to switch input devices.

3.2 Performance Data - Practice Tasks

In total, each subject completed two sets of 25 practice trials for each of the three input devices. Equipment problems caused practice data from five of the subjects to be lost. For the remaining 19 subjects a 3 (device) by 2 (set) within subject analysis of variance for the mean of each set of practice trials was performed. Main effects for device ($F(2,36) = 54.9$) and

set ($F(1,18) = 36.9$), and the device by set interaction ($F(2,36) = 10.2$), were all significant. Subjects were faster making selections with the touch panel and keyboard (0.8 and 1.1 secs. overall) than with the mouse (2.7 secs.). All devices showed improvement for second set over first, showing a strong practice effect. The difference between the mouse and the other devices was greater on the first set (1.0 and 1.2 for the touch screen and keyboard respectively and 3.3 secs. for the mouse) than the second set (0.7 and 1.0 secs. for touch panel and keyboard and 2.0 secs. for mouse).

3.3   Performance Data - Menu Tasks

Subjects completed the application tasks three times, once with each input device. Table 2 summarizes the total time to complete the 20 menu tasks for the three repetitions. Each block includes 10 tasks within each application. Note that subjects using one device for the first block used a different device on the second and third blocks.

		Block	
	First	Second	Third
Touch panel	1805.3	874.9	676.2
Keyboard	1862.1	991.8	808.5
Mouse	1884.5	1189.7	897.5

Table 2. Time in secs. to complete menu tasks.

There is a clear tendency to complete the task sets faster with experience. Subjects took over 30 minutes on the average to complete the first block of 20 tasks (10 calendar and 10 telephone tasks), and less than half that time to complete the tasks on the third repetition. This can be attributed to experience with the applications. Remember that the actual applications were new to the subjects, and the first block times include considerable learning times.

The times to complete the menu tasks were subjected to an analysis of variance. Presentation order of the devices was a between subjects variable with eight subjects in each of three device order groups (keyboard/touch panel/mouse, mouse/keyboard/touch panel, and touch panel/-mouse/keyboard). Each subject used three devices, two task types (selection only and selection with typing) and two applications.

Several of the main effects are not of particular interest here. While there is a significant difference between performance on the two applications ($F(1,21) = 59.9$, with the telephone task faster), the two task types ($F(1,21) = 152.7$, with selection only faster), and an interaction between application and task type performance ($F(1,21) = 48.8$), no attempt was made to control or equate these factors. The focus was on providing varied task types and applications, without studying the relative difficulty.

There is a significant difference in performance for the three input devices ($F(2,42) = 6.1$). Additional analysis shows a significant difference between the touch panel and mouse performance. No significant difference was found for comparisons of the keyboard with mouse or touch panel. Additionally there is no significant interaction between task type and device, application and device, or task by application by device (i.e. no difference in the pattern of the main effect of device for the different applications or tasks). Thus there is no difference in the device effects for different tasks or applications.

4. DISCUSSION

Both the subjective evaluations and the performance data suggest that the touch panel and the keyboard are better selection devices than the mouse. Performance measures in the applications showed an improvement of approximately 10% for touch panel over keyboard and 10% for keyboard over mouse. The difference was similar for selection only and mixed selection and typing tasks. For practice tasks, which were simple target selection tasks, the performance difference is much greater. However, it should be kept in mind that actual selection represents only a part of the application dialogue (it is estimated that selection time composed approximately 12 - 25% of the task time for the given experiment).

Several interesting considerations result from this work. Given that the subjects in this experiment were all skilled typists, and we assume also skilled pointers, it is perhaps not surprising to find a performance advantage for typed and hand pointing mechanisms. The mouse was a new device for all subjects (note that performance gains over the practice trials were greater for the mouse than for the other devices). The performance results are slightly different than those one might expect from the preference data. Even though the subjects stated a preference for keyboard entry in mixed entry tasks, the performance data shows an advantage for touch panel input.

Given the research reports of advantages of the mouse as an input device, the failure of the mouse in the current work is interesting. Three possible sources for this might be mentioned. The first possible factor is typing skill. Since the this study used only skilled typists, it may be that this biased the study in favor of the well known device (the keyboard). Additional studies should test both skilled and non-skilled typists in a controlled fashion. The second factor is sex of the subjects. This study involved mostly female subjects, and there has been considerable investigation of sex differences in spatial processing tasks. The manipulation of the mouse to control the positioning of a screen pointer can be considered as a spatial task. Further work should be done to examine male and female subjects. The third

factor is amount of practice. Even unskilled typists are far more familiar with the keyboard than they are with the mouse. While limitations on our experiment prohibit us from developing "mouse experts", we feel that additional information could be obtained by extending the amount of practice with each selection device.

It would be difficult to account for these findings within the framework suggested by Card et al. [2]. One way to account for the results of this study is to suggest that keyboard menu entry and mouse selection required additional cognitive processing compared to finger pointing. This would be consistent with the notion that touch selection is a highly automated skill for most humans, and that other techniques are less well learned. We do not suggest that this study renders previous findings invalid, only that more attention needs to be given to the nature of the dialogues for which the device is to be used, and the skills of the users. At the very least we must conclude that "unnatural" devices such as a keyboard, can in some circumstances both be preferred and lead to better performance than "natural" pointing devices such as a mouse. This study is part of a series being conducted to examine the issues raised.

REFERENCES:

1. Card, S. K., English, W. K., and Burr, B. J. (1978). Evaluation of mouse, rate-controlled isometric joystick, step keys, and text keys for text selection on a CRT. *Ergonomics*, 21, 601-613.

2. Card, S. K., Moran, T. P., and Newell, A. (1983). The Psychology of Human-Computer Interaction. Hillsdale, N.J.: Erlbaum.

3. Cooper, W. E. (1983). Cognitive Aspects of Skilled Typewriting. New York, N.Y.: Springer-Verlag.

4. Newell, A. & Simon, H. A. (1972). Human Problem Solving, Hillsdale, N.J.: Prentice Hall.

5. Shiffrin, R. M., and Dumais, S. T. (1981). The development of automatism. In J. R. Anderson, (Ed.), Cognitive Skills and Their Acquisition, 111-140, Hillsdale, N.J.: Erlbaum.

6. Shiffrin, R. M., and Schneider, W. (1977). Controlled and automatic human information processing: II. Perceptual learning, automatic attending, and a general theory. *Psychological Review*, 84, 127-190.

7. Whitfield, D., Ball, R. G., and Bird, J. M. (1983). Some comparisons of on-display and off-display touch input devices for interaction with computer generated displays. *Ergonomics*, 26, 1033-1054.

Human-Computer Interaction — INTERACT '84 / B. Shackel (ed.)
Elsevier Science Publishers B.V. (North-Holland)
© IFIP, 1985

THE EFFECTS OF INPUT MEDIUM AND TASK ALLOCATION STRATEGY ON PERFORMANCE OF A HUMAN-COMPUTER SYSTEM

Siu-Tong Lam and Joel S. Greenstein

Department of Industrial Engineering and Operations Research
Virginia Polytechnic Institute and State University
Blacksburg, Virginia
U.S.A.

The allocation of tasks between human and computer, and the merits of a dynamic approach to this allocation are discussed. Dynamic task allocation requires efficient human-computer communication. This communication may be accomplished in an implicit or explicit manner. A conceptual framework for the study of explicit human-computer communication is introduced and a study exemplifying the use of the framework is presented. This study investigated the effects of two input media and four task allocation strategies on the performance of a human-computer system. The task environment represented a simplified version of an air traffic control scenario wherein computer aid could be evoked by the human to accomplish task sharing between the human and the computer.

1.0 HUMAN-COMPUTER TASK ALLOCATION

Function allocation has always been central in the design of any complex human-machine system. Systems engineers distinguish between "function" and "task." "Function" is defined as "a general means or action by which the system fulfills its requirements" [1]. "Task" is described at the behavioral level, and is construed to be "a composite of related activities performed by an individual, and directed toward accomplishing a specific amount of work within a specific work context" [1]. Now that the computer is capable of human behavioral-like activities, allocation of responsibilities between human and machine can be extended to a lower system level. We should also consider task allocation between human and machine. For the sake of this discussion both function and task allocation are intermingled.

With the desire to enhance cost-effectiveness and productivity, past practice has been to mechanize everything possible. Mechanization extends the physical capabilities of the human, though it entails physical displacement of some workers. Despite human versatility, the bounds of human physical capabilities are extremely limited. Well-conceived machines can readily take over human labor, and even outperform the human in the physical domain, although the human is still prized for versatility and mental abilities. For such reasons, traditional task allocation between human and machine has been relatively straightforward. Rieger and Greenstein [2] outline some of the classical methods of task allocation and note certain limitations of these methods. In essence, the classical approach dissects system function into its constituents (other functions, tasks, and subtasks), and then allocates tasks to either human or machine according to some generalizations regarding human and machine abilities (e.g., Fitts' list; in [3]). This allocation is necessarily "static;" once implemented, it is largely situation-independent and unchanging over time.

Computerization has since increased in sophistication to a level capable of mimicking or enhancing some uniquely human functions. The implications for task allocation between human and machine are intriguing. First, the computer has not become the mental equivalent of the human; it excels in some abilities but is deficient in others. Automation entails some form of mental displacement. This occurs, for instance, when an operator is replaced by a computer and then becomes the supervisor of the computer. As a result, human involvement lingers on in the working loop. As the development of the computer continues, putting the human in the right place, in the right way, and at the same time providing for human needs is a particularly arduous endeavor.

Second, generalizations such as Fitts' list are becoming increasingly inadequate. They are non-quantitative, subjective, overly general [2]; they do not reflect other important situational considerations (e.g., trade-offs of the various costs, as related by Chapanis [4]); and they do not consider the integration and collaboration of human and computer [5]. Hence, systems engineers should exercise discretion when using these general guidelines as a basis for task allocation.

Third, most machines have traditionally been designed with a static role in mind, and have been used in relatively static environments. Because the machine performed only one function, static task allocation was adequate. However, the computer, with its abilities analogous to human cognitive abilities, can be more flexible in its role and in the kind of task it performs. Classical methods of task allocation do not permit systems engineers to exploit this flexibility.

Finally, allocation of functions in human-computer systems might in large part be determined by other considerations than the comparisons of Fitts' list. These considerations include social, economic, political, psychological, and philosophical criteria [4, 6]. It is not only a matter of which entity will perform the task better; there are larger issues beyond this. The systems engineer must be sensitive to these more encompassing organizational issues as well.

Various parties have voiced their approaches to this predicament (see, for example, Nickerson, et al. [6]). Despite different opinions on task allocation, there is a consensus that the human and computer relationship should be complementary (e.g., Licklider [7]; Jordan [8]; Hormann [9]; Rouse [10]). Rouse [11, 12] identified an approach to achieving an adaptive complementary relationship. It is important that responsibilities (functions, tasks, and subtasks) be dynamically allocated to the human or computer in multiple task situations where the entities possess overlapping capabilities. This is especially necessary for human-computer systems in the control of dynamic systems [12]. A dynamic approach allocates a particular task to the decision maker that has at that moment the resources available to perform the task. Dynamic allocation is adaptive in the sense that the allocation depends on the state of the system as well as the states of the decision makers. Rieger and Greenstein [2] showed that by incorporating dynamic allocation in the overall task allocation process, the systems engineer is able to tackle the allocation problem in a more flexible, comprehensive, and systematic manner.

Dynamic task allocation is advantageous from the system and human perspectives [10, 11]. The human and computer resources available within the system are more effectively utilized. This can be visualized using a queueing theoretic analysis wherein customers are more promptly served when servers can move freely among queues. With dynamic task allocation the human and computer are active simultaneously and each has knowledge about the other's present state. Systems with such parallel components are more fault-tolerant than those without them. Moreover, the human is not separated from some system subtasks; he is thus able to retain necessary knowledge and skill about system operation which can be evoked in case of need (e.g., upon computer failure or malfunction). This contributes to overall system fault tolerance and mitigates human motivational problems as well. The need for periodic retraining and the variability of human workload are also reduced.

2.0 HUMAN-COMPUTER COMMUNICATION

Allocation of responsibilities can be initiated by the human or computer, though intuitively it would be more motivating (but more work) for the human to assume the active role. In either case, human-computer communication is essential to inform the other party when and where one will allocate attention. Two types of communication can be utilized to convey the messages: implicit or model-based communication and explicit or dialogue-based communication [13].

Implicit communication uses models of human performance to enable the computer to work cooperatively with the human in a reasonably conflict-free fashion. The computer uses these models to predict what the human is likely to do next. The computer then attends to tasks which will be neglected by the human. Communication is implied, and the computer utilizes these implicit messages to complement the human by averting conflicting or redundant actions.

There is an important advantage to the design of a human-computer coupling such that the computer actively seeks to accomodate the human. The human retains the initiative and primacy of his/her role, and the computer remains the human's aide [14]. Rouse [12] provides two additional reasons for employing implicit communiction. The first is to avoid the extra human workload associated with explicit communication. Second, implicit communication may be useful for tapping information which the human is unable to supply explicitly. For instance, a model may be used to predict that the human will devote an inordinate amount of attention to instruments which are irrelevant to the current task set.

A series of recent studies illustrates some intriguing properties and the potential utility of implicit communication (Greenstein and Revesman [13]; Revesman and Greenstein, [15, 16, 17]). In a simulation investigation, Greenstein and Revesman [13] demonstrated: (1) the importance of the computer using the correct

algorithm to act upon model-based communication; choosing a poor algorithm can lead to poorer performance than that obtained with no model at all; (2) when an appropriate algorithm was used, system performance increased linearly with the predictive validity of the model; (3) for the conditions simulated, explicit communication achieved better system performance than implicit communication. However, as the time cost associated with explicit communication increased, implicit communication fared better, even when achieved via a relatively poor model. Greenstein and Revesman concluded that the trade-offs between the two types of communication in dynamic task allocation can and should be carefully considered. In the ensuing studies, Revesman and Greenstein [16, 17] further demonstrated the feasibility of model-based communication by the validation and implementation of their model in a process control environment.

Explicit communication focuses upon the process in which the human uses some kind of computer input mechanism to explicitly relate intentions to the computer. This form of communication is relatively simple to implement, and it averts conflicts of responsibilities between the human and computer with a high degree of certainty. In comparing implicit with explicit communication, the merits of one can be visualized as the demerits of the other. As mentioned earlier, Greenstein and Revesman [13] conducted a simulation study to investigate possible trade-offs between implicit and explicit communication. They note that implicit communication entails a time cost for development and verification of models, an ambiguity cost (the model will not be perfectly predictive of human performance), and an increased load on the computer (when the model demands a great deal of computation). It also requires that the computational complexity of the model is amenable to real time implementation, that the intricacy of the human behavior in question can be represented by a model, and that the parameters concerned are measurable (Rouse [12]; Rieger and Greenstein, [2]). Explicit communication entails direct entry time cost and extra load on the human. As Greenstein and Revesman [13] remarked, there are likely to be situations in which one kind of communication will be superior to the other.

3.0 A CONCEPTUAL FRAMEWORK

To better understand and utilize explicit communication for dynamic task allocation, one can study the factors that generally define interaction between human and computer. These factors include the human user, the computer and system, the task, the task environment, and the human-computer interface. The human-computer interface is of particular interest to system designers because in most systems the other factors are either given or relatively fixed; interface design becomes the most flexible tool for enhancing explicit communication.

The interface factor can be further delineated into four subfactors, each amenable to investigation and variation. These subfactors include the medium, the directly communicative hardware used in any human-computer interaction (e.g., dedicated function keys and voice recognition equipment); the mode, the directly communicative software used in the interaction (e.g., menu selection and command language); the style of information presentation used within a particular mode (e.g., color and formatting); and the strategy, the goal-directed decision and choice of action from among various alternatives. Strategies may be dialogue, task, or task allocation related. One dialogue strategy might be to provide the human with a set of possible messages, permitting a choice from this set. Task strategy pertains to the ways a given task and mission can be fulfilled by the human-computer system. Task allocation strategy concerns how tasks are allocated between human and computer and is particularly important to the specification of explicit communication for dynamic task allocation.

This framework provides a structure for systematic investigation. A four-dimensional array comprised of different combinations of the interface subfactors can be constructed. The goal is to identify those subfactor combinations which specify appropriate interface designs for a given application. A study was conducted (1) to exemplify the use of the framework to conceptualize and delineate the human-computer communication problem; and (2) to determine how system performance is affected by different media and task allocation strategies.

4.0 A STUDY OF INPUT MEDIA AND TASK ALLOCATION STRATEGY

4.1 THE EXPERIMENTAL TASK

A Generic ENvironment for Interactive Experiments (GENIE), designed for behavioral research on human-computer interaction in real-time multiple task situations was employed [18]. The task environment represented a simplified version of an air traffic control scenario wherein computer aid could be evoked by the human to accomplish task sharing between human and computer.

The primary display monitor showed a radar-like screen with moving aircraft, a guide path and runway, aircraft status, approach information, and remarks (Figure 1). Also displayed was feedback regarding the total number of planes landed and lost. Planes that followed the designated flight path and landed on the cross hatch were scored as successful landings. Planes flown out of the displayed control area were scored as lost. The dotted path served as a navigation guide for normal landings. A secondary display monitor was used to echo-print human command inputs, and to display messages from the computer (e.g., error messages and requested information).

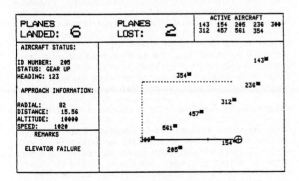

Figure 1 : The primary display

Planes entered onto the upper right corner of the primary display monitor at a predetermined rate. The subject was to direct and land these planes safely and efficiently onto the runway according to one of two landing patterns. Identification numbers of "normal"

planes were displayed in white (against a blue background) in the active aircraft window, and were to be landed adhering to the normal landing path. Identification numbers of planes encountering emergency situations were coded in red; these planes could abandon the guide path and land via the shortest route onto the runway. Ideally three "TURN" commands would be sufficient for each normal landing, and two for each emergency landing. In actual practice, more commands were typically necessary due to imperfect specification and timing of commands. In some of the conditions, computer aid was made available when the human issued specific "TAKE" commands. The computer-assisted planes would then be coded as round blips instead of square ones, and they would be landed without further human involvement.

In sum, the present scenario represented a high-workload, moderately complex, frequent (i.e., the tasks are performed frequently), open (i.e., the tasks are open to the influence of external parameters), and dynamic multiple task system.

Five male and five female students at Virginia Polytechnic Institute and State University participated voluntarily in this study, and they received $3.50 per hour. Students were considered ineligible if they were pilots or air traffic controllers, if they had extensive experience in playing video games, or if they had previous experience in similar kinds of studies. Prospective subjects were screened for corrected 20/20 vision using a Bausch & Lomb Ortho-Rater and were given a one-minute typing test. Those who could type at least twenty words per minute were accepted.

The basic hardware comprised a DEC GIGI terminal (model VK100), plus two Barco Model GD33 color monitors interfaced to a DEC VAX 11/780 host computer. The right monitor was the primary graphics display and the left monitor was the secondary command display. A protractor was attached to the terminal for directional aid. An intercom was available in case the subject wished to communicate to the experimenter. The sessions were closely monitored by the experimenter in an adjacent room using terminals slaved to the two task displays.

4.2 INDEPENDENT VARIABLES

In the context of our framework for the study of human-computer interfaces, the present study was two-dimensional in the sense that only input media and allocation stategies were investigated. Either dedicated function keys or the standard Sholes qwerty keyboard was used as the medium to input task commands (e.g., "TURN" and "SAY") and allocation commands (e.g., "TAKE").

Four allocation strategies plus a control condition were studied:
(1) Control condition, wherein no computer aid was available and the human performed all tasks.
(2) Assignment by designation, wherein the computer might be requested to take over certain tasks pinpointed by their associated identification numbers.

The human could issue, for example, the command "TAKE 200" to ask the computer to take control of the plane numbered "200." Up to four planes could be allocated to the computer at one time.

(3) Spatial assignment, wherein tasks within a certain spatial confine were assigned to the computer. The control area was partitioned into four indexed quadrants, and the human could issue, for example, the command "TAKE QUAD 1" to signify that planes within quadrant one were to be controlled by the computer. A maximum of two quadrants could be assigned at one time.

(4) Temporal assignment, wherein tasks occurring within a certain time frame were assigned to the computer. Using the "TAKE NEXT" command, the human could assign up to the next four planes entering the control area to the computer at one time.

(5) Contingency-based assignment, wherein responsibilities for certain contingencies (here, emergencies) were assigned to the computer. The "TAKE EMERG" command would effect computer control of all planes on the screen currently encountering emergencies.

It was hoped that this delineation of strategies might be generalizable to other multiple task situations. Clearly there are other possible strategies or combinations of strategies that might be incorporated in future studies. It shall be argued in the following discussion that there are important idiosyncratic differences in the selected strategies.

There were ten treatment conditions resulting from the crossing of two input media with four allocation strategies plus one control condition. Each of the ten subjects received all the treatments in a balanced Latin Square design.

4.3 RESULTS

Fourteen performance measures were metered on-line during the study. These measures can be grouped into five clusters, each reflecting a different aspect of system performance, as presented in Table 1. Analyses of variance revealed significant medium and strategy effects on a number of the performance measures. However, no significant interaction effects were found. Open-ended questions were also presented to the subjects at the end of the experiment.

Table 1
Performance Measures

Overall System Performance Measure:
% landed by system — The percentage of planes entering the control area that were landed by the human-computer system.

Human Performance Measures:
% landed by human — The percentage of planes entering the control area that were landed by the human.
% correct commands — The percentage of commands entered by the human that were syntactically correct.

Computer Performance Measures:
% landed by computer — The percentage of planes entering the control area that were landed by the computer.
# TAKE commands — The number of TAKE commands issued.
# planes to computer — The number of planes assigned to the computer.

Human Error Measures:
errors — The number of action and syntax errors committed by the human.
approaches missed — The number of landing approaches missed by the human.
syntax errors — The number of syntax errors committed by the human.

Human Workload Measures:
commands — The total number of commands issued by the human.
TURN commands — The number of TURN commands issued.
SAY commands — The number of SAY commands issued.
SHOW commands — The number of SHOW commands issued.

4.3.1 MEDIUM.

Table 2
Mean Performance Measures by Input Medium

Measure	Qwerty Keyboard	Function Keys	Percentage Difference	F Ratio	p
% landed by system	58.87	64.67	+9.85	4.60	.0353
% landed by human	32.33	37.80	+16.91	6.03	.0165
% correct commands	88.35	93.33	+5.64	38.98	.0001
% landed by computer	26.53	26.87	+1.26	0.02	.8785
# TAKE commands	4.98	5.30	+6.43	0.44	.5108
# planes to computer	9.88	9.68	-2.02	0.08	.7768
# errors	25.40	19.26	-24.17	15.06	.0002
# planes lost	4.70	3.18	-32.34	8.14	.0057
# approaches missed	5.66	5.60	-1.06	0.01	.9111
# syntax errors	16.50	10.54	-36.12	17.62	.0001
# commands	134.40	146.50	+9.00	10.08	.0022
# TURN commands	94.90	108.16	+13.97	16.36	.0001
# SAY commands	0.20	0.32	+60.00	0.80	.3750
# SHOW commands	17.66	22.06	+24.58	15.51	.0002

Table 2 summarizes the differences in performance obtained with the qwerty keyboard and function keys conditions. As was expected, there was a significant effect of input medium on performance. Both performance and subjective preference measures indicated that function keys were the more desirable tool for input communication. In general, when function keys were used, more planes were landed and fewer errors were made. The use of function keys had the greatest effect on human performance (and ultimately overall system performance). The effect on computer performance was not significant. Eight of the ten subjects preferred function keys, mainly for their keying efficiency. Subjects input commands at a faster rate, accomplished more tasks, felt a greater sense of control, and experienced less stress in the function keys condition. Subjects also issued significantly more commands using function keys. When function keys were used, subjects clearly exerted more frequent control of the tasks.

Function keys may represent a better input medium than the qwerty keyboard because they permit a faster input rate and convey structured input cues to the user that demand less cognitive processing. Function keys are especially desirable in situations where the tasks, subtasks, and commands are relatively simple, the number of possible commands is comparatively small, and the input rate is of considerable importance. When the task environment becomes more open and complex, and when the total number of possible commands increases, selecting and locating the correct function keys becomes taxing.

Subjects who preferred the qwerty keyboard mentioned its inherent flexibility. As the number of possible commands increases in a situation, there is likely a point beyond which the qwerty keyboard becomes a better input medium than function keys. Another comment made by those who preferred the qwerty keyboard was that the longer keying time imposed by it enabled them to contemplate the appropriateness of their command and objective before the command was issued. As a result, erroneous or inadequate commands could be averted. The enforced delay may be beneficial in that it increases the opportunity for cognitive participation.

4.3.2 STRATEGY.

Significant differences were noted in all but two of the performance measures. Post-hoc least significant difference tests were performed to determine the loci of significance. Representative results of these tests are presented in Table 3. As that table shows, the control condition, in which computer aiding was not available, resulted in the fewest planes landed and the most planes lost. This condition was also the least preferred by the subjects. Of the four different allocation strategies considered, spatial assignment (QUAD), contingency-based assignment (EMERG), and assignment by designation (ID) achieved the highest levels of overall system performance. Temporal assignment (NEXT) was significantly poorer in this regard, as Table 3 indicates. Subjective ratings revealed an overall preference for assignment by designation, followed by spatial assignment and contingency-based assignment. Subjects rated assignment by designation the most flexible strategy, while they considered spatial assignment to be the most powerful strategy.

The four different strategies studied possessed diverse characteristics; consequently they entailed dissimilar cognitive processing. First, the four strategies referred to different dimensions. Obviously spatial assignment concerned the dimension of space; temporal assignment, the dimension of time; assignment by designation and contingency-based assignment some particular cases within a certain time and space. The different reference dimensions varied in their degree of abstraction. Time would seem to be a more fluid and abstract concept than space, while referring to specific planes or contingencies is probably least abstract. If so, temporal assignment entailed manipulation of the most abstract concept.

Next, the four strategies differed in degree of specificity. Assignment by designation was the most specific strategy in that it could pinpoint particular planes for assignment to the computer. Temporal assignment and contingency-based assignment were the next most discriminative, and spatial assignment was the least.

With respect to flexibility, assignment by designation was the most flexible strategy in the sense that it could be used to assign virtually any subset of the planes currently on the screen to the computer. This was reflected in the comments of the subjects who participated in the experiment. Spatial assignment ranked next in flexibility, followed by contingency-based assignment and temporal assignment.

The four strategies also differed in power. This word is taken to imply the average number of planes that can be allocated at one time per command. Spatial assignment was the most powerful strategy in that it could be used to allocate the greatest number of planes at one time. This is reflected by the fact that while spatial assignment was among the strategies associated with the smallest number of TAKE commands, the percentage of planes landed by the computer was greatest in this condition. Depending on the total number of emergency planes on the screen, contingency-based assignment might have been equally powerful at times. Temporal assignment was not as powerful, and assignment by designation was least powerful. The powerful strategies tend to reduce the number of TAKE commands issued by the human.

Finally, because of its flexibility and specificity, assignment by designation may instill a greater sense of control in the human. This feeling of control diminishes as the human moves to spatial assignment, contingency-based assignment, and temporal assignment.

The results of this study tend to concur with some of the findings of Carroll and Thomas [19]. They discovered that spatial metaphor was more conducive to task performance than temporal metaphor. They postulated that space might be a better framework for reasoning than time since the temporal dimension is more abstract and spatial processing involves a larger number of special-purpose inference rules.

Temporal assignment possesses two additional shortcomings. It entails a break with time; the human does not know what will come next or what will be taken care of by the computer component. This might induce a diminished sense of certainty and hence control in the human. Further, a problem with temporal assignment may occur when the human believes that a command is still active (when in fact it is not) and that the computer will continue taking care of future tasks. When the tasks are not taken care of, the human will have a difficult time keeping up with the flow of tasks. Hence, using temporal assignment entails the extra labor of keeping track of the tasks assigned to the computer component to determine what has and what has not been done.

In sum, spatial assignment is the most powerful and least discriminative strategy. Assignment by designation is the most flexible and specific, and is also most preferred by subjects. In terms of system performance and system adequacy data the two strategies are comparable. Although no interaction effect was found between input media and strategies, it might be speculated that when the qwerty keyboard is used, spatial assignment may be the more appropriate strategy. This is because the qwerty keyboard is a slow

Table 3
Results of Selected LSD tests on Performance Measures

% Landed by System

Control	NEXT	ID	EMERG	QUAD
40.33	55.17	68.50	68.84	76.00

% Landed by Human

QUAD	NEXT	ID	Control	EMERG
22.33	33.50	38.00	40.33	41.17

% Correct Commands

Control	ID	EMERG	NEXT	QUAD
89.29	90.33	90.53	91.11	92.94

% Landed by Computer

NEXT	EMERG	ID	QUAD
21.67	27.67	30.50	53.67

TAKE Commands

EMERG	QUAD	NEXT	ID
4.40	4.85	6.05	10.40

Planes Lost

QUAD	ID	EMERG	NEXT	Control
2.35	2.75	2.85	3.75	8.00

Commands

QUAD	EMERG	NEXT	ID	Control
126.30	134.10	138.30	146.75	156.80

Bracketed means are not significantly different (*p* > .05)

input medium while the spatial assignment strategy is powerful requiring few invocations. In this instance, qwerty keyboard input and spatial assignment strategy may be complementary. However, when function keys can be used, assignment by designation may become the preferred strategy. Assignment by designation can be used in this case to boost the human's sense of control, with the increase in keying time compensated by the use of a faster input medium.

5.0 IMPLICATIONS

Given a set of constraints, the systems designer is responsible for identifying the most appropriate medium/strategy combination for human-computer communication and dynamic task allocation. The proposed framework serves as a guide for investigation and result interpretation. Future research may be directed toward the study of other factors and factor combinations defining human-computer interaction. In particular, the subfactors defining the human-computer interface (medium, mode, style, and strategy) are of interest to systems designers. For instance, one might probe into input media such as the voice recognizer and touch panel, and their interaction with various dialogue strategies. Research effort should also be directed toward the empirical comparison of implicit and explicit communication for dynamic task allocation.

ACKNOWLEDGEMENTS

This research was supported by the Office of Naval Research under ONR contract Number N00014-81-K-0143, and Work Unit Number SRO-101. The effort was supported by the Engineering Psychology Programs, Office of Naval Research, under the technical direction of Dr. John J. O'Hare.

REFERENCES:

[1] DeGreene, K.B. (Ed.), Systems Psychology (McGraw-Hill, New York, 1970).

[2] Rieger, C.A. and Greenstein, J.S., The allocation of tasks between the human and computer in automated systems, IEEE 1982 Proceedings of the International Conference on Cybernetics and Society, Seattle, Washington, (October 1982), 204-208.

[3] Fitts, P.M., Functions of men in complex systems, Aerospace Engineering 21 (1962) 34-39.

[4] Chapanis, A., On the allocation of functions between men and machines, Occupational Psychology 39 (1965) 1-11.

[5] Bainbridge, L., Ironies of automation, Analysis, Design, and Evaluation of Man-Machine Systems, IFAC/IFIP/IFORS/IEA Conference, Baden-Baden, Federal Republic of Germany, (September 27-29, 1982) 151-157.

[6] Nickerson, R.S., Myer, T.H., Miller, D.C., and Pew, R.W., User-computer interaction: some problems for human factors research. Cambridge, MA: Bolt Beranek and Newman Inc., Final Report No. 4719, (September 1981).

[7] Licklider, J.C.R., Man-computer symbiosis, IRE Transactions on Human Factors in Electronics 1 (1960) 4-11.

[8] Jordan, N., Allocation of function between man and machines in automated systems, Journal of Applied Psychology 47 (1963) 161-165.

[9] Hormann, A.M., A man-machine synergistic approach to planning and creative problem solving, part 1, International Journal of Man-Machine Studies 3 (1971) 167-184.

[10] Rouse, W.B., Design of man-computer interfaces for on-line interactive systems,. Proceedings of IEEE, Special Issue on Interactive Computer Systems 63 (1975) 847-857.

[11] Rouse, W.B., Human-computer interaction in multitask situations, IEEE Transactions on Systems, Man, and Cybernetics 7 (1977) 384-392.

[12] Rouse, W.B., Human-computer interaction in the control of dynamic systems, ACM Computing Surveys 13 (1981) 71-99.

[13] Greenstein, J.S. and Revesman, M.E., A Monte-Carlo simulation investigating means of human-computer communication for dynamic task allocation, Proceedings International Conference on Cybernetics and Society, Atlanta, Georgia, (October 1981) 488-494.

[14] Greenstein, J.S., The use of models of human decision making to enhance human-computer interaction,. IEEE International Conference on Cybernetics and Society, Cambridge, MA., (October 1980) 968-970.

[15] Revesman, M.E. and Greenstein, J.S., Human/computer interaction using a model of human decision making, IEEE 1982 Proceedings of the International Conference on Cybernetics and Society, Seattle, Washington, (October 1982), 439-443.

[16] Revesman, M.E. and Greenstein, J.S., An empirical validation of a model of human decision making for human-computer communication, Proceedings of the Human Factors Society - 27th Annual Meeting, Norfolk, Virginia, (1983), 958-962.

[17] Revesman, M.E. and Greenstein, J.S., Application of a model of human decision making for human/computer communication, Proceedings of CHI '83 Conference on Human Factors in Computing Systems, Boston, MA.,(December 1983), 107-111.

[18] Lindquist, T.E., Fainter, R.G., Guy, S.R., Hakkinen, M.T., and Maynard, J.F., GENIE: A computer-based task for experiments in human-computer interaction. Blacksburg, Virginia: Virginia Polytechnic Institute and State University, CSIE-82-10, (November 1983).

[19] Carroll, J.M., and Thomas, J.C., Metaphor and the cognitive representation of computing systems, IEEE Transactions on Systems, Man, and Cybernetics, 12 (1982) 107-116.

SPEECH INPUT AND OUTPUT

Human-Computer Interaction — INTERACT '84 / B. Shackel (ed.)
Elsevier Science Publishers B.V. (North-Holland)
© IFIP, 1985

SPEECH INPUT AS AN ADJUNCT TO KEYBOARD ENTRY IN TELEVISION SUBTITLING

*   **
R.I. Damper, A.D. Lambourne and D.P. Guy

Department of Electronics and Information Engineering,
University of Southampton,
Southampton SO9 5NH.

* now Oracle Teletext Ltd.
** Royal Navy.

This paper describes an investigation of the potential benefits of using automatic speech recognition in television subtitle preparation. Analysis of the subtitling task indicated that the principal benefits were likely to be obtained in spoken entry of subtitle 'style' commands. However, off-line subtitling trials showed that use of speech recognition increased preparation time by 9%. Speech input significantly reduced the time spent transferring between text and style entry but increased the time spent in other activities. The error rate for style entry by keypad was consistent and averaged 5% whereas speech recognition errors ranged from 5% to 15%. A valid comparison of the two modes of entry can, however, only be made with subjects having as much experience of voice entry of data as they have of keying.

1. INTRODUCTION:

At present, the amount of television material which can be subtitled for deaf viewers is limited for practical reasons by subtitle preparation times. Effective man-machine interface design has a crucial part to play in improving subtitlers' productivity and, thereby, the service to the deaf community. The paper by Lambourne et al gives a fuller account of work in this field, which culminated in the production and marketing of the NEWFOR rapid subtitling system. During subtitle entry, the information supplied by the operator is of two types; namely subtitle text and style parameters. "Style" relates to presentation factors such as text colour and on-screen position. The production version of NEWFOR uses a dual-area keyboard, comprising a QWERTY keyboard for text entry with a special function keypad for style selection alongside it.

Advances in automatic speech recognition led us to consider ways in which a speech-input channel might be of value in subtitle preparation. Because of current technological limitations, speech input is not a serious alternative to QWERTY keyboard entry as far as subtitle text is concerned. There did appear, however, to be some potential in using speech for the much more restricted task of style input. Work was therefore initiated to test the hypothesis that speech input of subtitle style would be of benefit in terms of increased input speed, lower error rates, improved subtitle "quality" or other advantages. Of course, any such benefits must be sufficient to justify the cost of the additional hardware and software.

2. THE SUBTITLING TASK:

It has been estimated that 4-5 million deaf and hard-of-hearing people in the UK would benefit from television subtitling [1]. Such subtitles are provided by the broadcast teletext services operated by the BBC (CEEFAX) and ITV (ORACLE). However, only about 5 hours of programmes a week are currently regularly subtitled, due mainly to the high cost involved. (It takes 20-30 hours to prepare subtitles in advance for a one-hour programme.) NEWFOR [2] (NEW FORmatter) is a computerised subtitling aid which operates in conjunction with the ORACLE service. By dividing the tasks involved in subtitling between the human subtitler and computer in an appropriate way, subtitle preparation time is reduced by some 40% compared to that using a conventional teletext page-editing terminal.

Using NEWFOR, subtitle text is entered by the operator using a QWERTY keyboard. The operator is also responsible for specifying colour and other style parameters using function keys. The computer is responsible for dividing the text into suitable lines (using linguistic and geometric rules to determine the best line endings), boxing the subtitle and inserting the teletext control characters necessary to produce the required display.

Subtitles can be input in two modes. In the off-line mode, used to subtitle recorded programmes for later transmission, the teletext-format subtitle is stored on a floppy disc. In the live mode, NEWFOR is linked to a teletext computer which inserts subtitles directly into the broadcast page sequence. The NEWFOR terminal VDU displays current operating mode, current and previous subtitle text, command menus, error messages and the currently selected display styles.

Four phases are involved in off-line subtitle preparation: (1) script preparation (2) text and style input (3) synchronisation to the programme videotape and (4) review and correction. The majority of data entry takes place in phase (2), which occupies about a quarter of the total preparation time, and this is where speech input could have an impact. The subtitle script, from which text and style are entered, is essentially an edited version of the programme script annotated with style parameter markings.

Subtitling in real-time presents considerable problems as phases (1) and (2), editing and data entry, must be performed virtually simultaneously. Two-person operation, with an editing interpreter dictating to a skilled keyboard operator, has been tried with NEWFOR; and use of pre-stored subtitle sequences can also be effective in some circumstances. NEWFOR offers a "shortform" facility which allows commonly encountered words or phrases to be entered as abbreviations which are detected and expanded by the computer. Even with these aids, however, the pressure of time is such that subtitle style is usually neglected, the most serious consequence being unsuitable positioning of a proportion of subtitles.

3. ROLE OF SPEECH INPUT IN SUBTITLING:

The advantages of speech input are now widely appreciated [3]. It is a very natural means of control, requiring little training, freeing hands and eyes for other tasks, and permitting multi-modal communication. Current recognisers are, however, limited in their capabilities: typically, they can classify only relatively few words, and often these words must be spoken in isolation by a user who has previously "trained" the system. In spite of these limitations, the undoubted benefits have led to widespread interest in speech input amongst commercial, industrial and military concerns [4]. Until recently, the high cost of recognition hardware has restricted applications to areas where the economic advantages are substantial and immediately apparent. This has usually meant cases where it is a serious disadvantage to switch attention, and move hands and/or eyes, from the primary task to perform data entry via a keyboard.

This situation has been changing over the last few years by the appearance of cheaper recognisers suitable for use with microcomputer-controlled systems. These low-cost devices have opened up a much wider range of applications for speech input, and made it worth considering in cases where the advantages are less immediately obvious - such as the preparation of television subtitles.

It is not usually easy to predict the effectiveness of speech input in any particular situation because of the number of factors involved [5, 6, 7]. The performance (error rate) of the recogniser used is of obvious importance, and this is strongly dependent on the size and phonetic composition of the vocabulary selected. Performance is also greatly affected by human factors, such as the experience and motivation of the users, and the amount of stress they are under. There are, however, many other influences on overall effectiveness, including task criticality, the degree of hand/eye occupation, feedback and prompting schemes, error correction procedures and recogniser response time.

Unconstrained speech recognition is currently an unsolved problem, and will remain so for the foreseeable future: typical low-cost, commercial recognisers have vocabularies of about 100 words. Accordingly, the scope for speech input of subtitle text is extremely limited. Speech input of style, however, appears feasible since it involves only a fixed, relatively small, vocabulary of spoken commands. Further, the task is non-critical since style defaults are available. Nonetheless, there are some counter-indications. Keypad entry of style can be very fast (requiring less than 3 keystrokes, and usually only one) and there is experimental evidence that, as far as a primary data-entry task is concerned, use of a keypad is considerably faster than speech input [8]. In the context of subtitling, however, the following considerations encouraged us to assess seriously the speech input of style parameters:

* manual entry of both style and text requires physical movement of at least one hand between keyboard and keypad in changing from one task to the other. This movement would be eliminated, reducing the time needed to transfer between tasks.

* it might be possible, provided both the operator and computer system could cope, to enter style and text concurrently. Speaking style parameters while typing text could reduce the effective time spent on style entry to zero.

* in a dual-task situation, the two tasks compete for central processing resources, resulting in mutual interference and a consequent performance loss in one or both tasks [9]. A major factor determining the extent of dual-task interference is the functional similarity of the tasks, and particularly whether or not they use the same physiological input/output channels [10, 11]. Thus, a change of output modality, from hands to speech, for one of the tasks could lead to a performance increment in both.

Taking these factors together, there seemed sufficient justification to investigate the benefits of speech input of subtitle style. In the first instance, off-line subtitle preparation was to be studied. The investigation was to focus on the relative speeds of keypad and speech entry, including the time spent transferring between tasks, and the error rates for the two entry modes. Later, if time allowed, live subtitling was to be studied.

4. SYSTEM CONSTRAINTS:

As NEWFOR is a commercially successful product, and the value of speech recognition in subtitle preparation is unproven, it was decided at the outset that any alteration to the NEWFOR system should be minimal. Accordingly, the speech input hardware and software was conceived as essentially additional to existing NEWFOR hardware and software, rather than requiring fundamental system modifications. Further, operating procedures with speech input were to be as close as possible to those employed normally. These decisions had important implications for the choice of recogniser and vocabulary to be used.

As far as the recogniser is concerned, then, it must be compatible with the standard NEWFOR terminal - the C. Itoh CIT-101 (DEC VT-100 equivalent) VDU. We also felt that the recogniser used should be reasonably cheap, as any performance advantage of speech input is likely to be marginal. Finally, in view of the potential importance of concurrent spoken style and keyed text input, the recogniser selected should ideally allow this. Only one available recogniser fulfilled all of these criteria - namely the Interstate VRT-300 [12]: a 100-word, speaker-dependent, isolated-word device. This recogniser is reasonably inexpensive and interfaces directly with the CIT-101 terminal. It also allows concurrent data entry from the terminal keyboard and the speech-input channel. The VRT-300 simply buffers and sends ASCII-coded strings to the host computer. Since the ASCII codes do not distinguish the source of the data, keyed and spoken information may be entered effectively simultaneously.

The constraint that NEWFOR software and operating procedures were to remain as little changed as possible had an impact on vocabulary selection. The choice of vocabulary is of importance for two reasons. First, recognition accuracy is highly dependent on the phonetic distinctiveness of the words used. Second, the vocabulary shapes the "dialogue" between man and machine. This dialogue must be as natural as possible, to promote acceptability and speed up data entry. Thus, the words chosen must be easy to say, come readily to mind, conform with prompting and feedback messages and be consistent in meaning with the responses they elicit. The following considerations applied to the choice of style command vocabulary:

* spoken commands should be the same as keypad command names (and the words employed for visual feedback of NEWFOR status).
* commands should be phonetically distinct. This clashes to an extent with the preceding consideration, because the style commands do contain some phonetically similar word pairs e.g. 'white'/'right'.
* recognition accuracy can be improved by "structuring" the vocabulary i.e. restricting the active words to a subset of the total vocabulary. This is essentially a primitive command syntax, limiting the range of legal word sequences. In practice, this would mean entering commands in a fixed order. (E.g. colour, then lateral position, then vertical position.) Further,

all would have to be specified whether or not the parameters were to be altered.
* no error correction words were thought necessary since a wrongly entered style parameter can be corrected by entering (i.e repeating - in the case of recogniser, rather than human, error) the required command.

It was decided that the need for consistency between keypad and spoken commands should take priority over the requirement to avoid phonetic similarity, and that syntactic division of the vocabulary should not be attempted because it interferes with a natural dialogue and forces the operator to give unnecessary commands. It was realised that these decisions would sacrifice some potential performance, and they might need to be reversed if subsequent recognition accuracy were unacceptably low. The 25-word vocabulary selected was:

White	Left	Zero
Cyan	Centre	One
Yellow	Right	Two
Green	Top	Three
Magenta	Middle	Flash
Blue	Bottom	Add-on
Red	Up	Clear
Black	Down	Send
On		

Although it violates the principle of consistency with keypad names, 'on' was chosen (in place of 'background') to select backgound colour since it allows use of the more natural construction <colour>'on'<colour>. Two control commands were included in addition to the style parameters: 'send' (corresponding to the 'end of subtitle' key) to allow subtitle entry to be completed by voice command or keystroke; and 'clear' (equivalent to the similarly-labelled key.)

5. EVALUATION OF THE RECOGNISER:

Before conducting subtitling trials, the VRT-300 was tested and assessed to find the optimum choice of recognition parameters and command vocabulary. Tests with 7 speakers (5 male and 2 female) showed that a recognition rate of 92-98% could be expected with the vocabulary listed above. Rejection and substitution error rates were similar. In these tests, the speakers only task was to repeat the vocabulary words as prompted visually. Analysis of the misrecognitions revealed that none of the vocabulary words were prone to misrecognition by more than a small proportion of the set of users. The severest confusion, 'white'/'right', affected only 3 of the 7 speakers. It was concluded that the vocabulary was satisfactory but that users experiencing problems with a particular word should be encouraged to re-train the word using a different pronunciation or even modifying it e.g from 'white' to 'whitey'.

Accuracy was found to be relatively independent

of the number of training passes: 3 passes were
subsequently used. Reject and delta-score
thresholds (see [12] for an explanation of these
measures) were investigated. It was found that,
ideally, the two thresholds should be chosen on
an individual basis but that, strictly, a
different pair of thresholds should apply to
each pair of vocabulary words. As the latter is
clearly impractical, compromise global values
were chosen by inspection of the results.

A number of other user-selectable settings and
variables were considered: these are described
fully elsewhere [13].

The influence of noise on VRT-300 performance
was not investigated quantitatively. However, it
was observed that impulse noise (e.g. from
slammed doors) frequently triggered the
recogniser.

6. SUBTITLING TRIALS USING SPEECH INPUT:

6.1 Experimental Details

A microcomputer was interposed between the
NEWFOR terminal and computer, to monitor the
subtitler's activity i.e. to record the times
spent by the operator on each of the various
subtitling activities. The monitoring program
considers the subtitler to be in one of five
states:

TEXT   : entering subtitle text
STYLE   : entering subtitle style
TRANSFER : transferring from text to
             subtitle entry or vice versa
BETWEEN   : between subtitles
IDLE   : not engaged in any of the above.

The measured timings were affected by the
interrupt-driven nature of character transfer
between NEWFOR terminal and host, but the
inaccuracies introduced were negligible. Errors
in text and style entry were also monitored, but
this was done manually. The NEWFOR terminal
visual display information was relayed to a
'trial controller' situated in another room, as
was an audio channel to allow speech recogniser
input to be heard. Both sound and visual
information were also recorded on a video tape
for subsequent verification of the controller's
error data after the trial.

Two programme scripts were produced for use
during the trials; one containing fifty
subtitles and the other thirty. The text was
taken from a real script, but the style
parameters were augmented to include examples of
all possible parameters in a representative
ratio. The longer script contained 100 style
commands and 294 words of text, the shorter 50
style commands and 112 text words. Five
subtitlers, all familiar with the NEWFOR system,
were studied. Three were professional subtitlers
from Oracle Teletext Ltd., all new to speech
input. The other two were experienced with
speech input, but not very practised typists.

Trials were carried out in pairs; each

consisting of the subject entering one of the
scripts by either voice or keypad input of
style, followed by entry of the other script
using the alternative mode of style input.
Twenty four such trials were conducted. To
obtain a direct comparison between keypad and
speech entry of style in a single-task
situation, three additional pairs of trials were
carried out. These involved the subjects
entering only style commands from the script
without any text using first the keypad and then
speech input. Subjects were instructed to
correct any errors that occurred.

Before starting trials, each subject completed a
voice test using the NEWFOR vocabulary. This
gave the three naive subtitlers some feel for
the requirements of voice input and allowed any
poorly-trained words to be identified. An
estimate was also made of the best reject and
delta-score thresholds for each subject, and
these were used subsequently.

6.2 Error Rates

The keyboard error rate was virtually unaffected
by use of speech input, averaging 1.6% whether
or not speech input was used. Curiously, this
error rate was very consistent over all
subjects, regardless of typing ability. Errors
in using the style keypad averaged 5%. VRT-300
recogniser performance was considerably worse
than that measured in prior evaluation and, as
expected, exhibited high inter-speaker
variability. One of the subjects suffered from
very bad performance, due partly to an inability
to adjust to the consistent pronunciation
required and partly to heavy-handed use of the
keyboard, the noise from which frequently
triggered the VRT-300. This highlights the
susceptibilty of the recogniser to impulse
noise, as noted in Section 5. Results for this
subject were excluded from the analysis since
they would have biased the conclusions
disproportionately.

Recognition accuracy for the other subjects
varied from 85-95% (c.f. 92-98% reported in
Section 5 above). The substitution error rate
was between 1% and 3% but the rejection rate was
very much higher — between 4% and 17%. Most of
the problem could be attributed to two causes.
First, a single rejection frequently led to a
string of similar rejections during which the
subject would make increasingly tense efforts to
get the VRT-300 to accept the utterance. All
subjects suffered at some time, but the worse
performers were affected much more, owing to
their naturally higher rejection rate. This
problem may be solvable with more sophisticated
error correction procedures than simple
repetition. Second, there was a tendency at the
start of the trials to speak two style commands
together, without the distinct pause
necessitated by the isolated word recogniser.
Subjects quickly learnt the need to pause but
the test sessions were short enough for this
factor to have affected overall rejection rate.

This difficulty probably also slowed down the average rate of input since it would take users some time to optimise their delivery rate, with most leaving a longer than necessary pause to be "on the safe side".

Results indicate that keypad entry is less error prone than speech input but this may be merely due to differences in familiarity with the two input modes. (Even the subjects experienced with voice input have infinitely more familiarity with keyboard entry.) Neither method, as implemented here, has any advantage over the other in terms of error correction, since all errors are corrected by entering the intended selection. However, the repetition of misrecognised spoken commands is unsatisfactory; thus, speech input requires more sophisticated error correction than does keypad entry.

6.3 Comparison of Keypad and Speech Input in a Single-task Situation

Keypad entry was 32% faster on average than spoken entry of style commands. This compares well with the results of Welch [8], who reported keyboard entry of alphanumeric data as 29% faster than voice entry. The speech input rate ranged from 30-35 words per minute (average 32 wpm). These figures compare with 27-36 wpm for the data entry task described by Bierfert et al [6], and the 39-63 wpm rate obtained by Cochran et al [7].

6.4 Comparison of Keypad and Speech Input During Off-line Subtitling

Figure 1 shows how subjects divided their time during off-line subtitling; and Figure 2 shows the increased time spent on each activity when speech input is used.

state	keypad entry (%)	voice entry (%)
TEXT	61	56
STYLE	8	10
TRANSFER	10	8
BETWEEN	16	15
IDLE	5	11

Figure 1: How subtitlers divide their time

The percentages are averages taken over all trials (but excluding one of the subjects) and both scripts. Note that the proportion of time spent entering style is far greater than would be observed in practice, because of the artificially high number of style commands in the scripts. As expected, individual figures varied considerably about the average: however, the trends identified were consistent for all

state	increase (%)
TEXT	+3
STYLE	+34
TRANSFER	-28
BETWEEN	+8
IDLE	+162
ALL	+9

Figure 2: Increase in time spent in each state when using speech input of style

subjects.

The results show that speech input of style increases total subtitle preparation time by some 9%. Although the premise that the time spent transferring attention for style to text entry and vice versa is correct, such transfer accounts for only 10% of the subtitler's time. Speech input not only increases the time spent inputting style but also increases time for apparently unrelated activities as evidenced by longer text-entry, 'between subtitle' and idle times. The increases in text and 'between' times were shown by all subjects but are small. It was originally thought (see Section 3 above) that speech input of style might facilitate text entry, by separating the output mechanisms used. In fact, the requirement to use an unfamiliar means of data entry appears to have increased dual-task interference but this effect might well disappear with practice. The increase in idle time (spent checking that text and style have been correctly entered) was very substantial. Apparently, checking of style is virtually neglected with keypad entry because of a high degree of confidence in this entry mode. This is not true of speech input where the user's expectation of errors leads to a large increase in time spent checking input, and hence in idle time.

Limited experience with speech input means that the small but consistent increase in subtitling time can safely be viewed as a worst-case result. Given practice, many subtitlers could undoubtedly achieve faster entry speeds using speech input of style than using keypad entry. It is clear, however, that no dramatic time saving can be expected.

6.5 Concurrent Entry of Style and Text

None of the subjects showed any natural inclination to speak style commands while engaged in text entry. When asked to attempt such concurrent input, all but one subject was unable to do so. The remaining subject, who showed some ability, was investigated as she attempted parallel text and style entry. About one-third of the style parameters were entered concurrently with text input. This reduced the time spent purely on style entry but total input time increased by some 10%, owing to a large increase in text entry time because of dual-task interference. Keyboard error rate also increased, with many errors occurring at times of speech input. Furthermore, VRT-300 performance was worsened by 10%, with a higher rate of both substitution and rejection errors. This can be partly attributed to increased stress affecting the subject's voice but also to impulsive keyboard noise introducing errors.

It was concluded that concurrent entry of style and text might lead to faster subtitling in some cases, but significant practice would be needed to develop the requisite skills. Also, some means of coping with the problems caused by keyboard noise would have to be found.

6.6 User Acceptability of Voice Input

One subject was effectively unable to use voice input because of very poor recognition accuracy. The remaining subjects found the chosen vocabulary easy to learn and use. Of the two Oracle subtitlers who obtained satisfactory speech-input performance, one said she found it more relaxing and would welcome it as an option. The other preferred keypad entry, citing the need to wear a microphone, the tedious recogniser pre-training and the tendency for rejection errors to occur in strings as negative factors.

7. CONCLUSIONS AND FUTURE WORK:

The work described here shows voice input of style increases total off-line subtitle preparation time by about 9% compared to keypad entry of style. The basis of comparison is, however, questionable since subjects naturally have far greater experience of keyboard and keypad input than of speech input. With sufficient practice, a saving in subtitle entry time could be expected but any saving is unlikely to be sufficient to justify the cost of the additional input channel. In any event, many subtitlers are likely to prefer continued use of keypad entry.

An investigation of use of speech recognition in live subtitling has commenced, but space precludes further discussion here. This is perhaps a more fruitful direction than off-line subtitling, since even a small time saving could allow more attention to be paid to style selection than is currently the practice, thereby improving live subtitle quality. There is also more scope for spoken text entry, particularly employing spoken shortforms.

8. ACKNOWLEDGEMENTS:

The authors are indebted to Oracle Teletext Ltd., who supported this work financially, and to our experimental subjects.

9. REFERENCES:

[1] Baker, R.G., ORACLE subtitling for the deaf and hard-of-hearing. Final Report to IBA/ITCA. Dept. of Electronics, University of Southampton (January 1982.)

[2] Lambourne, A.D., NEWFOR - an advanced subtitle preparation system. International Broadcasting Convention Proceedings, IBC 82, Brighton, UK. 269-272.

[3] Lea, W.A., The value of speech recognition systems, in Lea, W.A. (ed.), Trends in Speech Recognition (Prentice-Hall, Englewood Cliffs, 1980).

[4] Nye, J.M., The expanding market for commercial speech recognisers, ibid.

[5] Bierfert, H., Kirsten, M. and Lance, D., Some aspects of evaluating the performance of speech recognition systems in real applications, Proc. ICASSP 80 (1980), 186-189.

[6] Cochran, D.J. and Riley, M.W., An evaluation of the strengths, weaknesses and uses of voice input devices, Proc. Human Factors Soc. 24th Annual Meeting (1980), Los Angeles, 190-193.

[7] Lowerre, B.T., Removing gamesmanship from the performance specifications of discrete word recognition, VLSI in the Laboratory, Office and Home, COMPCON 81 (1981), San Francisco, 149-151.

[8] Welch, J.R., Automatic data entry analysis, Technical Report, Rome Air Development Center, TR-77-306.

[9] Kahnenan, D., Attention and Effort (Prentice Hall, New Jersey, 1972).

[10] North, R.A., Task functional demands as factors in dual task performance, Proc. Human Factors Soc. 21st Annual Meeting (1977), San Antonio, 367-371.

[11] Wickens, C.D., Vidulich, U., and Sandry, D., Factors influencing the performance advantage of speech technology, Proc. Human Factors Soc. 25th Annual Meeting (1981), Rochester NY, 240-242.

[12] Interstate Electronics Inc., VRT-300 Operations and Maintenance Manual (1983).

[13] Guy, D.P., The use of speech recognition in the preparation of television subtitles, M.Sc. Dissertation, Dept. of Electronics, University of Southampton (1983).

Human-Computer Interaction — INTERACT '84 / B. Shackel (ed.)
Elsevier Science Publishers B.V. (North-Holland)
© IFIP, 1985

THE USE OF SIMPLE SPEECH RECOGNISERS IN INDUSTRIAL APPLICATIONS

David Visick[*], Peter Johnson and John Long

Ergonomics Unit,
University College London

* now at Warren Spring Laboratory, Stevenage

This paper points out, and attempts to deal with, some of the problems that may be
encountered when using simple speech recognition systems in industrial applications.
An experiment compared a voice recogniser with a keyboard, as the destination input
device in a parcel sorting task. The task was represented first by a simple
laboratory simulation of the coding sub-task, and then by an authentic simulation
using real parcels on a sorting rig. Results showed that voice input may be quite
unsuitable for tasks having little or no manual content. Also, for tasks requiring
precise sequencing of operations, voice may offer inadequate intrinsic timing
feedback. Finally, a practical means of empirical vocabulary optimisation is described.

1. INTRODUCTION

In recent years, a great deal of research
interest has centred on the development of speech
recognition machines. The public and potential
users, however, remain largely unaware of the
current state of play. Large and sophisticated
systems such as HARPY (1) - capable of recognising sentences of continuous speech - have
received most attention, but the most cost-
effective uses of speech recognition technology
are probably at the other end of the spectrum,
where a simple discrete word recogniser may be
used to dramatically improve performance in a
routine industrial task.

Continuous speech recognisers have a harder job
to do because of the need to extract basic
phonemic information from speech, but deficiencies in this area can be overcome by their
ability to make use of syntactic features when
identifying words. Isolated word recognisers
normally have to store each word pattern as a
separate unit, and of course cannot make use
of syntactic structure to anything like the same
extent. However, the hardware required to store
and recognise 50 to 100 carefully chosen words
with reasonable accuracy is now readily
available.

There is a widely accepted list of potential
advantages to using speech as an input medium:
1) it frees the hands
2) it requires little concentration
3) practically no training is needed
4) it can be a more 'natural' communication
   medium than keyboards
5) it does not require vision
6) it provides an extra channel for complex
   systems
The first three factors seem to make speech the
ideal choice for the input medium in a parcel
sorting task: A task analysis of parcel sorting
using a PSM (parcel sorting machine) keyboard

as the destination input device was performed as
part of this study. The PSM keyboard, used in
most British sorting offices, contains 50 keys,
each one labelled with a single town name. This
analysis showed that the sorter performs an
almost completely serial task sequence: Parcel
selection is followed by manipulation until the
label can be read, and then a visually guided
keying procedure, during which the parcel is
held static, since it must not be disposed of
until the keystroke is complete. Only after the
parcel is disposed of is the next parcel selected.
According to currently popular theories of
attention (e.g. 2) a spoken destination code
would not interfere with parcel handling, since
it would not compete for the same mental resources, i.e. vision and limb control. Thus
faster sorting should result, since more
parallel activity could take place. Equally
importantly, however, it has been suggested that
voice can be faster where it removes the need
for translation into an intermediate code, e.g.
a number.

Accuracy is also a major criterion in parcel
sorting, and achieving low error rates with a
voice recognition machine (VRM) depends to a
large extent on vocabulary choice. In this
study, no attempt was made to optimise the
vocabulary, which contained many apparently
confusable words (e.g. Edinburgh and Peterborough)
since in real parcel sorting, there is not
normally a choice of vocabulary. This method
also permitted the analysis of a reasonably large
number of errors, enabling a methodology for
reducing them to be examined.

The principal object of the study, however, was
to isolate some of the factors influencing
performance and learning in a parcel sorting task
when using a VRM as opposed to a keyboard. This
was achieved by i) examining performance over a
realistically long training and testing period,
ii) representing the task in two forms - a 'pure'

sorting task with no manual component, and a
complete simulation of a real parcel sorting
task - and iii) extracting detailed time data
from individual time elements, although this
short paper does not report the results of this
exercise. Previous studies in this area (3)
have relied on relatively gross performance
measures, such as mean sorting rate, have used
only short testing periods, and have not directly
compared one input device with another.*

2. METHOD

The experimental design was similar throughout
the study. A mixed design was used, each subject
being tested on one device only, but over 12
sessions lasting about 45 minutes each. An
average of 48 hours elapsed between sessions.
Each session comprised a training period of 875
parcels, followed after a short interval by a
recorded test session of 500 parcels. The
independent variables were thus session number
(i.e. amount of practice) and device type (PSM
or VRM). A separate statistical analysis was
planned for each of the dependent variables,
sorting time and errors.

The experiment was divided into two phases, a
different set of subjects being used for each.
Phase 1 consisted of a laboratory task, in which
a random sequence of stimulus town names, drawn
from a set of 50, would appear on a VDT screen.
The subject's coding response would then initiate
the next stimulus, i.e. the task was self-paced.
For the VRM, the coding response would be the
town name spoken into a headset microphone. For
the PSM keyboard it would be the depression of
one of the 50 labelled keys.

Phase 2 was a simulation incorporating all
important aspects of real parcel sorting. A
stream of dummy parcels would flow down a ramp
to a sorting table, where the subject would
select a parcel and read the destination town
printed on the label. The parcel would then be
'coded' as described in Phase 1, after which the
subject would slide the parcel through a light
beam switch and into a bin. In the case of the
VRM, the sequence had to be reversed, the subject
disposing of the parcel <u>before</u> coding it. This
was because in preliminary trials, subjects
proved unable to judge when the VRM had finished
processing an utterance, and would often dispose
of a parcel before it had been coded. In addition to the suspected difficulty of judging
precisely the end of a spoken word, the VRM would
take 230ms to process an utterance, and subjects
would have had to estimate this interval as well.
This problem is discussed further below. No
immediate extrinsic feedback of any kind was
emloyed with the VRM or the PSM, since it was
intended to achieve the best possible sorting

rates, and it was thought probable that any
form of feedback would have slowed sorting.

Every response (keystrokes, processed voice
inputs, and light beam cuts) were recorded and
timed by a microcomputer to a resolution of 1ms,
in terms of time since last response.

Error counting and identification was possible
for individual items in Phase 1, as the identity
of each stimulus and response was known to the
computer. In Phase 2, a less accurate response
counting procedure was used, dependent on the
assumption (shown to be largely correct from
analysis of Phase 1 data) that as long as the
total error rate is quite low, exchange errors*
are rare.

3. RESULTS

<u>Sorting time</u>

The sorting time results are shown in Figures 1
and 2, for Phase 1 and Phase 2 respectively.
For the VRM it can be seen that there is little
difference between the two phases, mean sorting
times being approximately constant at about
1500ms. The only noticable difference is a
small learning effect over the first 2 sessions
of Phase 2, making session 1 significantly
slower than all the other sessions (t=1.81,
p<0.05). For the PSM keyboard, however, both
phases exhibit a clear learning effect, significant up to session 4 in Phase 2 (t=2.99, p<0.01
between sessions 3 and 4), and up to session 2
in Phase 1 (p<0.01, Newman Keuls' test).

Comparing Phase 1 with Phase 2, therefore, shows
that the two tasks give almost identical performance with the VRM on all sessions except
session 1, on which the Phase 2 task is about
300ms slower per parcel (or trial). For the PSM
keyboard, however, Phase 1 item times are faster
than Phase 2 item times by about 900ms over the
final 5 sessions, and by more than this over
earlier sessions. The learning curve in Phase 2
is also steeper than in Phase 1, and the point
at which the curve appears to asymptote occurs
sooner in Phase 1.

<u>Errors</u>

The error rate data were extremely clear-cut,
but varied widely between devices, and in the
case of the VRM had to be estimated in parts.
The data from both phases are portrayed in
graphical form in figure 3.

The PSM yielded mean error rates of about 1% in
Phase 1, and 1.5% in Phase 2. Neither result
showed much variation, and there was definitely
no systematic effect of practice.

---

* Note that while three keyboards were actually
tested in the study, only the PSM will be
discussed here. The complete set included a
QWERTY keyboard and a numeric (0-9) keypad.

* Exchange errors, in which A is coded as B and
on a later trial B is coded as A, are not detected by response counting, since they do not
affect the total number of each response.

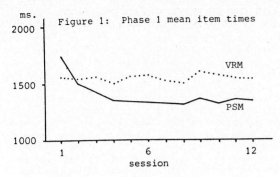

Figure 1: Phase 1 mean item times

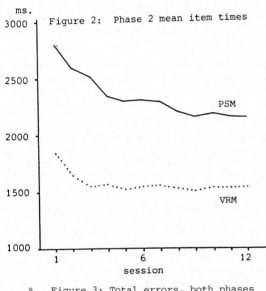

Figure 2: Phase 2 mean item times

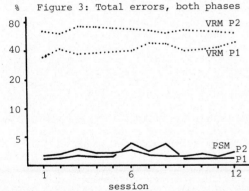

Figure 3: Total errors, both phases

The VRM error rates, as expected on grounds of vocabulary choice alone, were enormous by comparison. In Phase 1, total errors averaged over 40%, showing a slight upward trend over sessions. This figure was made up of approximately equal numbers of mismatches (one word being mistakenly recognised for another) and non-recognitions (words rejected as not matching any of the VRM's current vocabulary). Clearly in this task, mismatches are the more serious class of error, as they would result in parcels being sent to the wrong destination. Non-recognised parcels can be identified and

re-circulated, resulting in a comparatively small time penalty. In Phase 2, performance was far worse, the rate of non-recognitions alone being about 40%. This also meant that the procedure of measuring mismatches by counting the number of occurrences of each response broke down completely, since non-recognitions would remove unidentifiable responses from the count. It can reasonably be supposed that mismatches were also more frequent than in Phase 1.

4. DISCUSSION

One very interesting and important feature of the results was that voice input clearly offered no time advantage over the keyboard in the Phase 1 task. Even though PSM operators would conduct a visual search of at least part of the 50-key board before pressing a key, this apparently inefficient practice (compared with the 'blind' keying possible with many keyboards) was about 200ms faster than voice input. The reason is clearly that for the VRM, the time taken actually to make the response, after having selected it, was very long. The average utterance, being in this case 2.3 syllables, would take about 600ms to produce, and a further 230ms were required for machine processing. The time taken to physically press a key on the PSM, however, was of the order of 50ms. This meant that at least 780ms had to be gained during the pre-response period, for the VRM to even equal the performance of the keyboard.

In Phase 2, however, the addition of a manual component added an average 900ms to the mean sorting time per item for the keyboard. This would be predicted since for the keyboard, the sub-task of searching for parcel labels and reading them would completely interrupt the required visual search of the keyboard. For the VRM, however, two things were true: First, the act of verbal coding was not impaired by the process of parcel selection and manipulation, and second, the fact that both hands were always available for this meant that the disposal of one parcel could usually take place concurrently with selection of the next. This latter condition will not normally arise with a keyboard. The general conclusion to be drawn from this is that while voice input clearly exhibits the predicted advantage of not interfering to any significant extent with a manual task, and vice versa, it shows no advantage for a non-manual coding task, simply because the verbal response itself takes so long.

An additional point relating to this fact was brought up briefly in the Method section, and this concerns synchronisation of responses. In this type of task there must be a strictly preserved sequential relationship between coding responses (keying or speaking) and parcel registration via the light beam switch. This is necessary in order that the machine can associate a physical parcel with its code. In practice this means that with a keyboard, a parcel must not be disposed of until after its associated keystroke on each trial. This proved to be quite easy for keyboard users, even without the aid of any response completion feedback. Presumably the tactile feedback inherent in the task was sufficient. As explained briefly above, however, this procedure was unsuccessful for the VRM. Either subjects could not accurately tell when they had finished speaking a word, or they could not judge the machine processing time, or both. In any case the sequence had to be reversed, taking advantage of the fact that if the subject were to dispose of a parcel before, or even simultaneously with commencing an utterance, the long verbal response would reliably not be complete until after the disposal had been registered. While this is only one of several solutions, the problem itself is somewhat more general: It will arise whenever verbal responses are chained with other responses such as keystrokes, in such a way that timing or sequencing are important. This might be the case, for example, on a text editor using multi-modal input.

With regard to training requirements, the VRM performed as predicted, bearing in mind that minimal restrictions were placed on the manner in which subjects used the device. That is, they were not constrained in their pronunciation of words, beyond being asked to be as consistent as possible. Also, as described above, in Phase 2 every effort was made to avoid the need to train subjects to synchronise voice responses with other actions. For the PSM, it seems probable that much of the learning requirement stemmed from the need to learn the keyboard layout. The difference between the two devices thus reflected the fact that use of the VRM required no translation from one code to another, whereas the PSM required words to be translated into keyboard locations, i.e. a spatial code. Similar learning requirements could be expected with a VRM if an arbitrary or unfamiliar vocabulary had to be learned, in order to achieve acceptable recognition accuracy.

This brings us to a discussion of the factors contributing to the abnormally high error rates experienced with the VRM in this study. In the Phase 2 task, it is probable that at least two factors were at work which were not significant in Phase 1. First, the amount of physical activity involved in the Phase 2 task was considerable, and many subjects experienced difficulty in maintaining the headset microphone in a constant position. Changes in the relationship between mouth and microphone are bound to affect the characteristics of transmitted speech, particularly with the highly directional 'noise-cancelling' microphones typically used with VRM's. Second, in Phase 2 the voice pattern training of the machine (i.e. presenting the VRM with several examples of each vocabulary item from each subject) was a very different task from the actual sorting task. This was true to some extent in Phase 1, but the physical content of Phase 2 certainly added to the discrepancy,

since in both phases the subjects conducted machine training by responding to an ordered sequence of prompt words presented on a VDT. Green et al (4) have indicated that optimum recognition accuracy requires voice pattern training and recognition tasks to be as nearly identical as possible. In the Phase 2 task, this would have meant incorporating some substitute for the parcel sorting task in the machine training procedure, although this would have been very difficult, since the word expected by the VRM at any one point in the procedure could not be known, so the correct sequence of labelled parcels could not have been predetermined. In general, however, where the task contains a manual component, it will be essential to include a manual component at the machine training stage also.

Neither of the above mentioned problems was given explicit consideration in this study, and technical solutions to both would normally be possible. One factor which was specifically examined was that of long term drifts in voice quality. In the main experiments of both phases, no subject began his or her first test session less than 48hrs after training the machine. Thus there was no opportunity to look at changes in performance during this period. In Phase 1, therefore, an additional session was appended to the main experiment, in which each subject re-trained the machine immediately prior to a normal recognition test. The result of this was that while the mean rate of mismatches was slightly higher than previously, at 26%, the rate of non-recognitions was reduced dramatically to about 3%. The ratio between non-recognitions and mismatches can be controlled by means of a machine parameter, the reject threshold level (RTL). A high RTL will cause a high rate of rejections (non-recognitions), but of those accepted, few will be mismatched. The RTL could thus have been adjusted to reduce the mismatch rate to an acceptable level, while raising the less important non-recognition rate. In any case, regular updating of voice patterns is clearly highly desirable, although the optimum interval at which this should be done is not certain, and may be system and user specific.

The main factor ultimately determining recognition accuracy will often turn out to be vocabulary design, that is, the choice of a set of words that are maximally distinguishable from each other to the VRM. In Phase 1 of this experiment, it was possible to analyse systematically the patterns of confusions between words, to see if a method of error reduction could be found that would be more reliable than intuition.

In the whole of Phase 1, there were about 15000 mismatches out of a total of 72000 trials. A 50x50 matrix was constructed by the computer, in which each cell contained the number of times a given word (x) had been misrecognised as another word (y). This matrix thus showed not only the number of times each word had been mistaken for any other word, but also, by summing along rows, the total number of times each word was misrecognised. It is not possible to reproduce a matrix of this size here, but one or two examples should help to clarify its usefulness. First, it was noticed that Lancaster was identified as Manchester 173 times, while Manchester was identified as Lancaster only 39 times. Also, while Manchester was mis-identified as other items 379 times, Lancaster was misidentified 552 times. The matrix thus makes clear which of a pair of confusable words should be removed for maximum benefit (in this case Lancaster). Second, the matrix will aid identification of counter-intuitive confus-ions, such as Bristol being mistaken for Leicester (52 times), and Edinburgh being mistaken for Bedford (105 times). It would seem that in the event of a voice recognition system being able to provide accurate error data either before or after installation - as will normally be the case with any system controlled by a host computer - this method would provide a positive aid to vocabulary optimisation, independently of other performance factors.

5. CONCLUSIONS

The most important conclusion to be gleaned from this study is that any superiority of voice input over keyboard input is strongly dependent on the nature of the overall task. In the first place, voice input will only be faster if the task has sufficient manual content to effect-ively 'swallow' the relatively long response time required for speech. This may mean that voice input is not in fact very suitable for a range of wholly computer-based tasks such as word processing, data entry etc. Furthermore, it appears that spoken responses can be quite difficult to synchrosize or co-ordinate with other (e.g. manual) responses. Both of these considerations must be borne in mind when assess-ing an application for automatic voice recog-nition.

At a more particular level, this study illust-rates the seriousness of the problem of recognition accuracy, highlighting the import-ance of vocabulary selection, and pointing out some features of manual tasks which are likely to affect recognition accuracy.

REFERENCES

[1] Lowerre,B. and Reddy,R., The HARPY speech understanding system, in Lea,W.A. (ed.), Trends in speech recognition (Prentice-Hall, 1980)

[2] Allport,D.A., Antonis,B. and Reynolds,P., On the division of attention: A disproof of the single-channel hypothesis, Quarterly Journal of Experimental Psychology 24, p.225-35 (1972)

[3] Craft,A.M., Man-machine interaction in voice encoding applications: Experiments in isolated word recognition, U.S. Postal Technology Research Technical Note PTR-04-81 (1981)

[4] Green,T.R.G, Payne,S.J., Morrison,D.L. and Shaw,A., Friendly interfacing to simple speech recognisers, Behaviour and Information Technology 2 (1), p.23-38 (1983)

ACKNOWLEDGEMENTS

We would like to thank the Engineering Department of the British Post Office for funding this work, and for continual technical advice and assistance throughout the project.

Human-Computer Interaction — INTERACT '84 / B. Shackel (ed.)
Elsevier Science Publishers B.V. (North-Holland)
© IFIP, 1985

HOW SHOULD PEOPLE AND COMPUTERS SPEAK TO EACH OTHER?

M A Richards and K M Underwood

British Telecom Research Laboratories,
Martlesham Heath, Ipswich, England

Voice is becoming a more common mode of communication between man and machine. We
have previously shown that computer-naive users naturally adapt the way that they ask
questions in an information retrieval task when they think that they are addressing a
computer system, as opposed to a human (3). The present study investigates how the
content of the messages with which the computer system initially addresses the user
can further encourage behaviour that would be potentially useful for enabling
automatic speech recognition and analysis. Elements of 'politeness' and
'explicitness' in the system's initial message were varied, and the regularity and
conciseness with which users responded was studied. Several aspects of users'
behaviour were found to be affected, and age and learning effects were also observed.

1. INTRODUCTION

For many applications the most convenient means
of interacting with a computer is to use voice
as the communication medium. This allows the
computer operator to be mobile, for example, and
to have his hands and eyes free for other tasks.
Systems which permit the operator to speak to a
computer, using isolated word entry, and for the
computer to reply, are becoming more and more
widespread. Technological limitations in the
fields of voice recognition and synthetic speech
production determine that such interactions are
somewhat different from normal spoken exchanges
between people. The user's attitude towards the
computer can also help to determine the extent
to which his everyday skills in verbal communication are applied to interactions of this kind.
Bearing these factors in mind, but also anticipating the day when flexible and efficient voice
communication between a computer and its human
operator becomes a possibility, we need to know
how the computer should speak to the operator,
and how the operator should speak to the
computer.

2. DIALOGUE DESIGN

Most current speech recognisers can only achieve
an acceptable level of recognition performance
when words are spoken clearly, consistently,
and in isolation. This makes demands on the
speaker that cannot easily be compromised.
Whether or not people are naturally inclined to
speak this way, experience has shown us that
they are capable of doing so; even naive users
can successfully address a computer in this
manner after appropriate instruction (4).
Dialogues can be designed specifically to elicit
one-word utterances from the human operator, by
asking direct questions and giving the alternatives listed in an auditory menu. We must now
turn our attention to the possibilities of
designing more sophisticated dialogue structures,
if voice is to be fully exploited as a mode of

communication between man and machine.

2.1 System and User Limitations

Even the most advanced recognition systems will
continue to have limited capabilities in the
foreseeable future, such as limits to the
vocabulary size and syntax complexity that can
be accepted. However, as recognition systems
become more complex and flexible, their remaining limitations are liable to become more
difficult to define and explain to the human
user, at least initially. Between the basic
level of dialogue complexity that can currently
be achieved, using single word inputs, and the
vastly complex 'natural' dialogues that we
employ when communicating with one another, lies
an area fraught with difficulties. Dialogue
structures must be designed such that the
limitations imposed by the recognition system
are compatible with the ways in which humans
naturally speak or, at least, how they can be
easily encouraged to speak. Clearly, humans too
have limited capabilities. Thus we need to know
how people naturally communicate by voice when
performing tasks typical of those involved in
computer interaction, and how they might be
naturally inclined to speak to a computer.

2.2 'Natural' Dialogues in Information Retrieval
    Tasks

In a previous experiment (3) we investigated how
people normally express themselves when requesting information over the phone, using this
example of information retrieval as a typical
function of computer interaction. We were
interested to see to what extent speakers'
utterances were standardised, both in terms of
style and content, and would hence be amenable
to computer analysis. We also investigated the
extent to which speakers' responses would be
affected by the perceived nature of the system
they were addressing. Controlled experiments
were conducted in which computer-naive members

of the public were used as subjects. In one
case, subjects were told that they would be
addressing a human respondent, and in the other
that they would be addressing a computer. The
voices used by the respondent were, respectively,
a natural human voice and a synthetic-sounding
voice. However, the content of the respondent's
utterances (and also the intonation patterns)
were, as far as possible, the same; in fact, the
same individual played the part of the
respondent in both conditions, unaware of the
form in which her voice was being transmitted to
the subjects. Any differences in the subjects'
perceptions of the two systems would thus be
based primarily upon having initially been told
the general nature of the system (human or
computer-based), and the system's voice quality.

Regardless of the identity of the system, a good
deal of ritualistic and standardised verbal
behaviour was observed. For example, the order
of information volunteered by speakers was
similar across all subjects. Again, a tendency
towards politeness was observed in subjects
addressing either system.

In other respects, however, it was found that
the style and content of the subjects'
utterances were significantly affected by the
attributed nature of the system that they were
interrogating. For example, when addressing the
computer system, users spoke more slowly, used a
more restricted vocabulary, tended to use less
potentially ambiguous pronouns, and asked
questions in a more direct manner. In general,
the concessions made to the simulated computer
system were of a kind that would more easily
enable machine analysis.

3. AIMS OF PRESENT STUDY

Although unique in looking at how people address
a 'machine', the previous study is just one of
many that demonstrate that speakers' utterances
can be determined, in part, by the perceived
nature of the party with whom they are conversing, and hence the relationship that can exist
between them (2). The results demonstrate that
there is at least one way (ie through the nature
of the system's voice) in which users can be
encouraged to address an automated system at a
level more appropriate to the capabilities of
the foreseeable technology. However, there may
be many other, more subtle, ways of achieving
this end. In the present experiment, we
investigate how the manner in which the system
addresses the user can encourage him to respond
'appropriately'. The aspect of a verbal
dialogue with a computer which will have the
greatest impact in this respect is the system's
initial message - both what it says (eg including any description of its capabilities and
limitations) and how it says it (eg in terms of
the level of politeness used).

Two particular variables in the system's initial
message were studied, the 'explicitness' and the
'politeness' of the message. In the case of the

former, the system's message would either spell
out the form in which the user must address the
system (eg indicating what items of information
the system requires from the user), or else just
invite an enquiry. In relation to 'politeness',
the system would either include polite and
colloquial phrases to help 'personalise' the
exchange, or omit them. The initial messages
used, representing the four experimental
conditions of this study, are given in section
4.2. Specifically, we wished to know what types
of user responses would be elicited with and
without explicit instruction, and also whether
elements of informality introduced by the system
itself are responded to by the user.

4. METHOD

4.1 Procedure

A total of 48 subjects, computer-naive members
of the public ranging in age from 20-60 years,
were asked to carry out 6 tasks. These
involved obtaining train times from a time-table
service, accessed over the telephone. All of
the information necessary to complete the
requests (approximate time and place of arrival
and departure) was included in the written task
descriptions. Subjects were given the opportunity to volunteer all the relevant facts
immediately after the system's introductory
message, but were prompted by the system if they
failed to do so. The order in which these items
of information were included in the tasks was
varied between the 6 tasks.

The subjects were divided into 4 groups,
balanced for age and sex, all members of each
group receiving the same pre-recorded introductory message at the beginning of each call.
However, the introductory messages were
different for each group, as shown below (ie
conditions 1-4). All subjects were initially
told that the information service was to be
provided by a computer, and were addressed in
the same synthetic-sounding voice. Apart from
the introductory message, the conversations were
actually conducted 'live', as a simulation of an
automated service. The conversations were
recorded on tape for later analysis.

4.2 Variables

Condition 1. Explicit, polite.
"Hello. This is British Telecom's train time-
table service. Would you please tell me where
you wish to travel from, where to, and the day
and approximate time that you wish to travel."

Condition 2. Explicit, non-polite.
"British Telecom's train time-table service.
State where travelling from, where to, and the
day and approximate time of travel."

Condition 3. Inexplicit, polite.
"Hello. This is British Telecom's train time-
table service. Can I help you?"

Condition 4. Inexplicit, non-polite.
"British Telecom's train time-table service.
State your request."

5. RESULTS

The recorded conversations provided a rich
source of experimental data. Our initial
analysis concentrated on two particular aspects
that have direct implications for the possibilities of machine recognition; these concern the
regularity and the conciseness with which
subjects made their requests. The regularity of
the subjects' requests was investigated by
looking at the order in which items of information were volunteered, and the numbers and
combinations of items that were included in
separate utterances. To investigate conciseness,
we measured the total number of words used by
subjects in making their requests and related
this to the number of words that were non-
essential. Utterances that were not classified
as being strictly essential mostly comprised
repetitions, irrelevant information, or phrases
associated with politeness.

5.1 Regularity

Clearly, the recognition task would be eased if
the format in which information was requested
followed some reliable pattern, since the
probabilities of particular words occurring, in
a particular order, could be predicted and hence
the overall accuracy of recognition improved.
Such a pattern was indeed observed, and not just
for those conditions in which the information
required by the system was explicitly stated (ie
conditions 1 and 2). Though significantly less
pronounced in conditions 3 and 4, the trend
towards providing information in a particular
order (place of departure, place of arrival,
day, and finally approximate time of travel) was
nevertheless reliably found in subjects in all
four experimental conditions. In all cases the
finding was sufficiently well established to
provide for a potentially useful means of
improving recognition accuracy by allowing
recognition probabilities to be appropriately
weighted. The probability of each item of
information occurring in a particular position
within the user's initial question was around
0.9 for conditions 1 and 2, and 0.6 for
conditions 3 and 4. As a more minor effect,
there was also some indication that people were
more inclined to structure their questions in a
standard manner when the system's message was in
one of the 'non-polite' forms.

The greater the number of items of necessary
information provided to the system by the user
in a single complete utterance, the more rapidly
the dialogue could proceed; less 'hand-overs'
between system and user would be required,
points at which errors and misunderstandings are
particularly common in verbal exchanges. In
fact, subjects most commonly gave all 4 items of
information in one go, again regardless of
whether they had been explicitly instructed to

do so or not. In almost all cases where the 4
items were not given at once, 3 items were
included together and the fourth (usually the
approximate time of travel) had to be prompted.
Nevertheless, the tendency for all four items of
information to be given together was significantly greater when explicit instructions were
given (ie conditions 1 and 2).

5.2 Conciseness

As a measure of the conciseness of peoples'
expressions we calculated a ratio of non-
essential words/total number of words spoken
within the users' basic requests. A relatively
large proportion of inessential information
would suggest an informality of communication,
and this was found to be discouraged particularly
by the explicit and non-polite nature of the
message in condition 2. A significant learning
effect was found in all conditions, with users
stating their requests more concisely as they
gained experience of the system. However, the
single most important factor in determining the
conciseness with which people expressed themselves was their age, with subjects in the
highest age group (50-60 years) being
particularly verbose.

A considerable proportion of the 'inessential'
components of users' utterances were concerned
with politeness. It has previously been shown
that politeness from one party in a conversation
invites similar behaviour from the other (1);
the present results suggest that this is also
true in man-machine interaction, at least in
part. Polite responses tended to be more
commonly elicited from users when the system
addressed them with a polite, inexplicit
introductory message (condition 3) than when the
other messages were used. It was also in
response to this message type that users most
commonly corrected themselves, again suggesting
a certain informality and a preparedness to
speak without thorough preparation.

By explicitly stating its input requirement
(conditions 1 and 2) the system might suggest
to the user that it is less intelligent than is
the case when the user is apparently free to
address it as they please (conditions 3 and 4).
This would be useful if the user was otherwise
inclined to overestimate the system's capabilities, and address it in too complex a manner,
but counter-productive if users were discouraged from exploiting the level of intelligence
actually possessed by the system. Although
formal analyses of syntax complexity have yet to
be completed, there is no immediately apparent
evidence to suggest that the complexity of users'
expressions was generally affected by the
explicitness of the system's initial message.
However, it was noted that several people did
not provide the information requested in the
form of a sentence when replying to the
'explicit' messages, but justed listed the
requested items.

Neither explicitness nor politeness in the system's initial message alone had a significant effect upon the range of vocabulary adopted by users, but the politely phrased inexplicit message (condition 3) did tend to encourage the use of a wider vocabulary (around 150 different words between all speakers, compared with around 100 words in the other conditions).

6 CONCLUSIONS AND DISCUSSION

The findings of the present study complement those of an earlier investigation (3) into how naive users are inclined to interrogate an information service. From observations of their behaviour, we have found that most users are able to make reasonable judgements about the capabilities of a computer system with which they can communicate by voice, on the basis of some simple but fundamental cues (ie voice type and message content). Encouragingly, they appear to be capable of adapting their verbal behaviour in ways that are potentially useful for automatic speech recognition and dialogue control (eg by adapting the formality and conciseness of their expressions). Clearly, the success of communication with computers by voice will depend upon the way in which human users can and will speak to a machine. Since this can be significantly affected by the system's voice quality and the manner in which the computer initiates the dialogue, we must initially pay particular attention to how the computer should speak to the user.

In relatively strightforward tasks, such as this information retrieval task, the user is likely to adopt standard forms of expression, which are broadly common to all users. Although most users do this without explicit instruction, the more explicit system messages did elicit more uniform responses.

Politeness and informality in the system's messages appear to encourage similarly informal responses, particularly when the messages are also inexplicit in their demands of the user. The form of the exchanges tend to become more conversational, and potentially more difficult to process automatically. However, the factor which had the greatest effect upon how people expressed themselves was age: older people were more verbose and informal in their exchanges than younger people. This suggests that their understanding of the likely capabilities of computer systems, particularly in respect of voice i/o handling capabilities, is rather unrealistic. However, the finding that subjects in all age groups learned to speak more concisely as they gained experience of using the system underlines the importance of appropriate training and preparation.

The most helpful aspects of user-friendliness in communicating with machines relate to the under-lying compatability of the computer with the human user, and do not necessarily include the notions of friendliness (such as personal

familiarity and informality) that we associate with interactions between people. However, any reduction in 'politeness' on the part of the system, though it may lead to a useful degree of conciseness in the dialogue, must not be at the expense of creating negative reactions to the system as a whole. Although there was no clear evidence that users felt less comfortable or more alienated from the computer system when the 'polite' components of its messages were omitted in this study, the terseness of the interactions was remarked upon by several people.

As a general principle it must be better to study the natural inclinations of users in any particular interactive task, and to design the system around any standard forms of behaviour observed rather than to initially define the system's requirements and then to explicitly instruct the user on how to fulfil them. The same degree of recognition performance may be achieved, but in addition the dialogue will appear to be more natural to the user. Moreover, the user's memory will not be unduly loaded with formal instructions. The user may have the impression that he has a greater degree of freedom in expressing himself than may actually be the case, and this may lead to a more favourable impression of the system. In practice, the design of the man-machine inter-face will demand compromises between the natural inclinations of the user and the technical complexities of the system. We have shown that the content of the system's introductory message significantly influences a user's verbal behaviour, and these findings suggest means of achieving compromise solutions which could minimise the demands made of the user.

REFERENCES

(1) Clark, H.H. and Schunk, D.H., Polite responses to polite requests, Cognition 8 (1980) 111-143.

(2) Giles, H. and Powesland, P.F., Speech style and social evaluation (Academic Press, London, 1975).

(3) Richards, M.A. and Underwood, K.M., Talking to machines: how are people naturally inclined to speak?, Proceedings of the Ergonomics Society Annual Conference (1984).

(4) Waterworth, J.A., Interaction with machines by voice, Proceedings of the 10th Intern-ational Symposium on Human Factors in Telecommunications (1983) 263-270.

ACKNOWLEDGEMENT

Acknowledgement is made to the Director of Research of British Telecom Research Laboratories for permission to publish this paper.

Human-Computer Interaction — INTERACT '84 / B. Shackel (ed.)
Elsevier Science Publishers B.V. (North-Holland)
© IFIP, 1985

HUMAN FACTORS AND SYNTHETIC SPEECH

John C. Thomas and Mary Beth Rosson

Computer Science Department
IBM Thomas J. Watson Research Center
Yorktown Heights, NY 10598 USA

Martin Chodorow
Psychology Department
Hunter College, City University of New York
New York, New York

Recent advances in linguistics, speech science, psychology, and especially in computers have made unlimited text-to-speech conversion systems a practical reality. However, the use of audio output from a computer poses special problems in ergonomics, most of which have not been dealt with in the literature. In this paper, we review relevant findings in the literature and recent work in our own laboratory. We then provide some guidelines for good human factors in applications that use speech synthesis. These guidelines address both the process of development and suggestions for the end-product. The latter must be considered highly tentative due to the nascent nature of this research area.

1. INTRODUCTION

Recent advances in linguistics, speech science, and especially digital signal processing and computer power have made text-to-speech conversion systems a practical reality. Yet relatively little work has been done on the human factors of speech synthesis applications. Since products and applications are currently being used by real users, human factors personnel find themselves in the typical situation of having to give advice on the basis of scanty evidence. In this paper, existing findings on synthetic speech will be reviewed followed by the presentation of tentative guidelines in using speech synthesis.

Findings relevant to the human factors of speech synthesis can be classified into 1. those that evaluate the goodness of existing synthesizers, 2. those that attempt to understand the underlying processes of people understanding synthetic speech, 3. studies that parametrically compare options in synthesis to determine which options are best according to some objective or subjective criteria, and 4. those which specifically address how to use speech synthesis. Excluded from this review are the myriad of studies by linguists, phoneticians, and psycholinguists which use synthetic speech merely because it is a convenient way to prepare well-controlled stimuli for studies whose purpose and outcome are not directly relevant to human factors. Also excluded are the

many earlier studies on perceiving human speech in the presence of noise, although consideration of these studies has played a part in the tentative recommendations presented in section 3.

2. REVIEW OF RESEARCH

2.1. Intelligibility Studies.

Among studies in the first category, those done in David Pisoni's lab at Indiana are the most comprehensive. Anyone interested in the human factors of speech synthesis is referred to this work [1] which indicates the absolute and relative levels of intelligibility for various synthesizers under various conditions of semantic and syntactic predictability. For example, Pisoni [2] found that correct word recognition with the Harvard meaningful sentences was 93.2 per cent while performance for the Haskins "nonsense" (but syntactically correct) sentences was only 78.7 per cent correct with MITtalk (an excellent Text-to-Speech system).

Similarly, in the Modified Rhyme Test wherein the listener merely chooses which of several potential words was the one played out by the synthesizer, the average error rate on 50 monosyllables by 72 naive listeners was only 6.9 per cent. (Although natural speech produced only a .6 per cent error rate). However, when listeners were not given choices but had to transcribe each word after they heard it, the natural speech error rate rose to 2.8

per cent but the synthetic speech rate increased to 24.6 per cent. It should be cautioned that these results were obtained with MITalk and many commercially available synthesizers would produce higher error rates under these conditions. Qualitatively, the results indicate clearly that human listeners to some extent can compensate for problems in the acoustic signal when choice is restricted to known or inferred alternatives.

Another caveat in these studies is that they have been conducted with college students and the human factors engineer is encouraged to be cognizant of this. More recent work, however, has begun to extend this work to other subject populations. Work in Pisoni's lab also demonstrates that with about an hour's practice, one can expect comprehension of SAT reading questions with a good speech synthesizer to approach comprehension of the text read by human readers. It should also be noted, however, that even in cases where synthetic and natural speech produce equal recall performance, the synthetic speech requires more processing capacity and messages spoken in synthetic speech seem less credible.

Work in our laboratory replicates several of these findings. For example, after an hour's practice, personnel at the Watson Research Labs are able to transcribe simple predictable sentences in synthetic speech very well. Overall, subjects can transcribe the CHABA sentences well over 90 per cent word-correct [3]. Garden path sentences, however, like "The horse raced past the barn fell", [4] are transcribed at only about 50 per cent word correct when presented synthetically but at 97 per cent correct from human voice (with correct prosody).

It is important to note then that intelligibility exhibits a very wide range with existing synthesizers depending upon the predictability of the text. In addition, the size of individual differences in perceiving synthetic speech is quite large. For example, on one commercially available speech synthesis system, 15 naive subjects varied in the percentage of correctly transcribed CID-W22 words on first listening from only 40 per cent correct to 74 per cent correct. On a different synthesizer tested in our laboratory, six naive subjects varied from 0 per cent correct to 44 per cent correct on this same test of phonetically balanced monosyllables. These studies, though preliminary, should already be convincing enough to caution the evaluators of an application using synthetic speech that favorable results with a few subjects does not necessarily imply that the quality of synthesis will be acceptable to all potential users.

2.2. Studies of Perceptual Processes.

Studies that attempt to explicate how people perceive normal speech are legion and will not be reviewed here. Studies that attempt to understand the processes involved in perceiving and learning to perceive synthetic speech (from a human factors perspective) are few. One study in our laboratory indicates an interaction in phoneme transcription within a word. People tended to transcribe the entire word correctly (i.e., zero phonemes wrong), or they made multiple errors in transcribing the word (two, three or four phonemes wrong). Given the overall error rate in phoneme transcription, there were fewer than expected words with exactly one phoneme mistranscribed. We also attempted to adduce evidence for a short-term "tracking" perceptual process by which subjects "tune in" to the synthesizer. We examined word perception when prefaced by variable length non-informative introductions but found no effect of the length of the introduction. In this particular study, it should be noted that the subjects were already ready and waiting to listen to the synthesizer. Different results might be expected from subjects who were attending to different sensory channels. Then an acoustic preface might be critical in signaling an attentional shift.

On the other hand, the data of Simpson and Williams [5] cast doubt on even this speculation. Basically, they showed that an alerting tone increased response times to a warning message (produced by a VOTRAX VS-6 synthesizer); pilots were faster in responding to the message-alone warnings. But time to produce tone was included in response time measurement. They argue that because if the warning voice is qualitatively different from other speech sounds, it serves as its own warning, and additional alerting signals will be necessary only if the voice is to be used for other purposes in addition to warning messages.

Also, including extra semantic information, while it adds time, like the warning tone, does not increase response time, suggesting that it's a good idea. They also refer to previous work on the benefits of semantic context [6]:

By inference, several studies indicate a great deal of top-down processing in the perception of synthetic speech. However, one should not make the mistake of concluding that bottom-up processing is unimportant. For example, in one study done in our lab in order to understand the level at which learning to understand a speech synthesizer takes place, we found evidence concerning both general and specific learning. Furthermore, we found some low frequency words happened to be quite intelligible (e.g, gore, dire, elf, zeal, farce, and dirge!), at least on the synthesizer studied.

As a further investigation into the nature of top-down processing in the perception of speech, college students were given synthetic and natural voice sentences some of which violated syntactic or semantic constraints and which varied in word frequency. Again, natural speech was well transcribed under all conditions, but synthetic speech transcription varied from very good to quite bad. All the types of constraints contributed to intelligibility. Interestingly, subjects often tended to mis-write the preposition at the beginning of a prepositional phrase and once the beginning of a phrase was mistranscribed, the entire phrase was generally wrong.

2.3. Optimizing Synthetic Speech Output.

There have been few published studies that compare options in speech synthesizers. Experiments by Pisoni's lab and by Jenkins and Franklin [7] seem to indicate that prosody, at least at the level of accuracy available in commercially available synthesizers, has a negligible effect on sentence intelligibility. Our informal observations tend to corroborate this, at least with respect to fundamental frequency changes (monotone versus prosody switch). Several long-term listeners to speech synthesizers (blind people) have indicated a boredom with the repetitious prosody of existing synthesizers. Further work is clearly needed to demonstrate the objective and subjective value of prosody in synthetic speech.

Experiments with rate have indicated that maximum sentence comprehension with an existing speech synthesis system is considerably slower than the default rate. This might indicate that system designers should consider playing the system more slowly than the default, at least initially.

Another way of optimizing perception is not by manipulating the signal, but by manipulating the listener. Untested at this point are various possible conscious "strategies" that the listener might use. Anecdotally, it appears that during sentence perception it might be advantageous to "hold off" trying to form a Gestalt too quickly and "let the sentence emerge." At least these are comments from those subjects who did best at sentence transcription.

Individual differences are surprisingly large; strategy may play a part here. Other factors also need to be investigated. It has also been remarked that non-native speakers have particular difficulty with synthetic speech although it is not really known whether this is a true interaction or simply a by-product of having a more difficult time generally combined with the fact that natural speech has such a high quality signal that, in context, the somewhat higher error rate of the non-native speaker at the phoneme level does not impinge greatly on sentence perception.

There are probably other demographic or psychological factors that could predict which particular people would be good at listening to synthetic speech. Further research may be forthcoming in this area. The so-called normal presbycusis or other age-related effects may make synthetic speech relatively more difficulty for older listeners. Preliminary results (personal communication) in Pisoni's lab hint that children may be particularly good at perceiving synthetic speech.

Probably the biggest factor in improving the listener's performance is experience and learning. Even an hour's practice improves perception of synthetic speech remarkably. This has been shown in Pisoni's lab [2], by Jenkins and Franklin [7] and again in our laboratory. Although individual differences are also large in learning, an hour's practice increased the percentage of correctly transcribed monosyllable words from 70 to 80 per cent on one synthesizer. Carlson, Granstrom, and Larsson [8] found that performance increased from 55 to 90 per cent correct on sentences as listeners heard 200 sentences over a two week period. With even more extended practice, and with the ability to re-listen and, if necessary, spell things out, blind users of reading machines are essentially able to read (i.e., listen) with very accurate comprehension. I tested one such experienced listener, however, and found that for isolated monosyllable words without using the spell option, he still was only 60 per cent accurate. Clearly, much of the ability to get essentially normal performance on connected discourse is due to reliance on context and on the ability to skip back and spell when needed.

We are just beginning work in our laboratory to attempt to determine how to maximize the effects of practice and to understand what is learned when one adapts to synthetic speech.

2.4. Human Factors of Speech Synthesis Applications.

So far as we have been able to determine, the only studies directly relevant to how to use synthetic speech in an application are the informal studies done in the development of IBM's Audio Distribution System which used digitized human speech for messages. In that system we found it useful to play messages at different rates depending upon the user's preference or experience and to allow users to re-listen to a message, skip backwards or forwards, vary the rate and volume and to allow user's to skip to a particular message. A hierarchical set of markers to allow for intelligent skimming through long audio documents was seldom used, perhaps primarily because audio messages tended to be quite short.

In using the telephone keypad (which will be used in many speech synthesis applications), we found that verbal and spatial mnemonics were far superior to arbitrary number sequences for commands. Our experience with the Audio Distribution System also convinced us that, at least for office principles it is vital that they be able to learn the system within a very short period of time. We are currently engaged in exploring people's reactions in a qualitative way to the following applications: an audio on-line internal phone directory, an audio questionnaire facility, and a travel reservation system.

3. TENTATIVE GUIDELINES TO SYNTHETIC SPEECH APPLICATIONS.

3.1 Process Guidelines.

The guidelines that we feel most confident about are those that suggest how to manage the process of developing applications with synthetic speech. In general, these match the process guidelines in Thomas [9]. Space permits only the barest outline here. Basically, we believe that there is no "key" to good human factors. Rather, there are many ways in which human factors must be addressed and at each of several stages in the development process.

Our overall philosophy is that computer systems at this point must be evolutionary systems. We cannot design to a fixed point because the users, the tasks, the environment and the technology are all continually changing. This does not mean that we should not try to do the best possible job during initial design. But it does mean that the feedback process both within and between development cycles is even more important. "Initial" design needs to begin with feedback about other similar systems. During initial design, behavioral expertise should be involved and behavioral goals should be set. Fundamental questions need to be raised. For instance, should you even use voice output? If you are giving a limited number of signals to experienced users who should respond quickly, distinctive non-speech sounds may be better. Are the users going to have a choice about whether to use the system? In that case, aesthetic appeal as well as intelligibility is probably important. These are just two samples of the kinds of questions that must be asked. Generally speaking, everyone on the design team should

have thought completely about the users, their tasks, their goals, and their environment. One fundamental question is simply whether speech synthesis is really called for. Generally, speech synthesis is useful in four kinds of cases: 1. those in which people need remote access to information (because of the ubiquity of the telephone), 2. cascs in which the user cannot read due to age, training, or visual problems, 3. cases in which the user is already overloaded with visual stimuli and audition can provide an additional channel of information (e.g., air traffic controllers, CAI, CAD, computer operators), 4. cases in which audition provides special advantages due to its omni-directional character and attention-grabbing properties (e.g., warning messages, lathe operator instructions).

During implementation, a variety of methods should constantly provide feedback to the designers. For instance, before using real speech synthesis, it may be useful to simulate the system with human beings communicating via speech or speech in noise. Before incorporating an LPC fixed message speech system into your application, it would be good to use the more flexible text-to-speech system to determine which messages are understandable in content.

In any case, if you are designing a new application, a prototype will be highly desirable. In order to facilitate changing the prototype intelligently, program behavioral "hooks" into the system; i.e., code that keeps track of the frequency and order in which various functions are used. Find out users' objective and subjective reactions to the system.

On the basis of these data, you may decide not whether but how to change the user interface. This change will be much easier if the prototype is built with change in mind. One way to aid this change is to separate the code that carries out function from the user interface. For a fuller case history of a product developed under this philosophy the reader is referred to Gould and Boies [10],[11].

During the testing phase, people representative of intended users should be given tasks and their performance should be compared to the behavioral goals. To the extent possible feedback about the use of the application should be built into the design.

3.2 Product Guidelines

The reader is again cautioned that due to the very limited scope of research and practical experience in this area, these guidelines are to be viewed as very tentative. In addition, they can only be applied in a

Human-Computer Interaction — INTERACT '84 / B. Shackel (ed.)
Elsevier Science Publishers B.V. (North-Holland)
© IFIP, 1985

EXPERIMENTS IN SPEECH INTERACTION WITH CONVENTIONAL DATA SERVICES

Christopher Labrador and Dinesh Pai

BNR
P.O. Box 3511, Station C
Ottawa, Canada   K1Y 4H7

Access to conventional data services typically involves the use of a standard keyboard terminal over a data network. This paper discusses our experiments at BNR in using speech as an alternative. We used a text messaging service as the vehicle for our experiments to investigate the interaction between humans and computers over the telephone voice network using the telephone as a terminal. In our experiments, presentation to the user is accomplished using speech synthesis and user input is effected with DTMF (Dual Tone Multi-Frequency) signaling.

INTRODUCTION

The technological advances of today make a large number of computer based services accessible to us. Typically, to communicate with these services, users must interact with the computer at its level. That is, the dialogue of the transaction is fixed and information conveyed between the user and the computer must be in a machine-acceptable form. The user must ultimately accommodate the computer in order to effect a successful transaction.

Although progress in dialogue design is providing the user with "tolerant" and "friendly" interfaces, we are still faced with the issue of how the user and the computer convey information to each other. The mechanisms for human-computer communication have progressed substantially since the inception of the "punch-card" but, until recently, attempts to improve human-computer communication often resulted in little more than repackaging exercises. Instead of reinventing the terminal, we must incorporate human-like modes of communication into human-computer interaction.

Speech is an important component of communication among humans. There are also many practical benefits to be gained by using speech to communicating with computers [1]. By complementing the existing communication media with speech, alternate methods to access conventional data services become available. Furthermore, it may be possible to offer mechanisms for common access to multimedia services.

This paper details our experiments in using speech to interact with an electronic text messaging service. Because of the nature of the experiments, the results obtained are applicable to other text-oriented data services where control or selection is normally effected using a keyboard and the responses generated by the service are usually presented in a visual form.

A TEXT-TO-SPEECH MESSAGING EXPERIMENT

Our main interests involved investigating the issues concerned with managing the human-computer dialogue, handling data that was originally intended for visual presentation, and using the telephone as a terminal. We used an electronic text messaging service which provided us with the opportunity to obtain results in all these areas as well as to establish the viability of using speech in conjunction with conventional data services.

A Text Messaging Service

The service used in our experiments was Envoy 100[1] [2]. It is a store-and-forward text messaging service, designed to meet the needs of both the business and residential communities. Envoy 100 can be thought of as an electronic representation of various office components (e.g., mailboxes, files, bulletin boards). The commands and features of Envoy 100 allow the user to manipulate his electronic information in much the same manner as he would paper correspondence in the office.

Access to Envoy 100 is via Datapac[1], a
packet switching data network offered by
Telecom Canada. Using a standard terminal, Envoy 100 users access the Datapac
network and then provide the network
address for Envoy 100 in order to be
'connected' to the service.

Once a connection is established and a
user is authenticated, a typical Envoy
100 session might consist of reading
unread messages, retrieving previously
filed messages for review, or creating
and sending new messages. Messages can
also be disposed of or maintained for
future reference.

Envoy Voice Interface System

A requirement was that we could not
interfere with or modify Envoy 100 service throughout our experiments. To
achieve this, a front-end processor,
EVIS (Envoy Voice Interface System), was
used for all human-computer interaction.

EVIS connects to Envoy 100 via Datapac
and to the user via the standard telephone voice network using a telephone as
a terminal. To Envoy 100, EVIS appears
as a data terminal. To the user, EVIS
appears as a message attendant. Using
the text output from Envoy 100, EVIS
provides the user with synthesized
speech using the Prose 2000[2]
text-to-speech converter [3]. Input to
EVIS is accomplished with DTMF signaling, such as Touch-Tone[3]. Figure 1
illustrates the network configuration.

Implementation

Envoy 100 offers a large number of features of varying complexity. For our
experiments, however, we considered only
a subset of these features. Using EVIS,
an Envoy 100 user can be connected to
the text messaging service and, after
being informed of whether there are any
messages in his mailbox, he can perform
one of the following:

- determine whether there are messages
  in his mailbox or 'heard' file (an
  area independent of the mailbox that
  is used to store messages after they
  have been listened to);

- listen to, file, or dispose of messages from his mailbox;

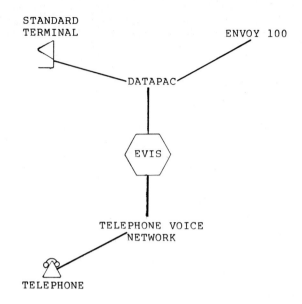

Figure 1. Envoy   100   and   EVIS
           network configuration

- listen to or dispose of messages
  from his 'heard' file;

- request assistance; or

- terminate the Envoy 100 session.

The user first receives information concerning his Envoy 100 environment, then
receives a prompt. The user then enters
one or possibly two DTMF keys to effect
a particular command. The user enters
one key to select from several possible
actions (e.g., listen to a message, file
a message). The user enters two keys
where the scope of the command is to be
specified or to ensure that the first
key was not entered accidentally.

We chose the command names and the keys
corresponding to the commands so that
the first letter of the command name
corresponded to one of the letters commonly associated with the DTMF key used.
For example, the 'FILE' command, which
is used to file messages in the 'heard'
file, is invoked by entering key '3'
which has the letters 'DEF' associated
with it.

RESULTS

Our experiments were concerned with
dialogue management, oral presentation
of textual information, and issues
relating to the use of the telephone as
a terminal for human-computer inter-

action. The results obtained provide us with the following details.

Dialogue Management

Quantity of Presented Information: Envoy 100 often uses visually formatted data to present information. It is relatively easier for a user to scan a table or view a hierarchical structure than to have a verbose description of the data presented to him. Visual effects, however, have little, if any, meaning when orally presented to the user. As a result, the information normally presented to the Envoy 100 user must be interpreted and described to the EVIS user. Furthermore, once this information is provided, it is no longer available for review unless the user explicitly requests that it be repeated. In contrast, a visual presentation is usually available for immediate review.

In transforming the text output from Envoy 100 into descriptions provided by EVIS we found that the user was being saturated with information which he could not effectively use. Phrases were needed to accurately describe individual table entries. Where each entry was used to describe a particular message attribute (e.g., originator, subject, length), several phrases were required to describe individual messages. Because of this, it was necessary to manage the tables and lists generated by Envoy 100 by decomposing them into logical segments, each embodying a portion of the originally intended information. These segments were then read to the user, providing him with a smaller, more manageable amount of information that could also be easily repeated. This mechanism was used to effect a sequential decision making process instead of a single step selection. In this manner, the user could hear and assimilate the information provided without having to remember a number of details regarding other pending transactions.

Quality of Presented Information: We found that the quality or naturalness of the spoken information as well as the prompt itself was an important factor in obtaining a response from the user. When the entire EVIS session was conducted using the same synthesized voice there was no subtle way to indicate to the user that they should pay particular attention to any specific portion of the speech output. Textual information often conveys secondary information relative to its location or format and it

is this coloration which was lacking in EVIS. Because of this, important information was sometimes lost and had to be repeated.

We investigated different aural cues to attempt to eliminate this problem. Statements issued by EVIS, which alerted the user that information of a particular significance was to follow, were used along with pauses and 'beeps'. This alleviated the problem somewhat, yet it added to the overhead in terms of total speech output. To improve upon this solution we varied parameters of the synthesized voice so that, depending on the context of the session, the pitch and rate of the synthesized speech were changed. This seemed to give better results. Fewer requests to repeat information were issued by the user because he was able to use these variations rather than the context of the speech itself as a cue to attribute different values to the perceived speech. In light of these results we felt that using stored-speech synthesis, which offers increased naturalness and intelligibility, for prompts and fixed information (e.g., online assistance, status information) would improve the situation even further. Preliminary results indicate that this is the preferred solution.

Feedback: Mapping a speech interface over the existing Envoy 100 text interface creates the problem of providing suitable feedback to the user. Typing in a command and pressing the enter key on a standard terminal repositions the cursor on the terminal and thus provides the Envoy 100 user with confirmation that his command has been entered. Unless oral confirmation is provided, the EVIS user cannot be sure that his command has been accepted by the system. Furthermore, even if the command is acknowledged, waiting for it to be processed often seems interminable, especially when Envoy 100 is slow to respond. To remedy this, EVIS provides the user with an oral acknowledgement of his input commands and also issues periodic 'beeps' to assure the user that the connection, and hence the session, is intact.

Oral Presentation of Textual Information

Text-to-Speech Problems: A major concern relates to the actual textual information that EVIS is expected to transform into speech. Since the Envoy 100 user is not restricted, he is able

to enter any characters in any order as
part of the message. Because of this,
EVIS is faced with the traditional
text-to-speech problems associated with
spelling errors, abbreviations and acronyms, and context-dependent pronunciation. Spelling errors are a particular
nuisance in that the energies involved
in trying to comprehend apparent nonsense sometimes detract attention from
the message and information is lost.
Even when a spelling error results in
another pronounceable word, the effect
can be the same. Similarly, abbreviations and acronyms might be considered
as spelling errors. Even though the
Prose 2000 text-to-speech converter is
programmed and can be tuned to handle
certain instances of specific abbreviations and acronyms, it cannot accommodate every conceivable one.
Mispronunciation of words that are
spelled correctly can similarly confuse
the listener.

Problems with Visual Effects: EVIS must
also contend with the problem of dealing
with messages that contain characters
that are used to generate visual
effects. Techniques such as underlining
and capitalizing, which are used to
highlight and emphasize the text, are
common. Diagrams, graphs, and charts
usually convey meanings independent of
the characters used to depict them. In
these instances, the messages are
intended to have a visual impact.
Humans can encode and decode information
in this fashion but, unfortunately,
there is no adequate algorithm that computers can use to establish the implied
meaning of the message. The easiest
solution to this problem would be to
discourage the use of such visual techniques but Envoy 100 users cannot be
expected to adhere strictly to a set of
message composition guidelines since
they will not necessarily know whether
their composed messages are to be read
or listened to. The ultimate solution
would be to provide a mechanism which
would extract the meaning from the message and convey this meaning to the EVIS
user without necessarily reading the
message verbatim.

As an intermediate solution, EVIS takes
into account the way in which Envoy 100
visually arranges the logical elements
of the message. In this manner, information pertaining to the 'envelope' of
the message is distinguishable from that
of the 'content'. Details regarding
each specific field of the 'envelope'
can now be provided to the user with the
'content' of the message being well
defined. Should user-generated 'pictorial' information be encountered by EVIS

within the 'content' of the message, no
attempt is made to interpret it. Currently, EVIS speaks each character of
the 'picture' as it processes the message.

Using the Telephone as a Terminal

By using the telephone and associated
network, EVIS can be made available to a
large user population and can be
accessed virtually anywhere. Furthermore, individuals who might otherwise be
intimidated by computers and their service offerings appreciate the convenience
of using a familiar and simple device
such as the telephone to conduct their
transactions.

Although not every telephone is equipped
with a Touch-Tone keypad, portable
hand-held units that generate DTMF signals are available. Use of the telephone, however, imposes a major
restriction on the input of alphabetic
data. Although possible, it is a
lengthy process that is prone to error.
Therefore input to Envoy 100 in the form
of actual message composition is not
realistic.

This limitation is further highlighted
by the fact that typical Envoy 100 users
are identified by names and passwords
that consist of alphabetic, numeric, and
punctuation characters. To overcome
this problem, EVIS users must first
undergo a validation process. At this
time, users' Envoy 100 identification
and password information is supplied to
EVIS and corresponding numeric codes are
supplied to the user. A user accessing
Envoy 100 via EVIS will supply the
numeric codes to EVIS, which in turn
will retrieve the corresponding Envoy
100 identification and password information and 'sign on' to Envoy 100 on
behalf of the user.

In general, noise, whether external,
background, or network is a major problem in using the telephone. The impact
on the EVIS user tends to be greater
than on a regular user because of the
reduced naturalness and intelligibility
of speech synthesized by rule.

USING SPEECH TO INTERACT WITH OTHER SERVICES

We found that speech output can be used

to interact with a conventional data service. Using a telephone, an EVIS user can access a text messaging service and obtain text messages as well as information pertaining to the disposition of his electronic mail. We contend that the methods incorporated in EVIS can also be used to access and interact with other data services.

Multidesk Syndrome

Many data services are characterized by their lack of consistency with regard to their human-computer interfaces. Furthermore, the functions afforded and data elements processed tend to be incompatible between these services. A user of different services must become acquainted with the peculiarities of each service. If he wishes to incorporate the results generated by one or several services as input to others, he must perform this interworking manually. We refer to this as the "multidesk syndrome".

A solution to the problems resulting from the multidesk syndrome is provided for conventional data services with iNet[3] (intelligent Network) [4]. This proposed Bell Canada service, currently under market trial, establishes connections between users and services and allows for the interworking of these services while providing a consistent human-computer interface. By combining the intelligence and techniques of both iNet and EVIS into a single system, a user could easily access a variety of data services using only a telephone.

Integrating Text and Voice Services

Another dimension of the multidesk syndrome becomes evident when using both text and voice services. Each of these services has fundamentally different types of data and mechanisms for their manipulation. As a result, the user must interwork manually between the two different types of service.

We find, however, an excellent opportunity to apply further the principles of iNet and EVIS to provide an integrated offering to the user in future integrated voice and data services. As an alternative to the existing methods of communication, a common channel and method of communication would be made

available with a consistent human-computer interface and interworking between the services. We feel that this is an initial step towards integrating text and voice services into a single service offering.

CONCLUSION

To interact effectively with computers and their service offerings, we must make greater use of human-like modes of communication. Visual methods should be complemented, not replaced, by the use of speech. Conventional data services will continue to exist and by providing the facility for speech interaction, they can be made available when textual or visual access is not possible or desired.

Developments in speech synthesis, speech recognition, system architectures, and artificial intelligence are providing us with more powerful tools and methods that can be used to achieve our goal of human-like human-computer interaction. It is only a matter of time before multi-media interaction with conventional data services and integrated text and voice service offerings are available to the user.

---

1   Trademark of Telecom Canada.
2   Trademark of Speech Plus Inc.
3   Trademark of Bell Canada.

REFERENCES

[1] D. R. Hill, "Using Speech to Communicate with Machines", *Infotech State of the Art Report: Man/Computer Communication*, 2 vols., Maidenhead, Berkshire, England: Infotech International Limited, 1979, vol. 2, pp. 193-221.

[2] *Envoy 100 User Guide*, Telecom Canada, Sept. 1983.

[3] *Prose 2000 Text-to-Speech Converter User's Manual*, Speech Plus Inc., Sept. 1982.

[4] I. Cunningham and J. Raiswell, "iNet: Gateway to Online Information Services", *Telesis*, vol. 10, no. 1, pp. 2-7, 1983.

Human-Computer Interaction — INTERACT '84 / B. Shackel (ed.)
Elsevier Science Publishers B.V. (North-Holland)
© IFIP, 1985

SPEECH – THE NATURAL MODALITY FOR MAN–MACHINE INTERACTION?

Prof. A. F. Newell
Microcomputer Centre,
University of Dundee
Scotland.

In recent years the use of speech as a man-machine interface has received considerable prominence. A number of systems have been developed which use speech output from machines, and speech input has been introduced in a small number of cases with rather less effectiveness. In those cases where it is impracticable to look at a display, or the hands are fully occupied, speech has obvious advantages, but often a major justification for the use of speech has been that is the 'natural' method of communication for man, and therefore must be the optimum solution. This contention, however, is a simplification of the situation, and, in general, much greater thought must be given to the choice of modality of input-output means than is implicit in justifications of this nature.

Introduction

Human beings have traditionally interacted with machines via their eyes and their hands. Recent technological advances in speech research, however, have provided the possibility of the use of the mouth and ears with the provision of speech communication with machines. This possiblity has excited technologists, and systems have been developed in which speech recognition is used for example in a parcel sorting situation. Similarly speech synthesis provides a very flexible speech output system and thus of potentially wider application than the well known recorded messages.

Speech is a very different modalitiy to a keyboard and visual display unit and thus the design of systems needs to be reappraised if this modality change is to be introduced. The use of speech seems to be a move in the right direction; for example, Nickerson (1969) commented that "the need for the future is not so much for computer-oriented people as for people-orientated computers", and in a similar vein, Jones and others have suggested that the human interface with the computer is best when it resembles human communication as much as possible

Computers, however, are very different sytems to human beings and this difference ought to be reflected in any communication with them. The Modus Operandi a person adopts when dealing with a person is usually very different from that which he adopts when dealing with a machine. In addition, when communicating with a machine, a person is usually concerned with transferring specific, relatively simple,

and unambiguous information, as this is all that the current generation of machines can cope with. In contrast human speech is at its best when it is used to convey complex, very subtle and often ambiguous information.

Talking and listening to Machines

There is currently little operational experience of talking to and listening to machines. The most wide spread examples are talking clock type services and telephone answering machines. It is significant that the talking clock recording makes it clear from the very beginning, and throughout the recording by its style that it is a "machine" which is giving the message. If this was not done the listening behaviour of the caller would have to be drastically modified.

The experience with answering machines is also significant. Maskery and Pearce have reported a study of the response of callers to an answering machine. This appears to be only a very simple task: to note that you are talking to a machine, and give a simple message. In practice, however, many people find it very difficult to adapt quickly to this situation and conclude the call without giving a message, or give a very garbled and hesitant message.

Spoken Orders

Although there is little experience of spoken communication with machines, there are instances where a human operator is used as a speech recognising intermediary between the initiator and a machine. The dictation of a letter is one example which will be discussed later, but other examples include the steering of a large ship.

The type of messages which are given are: "steer due north", "port the helm", "full steam ahead".

This method of communication with the ship was used in the early days of seamanship when great strength was needed to operate the wheel, and is still used for historic reasons and because the master needs to move about on the bridge. It should be remembered, however, that it is a reasonable and feasible method of control only because the time constant of the system which is being controlled is very long indeed. Compared to direct operation of controls - be they wheels, buttons, or pedals - the speech link is a very slow link indeed

In certain other situations the human recipient of a spoken message is expected to behave in a mechanistic fashion. The occasions when human speech is used in this way - to communicate very specific orders which are to be unquestioningly obeyed are few. In the main these are confined to the armed forces and sections of the servant owning classes.

Examples of such communications are: "Halt" - "right turn" - "whisky".

Thus:

a) when men control machines via speech they use a very formalised code and the information transfer rate is very slow, and

b) when an unquestioning response to a verbal message is expected, the message usually takes a very unnatural form, with none of the usual grammatical structure associated with speech. (In fact, in terms of both vocabulary and grammar, messages of this kind are as similar to natural spoken language as BASIC or Fortran.)

The Characteristics of Speech

What then are the characteristics of speech which it make it so popular for communication between people ? It is obviously easy to use, instantly available, and does not usually require extra equipment. In addition, however, the information contained in the spoken word can be a great deal more, and in some cases orders of magnitiude greater, than that contained simply in the words spoken. Speech is far richer than the words which are spoken and in normal circumstances a whole variety of extra information is transmitted.

This extra information includes:

a) The personality of the speaker,
b) his emotional state,
c) his geographic, ethnic and socio-economic background,
d) the relative status between him and the listener, and
e) changes of meaning which may sometimes be very subtle

The most obvious example of this increase in information can be found in the theatre. A script contains the words to be spoken: it is actor's job to add to those words an interpretation of the character. Thus, even in the case of a radio presentation where only the voice can be used, two companies will produce an entirely different interpretation of a play from the same script. In a more every-day context a wide range of meaning can be imparted to a spoken word by very subtle changes to the way it is pronounced. The word "no" can be made to mean anything ranging from "under no circumstances whatsoever" to "yes". With many other subtle variations.

The spoken word is very ambiguous and, in those human situations where one is concerned that the message be completely understood and obeyed "to the letter" - a written communication tends to be used if at all possible. Thus in those situations which are closest to man-machine interaction in terms of the information needing to be transfered, man usually prefers not to use the speech modality but to rely on paper transactions. Grant applications are not usually accepted on the basis of a verbal presentation alone, and the telephone has not removed the need for writing letters.

When information needing to be communicated has important emotional overtones, however, words are not sufficient and speech is written used. Thus a substantial, and often the most important part, of the information which men communicate by speech is information which is either not available to the current generation of "word recognition " machines and, even if it were, would not be usable by them. Fortunately, however, we do not have to stoop to pleading, or black-mail when communicating with machines - or at least it does not seem to have any noticable effect.

The effects of a modality change

It is also important to note that, in man-to-man interaction, changing the modality of an act of communication has substantial effects on the information communicated.

The effect of this is seldom appreciated. Man is usually able to choose the modality, and either consciously or subconsciously tries to select the one which is most appropriate to the particular information exchange on which he is about to embark. One of the causes of the problems people have with telephone answering machines is that communicating with a telephone answering machine is much nearer to writing a letter than talking to a person - there is no feedback from the recipient and the message is going to be stored, and can be replayed. Thus the person who suddenly finds himself talking to a telephone answering machine, has to adopt a style which is appropriate to a different modality. With this interpretation, it is not suprising that he may have difficulties.

When one examines interactions involving disabled people the effects of changing the modality are also more obvious. When either speech or hearing impairment removes the ability to convey information by voice, another modality has to be introduced and that is often writing (or typewriting). Examinations of interactions with disabled people reveal that there are substantial differences in the quality of the exchange, and in some cases the information conveyed is very different even though the words are the same.

For example, if a speech impaired patient writes to a nurse "you did not brush my hair properly this morning", this will often be interpret ed as a serious complaint - a similar comment passed by a speaking patient will be treated much less formally. This, however, is not only because of the modality change. In order for a simple text-to-speech device to produce the same message as the speaking patient, the patient would have to be able to produce a variety of sentences such as:

"you did not......but if you do it again I will be cross"
"you did not......and I am very cross with you about it"
"you did not......but it doesn't matter"
"you did not......and someone in your position should know better"
"you did not brush my hair properly this morning, but I still like you very much and it was just a small slip which I am mentioning to pass the time, although perhaps next time you will bear in mind that I have mentioned it"

The synthetic speech device is often an improvement for a speech impaired person, and in a number of nursing situations the use of synthetic speech has improved relationships between the disabled person and the nurse. The danger, however, is

that people have a whole range of expectations about voice, and may well misinterpret messages because of these expectations. (In this context it is interesting to note that many synthetic speech systems are rejected because they do not fit the clients self-image. For example, the sexual characteristics of the voice have to be correct, and the class must not be too different.)

Television subtitles for the deaf are another valuable source of data concerning the differences between the spoken and the written word, and this has been clearly pointed out by Baker et.Al. It is rarely good enough just to reproduce the words which are being spoken - and the subtitler is often faced with the conflicting goals of:
a) reproducing as accurate as possible a version of the words being spoken, or
b) reproducing the same impact as the spoken word, but in a written form.

This conflict occurs often, but is most obvious when expletives and words of abuse are used - these appear much more powerful when viewed as subtitles, than they do when they are heard in their spoken form.

A second justification, for the use of speech recognition and synthesis is an economic one based on a reduction in manning levels of machines. When this is proposed, however, care must be taken to ensure that the task actually will be performed quicker, and that any operator to be replaced is not performing a much more complex task than was anticipated by the technologist. Examples of possible problem areas can be found in proposed uses of both speech synthesisers and automatic speech recognition machines.

Talking Data Bases

Speech synthesis has been used for data base enquiry systems - train time tables being an example. Obviously there is a reduction in terminal cost - a loudspeaker or telephone handset rather than a visual display screen, but the overall system economics is less obvious. In this context Cox has commented that "if a service is already offered in an acceptable way which does not rely on voice input or output then care must be taken before changing to a speech system to ensure that such a change offers real benefits to the end user". Searching a data base using a voice synthesizer is not a trivial task and very inefficient compared to the use of the eyes. This is clear from current telephone based systems, and also has been studied in detail by King et Al. in their work concerned with access of blind people to data bases.

The listening typewriter

A favourite application area for speech recognition machines is for data input and a typewriter at which one can dictate. The effect of voice input on speed, efficiency and user satisfaction however is less than clear. For example Braunstein & Anderson reported that all their subjects preferred keying digits to speaking them, and also found reading digits aloud a very tiring task. Welch has also shown that skilled operators could key digits almost twice as fast as they could read them out loud.

At a more complex level Gould et Al. have produced a laboratory simulation of a "listening typewriter" by the use of a typist acting as a speech recognition machine. They found that with their listening typewriter, the dictation speed was of the order of half that of trad- itional dictation methods. The implication of this work, however, is that typists normally act, and are expected to act as very simple speech recognition machines. This may be the case in the laboratory, but is less likely to be true in real situations.

Verbatim reporting in the Law Courts

A well documented example of engineers failing to appreciate all the tasks perfomed by a "human speech recogniser" occurred in the Law Courts. Records of proceedings in the Law Courts are trad- itionally kept by a stenographer who takes down a shorthand note of what is being said. If an appeal is lodged, the writer produces a verbatim report from his/her shorthand note. In 1976, in the U.K., the Lord Chancellor's Office was pursuaded to begin to replace verbatim reporters by tape recorders and dictaphone typists. After only a relatively short period, however, tests had shown that the substantial capital investment had produced a signif- icantly inferior service with a higher running cost.

The problems which were produced by this "technological breakthrough" are obvious a posteriori, but were not anticipated by many of the people who agreed to the change. These problems included :
a) Any passages which were inaudible on the tape are not recoverable (a stenotypist would have stopped the court if she could not take a good note)
b) Lip reading plays a significant part in interpret ing speech in a noisy environment; thus, even given the same acoustic input, a stenographer would

produce a much more accurate note than a dictaphone typist. (In addition the stenographer has the advantage of stereophony to help discrimination)
c) Any important gestures are included in a stenographers note,
d) the stenographer's note includes an indication of who is talking; this is not always obvious on a tape recording
e) a "machine minder" is necessary in case of a fault occurring in the equipment and to keep a log of who was speaking
f) even with a machine minder, a duplicate system has still to be provided in case of technical breakdowns which could not be observed - e.g. a malfunctioning record head on tape recorder.

Admittedly the courts are a very harsh environment, nevertheless it is significant that even when replacing the stenographer by dictaphone typists, the results obtained were very dis appointing, and the running costs of the tape system were found to be approximately twice those of using stenographers. The Lord Chancellor's Office are now going to significant lengths to encourage and expand the use of court reporters even though they have made a substantial investment in audio recording equipment. Similar experiences have been noted in North America, and a number of judges insist on a reporter rather than relying on tape recordings of the proceedings.

The requirements of a listening typewriter

The listening typewriter does not usually have to perform in such a harsh environment as the Law Courts but, in order to be useful, it should perhaps be able to do those tasks which a reasonable typist does at present.

These tasks include;

a) correcting slips in English grammar,
b) automaticaly punctuating,
c) ignoring asides to other people in the environment or made by a visitor,
d) deleting unitentional comments (e.g."now what shall I say),
e) suggesting something to say - see (d) above,
f) discrimating between the tones of voice used to dictate, and to give orders (e.g. "leave a gap there" - "no, start again"),
g) filling in addresses, titles, headings etc., and
h) refering to details in previous letters.

A typing pool does not provide such a good service as that outlined above, but it is a very poor typing pool which simply provides a typewritten version of what appears on the dictaphone machine.

The listening typewriter will probably reduce dictation speeds and it is also probable that much more editing will be required of the output of such a device. It is therefore not at all obvious that the overall system will be any more efficent than using a typist for the first draft, and may well be much more expensive.

The disadvantages of speech

Speech is proclaimed as the natural method of communication, but what are its disadvantages - particularly if we are going to communicate with machines.

Some of the disadvantages of speech are that it is:

a) very slow compared with direct controls such as keys and visual display,
b) transitory - cannot be studied at leisure,
c) cannot be scanned - see King et al,
d) more error prone (miss-hearing, poor pronounciation, slips of the tongue, etc.), and it is
e) sometimes ambiguous.

There is no doubt that, in some circumstances, speech is an appropriate man-machine interface. At present, however, these are mainly situations where an auditory output, or a hands-free input is desirable. With the current level of speech technology, impressive though this is, it is not often appropriate to use speech simply on the grounds that it is the "natural means" of communication.

Conclusions

When we design systems and their man-machine interfaces we need to be keenly aware of the differences between modalities, and possible effects of changing the modality. The expectations and mores of the written word are very different to those of the spoken word and care needs to be taken to choose a dialogue system which is appropriate for the modality being used.

Speech is not the universal solution to improving man-machine interaction, and more valid justifications than "it is natural" must be found before speech is chosen as the modality for any particular situation. The current levels of speech technology, both speech synthesis and speech recognition, fall below normal expectations of natural speech, and current computer systems are not able to cope with much of the information which is normally transmitted in human-to-human speech communication.

Speech may be a "natural" method of communication between people, but the restricted speech codes that are applicable in current man-machine communication are not "natural". If we are to use the speech modality, we must recognise this and design our systems, and the dialogue types within them - not to imitate "natural" communications - but to be appropriate for the system we are designing. Otherwise we will be in danger of designing systems which will be ineffective and thus unnecessarily bias people against the use of the speech modality in the future.

* * * * * * * * *

Bibliography

[1] Nickerson,R.S. Man-Computer interaction: a challenge for human factors approach, Ergonomics, 1969, 12, 501-507

[2] Jones,P.F. Four principles of man-computer idalogue. Computer Aided Design, 1978, 10, 197-202

[3] Maskery,H.S. & Pearce,B.G., Telephone answering machines - an investigation into user behaviour. Proc. Int. Conf. Man-Machine Systems, Manchester, U.K. July 1982, I.E.E. publication 212, 258-261.

[4] Cox,A.C. Human Factors investigations into interactions with machines by voice, Ibid, 254-257

[5] Baker,R, Lambourne,A & Rowston.G., Handbook for Television Subtitlers, available from Engineering Division, I.B.A., Crawley Court, Winchester,Hants.

[6] King, R.W., Cope,N. & Omotayo,O.R. Videotex for the blind - design and evaluation of braille and synthetic speech. Proc.1st. I.F.I.P. Conference on Human-Computer Interaction, London Sept. 1984.

[7] Gould,J.D., Conti,J. & Hovanyecz, T. Composing Letters with a simulated listening typewriter. Proc. of Human Factors in Computer Systems, Gaithersburg, Maryland, March 1982. 367-369

[8] Braunstein,M. & Anderson,N.S., A comparison of reading digits aloud and key-punching. IBM Technical Report RC 185 Nov.1959

[9] Welch,J.R., Automatic Speech recognition - putting it to work in industry. Computer May 1980.

DIALOGUE INTERACTION

ANALYSING INTERACTIVE DIALOGUES

GRAPHICAL INTERACTION

Human-Computer Interaction — INTERACT '84 / B. Shackel (ed.)
Elsevier Science Publishers B.V. (North-Holland)
© IFIP, 1985

WINDOW-BASED COMPUTER DIALOGUES

S. K. Card, M. Pavel, and J. E. Farrell

Xerox Palo Alto Research Center   and   Stanford University
Palo Alto, California   Stanford, California

In recent years a number of systems have used windows as the basis for advanced user interfaces. Yet how exactly users benefit from windows or what features of windows are important for design is neither understood nor has it been studied. Current window designs are given a simple classification. Seven functional uses that have been identified for windows are described. The Window Working Set concept based on operating system theory is introduced for the an analysis of space constraints on window use.

The last several years have seen substantial advances in the design of human interfaces for computing systems. These interfaces, which use techniques of computer graphics, offer substantial promise for making computers easier to use and for extending the complexity of tasks that humans can perform. But, whereas there is considerable understanding of the basic perceptual requirements of displays, how to make dials easy to read, for example, there is very little systematic understanding of the interaction between the display and the user's ability to perform cognitive tasks. Yet such tasks are a central feature of most human-machine systems and increasingly more so. The general aim of the present research is to increase our understanding of the interplay between graphical interfaces and user cognition by studying one of these techniques.

WINDOWS

Central to the new techniques for interface design are "windows." Windows allow the user to interact with multiple sources of information at the same time, as if he had a set of CRT displays of different sizes at his work-station. It is this multiplicity of contexts, together with the graphical features of the display and the ability to use graphical input devices that is the source of the power of the new interfaces.

The basic idea behind windows is simple. A window is a particular view of some data object in the computer. In Fig. 1, the time of day is displayed in one window by the hands on a stylized clock, a LISP program is presented in another window as text on a piece of paper using different typographic styles to set off its parts. Still other windows are used to display subroutine calls among LISP routines as a horizontal tree (upper right), a data structure representing the geography of Europe as a map, the bitmap pattern for the letter A from some system font in enlarged pixels to facilitate editing, the parsing of an English sentence as a tree, and an array of bit patterns encoding a photograph as as a half-tone illustration. The figure shows some of the representation potential of windows: windows can depict data structures using different textual and graphic idioms and these can coexist together on the user's display popping into and out of existence, moving about, or changing shape and size according to the exigencies of the moment.

Fig. 1 is but one way to implement the notion of a window. There are many others and arguments about which design is the best (or merely about which are not the worst) are conducted among computer scientists with considerable heat. The current designs for window systems can be broken down approximately into four categories: (1) the familiar simple TTY windows, (2) time-multiplexed windows, (3) space-multiplexed windows, and a less certain category, (4) "non-homogeneous windows."

Fig. 1. Two and one-half dimensional windows in Interlisp-D

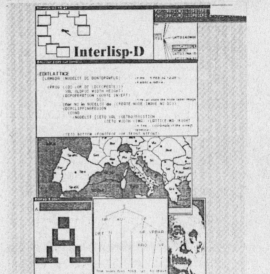

Simple TTY Windows.

These are the the familiar single windows with automatic single direction scrolling. The user types a command that appears in the bottom line of the window. The system response also appears on the bottom line(s) of the screen after first "scrolling" the screen up. Because this method imitates the mechanical flow of paper in a teletype machine it is sometimes called a "glass teletype."

Time-Multiplexed Windows.

The concept of windows can be extended by having the content extend virtually beyond the screen in various ways. One way is to think of the screen as a resource shared by different windows at different times—time multiplexed windows. Another way is to think of sharing the space on the screen more or less constantly among different windows—space multiplexed windows. Time-multiplexed windows themselves come in at least two forms, scrolling windows and frame-at-a-time systems.

Scrollable windows. Scrolling windows are often used with text-editors. The user edits his text in a window, but has available commands that can cause the text to move up, down, or to a certain place, as if the user had a movable window he could position in front of a long scroll. This is one way of using the display to show larger amounts of text frames by showing different parts at a time.

Frame-at-a-time systems. Using a menu, the user flips back and forth among a number of frames, but only one frame is visible at a time.

Space-Multiplexed Windows

Space-multiplexed windows may be grouped according to how many dimensions of the space there are and whether the windows are independent or part of a "split."

One-dimensional windows. Fig. 2 shows the screen for a text-editor called Bravo divided vertically into a number of separate parts. Those parts below a heavy black stripe are windows open to different files (one file in the figure is the text the user is editing, another is to the references of his paper, a third is to a file containing a table in the paper). The thin line separates two separate views of the same file (one part is looking at the front and one at the end). This is an example of a "split window."

Two-dimensional windows. Fig. 3, from the Cedar system[2] shows the screen divided into separate windows in two dimensions. The windows can change in size and they can move around, but they cannot overlap.

Two-and-a-half-dimensional windows. Fig. 1 was an example of an overlapped window system. Some windows appear to have been overlaid by others. Selecting a portion of an overlapped window causes it to appear on the top of the pile. Window placement is largely determined by the user.

Split vs. independent windows. Some windows display independent information. Others are "split" into smaller windows displaying closely related information. Changes to one of these split windows may cause changes reflected in another.

Fig. 2. One-dimensional windows in Bravo

```
READY: Select operand or type command
Last command was LOOK
{Referenc...}          {0.00in}              ()
paper 31.1·HPHP
```

```
[File PAPER-31.1-HPHP / August 23, 1983  12:26 AM]


              The Model Human Processor:

        An Engineering Model of Human Performance†


              Stuart K. Card and Thomas P. Moran

   SUMMARY

        This completes our initial description of the Model

   Human Processor.  To recapitulate, the Model Human

   Processor consists of (a) a set of interconnected memories
```
```
paper 31.refs[
```
```
                 References


AZIN, O., & CHASE, W.  Classification of three-dimensional structures.  Journal of

Experimental Psychology, 1979, 4, 397-410.
```
```
paper 31.table[
```

Typewriters	(msec/stroke)	
Best keying	60	Devoe (1962)
Typing text	158–231	Hershman and Hill x(1965)
Typing random words	200–273	Hershman and Hill x(1965)
Typing random letters	462–500	Hershman and Hill x(1965)

Non-homogeneous Windows.

Instead of displaying all the information on the display at the same level of detail, the detail may change whether within the same window or across windows. Icons, bifocal windows, fish-eye windows, and zooming are techniques for accomplishing this.

Fig. 3. Two-dimensional windows in Cedar

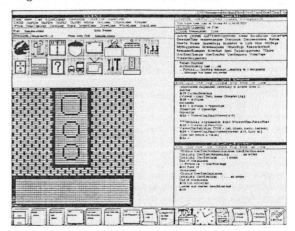

Icons. These are very small windows, generally represented on the screen by a small symbolic picture of some sort (e.g. the picture of an in-box for a mail window). The icon may be selected and expanded into a full-size window. Several icons are shown in the bottom of Fig. 3. Icons are a means for keeping reminders of a large amount of information on the screen without taking up much space.

Bifocal windows. Bifocal windows[3] are a related technique. Information is assumed to be organized hierarchically (e.g. journal, volume, issue, article). Information on one of these levels is displayed in full detail in the center. Related information, perhaps at a higher level, is displayed on the periphery in just enough detail to recognize it. Thus the user always has detailed display of some item of interest and non-detailed display of contextually related items.

Optical fish-eye window. Information in the window is compressed like the image of a convex mirror.

Logical fish-eye window. Information detail may be reduced according to its logical distance from some focal point. For example, a program listing may be completely displayed for some point of interest in the program, but only a single line devoted to other arms of a conditional statement[4].

Zooming window. Data in a window or the window itself gets larger or smaller in the manner of a zooming camera. This effect may involve changing type fonts, suppressing parts of the diagram, or even distorting parts that are salient (as on a road map).

The above is the beginning of a rough taxonomy of window designs. It shows some of the competing designs, whose relative merits we should be able to understand as a result of our analysis.

TASKS

The use of windows by a user depends heavily on the tasks the user is trying to accomplish. It is therefore impossible to accomplish an analysis of window and display design without careful consideration of the tasks for which windows are used. As a first step, we can categorize tasks by the functions windows seem to serve in accomplishing these. There are at least seven such functions:

1. More information. Window techniques may allow relatively rapid access to more information than would be possible with a single frame of the same screen size. For example, the Apple Lisa uses overlapped windows to compensate for small screen size.

2. Access to multiple sources of information. A task may require access to independently stored pieces of information. For example, a writer may need to refer back and forth to several parts of the text he is writing: a reference bibliography, a table, and possibly comments from readers and draft sections done by co-authors (see Fig. 3).

3. Combining of multiple sources of information. Information from different sources of information may need to be combined. Text from several electronic messages may need to be combined into a new message. This operation is simplified if the several sources of information are displayed simultaneously.

4. Independent control of multiple programs. A user may want to supervise or control the running of multiple programs. For example, he may use one window for the output of his program, another to control the debugger after a program error, a third to display and edit parts of the program code, a fourth to display the system stack, and others to display the state of various data structures. Several programs may run independently, each in its own window.

5. Reminding. Windows can be used to help the user keep track of information likely to be of use in the near future, but that otherwise he would need to expend some sort of effort to remember. For example, pop-up windows with menus of commands in them, a clock window giving the time, a history window containing the several commands most recently issued.

6. Command context/active forms. Windows can serve as a visible indication of a command context. They can be used to represent instances of objects. When the cursor is in the window, various commands and buttons can have different interpretations. This allows the command language to be simpler and more modular. A special case is the use of active forms. For example, in Fig. 1 there is a window containing the graph of a parse tree. Whenever the user points to a particular node in the parse tree, the user can give a command that attaches it to the cursor so it can be moved around. Because the window supplies a well-defined context for such an interpretation, this technique can be used to create, context dependent command languages. In fact, the need for typed-in commands can be eliminated.

7. Multiple representations. Windows can be used to display multiple representations for the same task. For example, in the Rabbit system[5] the user has three windows on view simultaneously, each with a different representation of his information retrieval task: a query command, a fragment of a network diagram, and specific instance. For a difficult query, the use shifts back and forth among these representations in a set of successive negotiations with the machine to satisfy his retrieval using the representation easiest at each point.

These seven functional uses of windows (as well as other functional uses that remain to be identified) warn that attempts to understand the merits of competing window designs must be clear about the function for which the windows are being used.

THE DISPLAY AS AN EXTERNAL MEMORY

Of course an analysis of windows also depends critically on an understanding of the user and how he is linked to the display. An understanding of the user must, of necessity, weave together, on the one hand, cognitive considerations of a user's goals and problem solving and, on the other hand, the perceptual and visual science issues of how he moves his eyes and what cues from the display affect his ability to locate and discover information needed for cognitive processing.

External memory

Our analysis of the effect of the human processor on window use begins with the proposition:

A fundamental constraint on users' cognitive performance arises from limitations of working memory.

The ability to do mental arithmetic is limited largely by difficulties in keeping track of the intermediate products and keeping one's place. In debugging a program, in writing a paper, in doing financial analysis of a firm, in attempting to reason about a machine, limitations on the number of mental things that can be kept track of lay a strong constraint on human cognitive capabilities.

The display of a computer provides the possibility of giving the user an *external memory* that is an extension of the user's own *internal memory*, one with which he can remember and keep track of more information than otherwise. (Of course, notes on paper scattered about a desk can serve a similar function, but they are not dynamic as with a computer display that can automatically graph in one window the data in another or always keep the listing of a program properly indented). And the computer display is not only an external memory that extends the user's internal memory, it is also (partially) shared with another active agent, the computer itself. This means that it is at once both memory and communications medium. Both the full power of the display as external memory and communications medium and the synergistic interaction between these are only realized when the display supports independent, but related, nodes or objects of memory and communication. It is for this reason that the windowing technique, with its emphasis on separate communication contexts, has become the harbinger of dramatic improvements in human-machine interfaces.

Window Working Set

The external memory i.e. the screen of the display is a resource with very definite constraints. Regardless of how advantageous it might be to display more to the human, there is only so much space. Using overlapped windows, for example, to expand the display is like placing pieces of paper on a desk. If the desk is small and the papers are numerous, the user may spend most of his time attempting to searching for his papers.

The situation is reminiscent of the design of demand paging algorithms for the virtual memory algorithms of operating systems.[6][7][8][9] Programs running on a computing system often have a virtual memory much larger than the physical memory available for the program, particularly when they run in a multiprogramming environment. During some interval of time, only a portion of the pages of the program's virtual memory are actually referenced. This set of pages is called the program's working set (to be defined more precisely later). If the number of pages in the program's working set is not greater than the number of pages actually available for the program to run, the program will run efficiently. If, however, the working set is larger, then the program will spend most of its time reading and writing pages back and forth from main memory to some secondary memory device, a condition known as thrashing.

The user might similarly be said to require during some interval of time a certain amount of screen area to present the displays he needs to accomplish his task, a window working set. If the screen size is too small he too will experience a phenomenon akin to thrashing.

Of course, in the human case there are additional complications. The user can decide he would rather not have a piece of information, possibly leading to errors later, than to churn his display to get it or he may choose an alternative, space-reduced, method of obtaining it. Nonetheless, the comparison suggests a rich set of analyses available to apply to the analysis of display space management and the effect of physical screen size. For example, an important property of program behavior is a statistical property called locality: within a short period of time, most programs tend to reference only a few pages, then move on to reference only a few other pages. This property seems likely to apply to window reference as well. Locality is a very important property in determining how much real memory is necessary to prevent a program with a certain virtual memory size from thrashing and there are technical indexes available for describing it. These could of course be applied to the analysis of window references and to the characterization of the time varying information needs of a user doing a task. An interesting possibility is that users can trade their own memory load off against using the display as an external memory. Hence it might be possible to see interesting trades between time plots of the user's internal memory load and the display loading.

WORKING SET ANALYSES OF USER BEHAVIOR

In this section we shall illustrate the usefulness of the working set idea for analyzing the space constraints operating on windows placed on the display screen. To do so we shall define the working set in terms of windows, describe a technique for data collection, and describe corresponding data analyses.

The user's interaction with a window-based interface at each instant of time is associated with a state, s. The state is identified by the particular window that is active at that time. Let S be the set of possible states. Define a reference string, R, as a list of pairs of the form

$$R = (S_1, T_1), (S_2, T_2), ..., (s_i, t_i)$$

where S_i is a random variable representing the state and T_i is a random variable representing the time when the user entered the state S_i.

The working set is then defined as a random variable $W(t, T)$ representing the set of states visited during a time interval from $t-T$ to T. More formally,

$$W(t,T) = \{s \mid S_i = s, \, t_i \in [t-T, t]\} \tag{1}$$

Thus the working set random variable depends only on (and can be computed from) the reference string and the working set size parameter T.

The working set notion is particularly convenient if the reference string has certain statistical properties. In particular, if the set of the states visited in a given interval T changes only slowly with time the working set provides a good description of the number of windows that should be displayed simultaneously on the screen.

Data Collection

We have observed users performing their usual work involving windows. User behavior is videotaped and users are encouraged to talk in order to gain access to the users' goals.

Experimental Setup: The following three types of records were collected simultaneously during a session.

(1) Video monitoring of the session using two cameras aimed at a slave terminal. One camera monitored the entire screen, the other camera monitored the portion of the screen that the user was attending to.

(2) Video monitoring of the user.

(3) A record of window activities consisting of lists of active windows recorded whenever a new window was created or an old window closed.

Data Analyses

The most important goal of the analyses is to characterize the computer-user interaction and separate it from the particular task domain (e.g. editing or debugging). The data analysis began by combining the different types of information into a coherent composite protocol. Using this composite protocol enabled us to construct *reference strings* from the observations. Each reference string consisted of a list of windows that the user was working on together with the corresponding time intervals.

The first step of the analysis is determination of the recurrence of the reference string process. Recurrence is a critical property of the computer-user interaction: If each window is unique and no window is used more than once, then one can do little to improve the interface design to avoid thrashing. This is because if the user continues to use new windows, he or she will eventually reach the memory limit imposed by the size of the screen. If, on the other hand, there are windows that are used repetitively (there are recurrent states) then one may improve the efficiency of the interface by choosing an optimal set size. The proportion of recurrent windows in our example was 71.2%. This value is sufficiently high to proceed with further analyses.

Given that a significant proportion of the windows were recurrent we were then able to examine the locality of the process. An important indication of locality is captured in a inter-reference distribution h.

$$h(x) = Pr\{T_{ir} = x\} \tag{2}$$

where T_{ir} is the time interval between two consecutive references to the same window. In practice an estimate of $h(.)$ is obtained by combining inter-reference intervals for all recurrent windows. The resulting inter-reference distribution in our example is shown on Fig. 4. This plot illustrates the number of times the windows were referenced as a function of the inter-reference interval. The locality characteristics is apparent on this graph as the prominent peak at the low values of inter-reference times. Thus if a particular window is used more than once it is likely to be used two or three events later.

Encouraged by these analyses we were able to study the locality in more detail by using the working set notions. In particular, we determined the number of distinct windows $k(t, T)$ at event t referenced during T previous events. Of course k is simply the working set size

$$k(t,T) = \|W(t, T)\|. \tag{3}$$

Fig. 4.   Inter-reference distribution

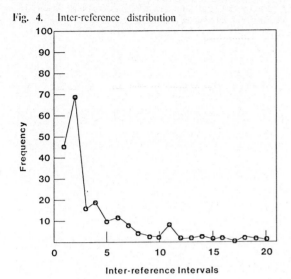

Fig. 5.   Variation of working set size with event number

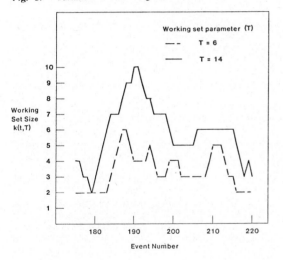

Fig. 6.   Window faults as a function of working set size

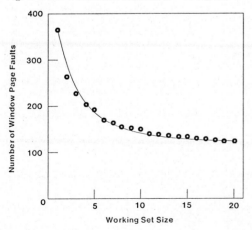

The choice of the parameter T determines the behavior of k for any particular reference string. An example of the behavior of k for two values of T is shown in Fig. 5. The interesting and potentially useful aspect of the this representation is in the relationship between the rapid changes in k and the tasks performed by the user at that time. In particular, as the user progresses through the various phases of his interaction, he may need different sets of windows. Thus the number of required windows is temporarily higher at transition between phases.

While the working set size is a useful measure of the number of windows required during various periods it is only an indirect indicator of how often a new window must be created (a *window fault*, similar to a page fault in a virtual memory system). To determine the window fault frequency or, conversely, the life-time distribution we determine from the reference string all instances when a new window is referenced based on the working set analysis. A window fault is generated whenever a window to be used is not in the working set at that time. The resulting distribution of the frequency of window faults f as a function of the working set parameter T is illustrated in Fig. 6. The locality of the string is exhibited by the rapid decay of f for small values of T. We then look at how fast the set of active windows changes over time. Whenever the change is slow (quasi-stationarity or locality holds), then the working set identifies the windows required to do the task.

DESIGN APPLICATIONS

The data presented in the previous section have been chosen to illustrate how we might begin to employ ideas from the analysis of operating systems to analyze the effect of the limited screen area resource on the use of windows. The analysis could be performed for different task domains or window system design and provides a method by which we can evaluate the advantages of particular window designs given the task demands. For example, rather than considering icons as an isolated technique, we might think of icons as external memory cues that have low space-time cost and that shift the window-fault curve favorably.

REFERENCES

[1] Newell, A.   Notes for a model of human performance in ZOG. Technical Report, Department of Computer Science, Carnegie-Mellon University, Pittsburgh, Pennsylvania (1977).

[2] Teitelman, W.   Technical Report, Xerox Palo Alto Research Center, Palo Alto, California, forthcoming.

[3] Spence, R. and Apperley, M.   Data base navigation: an office environment for the professional.   Behaviour and Information Technology 1 (1982) 43–54.

[4] Furness, G. The FISHEYE view: a new look at structured files. Internal Memorandum, Bell Laboratories, October, 1982.

[5] Williams, M. and Tou, F. Rabbitt: An interface for database access, in Proceedings of the 1982 ACM Conference, 1982 (Association for Computing Machinery, New York, 1982).

[6] Denning, P. J.   Virtual memory.   Computing Surveys 2, 3 (1970) 153–189.

[7] Hansen, P. B.   Operating System Principles (Prentice-Hall, Englewood Cliffs, New Jersey, 1973).

[8] Coffman, E. G., Jr., and Denning, P. J.   Operating Systems (Prentice-Hall, Englewood Cliffs, New Jersey, 1973).

[9] Denning, P. J.   Working sets past and present.   IEEE Transactions on Software Engineering SE-6 (1980) 64-84.

Human-Computer Interaction — INTERACT '84 / B. Shackel (ed.)
Elsevier Science Publishers B.V. (North-Holland)
© IFIP, 1985

Generic Commands

Jarrett K. Rosenberg

Xerox Office Systems Division
3333 Coyote Hill Road
Palo Alto, CA 94304

Thomas P. Moran

Xerox Palo Alto Research Center
3333 Coyote Hill Road
Palo Alto, CA 94304

A generic command is one which is recognized in all contexts of a computer system; examples from the Xerox 8010 Star system are **move, copy,** *and* **delete.** *They may be viewed as extremely general actions which make minimal assumptions about their objects, the particular interpretation of the commands depending on the contexts in which they are issued and the nature of the objects to which they are applied. Of the several tradeoffs involved in using generic commands, the primary one concerns having to design the objects in the system so as to efficiently use them.*

1. Introduction

Most computer systems consist of a collection of different application programs; thus a computer system contains various kinds of data objects and structures, various subsets of which define *contexts* for issuing commands. A *generic command* is one which is recognized in all contexts of a computer system; examples from the Xerox 8010 Star system are **move, copy,** and **delete.** A *pure generic command system* is then one in which all the commands are generic. (It should be noted that generic commands are different from what we will call *universal commands* which are ones claimed to be generic to all systems.)[1]

A number of designers have discussed the advantages of using generic commands, and there are both experimental and commercial systems designed around them ([1], [5], [10], [11], [12]). There are basically three interrelated advantages of generic commands:

- They reduce the number of commands and command names a user has to know, an advantage that increases in importance as the number of different contexts increases. This also serves to increase the functional efficiency of the system's command language, since in a pure generic command system, every command can apply to every object;

- They increase the consistency and predictability of a system by using a similar set of actions across different contexts; thus if users know how the commands work in one context, they can more easily predict how they work in another;

- They allow users to more easily map their everyday actions into the computer domain, a process described in [7] as external-to-internal task mapping. Furthermore, it has been found that people use high-frequency, and thus more general, words to describe a wide range of related computer actions ([2], [3]).

The idea of generic comands is thus attractive, but has not been deeply analyzed; this paper investigates the use of generic commands in several computer systems, and some of the design tradeoffs involved.

2. How generic commands work.

Generic commands may be viewed as extremely general actions which make minimal assumptions about their objects, the particular interpretation of the commands depending on the nature of the objects to which they are applied. This is why such generic commands are most aptly named with general words such as *delete*. An obvious sort of model for generic commands is one using frames, such as Fillmore's semantic case-frames [4] or Minsky's knowledge frames [6] (a somewhat different approach is given in [9]). In such a model,

---

[1] In some systems pointing is a sort of generic command. There are also generic meta-commands, such as **undo, stop,** and **again**.

one would say that generic commands are simple context-free semantic frames whose slots are constrained and filled differently in different contexts. The assumptions or constraints of a generic command may be about the number, type, and structure of its objects, their relationships, and the pre- and post-conditions surrounding the invocation of the command. Some examples are given in Figure 1. Consider, for example, the **delete** command: its frame has slots for two objects, the item to be deleted and the containing set from which it is to be removed. The pre-condition of the command's application is that the target item actually be in the containing set. Its two post-conditions are that the target item no longer be in the containing set, and that the containing set still exist. It is neutral as to whether or not the target still exists, or where it might be (in a buffer perhaps). It is also neutral as to the structure of the remaining items in the containing set: in a text-editor, one would want the remaining characters to close up; in a graphics editor, one would probably not want the remaining picture elements to close up.

Because so much of the meaning of a generic command is dependent on the object on which it operates, much of the power of generic commands derives from the structure of the set of objects in the system. All the objects in a given system may be viewed as forming a taxonomy. This taxonomy, which is often only implicit, is defined by the various properties that the objects share. An example of such a taxonomy is given in Figure 2. Objects higher in the hierarchy have fewer and more general features than their more specialized descendants (for example, a file might be simply defined as a sequence of bytes, while a mail file would have the additional features of having a certain structure and containing certain specific kinds of data). Equivalently, the nodes of the hierarchy define sets of features shared by the objects under that node.[2]

Given this taxonomy, it follows that "generic" is actually a relative rather than absolute property of commands. Every command is applicable to some subset of this taxonomy, and the higher in the taxonomy its applicability extends, the more generic the command is. For example, the **delete** command may apply to all objects, but the **run** command would only make sense for an object file. Hence **delete** would be more generic a command than **run**.

This variation in the scope of commands shows why it is virtually impossible to have a pure generic command system: it is inevitable that some command + object combinations will be either nonsensical or potentially dangerous to users, and hence not allowed (e.g., applying **run** to a text file). Conversely, to force a command to be generic (i.e., to violate its constraints or assumptions by applying it to inappropriate objects or situations) may lead to nonobvious interpretations or applications of it, as in the XS-1 system [1], where **up** can mean "end the parameter sequence of a command."

Thus what we have been calling generic commands are simply those commands which are at one end of this dimension of generality of application. A consequence of their extreme

---

Figure 1. Examples of Command Frames.

DELETE

Number of Args: 2
Arg1: Item-to-be-deleted
Arg2: Containing-set
Pre-condition: Arg2 contains Arg1
Post-condition: Arg2 doesn't contain Arg1
Post-condition: Arg2 still exists

PRINT

Number of Args: 2
Arg1: Item-to-be-printed
Arg2: Printer-specification
Pre-condition: Arg1 is readable
Post-condition: Arg1 still exists

RUN

Number of Args: 1
Arg1: File-to-be-run
Arg2: Printer-specification
Pre-condition: Arg1 is executable

---

[2] An important constraint on the features in the taxonomy is that it they be "monotonic", i.e., that additional features of an object not be opposite to those of its ancestors. This is because such an inconsistency would make the application of a generic command inconsistent. Consider the case of the **print** command in TOPS-20 (which is named **list**): it works as one would suppose on text files, except in the particular case of a text file whose extension is .LST; in that case it prints the file and then deletes it. Here a feature of a more specialized object (that it disappears after being printed) violates a constraint in the **print** command's frame.

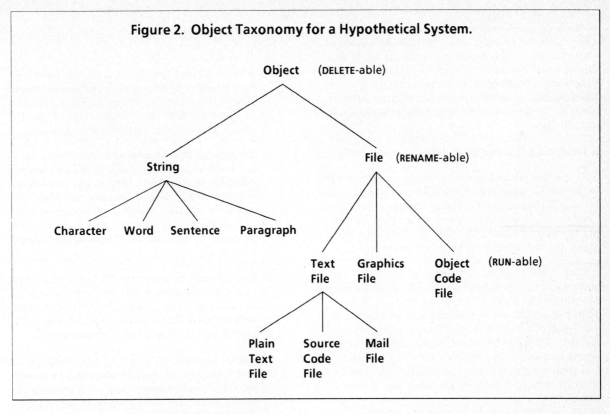

Figure 2. Object Taxonomy for a Hypothetical System.

location is that they must modify their behavior in different contexts: the distinctive features of an object cannot be ignored. This modification may involve adding further specifications or parameters to the command in particular instances, or specializing the objects further (as in Star). Inevitably, however, the users of a pure generic command system will want to have specialized commands available independently (cf. the EMACS editor). This then is an important tradeoff in the use of generic commands: for the sake of generality, specialization will be harder.

But as shown in Figure 3, there is another dimension involved besides that of generality of application. Generic commands also vary widely in the degree to which their meaning is determined by the disintinctive characteristics of their objects. The effects of some generic commands such as **rename** rely chiefly on the features which the relevant objects share, in this case, having a name. Others such as **delete** must take into account more of the distinctive properties of the object, for example, whether or not to close up the remaining items in the containing set. Finally, there are those generic commands, let us call them *interpretive generic commands*, whose effects are amost entirely determined by the properties of the object (cf. EVAL in Lisp). This is made use of explicitly in Star by the

use of *function objects* such as printers and outbaskets in conjunction with the **move** command (for example, to print an object one moves it to the printer icon). In such a case, the generic command **move** becomes almost totally syntactic in nature:

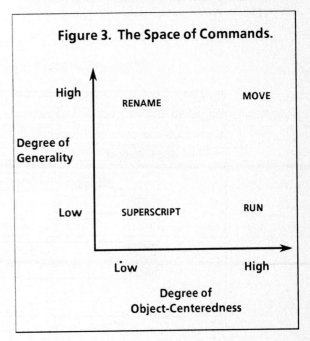

Figure 3. The Space of Commands.

its meaning is determined entirely by the semantics of the function object (printer, outbasket, document converter, etc.). An important consequence of this object-centeredness of interpretive generic commands is that they have potentially greater functionality. In order to make use of this potential, however, the objects in the system must be designed accordingly.

3. Designing systems with generic commands.

If we look at two systems which are the most ambitious in their use of generic commands, the Xerox 8010 Star system [10] and Beretta *et al.*'s XS-1 system [1], it becomes apparent that they have in fact specially designed the objects of the system to enable the widespread use of generic commands.

The XS-1 system. In the case of XS-1, the generic commands depend on the fact that the data structures have the same form: that of a tree. Hence, no matter what context the user may be in, the same set of tree-related commands may be applied. The drawbacks, of course, are that some objects and tasks may not be easily represented in that form, and that it may be difficult for users to map the external task space onto the system's internal one.

The Star system. The case of Star shows most clearly how the design of the rest of the system is crucial to the success of generic commands: there are several different aspects of the system's design which lend support to them. Chief among these are the replacement of specialized commands with specialized objects, and the extensive use of pointing.

- Every object in Star has properties, manipulated by two generic commands **show properties** and **copy properties**. These properties are the locus of an object's distinctive features and their manipulation.

- Displaying the properties of an object in a menu format (see Figure 4) allows menu selection to be used to change the properties, instead of separate commands and object or property specifications (for example, one selects the ITALICS property on a character's property sheet instead of issuing an **italics** command).

- In addition to data objects, Star also has function objects such as printers and outbaskets, thus replacing specialized commands with combinations of function objects and the interpretive command **move**.

- There is extensive use of pointing as a selection method, to eliminate the necessity for users to name every object and property in the system: the user simply points at the desired object, function, or property, and clicks a button on the mouse.

These observations suggest that other features are essential in Star's ability to successfully use generic commands. Without the function icons and property sheets, and the pointing to indicate objects

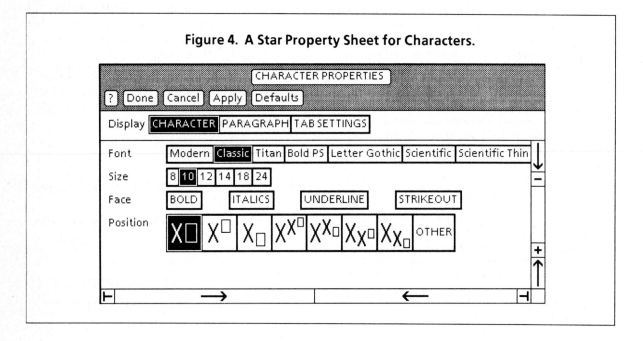

Figure 4. A Star Property Sheet for Characters.

and actions, it would be much harder to systematically apply even a small set of commands across such different contexts. The moral is thus that generic commands are not independent of the rest of the system, and that the attempt to use them will be most successful if the rest of it is designed accordingly.

4. Conclusions

As we have seen, there are several tradeoffs involved in using generic commands. One is that between the size of the set of generic commands and that of the set of system contexts. The fewer the number of generic commands the better, but the larger the number of contexts, the more likely that more commands will be needed. This is indeed a paradox, since the greater the number of contexts, the more valuable it is to have generic commands, but also the harder it is to have them.

A second tradeoff is that between the generality of generic commands and the need to specialize them. If the only commands are very general, then they will need to be modified or combined to apply them in specific instances (thus increasing the system's learning time; cf. [8]). If those specialized commands are used with any frequency, then one would want them to be available separately (as macros, say). But that will increase the number of commands to be learned.

However, the primary tradeoff is not that of number of commands vs. number of contexts, or generality of commands vs. their specialization, but the fact that to work successfully, generic commands require that the objects in the system be designed with them in mind, either in terms of generic properties (as in XS-1's trees), or in terms of increased specialization (as in Star's function objects). This implies that one cannot redesign an existing system's command language to use generic commands without also redesigning its objects to make effective use of them.

Acknowledgements. We thank Mike Williams and Bill Verplank for their comments in discussions.

References

[1] Beretta, G., H. Burkhart, P. Fink, J. Nievergelt, J. Stelovsky, H. Sugaya, A. Ventura, J. Weydert. 1982. XS-1: an integrated interactive system and its kernel. *Proceedings of the Sixth International Conference on Software Engineering*. New York: IEEE.

[2] Black, J. and T. Moran. 1982. Learning and remembering command names. *Proceedings of the Conference on Human Factors in Computer Systems*. New York: ACM.

[3] Dumais, S. and T. Landauer. 1982. Psychological investigations of natural teminology for command and query languages, in A. Badre and B. Shneiderman, eds., *Directions in Human/Computer Interaction*. Norwood, NJ: Ablex.

[4] Fillmore, C. 1968. The case for case, in E. Bach and R. Harms, eds., *Universals in Linguistics Theory*. New York: Holt, Rinehart and Winston.

[5] Lemmons, P. 1983. A guided tour of VisiOn. *Byte*, 8(6).

[6] Minsky, M. 1975. A framework for representing knowledge, in P. Winston, ed., *The Psychology of Computer Vision*. New York: McGraw-Hill.

[7] Moran, T. 1983. Getting into a system: external-internal task mapping analysis. *Proceedings of the CHI '83 Conference on Human Factors in Computing Systems*. New York: ACM.

[8] Roberts, T. and T. Moran, 1983. The evaluation of text editors: methodology and empirical results. *Comm. of the ACM*, 26(4): 265-283.

[9] Rosenberg, J. 1983. A featural approach to command names. *Proceedings of the CHI '83 Conference on Human Factors in Computing Systems*. New York: ACM.

[10] Smith, D., E. Harslem, C. Irby, R. Kimball. 1982. The Star user interface: an overview. *Proceedings of the 1982 National Computer Conference*.

[11] Tesler, L. 1981. The Smalltalk environment. *Byte* 6(8).

[12] Williams, G. 1983. The Lisa computer system. *Byte*, 8(2).

Human-Computer Interaction — INTERACT '84 / B. Shackel (ed.)
Elsevier Science Publishers B.V. (North-Holland)
© IFIP, 1985

TRANSACTION PROCESSING USING VIDEOTEX
or: Shopping on PRESTEL

John Long and Paul Buckley

Ergonomics Unit, University College London
26 Bedford Way, London WC1H 0AP

The suitability of videotex (VT) for supporting transactional services
(including shopping) was assessed, firstly by relating VT technology to a model
of transaction processing. Expectations regarding suitability were generally
confirmed by an observational study in which naive subjects ordered goods via
two different systems. Further assessment involved analysis of user
difficulties and errors. These were used to identify variables affecting
performance and were modelled in terms of a mismatch between a naive user's
incomplete representation of the system and inappropriate representations which
interfere with task performance.

1. SUITABILITY

Tex is the generic term for all forms of public
information service involving the display of
text and graphics on television screens. There
are two main sub categories: Videotex (VT), and
Teletext (TT). Tex systems differ in technology
and organisation which may affect their suitability for particular uses. A recent growth in
popularity of tex has encouraged commercial
concerns to use these systems for marketing
purposes, ranging from advertising to selling.
It is now possible to buy groceries and
holidays, and to order banking services, on
Videotex, using a television set and a local
input device. The suitability of particular
systems for supporting such transactions is
determined by: (i) the technology and
organisation of the system; and (ii) the
requirements of transaction processing.

Tex has been described in detail elsewhere [1],
[2], and in the discussion of suitability below,
only relevant features will be briefly
explained. First, however, we need to describe
what is involved in a transaction.

TRANSACTIONS: are defined as the activity of
exchanging resources between two transactors.
The activity is symmetrical in that each
transactor both gives and receives. The
resources transferred may be physical, eg
glasses; or informational, eg software.
Resources themselves may be transferred or they
may be substituted by symbols of resources, eg
credit card numbers. Before transfer of goods,
the transactors make an agreement concerning:
(i) the nature (design) of the goods; (ii) the
quantity of the goods to be exchanged; (iii) the
organisation of delivery. The model proposed
(see Figure 1) is a preliminary attempt to
specify transaction processing in terms of task
components and their relations.

The model is briefly described:
Criteria: Each transactor has a set of criteria
which are derived from the goal of the
transaction. "Make a profit" could be used by a

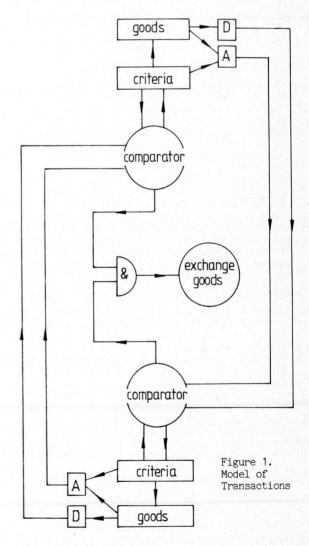

Figure 1.
Model of
Transactions

seller as a criterion. "I must have it
immediately" could be a criterion for a buyer.
Criteria determine which resources are to be

offered for exchange.

Goods: "Goods" are the specific resources to
be exchanged. Thus, while "credit" is a general
resource, "£5" is the particular goods. Both
transactors have their own kind of goods.

Design: Design constitutes a data base (D)
containing the specification of one transactor's
goods- its physical characteristics (if any),
etc. Examples of "Design" data are: a textual
description of a computer; a photograph of a
holiday resort.

Availability: Information such as delivery
times and quantities are represented in the
availability data base (A). These data are
derived from the goods. The data base A may
also contain information derived from the
transactor's criteria. This information is in
the form of transfer conditions, which specify
the conditions of exchange, a form of
specification of what is wanted. Prices are a
form of transfer conditions; the datum in A
could be a price ticket. An example of a
transfer condition for a bookseller might be:
Transfer: goods(book), if £5; and for the buyer:
Transfer: goods(£5), if book. Transfer
conditions are a partial re-description of
criteria, one that can be directly compared with
the other transactor's D and A; eg, the
criterion "a nice present" is not adequate as a
transfer condition, unless the other's D and A
represent goods in these terms (eg a section in
a catalogue called "nice presents"). Usually,
transactors need to derive a lower level
description for transfer conditions.

Comparator: Both transactors compare the
other's D and A with their own transfer
conditions in the Comparator. The output of the
comparator is normally FALSE. If the other's D
and A match the the transfer conditions, output
goes TRUE - a decision to exchange goods.
However, since transactions are symmetrical,
both sides must decide to exchange before
transfer can occur. The AND gate output
represents this mutual agreement. Only when
both comparators have TRUE outputs does the
transaction proceed to the exchange of goods.

Note that there is no need for the two
transactors to process data simultaneously, nor
in synchronisation, nor for the comparator
outputs to change state at the same time -
consider ordering by post. Should the other's D
and A not meet the transfer conditions (output
of comparator FALSE), then the model allows re-
specification of goods, and of D and the part of
A derived from goods, and the re-specification
of transfer conditions, although always within
the constraints of criteria.

Example: In order to illustrate the model,
it will be used to describe a typical shopping
scenario of buying a newspaper. The transactors
are the vendor (V) and the purchaser (P). The
criteria of V are that the transfer conditions
require the offer of the cover price, in cash,
for the comparator output to go TRUE. The
transfer conditions of P are that the newspaper
is called "The Times", it is dated today and is
in good condition. P and V criteria could be

perhaps: P- entertainment and information; V-
make a profit and sell all stock.

The design data base of the vendor's goods D(v)
is the representation of the newspapers for
sale. Typically, the actual goods are displayed.
Availability of V's goods (A(v)) is in the
presence of the newspaper, responses to queries,
etc. The transfer conditions are the cover
price of the newspaper. The other conditions
(cash, now) are not represented in A(v). In
order to drive the transaction to the exchange
of goods, both sides must produce a D and A in
order for both comparators to operate. In this
example, V has already issued D and A by
exposing the goods. P must also generate a D
and an A (D(p) and A(p)). This may be done by P
offering money and saying "Times, please". D(p)
is the amount of money in the hand; A(p) is
obviously "now" because the money is in cash.
The transfer conditions are contained in the
statement. Note how the transfer conditions act
as a specification of the required goods.

Both transactors compare the other's D and A
with their own transfer conditions. Agreement
to exchange goods is expressed in the model by
the output of the AND gate. Goods are
exchanged: the 20p passes from P to V, and the
"Times" passes from V to P.

SUITABILITY: This description of transaction
processing helps discussion of system
suitability by enabling exemplification of the
relationships between technological limitations
of tex and components of transaction processing.

Display Characteristics: The component of
transaction processing most affected by display
characteristics is the D representaion.
Restrictions on the text capacity of the screen
mean that descriptions have to be brief; and the
graphical resolution of most tex systems
(especially "alphamosaic" ones like PRESTEL)
means that pictorial representations are
normally poor.

Response facilities: Only VT systems have
response facilities. Information and
transaction services are provided by
"Information Providers" (IPs). Users respond
via "Response Frames" (RFs). In message sending
systems, like PRESTEL, the RF is transmitted to
and retained in the system page store until
accessed by the IP. It is likely that delays
may occur between the user sending a message and
the IP receiving it. The users are informed
only that a message has been sent, but not that
it has been received. Ordering via response
frames is similar to posting a coupon.
Transactions involving bartering cannot easily
utilise message sending systems. Transactions
involving criteria for time might not be
completed successfully on these systems.
Neither do these systems support users and
sources whose criteria are such that they
require extension of the D and A representations
before a successful comparison can occur.

"Interactive" systems provide a direct link from user to the IP's computer. Responses are generally much faster (being on-line), and inputs can be less sterotyped. Inputs are processed immediately and specific responses are received. This is in contrast to the (non-specific) "message sent" response to the sending of an RF on PRESTEL.

Updating data bases: Because the IP's own computer is accessed directly in "interactive" type systems, changes in the goods and in the transfer conditions may quickly be expressed in the D and A representations. For instance, a confirmed flight booking affects the availability of that seat. This change can be instantly registered in part of the A representation of seats. In PRESTEL type systems, the IPs must first access their pages from the system operator's data base in order to make alterations. These inherent delays, and operator charges, make it likely that the page could contain inaccurate information (poor D and A representations). When goods are changing fast, as in the travel industry, the risk of inaccuracy may not be acceptable.

It appears, then, that message sending systems, like PRESTEL, are suitable for transaction processing if: (i) the goods and the transfer conditions can be represented adequately on the tex page and the response frame or item; (ii) transactors do not require changes in the D and A information represented in the tex page during progress of the transaction; (iv) transactor's criteria are such that time is not an important transfer condition. "Interactive" or direct link systems are more suitable if: (a) i above holds; (b) time is an important transfer condition; (c) the transfer conditions and/or the goods are changing rapidly; (d) specific responses are required (eg on-line confirmation of booking).

2. OBSERVATIONAL STUDY

The observational study had two aims, first, to assess empirically the expectations concerning suitability which were derived from a consideration of VT in the light of the model of transaction processing. Second, to identify important variables of usability for future quantitative examination.

METHOD: The study was semi-naturalistic. Subjects were required to follow a set of shopping scenarios. They ordered goods via PRESTEL, and also via an "interactive" type service run by Great Universal Stores (GUS). For the GUS system, subjects were provided with a printed catalogue. The shopping tasks described various shopping situations. For instance: "It is your favourite aunt's birthday. She is especially fond of cut roses. You have decided to send her some." and: "Two of your friends are moving into their own home for the first time. Buy them a suitable housewarming present". There were eight

scenarios: roses, housewarming present, souvenir, video game, crystal wedding present, champagne, record, bedding. Only the eighth scenario involved GUS. Subjects were videotaped and verbal protocols were elicited during the selection of goods, and retrospectively, while subjects watched a mute videotape of their earlier activity. Also, there was a debriefing session during which subjects were interviewed about the tasks and shopping in general. The concurrent protocols were recorded together with the relevant screen display. Retrospective protocols were audio recorded. Each session lasted about 2h. There were 5 subjects, who were each given an imaginary credit card number and a credit limit of £500 for each scenario. No subject had ordered goods via VT previously.

DATA: Difficulties were widespread and common. As expected from the discussion of suitability, many problems arose because of poor quality graphical representations: eg "It was the first time I'd seen the graphics and they were appalling. I mean you couldn't tell what things are" (S2, crystal wedding). The subject appears to require, in terms of the transaction processing model, a richer D representation. Not surprisingly, the photographic representations in the GUS catalogue were preferred "I prefer it [the GUS system] a) because I have pictures...." (S3, interview).

As far as A representations were expressed via the system, the GUS service was also preferred, as it aided the correction of mis-specification of goods (inadequate statements of transfer conditions in the Response Frame). For instance, "I liked where I didn't give colour and it came back at me and said what colour do you want" (S3, interview). The system elicits the user's transfer conditions, part of the A data base. In the PRESTEL system, the only available response was "message sent". RFs that were incorrectly filled in were followed by the same sequence of responses as correct RFs. Because of this, subject 2 falsely believed he had sent an order because the IP followed RFs with a page stating "thank you for your order". Although he was satisfied at the time, the lack of adequate specification in the order would have caused problems later when no goods or incorrect goods would have been delivered.

The degree of interactivity in the GUS system seemed to allow for correction of incomplete messages. But why do the errors occur in the first place? One reason may be that subjects were sometimes required to fill in RFs with the reference numbers they had ignored during selection. "Reference number? I'll have to go back a page. <goes back> I've got to remember this.. R dot 322 <back to RF> <inputs R dot> <doesn't fit space> I know, they don't want the R dot.." (S2, housewarming). Some subjects were better prepared: "OK, reference number. It's a good job I wrote this down" (S3, record). The difference in behaviour of the two subjects above is not explained easily in terms of the

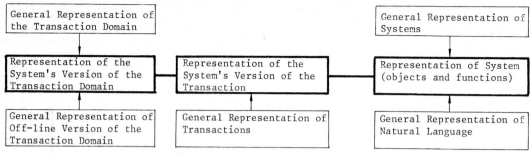

Figure 2. Usability Model

"suitability" constructs of Part 1. At best, we may describe the situation as "interactive systems can compensate for omissions in transfer conditions", but why and how the omissions should occur at all remains unclear.

Many other difficulties were found that do not sit easily within the "suitability" framework. These included misunderstandings of system terminology: "Message services and response pages. What does that mean?" (S3, champagne); not knowing how to fill in RFs: "Then what do I do? How do I make them know that's my card. Put a tick or circle it?" (S3, housewarming); false expectations of the system: "...when I first started I thought it was a system that was updated continuously, and if anything was in it, it was available" (S2, souvenir).

In general, then, expectations with respect to the suitability of PRESTEL for transaction processing were confirmed, at least for naive users. The system fails when the goods and transfer conditions are inadequately represented, either on the tex page (eg poor graphics) or on the RF. Users requiring more D and A information than is available fail to transact or transact unsatisfactorily. Difficulties and errors other than those predicted by a consideration of suitability, however, were also identified. A full report of the data assessing the suitability expectations and those difficulties and errors not predicted will appear elsewhere [3].

3. USABILITY

The empirical assesment of suitability was the first goal of the observational study. The second was to identify variables affecting the usability of the system for future and quantitative evaluation. "Variable" here is defined as a factor open to operationaliz-ation and to experimental manipulation. "Graphics resolution" might be such a variable, or "system response time". The variables identified in this study have been organized using a modified version of a method proposed elsewhere [4] for the structuring of variables underlying naive users views of an interactive data base interrogation system. The method was in turn based on a model of usability proposed earlier [5]. In summary, variables are associated with a set of representations which

are used to characterize successful and unsuccessful task performance.

The model is expressed as a set of represen-tations (figure 2). In the figure, the heavy boxes indicate the particular representations (ie knowledge) required by the ideal (or expert) user to complete a transaction successfully. The light boxes indicate other often more general representations which may in the case of the non-ideal user be needed to complete a transaction. They are recruited when the appropriate system-related representations are not available to the user. They may facilitate or interfere with the transaction depending on their overlap with the system-related representations. Interference can be thought of as a mismatch between system and user representations. Both difficulties and errors as they appeared in the protocols were categorized as "mismatches". A system will be usable if: (i) the user acquires all the system representations appropriately; (ii) the user's non-system representations overlap with (ie "match") and therefore facilitate the system representations.

Transaction: the transaction is the task. The two central "Transaction" parts of the usability model relate to the task model of transaction processing proposed earlier. These structures should reference the transaction entities D,A, and Criteria, and their relationship. Transaction domain: The domain here is "goods to be transacted" ie records, glassware, money etc. System: Systems include on- and off- line versions of transaction processing contexts. PRESTEL is an on-line transaction processing system; shops and catalogues/post are off-line versions. System objects are reference numbers, pages, menus etc.; system functions are select, go on to next page etc.

We exemplify the model by applying it to some of the user's difficulties. Where appropriate, variables affecting these difficulties are associated with the different types of representation. For instance, one subject did not realize the importance of reference numbers in specifying goods (issuing transfer conditions). In a shop environment, reference numbers are not normally used. In terms of the usability model, the subject recruited an

inappropriate General Representation of Systems.
The variable here could be experience of
catalogue shopping.

Another example involves a subject who is faced
with the option "key 1 to send, key 2 not to
send". Here, "send" means something like
"transmit the order from the user's terminal to
the PRESTEL computer". However, the subject
does not understand the function "send", but
thinks it refers to dispatching the goods:
"...well, I think if I bothered to buy this way,
I'd have it sent." (S4, housewarming). Natural
language, then, is used to interpret the system
term for a function- and inappropriately. The
variable here is knowledge of natural language.

As well as "system" representations (those on
the right), the model includes "transaction
domain" representations. These constitute a
capability for the interpretation of system
versions of the goods of the transaction. We
suspect an evaluation of D is necessary for
transactions to be processed. The PRESTEL
version of D is characterised by poor graphics
and short textual descriptions. This D would be
by definition completely adequate for the ideal
user. But not all users are ideal:
"<reads>"Roses size 60cm" That's big! Perhaps
it's the length " (S2, roses). The implication
is that the subject thought that 60cm described
the bloom size.

In the model, the inadequacy of the
Representation of the System Version of the
Domain meant that knowledge is recruited from
one or both of the structures feeding into it.
The subject may have used off-line (florist) or
general (garden) representation of the goods in
D. Stem length is normally hidden by paper,
vase, other plants. Typically, variables
associated with the representation were found to
be modality of expression (textual or graphical
representation) and image resolution.

The usability model will be used to
conceptualise the difficulties found in the
observational study and to structure the
relevant variables. The model may have to be
modified as a consequence of difficulties in
matching data to the existing representational
structure. Some modifications could lead to
clearer specification of the contents of the
blocks, as would an expansion of the transaction
Representations to include the elements of the
transaction processing task model.

Already, we feel a need to divide General
Representations of Systems into off-line and
on-line systems. This is due partly to data in
the protocols in which S4 incorrectly pressed 7
to return to the list of shopping services:
"...I was expecting something else. I was
expecting because it was 7 that got me the list
of shops before, I assumed it was going to be
the same" (housewarming). One interpretation
of this error is that the subject failed to
grasp that there were two representations for

each page in the system: (i) a page number- in
this case 55, obtained by keying the appropriate
command syntax (*55#); (ii) a number
associated with an option in a menu- in this
case (given the previous menu) 7.

It most likely that the subject assumed a one to
one relationship betweeen keyed numbers and
pages and failed to notice the real page
numbers. This relationship could have come from
books ("turn to page 7") or from telephone
numbers, house addresses etc., where the the the
number relation is fixed. This error probably
requires the new structure General
Representation of Off-line Systems in which
there are no variable object/number mappings.

CONCLUSIONS
In this preliminary report of the research, we
have shown how expectations concerning the
suitability of a transaction processing system
can be derived from a consideration of the
appropriate technology in conjunction with a
model of the task. An observational study
confirmed these general expectations while
providing a more detailed data base of user
difficulties and errors. We then showed how a
model of usability could be used to
conceptualise the data base and to structure
variables identified as affecting task
performance. This research preceeds controlled experimentation involving variables
affecting performance and the establishment of
guidelines for the designers of transaction
systems.

Acknowledgements
The research reported in this paper is part
of project GR/C/23032 "An evaluation of dialogue
forms for transaction processing in videotex
systems" funded jointly by the SERC and British
Telecom. The authors would like to thank Peter
Gilligan for designing and running the
observational study.

References
[1] Woolfe,R.,VIDEOTEX: the new television-
telephone information services (Heyden, 1980)

[2] Gilligan,P. and Long,J.B., Videotext
Technology: an overview with special reference
to transaction processing as an interactive
service, Behaviour and Information Technology,
1984 (in press).

[3] Buckley,P.K. and Long,J.B., in preparation

[4] Long,J.,Hammond,N.,Barnard,P.,Morton,J. and
Clark,I., Introducing the Interactive Computer
at Work: the user's views, Behaviour and
Information Technology, 2, 1 (1983)

[5] Morton,J.,Barnard,P.,Hammond,N. and
Long,J.B.,Interacting with the Computer: a
Framework, in Boutmy,E.J. and Danthine,A.(eds),
TELEINFORMATICS 79 (North-Holland, 1979)

Human-Computer Interaction — INTERACT '84 / B. Shackel (ed.)
Elsevier Science Publishers B.V. (North-Holland)
© IFIP, 1985

People Can Retrieve More Objects With Enriched Key-word Vocabularies.
But Is There A Human Performance Cost?

Louis M. Gomez   Carol C. Lochbaum
Bell Communications Research
Murray Hill, N.J., U.S.A.

ABSTRACT

Recent research using statistical data and models has suggested that information systems with many different and not necessarily unique names for each system object will dramatically increase the likelihood of finding a target object over more standard retrieval systems in which each object has only one or a few names. In the current experiment this conclusion was supported by observations of people using actual information systems to retrieve target objects. In addition, those people using systems with richly indexed vocabularies needed slightly fewer, rather than more, key-word entries to find a given target object.

INTRODUCTION

The promise of the information age is information, but with the promise goes the problem of easy access to that information. Students, consumers, and professionals of all types have an increasing number of information sources at their finger tips to browse and query. Key-word information retrieval systems are one way to provide access to large collections of information. In this paper we explore some system design issues which may influence user performance in key-word information retrieval environments.

To use a key-word information system successfully, a user must refer to a desired object by the same name given the object by the system designer. This can be an extremely difficult task for untutored users of reasonably large retrieval systems. One reason for this difficulty is that different people (sometimes the same person on different occasions) refer to the same object by many different names. The extent and nature of such verbal disagreements were recently studied by Furnas, Landauer, Gomez, & Dumais (1983). They analyzed data from several experiments in which subjects' task was to select words or short phrases to describe common objects. The subjects' goal in these studies was to generate descriptors which would be helpful to other people, who later would retrieve or identify the target objects. Data of this type simulate the performance of computer based information retrieval. Any pair of people providing descriptions of target objects is analogous to the situation in which a system user must refer to objects in the same terms used by the system designer. The probability that a system will return the desired object is a function of how often the user and designer refer to the same object by the same words. Furnas et al. estimated that in systems where each target object was referenced by only one name, a situation not unlike many key-word systems in use today, the probability that two people will use the same single word to describe an object is typically about .10 to .20. Verbal agreement at this low level clearly leads to unacceptably poor system performance.

The source of the problem is that each object in a data base has many aspects and dimensions, and different people choose different words to describe the same features. How can key-word systems be improved so users will be successful more of the time? Furnas et al. suggest "unlimited aliasing". Each object should be given several not necessarily unique names. Models of systems that recognize a large number of properly chosen names for each object predict a dramatic improvement in object recall. For example, in one of the data sets studied by Furnas et al., the simulated probability of successful retrieval reached .9 when the system stored an average of twenty aliases for each object.

The "unlimited aliasing" approach modeled by Furnas et. al. requires the system to recognize as a name for an object every word that any user wants to apply to it. This means, necessarily, that the same words must be permitted to apply to more than one object. As more people are allowed to nominate key-words, the chance that a given key-word will point to multiple objects increases. Systems designed in this manner carry a potential cost. The system may return many unwanted objects in response to each key-word entry. Thus the user's ability to differentiate desired objects from undesired ones may be impaired. On the other hand, the Furnas et. at. data show that "unlimited aliasing" adds, for the most part, many relatively rare words that tend to be applied very narrowly. This feature of "unlimited aliasing" could minimize the volume of unwanted objects returned in response to any given entry. Thus the cost associated with the user's ability to distinguish between wanted and unwanted objects may not be severe. Because the Furnas et al. work was based on statistical simulations of information retrieval situations, the net effect of the cost of ambiguity in relation to recognizing a significantly larger proportion of the user's key-word entries could not be evaluated with respect to people's performance using actual information retrieval systems.

In the experiment reported here, we observed people trying to find target objects with key-word information systems that varied in vocabulary richness. We also explore the value of an automatic word-aid list. The list was intended to provide users with an opportunity to choose entries from a menu-like addition to the key-word system. If recognition of words that specify the target objects is easier than the generation of those words, then the word-aid list may improve performance.

METHOD

Subjects. Sixty women from the Murray Hill, New Jersey, area, whose average age was approximately 46 years, served as paid participants. None of the subjects had any experience using computer based information retrieval systems.

Materials. Six data bases were used in this experiment. The data bases contained descriptor words provided by eight of the 24 subjects, (referred to here as the indexers) who had participated in a cooking recipe indexing study reported in Furnas et al. (1983). The eight indexers, all expert cooks, generated key-word descriptors for 188 recipes drawn from several cook books. They were told to choose descriptors that would be helpful to other people trying to locate the target recipes in a culinary index or information system. The indexers described each recipe with three to seven key-words. They were asked to generate the keys in order of importance, beginning with the most important.

The six data bases were constructed by combining only the first descriptor or all descriptors from two, four, or all eight indexers. The particular combinations of two and four indexers were chosen to maximize the total number of unique key-words and the number of key-words per recipe (number of aliases) in each vocabulary. Table 1 shows the number of key-word types in each data base, the mean number of key-word types per recipe in each data base, and the mean number of recipes per key-word type in each data base.

Table 1

Data Base Characteristics

Data Base Number	Number of Key-Word Types	Mean Number of Key-Words per Recipe	Mean Number of Recipes per Keyword
1.	180	1.96	2.04
2.	268	3.64	2.56
3.	305	5.41	3.33
4.	684	12.81	3.52
5.	884	22.60	4.81
6.	1064	31.63	5.59

Data Base One, formed by using the first words generated by two indexers, was the most impoverished; it had the smallest number of unique words, the fewest aliases per object, and the fewest number of recipes per key-word. The remaining five, numbered in order of increasing vocabulary richness, were composed of first words generated by four indexers, first words generated by eight indexers, then all words generated by two, four, and eight indexers.

Information retrieval system. Subjects used an experimental computer based information retrieval system to find one of 24 target recipes on each trial. In addition to the key-word vocabularies, the system recognized the numbers 1 to 188, which served as unique identifiers for each recipe in the collection. The system recognized two types of commands and issued one of four responses. When subjects entered a key-word, (Command Type 1) the system responded in one of two ways. If the word was not in its vocabulary, it responded "No recipes for this word". Otherwise, the system responded with the numbers of all recipes which were referred to by that key-word. When subjects thought they knew the identity of the current target, they entered a recipe number (Command Type 2). In response to a number entry the system replied "Right!" or "Incorrect guess; try again". Subjects were allowed a maximum of seven entries, either words or numbers, with the only restriction that the seventh entry be a number. The goal, of course, was to find the number of the target recipe, much the same as one would try to find a page number in the index of a book.

Procedure. Following a preliminary introduction to the use of the computer terminal, which included having the subjects type their names and some numerical identification information, subjects read the experimental instructions from the terminal, while the experimenter read them aloud. Next, subjects were given a two trial practice "walk through" of the entire procedure. During this period the experimenter interacted with subjects to correct any problems they had with the instructions or the task.

Subjects were then told they would use the key-word information retrieval system to find thirty targets. The targets were presented in five blocks of six targets each. Subjects were not informed that block one, a practice block, would not be counted.

Pilot experimental results had determined that it was necessary to develop a target specification technique which did not directly provide useful key-words. For example, if recipe targets had been specified by their title, subjects could use words from the title as key-word entries, leading to inflated success rates. Our target specification method was intended to approximate the amount and quality of information people have about a desired object in real information retrieval situations.

Each block had a study phase and a target retrieval phase. In the study phase, subjects became acquainted with six target recipes for that block. They were given six minutes to read and study the printed texts of the recipes, which had been typed on 8 1/2 X 11 inch paper and placed in a ringed binder. The binder was then removed, and the subjects were given six index cards and instructed to make notes about each of the recipes. They were told they would use these "reminder note cards" as an aid to generate key-words for recipe retrieval. The goal of this study procedure was to simulate an actual retrieval situation, in which the to-be-recalled object is represented in the subject's mind by remembered features, rather than by a literal copy of the target or its parts. After four minutes of note taking, subjects were given a two minute distractor task to reduce any surface memory representation of the recipes. The distractor task required simple arithmetic computations to convert ounces to grams.

Following the study phase, subjects were then asked to find the six target recipes one at a time. The orders in which the subjects studied and retrieved the targets were randomized separately for each block and for each subject. The experimenter was able to assign each of the note cards uniquely to one of the targets, which were specified by using the letters A-F. The terminal displayed "Your target is: Recipe A" for the first recipe to be retrieved. The subject was then given the index card containing her notes for the recipe coded "A". Subjects used TVI 920c terminals to interact with the retrieval system. All subjects completed the experiment within the maximum allotted time of three hours.

Half the subjects were provided with a word-aid list to the key-word system. A second terminal, an HP2621 without a key pad, displayed a list of candidate key-words. A new list was displayed after every word entry which returned one or more recipe numbers. The word-aid list was generated "on the fly"; that is, its contents were determined by the current key-word entry. The list contained words that were also keys to the recipes in the set returned by the entered key-word. For example, if the word "pasta" were entered, and it was a key-word for ten recipes, and those ten recipes had 40 other associated key-words, then those 40 words would comprise the word-aid list. The size of the word-aid list ranged from zero words to a maximum of 92, set by screen size limitations. In cases where the word-aid list contained more than 92 words, it was truncated. Member words of the truncated list were chosen based on precision. Precise key-words refer to few objects in a retrieval system, while imprecise key-words refer to many. For truncated lists, potential members were ordered from most precise to least precise. The words were then displayed by choosing words from both ends of the list until 92 words were selected, thus omitting medial precision key-words. Subjects were not required to choose their next entry from this list. They were told to use it if they felt the words suggested by the list would be helpful. The word-aid list was designed to provide an opportunity for subjects to select an entry that they might not have generated on their own.

RESULTS

Performance measures. We report several measures of performance (a) Proportion of Targets Correctly Identified, (b) Proportion of Word Entries that Returned the Target -- the proportion of word entries for which the target was a referent, (c) Mean Return Set Size -- mean number of objects returned per word entry, (d) Proportion of System Unrecognized Word Entries -- the proportion of word entries with null return sets, (e) Total Word and Number Entries, (f) Average Response Time per Word Entry -- the time subjects needed to generate a key-word, measured from the time a prompt appeared until the subject began typing a key-word, (g) Repeat Rate (Herdan 1960, Furnas et al. 1983) -- a measure of commonality of word usage for entered words. Repeat rate is an unbiased estimate of the probability that two random subjects will use the same word to indicate the same object.

Retrieval success. It is apparent from Figure 1 that subjects who used systems which recognized larger vocabularies were able to identify more targets, $F(5,20) = 35.81$, $p < .001$.

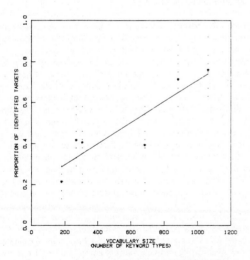

Figure 1   Proportion of Targets Identified as a Function of the Number of Key-word Types in each of Six Vocabularies

Figure 1 shows data from individual subjects in each vocabulary condition, condition means, and the linear fit to the data. The proportion of targets correctly identified ranged from .21 for the system with the fewest key-word types to .76 for the system with the most. The data in Figure 1 were well fit by a linear trend

when vocabulary size was used as a predictor of target identification success, $F(2,57) = 42.62$, $p < .001$. An analysis of the residual error gave no indication of significant higher order components; there was no reliable lack of fit to the linear model, $F < 1$. It is apparent from Table 2 that the proportion of word entries which returned the target, a measure of retrieval success that does not depend on target identification, also shows that enriched key-word vocabularies improved performance.

Table 2

Characteristics of Word Entries

Data Base	Proportion That Returned The Target	Proportion of Unrecognized Word Entries	Mean Return Set Size
1.	.12	.40	3.67
2.	.34	.24	6.69
3.	.34	.30	8.34
4.	.37	.16	9.82
5.	.69	.10	15.74
6.	.73	.10	18.81

For the system with the fewest number of key-word types, 12 per cent of all entries returned the target number, while for the system with the most key-word types, 73 per cent of all entries returned the target number, $F(5,20) = 125.74$, $p < .001$. This corresponds quite well to the simulation results reported in Furnas et al.

Subjects using the enriched systems identified more targets, but they also had to manage more information per entry. Entries made by subjects in the richest vocabulary condition returned an average of 18.81 recipes (see Table 2), while entries made by those in the most impoverished vocabulary condition returned only 3.67 recipes, $F(5,20) = 245.97$, $p < .001$. Table 2 also points out that, not surprisingly, subjects working with rich vocabularies used more system-recognized words. Only ten per cent of all entries went unrecognized by the system with the most key-word types, while 40 per cent of entries were not recognized by the system with the fewest key-word types, $F(5,20) = 38.96$, $p < .001$.

It was also clear that the word-aid list failed to improve target identification performance. People who received the word-aid list correctly identified 49 per cent of the targets on average, while those who did not receive the word-aid list identified 48 per cent, $F(1,4) < 1$. While the word-aid list failed to help subjects identify more targets, it did help them use words which the system recognized more often. Subjects who did not have the word-aid list entered words which the system did not recognize 26 per cent of the time, while subjects who had the aid used unrecognized words on 18 per cent of entries, $F(1,4) = 29.77$, $p < .01$.

Retrieval efficiency. Subjects who used the richer vocabulary systems needed somewhat fewer total entries to identify targets. Slightly more than 4.5 entries were generated in the two richest vocabulary conditions, while up to 5.5 entries were used in the leaner vocabulary conditions, $F(5,20) = 3.79$, $p < .05$. This result is contrary to the feared ambiguity cost of extended aliasing.

The word-aid list apparently caused subjects to spend more time generating key-words. Subjects who had the word-aid list took an average of 14.20 seconds to generate each word entry, while those who did not have the word-aid list needed only 10.35 seconds,

$F(1,4) = 250.89$, $p < .001$. This extra time was probably spent reading the word-aid list.

Word usage. One of the most striking aspects of the results reported by Furnas et al. (1983) was the extremely low agreement between people in the index words they used to describe objects, as measured by repeat rate. In their recipe data set, a superset of the targets used here, indexers used the same word to describe the same object only about one in 20 times.

The first three rows of Table 3 give repeat rates for the key-words subjects generated to find targets, the words subjects wrote on the reminder note cards, and the index words generated by the indexers in Furnas et al. for the same set of 24 targets used here.

Table 3

Repeat Rates

Words Generated For:	First-Word	All-Words
Retrieval Task	.71	.10
Reminder Cards	.50	.10
Indexing Task (Furnas et al.)	.22	.04
Blocked Re-indexing	.36	.04
Unblocked Re-indexing	.41	.02

In Table 3, repeat rate is reported for the All-Words and First-Word cases separately. In the All-Words case, repeat rate was calculated for all words that were generated to describe an object, while in the First-Word case, only the initial word generated to describe an object was considered. It is clear from Table 2 that a low level of inter-subject agreement similar to that observed by Furnas et al. was observed in the All-Word retrieval data. When only the first word generated was considered, inter-subject word agreement was much higher for the recipe finding subjects than for the original recipe indexers.

Perhaps this increased inter-subject word agreement was due to a task context effect. Generating key-words while doing an actual information retrieval task using a computer may initially make some aspect of a target more salient to subjects, thus encouraging higher First-Word agreement. However, it is also possible that the increased agreement was brought about because the subjects in this experiment had to consider 24 targets rather than the 188 considered by the original indexers. To study this possibility, we asked a new group of 22 subjects to generate index words for the 24 recipes used in this experiment. Ten of these subjects read and indexed the recipes in four blocks of six, just as the subjects who used the information retrieval system had done. The remaining subjects were given all 24 recipes at once. These data are also displayed in Table 3. These "re-indexers" had word agreement somewhat higher than the original indexers, but the level did not reach that achieved by the subjects who used the information retrieval system. Therefore, it seems likely that some aspect of actual retrieval promotes higher First-Word agreement than does a simple indexing task.

DISCUSSION

The data presented here clearly show that richly aliased key-word vocabularies lead to more successful information retrieval performance than do key-word vocabularies with limited aliases. Thus, the conclusions of Furnas et al. (1983) are confirmed by actual user performance. The data also showed that richly aliased vocabularies *did not* penalize users by causing them to use more entries to find a desired object. In fact, subjects using the systems with rich vocabularies needed slightly *fewer* entries to identify targets. In addition, contrary to some naive expectations, we have shown that providing users with a word-aid list did not improve target identification. The word-aid list did have a performance effect, albeit limited; in that the subjects who received it entered fewer words the system failed to recognize.

Rich aliasing. Subjects using the richest vocabulary system identified almost four times as many targets as subjects using the leanest key-word system. Why does vocabulary richness have such a potent effect on performance? The effectiveness of rich aliasing is due to the large number of dimensions by which any real object can be described. People, when they go to an information source to find an object, cannot be relied on to characterize the object consistently by one or few of its dimensions, or to describe its value on those dimensions by any one or few of the possible terms in the language. Richly aliased objects are known to the information system by many names; therefore, users are free to pick which of its many dimensions occurs to them, and to describe the object with their own words. The same person will often use a different word on different occasions to talk about the same object, simply because he or she is interested in the object for a different reason, or because of fluctuations in his or her personal production lexicons. Richly aliased objects, then, are found more often, because the system knows the object the user wants by the word or words the user wants to provide.

Subjects who worked with the most enriched vocabularies were not overwhelmed by larger return sets. Objects in the richest vocabulary were known by almost 32 names (see Table 1). The resulting performance benefit was not outweighed by the potential ambiguity cost of having each entry return almost 19 objects (see Table 2). Perhaps subjects were able to discriminate wanted items from unwanted ones by mentally constructing intersections from the numbers in the return sets to isolate likely target candidates. One way to measure the extent to which subjects were using intersections is to look at the proportion of times a number entry appeared in the return sets of the previous word entries on a trial. The data reveal that the proportion of times intersections were used was highly correlated with target identification, $r = .88$, $p < .001$. If the same objects continue to appear in the entries' return sets, then users may select these objects as solutions to the query. Thus, there is marginal evidence that subjects were able to avoid information overload by carrying out rudimentary logical operations on system return sets. Such operations may actually be thwarted by a system that fails to recognize most of the words entered by users. Users faced with great quantities of information from "real" or production information systems will, one hopes, have software tools to help perform such logical operations. But even automatic logic facilities will not help if the system does not know the terms the user gives it. In addition, production systems will certainly not have the minimal feedback we chose to give our subjects for methodological reasons. With enhanced system response to queries, (e. g. book titles, publication dates, and authors' names) users may be able to recognize from a set of objects returned the objects they want.

Why menus appear better. Menu based retrieval systems often seem easier to use than key-word information systems. The data from this experiment suggest at least part of the reason why menu systems give this appearance. The word-aid list was like a menu supplement to the key-word system in that subjects could choose a word from the list, rather than having to generate one. Subjects didn't identify more targets with a word-aid list, but they used fewer unrecognized words. Menus provide users with an aid to enter items to which the system can respond. People may find menu systems more friendly, because they rarely turn a deaf ear to users' entries.

Summary. The results show the clear benefit of extended aliasing for known-item information retrieval tasks, while not revealing any obvious human performance cost. However, the effect of rich aliasing on performance should also be explored when the users' task is an unknown-item-search. In a great many queries, the user doesn't know how many objects exist that solve a problem. It seems that an unknown-item-search would be made easier if the user sees as much of the relevant data base as possible. Richly aliased information systems will, on average, show the user more of the data base. It would appear that rich aliasing would help with problems of this class, but this conjecture should be investigated.

These results also should be replicated using a broader sample of information systems, especially those which give users more informative output; the number list used here provided only minimal feedback. We believe that more informative output will actually make rich aliasing more effective, because users will be better able to recognize desired objects.

Rich aliasing is probably an important technique for improving users' interactions with information systems. However, only additional research can determine how and in what situations it can best be used.

References

Furnas, G. W., Landauer, T. K., Gomez, L. M., & Dumais, S. T., Statistical Semantics: Analysis of the Potential Performance of Key-Word Information Systems, *The Bell System Technical Journal,* 1983, 1753-1806.

Herdan, G., *Type Token Mathematics: A Text Book of Mathematical Linguistics,* Mouton: S-Gravenhage, 1960.

Human-Computer Interaction — INTERACT '84 / B. Shackel (ed.)
Elsevier Science Publishers B.V. (North-Holland)
© IFIP, 1985

ACCESSING LARGE DATA BASES:
THE RELATIONSHIP BETWEEN DATA
ENTRY TIME AND OUTPUT EVALUATION TIME

Carla J. Springer and James F. Sorce
Bell Communications Research Inc.
Juniper Plaza, Route 9
Freehold, New Jersey   07728

The total time required for retrieving information from large data bases has two components: (1) the time spent entering the retrieval request and (2) the time spent evaluating all of the output that matches the request. There is an inverse relationship between these two components. This study assessed the particulars of this data-entry/output-evaluation trade off in the context of Directory Assistance. Results argue strongly that total retrieval time is reduced when output evaluation time is reduced even at the expense of increased data entry time.

1. INTRODUCTION

Since the number of large, computerized data bases is continually growing, the ability to retrieve information rapidly and accurately is becoming an important economic concern. The total time required for retrieving data base information has two components: (1) the time spent entering the retrieval request and (2) the time spent evaluating the output. In many cases, there is an inverse relationship between these two components since the less specific the information that is entered as the basis for the search, the more matching output that is produced for evaluation.

In providing directory assistance, operators search large, computerized data bases to retrieve directory listings for customers. Typically, operators use names, addresses and geographical locations as the data entered in their retrieval requests. Only a fragment of each type of information is entered in order to minimize data entry time. Indeed, minimizing keying time is viewed as a critical ingredient for minimizing the average work time per call, thereby reducing the overall cost of each call.

There is, however, one important consequence of the minimal keying strategy that has not been adequately assessed. As the amount of keyed information decreases, the number of potential data base matches increases. This, in turn, results in a larger number of retrieved listings for the operator to scan. When forced to evaluate more listings in order to locate the desired one, it takes a longer time and the desired listing may be missed. Therefore, the optimal strategy for minimizing average work time may be to minimize operator output evaluation time instead of operator keying (data entry) time.

The present study was designed to assess whether average operator work time could be reduced significantly by minimizing output evaluation, even at the expense of increased data entry time.

2. METHOD

In this experiment, operators used one of three data-entry strategies to retrieve listings from both business and residence data bases. The three strategies differed according to both the amount and type of information entered as the basis for the searches of the data bases. Specific directory listings were selected in order to vary the amount of output retrieved for operator evaluation for each strategy. The time required to complete data entry and output evaluation were measured for each retrieval.

2.1 Materials

Two directory assistance data bases incorporating the greater Indianapolis area were sampled: business and residence. These data bases were treated separately since operators typically enter different types of information for the two cases.

2.1.1 Business File.

For the business file, two different keying methods were evaluated: Method-5 and Method-7. Method-5 represented a minimal keying strategy frequently employed in Bell Telephone Operating Companies. It required the operator to enter a total of five characters -- the first four letters of the first word in the business name, and the first letter of the second word. Thus, to search for "Miller Discount Landscaping," MILL D would be keyed. Method-7 represented a more extensive keying method designed to reduce the number of listings retrieved, thereby reducing operator output evaluation time. Method-7 required operators to enter a total of seven characters -- the first four letters of the first word in the business name, the first two letters of the second word, and the first letter of the third word. Thus, to search for "Miller Discount Landscaping," MILL DI L would be keyed.

A total of 24 listings from the business data

base were selected to serve as test stimuli. The names differed according to where in the listing the uncommon element occurred. Importantly, half of the listings were names where there should be a benefit for minimal keying (Method-5). These would be listings where five keystrokes are sufficient to capture the uncommon aspect of the name.

The remaining business listings consisted of names where only the more extensive Method-7 keying strategy captured the uncommon element of the listing. See Table 1 for example listings.

2.1.2 Residence File.

For the residence file, three different keying methods were evaluated: Method-5, Method-7, Method-9. Method-5 again represented a minimal keying strategy frequently employed by Bell Telephone Operating Companies. The operator again keyed a total of five characters -- the first four characters of a person's surname and the initial of the person's given name, thus keying HARR M for the listing Margaret Harrison. In Method-7, the operator keyed a total of seven characters -- the first four characters of the person's surname, the first two characters of the given name and the first letter of the street name when it was provided by the caller. Thus HARR MA Q would be keyed for the listing

Margaret Harrison on Queen St. In Method-9, the operator keyed a total of nine characters -- the first six letters of the person's surname (when possible), the first two letters of the given name and the first letter of the street name when it was provided. Thus, HARRIS MA Q would be keyed for listing Margaret Harrison on Queen St. Method-7 and Method-9 were designed to reduce the number of listings retrieved, thereby reducing operator scanning time, but at the expense of increased operator keying time.

A total of 23 listings from the residence data base were selected to serve as test stimuli. Once again the names differed according to how far into the listing the uncommon element of the listing occurred, so that half of the listings should favor minimal keying while the remaining listings should benefit from extended keying. Sample listings are found in Table 2.

2.2 Design and Procedure

Fifteen operators with job ratings of satisfactory and six operators with job ratings of outstanding participated. Each operator was required to search for all of the business and residence listings. Seven of the operators were randomly assigned to each of the three keying strategies for residence listings (Method-5, Method-7, and Method-9), with the restriction

---

TABLE 1

Mean Total Time (in seconds) for Business Calls
as a Function of Keying Method and Listing Type

	Method-7 (Group 1)	Keying Method-7 (Group 2)	Method-5
Listings with an uncommon element toward the beginning: should favor minimal keying e.g. Grundy Memorial Chapel General Wine and Spirits	9.35	9.45	10.11
Listings without an uncommon element toward the beginning: should favor extended keying e.g. National Aviation Underwriters American International Underwriters	9.34	9.84	14.14
X=	9.35	9.65	12.13

that two of the operators with "outstanding" job ratings be assigned to each method. Operators retained the same keying method for business listings except that the Method-9 operators now keyed identically to Method-7 operators (thus serving as a replication group).

Each operator was tested individually in a private room on a terminal identical to those in their Directory Assistance office. One experimenter provided instruction and served as the caller during the test trials. A second experimenter focused on the operator's keying activity and recorded times at critical points during each trial.

First, the assigned keying method was introduced and the operator was given a number of practice listings in order to gain familiarity with the keying strategy. When Experimenter-1 judged that the method was being employed accurately, and when the operator reported feeling comfortable with the task, the test trials began. Eleven operators initially received a random ordering of listings from the business file followed by the randomized set of residential listings; the remaining ten operators received the listings in the reverse order. When all listings from one file were completed, the second data base was introduced along with another series of practice listings.

In the simulated calls, the experimenter who posed as the caller spoke through a telephone handset and the operator used a headset. An operator began each call with his/her typical greeting to customers after which the experimenter requested the listing for that trial. The operator then used the designated keying method to enter the appropriate characters, initiate the search, scan the retrieval listings, and either report the telephone number or initiate subsequent searches until either the appropriate listing or a "No Find" report was given. The trial was completed when the caller acknowledged the operator's report.

2.3 Dependent Measures

Four dependent measures were recorded for each call: data entry time, total call time, number of searches initiated, and whether an accurate telephone number report was given by the operator.

Data entry time was defined as the time from the beginning of the operator's greeting until the file key initiating the first search was depressed. Total call time was defined as the time from the beginning of the operator's greeting until the beginning of the caller's "thank you." When the operator did not find a listing after the initial search, the total number of

TABLE 2

Mean Total Time (in seconds) for Residence Calls
as a Function of Keying Method and Listing Type

| | Keying | | |
	Method-9	Method-7	Method-5
Listings with an uncommon element toward the beginning: should favor minimal keying e.g. <u>Sugars</u>, Fred <u>J</u>ohnson, <u>Z</u>ola	10.75	11.38	11.11
Listings without an uncommon element toward the beginning: should favor extended keying e.g. Arn<u>one</u>, Antonino Arno<u>ld</u>, <u>R</u>uth	11.71	11.58	17.37
X=	11.23	11.48	14.24

times subsequent searches were executed was recorded. Since all listings were potentially retrievable, the number of "No Find" reports was tabulated as an accuracy measure.

2.4 Apparatus

All retrievals were performed on a Computer Consoles Incorporated Directory Assistance System. The average response time of this system during average workday conditions was reported to be 0.5 to 0.6 seconds from the time a search is initiated by depressing a file key until all the listings on a screen are displayed. A maximum of 21 lines per page were displayed.

Times were collected with a Data Myte 900.

3. RESULTS

Residence and business calls were analyzed separately. However, in both cases, total time per call and data entry time were analyzed as functions of keying method and listing type (i.e., where in the listing the uncommon element occurred).

3.1 Business Listings

3.1.1 Time Measures.

A hierarchical repeated measures analysis of variance and a Newman-Keuls post hoc analysis were performed on total time per call. See Table 1. The two Method-7 groups did replicate each other, and were significantly faster than the Method-5 group by an overall average of 2.6 seconds, F (2,18) = 15.27, p < 0.01.

Importantly, for the two listing types where the maximum benefit of Method-5 was predicted, the difference between Method-5 and Method-7 did not reach statistical significance (less than 1 second). However, for the two listing types where the maximum benefit of Method-7 was predicted, a significant difference between the two keying methods favored Method-7 by over 4 seconds. These differences comprised a statistically significant interaction of Keying Method and Listing Type, F (6,54) = 3.18, p < 0.01. Thus, the additional keying in Method-7 resulted in shorter total times per call for the predicted listing types, while there was no total time advantage for Method-5 for any listing type.

In order to assess the difference between Method-5 and Method-7 in the time required for data entry, a hierarchical, repeated-measures analysis of variance was also performed on data entry times. The mean data entry time was 5.2 seconds per call and did not differ significantly between the two keying methods. Also, differences in keying time among specific listing types did not differ as a function of keying method even though there were more keys

depressed in the Method-7 and Method-9 strategies.

3.1.2 Other Measures.

The number of searches initiated by operators for each listing type was tabulated. For listing types in which the uncommon part of the business name was captured by using either keying strategy, typically only one search was performed by operators. Importantly, for the other two listing types, however, operators using only Method-5 required an average of two searches.

3.2 Residence

3.2.1 Time Measures.

A hierarchical, repeated measures analysis of variance and a Newman-Keuls post hoc analysis were performed on total time per call. See Table 2. The Method-7 and Method-9 groups did not differ from each other, but showed a statistically significant overall advantage of 3.5 seconds over the Method-5 group, F (2,18) = 14.66, p < 0.01. Importantly, for listing types where the maximum benefit of Method-5 keying was expected, the three keying methods did not differ statistically. However, the three remaining listing types, where the maximum benefit of extended keying was predicted, did show a statistically significant advantage of 5.7 seconds over Method-5 but did not differ from each other. These differences comprised a statistically significant interaction of Listing Type and Keying Method, F (8,72) = 8.30, p < 0.01.

In order to assess the differences among keying methods in the time required for data entry, a hierarchical repeated measures analysis of variance was performed on the data entry times. The mean data entry time was 6.4 seconds per call and did not differ significantly among keying methods. Also, there were no differences in data entry times among the five listings as a function of Keying Method.

3.2.2 Other Measures.

The number of searches initiated by operators for each listing type was tabulated. For listing types where the greatest benefit of minimal keying was expected, typically only one search was performed for all three methods. However, for listing types expected to benefit from more extensive keying, an average of two searches were performed by operators using only the minimal keying of Method-5.

4. DISCUSSION

The results of the present study argue strongly against the minimal keying strategy: keying time is cheap; output evaluation time is expensive.

Surprisingly, there was little difference in the time required for keying up to 9 rather than 5 characters. However, keying more characters resulted in a significant reduction in total work time per call due to substantial savings in output evaluation time. There was never an advantage of minimal keying for any type of listing tested while the overall advantage of extended keying averaged 2.6 seconds for business calls and 3.5 seconds for residence calls even though the more extended keying method was new to the operators.

The savings in output evaluation time resulted from the decreased number of listings retrieved under extended keying conditions. Output evaluation time proved to be sensitive to even small variations in the number of listings displayed to the operator. A subsequent analysis revealed that even when the desired listing appeared on the first display screen, extended keying required less scanning and resulted in an average output evaluation savings of 2.7 seconds per business listing and 4.5 seconds per residence listing. Under extended keying, operators had to scan only 1-2 lines to find the desired listing, while under minimal keying they were required to scan anywhere from 11-21 lines to find the desired listing.

The experimental requirement that Method-5 operators strictly adhere to the minimal keying strategy led to another interesting observation. Some operators reported feeling frustrated at not being allowed to key more information for their initial search. These operators predicted that too many listings would be retrieved with minimal keying. In fact, this was the case for many of the calls, and a subsequent search involving more keying was executed. However, operators varied considerably in their ability to judge which searches would benefit most from additional keying. This judgment is, in fact, a very difficult cognitive decision to make quickly; it may not be immediately obvious to the operator that the name "Antonino Arnone," for example, might be matched with the common surname "Arnold," if only the first four letters of the surname are keyed. Indeed, this type of situation may be a frequent one for directory assistance operators. For example, an examination of the Wichita, Kansas data base reveals that only 268 initial tetragrams account for 40 percent of the total data base listings.

The insignificant expense of increased keying was an unexpected finding in the present study. An analysis of keying time revealed a small increase between keying Methods 5 and 7 (0.78 seconds), but revealed no further increase under Method-9. This finding is the result of at least two factors. The cost of additional keystrokes may not be a linear function of the number of keystrokes. Also, it must be remembered that the directory assistance operator's task is not merely a typing task. It is a task involving listening, discriminating, cognitive processing and decision making. The time spent in these activities may be more important components of data entry time than the actual keystrokes.

Conclusion

Results of this study strongly support the hypothesis that total operator work time for directory assistance calls can most effectively be reduced by minimizing output evaluation time rather than keying time.

The conclusion that keying time is cheap while output evaluation time is expensive should apply to any situation that requires the quick retrieval of a unique item from a large data base. The savings which result may be expected to occur in such centralized services as reservations and scheduling, library cataloging, and customer or patient records.

Human-Computer Interaction — INTERACT '84 / B. Shackel (ed.)
Elsevier Science Publishers B.V. (North-Holland)
© IFIP, 1985

CONSTRUCTIVE INTERACTION:
A METHOD FOR STUDYING HUMAN-COMPUTER-HUMAN INTERACTION

C. E. O'Malley, S. W. Draper, and M. S. Riley

Institute for Cognitive Science, C-015
University of California, San Diego,
La Jolla, California 92093

In this paper we describe a promising technique for studying human-machine interaction (HMI) called Constructive Interaction. We describe two pilot studies from a set which explore its application to HMI. Constructive Interaction was developed by Naomi Miyake (Miyake, 1982). It consists essentially of recording sessions with two participants who are discussing some topic which they do not fully understand, in the hope of sharing their knowledge and arriving at a fuller understanding. Miyake was interested in what was revealed about the underlying schemas of the participants and how new schemas can originate in an interaction between two people. We are interested in what this basic situation can offer for the study of HMI.

Introduction

This paper describes some exploratory studies involving an observational technique called Constructive Interaction. This method is a variant of think-aloud protocol methods, the difference being that Constructive Interaction involves studying two people jointly trying to solve a problem. The method we adopted is based on some work done by Naomi Miyake, in 1982. We were interested in finding out whether or not the technique would be useful in studying human-computer interfaces, especially in cases requiring exploratory studies, where the domain is not very well understood, and therefore not amenable to laboratory-controlled studies requiring specific prior theories. We set out to apply this technique to several aspects of the UNIX user interface, by running several pilot studies, in which two participants were videotaped as they discussed some

This research was conducted under Contract N00014-79-C-0323, NR 667-437 with the Personnel and Training Research Programs of the Office of Naval Research. Work on Human-Computer Interaction was also supported by a grant from the System Development Foundation. Requests for reprints should be sent to the Institute for Cognitive Science C-015; University of California, San Diego; La Jolla, California, 92093, USA.

part of the system.[1]

The technique itself is very simple to set up and conduct:

1. Two subjects are needed, both of moderate experience and comparable expertise — that is, neither expert nor novice;

2. the subjects should have a shared problem, of a conceptual nature, and involving the system;

3. subjects should be encouraged to experiment with the system and use diagrams where possible;

4. subjects, screen, and diagrams are all videotaped;

5. the experimenter may be present to take notes, but otherwise intervenes as little as possible, unless the dialogue halts, at which stage subjects may be prompted with questions;

6. if necessary subjects may be asked to go over tapes and diagrams afterwards.

---

1. UNIX is a trademark of Bell Laboratories. The comments in this paper refer to the 4.2 BSD version developed at the University of California, Berkeley.

Constructive Interaction is a descendant of the more traditional types of protocol study in which subjects are asked to think-aloud while solving some problem. However, while these kinds of studies have proved useful, for example in problem solving, and in studies of novices learning how to use a text editor, we felt that there were several problems inherent in the method. One of these is already well known to psychologists, that is, the doubtful nature of the connection between verbal reports and **mental processes** — people tend to use implicit theories about themselves to infer causally their behaviour, rather than actually reporting on cognitive processes. It is also possible that having to make a verbal report changes the subject's task significantly and thereby invalidates any generalization of the findings to more naturalistic situations. In other words, the experimental situation may not be ecologically valid.

Both of the objections outlined above hinge on the fact that the verbal activity is not *intrinsic* to the subject of study. However, verbal data can be very useful, as long as one is aware of the factors which influence the way they are produced. In a two-person interaction the communication is not made for the investigator's benefit but for the benefit of the other participant. In other words, in a two-person interaction one may *capitalise* on the fact that communication takes place *between* people, rather than having it *interfere* with the object of study. Another advantage of two-person interactions is that, even if subjects are poor at expressing their knowledge they are likely to persevere in trying to communicate until their partner *does* understand, while in traditional protocol analysis the investigator is left with the choice of intervening further with requests for clarification or the choice of making inferences from the protocols.

Miyake's original study (Miyake, 1982) concerned the problem of understanding how a sewing machine could make stitches. Two subjects were videotaped as they tried to develop an adequate theory of the mechanism, chiefly by verbal discussion, but also using paper and pencil to draw diagrams, as well as using the sewing machine itself. Miyake used two people, neither of whom had a predominance of expertise, so that their uncertainty forced them to make explicit what they *did* understand, and to identify the points at which they *lacked* understanding. She had her subjects try out the system to provide evidence and counter-evidence

for their hypotheses about its mechanism. The theory developed by subjects was found to involve several stages, each of which solved the problem posed by the previous stage. The recordings were analysed to identify the points of transition when a new stage was reached for one or other of the participants.

At the end of the study, Miyake was able to construct a model of the structure of the subjects' knowledge of the topic in terms of its levels and connections. She was able to see subject's schemata or models changing, to see which questions "upset their understanding", and which explanations were effective in giving them new understanding. This method seems to be useful for extracting partial and tacit knowledge from subjects, where analysis of protocols can show both what utterances really seem to advance the hearer's understanding, as well as what problems are actually raised by learners.

First Study

Since we were interested in exploring the *potential* of Constructive Interaction for HMI studies, and in the *conditions* under which it might be effective, our studies involved different topics of discussion, and different mixes of participants, in terms of their prior knowledge of the topic. We present here two examples of two-person protocol studies, the first of which is a fairly straight-forward extension of more traditional studies; the second study we describe is, we feel, an example of true Constructive Interaction.

The first kind of study was a simple two-person interaction, concerning a tutorial session, in which a novice user, with very little prior experience with computers, was introduced to the system for the first time by someone who had considerable experience in using the system (although the subject was not a programmer). The session revealed some interesting sources of confusion for the novice, not unlike findings reported by Lewis and others in similar studies (cf. Lewis & Mack, 1982; Mack, Lewis & Carroll, 1982). However, the most striking feature of the session was the extent to which the tutorial was interrupted by questions concerning what was, to the tutor, irrelevant to the main theme — how to use the message system. Figure 1 shows schematically the interaction in terms of topics discussed (shaded areas) and number of utterances (to scale), where utterances refer to turns taken in the discourse. The total length of the scale is

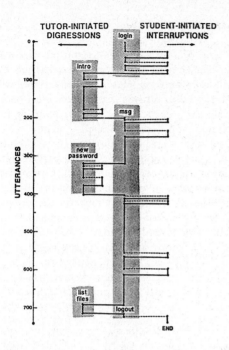

Figure 1. Diagram of tutorial session, showing main topics discussed (shaded portions). The scale refers to the number of utterances, in terms of turns taken in the discourse. The total length of the scale is roughly equivalent to one hour.

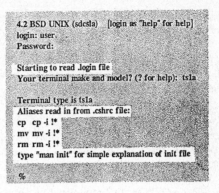

Figure 2. Diagram of the screen display showing the introductory messages for new users. Highlighted areas show the relevant messages.

roughly equivalent to one hour. This figure shows the proportion of student-initiated interruptions (dashed lines), as opposed to tutor-initiated digressions.

An example of a tutor-initiated digression (see "Intro" in the diagram) concerned some confusion created by a new system that had recently been installed for first time users. This system gave information about aliases — that is specially tailored commands — being read in from their *cshrc* and *login* initialisation files, and gave users instructions for where to find more information about changing their aliases. Figure 2 shows what appeared on the screen (the highlighted areas show the relevant messages). These messages had been put in deliberately as an attempt to solve another problem newcomers have: of never knowing of the existence of this file and of the initialization process. Without knowing, novices can never later think to ask about personalizing it; nor do they have a chance of understanding why a few commands (redefined via aliases in these initialization files) behave differently from what the documentation describes. The messages were intended as a reminder which, as they saw them every day, would

help create a more self-revealing and therefore accurate image of the stages involved in logging in. Since no response to this is needed it was assumed that this would be at worst neutral. This session showed the incorrectness of this. The information was confusing for the novice, who had no knowledge of the entities to which the information referred, and it was frustrating to the tutor, who wanted to deal simply with the process of logging in and reading mail.

Figure 1 demonstrates an apparent conflict between what the tutor wanted to convey — which was a basic ability to login to the machine and read electronic mail — and the questions of the *student*, which were largely driven by the screen display. Thus, in order to introduce the user to the message system, the tutor had to spend over half the session explaining various aspects of the system as a result of the user's queries about what was happening on the screen, much of which was in fact unnecessary for learning how to perform the basic task of reading and sending mail. In fact, about 55% of the tutor's utterances were in response to interruptions by the student for an explanation of low-level details concerning what was happening on the screen.

What was most striking about this was that it revealed the importance of low-level procedures to the first time user, procedures, for example, involving pressing the RETURN key after typing a command; when to take the initiative in interacting with the system; what a "prompt" is; what is status information and what is an instruction for the user to act upon, and so on. Users have even more problems with these kind of low-level procedures where they differ according to context, especially when, as novices, they have not yet been able to discriminate different contexts. These kind of discriminations tend not made explicit enough in most introductory manuals and tutorials. A majority of the pupils' questions, in all of these kind of studies, were directed at this level — a level that the tutor (like written tutorials) did not seem to anticipate having to focus upon.

These tutorial studies are similar to other forms of think-aloud protocol study, in showing the problems a novice can have with a system and with a tutorial; in revealing information about how beginners should be introduced — about what information it is relevant to explain initially, and what should be left out. In fact these kinds of study are probably closest in spirit to those of Lewis and others at IBM, in that they are exploratory studies. In studying tutorials given by people, clearly a two-person study is needed; in studying novices' problems with a system, a conventional one-person protocol study does as well, but it is probably much easier to get a novice to articulate questions to a tutor — who is obliged to try and give a useful answer — than to "think aloud" in a way that benefits the investigator rather than the subject.

Second Study

We would like to contrast the kind of study we have just described with another type, which we feel is much more characteristic of true Constructive Interaction studies. The study we describe was particularly interesting in that it revealed the potential of this method for exploring users' understanding of system concepts. The topic being discussed by the subjects in this study was the UNIX C-shell command interpreter and the rules governing when variable values will get passed to subordinate processes. The two participants both knew the system moderately well but were not experts. The study revealed that the subjects were seeking different *kinds* of explanation, based on different kinds of system models.

The subjects could use the system well enough for day to day business but there were various apparent anomalies they were interested in understanding: These concerned the fact that there are two distinct kinds of variable in the command interpreter (C-shell) used locally, with different

inheritance properties.

One of the subjects (A) started to construct an explanation of what the underlying job of the C-shell was, based on his programmer's knowledge of the system primitives for process creation called *fork* and *exec*, in the hope that the puzzling surface behaviour of the C-shell might become comprehensible. A substantial amount of time was spent in his working this out and explaining it to the other subject (B), who showed every sign of understanding and participating in the discussion. At one point, B suggested they try the experiment of explicitly executing an *exec* command from the C-shell. This turned out to be possible because the C-shell recognises *exec* as a command. As a control, they typed *lf*, the command for listing files, which listed the files in their current directory, and returned the normal shell prompt (the percent sign).

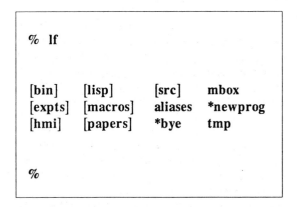

Figure 3. Screen display showing the result of typing the command *lf* (list files).

(See figure 3.) They then typed *exec lf*, which again listed the files, but instead of printing the usual shell prompt, it printed the login prompt (see figure 4). In other words, their session had been terminated and they were logged out.

This provoked laughter, but A quickly constructed an interpretation that fitted his model so well that the experiment served as an illuminating confirmation for him. (What happens is that the *exec* primitive overwrites the calling program with an instance of the new program. Thus in this case, the C-shell had overwritten itself with the directory listing program, which had run normally and terminated. The system had detected that there

```
% exec lf

[bin]     [lisp]      [src]      mbox
[expts]   [macros]    aliases    *newprog
[hmi]     [papers]    *bye       tmp

4.2 BSD UNIX (sdcsla)
login:
```

Figure 4. Screen display showing the result of typing the command *exec lf*.

were no more processes associated with that terminal and had prompted for a new login.) A offered this explanation to B, who did not fail to understand it, nor argue directly against it, but nevertheless refused to accept it fully, because of what was for him an overwhelming problem: In his model of systems, the command interpreter is a part of the operating system which can never die, nor allow itself to be replaced by some other program.

The rest of the session became devoted to talking about his model, with A taking pains to address the problems that B saw. However the acceptance by B of A's explanations was blocked by interference from B's model of how computer systems worked, which was imported in the absence of any readily available description in the documentation of how Unix is structured. This interference was interesting, in that it did not prevent B's apparent "understanding" of A's theory when described in and of itself: the trouble came in applying it to phenomena which B's model also addressed — that is, logging in, and the lifetime of the command interpreter. In practice B demanded an explanation of the visible events and objects — the tty, logging in, the duration of a login session, and so on — before being able to truly accept a description of the system primitives; although "logically" speaking, an explanation of the visible or surface events is based on these primitives.

This exploratory session showed for us a particular gap in the standard documentation, which does contain the actual information about system primitives such as *fork* and *exec*, but not in a form that is obviously related to visible system events and

objects. More interesting were the relationships that were revealed between aspects and stages of understanding in the subjects, which were also brought out in Miyake's original studies, and which we believe are relevant to what will succeed as an explanation for users, and hence are relevant to designing documentation.

Conclusions

The first kind of study we discussed — the tutorial session — is not remarkably different from other protocol studies, except that it involves two people rather than one. However, it may be contrasted with the study just described, which characterises much more the technique of Constructive Interaction. The advantage of Constructive Interaction is that the subjects reveal different points of view about a common problem. This difference between them forces them to articulate the rationale behind their hypotheses to each other, and to try and resolve a common ground between them. In the second type of study we described, only one of the participants (the novice) was interested in changing their point of view. In our view there are three main characteristics which distinguish Constructive Interaction from other kinds of two-person studies:

(1) the participants should have comparable knowledge about the topic (but not necessarily the same schema or model);

(2) they should want to solve the same problem;

(3) the emphasis should be on understanding or developing *concepts*, as opposed to learning *procedures*.

The studies reported on here, although exploratory, suggest that Constructive Interaction may be a useful technique to adopt in studying users' conceptualisations of computer systems. In allowing subjects to explore a problem and to develop the solution, without prompting or guidance, the investigator is able not only to observe the solution reached by subjects, but also to distinguish the *ways of expressing explanations* that proved effective for the participants, from amongst other less effective attempts. In Constructive Interaction studies one can not only observe what concepts users understand, and what models they have, but one can also observe them *changing* these ideas and concepts as they move between different levels of understanding the problem, and as they alternately pose and solve problems for their own and the other participants' hypotheses, rather than just observing them react to the situation.

References

[1]   Lewis, C. & Mack, R., *The role of abduction in learning to use a computer system* (Tech. Rep. No. RC 9433 (#41620)). New York: IBM Thomas Watson Research Center (1982).

[2]   Mack, R., Lewis, C., & Carroll, J., *Learning to use word processors: Problems and prospects* (Tech. Rep. No. RC 9712 (#42887)). New York: IBM Thomas Watson Research Center (1982).

[3]   Miyake, N., *Constructive Interaction* (Tech. Rep. No. 113). San Diego: University of California, Center For Human Information Processing (1982).

Human-Computer Interaction — INTERACT '84 / B. Shackel (ed.)
Elsevier Science Publishers B.V. (North-Holland)
© IFIP, 1985

SAYING WHAT YOU WANT WITH WORDS & PICTURES

Aart Bijl and Peter Szalapaj

EdCAAD, Department of Architecture
University of Edinburgh, UK

A logic modelling system for modelling descriptions of any kind of thing is
described. The system employs a symbolic representational structure that permits
integration of graphical and textual parts of descriptions, offering these as alternative means for depicting the same information. The goal is to represent knowledge
about drawings and words in computers in a way that will enable a computer to interpret intended meaning from human interactions, to understand what people want it to
know and do.

Human mind interacting with machine
intelligence, it is this interaction which is
central to computer aided design. We are here
less concerned with ergonomics, the physical
conjunction of people and artifacts, computers,
and we are less concerned with cybernetics,
people's control of system functions that have
been preordained in machines. We are more
concerned with artificial intelligence, the
representation of people's knowledge in
machines. The question we will explore is both
simple and fundamental – how can you describe to
a computer what you are thinking, so that the
machine will represent your thoughts in a manner
that you and other people will recognise? Can
we use computers to externalise knowledge
possessed by individuals, to support dialogue
between people?

Why is this question important to computer aided
design? Here we have to consider the nature of
design activity, particularly when aimed at
design artifacts that are not well defined, as
in the example of architecture. We have to
recognise a distinction between discipline based
activities and practice or experience based
activities, which rests on the answerability of
people engaged in an activity to other people
who have to validate results (Fig.1).

DESIGN: DISCIPLINE OR PRACTICE?

**KNOWLEDGE BASED
DISCIPLINE**

ACTIVITY: explicit
knowledge forms the
primary means for
progressing from
problems to solutions

ANSWERABILITY: to
peers who share a
common knowledge base

DISCIPLINE: formal
and detached, a shared
basis for assessing new
developments

PROCEDURES:
methodical and stable,
overt exclusion of
intuitive judgement

answerability

ACTIVITY

procedures

**EXPERIENCE BASED
PRACTICE**

ACTIVITY: relies on
explicit knowledge plus
intuitive judgement of
practitioners

ANSWERABILITY: to
public who do not share
a common knowledge base

DISCIPLINE: informal
and inconsistent,
practitioners must be
responsive to a
volatile world

PROCEDURES:
idiosyncratic,
ill-defined integration of
knowledge and experience

Discipline based activities, such as physics or
banking, are assessed within peer groups, among
people who share a common body of knowledge.
For such knowledge to be shared it has to be
overt, relatively stable and subject to explicit
procedures that are used to operate on the
knowledge. Correct use of procedures then plays
an important part in validating new
contributions to a body of knowledge.

Practice or experience based activities, such as
designing buildings, differ in that people
engaged in such an activity are answerable to
any other people. They have to meet divergent
and often undeclared criteria that do not
emanate from a shared and overt body of
knowledge. To a greater extent, we have to call
on intuitive knowledge and judgment of
individuals. Correct use of procedures
contributes little to the validity of a result.
The idiosyncratic nature of design procedures is
a necessary consequence of demands made by a
volatile world, and if these demands were not
volatile we would not need designers.

The search for some explicit and predictive
model of the design process which could be
acknowledged by different designers, and would
serve as a specification for a computer aided
design system that could be used by different
designers, has been found to be fruitless [1].
Instead, we need advances in computing
technology to progress from a predictive to a
descriptive mode of computing, so that we are
able to represent and operate with any current
state of thinking. The technology must permit
systems that have no inbuilt anticipation of
what people will think and do.

This need is not unique to designers, it arises
in all fields where work activity involves
interaction between varied people, ordinary
activity. We can express the goal in general
terms. More of the knowledge used by
programmers when they interpret end-user
requirements into available machine procedures
has to be transferred into computers. Computers

must be able to interpret demands directly from
users and automatically invoke appropriate
machine responses. Computers must be given the
base knowledge required to carry out this
interpretive role, and we need modelling systems
that permit users to describe to computers
anything they wish a computer to know and do.

This goal requires radical advances of the kind
highlighted by the Japanese Fifth Generation
Computer Systems project [2], and indicated by
the Alvey Programme [3]. We are here concerned
not so much with hardware technology, but with
advances in knowledge engineering that will make
new technology usable for an expanding
population of computer users.

LOGIC MODELLING SYSTEM

This paper outlines an early attempt to develop
a logic modelling system for modelling
descriptions of buildings, MOLE (Modelling
Objects with Logic Expressions). The logic
system exists in abstract, independently of its
machine implementation as a computer program,
and it is intended as a means for describing
anything. The system is implemented in the
Prolog logic programming language [4,5].

Prolog is as yet the only implementation of a
computationally treatable sub-set of symbolic
logic as a general purpose programming language
and, as such, it offers a computing environment
in which it is possible to maintain separation
between a logical representation of a user's
world and its corresponding physical
implementation in a computer. We may see Prolog
as a machine implementation of logic that
supports applications in text mode - logic can
be made to behave like grammatical rules which
enable people to extract meaning from
collections of words that pass between them,
where the "technology" of written words on paper
requires no anticipation of what will be said.

The approach taken at Edinburgh is to integrate
graphical and verbal descriptions into single
representational models. Text then contains
names given to instances of graphical primitives
and constructions made from collections of
primitives. The text also refers to other non-
graphical properties of things (objects, events)
that may be described. By such integration, it
becomes possible to interact with the graphical
part of a representational model by means of
text, or the other way round, and the system can
reveal consequences of interaction either
graphically or textually. The modelling system
has to possess the equivalent of grammatical
rules for interpreting intended meaning from
collections of graphical primitives, the system
has to reveal its current understanding at any
state of a graphical dialogue between a person
and a computer, and it must support continued
interaction to steer the machine's
interpretation towards the user's own intention.

ELEMENTS OF DESCRIPTIONS

MOLE employs the concept of a parts hierarchy in
which things are described by reference to their
parts, collections of parts forming
descriptions. The part/whole distinction is not
used; any whole is regarded as a temporal state
and is a candidate part of some other part.
Things may be described by reference to partial
descriptions of other things and links between
things may be preserved so that descriptions of
things may inherit changes to other things, thus
forming a variant hierarchy. The type/instance
distinction is not used; any instance may spawn
variants as further instances.

The favoured strategy is to name some thing and
then to describe what is meant by the name by
naming its parts, bottoming out with names that
are unambiguously understood in the knowledge
base of the recipient, either human or machine.
This is a top down approach. It is also
possible to first describe things and then
attach these descriptions to higher level
things, the bottom up approach.

The constituents of descriptions are kinds,
slots and fillers (Fig.2). Kind names refer to
any kind of thing, a concept, an event, a
function or an object. In this context,
drawings and drawing primitives are regarded as
objects. Kinds refer to something that is to be
described and which may form part of a
description of something else. Filler names
represent the parts of some thing that, as yet,
have no further description, the bottom level of
any current parts hierarchy. Slot names name
parts of a description and slots are the means
for attaching fillers to a kind. The system
then provides operators for linking these
elements in different ways to build up a
description of what you have in mind.

Kinds can be copied to other kinds, and
descriptions may arbitrarily have slots and
fillers added, replaced and deleted. The system
includes further operators to get it to reveal
names of existing kinds, fillers and slots, and
reveal virtual structures of existing
descriptions.

PARALLEL STRUCTURES OF THINGS AND DESCRIPTIONS

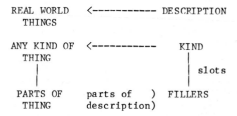

The naming conventions of the system are to use
upper case for kinds and fillers, and lower case
for slots. Kind and filler names may be defined

Fig. 2: LOGIC MODEL

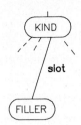

PART HIERARCHY

any kind of thing, objects events, functions ...,

slot

naming parts of kinds,

and

parts of descriptions of kinds.

KINDS — can inherit descriptions of other kinds;

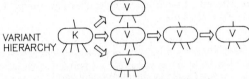

VARIANT HIERARCHY

slots can be added or deleted;
fillers can be replaced;
automatic update of kind names.

SLOTS — in combination, act like frames.

FILLERS — numbers;
words;
kinds;
references to parts of other kinds;
evaluable expressions.

by the user or the system; typically the system will assign names to empty fillers when they become kinds and receive their own further descriptions, taking the name of the slot that names the part which is the filler. Kind names are automatically given instance identifiers which are incremented whenever their descriptions are changed. Slot names are always declared by the user. Operators are generally represented by symbols, such as <+ for add to, <= for replace with or <~ to make a variant of.

WORKED EXAMPLE

We start with a simplified example using words to describe houses. The example illustrates the use of logical operators to link words that describe houses, as separate statements, and shows the use of relative naming to identify things and link each statement to other statements.

We have an architect who knows something about houses in general, and proceeds to tell the system what he wants it to know. We assume that the system starts off knowing nothing and no one has anticipated that the system will have to work with houses. Furthermore, we are not concerned whether the architect is telling the system the right things about houses; he decides that and he can change his mind.

Architect knows....

```
HOUSE <+ [accommodation,construction,
   frontage].
HOUSE:accom <+ [living-rooms,bedrooms,
   kitchen,bathroom,separate wc].
HOUSE:const <+ [walls=<BRICK,CONCRETE,
   TIMBER>,roof=<TILES,SLATE,SHEET>].
HOUSE <+ [frontage=<WIDE,NARROW>].
```

Now the system has been told that houses in general are things described in terms of their parts which are accommodation, construction and frontage and, in turn, these have further parts such as living rooms and walls. Note that parts can be described in terms of a range of further parts; walls are either brick, concrete or timber.

The architect then meets a client, John, who wants a particular house. The architect tells the system about the client.

Architect meets client....

```
JOHN <+ [family,site,likes].
JOHN:family <+ [spouse=WIFE,children=3)
JOHN <+ [site=NARROW].
JOHN:likes <+ [walls=BRICK,roof=SLATE].
```

John is described as something which has a family, a site for his house and he has likes or preferences. The family is described as something that has a wife and three children. John wants a house with brick walls and a slate roof.

The architect then describes John's house and describes his design to the system.

Architect designs John's house....

```
JOHN'S H <~ HOUSE.
JOHN'S H:liv rm <+ [number=1,size=LARGE].
JOHN'S H:bedrm <+ [number=4,bedrm1=DOUBLE].
JOHN'S H:accom <+ [garage].
JOHN'S H:const <+ [walls=BRICK,roof=TILES].
JOHN'S H <+ [frontage=[JOHN:site]].
```

John's house has one large living room, four bedrooms including one double bedroom, kitchen, bathroom, separate w.c. and a garage. Note that the system thus far knows of the kitchen, bathroom and w.c. only that they exist as parts of this house, but nothing more about them. The system knows this much because the architect has said that John's house is a variant of houses in general, and he has added the garage to the description of house accommodation. The design of John's house has brick walls and a tile roof; John cannot afford slate. John's house frontage is described by referring to John's site which is narrow, an example of indirection.

The architect meets another client, Mary, who

also wants a house but a different one. The
architect then tells the system about Mary and
his design for Mary's house.

>   Architect later designs similar house for
>   another client....

```
MARY <= JOHN.
MARY:family <+ [spouse=HUSBAND,children=2].
MARY'S, HOUSE <~ JOHN'S, H.
MARY'S, H:bedrm <+ [number=3].
MARY'S, H:accom <+ [workshop].
MARY'S, H:accom <- [garage].
```

He says that Mary is the same kind of thing as
John, but has a husband and only two children.
Mary's house is described as a variant of John's
house, which means that Mary's house inherits
the descriptions of John's house and houses in
general and will continue to inherit any
subsequent changes to the descriptions of these
other houses. If, later, it becomes
inappropriate for Mary's house to inherit
further changes to these other descriptions, the
architect can tell the system to stop making
Mary's house a variant of John's house (MARY'S, H
<\ JOHN'S, H). For the moment, Mary's house is
described as being different to John's in having
three bedrooms, a workshop and no garage.

The architect has been able to describe Mary and
her house by referring to knowledge the system
already possesses about John and houses. As the
system accumulates knowledge, the user needs to
say less and less to achieve more. But the user
may lose track of what the system knows, so the
user can use the "virtual" operator.

>   System knows about Mary....

```
MARY:
[family=[spouse=HUSBAND,children=2],
site=NARROW,
likes=[walls=BRICK,roof=SLATE],
house=[accom=[liv_rm=[number=1,size=LARGE],
            bedrm=[number=3,bedroom1=
               DOUBLE],
          kitchen=*,
          bathroom=*,
          sep, wc=*,
          wkshp=*],
      const=[walls=BRICK,roof=TILES],
      frontage=NARROW]].
```

The system reveals all that it knows about Mary
and her house. Equally, the architect could
have called for only part of this information,
for instance by asking "virt MARY's, H:accom" to
get only the description of accommodation. In
this example the asterisks opposite kitchen,
bathroom, wc and workshop indicate that the
system knows that accommodation has these parts
but does not yet know what they are, the parts
are empty and can be filled with anything at any
time.

Seeing this description of Mary, the architect
may want to modify parts of it, he may have
discovered more about Mary.

>   But Mary's husband is Fred and she cannot
>   afford a separate wc....

```
MARY:family <+ [spouse=FRED].
MARY'S, H:accom <- [sep, wc].
```

DRAWING DESCRIPTIONS

So far we have described Mary in words, but we
also want to be able to draw descriptions. We
want to draw the shape of Mary's house and we
want the shape information to form part of the
text description.

Drawings produced by people are instantiations
of descriptions that may consist of points and
lines where points establish location and lines
pass through points and have the attributes of
angle and length. The instances of location,
angle and length become facts as soon as
drawings appear on whatever medium is used,
paper or a computer graphics display; we may not
know the significance of these facts (are they
precise or final?) or how they relate to other
parts of a description, until we are told.

Interpretation of a drawing part of a
description in terms of the representational
structure of MOLE must accord with the goal of
the system to accommodate any different drawings
as parts of any other descriptions, and permit
any modifications.

REAL WORLD DESCRIPTIONS AND SYMBOLIC REPRESENTATION

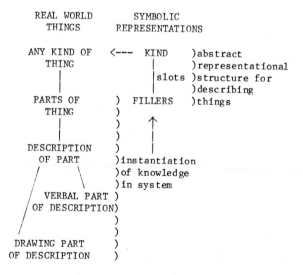

Real world here means anything outside a system
where system refers to knowledge contained
within the head of a person or within a
computer. Symbolic refers to a representational
structure that is not dependent on any

instantiation of things that are to be
represented, that can accommodate different and
unanticipated instances of things.

From MOLE's point of view, drawings produced by
people are real world objects just like the
things that drawings may describe. The system
then has to glean from facts provided by the
user, detectable from the process of
constructing a drawing and supplemented by the
user saying what is being drawn, sufficient
information to build up its own representation
of the drawing part of a description, and it
must be able to regenerate drawings to show
modifications to the description.

The parts of drawings that MOLE knows about are
construction lines (equivalent to pencil lines
in conventional practice), points at the
intersections of construction lines and finished
line segments (ink lines).

Construction lines are kinds with slots for
angle values, their fillers referring to some
angle datum (conventionally 0 for horizontal).
Points have slots for their construction lines,
and points become parts of a description in MOLE
only when they are used to delimit segments.
The coordinate value of a point is initially
taken from the space in which the drawing first
occurs (the display screen coordinate, suitably
translated into some real world value), but
thereafter coordinate values are calculated by
MOLE from information it knows about a current
(modified) description, from segment lengths and
construction line angles, related to some
coordinate datum. Finished line segments have
slots for their end points, length value and
sign (direction, from first point).

Construction lines and finished line segments
are MOLE's only drawing primitives in the sense
that these are used to build up further
descriptions of objects. Point coordinates in
the drawing system are used only to give a
single value to position a drawing shape, and to
calculate initial values for segment lengths
when segments first occur in a drawing;
coordinates are not used to manipulate a
description. Construction points are inferred
from construction lines and segments, and are
manipulated by the user saying things about
construction line angles and segment lengths.

Figure 3 illustrates the relationship between a
MOLE description and a real world drawing. For
convenience, MOLE's representation is presented
as a logic diagram of a virtual structure of
parts of Mary (the earlier example). Remember
that this is a virtual structure in the sense
that it is not a physical structure stored in
the computer. The structure is created by the
system from information contained in the
separate declarations of the user, in response
to the user invoking the "virtual" operator, and
the structure disappears when the user no longer
wants to see it. The diagram exists outside the
system and its purpose is solely to illustrate

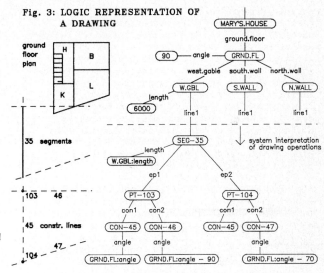

Fig. 3: LOGIC REPRESENTATION OF A DRAWING

to the reader the relationships between parts of
a description inside the system.

The drawing is shown in the process of being
constructed (from the bottom upwards), with
construction lines drawn first and then a
segment added, on the way to a ground floor plan
of a house. The segment forms part of the west
gable wall description. MOLE uses its knowledge
about drawings in general to build up its
representation of the thing that the particular
drawing describes, and the information it holds
is sufficient to regenerate the drawing.

In this illustration the description in MOLE
below the dotted line is generated automatically
by the system. Note that angle values are
established with reference to the user-declared
angle value for the ground floor (so that if the
completed ground floor part is later reused in
different orientations, relationships between
the drawing parts of the ground floor
description will hold true), and the length
value for segment 35 is overwritten by a user-
declared length value for the west gable wall
(affecting the position of lines that will
appear on a subsequent regeneration of the
drawing on the display screen).

CONCLUSIONS

We now have three primary elements of an
interactive system. A person who we normally
refer to as the user, a computer system for
executing drawing operations and the MOLE logic
modelling system. The drawing system can be
driven either by the user or MOLE and its role
is to serve as a dumb vehicle for transmitting
knowledge both ways between the user and the
modelling system. In this sense the drawing
system is analogous to systems that allow users
or programs to cause words to appear on a
display screen; words and drawings are
alternative ways of depicting information.

By integrating drawing and textual parts of descriptions in a MOLE representation, it is possible for a user to describe things including modifications to descriptions by using either words or drawings. Changes described in words, which have consequences on drawings, can then be seen in subsequent drawings generated by MOLE. Similarly, changes which a user may make to drawings can be viewed in subsequent verbal descriptions. Using a computer, the drawing system deals primarily with point locations in screen space, and the user and modelling system pick up information about lines as objects between or passing through points.

The drawing part of this logic modelling system is still at an early stage of development. We know that there is a whole range of operations on drawing objects that affect interpretation of intended meaning relevant to descriptions of things that drawings depict. One such operation refers to attachment facts, the nature of connectivities between parts of a drawing and parts of the thing a drawing depicts [6]. Another refers to post-hoc decomposition of drawings which becomes necessary as more parts are added or modified in a drawing. These topics are presently receiving urgent attention.

The logic modelling facilities of MOLE are intended to be capable of modelling any description and any change that may be made to a description. A problem then arises for the user in knowing how MOLE employs logic to represent what the user is thinking about; the user has to be aware of the knowledge about drawings in general that MOLE possesses, to know how MOLE will interpret particular drawings. This is a general problem that will probably require considerable investment by users in learning how to use this kind of system. Provided the power of the system, or any similar successor, is sufficiently general and not bound to any anticipation of a particular application, the investment would be worth while. We have the precedent of investment in learning how to use written language.

ACKNOWLEDGMENTS

The authors wish to acknowledge the SERC's continuing support for research at Edinburgh which is essential to the work described in this paper. Thanks are also due to all members of EdCAAD who sustain the environment in which this work can occur, and in particular to Sam Steel for lending us his logicians mind from the field of AI.

REFERENCES

[1] Bijl, A., Stone, D. and Rosenthal, D.S.H., Integrated CAAD Systems (EdCAAD, University of Edinburgh, 1979).

[2] Fuchi, K., Aiming for Knowledge Information Processing Systems, proc. Int. Conf. on Fifth Generation Computer Systems, Tokyo (Oct. 1981).

[3] Alvey Committee, A Programme for Advanced Information Technology (HMSO, UK, 1982).

[4] Kowalski, R.A., Logic for Problem Solving (Elsevier North Holland, 1979).

[5] Clocksin, W. and Mellish, C., Programming in Prolog (Springer-Verlag, 1981).

[6] Szalapaj , P. and Bijl, A., Knowing Where to Draw the Line, submitted to IFIP WG5.2 Working Conference on Knowledge Engineering in Computer-Aided Design, Budapest (Sept. 1984).

Human-Computer Interaction — INTERACT '84 / B. Shackel (ed.)
Elsevier Science Publishers B.V. (North-Holland)
© IFIP, 1985

CONCEPT REFINEMENT IN SOCIAL PLANNING THROUGH THE
GRAPHICAL REPRESENTATION OF LARGE DATA SETS

M. Visvalingam

Department of Geography,
University of Hull,
Hull, HU6 7RX.

Social planning is part of a process of arbitration. Empiricism is sought as a means
of reaching a decision even if not consensus. This paper argues that the prevailing
rule-based approach to the production of statistical evidence can confuse as much as
clarify social issues. A graphical information system, based on Advanced Information
Technology, can expedite concept refinement in complex problems, wherein the underlying assumptions remain implicit and vague rather than explicitly articulated.
However, this calls for changes in both the framework for and form of human-computer
interaction in computer cartography.

1.   INTRODUCTION

This conference seeks to promote ideas which
would make information systems "safe, more
useful, less tiring and easier to learn and to
use". This paper is particularly concerned
with the second objective and demonstrates how
the graphical interaction of man with computer
can extend human capacity for concept
formation and refinement in social planning.

Social planning is not an objective, rule-
based and value-free activity. Irrational
and primitive instincts are known to
influence both motivating beliefs and policy
decisions. Provisions for public participation
in planning recognise that there may be many
equally valid even if competing and conflicting
views of man-made reality, visions of the
future and claims for resources.

It is generally assumed that empiricism
provides hard evidence and impartiality in the
formulation, implementation and evaluation of
policy. It provides a means of reaching a
decision for instituting action, even if not
consensus. Information, however, is costly
and it is impractical to commission ad-hoc
surveys for each and every social issue.
Instead, planning agents usually rely on the
services of a primary sector within the
information industry, which collects and
disseminates 'raw' statistics on a variety of
social issues.

Whilst such independent observations, are
impartial, they do not preclude subjectivity
or arbitrariness in the selection and interpretation of welfare indicators. Applications
of inappropriate statistical methods have
become standard practice owing to the low
state-of-the-art of social indicator
development.

This mismatch between concepts and methods has
in part been caused by the enormity of the
data and the lack of an adequate human-computer
interface for exploration, cross-reference and
validation, in visual form, of both the data
and the information product. Computer cartography provides a powerful tool for validation
through visualisation. More recent exploratory
research, taking advantage of developments in
computer graphics, demonstrate that statistical
'evidence' can confuse as much as clarify
social issues. Graphical representations of
large data sets highlight important features
which are easily overlooked in detailed statistical tables and concealed by aggregate
statistics and conventional statistical
processing.

Methodological research is at present an
involved process on multi-user systems.
Scheduling priorities and offline operations
necessitate the dismembering and sequencing of
unified tasks. The resulting proliferation of
unnecessary activities and files is extremely
confusing to non-programming users.

Graphic workstations which support concurrent
processing and analog input are more conducive
to the development and use of graphical
information systems. However, the already
available but disparate items of software need
to be rationalised and presented through a
high-level user interface, which incorporates
graphics. Given the data and software functions
an information system should facilitate not only
the pre-planned production of information but
also an experimental approach to the evaluation
of the latent information potential and of
alternative information perspectives.

In Section 2, it is argued that currently
available software for computer cartography is
based on inadequate models of information flow
and that advances in IT offer some considerable
scope for extending these models and for
providing improved systems for human-computer
interaction in the procurement of statistical
evidence.

This is elaborated in Section 3 by reference to a published example (1), which demonstrates the potent value of graphics in making explicit many of the assumptions which remain implicit in current statistical analysis. The articulation of these assumptions fosters the concept of alternative information perspectives on a data-field, and stresses the need to relate perspective to purpose.

The concluding section discusses the wider implications of this project both with respect to practical social planning and other academic research.

2.   COMPUTER CARTOGRAPHY AND PLANNING

Although there has been significant develop-ments in computer graphics (2,3) the design of cartographic software has been limited by available technology and pre-computer era models of information flow in cartographic communica-tion (4). These associate with maps their traditional functions, regarding maps as media for the storage, dissemination and communica-tion of spatial information; for example, on absolute and relative location, direction, distance, gradient, shape, connectivity, contiguity and heirarchy. In this role, maps are not merely representations of data, but are models of reality itself although there are some considerable variations in concepts of reality and aims of map-making (3).

Information flow models are largely concerned with the processes by which the cartographer conveys his view of reality to the map-user. The flow is cyclic, since the latter can communicate his reading, analysis and inter-pretation of the map to the former so that noise factors in the encoding and decoding of the map medium could be recognised and eliminated where possible. This is an adequate schema of information flow in the production and use of some reference maps, for example those which convey some aspect of physical reality. Map-makers, such as the Ordnance Survey, are also collectors of the primary data, which have until very recently been made available only in printed map form; suitably structured digital maps are a recent phenomena.

Elements from reference maps are included in planning maps for purposes of orientation and location. The focus, however, is on the thematic content of the map, based on own-survey and other census data. General purpose census atlases, whether on population (5) or on disease and mortality (6), give some impression of prevalent social conditions but are insufficient for purposive studies. Policy researchers and implementers require greater detail and a different perspective or range of variables. Moreover, whilst maps are useful for focussing attention and deriving abstractions, policy analysts need to recover and process underlying statistics as prompted by map observation. Currently available

cartographic software facilitates the production of customised maps but does not allow the map maker-cum-user to use the medium to recover vital statistics.

Whilst, in theory, computer cartography offers some considerable scope for experimentation, commonly available command-driven packages inhibit data exploration. They offer a poor man-machine interface and assume that users have a programmer's mentality. Users generally tend to identify procedures which make the package work for them and then stick to this format, often through the use of front-end macros provided by someone else. This encourages a pre-planned approach to the production of cartographics. Ephemeral displays are generally used to check the product for errors in user input rather than to experiment via interaction. Even when there has been a man-machine interface lift, the intention has been to reduce the scope for erroneous input by altering the form of the dialogue. There has been little change in the framework for man-machine interaction, which remains inadequate.

This has in part been due to the limitations of yesterday's technology, which in practice is still in use. Multi-user systems are not conducive to speedy graphic interaction. Eight-bit micro-computers do not offer the memory and the screen-format convenient for planning applications which rely on large data sets.

However, the emergence of powerful single-user personal workstations with enhanced graphic facilities is just one of the developments which is likely to change the role of computer cartography in social planning. Such decent-ralised systems offer prospects for optimising all operations towards one application. They already feature high-resolution large-format screens. Further, developments in network technology permit rapid access to large, shared data sets on data servers or on systems else-where on a network.

These single-user systems already support concurrent processing, which considerably eases not just the development of complex graphical information systems but their use; parallel processing hardware is likely to upgrade speed rather than functionality in information systems. What is seriously lacking, and urgently needed, is a relatively inexpensive high-resolution colour capability.

Research and development in enabling technol-ogies will lead to the computerisation of many tedious cross-referencing functions in data exploration. These are only semi-automated at present, slowing down and often cutting out methodological research when confronted with planning deadlines. Future systems need new software concepts. We already have the necessary minimal capability to undertake investigations into high level cartographic software.

We, at Hull, are investigating the feasibility of a socio-technical system, wherein a set of maps can be used to a) stimulate insight, b) derive the perspectives on data which are most relevant to policy issues, and c) act as 'pointers' to data. This requires the transfer of the data storage function from the map to the computer, so that the map can be used for the functions that it is best suited for, namely the comprehension and customised communication of spatial relationships in a holistic form. The map can instead become part of the front-end to data base systems - a front-end which will include graphic query functions to retrieve 'raw' or related data in a natural way.

3. GRAPHICS FOR CONCEPT EXPLORATION

Maps as pointers to data and the notion of concept exploration through visualisation can be illustrated with a very simple example. Area-based policies often involve the identi-fication of priority or target areas, for example for purposes of positive discrimination or for product promotion. Target areas are usually identified with composite indices based on some forty or so variables. The method is extremely simple if we consider the bare bones of the approach ignoring sophistications.

Firstly, there is a need to specify the central concept - poverty in policies of social reform or market potential in product promotion. Such concepts are difficult to define precisely, let alone measure directly. Thus, surrogate measures such as income become candidate indicators of poverty and buying power. Data on income is not directly measured in many countries and is often suspect even when avail-able. Thus, proxy measures, such as data on unemployment, are used in their diagnostic, not descriptive, capacity (7).

Operational values are then derived from the selected data, for instance on male unemploy-ment. Policies directed at individuals and generally intended as relief measures feature statistics on the numbers unemployed; they are based on the concept of absolute deprivation. Policies of social reform, on the other hand, operate on the concept of relative deprivation and have traditionally used ratio indicators in the identification of priority areas.

Areas can now be sorted on these operational values and 'best' and 'worst' areas be identi-fied, using some system for determining cut-off values. The characteristics of extreme areas can then be assessed.

The following assumptions are implicit in this procedure. Johnston (8) argued that "spatial variations in the human condition can be measured on a generally acceptable metric, irrespective of how that metric is interpreted by the value system of the perceiver". Further, it is assumed that each surrogate or proxy measure, however crude, bears at the very least a monotonic relationship to a selected dimension of the underlying theme. Geographic areas, or for that matter any set of samples or sub-populations, can be deemed to be ranked unequi-vocally on a good to bad scale only if we accept the above assumptions.

It is widely known that absolute numbers are biased towards large populations and that ratio values tend to be more extreme in small populations. Choynowski (9) used maps to point out this ratio bias but this has largely been ignored in many sophisticated statistical analyses. Some have used population weighting to counteract this effect but this is not always adequate.

Editors of thematic atlases, on the other hand, have been forced to acknowledge and either camouflage or compensate for this bias, which is often obvious on maps. Dewdney and Rhind (10) omitted the most offending smallest populations from grid-square choropleth maps. Howe (6,11) tried to indicate the size of the base population with embellished or proportional symbols and shaded them according to their ratio class.

These approaches were influenced by the need to preserve the data storehouse function of the map so that map users could determine an area's data values or data class. This function of maps could be performed more effectively by other means when electronic publishing and teleconferencing come into everyday use (12). The above cosmetic changes, which are largely instituted within the secondary stages of information production, are also influenced by the need to preserve the aesthetic quality of maps in general purpose atlases. Even within the tertiary stages of graphic encoding, aesthetic quality is of secondary importance to information perception in planning maps (13). More importantly, the above procedures do not yield an acceptable technique for the ranking of populations.

The original colour versions of black and white geographic maps published elsewhere (1) can be used to demonstrate this known bias of both absolute numbers and ratios; male unemployment is suggested to be particularly serious in urban areas by the former and in rural and small populations by the latter. Other cartographic displays, such as a scatter-plot of percentage against number unemployed (Figure 2, Visvalingam, 1983a), not only high-light these two trends but also draw immediate attention to the existence of two outliers. It would be extremely useful if these various displays could be simultaneously viewed on a large screen and if the geographic areas which produce these anomolies could be rapidly identified. The graphical information system, which will allow the user to point to these outliers on the scatterplot and which will respond by indicating their location on the maps and by displaying the required statistics, would quickly locate the two outliers as being in areas which had male Borstals in 1971.

The propensity for a mismatch between many proxy measures and underlying concepts has already been documented by several workers (7). Data is more often than not sold in aggregate form to ensure confidentiality of personal and household information and to ease processing. Individuals and households are allocated to one of a finite number of mutually exclusive and together exhaustive classes. Even when categorisations are devised after consultation, categories of interest may include unwelcome elements particularly when a 100 per cent sample survey is undertaken. The onus is ultimately on the user to ensure the correctness and suitability of the data. A graphic interface is expedient for identifying and investigating outliers and deducing the proxy value of nominal classes; in some cases it provides the only means of detecting missing data (14).

Even more important than the differential bias is the lack of correspondance between operational definitions and issues of policy (1). Propositions concerning the equity and efficacy of area-based policies of positive discrimination (15) require the simultaneous consideration of three forms of concentration of deprivations, namely absolute, relative and density. Area-based marketing requires the same. Ratios and absolute numbers operationalise only one each of these requirements.

The signed chi-square measure (16) is capable of considering all three requirements simultaneously. The spatial pattern of male unemployment based on this measure is markedly different to that portrayed by ratios and numbers. Lorenz curves are useful for comparing these performance indicators. In Figure 1a, each Lorenz curve plots the cumulative proportion of unemployed males against the areas, ranked using the three indicators. Here, again it would be useful if a graphical information system enables the analyst to select cut-off values and responds with a tabulation of the specified characteristics of 'worst' areas on each indicator. At the worst end, signed chi-square produces a ranking which, even if not perfect, is intermediate to and more acceptable than ratios or absolute numbers.

However, studies which are more concerned with the 'best' end would find the Lorenz curves rather perplexing. The graphs instantly show that the best ten per cent of areas, using this measure, include some 13 per cent of the unemployed when some forty five per cent of

areas enjoy full employment as indicated by the curves for ratios and numbers. Again, it will be useful if the characteristics of these different sets of best areas can be retrieved by pointing to cut-off values. The statistics indicate that there are between 2 and 364 economically active males in the areas with full employment. Whilst full employment for 364 males is significant as an indicator of buying power, full employment for two is not worth considering, particularly since the addition of one unemployed school-leaver would cause a jump to 33 per cent unemployed.

Signed chi-square is thus a measure of the reliability of ratios and corresponds to the binomial test statistic in the two-category case. In areas with above expected levels of unemployment, the emphasis is on the unemployed; in areas with below expected levels, the focus is on the employed. This is obvious on Lorenz curves for employed males (Figure 1b). The best 10 per cent of areas, using the signed chi-square measure, include some thirty per cent of working males and are located in the relatively higher status areas in Humberside. In contrast, the 45 per cent of areas with full employment occur in dispersed locations and capture only some six per cent of working males.

It therefore appears that the signed chi-square measure may be more suitable for commercial purposes when there is a marked variation in sample sizes. Since the key issue in the use of probabilistic indicators is the formulation of expectation, it would be pertinent to consider the impact of alternative reference points. Performance indicators, based on statistical averages, summarise the net effect of past and prevailing processes; this is adequate for commercial ventures which merely seek to exploit the existing socio-spatial structure of society. It is not the overt intention of such programmes to change the existing fabric of society. Policies of social reform are construed as instruments of socio-spatial engineering. Thus it is necessary to investigate the utility of social or political norms, such as the level of unemployment considered to be tolerable in a given state of the economy. Other questions are prompted by graphical displays based on an expectation of full employment (1). Even with only two inversely correlated items of data per sample there are even further perspectives if we move to data for irregular units (16), such as enumeration and administrative districts instead of constant-area grid squares. The implications of such changes to perspectives have yet to be explored and clarified.

The derivation of performance indicators from descriptive statistics is only one process within the secondary stages of information production. The aim of our research is to equip the policy analyst with an environment wherein the impact of changes to the data content, processing, analysis and graphic encoding can be immediately assessed. An operator of the graphical information system will change the appearance and information impact of data in much the same way that a user of word-processing software alters the layout and appearance of text.

CONCLUSION

Statistical evidence can project a misleading perspective on even pertinent data; this may not always be intentional. A graphical information system will facilitate an experimental approach to the exploration of large quantities of relevant data and thereby promote the clarification of nuances in policy issues. At the very least, this requires friendly functions for retrieving selected statistics by pointing to maps and for cross-referencing elements in different displays. Within this context, existing cartographic software is excellent for the communication of well-defined perspectives but is inadequate for the formulation and refinement of concepts and methods.

The graphical information system will also expedite academic research into social measurement and cartographic communication, and could be linked to front-ends to demonstrate and teach the principles of cartography and basic statistical techniques. It may provide a working environment within which cognitive processes involved in the abstraction of knowledge from graphics can be studied.

REFERENCES

(1) Visvalingam, M, Area-based social indicators: signed chi-square as an alternative to ratios, Soc. Ind. Res. 13 (1983) 311-329.

(2) Dudycha, D.J., The impact of computer cartography, Cartographica 18 (1981) 187-213.

(3) Visvalingam, M. and Kirby, G.H., The impact of advances in IT on the cartographic interface in social planning, Dept. of Geography Misc. Series, Univ. of Hull (1984) in preparation.

(4) Board, C., Cartographic communication, Cartographica 18 (1981) 42-78.

(5) CRU/OPCS/GRO, People in Britain - a census atlas (HMSO, London, 1980).

(6) Howe, M.G., National Atlas of Disease Mortality in the United Kingdom (Nelson, London, 1970).

(7) Visvalingam, M., An examination of some criticisms of area based policies, Census Research Unit WP 22, Dept. of Geography, Univ. of Durham (1983).

(8) Johnston, R.J., On the nature of explanation in human geography, Trans. Inst. Brit. Geogr. NS5 (1980) 402-12.

(9) Choynowski, M., Maps based on probabilities, J. Am. Statist. Ass. 54 (1959) 385-388.

(10) Dewdney, J.C. and Rhind, D.W., People in Durham - a census atlas, Dept. of Geography, Univ. of Durham (1975).

(11) Howe, M.G., Mortality from selected malignant neoplasms in the British Isles: the spatial perspective, Soc. Sci. Med. 15D (1981) 199-211.

(12) Monmonier, M.S., Trends in atlas development, Cartographica, 18 (1981), 187-213.

(13) Kirby, G.H. and Visvalingam, M., The representation and use of multivariate data in graphic form, in Greenaway, D.S. and Warman, E.A. (eds.) Eurographics '82 (North-Holland, Amsterdam, 1982).

(14) Visvalingam, M. and Perry, B.J., Storage of the grid-square based 1971 GB census data: checking procedures, Census Research Unit WP 7, Dept. of Geography, Univ. of Durham (1976).

(15) Holtermann, S., Areas of urban deprivation in Great Britain: an analysis of 1971 census data, Social Trends 6 (1975) 33-47.

(16) Visvalingam, M., The operational definition of area-based social indicators, Environment and Planning A, 15 (1983) 831-839.

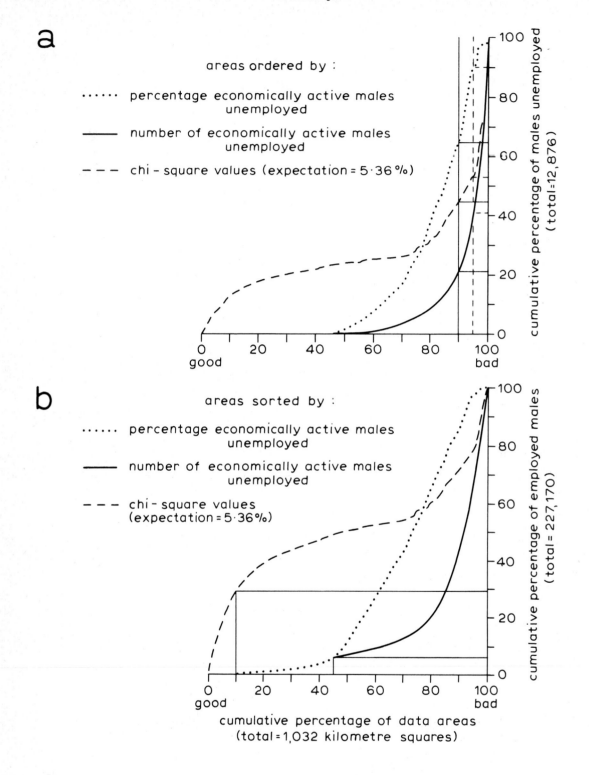

DIALOGUE INTERFACES

Human-Computer Interaction — INTERACT '84 / B. Shackel (ed.)
Elsevier Science Publishers B.V. (North-Holland)
© IFIP, 1985

USER REPRESENTATIONS OF ORDERED SEQUENCES OF COMMAND OPERATIONS

Phil Barnard, Allan MacLean and Nick Hammond

MRC Applied Psychology Unit,
15 Chaucer Road, Cambridge CB2 2EF, England

An experiment is reported in which users learned how to operate a "laboratory" system for handling electronic mail. Two variables were manipulated. Users were asked to learn one of two task structures involving eight operations. In one form the task was structured into a sequence of four pairs of semantically related operations (4x2). In the other, operations were structured into two groups of four on the basis of their abstract class. Two sets of command names were employed one being less discriminable than the other. Both variables were found to influence the ways in which users learned the system. The results suggested that users of the 4x2 structure were constructing mental representations in which individual operations were more semantically integrated than users of the 2x4 grouped structure.

INTRODUCTION

In learning any command-driven interactive system, users must acquire considerable new knowledge concerning system operation, its commands, and command sequences required to carry out specific tasks. Anecdotes and systematic evidence more than adequately illustrate the difficulties experienced and errors made in learning and use [5] [9] [10]. In spite of the difficulties, users obviously do learn. During the initial stages of acquisition they appear to build up a repertoire of knowledge 'fragments' concerning a system and its operation. This fragmentary knowledge may be inaccurate or based on inappropriate inferences [8]. Individual fragments may also be mutually inconsistent and resistant to change [6].

This paper will focus on two key aspects of knowledge acquisition in learning command-driven interactive systems. The first concerns the relationship between the nature of the command set and the development of mental representations of individual operations. The second concerns the development of a more superordinate mental representation which interlinks these commands into a coherent sequence.

The problems associated with command names have received some empirical attention eg [2] [3] [4] [7]. Although the evidence has yet to settle into a clear picture, the relative discriminability of the mapping from names to operations appears to be one critical factor determining how the learning of a system occurs [2]. With a discriminable mapping between names and operations, it should be easier for users to create new fragments of knowledge linking names and operations than when the mapping between names and operations is less discriminable.

Issues associated with the development of knowledge fragments linking individual command operations into coherent sequences have received much less attention. This has been due, in part, to an emphasis on text editing systems where the order of operations is determined by the text to be altered. It is well established in cognitive psychology that the order and organisation of information is a critical factor in determining how the information is understood, encoded in memory and subsequently recalled [1]. The presence of coherent organisational links within a sequence of command operations should thus facilitate the encoding and recall of that sequence.

The experiment reported below was designed to explore these issues empirically by monitoring users of a specially designed laboratory system for handling electronic mail.

EXPERIMENTAL DETAILS

The Message Processing System

In the basic experimental task users were required to deal with two kinds of electronic message – incoming and outgoing ones. Each item of mail required an ordered sequence of eight operations. The basic display is illustrated in Figure 1. On the left of the display there is an argument information panel. At the start of the procedure certain basic data appears in this panel automatically (eg incoming/outgoing; rate for pricing). In each task sequence users need to "establish" four other relevant pieces of information by issuing commands. These become arguments for four "actions" which need to be performed on each item of mail. The mail itself is displayed in the right hand panel. In this illustration, the company reference (dd/cat) has been established by the use of one command, and

Figure 1 The basic task display

```
┌─────────────────────────────────────────────────────────────────────┐
│  Type a command            - OR -    Choose an item from this list    │
│  COMMAND: dispatch█                  [NEXT to move arrow, CHOOSE to make choice] │
│                                      ) See list of commands           │
│                                      See details of task              │
│                                                                       │
│   ┌──────────────────────────┐   ┌──────────────────────────────┐    │
│   │     Office Records       │   │  To: Mr G. Nestor            │    │
│   │                          │   │      Office Furnishing Ltd   │    │
│   │   Message number: 1      │   │      Leeds         ref: kg/rec│   │
│   │   Message type: Outgoing │   │                              │    │
│   │                          │   │  Our records over the past fiscal year │
│   │    File number: kg/893   │   │  reveal three outstanding orders (refs │
│   │   Originator ref:        │   │  6942, 7038 & 8172). Attend to these. │
│   │      Mail point:         │   │                              │    │
│   │ Destination code: offlee │   │     From: Mr K. Grundle      │    │
│   │           Time:          │   │           Records Department │    │
│   │           Rate: regular  │   │           Matric Ltd         │    │
│   │    Company ref: kg/rec   │   │           Oxbridge           │    │
│   │       Register:          │   │                              │    │
│   │          Price: $13.10   │   │        Debiting complete     │    │
│   │                          │   │        Filing complete       │    │
│   └──────────────────────────┘   └──────────────────────────────┘    │
└─────────────────────────────────────────────────────────────────────┘
```

added to the letter concerned by another command. Similarly, the price ($13.10) has been established and the department sending the message has been charged; a file number has been established and and the letter itself filed; a destination code has been established and the final command in the sequence of eight (DISPATCH) is being entered in the command entry field at the top left.

From the top right hand corner of the basic task display users could access a number of help facilities. These were designed to assist in learning individual commands and the sequences required for incoming and outgoing mail. Command and sequence information were given in different panels. Selection of the "task" option resulted in a display of the eight steps to be taken, in the order to be carried out. Selection of the "command" option resulted in an alphabetical menu of all 12 command names. If after consulting either of these panels the users were still unsure, additional options enabled them to see how many task steps they had actually completed or they could access full descriptions of individual command operations. The help panels were organised in this way to enable empirical assessment of the precise nature of the user's uncertainty.

Task structure, operations and names

The mail system incorporated twelve different commands. Six of these were employed to establish information which could then be used by the other six commands to carry out some action to process the mail. The procedures for

handling incoming and outgoing mail each required a subset of eight of the twelve commands, four being used in both procedures and four unique to one of them. Each procedure required four "establish" and four "action" operations to be carried out. A command operation involved typing a command word and entering an argument in response to a prompt from the system. Users thus had to learn the commands, the subsets required for incoming and outgoing mail and the appropriate sequences in which to carry the operations out.

The structure of the sequences of operations was systematically manipulated. In one structure, users were required to carry out the four "establish" operations first, thereby completing the argument information panel, and then proceed to carry out the four "actions" to process the mail itself. The operations were thus organised into two groups of four (2x4) on the basis of their abstract class. In the other structure, the operations were organised into a sequence of four establish-action pairs (4x2). For example, the price of sending the mail would be established and the department sending the message immediately charged for it. The operations were thus organised into pairs on the basis of related semantic content. It was hypothesised that the presence of the semantic links between operations within a pair would facilitate learning relative to the grouped structure in which adjacent commands in a sequence were not directly related semantically. Table 1 shows the 2x4 grouped structure for incoming mail and the 4x2 paired structure for outgoing mail. Individual users had the same structure for both types of mail.

Table 1 The two alternative task structures

---

2 x 4 grouped structure (incoming messages):

*Establish the time at which the message arrived (6)
*Establish the originator reference of the sender (10)
*Establish the register number for keeping a copy (9)
*Establish the mail point of the recipient (8)

*Mark the message with its time of arrival (11)
*Acknowledge receipt of the message (to sender)(3)
*Keep a copy of the message in the register (12)
*Forward the message to the recipient's mail point (5)

4 x 2 paired structure (outgoing messages):

*Establish the company reference of the sender (2)
*Attach the company reference to the message (1)

*Establish the price of sending the message (4)
*Debit the department sending the message (7)

*Establish the file number for keeping a copy (9)
*Keep a copy of the message in the file (12)

*Establish the destination code for the recipient (8)
*Forward the message to the destination code (5)

Table 2 The Command Sets

	Discriminable Names	Confusable Name Pairs	Incoming Outgoing
1	APPEND	APPEND	Outgoing
2	AUTHOR	SHOW	Outgoing
3	CONFIRM	SEND	Incoming
4	COST	LIST	Outgoing
5	DISPATCH	DISPATCH	Both
6	DISPLAY	DISPLAY	Incoming
7	ENTER	ENTER	Outgoing
8	IDENTIFY	FIND	Both
9	INDEX	INDEX	Both
10	LOCATE	LOCATE	Incoming
11	STAMP	ADD	Incoming
12	STORE	INPUT	Both

The constitution of the command nameset was also manipulated. For one set an attempt was made, within the constraints of a task involving conceptually similar operations, to keep ambiguities in name-operation mapping to a low level. This nameset was formed from relatively discriminable lexical items. The other set was derived by replacing half of the names in the first set. Each replacement name was semantically similar to one of the remaining names (eg Display/Show; Enter/Input). This set of names should thus create additional difficulties for users in learning the appropriate name-operation mappings.

The two namesets are shown in Table 2 and the numbers used in this table are indexed to operations in Table 1. Confusion pairs were counterbalanced across the incoming/outgoing and establish/action distinctions. The arguments required for the establish commands were either obtained by reading the mail itself or were already present in the information panel. Arguments for the action commands were entered into the this panel as products of the establish commands.

Four independent groups each of 12 naive users from the subject panel of the Applied Psychology Unit took part in the experiment. Each group processed electronic mail under one of four conditions derived from the two command sets and the two alternative task structures. Each user attended for two sessions separated by a week. In the first session users had initial training involving the processing of

four items of mail. For the first two items advice was given if users attempted either to enter more than three erroneous commands or if they accessed more than three command descriptions. For the second two items users could only obtain information by accessing the HELP facilities in the system. In the second session users were asked to process eight more items of mail, relying solely on the help facilities in the system.

In both sessions incoming and outgoing items of mail were organised in pairs with matched randomisations of presentation orders across conditions. Users' performance on the task was monitored by keeping a session log of all actions and the time taken to carry them out. A short paper precludes full presentation of the data and the following section will be confined to representative results from session 2 in which much of learning actually took place. Unless otherwise specified, results summarised below were obtained from analyses of variance of these data.

RESULTS AND DISCUSSION

Overview

As with some other studies [2] [7], the total time taken to process each item of mail showed strong effects of learning but was not greatly affected by the structure of the task sequence or nameset. Users could, and some did, rely on a trial and error strategy for command entry. However, the vast majority in all conditions made use of the help facilities. The typical strategy involved finding out what to do from the task help and then, if still uncertain, proceeding through the command menu to the full description of the operation of a particular command. On 98% of the occasions when this latter facility was used, it was accessed indirectly via the task help rather than by a direct route.

Learning Command Sequences.

Organising the task into four pairs of
semantically related command operations (4x2)
clearly facilitated sequence learning relative
to the task involving two groups of four
operations (2x4) organised on the basis of
their abstract class (establish or action).

Figure 2 Mean number of operations entered
without help or error

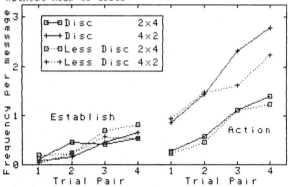

Figure 2 shows the frequency, for each item of
mail, with which commands were issued without
error or use of the help facilities. The
learning curves for establish and action
operations are shown separately and since four
operations of each type were required, the
maximum value on the ordinate is four. In
addition, learning across the eight items of
mail processed is averaged over trial pairs
involving one incoming and one outgoing
message. The performance advantage for the 4x2
structure is selective. Performance with the
establish operations was poor throughout and
was unaffected by the structure of the task
sequence. Performance with the action
operations was generally superior and
facilitated in the 4x2 structure (task
structure x operation type interaction
(F[1,44]=27.4; p<.001).

Further analysis showed that this advantage for
the action commands in the 4x2 task structure
could be entirely attributed to better
knowledge of what operation to perform next
rather than how to do it. With the grouped 2x4
structure, users accessed the task sequence
help facility on an action command step
(without accessing help on the command names)
more often than users in the 4x2 condition,
with no difference on establish operations
(interaction, F[1,44]=22.6; p<.001). When the
number of operations carried out without help
or error were added to those involving help
only on the sequence of operations, there were
no residual effects of the task structure
(F[1,44]<1).

Learning to assign command names to operations.

The relative discriminability of the nameset

did not give rise to a significant main effect
either on users' ability to proceed without
help or error (Fig 2) or on their rate of
entering erroneous commands. However, it did
affect their use of the help facility giving
information on individual command operations.
In this context, the equivalent of an "error"
is, for a particular command step, to obtain
help on a command name which would not have the
desired effect. Figure 3 shows these data.

Figure 3 Mean frequency of obtaining help on a
command name inappropriate for a particular
command step.

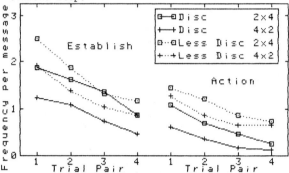

There were significantly more cases where a
wrong command name was tried in the help
facility with the less discriminable set of
names (F[1,44]=4.26, p < .05). There was also
evidence that users with the grouped 2x4 task
structure required more help on individual
commands for both namesets. This was of
marginal significance (F[1,44]=3.18, p=.08) for
the data shown in Figure 3, but the effect was
reliable for the total number of times this
help mode was entered (F[1,44] = 4.58, p<.05).

Representations of task sequence and operations

The fact that users were more able to carry out
an action step without help or error in the 4x2
structure than in the 2x4 groups suggests that
the 4x2 structure enabled them to create more
integrated mental representations of the
sequence of operations. Furthermore, the fact
that users of the 4x2 structure also tended to
require less access to the help facility for
individual commands would suggest that the
mental representation enabled them more readily
to interlink fragments of knowledge about what
to do next with fragments of knowledge enabling
them to narrow down the range of likely command
names for particular operations. Although
there was no overall difference in the level of
errors actually made between the discriminable
and less discriminable namesets, more detailed
analysis of the types of confusion error which
occurred furnished important clues about the
nature of the mental representations involved.

For example, with the less discriminable
nameset, users quite frequently entered one

member of a semantically confusing pair of names (display/show; add/append) in place of the other. However, these semantic confusions were more frequent (21.1% of all errors) in the 4x2 structure than in the 2x4 structure (13.7% of all errors). In terms of absolute numbers of errors, this difference was significant both across subjects (median test;chi-square=4.2 (df=1); p<.05) and across command names (F[1,15]=25.9, p<.001). This higher rate of confusion with the 4x2 structure suggests that performance in this condition was more likely to be mediated by semantic representations of the operations. This would give rise to difficulties in resolving which of the two related names carried out which operation. The more infrequent occurrence of these semantic confusions with the 2x4 grouped structure would suggest that users in this condition were more likely to construct mental representations involving simple lists of command names to use. In the absence of semantic mediation, words like display and show would be represented solely in terms of their phonological identity which is quite discriminable. If users of the 2x4 grouped structure were more likely to create these more superficial representations, it would also be expected that they would make systematic errors of transposition between the name of the first establish operation and the name of the first action operation. This type of error occurred nearly twice as frequently in the 2x4 grouped structure (70 errors) than in the 4x2 paired structure (36 errors). Furthermore, the pattern was the same for both incoming and outgoing mail. A low level of semantic mediation with the 2x4 task structure would also be consistent with their higher use of the help facility for information about the action of individual command names (fig 3).

CONCLUSION

Taken as a whole, the data suggest that the 4x2 task structure facilitated the construction of superordinate mental representations for the task sequences, involving four ordered components in which two constituent operations become semantically interlinked. Within each component, the establish constituent facilitates recovery of its related action and the semantic nature of the links precipitates semantic confusions in choosing the command name to suit a particular operation. In contrast, the data suggest that users of the 2x4 grouped structure were more likely to represent their task in terms of simple ordered lists of command names which need to be entered to complete a sequence. This kind of superficial representation seems less likely to precipitate certain kinds of semantic error and more likely to precipitate certain positional errors. Such a dichotomy obviously greatly oversimplifies the complex pattern of user performance in this kind of command dialogue. There are many different classes of errors and

it is their relative proportions which alter. However, the data presented serve to illustrate the wider implication that ease of learning and use is not simply a function of factors like the discriminability of the command names. Rather, performance and error patterns can only be fully understood by taking account of the cognitive structures which users develop - both superordinate structures which represent extended task sequences as well as the precise way in which individual commands are represented and incorporated into these structures.

REFERENCES

[1]   Baddeley, A.D. The psychology of memory. (New York: Basic Books, 1976)

[2]   Barnard, P., Hammond, N., MacLean, A. and Morton, J. Learning and remembering interactive commands in a text-editing task. Behaviour and Information Technology 1 (1982) 347-358

[3]   Black, J. and Moran, T. Learning and remembering command names. In Human Factors in Computer Systems, ACM: Washington (1982) 8-11

[4]   Carroll, J. Learning, using and designing command paradigms. Human Learning 1 (1982) 31-62

[5]   Hammond, N., Long, J., Clark, I., Barnard, P. and Morton, J. Documenting human-computer mismatch in interactive systems. In Proceedings of the Metropolitan Chapter of the Human Factors Society (HFS: New York, 1980) 35-54

[6]   Hammond, N., Morton, J., MacLean, A. and Barnard, P. Fragments and signposts: Users' models of the system. In the Proceedings of the 10th International Symposium on Human Factors in Telecommunications, Helsinki (1983) 81-88

[7]   Landauer, T., Gallotti, K. and Hartwell, S. Natural command names and learning: A study of text-editing terms. Communications of the ACM, 26, (1983) 495-503

[8]   Lewis, C. and Mack, R. Learning to use a text processing system: Evidence from "thinking aloud" protocols. In Human Factors in Computer Systems. (ACM: Washington, 1982) 17-24

[9]   Nickerson, R.S. Why interactive computer systems are sometimes not used by people who might benefit from them. Int. Journal of Man-Machine Studies, 15 (1981) 469-483

[10] Norman, D. The trouble with UNIX. Datamation, 27, (1981) 139-150

Human-Computer Interaction — INTERACT '84 / B. Shackel (ed.)
Elsevier Science Publishers B.V. (North-Holland)
© IFIP, 1985

THE ROLE OF PRIOR TASK EXPERIENCE IN COMMAND NAME ABBREVIATION

Jonathan Grudin
Wang Laboratories
Lowell, Mass., USA

Phil Barnard
MRC Applied Psychology Unit
Cambridge, England

ABSTRACT

An experiment is reported in which subjects previously naive to text editing are asked to generate abbreviations for a set of editing commands. We manipulated the degree of the subjects' experience with the editing task prior to the point at which they were asked to produce the abbreviations. We found effects of experience on both the length and the form of the abbreviations produced, with more experienced subjects inclined toward shorter abbreviations and, independently, toward truncation as an abbreviation scheme. We conclude that experimental paradigms previously used to investigate naming and abbreviation may have encouraged subjects to construe their task falsely as one in which they would be using abbreviations to reconstruct referent names, whereas the actual task involved recalling the abbreviation given recall of the referent object or its name.

INTRODUCTION

Abbreviation appears in various contexts in computing environments. Systems may require abbreviated forms of command names, or permit "terse" abbreviations of the full commands. Similarly, computer users often generate abbreviations for frequently used commands, command sequences, path routes, file and file directory names, and so forth. Macro names, indirect command file names, and aliases very often take the form of an abbreviated word or sequence of words.

In its most general sense, abbreviation is central to all communication, whether graphemic or iconic, auditory or gestural. The degree of reduction is determined by balancing the demands for efficiency and for intelligibility in communication. Efficiency can be increased through abbreviation, but at the risk of decreased intelligibility. In the computing environment, as well as in the realm of general communication, abbreviated words serve two quite different roles. In one role, intelligibility is at a premium; in the other, efficiency is stressed.

From abbreviation to word, phrase, or concept. If we read a reference to the chemical compound "KCl", our task is to recall the elements that "K" and "Cl" are abbreviations for. Given a listing of system commands, or of files in a directory, we may have to deduce what "ls", or "COMSUB.S1", stand for. In such situations, the abbreviation is confronted and the task is to use the abbreviation to construct or reconstruct the full word or phrase, perhaps as the first step in determining the referent object.

From concept, phrase, or word to abbreviation. In other situations, one has the object or name in mind and must recall and use the correct abbreviation. We wish to write "Potassium chloride" in abbreviated form. Will "li" or "ls" give us the listing we want?

What did we call those files of substituted command names?

The actual role played by an abbreviation may well determine the abbreviation form (truncation, vowel deletion, acronym, etc.) that will enhance performance. But also important is the preconception about that role in the mind of the abbreviation user or creator. An abbreviation may be used differently by different people. It may be used differently by the same person at different times. Thus, some foresight, as well as knowledge about the environment, may be necessary for making decisions about the creation and use of names and abbreviations. The designers and users of computer systems may not always exhibit such foresight. Subjects in the experimental paradigms used to investigate naming and abbreviation may have insufficient knowledge of the task before them, as well.

Past work on naming and abbreviation has often relied on verbal learning techniques and/or single-session experiments (e.g., Black and Moran [2]; Carroll [3]; Hirsh-Pasek, Nudelman, and Schneider [5]; Streeter, Ackroff, and Taylor [8]; Landauer, Galotti, and Hartwell [6]). Subjects who generated abbreviations did so without first using the unabbreviated forms. Typically (but with exceptions, such as Scapin [7]), interpolated distractor tasks in a single-session experiment simulated the much longer intervals that separate non-laboratory task sessions.

In practice, meaningful contexts and elapsed time seem likely to be key factors affecting performance in recalling names and abbreviations. In addition, the lack of initial experience, and the subjects' awareness of the single-session nature of the experiment, may influence the view of the role of the abbreviations subjects generate and use. The study reported here contrasted single-session abbreviation performance with behaviour in an editing task consisting of sessions separated by several days.

As part of a broader study of abbreviation, we examined the effect of prior experience on the design and use of abbreviation. In previous studies of abbreviations generated by individuals for their own use, subjects created their abbreviations at the outset of the experiment. They were thus relatively unfamiliar with the name set being abbreviated. In contrast, computer users may generate names or abbreviations in situations where the object or function being labeled is a familiar one. This distinction is critical, because it may affect whether subjects foresee their task as being one of reconstructing an (unfamiliar or forgotten) full name from the abbreviation, or of recalling the correct abbreviation given possession of a (familiar) full name or description. The abbreviation generated, and its subsequent efficacy, may depend on this perception. The unfamiliarity of the task to the subject at the beginning of an experiment may mask the fact that the subject could very soon be highly familiar with the objects and names in the experiment.

METHOD

The present study used the text-editing task developed by Barnard, Hammond, MacLean, and Morton [1], with minor modifications that are described in another set of experiments reported in Grudin and Barnard [4]. Subjects naive to text editing learned a set of eight editing and two file transfer commands, then used these commands to edit previously constructed text.

These ten commands were the basis for the abbreviation study. (They are shown in Table 1, along with the commands used in a replication described below.) We asked four groups of subjects to generate abbreviations for the command set, manipulating the prior exposure of the subjects to the editing task. Two of these groups performed a paper and pencil abbreviation exercise with differing instructions (no prior experience and vicarious experience, described below). The third group (passive experience) underwent a short computer-presented tutorial introduction to the command operations and their consequences. This simply involved pressing the space bar to advance a step-by-step demonstration of each command. The final group (active experience) underwent full training on the command operations and actually did some text editing.

No prior experience. One group of 8 subjects received lists of the command names with written instructions. The instructions indicated that the words were commands used in a computer text editing task, and asked each subject to write down an abbreviation, consisting of letters, for each word.

Vicarious experience. A second group of 7 subjects went through the same procedure, with expanded instructions. They were told explicitly that experienced users found it time-consuming to type in command names, and thus the abbreviations were specifically intended to reduce the number of keystrokes required to enter the commands.

Passive experience. One group of seven subjects was given a more extensive introduction to the editing task. These subjects sat before a computer terminal and went through the initial computer-assisted instruction and a step-by-step demonstration of each of the ten commands. The demonstration was self-paced, but was otherwise passive. Following this introduction, which took approximately ten minutes, a message appeared on the computer indicating that with growing expertise, typing time became a major factor in editing time, and that therefore the subject was asked to devise a set of abbreviation alternatives for the command set. The commands were presented one at a time, and when choices were made for all of them, the list was shown and the subject given a chance to change any of the abbreviations.

Active experience. Seven subjects were run as one condition in a larger experiment not reported here in full. These subjects underwent an expanded version of the computer-assisted instruction described above. In addition to reading a step-by-step description of the operation of each command, these subjects were stepped through an example, then given two further exercises to be carried out before proceeding to the description of the next command. Following that instruction, the subjects were introduced to the specific editing task. Upon completion of an editing session of approximately half an hour, the subjects were given the abbreviation construction task described above. A second editing session of the same length followed, and the subjects returned a week later for a third session. In the

Table 1   The Command Sets.

Experiment	Replication
front	first
back	last
insert	inject
delete	rubout
prefix	precede
append	suffix
merge	join
divide	split
fetch	bring
store	return

second and third sessions, each subject could use either the full command names the experiment had begun with, or the abbreviations generated following the first session. Following the final session, the subjects were once again asked to compose a set of abbreviations, drawing on the hindsight obtained from their experience with the first set.

The entire experiment was handled by the computer. For details on the editing task, see Grudin and Barnard [4]. The principal variations in this study were the compression of the three sessions into two days, and the response to the Help key: In the first session it produced the full list of command names; in subsequent sessions it produced first the list of abbreviations, then on a second striking the list of full command names.

RESULTS

The mean length of abbreviation was 2.35 letters for the subjects with no prior experience and 2.60 letters for the subjects with vicarious experience (those for whom the typing efficiency motivation for abbreviation was made explicit). An analysis by subjects showed that this difference was not significant $(T(13) = 0.77, p = .23)$. The passive experience group produced abbreviations averaging 2.36 letters, while the group with active experience averaged 1.57 letters after session one. The analysis showed that the abbreviations of the active experience group were significantly shorter than those of the other group (all T's > 2.4, $p < .05$ two-tailed), which did not differ among themselves (all T's < 1.0). An analysis over items confirmed that the abbreviations of the active experience group were significantly shorter than those of the other three groups. These data, with the two written instruction groups combined, are shown in Table 2.

Six of the seven subjects in the active experience condition produced abbreviations averaging under 2 letters in length, whereas only one subject in each of the other conditions did so. The exceptional subject in the active experience group was also anomalous in that for five of the ten commands, he replaced the command name with another word rather than abbreviating it (e.g., "merge" was abbreviated as "join"). Excluding that subject, the active experience group abbreviations averaged 1.35 letters.

When the active experience group created abbreviations for the second time, following the third session, they averaged 1.76 letters. This set was not significantly longer than their first abbreviation set $(T(12) = 0.5, p = 0.3)$, and in fact contained few changes at all. Therefore, the remaining analyses were done with the initial abbreviation set of this group.

Table 2   Results.

Mean length of abbreviations in characters, the proportion of abbreviations following a truncation rule, and the proportion of abbreviation characters that are vowels. The data for the no prior experience and the vicarious experience conditions are combined into an overall mean for written instruction conditions.

	Abbreviation (Length)	Truncation (Percent)	Vowels (Percent)
Written Instructions	2.47	55	20
Passive Experience	2.36	87	26
Active Experience	1.57	84	27

We looked for effects of experience with the command set on the structure of the abbreviations subjects created. First, we computed the proportion of abbreviations that could be explained as truncations of the full command name. (The instances noted above where the command was changed and not abbreviated at all were dropped from the analysis.) Within the active experience group, 84% of all abbreviations were truncations. The subjects with passive experience produced 87% of such abbreviations, while the subjects with written instructions averaged 55% truncations (see Table 2). The high percentage of truncations by the active and passive experience subjects is not completely explained by their increased use of initial letter abbreviations -- examining only 3-letter abbreviations, the figures were 100%, 91%, and 55% truncation abbreviations for the active, passive, and written instruction groups, respectively.

Looking for evidence of a vowel-deletion abbreviation rule, we calculated the proportion of vowels in each abbreviation set (Table 2). Despite the fact that 8 of 10 initial letters were consonants, which would contribute few vowels to the frequent single-letter truncation abbreviations in the active experience group, that group actually produced a higher proportion of vowels in its abbreviation set than did the subjects with written instructions. This indicates that the subjects in the written instruction conditions, who did not rely on truncation to as great an extent, were more likely to use vowel deletion as an abbreviation strategy.

Finally, we examined abbreviation consistency. Only 3 of the 29 subjects were self-consistent in abbreviation length: One subject in the active experience group used one-letter abbreviations throughout, and two subjects with written instructions produced two-letter sets of abbreviations. Only one of the three was completely consistent (a 2-letter truncation pattern), since the 1-letter set relied on some initial and some medial letters, and one of the 2-letter sets alternated between truncation ("fr" for "front") and other schemes ("bk" for "back").

REPLICATION

We decided to run a partial replication of this experiment, due to the limited number of command names and subjects involved. We found "synonyms" for the ten command names that preserved the average word length and word length distribution of the original set. (See Table 1 for the command names used.) Because the original set was generally selected to be the best fit of name to function, the synonym list unavoidably seemed somewhat inferior.

Three conditions were run: The two paper and pencil conditions, and one on-line, active experience condition. Each group had twelve subjects. The active experience condition was a modification of the full, three-session experimental condition, in that it was terminated during the second session. Subjects went through the full training, the first session, the abbreviation creation procedure, and one-fourth of the second session.

RESULTS

The mean length of abbreviation was 2.81 letters for the no prior experience group, and 2.73 letters for the vicarious experience group (for whom the typing efficiency motivation was made explicit). Abbreviations generated by the active experience group averaged 2.22 letters, half a letter shorter. An analysis by subjects showed no significant difference between the two groups with no active experience (T(22) = .468, p = 0.32 one-tailed). The abbreviations generated by the group with active experience were significantly shorter than those of the other two groups (T's > 1.95, p<.05 one-tailed). These differences remained significant in a related T-test over items.

Subjects appeared considerably more dissatisfied with this command set, frequently changing the command word before abbreviating it (for example, abbreviating "rubout" as "ers", with "erase" the apparent word they had in mind). Excluding such words from the analysis did not change the pattern of results.

One-third of the subjects in the active experience condition created abbreviations averaging 1.5 letters or less. No subjects in the other conditions averaged under 1.8 letters. These subjects accounted for most (but not all) of the mean group differences.

Once again, experience not only reduces abbreviation length, it also increases the likelihood of truncation as an abbreviation tactic. Truncation is used for 39% of abbreviations by the groups with no active experience and 69% of abbreviations in the active experience group. Nor is this simply due to the heavier reliance on initial-letter abbreviations in the latter group: 41% of three-letter abbreviations use truncation in the first two conditions, while 80% of the three-letter abbreviations in the active experience group rely on truncation.

Nine of the ten initial command letters were consonants. Despite this, the active experience, high-truncation group included proportionately more vowels, 23% to 18% in the other conditions.

In generating abbreviations, 33 of the 36 subjects were structurally inconsistent in that they created abbreviations which differed in length. Two of the three subjects using structurally consistent schemes were in the active experience condition; one followed a 3-letter truncation rule, the other used the initial and final letter of each command name. The third was in the no prior experience group and used a 3-character rule, but incorporated a digit into one abbreviation and changed four of the command words before abbreviating them.

DISCUSSION

The subjects' perception of the purpose of abbreviating command names changes as a result of experience with the editing task.

Even when told explicitly that the purpose of the abbreviaiton is to reduce typing time, inexperienced subjects produce longer abbreviations and rely more on vowel deletion. This suggests that they are creating intelligible, rather than efficient, abbreviations. Confronted with a large number of unfamiliar names, it may seem natural to look for abbreviations that reliably identify the referents. They may not fully realize that with experience, these referents will become highly familiar. Intelligiblity will no longer be an issue -- "p", "pre", "pfx", and so forth would all communicate "prefix" equally effectively to the expert. At that point, efficiency becomes central, ideally leading to short, easily remembered abbreviations.

Many experienced subjects appear to have understood some of this when they created their abbreviation sets. The shift to shorter abbreviations and to truncation was pronounced with both sets of words. The effect was stronger with the original command names: Those subjects were scheduled for more time, and may have reflected that they could be doing a lot of editing, or the subjects in the replication study with a less intuitive set of command names may have been more likely to hold on to "intelligible" abbreviations.

After three sessions, subjects did not select shorter abbreviations than after the first session. This may reflect that they became attached to their first choices, but it may also reflect that the abbreviations selected by the experienced editor users were not optimal, and caused them problems.

Problems with the novice and the expert abbreviation sets. In addition to being relatively inefficient, the consonant-heavy abbreviations generated by an inexperienced subject may be difficult for that subject to remember, particularly after a break in editing (see Grudin and Barnard [4]. This may be due to the lack of a coherent rule that would permit the reconstruction of the abbreviation given the full command name. Truncation is a solution to this problem, but if truncation is not applied uniformly, it leads to errors.

Although beyond the scope of the data reported here, it is important to note that the names or abbreviations generated by experts will be different, but not necessarily better, than those generated by novices. In particular, the high degree of familiarity with the computing context that leads the user to favor efficiency over intelligibility may be treacherous. Looking over a directory created months or years ago, trying to recall what is in our own cryptically named files, we may be forcibly reminded that what seemed very familiar at the moment was unfamiliar later.

But by being fully aware of the effects of context familiarity upon our naming behaviour, we may be able to find the right balance between efficiency and intelligibility.

ACKNOWLEDGEMENTS

The authors wish to thank John Dennett, Allan MacLean, and Nick Hammond for their help with all aspects of this study.

REFERENCES

[1] Barnard, P.J., Hammond, N.V., MacLean, A., and Morton, J. Learning and remembering interactive commands in a text-editing task. Behaviour & Information Technology 1 (1982) 347-358.

[2] Black, J. and Moran, T. Learning and remembering command names. Paper presented at the Conference on Human Factors in Computer Systems, Gaithersburg, Maryland (1982).

[3] Carroll, J.M. Learning, using, and designing filenames and command paradigms. Behaviour & Information Technology 1 (1982) 327-346.

[4] Grudin, J. and Barnard, P. The cognitive demands of learning and representing command names for text-editing with varying structural and semantic attributes. Human Factors (in press).

[5] Hirsh-Pasek, K., Nudelman, S., and Schneider, M.L. An experimental evaluation of abbreviation schemes in limited lexicons. Behaviour & Information Technology 1 (1982) 359-370.

[6] Landauer, T.K., Galotti, K.M., and Hartwell, S. Natural command names and initial learning: A study of text editing terms. Comm. ACM 26 (1983).

[7] Scapin, D.L. Generation effect, structuring and computer commands. Behaviour & Information Technology 1 (1982) 401-410.

[8] Streeter, L.A., Ackroff, J.M., and Taylor, G.A. On abbreviating command names. The Bell System Technical Journal 62 (1983) 1807-1826.

Human-Computer Interaction — INTERACT '84 / B. Shackel (ed.)
Elsevier Science Publishers B.V. (North-Holland)
© IFIP, 1985

COMMAND INTERFACES AND THE HIERARCHY OF NEEDS

JULIAN NEWMAN

City of London Polytechnic
Department of Information Technology
Old Castle Street
London E1 7NT
United Kingdom

Effective office automation must support integration between different areas of application, enhance the users' understanding of the system and its potential, and encourage them to develop their own applications on the basis of that understanding. Thus the design of the interface cannot assume a fixed prior classification of users and of applications with certain users being adequately served by hiding most of the facilities behind a restricted menu.

The degree and kind of protection to be afforded to users requires careful attention, if the motivation for user growth is to be sustained. Human beings have security needs, implying requirements for protection, but also needs to explore and to realise their potential, implying requirements for freedom. At different times, users will require a greater or lesser degree of protection.

The Unix concept of a command language as a set of software tools, provides the elements from which can be developed an interface that allows for user growth albeit that Unix as it stands is perceived as user-friendly only by professional programmers. This paper outlines the development of a set of Unix commands for office applications, designed to allow the user to gain confidence in the use of the system. Illustrative examples are given of problems in the original Unix commands and of the solutions implemented.

Introduction

The design of interfaces and the motivational aspects of job design have to a large extent been regarded as separate areas of concern in the Psychology of computer use. Eason & Damodaran (1) have come closest to bridging the gap, with their identification of four sets of user needs, which they term "psychological needs", "expectations", "support needs" and "task needs". Thomas (2) and Palme (3) have also argued that the user needs the capability to program the interface himself, in order to have a feeling of competence and power over the system.

Within the industry, there is certainly growing awareness that users' needs are important, but the underlying assumption is that those needs are a given, and that the task of the designer is to discover them and cater for them. Comparisons of command-driven and menu-driven user interfaces have tended towards identifying the suitability of one or other approach either for a type of user, or for a category of application, and there is a trend in office-oriented computer systems to hide the system behind a "shell" which is different for different categories of user, and in the case of users who are not programmers is usually menu-driven. The assumption is that good design of the menu interface will enable the user to interact with the computer satisfactorily, and that consequently the system qualifies for the accolade "user-friendly".

Knowledge work

Effective office automation, however, must support work involving a high degree of employee discretion. This requires both integration between different areas of application, and attention to the ability of users to grow in understanding of the system and its potential, developing their own applications on the basis of that understanding.

High-discretion work plays an increasingly central part in wealth-creation (4,5). The cost of employing professionals and managers is believed now to account for the majority of office costs (6,7), and they are certainly the fastest-growing section of the workforce: these are users who are paid to use their judgement, even though professionals may have to undertake some relatively routine tasks in interacting with the computer (8). However, the term "professional" should not be taken too literally: technical and organizational change is undermining boundaries and opening opportunities for high-discretion work to persons who are not professionally qualified in the traditional sense, at the same time as it limits opportunities for routine white-collar work.

A high degree of task structuring in a computer-based system may not therefore be in the interests of the organization which is paying for the system and for the work done on it. It has long been recognised that whenever we institute a formal organization, which is a set of secondary, designed social relationships, there emerges among its members an informal organization, a network of primary relations which is often the system that, by bending the rules, actually gets the job done (9,10). Jobs that permit their occupants little discretion may deny the organization the benefit of such initiative as the individual or the group possesses, as well as denying to the individual and to the group the opportunities for growth, learning and job-satisfaction which might have motivated them to contribute a greater effort towards the organization's goals.

The Hierarchy of Needs

Barriers to user growth may be accidental or deliberate. For example, a restricted task may be designed to protect the organization's resources, or to protect the employee against too much complexity. Limiting the employee's discretion was a fundamental idea of "scientific management": however, the attempt to specify with complete precision how a task is to be performed would lead to an infinite regress. At some stage it becomes necessary to depend on the employee's capacity to interpret the purpose of the task. With the progress of automation, the value of human beings as employees is seen to lie in their capacity to handle the exceptional. Thus the chief remaining argument for limiting the user's discretion is to protect him from exposure to greater complexity than he is capable of handling.

The degree and kind of protection to be afforded to users requires careful attention, if the motivation for user growth is to be sustained. The motivational theories of Maslow and Herzberg can provide guidelines for the interface designer: human beings have security needs, implying requirements for protection, but also needs to explore and to realise their potential, implying requirements for freedom.

The concept of a "Hierarchy of needs" is one of the most venerable parts of the psychology of motivation. It was introduced into the theory of motivation by Maslow (11) and has been subject to redefinition and re-working by Herzberg (12) and other writers. As Maslow himself conceded that there are many exceptions to the hierarchical principle, it is best taken as a sensitising concept rather than a predictive theory, and that is how it will be used below.

By contrast with theories that viewed higher-order motivation as learned on the basis of the reinforcement of the most primitive, biological drives, Maslow argued that it is only as the lower-level needs are satisfied that higher needs come to be felt. Thus social needs are not learned through the satisfaction of physical needs for nourishment and protection: rather, it is not until the physical needs are satisfied that social needs come into play. Similarly, social esteem is not sought as a means of gaining social acceptance, but the need for social esteem is felt once the need for social acceptance has been satisfied; at the highest level of Maslow's hierarchy comes the need to "self-actualise", to achieve a personal and individual standard of excellence.

Notice that as we ascend this hierarchy of needs there is a progressive movement away from concern with protection, be it physical or social, in the direction of exploration and growth. Consideration of Maslow's scheme might give us pause before we start to design an interface based on the assumption that protection from the complexity of the computer is the complete answer to to the needs of the non-programmer user: " .... the more structured the task, the less flexible the system needs to be; however, there are dangers in the literal interpretation of this statement because the provision for psychological needs may not be entirely compatible with the pre-definition of task needs." (Eason & Damodaran, op.cit.) At different times, users will be at different levels in the hierarchy of needs and so require a greater or lesser degree of protection.

Extensible Command Languages and Software Tools

The concept of a command language as a set of software tools, which is the basis of the Unix Shell command language, provides the elements from which can be developed an interface that allows for user growth. Unix as it stands is perceived as user-friendly only by professional programmers, for whom it was originally developed. The work of programmers is, however, paradigmatic of knowledge-work in that they need to be able both to share documentary and other information and to handle it in unpredetermined ways.

An Office User and Training Environment

The work described in this paper took place within the context of an installation designed to provide an office automation environment for a wide range of Polytechnic staff and students, the majority of whom have no knowledge of programming. There are approximately 450 users in the course of a year, of whom 200 are secretarial students, 100 are students of Information Technology, 30 are overseas graduates on business courses, 25 are teaching staff, 5 are administrative staff, and the remainder students on short courses or other degree courses. The modal user is thus not strongly computer-oriented, but needs to use the system as a tool for word processing and for information storage and retrieval. Electronic mail is also regularly used as a communication medium by both staff and students.

While the system is principally provided for teaching purposes, regular staff usage, particularly by teachers of secretarial skills, is essential to convincing the secretarial students of the relevance of computer techniques for their future employment; the teaching staff are therefore encouraged to explore and fully exploit the facilities of the system, and it is used to support the full range of activities related to course development and administration, for calendar management (both group and individual), and for the production of survey research instruments and research reports. Students are required to use the text processing facilities for preparation of reports, and are encouraged to use the system for any other purpose connected with their studies.

The hardware consists of two Onyx C8002 16-bit multi-user microcomputers (*), each with 1 mB RAM and 40 mB Winchester disk storage. Up to 14 users may be logged in at any one time. All terminals are cursor-addressable VDUs. Two types are in use: Visual 200 and Cifer 2605; the former provides 26 function keys when using the INed editor (see below), the latter has 14.

The principal software is the Unix (*) operating system (IS/1 variant of version 7), with the INed (*) screen editor which is the main Word Processing tool. The Uniplex Word Processor (*) and the Supercomp spreadsheet package (*) are also available. The availability of Unix, with its hierarchical file system and extensible command language, was the major reason for selecting the Onyx hardware.

The original Unix Shell command set has been supplemented by the development of an extended set of Unix commands for office applications, designed to allow the user to gain confidence in the use of the system. Associated with these is an evolutionary strategy of training and support. Problems in the original Unix commands have been progressively identified by observation and by discussion with users; the original commands have, generally, been left unmodified but new commands have been provided and introduced to existing users for a trial period, following which they are modified if necessary, and eventually incorporated into the training material. Some of the new commands are intended to replace the original commands, others to supplement them.

With the development of a range of made-in-house commands, the issue arises of bridging the user to standard Unix. Text of some of the made-in commands is used as teaching material as part of the training and evolutionary support strategy, and users are encouraged to try copying and modifying the simpler ones to form their own personal commands.

The Unix Shell

The Unix Shell command language (13, 14, 15) consists of nearly 200 different command names, each of which invokes a software tool that may have a large range of options and parameters. These tools perform a wide range of file manipulation and information retrieval functions. In addition to the names of commands, there are control constructs such as if ... then ... else, case, while, until, etc. There are string variables, some of which are predefined in the Shell, while others may be created by the user.

Each original command name is in fact the name of an executable file in the systems area of the filestore. Commands may be given by typing them at the keyboard one at a time, or they may be placed in a file which is passed to the Shell to read. Some of the original commands are binary programs, and some are written in the Shell command language. The system administrator can add further commands to the directories in the systems area, or can replace existing commands with variants for the installation.

The user may choose to have a "profile" of commands which will automatically be executed when he logs in. A profile might be used, for example, to make the Shell look for the user's own private version of a command in preference to the standard version. This would be done by changing the value of the variable PATH: normally, when a command name is typed on the keyboard or found in a command file, the Shell first looks in the current directory (i.e. the directory in which the user is currently working) for an executable file having the given name; if none is found, the search goes successively to two directories in the systems area, whose names are /bin and /usr/bin. This could be changed by a statement assigning a different value to PATH, e.g.

    PATH=:/u/Peter:/bin:/usr/bin

Such a statement could be issued at any time, but is most likely to be useful at the beginning of a session, which is most conveniently arranged by including it in a "profile" file.

A value may also be assigned to a variable by input from the keyboard, e.g.

    read a

or as the value of an argument passed to a command, etc.

A particularly useful feature of Unix, and central to the philosophy of "software tools" on which it is built, is the capacity to redirect input or output to or from a file instead of the terminal, or by setting up a pipeline, passing the output of one command to another, so that the second command "filters" the output of the first, for example

    di /u | grep MA | print

Here grep (get and report) filters the output of di (a directory-listing command), so that only lines containing the string MA will be output, while print takes the output of grep and queues it for printing. The ability to apply successive filters to a stream of output is extremely helpful in handling information in unpremeditated ways.

Problems in the original
Unix commands

One set of problems that readily comes to light when teaching Unix to naive users has to do with the discriminability of command names. For example, ls lists a directory, while l lists a file on the VDU screen. Users who are just beginning to get used to the difference between files and directories find their problem compounded by the difficulty of discriminating between these two similarly-named commands. The solution is to provide alternative names that invoke the same actual commands. This is readily done in Unix because the name actually belongs to a pointer to the command file, and an additional pointer, with a different name, can be set.

Choice of names in this case had to take into account the following constraints: no name of an existing Unix command should be used, and if possible there should be positive transfer from learning on other systems. Since a large proportion of users either had used CP/M, or would do so in the near future, dir which performs the equivalent function in CP/M, was chosen as the synonym for ls. However, the equivalent CP/M function for l is type, which was judged misleading in that the output is to be displayed on the screen and not as hard copy; therefore the name view was chosen as a synonym for l. This was intended to emphasise the function of "viewing" a file quickly, rather than through the editor, with the implication that one could only look at the file, not modify it.

A further set of problems involved the meaningfulness of original Unix command names.

Some are relatively straightforward, e.g.

who am I?

gives details about the user, while others, e.g. pwd (give pathname of working directory) or grep (get and report) appear obscure to the point of being offputting. Once again, the solution is to provide synonyms, in this case where am I? and report.

Unix is curt in its error messages, and generally does not give any prompts or help where the user has acted correctly. This is in part an expression of the very "software tools" philosophy that gives it such great potential: error messages are more readily devised where one is certain that the command will be issued from the terminal, in rather a restricted range of circumstances. However, the lack of intelligible feedback or prompts tends to inhibit initial learning, so that it is preferable in many cases to hide the original Unix command inside a less general tool which is more suitable for learning. For example, the Unix mail system uses the same command mail both for sending and for receiving electronic mail. Thus

mail Fred

indicates that one wishes to send mail to Fred, while

mail

indicates that one wishes to see one's own incoming mail. If (as would normally be the case) one wishes to read one's mail in chronological order, then one has to give an additional argument

mail -r

(-r presumably standing for "reverse", but actually meaning the opposite!)

The most common mistake with mail is for naive users to type their own login name after the command, when they want to read their own mail; Unix interprets this as a desire to send mail to oneself. As no prompt is given, the system awaits input from the user, while the user waits patiently for his mail to be displayed.

Another common problem arises when a user who is sending mail fails to terminate the message with the proper control character, and proceeds to issue "commands" which the system takes as part of the message text.

To avoid both these types of problem, the Unix mail command was hidden inside two new distinct commands, for the two different functions of sending and receiving mail. These were named sendmail and receivemail; "mail" could be omitted, or typed as a separate word from "send" or "receive". Also, for the benefit of those users who had had a progressive education, receive could be abbreviated as rec.

When receiving mail with the new command, the user is first shown a menu of the main commands recognised by the mail program; however, an option exists for an experienced user to turn this menu off temporarily or permanently. When sending mail, the user is prompted with a message saying to whom he is sending mail, and also reminding him to finish the message with a Carriage Return followed by Control-D. There is thus little chance of the user thinking he is receiving when he is actually sending. Both commands give the message "Mail program has finished" before returning to the Shell, to as-sist the user in learning to distinguish different system states.

One adverse consequence of embedding mail inside sendmail is that it is no longer practical to use the facility for redirection of input in order to mail a message previously composed in a file. With the original Unix command, one would simply do

mail Fred < file1

This is catered for in the new commands by

send file file1 to Fred

which may be contracted to

send file1 Fred

The price of this "naturalness" of expression is that one cannot mail a file called "file" to a user called "to".

A further problem for the naive user lies in the need to specify relatively obscure options: for example, the screen editor needs to know the name of a configuration file to describe the users's terminal. This is handled by embedding the editor call within a command that asks the user the terminal type, and selects the appropriate configuration file. In general, however, to allow for user growth it is preferable to introduce the user to the concept of options within commands, rather than to conceal their existence. Provided a graduated approach is used, the more adventurous user can gain in this way confidence in his ability to use software tools.

The screen editor INed (16) is not part of Unix, but is particularly well-designed to work within a Unix environment, and to enable the user to take advantage of the characteristics of Unix while editing. INed supports multiple windows, allowing the user to look at several files at once, or at several parts of the same file. Shell commands may be issued while editing, and may be used to process the text, or to retrieve or process information from other files and put it into a file that is being edited. This is particularly useful for authors composing at the terminal.

It is in fact possible to conduct a complete Unix session without ever leaving the editor. To assist users who wished to work in this mode, a number of modifications were made to the mail commands, to maintain maximum compatiibility with the processing of mail outside the editor; in particular, Shell commands were written to replicate the effect of those mail program commands which save and forward mail.

A shortcoming of the evolutionary approach, to which there is no obviously satisfactory solution, is that it tends to satisfice rather than optimise. There are certainly major remaining inconsistencies in the naming of the commands (for example, dir is an abbreviation of a noun, while view is a verb. Again, to what extent should users' difficulty in remembering the name of an original Unix command such as cp (to copy a file) be catered for? By tending to avoid abbreviations in the new command names, or to make them optional, one makes a mandatory abbreviation perhaps less friendly than it was in its original context. Designers do frequently show major inconsistencies in naming commands (17); but to attempt to be completely natural may be counterproductive. These issues are the subject of further investigation. However, it is argued that the use of the extensible command language provides the

user with greater opportunities for growth and development, and tends to "demystify" the computer, by contrast with the alternative option of hiding the system from the user behind a menu-driven shell.

----

* Onyx is a Trade mark of Onyx-IMI; Unix is a Trade mark of AT&T; IS/1 and INed are Trade Marks of Interactive Systems Corporation; Uniplex is a Trade Mark of Redwood Ltd.

----

1 Eason, K & Damodaran, L (1981) "The needs of the Commercial User" in Coombs, MJ & Alty, JL (eds) Computing Skills and the User Interface London: Academic Press.
2 Thomas, R C (1981) "The Design of an Adaptable Terminal" in Coombs, MJ & Alty, JL (eds) Computing Skills and the User Interface. London: Academic Press.
3 Palme, J (1975) Interactive Software for Humans. Stockholm: Swedish National Defence Research Institute (FOA). Report C10029-M3 (E5).
4 Stonier, T (1982) Wealth from Knowledge. Bradford: Sigma Technical Press.
5 Newman, R L & Newman, J C (1984) "Information Work: The New Divorce?" BSA Conference on Work, Employment and Unemployment, Bradford.
6 Doswell, A (1983) Office Automation. Chichester: Wiley.
7 Tapscott, D (1982) Office Automation: A User-Driven Approach. New York, N Y: Plenum.
8 Stewart, T F M (1976) "The needs of the Professional user" NATO ASI on Man-Computer Interaction, Mati, Greece.
9 Argyle, M (1974) The Social Psychology of Work. Harmondsworth: Pelican.
10 Gouldner, A (1954) Patterns of Industrial Bureaucracy. New York, NY: Free Press.

11 Maslow, A (1954) Motivation and Personality. New York, NY: Harper Row.

12 Herzberg, F (1966) Work and the Nature of Man. New York, NY: World Publishing Co.

13 Bourne, S R (1978) An Introduction to the Unix Shell. Murray Hill, NJ: Bell Laboratories.

14 Banahan, M & Rutter, M (1982) Unix: The Book. Bradford: Sigma Technical Press.

15 Gauthier, R (1981) Using the Unix System. Reston, VA: Reston Publishing Co.

16 Interactive Systems Corporation (1981) INed Interactive CRT Text Editor Reference Manual. Santa Monica, California: Interactive Systems Corporation.

17 Barnard, P, Jorgensen, A H, Hammond, N, & Clark, I A (1982) Naming Commands: An Analysis of Designers' Naming Behaviour. Winchester: IBM UK Laboratories, Report HF072.

Human-Computer Interaction — INTERACT '84 / B. Shackel (ed.)
Elsevier Science Publishers B.V. (North-Holland)
© IFIP, 1985

RECALL AS AN INDICANT OF PERFORMANCE IN INTERACTIVE SYSTEMS

Allan MacLean, Phil Barnard and Nick Hammond

MRC Applied Psychology Unit,
15 Chaucer Road, Cambridge, England

Recall measures are often used in the area of human computer communication as a quick means of obtaining an index of the 'goodness' of alternative command sets. However there is a rich assortment of additional information available to mediate use of an on-line system, which is absent in conditions under which recall is typically elicited. The present paper reviews a number of experiments in which both on-line performance and recall measures are available, with a view to determining the extent to which recall can be used to explore the user's representation of the computer system in interactive performance. In addition, it relates the phenomena observed to established findings from the psychological study of memory.

INTRODUCTION

The traditional psychological tools of free recall are often seen as quick and convenient ways of assessing users' ability to remember from one occasion to the next the functions implemented in a particular interactive system, and the commands required to execute them [3] [7] [16]. Since the ability to remember system actions is of crucial practical importance in assessing usability, it is equally important to establish whether or not there are any systematic relationships between simpler laboratory measures of memory and subsequent performance in interactive dialogue. The present paper explores some of the issues associated with this problem by examining evidence from a number of experiments for which simple recall and recognition measures were available, as well as a variety of performance measures obtained during actual system use.

In other areas, establishing the relationship between everyday performance and laboratory measures of memory has often proved problematic. For example, it is well established in the psychological laboratory that increased exposure to lists of items leads to better learning (see [1]). However, in real life, massive exposure may not always have the same consequence. For example, Bekerian and Baddeley [5] have shown that remarkably little learning occurred during a saturation advertising campaign to acquaint the public with changes in radio wavelengths, despite the fact that subjects were exposed to an average of 25 presentations per day over many weeks. It is therefore not sufficient simply to be repeatedly exposed to information to ensure that it is remembered [5]

Apparently minor changes in laboratory procedure can radically alter implications for real life performance. For example, Loftus has shown that after people are given new and misleading information about a previously seen incident they are often unable to remember the original incident accurately [15]. This result only holds if cues for recognition are presented in a random order. If cues are presented in the order they actually occurred, no memory loss is found in an otherwise identical laboratory task [6]. There are numerous examples of similar lack of success in attempting to relate performance in laboratory tasks to assessment of everyday memory (eg [2] [11] [12]).

These discrepancies can be partly understood by considering not only the precise task in hand, but also the context within which it is carried out and that in which recall is later attempted (see [2]). For example, it is well known that the precise conditions under which people learn even simple lexical lists, and the form of any cues they may be given during a later memory test are crucial in determining exactly what is recalled [18]. Similarly, the nature of the processing which takes place when information is encoded determines how well it will be remembered [13], as does the ease with which the subject can generate appropriate retrieval cues for himself [2]. Drawing parallels between the psychological literature and the way in which computer systems are typically used, we might expect relationships between laboratory measures of recall and actual system performance in interactive dialogue to be rather complex.

Although we have some idea of the factors which can influence memory, it is much more difficult to know which factors will be important in any specific situation, let alone how they will influence it. Given the relative lack of success in relating memory performance to everyday memory in more complex task environments, we should not expect it to be an easy matter to forge strong relationships between off-line measures of memory, using standard psychological paradigms, and actual use of an on-line system.

THE EXPERIMENTS

This paper will draw on illustrative examples from four experiments where we have obtained measures of recall of command names and operations, usually one to two weeks after initial training, as well as comprehensive measures of interactive performance. The detailed results are reported elsewhere, however the salient points are as follows. Three experiments (A, B and C) used a text editing task in which subjects had twelve commands available to enable them to correct a number of simple sentences. Attributes of the command sets were systematically manipulated. Experiment A looked at performance with general (eg TRANSFER, PUT) and specific (eg FETCH, SEND) command sets [3]. Experiment B examined the effect of mixing general and specific commands within the same set. Experiment C compared five command sets ranging from a specific vocabulary through a set which consisted of words which were unrelated to the operation they carried out (eg LIGHT, BRAKE), to a set consisting of random consonant strings (eg NRB, RCN) [10]. The fourth experiment (D) required subjects to learn an office message handling system consisting of twelve commands which were used to either ESTABLISH information about the message, or subsequently carry out some ACTION based on the previously established information. Two command sets were compared, one of which contained lexically confusable commands (eg SEND, DISPATCH) [4].

Table 1   The mean performance level (%) for each experiment, for each of the recall measures used.

	EXPERIMENT			
	A	B	C	D
Free Recall of Names	38	55	78	43
Free Recall of Operations	47	51	95	–
Recognition of Names	84	85	–	92

Table 1 indicates that experiments A,B and D had broadly comparable levels of performance on laboratory measures of memory. Experiment C shows considerably better recall than the others. However subjects in this experiment had more extensive training. Within each experiment there is further variation in performance depending on the structure of the name set, the nature of the operations and the way in which the system is used. We shall now discuss some of the more important implications of these studies with particular concern for relationships between patterns of performance and subsequent recall of command names.

STRATEGIC ASPECTS OF PERFORMANCE

In experiment A, performance in interactive dialogue suggested that the people who had the general command set adopted a relatively passive learning strategy compared to the specific group, and relied on help information much more frequently [3]. There was no significant difference in memory for command names between the two groups (44% correct for specific and 33% for general), but the specific group with the more active learning strategy were better able to define the operations (55% vs 38%). It is not clear from this whether the specific commands acted as better cues for recall of the operations, or whether that group relied more on a representation based around the operations, and therefore had them encoded better. Experiment B mixed specific and general commands within the same set. In this case on-line performance was very similar to the specific group and there was no overall difference in recall of either names (55% vs 50% correct) or operations (47% vs 45% correct) as a function of the type of command (specific or general). Superior recall of operations in experiment A cannot therefore simply be explained by the specific commands being a better cue for retrieval of the operations, but rather the structure of the command set as a whole determines performance. The general command set leads to a strategy which relies on help information to assist in resolving ambiguities. This in turn leads to the generation of a poorer cognitive representation of system operations as is reflected in later recall.

TRAINING AND PERFORMANCE

Unlike experiments A and B, experiment C gave subjects training on each command individually before the first on-line session to encourage more active learning of all the available operations and commands. As might be expected this extra training generally improved both on-line performance and recall the following week. However, one of the five command sets consisted of meaningless three letter consonant strings. In this condition, although the training had indeed led to relatively good recall of the system operations (88%), the level of recall of names was comparable to that of the general command set in experiment A (34%), as was the pattern of help use. Comparison of the patterns of data in these two conditions highlights the need to have a number of measures available to provide converging evidence. Had we only had the data from the patterns of help use and recall of names, we might have concluded that the consonant strings simply led to slower learning, and that the provision of appropriate training would give performance comparable to that obtained with the general command set. This is clearly not the whole story. The training has in fact given the consonant string group a good grasp of the system operations, but this is not sufficient in itself to allow them to build suitable mappings from the operations to the names. The full representational demands are quite different in the two groups.

FREQUENCY OF USE OF COMMANDS

In traditional psychological experiments, it is well known that amount of exposure to words is an important determinant of later recall (see [1]). In the domain of human computer interaction this tradition is continued in typical off-line studies based around verbal learning techniques, which present each potential command name the same number of times (eg [7], [16]). The frequency with which commands are used in a real interactive system, however, tends to vary both as a function of user preference and task requirements. For example in the text editing task, subjects often used INSERT/DELETE combinations to carry out the action of other commands and thus these commands were used three times more often than was strictly required. As might be expected, they were also the most frequently recalled (58%). It is not uncommon for a subset of commands to be used in this way in place of functions for which more specialised commands exist (eg [9]). The nature of the task and the set of functions available will determine the extent to which this is likely to happen, so assumptions about equality of exposure to commands in off-line studies are often liable to be unwarranted.

In experiment D, subjects were required to use some of the commands twice as often as others. This difference in required use was only reflected in recall when a less confusable command set was used (57% correct for more frequent commands vs 33% for less confusable set; 48% and 45% for confusable set). Subjects in the confusable set might have been expected to make more errors or more help requests for the less frequently used commands. This could have equated the overall exposure to the two groups of commands, leading to no difference in recall. There was in fact no evidence to support this hypothesis, so increased frequency of use does not always lead to better recall in use of an on-line system.

STRUCTURE OF NAMES - LEXICAL CONFUSION

A more detailed look at individual members of the command set throws light on other factors which can cause a mismatch between performance and recall. In experiment D confusable names (eg SEND, DISPATCH) were included in the command set. Although subjects in this condition showed poorer performance, as measured by the number of help requests they made, they tended to recall not fewer, but more

of these commands names than the subjects who used the less confusable command set. Scoring recall as correct only if both members of the confusable pair appeared in the recall list, they averaged 29% - against only 19% for the names of the same pairs of operations in the less confusable set. A similar phenomenon can explain the lack of discrimination in recall of command names between the general and specific command sets in experiment A - the general command set is more confusable than the specific, and subjects know which commands confuse them, but not what these commands do. They show poorer performance while carrying out the main task by having to refer to the help system to resolve ambiguities, but these very ambiguities provide links between command names in memory which can be beneficial in increasing the number of command names recalled. The interpretation of recall measures in isolation would be quite misleading in these circumstances.

STRUCTURE OF SYSTEM FUNCTIONS

Typically a computer system is organised so that certain groups of operations are more closely related to each other than to the rest of the system. For example, the commands in the text editing experiment are differentiated in that they consist of two housekeeping commands (HELP and CANCEL); two file handling commands and eight text manipulating commands.

Of particular interest in this section are the HELP and CANCEL commands. They were both entered in the same manner as the other commands and used more often than most - in fact HELP was used four times more frequently than even DELETE and INSERT - yet they were recalled much less frequently than would have been expected - CANCEL was the least well recalled of all the commands (21%), and HELP was recalled no more than average (33%). Indeed, subjects, when seeing these commands on the recognition list (the mean for these two commands was 89% correctly recognised) would often spontaneously make remarks such as "I forgot all about those ones". They had clearly retained some memory of them, despite having not spontaneously recalled them in free recall.

In experiment D, the help system dialogue was differentiated much more strongly from the rest of the system by using function keys marked NEXT and CHOOSE to point and select information from menus. It was extremely rare for either of these labels to be recalled as commands, despite the fact that for most subjects they were an essential part of the dialogue. In experiment A, a prompt for the HELP and CANCEL commands was always available on the screen and in D, NEXT and CHOOSE were prompted by the labels on the keys. In both experiments, there is therefore only a recognition demand on their use. In addition, they carry out functions which are clearly differentiated from the other operations in the system. Appropriate cues to assist later recall were therefore relatively unlikely to be generated.

A similar phenomenon is well documented in the psychological literature. If subjects are required to learn a list of words belonging to a number of discrete categories (eg animals, furniture, plants) they will later recall more words if given the category names as cues for retrieval. If they are not given any cues, they will recall fewer words but this is normally due to omitting entire categories rather than recalling fewer members of all categories [17].

USER CONFIDENCE

Users may "know" a command and be quite able to recall it, but may show little evidence of this knowledge in the way they use the system. In study A, subjects given the general command set remembered the same number of commands as those who had the specific set, whether measured by recall or recognition. However, in recognition the people who had the general set were less confident that they had correctly recognised many of the command names. This lack of confidence seems to be reflected in the greater use of the help facilities by this group.

We could not tell precisely why subjects used help in the text editing experiments, but it seems likely from the confidence ratings in the recognition data that some of the use may not really have been necessary, but simply reflected a lack of confidence rather than a real lack of knowledge. In experiment D where subjects had to specify the command for which they wished help, it was not uncommon (about 25% of operations) for subjects to request a description only of the correct command. This serves to provide some additional support for the idea that confidence plays a part in determining strategies of help use.

Lack of confidence due to errors in the use of individual commands can also reduce confidence in their use. In experiment A, we have evidence of commands being used quite correctly until for example, their range of applicability was overgeneralised. These commands were not used after that even in situations identical to those in which they had previously been correctly used. Sequences of DELETE-INSERT commands were used instead. In experiment C, some subjects correctly used an abbreviation; later made an error in entering the abbreviation, and thereafter apparently lost faith in their memory and used the help facility to check on the correct form of the abbreviation before using it subsequently.

A practical implication from these findings is that if the opportunity of making mistakes is minimised, users are likely to have confidence

in their knowledge of the system, and hence improved performance in using it. In this context it is interesting to note that protecting users from the consequences of erroneously using advanced functions in a word processing system has been shown to lead to improved learning [8].

STRUCTURE OF THE RECALL LIST

The previous section indicated that the cues which subjects generate to assist free recall are crucial in determining exactly what is recalled. If a subject is asked to recall all the command names remembered from previous use of an interactive system, we would expect the most salient memories of the system to be generated first, and therefore the associated commands would be likely to appear first in the recall list. In experiment A, the command for the DELETE function was recalled more frequently in the first position in the list than any other command (and six times more than the INSERT command). Despite the comparable frequency of use, and the relatedness of the DELETE and INSERT commands, only one sixth of the lists which had DELETE first had INSERT second. The system design was such that had the commands been used optimally, all commands would have been used equally frequently and no command would have been more useful than any other. The structure of the recall list, along with the tendency to use the DELETE and INSERT commands more frequently, shows that this was clearly not how users perceived or used the system – the DELETE command held a much more salient position than would have been expected.

There is a similar strong bias towards one command being more likely to appear first in the recall list in study D. This experiment required the entry of four pairs of commands, the second member of each pair acting on information which had already been established by the first. The command which was most frequently output first in the recall list specified an operation which was semantically closely related to the first operation which had to be done for that message. In the psychological literature, the primacy effect refers to the tendency for words presented at the beginning of a list to be better recalled than those in the middle (eg [14]). However, in this case the command which was recalled first occurred either second or fifth in the list. It appears that the sequence is marked not by the name of the first command to be entered, but by its underlying semantics. The first command in the sequence refers to an operation which had a similar function to five others in the system, and with which it tended to be confused in use. Hence the semantics of the first operation act as a better retrieval cue for the later command in the sequence since they are less ambiguously related to it. The structure of the recall list is far from random and can provide clues to salient aspects of the system when the nature of the retrieval cues which are likely to have generated the list are considered.

CONCLUSION

The factors which determine recall of the commands and operations which were previously used in an interactive system are many and varied. Psychological research has investigated many of the theoretical issues which appear to be important, but it is often problematic to see a priori which of these will be important in a given applied situation, and what their influence will be. This would suggest that any simple relationship between recall and the usability of a computer system is unlikely to be found. What then is the role of recall measures in understanding interactive performance? No one variable can be expected to adequately capture the richness of such a complex environment, but if some evidence exists for a particular form of user representation being important in determining performance, other measures can often provide useful converging evidence to form a more detailed conclusion. Recall measures can provide a useful source of such evidence. The relationship between recall of names and operations can provide useful insights into the nature of the user's representation, as can the order in which items are recalled and their likelihood of being recalled together.

REFERENCES

[1] Baddeley, A.D. The Psychology of memory. (New York: Basic Books, 1976).

[2] Baddeley, A.D. Domains of recollection. Psychological Review 89 (1982) 708-729.

[3] Barnard, P., Hammond, N., MacLean, A. and Morton, J. Learning and remembering interactive commands in a text-editing task. Behaviour and Information Technology 1 (1982) 347-358.

[4] Barnard, P., MacLean, A. and Hammond, N. User representations of ordered sequences of command operations. Submitted to INTERACT '84: First IFIP Conference on Human-Computer Interaction (1984).

[5] Bekerian, D.A. and Baddeley, A.D. Saturation advertising and the repetition effect. Journal of Verbal Learning and Verbal Behaviour 19 (1980) 17-25.

[6] Bekerian,D.A. and Bowers,J.M. Eyewitness testimony: Were we misled? Journal of Experimental Psychology: Learning, Memory and Cognition 9 (1983) 139-145

[7] Black, J & Moran, T. Learning and remembering command names. In Human Factors in Computer Systems, (Gaithersburg Maryland 1982) 8-11.

[8] Carroll, J.M. and Carrithers, C. Blocking user error states in a training system. Submitted to Commun. of the ACM (1984).

[9] Folley, L. & Williges, R. User models of text editing command languages. In Human Factors in Computer Systems, (Gaithersburg, Maryland 1982) 326-331.

[10] Grudin, J. and Barnard, P. The cognitive demands of learning and representing command names for text-editing with varying structural and semantic attributes. Submitted to Human Factors: special issue on text-editing (1984).

[11] Gruneberg, M., Morris, P.E. and Sykes, R.N. (eds) Practical Aspects of Memory (Academic Press, London, 1978)

[12] Harris, J.E. and Morris, P.E. (Eds) Everyday memory, actions and absentmindedness. (Academic Press, London, in press)

[13] Jacoby, L.L. On interpreting the effects of repetition: Solving a problem versus remembering a solution. Journal of Verbal Learning and Verbal Behaviour 17 (1978) 649-667.

[14] Jahnke, J.C. Delayed recall and the serial position effect of short term memory. Journal of Experimental Psychology 76 (1968) 618-622.

[15] Loftus, E. Eyewitness Testimony. (Cambridge, Mass. Harvard University Press, 1979)

[16] Scapin, D.L. Computer commands in restricted natural language: some aspects of memory and experience. Human Factors 23 (1981) 365-375.

[17] Tulving, E. and Pearlstone, Z. Availability versus accessibility of information in memory for words. Journal of Verbal Learning and Verbal Behaviour 5 (1966) 381-391.

[18] Tulving, E. and Thomson, D.M. Encoding specificity and retrieval processes in episodic memory. Psychological Review 80 (1973) 352-373.

Human-Computer Interaction — INTERACT '84 / B. Shackel (ed.)
Elsevier Science Publishers B.V. (North-Holland)
© IFIP, 1985

MAKING THE RIGHT CHOICES WITH MENUS

Gary Perlman

AT & T Bell Laboratories
Murray Hill, New Jersey 07974 USA

and

Cognitive Science Laboratory
University of California, San Diego
La Jolla, California 92093 USA

Menus provide a effective way to present a limited set of options to users. System designers have to decide how many options to present in what format, and how users will indicate their choices. Two experiments are reported that manipulate (1) menu size, (2) option ordering, (3) option selector type, and (4) selector/option compatibility. The results show (a) people use simple search strategies for ordinary menu sizes, (b) people are sensitive to menu length, (c) sorted menus are easier to search, and (d) letter selectors can produce the best or worst performance depending on compatibility. Some guidelines for menu design and suggestions for further research are discussed.

A menu is a list with a limited number of options, usually words or short phrases. Often associated with menu options are unique selector strings, sometimes the index number of the option or a letter abbreviation, sometimes the option itself. Some large systems create hierarchies of menus leading to sub-menus so that large menus or inappropriate menu choices are avoided. In this paper, I present results about how menus are searched and how options in menus are selected. I conclude with some guidelines for designing menus.

EXPERIMENT 1: Menu Search

In this experiment I study how people search through menus. I vary menu size, option order, and option type to see how these factors affect how long it takes people to find menu options.

METHOD

Conditions

Subjects saw menus on a CRT terminal with keyboard connected to a mini-computer. Menus were plotted on the left side of the screen with items vertically aligned and left justified. There were two *types* of menu lists: Arabic numbers from 1 to 20, and well known names of members of categories drawn from Battig & Montague (1969) such that the letters 'a' through 't' were covered. For each menu list type, four menu lists were made up of length 5, 10, 15, and 20, using the beginning of the menu lists. Four groups, eight undergraduates each, searched sorted words, sorted numbers, random words, and random numbers, respectively. Subjects were shown only one list ordering to try to force them into the best strategy for their list. All subjects searched though four list lengths, the order of which was controlled by a Latin square.

Procedure

On each trial, one of two randomly chosen arrows '<' or '>' appeared to the left of each item, and the item to be found, the *target*, was presented at the right of the screen at a constant location. The task was to find the target and indicate when it was found by pressing the arrow key next to the target. The subjects had their left fingers on the left arrow key and their rights on the right. It was thought that this response measure would add a constant to the search time independent of the experimental factors and make sure subjects were really finding the targets. To control the amount of practice subjects had with the lists, there were 60 trials per condition so subjects had practice ranging from three trials for the 20 long lists to 12 for the five long list. Subjects rested between different list length conditions, but within a condition, trials were continuous with two second pauses between.

RESULTS

The main results are shown in Figure 1. Finding words (1.89 sec) took longer than numbers (1.56 sec) ($F(1,28) = 11.7$, $p < .01$) perhaps because the numbers were shorter or more familiar. Sorted lists (1.45 sec) were easier to search than random (2.01 sec) ($F(1,28) = 10.05$, $p < .001$). There was no interaction between list type and order.

The length of the list had a reliable effect: 5 (1.26 sec) 10 (1.57 sec) 15 (1.84 sec) 20 (2.23 sec) so it took longer to find items in longer lists ($F(3,84) = 113.86$, $p < .001$). There was an interaction between list type and length ($F(3,84) = 4.50$, $p < .01$); words took longer per list item to find than numbers. More important, there was an interaction between list order and length ($F(3,84) = 18.28$, $p < .001$); random lists had higher slopes than sorted.

The data for the first three trials (the minimum amount of practice subjects had with all list lengths) showed similar trends for all the data. People got

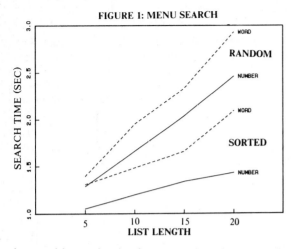

FIGURE 1: MENU SEARCH

better with practice, but it was not the only reason why they did better with the short lists with which they had more trials per item.

Error rates were lower than one percent of all trials and were nearly evenly distributed among conditions. This suggests that subjects were really finding the items and the left and right arrow key test to indicate *finding* worked properly. Reaction times for errors were non-significantly lower than correct trials. Errors did not play a large part in the experiment because subjects were instructed to be accurate.

DISCUSSION

The results of the experiment have practical applications and some interesting theoretical implications. In general, list length has a linear effect on the time it takes to find an item, and this effect is larger if the list is random. Randomness is in the mind of the person doing the searching. Usually, people searching though a list will be looking for a semantic match, not an exact match for what they have in mind. For example, a user might want to *print* a file, but the name of the command is *display*. So, in some cases, an alphabetically ordered list would not allow a fast search for what the person had in mind.

It is surprising that sorted lists show a time increase linear in list length; an optimal computer algorithm would produce a logarithmic function (Aho, Hopcroft, & Ullman, 1974). For lists of these lengths, the gains from a binary search strategy is not worth the cost of a more expensive comparison routine. An identity match is a fast operation for people while an ordinal judgement takes longer. Norman and Fisher (1981) found that alphabetic keyboards were not much easier for non-typists to learn, and this seems to be related to the findings here: making use of the ordinal information of an alphabetic keyboard is not worth the trouble because the extra computation is no match for

a simpler search and match strategy. One would expect that the comparison of numbers to be faster than words because they are shorter and their ordinal nature is much more practiced. There is some indication of this: longer lists of sorted words look like they have an increasing slope while longer lists of sorted numbers look like their's is decreasing. These trends are small and not reliable. Practically speaking, we can treat the lines as straight, though the theorctical implications of search strategies demand more experimentation.

Card (1983) concluded from his data that people search through menus with a random strategy and gradually memorize the position of the items. A fine grained analysis of the response times according to list position yielded some interesting results. For random lists, there were no reliable trends in the data suggesting that with lists they know to be random, people adopt a random strategy and perhaps try to memorize list position. This is what Card found.

For sorted lists, there was an advantage for the first few items for both words and numbers, and an advantage for the ends of number lists. With the longer sorted lists of numbers, there was an advantage for the middle of the list as well; apparently people could estimate that items were in the beginning, middle, or end of the lists and begin search in that region. This is true for lists of numbers, not words, an probably not phrases, so the practical implications must be qualified. Card found that with extensive practice, people were able to go directly to target options. This was not found in this experiment perhaps because subjects were not practiced enough.

With longer lists, people took longer to find the first list item. Even though they know that the first number is '1' and that it is at the top of all the sorted lists, they still take longer to find it. This suggests that people cannot ignore extra options added to menus.

EXPERIMENT 2: Option Selection

Once an option in a menu has been found, the next step is to select it. There are several mechanisms for selection: cursor movements, mice and joy sticks (see Card, 1983), touch screens, and even voice input, however the one most commonly used is typing a selection string, usually a character, to indicate a choice. This is primarily due to the lack of availability of more advanced technology, but selector strings can stand up to more advanced methods under certain conditions and can let users avoid moving their hands away from keyboards. When users are familiar with the available items but still want to use the menu selection scheme to abbreviate input, some selection schemes can support them and allow them to avoid menu search by using memorable selectors.

In this experiment, I recorded selection times for compatible and incompatible letter and number selectors. The experiment was motivated by an observation that menu systems using letter selectors a-z can have awkward pairings between selectors and options. Letters are attractive because there are 26 to choose from, but an ordered list of letter selectors might pair "print" with 'd' and users might type 'p' for "print." The following experiment quantifies this interference.

METHOD

Conditions

The apparatus was the same as in Experiment 1. The stimuli were eight computer terms beginning with the letters 'a' through 'h'. The terms were *assemble, buffer, compile, debug, edit, file, graph,* and *halt*. Pilot data showed that knowledge of the computer terms was not important for the task. Two types of selectors were paired with the computer terms: single letters between 'a' and 'h', and the digits 1-8. There were two compatibility conditions. A compatible letter is the first letter of the word it is paired with, and a compatible number is the ordinal alphabetical position of the initial letter of the word (e.g., 1-assemble, 4-debug). Incompatible selectors were chosen randomly so that no selectors were compatible. Incompatible letter selectors can occur when the letters 'a' through 'z' are used as menu selectors and get paired with words with different initial letters. Incompatible numbers served as a control condition.

Procedure

The left justified stimulus set of eight terms and their selectors were displayed vertically in the upper left corner for the duration of each condition. On each trial, a target word was presented at a fixed location in the lower right corner of the screen. Sixteen undergraduates were instructed to begin a trial by holding their preferred index finger away from the keyboard and then press the selector character paired with the stimulus target. Subjects saw all conditions, the presentation order of which was controlled by a Latin square. There were five trials per term per condition and about two seconds between trials; subjects were allowed to rest only between conditions.

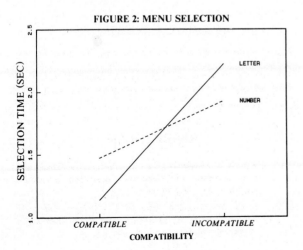

FIGURE 2: MENU SELECTION

RESULTS

The results are summarized in Figure 2. Compatible selectors were superior to incompatible ($F(1,12) = 107.9$, $p < .001$). Compatible letters were the best selectors (1.14 sec) followed by compatible numbers (1.47 sec) while for incompatible selectors, the trend was reversed. Incompatible numbers (1.93 sec) were superior to incompatible letters (2.22 sec) ($F(1,14) = 52.1$, $p < .001$). A 99 % Scheffe confidence interval showed all differences to be reliable.

Before each experimental condition, subjects were allowed to study the lists. Subjects spent more time (26 sec) looking at incompatible pairings than compatible (16 sec) ($F(1,15) = 14.9$, $p < .01$). There was no difference in viewing times between letter and number selectors.

Errors occurred in less than one percent of the trials and most could be attributed to hitting a key next to the one they were supposed to. The remaining errors were too few for meaningful analyses. Response times for for errors were longer than for correct trials.

DISCUSSION

Norman's (1981) theory of action slips predicts that competing activations between the initial letter of a word and an incompatible selector letter should result in more errors than other conditions. Because subjects were instructed to minimize errors, there were not enough for statistical analyses. Still, the interference is manifest in the selection times. If there were no competing activations, the differences between incompatible letters and incompatible numbers would not have been observed.

The application of the results to the design of menu systems is clear. The best that can be done is to use compatible letters as selectors, but this can only be done if the designer has full control over the contents of menus. If the pairing is done automatically, such as by a program to select files, then using letter selectors can lead to the worst case, incompatible letters, and numerical selection would be preferable.

GENERAL DISCUSSION

The effects observed in the two experiments suggest that one or two seconds can be saved every time a menu selection is made. The importance of the results depends on the frequency of menu use.

A menu is particularly useful when users do not know what options are available to them or if the contents of a menu change over time. For example, the commands available in a program (e.g., a mail program) are limited to a fixed set (e.g., print, delete, answer) and so can be presented to users in a menu. These commands do not change over time, and a menu of commands useful to a new user becomes a nuisance to moderately experienced users. A menu can be used to abbreviate user keyboard inputs, but sometimes this costs menu display time or lost screen space. The objects on which commands might operate (e.g., the messages) are constantly changing, but are usually limited, and therefore suitable for menu presentation. I call this a distinction between between *static* and *dynamic* displays (Perlman, 1981).

Experiment 2 demonstrated the best single character option selectors are initial letters, but in many cases, using initial letters is not possible; there may be more than one option beginning with the same letter. Static menus are more amenable to initial letter selectors because one of two options with the same initial letter can usually be renamed with a synonym. Dynamic menus are less predictable, and numerical selectors appear to be the best compromise. This reasoning was applied to the design of a menu based interface to a programming system's (static) programs and (dynamic) files (Perlman, 1981); letters selected programs and numbers selected files.

When menus are static, they should only be displayed to novice users, or on request. Even experienced users are not familiar with all parts of complex systems, and all users occasionally need their memories refreshed. The amount of space static menus take up on the screen should be minimized; one line menus should be considered. Dynamic menus can be useful to users of all levels of expertise because their contents are unpredictable and they can provide feedback about the outcome of operations.

Users should be allowed to make a system switch modes between automatically presenting menus and only on request. The most vocal critics of menus complain about systems that automatically take over the whole screen, use simple and inefficient display drivers, and force users to use menus. These are tedious and users must be allowed to avoid them.

Menus can be compared with *forms* because both are input mechanisms. Forms are *integrators* of information while menus are used to *discriminate* among alternatives. A *form* is a series of *fields*, and so can be viewed as a menu with access to items usually controlled by cursor movements on a screen. Using character selectors to access fields on a form is an alternative that allows random access of fields. Fields are used to specify a variable value, as are menus. The difference is that any value can be entered in a field (after which validation may take place) while the options allowed by a menu is finite and can be assumed valid.

FURTHER RESEARCH

The experiments described here do not help with the overall design of systems, but their results can aid low level implementation decisions. Higher level guidelines are discussed by Shneiderman (1983). One strategy for studying user interfaces is to compare complete systems while manipulating variables of interest. The problem with that strategy is that it is so costly to do, it is not clear how the results generalize to other systems, and often the differences between systems are confounded by their complexity. Problems with isolated experiments are that they may not apply to any real systems, and the relative importance of factors may not be apparent. For practical applications, isolated experiments appear more cost effective.

Several areas of generalization for experimentation are anticipated:

Vertical lists were studied here. Would the results apply equally well to items on one line? I suspect vertical lists are easier to search, but horizontal displays usually take up less room and so might be better for static menus.

A generalization of simple lists is tabular displays and how their format affects ease of finding items. Should items cycle by rows or by columns fastest, and how important is vertical alignment of items in different columns?

All the items to be found were in the lists, but in menu systems with networks, users sometimes are looking for an option in the wrong menu. An investigation of the search times to determine an item is *not* in a list might prove useful.

Finally, for searching through menus, the usefulness of various forms of highlighting should be determined. Attributes like capitalization, reverse video, underlining, color, and intensity are but some of the possible manipulations, though using all at once might cause confusing visual displays.

ACKNOWLEDGEMENTS

I thank Anne Sutter for collecting the data. This research was conducted in part under Contract N00014-79-C-0323, NR 667-437 with the Personnel and Training Research Programs of the Office of Naval Research, and was sponsored in part by the Office of Naval Research and the Air Force Office for Scientific Research.

REFERENCES

[1]   Aho, A. V., Hopcroft, J. E., & Ullman, J. D. **The Design and Analysis of Computer Algorithms,** Reading, Massachusetts: Addison-Wesley, 1974.

[2]   Battig, W. F. & Montague, W. E. *Category Norms for Verbal Items in 56 Categories.* **Journal of Experimental Psychology Monographs,** 1969, 80:3.2.

[3] Card, S. K. *The Evaluation of Pointing Devices.* **Digest of Papers, Compcon Spring '83,** San Francisco, 1983. New York: IEEE Computer Society Press.

[4] Card, S. K. *Visual Search of Computer Command Menus.* in H. Bouma & D. Bouwhuis (eds.) **Attention and Performance X: Control of Language Processes,** Hillsdale, New Jersey: Lawrence Erlbaum Associates, in press.

[5] Norman, D. A. *Categorization of Action Slips.* **Psychological Review,** 1981, **88,** 1-15.

[6] Norman, D. A. & Fisher, D. *Why Alphabetic Keyboards Are Not Easy to Use: Keyboard Layout Doesn't Much Matter.* **Center for Human Information Processing Report 8106,** University of California, San Diego, November 1981.

[7] Perlman, G. *The Design of an Interface to a Programming System.* **Center for Human Information Processing Report 8105,** University of California, San Diego, November 1981.

[8] Shneiderman, B. *Design Issues and Experimental Results for Menu Selection Systems.* **CS Tech. Report 1303,** University of Maryland Computer Science Department, July, 1983.

The author's new address is:
    Wang Institute of Graduate Studies
    Tyng Road
    Tyngsboro, MA 01879
    USA

ADDITION TO EXPERIMENT 1 DISCUSSION

The appended figure shows the mean search times for the first five items in sorted lists. Note that the time to find the first item increases with list length, even though the item is always at the same location on the screen. The effect, though small, is reliable, and similar effects can be seen for other items. Also note the list end advantage for the shortest list, indicating that people start their searches of sorted lists at the beginning or end. Eye movement apparatus would be necessary to decide this.

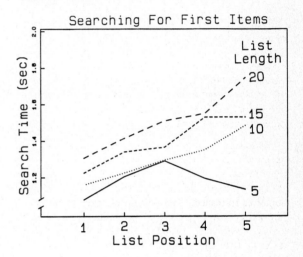

Human-Computer Interaction — INTERACT '84 / B. Shackel (ed.)
Elsevier Science Publishers B.V. (North-Holland)
IFIP, 1985

A COMPARATIVE EVALUATION OF MENU-BASED INTERACTIVE HUMAN-COMPUTER DIALOGUE TECHNIQUES

M.D. Apperley   and   G.E. Field
(Department of Computer Science)   (Department of Psychology)

University of Waikato,
Hamilton,
New Zealand

Menu selection is an often used type of human-computer dialogue. However, there is little data on the effectiveness, efficiency or merits of this technique. This paper describes an experiment designed to compare the utility of recently published intuitively derived techniques relating to the syntax of menu interaction with more conventional menu techniques.
This experiment is a complex problem solving task which involves retrieving a number of related items from a data-base using a menu dialogue. Subjects will be presented with a task for which they must access, interpret and relate information from several different pages of a Viewdata-like database. Traversal paths and time taken to achieve the goal, are monitored, to provide data with which to assess the effectiveness of the menu syntax.
It is anticipated that these results will be of significant interest to the designers of Viewdata systems, and to all people interested in human-computer interaction.

1. INTRODUCTION

Menu selection, in which the user is presented with a list of possible commands or items from which to choose, is a popular form of human-computer dialogue, particularly for unskilled users. However, little real data is available on the merits of this technique compared with other forms of dialogue (e.g. question-and-answer, imperative command), or on the effects of different forms of menu layout and control. This paper describes an experiment designed to compare the effectiveness of recently published intuitively derived techniques relating to the syntax of menu interaction (1) with more conventional menu techniques.

Other published results in this area (2, 3) present conflicting evidence on the influence of menu structure on effective search. These results have been based on experiments involving the search for a single identifiable goal; a command or target word. By contrast, the experiment described here is based on a more complex problem solving test. The goal is not directly evident from the menu per se, but involves retrieving a number of related items from a data-base using a menu dialogue. Thus it is not merely the ability of the subjects to identify goal words from within menus of various structures which is being assessed, but their ability to manoeuvre with confidence within a hierarchical information structure.

Subjects are presented with a task for which they must access, interpret and relate information from several different pages of a Viewdata-like database. Their traversal path through the tree structure is monitored, and together with the time taken to achieve the goal, this information is used to assess the effectiveness of the menu syntax.

It is anticipated that these results will be of significant interest to the designers of Viewdata systems, for which the problems of existing menu dialogue techniques have already been described. (4)

2. PREVIOUS RELATED EXPERIMENTAL STUDIES

As computers have become more prevalent in everyday activities, it has become increasingly important to pay attention to the interface by which users, now most often non-specialists, access them. Menu selection and form filling have generally been found to be the most satisfactory interaction techniques for novices and non-specialists, but are often found to be too slow and cumbersome for experienced operators. In spite of the widespread use of menu selection as a form of human-computer dialogue, the effects of menu structure on operator performance are not well understood. This area has not yet received the amount of experimental attention it requires, and deserves.

In an earlier experimental study of the depth/breadth tradeoff in menus, (2) four different hierarchical menu structures were used to access 64 goal items. These structures corresponded to one level (64 choices), two levels (eight choices at each level), three levels (four choices at each level) and six levels (two choices at each level). The goal items were identical for all four structures; a set of 64 common English words. For the three multilevel structures, the words were related by category names. The menus were displayed on a CRT screen and subjects indicated their choice using push-buttons mounted on the edge of the screen adjacent to the displayed items.

Use of the two-level eight-choice structure resulted in the fastest acquisition time and

the fewest errors, where acquisition time was
calculated as the sum of the individual response
times necessary to reach the goal. The acquisition time for the four-level structure was
similar, but the error rate was higher. It is
likely that this higher error rate can be attributed to the increased likelihood of cognitive
mismatch caused by choice of category names
with an increased number of levels rather than
any other inherent characteristic of higher-
level structures. Miller concluded that "for
systems of moderate size the number of hierarchical levels should be minimized, but not at
the expense of display crowding, for optimal
goal acquisition performance." (2)

More recently, however,(3) the validity of
Miller's results has been challenged. It was
suggested that the ordering of the goal items
and the means of selecting them in the case of
the one level (64 choice) structure had confounded Miller's results. Snowberry repeated
Miller's experiment, but used a keypad as a
means of user response (the user indicated the
number of the selection), and both random and
categorised groupings of the goal items for the
one-level structure. It was found that with the
categorised grouping, the one-level (64 choice)
structure showed both the fastest acquisition
time and the lowest error rate.

In the discussion of these results, it was
appreciated that ultimately physical limitations
would apply, and increasing the depth of the
hierarchy could become a necessity rather than
an option, as the required number of menu items
could no longer be displayed simultaneously.
As a consequence, Snowberry stated that "future
research should be directed both at determining
reasonable limitations of breadth and ways of
improving performance on relatively deep hierarchical menu structures." (3)

3.   AN IMPROVED TECHNIQUE FOR MENU NAVIGATION

Probably the most widely used application of
hierarchical menu systems is in the viewdata or
videotex public information utilities. In these
systems, many thousands of pages of information
are accessed by multiple level menus, usually
with only 8 to 12 choices presented at each
level. It has been suggested that the two most
significant obstacles in accessing the information in these systems are cognitive mismatch,
caused by the organisation and categorisation of
the information, and the difficulties encountered
in navigating within the complex menu structures.
(5) Although the first of these problems can be
studied using single goal acquisition experiments
such as those of Miller (2) and Snowberry (3)
studying the problem of menu navigation requires
more complex problems involving access to
several different parts of the structure.

A menu system has been recently described which
claims to resolve some of the navigation problems
traditionally associated with hierarchical menu
structures. (1) Essentially it provides the

user with some context for the current menu
frame, by including as part of the frame a trace
of the choices leading to it. By treating each
of the menu items as a *bistable* switch, the user
is able to cancel any previous choice and so
selectively backtrack or retreat through the
structure.

Because menu items have just two possible states,
active or *inactive*, they can be described as
bistable. Generally, those choices which have
produced the current frame are active (those
above the dotted line in Figure 1(b)). The
choices possible from this frame are normally
inactive. The two states can be represented on
a display screen by differing intensities -
bright for active and dim for inactive. The
same action that is used to select an inactive
button and render it active, can also be used to
cancel or deselect an active button and thereby
render it inactive.

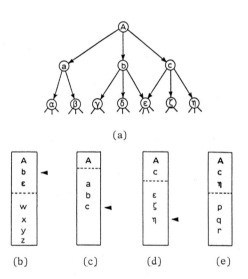

(a)

(b)   (c)   (d)   (e)

Figure 1 : (a) A typical hierarchical command
   structure; (b), (c), (d) and (e) show how
   the trace of choices and the use of bistable
   items allow for selective retreat and navigation through the structure. ◄ Indicates the
   choice leading to the next menu in sequence.

Consider the sample structure described by the
directed graph of Figure 1(a). The menu shown
in Figure 1(b) is the one which would be presented after *b* was chosen from the original menu
presented at *A*, and then ε chosen from the
subsequently presented menu frame. The user can
return to the original menu by cancelling the
choice from this menu (*b*). This will result in
the menu shown in Figure 1(c). A subsequent
choice of *c* will result in the menu shown in
Figure 1(d).

By this means the dialogue is made *stable*, in that any command can be reversed by repeating the action by which it was selected (incremental retreat), and at the same time provision is made for *selective* retreat, in that the user can return immediately to any menu frame along the path leading to the current one.

4. A COMPARATIVE EVALUATION OF TWO MENU TECHNIQUES

Although the menu structure just described may appear to have obvious advantages over conventional techniques, particularly in resolving the difficulty of navigation through the dataspace, as yet no real evidence of any measurable benefit has been produced. To this end an experiment has been designed to compare the proposed new structure with conventional menu techniques in accessing a viewdata-type data base. Because the benefits of the new structure are in navigation rather than isolated selection, rather than use a single goal acquisition task, the experiment involves the solution of a problem which requires several accesses to different parts of the data base.

A viewdata-type data base has been set up on a BBC model B microcomputer for the purpose of this experiment. This data base comprises approximately one thousand pages of information relating to a hypothetical city. The information is accessed using hierarchical menu frames after the style of Prestel, with the majority of the information pages located at the fourth or fifth level of the hierarchy. For example, initially the user is presented with a choice between six broad categories of information:

> Leisure
> News and Weather
> Business Information
> Travel
> Buying and Selling
> Employment

Selecting the "Travel" item would lead to the second-level menu frame offering a choice between modes of transport, rail, road, air and so on. If "Rail Travel" was the choice from this frame, the user would then be presented with the third-level menu frame listing options such as; timetables, station details, and booking information. Choosing "Timetables" would lead to the fourth-level menu frame presenting a list of destinations, and selecting the desired destination would in turn produce the fifth-level information frame containing a timetable for rail travel to the given destination.

Two separate programs have been written for accessing this data base. The first (Method A) presents the menus and the information as just described i.e. a conventional hierarchical menu system. The second (Method B) presents, in addition to the prescribed menu of choices from the current frame, additional menu items delineating the path taken to arrive at the current frame. These additional items can be cancelled to provide the user with a facility for incremental and selective retreat. Figure 2 shows such a modified menu for level 4 of the train timetable sequence described above.

```
 11   TRAVEL              Page 1411
 12   RAIL
 13   TIMETABLES
 ──────────────────────────────────
 Rail services from Central Carlton
 to destinations:

 1.  ABBEYWELL        5.   LAKEVIEW
 2.  CARLTON EAST     6.   NEWTOWN
 3.  DEANFORD         7.   RIVERSIDE
 4.  ENDERLEY

 Key each number for timetable.
 Key your selection here:
```

Figure 2: The modified menu providing a trace of the choices already made as used in Method B.

In the current experiment, subjects use one of these two menu systems to solve a multiple task problem. This problem can be described as follows. The subject is to meet a friend after work to see a particular film. After seeing the film they are to dine at a vegetarian restaurant. To solve this problem the subject must determine (a) at which cinema the film is showing, (b) the most appropriate method of travelling to this cinema, (c) a nearby vegetarian restaurant which is open after the film finishes, and (d) a means of travelling home after the meal. Appendix 1 shows the first page from the instruction sheet with which the subjects are provided. Appendix 2 shows a typical sequence of menu frames that a subject using Method A would encounter in seeking the answer to the first question; At which cinema is the film 'Breakout' currently showing?

As each subject sets about obtaining the required information, the computer records the time and nature of each of their choices. Thus it is possible to study the entire sequence of choices, including errors, made by each subject, to ascertain the time that each of these choices was made, and to determine the overall goal acquisition time. Additionally, information relating to the *process* of interaction, along the cognitive, behavioural and affective dimensions, is sought. As the problem is concerned with the subject's navigation through the database, the measure of confidence that the subjects have about the completeness and correctness of their answers, and the ease with

which their interaction is facilitated by each
menu type, are also significant factors.

To this end, a series of Rating Scale Checklists
are currently being devised, which will assess
some of the psychological aspects of familiarity,
confidence and facilitation, provided by different interactive systems.

5. SUMMARY

This paper has described an experiment designed
to compare a novel technique for managing
hierarchical menus with conventional menu techniques. To make this comparison it has been
necessary to resort to a more complex problem
than has been used by others in evaluating menu
dialogue techniques. It is appreciated that
the use of this complex problem may introduce
other effects (such as cognitive mismatch) which
may influence the results. However, it is felt
that without experimental evaluation, dialogue
designers will have to continue to use intuition
in deciding on appropriate techniques. The
experiment described is only the first in a
series which, it is hoped, will provide a
greater insight into the effective design and
use of menu based systems. In addition, some
initial work on the psychometric evaluation of
the cognitive, behavioural and affective factors
of human interaction with computers will be
completed. The information gained here should
lead to a more generalised assessment device
which could be related to other aspects of the
human-computer interface.

The experiment is currently underway, and results
will be shortly available. It is proposed to
make use of these results in planning and
devising the next experiment in the series.

6. REFERENCES

(1) Apperley, M.D. and Spence, R., Hierarchical
     dialogue structures in interactive computer
     systems, Software-Practice and Experience,
     13, (1983) 777-790.

(2) Miller, D.P., The depth/breadth tradeoff in
     hierarchical computer menus, Proceedings of
     the Human Factors Society, 25th Annual
     Meeting, (1981), 296-300.

(3) Snowberry, K., Parkinson, S.R. and Sisson,
     N., Computer display menus, Ergonomics, 26
     (7), (1983), 699-712.

(4) van Ness, F.L. and Tromp, J.H., Is view-
     data easy to use? IPO Annual Progress
     Report, 14, (1979), 120-123.

(5) Young, R.M. and Hull, A. Cognitive aspects
     of the selection of viewdata options by
     casual users, Proceedings of the 6th Inter-
     national Conference on Computer Communica-
     tion, London, (1983), 571-576.

APPENDIX 1: First page of the problem solving task to guide navigation through the Carlton database.

UNIVERSITY OF WAIKATO
Department of Psychology

Human Interaction with Computers

This is an experiment using a computer.

We want you to use the computer, in front of you, to solve a problem. You will solve the problem by making a series of selections from various lists that are displayed on the screen.

To make a selection from a screen, simply type the number that corresponds to the choice that you wish to make, at the place indicated at the bottom of the screen.

For example:

    If the following list were displayed:

        1. Leisure
        2. News and Weather
        3. Business Information
        4. Travel
        5. Buying and Selling
        6. Employment

and you wished to find out something about "Local Industry" you would key in the number '3' in response to the statement -

    Key your selection here:

Consider the following problem:

    'You work in Central Carlton at a bank, until 5.30 p.m. A friend has left a message to suggest that you meet to see a movie called "Breakout" and have a meal after the movie. Your friend is a vegetarian.'

    Using the information available in the computers memory store or database, determine:

A. 1. At which theatre is the movie showing?_____

   2. What district is the theatre in? _____

   3. Is there a screening at an appropriate time?_____

   4. If so, what session?_____

(Use the space provided for making notes if you wish)

Now you need to travel to the movie theatre.
Find out:

B. 1. What form of transport (Bus or Rail) will you use to get to the theatre?_____

   2. What time does your transport leave Central Carlton?_____

   3. What time does it arrive at, or near, the movie theatre?_____

APPENDIX 2:   Possible sequence of screen selections to answer Questions A1, 2, 3 and 4

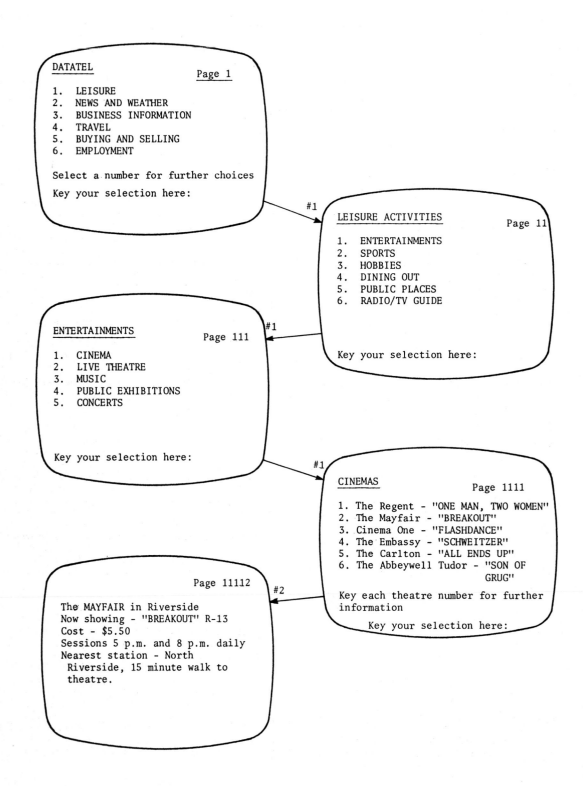

Human-Computer Interaction — INTERACT '84 / B. Shackel (ed.)
Elsevier Science Publishers B.V. (North-Holland)
© IFIP, 1985

GRAPHICAL SUPPORT FOR DIALOGUE TRANSPARENCY

J. Kaster and H. Widdel

Forschungsinstitut für Anthropotechnik
Wachtberg-Werthhoven, FRG

The development of a dialogue interface is described and general problems of a
design process are discussed. Principles of cognitive ergonomy lead to the graphical
representation of the menu hierarchy of the dialogue as realisation of its formal
transparency. The experimental set-up for investigating the influence of graphically
displayed dialogue structure on human-computer interaction of unexperienced users
is presented.

1. INTRODUCTION

Design of a human-computer-dialogue requires
some techniques of a problem solving process.
It is characterised as an interdependent procedure between distinct and well defined
development steps on the one side, and more
intuitive decisions of experts with various
experience on the other. The first aspect is
distinguished from the second by a high degree
of precision and objectivity in defining the
problem resources (1). The activities of
developing a dialogue include both strategies
showing a predominance of intuition and experience. However, at particular levels of
design evaluation analytical and experimental
methods can be used. In this case an experiment should be conducted to analyse a specific
dialogue characteristic. This attempt is
related to the first strategy, mentioned
before, and requires well defined variables to
be measured and systematically varied.

2. PROBLEM

2.1. Transparency

Before defining a variable the designer has to
come to the decision what design goal he wants
to realise. Generally, user-friendliness
represents a dialogue aspect of high significance. Descending to a lower operational level
of definition this variable is concentrated to
transparency of a dialogue system. Transparency can be interpreted as a subcategory of
self-descriptiveness (2).

Designers and programmers of interactive systems do not only delegate functional behavior
but also communicating behavior. They design
communication partners for the users, with
formal communication behavior. Transparency
can be defined in different ways one of which
is a well structured, consistent, and comprehensible appearance of the system for its
users (3). Realisation activities of transpar-

ency should provoke the consequence that users
can easily build up an internal model of the
relevant parts of a system, in the case in
point of a dialogue system. A transparent
dialogue system makes it easy for users, especially for naive users (4) or occasional users
(5), to create a mental model of the functions
the system can perform for them.

For the study presented in this paper transparency includes the dialogue functions but
not the problem solving functions. This variable to be investigated can be defined more
precisely as formal transparency. It is
related to the hierarchical structure of menus
and the work-path and position of the user in
this menu-tree.

2.2. Menu-based dialogue

Dialogue, as it relates to a human-computer
interface in the traditional sense, refers to
the computer system being used. Human-computer
dialogue has the two distinct functions: request informations from the user or from the
computer, and transmit information to the user
or to the computer. A combination of requesting and transmitting information is manifest
in a menu, which displays possible options and
then asks the user to choose one. In each of
these instances the user is interacting
directly with output generated from the software itself.

Generally, a menu presents a set of available
choices at any particular step in the user's
selection of computer functions. It includes
the title, the menu options, their selection
codes, and the query that the user should
answer by the choice of a selection mode. The
menu-based dialogue guides the user through
the numerous sequences of activities constituting the task. On the other side the selection of unappropriate alternatives is excluded
reducing the need for error correcting routines. In some limited amount the menu-method
reduces the demands for the memory of the
user.

These benefits emphasize that this type of interaction is well suited for unexperienced and casual users. However, menu-driven dialogues prove slow and frustrating for experienced users with a complete understanding of the system. In this case a dialogue is inadequate.

Application of menu selection operations refer to several types of interactive hardware, c.g., keys, mouse, rolling ball, touch input, to capture the required alternative on the screen. In a first development step of the present study we used the key input with a three-letter abbreviation (figure 1).

Bilder editieren

Text schreiben .... SCH

Linie/Rechteck zeichnen .... ZEI

Bild-Komponenten speichern ..... SPE

Bild-Komponenten löschen .... LOE

Bild-Komponenten auflisten ..... LIS

Eingabe: _ _ -

Figure 1: Example of menu

A particular aspect of the menu-structure related to the depth-breadth dimensions has been investigated in several studies. Savage et al. (6) found that people prefer shorter menus with more levels. Snowberry et al. (7) found a relationship between speed and accuracy using a dialogue and varying the breadth of menus. Additionally, the structure of the task itself may dictate a particular menu dimension in some cases. We decided to realise a balanced depth-breadth relationship in our investigation which does not focus on this specific question.

2.3. Cognitive representation of dialogue structure

When the designer wants to create a dialogue system he has to consider and to analyse characteristics of the user group the dialogue is addressed to. General knowledge of cognitive human behavior suggest that people build an image of a process and that they learn in structures. The topic of metaphor-based learning is crucial in software psychology and human factors (8). Carroll et al. (9) found that a spatially presented problem obtained better performance and faster solution times than a temporal presented isomorph problem. Under both conditions the problem solving process was favored by graphically displayed problem structures.

The graphical presentation as an integrated part of the dialogue and as a support for its users has to be focused on user characteristics. They are chiefly related to mental operations user interfaces should be assimilated to. Norman (10) is postulating three points of view embedding how people make use of computer systems. The analysis leads to three related concepts: (a) the designer's view of the system - the conceptual model, (b) the image the system presents to the user - the system image, and (c) the model the user develops of the systems mediated to a large extent by the system image - the mental model. The mental model of the user should be functional and refer to the dialogue structure but not to the realisation of internal computer processes.

In this study we created a spatially represented image of the menu-hierarchy. This approaches more to an interpretation of "gestalt"-theoretical provenience than to a pure associative learning. The paradigm of associative learing means in relation to software design a close connection of menu alternatives to the following menu unit. It reduces the knowledge of the context of the dialogue structure and of the work-paths and complicates the handling of the dialogue. On the other hand, the structural and "gestalt" learning forms a mental representation of metaphoric character of the dialogue structure including the whole of elements. An isomorphic relationship between dialogue structure and mental representation is realised.

The experiment conducted but not finished, yet, investigates the question if permanent graphical presentation of the dialogue structure will increase learning and performance of unexperienced users handling the computer system. This on-line assistance, as defined by Sondheimer and Nelles (11), is expected to be compatible with the above considerations.

3.   EXPERIMENTAL SET-UP

3.1. Graphical editor

For our study we designed a graphical editor as an example for a highly interactive process. This tool provides facilities to generate and manipulate synthetic graphical data. Subjects are told to draw several diagrams on an electronical colour display. The subjects have a number of facilities at their disposal, for example to generate and modify picture components or to manage a picture data base and the appertaining directories.

The following basic functions have been implemented for the realisation of the graphical editor:

- Generation and modification of picture elements (text and symbols)
- Combination of basic elements to form complex picture components
- Combination of different components to form consistent images
- Processing of a picture data base (e.g., insertion, deletion, grouping).

The editor functions are arranged in a tree structure as indicated in figure 2.

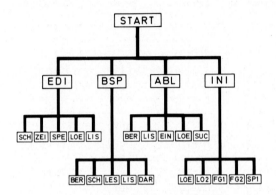

Figure 2: Hierarchical arrangement of dialogue functions

3.2. Menu realisation

A menu-driven interface was chosen as the form of man-computer dialogue where menus are arranged in a strictly hierarchical structure. This hierarchical structure is characterized by intermediate levels of breath and depth of menus as indicated in figure 2. This takes into account that menus have to be simple enough for easy and quick assimilation, and that, on the other hand, a deep menu organisation can lead to a loss of orientation of the users within a complex dialogue structure. Related options are semantically categorized and concentrated to facilitate acquisition.

The optimized hierarchical ordering of menus may be appropriate for the design of the user-computer interface in rather small and easy to survey dialogue systems. However, in more complex interactive systems, the number of nodes within this hierarchy becomes so large, that the implementation of a conventional menu technique is not effective. The increasing complexity will create major problems, especially for novices and and users with minimal training. This is mainly due to the fact that users might feel lost in nontransparent menu-driven systems and therefore might take excessively long to respond.

Figure 3 illustrates an arrangement of different menu fields. A response field is reserved below the various label fields. A "type-ahead" facility permits skilled operators to link responses and by-pass portions of the dialogue structure. The utilization of this capability requires an excellent knowledge of the dialogue architecture. Therefore the learning process has to be supported for an untrained user.

Bild-Speicher bearbeiten

Platz in der Bild-Ablage bereitstellen .... BER
Bilder in die Bild-Ablage schreiben .... SCH
Bilder aus der Bild-Ablage lesen .... LES
Bild-Komponenten der Bilder auflisten ..... LIS
Bilder auf dem Bildschirm darstellen ...... DAR

Eingabe: SCH_

Figure 3: Menu example with selected item "SCH"

As indicated before, the objective of our experiment is to investigate the effects of dialogue transparency on performance and learning of unexperienced user. Transparency is operationalized as the permanent graphical representation of the dialogue structure on an additional control monitor. The permanent presence of the system architecture marks additionally the actual position of the user within the system and suggests appropriate ways through the menu hierarchy. The graph which is generated according to the example illustrated in figure 4, is shown in the next diagram.

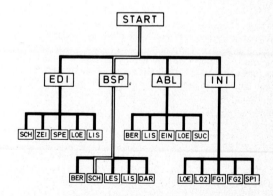

Figure 4: Control graph generated on an additional control monitor with highlighted pathway (START-BSP-SCH)

The actual navigation through the dialogue
structure – which was chosen in the menu "BSP"
by tying in the prompt "SCH" – is marked by a
colored pathway. Based on the previously indicated postulation of mental representation,
the hypothesis is that this additional information will help the user to keep track of the
current state (he knows <u>where</u> he is) and how
to navigate within the dialogue hierarchy (<u>how</u>
to get to another state).

3.3. Workstation

Figure 5 shows the experimental workstation
using three independent monitors. In a multi-
ple-window technique, the use of independent
windows permits the display of different
information categories, e.g., user data and
system control data.

In our approach, two colour TV monitors are
used, one for the display of the generated
picture and the other as control monitor for
the graphical representation of the dialogue
command structure. The subjects instruct the
computer system using the interactive terminal
with a keyborad as alphanumerical input
device.

Figure 5: Interactive workstation concept

4. DATA ANALYSIS

During all sessions a complete protocol of
subject's behavior was recorded by mapping
each subject's responses. Time was registered
for each command, each menu and for the whole
dialogue context. Separating the task section
from the dialogue, that means the performing
of the graphical editor, seemed to be reasonable. An example of a protocol chapter is
shown in figure 6.

The analysis of the dialogue system involved
the evaluation of an experimental comparison
of two alternatives. One presenting permanently the menu-hierarchy on the second TV monitor, the other not presenting this graphical
support. Time measuring has the advantage to
determine if an unusually large amount of time
was spent on a particular menu or command.

Additionally, deviation of the observed navigation to the optimal path, which is defined
as the shortest route to the desired function
or menu, represents a substantial measure of
performance. An expectation value for each
menu and each command can be performed regarding each point as a decision point. The analysis of the observed frequencies of specific
menus or commands point to communication problems.

duration	level 1	level 2	level 3
0.3	STRT		
2.6		BSP	
3.4			BER
9.2		BSP	
4.3			DAR
1.8		BSP	
1.2	STRT		
3.1		EDI	
2.7			ZEI
124.8		EDI	
2.4			SPE
6.4		EDI	
1.8			ZEI
63.5		EDI	
3.8			SPE
11.6		EDI	
3.7			LIS
4.2		EDI	
2.3	STRT		
3.1		BSP	
2.7			SCH
2.5		BSP	
9.1	STRT		

Figure 6: Protocol section of user
           activities

When having finished the experiments we expect
as result that the dialogue immanent support
which is realised as the permanently presented
menu-hierarchy will favor unexperienced users.
Interaction facility will increase and relevance of graphical presentation will diminish
when users become familiar with the system and
their cognitive representation of dialogue
structure has consolidated. Additionally,
navigation characteristics in the menu structure will represent resources for optimizing
the dialogue. The results of the actual
experimental investigation will be presented
at the conference.

REFERENCES

/1/ Thomas, J.C., and Carroll, J.M., The psychological study of design, Design Studies 1 (1979) 5-11.

/2/ Kaster, J., and Widdel, H., Grafische Unterstützung zur Selbsterklärungsfähigkeit eines Dialogsystems, in: Balzert, H. (ed.), Software-Ergonomie (Teubner, Stuttgart, 1983) 114-123.

/3/ Maass, S., Why systems transparency?, in: Green, T.R., Payne, S.J., and van de Veer, G.C. (eds.), The psychology of computer use (Academic Press, London, 1983) 19-28.

/4/ Thompson, D.A., Man-Computer system: toward balanced co-operation in intellectual activities, Proceedings: International Symposium on Man-Machine Systems (New York, 1969).

/5/ Hammond, N.V., Long, J.B., Clark, I.A., Barnard, P.J., and Morton, J., Documenting human-computer mismatch in the interactive system, Proceedings: Ninth International Symposium on Human Factors in Telecommunications (Holmdel, N.J., 1980) 17-24.

/6/ Savage, R.E., Habinek, J.K., and Barnhart, T.W., The design, simulation, and evaluation of a menu driven user interface, Proceedings: Human Factors in Computer Systems (Gaithersburg, Maryland, 1982) 36-40.

/7/ Snowberry, K., Parkinson, S.R., and Sisson, N., Computer display menus, Ergonomics 26(1983) 699-712.

/8/ Carroll, J.M., and Thomas, J.C., Metaphor and the cognitive representation of computing systems, IEEE Transactions on Systems, Man, and Cybernetics, 12 (1982) 107-116.

/9/ Carroll, J.M, Thomas, J.C., and Malhotra, A., Presentation and representation in design problem-solving, British Journal of Psychology, 71 (1980) 143-153.

/10/ Norman, D.A., Design principles for human- computer interfaces, ICS Report no. 8305, User Centered System Design (1983) 15-24.

/11/ Sondheimer, N.K., and Relles, N., Human factors and user-assistance in interactive computing systems: an introduction, IEEE Transactions on Systems, Man, and Cybernetics, SMC-12, 2 (1982) 102-107.

MONITOR. A SELF-ADAPTIVE USER INTERFACE

David Benyon

The design of a human-computer dialogue is widely recognised as being difficult, as it includes principles of graphics and information presentation underpinned by psychological factors such as closure and control over the system. This realisation has prompted the call for adaptive or self-adaptive user interfaces. Such systems need to maintain a model of the user and the dialogue so that the dialogue can be altered as users develop their skills.

MONITOR has been designed to provide a self-adaptive user interface. The system is flexible enough to cater for any dialogue, and a prototype system in the area of computer aided learning has been implemented. The prototype is seen as a contribution to the collection of research tools which are needed if a useable system is to be developed. The system is still unsophisticated in much of its operation but the design has proved itself to be a suitable and flexible representation of any problem which can be analysed along the user-task dimensions, and the feasibility of the system has been established.

1. Introduction

Any meaningful description of a computer system includes at least one human – the user. At any particular time the user is performing a specific task on the computer. This interaction between human and computer takes place in an environment and hence the Human-Computer Interaction consists of the three dimensions – User, Task and Environment.

In addition to such features as light, airiness, humidity, etc., the provision of documentation, education and training in the use of hardware and software effect the overall environment of the interaction. Damodaran and Eason[5] have emphasized the desirability of a complete "user support system" which would provide help and tutorial assistance and include a "local expert" who is highly knowledgable of the system. Maguire[12] also emphasizes the importance of this environment. However, the move towards more decentralised and personal computing makes it more difficult to maintain and hence the user becomes more isolated. Much of the user support system could be developed to accompany the software, but the problem arises of providing a level of support suitable for the user. A "HELP" system under the control of a system such as MONITOR would go some way to providing a suitable environment.

The User/Task analysis is presented by Moran[14] and others, particularly Shneiderman[18], Maguire[12] and James[11] Users are a heterogeneous group with differing levels of expertise, differing views of the system and varying degrees of frequency of computer use. Users are usually represented on an expert-novice continuum, but

it is often overlooked that an expert at one piece of software may be quite unfamiliar with another, hence this must be viewed in respect of each task performed. Moreover users do not occupy a static position on this continuum, but move along it as their expertise increases. The nature of the task changes as the user becomes more expert and empirical evidence suggests that users demand a faster response and more control over the system as their expertise develops.[12] Moran suggests that the user moves from a problem solving activity in the early stages of performing a task (characterised by a desire simply to get results) to a "routine cognitive skill" in the later stages (characterised by a desire for elegant or speedy solutions)[14] The outcome of this analysis is that the interaction must be flexible enough to provide for the changing desires of users.

The part of the system encountered most readily by users is the Human-computer dialogue (although the term "dialogue" must not be taken to imply a mutual understanding – this rarely, if ever, exists) and it is here that requirements differ most between expert and novice users. A novice user will require detailed help and hand-holding and will be unconcerned about response time; the novice will be content with a system-determined dialogue in the sense of Thimbleby.[20] The expert will require a user-determined dialogue and may be frustrated if the system does not perform well enough. Most users, of course, will require a dialogue somewhere between these two extremes. The problem is summed up by Maguire.[12] "Each specific application for an interactive situation is likely to consist of a unique combination of attributes which determines the nature of the dialogue required". How can we provide a

dialogue which adapts to different users performing different tasks at different times?

2.   The User Interface

Models of the User Interface have been developed
by several authors (e.g. Fitter[7], Edmonds[6] and
Innocent)[10] The definition of the interface varies
slightly between authors, but it is generally
agreed that it includes all points of contact
which the user has with the system. These may
be physical (e.g. input method or VDU design),
conceptual (e.g. the users view of how the hardware or software operates) or perceptual. It is
the perceptual and conceptual aspects of the
interface which concern us here.

In Edmonds' model (fig.1) a human designer
amends the interface according to data obtained
from a resident monitor module. Innocent goes
one step further in arguing that the interface
should be self-adaptive. The central part of
the intelligence is envisaged as a "frame type"
representation of the user - a "user model"
consisting of frames which are "user, system and
task dependent and have some correspondance with
user images in terms of their structure". He
suggests that the human designer/modifier in
Edmonds model could be replaced by an "expert"
system.

In short, the challange is to develop a piece of
software which will adapt the user interface
through controlling the dialogue and monitoring
the users performance.

It is important to see the user interface in the
context of the environment mentioned earlier.
The complete area of human-computer interaction
is shown in Fig.2. This specification has been
developed in another paper[2] and it is included

here in order to emphasize that we are dealing
only with the central part of a larger system.
The "workstation I/O" is the physical part of
the interface system, the "dialogue generator"
ensures a consistent and unambiguous format for
the dialogue and the "help" module provides the
user support. The "control" module activates
parts of the system as appropriate and "converter"
presents commands to the background system in a
suitable manner. The MONITOR system incorporates
the "user model", "expert modifier" and "monitor"
modules.

We have used the Innocent model as the basis
for the MONITOR system, but before specifying
it in detail, we need to consider how the user
and dialogue can be modelled.

Attempts to model the user have been made by
Rich[16] whose approach is to create an initial
model of the user by referring to a number of
predefined stereotypes. She defines a stereotype as "a collection of frequently occurring
characteristics" (p.339). In the case of a
dialogue, these are translated into allowable
tasks. The stereotype is incorporated into an
individual user model which is then refined in
the light of further information. In MONITOR
a stereotyped dialogue (a "script") is adapted
to the individual.

It has also been recognised that the user has a
conceptual image of the system which should be
made explicit. Carroll and Thomas[4] call this
the users metaphor. This philosophy has recently
been put into practice in the Xerox "Star" and
Apple "Lisa" systems. However, both of these
use the office metaphor to represent the
computer's operations and this will be quite
alien to many users. It follows that metaphors
should be available for different classes (or

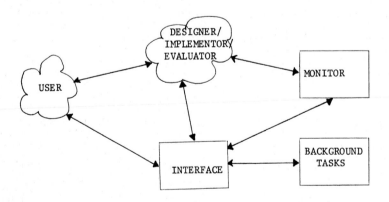

Fig 1. Edmonds' Model of user interface

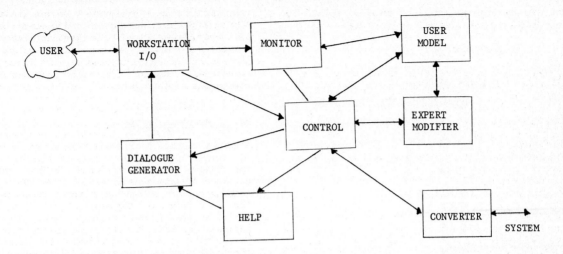

Fig.2. Components of a Knowledge Based Interface System (KBIS)

stereotypes) of users and possibly for different tasks as well. Whilst these ideas have been incorporated into the conceptual design of MONITOR, they have not been implemented as more research in this area is required.

The dialogue can usefully be represented as a transition network in which the nodes are points in the dialogue and the arcs are the allowable responses at each point. This representation has been recommended by several authors, and in particular the SYNICS system developed by Edmonds and Guest[18] is based on a transition network. More recently Alty[1] has shown how an algebra can be specified which assists in defining and controlling the dialogue.

The network representation provides a flexibility in the system because a node can be specified at any level which proves useful. Thus we can view tasks as nodes within the overall system and within each task each screen of information can be viewed as a node - each task then consists of a sub-network of nodes. Parts of the dialogue can then be enabled or disabled as required.

3. The Monitor System

The MONITOR system has been developed as an "expert" or knowledge-based system which will monitor, modify and maintain details of the User, the tasks performed, and the tasks available to the system. The design is applicable to any system as the tasks are defined at a level suitable to the system. A computer assisted training system has been used as the prototype, but this does not mean that this sort of system is particularly appropriate.

The claim that MONITOR is an expert system requires some justification. Buchanan[3] selects the three criteria utility, (high) performance and transparency as fundamental to an expert system, and Nau[15] argues that an explicit representation of knowledge is most important. Other authors point to the need to reason under uncertainty and to operate in a limited domain as principle features. Many of the earlier expert systems have been criticised for lacking this transparency and explicit knowledge representation(e.g. Stefik[19]) and so MONITOR has been designed in line with the architecture (adapted from Nau) as shown in fig.4. The prototype system developed does not meet the criterion of high performance, but otherwise it fulfills the requirements of an expert system.

MONITOR follows the architecture as shown in Fig. 3 using a combination of procedural and declaritive knowledge and maintaining an appropriate grain of knowledge through a system-defined hierarchy. The terms "frame" and "script" are used in line with Minsky[13] and Schank and Abelson[17] where a frame is a packet of data and procedures representing an event or object and a script represents a succession of events. A frame holds(or can obtain) various items of data and their values (sometimes providing default values) and terminates in an array of slots. For example, the remedial flag has a default

new tasks can be added through defining additional Task functions and the data stored against
each User can be extended without effecting
current processing. Before discussing the
implementation of the system we will examine a
machine and language independent model of the
components of the system.

3.1   Conceptual Design

A conceptual model of MONITOR is shown in fig.
4. Boxes represent the things of interest to
the system, and the relationship between these
entities are shown as diamonds. The "1" and "m"
should be read as "one" and "many" respectively;
thus each Task may have many Scripts, but each
Script relates to only a single Task. A dot
inside a box indicates that the entity must
participate in that relationship, but outside
indicates that the relationship is non-obliga-
tory. The notation follows Howe.[9] Thus a
Session must be related to a particular User,
but a User need not have participated in a
Session. The information content of each entity
is outlined below.

User - contains personal and computer-specific
knowledge of the User.
User-Task - contains performance details of each
Task attempted.
Task - contains details of each Task in the
system.
Session - records details of each attempt for
each User-Task.
Script - specifies allowable sequences of Nodes
for each Task.
Node - details of each Node
Text - actual text for display
Scheduled-dialogue - corresponds to the chosen
script.
Actual-dialogue - corresponds to a single session.
Stereotype - contains certain User knowledge
applicable to a category of User.
Metaphor - contains knowledge relating a
Stereotype to a Task.

3.2   Implementation

The conceptual model (fig.4) has been implemented
as a frame system written in INTERLISP. The
nature of LISP facilitates the frame representation as a frame can be implemented as a system
designed function or other s-expression. The
hierarchy implicit in the data model has been
represented as a nested list structure containing User, User-Task and Session details. Node
frames are supported by functions defining the
text content.

USER

The User frame is a nested list structure containing details about the User (name, occupation,
course (if occupation = student) and a remedial
assistance flag) and about the Tasks. Three

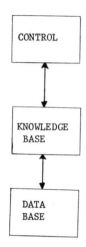

Fig.3. Architecture of a
knowledge based system

value of ∅ (meaning no remedial assistance is
required). The user frame has slots corresponding to the tasks and dialogues relating to that
user.

Knowledge of control is represented by the driver
program which allows the selection of tasks.
Finer grained knowledge of tasks is represented
by a program for each task which uses production
systems to select an appropriate dialogue. These
programs refer to the knowledge base.

The knowledge base maintains details of users,
tasks and the functioning of nodes. The users
performance is recorded and the user databse
modified by another rule-based program. Nodes
are frames linked into a network which facilitates their addition or modification. They are
formed into logical scripts. The knowledge base
thus consists of a mixture of procedures and
data.

The data base contains the data which it is
practical and desirable to separate from procedural knowledge. In our case this is the
details of users and the text content of the
nodes ,

Using the architecture outlined in fig.3 enables
the system to be easily modified or extended
as there is a high degree of program/data/
knowledge independence. The selection of Tasks
can be altered by amending the Modify program,

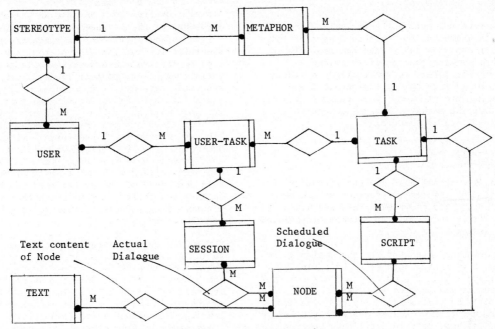

Fig.4.   MONITOR – conceptual design

lists contain the details of Tasks. The first
is a list of Tasks which the User is allowed to
undertake, the second is a list recording the
User's perfromance in those Tasks,and the third
is a list of Session details. Each element is
itself a list corresponding to the sequence of
nodes(i.e. the actual dialogue followed)in that
session. The first element of each session is
the session number.

Thus the LISP for the User frame is:-

CAR USER	user name
CADR USER	user's occupation
CADDR USER	user's course level or NONE
CADDDR USER	list of allowable Tasks
CADDDDR USER	list of task performance
CADDDDDR USER	list of Sessions
CAR (CADDDDDR USER)	Session number
CDR (CADDDDDR USER)	(first Node,2nd Node, etc....)
CADDDDDDR USER	remedial assistance flag

TASK

Tasks are functions which specify the conditions
under which each Script is selected. They contain knowledge of the parameters required by
each Script and control the updating of the
User frame when the Task is completed.

Scripts are functions containing knowledge about
a particular dialogue. They call Node frames
and direct the dialogue according to the value
returned by the Node frame. Scripts maintain
a record of the actual dialogue(i.e. Session)
and return this list as their value.

Node frames are functions containing knowledge
pertinent to the operation and information
presentation of that Node. For example Node
N1.4 requires the User to answer some questions
and contains knowledge about what to do under
the various circumstances - this may involve
providing extra assistance (enabling a sub-net),
suggested additional reading or proceeding
uninterrupted. Node frames call the text functions which simply contain the formatted text to
be displayed. This arrangement enables easy
modification of the text without disturbing the
logic of the Node.

For example, in the computer assisted training
prototype, the Task selects one of three Scripts
according to the type of User (M.Sc student,
HND student or Lecturer) and whether or not they
have attempted the task before. Each Script is
handed a number of parameters by the Task frame
which adapt the dialogue suitably (in particular
ones which indicate the number of taks attempts
to date, the level of the students course -
M.Sc students receive some additional information
- and that remedial assistance is required for

this user on certain topics).

The stereotype and metaphor entities have not yet been implemented, but must form part of the final system as inevitably they are implicit in any system. Making them explicit forces designers to consider the implications of their system. This first implementation has drawn attention to some problems, particularly the size and speed of the machine, but has demonstrated the possibilities of the design.

4. Conclusions

This paper has established the design and an implementation of the central section of a knowledge-based interface system. This has been achieved within the domain of a computer assisted training system.

Much attention has been paid to the design which was chosen principally because of it's flexibility and hence a high degree of program/knowledge/data independence has been achieved. This ensures that the system is easily modified and that knowledge is represented explicitly. Little attention has been paid to efficiency because the prototpye is not intended to be sophisticated enough to explore this area. Any Task could be defined in such a way as to fit into the MONITOR design. A Node is defined at a level which is suitable to the system at hand - in our example this was a section of the CAT material.

Similarly a Task may be defined at a logical level - in our example a Task corresponds nicely to a "unit" of the course. In a commercial environment, for example, a payroll clerk may have the following tasks defined; enter bonus payments, enter hours worked, enter days sick, print weekly analysis. Nodes would then correspond to the screen formats available. The User profile could easily be extended to include many other features - in the case of the payroll clerk these might be such things as security clearance, computer experience and so on.

Some of the desirable features of such a system have not been tackled. The user model is still rather crude and research needs to continue in order to establish what statistics should be gathered so that more sophisticated deductions can be made of the users performance. However, the design of the system can accommodate such extensions and indeed be used to experiment in this area.

A major problem with such a system is the amount of effort which must be expended in order to represent the dialogue in a suitable form. A MONITOR editing package would facilitate this, or it may be possible to use a dialogue generation system such as SYNICS[8] to provide output which would be picked up by MONITOR. The provision of easy authorisation is vital if the

system is to be readily usable.

A further problem - common to all expert systems - is the care which must be taken in defining the rules for modification of the user model i.e. to capture the expert's knowledge. In a real teaching environment factors such as the student's personal circumstances would be taken into account in deciding whether he can continue with the course. More expertise needs to be included to prevent the system from being too mechanistic in its decision making. At present only a few rules have been implemented to represent this knowledge, in a full version many tens or hundreds might be involved. The size and speed of the system need to be examined so that the interface remains in the background - controlling the user's interaction, but transparent to him.

MONITOR is currently the subject of a proposal to the Alvey Committee. In this further project, MONITOR will be enhanced to form the hub of an intelligent Computer Assisted Training system which will initially be implemented in 3 areas: statistical inference, learning Pascal and basic accounting. In all these areas, the interaction is characterised by infrequent computer users who require various levels of comprehension of the course material. The systems will be carefully monitored and in this way, knowledge of necessary user attributes can be gained. This protoyping approach to the development of knowledge-based interface systems is a vital part of research into this area as it provides a real world test bed and is flexible enough to accommodate any further theoretical findings.

Finally it is envisaged that the "Help" and "Coverter" modules of the completed KBIS will be KBIS's in themselves and thus the system will provide a suitable interaction environment as well as a personalised interface with a variety of tasks.

References

1.   Alty, J.L., Path Algebras: A Useful CAI/CAL Analysis Technique, Computer Education Vol.8.No.1 (1984) 5 - 13.

2.   Benyon, D.R., Justification and Outline of a Knowledgeable Interface System, M.Sc CCP paper, Dept. of Psychology, University of Warwick (Feb.1983).

3.   Buchanan, B.G. New Research on Expert Systems, Computer Jan.1982.

4.   Carroll J.M. and Thomas J.C., Metaphor and the cognitive representation of computer systems, IEEE SMC - 12,2 (1982)

5. Damodaran G. and Eason K., Design Pro-
    cedures for User Involvement and support,
    in Alty J.L. and Coombs M.J. (eds),
    Computer Skills and the User Interface
    (Academic Press, 1981).

6. Edmonds E.A., The Man-Computer Interface,
    International Journal of Man Machine
    Studies 16 (1982).

7. Fitter M., Towards more Natural Interface
    Systems, International Journal of Man
    Machine Studies 11 (1981).

8. Guest S.P., The Use of Software Tools
    for Dialogue Design in International
    Journal of Man Machine Studies 16(1982).

9. Howe D.R., Data Analysis for Data Base
    Design. (Edward Arnold 1983).

10. Innocent P.R., Towards Self-adaptive
    Interface Systems in International
    Journal of Man Machine Studies 16 (1982).

11. James E.B., The User Interface: How we
    may Compute, in Alty J.L. and Coombs M.J.,
    (eds), Computing Skills and the User
    Interface (Academic Press, 1981)

12. Maguire M., An evaluation of published
    recommendations on the design of man-
    machine systems., in International Journal
    of Man-Machine Studies. 16 (1982).

13. Minsky M., A Framework for Representing
    Knowledge in Winston P.H., Psychology of
    Computer Vision.

14. Moran T.P., An Applied Psychology of the
    User, Computer Surveys Vol 13 No.1(1981).

15. Nau D.S., Expert Computer Systems,Computer
    (Feb. 1983).

16. Rich E., User Modelling via Stereotypes;
    Cognitive Science Vol.3 No.2 (1980).

17. Schank R. and Abelson R., Scripts, Plans,
    Goals and Understanding (Lawrence Erbaulm
    1977).

18. Shneiderman B., Software Psychology
    (Winthrop 1981).

19. Stefik M., The Organization of Expert
    Systems, Xerox research paper VLSI⁻ 82-1,
    Palo Alto (1982).

20. Thimbleby H., Dialogue Determination,
    International Journal of Man Machine
    Studies 13 (1982).

Human-Computer Interaction — INTERACT '84 / B. Shackel (ed.)
Elsevier Science Publishers B.V. (North-Holland)
© IFIP, 1985

ADAPTIVE INTERFACES FOR NAIVE USERS - AN EXPERIMENTAL STUDY

H S Maskery

The HUSAT Research Centre
Loughborough University
Loughborough

An experimental study is described in which eighteen naive users used a developmental
adaptive interface. The subjects were divided into three groups who initially used a
statistical tool, either daily, weekly, or with a six weeks interval. A number of the
subjects progressed to using a graph-plotting tool. Conclusions included (1) that
weekly usage promoted better learning than daily usage, (2) that a break of five and
six weeks led to an initial decrement in performance followed by rapid improvement,
and (3) the change between dialogue styles must be predictable and consistent with the
system's previous behaviour.

INTRODUCTION

Adaptive interfaces are one solution to the
problem of building computer systems which can
be used by the wide variety of so-called naive
users. By providing different types of
dialogues, each of which is suited, for instance,
to different levels of experience or usage
patterns, a computer system should be more
acceptable to a larger range of users
(Shackel, 1969; Newman, 1978; Edmonds, 1981;
Bair, 1981; Eason, 1982).

The term 'naive' user covers a wide range of
computer users. Along with other terms such as
'casual', 'non-computer professional', and
'occasional', it is used to convey the attributes of a growing group of people who use the
computer as a tool. It is to these people that
adaptive interfaces offer the best chance of
realising the computer's potential to aid their
work.

Successful usage or full utilisation of a system
is dependent on many factors, the majority of
which interrelate. They can be conveniently
grouped under three main headings - the user,
the task, and the tool. The 'user' category
includes individual factors such as learning and
memory, motivation, previous computer experience,
position in organisation, degree of discretion,
attitudes and education. The category also
includes job-related factors such as pressure,
satisfaction, responsibility, work methods and
so on. The 'task' relates specifically to the
task which is being aided by the tool. Of importance in this category, are task-fit,
structure, frequency and the importance of that
task to the job. The 'tool' comprises those
factors which relate to the tool itself and
the system which provides it. This includes the
hardware and software aspects as well as accessibility, reliability, availability, support,
cost of usage, and training.

Thus it can be seen that the interface forms
but one part of a complex model of man-computer
interaction. This does not mean it is unimportant. Once the user has gained sufficient motivation to initially use the tool, it is the
interface which then allows the user to discover
whether the tool fits his task. Much has been
said in the human factors and computing literature about the attributes of a good interface
for naive users (Martin, 1973; Cuff, 1980;
Nickerson, 1981; Eason 1982). Many recommendations exist to guide the construction of such
dialogues and screens. There are also a multitude of 'horror' stories about the effects of a
bad interface or a mismatch between interface
and user. The immediate results can be non-use
or only partial use, and there can be long term
effects on the attitudes of those who experienced
the system, or gained 'second-hand' knowledge of
it.

ADAPTIVE INTERFACES

The interface is important in that it allows the
user and the computer to 'communicate'. There
are numerous papers which detail the characteristics and needs of naive users (Eason, 1979;
Cuff, 1980; Eason, 1982) and give guidelines to
match them to the different dialogue styles
(Martin, 1973; Eason, 1979; Hebditch, 1979).
The objective of this matching process, is to
create an interface which fits the user, allowing effective, efficient, beneficial, inter-
ference-free use of the tool.

With the increase in multi-user, multi-function
systems, and a growing awareness of the differing needs of different types of naive users, the
objective of matching interface to user is becoming more difficult. To avoid compromises
which may lead to non or partial usage, a number
of dialogue styles and levels must be available
at the interface. That interface must also be
able to change the dialogue styles according to
user changes. Only then will the interface fit
the user and not vice versa.

The achievement of 'adaptive interfaces' is
therefore a vital factor in meeting the variety
of human characteristics and needs. However,
before it can be achieved there are a number of
serious human factors' problems which must be
overcome.

RATIONALE FOR EXPERIMENT

Adaptive interfaces offer a solution to the
problems of providing the optimum user-interface
match for multi-user, or multi-facility systems.
Although many guidelines and recommendations
exist to aid designer of 'user-friendly' systems,
there is very little reported research on adaptive interfaces. It was decided therefore to
carry out an exploratory experiment which would
give insights into the problems of naive users
when faced by an adaptive interface. This would
then indicate the direction of future research.

OBJECTIVES

The main aim of the experiment was to study the
progress of naive users when interacting with a
computer based tool via an adaptive interface.
Particular interest was paid to the learning
aspects, the user's difficulties (if any), and
the reaction of the user to the adaptive interface.

Secondary objectives were to identify the more
specific aspects of transfer of learning both
between different tools interfaced by the same
adaptive interface. The effects of frequency of
use, and change in support needs were also of
important interest.

THE SYSTEM

The adaptive interface used in the experiment
was part of a suite of programs written specifically for 'naive' users. This package, called
Dialog, was available to staff and students at
Loughborough University - (Negus et al). It
offered a variety of statistical, mathematical,
and graph-plotting tools.

The interface was based on the 'instruction and
response' dialogue style (Hebditch, 1979), which
is considered 'suitable for less frequent users
of a system'. The adaptiveness was based on
three levels of the dialogue style. Using
Miller and Thomas' (1977) proposed classifi-
fation scheme, the three levels were

    1. System leads, user has forced choice
    2. System leads, user has free choice
    3. User leads, user has free choice

Detailed on-line help was available at all
levels.

Allocation to levels 1 and 3 was done by the
system following the users' responses to questions often calling-up the particular tool to be
used. Level 2 was reached after the user had

completed a task at Level 1 and typed in 'TERSE'
following instructions from the computer. When
users had completed a session at Level 3, the
system informed them of how to avoid the initial
questioning and to start immediately at Level 3.

Once the user was allocated to either the 'system
leads' or the 'user leads' levels, there was no
way of changing between the two styles. The
system alerted new users of level 3 that a change
had been made.

THE EXPERIMENT

Three experimental conditions were created using
the amount of usage and frequency of use as independent variables (See Figure 1). This was to
represent three types of naive user.

Condition	Amount of Usage (Sessions)	Frequency Interval	User Type
A	2	6 Weeks	Occasional
B	6	1 week	Inter-mittent
C	6	daily and 5 weeks	frequent then occasional

Figure 1. Experimental Conditions

Eighteen subjects who met the following conditions were used:

   - equal numbers of male and female
   - equal representation from each year of
      students
   - they were not studying for computer sciences,
      mathematics or statistics degree
   - they had a basic knowledge of descriptive
      statistics
   - they had not used Dialog before
   - they were not touch typists.

Each session followed a similar pattern and lasted approximately 30 minutes. The login procedure was completed before the subject arrived,
and the Dialog tool to be used was called up.
The subject then answered the systems questions
and completed the simple statistic problems
given. Those subjects who used level 3, were
given the system's information about providing
the initial questions. These subjects were then
told how to call-up the tool at the next session.
Three sets of statistics problems were used.
Starting with simple calculation of single
statistics, they moved to calculation of multiple
statistics, and finally had to edit some of the
data between calculations. When subjects had
completed the statistical problems, they were
transferred to a graph-plotting tool.

The subjects were told they may ask questions
providing they were not about actually using the

tool. If they experienced problems of this sort, it was suggested that they should first try the on-line help available. It this was not satisfactory, they could then ask the experimenter for help. Before the start of the first session, the subjects were briefly familiarised with the terminal.

The approach used in this experiment was subject to a number of problems. This is to be expected with a preliminary study and due allowance was made in interpreting the result.

Naive users do not generally use computer-based tools under the controlled conditions of a laboratory experiment. To reduce the effects, either positive or negative, of having subjects 'performance' tasks to order, it was decided to simulate a 'possible' working environment (i.e. the terminal was not placed on its own in an 'experimental cubicle'). There were also differences in the system response time due to the 'shared' nature of the system. These introduced unmeasurable differences, between sessions, the effect of which is not known, but the realism gained by them was felt to outweigh the disadvantages.

The second and possibly more important, potential source of distortion to the results, was attributable to the experimenter's presence throughout each session. It could have affected the subjects' confidence and speed with which they 'felt at ease' with the situation. It could also have caused subjects to be more or less 'adventurous' in their use of the tool. Finally, the experimenters' presence and ability to give help, may have kept a few subjects sitting in front of the terminal when they might otherwise have given up.

A large amount of data was collected, including time, errors, facilities use, dialogue level, and help needs.

RESULTS

Condition	System-led dialogue (means)			User-led dialogue (means)		
	Time (secs)	Conceptual errors	Calls for help	Time (Secs)	Conceptual errors	Calls for help
B	489	2.3	4.5	570	2.6	5.6
C	271	.16	1.6	661	3	9.5

Figure 3. Effects of Change between System-led dialogues and User-led dialogues (comparison with previous session to change)

		Condition		
		A	B	C
Session 1	System-led	6	6	6
	User-led	-	-	-
	express	-	-	-
Session 2	System-led	5	2	5
	User-led	1	4	1
	express	-	-	-
Session 3	System-led	-	1	2
	User-led	-	5	4
	express	-	-	-
Session 4	System-led	-	1	2
	User-led	-	2	3
	express	-	2	1
Session 5	System-led	-	-	-
	User-led	-	2	3
	express	-	4	3
Session 6	System-led	-	-	2
	User-led	-	-	4
	express	-	6	-

Figure 4. Number of users using each dialogue (excluding the graph plotting tool)

Conditon	Session 1		Session 2		Session 3	
	No of users	No of problems	No of users	No of problems	No of users	No of problems
A	6	3-5	5	1-3	-	-
B	6	1-6	2	1	1	3*
C	6	4-9	5	1-4	2	1

* Mistake at call-up

Figure 2. Number of problems completed before changing to dialogue level 2.

		Session 1	Session 2	Session 3
Dialogue level	No of Users	9	4	1
	System Led	8	–	1 (Mistake)
	User Led	1	2	–
	Express	–	2	–

Figure 5.   Users Choice of dialogues for each
            session with Graph-plotting Tool.
            (not including the sixth session of
            Condition C)

	Session 5 (secs)	Session 6 (secs)
Condition B	215	167
Condition C	185	335

Figure 6.   Time to complete first problem of
            session

DISCUSSION OF EXPERIMENTAL RESULTS

This paper presents some of the specific findings
from the study. For a full account of the
experiment and results see Maskery, 1981. As
this was a preliminary study, the discussion and
conclusions are based on the trends shown by the
data rather than statistical significance. For
this reason, little objective data has been
presented in this paper.

ADAPTIVE INTERFACES

The transfer between dialogue levels is one of
the key points in the design of an adaptive
interface. This experiment highlighted the user
difficulties which occur when an interface
changes or does something unexpected. The change
between levels 1 and 2 was accomplished by all
subjects. Some subjects in session 1 took much
longer before changing to level 2 (5 problems)
than others (1 problem) (see Figure 2). This
was to be expected. In later sessions subjects still using the system-led dialogues, made
the change much faster, i.e. after 1 problem.

The change between the system-led dialogues to
the user-led dialogue proved too great for easy
user-transference. Performance times, calls for
help, and error rates increased beyond that which
could be expected for the first problem of each
session (see Figure 3). The main impression that
users gave, was that they were dealing with something completely different. The majority of
users were not expecting the change, and were
not aware of what had caused the change.

However, it was also apparent from the learning
curves, that the majority of users learnt to
control the user-led dialogues quicker than the
system-led dialogues. Whilst part of this would
be due to basic familiarisation with the terminal
and its operation, this did not fully account
for the improvement. User comments suggested
the fact that previous experience with the tool
had been beneficial.

It took at least three sessions before users became aware of the relevance of the systems'
initial questions. When the role of these
questions was realised, the users made deliberate
decisions about which dialogue level they wanted
to use. This was particularly apparent in those
less confident in their ability to use the tool,
and in those subjects who had a five week interval following daily usage between the fifth and
last session.

In this particular experiment, the users would
have felt less unsettled if they had known what
was happening to the interface and why. In
general, naive users do not want to know technical details. In this case, if the users had
known how they got into level 3, and what the
difference was, the confusion would have been
less, and frustrating mistakes in answering the
system's questions in future sessions would have
been avoided. However, this is not the answer
for adaptive interfaces in the future.

FREQUENCY OF USE

Frequency of usage was a very important factor
in determining subject's ability by the end of
the experiment. The two groups who completed
six sessions, can be considered as representing
massed and spaced usage.

Those subjects who used the tool at weekly intervals showed better performance, less disturbance when errors occurred and decreasing refamiliarisation times, than did those using the
tool daily. This difference in and quality of
learning between the massed and spaced subjects,
is supported by Welford (1968) writing about the
acquistion of skill. Further work on this aspect
is particularly important as it has implications
for computer-based tools usage, and the training
given when implementing new technology.

In addition to the above beneficial effects of
spaced usage, the subjects appeared to have
greater confidence in their ability. They were
quicker to change to level 3 than did those in
daily contact with the tool (see Figure 4).
This may have been because the longer interval
allowed them time to think back over the first
session and internalise what occurred. When
faced by the system's questions at the second
session they had a clearer mental image of the
tool and therefore did not want the detailed
prompting offered by the system. They did not
know they would be allocated to level 3.

Those in daily contact with the tool did not change to level 3 until the third or fourth session. It was also noticeable from their performance decrement and increased calls for help, that they were less able to cope with the transition to level 3 than the weekly subjects. It is possible that by changing in later sessions, the learning associated with, and reliance on the system led levels had become more established and therefore caused more difficulties at changeover.

GENERAL ASPECTS OF USER-TOOL INTERACTION

When the subjects had completed the statistical problems, they were transferred to a graph-plotting tool. All but one of the nine subjects who reached this point started using the new tool with the system-led dialogue (see Figure 5). Of the four weekly subjects who transferred during either the fourth or fifth session, all chose the user-led dialogue for their next session. Performance comparisons are not possible between the two tools, other than that there was less reliance on the experimenter's help and more on the computers' help, and that familiarisation with the new tool was quicker than for the first tool. This suggests that experience of the first tool proved beneficial to subjects using a second, similar tool. The transfer between tools was accomplished with less disruption to task completion, than earlier transferances between dialogue levels. In addition subjects already had knowledge of the dialogue levels and how they were allocated to them, so changes between the levels were achieved more easily than before.

Long breaks between usage can be expected with some some computer-based tools. It was apparent from the experiment, that breaks of five or six weeks led to a longer refamiliarisation time than that of a week's break (see Figure 6). A break of a week or less seemed to have little effect especially in the latter half of the experiment as familiarity and experience grew. The weekly and daily subjects showed decreasing refamiliarisation times in later sessions.

With the breaks of five or six weeks, the subjects retained some memory of the tool. They felt that they might not remember the details. The refamiliarisation time was longer than for previous sessions during the period of intensive usage. However, in common with those subjects who only used the tool twice, the performance improved more rapidly than that of the first session, and a continuation of improvement was then shown.

The length of break also affected the subject's confidence in their ability to use the interface. Of the subjects who returned to the tool five weeks after the daily sessions, four chose to use the system-led dialogues (see Figure 4). All six of these subjects had previously been using the user-led dialogues. There was a strong possibility that these four users had only wanted to be reminded of the tool and would then have

preferred to take control of the interaction again. This did not appear possible with Dialog, although the system-led dialogues would have responded to the user taking control.

Finally, it was noticed that the support needs changed during the experimental period. Initially, the computer's on-line help was not able to aid the users when in difficulty. The experimenter was therefore necessary to provide help. On occasions, the on-line help got the user into greater difficulties. If the experimenter had not been there, one or two of the subjects would have walked out!

As the subjects's knowledge of the system and familiarity with the jargon increased, the on-line help proved more useful. The experimenter was then looked to, to provide reassurance that the subject was doing "the right thing" (this was not given). Towards the end of the experiment very little support was needed, either computer-based or human.

EVIDENCE RELATING TO USER FRIENDLY GUIDELINES

There have been many papers and books published which give guidelines to designers of naive-user systems. A number of these guidelines were supported by evidence from this experiment.

The adaptive interface poses a dilemma to the designer because of its ability to change. One of the strongest recommendations concerns the need for consistency and predictability in the computers' responses and actions (e.g. Gaines and Facey, 1975; Dzidaetal, 1978; Cuff, 1980; Nickerson, 1981). It was apparent from the subjects that Dialog did not meet this requirement. Some users experienced relatively large problems when the dialogue levels changed as it was unexpected. They did not know what they had done to cause this to happen. In one or two cases, this change was very unsettling and could possibly have led to a non-use situation in the 'real' world.

A minimum amount of keyboard use is recommended for naive users unlikely to have typing skills. (e.g. Dzidaetal, 1978; Cuff, 1980; Eason, 1982) This was supported by the levels of typing mistakes recorded, especially during the early sessions. Use of upper case characters in particular, caused some problems in those unused to using the 'shift' key (some subjects did not know how to obtain upper case characters). On occasions, typing mistakes landed the subject into greater difficulties as they spent time trying to work out what had gone wrong and what they should do about it. This typing problem was partially compounded by the unhelpful error messages. Several authors recommend the use of helpful and graded error messages so that first time users are not left in confusion and experienced users are not frustrated by redundant information (e.g. Kennedy, 1974).

Error tolerance is considered (e.g. Dzida, 1978; Cuff, 1980) one way of approaching the problem of typing mistakes. Dialog was not error tolerant and a great deal of frustration was caused as subjects had to retype, and retype, commands. An inexperienced typist is not capable of error-free typing, and the subjects were usually unaware of having made mistakes. The level of error tolerance allowable is difficult to determine; too much and the users will not be 'disciplined' to accuracy, with an increase in the potential for errors in data entered an outcome; too little tolerance and the user experiences frustration and increased likelihood of making further mistakes.

Cuff, (1980), makes reference to the naive users' limited ability to retain details of the interaction. This is supported to an extent by the experiment. The five or six weeks break was long enough for most users to feel they could not remember the details of the tool. However, refreshment of memory did not take long. Longer breaks may lead to greater memory loss with correspondingly longer refamiliarisation times. From users comments, it would appear that they would have preferred to take control of the interaction once they had refreshed their memory of the tool. This would have allowed them to achieve the preformance levels and ease of use which they had experienced before the break. Dialog, by not allowing this transferance, and the user's incomplete mental image of the interface structure, combined, to cause some degree of frustration to these users.

CONCLUSIONS

There are a number of interesting conclusions to be drawn from this study.

1. Transfer between system-led dialogues was easy for all subjects. Transfer between the system-led and user-led dialogues was much more difficult.

2. The relevance of the tool's initial questions (for dialogue allocation purposes) was not realised by subjects until at least the third session.

3. Not enough information was given to the user to explain what was happening to the interface. An easier transition between system and user-led dialogues was needed, rather than an increase in the amount of information given to the user.

4. Frequency of use was important in determining the user's ability by the end of the experiment. Weekly sessions rather than daily sessions created a better environment for learning.

5. Those subjects who had daily sessions, changed to user-led dialogues, later than those with weekly sessions. Daily users also experienced greater difficulties making the transition.

6. Use of the statistical tool proved beneficial when users changed to using a graph-plotting tool.

7. Breaks of five to six weeks led to a degradation of the subject's confidence to use the tool. The majority of users chose system-led dialogues following the five or six weeks break.

8. Support needs changed during the period of the experiment. Initially, the experimenter was a more useful source of help than the computer. By the end of the experiment, subjects were able to make use of the computer help.

9. Strong support was shown for the userfriendly recommendation of providing consistent and predictable interfaces.

10. High rates of typing errors were shown during initial sessions. This supports the need for minimum amounts of keying, and non-use of upper case characters.

11. Error tolerance to typing mistakes may help reduce the frustration and confusion caused in the inexperienced typist, naive user. It may lead to problems with accuracy in data entry.

ACKNOWLEDGEMENTS

I would like to acknowledge the large amount of help received from Dr Ken Eason, Nick Dawe, Sue Pomfrett, and HUSAT.

REFERENCES

1. Shackel, B, Man-Computer Interaction. The Contribution of the Human Sciences, Ergonomics, 12. 4 (1969) 485-500.

2. Edmonds, E., Adaptive Man-Computer Interfaces. In Coombes (ed.), 'Computing Skills and Adaptive Systems', (Academic Press).

3. Newman, I.A., Personalised user interfaces to computer systems. Eurocomp 1978, 473-486.

4. Bair, J.H., Automated Office System Design: Problems and Principles. Nat. Telecomm. Conference on Innovative Tecomm. - key to the Future., I.E.E.E., 1981.

4. Eason, K.D., Patterns of Acceptability: Problems and Solutions. HUSAT memo. No. 262 (1982), Department of Human Sciences, Loughborough University.

5. Martin, J., The Design of Man-Computer Dialogues (Prentice Hall, 1973).

6. Cuff, R.N., On Casual Users. International
    Journal of Man-Machine Studies, 12, (1980)
    163-187.

7. Nickerson, R.S., Why interactive computer
    systems are sometimes not used by people
    who might benefit for them. International
    Journal of Man-Machine Studies, 15, (1981)
    469-483.

8. Eason, K.D., A Comparative Analysis of the
    Needs of Computer Users. HUSAT memo.
    no. 186, (1979) Department of Human Sciences,
    Loughborough University.

9. Hebditch, D., Design of Dialogues for Inter-
    active Commercial Applications. Infotech
    State of the Art Report, 2, (1979)
    171-192.

10. Miller, L.A. and Thomas, J.C. Jr., Be-
    havioural issues in the use of interactive
    systems. International Journal of Man-
    Machine Studies, 9, (1977), 509-536.

11. Maskery, H.S., A Pilot Study to Investigate
    Factors Relating to the Learning and use of
    an Adaptive, Dedicated Computer Interface.
    B.Sc. Final Year Dissertation, Department of
    Human Science, Loughborough University,
    (May 1981).

12. Welford, A.T., Fundamentals of Skill.
    (Methuen and Co. Ltd., London, 1968).

13. Gaines, B.R. and Facey, P.V., Some Experi-
    ence in Interactive System Development and
    Application. Proc. I.E.E.E., 63, (1975)
    894-911.

14. Dzida, W., Herda, S. and Itzfeldt, W.D.,
    User-Perceived Quality of Interactive
    Systems. Compcom (1978) February 28 to
    March 3, San Francisco.

Human-Computer Interaction – INTERACT '84 / B. Shackel (ed.)
Elsevier Science Publishers B.V. (North-Holland)
IFIP, 1985

USE OF PATH ALGEBRAS IN AN INTERACTIVE ADAPTIVE DIALOGUE SYSTEM

J.L. Alty

Department of Computer Science,
University of Strathclyde,
Glasgow   G1   1XH

The CONNECT system - an adaptable dialogue delivery vehicle
- is briefly described.   The system casts interactive
dialogues in the form of a transition network.   Adaptability
is achieved through a production system which monitors user
transitions in the network and thereby enables or disables
transitions in the network.   A multilayered network
representation technique is described and an example of use
providing access to the CP/M operating system is outlined.
Some preliminary user experience of automatic adaptation is
reported.   The importance of the path algebra approach is
emphasised.

1.   Separation of Dialogue and Tasks

It is now generally accepted that separation
of the dialogue and task aspects of an interactive system is a desired objective [1].   Not
only can the resulting system be easily changed
as a result of user experience, but monitoring
can be effected and different views of the
system presented to users with differing
requirements.   Above all, such separation is
essential if truly adaptable interfaces are to
be constructed.

Systems constructed with a task-dialogue
separation architecture may be though of either
as interactive programming systems or as
dialogue delivery vehicles.   In the former
case the designer specifies the dialogue and
constructs the tasks.   He is essentially
programming the interface.   In the latter case
he constructs a front-end dialogue system onto
an existing application task.   The application
is not changed in any way but a richer dialogue
is constructed which is easier to modify, can
be monitored and can adapt to differing user
requirements.

There is however another important reason for
dialogue-task separation.   Systems constructed
in this way are amenable to analysis and may
form bases for interactive interface
specification.   Tools are urgently needed to
assist interactive designers not only in
specifying the interface but also in checking
its correctness and effectiveness.   The
approach presented in this paper could in our
view lay the foundations for a dialogue
specification and analysis tool.

Two common representation systems used for
dialogues are transition networks and
production rules.   Networks have been used in
such systems as SYNICS [2], STAG [3] and

CONNECT [4].   Networks have been used
to model concepts in a Computer Aided
Instruction system [5].   The production rule
approach has been used in other approaches [6],
[7].   Each approach has its advantages and
its drawbacks.   Networks are easily understood
by designers [8].   Furthermore they are
amenable to analysis by graph theory.   On the
otherhand they tend to be large and inflexible.
Production Rules are more versatile but are
difficult to check for correctness and cannot
be easily subject to theoretical analysis.

2.   The CONNECT System

In the CONNECT system we decided to use a network representation for the dialogue but to
allow the topology of the network to be changed
(during the interaction) via a production
system which monitors the user interaction
thereby enabling a degree of adapability to be
achieved [9],[10].   We then use graph theory
as an aid to dialogue design and to assist the
production system with its topology alteration
decisions.   An overview of the system is given
in Figure 1 below.

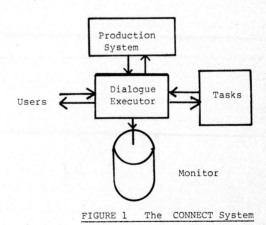

FIGURE 1   The CONNECT System

In the absence of a well defined user model we
use previous trajectories on the arcs as an
artifact of it.   These path fragments are very
important and constitute the major elements of
the IF parts of the production rules.

3.   Path Algebras

The networks are analysed using a technique
known as path algebras.[11].[12]   The technique
is discussed extensively elsewhere [9],[10] but
essentially a path algebra consists of

(a)   a set of labels for the network arcs
(b)   two operations called Join (V) and Dot (.)
        which respectively generate composite
        labels for alternative arcs and arc
        sequences respectively.
(c)   a zero element Φ and a unit element e
        defined respectively as

$$e.x = x = x.e \quad (e)$$
$$\Phi.x = \Phi \quad \Phi \ V \ x = x \quad (\Phi)$$

The label set and operations are chosen to solve
problems of interest.   Once chosen the
Adjacency matrix A is constructed using the label
set.   Matrices formed from the label set are in
fact elements of the algebra and can thus be
DOTted and JOINed.   Repeated DOTting forms
powers of the Adjacency matrix A^2, A^3 .... A^n
etc. which provide information about all paths
of order 2, 3 .... n in the network.

Algebras can be used to determine labelled paths,
steplengths, to separate nets into appropriate
subnets, identify loops, and to compute the
value of variables or functions over traversals
on the net.   This latter facility could be
particularly useful for specification checking
and will be discussed in more detail later in
this paper.

4.   Adaptability

As has already been stated, adaptability is
achieved by altering the topology of the dialogue
network.   In the extreme case this could
involve creating connections between existing
nodes or even new nodes.   However in order to
preserve the advantages of graphical analysis
and specification checking, and to minimise
complexity, we do not allow addition of arcs or
the creation of new nodes.   All options are
included in the network at the outset and
adaptability consists of opening or closing
existing arcs.   Furthermore, only certain arcs
(specified at the design stage) can be altered.

A dialogue network in reality consists of a set
of parallel networks, each providing a particular
representation or interface to the user.   Only
arcs which cause transitions between different
representations can be opened or closed.   A
typical arrangement is shown in Figure 2.

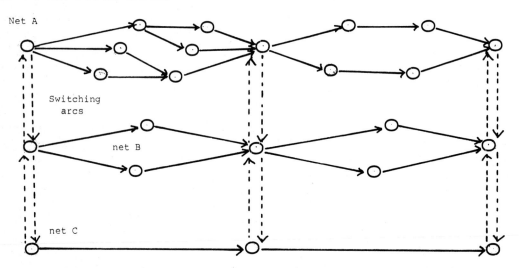

FIGURE 2   Network Layers

The multiple join of successive powers of A
usually exhibits Closure at some power

i.e. $$\bigvee_{K=0}^{n} A^K = \bigvee_{K=0}^{n+1} A^{K+1}$$

The closure matrix provides important information
about the whole network.

If the parallel network nodes are numbered within
discrete bounds, the adjacency matrix contains
the different networks about its diagonal.   The
off diagonal matrices are the switching matrices
between nets often, by carefully numbering, the
switching matrices can be made diagonal.   The
closure matrix can be computed from the
individual matrices which make up the adjacency
matrix [10] thus simplifying processing.   A
partitioning of the matrix for Figure 2 is shown
overleaf (Figure 3)

FIGURE 3 Adjacency Matrix for layered net

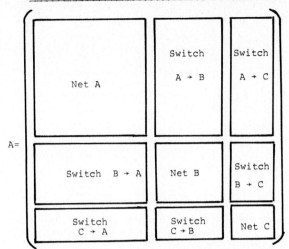

The production system controlling adaptability therefore alters the contents of the switching matrices depending upon past arc transitions and other user information of relevance.   Figure 4 below shows a two-level network which interfaces users to the operating system CP/M and provides two levels of representation.   The lowest level (Net C) looks identical to normal CP/M.   Net B however provides a help screen for selecting a command.   It then drives the user through a series of menu screens to build up the appropriate command.   It finally displays the result with additional information to assist the user.

Thus the user can be running simultaneously in different network levels for different commands. He may be competent in say, ERA and STAT so these commands will use net C, but he may be unsure of PIP so this command will operate in net B.   A series of successful users of PIP in net B will also fire the production rule and switch the user to net C.   The net will therefore automatically adapt.   Note the use of the common task between the networks.   The task knows which network has called it and always returns to it.   Nodes 1 and 5 will also use a common screen for display (actually just the CP/M prompt).

5.   User Experience

One key issue in adaptability is whether systems should be allowed to automatically adapt as a result of user activity.   It could be argued that such an adaptability will only serve to confuse the user's model of the system.   Even worse, the adaptability of users is well known and the user may begin adapting to the system whilst the system is trying to adapt to him. This has been described as "hunting" and is a common phenomenon in engineering design.   We have examined users interacting with our CP/M system.   As yet we have not collected enough statistics, or sampled enough users to draw any definite conclusions.   However some useful pointers already seem to be indicated.   Firstly users do get confused if the system begins to adapt particularly if this is a result of a mistake which the user knows that he has made (i.e. a simple typing error recognised after pressing return).   In such situations

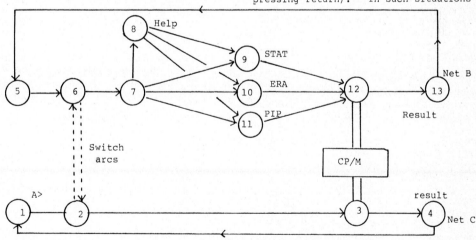

FIGURE 4   A Two-Layered CP/M Net

The two nets are connected by the switching arcs shown.   These arcs are enabled/disabled   at the switch nodes depending on the success of the command.   The production rules are of the form

IF at node 13 AND Command = STAT AND STATERR = 0
THEN enable switch at node 6 to net C, node 2

adaptability can be very irritating and frustrating with comments like "not that again. I don't want to be helped!"   On the other hand users with genuine difficulties appreciated the automatic provision of additional help particularly when they had found a reasonable model of the characteristics of adaptation.   It would seem that just as a good consistent simple model of the operation is required for naive users, so an equally simple model of the adaptation software of the interface is required. This implies that there should be few switching nodes at well defined logical switch points and bears out our original design philosophy that switching should be severely limited.

6.   Constructing the Networks

A key issue in setting up networks of the type we have described is how are the networks actually designed.   What underlying principles should be used to generate the set of parallel nets?   Certainly the idea of parallel representations is an attractive one, but what principles should govern the content of the different levels?   What is needed is an over-all view of the interaction.

We expect that some form of Command Language Grammar (CLG) similar to that proposed by Moran [13] could yield the structure of the different layers.   As stated in Moran's paper "to design the user interface of a system is to design the user's model", and a logical extension of this would be "to design an adaptable user interface is to design a set of possible user models". CLG describes the user interface by successively defining the conceptual, communication and physical components of the interface, each level being a refinement of the previous level .
These are in turn extended to embrace the Task, Semantic, Syntactic, Interaction, Spacial layout and device levels.   Our network levels would almost certainly be derived at the Task and Semantic levels.

Using CLC in conjunction with a path algebra approach could provide very powerful tools for man-machine interface design.

REFERENCES

[1]   Edmonds, E.A., The man-computer interface : note on concepts and design, Int.J.Man-Mach Studies 16 (1982), 231-236

[2]   Edmonds, E.A., Adaptive man-computer inter-faces, in Coombs, M.J. and Alty, J.L. (eds), Computing Skills and the User Interface (Academic Press, London 1981)

[3]   Bateman, R.F., A translator to encourage user modifiable man-machine dialogue, in Sime, M.E., and Coombs, M.J. (eds) Designing for Human-Computer Communications (Academic Press, London 1983)

[4]   Alty, J.L., Path Algebras : A useful CAI/CAL analysis technique, in Selected Proceedings from the Computer Assisted Learning 83 Symposium, P.R. Smith (ed.), (Pergamon Press, Oxford 1984), 5-13.

[5]   Feyock, S., Transition diagram-based CAI/ Help system, Int.J. Man-Machine Studies 9 (1977), 339-413.

[6]   Hopgood, F.R.A. and Duce, D.A. A production system approach to interactive program design, in Guedi, R.A., Tenhagen P.J.W., Hopgood, F.R.A., Tucker, H.A. and Duce, D.A. (eds), Methodology of Inter-action, (North Holland, Amsterdam 1980) 247-264.

[7]   Waterman, D.A. A rule-based approach to knowledge acquisition for man-machine interface programs, Int.J.Man-Mach.Studies 10 (1978), 693-711.

[8]   Guest, S.P., The use of software tools for dialogue design, Int.J.Man-Mach.Studies 16 (1982), 263-285

[9[Alty, J.L., The application of path algebras to interactive dialogue design, Research report No. 131 (University of Strathclyde, department of Computer Science). To be published in the Journal of Behavioural and Information Technology

[10]   Alty, J.L., The microcomputer and User friendly systems, Research Report No.134 (University of Strathclyde, department of Computer Science). To be published in the Journal of Microcomputer Applications.

[11]   Carre, B.A., An algebra for network routing problems, J.Inst.Maths Applic. 7, (1971), 273-294

[12]   Backhouse, R.C. and Carre, B.A., Regular algebra applied to path finding problems J.Inst.Maths.Applic. 15 (1975), 161-186

[13]   Moran, T.P., The Command Language Grammar, a representation for the user interface of interactive computer systems, Int.J. Man-Mach.Studies 15 (1981), 3-50

PERSONALISING THE SOFTWARE INTERFACE

ROBERTO SASSO

Oxford University Computing Laboratory
Programming Research Group

Humans communicate with (application) programs through a software (or logical) interface. We believe there should be a common framework shared by the interfaces of these interactive systems. A model of interaction is presented together with a formal specification using a notation based on set-theory. The implementation of this model allows users to interact with their system in a uniform and consistent way not only to make use of the facilities provided but also to "personalise it", that is, to redefine the external appearance of the system in order to suit their personal needs and desires.

Introduction

In our research project we are mostly concerned with the engineering aspects of building software interfaces. We are interested in interactive systems used by a large community of users for a wide variety of purposes. We recognise the individuality of human beings, the natural limitation of our short term memory, and, most importantly, the need to minimise the overhead cost (in time and effort) incurred in using interactive systems.

We have undertaken to build an adaptable software interface that demands minimum intellectual effort from its users. Therefore it must consist of a very small set of primitive operations, it must be the same for all their applications, it must offer the application's facilities in the amount and form required by each user, and adaptations of the interface must require no extra effort. In other words, the interface must not only be user and application independent but it must also be based on a few simple concepts.

The interaction between application programs and human users can, and has many times, been improved by advancements in the hardware (or physical) interface. Our claim is that our software (or logical) interface improves the interaction between users and their applications –for any available hardware– because:

- the system appears smaller, simpler and less demanding (friendlier system)
- due to the personalised appearance of the system, the user's attitude changes (friendlier users)

Like many engineers in the past, when faced with a difficult analytical problem we have reverted to mathematical modelling. Our general research approach therefore has been to formalise, implement and experiment.

Background

Anecdotes, horror stories and in general user complaints are a common finding in the literature [1], [2], [3]. Methods and techniques to avoid user complaints are also quite common [4], [5], [6], [7]. Some of them are intended to assist the user to overcome the natural limitations of his short term memory, while others are intended to enable the user to cope with an unnecessarily complex system.

The need for the interface to be considered as a separate component of the computer software has its basis in the well established principle of separation of concerns [8]. It has recently been advocated and supported by many: [9], [10], [11], [12], [13], [14].

The value of having flexible and/or adaptable interfaces has also been widely recognised [9], [12], [15], [16], [17], [18], [19], [20]. All the past approaches to producing adaptable or flexible interfaces present problems. Some require the actual construction of several interfaces (for the different types of users), some require too much time and effort from the user in order to make any adaptations, and some are self-adaptive, that is, they change on their own initiative (based on the patterns of use) and therefore presumably force the user to cope with an ever changing system.

The need to consider the interface in an application-free context was first mentioned in 1972 by Bennett [21]. Recently more specific engineering approaches have been put forward. Some of them stress the user's need to access several applications without having to learn different protocols [22], [23]; others stress the fact that building software interfaces is very expensive and therefore a substantial saving will be achieved if many applications share a single interface [24].

The new and interesting contributions of our project are:
- we include all the aspects mentioned above, so our interface is: composed of very few primitive operations, a separate piece of software, adaptable to different users, and usable by all applications
- adapting the interface is just as simple as using it
- the development of new interactive applications is considerably simplified, while adapting existing ones does not require too much extra effort.

Following is first an informal and then a formal description of a model of interaction which is the basis of an interface that allows users to interact with a system where:
- everything that is happening is visible (no hidden modes)
- one is offered only the facilities one is interested in (not the whole system)
- things appear where and how one wish them to appear
- what one sees is what one gets (no embedded control language)
- all actions have an inverse (they can be undone)
- all actions are uniform and consistent (similar things are always done in similar ways).

A Model of Interaction

Logging-in to an interactive computer system is like opening a door to a world of facilities. These facilities are a set of data (the collective result of all the previous sessions) and a set of processes (to process the data with). Let us define the system state as the total set of facilities (data and processes) available to the user at any one time.

Our proposed model of interaction is based on the simple concept of opening and closing doors. This concept is an extension of the fold/unfold principle of the OCCAM Programming System. We believe it to be powerful enough to allow users to easily visualise, understand, and control their system state.

Let us define an object as either a piece of data or a door, where a door contains a set of objects and denotes a process, and a process is a state-to-state transformation. When a door is closed, it is the only reference available to its contents and its denoted process. When a door is opened, its contents becomes available and the process is immediately initiated.

Together with the facilities to manipulate doors (create, change, delete, open, and close) we provide a library of primitive interaction processes (to handle, for example, the screen, the keyboard, and the tablet, with parameters stored in data objects).

For example: a door *log-in* can be created so that opening it will cause the user name and password to be input (and verified), and a menu of doors to be displayed (according to parameters stored in a data object). After logging-in the user might open the door *editor* and use the editor's commands (which are also doors) to change around the menu of doors (thereby changing the parameters), and save it, so that at next log-in the menu of doors displayed will be different.

The Formal Specification

Formal specification techniques have been used by software engineers for years in the development of compilers, in recent times these techniques are being used in the development of a wide variety of software, including interactive systems: [11], [14], [25], [26]. The need and the value of the formal specifications are agreed by all. Differences arise mostly on notation. Some notations are able to convey certain concepts more clearly than others. State transition networks give a clear view of a sequence of events, BNF-like notations give a clear view of the command syntax. Both notations however lose their clarity of expression as the system grows to any realistic level of complexity. One way of coping with complexity in the specifications is to introduce another level of notation, for example using path algebras to manipulate state transition networks [25]. Notations based on set theory, on the other hand, use familiar set-theoretic notation directly and only introduce new symbols to simplify presentation. The use of set theory allows to abstract away from operational detail, therefore making the presentation of large and complex systems more clear and concise.

In the formalisation of our model of interaction we use a mathematical model to indicate *what* the system is supposed to do, not *how* it is supposed to do it. For this reason we present the specification in a form that facilitates *reasoning* rather than *execution*. We therefore specify functions non-constructively, in terms of the relationship between their arguments and results.

The notation we use is based on modern set theory. It has been developed at the Programming Research Group during the last few years and has recently been referred to as *Schema Notation* (for reasons that will become apparent). At this point we strongly recommend that readers who are not familiar with this notation read the appendix before proceeding.

Due to space restrictions we are only able to present here a fragment of the complete specification of our model of interaction.

The building blocks in our specification are the sets of all possible objects, doors and data. We define the set of all possible objects as being partitioned by the set doors and the set of data.

OBJ, DOOR, DATA

```
┌─────────────────────────────────────────┐
│ OBJ = DOOR ∪ DATA                        │
│ DOOR ∩ DATA = ∅                          │
└─────────────────────────────────────────┘
```

Let us now refine the notion of system state. It is the set of accessible objects, the set of opened doors, a function *parm* that maps every known door to a set of data, and a function *content* that maps every known door to a set of objects.

```
┌─SYS_STATE────────────────────────────────┐
│ access:  IF OBJ                          │
│ opened:  IF DOOR                         │
│ parm:    DOOR ↦ IF DATA                  │
│ content: DOOR ↦ IF OBJ                   │
│                                          │
│ dom parm = dom content                   │
│ opened ⊆ dom content                     │
└──────────────────────────────────────────┘
```

In the initial state, when there are no opened doors, the only accessible object is the log-in door.

```
┌─ISTATE───────────────────────────────────┐
│ SYS_STATE                                │
│                                          │
│ opened = ∅                               │
│ access = {"login"}                       │
└──────────────────────────────────────────┘
```

At all other times, the set of accessible objects is defined as the set of opened doors and their contents.

```
┌─ASTATE───────────────────────────────────┐
│ SYS_STATE                                │
│                                          │
│ opened ≠ ∅                               │
│ access = opened ∪                        │
│             ∪{content d| d ∈ opened}     │
└──────────────────────────────────────────┘
```

So we can define the system state as:

STATE ≙ ISTATE ∨ ASTATE

The purpose of the function *parm* is to allow us to present the system to the user as an ordered sequence of objects. For this we define a function *layout* (fixed throughout the system) as function from a set of data and a set of objects to a sequence of objects.

```
┌──────────────────────────────────────────┐
│ layout : IF OBJ × IF DATA ↦ Seq [OBJ]    │
└──────────────────────────────────────────┘
```

The user view of the system can now be completely defined in terms of the system state, and therefore, in the rest of the specification we can refer only to the system state.

```
USER_VIEW_____
view : Seq [OBJ]
STATE
_____
view = layout (access, parms)
where
       parms = U{parm d| d ∈ opened}
```

A process is defined as a state-to-state transformation.

PROCESS ≙ STATE ⇸ STATE

Which process is associated with each door is not part of the system state. This is because we felt there is no need for a self-modifiable system, instead we define the mapping of doors to processes as follows:

```
DOOR_MAP_____
proc : DOOR ⇸ PROCESS
```

This mapping is not affected by the execution of processes (they cannot created or destroy doors). We can define the common part of the execution of all processes as follows:

```
ALL_PROC_____
d? : DOOR
ΔSTATE
DOOR_MAP
_____
dom proc = dom content = dom content'
STATE' = proc d? STATE
```

By introducing some restrictions (what we know about a process' behaviour) we can define particular processes as follows:

```
OPEN_DOOR_____
ALL_PROC
_____
d? ∈ access ∧ d? ∉ opened
opened' = opened ∪ {d?}
```

```
CLOSE_DOOR_____
ALL_PROC
_____
d? ∈ opened
opened' = opened - {d?}
parm'    = parm
content' = content
```

Since the system state can change in any way upon opening a door, we decided that an operation abort_door should exist to allow the user to undo the last OPEN_DOOR and return to the state before the door was opened. For this we had to modify slightly the specification of OPEN_DOOR and give a specification of ABORT_DOOR.

```
BACKUP_____
ALL_PROC
oldstate : STATE
```

```
OPEN_DOOR_____
BACKUP
_____
d? ∈ access ∧ d ∉ opened
oldstate = STATE
opened' = opened ∪ {d?}
```

```
ABORT_DOOR_____
BACKUP
_____
d? ∈ opened
STATE' = oldstate
```

Note that although OPEN_DOOR is more specific than ALL_PROC, it is still rather general: it does not specify what happens to the functions *parm* and *content*. To be able to specify exactly the system state that will result from opening a door, we need to know more about the door, namely, which process is associated with the door. For example, the process that simply displays the content of a door at the locations specified by the parameters:

```
DISPLAY_____
OPEN_DOOR
_____
parm'    = parm
content' = content
```

The process that replaces an object (contained in another door) for a new object and leaves it in the same location as the original one:

```
REPLACE_____
OPEN_DOOR
container? : DOOR
old?, new? : OBJ
_____
container? ∈ opened
old? ∈ content container?
parm'    = parm
content'= content ⊕ {container? ↦ newobj}
where:
newobj = content container? - old? ∪ new?
```

The process that moves an object (within the door it is contained in) to a new location:

```
MOVE_____
 OPEN_DOOR
 obj?      : OBJ
 container? : DOOR
 from?, to?: DATA
 _____
 container? ∈ opened
 obj? ∈ content container?
 from? ∈ parm container?
 content' = content
 parm' = parm ⊕ {container? ↦ newpar}
 where
    newpar = parm container? - from? ∪ to?
```

All other processes in the system can be specified in a similar fashion.

Finally, we present the operations used to create, change and destroy doors. They are the only way of modifying the mapping between doors and processes. First we define the common part of these operations :

```
DOOR_PROC_____
 ΔSTATE
 ΔDOOR_MAP
 d? : DOOR
 _____
 dom proc  = dom parm   = dom content
 dom proc' = dom parm'  = dom content'
 opened'   = opened
```

And now the operations:

```
MAKE_DOOR_____
 DOOR_PROC
 p?    : PROCESS
 obj?  : IF OBJ
 data? : IF DATA
 _____
 d? ∉ dom proc
 (obj?, data?) ∈ dom layout
 proc'  = proc ⊕ {d? ↦ p?}
 parm'  = parm ⊕ {d? ↦ data?}
 content'= content ⊕ {d? ↦ obj?}
```

```
INCLUDE_DOOR_____
 DOOR_PROC
 into?  : DOOR
 par?   : IF DATA
 _____
 d? ∈ access ∧ d? ∉ opened
 into? ∈ opened
 (newcont, newparm) ∈  dom layout
 parm'  =  parm ⊕ {into? ↦ par?}
 content'= content ⊕ {d? ↦ newcont}
 where
       newcont = content into? ∪ d?
```

The operation MAKE_DOOR' will normally be followed immediately after by INCLUDE_DOOR, so we could define a new operation to be the sequential composition of the two.

$$\text{MAKE\_AND\_INCLUDE} \triangleq \text{MAKE\_DOOR} \; ; \; \text{INCLUDE\_DOOR}$$

Note that except for "login" all doors must be included in the contents of at least one other door, because otherwise they could never be accessible. The door "login" is special in that it is not contained in any other door, and it is the only available object after executing the operation LOGOFF.

```
LOGOFF_____
 ALL_PROC
 _____
 opened' = ∅
 parm'   = parm
 content'= content
```

The operations that modify and destroy doors are defined as follows:

```
CHANGE_DOOR_____
 DOOR_PROC
 p?    : PROCESS
 obj?  : IF OBJ
 data? : IF DATA
 _____
 d? ∈ opened
 proc'  = proc ⊕ {d? ↦ p?}
 parm'  = parm ⊕ {d? ↦ data?}
 content'= content ⊕ {d? ↦ obj?}
```

```
KILL_DOOR_____
 DOOR_PROC
 from? : DOOR
 par?  : IF DATA
 _____
 d? ∈ access ∧ d? ∉ opened
 proc'  = proc \ {d?}
 parm'  = parm \ {d?} ⊕ {from? ↦  par?}
 content'= content \ {d?} ⊕ {from? ↦   d?}
```

At this point it is interesting to notice that the implementation of these last two operations may cause doors to be lost in the system (i.e. not contained in any other door), and therefore require some form of garbage collection.

From an engineering point of view, the exercise of formalising our specification has been most useful. It has given us a precise framework within which to discuss the design of the system. It has forced mathematical rigour into our design process and has allowed us to start with a very abstract specification (without any consideration of implementation constraints) and gradually refine it towards the actual implementation. In fact at each step of refinement we are forced to show that the new (detailed) specification is equivalent to the last (abstract) one, this means that design flaws are detected and correct before embarking on the implementation. Which obviously makes the implementation that much smoother and painless.

Design

Now we lower the level of abstraction and move closer to the implementation. Following is an informal description of the design of an implementation of the model. We are not able to include the formal specification of this design due to space restrictions.

When developing this design we had in mind a particular hardware to implement it on, the ICL PERQ, this machine was chosen for practical reasons:

- the machine is available
- access and replacement of the top level command interpreter (SHELL) is provided
- the high resolution screen and pointing device allow rich user-computer communication
- an advanced bitmap text and graphics editor is available on the machine

The ability to replace the top-level command interpreter is necessary to be able to implement a uniform method of accessing data and invoking commands throughout the system. The availability of the bitmap editor is important first as a development tool and second as a component of the interface. Whenever typing on a keyboard is involved, editing facilities should be available.

The system (interface) sits between the user and the rest of the system (application and systems programs). The user interacts with the interface by opening and closing doors, by typing text , and by drawing pictures.

Since we decided that the basic editing facilities must always be available, the top-level command interpreter is in fact an editor (with the ability to open and close doors) and therefore, the system state, the door-names, and the doors are all documents. A document is a sequence of objects (characters, pictures, and door-names).

At this point it is easy to (informally) show that this basic design is consistent with the formal specification we gave before. The users view of the system was defined as a sequence of objects, the system state has now been defined as a document which is a sequence of objects. The accessible document is what the user sees, and it is formed by all the accessible objects being organised in the sequence indicated by the parameters.

To make the interface usable, there is a minimum set of doors whose contents may not be changed, so that the processes invoked as a result of opening these doors is always the same. This minimum set includes: DELETE, INSERT, CUT, PASTE, LIFT, SAVE, SCROLL, PAN, PLACE CURSOR, PLACE MARK, and a door named OPENED which, when opened displays a menu of all those doors currently opened. If the contents of these doors may not be modified, then why are they doors? the answer is that they must be doors so that the way in which they are opened and closed can be defined in the same way as any other door.

Doors are opened either by pointing at the door-name and pressing one of the buttons on the mouse, or by pressing a function key. Doors can be closed either by themselves or by a subsequent pointing and pressing.

When a door is opened, first the door-name is removed from the screen and added to the set of opened doors, and then its contents is scanned line by line. If a line is associated with the attribute RUN, then the line (which must be a runnable process in the library) is imediately executed, otherwise the objects in the line are displayed according to the parameters contained in the parameter file (another document) associated with the door.

When a door is closed, the document is again scanned line by line. Lines that are associated with the attribute RUN are ignored and all the objects contained in all other lines are un-displayed according to the parameters. The door-name is removed from the set of opened doors and displayed again where it was before being opened.

So every door is a document and it has a door-name and a parameter file (both of which are also documents) which are linked together by the operation MAKE-DOOR. This operation includes the door and the door-name in their respective sets and creates the parameter file by example, that is to say, the user places the objects contained in the door at the locations where he wishes them to appear when the door is opened. These locations can be relative to the documents origin, or fixed at an absolute screen or keyboard address.

Implementation

The first application to be embedded within our framework was the editor itself. First, all the calls to the operating system were isolated and implemented in separate modules. The arguments used to call these modules are not hard coded in the calling module, instead they are contained in a door. These modules, which form part of the library of processes, include the display text or icons, input from the tablet, input from the keyboard, display cursor, and track cursor.

Developing interactive applications is simplified by the existence of the interface. The concept of detailed dialogue is replaced by the accessible document and the editing facilities. The application takes its input from the document and also places its results there. Since the document is made up of all the opened doors and their contents, and there is another document (the parameters) which indicated how the contents of each door is organised, then the applications programmer does not have to be concerned with how exactly the data is input and output.

Adapting existing applications to use the interface involves replacing the supervisor calls by procedure calls to modules from our library. If the application is not well structured, the process can be very tedious, and most probably will result in an under-utilisation of the facilities provided.

Both the users and the applications use doors to communicate. Doors have to be defined. Should they be defined by the programmer, by the user, or by some sort of interface administrator?. We think that this will probably be different from one installation to the next, the important thing is that the system structure provides the flexibility necessary to satisfy almost any user and any application.

Experiments

During the early stages of our project we considered designing an experiment to test whether users prefer personalised intefaces to standard ones, and whether personalised systems improve user productivity. To carry out such an experiment by tailoring interfaces would probably be more expensive than building an adaptable interface, and in any case, most people prefer personalised goods, why should computer systems be any different?

We believe that experiments designed to test the acceptability and/or the usability of a product can only be carried out in a live environment, and with users that have the prerogative of using the product or not.

At the time of writing the system has not yet been made available to a sizeable community of users from which experimental results could be obtained. This is mostly because the system (interface) at this point does not include enough applications to attract enough users.

In the near future, we will develop some new applications: a bibliographical referencing system, a mail service, and a schema handling system. These new applications together with the editor and the utilities will form a useful support system for a research environment like ours. We are confident that the development of these applications will be substantially simplified by the availability of the common interface, and that the total set of facilities then available will be enough to encourage a more substantial use of the system by a large number of users.

We are aware that the users' first encounter with the system is crucial and that therefore the set of default parameters could play an important role in certain environments. We are therefore designing an experiment to study the relationship between the users' background and his first reaction to the adaptable interface. We are particulary interested in determining how much emphasis should be given to the system's adaptability. Should the user be tempted or forced to make some adaptations on his first session, or should the adaptability be introduced gradually as the user gains experience?

For users who will only ever use one application to perform a specific task, adaptability might not be so desirable. The availability of the adaptable interface will enable us (or anyone else) to design experiments aimed at finding out which is the best interface for them. Users (in their live environment) could be asked to use a number of different interfaces (sets of default parameters) and measurements could be made on differences in productivity, and users' satisfaction.

References

[1] Nievergelt J., Errors in Dialog Design and How to Avoid Them, in Nievergelt, et al (eds.) Document Preparation Systems - A Collection of Survey Articles (North-Holland 1982).

[2] James E.B., The User Interface, The Computer Journal, Vol.23, No.1 (March 1980).

[3] Sime M.E., The Empirical Study of Computer Language, in Shackel, B.(ed.) Human Factor Aspects of Computers and People (Sijthof and Noordhoff 1976).

[4] Schneiderman B., Software Psychology, (Little, Brown & Co. 1980).

[5] Darlington J., Dzida W. and Herda S., The Role of Excursions in Interactive Systems, International Journal of Man Machine Studies, Vol.18, No. 2 (1983).

[6] Eason K.D., A Task-Tool Analysis of Manager-Computer Interaction, in Shackel B.(ed.) Human Factors Aspects of Computers and People (Sijthof and Noordhoff 1976).

[7] Martin J., Design of Man Computer Dialogues, (Prentice-Hall 1973).

[8] Dahl O.J., Dijkstra E.W. and Hoare C.A.R., Structured Programming (Academic Press, London 1972).

[9] Hayes P., Ball E., and Reddy R., Breaking the Man-Machine Communication Barrier, Computer (March 1981).

[10] James E.B., The User Interface: How We May Compute, in Coombs and Alty (eds.) Computing Skills and the User Interface (Academic Press, London 1981).

[11] Edmonds E.A., Adaptive Man-Computer Interfaces, in Coombs and Alty (eds.) Computing Skills and the User Interface (Academic Press, London 1981).

[12] Innocent P.R., Towards Self-Adaptive Interface Systems, International Journal of Man Machine Studies Vol. 16 (1982).

[13] Gaines B.R. and Shaw M.L., Dialog Engineering, in Sime and Coombs (eds.) Designing for Human-Computer Communication (Academic Press 1983).

[14] Jacob R.J.K., Using Formal Specifications in the Design of Human-Computer Interface, Communications of ACM, Vol.26, No. 4. (April 1983).

[15] Norman M.A. and Macauley L.A., Criteria for Adaptive Software Design: An Experimental Approach, Proceedings of the Ergonomics Society Conference (1983).

[16] Rich E., Users are individuals: Individualizing User Models, International Journal of Man Machine Studies, Vol.18, No. 3 (1983).

[17] Palme J., A Human-Computer Interface Encouraging User Growth, in Sime and Coombs (eds.) Designing for Human-Computer Communication (Academic Press London 1983).

[18] Mozeico H., A Human-Computer Interface to Accommodate User Learning Stages, Communications of ACM, Vol.25, No. 2 (February 1982).

[19] Bateman R.F., A Translator to Encourage User Modifiable Man-Machine Dialog, in Sime and Coombs (eds), Designing for Human-Computer Communication, (Academic Press London 1983).

[20] Edmonds E.A., The Man-Compute Interface, International Journal of Man Machine Studies, Vol.16, No.3 (1982).

[21] Bennett J.L., The User Interface in Interactive Systems, Annual Review of Information Science and Technology, No.7 (1972).

[22] Treu S., Uniformity in User-Computer Interaction Languages: A Compromise Solution, International Journal of Man Machine Studies, Vol.16, No.2 (1982).

[23] Robertson G., McCracken D. and Newell A., The ZOG Approach to Man-Machine Communication, International Journal of Man Machine Studies, Vol.14, No.4 (1981).

[24] Hayes P.J. and Szekely P.A., Graceful Interaction Through COUSIN Command Interface, International Journal of Man-Machine Studies, Vol.19, No.3 (1983).

[25] Alty J., The Application of Path Algebras to Interactive Dialogue Design, Proceedings of the Ergonomics Society Conference (1983).

[26] Sufrin B., Formal Specification of a Display-Oriented Text Editor, Science of Computer Programming 1 (North-Holland 1982).

APPENDIX

Schema Notation

First let us define some of the symbols used which might not be familiar:

$\mathbb{N}$	The set of natural numbers
$\mathbb{P}$	Powerset
$\mathbb{F}\ A$	The finite subsets of A
$A \nrightarrow B$	The set of partial functions from A to B
$[a \mapsto b]$	The function $\{(a,b)\}$
dom	The domain of a function
$\wedge$	Logical and

$\setminus$ Domain restriction

for $f: A \nrightarrow B;\ A : \mathbb{P}A$

$f\setminus A \equiv \{(a,b):f\ |\ a \notin A\}$

$\text{dom}\ (f\setminus A) = \text{dom}\ (f) - A$

$x \in \text{dom}(f\setminus A) \implies (f\setminus A)(x) = f(x)$

$\oplus$ Functional overriding

for $f,g : A \nrightarrow B$

$f \oplus g \equiv (f\setminus\text{dom}\ g) \cup g$

$\text{dom}\ (f\oplus g) = \text{dom}\ f \cup \text{dom}\ g$

$x \in \text{dom}\ g \implies (f\oplus g)(x) = g(x)$

$x \notin \text{dom}\ g \wedge x \in \text{dom}\ f \implies$
$\qquad\qquad (f\oplus g)(x) = f(x)$

The rest of the symbols utilised in the specification presesnted in this paper is considered to be "standard" set theory.

In this notation an entity can be named by placing the name on a box surrounding the term whose value is to be named. For example, to give the name PAIR to the set of pairs m, n of natural numbers for which m ≥ n, we write:

```
PAIR_____
| m,n : IN
|_____
| m ≥ n
|_____
```

We call such boxed signatures and their related predicates *schemas*. They indicate textual equivalence between their content and their name. The horizontal line between the signature and the predicate should be read "such that". Since the use of the schema name is equivalent to the use of its contents, schema names can be used in conjunction with quantifiers to denote sets, functions, relations, predicates etc.

The effect of decorating a schema name is to so decorate every component within it. Thus PAIR' denotes the schema

```
_____
| m',n' : IN
|_____
| m' ≥ n'
|_____
```

When a schema is included in the description of another; its signature and predicate join any others in the

enclosing schema with equal status. There is no implied hierarchical structure.

```
ΔPAIR_____
| PAIR
| PAIR'
|_____
```

is equivalent to writing

```
ΔPAIR_____
| m,n,m',n' : IN
|_____
| m ≥ n ∧ m' ≥ n'
|_____
```

Conventionally Δ schema represents the schema undashed as the initial state and the dashed schema as the final state. Similarly variables decorated with ? represent input and those decorated with ! represent output.

Operations may also be presented as schemas. The domain of an operation may include a schema together with any input parameters required:

```
PLUS_____
| ΔPAIR
| x? : IN
|_____
| m' = m+x?
| n' = n+x?
|_____
```

Human-Computer Interaction — INTERACT '84 / B. Shackel (ed.)
Elsevier Science Publishers B.V. (North-Holland)
© IFIP, 1985

THE DESIGN AND IMPLEMENTATION OF FLEXIBLE INTERFACES :
A CASE STUDY OF AN OPERATIONAL SYSTEM FOR ASSISTING THE DIAGNOSIS OF CEREBRAL DISEASE

Innocent, P.R., Plummer, D.*, Teather,D., Morton, B.A., Wills, K.M. and du Boulay, G.H.+

School of Mathematics, Computing & Statistics, Leicester Polytechnic,Leicester.
* Rayne Institute, University College Hospital, London.
+ National Hospital for Nervous Diseases, Queens Square, London.

The design of flexible user interfaces is discussed. An interface system for
constructing menu type dialogues is described. The interface system has been utilised
in the building of an extensive applications system to assist in the radiological
diagnosis of cerebral disease.

1. Introduction.

It is widely recognised that the user interface
is a major factor contributing to the ease of
use, ease of learning, and effectiveness of an
interactive system. A problem in the design of
such an interface is coping with the variety
of, and changes in, user requirements. A
number of strategies, e.g. Edmonds, (3), have
been proposed for achieving a sufficiently
flexible and adaptable interface.

This paper considers a study in which the user
interface was developed as a separate component
of the system. The advantage of this approach
is that, as a clear division is generated
between the interface and the application,the
interface can be specified in detail and made
available to a team of application programmers.
In addition the interface can be modified in
a coherent manner, should requirements change
during the development of the applications
system.

2. The Application : Cerebral Disease.

The application system being developed arises
as the result of a five year joint research
project between Leicester Polytechnic and the
National Hospital for Nervous Diseases, London.
A statistical database of nearly 1000 cases
of cerebral disease has been established as a
fundamental part of the research. This database
has been extensively analysed to determine the
features of the Computer Tomography (C.T.) scan
image that are important in differentiating
between different forms of cerebral disease
(Wills et al., (9); Wills et al. (10); Morton
et. al. (6); Morton et al. (7)). The analysis
has led to the development of a statistical
model to aid in diagnosis, and this model
is being implemented as part of an extensive
applications system for scan interpretation
(Wills et. al., (11); Innocent et al. (5)).
The system is Fortran based and runs on the
independent display consoles that are available
as "add-on" units for the C.T. scanner system.

To obtain advice from the system the radiologist
responds to a menu based dialogue to describe

the position and appearance of any
abnormality visible on the C.T. scan
image. These abnormalities are described
in terms of a number of defined signs.
A database of sample images, to illustrate
different signs, appearances, and diseases, is
available on-line and used as the basis for
extensive "show-me", "help" and "why" facilities.

Advice provided to the radiologist concerning
diagnosis is not simply "the most likely disease",
but is quantified in terms of the advice system's
error performance. The radiologist is also
informed as to which signs were most important
in reaching the stated diagnosis. In addition
any signs that conflict with the current
diagnosis are also indicated. Descriptions of
new cases are stored on the system and these
may be updated with the final confirmed "true"
disease of the patient, when this information
is available. This "data-capture" facility
permits detailed error analysis and further
analysis of patient profiles, to provide more
quantitative feedback to the radiologists.

If a preliminary diagnosis is made on the basis
of a plain scan, the radiologist must decide
whether or not to also obtain an "enhanced" scan.
Enhancement, in this medical application,
refers to the process whereby the patient is
injected with organic iodine, and then further
scan images obtained. The process is not
without risk or discomfort, and does not always
give extra useful information. The system is
able to provide advice, on the basis of a
description of a plain scan, as to whether
enhancement is likely to be of value. In
particular, the system is able to state the
chance that enhancement will lead to a change
in the diagnosis.

3. The System's Design Environment.

As stated above, the application system was
designed with the user interface as a distinct
component. A programming "environment" was
created in which the dialogue for the
application could be implemented, with ease and
in a uniform manner, by the applications

programmers (henceforth called programmers). This environment extends to the end-user, in our case the radiologist, (henceforth called the user) who consequently sees a standardised dialogue structure - even though several programmers are involved with the work.

This configuration creates a buffer between the programmers and "the world" (i.e. the user and the machine operating system), enabling them to take advantage of a range of powerful features without compromising transportability. It also standardises the interface to the users, isolating them from the "egos" of the various programmers. The "interface system" developed is not aware of the exact details of the actual application but rather functions as a utility for the generation of interfaces. By creating such flexible environments, applications can be made more transportable, and the effort of implementing a new application system or package can be reduced (Collard et al, (2), Hall et al, (4)).

4. Design considerations.

Two main factors controlled the design of the interaction between the system and the user. First the desire to provide a uniform user interface for which the learning curve would be very steep, and second the need for a means by which details of terminology and indeed natural language might be changed with a minimum of disturbance to the main code of the system.

If a user interface to a system is implemented in such a way that a small set of conventions and rules applies throughout the system, it is much easier for a user to adapt to the system, as experience gained in one section of the system can be applied in any other section. Specifically, conventions should be established for: default values, obtaining help, performing special functions etc. These should be generally meaningful rather than dependent on specific context. Such conventions, once learned, give users a sense of security which is most important in encouraging them to experiment and expand their horizons in using an information processing environment. For example, if typing interrogation mark as the response to a request always produces helpful text on the current status, and to where one might proceed, users will be less afraid of experimenting with unfamiliar operations. Similarly, if screen formats are standardised in such a way that similar information always appears in the same part of the screen, a sense of familiarity will be created which will also speed learning.

Many guidelines have been specified which support the implementation of the user interface in the system being developed. A summary of these guidelines is given in Shneiderman (8). In translating the

guidelines into practice, emphasis has to be given to the provision of adequate facilities for users to interact with confidence, and not be penalised for interrupted sessions.

4.1 User Sessions

Given the nature of the clinical environment, the ability to suspend and resume user sessions at will is a great advantage and also provides a measure of protection from system failure. This has been achieved by keeping a sessional record of interactions in a workfile. A workfile record is associated with the particular user and the patient being considered in the session. Thus a user cannot resume another users session. Workfile records only exist within sessions or for incomplete sessions. Once the user has successfully completed a session or decided to abandon a previously interrupted session, the workfile record is deleted from file.

In the case of the existence of a resumed session, it is necessary that the user be reminded of his previous interactions so that a decision to abandon or continue can be sensibly made. Thus the workfile record should be presented to the user in a form which reminds him of his previous responses. The design of the interface is such that the workfile record can be used to regenerate the states of the interface which resulted from the interactions of an interrupted session. Since there may be a considerable number of such interactions, it is tedious for a user to have to view them all if the user wishes to make an early decision not to resume. The system makes use of a series of "checkpoints" at which the user can make a decision as to whether to accept or amend previous inputs.

The workfile is implemented as an indexed sequential file. The primary key of workfile records is the concatenation of the user identification and the patient identification (both encoded for security). The index contains parameters which enable context information to be set up by the interface program, prior to using the workfile records for presenting or storing sessional interactions. Input and output is accomplished by calls to simple routines written in standard Fortran. This ensures that the system is portable and minimises storage requirements. Workfiles are deliberately simple in construction, and consist of a list of numerical "tokens", which represent both the questions posed by the system and the user response.

It is expected that most sessions will run to completion, at which point the workfile is used for creating a permanent record in the system. This permanent record can later be retrieved and used to remind the user of previous interactions and/or drive further features of the system.

5. Design of the User Interface.

The system under construction is directed at neuro-radiological centres in all parts of the developed world. For this reason it is important that local variations in terminology can be accommodated easily. As many users taking advantage of the facilities within the system will not have had a full exposure to international terminology, it is improbable that any standard set could be established even in the English speaking world. For this reason it is desirable that all messages be located centrally and be available for modification, preferably without the need to distribute system sources.

The design of the 'menu driver' for the system took place with all the design considerations described earlier, in mind. All data is presented as part of a screen or 'page' of text. A fixed number of pages is defined for the system, each of which has an independent description. Pages are logically divided into 'regions' each corresponding to a particular class of information. The principal such classes are: 'status' giving information on the current state of the system, 'menu' giving details of options available at this point, 'feedback' accumulating user input for the current operation, and 'prompt' being specific text for the current input request. All pages have a prompt region as some user input is always required before proceeding to the next page. Other regions are defined as needed, but most pages in the system use status, menu and feedback regions.

As the exact contents of many pages are context dependent, some mechanism was required for specifying additions and modifications to a basic page format. Text is divided up into two components, the basic page descriptions and additional messages which are identified by unique numeric 'tokens'. A message may be added to or deleted from a region by specifying its token number. Similarly, when an option is selected from an options list, the value returned to the applications program is the token value of the option string rather than the sequential option number typed by the user. This enables menu input to be performed in a highly context independent manner as the actual text of the questions displayed on the screen need not be known by the program at the time of input. Bramer (1) describes a similar processor using tokens to represent interactions; the work described here provides a significant extension to this concept.

Though the page and token mechanisms provide for the construction of a wide range of page formats, there was still a necessity to include numeric and text values, from the environment of the program, into the messages. This was achieved by placing the required integer, real or text values into elements of arrays of corresponding type and providing a mechanism for substituting a specified element from any of these arrays into any message in a page as it is displayed. By this means, patient numbers, numerical results etc. can be positioned as required in the output page.

5.1 Interface to the application programmer

The implementation of the menu driver at the level of the program consists of calls to display a specified page and then request a value of a specified type from the user. Calls are implemented to return: (i) text, or (ii) a numeric value or (iii) the token number associated with an option selected. A further call simply returns with no result when the user presses the return key. In the more complex case where a page is to be modified by the addition of messages, any of the above routines may be preceded by calls, first to load up the required page and then to add the messages as required by specifying their token numbers and the regions into which they are to be placed.

A simple menu description language was provided for the specification of page formats and the assignment of text to token numbers. This permits the information to be maintained in a readily comprehensible form which can be modified with a standard text editor and then compiled by a utility program into data files organised for optimal speed of access.

5.2 Interface to the user.

The style of interaction between the user and the system can have a big effect on its ease of use and speed of acceptance. Numbers should always be read in free format with leading banks ignored and decimal points required only when followed by one or more decimal places. In many cases standard FORTRAN input is insufficient to meet these requirements and we chose to write our own numeric parsing routines using a format input at the lowest level. An additional feature which can contribute greatly to speed of use is to permit future questions to be anticipated, and replied to at the same time as the current question. This avoids redundant page display and in many cases provides an alternative view of the command syntax as: 'command, argument-list'.

5.3 Application support and HELP functions.

A requirement of the application is that at any point in the dialogue the user should have access to a variety of information. This includes the output of files of descriptive text and of images to an associated display system. This was implemented via a generalised help facility. Any input line starting with

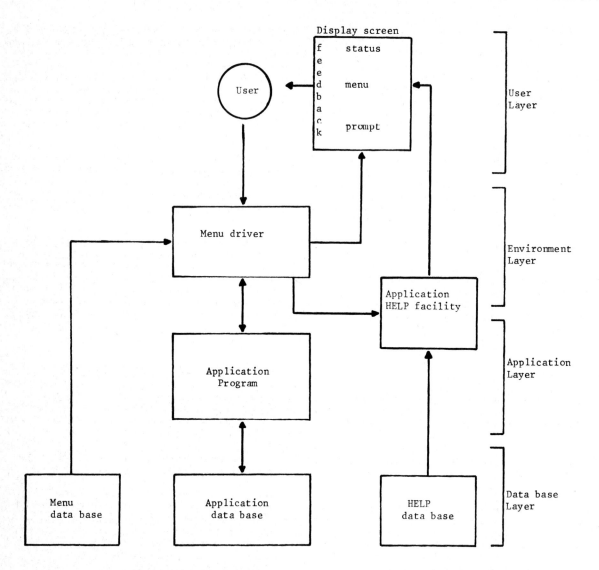

Figure 1 : Overview of system components

the interrogation mark character is interpreted
as a help line and is passed to the help
processor routine. This routine has access to
the menu driver environment and can thus
obtain information keyed by the current page
number. It can also map option numbers into
token numbers so that information associated
with a particular option can be accessed
using the token number as a key. Help text,
image numbers etc. are all associated with
page or token numbers and like the menu
descriptions are contained in a normal text
file which can be readily modified and
re-compiled into its runtime format. An
overview of the main components of the system
is shown in Figure 1.

6. Performance

The application system is currently implemented
on a 16 bit 32KW machine and has been
demonstrated to be transportable between
various 16 bit mini-computer systems. It is
written completely in FORTRAN but using the
INCLUDE and PARAMETER extensions found in most
modern compilers. In execution, even on
relatively slow disks, no appreciable delays
occur in displaying pages of text even though
several file accesses are often required. The
total quantity of textual information accessible

to the system is of the order of 100K characters, and in addition a large number of patient and example images may be viewed, this number being limited only by available storage space. Though the application system is still being developed, the menu driver has demonstrated itself to be a powerful and efficient programming tool.

REFERENCES.

1. Bramer, B.(1983). FORTRAN based Machine Independent User Input Processor, in Proceedings of Conference on "The User Interface: The Ergonomics of Interactive Computing", Sept. 1983, Leicester Polytechnic.

2. Collard, P., Plummer, D. Operating system requirements and user interfaces: IEEE Transactions on Nuclear Science. Vol. NS-29 No. 4, August 1982.

3. Edmonds, E.A. (1982). The Man-Computer Interface: A Note on Concepts and Design. Int. J. Man-Machine Studies, 16. p.p. 231-236.

4. Hall, D.E., Scherrer, D.K., Sventek J.S. A virtual operating system: Comm. ACM Vol. 22, No. 9, Sept. 1980.

5. Innocent, P.R., Teather, D., Wills, K.M., du Boulay, G.H., and Plummer, D. An operational system for the computer assisted diagnosis of cerebral disease: In Van Bemmel , J.H., Ball, M.J., Wigertz,O. Eds.: Medinfo 83, Amsterdam, North Holland, 1983, p.p. 467-470.

6. Morton, B.A., Teather, D., du Boulay, G.H., and Wills, K.M. The analysis of diagnostic data with application to the diagnosis of cerebral lesions. In, Van Bemmel, J.H., Ball, M.J., Wigertz, O. Eds: Medinfo 83, Amsterdam, North Holland, 1983, p.p.471-474.

7. Morton, B.A., Teather, D. and du Boulay, G.H. : Statistical modelling and diagnostic aids. Medical Decision Making, 1984 (to appear).

8. Shneidermann, B. Software Psychology, Winthrop Computer Systems Series, 1980.

9. Wills, K.M., du Boulay, G.H. and Teather, D. : Initial findings in the computer-aided diagnosis of cerebral tumours using C.T. scan results. Brit. J. Radiology, 54, 948-952, 1981.

10. Wills, K.M., Teather, D. and du Boulay, G.H. : An improvement in computer-aided diagnosis of meningiomas after C.T. Neuroradiology, 22, 255-257, 1982.

11. Wills, K.M., Teather, D., Innocent, P.R. and du Boulay, G.H. : An expert system for the diagnosis of brain tumours. Int. J. Man-Machine Studies, 16, 342-349, 1982.

ACKNOWLEDGEMENTS.

This work was supported in part by: International General Electric and by the Department of Health and Social Security.

TOOLS TO AID INTERFACE DESIGN AND PROGRAMMING

Human-Computer Interaction — INTERACT '84 / B. Shackel (ed.)
Elsevier Science Publishers B.V. (North-Holland)
© IFIP, 1985

AN ATTEMPT TO EASE AND SIMPLIFY THE DEVELOPMENT OF INTERACTIVE SOFTWARE: THE MENU SUPPORT SUBSYSTEM OF INTERPRO

Dimiter Novatchev, Yuly Gabrovsky

INTERPROGRAMMA - Sofia

A general method for dialog organisation, supported by the Menu Support Subsystem - MMS of an interactive environment INTERPRO, is described. The most distinguishing MMS features are pointed out. The Menu Description and Interpretation Language - MDIL and the Menu Interpreter - MINT are briefly examined, their use being demonstrated by a practical example. The authors argue that MMS can be regarded as a software engineering tool, aiding the design and partly the development of prototypes for interactive programs. They outline some basic directions for future work.

1. INTRODUCTION

The obvious cause of the currently witnessed great attention paid to dialog management and specification [1,2,8] is the interactive nature of the typical today's program product. The INTERPRO system is an example of a simple interactive programming environment, aiming to propose a solution to some of the problems of the design of interactive (conversational) software.

2. MSS ESSENTIALS

We propose a general method for dialog management which is supported by a set of tools, generally known as the Menu Support Subsystem (MSS) of INTERPRO, characterised by the following dialog organization: *messages, menu* and *help screens* are displayed on the terminal.

A *menu* is a basic unit of information the display of which allows the user not only to select a specific function as in [9] but also to enter the arguments of (already chosen) functions.

The screen display usually comprises constant and variable data, whose value depends on the specific user and/or on the system state. By definition these variable data are the values of the corresponding *dialog variables.* The variables whose value depends only on the system state ate called system functions. Most of the dialog variables have as their values the most recent user-entered data in a particular field of a given screen display. These values are saved in a special User Profile Table - UPT across user sessions. User-entered data on a particular screen display of a menu can be obtained only as the value of corresponding dialog variables. Moreover, when a menu is redisplayed the contents of the variable screen fields are taken from the corresponding variables. In effect this means that the most recent (correct, accepted by the system) user inputs are redisplayed in their fields. Menus are not "hardwired" in MSS - *menu descriptions* are used instead. They are kept on external files and are written in the Menu Description and Interpretation Language - MDIL. Menu descriptions contain all the information required by another MSS component - the Menu Interpreter - MINT to manage the dialog flow. A menu description has three basic sections of the following form:

'.SCREEN'
<SCREEN LAYOUT DEFINITION>

    defines the order, attributes and contents of the screen fields with constant fields containing text and variable fields - the name of the corresponding variable.

'.DECLARE'
<SYNTAX DEFINITION OF VARIABLES>

    for each variable the syntax (type,length,range and list of values), its initial value, any necessary transformations and other attributes are defined.

'.ACT'
<MINT COMMANDS>

    a series of commands, directing MINT exactly what actions and in what order are to be taken (display the screen, call a program, start the interpretation of another menu, etc.)

'.END'

Not intending to present MDIL in detail we should note that its constructs are quite similar to those in [3,4,5,6]. The difference from those systems lies primarily in the way MINT commands are defined and interpreted. We followed the principle that MINT commands (not the user's programs as in SPF [5,6]) should explicitly define most actions, needed for the dialog flow organization, leaving at the same time any operations, not directly concerned with the dialog to the user's programs. This can be compared with the electronic forms systems approach [3, 4,7] where most of the processing logic is concentrated in the form definition. Thus two results were obtained:

(1) Removing much of the dialog-related actions from user processing programs makes them significantly simpler and more easily understandable. There is no great necessity for writing special "interactive" programs instead of "batch" ones. Programmer productivity is increased.

(2) Defining as MINT commands only actions directly concerned with dialog management results in very simple "MINT programs", easily written and understood that need practilly no debugging.

A brief explanation of MINT commands is needed as a prerequisite for the understanding of the example, included in this paper. The following types of commands exist:

INIT PGM(pgmname); and
TERM PGM(pgmname);
specify a program to be invoked for initialization/termination processing.

EXIT;   causes the immediate end of menu interpretation.

PERFORM PGM(pgmname) 'parameters';   or
PERFORM MENU(menuname);
causes the invocation of the program or the interpretation of
the menu, specified in the command. Having processed a
PERFORM command MINT starts the interpretation of the
next command in the '.ACT' section.

TRANSFER TO PGM(pgmname) 'parameters';   or
TRANSFER TO MENU(menuname);
has a similar effect except that control never returns to MINT
for the next command's interpretation but to the point right
after the current menu's interpretation has been started. The
PERFORM and TRANSFER TO commands realize a transfer
of control with and without return, respectively.

DISPLAY;   or
DISPLAY FOR PGM(pgmname);
causes the formatting and display of the '.SCREEN' section,
and the analysis of the user's input. Only valid (according to
the '.DECLARE' definitions) input is accepted. When the second form of the command is used MINT invokes the specified program after a valid user's input, passing to it as parameters all variables of the current menu. A DISPLAY command of the first form is not meaningless as the (new) values
of the dialog variables may be accessed later by another command, such as:

SELECT:
WHEN   condition 1   command1;
....
WHEN   condition N   command N;
the choice and interpretation of a command out of a group
of alternatives is realized. The command of the first WHEN
clause, the condition of which is true, is chosen and interpreted.

Except the INIT and TERM commands which are interpreted
only once - at the start of interpretation and when the END
key is hit, all other commands in an '.ACT' section are interpreted in a wrap-around fashion - the first command is interpreted after the last.

Having provided the necessary basis we can now proceed with
the discussion of the

3. DISTINGUISHING FEATURES OF MSS

Keeping to the scheme outlined above and regarding its current implementation, the following MSS features can be pointed out:

(1) Use of EC-7927 (functionally equivalent to IBM-3270)
terminals. In fact we make only the following assumptions
about the terminal:
    - sufficient screen size (at least 24 lines of 80 characters);
    - the screen can be formatted into fields which may have
      the attributes of input protection and high or low dis-
      play intensity;
    - there is a set of special (program function) keys used
      for the most general operations (i.g. HELP, END);

(2) User personalization. Keeping the set of each user's variables values in a UPT leads to user personalisation that can
have great consequences. Firstly the text of one and the same
menu M displayed for any two users U1 and U2 can be different - the system communicates with the user in his own
terms. Secondly the values of some variables can be used to

determine differences between users and to group them into
specific classes. For example a variable could be introduced
whose value restricts the type of menu functions the user can
select;

(3) Keystroke minimization. By redisplaying the last user input in the appropriate screen fields the user is not forced to
type a field's contents all over again - he may overtype only
a part of his last input, or even leave it unchanged at all. Thus
user keystrokes when entering data in a menu display are minimized;

(4) Multilingual support. A special variable LANG has as its
value the language in which the text of menus, messages and
help screens should be displayed to a particular user. Using
this variable MSS decides which description of a menu M to
choose for a user U. Thus it is possible for example to display
the text of a menu M to two different users Ue and Ub in English and in Bulgarian, meaning our system is essentially multilingual;

(5) Decreased number of interactions with the system. Due
to the cycle of interpreting MINT commands the same menu
is displayed continuously to the user, allowing him the convenience of repeated selection of a function without exit to
an upper level menu. The user exits to an upper menu only
by ultimately hitting the END key;

(6) Ease of system extension. New menu descriptions, messages and help panels can easily be added to the system, using a text editor. Thus a whole new menu hierarchy can be
created. Its root menu can be connected to an existing menu
adding a PERFORM command for its interpretation. No
compilations or linkage-editings are required;

(7) Support for the design and execution of new interactive
applications. New interactive applications can easily be added
to the system by (iteratively) realizing the following steps:
(i) the necessary menu hierarchy is created and connected to
an existing menu; (ii) at this time particular screen displays
and the general dialog flow can be demonstrated to future
users; (iii) the necessary processing programs are developed.
The use of MSS is illustrated below.

4. AN EXAMPLE - THE SUBMIT FUNCTION OF
INTERPRO

This function realizes the creation of user jobs and their sub-
mittal for execution. It satisfies the following requirements:
(1) The user should be able to create an unlimited number of
jobs in a single invocation of the SUBMIT function;
(2) The system should automatically generate a unique job-
name and allow user modification of each job's jobcard;
(3) Each job may consist of an unlimited number of compilations (all standard language processors) and linkage-editing
steps;
(4) At the end of each job's creation the user should be given
a choice to view, edit, submit, or cancel it;
(5) The transfer of control between different menus should
be minimal.

The menu descriptions for that function are listed below.
The meanings of the special characters (logical attribute
bytes for screen fields) used are:
'&' , '$' - protected fields with high and low display inten-
            sity, respectively;
'%'   - input variable fields with low intensity (variable
           name follows);

(1)   MENU=JOB

.SCREEN
&PLEASE, VERIFY/MODIFY YOUR JOBCARD:

&===>%JCLCARD
.DECLARE
    JCLCARD CHAR(72) REQUIRED;
.ACT
    INIT PGM(ALLOCNTL);
    an initialization program which
    allocates a temporary dataset
    (TEMPCNTL) - any job's text is
    kept here.
    PERFORM PGM(NJOBCARD);
    generates a unique jobname and
    replaces it in the JCLCARD variable.
    DISPLAY FOR PGM(JOBCARD);
    the jobcard is displayed, any
    modifications are accepted and the
    program puts it down in the temporary
    dataset TEMPCNTL.
    PERFORM MENU(JOBSTEP);
    all jobsteps are created while
    interpreting this menu.
    PERFORM MENU(JOBOPTN);
    the user is given a choice to view,
    edit, submit or cancel the job.
.END

(3) MENU=JOB01
  .SCREEN
        &PLEASE, ENTER/VERIFY:

        $PROJECT&===>%ASPROJ $
        $LIBRARY&===>%ASLIB $
        $TYPE   &===>%ASTYPE $
        $MEMBER &===>%ASMEMB$

        $LISTING DATASET
        $OR &SYSOUT&===>%ASPDSN

        $ASSEMBLER PARAMETERS:
                &===>%ASPARMS
  .DECLARE
        ASPROJ IDENT REQUIRED;
        ASLIB   IDENT REQUIRED;
        ASTYPE IDENT REQUIRED;
        ASMEMB IDENT REQUIRED;
        ASPDSN DSNAME REQUIRED;
        ASPARMS CHAR(60);
  .ACT
        DISPLAY FOR PGM(WRTJOBST);
        this program substitutes
        variables' values in a special
        jobstep skeleton, and writes
        the resulting text into the
        TEMPCNTL dataset.
  .END

(2) MENU=JOBSTEP
  .SCREEN
            &PLEASE, CHOOSE NEXT JOBSTEP(1-6)
            &OR HIT THE END KEY TO EXIT
                    &===>%X$
    &1$- ASSEMBLY   &4$- PL1 COMPIL.
    &2$- COBOL COMPIL.   &5$- PASCAL COMPIL.
    &3$- FORTRAN COMPIL.   &6$- LINKAGE EDITING
  .DECLARE
        X FIXED(1,1:6) REQUIRED CURSOR;
  .ACT
      DISPLAY;
      SELECT:
        WHEN X=1 MENU(JOB01);
        WHEN X=2 MENU(JOB02);
        WHEN X=3 MENU(JOB03);
        WHEN X=4 MENU(JOB04);
        WHEN X=5 MENU(JOB05);
        WHEN X=6 MENU(JOB06);
        a menu for specifying additional
        data for the chosen step is selected
        and interpreted next.

  .END

(4) MENU=JOBOPTN
  .SCREEN
        &JOB FINAL PROCESSING
        &PLEASE, CHOOSE AN ACTION:
            &===>%SEL$
        &1$- VIEW THE JOB'S TEXT
        &2$- EDIT THE JOB'S TEXT
        &3$- CANCEL THE JOB
        &4$- SUBMIT THE JOB
    &HITTING THE END KEY CAUSES
    &THE JOB'S SUBMITTAL !
  .DECLARE
        SEL FIXED(1,1:4) REQUIRED;
  .ACT
      INIT PGM(CLSCNTL);
      before viewing or editing
      the TEMPCNTL dataset should
      be closed.
      DISPLAY;
      SELECT:
        WHEN SEL=1 PGM(BROWSE)   'TEMPCNTL';
        WHEN SEL=2 PGM(EDIT)   'TEMPCNTL';
        WHEN SEL=3 EXIT;
        WHEN SEL=4 TRANSFER TO PGM(SUBMIT)
                                'TEMPCNTL';

      an action is selected and
      interpreted according to
      the user's input.

  .END

5. CURRENT IMPLEMENTATION AND INTENDED FUTURE DEVEPOPMENTS OF MSS

MSS is currently being implemented as a major component of INTERPRO. As a whole the system will run on the EC or IBM computers under the control of TSO. The terminals supported are EC-7927 or IBM-3270.

As the dialog management approach employed in MSS is quite general and machine-independent, a major future effort to develop a portable version of MSS seems thoroughly justified. MSS portability can lead to a uniform user interface over a wide range of computers and terminals.

A second possible development touches an area in which we still have no results - the automatic generation of menu descriptions for a program, using its formalized external specification. Any results in this area will certainly lead to increasing the reusability of programs and the quality of their documentation.

6. CONCLUSIONS

MSS can be regarded as a software engineering tool supporting a general method for the development of interactive applications having the following main characteristics:

- External definition and run-time validation of dialog variables' syntax;

- Centralization of most dialog management functions in MSS, radically simplifying the application programs' logic;

- Simplicity of MDIL constructs, making system decomposition in the design stage and verifying each menu in the implementation most natural and straight-forward;

- Prototyping capabilities - displaying menu hierarchies to future users long before the respective processing programs have been coded.

REFERENCES

1. Botterill J.H., The design of the System/38 user interface, IBM Systems Journal, vol.21, no 4, 1982.
2. Dean M., How a computer should talk to people, IBM Systems Journal, vol.21, no 4, 1982.
3. Gehani N.H., An electronic form system - an experience in prototyping, Software Practice and Experience, vol. 13, 479-486(1983).
4. Gehani N.H., High level form definition in office information systems, The Computer Journal, vol.26, no 1, 52-59(1983).
5. IBM GH20-1638-1, TSO-3270 Structured Programming Facility(SPF) General Information Manual.
6. Joslin P.H., System productivity facility, IBM Systems Journal, vol.20, no 4, 388-406(1981).
7. Tsichritzis D., Forms management, Communications of the ACM, vol.25, no 7, 1982.
8. Proceedings of the Seeheim'83 Workshop on User Interface Management Systems - to be published.
9. Robertson G., D.McCracken and A.Newell, The ZOG approach to man-machine communication, International Journal of Man-Machine Studies, 14, 461-488(1981).

Human-Computer Interaction — INTERACT '84 / B. Shackel (ed.)
Elsevier Science Publishers B.V. (North-Holland)
© IFIP, 1985

THE SYNICS2 USER INTERFACE MANAGER

ERNEST EDMONDS AND STEPHEN GUEST

HUMAN-COMPUTER INTERFACE RESEARCH UNIT
LEICESTER POLYTECHNIC
P.O. BOX 143
LEICESTER, U.K.

SYNICS2 is a user interface management system. It is the latest development of the
family of SYNICS systems and incorporates graphics and logging facilities. The paper
provides a brief introduction to the concepts of the new system.

1. INTRODUCTION.

Ehrich (1983) has contrasted two extreme types
of interactive software. Computation dominant
software has its logic driven by computation,
with occasional and independent exchanges with
the user. Dialogue dominant software has its
logic driven by its exchanges with the user.
These classes can be seen as end points of a
continuum. In the case of a computation
dominant program, it is clear that a parser that
can be evoked to obtain and appropriately
transform a single input together with suitably
high level output primitives provides an
adequate tool to facilitate the implementation
of user-system dialogues. Such a facility,
however, does not provide enough help in a
dialogue dominant program. In the latter case
the tool needs to facilitate the dialogue
itself, including its control logic. As the
former is a special case of the latter it can
be seen that a dialogue manager provides the
more general tool for interactive software
implementation. In recent years many experts
have, indeed, advocated the structuring of
systems so as to isolate a dialogue, or
interface, module that mediates between the
user and the computational software (see, for
example, the discussions in Edmonds, 1981 and
Jacob, 1983). This module has become known
as a user interface manager.

The two main contrasting styles of notation that
have been used in interface managers have been
BNF-style ones and state transition style ones.
BNF is good for defining the parsing of a given
string and state transitions are clear in
defining the dialogue logic. Whilst a detailed
psychological study remains to be done, the
indications are that state transitions are
more acceptable (Edmonds, 1982 ; Jacob, 1983).
It should be noted that, BNF and recursive
state transitions are logically equivalent
(Lomet, 1973). The SYNICS/DDL system of Edmonds
and Guest (Edmonds, 1981) combined the two
notations, using recursive state transitions
to specify dialogue logic and, where simple
matching is not adequate, a BNF-like notation
for specifying and transforming individual
inputs. Experience has shown (Guest, 1982)
that users find it easiest to approach user
interface specification through the dialogue
logic, using at first only straightforward
matching of input strings. More complex
specification of inputs can be handled later as
the need and motivation arises. SYNICS/DDL has
been used successfully for some years (Allen,
1983).

2. CONCEPTS OF SYNICS2.

A user interface management system can be viewed
as an independent process that communicates with
both the user and the applications program. Its
role is both to pass information between the user
and the application and to control the dialogue.
It is convenient to think of the management system
as consisting of three components (ten Hagen et.
al., 1984). Nearest to the user is the
presentation system which maps logical input/
output events from or into physical events. At
the next level is the dialogue control system.
This controls the path of the dialogue and
performs appropriate transformations on the data.
The last part is the applications interface
model. This provides a logical description of
the objects and actions that constitute the
application. This last component need be no
more than a set of explicit conventions for
communication between the management system and
the application.

The user interface management system must
provide a facility for interface definition.
In SYNICS2 this is an interactive system
incorporating test facilities. The completed
definition results in the construction of
files that can be used by the user interface
management system to run the dialogue. The
applications program remains the responsibility
of the programmer and can be implemented in
any suitable language. Figure 1 shows the
relationships between these various components.

3. THE SYNICS2 LANGUAGE.

In SYNICS2, the interface is specified by
defining a collection of DIALOGUE EVENTS. A
dialogue event definition is headed by the
command   DIALOGUE EVENT   name
and concluded by
END EVENT.

FIGURE 1

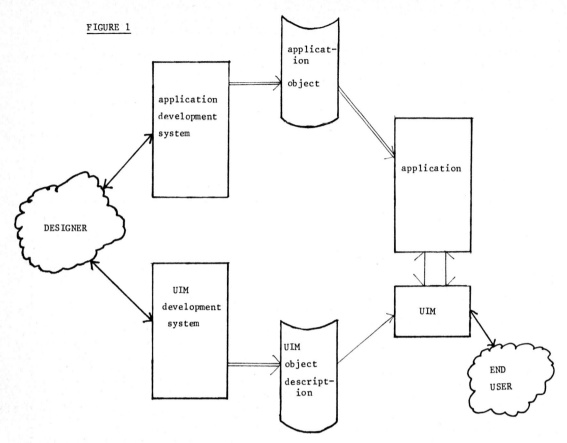

The first part of the definition consists of display commands. Commonly used ones are:-

> TEXT (x, y, message)

which outputs 'message' at screen location(x,y),

> ;message

which outputs 'message' on the next line,

> CLEAR SCREEN

and

> LINE (x1,y1,x2,y2)

which draws a line from (x1,y1)to (x2,y2). The full range of output commands is based upon GKS (ISO,1983) (Guest and Edmonds, 1984) and includes such operations as

> ENABLE CURSOR.

Following the output specification, the command

> INPUT FROM APPLICATION

may appear, in which case the event takes a string from the application and uses it to determine its actions. In the default case, without this command, input is taken from the user.

The body of a dialogue event specification contains an ordered set of rules of the form, in the general case,

> ENTER EVENT name IF
> device condition [application action]
>   <set variables>

where the 'condition' consists of a pattern to be matched with the input from the 'device'. If the match succeeds the 'application action'

is passed to the applications program for its attention, any variables are set as specified and the event 'name' is evoked. The minimum version of such a rule is the unconditional

> ENTER EVENT name.

The first successful rule is obeyed. In addition, sub-dialogues can be handled with

> CALL name parameter list

and

> RETURN.

The parameters can be thought of as text to fill slots in the sub-dialogue either in the display or the ENTER EVENT 'condition' components.

The 'condition' pattern can be specified as a simple literal match, such as 'BYE', or can be specified in terms of any defined context free language. Similarly, the 'application action' can either be a literal string, e.g. 'CLOSE FILE', or it can be a,possibly quite complex,transformation of the input. The details of this part of the SYNICS2 language are, in essence, the same as in SYNICS/DDL (Edmonds, 1981).

A help message can be associated with each dialogue event.

5. EXAMPLE OF A SPECIFICATION.

The following example shows a dialogue segment
in which the end user is allowed to draw a line
on a clear screen using the rubber band method.
The segment shown is a schema, which may be
called from a higher dialogue level.

```
DIALOGUE EVENT initialise

    CLEAR SCREEN
    ENABLE CURSOR

    ENTER EVENT start

END EVENT
-------------------------------------------------

DIALOGUE EVENT start

    ENTER EVENT line IF
        BUTTON ["start:" CURSX,CURSY]
            < SX=CURSX,SY=CURSY >
    REM when a button is hit send the cursor
    position to the application and store in
    local variables.  Otherwise re-enter this
    event.

    HELP: You have chosen to draw a line using
    the rubber band method.  Move the cursor
    to the required start point, using the
    mouse, then press one of the buttons

END EVENT
-------------------------------------------------

DIALOGUE EVENT line

    CLEAR SCREEN
    LINE(SX,SY,CURSX,CURSY)

        RETURN IF
            BUTTON [ "finish:" CURSX,CURSY ]
        ENTER EVENT end IF
            TEXT "cut" [ "cancel" ]
    HELP: Move the mouse until the line is
    correct, then press one of the buttons.
    To cancel type "cut".

END EVENT
-------------------------------------------------

DIALOGUE EVENT end

    CLEAR SCREEN

        RETURN

END EVENT
-------------------------------------------------
```

6. EXAMPLE OF A USER SESSION.

The following example incorporates the dialogue
defined in 4.

SCREEN 1:

```
    1. circle
    2. triangle
    3. hexagon
    4. straight line
    5. finish

    type in the number of your choice
```

INPUT: 4

SCREEN 2:

```
        straight line

    1. by end points
    2. rubber band
    3. drawn

    type in the number of your choice
```

INPUT: help

SCREEN 3 (help window appears):

```
    You may point to the two end points
    of the required line, point to one
    end and have a "rubber band" line
    displayed, which you can move until it
    is in the correct position, or you can
    draw a line which will be automatically
    straightened.
    Press "return" when you are ready.
```

Screen 2 is displayed again without the help
window.

INPUT: 2

SCREEN 4: The cursor now appears.

INPUT: help

SCREEN 5 (help window appears):

```
    You have chosen to draw a line using
    the rubber band method.  Move the cursor
    to the required start point, using the
    mouse, then press one of the buttons
    Press "return" when you are ready.
```

ACKNOWLEDGEMENTS.

The work reported in this paper has been partly
supported by the SERC under research grant
GR/B/99101 and contract N2A 3R 1613 for the
SERC's SIGTIP. Thanks are due to Richard
Hammond for his help in implementing this version
of the system.

REFERENCES.

1. Allen, G. "Impact of Industrial and Academy
    Collaboration on New Technology". Philips
    Lecture. Royal Society. 1983.

2. Edmonds, E.A. Adaptive man-computer inter-
    faces in Computing Skills and the User
    Interface. Coombs and Alty (eds.) AP.1981.

3. Edmonds, E.A. The man-computer interface -
    a note on concepts and design. IJMMS,16,1982.

4. Ehrich, R.W. DMS - A system for defining and
    managing human-computer dialogues. Proc.
    "Analysis, Design and Evaluation of Man-
    Machine Systems". IFAC/IFIP, Baden-Baden
    1983.

5. Engel, F.L., Anderson, J.J. and Schmitz,
    H.J.R. What,where and whence: means for
    improving electronic data access. IJM-MS,18,
    1983.

6. Guest, S.P. The use of software tools for
    dialogue design. IJM-MS, 16, 1982.

7. Guest, S.P. and Edmonds, E.A. Graphical
    support in a user interface management
    system. (To appear), 1984.

8. "ISO/DIS 7942 Information Processing -
    Graphical Kernel System (GKS) - Functional
    Description : GKS Version 7.2." (1982).
    ISO/TC97/SC5/WG2 N163.

9. Jacob, R.J.K. Survey and examples of
    specification techniques for user-computer
    interfaces. Naval Research Laboratory Report.
    Washington D.C. 1983.

10. ten Hagen et.al. Report on the Eurographics/
    IFIP5.2 Workshop on User Interface Management.
    (1984). To appear.

11. Lomet, D.B. A formalization of transition
    diagram systems. JACM, 21, 1973.

Human-Computer Interaction — INTERACT '84 / B. Shackel (ed.)
Elsevier Science Publishers B.V. (North-Holland)
© IFIP, 1985

A HUMAN-COMPUTER DIALOGUE MANAGEMENT SYSTEM

H. Rex Hartson, Deborah H. Johnson, and Roger W. Ehrich

Department of Computer Science
Virginia Polytechnic Institute and State University
Blacksburg, Virginia 24061, USA

The **Dialogue Management System (DMS)** of Virginia Tech is a comprehensive system for designing, implementing, testing, and maintaining interactive software systems with human-computer interfaces. A concept called dialogue independence, in which the dialogue component of a system is separate from the computational component, forms the fundamental philosophy of DMS. Dialogue independence is manifest at the highest level of DMS in three ways: by providing a comprehensive design methodology for the production of interactive systems, by providing separate sets of automated tools with which the dialogue and computational components are implemented, and by providing separate execution environments for each of the components.

1. INTRODUCTION

Poorly designed human-computer interfaces result in significant operational costs of computing systems due to many effects on the user, including extensive training requirements, high error rates, low productivity, and the poor emotional attitude of their users toward computers. Little theoretical guidance and few automated tools exist for building quality interfaces. In response to these problems, we have developed a holistic system development methodology, based on a theory of human-computer dialogue. We have also developed automated tools and environments to support the methodology and the model at both system design-time and execution-time.

The **Dialogue Management System (DMS)** of Virginia Tech is a comprehensive system for designing, implementing, testing, and maintaining interactive software systems with human-computer interfaces [1].

2. NEW CONCEPTS AND ROLES IN DMS

2.1 Dialogue Independence

In response to the need for improved human-computer interfaces, the concept of dialogue independence has developed as the underlying premise of DMS. **Dialogue independence** involves the separation of the dialogue component from the computational component of an application system. The dialogue component and computational component are brought together for execution of the completed application system. The interface between the dialogue component and computational component conducts an internal dialogue and the interface between the dialogue components and the user conducts an external dialogue. **External dialogue** is the traditional human-computer interface for the interaction between the user and the system. It is highly variable, limited only by the imagination of the person who creates the content of the dialogue component. **Internal dialogue**, on the other hand, has no direct connection to the user of the system, but serves as a link between the dialogue component and the computational component of a system. It must therefore be formally specified and is much less variable in its form.

Dialogue independence is manifest at the highest level of DMS in three ways: by providing a comprehensive design methodology for the production of interactive systems, by providing separate sets of automated tools with which the dialogue and computational components are implemented, and by providing separate execution environments for each of the components. The methodology assumes that the logically distinct components are to be developed by different specialists. The tools facilitate and encourage the creation of application systems with quality human-computer interfaces. The execution environment is based upon a multiprocess system architecture within which the logically independent components are also physically independent.

2.2 Dialogue Author

In order to emphasize the separation of dialogue and computational components of software systems, separate roles are responsible for each of the two components. An application programmer writes computational components, but writes no dialogue. In DMS, a new role, that of a **dialogue author**, has sole responsibility for developing the dialogue which comprises the human-computer interface of a system. The dialogue author is a person who is not necessarily a skilled programmer, but rather is oriented towards the human factors of human-computer interface development.

2.3 Human Factorability

The problem of building a human-computer interface requires bringing together the knowledge and techniques of the cognitive psychologist, the linguist, the human factors engineer, and the software engineer during the system design and implementation. Because the design of quality human-computer interfaces must necessarily be a process of iterative refinement, interfaces need to be easily and rapidly modifiable to meet their users' needs. In order to be made human factored, an interface must be **human factorable**, that is, easily modifiable and testable. Dialogue independence is a prerequisite for human factorability, especially when it is not always clear during the early stages of system design what is needed to make a system human factorable.

3. A HOLISTIC SYSTEM DEVELOPMENT METHODOLOGY

Creating an application system that has separate dialogue and computational components is different from the development of a traditional software system. Thus, a new, holistic methodology, called the **SUPERvisory Methodology And Notation (SUPERMAN)** [2] has been developed. Applicable to the modeling of any procedural system (software or not), SUPERMAN integrates many of the components of conventional methodologies (data flow diagrams, structure charts, and PDLs) into a single approach and a single design representation, throughout the software lifecycle. SUPERMAN is built around an automated programming tool environment, which also produces executable requirements specifications for rapid prototyping before any implementation code is written.

This methodology recognizes and addresses the fact that in order to deal effectively with dialogue, system developers must work with the entire system. SUPERMAN incorporates the dialogue management concept of dialogue independence into system design, and provides for effective interaction between the new role of the dialogue author and the traditional role of the application programmer.

3.1 Developing Interactive Software Systems

In SUPERMAN, the entire target interactive software system is represented with a **supervisory structure.** The supervisory structure is a hierarchy of **supervisory cells** (see Figure 1), each of which represents the subfunctions of a single supervisory function. The sequence of subfunctions is shown as a **Supervised Flow Diagram (SFD)**, shown in Figure 1, which indicates both control flow and data flow among the subfunctions.

A symbol having a circle inscribed in a box is a Dialogue-Computation (D-C) function; its SFD contains both dialogue and computation. A circle is a pure dialogue function and a box is purely computational. Each subfunction can then be a supervisory function of supervisory cells at the next level down in the hierarchy. Terminal nodes in the supervisory structure are called worker functions, which perform single dialogue or computational operations.

A key concept is that the administration of data flow and control flow among the subfunctions of an SFD is performed by the supervisory function of that SFD. A linear sequence, such as between subfunctions E and F in Figure 1 is accomplished by a simple sequence of two procedure calls in A, the supervisory function. Where alternate paths exist, such as coming from B to either C or D, the supervisory function, A, must evaluate a condition (e.g., with a "case" statement) to decide which successor to B should be called. Data flow can be represented in SFDs both through parameters and through data structures.

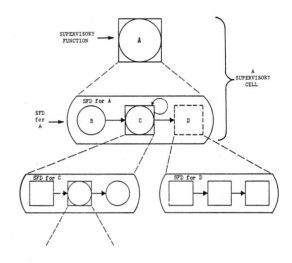

Figure 1 : Supervisory structure and cells

3.2 Structure of An Interactive System

The supervisory structure of a target application system can be divided into three components, as shown in Figure 2. The set of all D-C functions, plus the highest level pure dialogue and pure computation supervisors comprise the control structure of the entire target system. The dialogue component is the set of all dialogue functions (circles) and the computational component is the set of all purely computational functions (boxes). The dialogue and computational components will typically contain both supervisory and worker modules. Those same supervisory functions will also appear at the bottom of the control structure hierarchy.

The control component and the dialogue component, taken together, are the behavioral structure which determines the form, content, and sequencing of external dialogue at the human-computer interface. The computational component, via internal dialogue, sends data for displays and receives input values for computation. The behavioral structure can be prototyped, and system behavior demonstrated, before the computational component is implemented.

This is discussed further in Section 5 under the Behavioral Demonstrator.

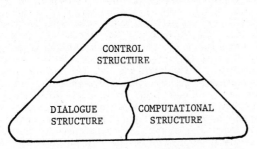

Figure 2 : Structure of an application system

The design lifecycle begins with a conceptualization of the problem and requirements specification. A systems analyst helps the designers, application experts, and users construct a "wish list." The human factors engineers and software engineers/systems analysts then structure the procedural parts of this list into a high-level supervisory structure, which is eventually expanded into the complete control structure, (using GPL, discussed in Section 5) with dialogue and computation functions as "stubs." This is a complete and precise statement of the system requirements (the logical system design). Because this structure is executable, there is no need for a translation step to design and implementation (as there is in most other methodologies), nor a need for verification that the design and implementation meet the requirements.

As the need for dialogue and computational functions becomes known, these are developed, respectively, by the dialogue author (using AIDE, discussed in Section 5) and the application programmer (using GPL, discussed in Section 5, and conventional programming). Dialogue independence allows these two components to be developed separately from each other and from the control structure.

4. A MODEL OF HUMAN-COMPUTER INTERACTION

Every exchange of information between a computer and its users follows a specific sequence. Under DMS, the exchange is called a dialogue transaction, and a human-computer interface is composed of many transactions. A **dialogue transaction model** is being developed as part of a theory of human-computer interaction to serve as a framework for the understanding and design of human-computer interfaces.

The dialogue of human-computer interfaces is typically conducted by means of a **transaction sequence**, (shown in Figure 3) based on an Input-Process-Output configuration [3]. A dialogue input transaction prompts the user and validates the resultant input. That input is passed to the computational component, where it is processed, and the results of this processing are displayed to the user via a dialogue output transaction. Each circle in every SFD is a

dialogue transaction of one of the types shown in Figure 3. The collection of all dialogue transactions for an application system is its dialogue component.

At the next level of abstraction down from the SFDs, one can observe the internal structure of a dialogue transaction. A **transaction** is a sequence of one or more interactions to extract an input and/or to produce an output. An input interaction is comprised of three **parts**: system **prompt**, followed by human **language input**, followed by system **syntactic confirmation**. Any of these parts may be implicit in a given interaction.

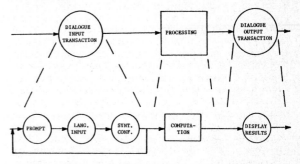

Figure 3 : A dialogue transaction sequence

Each prompt is a general display part and can be made up of various **pieces**, including pieces having these styles: list menu, labeled keypad outline, text, graphical objects, a form to be filled in, and voice output. Correspondingly, the language input definition can be composed of pieces featuring menu selection, keypad key selection, command string input, forms filling, and voice input. Confirmation parts are comprised of textual, graphical, and voice pieces.

5. DESIGN-TIME SUPPORT TOOLS

5.1 Graphical Programming Language (GPL)

The SUPERvisory Methodology And Notation is designed to be set in an automated programming environment. As the supervisory structure develops from an early representation of the basic functional system requirements to a complete system design, the SFD elements are considered to be symbols in a **Graphical Programming Language (GPL)**. In the implementation phase, the control structure and much of the computational component can be compiled directly from the GPL representation. Only the lowest level computational functions are programmed in the conventional sense, and even those lowest level functions can be implemented in the GPL. The graphical editor for the GPL, in addition to being an automated tool for production and maintenance of SFDs, also helps to manage the design by providing reminders to the system developers about incomplete components.

GPL is a highly sophisticated graphical editor

which, when completed, will contain an embedded database to track design progress and provide information services to the system implementers. For example, the database will record module histories, provide inter-team communication, and through split-screen displays will provide up-to-date information about documentation, global data structures, identifier references, and file and variable status. The database plays a critical role in insuring that every team member has all current project information necessary to make design decisions.

5.2 Behavioral Demonstrator

Since the sequencing of dialogue is tied to the logical control structure of the application software design, it is essential that the logical flow be tested as early as possible in the design process, to refine the specification of system requirements, and to identify and make changes to improve the resultant user interface. This need to visualize dialogue sequences continues all the way through the development process until the application system is implemented and operational, as well as later, during modification cycles. To meet this need, DMS provides a tool called the **Behavioral Demonstrator.** The Behavioral Demonstrator allows the execution of the automated control structure to be observed by the application end-users and studied by human factors experts to verify the fulfillment of their system requirements and to evaluate whether their requirements were complete and correct, all before any conventional program source code is written. Rather than being a specific phase near the end of the lifecycle, testing is distributed over all phases of the lifecycle.

As the need for changes inevitably arises, changes in the SFDs are easier to make than changes in partly coded systems. The Behavioral Demonstrator uses the GPL internal representation, but traverses it interpretively, rather than compiling it. An interface is provided to the user or human factors experimenter to capture design notes and suggestions as the application system is exercised.

The Behavioral Demonstrator is **not** a simulator. There is no mapping from a model to the real system as there is with simulation. No effort or code is discarded as there is when a simulation is completed and the design of the real system begins. In DMS the requirements specification and design evolve directly into the final system. The behavior of the target system can be demonstrated at any stage of its development. It begins as a finite-state model of control structure, and, as displays and language inputs become well-developed, the behavior which is demonstrated evolves gracefully into that of the finished product. Use of the GPL and the Behavioral Demonstrator continues through the maintenance phase. The SFDs are traversed as the Behavioral Demonstrator exercises the design representation, in order to locate the part of

the system needing modification. The GPL editor is then used to make the modifications and its effect can be immediately demonstrated.

Of all the supporting tools that will be implemented, the Behavioral Demonstrator is expected to have the most immediate and visible impact on the human factors people with whom we are working. In addition to providing early visualization of the logical sequencing of the system, it allows them to pretest the dialogues for their interactive experiments and make the appropriate modifications, rather than having to wait until the system is operational to discover that some aspect of it is not satisfactory for their needs.

5.3 Author's Interactive Dialogue Environment

The purpose of **AIDE** is to provide an automated set of tools for a dialogue author to use in creating human factorable human-computer dialogues. The current version of AIDE allows a dialogue author to develop static (non-changeable) displays consisting of any combination of menus, keypads, text, forms, and graphical objects; menu and keypad language inputs; and textual confirmations.

AIDE integrates a diverse group of interactive facilities for creating dialogue transactions. Such tools as a menu formatter, a forms formatter, and a touch panel display formatter are used to create the prompt/display and confirmation parts of a dialogue transaction. An example-based language definition tool in AIDE, called **Language-by-Example (LBE),** facilitates the design, specification, and recognition of the language input part of a transaction. By starting with a specific example of a language input (e.g., a command string), LBE guides the dialogue author through its definition, generalizing to a complete, stored definition of the language input.

The parts of a dialogue transaction (the dialogue elements) can be developed in any order, since AIDE is designed to allow the dialogue author to move freely among transactions, interactions, parts, and pieces. For example, if a menu is being designed, as each menu choice is added to the display, its (relatively simple) language input definition can be given (using LBE in AIDE) and the corresponding confirmation messages can be composed, if desired. Alternatively, the entire menu display can be designed and then the inputs and confirmations, in turn. Similarly, it is easy to move from one display piece formatter to another to combine, for example, a keypad, some text, and some graphics within the same display definition.

The output of the AIDE tools, the internal representations or definitions of the parts of a transaction, are held during their creation, modification, or execution, in a relational **transaction database (TDB),** which eventually contains all parts of all transactions for an entire application system. Each instance of a transaction (created using AIDE) has a definition for each of its parts (the output of AIDE) stored in the TDB, individually retrievable for modification or execution.

6. EXECUTION-TIME SUPPORT ENVIRONMENTS

6.1 Dialogue Executors

At execution-time, the form of the dialogue transaction model is built into the control structure of a **transaction executor.** This transaction executor is data-driven at run-time to instantiate a dialogue transaction, and to process the dialogue transactions of an applicative system interface. Each part of the transaction has its own executor, called by the transaction executor: a display executor to interpret the display definition and to produce a display; a language executor (DYLEX, discussed below) to interpret the language input definition and to accept, parse, and validate the user's input; and a confirmation executor to interpret the confirmation definition and to produce the system confirmation.

The key component for processing user language input parts at run-time is the **DY**namic character-at-a-time **L**anguage **EX**ecutor called **DYLEX** [4]. Invoked by the transaction executor, DYLEX uses the stored language input definitions, which were created using AIDE at design-time, to process each character which the end-user enters at run-time, with appropriate validation checks.

The approach taken in DMS dictates that wherever possible, validity checking is specified in the dialogue component as part of the syntax of the language specification, rather than in semantic routines in the computational component. That achieves two goals: validity checking is dynamic as a transaction progresses, and no programming is required. In order to accomplish these goals, DYLEX has a built-in repertoire of algorithms for the dialogue author to invoke at will. Some, such as token completion or spelling correction, are extremely sophisticated and beyond the normal skills of most programmers and dialogue authors. Others, such as format and range checking, are included because these capabilities are so frequently needed in human-computer interfaces. Other algorithms may need to be added in the future, and it is particularly important that these be added to DYLEX, rather than to application-specific computational modules. This permits them to be dynamic, and it makes them available to the dialogue author for use in future designs. Moreover, once the algorithms are refined, they never need to be reinvented.

6.2 Multiprocess Execution Environment

DMS uses a language-independent multiprocessing execution environment to support its tools (both design-time and execution-time), as well as the application systems created using the DMS tools. This multiprocessing enforces dialogue independence, by physically separating dialogue and computational components of an application system at run-time. It also allows possible dialogue and computational concurrencies that might not otherwise be feasible, provides a rather clean way of packaging large services such as embedded database systems, provides device independence, and allows multiple dialogue processes which facilitate the synchronization of multiple user requests for multiple devices. A task that might be conventionally implemented as a single program will, under DMS, be implemented as a set of independent communicating programs, each of which executes in a separate process. Such a set of communicating programs is referred to as a **program complex.** Within a complex, the computational component contains the control structure for the application. The dialogue component is in a separate process (or set of processes) containing a collection of dialogue transactions that do not call one another and which have no shared environment. The interrelationships among dialogue transactions are defined by the control structures in the computational programs that invoke the dialogue transactions.

7. SUMMARY AND FUTURE WORK

The Dialogue Management System (DMS) is an interactive system for developing human factorable human-computer systems. Future DMS research will include further dialogue modeling, enhanced versions of AIDE, GPL, and the Behavioral Demonstrator, metering capabilities, advanced database services, and empirical evaluation of DMS itself.

ACKNOWLEDGEMENT

This work is supported by the National Science Foundation under Grant MCS-8310414.

REFERENCES

[1] Hartson, H.R., R.W. Ehrich, and D.H. Johnson, "The Management of Dialogue for Human-Computer Interfaces," submitted to Human-Computer Interaction (1984).

[2] Yunten, T. and H.R. Hartson, "SUPERvisory Methodology And Notation (SUPERMAN)", in preparation (1984).

[3] Wasserman, A.I., "Information System Design Methodology," J. of the Amer. Soc. for Info. Science (January 1980), 5-24.

[4] Narang, P., R.W. Ehrich, and D.H. Johnson, "Dynamic Languages for Human-Computer Interaction," in preparation (1984).

Human-Computer Interaction — INTERACT '84 / B. Shackel (ed.)
Elsevier Science Publishers B.V. (North-Holland)
© IFIP, 1985

AN IMPROVED USER INTERFACE FOR PROLOG

Marc Eisenstadt
Tony Hasemer
Human Cognition Research Laboratory
The Open University, Milton Keynes, U.K.

Frank Kriwaczek
Imperial College, London

We have developed a series of prototype software environments for both beginning and
advanced Prolog users in an attempt to provide a consistent and powerful user
interface which is easy to understand, easy to use, and incorporates the best features
of several different dialects of Prolog. Our user interface is characterised by
Prolog-specific editing and debugging tools, and the ability of the user to interact
directly with the internal representation of the database in a manner which is
intuitive for beginners yet provides sophisticated debugging capabilities for experts.
Prototypes currently exist for most portions of the system, and run under Prolog-10,
POPLOG, and micro-PROLOG on a variety of machines.

INTRODUCTION

This paper describes our ongoing research into
the development of an environment to assist both
novice and experienced programmers working with
Prolog. The tools and other user aids we shall
provide will help in the easy development,
testing, debugging and understanding of Prolog
programs, based on a unified model of the way in
which such programs are executed.

Our work is new in that (a) it contains
Prolog-specific development and debugging tools,
most of them implemented in Prolog itself; (b)
it argues that by clear and consistent presentation of the underlying machine and the total
software environment, both novice and expert
users can benefit from similar tools; (c) it aims
to bring together developments in the Prolog-10,
micro-PROLOG, and POPLOG communities.

Prototypes exist of all of the facilities
described in this paper. Work is currently
proceeding at the Open University using the
POPLOG system [5] and Prolog-10 [1] and in
parallel at Imperial College where the main
supporting system is micro-PROLOG [2] running
on a Perq and on a North Star Advantage.

PROLOG SUMMARY AND OVERVIEW OF OUR SYNTAX

Prolog uses a modified predicate logic notation
to express facts, rules of inference, and
queries. Here are two facts, expressed in our
syntax, which is a derivative of micro-PROLOG
syntax:

(kisses Sue Tom)

(has-flu Tom)

The first fact can be regarded as meaning
"Sue kisses Tom," the second fact as meaning
"Tom has the flu." All of the symbols inside
the brackets are arbitrary tokens, so that the
second fact, for example, specifies 'has-flu' to
be a unary predicate. Upper and lower case
letters have no special significance in our
syntax. Our syntax requires even binary
predicates such as 'kisses' to be expressed in
the sequence (predicate argument1 argument2).

We eschew the 'naturalness' and 'readability'
accounts of infix notation (e.g. 'Sue kisses
Tom') on the grounds that (a) it would mislead
our students into thinking that the underlying
Prolog virtual machine understands more than it
really does; and (b) it would make the
introduction of n-place predicates, such as
(gives Tom money Fred) pedagogically more
difficult. We deviate from the predicate
argument structure of predicate calculus (e.g.
kisses(Sue,Bill)) in order (a) to reduce the
number of symbols to be typed, (b) to provide a
uniform internal list-structure representation
which makes the underlying Prolog virtual
machine easier to understand, and (c) to make
the structural scope of expressions easy to
perceive at a glance.

Here is an example of a Prolog rule:

(has-flu ?X) if
    (has-fever ?X) &
    (sneezing ?X)

Such a rule can be regarded as having both a
declarative and a procedural meaning in Prolog.
Declaratively, the rule states that "for all X,
if X has a fever and X is sneezing, then
conclude that X has flu". Procedurally, the rule
means "To prove that some person has flu, (1)
show that the person has a fever, and also (2)
show that the same person is sneezing." The
procedural interpretation is useful for
explaining order in Prolog, since the consequent
of a rule acts like the title line of a
procedure with parameters, and the antecedents

act like subroutine calls.

Queries are addressed to the Prolog interpreter in the following fashion:

(kisses Sue Tom)?

(kisses Sue ?X)?

The first query asks "Is it true that Sue kisses Tom?" The second query asks "Is it true that Sue kisses anyone (or anything)?" In both cases, the interpreter searches (sequentially) for facts or rules which can be used to deduce the truth of the query expression. In the latter case, it also shows the 'binding' (pattern match) of the variable ?X to the first possible item it matches against in the database of facts. We use the prefix character '?' to highlight the 'wild card' nature of the variable used during pattern matching. The same character also terminates a query. The everyday usage of the '?' symbol, combined with the positional information on the line makes its meaning unambiguous in both cases. The user can optionally obtain a printout of ALL possible matches in the second query, by typing in:

(kisses Sue ?X)??

Details of how Prolog copes with variable bindings, and how it undoes bindings upon failure of subgoals are beyond the scope of this paper. The interested reader is referred to excellent tutorial accounts in [3] and [2].

ENVIRONMENT OVERVIEW

All user-input is directed to one of three 'interface agents', which have distinctive visual representations/locations on the terminal display: (a) the DATABASE BROWSER, which is a sophisticated PROLOG-oriented screen editor; (b) the QUERY INTERPRETER, which is an ordinary PROLOG top level comparable to that of existing Prolog systems; (c) the DEBUGGER, which provides tracing, single-stepping, and source code analysis and highlighting facilities in a manner consistent with the conventions used by the DATABASE BROWSER and the QUERY INTERPRETER. Any fact or rule which is typed into the BROWSER is automatically 'known' to the Prolog interpreter as well, so that what you see is really what you get.

The normal screen layout of our system shows the DATABASE BROWSER occupying the top two thirds of the screen and the QUERY INTERPRETER occupying the lower third. Single-keystroke commands allow the user to move between these two indepentently-scrolling screen regions. On moving to the lower window the user receives an automatic 'Q:' (Query) prompt and may then type any Prolog query. In this case the <RETURN> key causes the query to be executed and the results

to be printed back, preceded by an 'A:' (Answer). For example, Fig. 1 shows the appearance of the screen with a particular portion of the database shown in the upper window. The cursor has been moved to the lower window, a suitable query entered, and an answer and new prompt diplayed:

```
-DATABASE: has-flu ------------------------|
|                                           |
| 1 (has-flu ?X) if                         |
|     (kisses ?X ?Y) &                       |
|     (has-flu ?Y)                           |
|                                           |
| 2 (has-flu ?X) if                         |
|     (has-fever ?X) &                       |
|     (sneezing ?X)                         |
|                                           |
|-QUERIES:----------------------------------|
|Q:(has-flu Sue)?                           |
|A:yes                                      |
|Q:█                                        |
|-------------------------------------------|
```

Fig. 1: Snapshot of display after a typical query. The cursor (█) is now sitting on the bottom line of the display.

The next two sections outline in turn the DATABASE BROWSER and DEBUGGER. The latter section will show portions of a trace which displays how the interpreter arrives at the answer to the query posed in Fig. 1.

DATABASE BROWSER

Ordinary users, especially beginners, view the database in terms of its internal organisation by predicate name, and don't work with traditional 'files' as such. This has the virtue of (a) being simple in conception, which is useful for teaching purposes, and (b) being very powerful for advanced users, since it gives them a window directly into the internal database, so that what the user sees on the screen is just what the user gets during execution-- if a fact or rule is visible, it is also known to Prolog. Analogously, assertions added during a running program will by default be displayed on the screen just as if the user had been adding them 'by hand' to the database (this facility can be supressed by a single keystroke).

Database items are indexed by predicate name and arity. Upon pressing a single 'visit predicate' key, the user is invited (on the top line) to supply the name of a predicate, followed by <CR>. A listing of the clauses for that predicate is then displayed in the upper screen. For predicates with multiple arity, the arity is displayed on the top line, and the user can specify alternatives if necessary (e.g., in the case of another has-flu predicate with three arguments, the specification would be 'has-flu/3'). The user can page through the clauses of that predicate, move one at a time

forwards or backwards, or move specifically to
the first, last or nth clause.

For convenience, and to provide some surrounding
context during browsing, the upper window can
grow to dominate all but the last line of the
display (which is kept so that there is always a
visible 'Q:' prompt for the user to move back
to). In addition, the upper window can be
subdivided into two parts. When a user is
investigating a particular clause of a
predicate, he can move the cursor through the
clause by character, word, literal (antecedent
condition), or whole line at a time. On wishing
to inspect the predicate in a particular
condition he can "zoom in" on this new
condition. The upper browsing region will then
display the clause that he was investigating,
with the condition in question marked by a "*"
symbol in the margin, and the definition of the
new predicate being explored will appear in the
lower half of the DATABASE BROWSER display. This
is illustrated in Figure 2, which shows a screen
snapshot taken after the user decides to 'zoom
in' on the 'kisses' predicate while browsing
through the first clause of 'has-flu':

```
|-DATABASE: has-flu{1} kisses ----------------|
|1 (has-flu ?X) if                            |
|*    (kisses ?X ?Y) &                        |
|     (has-flu ?Y)                            |
|2 (has-flu ?X) if                            |
|     ...                                     |
|                                             |
|     _____        |
|1█(kisses Sue Tom)                           |
|2  (kisses Fred Mary)                        |
|...                                          |
|-QUERIES:------------------------------------|
|Q:                                           |
|---------------------------------------------|
```

Fig. 2: Example of 'zooming in' on the
'kisses' predicate while browsing through
the first clause of 'has-flu'. Notice the
'zoom hierarchy' depicted on the top line.
The cursor (█) is positioned at the
beginning of the first 'kisses' clause.
The '...' symbol means that more exists
further 'down' in that region of the
database.

The user can move back from 'child' to 'mother'
clause, going on to other conditions of the
mother clause or to other clauses of the mother
predicate if so desired. A further zoom within
the child clause, however, will cause the
current child ('kisses' in Fig. 2) to scroll up
like a roller blind, so that it becomes the new
mother clause with a child clause of its own. A
record is kept of the history of the navigation
and displayed "ticker-tape" style on the top
line of the screen. This has the virtue of
providing surrounding context without requiring
the proliferation of new windows. By repeating
this process the user can navigate through the

clauses of a database, investigating how they
are related to one another. A predicate can be
'visited' at any time by (a) typing its name
after pressing the 'visit predicate' key; (b)
selecting it via cursor movement in the BROWSER
window for 'zooming'; (c) selecting it via
cursor movement in the top line 'ticker tape'
display.

At any time the user can employ the screen
editor to modify clauses, to add new clauses for
an existing predicate at any position relative
to the other clauses, or to add clauses for a
new predicate. Clause numbering along the left
hand margin is provided and updated
automatically, as is pretty-print formatting,
automatic syntax-checking, bracket-balancing and
spelling correction. If the user tries to
enter raw text to provide the definition of a
new predicate while browsing through the
definition of another one (e.g. trying to add
(kisses Sue Tom) in between the two has-flu
clauses in Figure 1), the browser display is
automatically updated to visit the region of the
database relevant to that predicate (e.g., as if
the user had pressed either the 'visit
predicate' button or the 'zoom' button).

More advanced users can work with ordinary
files, which may contain arbitrary text. In this
case, the top line of the diplay reads 'FILE:'
instead of 'DATABASE:', and the user must resort
to the more traditional edit/load/run cycle,
marking particular regions of Prolog code to be
loaded in on request. The disadvantage of this
style is that automatic database-updating and
clause numbering are lost (although in fact
these can be regained by reverting back to the
database browser to inspect the database at a
later time).

THE DEBUGGER

The debugger provides facilities for monitoring
the execution of a PROLOG program step-by-step,
as well as for static and dynamic analysis of
the user's code. It is invoked by pressing a
single keystroke, whereupon the 'QUERIES:' label
on the lower window changes to 'DEBUG:', and the
user supplies a query in the usual syntax,
followed by <CR>.

Stepping through code during execution is
conceptually similar (and uses the same
keystrokes as) the browse/zoom sequence during
editing. Consider the case of stepping through
the execution of the query (has-flu Sue) as
presented in figure 1. For this example, the
PROLOG database contains (kisses Sue Tom),
(kisses Fred Mary), (has-fever Tom), (sneezing
Tom), and the rules shown in the database window
in Figure 3:

```
|-DATABASE: has-flu ---------------------|
|                                        |
|>1 (has-flu ?X) if                      |
|      (kisses ?X ?Y) &                  |
|      (has-flu ?Y)                      |
|                                        |
|2 (has-flu ?X) if                       |
|      (has-fever ?X) &                  |
|      (sneezing ?X)                     |
|                                        |
| -DEBUG:---------------------------------|
|Q:(has-flu Sue)?                        |
|                                        |
|                                        |
|----------------------------------------|
```

FIG. 3: Screen 'snapshot' during
single-stepping through the query
(has-flu Sue). Execution has just
begun, with the interpreter
considering clause 1 of 'has-flu'.

The clauses of the first subgoal, or goal in the
case of an atomic query, are displayed in the
DATABASE screen. The stepper moves through the
clauses under variable-speed control from the
user, highlighting each with a ">" in the
margin, until a head can be matched. Any
variables in the head as well as in the
conditions of the clause, that have become
instantiated through this matching, are
displayed alongside the values that they have
acquired through the instantiation, using the
notation '?VAR:binding', e.g. ?X:Sue. The
stepper then flags the first condition of the
clause with a '?' in the left margin, and zooms
in on the definition of the condition predicate,
displaying it in the middle of the screen:

```
|-DATABASE: has-flu{1} kisses ---------------|
|>1 (has-flu ?X:Sue) if                      |
|?       (kisses ?X:Sue ?Y) &                |
|        (has-flu ?Y)                        |
|2 (has-flu ?X) if                           |
|        ...                                 |
|                                            |
|      _____|
|1    (kisses Sue Tom)                       |
|2    (kisses fred mary)                     |
|...                                         |
|-DEBUG:--------------------------------------|
|Q:(has-flu Sue)?                            |
|--------------------------------------------|
```

FIG. 4: The subgoal (kisses Sue ?Y)
is marked in the upper region, and
the 'kisses' predicate is displayed
in the middle.

Next, the matching fact (kisses Sue Tom) is
flagged with a '+', as is the corresponding
subgoal in the upper part of the screen. The
binding of the variable ?Y to Tom is also shown
in the upper region:

```
|-DATABASE: has-flu{1} kisses ----------------|
|>1 (has-flu ?X:Sue) if                       |
|+       (kisses ?X:Sue ?Y:Tom) &             |
|        (has-flu ?Y:Tom)                     |
|2 (has-flu ?X) if                            |
|        ...                                  |
|                                             |
|      _____|
|+1   (kisses Sue Tom)                        |
|2    (kisses fred mary)                      |
|...                                          |
|-DEBUG:---------------------------------------|
|Q:(has-flu Sue)?                             |
|---------------------------------------------|
```

FIG. 5: Successful match between current
subgoal and a fact in the database,
resulting in binding of ?Y to Tom.

After this, the next subgoal (has-flu Tom) will
be marked in the margin with a '?', and the
has-flu predicate will be (recursively) 'zoomed
in' in the middle of the screen, replacing the
'kisses' predicate shown in the middle of the
display in Figure 5. The stepping process
continues in the fashion through successive
subgoals, with each new subgoal scrolling up,
'roller blind' style, to the top part of the
screen, replacing the previous mother clause in
a manner exactly comparable to that described in
the BROWSER section for 'zooming'. This process
is repeated until the success or failure of a
descendant subgoal. On success, any
variable-instantiation will be reflected upwards
through the series of mother goals, and the
stepper will move to the next subgoal. On
failure, the stepper will backtrack
appropriately, undoing any instantiation that is
necessary, and will mark a clause that failed
before trying the next alternative subgoal, if
any.

Throughout the stepping, the top line gives
a history of the execution, also in
"ticker-tape" style, showing clauses with
numbers, and any variable bindings. At any time,
the user can review the steps by using a cursor
to move backwards from item to item in the top
line.

In our example, clause 2 of 'has-flu' will
eventually succeed for (has-flu Tom) because
both (has-fever Tom) and (sneezing Tom) are
stored in the database.

Although this stepper can be a most useful aid
in understanding the execution of a program, it
can also form a powerful debugging aid when
combined with the screen editor. While stepping
through a program in manual mode, the user can
backtrack through a specified number of steps
and employ the editor to modify the program or
add new clauses "on the fly". The system will
remember any changes made during the stepping
process, and afterwards the changes can be
incorporated permanently or forgotten.

The debugger internally stores the intermediate results of the stepping process, and from this store it is easy for the user to retrieve for example a list of failures, the hierarchy of goals, or suspect cases for further analysis. An implementation of this facility for Prolog-10 and POPLOG, with some automatic 'suspect code' analysis, is described in [4].

We do not expect novice users to take advantage of all these facilities. The important point is that the debugger display works in a manner consistent both with the way Prolog execution is explained to our students and with the way the browsing/editing facilities work. This means that advanced user aids can be selectively 'revealed' to the students as they become more proficient, without the attendant need to revise the description of the underlying virtual machine.

FUTURE DEVELOPMENTS

Prototypes of the BROWSER and the code tracing/ highlighting part of the DEBUGGER are at the time of writing fully implemented. Future work will concentrate on automatic - as opposed to user-operated - debugging. Our aim here is to provide intelligent knowledge based tools, implemented in Prolog, to detect and to report bugs. We are building on the work of (a) Shapiro [8], who developed a "divide and query" theory of algorithmic program debugging which was inherently well suited to (and in fact was implemented in) Prolog, (b) Laubsch and Eisenstadt [7], who investigated the symbolic evaluation of recursive programs involving pattern matching and assertional databases, and (c) Hasemer [6], who developed a suite of program analysis programs for the Open University's own in-house language, SOLO.

Our Shapiro-style debugger is expected to step through programs in an attempt to discover counterexamples, and will require the user to provide partial solutions to subproblems. Laubsch and Eisenstadt have already demonstrated the feasibility of symbolic evaluation techniques for various classes of the kind of programs with which our debugger will be faced, particularly those involving recursion and side-effects on data bases. Our Hasemer-style debugger is based on pattern matching and will look for near misses of frequently-occurring Prolog "cliches". It will also provide automatic or semi-automatic correction for a variety of mundane lexical and syntactic errors, and will be able to trap (and suggest remedies for) certain execute-time errors such as endless recursion.

REFERENCES

[1] Bowen, D. L. (ed), Byrd L., Pereira F.C.N., Pereira L.M. and Warren D. H. D. (1982) DecSystem-10 Prolog User's Manual. Edinburgh: Department of Artificial Intelligence, University of Edinburgh.

[2] Clark, K. and McCabe, F. (1984) micro-PROLOG - Programming in Logic. New York: Prentice-Hall.

[3] Clocksin, W.F. (1984) An introduction to Prolog. In O'Shea, T., & Eisenstadt, M. (Eds.), Artificial intelligence: tools, techniques, and applications. New York: Harper and Row.

[4] Eisenstadt, M. (1984) PTP: A Prolog Trace Package for the Prolog-10 Family. Technical Report No. 9, Human Cognition Research Laboratory, Open University, Milton Keynes, U.K.

[5] Hardy, S (1984) "A New Software Environment for List Processing and Logic Programming". In T. O'Shea and M. Eisenstadt (eds) Artificial Intelligence: Tools, Techniques and Applications. New York: Harper & Row.

[6] Hasemer, T. (1983) "A very Friendly Programming Environment for SOLO." in New Horizons in Educational Computing. M. Yazdani (ed). Ellis Horwood.

[7] Laubsch, J., and Eisenstadt, M. (1982) Using temporal abstraction to understand recursive programs involving side effects. Proceedings of the American Association for Artificial Intelligence (AAAI-82), Pittsurgh, PA.

[8] Shapiro, E. Y. (1982) Algorithmic Program Debugging. Cambridge, Ma: MIT Press.

Human-Computer Interaction — INTERACT '84 / B. Shackel (ed.)
Elsevier Science Publishers B.V. (North-Holland)
© IFIP, 1985

A SIMPLE USER INTERFACE FOR INTERACTIVE PROGRAM
VERIFICATION

R.J.R. Back[*]   P. Hietala

University of Helsinki   University of Tampere
Department of Computer Science   Department of Computer Science
Helsinki, Finland   Tampere, Finland

A prototype system for interactive program verification is described, with special emphasis on its user interface. The system supports incremental and iterative verification of programs, employing a spread sheet like paradigm of direct manipulation.

1. INTRODUCTION

We describe in this paper the user interface of the interactive program verification system I3V (Interactive system for Incremental and Iterative Verification of programs), which is currently being developed at the University of Tampere. The system assists the user in verifying the correctness of a given program, allowing the correctness proof to be constructed in an incremental and iterative fashion while the system records the proof being constructed and keeps track of the status of the proof (what has already been proved, what still needs to be proved and so on). I3V supports the verification of partial correctness, proper termination and the absence of run—time errors of a program.

One of the biggest obstacles to a more widespread use of program verification techniques seems to be the sheer amount of detail that has to be managed in carrying out a correctness proof. We therefore wanted to give the user a tool by which he can manage and control this wealth of detail during the verification process. Another motivation for the I3V system is that in our opinion the iterative nature of the program verification process has not been properly recognized in most of the existing verification systems. Programs intended for verification are usually not correct in the first place, or then the program invariants supplied for the proof are incorrect or incomplete. It takes a number of successive modifications in the program text and program invariants before these errors are removed and it becomes possible to prove the correctness of the program. In I3V the user constructs the proof interactively, sitting at a display terminal. The proof is built incrementally, piece by piece, and the user is free to go back and make changes to previously proved parts of the program, modifying proof of verification lemmas or making changes, additions or deletions in the program text or in the program invariants. The system will automatically adapt to these changes, generating

new verification lemmas when necessary and indicating those parts of previous proofs that need to be rechecked.

We will in this paper focus on the dialogue between the user and the system, emphasizing the interactive use of the display terminal. We want to exploit the advantages of merging two at present rather separated areas: user—machine dialogue and program verification. The user interface has traditionally not received very much attention in the design of program verification systems, where the main concern has been to automate as much as possible of the verification process. The program to be verified is therefore usually processed as a whole and reduced to a set of verification conditions, which are then supplied to a theorem prover or formula simplifier for verification. This approach is quite sensible, if all verification conditions can in fact be verified automatically. In practice this is not, however, usually the case, forcing the user to intervene and help the system in establishing the correctness of the more difficult verification conditions.

Rather than viewing the user as an agent which intervenes only when the automatic theorem prover or simplifier gets into trouble, we want to give the user the primary control over the the verification process, and consider the automatic theorem prover and formula simplifier only as convenient tools to be used when appropriate. Most proofs of verification lemmas are assumed to be carried out more or less manually. The user interface then becomes a critical issue in the design of a verification system, and ultimately determines the usefulness of it.

The significance of the interaction between programmer and program verification system was recognized already in the early seventies /4/. However, in spite of various recommendations on the subject (e.g. in recent workshops on formal program verification /15,16/), there are still only a few systems that allow a more flexible user interface, such as incremental development and verification of programs (the Gypsy system /6/), or help in reasoning about the effects of changes to previ-

---

[*]Present affiliation: Åbo Akademi, Department of Information Processing, Turku, Finland.

ously proved parts (the designer/verifier's assistant /9/), or provide facilities for interactive checking of proofs of verification conditions /12/. The rapid progress in the area of "direct manipulation" /13/, such as full-screen text editors, language-oriented editors, spread sheet manipulation programs and CAD-systems, has not aroused the attention in the verification community it deserves.

I3V is an attempt to apply the ideas of direct manipulation to the problem of verifying simple iterative programs. Program verification in the I3V system is done entirely within the context of the original program text. Errors and omissions can therefore be easily located, and once found, they can be fixed immediately. The effects of the changes (such as new verification conditions to be proved or proofs of old conditions that might have become invalid) propagate to subsequent parts of the program, in a manner similar to spread sheet computation. Being able to carry out the proof in the context of the original program text gives the programmer a better overview of the proof and its present status. This becomes particularly important when verifying larger programs.

The programming language that we use /2/ is a simple iterative one, with omission of all explicit loop control structures; all loops have to be made by jumps to specified labels, which also serve as program specification points to which the loop invariants are attached. This structure makes it easy to modify the program, and the proof rules become simple, while no expressive power is lost. The verification method used is symbolic execution, with forward generation of verification conditions. The programming language can be extended with procedure and data abstraction mechanisms without too much difficulty, and explicit looping constructs can also be added to the language if needed.

2. USER INTERFACE

We describe the user interface by dividing it into four components (following Newman and Sproull /10,11/): user's model, command language, information display and feedback. The first of these, the user's model, underlies the other three: it is the conceptual model that the user forms of the information he manipulates and of the processes he applies to this information. In our system the user is primarily concerned with locations in the program text, where a location is a position immediately preceding or following a program statement. With each location four pieces of information are associated: (1) the identifiers and their types that are accessible at the location, (2) user supplied or system generated assumptions that are valid at the location, (3) system generated lemmas that should be proved at the location, and (4) the proofs of the lemmas at the location. The last kind of information is provided by the user (possibly assisted by a theorem prover, formula simplifier or proof checker). In order to verify the correctness of a program, the user must supply a proof for the verification lemmas at every program location.

The command language of the I3V system allows the user to move around in the program text, search for information, compress and display it. He can also modify program text, invariants or proofs at specific locations. He has at his disposal a movable window into the program text which shows the information associated with a specific location in the program text. This window can be moved forward or backward in the text or directly to a specified location, with the information content of the window updated appropriately. The user can choose which kinds of information are to be shown in the window. The system then divides the window into subwindows, one for each kind of information. He can also choose to show no information at all, in which case the window degenerates to a single line which acts as a cursor in the text.

The proof status of a location is shown when the window is moved there. If the verification lemmas are displayed in the window, then there is an indication for each lemma whether it has been proved or not. Otherwise there is a mark after the location number indicating whether some, all or none of the lemmas there have been verified. To prove a verification lemma at the location, the user simply types in the proof (or modifies or extends the previously given proof at that location).

Example snapshots of a session with the I3V system are shown in Figures 1-4. In Figure 1 the user has his window at location 11. At this stage no information is shown in the window, which is therefore represented by a broken line. In Figure 2 the window has been expanded and shows the assumptions and lemmas at the same location. In Figure 3 the window has been moved one step forward to location 12. The same kinds of information are shown but now for the location 12. The lemmas here are only partially proved (indicated by the mark "+" after the location number: "*" denotes a completely unproved and a space an already proved location). In Figure 4 the window at location 12 has been expanded to also show the valid identifiers part and the proof part of the location.

One of the main problems we face in a design like the one described above is the limited size of the display screen (we use a 24 x 80 screen). The amount of information associated with a location will exceed the screen size already in small programs. This leads us to the crucial question of displaying appropriate information in a limited space (the third component of the above user interface classification). We have to provide facilities by which the information associated with a specific location can be selectively displayed. A simple approach is to have separate scrolling of subwindows. Another possibility is to compress the display in some suitable way. Language-oriented editors e.g. provide either automatic or user-controlled condensing of information. In the former, the refreshing algorithm (e.g. the PDE1L system /8/) decides what to display according to some weights assigned to the program constructs.

In many Lisp–editors and in the MENTOR system /3/ the user can define "the depth" of the structure displayed. In COPE /1/ the user has the possibility to compress the statements on the current line so that only the first one of them is displayed entirely. The modern workstation technology seems to offer many desirable features for the display problem (e.g. built–in windowing and high resolution) but basically the problems of a limited screen space remain the same.

```
LOCATION 11:

    var A : array [1..r] of integer;
    var r : integer;
    label exit : IsSorted(A,A0);
    decrease: (i,i-j+1);

ON ENTRY: (r >= 1) and (A=A0)

 1:  var x, i, j, k : integer;
 2:  label loop1: Perm(A,A0), 1<=i<=r, j=2,
          Ordered(A,i+1,r), Partitioned(A,i);
 3:  label loop2: Perm(A,A0), Biggest(A,j-1,k),
          1<=k<=j-1, j-1<=i<=r, x=A[k];
 4:  begin
 5:*     i:=r;
 6:      j:=2;
 7:*     goto loop1
 8:  # loop1:
 9:*     if (i > 1) then
10:*            k:=1;
---------------------------------------------------
11:*            x:=A[k];
12:+            goto loop2
```

Figure 1. Snapshot of a sort program, with the window acting as a cursor
(the broken line)

```
LOCATION 11:

 9:*     if (i > 1) then
10:*            k:=1;
----------------------------------------------------
ASSUME:                     :  PROVE:
                            :
 (1) A = A#,                :  (1) 1 <= k <= r
 (2) x = x#,                :
 (3) i = i#,                :
 (4) j = j#,                :
 (5) k = 1,                 :
 (6) r >= 1,                :
 (7) Perm(A#,A0),           :
 (8) 1 <= i# <= r,          :
 (9) j# = 2,                :
(10) Ordered(A#,i#+1,r),    :
(11) Partitioned(A#,i#),    :
(12) i# > 1                 :
                            :
----------------------------------------------------
11:*            x:=A[k];
12:+            goto loop2
13:      // (i <= 1) then
```

Figure 2. Expansion of the location window to contain also the assumptions and the
verification lemmas (an identifier with the mark "#" denotes a system
generated symbolic value)

```
 LOCATION 12:

10:*                 k:=1;
11:*                 x:=A[k]
 -----------------------------------------------------------------
 ASSUME:                          :   PROVE:
                                  :
   (1) A = A#,                    :   (1) Perm(A,A0)
   (2) x = A#[1],                 :   (2) Biggest(A,j-1,k)
   (3) i = i#,                    :   (3) 1 <= k <= j-1
   (4) j = j#,                    :   (4) j-1 <= i
   (5) k = 1,                     :   (5) x = A[k]            (OK)
   (6) r >= 1,                    :   (6) (i,i-j+1) <= (i#,i#-j#+1)
   (7) Perm(A#,A0),               :
   (8) 1 <= i# <= r,              :
   (9) j# = 2,                    :
  (10) Ordered(A#,i#+1,r),        :
  (11) Partitioned(A#,i#),        :
  (12) i# > 1                     :
                                  :
 -----------------------------------------------------------------
12:+                goto loop2
13:      // (i <= 1) then
14:*                goto exit
```

Figure 3. Moving the window to the next location; note that the contents are updated
          appropriately

```
 LOCATION 12:

10:*                 k:=1;
11:*                 x:=A[k];
 -----------------------------------------------------------------
 VISIBLE IDENTIFIERS:             :   ASSUME:
                                  :
   (1) A : array [1..r] of integer :   (1) A = A#,
   (2) r : integer                :   (2) x = A#[1],
   (3) x : integer                :   (3) i = i#,
   (4) i : integer                :   (4) j = j#,
   (5) j : integer                :   (5) k = 1,
 ..................................................................
 PROVE:                           :   PROOF:
                                  :
   (1) Perm(A,A0)                 :   Lemma (5) follows directly
   (2) Biggest(A,j-1,k)           :   from assumptions (1), (2)
   (3) 1 <= k <= j-1              :   and (5).
   (4) j-1 <= i                   :
   (5) x = A[k]            (OK)   :
 -----------------------------------------------------------------
12:+                goto loop2
13:      // (i <= 1) then
14:*                goto exit
```

Figure 4. Expansion of the location window to its full form; note that only part of
          the information fits in the subwindows

The I3V system supports the independent scrolling of subwindows. In addition, we have implemented a form of user-controlled information condensing: the user can compress the information by explicitly marking those parts he wants to display. (Automatic condensation is a possibility worth studying but the condensation of logical formulas seems to be more complicated than that of structured program text.)

Feedback (the fourth component in the user interface classification) is provided for every keystroke, either by a change in the display window or by echoing the command in a separate line. The user is also informed of the process of the computation when it takes a longer time. We try to give the user "immediate feedback", so that he feels better in control of the system, and thus is less prone to make errors /5/.

3. INCREMENTAL AND ITERATIVE VERIFICATION

The I3V system is based on the assumption that program verification is a process that takes a considerable amount of time. The proof has to be built up incrementally and many iterations are required to make it go through. Each iteration alters previous formulations of proofs, specifications or program text. In I3V the state of the proof can be saved and program verification can be resumed at the point it was last left. As the location proofs are supplied by using an editor—like facility, they are easy to write and change. Invariants are restricted to be in conjunctive normal form, and are modified by adding, deleting or rewriting conjuncts. The effect of a change is automatically propagated by the system, i.e. all the assumptions and lemmas depending on the modified invariant are appropriately changed. Proofs that are no longer necessarily valid after a modification are marked as such. Program text modification in I3V can be carried out by commands for deleting or rewriting statements or inserting new statements (similar to those in e.g. the Cornell Program Synthesizer /14/). The lemmas, assumptions and proofs affected by these changes are updated in the same manner as in the case of changing program invariants.

4. IMPLEMENTATION STATUS AND FUTURE PLANS

An I3V prototype system has been completed, and is running on DEC System 2060. It is written in SIMULA 67, and presently consists of about 8000 program lines. An earlier version is described in /7/. The current I3V verification system has been tested on a collection of smaller programs with encouraging results. More detailed user tests with larger programs will be carried out in the near future.

Three main extensions to the system are under study. First, a procedure mechanism will be added to the language. Second, the system will be extended to support the verification of ordinary Pascal—programs. Finally, a more selective invalidation of proofs after a modification will be implemented in order to minimize the need for reproving lemmas which actually remain valid in spite of the modification.

Acknowledgement

This work was supported by the Academy of Finland.

References

/1/ Archer, J.E., and Conway,R., COPE: a cooperative programming environment. Tech.Rep. TR81-476, Cornell University, Dept.of Computer Science, June 1981.

/2/ Back, R.J.R., Invariant based programs and their correctness. In Biermann, Guiho, Kodratoff (eds.), Automatic program construction techniques. MacMillan 1983.

/3/ Donzeau—Gouge, V., et.al., Programming environments based on structured editors: the MENTOR experience. Technical Report no. 26, INRIA Rocquencourt, France, May 1980.

/4/ Floyd, R.W., Toward interactive design of correct programs. Information Processing 71, North—Holland Publishing Company, 1972, 7–10.

/5/ Gaines, B.R., and Facey, P.V., Some experience in interactive system development and application. Proceedings of the IEEE 63, 1975, 894–911.

/6/ Good, D.I., and DiVito, B.L., Using the Gypsy methodology. Draft, Institute for Computing Science. The University of Texas at Austin, Texas, October 1981.

/7/ Hietala, P., An interactive program verification system: first version of the MESS environment. University of Tampere, Department of Mathematical Sciences, Report A97, February 1983.

/8/ Mikelsons, M., and Wegman, M., PDE1L: the PL1L program development environment — principles of operation. Tech. Rep. RC 8513, IBM T.J.Watson Research Center, Yorktown Heights, NY, September 1980.

/9/ Moriconi, M.S., A designer/ verifier's assistant. IEEE Trans. on Software Engineering, vol. SE–5, no.4, July 1979, 387–401.

/10/ Newman, W.M., Some notes on user interface design. In Guedj, R.A., et.al. (eds), Methodology of interaction, North—Holland, 1980, 325–326.

/11/ Newman, W.M., and Sproull, R.F., Principles of interactive computer graphics. McGraw—Hill (2nd edition), 1979.

/12/ Reps, T., and Alpern, B., Interactive proof checking. Proc. 11th ACM Symposium on Principles of Programming Languages, Salt Lake City, Utah, January 1984.

/13/ Shneiderman, B., Direct manipulation: a step beyond programming languages. IEEE Computer Vol. 16, No. 8, August 1983, 57–69.

/14/ Teitelbaum, T., and Reps, T., The Cornell Program Synthesizer: a syntax—directed programming environment. CACM 24, 9, September 1981, 563–573.

/15/ Workshop on Formal Verification (VERkshop), Menlo Park, April 1980. ACM SIGSOFT, Software Engineering Notes 5, 3, July 1980.

/16/ Workshop on Formal Verification (VERkshop II), NBS, Gaithersburg MD, April 1981. ACM SIGSOFT Software Engineering Notes 6, 3, July 1981.

Human-Computer Interaction — INTERACT '84 / B. Shackel (ed.)
Elsevier Science Publishers B.V. (North-Holland)
© IFIP, 1985

THE PROGRAMMER'S TORCH

T.R.G. Green and A.J. Cornah

MRC/ESRC Social and Applied Psychology Unit
The University
SHEFFIELD S10 2TN, UK

ABSTRACT

The Programmer's Torch is a projected
software tool designed to illuminate
the workings of programs by answering
maintenance-like questions about data
flow and the 'roles' of identifiers.
We describe the novel methods of
analysis used and the current state
of the project.

Experiments by the Sheffield group and others
(Sime et al., 1977; Sheppard et al., 1980;
van der Veer and van de Wolde, 1983) have
repeatedly shown that it is not enough for
information to be "logically" available in a
written program: it must be easily available.
Modern languages achieve some of these requirements by principles of information-hiding and
loose coupling between modules, but it is difficult to achieve all of the requirements merely
by clever notational design.

In any case, however inspired the next generation
of programming languages may be, history dictates
that for many years to come most programs will
continue to be written in antique languages -
Fortran, Basic, Cobol, which between them account
for a huge percentage of all programming teaching.
This is one motivation, the other motivation is
to increase our understanding of programmer
psychology.

Broadly speaking, a programmer puzzled by a
program should be able to put it into the
Programmer's Torch with no more fuss than putting
a text file into a spelling checker. The Torch
should get answers to such questions as "How
does identifier X get set? Is it safe to change
identifier Y here, or does something else use Y?
What is identifier Z for?" These questions can
be answered by various forms of static analysis
- preferably interactively, not by printing out
a great wodge of material to be digested.

By comparison, there are a number of 'programmer's
assistant' projects which aim to create an

intelligent tool capable of performing some
limited reasoning and problem-solving on its own
account (Rich et al., 1978): but we are instead
aiming solely to make it easier for programmers to
use their own intelligence - which is precisely
what a notational improvement is designed to do.
There are also projects aimed at demonstrating
what can be done to analyse and perhaps transform
programs, under the constraint that the programs
are written in specially-designed languages, which
are very clean and well-structured (Ruth, 1976;
Burstall and Darlington, 1977): however, we want
to see what can be done with an existing language,
to discover whether its problems are those we
predict.

Programs highly suitable for our purposes can be
found in the hobbyist pages of computer magazines.
They are written in Basic: they are short but
interestingly filled with logic: and they are
frequently quite inscrutable.

Who needs a Programmer's Torch?

Maintenance programmers - who frequently need to
probe into ill-documented programs written in
Cobol, Fortran, or assembler - are in great need
of software tools. (As a matter of fact, a small
industry is growing up around that need.) Our
project is intended to clarify the mental processes of someone in such a position, by discovering whether particular facilities would be useful
to them.

What information should a Programmer's Torch illuminate?

Consider the program of Figure 1. Experiments at
Sheffield and elsewhere have been interpreted as
indicating that it is fairly easy to obtain
sequential information from such a program: e.g.
for given X, Y, Z what will this program do? On
the other hand it is considerably harder to
obtain circumstantial information: under what
circumstances can line 60 be reached? (Answer:
X$ = JUICY or Y$ = TALL) Evidently, circumstantial information is one requirement. (Notice
that although the problems of extracting
circumstantial information are less acute in a
Pascal-like language, they do not disappear:
see Gilmore and Green, 1984).

FIGURE 1

```
10      READ X$, Y$, Z$
20      IF X$ = "JUICY" GOTO 60
30      IF Y$ = "TALL" GOTO 50
40      PRINT "FRY" : END
50      PRINT "ROAST"
60      PRINT "BOIL" : END
```

Now consider the slightly larger program of
Figure 2. According to many models of program
comprehension, not to mention folk wisdom, the
program has to be segmented and the data flow
has to be revealed. This will automatically
reveal whether a specified variable is 'live' -
that is, whether it has been given a value in
one segment that is used in a later segment -
or whether it can safely be re-used. A number
of existing static analysis programs perform this
job (Hecht, 1977).

FIGURE 2

```
999     REM --- Subroutine to count zeros in
        Array A
1000    INPUT "ACCEPT NEGATIVE VALUES?" : A$
1010    IF LEFT(A$,1) = "Y" THEN N = 1 : GOTO
        1030
1020    N = 0
1030    Z = 0 : T = 0
1040    FOR J = 1 TO C
1050    IF A(J) = 0 THEN Z = Z + 1 : GOTO 1090
1060    IF A(J) > 0 THEN GOTO 1090
1070    IF N = 1 THEN GOTO 1090
1080    A(J) = 0
1090    T = T + A(J)
1100    NEXT J
1110    PRINT "TOTAL=": T: "ZEROS = ":Z
1120    RETURN
```

Once segments or chunks are being displayed,
together with the data flow between them, it
becomes possible to attempt to recognise particular schemas. We use 'segment' to refer to a
passage of connected program text, and a 'schema'
for a set of related program statements that are
not necessarily continuous. Running program text
is constructed from interleaved schemas.

The empirical work of Mayer (1979) and Soloway,
Erlich and Bonar (1982), and the analytical work
of Waters (1982) indicate that it would be useful
to extract recognizable program schemas, although
empirical efforts to identify mental schemas have
not yet been wholly successful (Adelson, 1981;
McKeithen et al., 1981). Unfortunately the usual
techniques (e.g. Waters, 1979) are only applicable
to properly structured programs, since they rely
on extensive decoupling between components. As

amateur Basic programs are not noted for adherence
to the principles of structured programming, these
techniques cannot readily be applied.

Even if the schemas themselves cannot be recognized by program, it may be possible to identify
the roles of variables. In the program above, Z
has the role of a counter variable. Elsewhere in
the program, N has the role of a control variable
or flag. Identifying roles would possibly give
programmers substantial help in identifying the
enclosing schemas. We know of no empirical
evidence bearing on this possibility.

We chose as our targets, therefore, the presentation of the roles of variables, and the
analysis of circumstantial information. Although
the project has not reached a stage in which users
can interact with it, the aim would be to have
a very limited interface language, possibly
something like this:

```
User:       EXPLAIN  Z, LINE 1030, STATEMENT 1
Computer:   Z IS A COUNTER VARIABLE, THE COMPON-
            ENTS ARE:
   1030     Z = 0
   1040     start of loop
   1050     IF A(J) THEN Z = Z + 1
   1100     end of loop
   1110     PRINT Z
User:       COMEFROM, LINE 1090
Computer:   1090 COMES FROM:
   1040     ALWAYS: VIA:
      1050  IF A(J) = 0
      1060  IF NOT [ A(J) = 0 ] AND A(J) > 0
      1070  IF NOT [ A(J) = 0 ] AND NOT
            [ A(J) > 0 ] AND N = 1
      1080  IF NOT [ A(J) = 0 ] AND NOT
            [ A(J) >0 ] AND NOT [ N = 1]
```

The answer to a 'comefrom' question is strictly
textual - programmers will have to use their own
intelligence to deduce.

$$NOT [A(J) = 0] \text{ AND NOT } [A(J) > 0] \rightarrow A(J) < 0$$

The illustration takes the analysis back as far
as the nearest dominator, 1040 (a node through
which all paths to the target pass). Whether
this limited (but computationally cheap) analysis
will be useful is an empirical question.

The structure of Basic

A good many schemes for the analysis or transformation of programs require functional programming
languages, or at any rate emphasize the functional
aspects of whatever programming language is taken
as the source. Basic has hardly any resemblance
to a functional programming language.

To analyse amateur Basic programs at all, certain limitations must be accepted. For instance, programs containing the ON <expression> GOTO <line> command, which can branch to any line depending on the value of the expression, present difficulties. On the other hand, it should NOT be decided that only 'structured' programs will be acceptable. Behavioural evidence (e.g. Sheppard et al., 1979) is not wholly on the side of the angels - or puritans - and the mass of amateurs have voted with their feet to use whatever program construction discipline they choose.

The peculiarities of Basic encourage that. For instance it allows subroutines to be entered by GOSUBs to more than one line and also to be entered by 'trickling-through' from above or by a GOTO - from anywhere. Similarly they can be left by RETURN or by a GOTO addressed to the outer program: the subroutine return stack can then be updated by a POP command in some Basics. There are many similar features.

Amateur Basic programs do not often make extensive use of array manipulations. Since the present state of analysis of data flow in programs using arrays leaves much to be desired, this is fortunate for us.

A few Basics now include subroutines with parameters and local variables, but the textual scoping is still quite permissive even in these versions, so we shall not pay them any special attention. The Applesoft and Microsoft dialects have been taken as models.

Present State of the Project

An experimental program has been written by David Gilmore to extract circumstantial information from simplified Basic-like programs represented as semantic nets. However, the main thrust of our effort has gone into discovering the roles of variables, starting from real-life programs taken from computer magazines.

The program is written in early versions of Snap (Green et al., 1983), a language resembling POP-11, running on an Onix 16-bit micro under Unix V7. Initial processing is performed by the 'lex' and 'yacc' utilities, to build a flowgraph from the source text: virtually full Applesoft Basic can be accepted. Nodes certain descriptions of the variables used, arcs contain descriptions of variables defined and destroyed when control passes along the arc. This flowgraph is then passed to the segmentation phase, which forms higher-order graphs and classifies the segments. The final phase, which is not yet operational, will determine the roles of variables by parsing the pattern of use within the segments.

Segmentation

The segmentation phase aims to produce interpretable subgraphs from the program flow graph. This process is comparatively easy if the program is hierarchically constructed, but real Basic programs are sometimes quite tangled. To produce a useful form of analysis, it is no good limiting it to the easy bits - people can probably understand those without help!

Our initial attempts were based on intervals, which are maximal single-entry subgraphs. The work of Allen and Cocke (1976) shows how flow graphs can be constructed from intervals, and higher-order graphs can be constructed in turn.

FIGURE 3

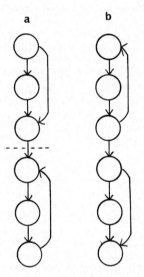

Conventional data-flow analysis is asymmetric: (a) forms two intervals, but (b) only forms one.

However, although intervals make data flow analysis very straightforward, they do not lend themselves to classifying the segments. Because of their property of maximality, too much gets included in each interval.

Instead, therefore, we classified segments as:

- Sequences - consecutive nodes with no branches entering or leaving the segment;

- Conditional structures - built out of IFs; usual definitions have been extended to allow STOP statements. A conditional structure has a head with multiple exit nodes, each of which is either the common tail statement (which is not a member of the case), a node with one entry and one exit to the common tail, or a node with one entry and no exit (i.e. a STOP).

- Loops - which have a head, which is entered by a back arc on a depth-first spanning tree, and members, which are nodes on any path from the head back to itself, provided that all their predecessors are already members of the loop. This definition prevents loops with multiple entries being classed as loops, and prevents outer loops from consuming inner ones.

- True subroutines - all heads entered only by
  GOSUBs, all exits by RETURN.

All segments that can be classified as sequences
(i.e. no branches) are replaced by a single
higher-order node: next all conditional structures (segments with no backwards jumps):
finally, loops. The analysis is performed
cyclically so that for instance a loop may
become one arm of a conditional which may then
become part of a sequence.

Unstructured programs

Programs which are not hierarchically constructed
will not be reduced to a single node by this
process. Our analysis then isolates, as far
as possible, the unstructured subgraphs. Earlier
algorithms (Williams, 1977, 1982; Prather and
Giulier, 1981) are liable to consume the entire
graph as one large unstructured subgraph in
certain cases, notably loops with multiple exits,
whereas in Figure 4 only nodes 1, 2, 3 and 4
should be classified as an unstructured component.

FIGURE 4

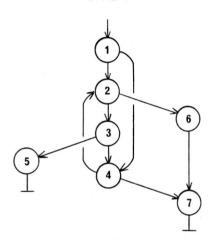

To achieve this, Prather and Giulieri's defini-
tion of a subgraph must be altered from "a set
S of nodes such that there is one entry node in
S and one exit node in S". Exits to STOP state-
ments must be allowed, and we must exclude from
S all nodes which have one entry from S and one
exit which leaves S, such as nodes 5 and 6 in
Figure 4.

The unstructured forms listed by Williams (1977)
and Oulsnam (1982) turn out to be equivalent.
Two of their forms, William's 'overlapping loops'
and 'loops with multiple exits' (= Oulsnam's LL
and BL and LD and LB), are fully analysable by
our scheme; the remaining forms, 'abnormal
selection' and 'loops with multiple entries'
(Oulsnam's DD and DL) are the two forms that we
leave as unstructured components.

The importance of extending analysis beyond the
realms of simple hierarchical structure is seen

if the program of figure 2 is slightly modified.
Change line 1080 to read

      1080 PRINT "Unacceptable negative" : RETURN

If a strictly hierarchical analysis is to be used
this small change has the profound result of
making the program unanalysable, since the loop
now has an extra exit. Yet from the programmer's
point of view, the change is very slight.

As an illustration, figure 5 describes the analysis of overlapping loops, a form of construction
widely cited as problematic (e.g. Fitter and
Green, 1979). In this figure, (a) presents the
original form; (b) shows the graph in depth-
first order. Nodes (1) and (2) will be recognized as loop heads but the loop with (1) as
head will have no members, because node (2) has
a predecessor (3) which is not already a member
of the loop. The loop with (2) as head will
have (4) and (3) as members, giving the graph
(c) from which we obtain (d).

FIGURE 5

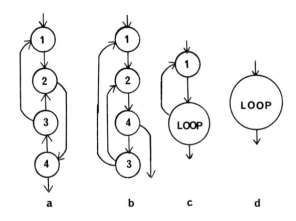

a   b   c   d

Roles of Variables

Using the classification of segment types, the
roles of variables can then be classified. All
classifications of variables can be made relative
to a certain structure, so that it is possible
to record that Z is a counter within a given
segment, such as a subroutine. The list below is
at present tentative, an indication of what we
expect to analyse, and the meta-language is very
informal.

- Constants: these are set once and never
  changed. Shape:

      set X: ... use X

- Counters: exactly one setting available to a
  loop head, updated to functions of themselves
  within the loop or within inner loops, and
  with exposed uses after the loop. In figure
  2 variables T and Z are examples. Archetypes

- counting, forming totals. Shape:

      set Z: ... [... Z = Z + expr : ...] ...
      use Z

- Loop counters: as counters, but tested by a
  conditional that leaves the loop and without
  exposed uses after the loop: e.g. J in
  Figure 2.

- "Best-of" holders: like counters, except that
  within the loop they are set within a conditional to a value which is related to the
  conditional expression. Archetype - finding
  a maximum. Shape:

      set MAX : ... [... IF expr > MAX THEN MAX
      = expr : ...] ... use MAX

- "Most-recent" holders: like "best-of" holders
  but not set to an expression that occurs in a
  conditional. Archetypes - find the index of
  the largest number in an array: pointer to
  previous element in a bubble sort. Shape:

      set LAST : ... [... set LAST : ... ? use
      LAST ...] ... ? use LAST

- Control variables: these decide the execution
  path from a test, and have several settings
  available to the test; e.g. N in Figure 2.
  Shape:

      IF expr THEN set FLAG ELSE set FLAG : ...
      IF FLAG THEN ...

- Subroutine variables: most Basics have poor
  facilities for subroutine communication, and
  variables must be explicitly passed.

  * Parameters: available to calls of the sub-
    routine and with exposed uses to a
    subroutine entry.

  * Results: available to a RETURN from the
    subroutine and having an exposed use at a
    call of the subroutine.

  * var parameters: these are 'call-by-reference'
    -like, and combine the conditions for para-
    meters and for results.

  * Locals: set within the subroutine, only
    the local settings used there, and the
    local settings not used after the RETURN.

Analysis in Action

The following program has been cited as an example
of a poorly structured, opaque amateur Basic program, that would be hard to comprehend or to
modify. It can readily be analysed using our
structures and the analysis corresponds closely
with the semantic sense of the program.

FIGURE 6

```
20 PRINT "TIME(S)","HEIGHT(M)","VEL(M/S)","FUEL(KG)","BURN(XG/S)"
30 GO=1.62\M=26000\D=10000\F=13000\T=1\T1=0\S=1
33 P=1125\R=3\V=100\U=100
40 PRINT T1,D,V,F,\INPUT B,D2\B=ABS(B)
45 FOR X=S TO D2 STEP S\R2=1.700000E+06
47 G=GO-2*D/R2\IF D<1.000000E+07 THEN 50\PRINT "TOO FAR OUT"\STOP
50 V=U+T*G-(B*P*T)/((M+(M-T*B))/2)\T1=T1+T
60 M=M-(T*B)\D=D-((U+V)/2*T)\U=V\F=F-B*T
65 K=K+(B*.23)-9.87854\IF P*B+G*100>250000 THEN 220
70 IF D<=0 THEN 110\NEXT X\IF K>2000 THEN 200\IF K>1500 THEN 210
75 IF F>=0 then 40
90 PRINT "OUT OF FUEL AT";T1\B=0\S=1.000000E-03\GOTO 45
110 PRINT "ON MOON AT";T1;"SECONDS.LANDING VELOCITY";V
120 IF V<10 THEN 160\IF V<20 THEN 170
130 PRINT "ALL CREW KILLED.BLASTED NEWCRATER ";V*11.78;"KM WIDE"\STOP
160 PRINT "SAFE LANDING"\STOP
170 PRINT "CREW INJURED "; INT(3.2*V/17.46);" BONES BROKEN"\STOP
200 PRINT "POWER TUBE BURN OUT";R-1;"LEFT"\R=R-1\IF R=0 THEN 207
205 P=P/(4-R)\GOTO 75
207 PRINT "ALL TUBES GONE"\S=1.000000E-03\B=0\GOTO 45
210 PRINT "POWER TUBES TOO HOT"\GOTO 75
220 Z=RND(0)*30\PRINT "BLACK-OUT FOR";INT(Z*D2);"SECS"
230 D2=Z\B=25\GOTO 45
```

The structure of Figure 6 turns out to be:

FIGURE 7

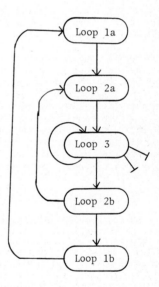

The program is a loop which follows the progress
of a moonlander for a period under given conditions (loop 3). This loop has various STOP
statements corresponding to different outcomes:
crashes, successful landings, and still going.
The program decides after completing loop 3
whether the crew still has control of the ship:
if not, the conditions are reset and loop 3 is
re-entered. This is loop 2, parts (a) and (b).
If the crew can still control the ship then the
player is asked to decide a course of action and
the descent continues: this is loop 1, parts
(a) and (b)

A typical item that could be extracted from this program would be the role of variable K, which is a counter set at RUN time (loop level 0), updated at statement 1 of line 65 (loop level 3), and used at lines 71 and 72 (loop level 2).

Empirical Assessment of Software Tools

Once it can be shown that the analysis technique will successfully classify the roles of variables in programs such as the Moonlander, it will be possible to test the utility of the Torch as a programmer's aid. At present our intention is to do this by 'paper software'.

With unlimited resources, we should construct a proper interactive interface between the programmer and the Torch, which would present the results of analyses in a clearly visible form and allow questions to be asked in a very simple manner (see above). Instead, however, the assessment will be made by analysing the target program in advance, storing the results of the analysis, and wheeling them out when requested by the programmer. By testing the ability of programmers to comprehend and modify real Basic programs, from the pages of hobbyist magazines, with and without the Torch as an aid, we shall discover whether it is capable of supplying a useful service.

Regardless of how far the particular facilities we have described turn out to be helpful in program comprehension, the investigation can be expected to throw light on the processes of comprehending programs. Other interactive software tools (e.g. Browne and Johnson, 1978; Masinter, 1980; Teitelbaum and Reps, 1981) should be empirically investigated from the same point of view and the results should be related to the growing body of theory on program comprehension.

REFERENCES

Adelson, B. (1981). Problem solving and the development of abstract categories in programming languages. Memory and Cognition, 9, 422-433.

Allen, F.E. and Cocke, J. (1976). A program data flow analysis procedure. Comm. ACM, 19, 137-146.

Browne, J.C. and Johnson, D.B. (1978). FAST: A second generation program analysis system. Proc. 3rd International Conference on Software Engineering, IEEEE/NBS/ACM.

Burstall, R.M. and Darlington, J. (1977). A transformation system for developing recursive programs. J. ACM, 24,

Fitter, M. and Green, T.R.G. (1979). When do diagrams make good computer languages? International Journal of Man-Machine Studies, 11, 235-261.

Gilmore, D.J. and Green, T.R.G. (1984). Comprehension and recall of miniature programs. International Journal of Man-Machine Studies, in press.

Green, T.R.G., Arblaster, A.T. McCluskey, T.I. and Cornah, A.J. (1983). Snap: A multipurpose programming languages for psychologists. MRC/ESRC Social and Applied Psychology Unit, Memo No. 621, University of Sheffield.

Hecht, M.S. (1977). Flow Analysis of Computer Programs. North-Holland.

McKeithen, K.B., Reitman, J.S., Reuter, H.H. and Hirtle, S.C. (1981). Knowledge organization and skill differences in computer programming. Cognitive Psychology, 13, 307-325.

Masinter, L.M. (1980). Global program analysis in an interactive environment. Report SS1-80-1, Xerox Corp., Palo Alto Research Center.

Mayer, R.E. (1979). A psychology of learning Basic. Comm. ACM, 4, (22), 589-593.

Oulsnam, G. (1982). Unravelling unstructured programs. Computer Journal, 3, 379-387.

Prather, R.E. and Giulieri, S.G. (1981). Decomposition of flowchart schemata. Computer Journal, 24, 258-262.

Rich, C., Shrobe, H., Waters, R. and Hewitt, C. (1978). Programming viewed as an engineering activity. MIT AI Memo 459.

Ruth, G.R. (1976). Intelligent program analysis Artificial Intelligence, 7, 65-85.

Sheppard, S.B., Curtis, B., Milliman, P. and Love, T. (1979). Modern coding practices and programmer performance. Computer, 12, 41-49.

Sime, M.E., Green, T.R.G. and Guest, D.J. (1977). Scope marking in computer conditionals: A psychological evaluation. International Journal of Man-Machine Studies, 9, 107-118.

Soloway, E., Ehrlich, K. and Bonar, J. (1982). Tapping into tacit programming knowledge. Proc. Conference on Human Factors in Computer Systems, ACM, New York.

Teitelbaum, T. and Reps, T. (1981). The Cornell Program Synthesizer: A syntax-directed programming environment. Comm. ACM, 24, 563-573.

Van der Veer, G.C. and van der Wolde, J. (1983). Individual differences and aspects of control flow notations. The Psychology of Computer Use. Academic Press.

Waters, R.C. (1982). A method for analyzing loop programs. IEEE Trans Software Engineering, SE-5

Waters, R.C. (1982). The programmer's apprentice: Knowledge based program editing. IEEE Trans. Software Engineering, SE-8, 1-12.

Williams, M.H. (1977). Generating structured flow diagrams: The nature of the unstructuredness. Computer Journal, 20, 45-50.

Williams, M.H. (1982). A commont on the decomposition of flowchart schemata. Computer Journal, 25, 393-396.

Human-Computer Interaction — INTERACT '84 / B. Shackel (ed.)
Elsevier Science Publishers B.V. (North-Holland)
© IFIP, 1985

A USER FRIENDLY EDITOR FOR THE PLATO SYSTEM FOR
FAULT TROUBLESHOOTING SIMULATIONS

Henry L. Taylor, William C. Entwistle, and Charles F. Ziegler, Jr.

Aviation Research Laboratory
Institute of Aviation
University of Illinois at Urbana-Champaign

ABSTRACT

A system editor was developed for the PLATO (Programmed Logic for Automated Teaching Operations) computer system to permit troubleshooting simulations to be created and edited. A user guide describes the system editor capabilities and discusses the editing options. To evaluate the user friendliness of the system editor, eleven subjects entered a troubleshooting simulation on PLATO. All subjects completed the task with some assistance from the experimenter. The subjects' responses to questions concerning the user friendliness of the editor were very favorable. They found the editor easy to use to enter the simulation and to correct mistakes. The subjects reported that the task of entering the simulation on PLATO was not difficult.

INTRODUCTION

Since 1976, the University of Illinois has been involved in a variety of computer-based, problem-solving research projects. During this period, a troubleshooting simulation named FAULT, an acronym for Framework for Aiding in the Understanding of Logical Troubleshooting, was conceptualized, developed, and evaluated; ten experiments were conducted using DEC-10 computer-based simulations (Hunt, R. M., 1979; Hunt, R. M. and Rouse, W. B., 1981; Johnson, W. B., 1981; Johnson, W. B. and Rouse, W. B., 1982,a; Johnson, W. B. and Rouse, W. B., 1982,b; Rouse, W. B. and Hunt, R. M., 1982).

In 1982 a FAULT simulation, "Truck Engine", which was first developed on the DEC-10, was transferred to the PLATO (Programmed Logic for Automated Teaching Operations) computer system (Johnson, W. B., Entwistle, W. C., and Gaddis, K. S., 1982). The objective of the PLATO FAULT simulation was for the subject to locate a single malfunction as quickly as possible while incurring minimum expense. The PLATO FAULT simulation presents information on a PLATO terminal about the system, the associated procedures, and the sequence of tests. The PLATO simulation displays such information as the system name, symptom description, gauge readings, troubleshooting actions, and options. Both free and expense options allow the troubleshooter to gather information about the problem, to act on the information, and to receive feedback on the action taken.

The present paper describes a system editor that can be used to create or edit a PLATO FAULT simulation. The paper also provides an overview of user procedures, and evaluates the user friendliness of the editor.

USER GUIDE TO PLATO FAULT SYSTEM EDITOR

The PLATO FAULT System Editor allows the user to create and maintain a total of 15 troubleshooting systems. Each system can contain a maximum of 99 parts, of which 10 can be gauges. A total of 128 connections and associated observations between parts, as well as up to 12 outputs from any specific part, can be created for each system. The editor permits the user to add and delete parts and gauges, edit all information associated with parts and gauges, add and delete connections between parts and edit observations associated with them, edit the system name, and delete the system. Information in the system for a part consists of the part number and name, an a priori probability of failure, observation cost, bench test cost, replacement cost, part description, system description, gauge reading, and bench test description. Information in the system for gauges consists of the gauge number, name, and description.

The FAULT System Editor provides on-line instructions for creating or editing PLATO FAULT systems. The user first selects the PLATO lesson, "faulted" (FAULT EDITOR). The editor then displays an index that lists the existing PLATO FAULT systems and two options. The options are (1) edit a system and (2) create a new system. The option to edit an existing system is selected by entering the number of the system, and the option to create a new system is selected by pressing SHIFT-LAB. In order to create a new system, the following three items must be created: (1) a nameset file to hold the system information, (2) a second nameset file to hold test results for the system, and (3) a common block to hold average problem statistics for the system. The editor instructs the user to have the content of the system specified and the information organized for entry before proceeding to create a system.

After these three items are created, the editor presents prompts that request the following information: system nameset name, system title, number of gauges, and number of parts. The program performs extensive checks on the validity of the information entered and advises the user of any problems encountered. If the information is valid, the system is created and the user is presented the index of editing options shown in Table 1.

Table 1
INDEX OF EDITING OPTIONS

1. Edit gauges
2. Edit parts
3. Edit connections/observations
4. Change system name
5. Delete entire system

The following paragraphs provide a detailed discussion of each editing option.

Editing Gauge Information

Selection of editing option 1 permits the user to create a gauge, delete a gauge, or edit the information associated with a gauge. Two items of information are required for each gauge: the gauge name and a short functional description of the gauge. Each gauge name can have a total of 24 characters and the descriptions can be up to 2 lines or about 120 characters. Gauge information should be entered before entering information on parts, since the gauge names appear when the gauge readings for any specific part are being edited.

Editing Part Information

Selection of editing option 2 provides the user with on-line directions for creating a part, deleting a part, as well as for editing the information associated with a part. The options and system limitations pertaining to editing a part are shown in Table 2.

Selection of part option 8, "Gauge Readings", in Table 2 permits gauge readings to be edited on a separate display that lists gauge number and name and the following six possible readings for each gauge: (1) normal, (2) zero, (3) low, (4) marginal, (5) variable, and (6) high.

Editing Connections and Observations

Selection of editing option 3 in Table 1 permits the user to create a connection, delete a connection, or edit the observation description associated with a connection. When editing connections and observations the top two-thirds of the screen is reserved for numerical listing of all the connections of the system;

the bottom third provides instructions to the user. Observation descriptions of five lines or about 300 characters can be entered. Normally, one observation description is entered for each connection in the system but sometimes there are connections for which no easy observation is possible. These observations are marked by an asterisk (*) by entering the connection and pressing SHIFT-DATA. If such an observation is subsequently selected during a troubleshooting simulation, the following message will be presented: "That observation cannot be made because of the nature of the parts involved." Observation descriptions for terminal parts, i.e., parts that have no output connection to any other part, can be created by entering a single part number.

Other Options

Selection of editing option 4 in Table 1 permits the user to edit the name of the system. System names can be 30 characters long.

A system can be deleted from the list of systems by selecting editing option 5 in Table 1. When this option is selected, a warning message is displayed on the screen and the user is required to press SHIFT-HELP to delete the system.

In addition to the five editing options (Table 1), the system editor displays a message indicating the action the user must take to allow student access to the system. When a system is first created, only authors and instructors are allowed access to the simulation. In order to make the simulation available to students, the author or instructor must access the Editing Options Index and press SHIFT-DATA. The use of SHIFT-DATA permits student access to be turned on and off as necessary.

EVALUATION OF THE PLATO FAULT SYSTEM EDITOR

Formative Evaluation

In order to evaluate the effectiveness of the editor, a content specialist with modest typing ability and substantial experience with PLATO, used the Editor to enter a FAULT system into PLATO. The system entered was the JT-12 Turbojet Engine that had been created by Johnson (1981).

The JT-12 system had been developed previously on the DEC-10 computer and the content specialist used information from computer printouts to enter the system on PLATO. Since the information on the printouts was in a format different from the PLATO format, the content specialist used screen copies of the PLATO Editor display to enter the JT-12 system

Table 2
PART OPTIONS AND SYSTEM LIMITATIONS

Options	System Limitations
1. Part Name	24 characters
2. Part description	2 lines or about 120 characters
3. Probability of failure	0 - .99
4. Observation cost	0 - $999,999
5. Bench test cost	0 - $999,999
6. Replacement cost	0 - $999,999
7. Symptom description	1 line or about 50 characters
8. Gauge readings	Normal, zero, low, marginal variable, or high
9. Bench test description	5 lines or about 300 characters

initially on PLATO. During the formative evaluation stage of the editor, the content specialist and the editor programmer worked together to identify and correct problems with the editor. A number of minor problems were identified and corrected using this procedure. As a result of the initial evaluation conducted during entry on PLATO of the JT-12 system, the following three major problems were identified and corrected:

1. The creation and deletion of parts caused the other parts in the system to be renumbered. For example, in a 30-part system, deletion of part 20 caused parts 21 through 30 to become parts 20 through 29; and any existing connections that involved original parts 21 through 30 became incorrect. The editor was reprogrammed to renumber the list of connections each time a part is created or deleted.

2. The creation or deletion of gauges caused the other gauges in the system to be renumbered and existing gauge readings became incorrect. The editor was reprogrammed to renumber the gauge readings associated with each part in the system each time a gauge is created or deleted. Whenever a gauge is deleted, the gauge readings associated with that gauge are also deleted from every part in the system.

3. The editor allowed only one user to create or edit a system at any given time. The editor was reprogrammed to allow more than one simultaneous user, as long as each user is editing a different system.

User Friendly Evaluation

In order to evaluate the degree to which the editor was user friendly, a group of 12 female subjects volunteered to use the editor to enter a system on PLATO. Four subjects were students; one of whom was unable to complete the task due to personal problems. Her partial results were not analyzed. Four subjects were clerical employees who did not routinely use a computer in their work. Four subjects were clerical employees who routinely used a computer; one of this group had some experience using PLATO as an editor. Five of the eleven subjects had previously used PLATO, five of the subjects had used other computer systems, but only one subject had previous programming experience.

Each subject reported her typing speed; the typing speeds for the eight clerical employees ranged from 100+ to 55 words per minute (WPM) with a median of 75 WPM. The three students reported typing speeds of 40, 25, and 10 WPM.

The content specialist developed worksheets that contained the requisite information for the gauges, parts, and connections. These worksheets were used by the subjects to enter the JT-12 system on PLATO.

In order to test the procedures for the experimental evaluation, a research associate with basic programmming skills and two years experience using computers for editing and word processing entered the JT-12 system on PLATO. As a result of this trial test, a number of minor changes were made in the experimental procedure.

During the experimental evaluation, each subject was scheduled individually for a block of time. Based on the trial run, the time to enter the JT-12 system was expected to vary between 2½ and 5 hours. Each subject received a PLATO sign-on and completed a short introductory PLATO lesson on key conventions. Next, the subject received a written set of instructions. The subject was informed that the task was to "create" a new PLATO FAULT troubleshooting system using the PLATO FAULT System Editor. The subject was given a set of file folders and informed that the information defining the content of the system was found in the folders and that the instructions for entering the information on PLATO were in the editor program. The subject was instructed to complete the task with a minimum of errors in a reasonable amount of time. The subject was also told to proofread and correct each display before going to the next display, and to avoid pressing any extraneous keys. The subject was informed that the time to complete the task would be recorded and the task would take several hours. In case of problems, the subject was instructed to consult the instructions on the screen, use the help reference section, refer to the written directions, and, if necessary, request help from the experimenter. The subject was instructed to start by pressing SHIFT-LAB to enter the following information: System Nameset Name: JT-12; System Title: JT-12 Turbojet Engine; No. of Gauges: 9; No. of Parts: 38.

The following data were collected for each subject: the number of times the subject had to be helped by the experimenter, the total time to enter the JT-12 system, the number of times the subject referred to the help section, and the number of operational and content errors. At the end of the experimental session, each subject completed a brief questionnaire.

All eleven subjects were able to complete the task of entering the JT-12 system in PLATO with minimal assistance from the experimenter. Some of the subjects asked questions concerning how to get started on the experimental task. Other subjects asked how to go on to the next option after completing the first option (editing gauge information). Other subjects interpreted on-line messages as directions that had to be followed instead of options available to them. The number of questions asked by the subjects ranged from 1 to 8 with a median of 4.

The time to enter the JT-12 ranged from 2 hours 34 minutes to 4 hours 47 minutes. The average time to enter the system was 3 hours 32 minutes and the median time was 3 hours 8 minutes. The average time for the clerical group that routinely used a computer in their work was 2 hours 46 minutes. The average time required by the clerical group that did not routinely use the computer was 3 hours 41 minutes and the average time for the three students was 4 hours 20 minutes.

Ten of the eleven subjects referred to the help section at least once; two subjects referred to the help section five times; the median was two.

Two types of errors were recorded—operational errors and content errors. An operational error was defined as a failure to properly use the system editor. The two most common operational errors related to connections with unavailable observations. The subjects either failed to mark these connections with an asterisk by entering the connection and pressing SHIFT-DATA, or they omitted the connections. The JT-12 system has fourteen connections for which observations are unavailable. Five of the eight subjects who made one of these two errors committed fourteen errors, i.e., they failed to either mark or enter all fourteen connections. Seventy-three or 93 percent of the total

operational errors were made in these two categories. The operational error category did not discriminate among the three groups.

Content errors consisted of omission errors (e.g., period, space, word(s), line(s), section) addition errors (e.g., space(s), word) confusion errors, 0 and 8, 1 and 1, capitalization errors, errors caused by entering the editing option in text, and miscellaneous typing errors. Two types of content errors were due to the PLATO system: entering a double letter due to key bounce and dropping a letter(s) due to a pause in the program.

Omission errors were common. Nine of eleven subjects omitted a word, seven a section of text, eight a period or space, and four a line. One of the subjects, who had good typing skills, omitted a space 47 times to account for 82 percent of the errors made in this category.

The addition of space(s) was a common error. Seven subjects committed this error; one subject consistently inserted spaces instead of typing text flush with the left margin, committing this error 98 times. Another subject committed the error 42 times; the combined errors of these two subjects accounted for 93 percent of the total errors in this category.

Ten subjects made errors due to a key bounce, and seven subjects made errors due to a pause in the program. Nine of the subjects recorded a total of 30 errors by entering the editing option in the text. Capitalization errors were minimal (a total of four errors were made by three subjects) as were errors due to addition of a word (a total of four errors by three subjects). All subjects combined made a total of 200 miscellaneous typing errors—the largest total number of errors of any category measured. The range of other typing errors was from 2 to 46 with a median of 18.

The clerical group with computer experience made an average of 34 content errors, the range of errors was 8 to 55. The clerical group with no computer experience made an average of 55 content errors, the range was 26 to 92. Two of the students made 49 content errors each and one student made 195 content errors. The latter student had very poor typing skills and most of the errors made were associated with the space bar.

Each subject completed a seven-item, five-point questionnaire with Strongly Agree = 1 and Strongly Disagree = 5. The subjects reported that the initial instructions were clear (mean response = 2.0); the introductory lesson on the PLATO keyset was helpful (mean response = 1.3); and the help sections in the editor were helpful (mean response = 1.5).

The subjects found that the editor was easy to use (mean response = 1.9) and that it was easy to correct mistakes (mean response = 1.8). The subjects thought that the task took a long time (mean response = 2.1). The subjects disagreed that the task was very difficult (mean response = 4.1).

DISCUSSION

The formative evaluation demonstrated the value of close interaction between the system editor programmer and the user (content specialist). A number of minor problems and three major problems with the editor were identified and corrected.

The user friendly evaluation clearly demonstrated that individuals with average to good clerical skills can use the editor to enter a troubleshooting system with minimum assistance. The questions asked by the subjects suggested the need to re-examine the initial training or instructions provided to the subjects. The only significant system editor problem related to marking and entering connections for which observations were unavailable. Content errors appear to be the major area of concern. Eight subjects with average to good clerical skills made an average of 44 uncorrected content errors. Almost half (41 percent) of these were miscellaneous typing errors. The results indicate that in order to create an error-free troubleshooting system, a significant amount of editing time will be required after the troubleshooting system is created.

The response of the subjects to a questionnaire concerning the user friendliness of the editor was very favorable. The subjects reported that the editor was easy to use and that it was easy to correct mistakes using the editor. The subjects reported that the task of entering a system was not very difficult.

REFERENCES

Hunt, R. M. A Study of transfer of problem solving skills from context-free to context-specific fault diagnosis tasks. Urbana, IL: University of Illinois, Coordinated Science Laboratory, Report No. T-82, July 1979.

Hunt, R. M. and Rouse, W. B. Problem solving skills of maintenance trainees in diagnosing faults in simulated powerplants. Human Factors, 1981, 23 (3), 317-328.

Johnson, W. B. Computer simulations for fault diagnosis training: an empirical study of learning transfer from simulation to live system performance (Doctoral Dissertation, University of Illinois). Dissertation Abstracts International, 1981, 41, (11), 4625-A. (University Microfilms No. 8108555).

Johnson, W. B. and Rouse, W. B. Analysis and classification of human errors in troubleshooting live aircraft powerplants. IEEE Transactions on Systems, Man, and Cybernetics, 1982, SMC-12, (3), May/June, 389-393 (a).

Johnson, W. B. and Rouse, W. B. Training maintenance technicians for troubleshooting: two experiments with computer simulations. Human Factors, 1982, 24 (3) 276-276 (b).

Johnson, W. B., Entwistle, W. C., and Gaddis, K. S. Development and Demonstration of a Laboratory Tool for Research in the Design of Games for Training of Troubleshooting Skills. Savoy, IL: University of Illinois, Aviation Research Laboratory, Technical Report, ARL-TR82-1, August, 1982.

Rouse, W. B. and Hunt, R. M. Human problem solving in fault diagnosis tasks: Final report for contract MDA 902-79-C-0421, July 22, 1979 - July 21, 1982. Submitted to ARI July 21, 1982.

ACKNOWLEDGEMENT

This research was supported in part by Contract, MDA 903-83-M-7611 from the United States Army Research Institute for the Behavioral and Social Sciences, Alexandria, Virginia. Dr. Douglas Bobko was the technical monitor. We are endebted to Mrs. S. Allen for manuscript preparation and to Dr. M. Weller for manuscript editing. Our thanks to the subjects who assisted in evaluating this editor.

Human-Computer Interaction — INTERACT '84 / B. Shackel (ed.)
Elsevier Science Publishers B.V. (North-Holland)
© IFIP, 1985

DESIGN CONSIDERATIONS OF AN INTELLIGENT TEACHING SYSTEM FOR PROGRAMMING LANGUAGES

Mark Elsom-Cook,

Department of Psychology,
University of Warwick,
Coventry, CV4 7AL, England.

The purpose of this research is to investigate the nature of the teaching interaction.
A system intended to guide a discovery learning interaction about the programming
language LISP is described.   Representation of domain knowledge, skills of interaction and knowledge about the pupil are discussed.

1. METHODOLOGY

The study is set within the framework of producing software capable of acting as a stand-
alone tutor for the programming language LISP.
The completed system is intended to be of practical use in teaching non-numeric programming
on an M.Sc course in Cognition, Computing and
Psychology which is taught in Warwick University Psychology department.   It is hoped that
the program will support the early stages of
learning, and will facilitate easy transfer to
normal programming environments once programs
become too complex for it to make a reasonable
teaching contribution.

This work embodies a specific model of the
teaching interaction.   Let us suppose that a
teacher has his own (usable) representation of
a domain of knowledge, and that the pupil also
has a representation of knowledge which may be
of relevance to the domain.   The goal of
teaching must be to provide the pupil with a
model of the domain (at least) as powerful as
that of the teacher.   This model will not
necessarily have the same internal form, since
it must be bound to differing cognitive structures in the two individuals, but both models
must be consistent with the real world.   A
"direct teaching" strategy involves the teacher
in translating his model into a suitable
external representation.   The learner then
attempts to integrate features of this representation with his preexisting cognitive
structures, and possibly to modify the form of
these structures.   One way of categorising
varieties of teaching interaction is by
locating the point in this "transfer of
knowledge" at which major reorganisation of the
knowledge occurs.   The following examples will
illustrate this;

In a traditional "chalk and talk" environment,
the teacher generates an external form from his
domain knowledge which is reasonably independant of the states of knowledge of the pupils
whom he is teaching - at best it is based on a
simple "prototypical" student model.   This
leaves the student to do all the work of
adapting the knowledge for his own under-

standing.   Another example of this would be in
learning from a book.

At the opposite extreme, the tutor devotes much
energy to developing an accurate model of his
pupil.   He then combines this model with his
domain knowledge to generate an individualised
course of tuition.   In this approach, the
tutor must constantly update his model and
reassess the presentation method.   The most
extreme example of this approach will be found
in the work of Jean-Jacques Rousseau (1).
Rousseau's philosophy is based on providing one
teacher per child who tries to model the child's
interests and readiness to learn, and ensure
that the appropriate experiences occur in the
environment to trigger each phase of learning.
It should be noted that it is actually possible
to exert complete control over the pupil by
this method, while maintaining the impression
of freedom.   Rousseau's own ideas of what is
"natural" have a great influence on what the
pupil is allowed to learn.

Between these extremes there is a continuum of
teaching styles.   The above framework permits a
definition of "good" or "bad" teachers and
learners.   A good teacher is one who successfully restructures information to make it easier
to learn before presenting it.   A good learner
is one who is capable of doing large amounts of
reorganisation of knowledge to make it fit into
his existing cognitive structures, and of
modifying those structures when necessary.
From these definitions, it is clear that good
learners are less dependant on the ability of
their teachers than are poor learners.

If we assume that the pupil has the clearest
idea of his current state of knowledge and that
the teacher has the clearest understanding of
the domain, then it is reasonable to suppose
that an optimal teaching interaction is one in
which the matter to be presented and the form
of it's presentation is decided by negotiation
between the two parties.   From this it follows
that a study of teaching should seek to identify the issues about which negotiation may take
place, and should investigate the form of that
negotiation.

1.1 Implications for user modelling

An examination of the teaching techniques applied in Intelligent Tutoring systems to date shows that they concentrate on producing a copy of the teacher's model in the head of the pupil. While this technique is the most straight-forward to study, it is a dangerous practical tool since it has a strong tendency to produce uniformity among the pupils to whom it is applied. It is also apparent that, unless much extra work is done by the pupil in integrating this knowledge with his existing structures, his model cannot be more powerful than that of the teacher. These techniques remain close to the "chalk and talk" methods of teaching.

In its most restrictive form this approach is manifest in Computer Aided Learning packages which make little attempt to adapt to the user. It is also apparent in Intelligent systems which use overlay modelling. In these, the user model is built as a subset of a model of an expert in the problem domain. The process of instructing the pupil involves finding discrep-ancies between the two models and attempting to remove them. These systems often use direct testing strategies to find evidence for the existence of units of the model. This should not be confused with systems which maintain a descriptive representation of an "expert" level of achievement. This is necessary for assess-ment of the pupil, but the details of the experts approach are not used in tutoring. In essence, this suggests that the teacher's expert knowledge of the domain should be regarded as a black box, and any glass box form which the pupil sees should be adapted to that individual.

An improvement of this type of model is to explicitly include representations of variations on the expert skill which are not actually used by the expert, but which reflect likely devia-tions from the model such as simplified versions of complex rules. The "bug" representation of systems such as Buggy (2) are examples of this category. This provides a better means of categorising the difficulties of a pupil, but does not affect the basic problem since these systems still have a goal of making the pupil into a copy of the expert.

In this system, an attempt has been made to avoid this restrictive aspect of the inter-action. The system maintains a descriptive model of expert competence in programming, and tries to detect discrepancies between this and a descriptive model of the pupil's programming. When an inconsistency is detected, the system brings it to the attention of the pupil so that the pupil may make appropriate corrections to her model. No particular model of expert problem-solving ability or bugs is explicitly maintained in the system for the purpose of tutoring. It is not yet clear whether this form of knowledge would have other, more reason-able applications in the system. This presents a topic for further investigation.

1.2 Educational position

Most Intelligent Tutoring systems make use of a highly constrained interaction such as Socratic tutoring (3). More recent systems begin to permit mixed-initiative interaction with a greater degree of freedom for the pupil, but they are still found to revert to their re-strictive form in difficult situations in order to tie people to the model which they know about. The method adopted in designing this system is to approach the problem from the other end of this Freedom-Constraint dimension.

The Educational Philosophy of "Discovery Learning" on which the child-centred education movement (and recent computer applications such as LOGO at MIT) has been based raises major issues about the degree and type of guidance which should be given to a pupil. In particular, it is generally acknowledged that totally "free" learning, in which a learner is simply left alone in an environment, is a very poor use of available resources, and unlikely to lead to high levels of attainment (4). It is interesting to note that although LOGO is often thought of as a free environment for learning, a case study of LOGO use at MIT (5) shows an interaction which is actually tightly con-strained in practical terms, and in which the pupil exercises virtually no control.

It is apparent that discovery learning offers advantages in terms of the motivation of the individual. If we consider the form of teaching which is necessary in "guided dis-covery" learning, we find that we can reduce the amount of detail involved in negotiating the course of teaching, since much of the learner's contribution can be in terms of actions in the environment. This reduces the amount of interaction needed between teacher and pupil, since the role of the teacher is now assessing the possible directions which the user could follow at a given point, and encour-aging those which it considers to be most pro-ductive. This leaves the major problem of assessing the likely value of a course of action.

It was decided to design a system which pro-vides an environment in which a pupil can "discover" the language Lisp. The system also contains a teaching program which monitors the interaction of pupil and environment, and attempts to make positive contributions to that interaction. The system has a goal of detect-ing skills which the user is ready to learn, and encouraging the exploration of those skills, either by manipulating the environment or by making direct "teaching statements" to the pupil.

2. OVERALL STRUCTURE OF THE SYSTEM

Conceptually, the system may be regarded as three separate entities. The first is the PUPIL, which is a system user plus various interfacing packages to enable him to interact smoothly with the system. The second is the ENVIRONMENT, which is the domain about which the pupil is trying to discover together with some tools to aid his exploration. In this case the environment is a LISP interpreter, and the tools are such things as Trace packages and Editors. The third item is the TEACHER, which is considered to embody the intelligent aspects of the system. The teacher monitors the inter-action between pupil and world, and attempts to build a user model which can be used to de-cide when to intervene in this interaction. It is also possible for the pupil to appeal directly to the teacher for aid.

2.1 An example interaction

Let us examine the action of the system when dealing with a specific problem. Assume that a task has been agreed between teacher and pupil which is to define a function to extract the second element from a list;

(FRED (QUOTE (A B C))) --> B

One correct solution would be

(DE FRED (X)
   (CAR(CDR X)))

and we will assume that the teacher is aware of this solution. Suppose that the pupil offers the following definition;

(DE FRED (X)
   (CDR (CAR (QUOTE X))))

The teacher executes the pupil's expression before it is completed in order to find possible errors. The teacher detects a violation of the semantics due to an inappropriate argument to CAR (i.e. X). It finds that there is one evaluation too few on the variable X (by com-paring this with the correct solution), and notes that removing QUOTE would correct this. The teacher makes a simple patch to get round this error and continues execution. A second error, due to an inappropriate argument to CDR is found. Comparison with the correct solution detects the differences in evaluation order, so this problem is also noted. It is important to note that, rather than being "the right solution" to the problem, what the system tries to generate is a solution using techniques which are currently at the boundary of the pupil's skill level, so the solution form is indirectly determined by the user model.

The comparisons of solutions are not done in the programming language itself, but rather in the underlying semantic representation. This enables the system to identify the reasons for a difference. These differences can be used to identify necessary changes in surface form, or can be discussed in their own right.

The teacher now compares the detected errors

with the user model. It finds evidence that this pupil has experience of the multiple-EVAL problem, but has had less experience of the EVAL-order problem. The teaching strategies use this to decide to make a simple statement of fact about the former difficulty, but pass control to a specialized teaching unit (a "talker") for a more detailed discussion of EVAL-order.

The EVAL talker waits until the problem becomes manifest to the pupil before doing anything. It takes this decision based on the evidence which the user model provides for the pupil's ability to deal with error situations, together with the pupil's experience of this type of problem. The pupil tests the function with '(D C A). An error results and the pupil immediately asks for help. The teacher decides to try the subproblem strategy, and asks "WHAT is (CAR (QUOTE (D C A)))", then "WHAT sort of argument does CDR expect". If this is insuffi-cient to cause the user to generate a correct answer then it uses a more informative technique.

2.2 Knowledge Sources

An attempt has been made to produce a clear separation between the knowledge sources in the system, so that the examination of the way in which they interact to produce a reasonable teaching sequence is possible. A further goal of this separation was to make the system capable of teaching different programming lang-uages with little overall modification. The success of this strategy will be discussed in the conclusion.

2.2.1 Knowledge about the problem domain

2.2.1.1 Syntax

In effect, problems of syntax have been bypassed in this system. The pupil works through a syntax-directed editor which is driven from a Backus-Naur form description of the language. The editor generates a parse-tree of any expression in the language, which is the form on which all other parts of the system act. This technique was originally investigated in the EMILY system (6). The current system was designed for novice programmer's rather than experts, so the constraints upon the editor design were different from those of Emily.

The boundary between syntax and semantics is not perfectly defined, and some problems are difficult to assign to either class. An example of this is the question of declaring variables before using them. While many systems assume this to be a high level of syn-tactic information (e.g. (7)), this system assigns it to the semantics, because it repre-sents an aspect of the language for which under-lying principles exist.

2.2.1.2 Semantics

An examination of standard techniques of program description showed that although they are well suited to mathematical manipulations, they are not the most appropriate representation for transferring a "psychologically reasonable" model of the language to a pupil. For this reason a different semantic representation was devised. This representation describes each statement in the language in terms of preconditions for it's application plus a body of commands to execute in order to achieve the appropriate effect. The commands are drawn from a set of about fifteen primitive operations which constitute the lowest level of semantic description in the system. This has similarities with certain aspects of Axiomatic and Operational semantics. In choosing this representation, some of the constraints of mathematical consistency and completeness for which other approaches have aimed, have been relaxed. The form used is a type of Direct semantics, so it is unable to handle unusual control flow features such as Jumps or Errors. Other limitations include an inability to prove termination of a program, and some limits involving aliasing of variables.

This declarative form of semantics is acted upon by different programs for each of the applications to which it is put in the system. The most obvious application is execution of expressions in lieu of an interpreter. The system is often able to execute incomplete expressions and ignore those errors which are due to the incompleteness. Describing statements of the language or behaviour of an expression is done by mapping the semantics onto some simple English descriptions of the primitive elements. Automatic generation of problems and problem-solutions using the semantics is an important area, but is not a major research goal in the design of this system, so it has not been examined in detail. The teaching methodology requires that the action of programs can be made visible in such a way as to avoid implying a particular mechanism, so some effort is devoted to providing the teacher with different ways of displaying information during execution.

2.2.1.3 Higher level structures

So far, the system has been applied to toy domains, so it is possible to detect correct problem solutions by exhaustive search. In real programming domains the search space will be too large to apply this technique, so the system requires the search to be constrained by likely solution forms. More importantly, the student is unlikely to discover such techniques as recursion by trial and error, so some representation of these must exist if the teacher is to guide the pupil towards them. These representations must include conceptual roles (such as "stopping condition") to which actual elements of the program can be assigned. A representation such as that used in the Programmer's Apprentice system (8) is envisaged,

though at present the system is being constrained to problems which can be tackled using only single plans.

Some "knowledge" about high level concepts of the language may be thought to reside in the descriptors of the domain, but this knowledge is not accessible to the reasoning components of the system. In fact, this knowledge is more about conventional methods of describing the units than about their actual semantic form.

2.2.2 Knowledge about the student

The user model of the system, which embodies all the information which the system has about the pupil, consists of four components;

1) Student History

The existence of a history of interaction in the system seems important for several reasons. Being able to refer back to recent events in the interaction helps provide a continuity to the teaching, and enables discussion of features which the English interface cannot handle. Exactly which past events can reasonably be referred to is not yet clear, and it is apparent that a principled solution to this problem must involve another level of user modelling. This may lead to a more selective form of history storage than is currently used.

It may prove necessary for the system to do some updating of the user model offline in order to maintain a reasonable interaction rate. What form this processing will take has not been examined, but it is certainly the case that human teachers consider problems which their pupils have presented them outside direct teaching time. It is likely that a teaching system capable of learning from experience would focus on this activity.

2) Apparent language

Part of the student model is maintained by building a language description corresponding to the language which the student thinks she is using. This is achieved by copying from the program semantics the most general form of a function description for which the student has had evidence. The copying rules allow variations such as specializations or overgeneral instances to be included in the user model. This provides an upper limit on the class of features which the pupil is able to use as a base for deductive reasoning. Attempting to solve problems using this version of the language can help the system to pinpoint likely areas of conflict between the user's model and the actual language.

3) Error handling

In knowing when to intervene, the system must have some idea of the pupil's ability to handle the problem with which she is currently confronted. In part this is achieved by examining the student's knowledge of the current problem area, but it also involves knowing about the pupil's ability to trace a bug from the sort of feedback which she receives. For this reason, the system monitors the effectiveness with which pupils can respond to error messages. A goal of the system is to improve this ability so that transfer to normal interpreters is fairly straightforward.

4) Rules of extrapolation

In the WUMPUS system (9), Goldstein identified a set of rules for approaching new knowledge in ways based on previous knowledge. These extrapolation rules identified possible forms of transition between "islands of knowledge" in the Genetic Graph. In this system, a similar approach is taken, with a fixed set of extrapolation rules being available to the system. A crude monitoring system attempts to assign "success values" to each rule depending on how well the systems goals are achieved if they are fired by that type of rule. More subtle techniques for exploring and modelling the pupil's own extrapolation rules should be investigated. It is interesting to note that there is a possibility of giving the system a goal of extending the pupil's rule set.

2.2.3 Knowledge about interaction

Unlike most Intelligent Tutoring systems, which are purely reactive, this system is intended to participate in a structured interaction with the pupil. Much of the work in this section makes use of recent progress in psycholinguistic models of conversation (10)(11). Control of the interaction is shared between three major units;

1) General interaction skills

These skills have the purpose of maintaining the consistency and smoothness of the interaction. They perform such tasks as marking subject boundaries, and adjudicating in the process of topic selection (by choosing a domain talker on the basis of a bid indicating the likely importance and relevance of the topic). Since these procedures make no assumptions about the particular actions of a domain talker, they can integrate linguistic and non-linguistic forms of interaction.

2) Descriptors of domain

Each concept about which the system is able to talk has a descriptor associated with it. This descriptor embodies all domain specific aspects of the concept, so it contains such things as outlines of various ways to present and discuss a topic. It also contains mechanisms to assess it's own importance at the current point in the interaction, and routines which enable it to make some assessment of it's own success in

modifying the user's model of the language. These mechanisms may contribute to the interaction by passing data to standard teaching strategies, or they may control an interaction specific to their own domain. These talkers may be thought of as including the tutorial goals of the teacher.

3) Teaching strategies

Teaching strategies are special conversation techniques which can be called by domain talkers. They are intended to represent those processes of communication which are common to all areas of the domain. They include such things as Socratic tutoring, giving examples, and direct statements of fact.

3 CURRENT STATE OF DEVELOPMENT

The user interface aspects of the system have been implemented, and have been used as a teaching tool on the M.Sc course (in conjunction with individual tuition). This work has been reported in an earlier paper. Most other aspects of the system have now been implemented in the form of demonstration packages. It is anticipated that implementation of a system which is robust enough to be used will be commenced in the near future.

REFERENCES

(1) Rousseau-Emile, J.J. (1762) (Everyman edition, 1974).

(2) Burton, R.R., Diagnosing bugs in a simple procedural skill, in Sleeman, D. and Brown, J.S. (eds.), Intelligent Tutoring Systems (Academic Press, 1982).

(3) Collins, A. and Stevens, A.L., Goals and strategies of interactive teachers. Bolt, Beranek and Newman report 4345 (1980).

(4) Dearden, R.F., Instruction and learning by discovery, in Peters, R.S. (ed.), The concept of education (1967).

(5) Solomon, C. and Papert, S., Case study of a child doing turtle graphics in LOGO, MIT AIM-375 (1976).

(6) Hansen, W.J., Creation of hierarchic text with a computer display, Ph.D. Thesis, Dept. of Comp. Sc., Stanford Univ. (1971).

(7) Teitelbaum, T., Reps, T., and Horowitz, S., The why and wherefore of the Cornell program synthesiser, ACM Sigplan notices Vol. 16, No. 6 (1981).

(8) Rich, C., Inspection methods in programming MIT AI-TR-604. (1981).

(9) Goldstein, I.P., The genetic graph: a representation for the evolution of procedural knowledge, in Sleeman, D. and Brown, J.S., (eds.), Intelligent Tutoring Systems (Academic Press, 1982).

(10) Power, R., The organisation of purposeful dialogues, Linguistics 17 (1979).

(11) Reichmann, R., Conversational coherency, Cognitive Science 2 (1978).

Human-Computer Interaction — INTERACT '84 / B. Shackel (ed.)
Elsevier Science Publishers B.V. (North-Holland)
© IFIP, 1985

DESIGNING AND EVALUATING COMPUTER AIDS IN STRUCTURED PROGRAMMING

HOC, J.M.
(Laboratoire de Psychologie du Travail de l'EPHE, ERA CNRS, Paris)

GUYARD, J., QUERE, M., JACQUOT, J.P.
(CRIN, Université de Nancy I, LA CNRS)

-=-=-=-=-

This research is supported by the "Agence de l'Informatique".

Presentation of the first stages of research work aimed at developping and evaluating a design language for structured programs and software aids, intended for experienced programmers.

In order to clarify some of the problems posed by programmer training, one of the targets of this research is to determine the variety of programming strategies employed by professional programmers.

INTRODUCTION

The research work presented here falls within the scope of the evaluation of programming methods and of software aid environments related to this activity. Purely syntactic aids (for example, those introduced by Teitelbaum and Reps, 1981 or Medina-Mora 1982) are not sufficient. However, within the framework of conventional programming languages, which involve implementation details often foreign to actual problem solving, it is difficult to go any further. The system being developped here goes beyond this context and is linked more particularly to such works as those of Rich et al.(1979) or De Goldberg (1982).

Pedagogical concerns often play a central role in this type of research (Miller, 1978). It follows, therefore that our research should emulate other works carried out in the area of programmer training : the study of the evolution of program construction strategies during the learning of top-down programming methods (Hoc, 1983) ; conception and pedagogical evaluation of the deductive programming method (Pair, 1979 ; Guyard et al.1981).

Evaluating programmer training poses two distinct problems :
    - the effectiveness of student guidance related to the programming methods in question ;
    - the relevance of these methods in professional situations.

This research concentrates on the second problem, the aim being to use experienced programmers in order to evaluate software aids and an implementation language for the deductive programming method.

The deductive programming method offers three main features :

    (a) it relies on a definitional language which, as a result, is more declarative than procedural. This language represents a departure from typical programming languages which encourage a mental execution strategy, largely used by beginners.

    (b) in addition, it favours a retrospective programming strategy in which the final results are defined from the intermediate results, which in their turn are defined from the data. This goes against the utilization of a mental execution strategy which beginners find very difficult to abandon.

    (c) finally, it imposes a program construction method using successive refinements starting from the basic construction of structured programming. This planning strategy also presents learning difficulties.

This research attempts to identify the conditions for implementing such a strategy and to devise suitable software aids when these conditions are not fulfilled by the experienced programmer. The current state of this research work and its advancement is presented here : the implementation of the language MEDEE and its editor, the composition of crucial problems for evaluation, and the aims of the experimentation in progress.

1. THE LANGUAGE MEDEE AND THE EDITOR MEDEDIT

1.1 The language MEDEE

Although this and procedural programming languages such as Pascal have some superficial analogies in common, MEDEE has been derived from an algebraic language which expresses mathematical relationships between objects. These relationships include the basic construction of structured programming. It is thus possible to give a modular structure to the algorithm.

The language is definitional, that is to say, the user defines objects rather than manipulating variables as in a conventional programming language. Each object can therefore be defined only once. Furthermore, these objects contain typed elements. They can be elementary objects such as integers strings, etc. or composed objects such as arrays where an indexation of the components is required. As a result, special operators have been introduced for composed objects.

Three kinds of definition are employed :

(a) Simple definitions which refer to logical and algebraic expressions, to readings, and to printouts.
Ex. a = b+c or a : data or a = output (b) linefeed output (c)

(b) Conditional definitions used when case analysis is necessary :
Ex. a : If (Condition 1) then a =
         If (Condition 2) then a =
                          else a =

(c) Iterative definitions : when the object is defined by a recursive formula :
Ex. x : INI for i in 1 to n repeat x = $@x + i$
(x is understood as x_i and $@x$ as x_{i-1} ; INI : x = 0)
Conditional and iterative definitions can imply the definition of several objects. In this case, everything on

the right of 'then' and 'repeat' is expressed separately in the form of explicit and labelled modules. Initializations are treated in the same way.

1.2 The MEDEDIT editor

The editor is stratified into four levels with different functions available at each level :

- Environment : manipulation of algorithms with possible access to a personal data base.

- Algorithm : manipulation of modules which correspond to sub-problems.

- Module : access to definitions.

- Definition : access to the components of a definition.

In order to avoid constant user reference to a menu for command selection, pre-defined programmable keys are preferred.

A multi-window screen is used. It has :

- a zone indicating the actual level

- a zone for any questions or messages generated by the system

- a temporary storage zone for a correct syntactic definition having just been created and being currently validated to deal with contextual errors

- a horizontal scrolling zone which displays the acceptable definition in the module

- a zone comprising objects used which have not yet been defined

- a zone where definition and information requested by the system are composed.

There are three main types of function:

(a) Editing function. These are directly under the user's control. He can create, restore or save an algorithm, scan the levels ; print, enter and modify definitions, etc. Syntactic errors are often corrected automatically.

(b) Control functions. These are executed automatically. By examining the context, the system can detect type inconsistencies, check that an object hasn't yet been defined etc.

(c) 'Clever' functions. These programming aid functions will, for the most part, be implemented following psychological analysis of the strategies employed. At present, the system helps the user initialize recurrent objects and executes automatic definition merging within the modules.

An example is given of the final state of an algorithm for calculating a mean, a standard deviation and a test group size, made up of three modules :

PRINCIPAL		
^{1}result=print(mean, stdev, size) ^{5}mean=total/size ^{7}stdev=sqrt((sqrs-(total pow 2)/size) /size) ^{9}total, sqrs,size:INI for x in data limit x=9999 repeat OBSERVATION	result (edit) ^{2}mean (real) ^{3}stdev(real):'standard deviation' ^{4}size(integer) ^{6}total(real):'sum of observations' ^{8}sqrs(real):'raw sum of squares' ^{10}x(real):'observation'	^{11}INI: 'initializes' ^{12}OBSERVATION: 'processes an observation'

^{13}OBSERVATION		
^{14}total= @total+x ^{15}sqrs= @sqrs+x pow 2 ^{16}size= @size+1		

^{17}INI		
^{18}total,sqrs,size=0		

The layout covers three columns : modules presented and defined (on the left), informal commentary and types of object (in the centre) and commentary on the modules (on the right). A purely retrospective strategy would mean that these texts are introduced in the same numerical order as in the table. At present, the order is only subject to two constraints :

- an object name employed in a definition which has just been entered, must be immediately commented and typed in the central column. The same applies to a module name which must be immediately commented in the right-hand column.

- a module 'son' cannot be defined before a module 'father'.

Finally, all the user's entries, definitions, comments, modifications, etc are automatically collected by a system combined with the editor.

2. COMPOSITION OF PROBLEMS CRUCIAL TO THE EVALUATION

2.1 Background

The programming situations referred to, are those usually encountered by professional users, and are situated between two extremes. It is thought more advisable to disregard these two extremes in this kind of evaluation:

- the problem does not consist of inventing an algorithm from scratch as such a method involves knowledge more directly related to the actual domain of the problem (mathematical or otherwise) than to informatics.

- nor is it just a simple process of encoding an algorithm known to the user, into a programming language.

The reference situations relevant here are those in which the algorithms, already partially known, must be combined and adapted so that they can

be implemented into a given programming
language. If, occasionally, algorithms
are indeed invented, they are relatively simple.

Even with this restrictive definition
of programming problems, according to
the central hypothesis, each professional programmer uses a variety of programming strategies which are dependant
on the characteristics of the problem.

For evaluation purposes, and rather
than choose problems at random as is
often the case, certain crucial problems have been constructed taking into account the conditions for implementing the strategies.

2.2 Method

To obtain relevant classification criteria, a method related to problem solving in physics, (inspired by the work
of Chi et al.1981) has been adopted .
Nine professional programmers were asked to participate volontarily in the
evaluation :

(a) to classify 27 problems, without solving them, according to the problem solving method they intended to
adopt. These problems were programming
exercises, used by a training establishment, which were thought to cover
the whole variety of problems met in a
professional setting.

(b) then, to characterize the different classes obtained from the classification.

(c) finally, to retackle each problem in an imposed random order so that
each one could be more precisely categorised in relation to its assumed
complexity and the strategy envisaged.

2.3 Results

The detailed data analysis is not discussed here as it is presented elsewhere (Hoc, 1983b). However, the principal
results are given.

There is little inter-individual
variability in the classifications carried out by the subjects. The classifications are not entirely coherent with
the degree of difficulty and the strategies envisaged. The problems tend to
be grouped according to their domain
(management, word processing, documentation etc.). Such sensitivity to the
different problem domains is probably
linked to transfer between problems
within the same domain. This point will
be discussed later.

A primary dimension of strategy classification concerns the bottom-up or
top-down nature of the approach. A
bottom-up approach involves program
construction which starts from the details and proceeds to the overall
structure. It can be carried out in
many different ways :

- preliminary execution of a procedure relating to specific data.

- program construction by mental
execution.

- preliminary restriction of the
problem to a simpler problem, etc.

This type of approach is employed all
the more frequently when the problem
is judged difficult.

On the other hand, the top-down approach (planning or successive refinements) is used for problems which
are deemed easy. It is frequently associated, however, with the subject's
possibility of transferring the plan
of the program (the overall structure) using a similar program that he
has already created.

A second dimension concerns the direction taken to write the program :

- prospective : the program is
established in the same order as execution - from data to results.

- retrospective : in the opposite
direction.

With students, it has been shown that
a prospective strategy is linked to
a bottom-up strategy and thus to the
difficulty of the problem (Hoc, 1981)
but with experienced subjects, this
is not the case. A prospective strategy is indeed envisaged when the
problem is considered difficult, although it is sometimes also contemplated in the opposite case, when the
relevant problems present one of two
characteristics :

- either the structure of the
process seems evident and is organised
in the order of execution, but at the
same time, the data and the results
have a weak structure, as for example,
in certain word processing problems
or ,

- the data have a strong structure from which the program structure
can be derived . This is often the
case for management problems.

The retrospective approach is preferred in two cases :

- either when the results have a strong structure or,

- when the construction of the results is based on a branch-like structure and complex strings of calculations with interaction between the procedures that are used to obtain each result, as for instance, in certain problems of statistical calculation.

An examination of the second dimension results in the introduction of a third which involves the form guidance takes in the planning, whether declarative or procedural. When guidance is declarative, the program can stem from either the data structure or the results. On the other hand, when the guidance is procedural, the plan derives from the structure of the process itself.

3. CURRENT EXPERIMENTATION AIM

The present experimentation has a dual aim :

- a detailed description of the variety of programming strategies employed by professional programmers and

- an evaluation of programming aids as currently available in the editor.

The subject's task is to construct programs directly into the system without using any external aids,(for example, paper and pencil). As already described, the editor contains a program which automatically collects all the subject's entries. The data analysis effected is thus similar to the analysis of individual problem solving protocols and aims at :

- providing a relatively detailed model of the programming strategies employed by the programmers,

- determining the implementation difficulties of these strategies so that improvements or additions to the editor can be suggested and a psycho-semiological evaluation of the language carried out.

The results presented above establish a link between the different strategy dimensions and the problem features. A given problem, however, cannot always be classified in one category alone as it may contain different types of sub-problem. Hence the reason for the choice of crucial problems - each

problem belonging to just one category.

The present position of the editor does not allow for the implementation of a top-down strategy, and so problems likely to provoke this strategy have temporarily been excluded. The problem types are defined by crossing the second and third dimensions already discussed : problem-solving direction (prospective vs retrospective)and planning guidance (declarative vs procedural). In each of the resulting, four categories two problems from different domains have been defined so that the inter-domain variability can be evaluated.

CONCLUSION

The general profile of this research work presents two aspects :

- the determination of the variety of strategies implemented by the professional programmer, in order to develop program software aids which are sufficiently defined so as not to discourage a potentially satisfactory strategy ,

- to fix training goals employing a relatively flexible method, which would allow for the inclusion of any satisfactory strategies employed by the experienced programmer.

The immediate effects of this research relate to software aids for experienced subjects. However, in the near future, it is hoped to adapt and extend these aids to provide programming tools for student guidance in Computer Assisted Instruction. To this end, the automatic data collection program must be improved to include a program which can determine the strategies evolved by the students and thus intervene in their development.

REFERENCES

Chi, M.T.H., Feltovitch, P.J., Glaser, R., Categorization and representation of physics problems by experts and novices, Cognitive Science, 5(1981) 121-152.

Goldberg, A., The smalltalk-80 system : a user guide and reference manual, Xerox, Palo Alto Research Center (1982)

Guyard, J., Kolmayer, E., Quéré, M., Souquières, J., Hoc, J.M., Une méthode de programmation déductive et son utilisation dans l'enseignement traditionnel ou assisté par ordinateur, Troisième

Conférence Mondiale sur l'Informatique
et l'Education, Lausanne (1981).

Hoc, J.M., Planning and direction of problem-solving in structured programming,
Int. J. Man-Machine Studies, 15(1981),
363-383.

Hoc, J.M., Analysis of beginners' problem-solving strategies in programming,
in Green, T.R.G., Payne, S.J., and van
der Veer, G. (eds), The Psychology of
Computer Use (Academic Press, London,
1983).

Hoc, J.M., Une méthode de classification
préalable des problèmes d'un domaine
pour l'analyse des stratégies de résolu-
tion, Le Travail Humain, 46(1983) 205-217

Medina-Mora, R., Syntax-directed editing:
towards integrated programming environments, PhD Thesis, Carnegie-Mellon University, Department of Computer Science,
Pittsburgh (1982).

Miller, M.L., A structured planning and
debugging environment for elementary
programming, Int. J. Man-Machine Studies,
11 (1978) 79-95.

Pair, C., La construction des programmes,
R.A.I.R.O.-Informatique, 13(1979) 113-137.

Rich, C., Shrobe, H.E., Waters, R.C.,
An overview of the programmer's apprentice, Proc. sixth IJCAI, Tokyo (1979).

Teitelbaum, T., Reps, T., The Cornell
Program Synthesizer : a syntax-directed
programming environment, Communications
of the ACM, 24(1981) 563-573.

Human-Computer Interaction — INTERACT '84 / B. Shackel (ed.)
Elsevier Science Publishers B.V. (North-Holland)
© IFIP, 1985

TRANSFERRING USERS' RESPONSIBILITIES TO A SYSTEM:
THE INFORMATION MANAGEMENT COMPUTING ENVIRONMENT[1]

Robert Neches,
Bob Balzer, Neil Goldman, David Wile

USC / Information Sciences Institute
Marina del Rey, CA, USA

User difficulties in developing and using a useful system model appear to depend both on the number and complexity of rules they must learn, and the memory load of building and applying the required set of rules. The **Information Management** computing environment, by presenting several non-traditional capabilities based on a fusion of AI and database technology, may help ameliorate some of these difficulties. The key concepts of the system consist of a uniform underlying database representing all information in the environment, support for retrieval of information objects by description, and the explicit specification of *rules* telling the system how to take over responsibility for consistency maintenance and routine user actions.

1 INTRODUCTION

Successfully interacting with any system requires that its users can acquire a useful model of that system, and can apply that model in practical situations without suffering from information overload. Facilitating this requires modifying the *division of responsibilities* between users and computer systems, particularly regarding what information will be maintained by the users and what information will be maintained by the system.

We will start by discussing the nature of users' system models and the information processing required to interact with a computer system. Then, we will present the Information Management computing environment (IM), along with two services provided within it: an employee information database and an electronic mail facility. After that, we will consider how the IM system design attempts to respond to issues raised in the first section, using the services and their evolution to provide illustrative examples. Finally, we will critique the system, based on our experiences with a prototype.

2 ACQUIRING AND USING A MODEL OF A SYSTEM

2.1 The contents of a model

In order to use a system, a user must have a knowledge base in which a number of different kinds of information are represented. The most commonly cited are the GOMS model of Card, Moran, and Newell [3]: *goals*; *operators*; *methods*, sequences of operators for acheiving common goals; and *selectors*, policies for choosing between alternative methods. In addition, the knowledge base must represent possible *states* (both desirable and undesirable) that the system can enter, and *constraints*, rules that map states into goals. Each of these concepts is really a collection of information rather than a single unit. Goals have conditions on when they are useful, preconditions on when they can be attempted, durations over which they must be satisfied, and so on. Operators similarly have applicability conditions and prerequisite conditions. States have (or at least should, for an effective user) likelihoods associated with them, as well as external indicators -- i.e., the factors one should be able to observe that indicate when the system is indeed in that state.

In addition, it is necessary for a user to have at least implicit procedural knowledge capturing Moran's [8] notion of "external-to-internal task mappings". This refers to knowledge about how tasks in the semantically meaningful domain of interest map into goals allowed in the version of that domain that uses the computer as a tool.

Also critical is the form in which all of the above knowledge is represented. It is not sufficient simply to have all of this information stored as declarative knowledge, since the user must be able to evoke this knowledge at appropriate times -- that is, the knowledge must be stored in a form that supports both recognition and recall.

2.2 The acquisition of a model

At this point in time, cognitive scientists have identified four complementary learning processes that play an important role in acquiring a model of a system: rule induction, analogy, abduction, and "knowledge compilation".

Rule induction [6] refines the conditions under which beliefs are asserted or actions taken by generalizing the conditions to cover cases where the outcome is known to be valid, then restricting the conditions to exclude cases where the generalized conditions predicted that outcome and it turned out to be invalid. One vulnerability of rule induction is that limited memory and understanding for a sequence of rules may make it difficult to determine which one to modify when feedback can only be given about the outcome of the whole sequence. Another vulnerability is combinatoric explosion; conditions can be generalized and restricted in many different ways, and people cannot easily keep track of all possible variants.

[1]This research was funded by the Defense Advanced Research Projects Agency (DARPA), contract MDA-903-81-C-0335.

Analogies serve as both help and hindrance in mastering a system. One of the more interesting analyses of this issue is Douglas and Moran's [4] technique of identifying analogous operators by looking at similarities in their effects, then predicting confusions on the basis of differences between those operators in their application conditions or side-effects.

Abduction is the generation -- and often, unfortunately, the acceptance -- of hypotheses that explain a set of observations [7]. It is a dangerous mode of reasoning, but necessary because it creates initial hypotheses that are refined by other learning processes.

Knowledge compilation [10] may apply to transforming knowledge from an initial declarative form into a form suitable for both recognition and recall. It is a process of generating new rules by combining the specific conditions that led to an information retrieval attempt with the results of processes invoked to obtain that information from long-term memory or external information sources. This is necessarily a slow, incremental process. Memory limitations make it impossible to retain the information about sequences of mental actions that would be needed to apply knowledge compilation to anything other than processes with fairly direct links to each other.

All of these processes rely heavily on mental search and comparison of complex knowledge structures. They are therefore highly vulnerable to memory failures in which the information needed in working memory during processing exceeds the limited capacity of that memory. To facilitate learning, therefore, we must reduce the amount of information needed in working memory -- either by simplifying things so that less information is needed, or by providing external memory aids so that not all of the information has to be held in human memory.

2.3 The application of a model

Memory demands are also an important factor in the application of a model to using a system in order to accomplish some task. In order to actually use a system, users must engage in planning at two rather different levels. At the conceptual level, they must figure out what they want to accomplish both in terms of their system-independent conception of the task, and in terms of their model of the system's conception of the task. At the communications level, they must plan how to tell the system about the entities they wish to manipulate, and the operations that they wish the system to perform upon those entities. Memory demands grow as a function of how much of those plans must be worked out before the interaction can begin. Once the interaction has started, further memory demands may be imposed by the necessity of keeping track of which portions of these plans have been executed, and which still remain. This information is critical not only to correct execution of any plan, but also to maintaining an accurate model of the state of the system during and after the interaction. That state information, in turn, represents yet another potential burden on the user's working memory.

3 THE INFORMATION MANAGEMENT SYSTEM

3.1 Overview of the IM system

The Information Management computing environment [1,2,9] is designed for high-performance personal work stations. The current implementation is written in an extended-LISP language called AP3 [5], and runs on Symbolics 3600 Lisp Machines using Symbolics Corporation's Interlisp Compatibility Package.

The key notion of the IM system is the use of a uniform representation in a persistent, underlying database of all information contained within the system. Rather than interacting with a disparate set of services, in IM one interacts with a *domain* that consists of *type definitions*, *object instances*, and three types of *rules*. Part of a type definition is a specification of the actions applicable to objects of that type. A traditional service, such as electronic mail, is simply some subset of type definitions, object instances, and rules in the database.

End users deal primarily with object instances -- creating or deleting them, applying actions relevent to them, or modifying attribute values associated with them. Since the system is self-describing, service builders also deal with object instances. However, some of the instances that they deal with represent type definitions and rules, and their actions may include "installing" those definitions and rules (thereby augmenting the range of capabilities represented in the system).

Objects are conceptual units located within a type lattice. Attributes may be associated with a type of object either through explicit statement in a definition, or through implicit effects of inheritance or definition of other types. Definitions specify restrictions on type and number of values for an attribute, and indicate the source of intial values upon creation of a new object instance (i.e., by explicit assignment, default values, inheritance, or derivation from other values).

Definitions also associate actions with object types, and may specify restrictions on when they should be available to users. (For example, there might be a "send" procedure applicable to draft messages, which is only to be presented to users when they are considering a message that has not already been sent.) Since there is inheritance through a type lattice, all types of objects inherit a set of generic actions defined for the top-most type of object, called "ENTITY". The generic actions provide the ability to create and destroy objects, and to add, delete, or replace attribute relations between objects.

Access to an object can come in three ways: reference by pointing to its screen display (thereby allowing associative browsing through the database), by use of its name if that is known, or by giving a *description*, which may be an arbitrarily complex pattern. Descriptions are similar to database queries, except that they may also be used to create new objects as well as to retrieve existing objects.

Rules specify, either explicitly or implicitly, actions that the system is to perform under certain conditions. IM *automation rules* explicitly indicate actions which are triggered by some event. *Co-ordination rules* specify relationships to be maintained between data items; implicitly, this entails actions which are triggered when a relationship is violated in order to "repair" the damage to the relationship. In the general case, these actions are specified as annotations to the co-ordination rule that we refer to as "repair rules".

One of our goals is for the system to be completely self-describing. This means that, among other things, type definitions and rules are themselves **IM** objects which can be accessed and manipulated in the manner described above. Thus, for example, one can find rule instances pertaining to a particular type or attribute by browsing or descriptive retrieval, and can modify those rules by applying generic actions to the rule objects or their attribute values.

3.2 The user interface

The user interface makes use of the mouse handling and large-screen bit-map display provided by the LISP Machines. In a typical configuration, the screen is divided into four non-overlapping windows. The *main window* displays the most recently touched **IM** objects, each represented as a line of descriptive information followed by a list of attribute/value pairs. An *overflow window* displays a list of identifiers for less recent objects that do not fit in the main window. An *editor window* allows users to examine and possibly modify any **IM** object(s) with textual representations, such as mail messages or co-ordination rules. Finally, an *interaction window* displays all messages output by the system and records all inputs from the user. The interaction window is scrollable, so that users can review the entire transcript of their session.

As far as possible, we attempt to blur restrictions on the mode of input. Users can reference objects or commands either by typing their names or by pointing with the mouse. Whenever the mouse's cursor is placed over an object, the user may obtain a pop-up menu of the commands applicable to that type of object in the current context. Objects or actions selected by pointing are echoed in the interaction window more or less as if they had been typed in.

Prompts issued by the system may be ignored by users, who may issue any number of commands until they are ready to respond to the prompt. Since this is handled through recursive calls on the system, users may stack up unanswered prompts to arbitrary depths. The system keeps track of its unanswered questions, and repeats them when interaction returns to the point at which they were originally asked. The display in the interaction window takes account of such unfinished interactions, so that users have that information available to them if they review the session transcript represented in the interaction window.

4 DEVELOPMENT AND USAGE OF SERVICES

The IM system provides a framework for implementing facilities of a computing environment. This section describes two: a database of information about employees at our research institute and an electronic mail system.

The employee database is the IM version of an in-house phone list, which previously had been maintained as an on-line text file. Like that phone list, the intended purpose of the database was simply to provide the information needed to contact co-workers. The information therefore included names, office numbers, phone extensions, back-up phones

(where messages can be left if employees don't answer their primary phones), and computer mail addresses. In IM, these are represented as instances of types rather than as text. PERSON is a type of object, with EMPLOYEE a sub-type. Names, offices, phones, and so on, are attributes of these types. Some of these attributes are also structured objects. For instance, computer mail addresses consist of an account name and a machine identifier.

Making these explicit permits stating rules about them, which capture implicit relationships previously known only to the text file's maintainer. For example, a co-ordination rule states that an employee's phone should correspond with the phone in their current office. If an employee moves to a new office, the rule tells the system that the phone has changed also. Another rule states that, for those employees who have project assistants, their back-up phones should correspond with the primary phone of their project assistant. This rule automatically updates back-up phones if a project assistant changes phone extensions, or if a project gets a different assistant. IM takes responsibility for chaining through its rule set to propagate implications of a change. Thus, if a project assistant moves to a new office, the two rules cause the system to update the back-up phones of the employees on that project.

Since employees and mail addresses were already represented in the system, adding electronic mail consisted primarily of defining object types for draft messages and received messages, along with actions that applied to them. Some attributes of messages have composite value restrictions; the TO and FROM headers of a received message, for example, can refer to employees, mail addresses, or strings. Some other attributes refer to a restricted set of possibilities. The STATUS of a draft message, for example, is one of the set {SENT, UNSENT, FAILED}. Rules govern the consistency of a number of items.

Although specific actions had to be defined for mail-related functions such as sending, forwarding, and replying, much of the "mail service" relies on generic capabilities of the system. For example, there are no special commands for adding or deleting recipients of a message, or for editing the SUBJECT field or body of a draft message. These are simply attributes of an object, and the generic commands for modifying values and editing text apply. The generic capability provided by descriptions is also incorporated in the mail system; messages addressed to descriptions are interpreted as being addressed to all objects that satisfy the description. There is a certain degree of flexibility in the order in which actions are applied because of IM's capability for handling embedded interactions. This is illustrated in Figure 1, which shows an annotated record from the interaction

(1) Send this message?...
   Selected menu item: Add Attribute
 (2) attribute... *cc*
 (2) attribute value...
   Selected menu item: View Object (R. Neches)
 (2) attribute value...
   Selected menu item: View Object (A. Neches)
 (2) attribute value... *R. Neches*
(1) Send this message?... *yes*

Figure 1: Sample of recorded interaction

window for a user who has started to specify a recipient for a message, realized that he is not certain who to send it to, and inspected the database in order to decide before finally responding to the original prompt.

IM services are meant to be extendable through augmentation of the database. One of us, for example, has personalized the mail service in his copy of the database. His extensions define "message-class" as a type of object, and specify rules that automatically sort incoming messages into classes and display them graphically. Figure 2 shows some of the message classes and the keywords used by the rules to identify messages as belonging to one of those classes. The ability to specify rules in IM has enabled the user to turn over responsibility to the system for examining each message to decide how to classify it.

PublicationGroup	(PUBLICATION PUBLICATIONS)
Engagement	(LUNCH DINNER)
RequiresAnswer	RSVP
RequiresAction	URGENT
Business	(HEALTH VISITOR)
ARPA	(OHLANDER SQUIRES SEARS KAHN)
Personnel	(TERMINATION HIRE WELCOME)
Paid	VACATION
JunkMail	("Files restored to disk"
	"Migrated files"
	"Thursday Internet Seminar")

Figure 2: Sample message classes
and identifying keywords

5 DESIGNED-IN SUPPORT FOR USER MODELS

We'd like to examine the extent to which IM provides aid and comfort to the user, in light of our beliefs about the nature and application of users' models. First, this discussion considers aspects of the system that might reduce the difficulty of building/updating a mental model. Second, the discussion considers aspects that might reduce the difficulty of applying a model.

5.1 Building mental models

At the conceptual model level, IM provides several facilities intended to reduce the number of rules and facts required to comprise an adequate model of the system.

The uniform underlying representation of information enables unification of concepts that otherwise could have multiple instantiations. Operations that would normally use special-purpose functions can instead be accomplished by generic functions that only have to be learned once. For example, the basic function for modifying an attribute value serves both to change the name of an employee and modify the address list of a message. Data concepts can also be unified because different services share a common database. Thus, knowledge about how employees are represented is equally effective for the mail system and for the employee database.

"Browsing" and descriptive retrieval facilities permit access to items whose names would otherwise have to be memorized. These mechanisms allow users to access and modify information objects -- not just data objects, but also rules and programs -- without requiring full knowledge about the form or content of the object sought.

IM co-ordination rules respond to implications and side-effects of actions that users would otherwise have to learn to predict, recognize, and handle. Automation rules respond to events for which routine actions are required, thereby relieving users of the responsibility to do so. Together, the rules give IM the feel of a VISICALC for non-numeric data by automatically changing related parts of a knowledge base affected by an externally introduced change. Their presence helps users avoid the difficult task of knowledge compilation, because they have less need to learn when to apply knowledge about relationships. For example, users need not remember to find and update the back-up phones of employees with a particular project assistant when the phone in that project assistant's office changes; IM rules have taken care of the responsibility.

Another advantage of the presence of IM rules is that, by hiding the distinction between stored and computed data, they reduce the level of detail at which users must model the system.

Rules are user-accessible objects in the IM database. Like all other IM objects, they can be found by browsing or descriptive retrieval. The ease with which they can be found and examined facilitates learning by allowing users to compare their emerging mental models of the system with an explicit external representation. Because the rules are represented externally, and therefore do not have to be held in memory by the users, we would expect reduced memory demands for learning.

5.2 Applying a model

At the communication level, the system provides several facilities intended to reduce demands on users' memories by providing an external representation for information which users must normally keep in working memory or retrieve from long-term memory. For example, dynamically computed pop-up menus remind users what commands are available by showing only those commands that are applicable in the current context.

Unlike many menu systems, where all record of a menu selection disappears after an item has been selected, IM does not force users to rely wholly on their own recall for past actions. Instead, it provides external memory support by recording each interaction in a scrollable display window that allows users to review their session history -- regardless of the original mode of input. The capability of mixing type-in with mouse pointing in communicating with the system gives users more freedom in identifying objects to the system, thereby reducing the amount of planning that has to go into deciding how to say something to the system.

The amount of pre-planning that has to go on before initiating interaction with the system is also reduced by IM's ability to accept digressions. Since users may ignore a system request for information without aborting the operation that produced it, they do not have to account for as many order dependencies in planning their instructions to the system. Instead, they can rely on knowing that they have an opportunity *at the time the need arises* to order the computations needed to produce any information requested by the system that they had not prepared in advance. The list of unfinished interactions, displayed as part of the record of the session, provides an external memory representation for incomplete goals; this further reduces the memory load of planning and executing interactions with the system.

6 CRITICAL EVALUATION

It is important in evaluating the interaction between humans and computers to distinguish between deep and shallow levels of interaction, and to evaluate a system separately along these two dimensions. In consonance with the theme of this paper, the discussion following emphasizes the deep level. At that level, we have noticed three major problems in our prototype system.

6.1 Inadequacies in the recording of history

A common-sense test of user-friendliness is to ask: *What happens if the phone rings?* The answer tells us how well the system functions as an external memory for the user. A system should help the user to determine the current state of the system, the sequence of operations that brought it to that state and the higher-level plan currently being followed. The system need not represent all this information explicitly, but it should retain enough to enable its users to reconstruct their mental states as well as the system's state.

IM takes two steps in this direction by extending its recording of previous actions to include menu selections, and by allowing embedded interactions. The former makes the history more complete. The latter captures at least one common sort of plan, in which prerequisite conditions must be satisfied or inputs must be supplied in order to enable the execution of an operation. These two steps alone, however, turn out to be insufficient.

One problem is that the current history does not record enough of the interaction. It tells what action was executed, for example, but not what context it was executed in. For example, it does not record information about alternative choices that would enable a user to find where a wrong selection was made.

Another problem is that the history is only recorded at the interface level, and does not indicate database changes that occured as side-effects of interactions (i.e., as the results of rules that applied during the transaction).

A third problem is that the history is not organized for arbitrary inspection. Currently, one can search it only by scanning line-by-line, and cannot request different presentations of the history. This problem can be expected to worsen as the first two problems are solved. Solutions to those problems would add information to the history that users would only sometimes want to see. One possibility is to represent some aspects of the history as objects in the IM knowledge base, allowing examination with the power of browsing and descriptive retrieval. This must await a better IM representation of the information displayed to the user; otherwise the history would inaccurately show objects in their current states, rather than in the state they were at the time recorded.

6.2 Human interface vs. code interface

The ability for users to specify rules that allow transfer of their responsibilities to the system is an especially important feature. However, currently this requires users to master two models: one for their own interaction with the system, and another for code that they write to extend it.

The problem is that the interface can provide access to the underlying functions in packagings more attractive than the original -- and certainly more familiar. These packagings often conceal the names of internal system functions from the user, but they also can form compositions of functions, provide default values for arguments, invoke functions conditionally, and so on. If those packagings are only accessible through the modalities provided by the user interface (i.e., by selecting menu items using a mouse then responding to prompts from the system), then users lose the ability to take advantage of them in trying to state rules for their behavior to the system.

We are now exploring a two-pronged solution to this problem. First, we are creating defining forms for interface procedures that will automatically generate a corresponding procedure suitable for non-interface invocation (and vice versa). Second, we will provide a representation of the interface itself in the IM database. For efficiency reasons, the system cannot, of course, run off of that representation. However, by having a representation in the database, users can use the power of the IM mechanisms for browsing, descriptive retrieval, and inspection to find the functions that they would like to utilize in expressing their rules.

6.3 Changing the world model

The power of the system lies in the fact that more about its world has been explicitly expressed and is therefore available for inspection. On the other hand, the more that has been expressed, the more that needs to be modified when users try to change some aspect of the system.

We have found that the problem arises in its most serious form when a service builder would like to extend the system by modifying a pre-existing type definition, even in as simple an aspect as changing the name of a type or attribute. When a type definition is changed in any way, virtually every component of the system is vulnerable to the effects. Previously created instances of the type may be inconsistent with the new definition. System and interface functions that dealt with the type or its instances may have been written with assumptions that are no longer valid. Rules may also contain assumptions that are now inappropriate, and the code generated to implement rules may also have been invalidated.

If the user has the full burden of re-establishing consistency after a change to the database schema, then the effort entailed in checking all of these factors drastically discourages making many changes. The solution seems to lie in stating rules that transfer some of the responsibility over to the system.

As objects and their type definitions are represented in the IM database, we should not have major difficulties in stating rules that detect when a change to a type definition has invalidated instances of the type. We expect to automatically repair many of the cases, although there are some which involve case-by-case decisions that will have to be passed to the user. Even in those cases, rules will still be helpful because **IM** will take over responsibility for finding the objects requiring an update.

There are more challenges and opportunities with **IM** rules handling changes to type definitions that affect rules, system code, or interface functions. Still, the problem appears manageable. We expect to automate a subset of cases, and to have the system take over responsibility for locating expressions that reference the modified type and that therefore require examination. We may be able to do more, by stating rules containing heuristics based on limited code analysis. For example, expressions that access values of an attribute are vulnerable to changes in the number of values allowed, while expressions that are conditional on the type of an attribute value are vulnerable to changes in the type restrictions for that attribute. To the extent that we can work out the details of such heuristics, the rules can either automate the repair process or at least filter out a large number of cases that will not require action and therefore do not require examination by the user.

7 SUMMARY

The **IM** system is founded upon notions of a uniform underlying database of information, the capability of accessing objects in that database by description rather than by name, and the capability of expressing rules telling the system how to act as an agent for users in manipulating database objects. We have argued that systems built on these notions could simplify the task users face in developing and using a system model. Several of the current prototype's limitations might be eliminated by providing building more information and rules about the system itself into its database.

REFERENCES

1. Balzer, R., Dyer, D. Morgenstern, M., and Neches, R. Specification-Based Computing Environments, in *Proceedings of the National Conference on Artificial Intelligence*, AAAI, 1983.

2. Balzer, R., Goldman, N., and Neches, R. Specification-Based Computing Environments for Information Management. To appear in *Proceedings of the Computer Data Engineering Conference*, April, 1984.

3. Card, S.K., Moran, T.P, and Newell, A. *The Psychology of Human-Computer Interaction*. Hillsdale, NJ: Erlbaum, 1983.

4. Douglas, S., and Moran, T.P. Learning Text Editor Semantics by Analogy. In *Proceedings CHI'83 Human Factors in Computing Systems* (Boston, December 12-15, 1983), ACM, New York, pp. 207-211.

5. Goldman, N. *AP3 Reference Manual*. Information Sciences Institute, Marina del Rey, CA, June, 1982.

6. Langley, P., Neches, R., Neves, D., and Anzai, Y. A Domain-independent Framework for Procedure Learning. *Policy Analysis and Information Systems*, vol. 4, 1980, pp. 163-197.

7. Lewis, C., and Mack, R. *The Role of Abduction in Learning to Use a Computer System*. Yorktown Heights, NY: IBM Watson Research Center, Research Report RC 9433 (# 41620), 1982.

8. Moran, T.P. Getting Into a System: External-Internal Task Mapping Analysis. In *Proceedings CHI'83 Human Factors in Computing Systems* (Boston, December 12-15, 1983), ACM, New York, pp. 45-49.

9. Neches, R., Balzer, R., Dyer, D., Goldman, N., Morgenstern, M. Information Management: a Specification-Oriented, Rule-Based Approach to Friendly Computing Environments, in *Proceedings of the IEEE Conference on Systems, Man, and Cybernetics*, Bombay, India, December, 1983.

10. Neves, D., and Anderson, J.R. Knowledge Compilation: Mechanisms for the Automatization of Cognitive Skills. In J.R. Anderson (Ed.), *Cognitive Skills and Their Acquisition*. Hillsdale: Erlbaum, 1982.

Human-Computer Interaction — INTERACT '84 / B. Shackel (ed.)
Elsevier Science Publishers B.V. (North-Holland)
IFIP, 1985

COMPUTER-SUPPORTED PROGRAM DOCUMENTATION SYSTEMS

GERHARD FISCHER and MATTHIAS SCHNEIDER

Project INFORM, Department of Computer Science, University of Stuttgart
Herdweg 51, D-7000 Stuttgart, Fed. Rep. of Germany

One of the most neglected research areas in computer system development is how to produce effective materials and reference information. Beyond the design principles developed for printed materials, there are documentation opportunities unique to interactive systems that we do not yet understand how to exploit effectively.

Program documentation systems with a high-bandwith user interface in connection with program analysis systems are necessary tools for program designers and users because they allow the monitoring of both the program and its underlying design principles and ideas.

1. Introduction

Documentation was once defined as printed matter that describes or explains how a system of some kind works or should be used. The documentation was necessarily separate from the system unless the system itself was something printed on paper. In the context of the computer, however, documentation can be part of the system it describes.

Recent experiences indicate that computer-based documentation has advantages over print-on-paper documentation even if the system itself is not a computer program. For example, computer-supported documentation about a large car manufacturing system facilitates the collection and maintenance of important information and guarantees that every person working with this documentation can get the same version.

When a computer system offers the information to a user we are able to tailor it for a specific user, for a specific problem and for a specific purpose and methods or tools to present documentation at the right level of abstraction can be provided.

More support can be obtained if the system to be documented is itself a computer program. Changing a huge program is currently a painful, often impossible task. Static comments and documentation help, but require manual updating whenever the program changes. Dynamic information (e.g. the overall structure indicated by the calling structure, the visual representation of the data structures) can be computed by the program itself, will change automatically with the programs executable code and will contribute to keep system and documentation consistent.

The user can get information that is specific to his problem and his level of experience. Modern Human-Computer Communication (HCC)

– techniques can filter out the necessary information, show different aspects of the situation and simulate the effects of changes in the user's program. The availability of undo-mechanisms allows the user to explore the behaviour of the system instead of analyzing its static description.

2. The role of documentation in software engineering

A large number of problems to be solved with the help of computer systems are ill-structured. Their solution requires incremental design processes, because complete and unchangeable specification are not available. An adequate design methodology must be based on a rapid prototyping approach to support the coevolution of specification and implementation. Communication between clients and designers and communication between the humans and the knowledge base in which the emerging product is embedded are of crucial importance. Program documentation systems are major components of systems that support knowledge-based human-computer communication (HCC) in software engineering.

2.1 Our view of the software engineering process

In software engineering we can differentiate at least between the following three different phases:

* developing an intuitive understanding of the problem to be solved; the communication between the client and the designer is of crucial importance in this phase
* designing a system intended to solve that problem; the designer will look at previous solutions to similar problems and will try to find modules which can be used in the design

* programming an implementation of the design; the implementor will try to show that his implementation is consistent with the specification.

In practise, these concerns are never totally separated nor entirely sequential. Life cycle models (Howden 82) have played an important role in software engineering but they rest on the assumption (which is unproven for many classes of problems) that at the beginning the requirements can be stated in a precise way and that the implementation can be derived from them relying primarily on formal manipulations.

2.2 Capturing the Intent of the System Designers

Most program systems are developed through efforts to improve existing systems, and those that do not are developed from some kind of design activity in the minds of system designers. The intentions of the designers and programmers are of crucial importance to understanding what the systems do, how they work, and how they should be used but they are very rarely documented. The documentation of a computer program usually tells how to do something, not what it is that is being done, and it is very difficult to reconstruct the programmer's intentions from the program. An alternative view on documentation is necessary. The right approach may be to create computer-based design systems to give designers continuous documentation support, with as much emphasis on recording intentions and goals as on devising the means for achieving them.

2.3 What can we do without complete specifications?

In an environment that supports a rapid prototyping style of programming (Sheil 83) it is necessary to document each step of the design process to support the designer during his work. Documentation should not be done at the end of seperate design phases but be strongly interwoven with the other design activities (see section 2.1). The resulting document supports the designer on further development cycles as a driving force to find new ideas and to implement alternative solutions.

Ill-structured problems are typical for situations where the client cannot provide detailed and complete specifications. The development process itself changes the user's and designer's perceptions of what is possible, increases their insights into the application environment, and often changes the environment itself. This incremental, evolutionary development should be supported by a suitable computer system.

The following methodologies exist to cope with incomplete specifications:

* Experimental programming systems which support the coevolution of specifications and implementations (Sheil 83; Deutsch, Taft 80); an existing, prototypical implementation allows us to replace anticipation (i.e. how will the system behave) with analysis (which is in most cases much easier).
* Heavy user involvement and participation in all phases of the development process; the user should be able to experiment with the existing system and to discuss the design rational behind them; an existing prototype makes this cooperation much more productive, because the user is not restricted to reviewing written specifications to see whether or not they might satisfy his needs for the right functionality and ease of use.
* Development of systems by the end-users themselves; this eliminates the communication gap altogether; it allows that a person is not separated from the semantics of his work and it eliminates the necessity to anticipate all possible future interactions between users and the system.
* We have to accept changing requirements as a fact of life and should not condemn changes as a product of sloppy thinking; we need methodologies and tools to make change a coordinated, computer-supported process.

The importance of documentation for a rapid prototyping environment stems from the large range of different tasks a documentation is useful for:

* to enhance the designers understanding of the problem to be solved and to assist him in improving the problem specifications
* to support the designer during the implementation of his solution
* to enable a programmer to reuse a program and to extend existing systems to tool kits
* to maintain a programming system
* to help end-users to understand and use a program
* to make a program portable and sharable in a larger community

3. Program documentation systems

A program documentation system is the kernel of a software engineering environment. It should be constructed as a knowledge base containing all the available knowledge about a system combined with a set of tools useful for **acquiring**, **storing**, **maintaining** and **using** this knowledge. It serves as the communication medium between system designers, clients and the knowledge base of the system throughout the entire design process. A valid and consistent documentation **during** the programming process itself (compared to one which is not produced until the end of the whole process) is of special importance in incremental design processes to provide answers to the questions: what has be done, what is the next thing to do, how does the current implementation compare with the the specifications, etc.

The amount of work that has to be done to keep the documentation of a large program up-to-date during incremental changes is far too large to be done manually by the designer. It is necessary to support the programmer by creating information about the structural properties of his system and by keeping the whole documentation consistent. Only if the information in the knowledge base is consistent with the existing program code at all times we gain the full benefit of the documentation as the base of the communication processes among designers and clients.

DOXY (Lemke, Schwab 83) (developed over several years within our research project INFORM) is a program documentation system that supports designers to create documentation which supports the incremental change of their programs and users to utilize the existing documentation of a system.

3.1 The Knowledge Base

Conventional documentation takes the forms of natural language text, diagrams, sketches, pictures, and tables; it is designed exclusively to be read by eye. New forms of documentation are becoming essential: pointer structures, semantic networks, procedural networks, and production rules. Documentation designed to be interpreted by computer programs offers the possibility to create a strongly connected network of knowledge, have the computer update this knowledge base and create user-tailored and situation-specific documentation.

The knowlege base is

* in part interpreted by the computer to maintain the consistency of the acquired knowledge about structural properties;

* in part only useful for the user, i.e. not directly interpretable by the machine. In this case the computer serves as a medium for structured communication between users and the knowledge base. The computer can support the user to maintain the consistency of non-interpretable information in the knowledge base (i.e it can suggest possible changes or drive an editor to places where changes are required).

DOXY's knowledge base is implemented in OBJTALK (Rathke, Laubsch 83), a object-oriented knowledge representation language. Object-oriented knowledge representation has the following advantages over conventional representation styles:

* it reflects the internal structure of a documentation; the knowledge is centered

```
Sample Data Structure
(defobject prem
  (name prem)
  (super function-description)
  (status ANALYZED)
  (code
  (def prem
    (lambda (key1 key2)
     (let ((i (phashit key1 key2)) (a nil))
       (setq a (passociation i key1 key2))
       (cond (a
              (store (put-get-hash-table i)
                     (cond ((eq
                             (car (put-get-hash-table i))
                             a)
                             (cdr (put-get-hash-table i)))
                            (t
                             (delq
                              a (put-get-hash-table i)))
                     )))))))))
  (in-package pputget)
  (is-called-by)
  (calls passociation phashit)
  (type function)
  (parameters ((key1) (key2)))
  (local-variables (i (TYPE NUMBER))
                   (a (TYPE NUMBER)))
  (free-variables)
  (see-also (pputget-description))
  (history ((DEFINED 10/14/1983
             (programmer HDB)
             (reason
              " "))
            (MODIFIED 12/12/1983
             (programmer HDB)
             (reason
              "prem didn't work if the property
               to be deleted was the CAR of the
               appropriate bucket"))))
  (version 2)
  (side-effects (PUTACCESS put-get-hash-table))
  (purpose "removes properties from the hashtable")
  (description
   "this function removes the appropriate association-list
    entry from the hashtable. If the right entry is the
    first entry of the association-list, delq won't work,
    so catch this event first.")
  (scratch-pad " "))
```

Conventions
1. Reverse Video: slot names of our knowledge units
2. Underlined: data that can be interpreted, used and updated by the system
3. Normal font: knowledge generated by the user, commentaries etc.
4. CAPITALS: system-generated information

Figure 3-1: A sample function-description

around objects (like functions, variables, packages, plans) which have links to other objects to show the dependencies.

* inference mechanisms to deduce properties of the program are bound to objects by means of methods; therefore the effects of these inferences can be kept local and reduce the complexity of the deduction process

* effects of changes are kept local by using the same technique of defining methods to propagate necessary changes to other objects

* objects own methods that define different views on their knowledge; new views on a knowledge unit which fit the needs of a user are created by defining other methods by the user himself.

OBJTALK is a good descriptive mechanism to model our problem domain (documentation of

LISP-programs). The basic units are frame-like
structures (Minsky 75) that incorporate different kinds of knowledge about the analyzed
items. Information is organized around the
concepts of packages (the largest package being
the entire system) and functions. Additionally
there is a concept called a filter (see section
3.4) which provides the user with the possibility to create his own filtered views on
the information units. Figure 3-1 shows a
sample knowledge unit for an analyzed and documented function.

3.2 Knowledge Acquisition and Maintenance

The knowledge collected in the knowledge base
comes from two sources:

* the analyzing system PAMIN (Fischer et al.
  81; Kohl 84) provides information about the
  structural properties (cross references,
  side effects) of a program. This system's
  functionality is similar to the one of
  MASTERSCOPE (Masinter 79).
* the programmer has to provide semantic information about the different parts of the
  program, information about the internal
  (semantic) structure of his system, descriptions of the used algorithms etc.

Most of the analysis done by the system is
done at read-time (see Figure 3-2) which implies that we have to redo the analysis after
each alteration of the program code. The system knows about possible dependencies between
knowledge units and , if necessary, reanalyzes
the units in question. It informs the programmer about possible inconsistencies in the
knowledge base caused by a change of the
program code or knowledge units in the
database. These techniques help us to maintain
the consistency between different representations of the information.

The system updates its knowledge units in the
following way:

* it changes certain structural information
  (e.g. calls - is-called-by relations)
  automatically and it is able to alter information by using its cross-reference
  knowledge. This knowledge can also be used
  to guide the user to places where he possibly wants to change information.

* for each unit the user can provide a list of
  other knowledge units he wants to inspect
  and possibly alter if a unit has been updated (see the "see-also"-slot in Figure
  3-1; this information cannot be created by
  automatic inspection of the code.)

prem (FUNCTION) FILTER: normal
in-packages:
  pputget
callers:

callees:
  phashit passociation
purpose:
  removes properties from the hashtable
description:
  this function removes the appropriate association-list
  entry from the hashtable. If the right entry is the
  first entry of the association list, delq won't work,
  so catch this event first.
code:
(def prem
  (lambda (key1 key2)
    (let ((i (phashit key1 key2)) (a nil))
      (setq a (passociation i key1 key2))
      (cond (_
see-also:

Figure 3-2:   Documentation during
                   programming

When the user starts to define a new function
(or package) the system creates a new knowledge
unit (as shown in Figure 3-1) and inserts inferred information as soon as possible. If the
user deletes program code the system deletes
the information derived from this piece of code
(Lemke, Schwab 83)

3.3 Using the available knowledge

The quality of a documentation system is
largely influenced by the user interface that
is available for the use of the collected
knowledge. The user has to be able to access a
consistent and valid documentation at any time.
He should be able to get the knowledge in a way
that supports his specific task.

Program documentation has to serve different
groups who perform different tasks. Therefore
the information offered to these groups has to
be different. We distinguish the following
groups and their tasks:

* the designer of a system during the programming process (see Figure 3-2). He has to
  have access to his design decisions and the
  different versions of the system. He also
  needs information about the state of his
  work in the whole design process.

* the programmer who is trying to reuse or
  modify a program that he does not know yet.
  He first wants to understand the purpose and
  algorithms of the program to decide which
  parts of it have to be changed to fit his
  needs. He needs information about design-
  decisions (in order to avoid known pitfalls)
  as well as a thorough documentation of the
  existing code.

* the client who is trying to find out whether
  the implemented system solves his problem.
  He wants to improve his own understanding by
  working with a prototypical version of the

system and is therefore not interested in any programming details but in design decisions.

* the user wants to see a description in terms of "What does it do? How can I achieve my goals?"; for end-users the documentation has to offer different views of the system: a primer-like description for the beginner and manual-type explanations for the expert (see Section 3.4, Figure 3-2 and 3-4).

3.4 HCC-Tools to enhance program documentation

In our research on Human-Computer Communication we have developed the following tools to deal successfully with documentation systems:

High-bandwith user interfaces:
The information which has to be transferred between the user and the documentation system cannot be displayed with conventional user interfaces. We need high-resolution bitmap displays to mix graphics and text and pointing devices for selecting objects displayed on the screen. In the future voice input and output enhances the quality of the transferred information.

Window-systems:
Multiple windows are used to support different contexts and to show different perspectives of the relevant knowledge.

Editors and text formatters:
The user of a documentation system should be able to edit the knowledge in the knowledge base when he thinks that an alteration is appropriate. The system should offer him help to find the relevant information units (see Fig. 3-4 for an example where the documentation system shows the user all the places where he should edit his code) and support him during the editing process.

Textformatters are necessary to make text more readable both on the screen and as copies on paper. They should create cross references, indexes and a table of contentsautomatically (SCRIBE (Reid, Walker 80)) provides a good example for support in writing large documents).

Access tools for the knowledge base:
Since the amount of knowledge in the knowledge base is far too large to be shown to a user entirely it is necessary to support the user on retrieving the knowledge that is relevant to his problem. Browsing tools (Goldstein, Bobrow 81) enable the user to explore the contents of a knowledge base (see (Williams et al. 82) for an example).

Filters to hide complexity:
The scarce resource in information processing is human attention, not the amount of available information. It is necessary to hide

irrelevant information. Filters that can be defined by the user (see Fig. 3-3) generate context-specific information structures of reduced complexity.

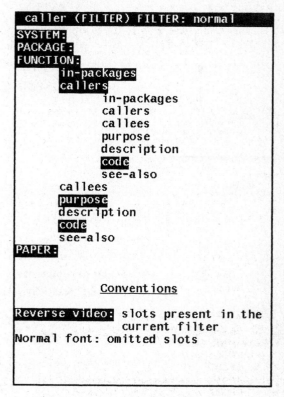

Figure 3-3: Definition of a filter

The user can create his own views of a knowledge unit. In the example given the user wants to see information about called functions (Lemke, Schwab 83).

Creation of alternative views for different user groups:
The display of the relevant knowledge may be different for different user groups (see Fig. 3-5 for an example of an alternative display of LISP-code).

Creation and display of implicit knowledge structures:
It is impossible to store all of the knowledge that might be of interest to the user. However, it is possible to make knowledge explicit that is usually spread over the knowledge base (e.g. to create the calling structure from the knowledge about the functions of a program).

```
passociation (FUNCTION) FILTER: caller
in-packages:
  pputget
callers:
  pput :
    code:
    (def pput
      (lambda (key1 key2 value)
        (let ((i (phashit key1 key2)) (a nil))
          (setq a (passociation i key1 key2))
          (cond (a (rplaca (cddr a) value))
                (t (store (put-get-hash-table i)
                          (cons (list key1
                                      key2
                                      value)
                                (put-get-hash-table i))
          ))))))
  pget :
    code:
    (def pget
      (lambda (key1 key2)
        (let ((a (passociation (phashit key1 key2)
                               key1
                               key2)))
          (cond (a (caddr a))))))
  prem :
    code:
    (def prem
      (lambda (key1 key2)
        (let ((i (phashit key1 key2)) (a nil))
          (setq a (passociation i key1 key2))
          (cond (a (store
                    (put-get-hash-table i)
                    (cond
                      ((eq (car (put-get-hash-table i))
                           a)
                       (cdr (put-get-hash-table i)))
                      (t (delq a
                               (put-get-hash-table i)))
          )))))))
purpose:
passociation returns the property key2 of key1 in bucket i
or nil if no such property exists
code:
(def passociation
  (lambda (i key1 key2)
    (do ((ass (cdr (put-get-hash-table i))
              (cdr ass))
         (a (car (put-get-hash-table i))
            (car ass)))
        ((or (null a)
             (and (eq (car a) key1)
                  (eq (cadr a) key2)))
         a))))
```

Figure 3-4:   A filtered view on a function

After having defined a filter for a knowledge unit (see Figure 3-3) the system generates a representation of the information structure showing the code of the function and its callers. This view allows the user to easily alter the name or parameters of the described function (Lemke, Schwab 83).

Program Visualization, Dynamic Graphics, Simulation Kits:

Program visualization offers new possibilities to support programmers during their work. The computer is capable of displaying representations of its own internal operation. It can present sequences of symbols representing the program that is being executed and the data on which the program is operating (see Fig. 3-6). Alternatively, it can present graphs, diagrams, and pictures to indicate what the program should be doing and what it is in fact doing. This latter ap-

proach to documentation, which requires sophisticated graphic display not widely available in the past, is now economically as well as technically feasible. Iconic representations may be superior to symbolic representations in helping people to understand the intrinsic complexity of computer programs. With the iconic approach, it may be possible to provide something analogous to a zoom lens, which helps to monitor and control the broad picture as long as everything proceeds according to plan but focuses on the offending details as soon as trouble arises (see Fig. 3-6).

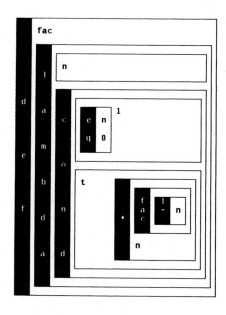

Figure 3-5:   Alternative Code-Display

Alternative program displays direct the user's attention to specific properties of the code (e.g. to the scope of variables or local functions) and hide structural difficulties from novice users (Bauer 84).

4. Conclusions

Documentation systems, equipped with excellent HCC-tools and methods will be necessary components of future programming environments. We have developed several components of documentation systems to pursue some of the stated problems. Many parts of the knowledge structures used in our documentation system are not interpreted by the computer but are presented to the human at the right time, under the desired perspective and with the appropriate level of detail. We have moduls which automate some of the knowledge acquisition (mostly by analyzing the program code) and we have simple

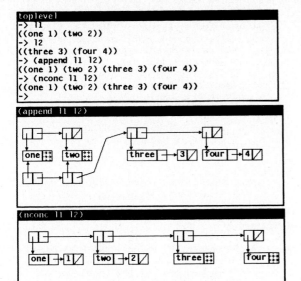

```
toplevel
-> l1
((one 1) (two 2))
-> l2
((three 3) (four 4))
-> (append l1 l2)
((one 1) (two 2) (three 3) (four 4))
-> (nconc l1 l2)
((one 1) (two 2) (three 3) (four 4))
->
```

Figure 3-6: Visualization of internal structures

KAESTLE (Nieper 83) offers graphic representations of a program's internal data structures and their changes during the interpretation of the code. The dynamic creation of graphical data descriptions allows to suppress details of the structures. With the help of KAESTLE the user can get graphic representations at arbitrary levels of detail.

mechanisms to maintain the consistency among different representations. All components are embedded in a LISP environment and can be accessed by a uniform, high-bandwith interface using windows, menus and a pointing device.

In our work we have found out many differences between conventional documentation techniques and our approach of computer-supported documentation which are shown in. Fig. 4-1.

To investigate the real potential of our approach many more problems remain to be solved. To mention some of the important ones:

* more parts of our knowledge structures must be formalized that they can be manipulated by the computer

* evolutionary, incremental development and modification must be supported by the computer (e.g. a dependency network must propagate the implications of a small change of our knowledge structures)

* the computer needs more knowledge about: specific subject domains, design, programming, users and communication processes; more support is necessary to acquire, represent and utilize this knowledge.

We hope to contribute with our work to the solution of a major problem in computer science: to help programmers and users to maintain and use large computer programs in an environment that is tailored to their needs.

	Documentation on paper	Online-Documentation
Knowledge	linear; reference tables; static knowledge only;	semantic networks support different access routes to the important knowledge; knowledge base reflects the complexity of the knowledge; static and dynamic knowledge; (see section 3.1)
Knowledge Acquisition	mostly handwritten; has to be done manually	automatic acquisition of knowledge about structural properties semantic knowledge from the programmer;
Knowledge Updating	no support, has to done manually	mostly done by a documentation-system, other parts updated with computer support;
Consistency	difficult (impossible) to maintain	guaranteed for knowledge about structural properties; computer-support for semantic knowledge (see section 3.2)
Knowledge Use	readable material; no support for different user groups or purposes	filters for different user groups and purposes; (see Fig. 3-3) situation-specific user support; can be machine-driven
Availability	only after the system is fully implemented; no support for designers	during and after the implementation process; useful for designers and users; (most of the work done by the computer)
	remote from the computer and the system;	within the system that the user wants to understand; can't get lost;
	for one user at a time; may be read off-line	for many users; can't be read without the computer

Figure 4-1: Documentation on paper vs. Online-documentation

References

(Bauer 84)
   D. Bauer: "Wissensbasierte
   Programmrepräsentation". Studienar-
   beit, Institut für Informatik,
   Universität Stuttgart, 1984.

(Deutsch, Taft 80)
   P.L. Deutsch, E. Taft (eds.):
   "Requirements for an Experimental Programming Environment". Xerox Corporation, Palo Alto, California, 1980.

(Fischer et al. 81)
   G. Fischer, J.R. Failenschmid, W. Maier,
   H. Straub: "Symbiotic Systems for Program
   Development and Analysis". MMK-Memo,
   Institut für Informatik, Stuttgart,
   1981.

(Fischer, Schneider 84)
   G. Fischer, M. Schneider: "Knowledge-
   based Communication Processes in
   Software Engineering". In Proceedings
   of the 7th International Conference on
   Software Engineering. Orlando,
   Florida, March, 1984.

(Goldstein, Bobrow 81)
   I. Goldstein, D. Bobrow: "An Experimental
   Description-Based Programming Environment: Four Reports". Xerox Corporation, Palo Alto, California, 1981.

(Howden 82)
   W.E. Howden: "Contemporary Software
   Development Environments".
   Communications of the ACM 25(5), pp
   318-329, May, 1982.

(Kohl 84)
   D. Kohl: "Ein Modul zur Analyse von LISP-
   Programmen". Studienarbeit, Institut
   für Informatik, Universität Stuttgart,
   1984.

(Lemke, Schwab 83)
   A. Lemke, T. Schwab: "DOXY:
   Computergestützte
   Dokumentationssysteme". Studien-Arbeit
   Nr. 338, Institut für Informatik,
   Universität Stuttgart, 1983.

(Masinter 79)
   L. Masinter: "Global Program Analysis in
   an Interactive Environment". PhD
   thesis, Stanford University, 1979.

(Minsky 75)
   M. Minsky: "A Framework for Representing
   Knowledge". In P.H.Winston (editor),
   The Psychology of Computer Vision, pp
   211-277. New York, 1975.

(Nieper 83)
   H. Nieper: "KÄSTLE: Ein graphischer
   Editor für LISP-Datenstrukturen".
   Studienarbeit Nr. 347, Institut für
   Informatik, Universität Stuttgart,
   1983.

(Rathke, Laubsch 83)
   C. Rathke, J. Laubsch: "OBJTALK: Eine Er-
   weiterung von LISP zum objektorien-
   tierten Programmieren". In H.Stoyan,
   H.Wedekind (editors),
   Objektorientierte Software- und
   Hardwarearchitekturen, pp 60-75.
   Stuttgart, 1983.

(Reid, Walker 80)
   B.K. Reid, J.H. Walker: "SCRIBE Introduc-
   tory User's Manual" Unilogic, Ltd.,
   Pittsburgh, 1980.

(Sheil 83)
   B.A. Sheil: "Environments for Exploratory
   Programming". Datamation , February,
   1983.

(Williams et al. 82)
   M.D. Williams, F.N. Tou, R. Fikes,
   A. Henderson, T. Malone: "RABBIT: Cog-
   nitive Science in Interface Design".
   In Proceedings of the Cognitive
   Science Conference. Ann Arbor,
   Michigan, 1982.

LANGUAGE DESIGN AND COMPREHENSION

Human-Computer Interaction — INTERACT '84 / B. Shackel (ed.)
Elsevier Science Publishers B.V. (North-Holland)
IFIP, 1985

THE ANALYSIS AND UNDERSTANDING OF AN OPERATIVE LANGUAGE

Pierre FALZON

Institut National de Recherche en Informatique et en Automatique
Domaine de Voluceau, B.P. 105, 78153 Le Chesnay, France

When the operators of a system have to communicate verbally, they tend to build operative languages, molded by the characteristics of the task and its objective. A better
knowledge of these languages could provide guidelines for the design of computer command languages. A method of analysis of such an operative language is presented, based
on schema theory. Within each category of command messages, the different expressions
are considered as a collection of different instances of a single underlying schema.
Their analysis provides a description of the schema, and allows the elaboration of a
dictionary of words. Given the knowledge of the schemata, the understanding process can
rely on a very limited syntax and on a very small dictionary in which all words are
monosemous. This hypothesis has been tested by implementing these principles in computer programs. Results of an evaluation of the programs are presented and discussed.

When the operators of a system have to communicate verbally, they tend to build specific languages, molded by the characteristics of the
task and its objective. These languages are restricted, as compared to natural language, in a
number of domains: vocabulary, syntax, field of
discourse are a few. They have the powerful
capabilities of natural language (they can give
commands, request or give information, comment
on the situation, etc.), while avoiding its possible ambiguities. Sailors, for example, or sur-
gical teams, have elaborated operative languages
(in the sense of Ochanine, (6)) specific to
their domain, laconic and functionally distorted
(1). In fact, even subjects allowed to use natural language in typing instructions to a computer have been observed to gradually restrict
their expression, i.e. to begin to build an operative dialect. In that perspective, natural
language cannot be considered as a natural command language.

The study of these languages would be helpful
for the design of computer command languages, in
two different ways:
- first, for a given domain, by providing the
  vocabulary and the forms of expression appropriate for the computer version of the task;
- second, and whatever the domain, by providing
  indications on the elaboration of these languages, and particularly on the natural rules
  of restriction.

This approach will be illustrated by the study
of a specific language, used by Air-Traffic Controllers (ATCers) in their communications with
aircraft pilots.
A first study (3) has shown two important points:
- this language uses a limited number of words.
  Moreover, it is possible, starting from this
  lexicon, to design an even more restricted
  vocabulary, still allowing to take into account a large number of messages.
- most messages begin with a "command" word:

this command word is enough to categorize the
messages. Moreover, in each category, the
possible constituents of the messages are
highly predictable.

In other words, as soon as the command word is
understood by the expert, a specific body of
knowledge can be activated, allowing expectations on the following information. Schema
theory (5) provides a framework for this process.

The messages of a category can be considered as
a list of different instances of a common underlying schema, as different actualizations of a
single schema. Each schema is a pre-defined frame which slots require to be filled with specific pieces of information. The understanding of
a message can be described as a process which is
first data-driven (a schema is activated by some
schema-associated word) then conceptually-driven
(the schema is then instantiated, i.e. the slots
of the schema are filled with the information of
the message).

These observations allow the following hypotheses. In this operative language:
- a limited vocabulary is sufficient to understand a large number of messages: the vocabulary is composed of a small number of words
  and each word has a single definition (no polysemy);
- to a large extent, and given the knowledge of
  the schemata, syntax can be neglected. The
  only assumption needed is that most messages
  begin with a schema-associated word.

These hypotheses have been tested by the following method:
- for each category of command messages, the
  underlying schema is defined; a method of
  schema abstraction has been devised. The same
  method allows the choice of the necessary

words and of their definition.
- this schematic knowledge is then implemented in programs, which must be able to understand (typed) messages in the operative language under study.
- the programs are tested on a sample of communications (different from the corpus used to build the schemata and the dictionary); the understanding performance of the programs allows an estimation of the validity of the approach.

SCHEMA ABSTRACTION AND THE DESIGN OF THE DICTIONARY

The knowledge base of the system is composed of two dictionaries: a dictionary of schemata and a dictionary of words. In order to elaborate these dictionaries, a first corpus of 8 hours of controller-pilot communications has been used. The messages emitted by the controllers have been extracted from this corpus, and categorized. The analysis has then been focused on the command messages.

Schema abstraction

The methodology used to define the schemata is based on the analysis, within each category of messages, of the paraphrases and of the meaning overlaps. It will be illustrated by the study of a specific category, dealing with instructions of modifications of the level of the aircraft. The schema for this category will be built step by step.

    [1] climb level 330
    [2] descend level 330
    [3] leave 290 for 330
    [4] climb level 330 at pilot's discretion
    [5] climb to the flight level 330
    [6] climb 330

The schema will be called CHLVL (for CHange LeVeL). By definition, we know that the action (Act) will concern the vertical dimension (VE), and that the nature of the action (Nat) will concern the level (as opposed to the rate of climb or descent).
We then have:

    CHLVL : ((Act : VE) (Nat : LVL))

Consider now message [1] and [2].
They show that a first element is missing in the schema : the level to be reached, which will be coded P (for parameter). Moreover, messages [1] and [2] do not indicate the same type of relation between the present level and the level to be reached. The schema must include two possibilities: a positive or a negative relation.

    CHLVL : ((Act : VE) (Nat : LVL) (Rel : (+ -))
             (To : P))

In message [3], a new information appears : the present level. This information was omitted in

messages [1] and [2], which could be re-written "from your present level, climb/descend level 330". The schema is then modified to include this piece of information.

    CHLVL : ((Act : VE) (Nat : LVL) (Rel : (+ -))
             (From : (PV P)) (To : P))

PV stands for "present value". In message [4], the expression "pilot's discretion" has several implications, concerning the time of execution of the action and the way it is to be performed. If this information is not specified, the pilot must assume by default that the action must take place now. The schema is modified accordingly.

    CHLVL : ((Act : VE) (Nat : LVL) (Rel : (+ -))
             (From : (PV P)) (To : P)
             (Time : (def NOW PD)))

"def" stands for "default", meaning that the default value of the "Time" slot is the following element. "PD" stands for "pilot's discretion".

All the schemata are built according to this method. Each schema has specific procedures attached to it, allowing different checks and some (limited) inferential capabilities. A schema is then a data structure plus a set of operations.

A dictionary of words

Messages [5] and [6] are paraphrases. From their examination, it can be inferred that some of the words are not needed to understand the messages. The information given by "to the flight level" is not useful : the word "climb" is sufficient to evoke an instruction of modification of the flight level. Therefore, the analysis of the different forms of expression allows the definition of the necessary words, which will be part of the dictionary.
The words are defined using the same elements that have been used in the definition of the schemata. For example, climb is defined as:

    ((Act : VE) (Nat : LVL) (Rel : +) (From : PV))

Some of the words have a special property : they are associated to some schema, i.e. when they appear, a specific schema is triggered. In the example we have studied, "descend", "climb" and "leave" evoke the CHLVL schema.
75 words are defined in the dictionary. 33 of these 75 words are schema-associated. On top of these words, the system knows a set of locations, and it is able to spot the numeric parameters (which are given in digits, not spelled).

THE UNDERSTANDING SYSTEM

Only a very brief presentation of the system will be given here (a more detailed account can be found in (4)).
The system is composed of two sets of programs:
- "understanding" programs : these programs are

able to process (typed) ATC communications, evoking appropriate schemata, filling their slots with the information of the messages. The system is able to infer some missing information by consulting its memory of past instantiated schemata.
- "planning" programs : these programs process the output of the understanding programs, i.e. instantiated schemata. The task of these programs is to transform these schemata into sequences of actions.

The evaluation has been focused on the understanding programs. They have been tested on a corpus of 4 hours of ATC communications, recorded in different work situations. These 4 hours represent 554 command messages.

RESULTS

There are 4 possible outputs to the programs:
- the appropriate schema is evoked and the instantiation is correctly performed: the system has understood;
- the appropriate schema has been found, but the instantiation is incorrect: the system has understood partially;
- an inappropriate schema has been evoked, and then instantiated: it is a false comprehension;
- nothing is understood by the system, either because no schema has been evoked, or because an incomplete instantiation forbade its storage.

Table 2 presents the understanding performances of the system according to these four possibilities.

		yes	ii	is	no	Tot.
Messages	N	433	42	10	69	554
	%	78.2	7.6	1.8	12.4	100

yes : correct schema evocation and correct instantiation
ii : correct schema evocation and incorrect instantiation
is : incorrect schema evocation
no : nothing is memorized

Table 2 : Understanding performances of the system for the command messages

78% of the messages are correctly understood, which is an interesting result considering the restrictions on the size and content of the dictionary and the virtual absence of syntactical parsing. The hypothesis according to which the knowledge of some schema-associated words is sufficient to trigger the appropriate schemata is verified for 85,8% of the messages (yes + ii).
However, these results only present the overt

behavior of the system, its output. It is more fruitful to consider the errors not in terms of their consequences, but in terms of their causes. This is particurlarly true because a given cause of error may have different consequences according to the messages, and because a given consequence may be originated by different causes. The causes of errors can be classified into two main categories : limitations of the knowledge base and limitations of the system's processing abilities.

Limitations of the knowledge base

The knowledge base has been elaborated by the analysis of the first corpus of controller-pilot communications. All the words and schemata which happened to be absent of this corpus are then absent of the knowledge base. This causes two types of errors :
- The schema is unknown to the system. For example, an aircraft approaching an airport can be guided relatively to another aircraft. The corresponding form of expression can be: "Follow the B747 ahead". Since this category of messages did not appear in the first corpus we studied, the schema does not exist in the knowledge base. This error is always associated with the absence of the command word from the dictionary.
- The schema is defined in the system, but it is incomplete, and does not allow a specific modality. For instance, the system is able to understand [7], but not [8].

[7] "cross Avenal at 10000 feet"
[8] "cross 10 miles east of Avenal at 10000 feet".

The structure of the schema causes the system to expect a waypoint, and not a location relative to a waypoint. This type of error is the most frequent among the instantiation errors. Again, it is often associated with the absence of definition of some words in the dictionary.

Errors caused by limitations of the knowledge base can be reduced by the use of a larger corpus.

Limitations of the system's processing abilities

This second category of causes of errors does not deal with limitations of the knowledge base, but with limitations caused by some design assumptions. Four types of problems can be differentiated.
The first problem concerns the messages in which some information appears before the schema-associated word : since the system assumes that a message begins with a command word, it does not consider any information emitted before the evocation of a schema. For example, the system will correctly understand message [9] but will miss the "Time" information in [10].

[9] "descend and maintain 270 at pilot's dis-
     cretion"
[10] "at pilot's discretion descend and maintain
     270".

A second type of problem concerns the repetitions (with or without modifications) and the
alternatives. Messages [11] and [12] are two
examples of repetitions: [11] is a simple repetition, [12] is a repetition with modification.

[11] "descend and maintain 230 verify yeah 230"
[12] "turn left heading 180 let's make it 190
     sir"

Messages 13 and 14 represent two different kinds
of alternatives: [13] is a simple alternative,
[14] is a program of action.

[13] "contact Oakland center 125.45 or 357.6"
[14] "proceed VFR if unable proceed to Shabo
     intersection.

A third type of problem is caused by one of the
assumptions of the systems, according to which
words are monosemous. Four words at least seem
to contradict this hypothesis: "stay", "approach", "departure", "speed".
In fact, these four words pose two different
problems. The problem with the word "stay" is
not so much that it has two different meanings
but rather that its definition in the system's
dictionary is wrong. "Stay" is schema-associated
and activates the "Radio frequency instruction"
schema, as in "stay with me". It is however used
also in a different context: "stay with the
right" (meaning: "stay with the runway on the
right"). "Stay" should in fact be associated to
the "maintain parameter" schema, which already
exists in the system and which can have different application domains.

For the other words, a different kind of problem
appears. The words "approach" and "departure"
have a variety of meanings: control center (e.g.
"contact approach"), flight procedure (e.g.
"intersection departure") or step in a procedure
(e.g. "final approach"). The word "speed" is
used with two different meanings in the same
message:

[15] keep your speed up to the high speed.

"High speed" stands here for "high speed turn-
off". The word "turn-off" is omitted in most cases.
The problem with the words "approach", "departure" and "speed" is a problem of category ellipsis (2). The message "contact approach" is an
abbreviation of "contact the approach control
center", in the same way as "high speed" is an
abbreviation of "high speed turn-off". These
words in fact do not pose a problem of polysemy,
but a problem of ellipsis.
This phenomenon of ellipsis is very general: in
fact, some words are omitted so often that they
do not even appear in the system's dictionary.

For example, the word "taxi" is not in the dictionary, because the message "taxi into position
and hold" is always abbreviated into "position
and hold".

These considerations bring us to the fourth type
of error causes, the ellipsis of the command
word. This category is by far the most frequent
single cause of error, representing 32% of the
understanding problems.

The first situations in which ellipses occur are
repetitions of a message, following wrong (or
incomplete) readbacks by the pilots, as in [16].

[16]   (C: Controller -P: Pilot)
[16a] C - Republic 343, reduce speed to 210,
          contact Bay approach 135.65
[16b] P - Republic 343?
[16c] C - Republic 343, affirmative, 135.65,
          reduce to 180
[16d] P - Slowing to 180, and say again the fre-
          quency?
[16e] C - 135.65, Republic 343

The striking fact in this conversation is the
gradual contraction of the controller's expressions. From message [16b], the controller has
inferred first that the pilot has not immediately understood that the preceding communication
[16a] was addressed to him, but also that he
probably has understood part of that communication, i.e. that the schemata have already been
triggered. The controller then assumes (in 16c)
that he only has to repeat the frequency parameter ("135.65"). Notice that the speed instruction ("reduce to 180") is only slightly abbreviated, probably because the controller has
changed the speed value between the emission of
[16a] and [16c]. In [16d], the pilot explicitly
specifies that he has understood the schema to
be triggered, but not the value of the frequency
parameter slot of the schema. Consequently, the
controller only has to fill this slot, by uttering the appropriate number [16e].

Suppressions of the command word occur also when
the controller knows that the situational context is so constraining that the pilot is expecting a given type of message. In other words,
the schema is evoked, not by a command word, but
by the context. Messages 17 and 18, in which the
omitted words are bracketed, are examples of
these cases.

[17] [runway] 28 left
[18] [contact] Bay approach 135.65

Messages like [17] are frequently emitted
towards the arriving or departing aircraft, in
order to avoid errors. In these situations the
possible movements are very constrained: on the
ground, or in the air, the aircraft are limited
to a few patterns of evolution, and they all
share the same goal: to reach a runway. In
these conditions, it is possible to shorten the
message indicating the runway to be reached

[17] without impairing the pilots' understanding.

In the same way, the occurrence of message [18] is quite predictable: the pilot knows when he is about to have to contact another control center, and he is expecting to be given a new frequency. Again, the context determines some expectations about the possible schemata. Understanding should be guided in these cases by some higher-level scripts.

CONCLUSION

The global performance of the system is quite satisfying: the programs are able to recognize much of Air Traffic Control instructions, and this despite the fact that the system has no syntactical knowledge, a limited dictionary, and a single definition for each word of the dictionary. The results give some indications as to possible improvements: a larger knowledge base, an ellipsis detection device and some script information would certainly increase the understanding performance of the system.

Still, the present programs are quite certainly not powerful enough to understand all possible Air Traffic Control messages. Although the human operators are willing, because they are operators, to restrict themselves to some standard phraseology most of the time, they still have the possibility, because they are human, to switch back to the use of natural language, when they want or need to do so (for example, in case of a low workload, or when the situation is rare, so that there is no adequate usual phraseology). In such cases, a more elaborate system would be necessary in order to understand the communications. Does this mean that this approach is useless? Certainly not.

The language under study is not homogeneous. Most of the time, it is a technical dialect, which vocabulary and syntax are highly restricted. However, other expressions and a different vocabulary may be used in less usual situations. The fact that the programs are not able to understand all of what is said is a consequence of the use of two different modalities in the communications to the pilots, for which different analyses must be performed. One interest of our approach is precisely its focus on that large part of the communications in which the operators use an operative dialect.

ACKNOWLEDGEMENTS

This research was supported by a grant from the INRIA (Rocquencourt, France), and completed at NASA – Ames Research Center (Moffett Field, CA, USA). Rob Flanagan helped transcribing the ATC tapes. The author wishes to thank Charles Billings, Renwick Curry and Everett Palmer for their help and support in this work.

REFERENCES

[1] BISSERET, A. Psychology for man computer cooperation in knowledge processing. In Mason (Ed.), Information Processing 83, Proc. of the IFIP 9th World Computer Congress (North Holland, Amsterdam, 1983).

[2] CARROLL, J.M. Nameheads. Cognitive Science. 7 (1983) 121-153.

[3] FALZON, P. Les communications verbales en situation de travail: analyse des restrictions du langage naturel. Technical Report INRIA CO 8211 R70, (1982) Le Chesnay, France

[4] FALZON, P. Understanding a technical language. A schema-based approach. Research Report INRIA. 237 (1983) Le Chesnay, France.

[5] NORMAN, D.A., RUMELHART, D.E. Explorations in cognition (Freeman and Co, San Francisco, 1975).

[6] OCHANINE, D.A. Recueil d'articles, Actes du Séminaire "L'image opérative", 1-5 juin 1981 P. CAZAMIAN (ed.), Paris I University (1981)

Human-Computer Interaction — INTERACT '84 / B. Shackel (ed.)
Elsevier Science Publishers B.V. (North-Holland)
IFIP, 1985

443

TRANSFORMATIONS OF SOFTWARE DESIGN AND CODE
MAY LEAD TO REDUCED ERRORS

Edward M. Connelly

Performance Measurement Associates, Inc.
Vienna, Virginia 22180

This research investigated the capability of programmers and non-programmers
to specify problem solutions by developing example-solutions and also for the
programmers by writing computer programs; each method of specification was
accomplished at various levels of problem-complexity. The results, which
showed the superiority of using example-solutions with inductive feedback over
writing code, suggests that the transformation process provided by the induction
might be applied analogously to software development. Considering designs and
code in multiple transformed forms may reduce software errors to a level found
for example-solutions.

INTRODUCTION:

Six experiments were conducted, with the same
problems used in all experiments. The ability
of the participants to develop example-solutions
was evaluated as a function of the participant's
background and experience, the complexity of
the problem to be solved, the level of inductive processing provided by the computer,
and the level of feedback-aids, when aids were
available.

THE TASK:

The experimental task required the specification of a ship selection logic (SSL) for a
hypothetical Navy task force. This involved
choosing ships from a list which identified
ship type, the transiting time from present
position to desired site, and the time each
ship could remain on duty, called stationing
time. For each problem, the participant was
required to specify example ship combinations,
from three combinations in the simplest problem to 14 in the most difficult. In addition,
the participant had to specify the desired
range (minimum to maximum, or MIN/MAX)
of transiting and stationing times for each ship
and combination of ships.

The example ship combinations entered were
analyzed by an inductive processor to form a
generalized ship selection logic which was fed
back to the participant. The participant would
view the selection logic and delete existing or
input additional example-solutions to further
refine or correct the logic.

Further, each participant was required to deal
with various levels of inductive processor
complexity. At one level, the processor would
generalize transiting and stationing times over
particular ships types only. At another, it
would generalize over all ship types in a
particular combination. The participant did
not know beforehand what level of processor
complexity would be used to interpret the
example-solutions the participant provided.

EXPERIMENTS:

Experiments 1 and 2 were designed to investigate the ability of expert programmers and of
bookkeepers/accountants who were not expert
programmers to develop example-solutions for
the hypothetical Navy task-force problem. The
experimental variables for both experiments
were problem-complexity and inductive processor complexity, i.e., the amount of machine
processing of user inputs.

Several results of the first two experiments
were used in the subsequent experiments.
First, as expected, more errors occurred with
more complex problems; but, the level of
processing or generalization (see Connelly, et
al. (1981) for definition of problem complexity
and level of generalization) of the example-
solutions was found to be an important factor,
i.e., a significant reduction in errors occurred
when data from example-solutions were processed into a standard form and presented to
the participant.

A second and perhaps the more important
result was that participants in both categories

who performed well tended to use a systematic, step-by-step strategy by considering example-solutions involving all combinations of a subset of all variables (ship types) before considering combinations of other variables. This strategy termed "Partial Enumeration" involves considering a set of example-solutions in which 2 or 3 variables are changed to produce all possible combinations of them while holding all other variables constant. Then after all those combinations have been considered (i.e., entered as example-solutions or not), a new variable that was previously maintained as a constant is modified and all combinations of the original subset considered again.

This result together with the first, noted above, suggested that feedback aids might be designed to assist participants to use a systematic strategy by processing their example-solutions and feeding back the resultant data to suggest possible additional inputs.

Yet another result of the first two experiments was used in the subsequent experiments. The number of years of advanced education (i.e., beyond high school) and the number of years of professional experience were found to be unimportant factors regarding performance. As a consequence of this result, additional demographic factors were evaluated for the participants in the subsequent experiments in an effort to find important demographic predictors of performance.

An additional result considered in the subsequent experiments was the observation that only a few errors-of-commission occurred in generation of the example-solutions. This intriguing result influenced the design of one experiment where FORTRAN IV code was written to solve the same problems used in Experiments 1 so that a comparison of error rates would be possible.

Experiments 3 and 4 were designed to investigate the ability of expert programmers and non-programmers to develop accurate and complete example-solutions using various feedback-aids at various levels of problem-complexity. Experiment 5 was designed to investigate the capability of expert programmers to revise problem-solutions' specifications in the form of example-solutions in which various numbers of initially-incorrect entries had been introduced, using the feedback-aids developed in Experiments 3 and 4.

Finally, Experiment 6 called upon expert programmers to develop computer code written

in FORTRAN IV for various levels of data input-a design intended to be analogous to the design of Experiment 1. The results of Experiment 6 were sub-routines written in FORTRAN IV that should accept or reject a ship combination, as that combination was correct or incorrect.

The performance measures used in the experiments consisted of error-measures and strategies-measures. Three error-measures were:

  a. P_T, the probability that a given ship-combination was correctly classified as acceptable or unacceptable.
  b. P_C, the probability that a correct ship-combination was accepted.
  c. P_{IC}, the probability that an incorrect ship-combination was rejected.

In addition to the error-measures above, relative error-measures were used. A relative error-measure was defined as a participant's error-score (P_T, P_C, P_{IC}) on an experimental problem minus his/her error-score on the pre-test problem. The relative error-measures thus tended to remove the effect of the participant's innate capability, and, as a result, were more sensitive to experiment factors than were the error-measures alone.

Two strategy-measures were used to detect the frequency with which participants used specific strategies. One strategy-measure, the combinational-measure, detected the frequency with which a participant changed only one component at a time of each successive example-solution. Another strategy-measure, a sequence-measure, detected the use-patterns of the various feedback-aids.

Results of Experiments 1, 2, and 3 in which programmers and bookkeepers/accountants provided example-solutions are compared with the results of Experiment 6 where experienced programmers wrote FORTRAN IV program code for the same problems. Results of the other experiments can be found in Connelly (1982 a,b).

DESIGN OF THE EXPERIMENT:

The experiment used a repeated measures Latin Square design (Plan #9 cited in Winer, 1971, pp. 727-736). The factors investigated were:

  1.   Three levels of problem complexity as measured by Halstead's E Metric (Halstead, 1977), where each level

required a different amount of effort to correctly specify a problem solution.

2. Three levels of feedback-aids.
3. Two participant populations: expert computer programmers and bookkeepers/accountants.

Each factor was fixed, but the groups and participants within the groups were random factors. A pre-test was used to screen the participants for their ability to understand the instructions.

A pre-test and 3 experiment problems were used. The least complex (used in the pre-test) required specification of 3 different ship combinations each involving 4 types of ships. The next required 6 ships combinations; then, in order of increasing complexity, 9 combinations, and finally, 14 combinations. The problem complexity, a function of the number of correct solution combinations, was quantified by Halstead's E Metric.

The participants had various feedback aids to use. It should be understood that the aids did not make use of any knowledge of the "correct solution", in fact, no information regarding the correct solution to each problem was entered into the computer for the experiment trials. One aid #1, shown in Table 1, provides a display of the ship selection logic (SSL) including: ship types, MIN/MAX for transiting times, and MIN/MAX for stationing times for each ship combination.

Table 1 Example of Feedback Aid #1.

"Ship Selection Logic (SSL)"

Ship Type	Ship Type	Transit Time MIN	MAX	Stationing Time MIN	MAX
CVAN*	0				
CVA	1	1	5	10	50
CA	0				
CGN	0				
CG	0				
DD	4	1	5	10	50
SSN	0				
SS	2	1	5	10	50
AO	1	1	5	10	50
TOTAL:	8				

*CVAN	Aircraft Carrier (Nuclear)
CVA	Aircraft Carrier
CA	Heavy Cruiser
CGN	Guided Missile Cruiser (Nuclear)
CG	Guided Missile Cruiser
DD	Destroyer
SSN	Submarine (Nuclear)
SS	Submarine
AO	Oiler

Another feedback aid #2 presented the participant's solutions ordered according to ship type. Table 2 is an example of ordered display. Each row shows a combination that the participant previously entered. The numbers indicate how many of each type of ship are in that combination. This aid is intended to help the participant to generate all necessary combinations by organizing them in a systematic way.

Table 2 Example of Feedback Aid #2.

"Ships Ordered According to Ship Type"

CVAN	CVA	CA	CGN	CG	DD	SSN	SS	AO
1	0	0	2	0	3	0	2	2
1	0	0	0	2	3	0	2	2
1	0	0	1	1	3	0	2	2

The third type of feedback aid #3 utilized an algorithm to form suggested next logical combinations for the participants to consider. Table 3 shows an example of feedback aid #3. Based on the computer's inductive interpretation of the participant's input examples, the computer identifies incomplete ship combination patterns and displays suggested combinations for consideration. For instance, if the previous inputs have included combinations 2 SS and 0 SSN, and 1 SS and 1 SSN, the computer would suggest 0 SS and 2 SSN. Again, note that the suggested combinations developed by the computer are not based on any data regarding the correct solution – the suggestion is made only on the detection of incomplete combination patterns of the participant's previous inputs.

Table 3 Example of Feedback Aid #3.

"Next Suggested Combination"

Your previous inputs* have suggested the following ship combinations should be considered:

Number of ships of Each Type

CVAN	CVA	CA	CGN	CG	DD	SSN	SS	AO
2	0	0	0	0	0	0	2	1
0	2	0	0	0 .	0	2	0	0

Three feedback aid levels were used: F_1 which consisted of aid #1 i.e., SSL; F_2 which consisted of aids #1 and #2, i.e., SSL and "ordered examples inputs"; and F_3 which consisted of aids #1 and #3, i.e., SSL and "suggested combinations."

RESULTS:

Several breadth vs. depth-of-experience results of Experiment 1 and 2 impacting on the subsequent experiments were discussed previously. All results of the experiments are given in Connelly 1982 a, b. The results of interest here are the analysis of data from Experiments 1, 2, 3 regarding the relationship of demographic factors, and the comparison of rates of errors-of-commission when specifying selection logic by example-solutions and by writing program code.

One result of the first two experiments was that the number of years advanced education (i.e., beyond high school) and the number of years of professional experience were found to be relatively unimportant factors in predicting performance.

The lack of a strong predictive relationship between years-of-higher-education or years-of-experience and performance may come as a surprise to educators and directors of personnel departments. This result was found in all of the experiments, so that very strong evidence is avaialble to support the assertion that years-of education and relevant work-experience are not good predictors of this type of problem-solving performance. Additional results suggest that the "number of programming languages (used to write 1 or more programs)" and "number of operating systems used" are better predictors of the capabilities of computer users/programmers.

Both of these factors explain different variance (i.e., a multivariate regression using both variables as independent variables explains a percent of variance that is the sum of the variance explained by univariate regressions using each variable separately). Further, the factor "number of programming languages used to write 1 or more programs" explained more variance than did "the number of programming languages used to write 11 or more programs." This suggests that "breadth of experience" is important and depth of experience in programming languages is not as important to the problem solving performance.

Low Frequency of Errors-of-Commission:

Another result applied to the subsequent experiments was the observation that only a few errors-of-commission occurred during the generation of the example-solutions. The majority of errors that did occur were errors-of-omission. This intriguing result influenced the design of Experiment 6, where FORTRAN IV code was written to solve the same problems used in Experiment 1, so that a comparison of error-rates would be possible.

Results for Experiment 6:

Two types of errors were analyzed. One type, termed an "error-of-omission", referred to an error that resulted in a failure to accept a correct entity (e.g., ship combination). When specifying a problem solution with example-solutions, an error-of-omission could be directly traced to a failure to enter an example of a suitable entity (ship combination). The second type of error considered was an "error-of-commission." When example-solutions were used to specify a problem solution, an error-of-commission corresponded to an incorrect example entered into the processor which was then treated by the processor as a correct example. An error-of-commission resulted in erroneously accepting incorrect entities (ship combinations). There was little difference in the effect of problem-complexity on errors-of-omission between the two methods of specifying problem solutions, i.e., by example-solution or by FORTRAN IV subroutines.

Errors-of-Commission:

When generating example-solutions without feedback-aids, the rate of errors-of-commission increased sharply at a problem complexity-level near 20,821, as measured by Halstead's E Metric (Connelly, Comeau, & Johnson 1981). But, given a suitable feedback-aid environment, such as in Experiment 3, this problem-complexity limitation could be eliminated, as evidenced by the Experiment 3 data in which performance degradation did not appear.

The most important result regarding errors-of-commission was that specification by example-solutions was superior to specifications by program code. Analysis of the mean scores from Experiments 1, 2, and 3 provided strong evidence that using example-solutions substantially reduced errors-of-commission compared to using FORTRAN IV program code. The 3% rate for errors-of-commission with example-solutions compared favorably with 18% for program code.

Three hypotheses concerning the superior performance of the example-solution method seem plausible:

1. It was working with examples and dealing with each individual combination of items one-at-a-time that resulted in a low rate of errors-of-commission.
2. It was the specification of each combination one-at-a-time that alone was important. Consequently if a computer programs were developed to specify each solution combination one-at-a-time, the rate of errors-of-commission would be low.
3. The success of the example-solution method was due, in part, to the transformation of example-solutions from one logic form into another, such as the ship selection logic (SSL), or into several different forms, such as the feedback-aids. Thus, it was the transformation of logic which enabled the user to view the problem in more than one way and that resulted in a low rate of errors-of-commission. Consequently, if program code entered by the user were transformed into a different logic form and fed back to the user for approval, a low rate of errors-of-commission would be obtained.

These hypotheses are not alternative hypothesis; all could be true. If the second is true but not the third, program-design and coding methods could be adapted to a more combination-dependent structure. And finally, if the third hypothesis were found to be true, pre-compilation aids could be designed to convert the user's program code into another form (while maintaining the same program logic) for feedback to the user.

CONCLUSIONS:

1. The lack of a strong relationship between "years-of-higher-education", "years-of-experience" and performance, coupled with the strong relationship between "number of computer languages" known and "number of operating systems" used, suggests that education and experience should not be used as performance indicators. Instead the number of operating systems used and number of languages known, which are better performance predictors, should be used until the underlying factors included in each are discovered.
2. Apparently, the depth of an individual's experience is not as important to performance as is breadth of his experience.
3. A possible common underlying experience-related factor is the ability to view problems from alternative viewpoints, or the ability to develop alternative approaches to problems – an ability that might be enhanced with feedback-aids.
4. The performance-prediction capability of strategy-measures, developed as moment-to-moment measures, not only clearly demonstrates that systematic strategies were used by successful participants (which led to the design of the feedback-aids), but also convincingly demonstrates that moment-to-moment measures provide the sensitivity to explain considerable performance variance (approximately 60% in Experiments 1 thru 4.)
5. The superior performance (fewer errors-of-commission) achieved when using example-solutions and inductive processing to specify problem solutions over the performance achieved when using FORTRAN IV code may provide a basis for determining the underlying mechanism for that success and a means for incorporating that mechanism into program designing- and coding-aids. Apparently, superior performance was obtained either because each combination of the input variables was treated individually and/or because the example-solutions were transformed into another logic form -- the ship selection logic (SSL). If the former is a significant factor, then aids described in Connelly (1982 a, b) should be adapted to program designing- and coding- aids. If the latter is a significant factor then designing- and coding-aids should be developed to transform the logic provided by the user into another form which is then fed back to the user for his review. Such a transformation might present the program's equivalent logic.

REFERENCES:

Connelly, E. M. A comparison of the accuracy
and completeness of problem solutions produced
by example-solutions and program code.
(Technical Report 82-362).   Performance
Measurement Associates, Inc. September
1982 (a).

Connelly, E. M. Accuracy & completeness
of problem solutions with example-solutions.
(Technical Report 82-363).   Performance
Measurement Associates, Inc. November
1982 (b).

Connelly, E. M., Comeau, R. F., &
Johnson, P. Effect of automatic processing
on specification of problem solutions for
computer programs. (Technical Report
81-361). Performance Measurement
Associates, Inc. March 1981. AD A108570

Halstead, M. H. Elements of software
science. New York: Elsevier, 1977.

Winer, B. J. Statistical principles in
experimental design. (2nd ed. pp. 727-736).
New York: McGraw-Hill, 1971.

The research reported here was supported
by the Engineering Psychology Programs,
Office of Naval Research. The views,
opinions and findings are those of the author
and should not be construed as an official
Department of the Navy position, policy,
decision.

Human-Computer Interaction — INTERACT '84 / B. Shackel (ed.)
Elsevier Science Publishers B.V. (North-Holland)
IFIP, 1985

449

Flip and Luciflip : A "tree" programming language and a "tree" editor for introducing novices to structured programming

Alain GIBOIN and Alain MICHARD

Institut National de Recherche en Informatique et en Automatique
Sophia Antipolis, France

Two empirical studies are presented which show that the simultaneous use of a small programming language, called *Flip*, and of its syntax editor, called *Luciflip*, by inciting the handling of a known metaphor - the *tree diagram*, constitutes a meaningful and refined environment to introduce novices to the basic notions of structured programming (mainly, stepwise refinement [or] top-down development, and modular development) : the syntax editor allowing to ignore programming syntactic details and to focuse on semantic features of programming -which are the most important.

1. Introduction

Among the different steps involved in computer programming, coding is not considered, nowadays, as the most important one. It is the "preparatory work" (Schneider, Weingart and Perlman, 1978) *developing algorithms*, or, more generally said, *planning or designing a solution*, which is considered as so. A method proposed to help the programmer to do it is called *structured programming*.

1.1. Structured programming

Structured programming can be understood as "the application of a basic problem decomposition method to establish a manageable hierarchical problem structure" (Jensen 1981, p. 31; see also Dijkstra 1970, Wirth 1974). In the basic structured programming procedure, program construction consists of a sequence of refinement steps. Each step of the construction consists of breaking a given task into a number of subtasks (Wirth 1971). So structured programming is also called *stepwise refinement* or *top-down development*. In fact, the process of breaking down a given task into subtasks has not, each time, to be carried on to the very end, because some subtasks of the task have been already refined by other programmers or by oneself, so that it is possible to use them as primitives. What is important is to design and to recognize well-defined and distinct functional units.

This is why structured programming is also referred to, but sometimes distinguished from, *modular development*. This technique "partitions a program into units -modules- which perform defined tasks and can be coded, compiled, tested, and executed as independent subprograms" (Lemos 1980, p. 59).

The purpose of structured programming is to make programs easier to design, to read or to understand, to debug, and to maintain. Therefore it is recommanded, therefore it is taught. However, the environment chosen to teach it do not met always learners' requirements.

1.2. Learning structured programming

To design an effective learning environment for introducing novices to the structured programming method, we started from a model of the psychological processes involved in learning : the theory of *meaningful learning* (Bransford 1979; Mayer 1981; Carroll and Thomas 1982). (a) Meaningful learning is a process, called *assimilation*, in which the learner connects new knowledge with knowledge that already exists in memory, called "knowledge structure" or *schema*. (b) This schema is used as a "structural template for further learning" (Thomas and Carroll 1981, p. 239). This leads to generation of new cognition structures by metaphorical extension.

To make easier the learning of structured programming, one has to use an adequate metaphor for representing it to the novice. A representation often related to structured programming procedure is the *tree diagram*, which is emphasized as the "most effective technique [or] program development tool", for it "provides a clear graphic representation of the program structure and a notation amenable to the stepwise refinement process" (Jensen 1981, p.43). We have proposed, to 11-13 years old secondary school students, the tree diagram as a metaphor for learning structured programming, a diagram they handled through meaningful tools : (1) a hierarchical (or "tree") language : *Flip;* and (2) its hierarchical (or "tree") syntax editor : *Luciflip.*

2. The tree diagram used as a schema for structured programming learning

2.1. Tree definition

Generally, *tree* means a "branching" relationship between nodes. Formally defined, a tree is a structure consisting of a *node*, called the *root* of the tree, and of a finite set, eventually empty, of trees, called *subtrees* of the tree. This definition is recursive, i.e., the tree is defined in terms of trees. By analogy with the family trees, a subtree of a tree is also called his *son;* the former is inversely called the *father* of the latter, and two subtrees of the same tree are said *brothers* (Knuth 1973, Meyer and Baudoin 1978).

2.2. Tree representation : the tree diagram

Generally a tree is represented by a figure called *tree diagram*. There are many ways to draw diagrams of trees. We will consider two types of such diagrams that we will call (a) *graphic tree* (see figure 2) and (b) *word tree* (see figure 3), in which indentation is used to highlight the tree structure.

2.3. Previous knowledge of the tree diagram

The tree diagram is a knowledge that already exists in the memory of most individuals who met it in everyday life's activities : reading tables of contents in books, reading a royal family tree in a magazine or in a history book, parsing during a grammar exercise, and so on. Anyway, we have observed in the two studies reported below that the novices was accustomed with this diagram and the terminology related to it.

Moreover, in the first of these studies, learners, because they had to communicate their programs to the computer, were first accustomed to some rudimentary notions of the Unix operating system they used, mainly that of "file system". A Unix file system can be represented as a tree, or a hierarchy of directories (Thomas and Yates 1982, p. 74). So, thanks to the tree diagram, novices understood quickly the meaning of the Unix file system and they visualize how to move in the hierarchy of the directories. We then considered that the Unix tree belonged to the novices' previous knowledge of the tree diagram, that it represented for them another instance of the tree schema.

The tree diagram then served as a structural template for structured programming learning.

3. Flip as a tool for learning structured programming

To learn the basic of the structured programming method, novices were invited to program the computer to design *flips* (i.e., color transparancies) by using a programming language called Flip (Kahn 1981).

3.1. Presentation of Flip

We have chosen Flip because : (a) it is a small language which emphasizes hierarchical planning (or structured programming) in terms of manipulation of trees and which saves notions such as "variable", "type", "procedure", and so on; (b) it is a declarative (Du Boulay, O'Shea and Monk, 1981) or a descriptive (Green, 1980) language, as opposed to a procedural language, what meets the psychology of novices who had been showed to prefer instructions written in the form of a statement of the goal (e.g., "put all red things in box 1") rather than a procedure to achieve it (e.g., "if thing is red then put it in box 1") (Miller, 1975, cited by Du Boulay *et al.*, 81); (c) it exists a syntax editor of Flip programs (see later).

With Flip, one can design "flips". In its simplest form, a flip is one rectangle with some graphical attributes (mainly, a frame-color, a ground-color, a text-color, a size, or an orientation). In figure 1.a is a simple flip with two graphical attributes : a black frame and a black text. More complex flips are composed of a set of horizontal, vertical, or superposed flips, as in figure 1.b. So a flip can be defined recursively as a tree : A flip tree is a structure composed of a flip and of a finite set, eventually empty, of other flip trees, called flip subtrees. Subtrees are delimitations. Leaves are graphical attributes. End leaves are text declarations.

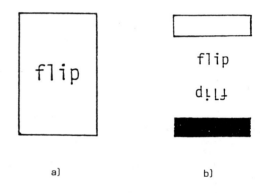

a)   b)

Figure 1.- *Examples of Flips.*

3.2. Using the structured programming method to design a Flip program

The logic of the Flip programming language induces the programmer to think in a hierarchical manner and to use the tree schema as we shall see by exposing the steps involved in Flip programming :

(1) *Defining the problem.-* The novice programmer has first to state the flip he wants or the teacher wants the computer to perform, e.g., the flip shown in figure 1.b.

(2) *Planning the solution : designing the Flip graphic tree.-* In the Flip context, the novice can see the sense of *stepwise refinement*. In fact, designing a flip consists of determining a hierarchy of declarations, precisely : (a) delimitations of horizontal, vertical, or superposed rectangles; (b) insertions of graphical attributes into the rectangles. For instance, if he wants to program the flip in figure 1.b, the programmer has to follow the process represented in figure 2.a and 2.b.

At the end of the decomposition process, the flip is viewed as a hierarchy of structurally nested declarations.

Moreover, in the Flip context the novice can see also the sense of the *modular programming*. Because it is possible to split the flip into subflips already programmed. Call (insertion) of flips inside a flip is possible, so that recursion (insertion of a flip in itself) is, in a way, possible.

a)   Hierarchical delimitation of rectangles   b)   Hierarchical insertion of attributes.

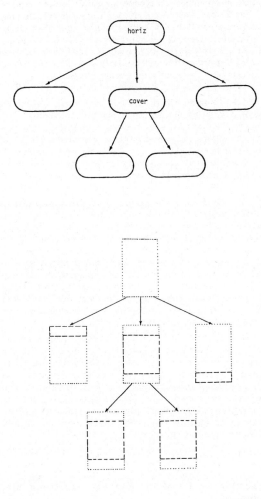

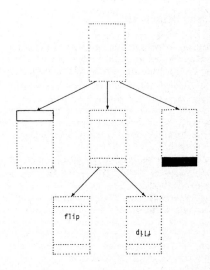

Figure 2.- *A Flip graphic tree.*

(3) *Coding : designing the flip word tree.*- The program-mer writes his solution in the Flip programming language. In other words, he transforms his graphi-cal tree in the word tree (see figure 3).

(4) *Editing and syntactic debugging.*- The programmer communicates the Flip word tree to the computer via an editor. Then he tests it for its syntax, thanks a "pretty-print" program which allows him to get his program in the correct indented form; in other words, to have the correct word tree. If necessary, he makes corrections to the program.

(5) *Execution and semantic debugging.*- Finally, the novice programmer asks to the computer to execute the program on a plotter or on a color screen. If necessary, he modifies the program to have a con-venient graphic tree.

```
horiz
  1:
    frame black
    -
    frame_end
  4:
    cover
      write black
      -flip
      -
    with
      rotate
      rotate
      -flip
      -
    end
  1:
    paint black
    -
    end
end
```

Figure 3.- *A Flip word tree.*

3.3. A preliminary study of the effectiveness of Flip as a tool for learning structured programming

This study consisted of an observation of the effectiveness of Flip for novices to acquire the structured programming procedure.

Method

Subjects were 3 secondary school girls (12-13 years old) who had no previous experience of computer programming.

Materials.- We used a 68000 based microcomputer with a Unix operating system, a 8-color graphic plotter and a 8-color screen for flip output, and an Emacs-like video terminal for editing. We used also manuals and plates.

Sessions.- During collective sessions, beginners learned theoretically and practically the different operations needed by the Flip programming activity, as described above. Thinking in terms of tree manipulation was emphasized.

Results and discussion

We will consider successively : (1) understanding of stepwise refinement or top-down development, and (2) understanding of modular development.

(1) *Understanding of stepwise refinement or top-down development* is revealed here by the ability to decompose the flip drawing into hierarchically nested rectangles with their respective graphical attributes. This ability can be broken down into two main aspects :

(a) An ability to dissociate the delimitation phase from the insertion phase, that is to say, an ability to abstract the rectangles as the units which will compose the hierarchy. Results showed that all subjects are able to dissociate the delimitation phase from the insertion phase. However, it must be noted that, at the beginning of learning, they confused delimitation of rectangles and frame insertion : they confused drawing of limits with dotted lines and drawing a frame. For instance, one subject believed that she would obtain a frame only by delimiting a rectangle. This was because we had not emphasized enough the "invisibility" of dotted lines which delimit the rectangle.

(b) An ability to hierarchize the declarations of delimitations and to nest them. Results proved subjects were not able immediately to hierarchize delimitations and to nest them. In the first times, we observed that the delimitations were juxtaposed instead of nested. In the case of the graphic tree, subjects drew juxtaposed graphic trees instead of a unique tree. In the case of the word tree, subjects did not succeed to indent the coded program to form hierarchical and nested blocks.

To find the hierarchy of delimitations was all the more difficult since it revealed a dissymmetry. In this case, subjects preferred to bypass the difficulty instead of overcoming it, by modifying their flip so that it revealed a symmetry. However, this difficulty was surmounted whenever we asked the learner to

apply really top-down development by really decomposing the flip into subflips.

However, learners were progressively able to hierarchize, for they designed more and more complex Flip programs. But they wanted to stop when they judged the task too difficult and a work rather than a game. The more complex Flip programs they designed were of 3rd-order. Difficulty mainly stayed in the boring aspect of the coding and editing phases.

(2) *Understanding of modular development* is revealed here by the ability to design independent Flip programs and to call them in a bigger program. Indicators are : call of flips and names given to program files (some of these names must denote a part of a bigger program file). We observed that all subjects understood call of flips, although they used it little.

An obstacle : the coding and editing phases.- Results showed that novices mixed up graphic tree and word tree syntax. So we can say that, when they were designing the graphic tree, they were anticipating and preparing the coding and editing phases. We can say also that these phases put a brake on the novices' activities, hence on their interest or motivation. The learner has to respect the syntax of the Flip programming language, what was not necessary in the planning phase, without being prevented from lexical and syntactic errors.

Coding and text editing favours also a linear mode of thinking. Subjects composed their programs line after line, not in a structural way. The "fliprint" program was little used to verify the correctness of indentation, but often to verify if the program will run or not. Coding and editing phases distracted novices from the main features of the method we wanted to teach them. They consumed time and reduced interest.

4. Luciflip as a tool for learning structured programming

In order to remove the syntactic obstacle, we decided to use a syntax editor of Flip programs : Luciflip (actually, a mode of a general system for manipulating hierarchies called Ceyx [Hullot 1982, 1983a and b]). With a syntax editor, editing can be similar to structured programming's stepwise refinement because it uses the syntactic structure or *"tree form"* of the programs "to direct their creation or alteration" (Allison 1983, p. 454; see also Teitelbaum and Reps 1981, Ince 1983). Syntax editing serves the learners as a mean of perceiving what programming and program structure should be like.

4.1. Using the structured programming method to edit a Flip program via the Luciflip syntax editor

Because the syntax editor forces the programmer to enter the program according to sentential forms (indentation being automatic), it is not possible to enter a syntactically incorrect program, which allows the programmer to never get lost in syntactic details. So it makes implicit the coding phase and enhances the planning phase.

Stepwise refinement or top-down development.- Luciflip is an aid for the beginner to better understand the sense of stepwise refinement, for programs are created top-down by inserting declarations at a cursor position.

Luciflip maintains a pointer to the current node; the pointer moves within nodes, in terms of the branches of the tree. There are one-letter to three-letter commands to move, to create nodes, and to define graphical attributes. Moreover, at the execution phase, not only the whole Flip tree can be executed, but any Flip subtree can also be executed. It can be noted here that execution can follow editing without delay, for the program is interpreted during editing.

Because portions of the program can be left out and filled in later, the novice can firstly design the hierarchy of delimitations of rectangles and, to see if this has been done well, ask to the computer to draw them. Secondly, he can insert the attributes into the rectangles. Figure 4 shows the Luciflip word tree got after designing and editing the program of the flip given in figure 1.b. [For lack of place, we cannot put here the figure representing a Luciflip editing session.]

```
(horiz
  (frame black
    (align))
  (% 4
    (cover
      (write black
        (align
          "flip"
          " "))
      (Rot 2
        (align
          "flip"
          " "))))
  (paint black
    (align)))
```

Figure 4.- *A Luciflip word tree.*

Furthermore, a feature of the editor allows the learner to see the subtree being edited and its context (father and brothers). This is *holophrasting.* Luciflip maintains on the screen an holophrasted representation of the hierarchy manipulated, i.e., it provides "an overall view of the program by *unparsing* or displaying text down to a certain level of detail and eliding the rest. The user may then select a smaller area to zoom in on" (Allison 1983, p. 457).

Modular development.- In the context of Luciflip editing, the beginner can see the sense of the modular programming technique. He can design modules in different buffers, then call for these modules when editing the definitive program. Later, when holophrasting his word tree, the learner can see his program as a set of modules because nodes are named, i.e., they appeared with the form : "&name".

4.2. A preliminary study of the effectiveness of Luciflip as a tool for learning structured programming

This study consisted also of an observation of the effectiveness of the Luciflip "syntax editor" for introducing beginners to structured programming method.

Method

Subjects were two of the three subjects of study I and a new one (11 years old).

Materials.- The Ceyx environment is implemented on a Multics operating system. It can be noted that Multics files are hierarchically organized just as are the Unix files. So our "old" subjects were not disorientated by the Multics context.

Sessions.- The "old" students continued their course with the syntax editor, the "new" one was introduced to the course directly with Luciflip. Subjects were taught how to edit with Luciflip using the family tree terminology. They were invited to edit their programs immediatly after having planned it.

Results and discussion

Subjects programmed more effectively with the syntax editor than with the classical text editor. They designed not only more programs, but more complex programs : in the Luciflip session, the "old" novices wrote, on average, 5 Flip programs -among which the most complex was of 4th-order- whereas in the best of the Flip sessions they wrote, always on average, 2 Flip programs -among which the most complex was of 3rd-order; for its first contact with Flip and a computer, the "new" beginner designed 5 Flip programs, one of which was of 5th-order, and embodied all the variety of declarations of delimitation and of insertion.

The reasons for this improvement lie in the fact that syntax editing allows (1) to ignore programming syntactic details and (2) to focuse on semantic features of programming -which are the most important.

(1) Indeed, subjects greatly appreciated that Luciflip suppresses the "clerical" aspect of editing (it reduces the number of touches, it prevents from syntactic mistakes, and so on). It can be noted that novices were not disturbed by the change in the concrete syntax of the language. Another aspect of the syntax editor which was appreciated, is that it eliminates delay between edition and execution of programs. The fact that execution of a flip immediately follows its edition, does not tax novices' attention. Consequently, subjects found the syntax editor easy-and-satisfactory-to-use.

(2) Because editing of a Flip program with Luciflip involves, we assume, cognitive representations and treatments near to the cognitive representations and treatments involved in planning the Flip program, it illuminates the basic aspects of structured programming : stepwise refinement/top-down development and modular development.

Because of lack of time, modular development was little used in the context of Luciflip : only the two "old" subjects used it, each in one of their programs. Nevertheless, the subjects who develop their program in this way clearly perceived why the editor displayed "&name" when they inserted an already designed Flip program in the program they were going to plan.

Concerning stepwise refinement and top-down development, we have to emphasize that beginners did not think editing in linear terms but in structural terms. They thought editing in terms of planning through their manipulation of Luciflip trees. On this subject, it can be noted that : (a) "Old" subjects referred explicitly to the way they "travelled" in the Unix tree to travel in the Luciflip trees. (b) At the beginning, all the three novices did not succeed to move in the Luciflip word tree because the orientation to move in it is not always the same as the orientation to move in the graphic tree (e.g., sometimes to go down in the graphic tree means to go right in the word tree). It follows that some confusions occurred. They were avoided later because subjects, when they moved in the word tree, had in mind a representation of the graphic tree. (c) Holophrasting was well understood. Beginners saw that the "&" sign represents a subtree which, eventually, contains other subtrees. So that, when they wanted to modify a Flip program, they succeeded to localize and to retrieve the subtree concerned by the modification, even though the program appeared to them in an holophrasted form.

Actually, it was reasonable to think that editing of a Flip program involves a cognitive mechanism near to the mechanism involved in planning the Flip program. Besides, so near seem to be these mechanisms that one subject decided and succeeded to edit directly a program, in other words to edit it while designing it.

5. Conclusion

The didactical environment we have proposed here seems to be adapted to novices of age 11-13 years, as confirmed by the two observations performed to see of how well those beginners used the environment, i.e., if they managed to apply the basic notions of structured programming. We can say that the simultaneous use of Flip and of its syntax editor, within the context of the tree diagram, delimits the basic notions of structured programming. It constitutes a refined environment to introduce novices to these notions. But this conclusion is limited to 11-13 years old secondary school novices. More systematic studies (Sheil, 1981) have to be performed to determine, for instance, individual differences in the adaptability of this introductory environment, or to see if the beginners so introduced to programming will transfer the structured programming method to any language.

References

[1] Allison, L. Syntax directed program editing. *Software-Practice and Experience.* 1983, *13*, 453-465.

[2] Bransford, J.D. *Human cognition: Learning, understanding and remembering.* Belmont, California: Wadsworth, 1979.

[3] Carroll, J.M. and Thomas, J.C. Metaphor and the cognitive representation of computing systems. *IEEE Transactions on Systems, Man, and Cybernetics.* 1982, *12*, 107-116.

[4] Dijkstra, E.W. *Notes on structured programming.* T.H. Report 70-WSK-03, Technological University Eindhoven, Netherlands, 1970.

[5] Du-Boulay, J.B.H., O'Shea, T. and Monk J. The black box inside the glass box: presenting computing concepts to novices. *International Journal of Man-Machine Studies.* 1981, *14*, 237-249.

[6] Hullot , J.M. *CEYX : fils de LUCIFER, manuel de référence.* Rapport informatique, I.N.R.I.A., Rocquencourt, 1982.

[7] Hullot , J.M. CEYX : A multiformalism programming environment. In *Les éditeurs dirigés par la syntaxe.* I.N.R.I.A., Aussois, 1983a.

[8] Hullot , J.M. *CEYX, a multiformalism programming environment.* Paper presented at IFIP 83, 9th World Computer Congress, International Federation for Information Processing, Paris, 1983b.

[9] Ince, D.C. A software tool for top-down programming. *Sotware-Practice and Experience.* 1983, *13*, 687-695.

[10] Jensen, R.W. Structured programming. Tutorial series 6, *Computer.* 1981, *14*, 31-48.

[11] Kahn, G. *Flip : Manuel de référence.* I.N.R.I.A., Rapport technique No 2, 1981.

[12] Knuth, D.E. *The art of computer programming.* Vol. *1/ Fundamental algorithms.* Second Edition, Reading : Massachussets, Addison-Wesley Publishing Company, 1973.

[13] Lemos, R.S. Methods, styles, and attitudes in the programming language classroom. *Computer.* 1980, *13*, 58-65.

[14] Meyer, B. and Baudoin, C. *Méthodes de programmation.* Paris, Eyrolles, 1978.

[15] Schneider, G.M., Weingart, S.W. and Perlman, D.M. *An introduction to programming and problem solving with PASCAL.* John Wiley & Sons, New York, 1978.

[16] Sheil, B.A. The psychological study of programming. *Computing Surveys.* 1981, *13*, 101-121.

[17] Teitelbaum, T. and Reps, T. The Cornell Program Synthetizer: A syntax-directed programming environment. *Communications of the ACM.* 1981, *24*, 563-573.

[18] Thomas, J.C. and Carroll, J.M. Human factors in communication. *IBM Systems Journal.* 1981, *20*, 237-263.

[19] Thomas, R. and Yates, J. *A user guide to the UNIX system.* Osborne/McGraw-Hill, Berkeley: California, 1982.

[20] Wirth, N. Program development by stepwise refinement. *Communications of the ACM.* 1971, *14*, 221-227.

[21] Wirth, N. On the composition of well-structured programs. *Computing Surveys.* 1974, *6*, 247-259.

Human-Computer Interaction — INTERACT '84 / B. Shackel (ed.)
Elsevier Science Publishers B.V. (North-Holland)
© IFIP, 1985

A COGNITIVE ACCOUNT OF 'NATURAL' LOOPING CONSTRUCTS

Marc Eisenstadt

Human Cognition Research Laboratory, Open University (U.K.)

Joost Breuker

Department of Social Studies and Informatics, University of Amsterdam

Rick Evertsz

Human Cognition Research Laboratory, Open University (U.K.)

We describe an investigation of the everyday skills which underlie a person's ability to write iterative programs. We look at the strategies used by naive and experienced programmers to perform repeated processing in both 'natural' and 'computer-like' settings, and develop a production system simulation of our subjects' performance. Our data suggest an overwhelming preference on the part of naive and experienced programmers alike to think in terms of function application to aggregate data objects rather than control flow and temporal sequence. Our model explains why this is so, and demonstrates that the various components of everyday knowledge which enable everyone to perform our tasks can be combined in systematic ways to account for some of the difficulties encountered by students of programming.

1. INTRODUCTION

What are the basic skills underlying a programmer's ability to write iterative programs? We know from the work of Sime, Green, and Guest (10) and Soloway, Bonar and Ehrlich (11) that the flow of control constructs available in popular programming languages such as Pascal may not work in precisely the way a novice programmer thinks they ought to work. But what is it that people know about looping and flow of control that makes them think a construct 'ought' to work in some particular way in the first place? Our aim is to investigate the knowledge involved in performing 'everyday' iterative tasks in an attempt to understand how it affects the code-writing behaviour of naive and experienced programmers.

In order to study this everyday knowledge of iteration, we ask subjects to perform several iterative tasks in a real-life context: finding the average value of a pile of bank cheques. We collect detailed behavioural protocols of subjects performing this task, then construct a simulation model of their behaviour by decomposing the knowledge required to perform the task into several discrete components: knowledge of how to generate sequences of items, knowledge of how to select items which meet a certain criterion, knowledge of how to find the sum of a set of numbers, and knowledge of how to tally the number of items in a set. We examine the difference between naive and experienced programmers on this task, to see how the distinct components of knowledge are composed together.

In order to study how everyday knowledge of iteration maps onto code-writing behaviour, we ask the same subjects to perform iterative tasks in a 'computer-like' context: finding the average value of a pile of bank cheques with the constraint that only one card may be processed

at a time, after which it must be thrown away. The purpose of this constraint is to approximate the constraints which programmers have to reason about when thinking about how their programs will perform related programming tasks. Our analysis of subjects' performance on this task allows us in turn to account in a principled way for the errors people make when writing iterative programs.

Section 2 describes our experiment, analysis techniques and results. Section 3 describes our simulation model. Section 4 discusses the implications of our data and model for understanding the behaviour of computer programmers.

2. AN EXPERIMENT ON PERFORMING ITERATION

Method

16 University students with no prior programming experience ('naive') and 10 with over 1000 hours of programming experience ('experienced') were instructed to compute the mean of a set of numbers printed on index cards. Each card represented a bank cheque, with the name of a payee on it, the date and the amount. The cards were placed in chronological order in a pile, with the oldest cheque on top. Subjects had at their disposal a pen and a sheet of paper, on which they could write whatever they wanted, and a simple four function pocket calculator. The subjects received three warm-up problems in which they had to compute the mean of a written list of numbers. Then the experimental problems were presented. For the unconstrained problems, the subjects were instructed that they could handle the pile of cheques in whatever way they wanted. The constrained problems required the subjects to process the cheques strictly sequentially: after taking a cheque from the pile it had to be deposited in a box so that it no longer could be read.

The problems involved either simple 'generation' of a sequence of cheques (i.e. only cheques from the year shown on the top card had to be processed), or a combination of generation and filtering (i.e. for a particular year, only cheques for a given payee were relevant). The sequence of instructions was counterbalanced for order effects. In the event of a false start, the problem was re-initialized by the experimenter. Each subject's behaviour was coded in real time by the experimenter, who simply ticked off arcs in a transition network diagram.

Results

Four different operations were observed: Generating a sequence of cheques, filtering out cheques which did not have the appropriate payee name, summation of the amounts and tallying the number of cheques. (This analysis ignores the inevitable final action of computing the mean from the sum and the tally).

A simple but informative way of comparing conditions and subject groups is to count the number of passes made by each subject through the pile of index cards, because this is a direct indicator of the way in which the subject's processing operations are combined. Thus, the 'four passes' category invariably means generation followed by filtering, followed by either tally-then-sum or sum-then-tally. 'Three passes' means generation, tallying, and summing in separate passes. 'Two passes' mean that as each card is generated, it is also tallied or summed at the same time, and the left over operation (tallying or summing) is saved for a final independent pass. 'One pass' means a single (Pascal-like) loop, involving generation of the next card, filtering (if appropriate), increasing the tally, and increasing the sum (or possibly sum-then-tally), before going on to the following card. Figure 1 shows the frequency of occurrence of these four categories on each of the four tasks for naive and experienced programmers (order of presentation had no effect).

Most obvious is the expected overall difference in number of passes between the constrained and unconstrained condition (X^2=110.24, df=3, p<.001). In general in the constrained condition only one pass is taken; in the unconstrained condition the modal category is 3 passes. There is a clear difference between experienced and naive subjects, both overall (X^2=18.72, df=3, p <.01) and, particularly, in the unconstrained condition (X^2=5.72, df=1, p <.05). In this condition, experienced programmers tend to require fewer passes than do naives.

Three of the 16 naive subjects found it necessary to perform even the constrained task in multiple passes, writing down the numbers on the first pass so that later passes could be performed. For two of these subjects this was the consequence of a false start in which they realized half-way that they had forgotten to tally: a clear indication of a buggy model of the constrained version of the task. Four other naive subjects, who chose not to write down the numbers, had similar false starts, which means that in total 6 out of 16 naive subjects started with an inappropriate mental model of the constrained task. For the experienced subjects this ratio is 1 out of 10.

In Figure 1 only the last trials are taken into account: it shows, not surprisingly, that every subject can correctly perform the task albeit that 1 experienced and 6 naive subjects had to back up.

3. A SIMULATION MODEL

We postulate that the four processing operations described above (generate, filter, sum, tally) can be modelled as autonomous bundles of expertise, and combined in principled ways to account for all of the observed behaviour. To do this, we model each of the operations as a self-contained packet of production rules (Newell and Simon (7)). Packets are either 'active' in which case they occupy processing resources, or 'inactive' in which case they simply reside in long-term memory. In the sense that packets restrict the currently active productions, enabling the use of a hierarchical control structure, our interpreter is akin to goal-oriented production system interpreters such as GRAPES (Sauers and Farrell, (9); however, we do not refer to packets as 'goals' because, in our system, there is no notion of the 'success' or 'failure' of an invoked packet. Details of the running simulation are available in Eisenstadt, Breuker, and Evertsz (3). For expository purposes, we present a simplified English-like version of the rules. Note that if a rule has several actions on the right hand side (separated by semicolons), the actions are applied sequentially in the order shown.

		NAIVE				EXPERIENCED			
Number of passes:		1	2	3	4	1	2	3	4
CONSTRAINED	CONDITION								
	Generate	13	–	3	–	10	–	–	–
	Generate + Filter	13	–	3	–	10	–	–	–
UNCONSTRAINED	Generate	–	1	14	1	1	6	3	–
	Generate + Filter	1	1	9	5	1	4	4	1

Figure 1: Frequency of occurrence of the four possible strategies (1,2,3, or 4 passes)

Here,then, are the four packets needed to model performance in our task domain:

PACKET G: "GENERATE"

G1: terminating symbol
visible   => pop

G2: cards remaining
& terminating symbol
not visible   => remove top card

NC:no cards remaining   => pop

PACKET F: "FILTER"

F1: criterion met   => remove top card

F2: criterion not met   => discard top card

NC: no cards remaining   => pop

PACKET S: "SUM"

S1: just begun   => press 'all clear'

S2: (amount is A)   => enter A;
press '+';
remove top card

NC: no cards remaining   => pop

PACKET T: "TALLY"

T1: just begun   => (counter is 0)

T2: cards remaining
& (counter is C)   => (counter is (C+1))
remove tope card

NC: no cards remaining   => pop

In addition, we assume that the subject's understanding of the problem statement causes him to formulate a simple plan specifying the sequence of packet execution. This sequence is stored in working memory as an ordered list, e.g. (G F S T).

This representation places a very minimal load on working memory: only the symbols denoting the packet sequence and the current packet need to be 'active' at any one time. When a given packet is finished, the 'packet sequence' order stored in working memory is sufficient to ensure that the next packet gets instantiated appropriately to carry out the next phase of the plan.

A three pass strategy on the unconstrained task without filtering and a four pass strategy on the same task with filtering can be modelled simply by invoking each of the relevant packets in the appropriate sequence. In fact, these rules are sufficient to account for the card-moving actions and calculator keystrokes of all 26 subjects on the unconstrained task.

How, then do we account for the performance of experts on the unconstrained task, for which they required fewer passes? We hypothesize that the programming expert can merge together several packets by application of the following rule: If packets X's output is packet Y's input, then instead of first applying X to all of X's input then Y to all of Y's input (two passes) we can apply the sequence (X Y) to the same input (one pass). In other words, if you can do on one pass what you've been doing on two, then do so. Experienced programmers will have seen multi-statement blocks of code with iterative loops many times in their careers, and this can be regarded as a well-known schema or single 'compiled away' chunk of expertise. Our model predicts that this expertise will therefore influence their performance on a real-world (non-programming) task. The experiment supports the prediction: experts perform the unconstrained task in fewer passes than naives ($X^2 = 5.72$, df=1, $p < .05$). This is the first time to our knowledge that the effect of programming on a non-programming task has been clearly demonstrated in the literature.

We now need to model the 'one-pass' performance of our naive subjects on the constrained task. Once again, we assume that during the interval between reading and performing the task, a subject decides that knowledge of GENERATE, FILTER, SUM, and TALLY are relevant. This time, however, the rules of the constrained task specify that once processed a card must be thrown away forever. In our model, we represent this constraint as a requirement that rules which pertain to dealing with the contents of a given index card must all be active at once. In other words, formulating a plan is no longer a matter of straightforward sequencing of relatively simple packets: rather, it is now a question of imposing some order on the firing sequence of production rules. The end result of this planning is a single active packet with the following rules (notice especially the symbols in quotes which are arbitrary sequencing symbols which get added into working memory):

```
G1:    terminating symbol
           visible              =>   pop

NC:    no cards remaining       =>   pop

F1:    new card visible &
           criterion met        =>   'good'

F2:    new card visible &
           criterion not met    =>   discard top
                                     card

S2:    'good' &
       (amount is A)            =>   enter A;
                                     press '+';
                                     'just did sum'

T2:    'just did sum' &
       (counter is C)           =>   (counter is
                                      (C+1))
```

The need to keep this entire packet active
throughout the performance of the experimental
task is precisely the extra processing burden
which brings about false starts by our naive
subjects (e.g. forgetting rule T2, which
performs the tally). We believe that it also
accounts for much of the difficulty non-
programmers have in visualising an iterative
programming task with the precision required
for error-free computer implementation.
Experienced programmers, in contrast, can use
their familiarity with iterative constructs,
conditionals, and subroutines, to collapse
together the cumbersome signalling sequence
which is used to trigger the actions
associated with rules F1,S2, and T2; these can
all be composed to form a single rule, with a
consequent reduction in processing load.

4.   DISCUSSION

Of primary importance to us is an understanding
of the nature of the strategies employed by
our subjects, and the way in which these
strategies might influence the way in which the
same subjects would write a program to perform
a comparable task. We argue that a novice
programmer faced with a coding task involving
iteration first goes through a planning phase
in which a mental model of the execution
sequence must be constructed. This mental model
will be guided by the novice programmer's
everyday experiences with iterative tasks. In
trying to force such experiences into the
appropriate (constrained) framework of a
programming language, the programmer will have
to go through reasoning closely related to that
involved in performing a real-world iterative
task under restrictions such as those imposed
by our 'constrained' experimental condition.
This process is cumbersome and unnatural
precisely because of the idiosyncracies of the
virtual machine underlying iterative constructs
in Pascal-like programming languages.

Soloway et.al. (14) have shown convincingly
that there is an inherent mismatch between the
way novice programmers think about repeating a
'read-then-process' sequence and the way in
which typical Pascal WHILE loop imposes a
'process-then-read' ordering. We take their
argument one step further: rather than
enhancing the WHILE construct to provide a
better 'cognitive fit', we feel that the
entire underlying virtual machine needs
rethinking. Iterative loops in programming
languages such as Pascal are traditionally
thought of in terms of a sequence of steps,
performed repeatedly over time. An alternative
view, exemplified by the work of Wulf et.al.
(13), Waters (12), and Rich (8), is that the
temporal sequence is really irrelevant to the
essential meaning of most loops. This meaning
is more properly characterized in terms of
performing some operation on a set of objects,
without regard to the (boring) detail of how
that set is sequentially generated. The notion
of operations applied to a set **is** referred to
by Waters and Rich as 'temporal abstraction',
because it abstracts out the meaning, in
declarative terms, without worrying about
precise implementation details.

We contend that novices tend to think naturally
in terms of temporal abstraction, and that the
use of generators and aggregate data objects
(without the terminology, of course) is far
simpler for them than the confusing detail
required by having to specify temporal
sequence. This view enables us to pinpoint an
important source of confusion in students
learning to write iterative Pascal programs:
the natural sequence of function application
to aggregate data objects is totally
destroyed by iterative constructs - destroyed
in a way which forces the novice to pull out
orthogonal slices of each successive function
to be applied.

Our experiments show that subjects
overwhelmingly prefer to perform an iterative
task in multiple passes over successively
smaller sets of data. Each of the observed
processing operations (GENERATE, FILTER, SUM,
and TALLY) can easily be mapped onto a function
which can be applied to an appropriate aggregate
data object. Consider the task of finding the
mean of all 1981 cheques paid to Jones. A
functional representation of the solution looks
like this:

MEAN(CHOOSE("JONES",(READTILL("1982",CARDS))))

MEAN (X)≅SUM(X)/TALLY(X)

The function CHOOSE(ITEM,SET) is a filter which extracts only those elements of SET containing ITEM. READTILL(ITEM,SET) is a generator function which returns a subset of SET, i.e. the first elements of SET up to, but not including, the one containing ITEM. Since function application proceeds from the inside out, this solution is isomorphic to the modal strategy used by our naive subjects on the unconstrained problems.

Our point is that iterative operators such as WHILE and REPEAT force people to merge together isolated snippets of their mundane expertise in such a way that tasks for which algorithm-design ought to be easy suddenly become very hard. Planning and imagining the execution of a Pascal WHILE loop ought to involve most of the same processes we posited for performing mundane iterative tasks, and is therefore vulnerable to the same kinds of processing overload as our simulation model. Additional programming errors arise because of the inherent difficulty of mapping interrupt-driven termination (e.g. our rule G1) onto WHILE loop termination, with the result that such loops often cycle once too often (cf. (10)). Our experiment suggests that the powerful abstractions being studied by Waters, Wulf, et.al., and others are the most natural way of expressing iteration. Our intuition is that such abstractions can be presented in a form which is palatable to novices, and we look forward to empirical studies which pursue this train of thought.

Much work still needs to be done on understanding the processes involved in code generation. We see the work of Brooks (2) and Anderson et.al. (1) as important steps in this direction. Kahney (4,5) has explored the way in which complicated world knowledge influences novices' understanding and solution of recursive programming problems. We see all of this research leading ultimately to the point where we can state with confidence what it is that people do when they plan, write, and debug programs. This in turn will help us to provide languages and environments which mesh appropriately with their users' preferred manner of thinking.

REFERENCES

(1) Anderson, J.R., Farrel, R., and Sauers, R. Learning to plan Lisp. *Cognitive Science*, in press.

(2) Brooks, R. Towards a theory of the cognitive processes in computer programming, *International Journal of Man-Machine Studies*, 1977, 9.

(3) Eisenstadt, M., Breuker, J., and Evertsz, R. Naive Iteration: an account of the knowledge needed to write iterative programs. Technical Report No.9. Human Cognition Research Laboratory, The Open University, Milton Keynes, England, 1984.

(4) Kahney, J.H. Problem solving by novice programmers. In T.R.G. Green, S.J.Payne, and G.C. van der Veer (Eds.) *The Psychology of Computer Use*. London: Academic Press, 1983.

(5) Kahney, J.H., & Eisenstadt, M. Programmers' mental models of their programming tasks: the interaction of real-world knowledge and programming knowledge. *Proceedings of the Fourth Annual Cognitive Science Society Conference*, Ann Arbor, Michigan, 1982.

(6) Mayer, R.E. A psychology of learning BASIC. *Communications of the ACM*, 1979, 22, 589-593.

(7) Newell,A., & Simon, H.A. *Human problem solving*. Englewood Cliffs, N.J.: Prentice-Hall, 1972.

(8) Rich, C. Inspection methods in programming. Technical Report AI-TR-604. Cambridge, MA: MIT Artificial Intelligence Laboratory, 1981.

(9) Sauers, R., & Farrel, R. GRAPES reference manual. Pittsburgh, PA: Department of Psychology, Carnegie-Mellon University, 1983.

(10) Sime, M.E. Green, T.R.G., Guest, D.J. Psychological evaluation of two conditional constructions in computer languages. *International Journal of Man-Machine Studies*, 1973, 5 123-143.

(11) Soloway, E., Bonar, J., & Ehrlich, K. Cognitive strategies and looping constructs: an empirical study. *Comm.ACM* 26 (11), 1983, 853-860.

(12) Waters, R.A. A method for analyzing loop programs. *IEEE Transactions on Software Engineering*, SE-5:3, May, 1979.

(13) Wulf, W.A. London, R.L. & Shaw, M. An introduction to the construction and verification of Alphard programs. *IEEE Transaction on Software Engineering*, SE-2:4 December, 1976.

Human-Computer Interaction – INTERACT '84 / B. Shackel (ed.)
Elsevier Science Publishers B.V. (North-Holland)
© IFIP, 1985

THE COMPREHENSIBILITY OF PROGRAMMING NOTATIONS

D.J. Gilmore and T.R.G. Green

MRC/ESRC Social and Applied Psychology Unit
The University
SHEFFIELD S10 2TN, UK

Empirical comparisons of the comprehension of four miniature programs were used to contrast the notational structures of four programming languages, concluding that an important determiner of comprehensibility is the match between notational structure and the task being performed by the programmer. None of the four languages was consistently the most comprehensible: the procedural notations (e.g. Pascal-like) were best suited to answering sequential questions and the declarative notations (e.g. production systems) to answering circumstantial questions. Software complexity metrics, like many models of program comprehension, do not allow for such structural and contextual effects and their validity is brought into question.

INTRODUCTION

Individual programs clearly differ in comprehensibility ([1], [3]). So do the programming languages themselves. For language designers, for the teaching of programming and for the development of "programmers' assistants" we need to understand the sources of comprehension difficulty. Languages are frequently contrasted in terms of their facilities – e.g. the presence of certain data features, such as complex reals – but they differ also in the design and presentation of those facilities that are present. Both these aspects can affect comprehensibility. For the latter aspects, which would not be changed merely by adding new features such as complex reals, we shall use the term 'notational structure'. Some notational differences imply differences in the 'underlying machine', for example the difference between a goto machine and a nested-conditional machine; other differences are presentational. We shall not distinguish between these kinds, preferring to concentrate on the psychological effects as a whole.

We have recently conducted an experiment which addresses the problem of notational comprehensibility and which demonstrates that it varies according to the purpose for which the program is being read. Our hypothesis is that comprehensibility depends upon the match between the notational structure and the information required to perform the task. We shall present the experiment first, followed by a discussion of its implications for models of program comprehension.

AN EXPERIMENT

Forty non-programmers answered four types of comprehension question about a short program which contained four conditionals and two loops. The questions were not difficult, but they could not be answered without some understanding of both the languages and the program. The programs described the route and distance travelled by a group of thieves before they buried their loot. The programs were written in two types of languages, procedural and declarative, where the former is assumed to highlight information about the order of events and the latter the conditions under which events occur. There were two languages of each type, one containing cues to the unhighlighted information and one without cues. For example, the procedural language without cues resembled FORTRAN and the procedural language with cues resembled Pascal. The questions asked about different types of information, in ways which reflected the sorts of problems faced by programmers. These questions were labelled "sequential" and "circumstantial", after Green ([6], [7]). For example a question could ask either 'What happened next?' (sequential), or 'Why did event X happen?' (circumstantial). There were two types of sequential question (next and previous) and two types of circumstantial question (positive and negative).

Our prediction, based on Green ([7[), was that the procedural languages would be easier for 'matched' sequential questions, but harder for 'unmatched' circumstantial questions. This contrasts with the possibility that comprehensibility might depend solely on features of the language and not on the context, in which case one of the languages would be consistently easier across all types of question. This is the result that would be predicted by current models of program comprehension and by the use of metrics of program complexity.

The experiment contained two distinct stages. First subjects answered the questions by examining the program text and then the program was removed without warning and similar questions had to be answered from recall. Stage 2 was included because of the possibility that comprehensibility from recall need not be equivalent to comprehensibility from the original text. During stage 1 both time and accuracy were measured, while accuracy was the main measure of performance in stage 2.

Stage 1:

If comprehensibility is an independent feature of a program or programming language then a more comprehensible program should be consistently more comprehensible across different tasks, or different types of comprehension question. The first stage of our experiment shows this view to be wrong.

FIGURE 1

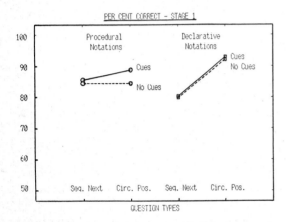

The results show that performance was best when the language matched the information required by the question (see Figure 1). There is a significant interaction between language and question type for both measures of performance (F [9,108] = 5, p < 0.001; F [9,108] = 3.1, p = 0.0025). Subjects using the declarative languages took 15% longer to find an answer to a sequential question, while those using the procedural languages took 110% longer for circumstantial questions. Also the procedural languages produced 24% fewer errors on sequential questions, but 94% more on circumstantial questions. The perceptual cues in the procedural language led to improved performance on circumstantial questions, but not up to the level of the declarative languages. The cues in the declarative language did not affect performance in stage 1. In order to explain these results, we must consider language comprehensibility as a feature of both the language and the context.

Stage 2:

According to current models of program comprehension there is a single semantic mental representation of the program, and therefore whatever the differences in stage 1, the results of stage 2 should reflect the general level of comprehension attained during stage 1. Alternatively, recall performance may reflect the structure of the original program, and therefore results in stage 2 will resemble those of stage 1.

The results for the languages without cues were surprisingly similar to those of stage 1 (see

Figure 2). Performance declined by approximately 20% across both languages and question types. The question by language interaction was still significant (F [9,108] = 2.4, p = 0.018). The procedural language produced 19% fewer errors than the declarative language on sequential questions, but the declarative produced 20% fewer on circumstantial questions. This indicates that the mental representation is not a semantic abstraction of the original program, and that it must preserve at least some features of the original.

FIGURE 2

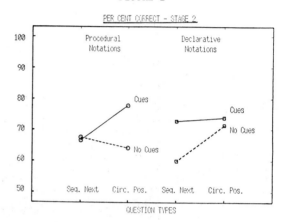

The cued languages produced very different results. Performance declined similarly by about 20%, except for the questions about the cued information, where performance declined by under 10%. This is particularly striking since this represents a difference between the two declarative languages where there was no difference in stage 1. This would suggest that language features can increase comprehensibility in limited, rather than general ways; i.e. the cues to sequential information in the declarative language were of little benefit when answering questions from the text, but when working from recall they led to improved performance.

Consistency within subjects was tested by Jonckheere's homogeneity test, measuring the conformity of each individual to the group's pattern of scores, and by analysing 'robust' means to reveal the presence of abnormally influential outliers. There was no evidence that individuals differed significantly from each other or from their group's overall pattern of results.

Summary

1   A language is comprehensible not by virtue of some feature it does or does not possess, but by virtue of the match between it and the information which must be extracted from it.

2 Memory for a program consists not of a single semantic representation of it, but of a variety of different aspects of it.

3 Features of a language which affect performance of a task under certain conditions need not affect performance of the same task under different conditions.

Although these results were obtained from small programs, written in miniature languages, this in no way prevents them from being used to invalidate existing theories. They might not support the building of a theory, but they do provide restrictions on what such a theory must be able to explain.

THE MEASUREMENT OF PROGRAM COMPLEXITY

Software metrics have been developed to measure the comprehensibility of particular programs, and they are usually calculated by counting the occurence of particular syntactic features in the program. As such they tend to ignore differences of notational structure, except through their effect on the syntactic features of the particular program being studied. Thus, Welsh, Lister and Salzman ([15]) compare two different notations for expressing concurrent processes by calculating Halstead's metric ([8]) for a variety of programs written in both notations, and then comparing the results. In this way, comprehensibility is assumed to be an aggregate of the comprehensibility of a variety of programs, which implies that it is determined by the language's effect on the program structure. This underlying philosophy of software metrics is contradicted by the above results.

However, it is not new to find problems in the development of software metrics, and recently there has been much discussion on the psychological validity of such metrics. Curtis ([4]) criticises Halstead's measures on the grounds that they only reflect very low-level features of a program, whereas the available psychological evidence suggests that programmers chunk programs into more meaningful structures. They emphasise the role that data flow plays in program complexity and develop a metric which takes account of chunks and data flow. This may be an improvement on the counting of operators and operands ([8]), but our results suggest that ANY complexity metric which postulates a single number based solely on the program text is in doubt. Only an average over the range of programmer's tasks, weighted as appropriate (like an economist's basket of goods) could be used as an effective scalar complexity index; and even that would fail to take into account the context in which the program is understood.

The study of readability indices for prose reached in a similar conclusion as the role of context in reading became apparent. In the early 1950's many different formulae were proposed for measuring text readability. Klare ([10]) reviewed these formulae and concluded that they were too syntactical and structural and he predicted that future research would assess and measure the role of text content on comprehension. These predictions were never fulfilled as the importance of context, of which readability was a part, became the dominant theme in research. Thus, Gibson and Levin ([5]) discuss readability indices as one factor among many which influence reading success.

This overview is not intended to devalue the use of such complexity metrics, but simply to put them in perspective as one component of programming success, a view which is forced upon us by the results of our experiment. This variation in the comprehensibility of notational structures has been summed up by Wright ([16]), who concluded that applied research into issues of language comprehension should "specify the comprehension of what, by whom and for what purpose".

MODELS OF PROGRAM COMPREHENSION

Existing models of program comprehension make little allowance for these factors. Bottom-up models (e.g. [13]) are concerned only with notational aspects of programming and not with the effects of different tasks on comprehension. Similarly, the concept of "natural looping strategies" ([14]) does not allow for the possibility that programming strategies may, at least in part, be determined by the requirements of the task being performed.

The model of Brooks ([2]) is a top-down, hypothesis driven process which assumes that the programmer has an initial hypothesis about the program's function, and that this either generates sub-hypotheses, or directs a search for confirmatory (or disconfirmatory) beacons in the program text. Brooks does not discuss how languages differ in comprehensibility, but it is probably fair to say that he assumes it depends on the ease with which a programmer can find a beacon in the text. But, since he fails to discuss how beacons are detected, this is of little practical use. No predictions are available from this model since it is only concerned with high-level integrative processes, rather than with the low-level comprehension of program details. Hence this model is neither confirmed nor disconfirmed by the results. Instead the experiment has provided some indication of how complex the processes of beacon-detection might be.

Atwood ([1]) applied Kintsch's propositional analysis of texts ([9]) to the comprehension of programs, which proposes that texts are read as a series of micro-propositions and rapidly chunked (to avoid memory limitations) into a coherent set of macro-propositions. Atwood argued that expert programmers are able to construct and manipulate more complex macro-propositions. Thus comprehensibility will be affected only by those features of the language which influence the extraction of propositions, which has been contradicted by the results above. Also, propositional analyses assume that memory for a program will consist of the macro-propositional structure which is formed by the process of comprehension, another assumption which is shown to be wrong by the above results.

CONCLUSIONS

Many current models of reading comprehension adopt the concept of interactive processes ([11], [12]). In these models cognitive processing may proceed either top-down or bottom-up depending on the information which is currently available from either internal (memory) or external (textual) sources. In order to allow for contextual effects in program comprehension it is necessary to develop models which are neither top-down nor bottom-up, but which include interactive cognitive processes.

A contender for a possible model would be a combination of Brooks' hypothesis forming processes and some language specific ones which control the search for beacons. These two types of process could then interact in different ways. According to Brooks' theory, comprehension could begin with a hypothesis which would direct the language specific processes to search for a beacon, or conversely, the language specific processes could pass information up to a guide the creation of hypotheses.

Returning therefore to our initial question about what makes a programming language comprehensible, we have shown that comprehensibility is not a constant feature of a programming language, but something that varies according to the language's match with the information demanded by the task. This is contrary to existing models of program comprehension, and contrary to the philosophy of software science, which assume that comprehensibility is an unchanging feature of a language, usually determined by the language's relationship to cognitive processes.

REFERENCES

[1] ATWOOD, M.E., TURNER, A.A., RAMSEY, H.R. and HOPPER, J.N. (1979). An exploratory study of the cognitive structures underlying the comprehension of software design problems. Tech. Report 392, Army Research Institute, Alexandria, Virginia.

[2] BROOKS, R. (1983). Towards a theory of the comprehension of computer programs. International Journal of Man-Machine Studies, 18, 543-554.

[3] CURTIS, B., SHEPPARD, S.B., MILLIMAN, P., BORST, M.A. and LOVE, T. (1979). Measuring the psychological complexity of software maintenance tasks with the Halstead and McCabe metrics. IEEE Transactions on Software Engineering, SE-5, 96-104.

[4] CURTIS, B., FORMAN, I., BROOKS, R., SOLOWAY, E. and EHRLICH, K. (1984). Psychological perspectives for software science. Information Processing and Management, 20, 81-96.

[5] GIBSON, E.J. and LEVIN, H. (1975). The Psychology of Reading. MIT Press, Cambridge, Massachusetts.

[6] GREEN, T.R.G. (1977). Conditional program statements and their comprehensibility to professional programmers. Journal of Occupational Psychology, 50, 93-109.

[7] GREEN, T.R.G. (1980). IFs and THENs: Is nesting just for the birds? Software - Practice and Experience, 10, 373-381.

[8] HALSTEAD, M.E. (1977). Elements of Software Science. Elsevier, New York.

[9] KINTSCH, W. (1974). The Representation of Meaning in Memory. Lawrence Erlbaum Associates, Hillsdale, NJ.

[10] KLARE, G.R. (1963). The Measurement of Readability. Iowa State University Press, Ames, Iowa.

[11] LESGOLD, A. and PERFETTI, C. (1981). Interactive Processes in Reading. Lawrence Erlbaum Associates, Hillsdale, NJ.

[12] RUMELHART, D.E. (1977). Toward an interactive model for reading. In S. Dornic (ed.), Attention and Performance VI. Lawrence Erlbaum Associates, Hillsdale, NJ.

[13] SHNEIDERMAN, B. and MAYER, R.E. (1979). Syntactic/semantic interactions in programmer behaviour: A model and some experimental results. International Journal of Computer and Information Sciences, 8, 219-238.

[14] SOLOWAY, E., BONAR, J. and EHRLICH, K. (1983). Cognitive strategies and looping constructs: An empirical study. Communications of the ACM, 26, 853-860.

[15] WELSH, J., LISTER, A. and SALZMAN, E.J. (1979). A comparison of two notations for process communication. Proc. Symp. on Language Design and Programming Methodology, Sydney, 1979.

[16] WRIGHT, P. (1978). Feeding the information eaters: Suggestions for integrating pure and applied research on language comprehension. Instructional Science, 7, 249-312.

Human-Computer Interaction — INTERACT '84 / B. Shackel (ed.)
Elsevier Science Publishers B.V. (North-Holland)
© IFIP, 1985

THE NATURE OF EXPERTISE IN UNIX

Stephen W. Draper

Institute for Cognitive Science, C-015
University of California, San Diego,
La Jolla, California 92093

This paper discusses the nature of expertise in Unix, arguing that in certain senses of the word there are no experts. The consequences for interface design of revising the common-sense notion of expertise, particularly with respect to designing help facilities, are then discussed.

1. Introduction

A frequently encountered common-sense view holds that in a computer system such as Unix[1] there are experts and novices, experts being people who know more and can do more than novices. As novices learn, they gradually become expert. There is an apparently natural set of beliefs along these lines:

Experts know more than novices (definition)
Experts know things that novices do not
(logically entailed)
* Experts know everything that novices know
* A system can be optimized for experts or
novices but not both
* A system should have two modes—a novice
mode and an expert mode
* Novices need more help than experts
* Novices will use the help facilities more

In addition to the help of my colleagues in the UCSD HMI project at all stages, I should like to acknowledge the comments of Gary Perlman which contributed substantially to this version.

This research was conducted under Contract N00014-79-C-0323, NR 667-437 with the Personnel and Training Research Programs of the Office of Naval Research. Work on Human-Computer Interaction was also supported by a grant from the System Development Foundation. Requests for reprints should be sent to the Institute for Cognitive Science C-015; University of California, San Diego; La Jolla, California, 92093, USA.

1. UNIX is a trademark of Bell Laboratories. The comments in this paper refer to the 4.1 BSD version developed at the University of California, Berkeley.

This paper will argue that most of the above notions are wrong: that the apparently common-sense notion of "expert" does not provide an adequate analysis of the nature of expertise in systems like Unix, and hence does not provide a sound basis for designing help facilities.

2. Command usage data

Over a period of 8 months data on the commands used on our system were collected: specifically how frequently each person used each command. The main measure extracted from this was each person's command vocabulary: the number of distinct commands that that person used at least once. The aspect of expertise reflected in this measure does not fit in with the above simplistic picture.

2.1 The data set

The data was collected over 8 months from a total of 94 people. They had about 570 commands available to them (the precise number fluctuates a little as new ones are added), of which only 394 were recorded as used at least once by at least one person. The largest vocabulary recorded for a single individual was 236. The data recorded the usage of our laboratory computer whose user population includes programmers, psychology researchers (faculty, postdocs, and graduate students), and administrative staff. Most users use (some of) the word processing facilities, a minority use data analysis facilities, another overlapping minority use programming facilities. The computer ran 4.1 Berkeley Unix, and in addition a substantial set of locally developed programs.

Its basis was the Unix system accounting facility which records every process run and who ran it. Nightly this is collapsed, and for this purpose a cumulative record was created equivalent to a 2-D matrix of individuals versus commands with each cell recording the number of times that individual had used that command since the start of record-keeping. (This data collection is based on the same facility as that reported in [1]; however here the collection was for a much longer period, and we use a different analysis in order to examine individual vocabulary sizes.)

This provides an easy method of mass data-gathering, but as we shall see there are a number of drawbacks inherent in this source of data which limit the conclusions that can be drawn from it. The first is that it records Unix processes run, not user commands issued. Thus it records some processes that the user is unaware of having started (since they are called indirectly). This was largely corrected for by a filter to eliminate those processes known to be called indirectly in almost all cases (e.g the mail delivery program, as opposed to the program providing the user interface to the mail system) and also any processes not publicly available (e.g. private programs). This probably correctly eliminated over 90% of programs called indirectly at the cost of losing rare cases of individuals calling these programs directly.

A second consequence of recording processes not user commands is that this source of data misses all use of the 51 commands built into the shell (command interpreter) and not implemented as separate programs. There is reason to believe that this does not distort the trends in the data on which the arguments below depend, even though the built-in commands include some common commands, because the use of the built-in commands is typically tied to patterns involving recorded commands. For instance the most common built-in command is probably "cd" (change directory). New users will not use this at first because they will not at first have created any subdirectories to move among. When they do begin to use it, they will also almost certainly begin to use the command "pwd" to show which directory they are currently in, and that is not built-in. Thus the overall trends and relative vocabulary sizes from this data are probably representative.

There are twin potential problems with estimating command vocabulary from such data, that is with equating observed use with the vocabulary known by the person. The first is with commands known but not used: a user might not use all the commands they know within the period observed. For instance a researcher would only use data analysis tools in bursts at a particular stage of research. The long period of data collection (8 months) should however have compensated for this to a great extent. The inverse problem is with commands used but not known: perhaps invoked accidentally. No good filter for this based on frequency of use of each command by each user seems possible since on the one hand a persistent typing error could generate repeated erroneous calls, and on the other there are commands which would naturally only be called infrequently. However there is no obvious reason to anticipate a systematic error of a kind to invalidate the arguements made below.

Another problem is with data from the "superuser". There is a special privileged user ID (the "superuser"), which is used both to run system utilities and to give special privileges to one or two users for fixing up problems. Thus the system administrator (an "expert") runs part of the time under this ID. All data relating to this ID was discarded to avoid attributing automatic utilities to a person. The danger is that a considerable part of the expert's commands were also discarded. Since the expert however also runs under his own personal ID much of the time, it is probable that the size of his command vocabulary is accurately recorded even though the frequency of use of each command is underestimated.

Finally there is the problem of equating command vocabulary with expertise. Later in this paper the question of the nature of expertise is discussed. For now, it seems reasonable to take vocabulary as a good, though partial, indicator of expertise. It is especially appropriate in considering the help individuals may need which is so often information about the existence and name of commands.

2.2 Observations

The data make it clear that there were no experts on our system in the sense of individuals who used all the commands. There were a substantial number of commands never used by anyone (about 175). Furthermore, of the 394 commands used at least once by someone, the highest individual vocabulary observed was 236 or 60% of the total.

Next, the common-sense division of all users into novices and experts implies a bimodal distribution of expertise (here equated with the number of commands known) of which there is no trace in the data. Figure 1 shows the number of users in each division of vocabulary size. There is a

USER VOCABULARY SIZES

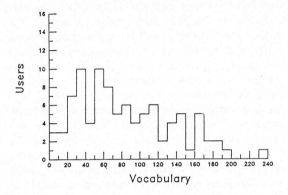

Figure 1.

fairly smooth distribution of vocabulary size across our user population with perhaps a single slight peak in the lower half around a vocabulary size of about 45. The expectation of a bimodal distribution is of course a naive interpretation of the categorization, but note that the proposal to have a system with two levels of friendliness for the two levels of expertise is naive to just the same extent.

A more important observation comes from examining the extent to which one user's vocabulary overlaps another's. The common-sense model of expertise in which there is a single body of knowledge to be learned, and an expert simply knows more of it than a novice, would lead to the set of commands used by a user with a small total vocabulary (a novice) being a subset of the set used by a large vocabulary user. (We can call this the strict subset model of vocabulary knowledge.) This was not observed: on the contrary, each user's knowledge overlaps other users'. A useful image that conveys a picture of the situation is to imagine a Venn diagram of the sets of each user's commands looking like a flower with radiating petals: overlapping all others in the center, completely non-overlapping at the periphery, and with partial overlap of nearest neighbours in between (see fig. 2). While users vary a lot in the size of their vocabulary (the petals are of various sizes), small users show the

A METAPHORICAL PICTURE OF THE DATA: OVERLAPPING OF USERS' VOCABULARY

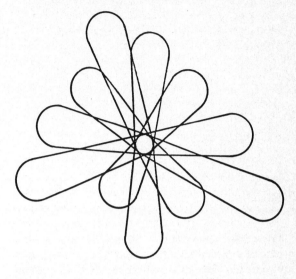

Figure 2.

same pattern as large users: they use one or two commands used by almost all other users, one or two that no-one else uses, and in between commands with all degrees of shared usage. In fact, as far as I know, you cannot usefully plot the data as a Venn diagram because there is no way to plot the commands as points on the plane such that each user's set can be plotted as a simple closed curve (e.g. an ellipse). The important features of the distribution can however be perceived by considering the following.

If knowledge of commands were completely randomly distributed then the number of users per command would be approximately constant for all commands (a normal distribution around the mean of 20.4 users per command). Clearly this is not the case (see fig. 3). On the other hand neither are commands acquired according to the strict subset model so that a large vocabulary always contains the commands in another user's smaller vocabulary. If that were so then the largest individual vocabulary (236) would be the same as the total combined vocabulary of the population (394).

In fact a substantial number of people know commands that no-one else knows (whereas that would only be true of the largest vocabulary user in the strict subset model). There were 40 commands which only 1 user knew, and 18 individuals (rather than 1) each knew one or more of these

COMMANDS GROUPED BY NUMBER OF USERS

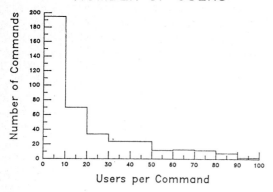

Figure 3.

idiosyncratic commands. (Remember that private commands have been filtered out — only commands in public directories are included.) Similarly, taking the group of commands used by 5 or fewer people, there were 128 such commands and 64 individuals with vocabularies spread evenly from the maximum (236) down to 25 each used one or more of them, but obviously the strict subset model would predict exactly 5 such individuals (those with the 5 largest vocabularies). In other words two thirds of the population used at least one "rare" command.

Thus the picture suggested by this data is that instead of there being a common body of known commands with users differing in how much of it they know, each user is an expert — or rather specialist — in a different corner of the system, even though the quantity of knowledge at least as measured by the number of commands certainly varies a lot. This is consistent with the familiar concept of specialists — that expertise is not concentrated in any one person but is distributed throughout the community, so that the physician (medical expert) is not the expert on, say, the law.

This suggests that a more fruitful way of viewing a system's users is that they are all in essentially the same general situation of knowing some things and being ignorant of (and therefore sometimes needing help with) others. It follows that although a given individual in a particular context may need either complete, partial, or no help depending on their knowledge of that part of the system, the kind of help needed will not be a stable characteristic of that individual i.e. that from the point of view of providing help, "expert" and

"novice" are labels for contexts not for individuals. Thus any scheme, such as Schneider [2] proposes, for classifying different levels of user skill, should not be applied uniformly for a given user but made specific to the command or context in question.

3. Help for users

Scharer [3] points out that users in general typically don't use manuals: at most they use one-sheet summaries, and they prefer to consult the local "expert". (We are now considering another aspect of the notion of expert — someone consulted by others.) Often this expert does not know the answer but does know how to use the documentation in order to extract the answer. This not only confirms the idea that experts do not know everything that even novices may want to know, but suggests that the help facilities provided with the system (manuals) are more heavily used by experts than by novices. This is borne out by informal observation on our system — the resident expert is indeed by far the heaviest user of the printed manual, while novices seldom use it, and roughly speaking manual use is proportional to knowledge of the system and not inversely proportional as might have been expected. We also found this pattern in the data: we compared the number of calls each individual made to the on-line manual (the "man", "apropos", and "whatis" programs) with their command vocabulary: the correlation was positive with a value of 0.72.

Does high manual use cause a large command vocabulary, or conversely does the latter cause the former, or are both due to a separate common cause? The first alternative sounds plausible initially: that those who use the on-line manual expand their vocabulary, so that high manual use causes high vocabulary. However in a given period only learners should have both high manual use and a high accumulated vocabulary; people who already had a large vocabulary at the start of the observation period would not be expected to show high manual use on this hypothesis. Unless most high vocabulary users were "learners" in this period, the correlation suggests a different causal relationship.

It could be that a high vocabulary causes high manual usage because the more commands you use the more commands there are whose details you could need reminding about, and the less likely you are to remember each accurately. This is possible, though perhaps not likely as the major cause of the correlation.

Finally, the correlation may be due to a common cause. One possible such cause is the person's social role as consultant, whether this is formal or informal. (Scharer observes that in the absence of an official "expert" an unofficial one usually emerges in any given user group.) Furthermore, apart from the role of giving advice, there is often a person or persons whose job it is to solve problems others cannot solve, and to bring into effective local use new facilities which were hitherto non-existent, non-functioning, or unknown locally. These people are naturally those with the most knowledge; yet because their job is to tackle new things, equally naturally they need "help" from documentation. These are the people who in fact therefore need the most help from the system at least in the sense of new information of the kind traditionally enshrined in documentation: system designers should presumably therefore be tailoring a large part of the help facilities for them. These people in fact may represent the only kind of general expertise actually observed: the ability to extract information from the system and its documentation rather than relying on other people. They have "manual dexterity" in Pat Wright's phrase [4]. Their skills include knowing how to get information by experimenting with the system, an ability to use other sources of information such as source code, and knowing whom to ask. (All these skills, including the last, are observed in the highest degree in our local consultant, even though he is the one other people ask.)

The above amounts to arguing that the correlation stems from a quality of expertise (causing both high vocabulary and high manual use) derived from performing the role of expert or consultant. Another analysis of this quality might be that the successful extraction of information from the manual itself requires special knowledge. Put bluntly, perhaps the present manual is of little use to non-experts. A variant on this is the idea that while vocabulary is a surface manifestation, "real" expertise depends on understanding core concepts of the system, and that this is a prerequisite for understanding the manual. Another variant, developed below, is that using the manual is a special skill that takes time to acquire, and is broadly correlated with vocabulary since both are indices of how much you have learned about the system.

4. An Interpretation

The data on command vocabulary showed a pattern more like specialization than omniscient expertise. At least with hindsight, we can see that it should have been expected in a large system (one with many commands), partly because different users have different tasks (specialization), and partly because for many tasks there will be more than one way to do it and different people pick different ones. Thus in a system with a small command set you would not expect to see it, but in other large systems you would. One such is the Unix editor "vi", which has about 110 commands (cf. the approximately 600 Unix commands at the shell level). Data was collected on its use from the same population, and a qualitatively similar pattern of command use was seen, especially when the use of compound commands is examined (e.g. "dw" for delete-word is a compound from the delete command, and the move-to-next-word command).

In addition to the tendency to specialization, we should anticipate many distinct kinds of user expertise. In fact every case of command use and the associated possible need for help is different — a unique combination of task and user experience, where that experience has a number of relevant components that cannot be properly compressed on to a single dimension. These components include knowledge:

- of using this system for this task
- of this task independent of any computer system
- of this computer system (independent of this task)
- general knowledge of other similar systems.

plus

- knowledge how to acquire information on this system

The kind of help most appropriate will in principle vary with all these components.

This is not to say that there is no sense at all in which individuals may acquire a general expertise in a system. Apart from the probable importance of factors such as learning about core system concepts, the pattern of on-line help usage suggests that the user's knowledge of how to acquire information on this system is especially important and will largely cut across specialization boundaries. This leads to the suggestion that expertise in Unix is different in nature from what is sometimes tacitly assumed.

Consider for a moment your expertise in arithmetic. It is probably true that, although there are wide variations in speed and accuracy, most readers could solve any problem in simple arithmetic given only pencil and paper. If a particular fact (such as the product of 7 and 9) is forgotten, it can be regenerated with a little effort from other knowledge (for instance by multiplying 7 with 10 and subtracting 7). Thus a comprehensive overall ability that can be called expertise is maintained by exploiting the redundancy of internal resources. In contrast, in a system like Unix it seems that experts systematically supplement their knowledge by using external sources of information. Again this yields a comprehensive overall ability, but the foundations are significantly different. This corresponds with a librarian's expertise: although many readers use the catalog, its heaviest users are librarians, and if users have trouble they ask a librarian to help them with it; they do not expect the librarian to know the answer from memory. Thus on the one hand there is a familiar kind of expertise in Unix, but on the other hand it is not the same as every other kind of expertise, and not all apparently common-sense conclusions will be valid.

5. Conclusion

Command sets as large as in our Unix system or in the **vi** editor are just too large for anyone to learn in their entirety, and there are not strong constraints common to all users on the order in which commands will be learned. Thus you should expect specialization not general expertise at this level of knowing commands. This conclusion appears to be established by the command vocabulary data despite its imperfections. At a more general level of knowing how to find things out about the system, the common-sense one-dimensional notion of expertise is more nearly applicable. This fits Scharer's experience; it means documentation is used most by experts, and that expertise in Unix relies on external information sources just as a librarian does. This conclusion is supported by the observation of high manual use by experts independently of the correlation of manual use and vocabulary, and is consonant with the picture of Unix as a city too large to be known entirely in practice.

The simple observations and data gathering described above thus lead to a quite different (though in retrospect not so surprising) view of user knowledge and expertise than the one based on the

common-sense notion of an expert. The nature of expertise in Unix does have parallels, but we must be careful in which comparisons we draw. There is specialization rather than comprehensive knowledge (comparable to specialization in traditional professions); and expertise relies not just on internal resources but on external information (just as a librarian does). There are no experts in Unix in the sense of people who know all the commands. While there are certainly some users with a larger command vocabulary than others, experts' real skill seems to lie less in familiarity with the whole command set than in discovery skills that allow them to find answers to the questions they cannot answer from memory.

To return to the common-sense beliefs listed in the introduction, we may now argue that in reality "novices" on a system like Unix may know some things that "experts" do not; that optimizing or having alternative modes for novices and experts is unlikely to be generally useful since an individual's knowledge varies across parts of the system in an idiosyncratic way; that experts use the help facilities more than novices, and to the extent that their job entails answering questions or path-breaking for the local user community, they need the help (from the system) more than novices.

Implications for help

What does this mean for providing help? It seems that in designing a system (and especially its help and documentation facilities) to match the expertise of its users, one should expect a user community, no matter what the overall expertise of its members, to contain users in all states of knowledge of any particular command or area, and furthermore that it will not be possible to predict a given user's expertise in one area on the basis of their overall knowledge of the system. All users will be experts in relation to some parts of the system, novices in relation to other areas they have never used, and intermediate elsewhere. In a utopian future (perhaps not very distant) we may have help systems that do take some of this into account usefully. For instance we could monitor command usage so that the help system would know at the time of a request whether that user had ever used that command before; and, more difficult, if we keep a database of how closely different commands or help topics are related semantically, we might make more sophisticated inferences from the user's history of command usage.

We saw that currently "experts" use the manual more than novices. A conservative attitude would then tell manual writers to forget novices and concentrate on their present audience of experts. However if you believe either that the correlation was caused by the opacity of the present manual or, as argued above, that expertise in Unix intrinsically depends on external information, then we should focus on the central skill of manual use as more important to all users than any other single piece of knowlege about the system.

There are two possible responses to this. The first is to take seriously the idea that the first and most important thing a new user must be taught is how to get help. This does not just mean giving them the manual or the name of the help command, but explicitly teaching techniques for using it (I only recently learnt from our local expert the importance of using the permuted index to the manual — I had preferred to muddle around in other ways before), alternative strategies when the first attempt fails, and whom to ask. (John Seely Brown has suggested that the single most important thing in introducing secretaries to a computer system is to have them work within sight of someone else so that they can see and so really believe how integral a part of using the system asking other people for help is.)

A second approach is to accept that the first may have failed and to provide backups. A concrete example is "usage" notation: a compact notation for expressing the syntax of commands. In Unix this is used to give a summary at the head of each manual entry, and is also used in brief help messages printed by many commands if they are called with wrong or missing arguments. Many other systems use versions of this technique. Its advantage is its compactness and ability to express the whole range of possibilities precisely (which a concrete example cannot). However the notation is not self-explanatory, so that much of such "help" is useless for people who have not learned to decode it. Some large manuals acknowledge this problem by providing alternatives. For instance the latest edition of the SPSS manual [5] (which its preface claims "is the most user-designed document in the industry", reflecting iterations over 17 years and 2 complete previous editions) provides both syntax summaries for users familiar with the notation, and full page annotated examples for conveying what is largely the same information to "documentation novices". Similarly the Los Alamos National Laboratory's computing division's plan for user documentation [6] distinguishes, in its set of "user attitudes", between "know what I want" users who

in general know where to find the information they need, and "no time to learn" users who do not and yet still need a quick reference facility.

This kind of awareness of the level and range of documentation expertise in users is needed in designers of help systems, especially on systems where no systematic attempt is made to train users in the acquisition of information. Currently Unix is one such system, where documentation is provided on the tacit assumption that users can at least "read the manual", even though nowhere is there help or tutorials for learning this complex skill. In practice however being able to "read the manual" usefully includes the decoding of special notation and the intelligent use of coordinated inquiry strategies perhaps involving the index, several entries, cross-references etc. Since "experts" are seen to use such strategies, the problem seems not so much to be that novices lack the concepts referred to in the documentation (in which case the problem will vanish when they "know the system better") but that they lack the ability to track down all the information they need i.e. they are "documentation novices".

References

[1] Kraut R.E., Hanson S.J., Farber J.M. "Command Use and Interface Design" in *Proceedings of the CHI '83 Conference on Human Factors in Computing Systems* (Boston, MA. 1983) pp.11-18

[2] Schneider M.L. "Models for the design of static software user assistance" in Badre and Shneiderman (eds.), *Directions in Human Computer Interaction* (Ablex 1982) pp.137-148

[3] Scharer, L.L. "User training: Less is more" *Datamation,* vol.29 (1983) pp.175-182. Directions in Human Computer Interaction

[4] Wright, P. "A user-oriented approach to creating computer documentation" in *Proceedings of the CHI '83 Conference on Human Factors in Computing Systems* (Boston, MA. 1983) pp.11-18

[5] SPSS Inc., *SPSS X User's Guide* (McGraw-Hill 1983)

[6] Los Alamos National Laboratory Computing Documentation Group C-2 *Computing Division Plan for User Documentation* (1983) LA-9807-MS

Human-Computer Interaction — INTERACT '84 / B. Shackel (ed.)
Elsevier Science Publishers B.V. (North-Holland)
© IFIP, 1985

NOVICE-EXPERT DIFFERENCES IN SOFTWARE DESIGN

Adelson, B., Littman, D., Ehrlich, K., Black, J. and Soloway, E.

Cognition and Programming Project
Department of Computer Science
Yale University
New Haven, Connecticut 06520

In this paper we describe the results of analyzing protocols of expert and novice software designers as they performed a novel, non-trivial design task from a domain with which they were familiar. The protocols allowed us to develop a model which can account for several interesting and recurrent expert behaviors such as constraint gathering, balanced development, and the building and running of mental simulations of partially completed designs. We have also found what look like systematic differences between our novices and our experts.

1. Motivation and Goals[1]

In this paper we discuss the protocols we have collected from novice and expert designers as they designed an electronic mail system. We will also present a cognitive model of expert design which we have developed as a result of analyzing our protocols. Two goals motivated this work: The first was to see novice and expert designers solving problems which called upon their problem solving abilities, as well as their "routine cognitive skills". The second was to create a situation in which general problem solving operators could be seen to interact with whatever knowledge bases existed for our subjects.

2. Methodology

Subjects. Three expert and two novice designers. Each of our experts had worked for at least eight years in commercial settings designing a wide variety of software whereas each of the novices had worked for several years as programmers but for less than two years as designers.

Procedure. We presented each of the designers with the following design task to work on.

> TASK -- Design an electronic mail system around the following primitives: READ, REPLY, SEND, DELETE, SAVE, EDIT, LIST-HEADERS. The goal is to get to the level of pseudocode that could be used by professional programmers to produce a running program. The mail system will run on a very large, fast machine so hardware considerations are not an issue.

The task we gave our subjects had several important properties: It was non-trivial, requiring close to two hours of our subject's time. It was novel, none of our designers had designed a solution to the problem previously. These two properties meant that for both the novices and the experts we would not be seeing only "routine cognitive skill", but some problem solving as well. In addition, the problem we chose was similar to the type of problem which our subjects had to deal with professionally. Therefore, although none of our subjects had designed a mail system before, whatever experience they did have was concerned with designing other types of communications systems and so we would be able to observe them in a situation where they could turn to whatever knowledge bases they had previously developed.

Organization

In Section 3 we present our model of expert design. We will use the model as a framework for interpreting recurrent expert behavior. We will also present recurrent novice behavior and compare it with that of the expert. This will be done in Section 4. Next we discuss our model in relation to novice design. In Section 6 we present questions raised by our data.

3. The Model

3.1. Components of the Model

Our model of the experts' design process contains four major elements:

- A Design Meta-Script. The function of the Meta-Script is to drive the design process by setting three general goals:

  1. To check the current state of the design for sufficiency. This means that all of the elements needed to specify the design at the current level are present.

[1] This work was sponsored by a grant from ITT, Shelton, CT.

2. To check the current state of the design for consistency. This means that all elements of the design are compatible at the current level of specificity, and that no element causes an inconsistency with currently known constraints both at higher and at lower levels.

3. To expand the design from its current level of specificity into the next level of specificity.

The main operator used to achieve these goals is the running of mental simulations of the partially completed design. The function of these simulations is explained in the next section which describes how the elements of the model function.

- A Sketchy Model. The Sketchy Model resides in working memory and as the design process proceeds the model becomes increasingly less sketchy. The model is initially sketchy in that the expert does not yet understand its functionality down to a level of detail which would be sufficient to produce an implementable program. In addition, the constraints or assumptions of the design are not entirely understood. One way of picturing the model is as a tree that grows in both depth and breadth as the expert's understanding of the problem specification increases (Jeffries et al., 1981; Atwood, Turner, Ramsey, and Hooper, 1979.)

- The Current Long Term Memory Set. This is the set of long term memory elements that are currently under consideration. This set would consist of all of the known solutions appropriate to the aspect of the design that is currently being worked on. Choosing an element from the set currently under consideration allows the expert's model to become less sketchy because the element selected from long term memory is now added to the model in working memory. It also causes a different long term memory set to be considered on the next iteration of the design process.

- The Demons. These contain the expert's notes to himself. The notes are things to remember such as constraints, assumptions, or potential inconsistencies. A note will be placed in a demon if it is: a. too concrete to be resolved at the time that it is thought of and b. needs to be considered when the expert's model has reached a level of concreteness that matches the note. The demons are able to monitor the state of the Sketchy Model. When the level of detail of the Model is equal to the level of detail of the note the demon calls attention to itself. (The reader will notice that our demons are rather unusual in that they are active information gatherers.)

Summary of the Model

At the most abstract level, the experts were performing a means-ends analysis driven by the Meta-Script. In this means-ends analysis the goal state was an implementable design specification and the current state was the expert's increasingly detailed Sketchy Model of the problem solution. The expert moved towards the goal state by repeatedly simulating executions of their incomplete models. For all of the experts observed, this appears to be the most powerful and frequently used operator in the means-ends analysis. However these simulation runs of the partial models served to decrease the gap between the current and goal states in a number of ways. This will be expanded upon in the next section where we present portions of both novice and expert protocols. These quotes taken from the expert protocols will help to give the reader a clearer picture of how the model functions. They will also bring out some of the interesting interactions among the components of the model. In addition, the expert protocols form an interesting comparison with those of the novices.

4. Recurrent Behavior Accounted for by the Model

Here we present behaviors which we found were repeatedly exhibited by our novice and expert subjects.

Observation I. How the Design Proceeded

There was a surprising degree of similarity in the time line of the expert subjects. As illustrated in the figure below, first the experts described how a user would view the mail system, then they expanded upon the various assumptions and constraints of the problem (e.g, E1: "We will assume dumb terminals", E2: "the number of users will not be fixed"). Only then, approximately 20 minutes into the session, did the experts begin to construct a working model of the mail system. This model also changed over time in that it began as a very skeletal version of a mail system and then became increasingly concrete as the design progressed. On the other hand, the novices began by designing solutions for specific functions. A comparison of the novice and expert protocols illustrates this difference.

```
EXPERTS:

Start                                           Finish
user....assump-....abstract........concrete...discussion
model    tions      models of         design
                    mail system

~10 mins ~10 mins              ~80 mins        ~10 mins

NOVICES:

.............. concrete design................discussion

                ~100  mins                    ~10 mins
```

Figure 1: Timeline for Novice and Expert Subjects

The following quote from designer E2 illustrates the progression from an abstract to a concrete model.

At 20 minutes into the task expert E2 said:

In the above quote from N1 we see that save suggests a particular operation, open a file and write to it. Although this is an appropriate operation for a save function it is at a fairly low level, and certainly more concrete than the representation that our expert subjects had developed at this point.

Observation II. Maintaining Balanced Development

The expert designers always followed a course of *balanced development*. Our experts attempted to develop each of the components of the design so that none of them acquired significantly more detail than any of the others. The following quote is representative of this behavior. Its significance becomes clear when we consider the next observation, *Simulation Runs of the Sketchy Model*.

> E3: ...you've never got so deep in that you can't improve it taking account of something you think of later... No, oh no I'm not going to take something down to its itty bitty conclusion because bet you I'm going to have to change it. When I take something else out and say (echh??) there's no logical consistency between that, remembering that mail is a two way thing. I'm going to have to reply to it and I may have to use this information to construct a message back ... I can see too many possible interactions between the pieces so it would be nicer if they all had some logical similarity.

There is a marked difference between the novices and the experts here. Once the novices had begun work on a function they continued until they had finished it. Additionally, the novices did not consider how a given element would interact with the others, whereas the experts repeatedly did so. This point will also be discussed in relation to the next observation.

Observation III.
Simulation Runs of the Sketchy Model

We observed all of our expert subjects repeatedly conducting mental simulation runs of their partially completed designs. The experts would consult the state of the Sketchy Model and then conduct a simulation of the model at its current level of abstraction. Thus we observed simulations which became increasingly concrete as the design progressed. For example, in E3's early simulation he saw the mailer as "information flowing through a system", whereas in a later simulation when considering his module for the READ function, E1 drew a state diagram for all of the states which could be reached from READ. What is the function of these simulations, which appear in our protocols and in those of Kant and Newell (1982)? Recall that the design process is driven by the Meta-Script. The goals of the designer's Meta-Script are to check the current Sketchy Model for consistency and sufficiency and if these criteria are met the next goal is then to try to expand the Model. Therefore, in order to meet the goals of the Meta-Script a simulation run of the Sketchy Model in its current state is conducted (e.g. E1 draws a state diagram for the current READ module to see how it behaves at this point in its development). We can now see why the experts maintain balanced development; *it would be difficult to run a simulation with elements at different levels of detail.*

Recall that the other goal of the Meta-Script was to

We can now start thinking about what type of processing structure is required for implementing (the mail system). In order to get the idea about the structure, we can see some kind of a state diagram which shows the dynamics of the system.... What we can see here is one state (accessing) several other states and after the operation is completed, control of the state transition going back to the initial state. This will help us structure our solution to the problem at a higher level. Then we will go into each one of the building blocks that help us write the processing step at each step in the state diagram.

The following quotes were taken from novices and experts at three minutes and 10 minutes into the task, they represent the observation that novice and expert subjects dealt with very different types of issues at each of these points:

At 3 minutes into the task, novice N1 said:

> (Writes SAVE) "To save I have to open a file and then write to that file... If I have 5 or 6 messages I have to consider if I want to save all of them or whether I should save a specific one and specify which one I am saving."

At 3 minutes N1 also wrote pseudocode to accompany these statements such as, "OPEN FILE" and "READ FILE".

In comparison to the above
at 3 minutes into the task, expert E3 said:

> "I guess I have to establish a set of assumptions of my own"

At 10 minutes into the task, novice N2 said:

> "The number of the message line has to be specified... In order to get the message,.. if I have 4 messages, I need to know which lines I'm going to take if the user only wants to save one message.."

At 10 minutes into the task we again find a novice-expert difference, here expert E1 said:

> "It is critical to define this user view. It is the foundation of this whole system... The issue is much less a program design issue than a human design issue. I would be much more concerned about issues such as what is the correct functionality to provide them with as opposed to how could I design the program. The program design gives me no cause for concern at all."

Why did the experts spend the first twenty minutes of the session gathering information? The answer is not that they were hesitant over their competence. As illustrated in the quote above, E1 showed (an appropriate) lack of concern over the design issues of the system. However, the answer does seem to have to do with the experts' strategy for searching memory. As discussed in the previous section, the expert designers search long term memory for stored solution elements. An effective search results from first choosing the right set of memory elements and then choosing the right element from among the set. This type of choice would be aided by having a sufficiently rich set of constraints and assumptions and it seems that experts do not begin their search until this information has been obtained.

expand the Sketchy Model. The simulation is used in this process as well. It points out an element of the Sketchy Model that needs expansion and the expert then accesses the appropriate long term memory set in order to choose how the expansion should proceed.

Once again we find a sharp contrast between the novices and the experts. The experts continually and explicitly conducted mental simulations at different levels of concreteness. As mentioned above the novices did not maintain balanced development and so conducting a simulation would have been difficult. In fact we observed only one occurence of what might have been the beginning of the use of simulations by our novices. This occurred when N2 said that she would work on DELETE and SAVE because they followed from READ, which she had just completed. However, from the following quote it seems almost accidental that N2 was conducting a simulation run of her design, whereas the experts consistently relied on this tool.

> N2: Following READ maybe I'll think about DELETE or SAVE.
> Experimenter: Why?
> N2: um, because, um, well, because usually people will have this action after he or she reads the mail.

We saw one bug which would have been caught had N1 been able to use simulations in order to check for consistency. This bug resulted from N1 having conflated two possible meanings of READ, i.e. having the user read a message and having the operating system read a command from the user to the mail system. It wasn't caught until late in the design session since N1 did not have the tools of balanced development mental simulation to point out the inconsistency.

Without having the simulations as a tool how did the novices decide what element of the design to work on next? Both N1 and N2 stated at least once that they were choosing to work on easy elements before difficult ones. This can be compared to E1's statement that at one point he chose to work on a module because it was difficult with respect to its interactions with the others. Additionally N1 and N2 both seemed data driven in that the first element they both chose to work on was the first element listed in the problems statement. In fact at one point N1 stated that she was working on READ "because it was first".

Observation IV. Notes and Interrupts

We found that the expert designers would frequently make "notes" to themselves about things to remember later in the design process. These notes had to do with constraints or partial solutions or potential inconsistencies which needed to be handled in order to produce a successful design. The reason that these notes were not handled immediately was that they were concerned with a level of detail which was greater than the level of detail of the current state of the Sketchy Model. This means that incorporating them into the design when they were thought of would have violated the principle of balanced development. This in turn would have interfered with the process of running simulations, which, as mentioned above, was a process upon which the experts rely quite heavily.

We also found that the expert designers would be reminded of previously made notes once the current state had reached a level of detail which would allow the note to be incorporated into the design without violating balanced development. Data of this sort is what led us to posit the existence of demons which were able to monitor the state of the Sketchy Model in order to interact with the design process without disrupting it.

Both N1 and N2 did, at one point make notes for themselves. These notes seemed more data driven than those made by our experts. This is because both of these notes were made while considering the problem statement we had given them.

> N2: (Pointing to READ on the sheet where the problem statement appeared) For READ I have to put the mail box in a good directory. I have to find somewhere to put the user's mailbox...so I'll have to study the operating system and the file system.

This is in contrast to the notes made by the experts, which were usually formed while talking aloud about the properties of the module they were currently considering. A novice-expert difference appeared not only in what prompted the designers to make a note, but also in the functioning of the demons which lead to resolution of the notes. Although we have only two instances to draw from we were not able to find the novices making use of their demons in the way the experts did. N1 attended to the note almost immediately whereas N2 did not return to the above described note at all. More controlled experimentation is needed here but our observations suggest that the novices do not have demons which are effective as those of the experts.

5. Overview of the Novices

In this section we discuss the extent to which each element of the expert model could be used to describe novice behavior.

- The Sketchy Model. The novices always considered functions one at a time, this suggests that although the novices may have understood each function in isolation, they did not have a global view of them as inter-related elements. Additionally, the novices view of the problem began at a concrete level, rather than going through several iterations in order to reach one. Both observations suggest that the novices did not have Sketchy Models, since two central properties of a Sketchy Model are that it relates the elements of the design and that it begins at an abstract level and gradually becomes more concrete. It seems that the novices placed a single current item into working memory and did not have any sort of "retrieval structure" in which to store intermediate results (Chase and Ericcson, 1981).

- The Notes and Demons. The novices do makes notes, which is not surprising since this is a general activity, rather than one specific to design. However for the novices, note making is data driven rather than conceptually driven. It seems that conceptually driven note making awaits the accumulation of more task specific knowledge (about design and/or about communication systems) This will then allow the general operation of note making to interact with better articulated knowledge structures and will result in conceptually driven notes.

- The Meta Script. The goals of 1. checking that no element of the model has been forgotten and 2. expanding the model, do exist for the novices. However, we did not find evidence of checking for consistency (this would be difficult to do without a Sketchy Model to organize such a check and without elements of equal detail).

- Long Term Memory Sets. The novices seem to retrieve only pseudo-code from long term memory. This suggests that they have less abstracted memory libraries to turn to. However it is also known that novices frequently are unable to use what they know in a way that produces information directly relevant to current needs (Chi, Glaser and Rees, 1981; Larkin, 1981). So it is possible that the novices have knowledge which they cannot access. A clear example of this occurred with N1. At one point after she had written correct pseudo-code for the READ function she decided that she should restructure her design. As a result of this restructuring she created a module, PRINT, which replaced the READ module. She stated that the READ module was no longer needed since PRINT had the same functionality and then crossed out the code for READ. What she did not seem to realize was that she could take the code she had written for READ and now use it for PRINT. Both N1 and N2 failed to see the relationship between the SAVE and DELETE functions (even when N1 wrote them one after the other on the same page), whereas the experts actively tried to find such relationships. These two examples suggest that the novices have less than full access to their knowledge and are unaware that this is the case, whereas the experts have heuristics for maximizing the probability that they can find and use what they know.

We see the beginnings of the expert model in some of the novice behavior, such as note making and the running of the one rudimentary simulation described above. Therefore, although we would not want to use the same model to describe both types of subject we can begin to see the mapping between novice and expert.

6. Open Questions

Three issues of theoretical significance are raised but not settled by our observations.

- Are the novice demons faulty or are they unable to fire because they are monitoring Sketchy Models that are not sufficiently well structured?

Although our sample size is small enough to warrant caution, in our data the novices' demons did not interrupt them at the appropriate time, whereas the experts' demons did seem to do so more reliably.

- Where do novice bugs come from? We saw one bug which resulted from N1 having conflated two possible meanings of read, i.e. having the user READ a message and having the operating system read a command from the user to the mail system. It wasn't caught until late in the design since N1 did not have the tool of mental simulation to point out the inconsistency. However we still wonder about the etiology of novice bugs. Do they arise only from misconceptualizations, or from lack of consistency checking and demons that do not fire?

- What drives the generation of the novices pseudo-code? The pseudo-code we saw appears to consist of plans for simple programming actions; here N1's plan for READ is: open a file, read it and then close it. This is in contrast to the conceptually based plans of the expert (Soloway, Ehrlich, Gold and Littman, 1983; Adelson, 1981). This issue also touches on the question of novice search. It seems that the functions of the mail system caused the novice to access some appropriate programming statement, such as SAVE and open a file. This then led to retrieving some larger piece of stereotypic or plan-like pseudo-code.

7. Concluding Remarks

We have chosen a complex and novel design task for our subjects from a domain with which they were familiar. This allowed us to develop a model which can account for several interesting and recurrent expert behaviors such as constraint gathering, balanced development, and the building and running of simulations of partially completed designs. We have also found what look like systematic differences between our novices and our experts. Most strikingly in our experts we find an effective interplay between meta-knowledge about design and content specific knowledge about communication systems. Our novices of course have more limited domain specific knowledge as well as less well developed meta-knowledge. Additionally they seem to have less well developed strategies for using whatever knowledge they do have and less effective ways of integrating their knowledge and their processes.

Acknowledgements

Thanks to Ruven Brooks and Valerie Abbott for their time and thought.

8. References

Adelson, B. Problem solving and the development of abstract categories in programming languages. *Memory and Cognition*, 1981 9(4), 422-433.

Atwood, M., Turner, A., Ramsey, R., and Hooper, J. An exploratory study of the cognitive structures underlying the comprehension of software design problems. ARI Technical Report 392. SAI-79-100-DEN. 1979.

Chase, W. and Ericcson, K. A.   In Anderson (Ed.) *Cognitive Skills and Their Acquisition*:   Hillsdale, NJ: Lawrence Erlbaum Associates, 1981.

Chi, M., Glaser, R. and Rees, E. Expertise in Problem Solving.   In *Advances in the Psychology of Human Intelligence*. Vol. 1.   Hillsdale: N.J. Lawrence Erlbaum, 1981.

Jeffries, R., Turner, A., Polson, P. and Atwood, M. The processes involved in designing software. In Anderson (Ed.) *Cognitive Skills and Their Acquisition*:   Hillsdale, NJ: Lawrence Erlbaum Associates, 1981.

Kant, E. and Newell, A. Problem Solving Techniques for the Design of Algorithms.   Tech Report No. CMU-C S-82-145 1982.

Larkin, J. Enriching Formal Knowledge. In Anderson (Ed.) *Cognitive Skills and Their Acquisition*:   Hillsdale, N.J.: Lawrence Erlbaum Associates, 1981.

Soloway,   E.,   Ehrlich,   K.,   Gold,   E.,   Littman, D. Programming Expertise: Theory and Experiment, in *The Nature of Expertise*, Chi, M., Glaser, R., Farr, M., (Eds.), 1983, in press.

KNOWLEDGE BASED TECHNIQUES

APPLICATION DOMAIN MODELLING BY KNOWLEDGE ENGINEERING TECHNIQUES

Wolfgang Dzida und Wilhelm Valder

Gesellschaft für Mathematik und Datenverarbeitung
D-5205 St. Augustin 1, P.O.Box 12 40

From an ergonomist's point of view it is important to understand the tasks and objectives a user is concerned with. Before a systems designer starts developing an application system his understanding of the application case can be facilitated by means of a knowledge base. To provide this knowledge an ergonomist may help, since work-analysis is his professional research field. This paper is intended to illustrate how work-analysis and user participation may contribute to the development of applications systems so that some ergonomic design principles may be considered during the software development process. Our approach is not focussed on modelling application domains in manufacturing but in business context.

"A business systems analyst is a common term to describe a person whose job it is to talk to the end-user of a computer system, and to document that user's needs so that an appropriate computer system can be developed" [1]. In other words, the analyst's duties are to interact with the customer and to document the application case in such a way that the customer can verify the problem representation; the representation is also expected to enable the systems designer to specify the software system. Systems analysis usually starts with deliberations about the application domain of a company. A systems analyst and the potential customer communicate about objectives and activities of the company so as to find out where the implementation of application software is suitable and beneficial. The problem domain has to be presented in the user's terminology as well as in terms of abstractions, with both of them enabling the systems developer to transform the problem representation into a technical concept. Of course, there is nothing gained by a one-to-one mapping; we are in favour of creatively developed software products. The traditional approach of this creative activity, however, is insufficient.

The systems analyst is inclined to understand the application problem on the background of his implementation expertise. Hence, his understanding is in danger of turning into a bias, particularly during the elicitation of vague facts and professional heuristics which are peculiar to the application field under study.

In order to avoid a biased understanding of the problem we suggest determining a problem representation by use of a DIALECTIC PRINCIPLE of understanding: the application domain has to be described independently of the systems analyst's diagrams so as to find out contradictions between both kinds of representations. If a mismatch appears one should seize the opportunity to elaborate a deeper understanding of the application case [2].

1. Advantages of two sources of knowledge

During the deliberation process between customer and systems analyst the major concern is not HOW to design and implement application software but WHAT has to be designed. As a matter of fact, application domain analysis is distinct from the implementation process. At least two sources of knowledge determine the analysis of potential benefits of application software: 1. the customer's expertise in the application field, and 2. the engineer's experience with the possibilities of a new technology.

An idea for a product of improved quality or even an innovative one might be evoked from a deeper insight into both the customer's understanding of his application field and the engineer's experience in what is feasible. Innovative products are evoked usually under conditions which govern intellectual creativity:

double-representation of information in human memory. Klix [3] has provided some empirical evidence for that explanation in the case in which a complex logical structure may be given a simple visual representation. "The transposition of one kind of representation into the other makes the structural identification possible, reveals possible transformations which could not be disclosed from the other one" (p. 6).

This paper is intended to introduce a computer assisted work analysis method which may be applied just at the beginning of the re-quirements analysis. We suggest to compare the results of our method with representations gained for example by SADT [4]. Contradictions between user requirements and the software design should be recognized early in the softwa-re development process. Thus, contradictions may contribute to uncover dialectic barriers so as to overcome them.

The effect of double representation may be that the user's requirements will be formulated more precisely, since a better understanding of the application problem can be achieved. This strategy contrasts sharply with formulating the requirements on the basis of certain design or implementation decisions.

Swartout and Balzer [5] have pointed out that specification and implementation are inevitably intertwined. Designers are overly naive who believe in an absolute separation of specifica-tion from implementation. "This partitioning is entirely arbitrary... Rather than providing an implementation of the specification, they knowingly redefine the specification itself" (p. 438). There is no doubt about the validity of this observation. A theoretical basis for this may be the TOTE model which describes the user's refinement of tasks in terms of intermeshed feedback circuits: refinement of tasks using a well-known repertoire of tools [6].

The approach of intertwining specification and implementation, however, is predicated upon the assumption that the problem to be specified is already sufficiently defined. This situation is described by Dörner [7] as a type of problem in-volving an INTERPOLATION BARRIER : To satisfy well-defined requirements a set of well-known means of solution is available; then it is up to the problem solver to establish an adequate sequence of operations to interpolate between the initial state of a problem and the goal sta-te, with both states being already determined.

It is generally accepted that at the beginning of software development the user requirements are by no means well-defined. The purpose of problem analysis is to formulate the re-quirements properly while the developer aims at elaborating an understanding of the problem domain. This situation is described by Dörner [7] as a type of problem involving a DIALECTIC BARRIER : Although the requirements are still

vaguely defined a set of means of solution is supposed to be well-known. In this situation the problem analyst should concentrate on objec-tives involved in an application domain, and he should attempt to uncover contradictions between his provisional understanding and the user's vaguely communicated requirements, rather than definitely representing the application case in terms of, for instance, SADT diagrams. Problem analysis is aimed at a valid understanding and representation of the application domain. Validity must be tested in the course of USER-DEVELOPER COMMUNICATION, provided that a re-presentation of the application domain is established enabling both the user and the developer to check the requirements.

For systems analysis purposes it is highly desirable to provide for a transfer of the user's knowledge into a representation that is suited to the design task of the systems engineer. Two problems are associated with this methodical requirement: 1. many existing work analysis methods which may be useful in re-presenting the customer's knowledge are not applicable because of formal deficiencies, 2. current systems analysis methods do meet the designer's needs. However, these methods are not intended for the purpose of problem representa-tion of a user's application field.

In order to fill this gap in methodology, we are attempting to introduce an approach which is both capable of representing an application field, so as to facilitate the user-developer communication, and formally sophisticated enough to satisfy the designer's needs.

2. The knowledge engineering approach

"The fundamental method of systems analysis is to apply common sense to a complete statement of a problem. Large systems tend to frustrate analysts who take this approach because it is hard to obtain a complete statement of the pro-blem or even the objectives of the problem solu-tion" [8]. We take into account that the compu-ter systems analyst is usually not an expert in the application field. If one accepts that the users and the customer are the real experts in an application domain, it is natural to use tho-se techniques during systems analysis that have been proven helpful in the knowledge elicitation for expert systems. The systems analyst should take the role of a knowledge engineer [9]. In Artificial Intelligence Research (AI) systems analysis is explicitly called knowledge engineering. We intend to apply knowledge engineering techniques to the systems analyst's traditional task, namely the analysis of an application domain and its problems.

2.1 Advantages of a knowledge base

The main problems in systems analysis are that

- the engineer is faced with an incomplete problem description,
- this problem description may be manipulated by a bias (as described above),
- the customer's requirements change, and
- the customer (user) usually knows more than he is aware of knowing.

The major advantage of a knowledge base is that it enables the systems analyst to handle an incomplete problem description, since he does not need to know exactly what to ask for and what to do with the results — as would be typical in the use of conventional database systems. An inference mechanism will enable him to apply all the heuristics that have been aquired from the user so as to get a more complete insight into the application domain. In turn, the designer can ask the knowledge base to explain the reasons for the customer's (user's) requirments, in order to get insight into the heuristics that govern the activities in the application field. This is particularly helpful in all cases of exception handling.

In conventional diagrams provided by a systems analyst the knowledge about the application is scattered throughout the high level description code, and changing a single fact may result in a change of dozens of diagrams. In a knowledge base, however, the knowledge is explicitly represented; furthermore, the inference engine does not change when a new piece of knowledge is added to the system [10].

2.2 A formal representation of an application domain

A user's WORK is composed of individual tasks to be performed regardless of the sequence of tasks.

$$work = \{task_1, task_2, \ldots , task_n\}$$

In turn, a user's TASK may be defined by a part of his/her work.

An ACTIVITY is here defined as a structural component of a task (fig.1), commonly communicated in the user's terminology, usually composed of a verb and a noun, for instance, "write a letter".

An ACT represents the structural aspect of work defined by a 5-tuple (fig.1):

$$act = (resultant\ object,$$
$$activity,$$
$$initial\ object,\ tool,\ parameter)$$

A TASK is the representation of an act from an abstract point of view, with the detailed components of an act beeing neglected. This abstraction is convenient for recording conversation between user and developer, for example in the case of an interview carried out by the knowledge engineer in the user's application field.

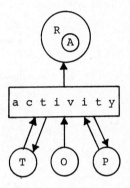

Figure 1 : Components of a work act; T-tool, O-object, P-parameter, R-result, A-attribute

PERFORMANCE represents the procedural aspect of work defined by a sequence of tasks.

$$performance = task_1, task_2, \ldots , task_n$$

We distinguish two types of OPERATORS: 1) a tool that provides properties of an object, with the properties being typical to the application of that tool, 2) a 'parameter' that provides attributes of an object; the value of the parameter has to be set by the user of the corresponding tool.

Example: A secretary uses a typewriter (tool) to print a column of numbers (=result) on a paper (=object); she sets a tabulator (=parameter) on a certain position (=value of the parameter), in order to type the digits more reliable into the column (=attribute of the resultant object). It is worth mentioning that attributes are mostly related to those user requiremets which are significant from an ergonomist's point of view.

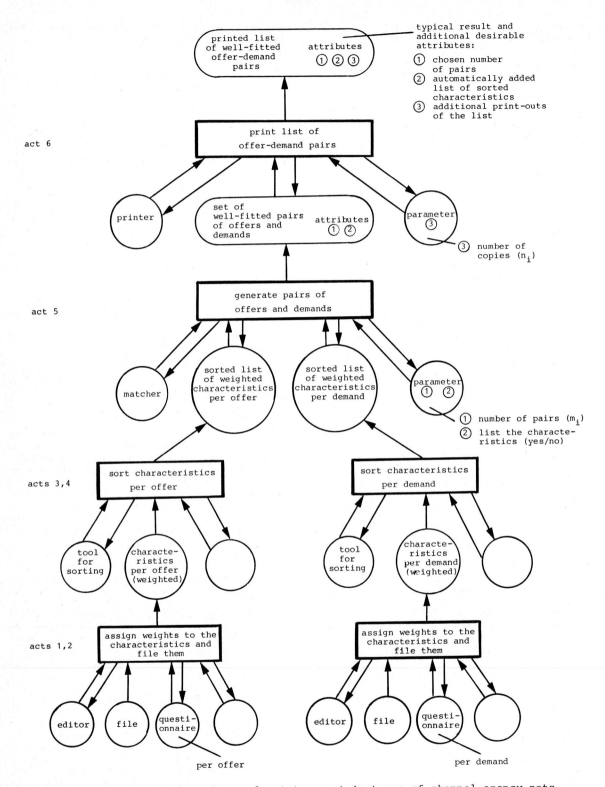

Figure 2: Six activities of a real estate agent in terms of channel-agency nets

A state (S) may be defined as a set consisting of 2-tuples of objects (O) and properties (P).

(1) $S = \{(O,P)^+\}$

Operators that transform a state of an object into a subsequent state may be represented as functions that are defined in the domains of states. One function is defined with respect to the tool (t), additional functions may be defined with respect to each value (v) of a 'parameter' (pa_v).

(2) $t \quad : S \longrightarrow S$
(3) $pa_v : S \longrightarrow S$

Figure 2 illustrates a set of work acts (acts 1 to 6) of a real estate agent.

The INITIAL STATE (S_I) of each work act is indicated as a set of pairs of initial objects (O_{I1}, O_{I2}, ... , O_{In}) associated with properties (P_{I1}, P_{I2}, ... , P_{In}):

(4) $S_I = \{(O_{I1}, P_{I1}), (O_{I2}, P_{I2}), \\ \dots , (O_{In}, P_{In})\}$

Example: For act 5 (fig. 2) the inital state may be represented as:

(5) $S_I = $ {(list of characteristics
per offer, P_{I1}),
(list of characteristics
per demand, P_{I2})} .

PROPERTIES of an initial object may be divided into two classes

- depending on whether the properties are required by the tool to work properly (necessary properties, P_n), or
- depending on whether an object has additional properties that result from former working steps (additional properties, P_a).

Additional properties are not required by the tool, but they also have no definite influence on the application of the tool.

Consequently, properties of an initial object may be represented as 2-tuple:

(6) $P_I = (P_n, P_a)$

Example: for act 5 (fig.2) the properties of the initial objects may be represented as:

(7) $P_{I1} = (\{$ weighted $\}, \{$ sorted $\})$
$P_{I2} = (\{$ weighted $\}, \{$ sorted $\})$

The matcher as a tool requires objects involving necessary properties, i.e., "weighted characteristics"; the additional properties, i.e., "characteristics being sorted" are indifferent to the application of the matcher.

The GOAL STATE (S_R) consists of the set of pairs of resulting objects ($O_{R1}, O_{R2}, \dots , O_{Rn}$) associated with properties ($P_{R1}, P_{R2}, \dots , P_{Rn}$):

(8) $S_R = \{(O_{R1},P_{R1}),(O_{R2},P_{R2})\}$

Example: for act 5 (fig.2) the goal state may be represented as:

(9) $S_R = $ {(set of pairs of offers
and demands, P_R)}

The set of properties (P_R) of a resulting object may be divided into three classes:

P_C CHARACTERISTIC PROPERTIES of a resulting object; these properties are defined by means of the "instrumental relationship" that holds between the tool and the result of its application;

P_A the ATTRIBUTES of a resulting object; they are determined by the "instrumental relationship" that holds between the given parameters of a tool and the result of its application.

P_H HEREDITARY PROPERTIES; this set of properties is a subset of the set of additional properties (P_a) pertaining to the initial object. Whether they are inherited depends on the "productive relationship" that is defined between the initial object and the resulting object, indicating such properties which are propagated unchanged (or reproduced) .

From this it follows:

(10) $P_R = (P_C, P_A, P_H)$ with $P_H \subseteq P_a$

Example: for act 5 (fig.2) the properties of the resulting object may be represented as:

(11) $P_C = \{$ well fitted $\}$,
$P_A = \{$ chosen number of pairs,
automatically added list
of characteristics $\}$
$P_H = \{$ sorted $\}$

The resulting object of act 5 (fig.2) involves one hereditary property due to the "productive relationship" between the initial object(s) and the resulting objects(s). One type of productive relationship is indicated by the fact that the sets of properties are not disjoint. Thus, the set of hereditary properties has to be represented explicitly by means of a productive relationship.

According to these definitions the tool and the parameters of a task may be defined as functions that transform states. The tool establishes a function that relates an initial state (S_I) to an INTERMEDIATE STATE (S_R'). It is important that this intermediate state is not the goal state because the effect of the parameters has not yet been taken into consideration. The parameters establish an additional function for each of its values that relate an intermediate state (produced by a tool) to a goal state (S_R).

$$
\begin{aligned}
t: S_I &\longrightarrow S_R' \\
t(S_I) &= S_R' \\
t(S_I) &= t(\{(O_I, P_I)\}) \\
&= t(\{(O_{I1}, (P_{n1}, P_{a1})), ==> \text{matcher}(\{(\text{list of characteristics per offer}, \\
&\qquad\qquad\qquad\qquad\qquad\qquad\qquad (\{\text{sorted , weighted}\})), \\
&\quad (O_{I2}, (P_{n2}, P_{a2}))\}) \qquad (\text{list of characteristics per demand}, \\
&\qquad\qquad\qquad\qquad\qquad\qquad\qquad (\{\text{sorted}\}, \{\text{weighted}\}))\}) \\
&= \{(O_R, (P_C, \emptyset, P_H))\} \quad ==> \qquad \{(\text{set of pairs of offers and demands}, \\
&\qquad\qquad\qquad\qquad\qquad\qquad\qquad (\{\text{well fitted}\}, \\
&\qquad\qquad\qquad\qquad\qquad\qquad\qquad\quad \emptyset , \\
&\qquad\qquad\qquad\qquad\qquad\qquad\qquad \{\text{sorted}\}))\} \\
&= S_R' \qquad \text{with } S_R' \text{ beeing an intermediate state.}
\end{aligned}
$$

Taking into account the effect of the parameter values it follows:

$$
\begin{aligned}
pa_v &: S_R' \longrightarrow S_R \\
pa_v(S_R') &= S_R \\
pa_v(S_R') &= pa_v(\{(O_R, (P_C, \emptyset, P_H))\}) \\
&= \{(O_R, (P_C, P_A, P_H))\} \quad ==\} \quad \{(\text{set of pairs of offers and demands}, \\
&\qquad\qquad\qquad\qquad\qquad\qquad\qquad (\{\text{well fitted}\}, \\
&\qquad\qquad\qquad\qquad\qquad\qquad\qquad \{\text{choosen number of pairs}\}, \\
&\qquad\qquad\qquad\qquad\qquad\qquad\qquad \{\text{sorted}\}))\} \\
&= S_R \qquad \text{with } S_R \text{ being the goal state.}
\end{aligned}
$$

The whole application of a tool, i.e., the execution of an activity may be described as the concatenation of the functions mentioned above.

$$
\begin{aligned}
a_v &= pa_v \circ t: S_I \longrightarrow S_R \\
a_v(S_I) &= (pa_v \circ t)(S_I) \\
&= pa_v(t(S_I)) \\
&= pa_v(S_R') = S_R
\end{aligned}
$$

The formal representation of the structural aspect of work provides the data base which is available for an inference mechanism. Additionally, the user knows a lot of heuristics that are worth representing in a "knowledge base". This kind of knowedge helps to ask for the reasons of a real estate agent's requirements. Rules representing heuristics of his exception handling can be formulated. A general rule (R1) for EXCEPTION HANDLING may be described by the real estate agent as follows:

R1: IF an exception with reference to a requirement exists,
THEN precautions have to be taken to handle the exception with reference to that requirement.

Rules (R2, R3) for a specific kind of exception may be formulated:

R2: IF no demand has been found for an offer during a fixed period of time
THEN an exception exists with reference to the requirement that offers must be negotiated in a short time.

R3: IF precautions have to be taken to handle the exception with respect to the requirement that offers must be negotiated in a short time
THEN try to attract demands by means of an advertisement, OR
simulate the offer's characteristics in order to find fitting demands.

Further alternatives of exception handling may be added during the problem analysis of the application domain. Another case of exception handling may result into rules as follows:

R4: IF no offers have been found for a demand in a fixed period of time

THEN an exception exists with reference to the requirement that the real estate agent wants to refer back to the client if the demand dates to a certain time in the past.

R5: IF precautions have to be taken to handle the exception with respect to the requirement that the real estate agent wants to refer back to the client if the demand dates to a certain time in the past

THEN ask for offers that fit to a certain degree, AND deliver these offers to the client in order to refer back.

The knowledge engineering approach implies no preferences for rules to be assembled. Even contradictory rules are not prevented from entering the knowledge base. Thus, the knowledge engineer has the opportunity to gather various facets of a problem domain without prejudice to a later design decision.

2.3 The procedure

The knowledge engineering approach comprises knowledge acquisition, knowledge representation and knowledge maintenance as tasks to be performed. Knowledge is manufactured by means of techniques. Firstly, one needs a technique to elicitate the expert's knowledge. "Experience has also taught us that much of this knowledge is private to the expert, not because he is unwilling to share publicly how he performs, but because he is unable. He knows more than he is aware of knowing." [9]. The same is true to the user as an expert of an application domain.

Therefore, we INTERVIEW him about those facts which are relevant to our model of the structural aspects of a work act. The model of a work act serves as a practical guide to organize the interviews. The interviewer needs a multi-level strategy for interviewing, so as to prevent himself from being overwhelmed by minor facts. Usually, the user tells about work activities in terms of verbs and nouns on different levels of abstraction. The interviewer asks for preconditions and postconditions of work activities so as to establish a link between these facts which refer to a productive relationship. Additionally, the interviewer tries to gather further facts associated with each work activity: tools, parameters, properties,

attributes; he thus gathers data that refer to instrumental relationships. The raw material consists of all these data. They can be submitted to a data base.

If the user explains certain attributes of result objects we ask him for relationships which may exist between attributes and objectives of his company or his department, since attributes mostly reveal hidden strategies of the user to cope with the requirements of his organisational environment. Of particular interest are strategies for exception handling (heuristics). This knowledge will be represented in terms of rules and submitted to a knowledge base.

It is not difficult to elicit what the user does as his daily routine. Essentially, however, his expertise is characterized by knowledge about tricks and coping strategies for extraordinary work situations. The advantage of the knowledge engineering approach is that it is concentrated on this expertise. Besides the representation of typical work situations a large number of variants of these situations will be gathered and represented in terms of the parameters and values assigned to the tools. While discussing these cases with the user, further heuristics can be elicitated. They will also be represented in terms of rules. In contrast to the traditional approach that mainly analyzes the typical work flow, the knowledge engineering approach facilitates dealing with vague facts and peculiarities of a complex application case. Thus, the analysis of user's requirements can be improved.

Knowledge engineering is difficult. It is even almost impossible, if the knowledge engineer can not apply a model to map the gathered facts. Our paper is intended to provide a model for the DECLARATIVE DESCRIPTION of structural components of work acts to be assembled in a database. Relations between these facts are represented explicitly, so as to elicitate the user's heuristics. Supplements to the data base and the knowledge base are added without claiming to represent the application case completely.

3. Discussion

A formal representation as such does not automatically imply that the collection of facts is biased due to the analyst's point of view, for instance, the implementer's view. As a matter of fact, the underlying representation method has the most important influence on the validity of an analysis. The validity may decrease, if a method that suits to systems analysis is applied to problem analysis. The model of a working act as defined in section 2.1 is designed for psychological task analysis purposes, whereas techniques such as SADT, HIPO, PSL/PSA are intended to systems design. We suggest to separate task analysis from systems analysis.

We suggest to call our approach APPLICATION DOMAIN MODELLING instead of "systems analysis", since we claim to represent a significant part of the customer's/user's reality for the sake of user-developer communication. Significant are facts and heuristics of day-to-day work, particularly those requirements of ergonomic value. These data may provide a knowledge base helping the systems designer in his understanding of the application case. In addition, knowledge engineering may help the customer/user to formulate his requirements more precisely. This improves qualitatively the communication between users and designers.

The representation of user's work by knowledge engineering techniques is not intended to cope with one specific type of design or programming style, such as functional programming or object oriented design. However, we have not yet examined thoroughly whether our knowledge base really enables the designer to improve his understanding of an application domain. We do not know enough about the circumstances during a design process that make a knowledge engineering approach to modelling an application domain useful. These problems are for further investigations in existing project teams.

Another problem is whether our approach is cost effective. From expert systems development we know that knowledge acquisition is a very time-consuming task. However, we suppose that the additional effort caused by our knowledge engineering approach is justified through the predicted effect that the validity of application programs will be significantly improved. Currently, it is generally accepted that software products often do not meet the user's/customer's requirements.

Furthermore, benefit may accrue to both the developer and the customer in that an existing knowledge base is available for maintenance purposes as well as for the adaptation of the software to future requirements. It is well known that maintenance engineers have severe difficulties with the reconstruction of design decisions.

Knowledge representation can be assisted by software tools and methods that are available in the Artificial Intelligence Research community. This contrasts with a lack of DP tools to support conventional systems analysis. One may argue that a knowledge base implemented at the designer's work station can be more easily adapted to his needs than conventional diagram sheets.

The traditional approach to the design of computer systems rests with a group of EDP specialists. By means of computer assisted knowledge engineering techniques the customer and the potential users of a system can be better involved in the decisions about requirements. USER PARTICIPATION has been generally requested by most ergonomists. However, one has to provide a means for it.

4. References:

[1] Yourdon, E. and Constantine, L.J., Structured Design. Fundamentals of a Discipline of Computer Programs and System Designs (Prentice-Hall, Englewood Cliffs, 1979).

[2] Dzida, W., Valder, W., Advantages of work analysis during software development, Angewandte Informatik - Applied Informatics, (Vieweg Verlag, Braunschweig, 1984, to appear).

[3] Klix, F., On interrelationships between natural and artificial intelligence research, in: Klix, F. (ed.), Human and Artificial Intelligence (North-Holland, Amsterdam, 1979).

[4] Ross, D.T., Structured Analysis (SA): A language for communication ideas, IEEE Transactions on Software Engineering, Vol. SE-3, No.1 (1977) 16-34. [5] Swartout, W. and Balzer, R., On the inevitable intertwining of specification and implementation, Communications of the ACM (1982) 438-440.

[6] Darlington, J., Dzida, W. and Herda, S., The role of excursions in interactive systems, International Journal of Man-Machine Studies (1983) 101-112.

[7] Dörner, D, Problemlösen als Informationsverarbeitung (Kohlhammer, Stuttgart 1976).

[8] Aron, J.D., The Program Development Process, Part II, The Programming Team (Addison-Wesley, Reading, Massachusetts, 1983).

[9] Feigenbaum, E.A., The Art of Artificial Intelligence: I. Themes and case studies of knowledge engineering, Proceedings of the 5th International Joint Conference of Artificial Intelligence (1977) 1014-1029.

[10] Sowa, J.F., Conceptual Structures: Information Processing in Mind and Machine (Addison-Wesley, Reading, Massachusetts, 1984).

Human-Computer Interaction — INTERACT '84 / B. Shackel (ed.)
Elsevier Science Publishers B.V. (North-Holland)
© IFIP, 1985

KNOWLEDGE ENGINEERING FOR EXPERT SYSTEMS

Mildred L. G. Shaw

Department of Computer Science, York University,
4700 Keele Street, Downsview, Ontario, Canada M3J 1P3

The Japanese fifth generation computer development program is targeted on knowledge processing rather than information processing. Expert system developments have demonstrated that knowledge can be represented and processed to replicate human skills, but have also focused attention on the difficulties of knowledge engineering, of eliciting and representing human knowledge and its processing. This paper presents a system for interactive elicitation of expert knowledge that is based on a systemic psychological model of human knowledge acquisition and processing. The need for normative tests of such methodologies is emphasized and an experimental study studies on reproducing a standard business record-keeping methodology is described.

1. KNOWLEDGE ENGINEERING

The human-computer interface (HCI) plays an ever more important role in computer system design. In particular, the Japanese **Fifth Generation** proposal stresses the transition from information systems used by specialists to knowledge systems accessible by everyone [23]. This emphasis shows in the "conceptual diagram" of fifth generation systems with its 3 rings of hardware, software and human applications [23 p.29]. However, as Gaines [10] remarks in these Proceedings, one notable feature of this diagram is that the hardware and software rings are full of detailed architecture, but the human ring is not. Logically, that ring should contain a psychological architecture of the person that is relevant to HCI. It does not, probably because we have no such definitive structure. There is much candidate material in human information processing studies [20] but Norman, in summarizing the current state of **cognitive science**, notes that there are major gaps in the underlying theory [24].

There is already evidence that the fifth generation objectives are reasonable. Expert system developments have led to a number of reasonably domain-independent software support systems for the encoding and application of knowledge [22]. However, the lack of detail in the third ring, of an account of human knowledge acquisition and processing, has created problems in what Feigenbaum [6] terms **knowledge engineering**, the reduction of a large body of knowledge to a precise set of facts and rules. As Hayes-Roth, Waterman and Lenat note:
"Knowledge acquisition is a bottleneck in the construction of expert systems. The knowledge engineer's job is to act as a go-between to help an expert build a system. Since the knowledge engineer has far less knowledge of the domain than the expert, however, communication problems impede the process of transferring expertise into a program. The vocabulary initially used by the expert to talk about the domain with a novice is often inadequate for problem-solving; thus the knowledge engineer and expert must work together to extend and refine it. One of the most difficult aspects of the knowledge engineer's task is helping the expert to structure the domain knowledge, to identify and formalize the domain concepts." [16].
We need to understand more about the nature of expertise in itself [15] and to able to apply this knowledge to the elicitation of expertise in specific domains.

The problem of knowledge elicitation from a skilled person is well-known in the literature of psychology. Bainbridge [1] has reviewed the difficulties of verbal de-debriefing and notes that there is no necessary correlation between verbal reports and mental behavior, and that many psychologists feel strongly that verbal data are useless. However, this remark must be taken in the context of experimental psychologists working within a positivist, behavioral paradigm. Other schools of psychology have developed techniques for making use of verbal interaction, for example through interviewing techniques that attempt to by-pass cognitive defenses, including those resulting from automization of skilled behavior. Welbank [38] has reviewed many of these techniques in the context of knowledge engineering.

This paper describes systemic and psychological foundations for a model of human knowledge representation, acquisition and processing, that can be used to fill in the third ring, and has been made operational through computer programs for interactive knowledge elicitation. Some experiments on validating these techniques applied to knowledge engineering for business record keeping are briefly described.

2. DISTINCTION-MAKING AND PERSONAL CONSTRUCTS

Clinical psychology is the prime source of literature on techniques for by-passing cognitive defenses. In particular, Kelly's **Personal Construct Psychology** (PCP) is significant because it develops a complete psychology of both the normal and abnormal, which has strong systemic foundations [11] and has been operationalized through computer programs [29]. PCP models a person as using **personal constructs** as distinctions made about experience:

"transparent templets which he creates and then attempts to fit over the realities of which the world is composed." [17]

and emphasizes the fallible use of constructs as a basis for knowledge acquisition:

"Constructs are used for predictions of things to come, and the world keeps rolling on and revealing these predictions to be either correct or misleading. This fact provides a basis for the revision of constructs and, eventually, of whole construct systems." [17]

In 1955 when Kelly developed his theory there was neither the mathematics to formalize it nor the computer technology to operationalize it. Despite this, PCP has developed to become a major psychological theory [21] and to provide a variety of techniques [30] used in clinical [35], educational [26] and managerial [29] psychology. In recent years strong links with system theory have developed that give formal foundations for PCP. Brown bases his logical system in **Laws of Form** on the notion underlying personal constructs of **making a distinction**:

"The theme of this book is that a universe comes into being when a space is severed or taken apart...By tracing the way we represent such a severance, we can begin to reconstruct, with an accuracy and coverage that appear almost uncanny, the basic forms underlying linguistic, mathematical, physical and biological science, and can begin to see how the familiar laws of our own experience follow inexorably from the original act of severance." [3].

Gaines derives the foundations of system theory using a similar approach:

"A system is what is distinguished as a system... In this lies the essence of systems theory: that to distinguish some entity as being a system is a necessary and sufficient criterion for its being a system and this is uniquely true for systems... The Oxford English Dictionary has it that a system is 'a group, set or aggregate of things, natural or artificial, forming a connected or complex whole.' One set of things is treated as distinct from another and it is that which gives them their coherence; it is that also which increases their complexity by giving them one more characteristic than they had before - that they have now been distinguished." [8].

Varela [37] extended Brown's logic to cover self-referential systems using a construction based on Russell's paradox. Kohout and Pinkava [19] showed that both systems could be embedded in a logical system that was consistent and complete. Gaines [9] has given a framework for these systems that encompasses modal, probability and fuzzy logics, and does not lead to inconsistency when unrestricted predication is allowed in set theory [39]. Quinlan [27] has shown recently that the constraint systems of such non-truth-functional logics may be used as a basis for improved inference in expert systems using uncertain rules and data.

Distinctions are not just static partitions of experience. They may be operations: actions in psychological terms; processes in computational terms. This shows in Goguen's [13] category-theoretic formulation of the logics, Ralescu's [28] application of these to a general theory of modeling, and Goguen's [14] development of a **OBJ**, a category-theoretic programming language. The role of distinctions at the base level of all models is evident in Klir's [18] hierarchy of modeling:

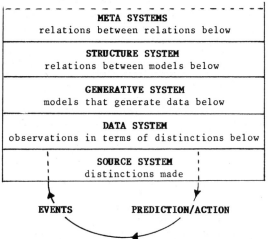

Fig.1. Epistemological hierarchy of a personal scientist

The loop from events through distinctions up through the modeling hierarchy and then down again to predictions and actions is one that I have termed the **personal scientist** [29]. Note that the upper levels of modeling are totally dependent on the system of distinctions, or personal constructs, used to express experience through the source system. Klir developed this hierarchy for work on symbolic modeling systems and Gaines [7] has shown that it forms a basis for general knowledge acquisition algorithms.

These systemic, psychological and computational foundations for a model of human cognition based on personal constructs lead to the hypothesis that the key to expertise is in the distinctions which the expert is making. The following sections examine techniques for eliciting these distinctions.

3. ELICITING CONSTRUCTS: SOFT SYSTEMS ANALYSIS

The difficulty with eliciting the hierarchy of distinctions, or constructs, of an expert is the lack of a conceptual framework that can be expressed and used in a dialog between expert and knowledge engineer. Checkland [4] has termed this a problem of **soft systems analysis** and emphasized the importance of the analyst not bringing his own preconceptions to the problem domain. He has developed a number of techniques for soft systems analysis, starting with a structuring of the stages involved:

1: **The Problem Situation - Unstructured**
2: **The Problem Situation - Expressed**
3: **Root Definitions of Relevant Systems**
4: **Making and Testing Conceptual Models**
5: **Comparing Conceptual Models with Reality**
6: **Determining Feasible, Desirable Changes**
7: **Action to Improve the Problem Situation**

Fig. 2. Stages in Soft Systems methodology

Checkland's study of Stage 3, **root definitions** of relevant systems is particularly interesting because it emphasizes the pluralism of systems analysis, what Kelly has termed **constructive alternativism**, that it is important to examine the problem from a number of viewpoints. These may be seen as forming a nested set to which Checkland gives the mnemonic CATWOE:

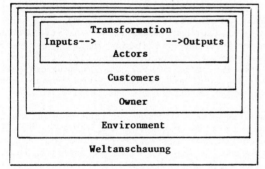

Fig. 3. Root Definitions of Relevant Systems

The system is defined through a **Transformation** carried out by people who are the **Actors** within it; it affects beneficially or adversely other people who are its **Customers** and there is some agency with power of existence over it who is its **Owner**; it has to exist within outside constraints forming its **Environment** and the whole activity of system definition takes place within an ethos or **Weltanschauung** that affects our views of it. Basden [2] has noted the utility of Checkland's analysis in developing expert systems, and I have shown how the techniques outlined in this paper may be applied to operationalizing it [33].

Applying the analysis to an expert system for oil exploration, we consider a **transformation** to which the **inputs** are survey data and the **outputs** are decisions to drill. The **actors** are

experts concerned with making these decisions. Their **customers** are oil companies. The **owner** of the problem represents the value system and, as usual in soft systems analysis, there are several choices: the managers, directors and owners of the oil company are possibilities, as are its customers and the government that taxes it. They have differing perceptions of the problem, risk/reward ratios, and so on. The **environment** is the physical, geographic and economic world within which oil extraction takes place, and the **weltanschauung** consists of energy policies, pollution concerns, and so on. These are the considerations which knowledge engineering has to take into account.

Checkland's methodology structures the task of knowledge engineering and provides techniques that are widely applicable. However, it leaves the burden of analysis with a person, and has no obvious operational form as a computer program. The next sections show how the analysis can be given these features.

4. ELICITING CONSTRUCTS: CONVERSATION THEORY

What is required to operationalize soft systems analysis is a theory of the way in which different viewpoints at different levels come together in an overall system of knowledge. Pask's **conversation theory** provides the basis for this and has been applied by Coombs and Alty [5] to the development of expert systems. Pask introduces the notion of a **P-Individual** or **psychologically characterized individual** in distinction to that of an **M-Individual** or **mechanically characterized individual**. He notes that an M-Individual is:
    "a human being (or his brain) as a
    biologically self-replicating system",
whereas:
    "a P-Individual...has many of the properties
    ascribed by anthropologists to a role, in
    society or industry, for example. A P-
    Individual is also a procedure and, as such,
    is run or executed in some M-Individual" [25]
He notes that while **an M-Individual may support many P-Individuals**, i.e. a person may play many roles, **a P-Individual may also be distributed over many M-Individuals**, i.e. a social unit may require the interplay of several persons.

In terms of the discussion of Sections 2 and 3 we may view P-Individuals as cross sections of modeling hierarchies interfaced to the world through personal constructs. This gives a coherent systemic framework for the relations between the multiple viewpoints discussed in Section 4. For example, Fig. 4 shows John, a person with a number of roles. He has formed P-Individuals as a husband, a sales VP of his company, a backpacker and a fisherman. The **personal scientist** or process which is John as a husband, uses operators to make construct-forming distinctions. They are distinctions about perception, about models, about values, about action. It is with the formation of these constructs that a P-Individual comes into being. John uses different constructs when he is in the role of husband from when he is in the role of fisherman, but some of the constructs he uses in the role of fisherman are also used in the role of backpacker and we show this as overlapping P-Individuals.

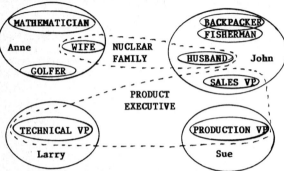

Fig. 4: P-Individuals formed by Groups

Fig. 4 includes some of John's associates: Anne is his wife, a mathematician and a golfer; Larry is the technical VP in John's company, and Sue is production VP. Sometimes John is acting with the others as a joint P-Individual that has some constructs shared between them and others that arise from only one. For example, John and Anne form a nuclear family: a P-Individual which has legal rights, behavior, concepts and language which are not those of either party alone. The product executive of the company is a P-Individual which has behavior, authority, responsibility, and language which is unique to the entity and not that of any one of its participants.

As expected from soft systems analysis, Pask's theory of multiple-person P-Individuals shows that expertise may not reside in one person. In developing an expert system for product development in a company we have to take into account all the actors shown in the product executive of Fig. 4, the objectives set by the problem owner, the constraints of the environment in which they operate, and the overall ethos for the development.

I have shown the interaction of conversation theory and soft systems analysis with personal construct psychology and how this provides a basis for computer programs for knowledge elicitation. The next section outlines briefly some computer techniques for doing this.

5. ELICITING CONSTRUCTS: PEGASUS AND SOCIOGRIDS

PLANET [31] consists of a suite of programs for eliciting personal constructs, analysing construct systems, and the common and disparate aspects of the systems of a number of people. PEGASUS [29] asks the user for a purpose and for elements that relate to it, and elicits different ways of construing these elements. It analyses the construct system continuously and feeds back enquiries based on this analysis

to elicit further elements and constructs. The programs have been used for a wide variety of studies in management, education and clinical psychology [26,29,30,35] and recently for knowledge engineering for expert systems [34].

One of the problems of evaluating any methodology for knowledge engineering is to have some clear-cut test cases where the conceptual framework of experts has been both elicited and validated. Sowa [36] describes one such case where the record keeping needs of a business can be prescribed through the BIAIT analysis technique based on seven features of the form:

Does the supplier bill the customer, or does the customer pay cash?
Does the supplier deliver the product at some time in the future, or does the customer take the order with him?

He notes that these features "seem almost obvious once they are presented, but finding the right features and categories may take months or years of analysis."

Experiments have been done with businessmen and students at different stages in accountancy careers to determine whether PLANET elicits the BIAIT structure. The purpose of the elicitation was "Examining business record keeping". Typical elements were "Selling car insurance" or "Being agent for home purchase." The constructs elicited included all those of BIAIT such as "take -- deliver", but also other such as "low-cost -- expensive." A SOCIOGRIDS analysis of the preliminary results has been used to determine whether the BIAIT construct system is construed more readily by those with more business and accounting experience, and this shows up clearly in the results [32].

Thus, empirical studies indicate that personal construct elicitation methodology is an effective knowledge engineering technique. An experiment is now being carried out using fuzzy entailment analysis [30] to generate decision trees for record keeping from the data.

6. CONCLUSIONS

The term **expert system** has come to be applied to interactive systems which provide one person with access to another person's skills encoded in some way. Although the concepts and terminology are of recent origin, many interactive computer systems in the past have been developed with these objectives in mind and the recent focus of attention in this area is the culmination of much HCI research [12]. This paper has noted the relatively weak foundations for describing the human part of systems compared with those for hardware and software. It has outlined systemic, logical, psychological and computational approaches to providing these foundations, which have been used to develop interactive computer programs for knowledge engineering.

7. REFERENCES

[1] Bainbridge, L., Verbal reports as evidence of the process operator's knowledge, **International Journal of Man-Machine Studies**, 11(4) (1979) 411-436.

[2] Basden, A., On the application of expert systems, **International Journal of Man-Machine Studies**, 19(5) (1983) 461-477.

[3] Brown, G.S., **Laws of Form** (George Allen & Unwin, London, 1969).

[4] Checkland, P., **Systems Thinking, Systems Practice** (Wiley, Chichester, UK, 1981).

[5] Coombs, M. and Alty, J., Expert systems: an alternative paradigm, **International Journal of Man-Machine Studies**, 20(1) (1984).

[6] Feigenbaum, E.A., Knowledge Engineering: the Applied Side of Artificial Intelligence, **Report STAN-CS-80-812** (Department Computer Science, Stanford University, 1980).

[7] Gaines, B.R., System identification, approximation and complexity, **International J. of General Systems**, 3 (1977) 145-174.

[8] Gaines, B.R., General systems research: quo vadis ?, in Gaines, B.R. (ed.), **General Systems 1979** (Society for General Systems Research, Kentucky, 1980) 1-9.

[9] Gaines, B.R., Precise past - fuzzy future, **International Journal of Man-Machine Studies**, 19(1) (1983) 117-134.

[10] Gaines, B.R., From ergonomics to the Fifth Generation: 30 years of human-computer interaction studies, **Proceedings of INTERACT'84** (North-Holland, Amsterdam, 1984)

[11] Gaines, B.R. and Shaw, M.L.G., A programme for the development of a systems methodology of knowledge and action, in Reckmeyer, W.J. (ed.), **General Systems Research and Design: Precursors and Futures** (Soc. Gen. Systems Research, 1981) 255-264.

[12] Gaines, B.R. and Shaw, M.L.G., **The Art of Computer Conversation: A New Medium for Communication** (Prentice Hall, New Jersey, 1984).

[13] Goguen, J.A., Concept representation in natural and artificial languages: axioms, extensions and applications for fuzzy sets, in Mamdani, E.H. and Gaines, B.R. (eds.), **Fuzzy Reasoning and its Applications** (Academic Press, London, 1981).

[14] Goguen, J.A. and Meseguer, J., Programming with parametrized abstract objects in OBJ, in **Theory and Practice of Programming Technology** (North-Holland, Amsterdam, 1983).

[15] Hawkins, D., An analysis of expert thinking, **International Journal of Man-Machine Studies**, 18(1) (1983) 1-47.

[16] Hayes-Roth, F., Waterman, D.A. and Lenat, D.B. (eds.), **Building Expert Systems** (Addison-Wesley, Massachusetts, 1983).

[17] Kelly, G.A., **The Psychology of Personal Constructs** (Norton, New York, 1955).

[18] Klir, G.J., Identification of generative structures in empirical data, **International Journal of General Systems**, 3 (1976) 89-104.

[19] Kohout, L.J. and Pinkava, V., The algebraic structure of the Spencer Brown and Varela Calculi, **International Journal of General Systems**, 6(3) (1980) 155-171.

[20] Lindsay, P.H. and Norman, D.A., **Human Information Processing** (Academic Press, New York, 1977).

[21] Mancuso, J.R. and Adams-Webber, J.R. (eds.), **The Construing Person** (Praeger, New York, 1982).

[22] Michie, D. (ed.), **Expert Systems in the Micro Electronic Age** (Edinburgh University Press, Edinburgh, 1979).

[23] Moto-oka, T. (ed.), **Fifth Generation Computer Systems** (North-Holland, Amsterdam, 1982).

[24] Norman, D., Twelve issues for cognitive science, **Cognitive Sci.**, 4(1) (1980) 1-32.

[25] Pask, G., **Conversation, Cognition and Learning** (Elsevier, Amsterdam, 1975).

[26] Pope, M.L. and Keen, T.R., **Personal Construct Psychology and Education** (Academic Press, London, 1981).

[27] Quinlan, J.R., Inferno: a cautious approach to uncertain inference, **Computer Journal**, 26(3) (1983) 255-269.

[28] Ralescu, D., A system theoretic view of social identification, in **Improving the Human Condition: Quality and Stability in Social Systems** (Society for General Systems Research, Kentucky, 1979).

[29] Shaw, M.L.G., **On Becoming a Personal Scientist** (Academic Press, London, 1980).

[30] Shaw, M.L.G. (ed.), **Recent Advances in Personal Construct Technology** (Academic Press, London, 1981).

[31] Shaw, M.L.G., PLANET: some experience in creating an integrated system for repertory grid applications on a microcomputer, **International Journal of Man-Machine Studies**, 17(3) (1982) 345-360.

[32] Shaw, M.L.G., Interactive knowledge elicitation, **Proceedings of Session 84** (Canadian Information Proc. Soc., 1984).

[33] Shaw, M.L.G. and Gaines, B.R., Eliciting the real problem, in Wedde, H. (ed.), **International Working Conference on Model Realism,** (Pergamon Press, Oxford, 1983) 100-111.

[34] Shaw, M.L.G. and Gaines, B.R., A computer aid to knowledge engineering, in **Proceedings of Expert Systems 83** (British Computer Society, London, 1983) 263-271.

[35] Shepherd, E. and Watson, J.P. (eds.), **Personal Meanings** (John Wiley, London, 1982).

[36] Sowa, J.F., **Conceptual Structures: Information Processing in Mind and Machine** (Addison-Wesley, Massachusetts, 1984).

[37] Varela, F.J., A calculus for self-reference, **International Journal of General Systems**, 2 (1975) 5-24.

[38] Welbank, M., **A Review of Knowledge Acquisition Techniques for Expert Systems** (Martlesham Consultancy Services, BTRL, Ipswich, 1983).

[39] White, R.B., The consistency of the axiom of comprehension in the infinite-valued predicate logic of Lukasiewicz, **Journal of Philosophical Logic**, 8 (1979) 509-534.

Human-Computer Interaction — INTERACT '84 / B. Shackel (ed.)
Elsevier Science Publishers B.V. (North-Holland)
© IFIP, 1985

MAPS FOR COMPUTER WAYFINDING

Ila J. Elson

IBM Entry Systems Division
P.O. Box 1328
Boca Raton, Florida 33432

The purpose and design of a knowledge based system is described and
compared to previous styles and methods for helping computer users.
This expert system answers a user's questions about the various
software entities stored in his computing environment.

1. INTRODUCTION

Maps enable people to operate efficiently
in spatial settings. They tell us where
certain valued things are and how to get
to where they are. The New York City
subway system is a spatial setting in
which the users acquire most of their
information through a map [1]. The
effectiveness of this system depends on
the ability of its users to determine
their own location and the pattern of
actions necessary to take them to their
destination. This can be a difficult
spatial orientation task because the City
has constructed many miles of route,
hundreds of subway stations, and dozens
of train routes and transfer points.

Computer users also enter a spatial
environment with complex properties.
This spatial environment stores numerous
programming products, databases and other
useful tools in various forms. The
usability of the total system depends on
the ability of its users to determine what
the valued things are and how to get
access to them. In contrast to the subway system, users in this spatial
setting acquire most of their information
through communication with others. There
are no maps.

The purpose of this paper is to encourage
development of software maps for computer
systems. This is accomplished in three
ways. First, I describe what a software
map is by illustrating how it differs
from other styles and methods for helping
computer users. Then several computing
environments and software products are
identified as excellent recipients for
software maps. Lastly, the map system
design is discussed. This knowledge
based system is predicated on the needs
and characteristics of people reaching
destinations.

2. WHAT IS A SOFTWARE MAP?

Wayfinding refers to the process involved
in reaching a destination. For a computer user this process is described via
a software map. This type of information is not found in other help systems
(see [2] for a review of online help
systems). They generally instruct the
user in the usage of specific commands
or sections of a particular programming
product. A wayfinding help system
(software map) instructs the user in the
usage of the total computer system by
relating the various software products
and databases. This is the major
difference between a software map and
other help techniques. This distinction
is reflected in Table 1 as the user's
computing environment or scope of operation. In other words, a software map
gives locations and attributes of various
software entities in a homogeneous
computer network.

A software map can differ from other
help techniques with respect to style
and method too. The evolving styles and
methods for helping computer users are
illustrated in Table 1. Style simply
refers to the manner of expressing help
while method refers to the procedure or
process for attaining that help. A
software map, then, is a future user
interface technique that can be
characterized to have a natural style
using an expert system methodology [3].

3. TRENDS IN THE PERSONAL COMPUTING
MARKET

There are several applications for
software maps. The reason for this is
primarily due to the recent trends in
the personal computing market. The
increased interest in personal computing
and communications is leading to

Table 1

STYLES AND METHODS FOR HELPING COMPUTER USERS

| User's Computing Environment (scope) | User Interface Techniques | | | | | |
| | Past | | Present | | Future | |
	Style	Method	Style	Method	Style	Method
Application software	terse	one-line message	friendlier	2-3 line meaningful messages		
				graphics, icons		
			structured	indexes, menus, query by depth and by example		
			tutorials	exercises, question and answer		
			consistent	integrating major tasks in one product	innovative	
System software	terse	one-line message	coordinated	high-level managers and shells	simpler	macro user interfaces
			flexible	windowing display technology		
Homogenous computer network (e.g., a business, a university, a public data service)	few online techniques		informative	news facilities	natural	expert systems
			exhaustive	online documentation	selective	dynamic books
					appealing	animation, graphics
Heterogenous computer networks	few online techniques		incompatible	gateway facilities (mostly experimental)	unified	intelligent gateway facilities

increasing numbers and varieties of software products, networks and informational
databases. In other words, complex
spatial environments are beginning to
emerge.

Two computing environments that would
benefit from the installation of a software map are universities and corporations.
Two software products that need this help
system are communications networks and
videotex services. Researchers in these
areas [4,5] have recognized the need for
software maps and are pursuing solutions.
This paper now discusses one method of
solving the computer user's wayfinding
problems.

4. MAP SYSTEM DESIGN

Wayfinding can be viewed as being composed of three major cognitive processes:
first, a process leading to spatial
information comprising the various aspects
of obtaining, accumulating and structuring
information; second, a process leading
to plans of actions in the form of decision
plans; and third, a process leading to
spatial behavior [6]. There is little
empirical research into the wayfinding
problems of users in a computing environment. Rather, most empirical work has
focused on the wayfinding problems that
people experience in natural settings,
like cities, subway systems or the
wilderness. Still, the conclusions from
these studies [7] are helpful in understanding in general the needs and
characteristics of people reaching
destinations. The extrapolated findings
of these studies indicate that a knowledge
base for a software map must contain two
basic and complimentary types of information. These are the locations and the
attributes of software entities. The
locational information is designed to
answer the question, where are these
entities? The attributive information
tells users what kinds of entities are
available and why one would want to use
them. This is the kind of approach that
is needed to build a useful knowledge
based system with a natural language
interface.

Walker and Porto [8] have demonstrated
the feasibility of building useful
knowledge bases in the programming
language Prolog [9]. Their expert system
is designed to answer English questions
about some of the products supplied by a
garden store. This system thus tries
to match the knowledge of a storekeeper
who sells products such as domestic
pesticides and weed killers. The user of
this system gets answers to his questions
within one second. Some typical
questions are:

what products do you sell?
what is each product that you sell for?
what can I use to kill snails?

The job of a computer operations
assistant in a computing environment is
similar to that of a salesman in a garden
store. In this case, the products being
discussed are software housed in a computer. The user of this expert system,
dubbed the Wayfinder, could ask questions
of the following nature:

what software do you have?
what is each product for?
what can I use to write reports?
what can I use to keep a calendar?
where is product A stored?
who is an expert on product A?

These questions garner the basic types
of information that users need in
computer wayfinding.

The Wayfinder prototype system is being
implemented on the IBM Personal Computer
using micro-Prolog. Its job will be to
help people find their way around the
computing environment at the IBM
Boca Raton computing center. The internal
design of the syntactic and semantic
components of the English interface of
Wayfinder is modeled after the work of
Walker and Porto [8].

5. CONCLUSIONS

As computers become more powerful and
commonplace, wayfinding help systems
will become necessary for efficient
operation. All computer users, from
the novice to the veteran, can benefit
from the development of software maps
for computer systems.

6. REFERENCES

[1] Bronzaft, A. L., Dobrow, S. B.
and O'Hanlon, T. J. Spatial
orientation in a subway system,
Environment and Behavior, 8(4)
(1976) 575-594.

[2] Houghton, R. C. Online help
systems: A conspectus,
Communications of the ACM, 27(2)
(1984) 126-133.

[3] Walker, A. Data bases, expert
systems and Prolog, IBM Research
Report RJ 3870 (1983) San Jose, CA.

[4] Huckle, B. A. A proposal for
improving access to heterogeneous
computer networks, in Williams, M.
B. (ed.), Proceedings of the 6th
International Conference on Computer
Communications (North-Holland,
Amsterdam, 1982) 589-593.

[5] Engel, F. L., Andriessen, J. J. and
     Schmitz, H. J. R. What, where and
     whence: Means for improving
     electronic data access, Int. J.
     Man-Machine Studies, 18 (1983)
     145-160.

[6] Passini, R. Wayfinding: A
     conceptual framework, Man-
     Environment Systems 10(1) (1980)
     22-30.

[7] Downs, R. M. and Stea, D. Image and
     Environment (Aldine, Chicago, 1973).

[8] Walker, A. and Porto, A. KB01, a
     knowledge based garden store
     assistant, IBM Research Report
     RJ 3928 (1983) San Jose, CA.

[9] Clocksin, W. F. and Mellish, C. S.
     Programming in Prolog (Springer-
     Verlag, New York, 1981).

Human-Computer Interaction — INTERACT '84 / B. Shackel (ed.)
Elsevier Science Publishers B.V. (North-Holland)
© IFIP, 1985

TASKS, SKILLS AND KNOWLEDGE: TASK ANALYSIS FOR KNOWLEDGE BASED DESCRIPTIONS

Peter Johnson, Dan Diaper and John Long

Ergonomics Unit, University College London, 26 Bedford Way, London WC1, England

A method for deriving descriptions of knowledge from tasks is described. Knowledge descriptions constitute the basis of a syllabus specifying the training requirements of Information Technology (IT). Task analysis for Knowledge Descriptions (TAKD) is a method which is first used to generate descriptions of tasks, and then to reexpress the descriptions in terms of knowledge. The resulting knowledge descriptions consist of action/object pairs that when combined represent the knowledge content of tasks. The potential application of TAKD to other design problems is discussed and in particular to the design of the Human-Computer Interface and Intelligent Knowledge Based Systems.

1. Syllabus creation; the origin of a method

As part of research, designed to specify the training requirements of Information Technology (IT), we have developed a method for producing descriptions of knowledge. The aim was to create a unitary framework for an IT syllabus that nevertheless allowed trainers the necessary flexibility to design their own courses and materials. A more theoretically driven and empirical approach to syllabus design was desired, rather than a desk top exercise or committee decision. Emphasis was placed on the need to identify the kinds of IT tasks currently performed in training centres and at work and the knowledge needed to perform such tasks. Criteria applied to the syllabus included: variable training resources; varying trainee ability; differing levels of course; complete coverage of IT and; coherence across training centres (see Johnson, Diaper & Long; 1984, for a full discussion). Note that specifying the syllabus as a set of training tasks could lead to a prescription for a course that would not allow course designers the necessary flexibility to deal with varying local conditions. Identifying and describing the knowledge required to carry out IT tasks offerred a solution to this problem. Knowledge descriptions are not necessarily task prescriptive, since similar knowledge may be required by different tasks. Further, it can be assumed that transfer of training beyond the immediate training environment can be facilitated if the training involves similar knowledge common to a wide range of tasks. Knowledge descriptions, based on real tasks offer an alternative to subjective, expert or committee decisions which lack all empirical justification. Since knowledge underlies task performance, these descriptions can serve to generate varying tasks on different equipment, for students of all abilities. They provide a basis, given an appropriate psychological model, (Diaper, Johnson & Long; 1984), for predicting transfer of training. The procedure used to produce this knowledge based

syllabus was: (i) classify existing IT training material to find the range; (ii) interview employers, trainers and IT specialists to identify gaps in the range; (iii) select tasks to exemplify IT skills; (iv) analyse tasks; (v) identify the underlying knowledge in terms of actions and objects; (vi) classify the action and object knowledge; (vii) identify the classified action/object knowledge pairs used in each step of the tasks and; (viii) construct a syllabus composed of action/object knowledge specifications (n.b. objects include both physical and informational objects such as tools and commands; actions can be overt or covert such as keystrokes or decisions). The original task descriptions produced in step (iv) were in the form of a sequential plan, for example:

- turn on microcomputer.
- insert floppy disc into drive 0
- load the data-base program

A detailed specification of the action and object knowledge was derived from these plans. These descriptions were then combined to form generic lists of actions and objects. e.g.:

Actions	Objects
Insert..to, a, with	Computers
Select..a, from	Electronic Components
Check...a, with	Help Facilities

The actions and objects were then paired according to the requirements of a particular task statement. This syntax of action/object (A/O) pairs describes the knowledge requirements of each task statement. This formed a grammar like expression of the knowledge requirements of the tasks. e.g.

Task statement	A/O knowledge descriptions
-insert a floppy -->	insert a storage media
disc to drive 0	insert to a storage device
	select a storage device
	check a storage device

This approach to syllabus design led to a method of Task Analysis for Knowledge Descriptions (TAKD). The benefits of TAKD in this application were: (i) that it was able to specify explicitly the knowledge requirements of a particular task;

(ii) these descriptions were capable of being mapped on to other tasks; (iii) there was no prescription for training on a particular task; (iv) syllabus creation had an empirical basis; (v) because of (ii) above, in conjunction with a psychological model, it provided a basis for predicting how transfer of training could be maximised. The remainder of this paper identifies further potential uses for TAKD and discusses the relationship between TAKD and other methodologies that reference theories of knowledge. A method for carrying out the analysis is described and different methods of presenting the knowledge descriptions are cited.

2. The need for task descriptions.

The syllabus example shows one need for TAKD and one that can benefit training course designers. This section considers the needs of other kinds of designers. These include: the design of teams in which functions are allocated to different persons and; organizations in which functions are allocated to different sections. More recently, designers of interactive computer systems have shown a need for descriptions of tasks in order to design and evaluate systems and to ensure good human-computer interaction. Task descriptions are required at different stages in the system design cycle from evolving the user-supplier dialogue to maintaining and supporting the system. The evolution of computer applications and the need for good human-computer interaction has created a demand for knowledge based descriptions of human task performance.

2.1 Application changes. The use of computers in tasks is changing (e.g. control, design, manufacture, education and consultancy). Furthermore, within the range of applications, the nature of the tasks performed by computers varies considerably. Moreover, computers place varying demands on their users. There is a general trend for computers to carry out more of the routine parts of a complete task, leaving the user more time to devote to the less routine, more creative, imaginative or supervisory aspects. This trend places additional requirements on the designer for more efficient human-computer interfacing because the more creative aspects of tasks are usually more difficult to define explicitly. The aim of the designer is to produce a machine that performs its task well, enables the user to perform his/her tasks better and allows the user to interact with machines with minimal effort, time and error.

2.2 Better systems design. A system that offers good human-computer interaction requires the designer to take account of the users' model or image of the system. However, the reality is more complex. The designer needs to model the tasks performed by the computer system, the users and their interaction. Consequently, the designer requires a full description of the total task requirements of the computer, the users and the interaction of humans with the computer. With these descriptions the designer is then in a position to take account of the computer's and the users' tasks in his design of the interface. This will facilitate good human-computer interaction.

3. Why knowledge based descriptions?

In a training context, knowledge based descriptions provide a general, task independent specification of syllabus content. Task performance can be described in many different ways. Psychological descriptions of human abilities required by particular tasks are commonly used by the U.S. military in personnel selection. In contrast, "job analysis" focuses on the components of jobs and their requisite skills by classifying the basic or "generic" skills of a particular job. The main purpose of ability and job analyses is to provide a means of selecting or distinguishing people for specific tasks. The utility of such descriptions for other purposes, such as generating training courses or designing computer systems, may, then, be low. The system designer is not directly concerned with job or ability profiles although the latter may constrain the design. Of more utility, are descriptions of tasks that identify: the plan for carrying out a task; the concepts or knowledge required and; the interaction of different kinds of knowledge. This type of description enables the designer to identify explicitly how tasks are performed and what commonality exists between tasks in terms of their knowledge requirements and their plans for execution. This is the advantage of knowledge descriptions.

3.1 Changes in task requirements. A consequence of the increase in the application of computers to human tasks is that the types of tasks being undertaken by computers are becoming more complex and more cognitive. For example, the electronic typewriter was developed to make the manual activities of typing on a mechanical device less effortful and thus improve overall typing efficiency. Recently, the word processor's capability to manipulate text, has further reduced the effort of document production. The design of the electronic typewriter was based on a model (perhaps implicit and ill-defined) of the biomechanical and anthropometric features of the hand plus some knowledge of digraph frequencies. Word processor design extended this model to include some knowledge of composing and editing different kinds of textual documents. Designers are implicitly extending this model to include the use of graphical information in documents.

These changes and extensions in the applications of computers represent a different class of tasks that require different kinds and levels of descriptions. For example, in a document creation task one level of the task might be to restructure the document by moving a paragraph from the begining to the end of the document, while a lower level description might be typing the appropriate commands on the word processor. Such descriptions essentially reflect different levels of a task's hierarchy.

3.2 Knowledge descriptions. For our research on syllabus creation, a particular form of task description was developed. This section considers other forms of task descriptions with respect to their ability to provide knowledge descriptions. Descriptions in terms of skills that are usually only adjectival (e.g. ease, effortlessness, fluency etc.) fail to identify the knowledge or the execution plan. Furthermore, describing a particular task's demands is too specific. Knowledge requirements are more appropriate and they generalise to other tasks. In the syllabus creation study, the action/object knowledge descriptions explicitly identified the conceptual requirements of the task. Taking another task, for instance, in the joinery industry, sand finishing the component parts of a staircase is a semi-automated process in which the operator is responsible for manually setting the sanding machine and feeding in the timber, checking its progress through the machine and then collecting the wood for further sanding or passing it on along the process line. Suppose the task demands are that the operator has to take off 80mm from the depth of an end rail and 1200mm of its width. To do this, the operator needs to be skilled at recognising the types of wood, judging the amount of wood to be sanded, identifying the appropriate grain of sanding belt, adjusting the position of the sanding bed etc. Such descriptions of the task are not sufficent to enable another (untrained) person to learn the task, since neither the concepts, nor their relations and execution plan, are identified. For similar reasons, a system designer would not be able to develop a machine to carry out all or part of the task currently performed by the human operator from these descriptions. Nor would such descriptions allow a similar task to be performed with different components of a staircase requiring a different degree of sanding and perhaps a different type of wood; in short, the task description is not generalisable. Instead, identifying the knowledge requirements and their relations for each element of the task plan would explicitly specify how the task could be performed and would generalise to other settings and finishing sizes of timber etc.

3.3 The development of IKBS's. A further development in computer use is the introduction of Intelligent Knowledge Based Systems (IKBS's). These are computer systems that possess a limited amount of intelligence in a particular domain of knowledge. One of the greatest potentials for TAKD is the development of IKBS's because TAKD produces knowledge descriptions that could be incorporated into an IKBS. In designing an IKBS, the designer and system builder must be able, at an early stage, to specify the knowledge to be incorporated in the IKBS. The system might be: a process plant controller; a decision support system; a diagnostic aid for the medical profession; or a computer based training facility in any number of areas. Ideally, as full an account as possible of the knowledge requirements for tasks within a domain is necessary. There are different approaches to this: protocol analysis; walk throughs; questionnaires (see Wellbank, 1983 for a review). The general problem of knowledge elicitation, is that of identifying the concepts and relations and how these are used to perform various tasks. This is what TAKD produced in the syllabus creation study. TAKD offers a unified approach that is suitable as an aid to IKBS design and development. Hakami & Newborn (1983) provide a good example of a case study of the development of an expert system for fault diagnosis in a process control application within a British Steel Corporation plant. The reported steps in the development of this system (known as ICLX) were : (i) the collection of actual fault data and the construction of a fault/symptom matrix; (ii) the development of a knowledge refining program; (iii) collecting further fault/symptom data by interviewing human experts; (iv) implementing the knowledge refining program and the fault/symptom data-base in a running system; (v) allowing human experts to interact with the system to enhance and increase the fault/symptom data-base and further evaluate the knowledge refining program. This is a well documented case history in which the importance of describing and evaluating the knowledge requirements of the domain are crucial at stages (i), (ii), (iii) & (v) above. The whole system ultimately depends on the success of this process. However, no formal methods appear to have been used or proposed.

4. Task Analysis in Perspective.
Given the importance of Task Analysis (TA) in the syllabus creation study and the development of TAKD from it, a brief discussion of TA follows. A perspective on TA can be obtained by considering the relationship between tasks, skills and knowledge and identifying the different elements in task descriptions. Finally, a relation between task analysis and knowledge descriptions is made.

4.1 Tasks, skills & knowledge. Task performance is often described in terms of skill and is usually an adjectival description of performance (e.g. smoothly, effortlessly etc.). Thus skills describe the quality of performance. Knowledge descriptions, as shown in the syllabus application, specify the concepts and plans necessary for carrying out a task. It is possible for the same task to be performed in a variety of ways and similar performance to be based on different knowledge. For example, in order to escape from a currently running program on a computer the user can press the <BREAK> key, issue a <QUIT> command or turn the machine-off. Each of these will achieve the objective of escaping from the current program, but the appropriateness may differ according to the particular circumstances. In order to be able to execute any of these operations, the user should ideally have knowledge of the operation, its consequences and the circumstances in which it can be appropriately applied.

4.2 Task Components. A job consists of a number of tasks that must be performed in order to achieve certain goals. For example, some of the tasks a doctor might perform include: diagnosing illnesses; prescribing treatments; and assessing recovery. Tasks are goal oriented behaviours that require the performance of certain actions with respect to particular objects in order to achieve goals. In diagnosing an illness then, a doctor may take a patient's temperature, blood pressure and ask questions about symptoms. Such activities involve sub-goals and sub-tasks so that when taking a person's blood pressure, the pressure cuff must be applied in the correct place, it must be pumped to an appropriate pressure and a reading must be taken. Consequently, there is a hierarchy of sub-tasks each requiring a particular activity to be performed. Duncan and Kelly (1983) refers to sequences of activities as the task plan. These plans, in some cases, may be well specified or invariant, with respect to the sequence of actions. However, even in such cases, it may still be possible to develop different strategies for executing the same plan. For example, a plan might involve moving a cursor to a particular point on a VDU screen. Different routes or ways of moving the cursor would involve different strategies to carry out the same plan. The individual elements of a plan can be represented as action/object mappings which are the concepts or knowledge necessary for performing an activity.

4.3 Task Analysis for Knowledge Descriptions.
This section discusses the relationship between TAKD as used in the syllabus creation study and a more general view of knowledge. Task analysis is one way of modelling behaviour that can be applied to many situations. For some purposes, such analyses need to contain descriptions of the knowledge required to perform the task. For example, in the syllabus creation study the training syllabus had to be independent of local resources and facilities and therefore could not be task specific. This was achieved by specifying the knowledge requirements from representative, exemplar tasks. In designing a human-computer interface, a well defined description of the human-computer interaction is required. This should be based on what the user and/or system must know in order to accomplish the task goal. For instance, the user might be expected to know how to use a mouse or a set of commands to achieve his/her goal of, for example, accessing a document in an office system. Thus, in order to access a message file, at an integrated office work station, the user may have to issue a series of commands to access the system, use a mouse to 'window' the message facility, and then issue further commands to access a message. The success of the human-computer interface is determined by the adequacy of the initial model of the knowledge requirements of the interaction and these can be identified and provided by task analysis. Knowledge can be expressed in different ways, such as procedural and declarative types of knowledge (Anderson, 1980). Procedural knowledge is taken to be knowledge about what to do with objects. For example, in operating a word

processor, procedural knowledge might be about how to: access a file; how to add or delete text and; how to move blocks of text about. In contrast, knowledge about the nature and contents of files or blocks of text would be classed as declarative knowledge. We question, however, whether people really possess declarative knowledge independently of their use of such knowledge (i.e. independent of procedural knowledge). An alternative view of knowledge adopted in TAKD, is to specify knowledge as comprising of actions and objects such that action/object pairs become operationally combined as the knowledge items. This can be likened to the view taken by Hayes-Roth, Klahr & Mostow (1981) in which "advice" is considered to consist of "concept definitions, behavioural constraints and performance heuristics". Concept definitions describe the elements of a problem domain and consist of actions or objects and their properties. Behavioural constraints are rules governing behaviour in a problem domain and performance heuristics describe ways of approaching a problem domain. There is a parallel here between Hayes-Roth et al's view of advice and the view of knowledge in TAKD described earlier. Action/object pairs are equivalent to concept definitions. Plans are similar to behavioural constraints and performance heuristics can be thought of as strategies that influence behavioural constraints. For example, in describing a game of cards, objects might include: deck; card; hand; suit etc. The actions might include: deal; take; follow etc. The action/object pairs would then specify the knowledge (concept definitions) by such combinations as: deal card; follow suit; take card etc. Plans (behavioural constraints) in Whist, for example, might include take all tricks, whereas strategies (performance heuristics) would be more involved with the order of playing the cards (e.g. trump cards first).

5. Methods of analysing tasks.
In the syllabus creation study, a particular technique of task analysis was employed. In this section, this technique is developed further. In a task analysis, the observer is faced with three major issues: what information is needed; from where can information be obtained; and how can information be obtained? A general strategy is for the observer to approach each source with a view to supplementing, confirming or amending information gathered elsewhere. The main source from which information about tasks can be obtained is a set of people. Other sources include manuals, training course material and case histories. The people may include trainees, experienced workers, trainers, supervisors, although not all of these may be present or relevant to a particular domain. However, as many sources as possible should be sampled since it is often the case that different classes of people will be able to give different levels and types of description. For example, an electronics trainer might have a

clear view of the general plan for say designing a circuit board but not what the various deviations from that plan are nor in what circumstances they occur. An experienced electronics technician might have the latter but not the former. The techniques of gathering information are, of course, not independent of the source or type of information. However, the approaches that might be required in any situation include: structured interviews; direct observation of tasks; structured demonstrations; protocol analysis; and problem manipulation. Audio and video recordings should be taken wherever possible. The types of information for which the observer searches should include: the objectives of the task; the procedures used; the actions and objects involved; the time taken; the frequency of operations; the occurrence of errors; the involvement of sub-ordinate/super-ordinate tasks etc.

6. Ways of describing Tasks
Having discussed different ways of analysing tasks, we now consider alternative ways of describing tasks. The simplest way, perhaps, is as a list of statements that describe the sequence of events within any task, for example:
-load disc into disc drive
-type in command to list directory
-type command to LOAD appropriate file
However, this does not indicate at what point(s) decisions or choices are made or recursion occurs. A flowchart is claimed to be more effective in capturing these aspects of a task, for example:

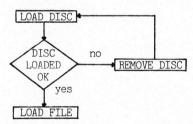

Other alternative ways of describing tasks include the use of logic trees (see Bainbridge, 1978, for application to process control operations), and formal or semi-formal grammars (Moran, 1978; Reisner, 1981, for application to human-computer interaction). It is likely that some forms of task description will serve some purposes better than others. However, no systematic comparison appears to have been made so far.

7. Ways of describing knowledge
The above task descriptions do not, of course, constitute descriptions of knowledge. Further, we are unaware of any formal method of describing knowledge derived from task analysis other than the one we have proposed for the use of TAKD in syllabus creation (with the exception, perhaps, of Hayes-Roth et al). We conclude this paper, then, by summarising this method. From descriptions of tasks, individual actions and objects are identified. These are

then classified as generic action and object lists. The knowledge required in each task sequence is then identified by assigning action/object pairs to the task descriptions. The resultant knowledge descriptions for each sequence of the task are a combination of all the action/object pairs required by the particular task sequence. This method of describing the knowledge requirements of a task has been shown to be of use in designing training syllabi. We have argued that TAKD would appear to be equally appropriate for other types of design including that of human-computer interfaces and IKBS's.

REFERENCES
Anderson, J.R. Cognitive psychology and its implications, (W. H. Freeman; S.F., 1980).

Bainbridge, L., The process controller, in Singleton, W.T. (ed.), The analysis of practical skills. (M.T.P., Lancaster, 1978).

Diaper, D., Johnson, P. & Long, J., A psychological model of knowledge suitable for educational and training applications. B.P.S annual conference (1984).

Duncan, K.D. and Kelly, C.J., Task analysis, learning and the nature of transfer, M.S.C. Training studies (1983).

Hakami, B. & Newborn, J., Expert systems in heavy industry, ICL technical jrnl. (1983) 346-359.

Hayes-Roth, F., Klahr, P. & Mostow, J., Advice taking and knowledge refinement. in Anderson, J.R. (ed.) Cognitive skills and their acquisition (Erlbaum., N.J., 1981).

Johnson, P., Diaper, D. & Long, J., Syllabi for training in information technology, in Megaw, E. (ed.) Procd. of the Ergonomics Society Conference (Taylor & Francis, London, 1984).

Moran, T.P., Introduction to Command Language Grammar. XEROX Rpt SSL-78-3, Palo Alto (1978).

Reisner, P., Formal grammar and human factors design of an interactive graphics system, IEEE Transactions on software engineering, SE7 (1981) 229-240.

Wellbank, M. A review of knowledge acquisition techniques for expert systems, B.T. Ipswich (1983).

MODELLING USERS AND USER INTERACTIONS

FOUR STAGES OF USER ACTIVITIES

Donald A. Norman

Institute for Cognitive Science, C-015
University of California, San Diego,
La Jolla, California 92093

When a person interacts with a computer it is possible to identify four distinct stages in that interaction: *Intention, Selection, Execution,* and *Evaluation.* Each stage has different goals, different methods, and different needs. It is well-known that the task and class of user affects the requirements for an interface. In this paper I emphasize that these requirements vary according to the stage of the interaction, even for an individual user working on a single task. The analysis of these four stages shows that different support is required at different times within an interactive session.

Stages of Interaction in the Use of a Computer System

When a person performs an action, an iterative cycle of activities is usually invoked. It is useful to identify four different stages of this activity cycle: the formation of an *intention*; the *selection* of a method; the implementation or *execution* of that selection; and finally, the *evaluation* of the resulting action. The evaluation can lead to a reconsideration of the intention and the resulting cycles of activity continue until either the person is satisfied, the activities temporarily suspended, or the intention abandoned. The purpose of this brief paper is to argue that each stage of the cycle has different implications for the design of a computer system, for each requires different support and has different implications for the needs of the user.

This analysis of the human action cycle is not intended to reveal dramatic new truths: the division into these four stages is straightforward. Similar divisions have been noted before (see Card, Moran, & Newell, 1983: Chapters 5 and 11). What is new, however, is the analysis of the kinds of implications the stages have for design of systems. But first, let us examine the four stages.

Part of this paper was presented at the *Workshop on Intelligent User Interfaces,* October 1983, Jackson, New Hampshire (USA) and is included within Norman (in press). The ideas result from the interactions with the UCSD Human-Machine Interaction project, including Liam Bannon, Allen Cypher, Steve Draper, David Owen, Mary Riley, and Paul Smolensky. Danny Bobrow, Sondra Buffett, Nancy Casey, Jonathan Grudin, Peter Jackson, Allen Munro, and Julie Norman provided useful suggestions.

This research was conducted under Contract N00014-79-C-0323, NR 667-437 with the Personnel and Training Research Programs of the Office of Naval Research and by a grant from the System Development Foundation. Requests for reprints should be sent to Donald A. Norman, Institute for Cognitive Science C-015; University of California, San Diego; La Jolla, California, 92093, USA.

I define *intention* as the internal, mental characterization of the desired goal. Intention is the internal specification of action responsible for the initiation and guidance of the resulting activity. Although intentions are often conscious, they need not be. *Selection* helps translate the intention into one of the actual actions possible at the moment. The mental specification of the desired action is unlikely to be couched in terms that translate readily into the actions that the computer system can carry out. Therefore, to go from intention to action, the person must review the set of computer operations that are available and select those that seem most auspicious for the satisfaction of the intentions. Then, having mentally selected, the actual command sequences must be specified to the computer. I call the determination of a particular command or command sequence *selection* and the act of entering the selections into the system *execution.* Note that *intention* and *selection* are mental activities whereas *execution* is a physical act of entering information into the computer. These activities do not complete the activity: the results of the actions need *evaluation*, and the feedback from that evaluation is used to direct further activity.

Perhaps the best way to understand the differences among the stages is to look at a simple example. Consider the computer user who continually confuses the file names in a directory. Suppose the name confusion results in the following intention: *change the name of file α to a new name, β.* The mental intention must now be translated into a possible command sequence. To do this, the user has to choose an appropriate set of operations from those available on the computer. Suppose that the user chooses to rename the file by following the (extremely) conservative strategy of first making a copy of file α (calling the copy β), then examining β to verify that the copy is correct, and then deleting the original file, α. That is, the selected actions are:

> *COPY from* α *to* β
> *LIST* β *(terminate when satisfied)*
> *DELETE* α

This selection of command sequence must then be executed. The exact method of entering the commands into the system depend, of course, on the particular facilities of the system. If the computer system requires use of a command language, then execution involves typing the appropriate commands into the system. If the computer uses a pointing system with icons or menus, then execution involves manipulating the icons or menu entries representing the files.

Note that the stages need not proceed in order. In this example, the *evaluation* stage occurs after each command execution as the user considers the effect of the action. Evaluation allows the user to determine whether the effect was expected, unexpected, useful, or not, and as a result, determines how next to proceed. Finally, the user evaluates the end result to see if the original intention has been satisfied. Thus, for this example, the sequence of stages is something like this:

> Intention
> Selection
> Execution—Evaluation Cycles:
>   Execute and Evaluate *COPY*
>   Execute and Evaluate *VERIFY*
>   Execute and Evaluate *DELETE*
> Evaluation *(of overall intention)*

Stages as Useful Approximations

Before we continue, a caveat on the nature of these stages: although the identification of the stages is useful, it is important to note that they are only convenient approximations to the actual interaction. People are not serial-processing mechanisms, they do not have well-defined stages of decision processes or action formation, and they are often not conscious of the reasons for their own actions. People are best viewed as highly parallel processors with both conscious and subconscious processing, and with multiple factors continually interacting to bias activity (see Norman, 1981a, b; Rumelhart & Norman, 1982). Nonetheless, the

approximations used by this analysis appear to yield relevant and worthwhile results and to identify important design considerations.

Implications of the Four Stages

Many of the existing controversies over design techniques actually result from different assessments of the value of support for different stages of activity. In an earlier paper (Norman, 1983), I argued that many design decisions involve *tradeoffs*, where each method has some virtues and some deficits. In that paper I considered only issues that affected screen layout or ease of operation, but it seems clear that the same argument can be applied to the stages of interaction. A design that enhances operation for one stage may detract from operations at another stage. The result is that the designer is faced with a series of tradeoffs.

The user support relevant to each stage is summarized in Table 1.

Table 1

DESIGN IMPLICATIONS FOR THE STAGES OF USER ACTIVITIES	
STAGE	**TOOLS TO CONSIDER**
Forming the Intention	Structured Activities Workbenches Memory Aids Menus Explicit Statement of Intentions
Selecting the Action	Memory Aids Menus
Executing the Action	Ease of Specification Memory Aids Menus Naming (Command Languages) Pointing
Evaluating the Outcome	Sufficient Workspace Information Required Depends on Intentions Actions Are Iterations toward Goal Errors as Partial Descriptions Ease of Correction Messages Should Depend upon Intention

Design Issues for the Four Stages of User Activities

The intention stage. Formation of the intention requires knowledge about the system and oftentimes considerable planning (Riley & O'Malley, 1984). Thus, the decision to change the name of a file requires knowledge of other existing names, the set of possibilities, and the fact that name changes are permissible. In general, intentions are formed as the result of evaluation of information available from previous uses of the system.

For many tasks, especially complex ones, the user's activities have structure. If only this structure were known, the system could provide intelligent assistance. This is where knowledge of intentions is most useful. Indeed, one could argue that all assistance (including help and error messages) requires knowledge of user intentions in order to be maximally effective (see Johnson, Draper, & Soloway, 1983). Thus, the formation of the intention interacts with all the other stages in that if only the intentions were known, one could better provide information relevant to selection, execution, and evaluation. However, it is going to be hard to determine a user's intentions. In some cases, the user can simply be asked. In others, it may be possible to infer them. Unfortunately, in many cases it simply won't be possible.

Commands often combine intentions and action execution. Thus, commands to *logout* or to *list* or *print* a file might better be thought of as specifying an intention rather than as a specific action that is to be performed. This way, if the system determines that there is some reason not to carry out the action, it could be helpful rather than obstinate. The system could explain the problem, remind the user of the relevant system state, give a set of alternative actions, and provide the tools for each alternative, all the while retaining the intention.

The intention stage is supported by anything that can structure the activities, by memory aids, and by messages and interactions that take into account the intentions of the users. It may be difficult to determine these intentions, but the more that can be done, the better.

The selection stage. Some intentions might map directly onto a single action, others might require a sequence of operations. In either case, the selection of an action sequence can require considerable knowledge on the part of the users. Consider how users decide upon what commands to invoke or files to use. How do they know what is possible at any moment? There are only three ways:

1: They could remember;

2: They might be told (or reminded);

3: They might be able to construct or derive the possibilities.

In the first case, no external information is required. Recall memory is used to identify the desired item. In the second case, some external source of information is required, either to inform or to remind. Then, recognition memory is used to identify the desired item from the list or description of the alternatives. In the third case, the user engages in problem solving, perhaps using analogy, perhaps eliminating possibilities.

Support for the selection stage comes principally from memory aids (menus, help commands, icons, manuals — all on-line support) that allow the user to determine the range of possible commands and their mode of operation, prerequisites, and implications. Selection can be enhanced by "workbenches" that collect relevant files and software support in one convenient location. Other methods of structuring groups of commands and files dependent upon the user's intentions need to be explored (for example, see Bannon, L., Cypher, A., Greenspan, S., & Monty, M. L., 1983).

The execution stage. There are only two major classes of procedures that can be used in specifying an action: *naming* and *pointing*. Naming is the standard situation for most computer systems. The designer provides a command language and the users specify the desired action by typing the appropriate command language sequences. Execution by naming provides the designer with a number of issues to worry about. What is the form of the command language? How are the commands to be named, how are options to be specified? How are ill-formed sequences to be handled? How much support should be provided the user?

It is quite possible to provide little or no support at this stage; that is, users might be expected to have learned the appropriate command sequences so that the move from intention through selection takes place without interacting with the system, save possibly to refer to reference or instruction manuals. Then the execution is judged either to be legitimate (and therefore carried out) or erroneous (and an explanation presented to the user). It is also possible to provide considerable support: telling the user what actions are available and how to execute them. This is usually done with menus, oftentimes abbreviated and restricted in content, serving primarily as reminders of the major actions available.

Execution of an action by pointing means that the alternative actions are visually present and that the user physically moves some pointing device to indicate which of the displayed actions are to be performed. Although the prototypical "pointing" operation is to touch the desired alternative with a finger or other pointing device, the definition can be generalized to include any situation where a selection is made by moving an indicator to the desired location.

The set of alternative actions can be indicated by numerous methods, from such mundane techniques as printed labels or lists displayed on a terminal screen, to more unfamiliar and unusual ones. It is even possible not to label them, the user being required to learn the appropriate spatial position for each action (such as with electronic devices that have unlabelled—or illegible—panels). Each action could be described rather completely or just hinted at with simple abbreviations or short words. Actions can also be labelled by pictures ("icons") that are intended to illustrate some aspect of the action, a method widely used on electronic equipment and just beginning to be applied to computer systems. These choices of execution are analogous to the choices offered in the design of command languages and in the naming problems faced when actions are specified by names.

The evaluation stage. Evaluation requires feedback, whether the operation has been completed successfully or whether it has failed. For full analysis, the user must know a number of things:

- What the previous state of the system was;
- What action was specified;
- What happened;
- How the results correspond to the intentions and expectations;
- What alternatives are now possible.

The evaluation of an action depends upon the user's intentions for that action. In cases where the operation could not be performed properly, either because it wasn't properly specified or because some necessary precondition was not satisfied, the user will probably still maintain the same intention but needs to correct whatever was inappropriate about the previous attempt. It would be useful to provide the user with the information and tools necessary to do this with minimum disruption. Once again we see the desirability of having the system knowing intentions.

One useful viewpoint is to think of all actions as iterations toward a goal. Ill-formed commands are to be thought of as partial descriptions of the proper command: they are approximations. Error messages should take this into account and, wherever possible, provide assistance that allows for modification of the execution and convergence upon the proper set of actions. This means, of course, that feedback must be sensitive to the intentions of the users.

Examples

Intention and evaluation: Video games. Video games are perhaps the best example of systems that support a particular class of intentions and evaluation. Video games usually are structured around goals and intentions (provided by the game designer and presumed to have been acquired by the player), coupled with immediate, high-quality graphics that provide excellent support for the evaluation stage. The user usually knows how well (or poorly) the performance is, as well as how well the intentions are being satisfied. Oftentimes the set of selections is not obvious—either the selections aren't emphasized or, in some cases, discovery of the selections is one of the subgoals of the game—and the execution may or may not be easy. The result is that the games are fairly easy for both novice and expert to watch, but not particularly easy to play. I myself have attempted several of the latest laser-disc games, finding myself frustrated by my inability to determine what the response choices were or, when several were explained to me, to figure out how to execute those choices. Veteran players explained that you had to "work at it," spending considerable time (and money) to build up the necessary experience. I therefore classify these as excellent examples of design at the intention and evaluation stages. (The difficulty of the selection and execution stages is, of course, deliberate, for the whole purpose of the game is to create a challenge to the player.)

Intention and evaluation: VISICALC. VISICALC (and spreadsheets in general) do an excellent job of matching the intentions of the bookkeeper to the format of the display and the operations. Feedback is immediate and relevant to the task; evaluation is supported in a strong and natural manner. However, the selection and execution stages are not necessarily supported well (some spreadsheets do better than others), and so the systems are not particularly easy to learn or to use. Moreover, if one wishes to do some novel task on them, then considerable effort may be required—the match with intentions is no longer so good.

Selection: Xerox Star and Apple Lisa. The Xerox Star computer systems (and Apple's related Lisa and Macintosh) are good examples of support at the selection stages. There is a visual display of the possible activities at every stage. This, of course, is a feature in common with most menu-based systems. The user, however, is not aided in transforming intentions into the set of available actions, and evaluation depends upon the quality of the particular program being executed. For some activities ("opening" or manipulating an icon), evaluation is immediate and direct; in other activities, it is not so obvious.

Execution: UNIX. I have often criticized UNIX, the Bell Laboratories' operating system, for its lack of support for the non-expert user (Norman, 1981). With this new perspective of four different stages of interaction, I now realize that the problems are a result of concentration upon one stage to the neglect of the others. Because the designers of UNIX were aiming the system at the expert user, they emphasized the *execution* stage, producing a system that allows one to specify exactly and precisely what actions are to be performed. There was little attempt to provide support for any other stage: neither help in getting from intentions to selections, nor help in figuring out what the selections are, nor feedback that might help in the evaluation stage. UNIX has computational power and flexibility. However, lack of support for mapping intentions to selections makes it difficult for novices to learn (and for experts to use when in an unfamiliar part of the system). The evaluation stage is also not supported, in part because of the desire to minimize messages from the system to the user, in part because the messages that do exist are almost always at the wrong level, either unintelligible for many users or too general.

Summary and Conclusions

A major moral of this paper is that it is essential to analyze separately the different aspects of human-computer interaction. In a related paper (Norman, 1983), I discuss a formal method of evaluating tradeoffs among interface techniques. In that paper I argue that each of the known techniques for human-computer interaction has different virtues, different deficiencies. Any single design decision is apt to have its virtues along one dimension compensated by deficiencies along

another. Each technique provides a set of tradeoffs. Each stage of human-computer interaction requires different methods and, therefore, has different tradeoffs to be considered. The designer must choose from among the tradeoffs. The final choices depend upon the technology being used, the class of users, the goals of the design, and which aspects of the interface are to be sacrificed for the benefit of the other aspects. Thus, the tradeoff analysis, coupled with the issues raised in this paper, emphasizes that the design problem must be looked at as a whole, not in isolated pieces, for the optimal choice for one stage of the interaction probably will not be optimal for another.

References

[1] Bannon, L., Cypher, A., Greenspan, S., and Monty, M.L., Evaluation and analysis of users' activity organization, *Proceedings of the CHI 1983 Conference on Human Factors in Computer Systems* (Boston, December 1983).

[2] Card, S.K., Moran, T.P., and Newell, A., *The psychology of human-computer interaction* (Hillsdale, New Jersey, Erlbaum, 1983).

[3] Johnson, W.L., Draper, S., and Soloway, E., *Classifying bugs is a tricky business*, RR#284, Dept. of Comp. Sc., Yale Univ. (1983).

[4] Norman, D.A., Categorization of action slips, *Psychological Review, 88* (1981a) 1-15.

[5] Norman, D.A., A psychologist views human processing: human errors and other phenomena suggest processing mechanisms, *Proceedings of the International Joint Conference on Artificial Intelligence* (Vancouver, 1981).

[6] Norman, D.A., The trouble with UNIX: the user interface is horrid, *Datamation, 27* (1981) 139-150.

[7] Norman, D.A., Design issues for human-computer interfaces, *Proceedings of the CHI 1983 Conference on Human Factors in Computing Systems* (Boston, December 1983).

[8] Norman, D.A., Stages and levels in human-machine interaction, *International Journal of Man-Machine Studies* (in press).

[9] Riley, M.S. and O'Malley, C., Planning nets: a framework for studying user-computer interaction, *Proceedings of the First IFIP Conference on Human-Computer Interaction* (London, September 1984).

[10] Rumelhart, D.E., and Norman, D.A., Simulating a skilled typist: a study of skilled cognitive-motor performance, *Cognitive Science, 6* (1982) 1-36.

Human-Computer Interaction — INTERACT '84 / B. Shackel (ed.)
Elsevier Science Publishers B.V. (North-Holland)
© IFIP, 1985

PLANNING NETS:

A FRAMEWORK FOR ANALYZING USER-COMPUTER INTERACTIONS

Mary Riley and Claire O'Malley

Institute for Cognitive Science, C-015
University of California, San Diego,
La Jolla, California 92093

During the course of interacting with a computer, a user has goals that correspond to tasks to be performed and must plan how to achieve those goals with the available commands. We present a framework for analyzing user goals, the mapping between those goals and available commands, and the factors influencing the success and efficiency of the resulting plans. We discuss the implications of our analysis for the development of principles for improving user-computer interactions.

Introduction

During the course of interacting with a computer, a user has goals that correspond to tasks to be performed and must plan how to achieve those goals with the available commands. We present a framework for analyzing user goals, the mapping between those goals and available commands, and the factors influencing the success and efficiency of the resulting plans. We discuss the implications of our analysis for the development of principles for improving user-computer interactions.

Our analyses so far have focussed on learning and performance in the context of a single editor. However, an important objective of our approach is that these analyses achieve a level of description that will enable principles developed in this context to be extended to the instruction, design, and evaluation of editors in general, and eventually to other areas of the interface.

Theoretical Framework

The general form of our analysis is shown in Figure 1. The figure presents a typical planning episode in the form of a hierarchical goal structure — or *planning net*. At the higher levels of the planning net are global goals. Here the global goal is to edit a paper which in turn generates the additional goal to transpose two words. Since this goal does not correspond to an executable action, further goal specification and planning is required. *"Transpose two words"* is broken down into the subgoals *"delete word1"* and *"insert word1 after word2"*, which

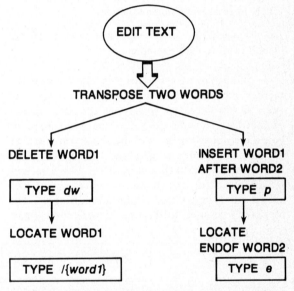

Figure 1. Planning net for the task *Transpose two words*.

correspond to the actions of typing *"dw"* (delete word) and *"p"* (put), respectively.

Planning does not necessarily stop with the selection of the primary actions. Associated with actions are requisite conditions that must be taken into account in the planning process:

Prerequisites are conditions that must be satisfied before an action can be performed. Referring to the figure, the prerequisite of *"dw"* and *"p"* is that the cursor be at the appropriate location. Therefore additional goals are generated to ensure that those prerequisites are satisfied.

Consequences are the changes that result from performing an action. In the above example, the consequence of *"dw"* is that the word is deleted from the text and placed in a buffer. The consequence of *"p"* is to put the contents of the buffer at the location of the cursor. These consequences define the *order* in which *"dw"* and *"p"* must be executed and, furthermore, place restrictions on interleaving plans. For example, other commands, such as *"insert,"* also have the consequence of changing the contents of the buffer — if one of these commands were executed between *"dw"* and *"p,"* the consequence of *"p"* would be different (in this case *"p"* would be inserted as text).

Finally, some commands also have *postrequisites* — conditions that must be satisfied after performing an action. For example, the action of inserting text must be followed by pressing the ESCAPE key, to return to command mode.

Figure 2 shows an expanded version of the planning net for this example.

An important component in determining the success and efficiency of a planning episode like the one above is the mapping between the user's *mental model* of a command (the user's representation of how a command works), and the *conceptual model* of a command (how a command actually works). Furthermore, the likelihood that the user's mental model will correspond to the conceptual model is to a large extent a function of the *system image* — the feedback presented to the user before, during, and after the command is executed. (See Norman, 1983, for a more complete discussion).

The importance of the mapping between a user's mental model of a command and the conceptual model has been emphasized in several recent analyses (e.g., Card, Moran, & Newell, 1983; Kieras & Polson, 1982; Moran, 1983; Roberts & Moran, 1983; Young, 1983). However, the role of the *system image* has not been systematically distinguished from the conceptual model in these analyses. In our analysis we emphasize this distinction, showing how the feedback explicitly presented to users — especially in the learning phase — accounts for a large number of users' errors and misconceptions, independent of the command's conceptual model.

Empirical Study

Preliminary support for the usefulness of this framework has come from an empirical study of new users learning to use a text editor for the first time. The text editor used in this study was the UNIX [1] screen editor *"vi."*

Procedure

Subjects were six undergraduates who had never used a word-processor before, and who had minimal experience with computers in general. Subjects were studied individually approximately twice a week for a total of 4-5 sessions, each session lasting one hour. A typical session involved having sub-

GOAL	GOAL	PREREQ	ACTION	CONSEQUENCE	
				system image	conceptual model
	Transpose 2 words	Locate word1			
SUBGOALa	Locate word1		Type "/{word1}"	Cursor at beginning of word	Cursor at beginning of word
SUBGOALb	Select delete operation		Type "d"		Delete operation selected
SUBGOALc	Mark range of operation		Type "w"	word1 deleted	Text deleted and placed in buffer
SUBGOALd	Replace word	Locate end of word2			
SUBGOALe	Locate end of word2		Type "e"	Cursor at end of word	Cursor at end of word
SUBGOALd	Replace word1		Type "p"	Word1 replaced	Word1 replaced from buffer

Figure 2. Expanded version of a *planning net*.

jects pace themselves through a written tutorial in the presence of an experimenter trained in taking protocol observations. Subjects were encouraged to think aloud while reading through the tutorial and performing the exercises. Audio, video, and keystroke information were recorded for each session and for the test that followed the instruction.

In the test phase, subjects were given a file to edit, which they were told contained several mistakes. They were also given a printout showing what the final version should look like. They were instructed to work through the file, taking as long as they liked, and to correct each of the mistakes they found. The corrections consisted of various core editing tasks (cf. Roberts & Moran, 1983) that required applying basic text editing operations (insert, delete, replace, transpose, or merge) to basic text objects (characters, words, lines, paragraphs). Subjects were also given a quick reference sheet, which contained a list of the basic editing commands which they had learned. (This was to ensure that we were not simply testing subjects' memory for the names of the commands.) Subjects were instructed to think aloud, telling the investigator what it was they were planning to do in solving the problems. The test lasted until the subject had completed all the tasks, or until one hour was up.

Results

Our initial analyses have focused on subjects' test performance, relying mainly on protocol transcripts from the audio-visual tapes, rather than the keystroke data. Overall results showed that subjects were correct on only 60% of the editing tasks, in spite of the fact they had practiced all the commands previously and had the list of commands available at all times. We grouped subjects' errors into three major categories, reflecting the stage in the planning process at which the errors occurred. These categories correspond closely to Norman's analysis of the stages involved in users' activities (cf. Norman, 1984).

The first category includes errors made during the formation of goals, or what Norman refers to as *intentions*. Approximately 15% of errors fell into this category. The second category includes errors made in the *selection* and/or *execution* of actions to achieve the specified intentions. Approximately 58% of errors fell into this category. In the third category we included errors that resulted from an *incorrect evaluation* of the outcome of performing an action. About 27% of the errors were of this kind.

These categories oversimplify what is really a *complex* and *interactive* planning process, and the errors we discuss reflect this. For example, many errors in forming intentions or in selecting actions were clearly the result of errors in evaluation from previous cycles of activity. Nevertheless, the categories are useful for identifying the stages of user activity that are not well supported by the system, and for suggesting specific changes to improve either the interface itself, or the instructional material.

Errors in the Formation of Intentions

Subjects often revealed very vaguely specified plans or intentions. We characterize this kind of error as a "fuzzy plan." (This finding is similar to what Lewis & Mack call "abduction" — Lewis & Mack, 1982). This captures the fact that a general intention is formed but there is no specification of that intention beyond this stage, and subjects can find no executable action that corresponds to that intention.

Example: The task was to insert a line of text above the first line, on which the cursor was positioned. The subject used the command *"i,"* correctly, in order to enter insert mode. She then typed the text she wanted, but realized, when she got near the end of the line, that the "old" text [2] had to be put on the next line. This could have been achieved by typing RETURN but this did not occur to the subject. She pressed the ESCAPE key to leave insert mode, then tried to think of a way to get the "old" text onto the next line. She could only come up with a very vague (or "fuzzy") plan for achieving this. She seemed to have the plan of copying the text that was on the current line onto the next line (a generalization from the commands *"yank"* and *"put,"* as a way of copying text):

> S: *I know you can copy buffer, right? Or can I just delete it then add? I know there's some way we can erase it, then tell it to go somewhere else. Then push a button, and everything will be back.*

Other examples of problems at the intention stage included inefficient, or overspecified, plans. Even though subjects performed correctly on 60% of the tasks, about half of their correct responses were counted as "inefficient" plans. In other words, subjects tended to overspecify their intentions, so that they were operating with very primitive commands, rather than with the compound commands which would have achieved the same solution more efficiently. (This is consistent with findings from, e.g., Folley & Williges, 1982, and Robertson & Black, 1983).

Errors in the Selection and Execution of Actions

There were three main types of errors in this category: errors in predicting the scope of a command's consequence, errors in syntax, and errors in selecting text objects. An example of each of these errors is given below:

Example (Scope Error): The task was to delete to the end of the line, including the punctuation. There were five words on the line, and the subject typed *"d5w"* (delete five words). However, she did not realize that the text object *"w"* does not include punctuation, so she had an extra task of deleting the punctuation.

Example (Syntax Error): The task was to replace two words with three words. The subject forgot how to specify the object to the *substitute* command. He was confused about the syntax of the command, and gave the argument as the number of spaces for the "new" text (three words), rather than the number of spaces of the "old" text (two words).

Example (Text Object Error): The task was to delete to the end of the line. The subject typed *"ds,"* for "delete sentence" — generalizing from *"dw,"* for "delete word." The correct command, however, is *"dd"* (which is of course inconsistent).

An important feature of each of the examples in this category is that the fact an error has been made is immediately reflected by the system image — text intended for deletion remains on the screen (first example), text intended to remain on the screen is deleted (second example), or the system gives audible feedback when a text object is incorrectly specified (third example). As a result of the immediate feedback, many of these errors were corrected or the subject was able to ask for help. The next category also includes errors in selection, but the fact that an error has been made is not immediately reflected by the system image and therefore is not easily evaluated and corrected.

Errors in Evaluation of Actions

The success and efficiency of the subjects' plans was to a large extent a function of the mapping between the "conceptual model" of a command and the "system image." Difficulties arose when the system image failed to reflect important information about the *prerequisites* for selecting a command or about the *consequences* of executing a command.

(i) *Prerequisites:* There were three main types of errors involving prerequisites — the user either neglected to take into account a necessary prerequisite of an action, had an unnecessary prerequisite, or had a wrong prerequisite.

Example (Violation of Prerequisite): The subject's goal was to search for a pattern (achieved by preceding the string with "/"). However, she forgot to type the search command, thus the prerequisite of the action was violated, and this was not noticed by the subject (even though the system image revealed it). The error was compounded because the next two characters typed were "la." The problem was that "a" is the "append" command, which results in insert mode. This was not noticed by the subject — in fact the first time she noticed the error was when the next character "w" was echoed on the screen. This was an example of an error resulting from neglecting to take into account a necessary prerequisite of an action. In this case the subject was not aware of the mode she was in. The example illustrates how errors in evaluation can still occur even where the system provides the appropriate feedback. It also illustrates how errors can be compounded.

Example (Unnecessary Prerequisite): An example of an unnecessary prerequisite occurred when a subject thought that she had to be at the end of the line before giving the command *"dd"* to delete the line. (The cursor may be anywhere on the line in this case.)

Example (Wrong Prerequisite): Finally, an example of wrong prerequisites involved a subject who was aware of what mode she was in (she was typing in text) but chose a command whose prerequisite was that of being in command mode.

(ii) *Consequences:* In some cases a single action has more than one consequence, only one of which may be visible to the user. As a result, subjects often associated an action with only one of its consequences.

Example: The subject's goal was to delete a character at the end of a line. She chose the command *"A,"* in order to move the cursor to the end of the line. However, this also put her in insert mode, which she did not know, and could not evaluate because the consequence of being in insert mode was not made visible. In this case the error was both in selecting the wrong command as a result of learning only a partial consequence of the command *"A,"* and in evaluation, since the consequence of typing *"A"* was invisible.

Example: Another example was where the subject typed *"O"* to get a new line and then typed *"a"* to get into insert mode. The error in this case also resulted from the subject learning a partial consequence of a command: typing *"O"* does open up a space, but it also results in insert mode, but not realizing this, the subject then typed the command to enter insert mode. This error therefore also resulted from not being able to evaluate the consequences of an action since they were invisible, and from the subject learning only a partial consequence of the command *"O."*

Another example is where the wrong action is associated with a consequence, as a result of *delayed* consequences:

Example: For example, since the consequence of backspacing while in insert mode was delayed until after ESCAPE was pressed, the subject thought that it was ESCAPE that deleted the text, whereas it was the compound of backspace and ESCAPE that performed the action. Delayed consequences, therefore, caused the error of associating the most recent consequence with the most recent action. In this case, ESCAPE was a *postrequisite* for the action of erasing while in insert mode.

Subjects were also confused when the *intermediate* consequences of performing an action appeared to violate other goals: for example, the action of typing text while in insert mode has the consequence of typing over existing text until a special key (ESCAPE) is pressed to terminate the input mode. Again, in this case, the pressing of ESCAPE is a postrequisite for insertion of text.

In summary, we have identified some of the difficulties experienced by users in learning how to use a text editor, and we have related these difficulties to specific stages in the formation and execution of plans. In the next section we discuss the implications of our analysis for improving user-computer interactions. Our focus is mainly on the problems in evaluation, since they highlight the importance of the system image.

Implications

Intention errors: The errors in the intention category revealed that novices sometimes have problems in mapping their general plans or high level goals into executable actions. At other times they overspecify their goals into very primitive units. Our analysis does not provide any specific recommendations about what might be the right level at which to implement operations that would more directly map onto users' intentions. More research is needed to determine this.

Selection/Execution errors: The errors found in the selection/execution stage imply that instructions should make more explicit such things as the scope of a command, and the rules for generating commands (for example cross-product rules). Moreover, such rules should be consistent.

Evaluation errors: More direct implications for improving the interface come from the analysis of errors occurring at the evaluation stage. Difficulties in evaluation occurred when the system image failed to reflect important information about the prerequisites for selecting a command or about the consequences of executing a command. The direct suggestion for improving the interface is to make this information visible to the user. For example, many of the subjects' problems involved either not knowing which mode they were in before executing an action; knowing the current mode, but selecting a command which required being in another mode; or not realizing that an action resulted in a mode change. Here the implications for improving design are that an explicit indication of mode change should be provided, and furthermore, that any such indication should be salient to the user.

One way to make prerequisites more salient is to have error messages explicitly reflect which prerequisites are being violated instead of, for example, simply giving audible feedback to indicate that the command cannot be executed.

Other difficulties in evaluation occurred because subjects only learned the consequences that were made visible and failed to acquire those that were left invisible. Again, this suggests that the consequences of actions (for example, changes in mode, the contents of the buffer) should be visible. Making things visible not only gives users explicit feedback, but also encourages the development of a more coherent model, allowing users to predict, explain, and evaluate the behaviour of the system.

Our analysis also suggests that not only should consequences be made visible, but to be associated with the correct action, they must be made visible immediately after performing the action (or at least before another command is executed).

Summary and Conclusions

We have suggested in this paper that difficulties in learning to use a text editor may be accounted for in terms of specific mappings and mismappings between the conceptual structure of a command, how that conceptual structure is reflected by the system image, and how users interpret that system image in terms of their mental models. These analyses suggest certain hypotheses about the knowledge required to generate efficient plans, how this relates to users' initial knowledge, and possible ways of helping users acquire more skilled levels of performance. Further theoretical and empirical work is required to test and extend our hypotheses. Nevertheless, results of this exploratory study support our idea that a planning framework is useful as a basis for developing general principles for instructing, designing, and evaluating features of an interface.

References

[1] Card, S.K., Moran, T.P., & Newell, A. *The Psychology of Human-Computer Interaction*. Hillsdale, N.J.: Erlbaum Associates (1983).

[2] Folley, L., & Williges, R. User models of text editing command languages. *Proceedings of the Conference on Human Factors in Computer Systems*. Gaithersburg, Maryland. (1982, March).

[3] Kieras, D.E., & Polson, P.G. *An approach to the formal analysis of user complexity*. Project on user complexity of devices and systems, working paper no. 2, University of Arizona (1982).

[4] Lewis, C., & Mack, R., *The role of abduction in learning to use a computer system* (Tech. Rep. No. RC 9433 (#41620)). New York: IBM Thomas Watson Research Center (1982).

[5] Moran, T. P. Getting into a system: External-internal task mapping analysis. *Proceedings of the CHI '83 Conference on Human Factors in Computing Systems*. Boston, MA. (1983, December).

[6] Norman, D.A. Some observations on mental models. In D. Gentner & A.L. Stevens (Eds.) *Mental Models*. Hillsdale, N.J.: Erlbaum Associates (1983).

[7] Norman, D.A. Four stages of user activities. *Proceedings of the First IFIPS Conference on Human-Computer Interaction*. Imperial College, London (1984, September).

[8] Roberts, T.L., & Moran, T.P. The evaluation of text editors: Methodology and empirical results. *Communications of the ACM, 26* (1983).

[9] Robertson, S., & Black, J. Planning units in text editing behavior. *Proceedings of the CHI '83 Conference on Human Factors in Computing Systems*. Boston, MA. (1983, December).

[10] Young, R.M. Surrogates and mappings: Two kinds of conceptual models for interactive devices. In D. Gentner & A.L. Stevens (Eds.) *Mental Models*. Hillsdale, N.J.: Erlbaum Associates (1983).

Footnotes

This research was conducted under Contract N00014-79-C-0323, NR 667-437 with the Personnel and Training Research Programs of the Office of Naval Research. Work on Human-Computer Interaction was also supported by a grant from the System Development Foundation. Requests for reprints should be sent to the Institute for Cognitive Science C-015; University of California, San Diego; La Jolla, California, 92093, USA.

1. UNIX is a trademark of Bell Laboratories. The comments in this paper refer to the 4.1 BSD version developed at the University of California, Berkeley.

"Vi" is a screen oriented (visual display), command driven editor, based on "ex."

2. As "new" text is inserted in front of text that already exists, the "old" text is pushed along in front of the cursor.

Human-Computer Interaction — INTERACT '84 / B. Shackel (ed.)
Elsevier Science Publishers B.V. (North-Holland)
© IFIP, 1985

PREDICTING EXPERT SLIPS

T.R.G. Green, S.J. Payne, D.J. Gilmore and M. Mepham

MRC/ESRC Social and Applied Psychology Unit
Department of Psychology
The University
SHEFFIELD S10 2TN

Although there has been considerable progress in identifying the features that make command languages hard to learn there has been less attention paid to the features that make them easy to use in the long term. In this paper we shall look at the possibility of predicting from the design of a language where experts will make slips: with the ultimate aim of making it possible to design 'non-slip' languages.

We shall describe a theory of slips which relates their occurrence to the mapping between the task structure and the language; the frequency of particular tasks; the internal representation of the language in long term memory; and to the characteristics of the user as an information-processing system. In so doing we are building on a tradition of work whose notable exponents include Reason, whose analysis of slips as the price of automaticity has been widely influential, Norman, whose philosophy of 'cognitive engineering' brought slips to the notice of human computer interactionists, and Anderson, who has successfully created a theory describing both the performance and the acquisition of cognitive skill.

What are slips?

We must distinguish between slips and mistakes. Slips have been defined as "actions not as planned" (Reason, 1979); or as "the error that occurs when a person does an action that is not intended" (Norman, 1981). When the plan or intention is wrong, that is a mistake. It is possible, of course, for both to occur at once.

Everyday observation suggests that some computer systems entice their users into slips more often than others. (Try counting how often you hear "dear me, I'm always doing that". Add points for vehemence.) Since it is well-known that the designers of all systems are well-intentioned men and women, doing their best for their users, presumably it is difficult to see in advance what parts of a computer system will turn out to be slippery.

The nature of slips

After classifying the slips recorded in everyday actions by a panel of volunteers, under such headings as 'discrimination failures', 'program assembly failures', 'test failures', etc. Reason (1979) established three very important facts. (1) "These lapses are characteristic of skilled rather than unskilled activity. This is an interesting departure from the normal expectation that errors decrease with the acquisition of skill"; (2) "A large proportion of these slips appear to have resulted from the misdirection of focal attention"; and (3) "Far from exhibiting novelty, these departures from intended action usually took the form of some frequently and recently performed behavioural sequence." (p. 83).

It is widely accepted that motor learning is accompanied by a gradual shift from closed-loop control to open-loop control, or from 'controlled' to 'automatic' processing. To explore slips, Reason considered the detailed consequences of that shift. When an open-loop program has been initiated, the central processor will engage in parallel mental activity. Consequently, skilled performance involves continual switching between the open-loop and closed-loop modes. "During the execution of any sequence of planned actions, no matter how familiar or well-practised they may be, there are critical decision points in which the closed-loop mode of control is necessary to ensure the intended outcome. The matter is neither as simple nor as obvious as it might at first appear since there are clearly moments during the performance of a well-practised task when close attention to the component actions, far from being essential, has a profoundly disruptive effect. "In view of the adverse consequences of an untimely switch from the open-loop to the closed-loop control mode, the question of when such a switch is necessary becomes central to our understanding of skilled performance" (p. 76).

Test failures, Reason predicts, will occur when the open-loop mode of control coincides with a decision point where the strengths of the motor programs are markedly different, when the stronger program can capture the weaker. Discrimination failures occur because during open-loop control, 'crude approximations to the desired stimulus configuration' will be acceptable. Another type of error, forgetting previous actions, can be caused by switching from open-loop to closed-loop during a critical counting phase of the sequence. Finally, omissions tended to occur when unexpected events took the place of expected ones.

Norman (1982, 1983), building on the work of Reason, Fromkin, and others, developed the ATS (activation-trigger-schema) system as a theoretical account of the origin of slips, which have been extensively collected in his group (Grudin, 1983). In this model, first developed to describe skilled typewriting, a skilled sequence starts with a parent schema, representing the initial goal, which can invoke child schemas as required to achieve subgoals. Each schema is provided with an activation level and with a set of specific conditions that are required for it to be triggered, although an exact match is not required. At any one time during the execution of a high-level skill, many schemas will be active, competing with each other. As he disarmingly remarks (p. 3), "the ATS model is novel only in its combination of previously unstated ideas; all the components of the model have been stated elsewhere, though not in this combination and not for this purpose", but it has proved able to simulate a typing session (Norman and Rumelhart, 1983).

The ATS analysis is most at home in explaining capture errors: these occur "when there is overlap in the sequence required for the performance of two different actions, especially when one is done considerably more frequently than the other". In a well-known text editor, "the command ':w' means to write the file. ':q' quits the editor ... and the combined sequence ':wq' writes, then quits". The ':wq' soon gets automatised and captures the ':w'. A solution would be to use a completely different sequence. Capture errors are quite frequent, not only with very short action sequences but also in longer sequences such as dialling phone numbers or (a classic example, from William James) starting to change for dinner, undressing, and then going to bed by mistake.

The competition between simultaneously active schemas, each trying to trigger its own actions, results in the omission of fragments of sequences or branching off into unintended continuations, giving typical capture errors.

Reason and Norman have shown that it is possible to integrate slips into current cognitive theory, on the one hand, and current theories of skilled performance on the other. The sharp differentiation between automatic and controlled behaviour finds many echoes in the literature. However, many of Norman's classifications, although implying a causal account, need considerable development. It can also be observed that Norman's account does not cope with one of Reason's major assertions: that slips occur at moments when

open-loop control gives way to closed-loop. Moreover, although the ATS system is sufficiently powerful to simulate a typing session (Norman and Rumelhart, 1983), it is difficult to see how in its present form it could move to the more complex world of text-editing, where the tasks are more diverse, the system state changes after commands, and a degree of problem-solving ability is required.

In an impressive development of ideas similar to Norman's ATS, Anderson (1982, 1983; also Nevers and Anderson, 1981) has combined a theory of human associate memory with a theory of problem-solving. The resulting system is well able to simulate a text-editing system. Anderson (1983, p. 36) claims that the most recent version, ACT*, can explain "many errors in performance of a skill (Norman, 1981)", since it allows partial matches in productions.

In ACT, the mechanisms of skill acquisition – and, by extension, of automaticity – are explained by two processes of 'knowledge compilation'. The first process is composition, in which productions that repeatedly follow each other are joined into one macro-production which combines their LHSs and RHSs. (Anderson, 1982, p. 385, defines more closely the conditions under which composition can occur and the exact form it takes.) The macro-production might be this, combining two previous productions P1 and P2 (LV stands for Local Variable):

P1&P2:

    IF   the goal is dial LVtelephone-number and LVdigit1 is the first digit of LVtelephone-number and LVdigit2 is after LVdigit1,

    THEN dial LVdigit1 and then LVdigit2.

The macro-production P1&P2 still has to retrieve information from long-term memory to fill in the digits in the local variables. But when a particular number is repeatedly dialled, a production can be set up in which the bindings of the local variables are permanently stored. Anderson uses the term proceduralisation for this process. For instance, if Mary's number, beginning 43..., is repeatedly dialled, this production will be created:

P1&P2*:

    If   the goal is to dial Mary's number,

    THEN dial 4 and then 3.

Repeated application of composition and proceduralisation can build up a production that dials the full number:

P*:

    IF   the goal is to dial Mary's number,

    THEN dial 432-2815.

Anderson's system gives a very plausible account of many phenomena, but capture errors do not seem to be explained. If I wish to dial a number similar to Mary's, say 432-2873, how can the fully-proceduralised production P* capture the sequence? A second problem is that the well-known prevalence of certain types of motor error (reversals, incorrect doublings, etc.) cannot be explained, since the action sequences possess no internal structure.

EXTENDING THE TRADITION

The three analyses agree with the present dominant cognitive model that closed-loop control can be distinguished from open loop, that the user's long term knowledge can be regarded as a semantic network, and that the knowledge is used by a 'cognitive processor' component which can be modelled as a production system. Within that cognitive processor, multiple goals can be simultaneously active and productions can be assigned varying strengths.

The analyses go a long way toward classifying and understanding slips, but not far enough. Ultimately, one wishes to be able to <u>predict</u> the slipperiness of a system, but analysis will have to go considerably deeper first. As a step on the route we propose certain extensions to the story so far. Our extensions can be summarised:

1   The user's long-term knowledge of the interaction language is internalised in the form of rule-<u>schemas</u>, not individual rules: each 'simple' task is associated with a rule schema and is marked with features. The user's combined knowledge of the task and the interaction language forms a 'task-action grammar' used by the cognitive processor. Mistakes in the matching of features will cause characteristic types of slip.

2   Automaticity of performance can be represented by direct associations from the right-hand side of one production to the right-hand side of another that frequently follows it. These right-hand side associations are created to economise on the firing of productions which examine the state of the world (i.e. use closed loop). Tasks in which simple right-hand side associations will often but not always succeed are primary candidates for mode errors.

3   RHS sequences are structured into <u>patterns</u> which can possess very extensive <u>internal</u> structure. (Presumably action sequences are structured in order to assist recall or to economise on effort in some way.) These structures can potentially clash with those of the interaction language and the task-action grammar.

4   The cognitive processor can not only activate several goals, but also it can reach the same goal by multiple routes simultaneously. When several chains of productions converge on the same action, it is highly likely to fire; but when simultaneous chains diverge and lead to different actions there will be intense response competition.

Representation of the Command Language

Norman (1982, 1983) relates 'description' errors to lack of <u>consistency</u> in the command language. One of the most important contributions of our model is to move the notion of consistency to a more formal and less intuitive level, building on explanations originally proposed to account for difficulties in learning command languages.

In a highly consistent language, it is possible to infer or reconstruct one rule of syntax from the remainder, because the rules share patterns of family resemblance. If the family resemblances are perceived by the user then the language will be easier both to learn and to use (Reisner, 1981; Green, 1983). Green and Payne (in press) present a list of 'guiding principles' which have been shown to help the learning of command languages, amongst which was the principle that grammar was easier to learn if it possessed an organising principle allowing one rule to be inferred from others; and they report a controlled experiment demonstrating that a command language with two conflicting organising principles was hard to learn.

A 'consistent' language will allow users to develop a highly developed internalised structure in which the family resemblances between rules are fully exploited. A model of the user's knowledge of the command language was presented by Payne and Green (1983).

But it is not sufficient only to account for the knowledge of the language: for an adequate explanation of user behaviour, including slips, the relationships between the language and the task must also be considered. We introduce here a theory of representation based on the 'task-action grammar' (Payne, 1984) which maps 'simple tasks' — the abstract syntax of the command language — onto their associated linguistic actions, illustrated by the following fragment of an editing language:

```
ctrl-C    move pointer forward a character
meta-C    ditto backwards

ctrl-W    move pointer forward a word
meta-C    ditto backward
```

The user's representation will contain concepts and rules:

Concepts:

"Simple tasks":

    e.g. move pointer forward a character
    {direction = forward, unit = character}

Symbols:

    ctrl {direction = forward}
    meta {direction = backward}

Letters:

    C {unit = character}
    W {unit = word}

Rule Schemas:

    move cursor: [direction, unit] - >
    symbol [direction] + letter [unit]

These rules are then interpreted by the 'cognitive processor', (Card et al., 1983) term, which has a learnt task structure possibly as follows:

    IF   a goal is to correct a word

    AND the word is to the right of the
          cursor on the same line

    THEN move forward word

These intentions will be interpreted according to the rules above:

    move [forward, word] -> symbol [forward] +
    letter [word] -> ctrl + W

Errors can occur when the system accepts a partial match. One will then find oneself moving the cursor by the wrong size unit, or deleting instead of moving. In a language which is 'inconsistent' the linguistic rules will be organised into rule-schemas in more than one way, and the cognitive processor will generate diverging chains of productions which will sometimes fire the wrong action.

It has been shown by Bock (1982, p. 34) that essentially the same error mechanism that we propose will also account for one of the more puzzling phenomena of verbal slips, the Spoonerism, in which characteristically the two words that are exchanged have the same form class; "give my bath a hot back" (Garrett, 1975), not "give my hot a bath

back". While we obviously cannot pursue this question here, we regard it as important that a model of the cognitive origins of slips should extend to verbal slips.

Automaticity

Automaticity is perhaps more of a problem than it may first appear, since none of the analyses above seems to be fully satisfactory. It is hard to see how capture errors can occur unless there is some way in which action sequences can become associated, both at a high level (going to bed instead of changing for dinner) and at a low level (typing :wq for :w).

Following the lines of ACT's mechanisms, it appears that the RHSs of consecutive productions can become directly associated. So if two productions are

    P1   IF a THEN do p
    P2   IF b THEN do q

and these two fire consecutively, the following production would be added:

    P3   IF p has just been done THEN do q

The new production would be added with a very low initial strength. Each time the RHS sequence p-q occurred, P3's strength would be increased; ultimately, it would become strong enough to capture other sequences in which the RHS 'p' occurred and divert them willy-nilly toward the 'q'.

Equally, each time 'p' was followed by a different RHS, the strength of the p-q association would be reduced. The association between p and q can only become sufficiently strong to capture other sequences if other sequences are comparatively rare.

The effects of proceduralising knowledge are more far-reaching than those in ACT. We know that as a skill becomes automatised, its control moves towards the open loop; and the straightforward association of the RHSs is one way to model that process. But not all task structures permit complete open-loop control. We propose, therefore, that the process of proceduralising knowledge is prevented by productions whose left hand sides require an unavoidable peek at the state of the world. In some cases - very frequent ones, when using a text-editor - the novice's original knowledge system requires peeks which the expert can dispense with, at the price of keeping an extra item or so in working memory (e.g. "Is the system currently in command mode?"). We distinguish therefore between productions which can be totally automatised; productions which can be automatised at the cost of working memory load; and productions which contain unavoidable peeks.

Unlike ACT, this mechanism would explain the occurrence of capture errors and also Reason's observations about open and closed loop control. It would also invoke a substantial literature on response-response learning. There is no requirement that the RHSs should be low-level motor actions: they could equally well be at a considerably higher level.

Sequence patterning

It is inconceivable that chains of RHS associations are formed with no internal structure, like rows of beads. Numerous studies have demonstrated that patterning is swiftly perceived in a variety of contexts, and numerous attempts have been made to characterise the underlying psychological processes. For instance, Restle (1970) developed a theory of hierarchical representation. Given an alphabet 1-6 and the basic sequence X = (1, 2), the operation R ('repeat of X') produces the sequence 1 2 1 2, the operation M ('mirror') produces the sequence 1 2 6 5, and the operation T ('transposition') produces 1 2 2 3. Then M(T(R(T(1)))) describes the sequence 1 2 1 2 2 3 2 3 6 5 6 5 5 4 5 4. Simon (1972) has shown the essential equivalence of many theories, and Deutsch and Feroe (1981) have developed the theory in connection with tonal music.

Anderson's analysis leaves no room for internal structuring of response patterns, even though his own example of proceduralisation, the telephone number 432-2815, obviously starts with a descending sequence 4-3-2 and then a repetition of 2. The ATS typing model of Norman and Rumelhart contains provision for 'repetition' and 'alternation' operators, but it is evident that much more advanced patterns are frequently formed.

Response conflicts and converging production chains

Since multiple schemas can be simultaneously active, it is possible for them to converge on a single response. When that happens the response will have no competition and will fire unproblematically. The role of the internal structurings of the prior section, in a well-designed language, will be to support other chains of productions, so that the correct response is activated by two or more different sources.

But in a poorly designed language the internal structurings may diverge from the true chain. To take an extreme example, if sequence of actions needed is:

   A A B B C C D E E F F

probably there would be great temptation to repeat the D. Less extreme examples can easily be found. In these conditions the true response will conflict with the response indicated by the pattern of the sequence as a whole.

No doubt designers of command languages would expect their users not to pay attention to such distractions as the internal patterning of response sequences. Unfortunately this is not easy, and as a skill becomes automatised it is likely that the patterning will make itself felt.

SOME EXAMPLES

Although we have no firm empirical data, it is interesting to make predictions for future testing. All the systems described below are commercially available CP/M systems which have actually been used by us.

Example (i)

Consider a display editor with two modes. Command mode includes commands to get and save files, commands for coarse cursor positioning, and a command to change mode. Edit mode allows text input and deletion, fine cursor positioning, and mode change. To maximise the usable screen area, the system feedback consists of only a single status line at the top of the screen. To reduce the number of commands to be learnt, the same command has been used for mode change in each mode - so ctrl-Q say, toggles between command and edit modes. What will be the result?

In a typical task, the user repeatedly does

   1)   position cursor coarsely

   2)   position cursor exactly

   3)   insert/delete

Step 1, however, will not always be necessary, since the cursor may already be in the appropriate area.

Since this is a two-mode system, it would be efficient to automatise the mode change, so that the sequence of actions becomes

1   (a)   change to command mode
    (b)   position cursor coarsely

2   (a)   change to edit mode

    etc.

Although more keystrokes are used, fewer decisions are then required (cf. Card et al. (1983) for analogous predictions). Moreover, automatising the sequence avoids consulting a status line which is poorly placed (top left hand corners are hard to read) and which breaks the rule of 'no significant omissions' (Green, 1980) because it indicates command mode by <u>not</u> saying EDIT. Thus there is strong pressure to automatise that sequence. But because the mode control is a toggle, the result will be frequent mode errors: if step 1 is unnecessary, the result of step 2a will be a change to the wrong mode.

The problem arises because (1) the mode must be changed sometimes but not always, (2) the system feedback is poor, and (3) the mode switch is a toggle. Altering any one of these would solve the problem. E.g., by simply switching to distinct commands for the two modes, the automatised sequence would become correct and the system would become much more usable.

Example (ii)

In a second text-editor, distantly related to TECO, the commands in command mode include the following:

V   B   F...$ S...$...$

These respectively switch mode, find the beginning of the text, find a specified string terminated by the $ symbol, and substitute one string for another – each of them terminated by $. Commands can be strung together, so that 'BFa$Sunix$TOPS-20$$' is a command string to start at the beginning, find a letter 'a', and then find 'unix' and change it to 'TOPS-20'. Each command string ends with two $ symbols and needless to say this fact rapidly gets automatised, since direct repetition of symbols is a powerful component of internal structuring of sequences.

The effect of this automatisation is to distort the grammar. Insofar as the designers ever thought about the language structure, which is probably not far, they may have imagined it like this:

    command-string -> command* + last-command $

    command -> V | B | F..$ | S..$..$

    last-command -> V$ | B$ | F..$ | S..$..$

The effect of the distinction between 'command' and 'last'command' is to allow the inconsistency in the use of $ to be cleared up. Unfortunately, the majority of command strings contain only one command, terminated of course by $$; and the $$ becomes automatised and converted into a single complex symbol meaning 'end of command string'. (This analysis is purely introspective, of course.) The language structure is therefore:

    command-string -> command $$

    command -> V | B | F.. | S..$..

Needless to say, this distorted version of the language creates difficulties when commands have to be strung together.

The problem in this case could readily have been avoided by using a separate symbol to terminate the command string. Direct repetition would not then take place, and the automatisation would not distort the grammar.

Example (iii)

Here we give three related cases. The editor of example (ii) allows commands to be enclosed in brackets.

    100[sCP/M$MS-DOS$]$$

meaning "do 100 times: change the next CP/M to MS-DOS". Problems at the end of the string, with the 3 terminators $ -] - $$, are so frequent that the user's manual explicitly warns against them (always a sign of design problems!).

The Unix editor 'ed' in its original form used this command to make a substitution:

    s/ed/vi/

Again, users very frequently forget the final /. And thirdly, it is a common observation that closing keywords of programming language constructions are frequently omitted when several endings coincide.

What makes these particular slips so common, according to our model, is that several levels of syntactic construction are being closed, one after the other. Each construction is strongly marked with the feature 'ending', and the response competition between competing productions allows the wrong one to fire.

CONCLUSIONS

Simplistic advice to designers (eg 'be consistent') is likely to be premature, not to say glib. Nevertheless our extensions to the existing analyses of expert slips may lead to sharper understanding of their nature and we hope to collect empirical data against which to make tests. Perhaps it will soon be possible to foresee some of the 'hotspots' where slips frequently occur. At the least, one hopes that designers will avoid the particular hotspots isolated in our examples.

REFERENCES

Anderson, J.R. (1982). Acquisition of cognitive skill. <u>Psychological Review</u>, <u>89</u>, 369-406.

Anderson, J.R. (1983). <u>The Architecture of Cognition</u>. Harvard University Press.

Bock, J.K. (1982). Toward a cognitive psychology of syntax: Information processing contributions to sentence formulation. Psychological Review, 89, 1-47.

Card, S.K., Moran, T.P. and Newell, A. (1983). The Psychology of Human-Computer Interaction. Hillsdale, NJ: Erlbaum.

Deutsch, D. and Feroe, J. (1981). The internal representation of pitch sequences in tonal music. Psychological Review, 88, 503-522.

Garrett, M.F. (1975). The analysis of sentence production. In G.H. Bower (ed.), The Psychology of Learning and Motivation, Vol. 9. New York: Academic Press.

Green, T.R.G. (1980). Programming as a cognitive activity. In H.T. Smith and T.R.G. Green (eds.), Human Interaction with Computers. London: Academic Press.

Green, T.R.G. (1983). Learning big and little programming languages. In A.C. Wilkinson (ed.), Classroom Computers and Cognitive Science. New York: Academic Press.

Green, T.R.G. and Payne, S.J. Organisation and learnability in computer langues. International Journal of Man-Machine Studies, (in press).

Grudin, J.T. (1983). Error patterns in novice and skilled transcription typing. In W.E. Cooper (ed.), Cognitive Aspects of Skilled Typewriting. New York and Heidelberg: Springer-Verlag.

Lewis, C. (1981). Skill in algebra. In J.R. Anderson (ed.), Cognitive Skills and Their Acquisition. Hillsdale, NJ: Erlbaum.

Neves, D.M. and Anderson, J.R. (1981). Knowledge compilation: Mechanisms for the automatization of cognitive skills. In J.R. Anderson (ed.), Cognitive Skills and Their Acquisition. Hillsdale, NJ: Erlbaum.

Norman, D.A. (1981). Categorization of action slips. Psychological Review, 88, 1-15.

Norman, D.A. (1983). Design rules based on analyses of human error. Communications of the ACM, 26, 254-258.

Norman, D.A. and Rumelhart, D.E. (1983). Studies of typing from the LNR research group. In W.E. Cooper (ed.), Cognitive Aspects of Skilled Typewriting. New York and Heidelberg: Springer-Verlag.

Payne, S.J. (1984). Task-action grammars. MRC/ESRC Social and Applied Psychology Unit, The University, Sheffield, S10 2TN, Memo No. 639. Submitted to Interact '84.

Payne, S.J. and Green, T.R.G. (1983). The user's perception of the interaction language: A two-level model. Proc. CHI 83 Human Factors in Computing Systems. Boston. ACM, p. 202-206.

Reason, J. (1979). Actions not as planned: The price of automatization. In G. Underwood and R. Stevens (ed.), Aspects of Consciousness. Vol. 1. London: Academic Press.

Reisner, P. (1981). Formal grammar and human factors specification of an interactive graphics system. IEEE Trans Software Engineering, SE-7, 229-240.

Restle, F. (1970). Theory of serial pattern learning: Structural trees. Psychological Review, 77, 481-495.

Roberts, T. L. and Moran, T.P. (1983). The evaluation of text editors: Methodology and empirical results. Communications of the ACM, 26, 265-283.

Simon, H.A. (1972). Complexity and the representation of patterned sequences of symbols. Psychological Review, 79, 369-382.

Human-Computer Interaction — INTERACT '84 / B. Shackel (ed.)
Elsevier Science Publishers B.V. (North-Holland)
© IFIP, 1985

TASK-ACTION GRAMMARS

Stephen J. Payne

MRC/ESRC Social and Applied Psychology Unit
Department of Psychology, The University
SHEFFIELD S10 2TN, UK

PRELIMINARIES

Task languages

A task language is the language used to interact
with the machine. Task language is used rather
than the more usual 'command language' to show
that the ideas refer to menu and icon systems,
as well as to conventional command systems. The
analysis may also apply to programming languages
but in this paper I will restrict myself to
single-transaction languages.

Mental models

Payne (1984) describes a user's mental model of
a machine as consisting of two components, a
model of the task language and a model of the
underlying system. The mental model of the task
language is assumed to be a linguistic, grammatical, representation, which generates action
specifications from "simple tasks". TAG is a
theory of the mental representation of task-
action grammars.

THE TAG THEORY

Overview

TAG is a meta-language for defining task
languages. Any given TAG description may not
correspond to a particular user's task action
grammar, but TAG does purport to represent the
operations and structures that a user may call
on to encode information about a language. As
a model of the user's perception and memory of a
task language, TAG is bound to be over simple.
At the current moment it is also underspecified
- this paper is a window on an ongoing project.
Nevertheless, I hope to demonstrate that TAG is
an applicable model which has merits for design
despite any potential psychological shortcomings.
In this sense TAG shares the spirit of GOMS, and
other models presented by Card, Moran and Newell
(1981).

Tag has two levels of description, concepts and
rule-schemata. The dictionary of concepts models
the mental representation of the grammatical
objects in the task language, including the
"simple tasks" (ie tasks that the user can
routinely perform). The rule-schemata model the
mental representation of the mappings from task
descriptions to action specifications. A full
description must include schemata for mapping
commands onto their names (in a command language)
and schemata capturing the syntactic rules of
the language.

An example

To help explain the TAG theory and to demonstrate that the ideas have a potential applicability, I have included a TAG description of a
simple fragment of a task language. The conventions of the meta-language are very straightforward - for ease of reading I have adopted as
many of the conventions of BNF as possible, so
are the systems that are being described. TAG
can easily be extended to larger, more complex
systems; these small examples should convey the
essential qualities. Featural descriptions are
denoted by curly brackets, features being associated with particular values by the '=' symbol.

Figure 1:   Cursor control in an experimental text
            editor (from Green and Payne, 1983)

Four example commands:

```
move cursor one character forward     ctrl-C
move cursor one character backward    meta-C
move cursor one word forward          ctrl-W
move cursor one word backward         meta-W
```

CONCEPTS

Simple tasks:

```
move cursor one character forward
     {direction=forward;  unit=char}

move cursor one character backward
     {direction=backward; unit=char}

move cursor one word forward
     {direction=forward;  unit=word}

move cursor one word backward
     {direction=backward; unit=word}
```

Symbols:

```
ctrl {direction=forward}
meta {direction=backward}
```

RULE SCHEMATA

```
s.t. [direction,unit] → symbol[direction] +
     letter[unit]
letter[unit] → first letter of unit name
```

The dictionary of concepts

TAG has a mental dictionary consisting not only
of the terminal vocabulary of the language, but

also of primitive task concepts, called "simple tasks", and of intermediate concepts specifying non-terminal symbols (where necessary). Simple task concepts serve two separate basic functions: they are manipulated by the user to perform goals to solve problems, and they are the "distinguished symbols" in the rule-schemata, allowing action specifications to be generated. For each purpose a different form of mental representation is posited.

For use in the rule schemata, task concepts are represented by feature-sets (as illustrated in figure 1). Featural descriptions of concepts have a rich history in linguistics and psychology. Features and featural descriptions can be defined in precise mathematical terms (see Rosenberg, 1982) but for our present purposes an intuitive introduction will suffice. A feature is anything that has a value with respect to an object. Often, useful features will be binary and so will be limited to two values, presence or absence. A feature-set description is simply a collection of features, and their values with respect to the described object. For problem solving, the representation of concepts is less well defined, but two ideas are crucial to the TAG model. Firstly, there is a wealth of evidence that concepts can be organised according to "plans" (Brewer and Dupree, 1983; Rabinowitz and Mandler, 1983). TAG must support this phenomenon. Secondly, the conceptual representation of the tasks can form a point of contact with a mental model of the underlying system (Payne, 1984). Thus, users with rich mental models of the computer system may be able to represent simple task concepts in terms of their effect on a conceptual machine.

It is worth stressing that the multiple representation of task concepts proposed by TAG is justified on theoretical grounds by the different functions that the representation serve (see Anderson, 1983), and is supported by recent empirical evidence on natural concepts (Armstrong, Gleitman and Gleitman, 1983).

The remaining (non task) concepts, such as the actions, and various non-terminal phrases, are represented in terms of their featural constitution. This is the ONLY form of representation of these concepts that is used by TAG currently, as these concepts only perform a function in the rewrite schemata.

The conceptual dictionary is the only representation of semantics in the TAG model. It is clearly related to Newell's notion of a "vocabulary model", as described by Young (1983).

The rules

TAG has rewrite rules in the standard phrase structure grammar sense, but the rewrite rules are in the form of schemata operating on SETS of concepts, and have featurally based restrictions on the selection of dictionary items. These

rewrite schemata are identical in function to those in the set-grammar model (Payne and Green, 1983), but the role of "selection rules" has been developed by featural specifications. Items in schemata can be tagged with valued or non-valued features. Any non-valued feature present in a schema must be instantiated with the same value throughout the schema. By the selection of a particular value, a set-descriptor can be replaced with a single grammatical object, thus generating a single-level rule from the schemata. Rule-schemata are similar to hyper-rules in van Wijngaarden grammars (see Green and Payne, 1984). Through the device of featural selection TAG enables specifications of simple tasks to be rewritten into syntactically correct action sequences. All the possible action sequences can be generated by TAG, just as all the sentences of a context-free language can be generated by standard phrase structure models. TAG makes no assumption about the architecture of the "grammar-runner" that is the program that interprets the grammar and actually generates actions from task specifications, but a production system architecture could be adopted (see Green, Payne, Gilmore and Mepham, 1984).

EMPIRICAL PREDICTIONS

Concepts

TAG makes many contentious claims about the representation of task language concepts. Many of these are offered some support by the literature on natural categories, but little research has been done on the sort of concepts of interest here, and many empirical questions remain to be addressed. Do users categorise task concepts? TAG predicts they do. Do users employ plan organisations when recalling task concepts? Again, TAG predicts yes. Do models of the underlying system help in problem solving, yet have little effect in routine use? TAG predicts this, and is supported by the preliminary data of Halasz and Moran (1983), who studied people using calculators.

Rules

If rule-schemata are used to encode syntactic regularity, then languages which can be generated by fewer schemata might be expected to be easier to learn. Two experiments testing this hypothesis have been performed; I report the most direct and conservative test.

Twenty subjects each learnt one of two experimental languages. The languages could both be defined by finite-state grammars, and both consisted of the same, eight item, single-letter vocabulary. Both languages shared a common core of five sentence types. Language B (for hypothesised bad) contained an additional two sentence types, of similar complexity to those in the core. Language G (hypothesised good) contained an additional four sentence types, but these all bore a simple family resemblance to the sentence types in the core, and could there-fore each share a schema with the corresponding core sentence type. For example, one of the sentence types in the core grammar was H S* X S - meaning that any sentence starting with H followed by any number of Ss and finishing XS would be a legal sentence. One of the additional sentence types from language G was H R* X R. These two sentence types can be represented by the schema: H C[i]* X C[i]. Where C stands for a category which can take the value S or R. By a schema analysis, language G consisted five schemata, language B seven. By a phrase-structure grammar analysis, language B contained fewer rules. Other obvious analyses, such as the number and frequency of letter diagrams, failed to distinguish between the languages.

Subjects were given sheets of example sentences, and allowed to study them while completing two tests: cloze tests, requiring the insertion of randomly deleted letters into otherwise legal strings, and well-formedness tests in which subjects had to judge the grammaticality of sentences, half of which were in fact illegal (created by inserting a bogus letter into a sentence generated by the core grammar). The example sheets were taken away, and the tests repeated. The results indicated clear support for the schemata hypothesis. Subjects using Language G scored significantly higher on all tests despite the fact that their target language contained more sentence types.

This experiment has clear implications for syntax design in task languages. Payne and Green (1983) have shown how the results of Reisner (1981) and Barnard et al. (1981) can be partly predicted from the number of rule-schemata in set-grammar descriptions of the experimental languages, and these demonstrations are equally straightforward using the TAG model. TAG has many further implications for HCI issues both for initial learnability and long term use (see Green, Payne, Gilmore and Mepham, 1984). Rather than attempting a too-brief survey, one more example will be presented in a little detail.

Command naming

An important decision in the design of human-computer interfaces is the choice of command names. This has become a popular issue with human factors researchers, and many well documented results can be found in the literature. A first attempt at bringing together the various findings was made by Rosenberg (1982), using featural analysis of names and operations as a theoretical base. TAG can extend Rosenberg's framework by associating rule schemata with featural descriptions. By so doing, the problems of Rosenberg's model are, I believe, circumvented, and a truly general model for command naming can be proposed.

Rosenberg's model is based on Tversky's featural theory of similarity. The essential notion of this approach is very simple. Given featural descriptions of two objects, their similarity can be calculated from some linear combination of their common features (those having the same value for both objects) and their distinctive features (those having different values). The precise nature and justification of the combina-trial equation need not concern us here. Rosenberg argues strongly that the "suggestive-ness" of a command name can be assessed from the featural similarity between the name and the operation it refers to. Rosenberg (1983) suggests that an optimal nameset will maximise the similarity between each operation and its name, and minimise the similarity between different names (increase the distinctiveness of names).

This heuristic seems eminently reasonable, but is flawed, as the experiment of Green and Payne (in press) demonstrates. They compared the learna-bility of four different namesets for 26 simple word processing commands, using a simple paired associate learning paradigm. A snippet of one of the four languages has already been shown; figure 2 shows a different snippet from two other namesets. From this small snippet, it is clear that the names of language L2 are more suggestive of the operations than are those in language L1. Furthermore, the names in language L2 use exactly the same number of symbols as those in L, and presumably are equally distinc-tive. According to Rosenberg's heuristic L2 should be the easiest nameset to learn, but it proves significantly harder. The reason (as discussed in detail by Green and Payne) cannot be explained in terms of the relationship between operations and their names, nor between different names. It hinges on the different rules that a user can adopt for matching names with operations.

Figure 2: Fragments of the namesets used by Green and Payne (in press)

Operations (simple tasks)	L1	L2
move pointer a character forward	ctrl-L	ctrl-F
move pointer a character backward	meta-L	ctrl-B
move pointer a word forward	ctrl-E	meta-F
move pointer a word backward	meta-E	meta-B
view next screen	ctrl-C	ctrl-V
view previous screen	meta-C	meta-V

A similar phenomenon was demonstrated by Carroll (1982) and labelled "congruence". Rosenberg discusses Carroll's work with regard to his featural framework, but is unable to incorporate it into a general heuristic. TAG allows this to be accomplished. TAG treats naming in exactly the same way as it treats syntax, as a stage of the mapping between simple tasks and action specifications. Command naming is represented by rule schemata in which the left hand sides specify one of several operations, and the right hand sides specify the names. In this view the optimal naming scheme will be one that allows the most economical TAG description, by

enabling powerful naming schemata. Thus the
nameset of L1 can be generated by the following
schema:

Simple-task[direction,unit] → symbol[direction]
+ letter[unit]

This schema can be compared to that in figure 1.
Note that this schema assumes that users have
learnt the concepts relating the symbols to
directions and the code letters to units. The
language described in figure 1 has the added
advantage of a schema for associating letters
with units. L2 does not allow any such schema
to be used for generating names - symbols can
not be associated with directions, and letters
cannot be associated with units.

COMPARISONS WITH OTHER MODELS

1   ACT* (Anderson, 1983)

Anderson's ACT* has a central tenet that
declarative and procedural knowledge should be
separated; Anderson therefore uses a production system to encode procedural knowledge and
a semantic network to encode declarative knowledge. TAG resembles ACT by having one purely
declarative component, the representation of
concepts. The rewrite schemata could be
compared to ACT's productions, but the comparison would be shaky as I am conjecturing that the
rewrite schemata of TAG are sometimes accessible
to conscious processes in a way that Anderson's
procedural knowledge is not, by definition.
The rewrite schemata are a sort of intermediate
knowledge not present in ACT. They can be
interpreted by a production system-like architecture, whereas ACT specifically disallows
productions to look at each other. Yet they
represent knowledge about rewriting and pattern
generation in a manner very similar to some of
ACT's productions. Perhaps the concept of rule-
schemata can be seen as a modest move toward a
reconciliation of schema-based theory with the
computationally more precise but empirically
weaker production system models.

Linguistic models

1   Case grammar (Fillmore, 1968)

The use of semantic features in syntactic rules
originates in case grammar. The features used
in TAG are very different to cases however.
Cases are designed to illuminate natural
language sentence structure and are not at all
task oriented. It is worth noting that the LNR
model of long term memory (Rumelhart, Lindsay
and Norman, 1972) initially adopted a case-
grammar-like representation of facts, before
moving to a more conceptually oriented approach
(following Schank, 1972). TAG's use of
featural AND schematic representations reflects
the fruitfulness of this approach.

2   GPSG

The use of schemata in a grammar in place of
simple rewrite rules can be compared with the
use of meta-rules in Generalised Phrase Structure Grammar (eg Gazdar, 1983); and with the
use of hyper-rules in the computational fore-
runner of GPSG's meta-rule idea, van Wijngaarden's
two-level grammar. In all three systems the
higher-order rules can themselves generate
standard phrase-structure rules. In GPSG this
works by defining meta-rules in terms of rules
eg "for every rule A → B, add the rule A/N →
B/N". In W-grammars the single level rules are
generated by uniform replacement of meta-
concepts throughout a hyper-rule, according to
the definition rule for the meta-concept. In
TAG single level rules are generated by the
selection of objects matching the featural
restraints on the rule-schemata.

3   Lexical functional grammar (Bresnan and Kaplan, 1983)

TAG clearly gives a lot more grammatical power
to the lexicon than a standard phrase structure
would allow. In this way it is similar to
lexical functional grammars. The matching of
features when selecting objects for rule-schemata
can be compared to evaluation of the lexical
equation in lfg, which also uses features,
similar to notion of case discussed above.
However, in lfg all the features are entirely
lexically based, the use of conceptual representations is not found. Furthermore, the
purposes of the two grammars are so different
as to render any more detailed comparisons
invalid.

Models from HCI

1   CLG (Moran, 1981)

Moran's command language grammar was the first
serious attempt at cognitive modelling in HCI,
and shares the credit for inspiring the current
work with Reisner (1981), Young (1981) and
Green (1983). CLG concentrated on full specifications at the various levels that Moran
identified: Task, Semantic, Syntactic and
Interaction, whereas TAG concentrates on
defining the mappings between these levels, and
leaves the knowledge at each level much more
loosely defined. By this change of emphasis
TAG is able to adopt a much less verbose
notation than CLG, which is somewhat unwieldy.

2   Task-action mappings (Young, 1981)

Young's (1981) adaptation of Moran's ideas
pointed to the importance of the mappings
between the knowledge levels. However, Young
offers no general model in which users' knowledge can be represented, merely a framework in
which such models might be built. TAG may be
thought of as a specific instantiation of
Young's proposed framework.

3   ETIT analysis

Moran (1983) has also developed Young's ideas, although not into a cognitive model. He has put forward a novel task analysis technique designed to evaluate the difficulties of "getting into a system". ETIT analysis assumes users comes to a new system with a clear specification and structuring of the task domain. The first problem is to learn the mapping between their own task structure and the one inherent in the design of the machine (ETIT stands for external -internal task mapping).

The problem with ETIT analysis is that it is impotent in situations where the user does not possess a coherent model of the task domain prior to using the computer system. Moran appears to assume that such situations do not arise. TAG theory makes no such assumption. In cases where Moran is right, then the TAG view of initial learning is very similar to that embodied by ETIT; the user already has the simple task concepts, and must learn the mapping onto actions. A first step in this mapping will be the mapping onto intermediate "internal task" concepts. TAG differs by expressing this mapping by schemata, rather than the simple one-to-one pointers that Moran adopts. In cases where the user does not possess a coherent task-model, the initial learning problem has two components which are likely to proceed in parallel. Users will have to develop conceptual representations of the simple task domain - which in these situations will be the ABSTRACT SYNTAX of the task language. And they will have to learn the rule schemata for mapping these simple task concepts onto action specifications. An important part of TAG's view of learning is that it is ongoing: the simple task concepts change as a user's task-action grammar evolves. When a new task is undertaken, it must be decomposed into simple tasks before it can be accomplished. If the task is often encountered it may become absorbed into TAG and itself become a simple task. This conception allows TAG consistency with the mature literature on problem solving and on experts' "chunks" (eg Chase and Simon, 1973).

CONCLUSIONS

A model of the user's knowledge of task languages has been presented and discussed. The case for progress rests on three propositions. Firstly the model can be developed into a metric which can be applied to designs in advance of implementation and allow the prediction of learnability and usability. Thus, counting the rules in the TAG definitions of the experimental languages used in the experiment mentioned above predicts the speed with which the languages are learnt. Secondly, the model allows empirical findings and common sense notions to be generalised into broadly applicable heuristics. Thus the rather surprising results from the command naming experiment of Green and Payne (in press) can point the way to a generalised naming heuristic. Thirdly, models that can be expressed as computable procedures, and that are consistent with the progress of cognitive science, are necessary to enrich our understanding of computer use.

Acknowledgements

Thomas Green has inspired and encouraged all of the ideas presented here. Many of them (as the references will show) arise from joint work.

References

Anderson, J.R. (1983). The Architecture of Cognition. Harvard University Press.

Armstrong, S.L., Gleitman, L.R. and Gleitman, H. (1983). What some concepts might not be. Cognition, 13, 263-308.

Barnard, P.J., Hammond, N.V., Morton, J., Long, J. and Clark, I.A. (1981). Consistency and compatability in human-computer dialogue. International Journal of Man-Machine Studies, 15, 87-134.

Bresnan, J.W. and Kaplan, R.M. (1983). Lexical-functional grammar: A formal system for grammatical representation. In Bresnan, J.W. (ed.), The Mental Representation of Grammatical Relations. Cambridge, Mass: MIT Press.

Brewer, W.F. and Dupree, D.A. (1983). Use of plan schemata in the recall and recognition of goal-directed actions. Journal of Experimental Psychology: Learning Memory and Cognition, 9, 1, 117-129.

Card, S.K., Moran, T.P. and Newell, A. (1983). The Psychology of Human Computer Interaction. Hillsdale, NJ: Erlbaum.

Carroll, J.M. (1982). Learning, using and designing command paradigms. Human Learning, 1, 31-62.

Chase, W.G. and Simon, H.A. (1973). Perception in chess. Cognitive Psychology, 4, 55-81.

Fillmore, C.J. (1968). The cases for case. In E. Bach and R.T. Harms (eds.), Universals in Linguistic Theory. New York: Holt, Rinehart and Wilson.

Gazdar, G. (1983). Phrase structure grammar. In P. Jacobson and G.K. Pullum (eds.), The Nature of Syntactic Representation. Dordrecht: Reidel.

Green, T.R.G. (1983). Learning big and little programming languages. In A.C. Wilkinson (ed.), Classroom Computers and Cognitive Science. New York: Academic Press.

Green, T.R.G. and Payne, S.J. Organisation and learnability in computer languages. International Journal of Man-Machine Studies, in press.

Green, T.R.G., Payne, S.J., Gilmore D.J. and Mepham, M. (1984). Predicting Expert Slips. Submitted to Interact 84.

Halasz, F.G. and Moran, T.P. (1983). Mental models and problem solving using a calculator. Proc. CHI 83 Human Factors in Computing Systems, Boston, ACM, 212-216.

Moran, T.P. (1981). The command language grammar. International Journal of Man-Machine Studies, 15, 3-50.

Moran, T.P. (1983). Getting into a system: External-internal task mapping analysis. Proc. CHI 83 Human Factors in Computing Systems, Boston, ACM, 45-49.

Payne, S.J. (1984). The role of mental models in user computer interaction. MRC/ESRC Social and Applied Psychology Unit, University of Sheffield. Memo No. 638.

Payne, S.J. and Green, T.R.G. (1983). The user's perception of the interaction language: A two-level model. Proc. CHI 83 Human Factors in Computing Systems, Boston, ACM, 202-206.

Rabinowitz, M. and Mandler, J.M. (1983). Organisation and information retrieval. Journal of Experimental Psychology, Learning, Theory and Cognition, 9, 430-439.

Reisner, P. (1981). Formal grammar and design of an interactive system. IEEE Transactions on Software Engineering, 5, 229-240.

Rosenberg, J. (1982). A psycholinguistic model for command names. Technical Report C15-14 Xerox Palo Alto Research Center.

Rosenberg, J. (1983). A featural approach to command names. Proc. CHI 83, Boston, ACM, 116-119.

Rumelhart, D.E., Lindsay, P.H. and Norman, B.A. (1972). A process model of long-term memory. In E. Tulving and W. Donaldson (eds.), Organization of Memory. New York: Academic Press.

Schank, R.C. (1972). Conceptual dependency: A theory of natural language understanding. Cognitive Psychology, 3, 552-631.

Young, R.M. (1981). The machine inside the machine: Users' models of pocket calculators. International Journal of Man-Machine Studies, 15, 87-134.

Young, R.M. (1983). Surrogates and mappings: Two kinds of conceptual models for interactive devices. In D. Gentner and A. Stevens (eds.), Mental models. Hillsdale, NJ: Erlbaum.

Human-Computer Interaction — INTERACT '84 / B. Shackel (ed.)
Elsevier Science Publishers B.V. (North-Holland)
© IFIP, 1985

REPRESENTING THE USER'S MODEL OF AN INTERACTIVE SYSTEM

Marion Wells

Keith London Associates, Welwyn Garden City
Hertfordshire, U.K.

With the very rapid increase in the development of interactive systems the traditional data flow diagrams produced using structured methods are becoming less than adequate as a basis for obtaining user acceptance of a proposed software system. Enhancement of such diagrams with screen or report layouts and input forms, can only hope to present static models of the proposed system. The user's conceptual model of the dynamic nature of the system should form an essential ingredient of the design process, and to this end a notation ·has been devised which can be directly integrated with traditional data flow diagrams. The paper describes the notation and its application in a dialogue prototyper.

1.   INTRODUCTION

The very rapid increase in the development of interactive systems has blurred the distinctions between the stages of systems analysis, systems design and software design within the life cycle of a computer system. The overlapping roles of systems analyst, systems designer and programmer are shown in Fig 1.

CURRENT PHYSICAL SYSTEM

                Systems Analyst

CURRENT LOGICAL SYSTEM

                Systems Designer

NEW LOGICAL SYSTEM

                Programmer

NEW PHYSICAL SYSTEM

Figure 1 : System life cycle

Traditionally the systems designer has been able to describe a new logical system in terms of the functions that will be performed, the data that passes between functions, samples of input and output layouts and the files required to support the functions. Such a description is presented to the proposed user of the system and if acceptable is then passed to the programmer who is responsible for the creation of the new physical system.

Where the system is to include interactive facilities the decisions about possible routes through the software system and the man-machine interface are entirely the responsibility of the programmer who may never meet the proposed user to discuss his preferences. Thus current descriptions of a new logical system can only hope to provide a static model of the proposed system for the user to consider. When interactive systems are under consideration it would seem appropriate that the dynamic nature of the system should form an essential ingredient of the design of the new system.

Attempts to rectify this deficiency have been made by some designers who present 'mock-ups' of the new system using prototyping, or less commonly, simulation techniques so that the proposed users can obtain a feel for what the system will be like to use. These techniques usually do not constitute part of a formal method or set of documentation standards from which the programmer can develop the new physical system.

However, considerable research has been undertaken into representation techniques for man-machine dialogues for the purposes of evaluation and simulation. These techniques may be adapted to provide the formalism required to specify the user's model of the dynamic aspects of a system. Once formalised the model is then available for simulation, prototyping, modification by the user, and implementation by the user.

2.   MAN-MACHINE DIALOGUE REPRESENTATION

A number of approaches have been taken to represent man-machine dialogues.

Production systems were first described
by Newell [1], Davis and King [2] and
Anderson and Gillogly [3]. Waterman [4]
and Hopgood and Duce [5] describe their
application to man-machine dialogues.
The production system approach enables
dynamic adaptation of the production
rules thus lending itself to machine-
adaptable user interfaces based on knowledge acquired about the user during his
use of the system. However production
systems do not provide a readily comprehensible model of the dynamic nature of
a dialogue for user assessment purposes.

The use of directed graphs or state
transition diagrams as a means of evaluating interactive interfaces before
implementation can be attributed to
Parnas [6]. Edmonds [7,8] and Guest [9]
have extended this notation to enable
interactions between the dialogue and
main processing tasks to be modelled.
Alty [10] has adopted a similar approach
enabling conditional iteration within a
network to be modelled.

A formal notation for the description of
state transition diagrams has been defined by Reisner [11] and Schneiderman
[12] using Backus-Naur Form. Jacob [13]
has compared the use of BNF and state
transition diagrams and concludes that
although they are formally equivalent
BNF does not readily demonstrate sequences in the behaviour of an interactive
system and are thus less readily understood.

The techniques used to represent man-
machine dialogues do not appear to have
been incorporated into any existing
methods to enable the dynamic aspects to
be included in the design stage of the
system. The reason for this might be
that the systems designer sees his job
as being the production of a specification for a new logical system and using
traditional methods such a specification
is identical for a system whether it is
to be implemented in batch and/or on-
line modes. As stated earlier, however,
it would seem essential that the
designer concerned himself with the
dynamic properties of an interactive
system in order to fully satisfy customer and user requirements.

3.   THE DESIGN OF INTERACTIVE SYSTEMS

Feldman and Rogers [14] describe the
development of an interactive system as
a top-down process involving four stages
of design: conceptual, semantic, syntactic and lexical. The conceptual model
involves the designer in understanding
the entire systems requirements.   The

semantic model is then developed which
describes the set of sub-tasks as perceived by the end users as a logical
decomposition of the overall task, each
requiring a few user supplied inputs.
The syntactic model describes the network of these tasks, with transitions
caused either by user inputs or by
results from processing. Finally, the
lexical design describes the input and
output devices to be used and the style
and format of all user inputs and outputs.

This paper proposes that in order to
adopt this top-down approach to interactive systems design, it is necessary
to integrate it into traditional structured techniques such as those of Gane
and Sarson [15], DeMarco [16] etc. The
starting point must be the logical model
of the new system produced as a result
of applying structured systems analysis
techniques.   Although this new logical
model is identical for both batch and
interactive implementations of the
system, it can be extended to become
Feldman and Roger's semantic model of
the system by identifying user inputs
and outputs for each of the sub-tasks.
These sub-tasks can then be connected
together to produce a dynamic model of
the system using a graphical notation
based on state transition diagrams. By
adopting a slightly different notation
to those described earlier it is possible for both the syntactic and the
lexical details of the system to be
defined simultaneously.

4.   GRAPHICAL NOTATION FOR INTERACTIVE
      SYSTEMS

The symbols shown in Figure 2 are taken
from [15] and are used to represent the
logical model of the new system. From
such a model the interactive parts of
the system are identified by drawing
dotted dividing lines between the proposed batch and interactive sections.

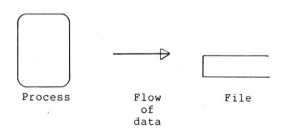

Process   Flow   File
                    of
                   data

Figure 2:   Structured Analysis notation

For each interactive section the inputs and outputs to the user are defined using data dictionary notation. The functions to be performed are divided into a number of sub-tasks. One or more data flow diagrams for each section are then produced and since the inputs and outputs to the user have been identified this description is equivalent to Feldman and Roger's semantic model of the system.

The sub-tasks are then connected together showing both inputs and outputs to the user and the tasks and files that are involved in the processing. Inputs and outputs are commonly portrayed using a screen symbol. (Figure 3)

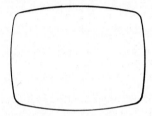

Figure 3 :   Screen notation

The control paths within the network of sub-tasks are defined either by user inputs or the results of a process. The paths are represented using an adaptation of the select, case and iteration notation used in BS6224: Design Structure Diagrams [17] as shown in Figure 4 and Figure 5.

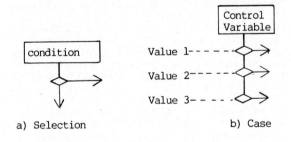

a) Selection   b) Case

Figure 4 :   Route selection

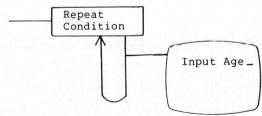

Figure 5 :   Route iteration

Using the notation described it is possible to construct a dynamic model of a man-machine dialogue which shows both its syntactic and lexical details and also includes the processes identified at the logical model design stage.

An application of the notation is shown in Figure 6 and also in [18].

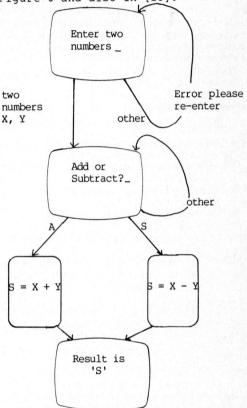

Figure 6 : Model of simple interactive process

5.   DIALOGUE PROTOTYPING

A simplified notation showing only inputs and outputs to the user has been used by the author to describe man-machine dialogues. Once described in this notation the dialogue description is entered to a dialogue simulator (DS) which has been designed and developed by the author. DS is currently in use by ergonomists who are involved in the design and evaluation of man-machine dialogues.

The limitations of a simulated dialogue are significant when a meaningful system has to be demonstrated to potential users since DS does not incorporate facilities which enable 'background' processing tasks to be carried out during the simulation.

One of the most interesting results to come out of the development of DS was that non-computer specialists such as psychologists were able to use the notation to describe a man-machine dialogue.

This feature has been incorporated into a Dialogue Prototyper (DP). DP employs the Dialogue Simulator's user-friendly techniques which enable the specification of man-machine dialogues by non-computer experts and additionally enables programmers to describe the processes carried out between inputs, outputs and files.

DP can be used in one of two modes:

DESIGNER MODE -

The analyst/designer/user of an interactive system is able to enter and modify the details of an interactive system in terms of:-

    o inputs from the user

    o outputs to the user

    o processes to be carried out on inputs in a BASIC type of language

Once entered such a description is 'compiled' and any errors or inconsistencies are reported.

USER MODE -

A user may select and execute an interactive system which has already been entered to the DP. The user has controlled access to some of the editing routines available in designer mode so that he can modify the man-machine dialogue format and mode to meet his own requirements.

Although similar to some program generator systems the overall advantages of DP are:

o Design and development are concentrated on user involvement.

o Rapid prototyping of the most important aspect of an interactive system, its man-machine dialogue, is facilitated.

o Users are able to modify a dialogue to meet their own requirements, with no programming expertise at all.

This paper proposes that this last feature of DP is the most significant.

Considerable research is currently being carried out into adaptable/modifiable interfaces including the use of expert systems [19] but it would seem that a user-modifiable interface offers the best solution to the problem of individual differences between users. Traditionally programming skills are essential for this to be carried out but DP offers a readily acceptable alternative.

A prototype DP has been developed, using a disc based BBC microcomputer system, which enables the entry and modification of simple interactive systems by users.

More sophisticated facilities for a DP are to be proposed in the light of experience with Mark I, such facilities may include:-

o An expert system to aid effective dialogue designs (e.g. screen layouts, input techniques).

o A range of input/output device techniques (e.g. colour, graphics, touch screen, mouse).

o Collection of evaluation data during execution of an interactive system, to enable experimentation with proposed systems.

6.   CONCLUSIONS

The techniques outlined in this paper to describe the dynamic model of an interactive system provide an invaluable tool for the designer to use to present a more meaningful model of a proposed system to the user. Such representation techniques may be applied to the logical design which results from the use of structured methods.

The definition of the dynamic model of the system is sufficiently comprehensive to form the basis of a description of the system that can be entered to the Dialogue Prototyper. The ease with which dynamic models can be described and entered to the DP enables users to modify the man-machine interface of the system. The user is therefore able to represent model of the interactive system.

The Dialogue Prototyper demonstrates a user-centred development system for interactive systems which have been specified using the extended structured notation. It also demonstrates user modifiable dialogue facilities which require no computer or programming expertise.

REFERENCES :

[1] Newell, A., Human Problem Solving, 1972, Prentice Hall.

[2] Davis, R. and King, J., An Overview of Production Systems, 1975, Stanford University Report STAN - CS - 75 - 524.

[3] Anderson, R. and Gillogly, J., RAND Intelligent Terminal Agent : Design Philosophy, 1976, RAND report No. R - 1809 - ARPA

[4] Waterman, D., A rule based approach to knowledge acquisition for Man-Machine interface programs, International Journal of Man-Machine Studies, 1978, 10, 693 - 711.

[5] Hopgood, F. and Duce, D., A production system approach to interactive graphic program design, in Methodology of Interaction, Guedj et al. Eds, 1980, North Holland Publishing Company.

[6] Parnas, D., On the use of transition diagrams in the design of a User interface for an interactive computer system, Proceedings of ACM National Conference, 1969.

[7] Edmonds, E., Adaptive Man-Computer Interfaces, in Coombs, M. J., and Alty, J. L., Eds - Computing skills and the user interface, 1981, Academic Press.

[8] Edmonds, E., The man-computer interface : a note on concepts and design, Int. J. Man-Machine Studies, 1982, 16, 231-236.

[9] Guest, S., The use of Software tools for dialogue design. Int. J.Man-Machine Studies, 1982, 16, 263-285.

[10] Alty, J., Path Algebras - a useful CAI/CAL analysis technique 1983. Research Report No. 125, University of Strathclyde.

[11] Reisner, P., Formal Grammar and Human Factors Design of an Interactive Graphics System. IEEE Transactions on Software Engineering, 1981, SE-7 229-140.

[12] Shneiderman, B., Multi - Party Grammars and Related Features for Defining Interactive Systems. IEEE Transactions on Systems, Man and Cybernetics, 1981.

[13] Jacob, R., Using Formal Specifications in the Design of a Human-Computer Interface. Proceedings of Conference on Human Factors in Computer Systems, 1982, 315-321.

[14] Feldman, M. B., and Rogers, G. T., Toward the design and development of style-independent interactive systems. Proceedings of Human Factors in Computer Systems, 1982, 111 - 116.

[15] Gane, C., and Sarson, T., Structured Systems Analysis : Tools and Techniques, 1979, Prentice Hall.

[16] DeMarco, T., Structured Analysis and System Specification, 1979, Yourdon.

[17] Design Structure Diagrams. BS6224, British Standards Institute, 1982.

[18] Wells, M., Modelling the user's view of interactive systems, in Bytheway, A. (ed), State of the Art Report on Structured Methods (Pergamon Infotech, 1984).

[19] Alty, J. L., The Application of Path Algebras to Interactive Dialogue Design, 1983, Research Report No. 128, University of Strathclyde.

Human-Computer Interaction — INTERACT '84 / B. Shackel (ed.)
Elsevier Science Publishers B.V. (North-Holland)
© IFIP, 1985

ON THE MODELLING OF HUMAN-COMPUTER INTERACTION AS THE INTERFACE BETWEEN THE USER'S WORK ACTIVITY AND THE INFORMATION SYSTEM

Juhani Iivari and Erkki Koskela
(Authors in alphabetical order)

Institute of Data Processing Science, University of Oulu,
Linnanmaa, SF-90570 Oulu 57, Finland

This paper analyses human-computer interaction and its design as an integrated part of an information system design methodology, paying principal attention to its role as the interface between the user's work activity and the information/data system. It is also pointed out that due to the great number of factors influencing human-computer interaction design, this should be layered in a way which is consistent with the whole information system design process.

1. INTRODUCTION

Even though (computer-based) information systems are becoming increasingly interactive, the design of this user-computer interaction is not an integral part of most information systems design methodologies (cf. the CRIS methodologies in [20]). On the other hand, we have a growing body of research into human-computer interaction, research which typically studies this interaction as being quite isolated from the rest of the information system, and especially from its design process.

The design of user-computer interaction should take into account the requirements and possibilities related to four categories of factors:
1. the user's personal characteristics (e.g. cognitive factors)
2. characteristics of the user's activity and work environment
3. characteristics of the information system (its contents and logic)
4. the available technology.

From the viewpoint of the information systems design methodologies, it is furthermore important to distinguish
- general factors which can be built into methodologies or the hardware/ software products to be used, and
- specific (to the application domain) and situational factors which must be analyzed separately in each specific design situation.

We shall pay most attention here to the second and third categories, those which are specific to each application domain, and more specifically to their role in and impact on the design of human-computer interaction as the interface between the user's work activity and environment and the information system. The analysis is based on the PIOCO model for information systems development.

PIOCO is an acronym for the three levels of abstraction, Pragmatic, Input-Output and Constructive-Operative (see [14],[7]) used in the modelling of information/data systems.

Briefly, the pragmatic (P) level views an information system as a structural element in organizational design or development, the input-output (I/O) level corresponds to information systems specifications and the constructive-operative (C/O) level to the architectural and detailed (technical) design of the information/data system (cf. [4]). These levels are defined more formally in the PIOCO metamodel for an information/data system ([8],[7]).[1]

In the following we analyse human-computer interaction design in the framework of these three levels of abstraction, which lead to a view of human-computer interaction design as a gradual refinement process which proceeds through the following levels (cf. [18]):

Pragmatic (P) level
- definition of the requirements for the interaction imposed by the host system, and especially the user's work activities.

Input-Output (I/O) level
- identification of the requirements imposed by the detailed contents and logic of the information system (semantic sub-level)
- specification of the logic of the interaction, describing the interaction in an 'ideal' error-free world and including specification of the sequences of primary functions, dialogue techniques and screen layouts (syntactic sub-level).

Constructive-Operative (C/O) level
- specification of exception handling features, e.g. error processing and HELP routines, etc. (functional sub-level)
- specification of the features of interaction related to the details of software and hardware (implementation sub-level).

In accordance with the title of our paper, principal attention is paid to the first two main levels, which are illustrated using the PIOCO description languages. Particular emphasis is placed upon interaction (IA) graphs, which form a 'fascade' language describing the information system as the user sees it.

2. HUMAN-COMPUTER INTERACTION DESIGN AT THE PRAGMATIC LEVEL

We emphasize in our definition of an 'information system' that it has a certain organizational context. This context is to some extent controllable and subject to design when the information system is viewed as a structural element in organizational design or development.[2] Reflecting this view, the pragmatic (P) model for an information system can be defined as follows ([8]): The P model is the development model for the long-term production factors associated with the utilizing host system (enterprise or the like), describing a planned change and forming one investment entity.

In order to facilitate the P design of an information system we have developed a graphical description language HSL (Host System Language), which supports an integrated description of the host system ranging from its overall description to very detailed descriptions of individual programmes (work routines) by means of three basic types of graph ([11]). Due to the limited space available, we provide only a simple example of certain HSL graphs (Figure 1). The first graph (HO graph, 1.a) describes the internal and external units of an inventory system and their relations (information, material and money flows). This graph could be refined down to the level of individual positions and their occupants. The second graph (HS graph, 1.b) describes the functions of the 'Inventory' unit. The small letters in circles (e.g. a) denote trigger types, e.g. specifying that a customer order triggers the selling function and the selling function the customer delivery function by means of the delivery order. The larger circles denote state information types as distinct from flow information types. The third graph (HP graph, 1.c) describes the programme related to the selling function. The structure nodes ⊗ = 'AND', ⊕ = 'FOR EACH' and ⊕ = 'OR' are from SREM ([2]). Before we proceed to the fourth graph (1.d) it is time to describe briefly our use of HSL for the delimitation of the information system.

From the viewpoint of the information system, the P model delimits its boundary. This includes three steps
1) the assignment or delegation of selected systematizable information processing functions to the information system (cf. [19])
2) identification of the input and output users
3) definition of the user-computer interaction by means of input and output information types and their relationships to the users' activities (functions and programmes, cf. HS and HP graphs).

In the assignment or delegation of the selected information processing functions to a (computer-based) information system, we see the computer as a technological (adp) device which is able to provide information services (state and flow information types). After that preliminary

assignment we make a synthesis of the information system in order to understand its nature as a system and its role in the host system.

This first step gives the output users of the information system (which may not yet be defined at the level of individual positions or persons). In the case of the input users we must accept the possibility that we are not able to see all the inputs necessary for the outputs. These precedence relations are specified in detail at the I/O level.

In step 3 we begin to view the computer-based information system as a communication partner ([19]). At the P level we do not necessarily require the semantics of the input and output information types to be precisely defined. Instead they may be proconcepts in the terms of Langefors ([15]). Our interest at this level is restricted to primary communication, i.e. we do not specify the metacommunication ([19]). The refinements needed in order to specify the semantics and syntax of user-computer interaction are made at the I/O level, to be discussed next.

Figure 1.d describes a selling programme from the viewpoint of a salesman as the result of the three steps detailed above. It shows that the maintenance of the state information types: 'customer info', 'store info' and 'open order info' and the performance of the operation type 'give a delivery order' are delegated to the computer-based information system under development. The communication process type 'customer info' between the user and the information system can be refined using IA graphs (see section 3.2).

3. HUMAN-COMPUTER INTERACTION DESIGN AT THE INPUT-OUTPUT LEVEL

The I/O model determines the primary information (data) and its processing rules at the infological (i.e. conceptual and linguistic) level and the external behaviour of the system.

From the viewpoint of user-computer interaction design, this definition includes two levels, the semantic level, corresponding to the determination of the primary information (data) and its processing rules at the infological level, and the syntactic level, corresponding to the external behaviour of the system. We describe these two levels separately in the following.

3.1 The semantic level

At the semantic level we define the detailed contents and logic of the information system. This includes
- specification of the information types included in the information system at the infological, i.e. conceptual and linguistic, level (information model)
- specification of the derivation rules for the non-initial information types and the

related control, i.e. qualifier and trigger
types (<u>information process model</u>).[3]

The semantic specification takes place in two
steps. First we have a <u>user-oriented I/O speci-
fiation</u> for each user or user group, in which we
<u>define</u> in detail the inputs and outputs related
to the user. This includes a specification of
the precise contents of the inputs and outputs,
their underlying concepts and potential derivation rules (conceptual level), and also the
names and other vocabulary of the inputs and
outputs (linguistic level).

In the second step we consolidate the local I/O
specifications into an integrated model for the
information system. This step does not directly
concern user-computer interaction, but potential
conflicts between the specifications of individual users, for example, may imply reformulation
of the users' specifications.

The Input-Output Specification Language (IOSL)
includes three types of graph for the semantic
specification of the information system.[3] Figure
2 illustrates the use of these graphs in the
case of an inventory control information system
(see [12] or [10] for detailed specification of
the IOSL). The information system (IS) graph
(2.a) gives an overall description of the information system. It identifies the information and
information process types, and specifies their
couplings and control, i.e. the qualifiers,
notes and trigger types. The latter are presented using notation of the same kind as in HS
graphs. Information type (IT) graphs (2.b) specify the contents of the information types and
information process type (IP) graphs (2.c)
define the logic of the process types. IP graphs
specify the derivation operations and conditions, and give derivation rules for each
separate trigger type (which causes different
responses in the process type) using "AND",
"OR", and "FOR EACH" nodes, as in HP graphs.

3.2 The syntactic level

At the syntactic level we define the detailed
logic of user-computer interaction in an 'ideal'
error-free world. This level is formally defined
(using a modified BNF notation) in the <u>interac-
tion model</u> ([9]). It describes interaction process types, consisting of communication process
types and the trigger type. The triggering may
be automatic, being performed by the system or
it may be done by the user. The communication
process type can be described using a hierarchical decomposition (cf. [3], [23]). The elementary communication process types correspond to
simple transaction types which may be primary or
dialogue ones. The former correspond to the
information types described in the information
model and the latter ones support the communication process (cf. metacommunication in
[19]). The transaction types are specified by
describing the transaction object type, i.e. the
transaction information type and its layout, and
the transaction requirements, such as timing,

media (text, graphics, voice, pointing, etc.)
and access control requirements. The description
of the transaction types, together with the
structure of the communication process type
(sequence/selection/iteration), defines the
dialogue technique in the sense of Martin ([26])
and a grammar for the dialogue by describing the
messages (transactions) and the sequences of
these which are acceptable during a dialogue
(cf. [5], [6]).

Corresponding to the interaction model outlined
above, we have proposed a special language,
interaction (IA) graphs ([12]), the symbols of
which are presented in Figure 3.a. In a formal
sense, IA graphs are based on PETRI nets ([21])
and more specifically on R nets in SREM ([2]),
which can be interpreted as modified PETRI nets.
IA graphs are like R nets in which only the
external interfaces (cf. interaction points in
[3]) are described.

In addition to PETRI nets, techniques for the
description of human-computer interaction (cf.
[13],[22]) are generally based on state transition diagrams (e.g. [3],[23]) and BNF notation. Referring to Jacob ([13]), we can say that
these techniques are in most cases formally
equivalent, but due to surface differences the
state diagrams are preferable, since they capture the surface structure of the user interface
more perspicuously.

We can treat IA graphs as structured state transition diagrams of a kind (cf. [1]) which,
contrary to the general custom (cf. e.g. [3]),
describe explicitly the inputs causing the state
transitions and the outputs reflecting the
current state and only implicitly, by comments,
the states themselves. Due to this modification,
IA graphs capture the surface structure of the
user interface still more realistically than
ordinary state diagrams. Another reason for this
modification is that users normally view human-
computer interaction as action performed within
a certain state (mode) rather than as a transition between states (cf. [6]).

Figure 3 also includes examples of IA graphs
identifying the main communication process types
(3.b) and describing some sub-process types of
customer order processing dialogue. These
examples show how we can describe different communication techniques (command language (3.b),
simple question-answer technique (3.c), menu
selection (3.d) and form-filling technique
(3.d)).[4] The IA graphs can be supplemented with
layout descriptions of the transaction information types and the related screens and windows.

4. HUMAN-COMPUTER INTERACTION DESIGN AT THE
   CONSTRUCTIVE-OPERATIVE LEVEL

The C/O model determines the internal structure
and action of an information (data) system, i.e.
the primary data and its processing rules at the
datalogical level, the control and supporting

activities and the organization of the data
system (see [8], [7]). It is divided into three
sub-models: the primary action model, the
control and supporting action model and the
organization model.

It is clear that most decisions concerning the
C/O model affect user-computer interaction in
some respect, at least its response times (cf.
requirements expressed in the iteration model).
In the following we outline user-computer interaction design at the C/O level more specifically, making a distinction between two levels,
i.e. the functional and implementation levels,
reflecting the major two steps of the C/O
design.

4.1 The functional level

At the functional level we define 1) the functional division of labour between the storing,
processing and transmission of data including
the storing, processing and transmission
necessitated by the control and supporting activities, and 2) the general technical solutions
for these functions. These solutions are general
in the sense that they should not include specific features of any hardware or software products.

The control and supporting activities to be
incorporated include (see [8], [7])
-   the external control support, producing
    feedback on the operation of the data system
    and its use to the external control respon-
    sible for the maintenance of the system
    (e.g. logging of selected features of user-
    computer interaction)
-   the internal control, taking care of proper
    scheduling of processes and the run-time
    allocation of resources (e.g. dialogue
    control)
-   quality monitoring, including
    -- error prevention in storing, processing
       and transmission (e.g. data validation,
       concurrency control, access monitoring)
    -- failure treatment, i.e. back-up, recovery
       and by-pass activities (e.g. informing
       the user about a failure situation)
-   system aid facilities (e.g. help functions,
    documentation administration, query language
    processing).

Refinement of the user-computer interaction
defined at the syntactic level by user-visible
features of the interaction at the functional
level is formally quite a straightforward exercise, including identification of the additional
transaction types (imposed by control and supporting activities) and their incorporation in
the main stream of information. This can be
depicted using a language very similar to IA
graphs.

4.2 The implementation level

At the implementation level we fix the hardware
and software resources to be used in the tech-

nical implementation of the data system and
adapt the general technical solution achieved at
the functional level to the specified hardware/
software environment. This design level likewise
concerns user-computer interaction, i.e. we fix
the devices and software implementing this
interaction.

5. SUMMARY AND FINAL COMMENTS

We describe the human-computer interaction
design here as an integral part of the PIOCO
model which is a methodology for information
systems design under development at the University of Oulu in Finland. The interaction design
is structured into three hierarchical layers,
the pragmatic (P), input-output (I/O) and
constructive-operative (C/O) levels, the linear
order of which defines the logical relations of
user-computer interaction design. It is beyond
the present scope to discuss more detailed
alternative ways to incorporate user-computer
interaction design in the total process of
designing the information system, but in accordance with our basic contingency assumption we
wish to emphasize their situation dependency. It
should also be recognized that in the PIOCO
model for information systems analysis and
design these levels are interwoven into a non-
linear structure ([7].)

ACKNOWLEDGEMENTS

This work was supported by the Academy of
Finland. We are also grateful to our colleagues
Jouni Similä, Reino Viippola and Pasi Kuvaja for
their participation in the development of the
graphical description languages introduced in
this paper.

FOOTNOTES

1. The PIOCO model described as a whole in [7]
    includes four components:
    1) the PIOCO metamodel for a data system
    2) the PIOCO description languages
    3) the PIOCO model for systems analysis and
       design and
    4) the PIOCO model for choice and quality
       criteria

2. The need for this level is being increas-
    ingly recognized, especially in implementa-
    tion research (e.g. [16]).

3. We omit here the object system model which
    specifies the structure and behaviour of the
    UoD underlying the data system, and the
    corresponding description technique.

4. We should note that description techniques
    like IA graphs are of greatest value in
    cases in which the dialogue pattern is quite
    closed, i.e. predefined and structured
    ([1]). In open, unstructured situations,
    e.g. queries using some query language, the
    communication process types consist of a
    sequence of transaction types in which each

transaction information type is defined by any expression allowed by the query language (and access control requirements).

REFERENCES

[1] Brown, J.W., Controlling the complexity of menu networks, Communications of the ACM, Vol.25, No.7 (1982)

[2] Davis, C., Vick, C., The software development system, IEEE Transactions on Software Engineering, January 1977

[3] Denert, E., Specification and design of dialogue systems with state diagrams, In Morlet, E., Ribbens, D. (eds.), International Computing Symposium 1977 (North-Holland, Amsterdam, 1977)

[4] Freeman, P., Wasserman, A. (eds.), Tutorial on software design techniques (IEEE, New York, 1980)

[5] Gaines, G.R., The technology of interaction-dialogue programming rules, International Journal of Man-Machine Studies, Vol.14, No.1 (1981)

[6] Hägglund, S., Tibell, R., Multi-style dialogues and control independence in interactive software, Software Systems Research Center, Linköping Institute of Technology, Research Report LiTH-MAT-R-82-40, (Linköping, 1982)

[7] Iivari, J.: Contributions to the theoretical foundations of systemeering research and the PIOCO model, Acta Universitatis Ouluensis, A150 (Oulu, 1983)

[8] Iivari, J., Koskela, E., PIOCO model for a data system, In Lyytinen, K., Peltola, E. (eds.), Report of the Third Scandinavian Research Seminar on Systemeering Models (Jyväskylä, 1980)

[9] Iivari, J., Koskela, E., A revised I/O meta model for a data system (Working paper, Oulu, 1982)

[10] Iivari, J., Koskela, E., An extended EAR approach for information system specification, In Davis, C.G., Jajodia, S., Ng, P.A., Yeh, R.T. (eds.), Entity-Relationship Approach to Software Engineering (North-Holland, Amsterdam, 1983)

[11] Iivari, J., Koskela, E., HSL: a host system language for the pragmatic specification and host system descriptions in the data system development, In Nurminen, M. et al (eds.), Report of the Sixth Scandinavian Research Seminar on Systemeering (Bergen, 1983)

[12] Iivari, J., Koskela, E., Similä, J., Viippola, R., IOSL: An infologically oriented input-output specification language for data systems, In Goldkuhl, G., Kall, C-O. (eds.), The Report of the Fifth Scandinavian Research Seminar on Systemeering (Stockholm, 1982)

[13] Jacob, R.J.K., Using formal specifications in the design of a human-computer interface, Communication of the ACM, Vol.26, No.4 (1983)

[14] Kerola, P., Järvinen, P., Systemointi II (Gaudeamus, Helsinki, 1975)

[15] Langefors, B., Control structures and formalized information analysis in an organization, In Grochla, E., Szyperski. N. (eds.), Information Systems and Organizational Structure (de Gruyter, Berlin, 1975)

[16] Lucas, H.C., Jr., Implementation, The key to successful information systems (Columbia University Press, New York, 1981)

[17] Martin, J., Design of man - computer dialogues (Prentice-Hall, Englewood Cliffs, New Jersey, 1973)

[18] Moran, T.P., The Command Language Grammar: a representation for the user interface of interactive computer systems, International Journal of Man-Machine Studies, Vol.15, No.1 (1981)

[19] Oberquelle, H., Kupta, I., Maass, S., A view of human-machine communication and co-operation, International Journal of Man-Machine Studies, Vol.19, No.4 (1983)

[20] Olle, T.W., Sol, H.G., Verrijn-Stuart, A.A. (eds.), Information System Design Methodologies: A Comparative review (North-Holland, Amsterdam, 1982)

[21] Peterson, J., Petri nets, Computing Surveys, Vol.9, Sept 1977

[22] Shneiderman, B., Software psychology; Human factors in computer and information systems (Winthrop Publishers, Cambridge, MA, 1980)

[23] Wasserman, A.I., USE: a methodology for the design and development of interactive information systems, In Schneider, H-J. (ed.), Formal Models and Practical Tools for Information Systems Design (North-Holland, Amsterdam, 1979)

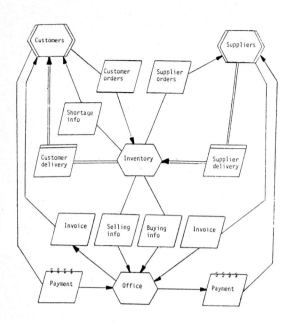

Figure 1.a: HO graph: internal and external units of an inventory system and their relations

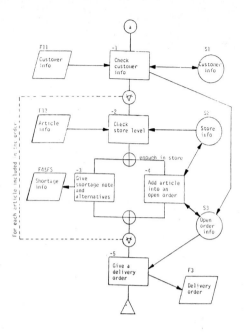

Figure 1.c: HP graph: Programme related to the selling function

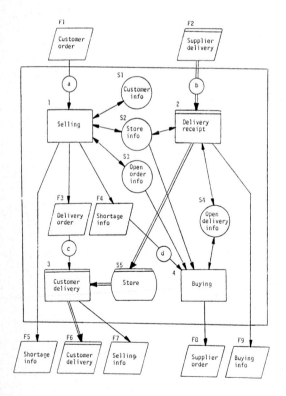

Figure 1.b: HS graph: Functions of the 'inventory' unit

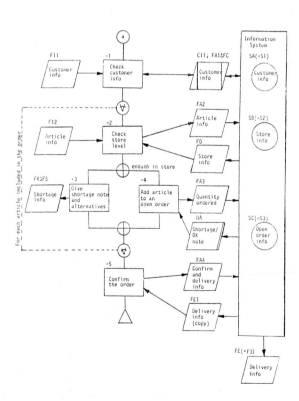

Figure 1.d: HP graph: A selling programme from the viewpoint of the salesman

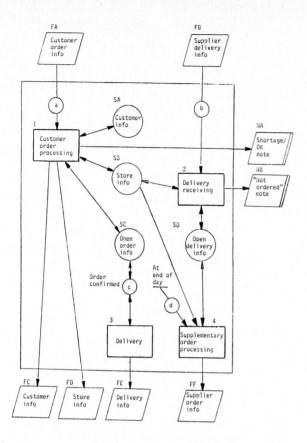

Figure 2.a: IS graph: Overall description of the information system

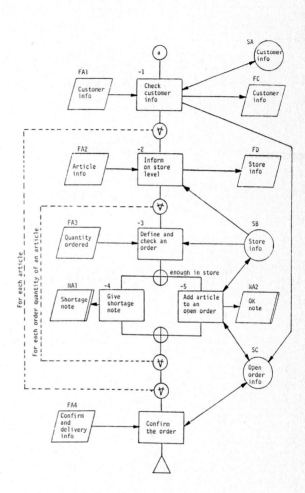

Figure 2.c: IP graph: The logic of the process type 'customer order processing'

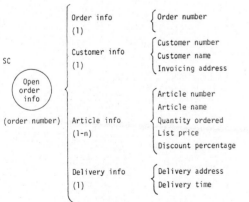

Figure 2.b: IT graph: The contents of the information type 'open order info'

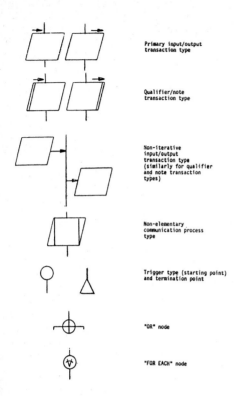

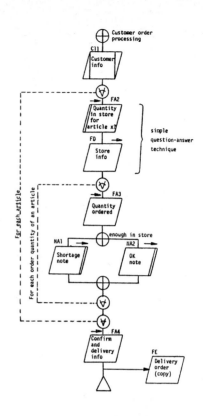

Figure 3.a: Symbols used in IA graphs

Figure 3.c: IA graph: The communication process type C1: 'customer order processing'

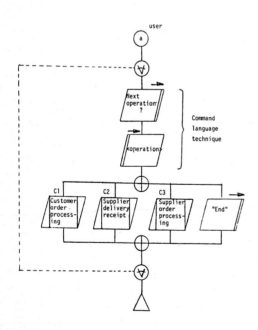

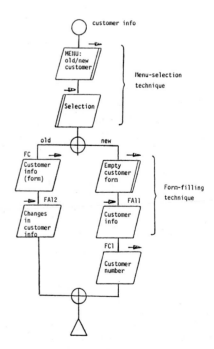

Figure 3.b: IA graph: The main communication process types in the information system

Figure 3.d: IA graph: The communication process type C11: 'customer info'

Human-Computer Interaction — INTERACT '84 / B. Shackel (ed.)
Elsevier Science Publishers B.V. (North-Holland)
© IFIP, 1985

AN OPERATIONALIZED MODEL FOR SUCCESS IN THE USER ROLE

Jouni Similä and Risto Nuutinen

Institute of Data Processing Science, University of Oulu
Linnanmaa, SF-90570 Oulu 57, Finland

The paper presents a conceptual model for success in the user role and operationalizes it in a longitudinal case study of adp systems implementation in a large Finnish chemical enterprise. The model is based on a general conceptual SROE - subject, role, object, and action environment - framework. An analysis is made of the role and systems hierarchy associated with the use of data systems in order to identify the relevant role, object and action environment combinations. Success in the user role is defined to consist of three conceptual components: (1) the degree to which the data system satisfies the information needs associated with the user role, (2) the individual's demands and desires towards acting as a user and his experiences of being a user, and (3) the organization's demands and desires towards the users and the corresponding experiences from the organizational point of view. A preliminary causal model for success in the user role is defined in terms of independent and dependent variables. The operationalization is presented in the context of the case study. The validation and generalizability of the model is briefly discussed.

1. INTRODUCTION

The dismal state of the implementation of adp systems is noted by several authors. Turner ([27]) estimates that somewhere between one third to a half of systems that survive feasibility study never complete implementation or have negligible use two years after their completion. Lucas ([17]) argues that our understanding of how to successfully implement information systems lags far behind our understanding of their technology.

Ives, Hamilton and Davies ([10]) made a wide survey of MIS doctoral dissertations in the U.S. and concluded that there is a clear lack of and a need for research on IS performance measures. They also classified research studies into five types by considering three variable groups: variables measuring environment characteristics, variables measuring information systems characteristics and process variables. They emphasized that contingency approaches to IS design should be directed to studies which at the same time deal with one or more variables from each of the three variable groups. Furthermore, Ives et al. noted that only one of the reviewed dissertations employed action research as a part of the case study.

It is our conviction that these practical and scientific problem groups are related. Implementation of adp systems in practice is in clear need of performance measures which to be relevant may only be developed in rich research settings. The model for success in the user role presented in the paper is closely related to information system use measures, user information satisfaction (UIS) measure to be specific (cf. for example Pearson [23] and Bailey and Pearson ([1]), and the case study offers the

desired characteristics from the research point of view.[1] Ives, Olson and Baroudi ([11]) have recently reported on further development of Pearson's UIS measure. In Finland the research in the implementation field is in its early phases (cf. however Järvinen [12] and Koiranen [16]) and in the field of IS performance measures nearly non-existent.

The concept of implementation success may be approached from several viewpoints. Kling ([15]) has classified studies of automation from a sociological perspective into two main groups: studies representing systems rationalism and segmented institutionalism. The demarcation line is formed by the standpoint on consensus and conflict - may consensus always be reached or is conflict inevitable. Systems rationalism is further divided into three subsets: rational, structural and human relations; and segmented institutionalism into three: interactionist, organizational politics and class politics. The theoretical background and the experiences of the case study place us at the present in the territory between human relations and interactionist groups, however on the consensus side (for conflict approaches cf. e.g. Ciborra [4]). This leads to a model for success in the user role consisting of two viewpoints which are assumed to reach equilibrium. The model owes much to Mumford's and her co-researchers' framework of job satisfaction ([19], [20]).

Lucas ([17]) and also Turner ([27]) analyze implementation research from the process perspective and the consequences or factor research perspective. Even though the case study offers wide research possibilities, this report does not explicitly deal with the process of implementation and neither with implementation process measures (cf. however later Nuutinen

[21], Nuutinen and Similä [22]). The model for success in the user role offers however an explicit measure for implementation success from the viewpoint of the ensued success of use. The model is used for investigating and measuring issues at the level of user interaction with adp systems as well as to a certain degree operator interaction with the terminal.

2. SUCCESS IN THE USER ROLE - A CONCEPTUAL ANALYSIS OF THE MODEL

2.1 A conceptual framework for role analysis (SROE)

The general conceptual SROE framework is depicted in Figure 1. Each logical role R is associated with a certain action environment E, and as a part of the environment with a certain set of objects O that the subject S who is occupying the role is interested in. The logical role is comprised of a set of acts which may be directed at the object (manipulative and observative acts, cf. Iivari [8]) or the environment (merely observative acts).

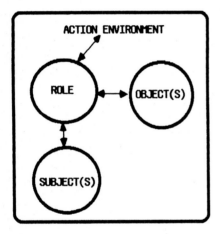

Figure 1. The conceptual SROE framework

The concept of role has been a dominating and to a great degree taken-for-granted basis for the Anglosaxian and Scandinavian social sciences. From a Marxian point of view the role theory has been criticized for its passivating and controlling aspects (cf. e.g. Forsen [5]). The criticism is well-warranted. However it seems to be directed at the manipulatory aspects which become apparent when practical inferences are made on the basis of scientific results. Basically then it is a question of the nature of scientific interest (cf. Habermas [7]). A more modest approach to conceptual frameworks is to consider their usefulness as the primary criteria (cf. e.g. Bunge [2], also Iivari [8]; note that even this of course returns the question to the scientific interest - useful for what?).

The approach may be characterized as phenomenological. It attempts to penetrate the rather confusing surface of data processing practice and to find certain logical elements which comprise part of the basic structure underneath the surface. It is postulated here that systematic information activities may usefully be analyzed with a conceptual framework comprised of subject-object interaction (cf. e.g. Similä and Nuutinen [25], Iivari [8], Goldkuhl and Lyytinen [6]) and that the concept of role enlargens and also focuses the necessary conceptual framework.

The approach does not prescribe a division of tasks among several people. Each person is postulated to occupy a multitude of logical roles which are in effect theoretically formed logical groupings of tasks. The person may or may not be aware of the logical roles he/she occupies.

2.2 Systems and role hierarchy in the use of data systems

In data processing science it is typical to divide the lifecycle of a data system temporally into the building and use phases. Furthermore, there seem to be two distinguishable approaches to the building of data systems. Especially in the Scandinavian countries systemeering is defined as the comprehensive set of activities associated with building a data or information system (cf. e.g. Kerola and Taggart [14], Iivari and Kerola [9]). Implementation of information systems is either referred to as the whole ongoing process which includes the entire development of the systems from the original suggestion to the final installation or only as the final stage of systems development (cf. Lucas [17]). In the producer - user conceptual pair it seems nevertheless valid to distinguish the approaches in such a way that the systemeering approach emphasizes the producer (or systems development environment) point of view and the implementation approach the user (or use environment) point of view.

The systems and role hierarchy in the utilization of data systems is described in Figure 2 (cf. also Kerola and Taggart [14], note that the figure omits an organizational view of the information activities). The main interest in the activities of a utilizing system (a firm for instance) is in its systematic information activities which are distinguished from non-systematic information activities in that there are predestined rules and regulations for the carrying out of the activities (cf. Iivari [8] for more accurate description of criteria).

Systematic information activities are divided logically into use of data systems and into other systematic information activities which include e.g. systemeering or implementation activities associated with the data system (cf. Kerola [13] for the analysis of the information function). Data systems are further divided into adp systems and manual systems where the dividing criteria is current state of automatization.

User role is here defined as the user of the data produced by a data system which may or may not include an automatic subsystem. For practical purposes we delimit the study to such systems which include one or more ADP subsystems.

The primum mobiles for data systems - their use and incidentally also for their development - are the information needs of the user. The information needs are directed at a certain part of the universe of discourse (not depicted in Figure 2, e.g. sales activities of a firm). The data system aims at satisfying these needs systematically directly in the form of adp system outputs (print-outs, terminal screen output etc.) or through some further processing performed in the manual system. Later we also use the term output user to refer to the concept of user.

The principal objects of the user role are then

- the object in the universe of discourse of which the user is interested, and
- the system which produces systematic data of the original object of interest in order to satisfy (partially) the information needs of the user.

The input user (and the original data source) provides the data either directly in the form suitable as input to the adp system or through some manual processing phase (cf. the terms output user and input user also in Goldkuhl and Lyytinen [6] and Sundgren [26]).

The operator refers to the role which entails direct operation of adp equipment. The primary operator or terminal operator which is usually combined to the output or input user role may be distinguished from the secondary operator or console operator.

The processor role represents the innate conviction that although a great deal of a data system may be potentially automatizable, there are tasks which are genuinely nonautomatizable. The manual data processing may occur in the input phase, in an intermediary phase when the adp system has produced intermediary results which are not yet ready for the output user but which must be manually processed somehow before the adp system may resume operation, and finally in the output phase. It must be noted that interpretation of data which must always occur before data is transformed into information is not conceptually a part of the processor role but a part of the output user role. The difference between the output user and the processor in this sense is that the former interprets the final products of the data system, the latter the intermediary products and processing rules of the data system. Concep-

tually the term information system comprises in Figure 2 the data system(s) and the two user roles: input user and output user.

These roles are critical in the use of data systems; higher in the system hierarchy the utilizer role must be noted. The utilizer encompasses the overall responsibility for the activities during the lifecycle of the data system and is exhibited through the decision making and control activities.

The roles are indeed logical, in practice two role combinations are typical. One of them is the combination output user/operator, the other input user/operator (cf. Similä and Nuutinen [24] for more detailed analysis). The term end-user refers in this framework to the same set of activities as the output user. Regrettably it seems that the common usage of the term is quite indecisive with respect to the axis output user - operator and overemphasizes the connection to the adp subsystem.

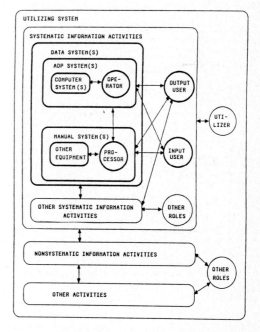

Figure 2. Systems and role hierarchy in use of data system

Sociologically it is also desirable to combine these logical roles in practice according to the principles of a good job to avoid negative effects. It must be noted that especially the roles of processor and operator will not exist in the future by themselves but are combined to other roles. Furthermore, the development of information technology is continually changing the internal structure of a job of adp employees in terms of these roles. Certain typical processor, operator and input user tasks will be automatized already in the fifth generation computer systems. Nevertheless the logical tasks themselves do not disappear.

2.3 A conceptual model for success in the user role

At the highest level <u>success in a role</u> may be defined as

$$SUCCESS = rel (R, (S, O, E))$$

to denote the role-centeredness of the approach. When the action environment is an organization and the (output) user role is the object of the analysis a first-level conceptual model depicted in Figure 3 may be presented. The systems and role hierarchy presented earlier is supplemented by an organizational view which necessiates the inclusion of user's organizational unit and adp support function into the figure.

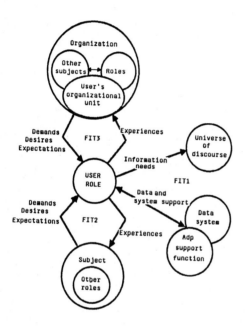

Figure 3.   Success in the user role - three fits

In Figure 3 three fits are presented (note the similarity to Mumford's job satisfaction and effective relationships approach, cf. e.g. Mumford [19]):

<u>FIT1</u> = the degree to which the data produced by the data system and other systems support satisfy the information needs of the (output) user

<u>FIT2</u> = the fit between the individual's demands, desires and expectations towards and experiences of the user role

<u>FIT3</u> = the fit between the user organizational unit's demands, desires and expectations towards and experiences of employees fulfilling the user role.

The core for the success in the user role is formed by FIT1. In the literature this is often commonly called <u>user information satisfaction (UIS)</u> (cf. e.g. Ives, Olson and Baroudi [11], Bailey and Pearson [1], Cheney and Dickson [3]). FIT2 and FIT3 offer two perspectives which in a consensus approach may be combined and in a conflict case remain apart (cf. Kling [15] for a more accurate classification).

There is on a conceptual level a causal link and a weaker feedback loop from FIT1 through FIT2 to FIT3. Additionally FIT1 may directly affect FIT3. It may be argued that the data system must satisfy the information needs associated with the user role before an individual may experience a successful fit of acting in the role. Furthermore FIT1 and also for the major part and for most individuals FIT2 must be successful before FIT3 may reach a successful level.

Figure 3 does not yet explicitly distinguish between dependent and independent variables (also intervening variables and feed-back loops may be present). The model may in this distinction be defined on a <u>conceptual</u>, <u>operationalized</u> and <u>validated</u> level, perhaps also preferably in this order.

On a conceptual level <u>success in the user role has been defined as the dependent variable.</u> The independent and intervening variables affecting success in the user role are described in Figure 4.

On the operational level each variable group involves a selection of relevant variables and their measurement methods. The reasoning for the independent variables is based on the SROE framework in its general sense where the subject and other subjects fulfill also other roles in addition to the user role. Interaction-determined characteristics include all variables which do not measure any of the other components but rather their interaction. These characteristics must be noted to contain also the individual's own success in the operator role if he/she is acting in that role (accordingly though weaker also processor and builder roles as well as general success in the worker role (= job satisfaction)). The analysis resembles somewhat Markus' ([18]) distinction between people-determined, system-determined and interaction-determined factors affecting implementation success.

The operationalization of the three fits, especially FIT1, involves a selection based on the characteristics of the different components of the model. In effect this means "tuning" of the model to suit the empirical case. At the present the most important and also only selection with respect to the dependent variables is based on the characteristics of the adp systems. Lucas ([17]) classifies adp systems into voluntary and involuntary systems and recommends actual use-measure for the former and satisfaction-measure

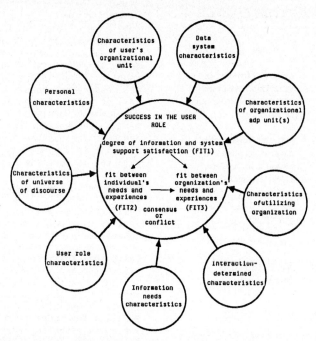

Figure 4. A conceptual model for success in the user role

for the latter. The adp systems in the case study are for the most part transaction processing systems and definitely involuntary for all but a few users on higher organizational levels who receive only summary reports from the systems. Consequently satisfaction is adapted as the performance measure in this study. The choice is made already on a conceptual level.

3. A LONGITUDINAL CASE STUDY OF ADP SYSTEMS IMPLEMENTATION - AN OPERATIONALIZATION OF THE MODEL

3.1 Integration of practical and research problems in an action research framework

The case study concerns one of the largest Finnish chemical enterprises which is currently nearing the conclusion of a massive implementation of distributed adp systems to the local factory level. The researchers have had the fortunate opportunity to closely follow and also offer consultation aid during the whole project.

The action research framework has been substantiated in the form that the researchers have weekly participated in the coordinating sessions of the implementation project on a local factory level. This type of participation has occurred from the early fall of 1982 until the present. The action research will be reported elsewhere (cf. Nuutinen and Similä [22], Nuutinen [21]).

In addition to the action research which has produced a great deal of qualitative data along with some quantitative data, the researchers have constructed a five-round interview, questionnaire and self-appraisal research set-up, of which the first two rounds have been implemented.

The research areas in the case study may be divided into two which are nevertheless intimately intertwined. The first concerns the effects of adp systems implementation on work and general job satisfaction and relies heavily on utilizing and operationalizing Mumford's job satisfaction framework. The second and also the topic of this paper concentrates on developing performance measures and ultimately a causal success model for the use of data systems. The topic deals closely also with implementation success studies and especially rather with factor studies than process studies in Lucas' distinction (cf. Lucas [17]).

The research problems have been stated earlier as follows (cf. Similä and Nuutinen [24]):

RP1 How is the success in the user role operationalized [with respect to the five contractual areas and the two fits in Mumford's framework]?

RP2 Which contingency factors have a major effect on the success in the user role?

RP3 What effect does acting in the adp systems user role have on work and general job satisfaction?

The problematization for the five phases of research is described in Table 1.

PHASE	RP1 AND RP2	RP3
I	Background analysis of certain contingency factors (cf. Similä and Nuutinen (24))	Analysis of the start-up situation of the workers' needs and experiences (job satisfaction)
II	Operationalization and analysis of organization's demands towards the user role (part of FIT3)	Analysis of organization's demands towards and experiences of workers (effective relationships)
III	Operationalization of success in the user role from the individual's point of view (FIT1 and FIT2)	Replication study of job satisfaction
IV	Replication study of Phase III	Replication study of job satisfaction
V	Operationalization and analysis of organization's experiences of the users (part of FIT3)	

Table 1. Five-phase interview, questionnaire and self-appraisal research process

3.2 Operationalization of the conceptual components of the model

Table 2 presents the first operationalization of the model in terms of the independent, intervening and dependent variables. The table also connects the measurement of the variables to the research phases (cf. Table 1).

The present operationalization of the model represents a synthesis of a wide reference basis: Mumford ([19]) and her coworkers, Bailey and Pearson ([1]), Iivari ([8]) and SYKE research group (internal working papers). The presented model hypothesizes numerous causal relationships. Validation of the model with empirical measurements will no doubt result in the elimination of several of these.

The core of the model is formed by FIT1 in the operationalization of which we have relied heavily on Bailey and Pearson. The conceptual analysis of Pearson's UIS measure has however resulted in a certain regrouping. The instrument is nevertheless fully included in the research program for replication, validation and standardization purposes. Iivari's conceptual framework (earlier not operationalized) is partly overlapping with Pearson's UIS measure and is included here for control purposes. Mumford's job satisfaction and effective relationship approach has formed a very useful conceptual basis, extensive work has however been required to make it suitable for the analysis of the user role. The parts of the model which bear no reference basis are the work of the authors.

4. CONCLUSIONS

The present model for the success in the user role represents the first theoretical results of an explorative case study. The validation of the model will take place in the subsequent empirical measurement phases during the spring and fall of 1984, however in such a way that the model may be analyzed already after the measurement in the spring. The results will bring evidence to the hypothesized causal relationships and also to the methodological issues associated with the measurement of the variables.

The research replicates the validation of Pearson's UIS measure in a Finnish transaction processing system environment along the guidelines of Ives et al. ([11]). Pearson's UIS measure is conceptually reorganized in the applied SROE framework where the major part of it indeed falls into the core of the model, the data and system support satisfaction section. The measure is however extensively supplemented with the inclusion of the individual's and the organization's viewpoints to the success measure. In addition the model is regrouped to reveal the variables affecting the success measure. The lack of adaptive data system use measures and also an understanding of the causal relations involved has notably been the concern of recent research. The present research setup has been constructed in such a way as to utilize the research possibilities of the case study. The generalizability of the model will depend on the statistical strength of the revealed relationships and will be discussed in later reports.

ACKNOWLEDGEMENTS

This work was financially supported by the Academy of Finland. We gratefully acknowledge Professor Kerola for his theoretical contributions and managerial support as well as Pirjo Keinänen and the other members of the research project SYKE for their constructive commentary.

FOOTNOTES

1.   The case study is part of a three-year research effort SYKE financed by the Finnish Academy and headed by professor Pentti Kerola at the University of Oulu, Finland.

REFERENCES

[1]   Bailey, J.L. and Pearson, S.W., Development of a tool for measuring and analyzing computer user satisfaction, Management Science, Vol. 29, No. 5 (1983) 530-545.

[2]   Bunge, M., Scientific research I, The research for system (Springer-Verlag, Berlin, 1967).

[3]   Cheney, P.H. and Dickson, G.W., Organizational characteristics and information systems: an exploratory investigation, Aca-

INDEPENDENT AND INTERVENING:

USER ROLE
Type, Amount (Phases III and IV)

PERSONAL

Age, Sex, Education, Handedness, HIP-style(3 tests), Talent factors (2 tests), Knowledge of adp in general, Knowledge of adp implementation project, Attitudes towards adp in general, Attitudes towards adp implementation project, Participation in the adp implementation project, Organizational position, Experienced organizational position, Employment time, Hobbies, Social activity (Phases III and IV)

> (SYKE-reseach group:
> Kerola, Weckroth, Keinänen, Komulainen, Nuutinen, Pankkonen, Similä, Tahvanainen)

Understanding of systems (Phases III and IV)
> (Bailey and Pearson)

UNIVERSE OF DISCOURSE

Content, Temporal change, Complexity, Demarcation with organization (Phases III and IV)

INFORMATION NEEDS

Time dependence, Temporal focus, Stability (Phases III and IV)

DATA SYSTEMS

Response/turnaround time, Convenience of access, Language, Flexibility of systems, Integration of systems (Phases III and IV)
> (Bailey and Pearson)

Effectiveness, Accessibility (partly), Adaptibility, Efficiency (Phases III and IV)
> (Adapted from Iivari)

ORGANIZATIONAL ADP UNITS

Priorities determination, Technical competence of the EDP staff, Attitude of the EDP staff, Organizational position of the EDP staff (Phases III and IV)
> (Bailey and Pearson)

USER'S ORGANIZATIONAL UNIT

Top management involvement (Phases III and IV)
> (Bailey and Pearson)

Organizational department, Use of technical appliances (Phases III and IV)

UTILIZING ORGANIZATION

Product market, Technology, Administrative structure, Organizational culture (Phases II and V)
> (Adapted from Mumford)

INTERACTION-DETERMINED CHARACTERISTICS

Organizational competition with the EDP unit, Relationship with the EDP unit, Communication with the EDP staff, Feeling of participation, Feeling of control (Phases III and IV)
> (Bailey and Pearson)

Job satisfaction and effective relationships (= Success in the worker role) (Phases I, II, III, IV and V)
> (Adapted from Mumford)

Success in the operator role, Success in other dp roles, Complexity difference between the subject in the user role and the various objects associated with the role (Phases III and IV)

DEPENDENT: SUCCESS IN THE USER ROLE

FIT1 = THE DEGREE OF DATA AND SYSTEMS SUPPORT SATISFACTION

DATA PRODUCT
Accuracy, Timeliness, Precision, Reliability, Currency, Completeness, Format of output, Volume of output, Relevancy, Expectations (also for systems support), Perceived utility (also of systems support) (Phases III and IV)
> (Bailey and Pearson)

Relevance of information structure, Recentness, Reliability of information, Interpretability (Phases III and IV)
> (Adapted from Iivari)

SYSTEMS SUPPORT

Schedule of products and services, Time required for new development, Processing of change requests, Vendor support, Error recovery, Security of data, Documentation, Confidence in the systems, Degree of training (Phases III and IV)
> (Bailey and Pearson)

FIT2 = THE FIT BETWEEN THE INDIVIDUAL'S DEMANDS, DESIRES AND EXPECTATIONS TOWARDS AND EXPERIENCES OF THE USER ROLE

Job effects (Phases III and IV) (Bailey and Pearson)

KNOWLEDGE CONTRACT
Use of knowledge, Self-development (Phases III and IV)

PSYCHOLOGICAL CONTRACT
Status, Responsibility, Recognition, Job security, Social relationships, Promotion, Achievement (Phases III and IV)

EFFICIENCY CONTRACT
Salary, Amount of work, Standards, Controls, Supervision (Phases III and IV)

TASK STRUCTURE CONTRACT
Work variety, Initiative, Judgement and decisions, Pressure, Targets, Dependency on others, Autonomy, Task identity (Phases III and IV)

ETHICAL CONTRACT
Company ethos, Communication, Consultation (Phases III and IV)
> (Adapted from Mumford to fit the user role)

FIT3 = THE FIT BETWEEN THE USER'S ORGANIZATIONAL UNIT'S DEMANDS, DESIRES AND EXPECTATIONS TOWARDS AND EXPERIENCES OF EMPLOYEES FULFILLING THE USER ROLE

KNOWLEDGE CONTRACT
Skills and knowledge requirements, Labour market, Recruitment, Training (Phases II and V)

PSYCHOLOGICAL CONTRACT
Management philosophy, Personnel administration, Motivation (Phases II and V)

EFFICIENCY CONTRACT
Salary, Organization of work, Control (Phases II and V)

TASK STRUCTURE CONTRACT
Technical limitations (Phases II and V)

ETHICAL CONTRACT
Company values (Phases II and V)
> (Adapted from Mumford to fit the user role)

Table 2. Independent, intervening and dependent variables in the model of success in the user role

demy of Management Journal, Vol. 25, No. 1
(1982) 170-184.

[4] Ciborra, C.U., Information systems and
organizational exhange: a new design
approach, in Bemelmans, Th. M.A. (ed.),
Beyond productivity: information systems
development for organizational effectiveness (North-Holland, Amsterdam, 1984).

[5] Forsen, B., Kritik av rollteorin (Bokför-
laget Korpen, Göteborg, 1978).

[6] Goldkuhl, G. and Lyytinen, K., A disposition for an information analysis methodology based on speech-act theory, in Goldkuhl, G. and Kall, C-O. (eds.), Report of
the fifth Schandinavian research seminar on
systemeering (Gothenburg, 1982).

[7] Habermas, J., Erkenntnis und intresse
(Suhrkamp, Frankfurt am Main, 1968).

[8] Iivari, J., Contributions to the theoretical foundations of systemeering research
and the PIOCO model, Ph.D Thesis (Acta Universitatis Ouluensis, Series A, No. 150,
Oulu 1983).

[9] Iivari J. and Kerola, P., A sociocybernetic
framework for the feature analysis of
information systems design methodologies,
in Olle, T.W., Sol, H.G. and Tully, C.J.
(eds.), Information systems design methodologies: a feature analysis (North-Holland,
Amsterdam, 1983).

[10] Ives, B., Hamilton, S. and Davis, G., A
framework for research in computer-based
management information systems, Management
Science, Vol. 26, No. 9 (1980) 910-934.

[11] Ives, B., Olson, M.H. and Baroudi, J.J.,
The measurement of user information satisfaction, Communications of the ACM, Vol.
26, No. 10 (1983) 785-793.

[12] Järvinen, P., A role of a user in the development and maintenance of an information
system: empirical and theoretical findings,
in Kerola, P. and Koskela, E.(eds.), Report
of the fourth Scandinavian research seminar
on systemeering (Oulu, 1981).

[13] Kerola, P., On infological research into
the systemeering process, in Lucas, H.C.
jr., Land, F.F., Lincoln, T.J. and Supper,
K. (eds.), The information systems environment (North-Holland, Amsterdam, 1980).

[14] Kerola, P. and Taggart, W., Human information processing styles in the information
systems development process, in Hawgood, J.
(ed.), Evolutionary information systems
(North-Holland, Amsterdam, 1982).

[15] Kling, R., Social analyses of computing:
theoretical perspectives in recent empirical research, Computing Surveys, Vol. 12.,
No. 1 (1980) 61-110.

[16] Koiranen, M., The development dimensions of
a computer-based management information
system: a study of systems effectiveness
and information management, Ph.D. Thesis
(Acta Universitasis Tamperensis, Series A,
No. 146, Tampere, 1982).

[17] Lucas, H.C. jr., Implementation: the key to
successful information systems (Columbia
University Press, New York, 1981).

[18] Markus, M.L., Power, politics, and MIS
implementation, Communications of the ACM,
Vol. 26, No. 6 (1983) 430-444.

[19] Mumford, E., Job satisfaction (Longman,
London, 1972).

[20] Mumford, E. and Weir, M., Computer systems
in work design - the Ethics method, Effective technical and human inplementation of
computer systems (Associated Business
Press, London, 1979).

[21] Nuutinen, R., Report of an adp implementation project: a case study of action
research from the viewpoint of an information systems architect, a paper to be
presented in the seventh Scandinavian
research seminar on systemeering.

[22] Nuutinen, R. and Similä, J., A longitudinal
case study of the effects of adp systems
implementation on work and job satisfaction, a paper accepted to the NordDATA '84.

[23] Pearson, S., Measurement of computer user
satisfaction, Ph.D.Thesis, (Arizona State
University, Tempe, 1977).

[24] Similä, J. and Nuutinen, R., On the analysis of the user role in the context of ADP
systems implementation: theoretical, methodological and operational aspects and the
first results of a case study, in Ross,
C.A. and Swanson, E.B. (eds.), Proceedings
of the Fourth International Conference on
Information Systems (Houston, Texas, 1983).

[25] Similä, J. and Nuutinen, R., On the image
of man and its implications for systemeering and systemeering research, a paper
presented in the sixth Scandinavian
research seminar on systemeering in
Øystese, Norway, 8.-11.8.1983, to appear.

[26] Sundgren, B., An infological approach to
data bases, Ph.D. Thesis (Statistiska
Centralbyrån, Skrifts No. 7, Stockholm,
1973).

[27] Turner, J., Observations on the use of
behavioral models in information systems
research and practice, Information & Management, Vol. 5, No. 4-5 (1982) 207-213.

Human-Computer Interaction — INTERACT '84 / B. Shackel (ed.)
Elsevier Science Publishers B.V. (North-Holland)
© IFIP, 1985

A MODEL OF THE ENGINEERING DESIGN PROCESS DERIVED FROM HEARSAY-II

Andy Whitefield

Ergonomics Unit
University College London
London, England

A model of the engineering design process is proposed. The framework for the
model is derived from the Hearsay-II speech recognition program, and therefore
consists of a set of knowledge sources communicating via a central blackboard.
Changes to the framework for the purpose of this model are outlined. The content
of the model comes from an analysis of the verbal protocols of four engineering
designers. A total of twenty knowledge sources are described, with examples from
the protocols. The uses of the model in comparing computer aided and unaided
design, and in the design of CAD system interfaces, are discussed.

1. Introduction

Understanding the design process at the level
of the individual is an important task in the
study of human-computer interaction. This is for
two main reasons: it could provide a valuable
input to software design methodologies, and it
would provide a basis on which to develop
appropriate computer aids for activities which
include a design component. The latter is the
focus of this paper. The obvious examples of
activities which both involve design and make
use of computer aids are programming,
architecture and engineering design. But design
also occurs in a range of other activities which
do or could benefit from computer aids, such as
graphic art, document creation and management
planning.

This paper presents a descriptive model of the
design process in the area of mechanical
engineering. The model is not intended to be
psychologically valid. Rather it is intended to
be useful in comparing computer aided and
unaided design, and in specifying interfaces for
computer-aided design (CAD) systems. Part 2
describes the derivation of the model's form.
Parts 3 and 4 describe data collection and
analysis. Details of the model are given in part
5, and the paper concludes with a discussion on
the uses of the model.

2. Derivation of the model

The framework for the model is derived from the
Hearsay-II speech recognition program. An
introduction to this is given in Erman and
Lesser (1980). There are several features of the
framework of Hearsay which make it a potentially
fruitful way of modelling design. Principal
among these are: that its hypothesise and test
paradigm is analogous to the notion of designers
focusing on the solution to a problem (Lawson,
1979); that its data-driven, opportunistic mode
of operation allows for design which is not
rigidly top-down; and that it is devised to deal
with the cooperation between diverse sources of
knowledge, something common in design problems.

Hearsay consists of a set of knowledge sources
(KSs) communicating via a central blackboard.
The blackboard is a data structure with three
dimensions: time within the utterance,
information level (e.g. word, syllable, phone)
and alternative hypotheses. It contains only
hypotheses about the identities of portions of
the speech signal. Related hypotheses are linked
together e.g. a particular word hypothesis
supported by certain phonetic interpretations.
In this way, the current state of the problem
solution is represented as a set of linked
hypotheses on the blackboard. Each hypothesis
has a uniform attribute-value structure. This
means that the blackboard has a single
representational form. Each KS can communicate
only with the blackboard, rather than with all
other KSs. This prevents an excessive growth of
communication channels and allows the creation
and modification of KSs to be carried out
independently of each other.

The KSs can only communicate with each other
indirectly by reading from and writing to the
blackboard. Each KS contains a precondition and
an action. This can be thought of as equivalent
to a production rule although Hearsay was not
originally written as a production system.
Effectively a KS scans the blackboard looking to
see if its preconditions are met. If they are,
the KS attempts to apply its action to the
blackboard. This action will be either to create
a new hypothesis or to modify links between
existing hypotheses. Whether or not a KS will be
allowed to act is determined by the scheduler,
which chooses between those KSs whose
preconditions are currently met. The scheduler
is a formula which calculates a priority for
each waiting KS action and selects the one with
the highest priority for execution.

In utilising the Hearsay framework to build a
model of design, changes of three kinds have
been incorporated. The first kind are those
changes appropriate to the different problem
area. These include: the time dimension of the

blackboard has been replaced by a space dimension; all the KSs are of course different; and the third blackboard dimension of alternative hypotheses has been dropped.

The second set of changes concern the purpose of the model. With Hearsay, the purpose was to produce a program with certain performance characteristics. The aim here is to describe the designers' behaviour in a way that allows for discussion of the human-computer interface. The major change here has been to simplify the model by reducing the number of blackboard levels from the six contained in Hearsay.

The third change is intended to strengthen one of the weak points in the Hearsay framework. This is to replace the scheduling formula as a means of controlling the application of the evoked KSs. Although this formula contains clear criteria for the assignment of priorities, it does still constitute control knowledge which is hidden within the program architecture. This means that it is difficult in Hearsay to implement strategy changes while the program is running. This can be seen from the need for, and the ad hoc nature of, the 'policy module' to do this job (Hayes-Roth and Lesser, 1977). The notion of meta-knowledge has been proposed by Davis (1980) as a solution to the problem of control without burying inaccessible knowledge in the program architecture. Meta-knowledge (i.e. knowledge about object-level knowledge) has the advantages that it is explicit, flexible, represented in the same form as the object-level knowledge, and is accessible to the program, making possible a hierarchy of strategies. It acts on the set of evoked object-level KSs, and makes conclusions about their likely utility, either in isolation or relative to other KSs. These conclusions are then used to order the application of the object-level KSs. The notion of meta-knowledge has been used as the means of incorporating control information into the framework for the model of design.

Given these changes, the framework consists of a central blackboard, with dimensions of spatial location and information level, which is read from and written to by a variety of object-level knowledge sources. These KSs can be thought of as containing knowledge in the form of production rules. The blackboard contains hypothesized solution elements, with related elements linked together. The KSs scan the blackboard looking for the conditions that will evoke their actions of creating or modifying blackboard elements. The order in which the evoked KSs are allowed to act is controlled by meta-level KSs. This facilitates both the clear expression of control knowledge and strategic changes as the design develops.

3. Data collection
Given this framework, the content of the model comes from the verbal protocols of four designers. Using a conventional drawing board,

each designer worked on one of two problems. The problems were posed at the level of layout design, rather than concept or detail design. That is, the subjects were asked to produce a general arrangement drawing showing the sizes and positions of the various components. One problem was to design a casing for a television monitor, and the other to design a casing for an electronic keyboard, in each instance given internal components of certain dimensions. Each subject was observed for one session of about two hours. In addition to the verbal protocol, each session was recorded on videotape. The sessions were conducted at the subjects' place of work.

The four subjects were practising mechanical engineering designers working in industry, who spent most of their time working on this sort of packaging problem.

4. Data analysis
The analysis so far has been concerned only with the verbal protocols. Having been transcribed, the protocols were analysed in the following way. Each was classified twice. One classification was to class each utterance in the protocol as belonging to one of the following five categories: generation of hypotheses; evaluation of existing hypotheses; reasoning behind hypothesis generation or evaluation; statement of conditions or existing hypotheses; or meta-statement about control. This classification was devised as a means by which the data could be used to fill in the details of the framework. It was derived from a combination of those distinctions commonly found in the design literature (e.g. generation/evaluation) which are appropriate for this framework, along with those distinctions necessary to utilise the framework (e.g. object knowledge/meta-knowledge). It is thus driven by assumptions about the suitability of such a framework. The classification is not absolute either in the sense that it is the only one suitable for this task, or in the sense that everyone using it would be bound to arrive at the same result. Assignment of utterances to categories is to some extent a matter of judgement.

What might be called the arguments of the generation and evaluation types constitute the individual KSs. For example, the subject might generate an arrangement of the internal components, or a certain type of fixing to mount a component in the case. The associated utterances would be taken to indicate the presence of KSs concerned with these aspects of the design. Similarly, parts of the design might be evaluated against criteria of maintenance or cost, and these utterances would be evidence for KSs dealing with these aspects. The number of KS distinctions that it is reasonable to make here is again a matter of judgement.

Each class of utterance provides a different kind of information for the model: generation

utterances indicate KSs which create new
hypotheses either within or between blackboard
levels; evaluation utterances indicate
within-level KSs which modify existing
hypotheses; reasoning utterances show part of a
KS's content; statements describe hypotheses on
the blackboard; and meta-statements are taken as
evidence of control processes.

The second classification divided the protocol
according to what was inferred to be the current
problem on which the subject was working. This
involved a hierarchic problem breakdown. This
breakdown was not predetermined, either in terms
of levels or content, but arose from the
combination of what the subject said and the
researcher's understanding of the problem. The
purpose of this second classification was to
allocate to levels on the blackboard the KSs
arising from the first classification. In so
doing, it also determined the number of
blackboard levels in the model. So, KSs were
taken as acting at the level on the blackboard
as indicated by the concurrent level in the
problem classification. The classification
resulted in only a three-level problem
breakdown. The model therefore contains three
blackboard levels. These were called the group,
component and detail levels.

This classification also involved a meta-level,
where the current problem might be said to be
'manage the task appropriately'. This was used
when the subject was not concerned with a
particular problem, but with, for example, which
problem to work on next. Some KSs appeared in
the protocol only when the current problem was a
meta-level one. Such KSs could not be allocated
to a blackboard level.

Using this dual classification scheme, one
subject's protocol has been analysed
exhaustively, and the other three selectively.

5. Details of the model
 The protocol analyses produced a total of 20
object-level KSs operating on a three-level
blackboard. This is illustrated in Figure 1,
using a similar representation to that used for
Hearsay (e.g. Erman and Lesser, 1980, Figure
16.1). The circles represent the level of input
to a KS, and the arrows its level of output. A
list of the KSs of each type is given in Table
1. Those KSs that are given as being of two
types (e.g. A and B) are those that were found
under two levels in the problem classification.

KS types C and D can be seen to operate only
within a level, and these arise from the
evaluation category. Types A and B, however,
which are generative, can operate either within
or between levels. Type E KSs are slightly
different from the others in that they read
from, but do not write to, the blackboard. They
take blackboard entries and translate them into
drawn objects, either on rough sketches or on
the finished drawing.

A brief description of each KS, with some
illustrative examples from the protocols, is as
follows:
 a) parts arrangement (types A & B): generates
spatial arrangements of the internal components;
particularly relevant for the monitor problem;
the arrangements are either general ("I would
expect to see the printed circuit board sitting
at the bottom there") or more specific ("We'll
decide then to keep the printed circuit board
back about 3mm from the front").
 b) fixing methods (A & B): generates methods
for mounting the internal components to the

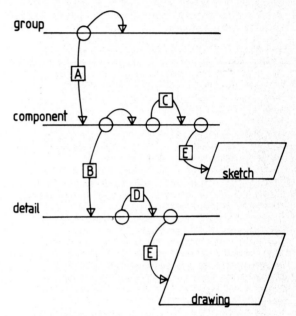

Figure 1: Blackboard levels and knowledge
 source types

Type A & B - parts arrangement; fixing methods;
 casing parts

Type A - materials

Type B - wiring connections; unspecified parts
 details

Type C & D - appearance; size; support

Type C - maintenance; usability; cost; moulding
 production; safety

Type D - assembly; environmental hazards

Type C or D (see text) - ventilation; market
 acceptance

Type E - drawing production; drawing management

Table 1: Knowledge sources belonging to each
 type indicated in Figure 1

case; similar to the above it can be general or specific ("I would expect to see some sort of metal clamping strip, probably in two halves, going round there, clamping through. Yes, to clamp the CRT"; "If we thicken that at that point, to something in the order of 5 or 6mm").

c) casing parts (A & B): generates the individual sections of the casing ("I would like to see the sides of the box slightly radius rather than straight sides"; "If we set a nominal thickness of the front panel at 3mm").

d) materials (A): is used early in choosing the materials from which to make the case, as this has consequences for the way the object is designed ("I would start off by assuming that we're going to have some sort of plastic moulded case for the thing").

e) wiring connections (B): the way in which the internal components are connected together places constraints upon their arrangement; ("And obviously at the back you've got to have a flying lead for your mains coming in").

f) unspecified parts details (B): in a layout design, where not all the components are fully specified, the designer sometimes has to generate missing details ("They're usually about... a centimetre, no, a centimetre and a half in diameter").

g) appearance (C & D): parts of the design are evaluated on appearance grounds, either based purely on personal feeling, or on more specific criteria; ("But I think the trouble is there, that the screen would look odd").

h) size (C & D): evaluates the design in terms of both the total size and the efficiency with which the space is utilised; can be general or specific; ("..front view of something like 440mm by 360mm. Not unreasonable at the moment"; "That's something in the order of 40mm, that's rather a long boss").

i) support (C & D): evaluates the stability of the whole or parts ("I would like to have seen another support on the CRT"; "That should be man enough for that, to take that").

j) maintenance (C): various factors are important for maintenance; ("If someone had to work on it, you'd want to be able to see it. You don't want it buried up inside where there's no way you can get at it"; "Again, you'd have to use inserts, it's no good having self-tapping screws or anything like that, due to the servicing of the thing"). This was considered by the subjects to be very important.

k) cost (C): evaluates solutions on cost grounds ("..it's not really worth making guides and sliding these in runners or anything. Because of the extra cost of all that"). This KS is an example of an evaluation KS which it is easy to imagine working at both the component and detail levels, but the only examples of which in the protocols are at the former level.

l) usability (C): perhaps more rarely than we would like, the subjects do occasionally evoke knowledge of usability in evaluating solutions; ("I suppose they ought to go on the front. Because that's where people will be").

m) moulding production (C): knowledge of how moulds are made is an important determinant of the size and shape of the case parts; ("I don't think that would be too big to mould... The biggest problem would be the tooling for it").

n) safety (C): this evaluation did not occur often, perhaps because monitors and keyboards do not have many moving or dangerous external parts. One subject used this as a reason for putting a bottom cover on the keyboard ("I think we should cover these up. It's easily lifted up and people poking fingers in").

o) assembly (D): evaluates the ease with which the parts can be assembled, an important factor in the production process; most relevant to the details of the fixings.

p) environmental hazards (D): the particular hazard with which one subject was concerned was dust. But others might be equally applicable, such as temperature and humidity.

q) ventilation (C or D): further grounds for evaluation. This and the next KS are not allocated to levels because under the problem classification, they were evoked only at times when the current problem was a meta-level one.

r) market acceptance (C or D): evaluates the product according to its marketability ("..and if we're looking at the TV market, no-one's going to buy a square box. They want something for their money").

s) drawing production (E): this is responsible for producing both freehand sketches, at the component level, and formal drawings, at the detail level. It contains knowledge of how to represent and draw parts in orthographic and perspective projections.

t) drawing management (E): chooses the views to be shown, their arrangement on the sheet, the scale of the drawing, and so on; ("Just from the layout point of view, we're doing a front view, side view and a rear view, to give us the positions of what we're going to put in it"; "..I think I'll have to cut it down.. probably go down to half size"). It also contains techniques for maintaining a 'clean' drawing, such as drawing parts on different sheets and moving them around to get a satisfactory arrangement, or drawing in light lines early on when things are more likely to be rubbed out.

The meta-level KSs concerned with control are currently one of the least elaborated parts of the model. They constitute the strategic and tactical knowledge of the model. They are thus responsible for deciding when to switch between problems, which problem to take up next, when to start drawing, the relative priorities of conflicting evaluations, for identifying missing knowledge and so on. At the moment the model contains a single meta-level, but it could probably be usefully divided into at least two levels, with strategic KSs scheduling tactical KSs, which themselves schedule object-level KSs.

Examples of meta-level statements from the protocols are: "Having got the rough position of where I want to put the things inside, I can now start to think about the case itself"; "I'll worry about that bit in a minute.. How the thing fixes together"; "The biggest problem, as I see it, apart from the shape of the box or whatever we're going to put it in, the biggest problem is mounting the CRT"; "I think that would be small price to pay for making the thing look a bit better on the front. So we'll settle for that one"; "If I have a look and see what happens when we come round to a side view".

The operation of such a model would be as follows. The problem statement places certain items on the group level of the blackboard. Generative KSs use these as input and produce approximate solutions, which are placed on the component level. These are then either modified by evaluation KSs, or used to generate detail level solutions. The drawing is equivalent to an instantiation of the blackboard's detail level, and can be used as KS input in the same way. Similarly with the sketch at the component level. The control KSs choose at any point which of the evoked KSs will be allowed to act.

Rather than always proposing a specific solution, one way in which the KSs can operate is by the use of constraints as partial descriptions of solutions (Stefik, 1981). That is, the designer can state a constraint within which a value must fall. For example, rather than locate exactly the position of the power supply, the designer might decide that it should not protrude beyond the rear of the CRT. Used in this way, constraints allow particular decisions to be delayed until more information is available, and combining constraints across sub-problems can reduce the range of possible solutions.

6. Discussion

As stated earlier, the model outlined above is not intended to be psychologically valid. It is intended as a descriptive model with two aims. The first is to use it as a means of comparing computer aided and unaided design. The second is to use it in designing CAD system interfaces.

Concerning the first aim, protocols of subjects using a CAD system on the same problems have yet to be analysed. Without anticipating the outcome of those analyses, there are several ways in which the two processes could differ in terms of this model. The number and identities of the KSs could vary. This will certainly be the case for drawing knowledge, since using a CAD system necessitates that the designer learn a range of skills for 'navigating' around the drawing. More importantly, it could also be the case for both generative and evaluative KSs, depending upon the use the system makes of libraries of pre-drawn parts or evaluative routines.

Another point of difference could be the contents of any KS. Again, this will clearly be found with drawing knowledge. For example, the knowledge required to scale a drawing on paper will no longer be necessary, as CAD drawings are almost always drawn on a 1:1 scale. Also, the techniques mentioned above for maintaining a clean drawing will not be suitable for use with

CAD, and might be replaced by dividing the drawing between different layers.

Even if all the KSs were to remain exactly the same, there would still be a third difference, and that is in the control knowledge. Due both to the restricted amount of the drawing that can be seen at any time with CAD, and to the greater precision with which lines are drawn, KSs are likely to be evoked at different times. This is likely to include KSs that might be more appropriately left to the next stage of the design, i.e. detailed rather than layout drawings. These differences in KS evocation will demand a change in control to achieve the same ends. Related to this is the possibility that analysis of the aided protocols will produce a different number of blackboard levels, as problems may be considered in greater detail.

The second aim of the model is to use it in designing CAD system interfaces that are appropriately suited to the design process. This will be the next phase of the research. It will involve implementing different interfaces on a CAD system, and examining the ways in which designers interact with them. Any differences in the evocation and control of KSs will be related to the functions of the system and the knowledge embedded in these functions. Two aspects of particular interest here are the extent to which the system knowledge and the model are organised compatibly, and in what ways KS control might be affected by the facilities available, especially the navigational ones. These aspects relate to the identities and control of KSs respectively.

There are, for example, various methods already used in extant systems for incorporating the sort of knowledge outlined here. These include libraries of pre-drawn parts, previous designs to which to refer, and generative routines for creating common parts within certain standards. These may or may not be well organised with respect to the KSs described here. Concerning control, it has been suggested above that the nature of the drawing will lead to differences in KS invocation with CAD. The question to be asked here is how navigational and other facilities can subserve good control of KSs.

References

Davis, R. (1980): Meta-rules: reasoning about control. Artificial Intell., 15, 179-222
Erman, L.D. and Lesser, V.R. (1980): The Hearsay-II speech understanding system: a tutorial. In W.A. Lea (ed): Trends In Speech Recognition. NJ: Prentice-Hall
Hayes-Roth, F. and Lesser, V.R. (1977): Focus of attention in the Hearsay-II speech understanding system. Proc. 5th IJCAI, 27-35
Lawson, B.R. (1979): Cognitive strategies in architectural design. Ergonomics, 22, 59-68
Stefik, M. (1981): Planning with constraints. Artificial Intelligence, 16, 111-140

Acknowledgement: this work was supported by a research studentship from the SERC.

DESIGN — APPROACHES AND METHODS

Human-Computer Interaction — INTERACT '84 / B. Shackel (ed.)
Elsevier Science Publishers B.V. (North-Holland)
© IFIP, 1985

DEFINING INFORMATION TECHNOLOGY SYSTEMS FOR ELECTRICITY SUPPLY DISTRIBUTION

J C Gower and K D Eason

HUSAT Research Group
Loughborough University of Technology

ABSTRACT

This paper demonstrates a methodology for the introduction of Information Technology to the Electricity supply industry.

A socio-technical systems analysis is made of the engineering function of the District office of an Area Board. This is used to identify areas where the introduction and application of information technology could be beneficial and generalisable to other District offices and other Area boards.

The development of a pilot system, using the stated needs and requirements of the potential users as a basis for the specification is also described.

1. INTRODUCTION

The potential of Information Technology is often squandered when organisations are steered towards "technology-led" applications. There is a tempting tendency to be deluded by salesmen's promises or glossy literature and be seduced into the belief a certain type of application will be valuable within a particular organisation.

The damage which this type of approach can cause is more serious than just the under-use of expensive systems. Undesirable consequences may also arise within the organisation. For example, personnel may become resistant to change and be unwilling to accept further system developments.

To avoid this problem the application of Information Technology should be preceded by the examination of the real business problems of an organisation. Unfortunately, there are few methodologies which enable us to follow such a 'business problem led' approach. This paper describes a case study of an attempt to establish such a methodology, and then to use it to identify and specify information Technology systems.

2. ELECTRICITY SUPPLY DISTRIBUTION

The Electricity Supply Distribution network is administered by fifteen autonomous Area Boards. The aim of the project described here was to define useful Information Technology applications which would be generalisable across the industry. The target was the engineering function of a District office of an Area Board. At this level the engineering function is responsible for maintenance and development of the supply to consumers.

The information technology supply specified as a result of this project was to be of generalisable value to other Districts in other Boards. The major difficulty was the wide diversity which existed between the methods of working and philosophies of the various Boards. There were differences in the types of consumers served, for example, industrial, commercial, domestic or agricultural, and in the topography of the office - whether urban or rural etc. It seemed likely, therefore, that whilst the basic functions would be the same in each District office, there would be differences in the problems encountered.

3. THE STRATEGY

Socio-technical systems analysis was used to define the basic functions and problems of a District office. These functions and problems were then compared to those encountered in other offices in other Boards.

When this had been achieved a second phase of the programme was to be the specification of generalisable information technology systems. The next stage was to specify a pilot system based on the most pressing needs perceived in the previous phase. We then aimed to implement the pilot system and evaluate it thoroughly in order to learn what could be generalised to other Boards. A programme of information dissemination was then planned to ensure that the benefits of this project were communicated to the industry as a whole.

The process of defining pilots, evaluating them, and then disseminating the knowledge gained would then be repeated for the other information technology possibilities. This paper is concerned primarily with the initial phases of this work: leading up to and including the development of a pilot system.

4. SOCIO-TECHNICAL SYSTEMS ANALYSIS

The methodology for this project is derived
from socio-technical systems theory: an
approach developed in the 1950's by the
Tavistock Institute of Human Relations.
(Emery: 1959, Trist et al 1963). A summary of
a modified version of the original approach is
presented here and is depicted in Figure 1. A
more detailed account is given in Eason and
Harker (1979). This theory views a work
organisation as an open system in continuous
transaction with its enviroment. Inputs from
the environment are taken and transformed into
outputs which fulfil the system's objectives.
To do this effectively the system has to cope
with turbulance in its relevant environment.
This way mean that the inputs vary, the
conditions under which it has to work vary, or
the demands for its outputs vary. The nature of
the inputs and outputs establishes the basic
requirements upon the system. It also
establishes the functional needs which the
system must meet to achieve its objectives
effectively.

Functional needs are met by a specific "work
performing system" which is a socio-technical
system: it has a social system of people working together in a co-ordinated set of work roles
and a more or less integrated technical system
which consists of tools and techniques relevant
to the work to be done. Socio-technical systems
theory predicts that optimum performance of the
total system is dependent on the co-optimisation
of the two subsystems.

In this context we need to establish whether
enhancing the information technology component
of the technical system could usefully

contribute to the co-optimisation of both
systems, and thus an improvement in overall
performance.

5. METHODOLOGY

The socio-technical systems analysis was undertaken by examining one District office Engineering function in considerable detail. Two
further District offices were then examined, in
less detail, in order to verify whether the
description of the major functions obtained
from the first District office was a good
explanation for the activities of other offices.
In particular it was necessary to check whether
the critical problems warranting information
technology solutions identified in the first
District office could be generalised with advantage to the other offices.

Semi-structured interviews with senior staff
were used to determine the overall description
of the aims and functions of the District office.
The study then descended through the levels of
the organisation to obtain more detailed descriptions of how function requirements were
operationalised. Subsequently, when it was
necessary to examine the way in which particular functions were handled, a mixture of semi-
structured interviews and tracer techniques was
used.

6. A SOCIO-TECHNICAL SYSTEMS DESCRIPTION

For the purposes of this paper the description
of the District office as a socio-technical
system is fiven in summary form only and is
presented in Figure 2. This reproduces the
structure from Figure 1 and now adds in the
principal features of the District office.

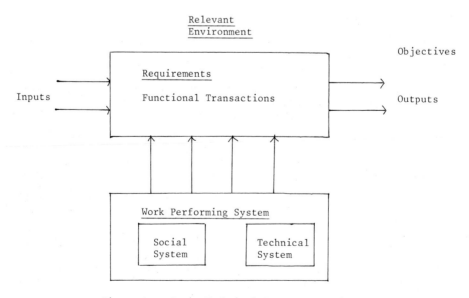

Figure 1:   Socio-Technical System Analysis.

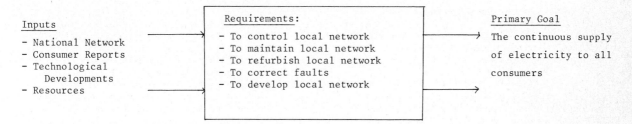

Relevant Environment

Weather, geography,
Local utilities

Inputs

- National Network
- Consumer Reports
- Technological
     Developments
- Resources

Requirements:

- To control local network
- To maintain local network
- To refurbish local network
- To correct faults
- To develop local network

Primary Goal

The continuous supply
of electricity to all
consumers

Structural Problems

1) Planned work vs emergency work
2) Continuous supply vs minimising resources
3) Integrated control vs geographical distribution
4) Operational action vs maintenance of records

Figure 2:   A Socio-Technical Systems View of the Engineering Function of a District Office

The statutory duty of the engineering function is to maintain a continuous supply of electricity to all consumers on the network. This can be separated out into a number of requirements: for example it is necessary to maintain a continuous supply now and to sustain that supply in the long term. Faults which occur on the network must be corrected quickly with the integrity of the entire network in mind and the safety of staff and the public as a major consideration. All of these requirements must be undertaken whilst making effective use of a limited pool of resources. Thus, it is evident that there may be problems in any office with these functions in trying to achieve all of these goals simultaneously.

The inputs to the system are from a number of sources. These include:

° Consumer reports of faults and requirements for network developments.

° The link to rest of the network. The fact that the District office controls one part of a highly integrated national network of electricity supply means that this link is crucial.

° Knowledge of the human technical and informational resources which are available to undertake these activities.

° Environmental factors such as the weather, which may cause changes in the state of the network as well as making it difficult to correct faults.

° The nature of the local geography is another important input, particularly when, in combination with bad weather, some parts of the network are rendered fairly inaccessible. It is also important in the sense that in an urban environment the supply network is principally underground cabling and thus fairly immune to the elements. If it is a rural environment the supply is principally overhead and thus susceptible to storm damage.

° The mix of consumers within a District can dictate the type of work and the nature of the problems which arise. There will be different demands from an area which principally contains large industrial consumers to that which has principally domestic or agricultural consumers.

° The work of the District is also dependent upon the other services and utilities present. In many cases permission has to be sought from, or notice given to, the Local authority, the Gas Board, the Water Authority and British Telecom as well as any private landowners, before work can commence.

These inputs or external influences place demands upon the engineering function and its performance. If we now look inside the function itself, a number of separable functional requirements can be identified. These have been listed in Figure 2 and are reiterated below:

° To control the local network

° To maintain the local network

° To refurbish the local network i.e. to over-
  hall it to meet current standards

° To correct faults on the network

° To develop the network by means of the
  addition of new consumers or the extension
  of existing supplies.

These functional requirements were examined in
some detail in an attempt to establish the
basic task sequence necessary to satisfy them.
We were particularly concerned to establish
whether the achievement of one requirement
affected the achievement of other requirements.
This analysis revealed certain structural
problems. These emerge from the conflicts
endemic within the organisation because it is
attempting to achieve different goals
simultaneously, with limited resources. Our
concern was to separate the problems which were
specific to this particular engineering
function - in respect of the way in which it is
organised, or the management style adopted -
from those problems which could be generalised
to many other District engineering functions.

We anticipated that the problems which were a
result of structural conflicts would reappear
elsewhere, perhaps in slightly different forms
because of the different ways in which they
were being handled. Four structural problems
have been identified in Figure 2; they are
discussed further below:

i)   Planned work versus emergency work:

     During normal day to day activities it
     is necessary to maximise resource
     utilization by means of careful forward
     planning. When an emergency occurs
     considerable resources are required
     quickly in order to restore the supply.
     The planned work schedule is then
     disrupted because the District office
     in question does not sustain a body of
     'floating' resources which could react
     to emergencies.

ii) Continuous supply versus minimising
     resources:

     Because there is a requirement to
     minimise the amount of resources used
     there is a tendency to reduce the amount
     of cover. Thus, there may occasionally
     be 'no supply' situations which cannot
     be dealt with promptly because resources
     are already stretched.

iii) Integrated control versus geographical
     distribution:

     There have to be formalised rules for
     working on the network and a form of
     central control to ensure that work
     done is co-ordinated and in the interests
     of the integrity of the entire network.
     However, engineers also need a degree of
     local discretion to enable them to cope
     with unexpected events. This produces
     arguments in favour of both centra-
     lisation of control: there were many
     views and variants on this within the
     engineering function.

iv) Operational action versus maintainance of
     records:

     It is necessary for the engineering
     function to maintain a large, up to date,
     database which must indicate the status
     of the network and precisely where every
     part of it is situated. It also includes
     an extensive list of engineering guide-
     lines and regulations.

     This necessity to maintain an up to date
     database conflicts with the need for
     operational action on the network.
     There is an inclination to take action
     where necessary, particularly in emerg-
     encies, and then to tidy up the files
     and leave the record straight after the
     event. It is very important, within
     this function, that the records of
     changes made are updated immediately
     because of the potential dangers which
     inaccuracies of the record could cause.

7.   POSSIBLE INFORMATION TECHNOLOGY SYSTEMS

The socio technical systems analysis outlined
above was then used as starting point to
investigate the possibilities for the application of information technology. Where
problems which were significant to the performance of the engineering function were
identified it was hoped the information
technology support systems could be specified
- both for the particular District offices
which we investigated, and other, similar
District offices. We did not feel that the
solution to all the problems would be Information Technology. Indeed, for particular problems
it is though to be likely that the solution lies
in another form of technology or some other
organisational structure. However, the
information technology possiblities are listed
below in Table 1.

Problem Area	Information Technology System Possibilities
1. Planning and Re-planning Resource Allocation	Resource Scheduling System
2. Integrating and Updating Large Information Bases	A 'Front End' Unified Information System
3. Communications with Staff in the Field	Mixed Media, portable Communications System
4. Fault Reporting and Diagnosis	Fault Reporting and Diagnostic System

Table 1: Potential Information Technology Support Areas.

1) In all the Districts which we listed there was already some means of computer aided resource planning or allocation. What was missing was a flexible and easy way of rescheduling disrupted resources. Thus, a system which could aid in rescheduling resources was seem to be appropriate for further development.

2) Several computer based databases were in existence in the District offices visited. The problem for engineering staff was that although data was available to them, it was not in an integrated or co-ordinated form. A 'front end' information system was therefore proposed to bring together all available information. Ease of use and updating would be major requirements of such a system.

3) The difficulties of centralised control and decentralised action require improved communications. Problems arise when staff in centralised control rooms try to communicate with field staff. Often they are away from their vehicles; in fields or next to overhead line towers or in substations. Mixed media communication facilities which allow the transmission of graphics, text and numerical information as well as speech, in a portable form, may be one solution.

4. Fault reporting and fault handling forms the first part of the fault correction procedure when emergencies occur. The most frequent way for a District office to be

aware of a fault at the consumer level of network, is if a consumer reports an interruption in supply. There is therefore a dependence upon the ability to receive calls from consumers and relate the consumer's address to the point on the supply network where the fault has occurred. Thus, the fault reporting procedure must ensure that information is collected reliably and the diagnostic procedure must be able to identify the nature, cause and location of the fault.

In practice, the procedures are limited and may fail, especially during emergencies when the volume and frequency of incoming calls from consumers is too great. Also, there is no readily available link between the consumer's address and the network diagram.

These potential areas for development of information technology support systems were presented to members of the Area Board in which the major study has been carried out and also to members of the Electricity Council. The priorities for system development were established after some debate.

First priority was given to the development of a fault reporting and diagnostic system. The second area for development was to be the provision of better communications between staff in the field and staff in control rooms.

At the present time the pilot system for fault reporting and diagnosis has been developed. It is hoped that this will shortly be implemented and tested. A more detailed socio-technical investigation of the communication problems is also being undertaken. The remainder of this paper describes the development of the fault reporting and diagnostic pilot system.

8. PILOT SYSTEM DEVELOPMENT

It was agreed that the aims of the pilot system would be to record fault information, assist in diagnosis of the fault, inform the consumer of the progress of the fault (if necessary) and to provide a record of the fault. These aims are shown diagrammatically in Figure 3.

Tracer analysis of the fault recording and diagnosis activity revealed many issues. When faults are reported it may be necessary for the office to deal with floods of information which may be incomplete or needs sorting. There is also a problem of passivity: Is it necessary to rely upon consumer reports? Should tele-control be extended? To diagnose the fault it is necessary to know whether it is new fault, where it is, both geographically and in relation to the supply network. It is also helpful to know whether there is any history of such faults, and which engineer has responsibility for dealing with them. The amount of accessible

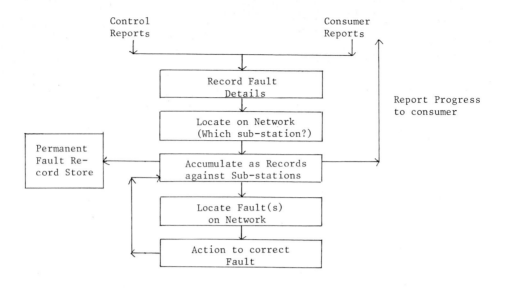

Figure 3.   Fault Reporting and Diagnosis System

information and the ability to act on it may depend upon the time of day, the weather, the degree of co-operation between the control room staff and the engineers and the experience and expertise which is available.

These issues provide the basis for a specification for a fault reporting and diagnosis system which would assist with data collection from consumers and cope with sudden increase in the number of reports received. The diagnostic system would assist with the provision of information about faults and give current/accumulating evidence as well as historical and geographical information about the network.

The pilot system has been developed in close collaboration with management services staff at the Area Board Head office. If effect, the system is a development of the existing consumer records system, extended to be linked to the plant maintenance computer file. It is also intended that the system will provide the link between the geographical location of the fault and its location on the network. Development of the system has included demonstrations to potential users which have precipitated some design changes. We have suggested some other changes, in terms of the design of the interface between the users and the system, for example: screen formatting and dialogue design.

There have also been discussions concerning the preparation of the organisation for the introduction of the pilot system. Issues such as who should use the system? who should have access to it? and who should have responsibility for it need to be hammered out before the system is introduced. Also, the process of consultation and negotiation with Trades Unions is now under

way and has to be completed before the pilot system can be implemented.

9.   CONCLUSIONS

This paper describes a case study in defining information technology systems within the electricity supply industry. The aim of the investigation was to find applications for systems which would have generalisable value despite the diversity which exists within the industry. The process by which we attempted to achieve this was by means of socio-technical systems analysis of the engineering function of an Area Board District office.

This analysis helped to highlight certain issues which appeared to be structural in nature: that is "problems which did not go away". One of the most critical of these was the ability to cope with faults and crises occurring on the network. Consequently, it was anticipated that an information technology system to support fault handling would be beneficial.

The methodology which we have discussed analyses the functions which the organisation must fulfil, rather than concentrating on the particular organisational idiosyncrasies. The pilot system which has been developed as a result of this methodology has several advantages. The staff who will use it are committed to it: they identified the need for such a system. The system will need refinement, amendment and, probably, extension, but the basic specification was drawn up by users so its potential utility is not in doubt. The Area Board staff do not need to be convinced of the efficacy of socio-technical systems analysis as a methodology: they recognise the enthusiasm and interest of

the potential users. Also, the pilot system is
not an end in itself, it provides the starting
point for the integration of other systems or
the addition of other databases

At the beginning of this paper we discussed
some of the disadvantages of ill-considered
technology -driven applications of information
technology. This paper demonstrates some of the
advantages of analysing business problems
before the specification of an information
technology support system.

10.   REFERENCES

1.   Eason, K.D. and Harker, S.D.P.,
      Ergonomics and the Nature of Tasks.
      HUSAT Memo no. 178, March 1979,
      Department of Human Sciences,
      University of Technology, Loughborough.

2.   Emery, F.E., (ed) Systems Theory,
      Vol. 1, Vol. 2, (Penguin 1981, 2nd
      Edition).

3.   Trist, E.L., Higgin G.W., Murray, H. and
      Pollock, A.B., Organisational Choice,
      (Tavistock London, 1963).

Human-Computer Interaction — INTERACT '84 / B. Shackel (ed.)
Elsevier Science Publishers B.V. (North-Holland)
© IFIP, 1985

System ABC:
A Case Study in the Design and Evaluation
of a Human-Computer Dialog

Catherine R. Marshall

AT&T Bell Laboratories, Summit, N.J.

ABSTRACT

Human factors specialists concerned with the human-computer interface live in two worlds. In the world of theory we are concerned with the properties of the ideal interface -- one that is easy to learn and use, and results in performance that is efficient and error-free. In the world of practice we must design working systems in the presence of many constraints. This paper presents a case study in the design and evaluation of a human-computer dialog in a constrained environment. It also discusses the relationship between theory and practice in interface design, with particular emphasis on the role of standards and guidelines.

1. INTRODUCTION

System ABC (a fictional name) is a combined hardware and software system that automates part of the configuring and maintenance of telephone-circuit transmission characteristics. The actual architecture of System ABC is complex, but for our purposes we can treat it as a black box containing a computer. The user connects to this computer with a standard asynchronous terminal, and interacts with the system via a "dialog" (defined here as everything the user types in and everything the system prints out).

The design of the ABC dialog was constrained by several factors: (1) The amount of memory and processing capacity available for the dialog software was limited both by the small size of the main processor and by the resource requirements of other software modules; (2) a wide variety of different terminals (CRT and hardcopy) would be used; (3) System ABC had to be compatible with several other related systems; (4) training and start-up time for users had to be minimized; and (5) the dialog had to be designed in accordance with the Man-Machine Language (MML) standard of the International Consultative Committee for Telephony and Telegraphy (CCITT) [1].

The final design of the ABC dialog was the responsibility of a team containing a software developer, a systems engineer, and a human factors specialist. The role of the human factors specialist was to make sure that the system would meet the needs of users, with special emphasis on minimizing training needs, maximizing initial user performance, and contributing to job satisfaction.

2. THE DESIGN PROCESS

The software development cycle for System ABC can be characterized in terms of the following stages:

- Product Definition
- Design
- Implementation
- System Test
- Field Test
- Product Delivery
- Product Support

The design phase, which is the subject of this report, can be further broken down into the stages of:

- Design Requirements
- Prototype Construction
- Prototype Evaluation
- Prototype Refinement
- Design Specification

The overview of the design process described above is somewhat idealized, reflecting a *post hoc* understanding of what happened rather than a pre-existing plan. Indeed, the most important lesson learned from our work on System ABC was how to approach the design of a human-computer dialog systematically. To allow others to capitalize on our experience, the following sections describe the stages of the design process in more detail, and, where appropriate, offer advice on how best to proceed.

2.1 Design Requirements

To determine design requirements for the ABC dialog, we first tried to discover as much as possible about the potential users, the tasks they would be performing, and the environment in which they would be using the system. To gather this information, members of the project team made field visits to potential installation sites, observed work operations, and talked with on-site personnel. These informal investigations revealed that the typical users of System ABC would be skilled technicians, male, aged 25-55, with 12 years of education, no typing skills, and little or no prior exposure to computerized systems. In a typical day, these technicians would perform a variety of tasks, only a fraction of which would involve work with System ABC. This work would take place in telephone central offices, which are often noisy and crowded with equipment, on a terminal located close to the physical equipment for System ABC. In light of these facts, a structured dialog with menus and prompts seemed most appropriate.

The main pitfall of this analysis, however, is that it fails to take into account the impact the introduction of System ABC would have on the users, the work, and the environment. By automating certain tasks previously performed manually and allowing equipment to be controlled remotely, System ABC encourages changes in telephone company work operations. As a result, certain technicians may specialize in the operation of the system, thereby becoming frequent rather than occasional users. Ultimately, the more routine operations may be performed from a distance in regional centers, where the typical user might be an entry level employee, male or female, aged 19-30, with 12 or more years of education, good typing skills, and trained in the operation of computerized systems.

Looking to the future, we thought it important to design a user interface that could be easily modified in later versions of the system. We also thought it wise to provide the initial version of the system with an interface that would allow the user to move in stages from a highly structured, menu- and prompt-driven dialog to a more efficient, command-style dialog.

2.2 Prototype Construction

Previous work has demonstrated the value of prototyping [2], and our experience confirms this. Having an early prototype allowed us to evaluate the human-computer dialog before we were committed to any particular design. Prototyping also proved to be a valuable design tool, because it forced us to think about details that might otherwise have been glossed over. Also, having a concrete model to manipulate sometimes revealed the shortcomings of ideas that seemed fine in the abstract.

However, the prototype construction phase did not pass without difficulties. Our first prototype was based on a very early design specification. Because we knew the design would change, the prototype was constructed with the aid of a database system that would, we hoped, make modifications easy to implement. As it turned out, some modifications were easy to make, but others required a great deal of effort. To understand the problem, imagine the entire dialog as a connected graph in which each prompt or menu, with its associated error and help routines, is a node. In our prototype, it was easy to change the content of a given node, but changing the structure of the graph itself (nodes and arcs) required changes to many different sections of the code. What we needed was a prototyping tool that would allow us add and change nodes as well as to change the content of a given node. Today such tools exist for a number of different operating systems, but they were not available when we were prototyping System ABC. However, we were able to create a program that did provide the flexibility described above, and this became the basis for all subsequent prototyping.

2.3 Prototype Evaluation

Once a working prototype had been constructed, members of the design team tried it out and made suggestions for changes. This part of the evaluation was informal, and served primarily to improve the internal consistency of the prototype.

The next stage of the evaluation was more structured. Six telephone company technicians drawn from our target user population came into the laboratory to work with the prototype for one day. They were asked to perform a set of tasks that would exercise a subset of System ABC's capabilities, and to "think aloud" while they worked [3]. An observer recorded their comments, and an on-line record of their interactions with the prototype, with field-by-field time stamping, was kept for later protocol analysis.

The evaluation study just described had two limitations. First, our subjects' exposure to the system was brief. As a result, we only saw how well the dialog suited naive users working in the structured menu-and-prompt mode. Second, this study only allowed us to evaluate a "snapshot" of the dialog. It provided no information about the impact of changes we might make.

In the third stage of the evaluation, we partially overcame these limitations. First, to study user performance over time, we arranged for four volunteers to interact with the prototype regularly over a period of several months. These volunteers were not very representative of the target user population, but analyzing their protocols did allow us to monitor changes in style of interaction as a function of experience. Second, to allow testing of incremental changes to the dialog, a dial-in demonstration facility was created. This gave a wide variety of potential users and customers access to the prototype; again, record files were kept for protocol analysis. In addition to helping us tune the dialog design, this dial-in facility was popular with our marketing and customer support people.

2.4 Prototype Refinement

Results from the prototype evaluation led to changes in the ABC dialog. In some cases features were added or modified in response to users' problems. For example, the on-line help facility was changed so that pressing the "?" key at any point would immediately produce a help message. In the initial version of the prototype, help was provided only if the "?" was typed as the first character in a response field. This proved to be unsatisfactory because our subjects tended to produce strings like "/?" and "//--?" while trying to request help. (The "/" results from a failure to shift, and the "-" represents a failed attempt to use the underscore, which is specified by the MML standard as the character delete for printing terminals.)

It is often the case that human factors evaluations lead only to suggestions for additions or changes that increase a product's cost. One benefit of our evaluation study was that it led us to eliminate features that proved to be unnecessary, and thereby to reduce costs. For example, a feature that allowed users to back up through prompts one at a time was removed after we discovered that it was seldom used and that many people found that it simply added to the complexity of the system.

2.5 Design Specification

One of the problems we grappled with during the entire design phase was how to specify the design of the user interface. Several methods were experimented with, none of which proved to be entirely satisfactory. In constructing the prototype, the author used a transition network model to describe the overall dialog structure. In addition, descriptor sheets for each node in the network specified the detailed semantic content of the dialog. This type of specification worked well as a design tool, but was not useful for communicating with those not familiar with the notational system used. For this purpose the prototype itself was more useful.

3. THE ROLE OF STANDARDS AND GUIDELINES

The design of System ABC was influenced by the CCITT MML Standard and by various design guidelines. Ideally, standards and guidelines bridge the gap between theory and practice, and allow us to design better products in a shorter period of time. In our experience, however, this was not always the case.

3.1 Problems with the MML Standard

The purpose of the CCITT MML standard is to provide a syntax, a vocabulary, and a set of formatting conventions for all languages used for human-machine interaction in the operation or maintenance of a telephone network. Because today's telephone networks are supported by a variety of computerized systems, such standardization is desirable as an effective means of reducing operator training time and minimizing errors caused by "negative transfer" of learning between systems.

In view of these benefits, we attempted to implement the MML standard in the design of System ABC. In doing this, we encountered a number of difficulties that are characteristic of standardization efforts. For example, we were forced to use a different format for dates than is customarily used in the United States, and this led to some complaints from our customers. While problems of this sort are real (and sometimes serious), standardization is seldom achieved without them.

However, our case study illustrates a more fundamental problem. This problem, which I will call "model incompatibility," stems from the fact that System ABC and the MML standard are based on different models of the user interface.

3.1.1 The System ABC model. The ABC model defines four levels of user input: characters, fields, lines, and procedures. The most basic of these is the field, which consists of a string of characters (usually fewer than seven) followed by a field terminator (e.g., a comma or a carriage return). To provide a structured dialog, the ABC system prompts the user for each field of input. Associated with each prompt are:

- an optional menu,
- a help message,
- a series of validation routines and error messages, and
- a set of branching instructions that interpret the current field and use it to determine the next prompt.

In keeping with this model, the ABC system examines the user's input one character at a time. If a character is special (e.g., "?") the system immediately takes an appropriate action. Otherwise, the input is buffered until the user enters a line terminator (e.g., carriage return). A line of input may consist of a single field, or the user may "type ahead" and enter several fields. If a line of input contains several fields, the system evaluates it one field at a time and suppresses prompts for those fields entered by "typing ahead." The ability to enter several fields on a line allows users to "chunk" together input in a flexible way. As the user becomes experienced in the use of the system, we would expect those chunks to map onto "procedures", here defined as a series of input fields containing sufficient information to initiate a specific system action. In this way, the user moves from a structured, menu- and prompt-driven dialog to a more efficient, command-style dialog.

3.1.2 The MML model. The MML model defines three levels of user input: characters, lines, and commands. The basic level is the command, which consists of a command code plus parameters. The command code, in turn, consists of a command verb plus one or two optional command qualifiers. Parameters may be defined positionally, in which case they simply consist of a parameter value, or they may be defined by keyword, in which case they consist of a name plus a value. The syntax of MML requires that the command verb and qualifiers be separated from one another by hyphens, and that the command code be separated from the parameters by a colon. In addition, parameters are separated from one another by commas, and the equals sign is used to separate parameter names from parameter values. As this description illustrates, the structure of an MML command is potentially rather complex.

The MML model assumes that in the typical case a line of input will correspond to a command. However, the standard also allows a command to be assembled from several lines of input. Furthermore, help messages, prompts, menus and form-fill blocks can be provided to aid the user in constructing a command.

3.1.3 The consequences of model incompatibility. At first glance it may seem that the two models described above are similar enough to allow the MML standard to be applied to the ABC dialog with little difficulty. In practice, this turned out not to be the case. The nature of our difficulties is illustrated by problems we had concerning the use of the "?" character.

The MML standard specifies the use of the question mark as a character to request an explanatory help message, a menu, a prompt, or a form-fill block. In the context of the MML model, this use of the question mark is coherent and consistent. In the context of the ABC model, however, it makes little sense to use the question mark to request menus or prompts since these are automatically provided. Nevertheless, a strict reading of the standard would seem to mandate the use of a question mark to terminate each line of input, unless the last field in that line marks the end of a procedure. Doing this, however, makes it impossible to respond immediately to the "?" character with a help message. It also makes it impossible to have a null field indicate acceptance of the default value for a prompt. Consequently, we chose to use the carriage return as a

line terminator, a choice that may not be consistent with the MML standard.

Needless to say, we were not aware of the nature or consequences of the model incompatibility described above when we formulated our initial design requirements. Had we been, we might have attempted to make our design fit the MML model. However, it is not clear that we would have been able to meet the needs of our user population as well with a dialog based on this model.

3.2 Problems with Design Guidelines

There is no doubt that some of the guidelines available to us were quite helpful [4,5,6]. Nevertheless, we experienced some difficulties in using these and other guidelines, the most significant of which are described below.

3.2.1 Vague or unsupported advice. A number of design guidelines advise that a user interface should be easy to learn, easy to use, powerful, flexible and fun to work with, that error messages should be informative but short, and that help messages should be designed to answer whatever question a user has in mind at a given time. While these are certainly nice principles, such advice is so vague as to be useless in the context of real design work.

At the other extreme, guidelines sometimes offer advice that is very specific but unsupported. For example, an in-house set of guidelines we used recommended that individual menus contain no more than seven items. No rationale for this rule was provided in the guidelines, nor am I able to supply one. It may be a valid rule in specific circumstances (e.g. for menus presented auditorily over a telephone), but it seems too restrictive for the general case.

3.2.2 Failure to address trade-offs. Another problem with existing design guidelines is that they fail to address the problem of trade-offs. Consider the following advice, again drawn from in-house guidelines:

> "If a terminal's output speed is
> less than normal human reading speed
> (average = 250 wpm) form more compact
> messages (both prompting and error).
> If the speed is greater, use the
> full natural language of the user."

What rule does one follow for a system like ABC which must support a variety of terminals? Our approach typically was to find a compromise solution. In some cases, however, such a solution seemed intuitively wrong. Recently Norman [7] has addressed the question of trade-offs in interface design. His analysis suggests that in certain cases a "compromise" is the worst design solution. At present, the techniques proposed by Norman are not sufficiently well-developed to be of practical use, though they may someday provide the basis for a useful design tool. In the meantime, empirical studies contrasting alternative solutions to trade-off problems would be instructive.

3.2.3 Lack of a clear model. The final difficulty we experienced with most design guidelines is that they take a fragmented approach to the problem of dialog design. Aspects of the design such as menu hierarchies, screen displays, and error diagnostics are considered without reference to any coherent model of the dialog as a whole. Our difficulties with the MML standard illustrate the importance of models in user-interface design. We would have benefited greatly from guidelines that described alternative models, provided advice on selecting an appropriate model, and gave specific design rules tailored to a particular model.

4. CONCLUSION

The case study described above shows how human factors specialists can make an effective contribution to the design of a real system. It also allows us to examine the relationship between theory and practice in human-computer interface design. The initial design of the ABC dialog was guided by existing standards and guidelines. Nevertheless, many questions arose for which there were no clear answers. In particular we found that the constraints described earlier often forced us to make trade-offs between various human factors design principles. Existing guidelines provided little assistance in making such decisions. Thus the prototype evaluation study played an important role in shaping the final design of the ABC dialog.

In working on the ABC dialog we also found that the MML standard often made it difficult for us to design a system that would meet the needs of our users. Since design guidelines and standards play an important role in bridging the gap between theory and practice, it is crucial that they be as correct, complete, and usable as we can make them. For this reason, guidelines and standards should be subjected to empirical evaluation and the test of practice whenever possible. Case studies can make a valuable contribution to that enterprise.

5. ACKNOWLEDGMENTS

The work described in this report involved the efforts of a great many people. While space does not allow a complete description of each person's work, the following people deserve a special acknowledgment: J. Donegan, who managed the human factors effort on System ABC; D. T. DeBaun and G. A. Kohl, who conducted field visits and provided information needed to formulate design requirements; D. N. Koppes, who provided valuable advice on the initial design of the dialog prototype; J. A. Collins and M. T. Moravec, who programmed the first version of the dialog prototype; L. J. Currence, who helped to program the prototyping tool used for later versions; and G. E. Strohl, who provided systems engineering expertise for the dialog design. Finally, the author wishes to extend a special acknowledgement to L. R. Satz, who collaborated in the design of the ABC dialog and ultimately assumed responsibility for its specification and implementation.

REFERENCES

[1] CCITT Man-Machine Language, *Yellow Book,* International Telegraph and Telephone Consultative Committee, Vol. VI.7, Recommendations Z.311-Z.318 and Z.341, 7th Plenary Assembly, Geneva, 10-21 November, 1980.

[2] Hemenway, K. and McCusker, L. X. Prototyping and evaluating a user interface. In *Proceedings of COMPSAC82,* New York: IEEE Computer Society Press, 1982.

[3] Lewis, C. H. Using the "Thinking Aloud" Method in Cognitive Interface Design. IBM Research Report, RC-9265, 1982.

[4] Martin, J. *Design of Man-Computer Dialogs.* Englewood Cliffs, NJ: Prentice-Hall, 1973.

[5] Shneiderman, B. *Software Psychology Human Factors in Computer and Information Systems.* Cambridge, MA: Winthrop, 1980.

[6] Smith, S. L. *Requirements Definition and Design Guidelines for Man-Machine Interface in C3 System Acquisition.* ESD-TR-80-122, Electronic Systems Division, Air Force Systems Command, United States Air Force, June 1980.

[7] Norman, D. A. Design Principles for Human-Computer Interfaces. In *Proceedings of the CHI 1983 Conference on Human Factors in Computer Systems,* New York: Association for Computing Machinery, 1983.

Human-Computer Interaction — INTERACT '84 / B. Shackel (ed.)
Elsevier Science Publishers B.V. (North-Holland)
© IFIP, 1985

BUILDING A USABLE OFFICE SUPPORT SYSTEM FROM DIVERSE COMPONENTS

Nancy C. Goodwin

The MITRE Corporation
Bedford, Massachusetts
USA

Organizations interested in providing computer-based office support systems now have
several choices. They can select an integrated system that uses new equipment or that
uses equipment already in-house, or they can select components from diverse sources
and build their own system. The latter approach enables an organization to introduce
office systems without major disruption to existing services, but requires a strong
awareness of user-oriented issues. Among these issues are user-system interface
design, text editing, data transfer requirements and user support requirements. The
success of the system will depend on the organization's commitment to resolving these
issues.

1. INTRODUCTION

Computer-based office support systems provide
users with information management tools in an
office context. They may include some data
manipulation tools (e.g., spreadsheets), but
generally do not provide large scale data processing support. Basic tools and applications
designed around those tools together comprise an
office support system. For example, a word processing system is a tool. Its use to create
project records is an application of the tool to
an office management task.

Office support systems are usually intended for
use by people who are not computer experts.
Managers, administrators, technical staff, secretarial and clerical support personnel are all
potential system users. They approach the system as a tool, and will use it if it helps them
accomplish their tasks. They will reject a tool
if it is too difficult to use and appears to
complicate or slow down their ability to work.
It is therefore especially important that office
systems be easy to learn and to use.

Many organizations interested in implementing
computer-based office support are already using
computers for other purposes. There are several
ways these organizations can choose to provide
office support. They can select an integrated
system that uses hardware and software different
from present installations, select a system
offered by one of the vendors whose products are
already in use, or select a variety of tools
from different vendors and add them to existing
facilities. For many organizations, previous
investments preclude acquiring a new, different
system. Instead, they would prefer to add
office support tools to existing facilities.

At The MITRE Corporations's Bedford Operations
(MITRE-Bedford), we have an established computer
center. This center provides services with
computers from two different manufacturers

running three different major operating systems.
We have significant investments in software
development and user training for these systems.
When we decided to increase our computer-based
office support we did not judge that any of the
new integrated office systems offered sufficient
overall functionality to justify changing our
current services. We did not judge that any
single vendor offered sufficient functionality
in a system that could be added to our existing
equipment to justify limiting ourselves to their
products. Therefore, we chose to devise techniques for adding and integrating tools from
various sources. Using this approach we could
pick the best of the available tools for our
applications. In addition, we were not dependent on the success or responsiveness of a single
vendor; if dissatisfied with one of the tools,
we could replace it without a major change to
the entire system.

This paper discusses some of the issues that had
to be confronted for this approach to succeed,
and some of the lessons learned along the way.
To provide context for this discussion, the
computing environment will first be described.

2. MITRE-BEDFORD COMPUTER FACILITIES

At MITRE-Bedford, data processing and office
support computing facilities are provided by the
Bedford Computer Center (BCC). There are two
IBM computers. One (an MVS/TSO system) provides
data processing support for the Corporation's
finance and accounting needs and for various
projects. The other (a VM/CMS system) is now a
primary host for office support systems but is
also used for program development. Four DEC
computers host a time-shared word processing
system (WORD-11). Another DEC computer (running
UNIX[1]) is used as a program development facility, a gateway for the ARPANET, and some "end
user" applications. Various other computers
serve special needs.

Most users access these computers via a local area network; they either go directly to the desired host or through a switch that offers access to these hosts. In addition, there are some terminals directly connected to the switch, and a few directly connected to the IBM systems. The majority of the users have multiservice terminals, DEC VT100s or equivalents, that can be used with any of the hosts. (Full screen access to the IBM hosts is provided by a Series/1 with a terminal emulation program.) Other types of terminals include printers, personal computers and terminals used from offices, homes or on trips.

At present, there are approximately 500 VT100/VT103 and 60 IBM terminals in use. In addition, approximately 70 local printers are used with the various systems. And, there are approximately 70 personal computers; a small number of these access the centralized computers. Approximately 550 people have time-shared word processing accounts, and nearly 500 people have accounts on the VM/CMS system. Many of these people have accounts on several of the systems.

3. HISTORY OF OFFICE SUPPORT AT MITRE-BEDFORD

Computer-based word processing, in one form or another, has been available at MITRE-Bedford for about 10 years. It began with text processing software on an IBM host and grew to include the four DEC hosts mentioned above. We also have approximately 150 standalone word processors. Almost all secretaries use some form of word processing for longer documents.

Electronic message handling began with a pilot program on the UNIX system. When this grew in popularity, it was decided to explore other alternatives to find more usable and functional software. This effort led to our overall approach to office support systems.

Because of investments in hardware, software, and user training, we were reluctant to abandon our word processing system, but could not at that time find a suitable electronic message system to add to it. Therefore, we decided to select the best electronic message system that we could find for our VM/CMS system and to consolidate additional office support applications on that host whenever possible.

The VM/CMS and WORD-11 systems are our primary office support hosts, and we have concentrated our efforts on them. If we need a tool, such as a spreadsheet, and there is not a suitable one available for the VM/CMS system, then we put it elsewhere. If we have an application, such as on-line vugraph production, that will be used mostly by secretaries, then we put it on the word processing hosts. Otherwise all new office support applications are placed on the VM/CMS system.

For this approach to succeed, we had to deal with a number of issues. Among them were: user system interfaces, text editing, document and data transfer, and user support.

4. USER SYSTEM INTERFACE

4.1 Software Issues

An advantage of using a system provided by a single vendor should be that there is a consistent user interface to all the applications. That is, the basic command entry technique should be the same, terminology across applications should be the same, display formats should be similar, etc. In practice, depending on the vendor and their approach to providing tools, the user interfaces may or may not be consistent. Because we were dealing with multiple vendors for hosts and tools, the user interfaces were definitely not the same.

One of the key elements of office support is word processing. The word processing system we use is menu-driven. After logging on and receiving a system broadcast message, users are presented with a list of choices. A selection is made by entering a two-letter code. This results in display of another menu, where a single letter code is entered to indicate the type of activity a user wants to do, such as creating, editing, or deleting a document. Editing within a document is done with function keys. Cursor movement is accomplished with advance and backup keys. At the menu level, commands can be edited using the same function keys (rub word, rub character) used within a document. Many people use this system and are comfortable with the menu interface.

We selected the VM/CMS system to be the main host for our non-word processing office support applications. On VM/CMS, after logging on a user is presented with some cryptic system messages, and a blank screen. Then the user enters a command to invoke the desired application, such as "InfoMail" to get to the electronic message handling system, or "flist" to get to a file management application.

To provide more consistency between the systems, we decided to build a menu-driven interface to applications on VM/CMS. The menu formats are not exactly like the word processing menus, but they do provide a familiar style of interaction for people accustomed to the WORD-11 system: users can make their selections using typed letter codes and step through the menus until they find the option they want. We added capabilities so they can also use programmed function keys (pfks) or enter codes representing the pathnames to go directly to a choice. With this interface, users never have to receive a blank screen after logging on; they can receive a list of choices and use their own preferred selection technique to proceed.

Another characteristic of VM/CMS applications was that in many cases, different tools used different programmed function keys for similar functions. For example, our electronic message system uses pfk 9 to page forward, while a file management system uses pfk 8 for that purpose. While we were not always able to change function key assignments for tools that other vendors supplied, we did control applications using tools developed in-house.

We developed guidelines for assigning sequence control options to function keys, so that menu panels and applications we developed ourselves would be consistent. And, in one case where a vendor-supplied tool has different function key assignments, we display a reminder to users as they access it. The reminder tells the user that its function key assignments are different from those of the menu system.

As individual packages, tools may be well designed; however, additional tailoring may be needed to enable applications to function well as parts of a whole system. For example, the electronic message system we selected required users to log on to it explicitly. It provided facilities for importing, exporting, and printing documents, but these were limited to the interface between the message system and the operating system. In other words, a user had to remember to execute a second print command after leaving the message system to cause a document to actually be printed. We found the requirement for an additional logon tedious, and built an "envelope" (some CMS execs) around the tool so that users do not have to log on again. Our envelope also provides automatic handling of commands such as print commands, so users do not have to execute them twice, once within the message system and another time outside the system.

4.2 Hardware Issues

If an office support system were acquired from a single vendor, one would expect to use a single terminal for all applications. There would be a single keyboard layout, and function keys would have the same meaning throughout the system.

At MITRE-Bedford, most users have VT100 (or equivalent) terminals that can be used to access any of the systems. However, the IBM and DEC hosts interpret the function keypad layouts differently. The VT100 keys are engraved with a layout for DEC systems. Unfortunately, the pfk assignments for IBM applications are almost just the opposite. The confusion is compounded because in the alphanumeric keyboard the key labeled RETURN for DEC systems is labeled ENTER for IBM, and on the keypad the key labeled ENTER for DEC is used as CLEAR for IBM. A new user on the IBM system, instructed to hit ENTER, is likely to hit a key that will be interpreted as CLEAR. The result is often destructive.

We have taken several steps to help overcome this problem. We supply users with a set of adhesive labels so that they can relabel the VT100 keypad. We supply clear plastic "gloves" that fit over the keypad. The gloves can be labeled and changed as a user switches systems. We provide a template showing the key assignments (along with other helpful information particular to a system) to remind users of the different key arrangements. For applications we develop ourselves, we take care to use appropriate terminology for the RETURN key. Our prompts often say "Hit the RETURN key on VT100s (ENTER on IBM 3270s)" to remind users of the differences. While these steps are not as satisfactory as using a truly compatible terminal, they reduce errors and frustration considerably, and are clearly better than having different terminals for the different systems.

4.3 Communications Paths

In a multihost environment, it can be confusing for people to move from one host to another. We have made it possible for users to request each host by name (e.g., VM) rather than number or communications path.

One feature offered on our VM system is the ability to "pass through" and log on to other IBM hosts. Rather than requiring users to learn the communications paths and commands needed to move from one host to another, we built an application to handle this automatically. We also have in progress another automatic logon capability, so that users will be able to move from an application on one IBM host to an application on another IBM host without logging on to the second host.

While we will not be able to achieve the same transparency between IBM and DEC word processing hosts, we have made the techniques for using these two hosts as similar as possible, and have protected users from the differences whenever we can.

Making communications paths transparent to users has mixed results. When all goes well it is much easier for users; when something goes wrong it is more difficult to identify or locate the source of the trouble. Users identify the problem with the host system, when in fact it may be part of the communications path that is causing trouble. Dealing with user problems thus requires user support staff to have a good understanding of the entire system, not just individual applications.

5. TEXT EDITORS

Text editing techniques are especially important, for they pertain not only to entry of large amounts of text, but also to entry and editing of typed commands. Cursor movement, character and line deletion, and character insertion techniques all apply to command, data, or text entry in all applications. In an integrated system one would expect the same text entry and editing techniques to apply throughout.

Perhaps the most critical problem we faced was the difference between WORD-11 and XEDIT, the text editor on the VM system. Different function keys and different names were used for similar functions on the two systems. In XEDIT assignments of functions to keys were not displayed on the screen or keyboard. Many XEDIT functions were accomplished using typed commands rather than function keys. On WORD-11 all editing is done on the bottom line of the display; XEDIT provides full screen editing. Formatting controls are quite different for the two systems.

While there were many features we could not change, we were able to tailor XEDIT so that it would be more familiar to WORD-11 users. A basic set of editing functions was implemented on function keys, with the key assignments shown on the display as an additional help for users. We designed and named some functions ourselves, so that CUT and PASTE, for example, exist and do similar things on both systems. While the result does not look like WORD-11, for people who use both systems our version is more usable than the standard XEDIT.

Although we were able to tailor XEDIT, we found that with other vendor-supplied tools still different editors were used. We worked with the vendors to be able to use our own editor, with moderate success. The ability to specify a standard system editor is now considered to be a critical issue when selecting tools. The most simple tasks become difficult if one does not know how to enter text or make basic corrections to errors, or if the commands or function keys used are different from the system standard.

6. DATA TRANSFER

Regardless of the approach taken, it is especially important that documentation or data created in one part of an office support system be usable in other parts. Without the ability to move data from one application to another, system utility is severely limited. For example, it may be necessary to manipulate some data using a spreadsheet, incorporate the results into a document, and distribute it using electronic message handling. With a truly integrated system these functions should be easy to accomplish. Working across several hosts it is more difficult.

We established communications paths among the hosts, and installed software to transfer documents and data in usable formats. We built user interfaces to the document transfer software so that users could accomplish the transfers without learning technical details of

communications paths or techniques. On WORD-11, users answer a series of computer-generated questions about the name of the document, the target host, and the target account. On VM/CMS, users fill in the blanks of a computer-generated form to provide that information. Document transfers usually occur within minutes of the request, so that by the time a person has logged off of one system and on to another, the document has been delivered.

Enabling users to move data easily from application to application, regardless of the application's host, is a critical issue. Unless this problem can be solved, it is unlikely that distributed functions can be used effectively.

7. USER SUPPORT

As office systems provide more extensive applications, the user support required becomes more complicated. In addition to increased demand for formal training courses and seminars, there is an increase in the number and types of questions from users.

When we introduced WORD-11, the BCC established a Word Processing Training Center to offer formal training courses to clerical and secretarial staff. This soon became a User Training Center with courses and seminars for applications other than word processing. This facility has since evolved into a User Support Center, formal training is just one of many services it provides. In addition to training sessions, the User Support Center is responsible for staffing a "hot-line". There is a single telephone number for users to call with all questions, from requests for terminals or accounts to problems using a system. This simplifies the user's search for help, and enables us to keep track of the types of problems and questions people have. If the person who answers the telephone cannot answer the question, it is referred to an appropriate system expert.

The User Support Center also distributes system documentation, writes newsletters announcing new features or changes to the systems, and writes system documentation tailored to our own environment. It handles system administration, discussed below. The USC is currently staffed by six people.

8. SYSTEM ADMINISTRATION

In addition to technical problems, a distributed office support system presents some administrative problems. Users must have accounts on each of the computers whose applications they need. This can create problems for both users and system administrators. Often different operating systems have different requirements for logon names and passwords. This makes it harder for users when logging on. System administrators also have to keep multiple sets of records; coordinating these records can be tedious.

Other administrative problems occur when users change projects, want to have different accounts charged to different projects, move from department to department, or leave the company. These changes can result in significant bookkeeping headaches for a system administrator.

We took several steps to alleviate these problems. We established guidelines for assigning user identifications and aliases so that there would be some common data to identify users on all systems. All account management is handled by the USC. Users only have to deal with one person to set up all accounts, and that one person can coordinate a user's accounts. We established guidelines for selecting passwords; if they want, users can have the same password on all systems. We also established a centralized data base with account information for all employees for all systems. This makes it easier to check information for users as well as systems, and to keep department and project data up-to-date.

9. SYSTEM SECURITY

There is a tradeoff between system usability and system security. The more usable a system is, the less likely it is to offer safeguards for security and privacy. If a system requires only one password to give access to all its facilities, compromising that password compromises a user's entire data base. If different passwords are needed for different tools, then their applications become more difficult to use.

Our distributed system gives users a choice of having the same password for all their accounts, or different ones for each account. Many users elect to have different passwords for their word processing accounts which may be shared with other personnel, and their office system account where electronic message handling resides.

Passwords should be changed periodically. We have made it possible for users to make those changes themselves rather than having a system administrator handle it for them on both the VM/CMS and on WORD-11, users can make a menu choice that will guide them through the password changing process, and make the changes accordingly. We provide guidelines and recommendations for characteristics of a "good" password (not their initials, not their first name, etc.). It is up to each user to decide if they want one password for all systems or different ones for each.

10. DISCUSSION

Creating a usable office support system from diverse components is feasible. It requires an awareness of user-oriented issues beyond the basic questions of functionality. For each component it is necessary to evaluate the user interface and its compatibility with other applications. This evaluation must consider how the application looks to the user, and also how it can be interfaced with other applications.

It is necessary to have a strong organization to support users. Training and problem solving become more difficult as the number of applications grows, and as different types of people use the system. User support personnel must be able to understand the system from the users' view, but also have a good understanding of the underlying structure of the system. They must be able to translate users' questions from the users' descriptions of what happened so that a helpful answer can be given. (For example, a user might call to say that the word processing system is down, when they are really having a problem with a communications path.)

Using diverse components also requires a strong system support staff. Interfaces between applications must be built and maintained, and new applications may be created when none are available on the marketplace. Although this was not discussed above, it is an important factor to consider when deciding on an approach to providing office support. The system staff must work closely with the user support staff, so that user concerns are considered during application design.

Taking a distributed approach to providing office support can be more difficult than buying a single, integrated system. Why do it? For organizations that can afford the support, this approach enables them to introduce office systems without causing a major disruption to existing facilities. Applications can be added as they are needed, and often can be tailored to specific organizational requirements. This can be done without becoming dependent on a single vendor, and thus offers a degree of flexibility and security that may not be available when a single system is used.

Gradually introducing various applications also gives an organization an opportunity to learn about office support requirements and utility before a major investment is made in user support, software, and hardware. It can lead to changes in perceptions of what is useful, and to changes in priorities for applications. It can also lead to new requirements as people learn what a system can or cannot do for them.

In the long run, a fully integrated system is more desirable than one built from diverse components. It is very difficult to mask system differences, particularly when dealing with very different host computers. The learning process is valuable, but is achieved at some cost. A system built from diverse components can be more difficult to use, and require an investment in strong system and user support staff.

[1] UNIX is a trademark of Bell Laboratories.

Human-Computer Interaction — INTERACT '84 / B. Shackel (ed.)
Elsevier Science Publishers B.V. (North-Holland)
© IFIP, 1985

Task and User Adequate Design of Man—Computer Interfaces in Production

H.-J. Bullinger, K.-P. Fähnrich, C. Raether

Fraunhofer Institut für Arbeitswirtschaft und Organisation (IAO),Stuttgart, Germany

The interface of the man-computer interaction for CNC-control has been according to software-ergonomical principles. The design was based upon a layered man-computer interface model and an overall interface design methodology. With the incorporation of an object oriented design and programming methodology, a large degree of freedom is won in the design of several interface parameters (e.g. colour coding) Thus, at a relatively early stage an evaluation of the man-computer interface can take place due to the rapid prototyping approach chosen.

1.Introduction

For a long time the major area of interest in human factors research and especially ergonomics, has lain in the production area. Due to the changing economic situation and the emergence of new information technologies, the interest has shifted towards cognitive tasks allocated in the office. In any case it can not be neglected that in the production area and associated technical offices too new computer based technologies are spreading quickly. Examples are CAE/CAD/CAM-systems, production control systems, robots, flexible manufactoring systems and CNC tools. The associated man—computer interfaces, are of specific interest for human factors research because:

o A considerable number of tasks dissapeared from the production area often due to unadapted design of new information technologies.
o The necessity for high qualified work elements (planing, programming etc) for the remaining workers was thus often reduced.
o Often the computer oriented work elements are not task defining. They nevertheless form a bottleneck in the work process due to their

importance. A qualified worker in production now is in an ambiguous situation: His role can not be described adequately by terms like skilled - unskilled in an overall way.

The development of man-machine interfaces must be seen in the light of fast developing production- and associated IT-technologies. The main concepts used in association with CNC-machine tools are:

o Interlaced concepts (centralized and decentralized solutions).
o Standardized concepts (usage of standard IT-components)
o Functional integration (machine programming, company data collection, control of peripheral systems)

In the light of this development, the discussion as to whether programming should take place in the vicinity of the machine, or in the job planning which has become dominated to a certain extent by emotions, will have to be altered - at least where future-oriented concepts are involved. Important for the future is going to be much more the concept of compatibility with its dimensions:

Vertical compatibility between the various layers in the development of a program (workshop, job planning, planning department).

Horizontal compatibility between various machining methods (drilling milling, nibbling etc.) and differing producer systems. Therefore it is necessecary to create compatible interactive dialogue processors, which can be used, due to their

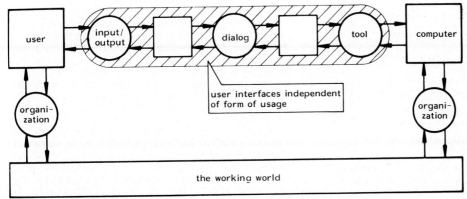

Figure 1: A Model for Man—Computer Interfaces

basic structure, either close to the machine or further away. They should be adaptable to differing user groups and for different task areas.

2. Man-Machine Interface Architectures

As a basis for discussion, the following model /3/ of a user interface emerges (cf. Fig.1). A generalized version and a discussion of it can be found in /11/. Here the input/output-interface has the closest relationship to the user. Various methods of input such as keybord input, voice input, input with pointer instruments (light pen, mouse etc.) are transferred into a unified form on this level and are made available to the following software layers in a generalized form. Output from the dialogue system is transferred to the output devices. According to the task at hand, user group and level of training, various dialog methods and techniques can be put into practice. These are made available at the dialog interface and also transferred for lower layers into a generalized function oriented form. The tool interface structures the way the user deals with the software tools and data. The relationship between the user's tasks and the tasks of other users is established down by the organizational interface. A software architecture directed by this approach consists in the overriding principles modularity, compatibility and adaptability. These principles can be achieved at economically reasonable conditions. Later modifications due to technical improvements can be integrated. An overall interface design methodology is given in figure 2.

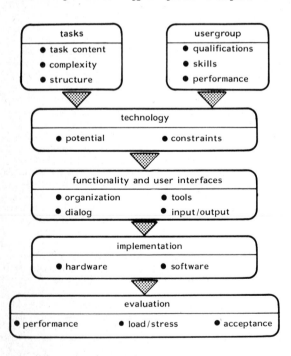

Figure 2: Method of Interface Design

3. An Interactive Processor for CNC-Programming

According to the methodology introduced in chapter two and taking the interface model as a basis for the software design a prototype laboratory processor has been constructed.

3.1. Task at Hand

With the usage of CNC-machine tools, the range of tasks is moving away from handling and physically demanding tasks to planning, programming and supervisory, that is, mentally demanding tasks due to the increasing degree of mechanization or automation. The scope of tasks can be structured as presented in Fig. 3.

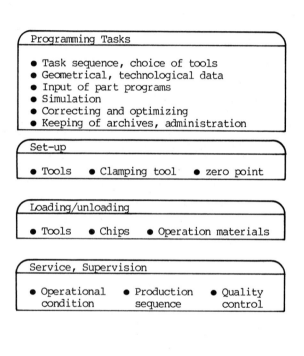

Figure 3: Task Scope at CNC-Machines

According to different organizational forms of programming (workshop programming, job-planning department programming, programming department etc.) and the complexity of the work pieces, several of those task areas are involved in a different way. Programming near to the machines causes bottlenecks when carrying out the task. Special consideration must be given to timely error detection and their correction, as time-intensive corrective and optimizing methods reduce the productive machining times. An increasing level of stress on skilled employees because of having to serve several machines, multi-axle-programming, parallel programming and the programming of periphery systems must be taken into account /4/ /5/.

3.2. User Profile

The observed work tasks were carried out by varying user groups. Fig. 4 shows the assignment of tasks to operators in the field of programming tasks /6/ /7/.

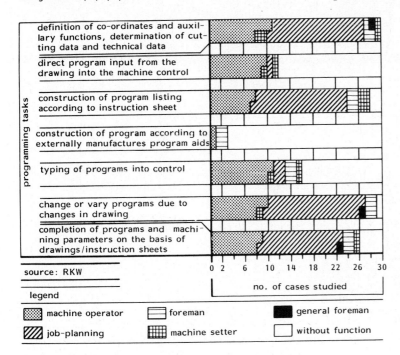

source: RKW

legend

- ▓ machine operator
- ▨ job-planning
- ▭ foreman
- ▦ machine setter
- ■ general foreman
- □ without function

Figure 4: Assignment of Functions to Users in the Area of Programming Tasks

On-the-spot investigations have shown that it is not possible to assign rigidly any task content to a particular user group. This is also reflected in the heterogeneity of the organizational model. Therefore it is essential to create an interactive processor which takes the qualifications and skills of all relevant user groups into account.

The users work with real objects and are used to pictorial representation (finished part, construction drawings). For this reason a visual task representation is more appropriate for them than algorithms. The machine language laid out in DIN 66025 (G-functions) is an extremely restrictive programming language for this user group as it is not adapted to users.

3.3. Technological Potential and Constraints

Due to the decreasing costs in the field of hardware and the continued development of standardized and modularly constructed software components, conceptions which, up to now, have see-

med too large-scale, are being realized more and more often. From the hardware aspect, configurations of multi-processors, enlarged program storage, colour videos capable of presenting graphics and with more coding methods have become possible. On the software side of the matter, standardized operating system components and the increased usage of utility programs such as for example comfortable editors, prevail.

Due to the present market situation and the predominating price pressure, manufacturers of control systems are forced to produce these new forms of technology economically and use them in such a manner so as to justify their additional value.

3.4. Functionality and Dialog Processors

3.4.1. Organizational Interface

Apart from the description of the division of tasks between the individual users, the organizational interface must determine the distribution of the complex of functions between the control and the user as well as between the system components.

In the determination of the division of tasks between man and machines, processes which can be automated, such as cutting data definition, simulation of collisions and various suggestions on the choice of tools and macros must be taken into consideration in the future (cf. Fig. 5).

3.4.2. Tool Interfaces Design

For the design of the programming language, the objective was to have a defined structure for the formulation of part programs into rough and final geometrical data input, as well as the determination of technological characteristic data and the work sequence. In this manner, data turning up during the construction and work preparation processes can be included without any difficulty. So the designed user interaction mode does not conflict with the layout of the next generation of automation systems. In extension to this, a macro-oriented command language was defined /8/ (cf.Fig.6).

Other software-tools for the graphic simulation of parts or of the entire manufacturing process are waiting for introduction. Comfortable video-display-oriented editors, which can also work with graphics, are another focal point.

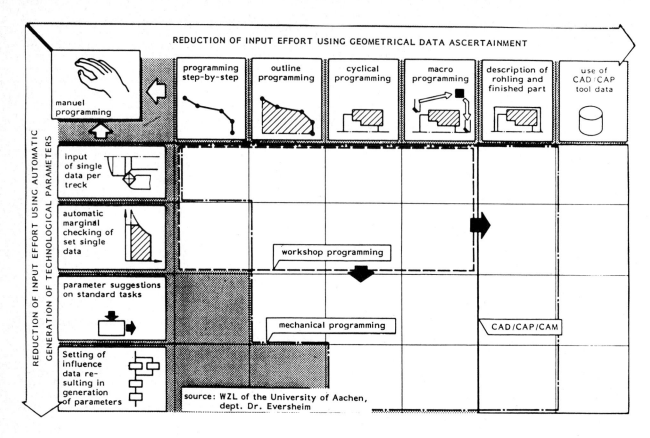

source: WZL of the University of Aachen,
dept. Dr. Eversheim

Figure 5: Automation Potentials of
CNC-Machines

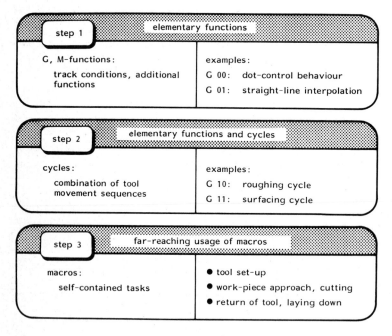

Figure 6: Three Steps of Complexity in the Construction of Part Programs

3.4.3. Dialogue Design

At present, there are six important criteria under discussion which are used to judge the quality of the dialog design. These criteria are based on a broad empirical study:

o appropriateness for the problem
   at hand
o controllability
o reliability
o self-explanatoryness
o learnability
o error tolerance

A thorough discussion can be found in literature /2/. For the realized system a combined mask/menue-system has been chosen and designed according to the above mentioned principles.

Figure 7 shows some design principles for mask/menue systems:

APPLICATIONS	Appropriate for inexperienced users. Good user guidance, more efficient forms of interaction for experienced users.
STRUCTURE	A homogenous structure is desirable (breadth and depth balanced).
	Minimizing of the path to be taken within the context of one task in the menu tree.
	Put semantically similar elements on one menu level.
	Do not have the length of the lists longer than 5-7 elements.
COMPLEXITY OF MENU STEPS	Totally hierarchical systems cause menu paths which are too long: use therefore a mixture of menu and from techniques.
	Universal commands which are often used to be reached easily e.g. with funktion keys.
	Commands which are local and often used in the present context are to be made available with soft keys.
INTERACTION IN MENU SYSTEM	Parallel choice by identifier, cursor or short commands.
	Unavoidable interactive sequences can be controlled with interactive forms initiated by the computer.
	In the case of large menu systems define pre-set entry points.
	In complex menu structures navigational alternatives should be displayed.
PRESENTATION OF INFORMATION	Give preference to vertical arrangement of the elements.
	Coding of particular list elements e.g. by invers video, colour or graphic aids.
FUTURE DEVELOPMENTS	Browsing in window-orientated systems.
	Self-adaptive menus.
	Usage of concepts above and beyond tree structures.

Figure 7: Design Principles for Menue/Mask Systems

3.4.4. Coding and Organization of Information

High-resolution CRTs, capable of presenting graphics, aid in extending the range of ergonomically worthwhile coding possibilities. Graphical presentation should support programming on as many levels as possible.

In order to draw attention to particular information (warnings, parameter values to be inserted), extra coding is used (cursor in differing forms and colours, inverse video, two brightness levels, blinking colour-bordered areas). A mixture of type is preferable to the exclusive use of capital letters in this field of application.

In comparison to the division of the screen by lines, due to the influence of EDP, the entire display area should be used to its full extent as a two dimensional medium. Certain categories,

such as status displays, menus, error messages etc. are to be designated to defined areas of the screen.

For the implementation of the system, a rapid prototyping approach was chosen, generating early user participation and theory hypothesis formulation for later empirical evaluations.

The development system was programmed in an object oriented approach. The object structure for a typical mask is given in Figure 8.

According to this system structure, the design methodology for interaction parameters was chosen. This methodology is demonstrated for the colour coding problem:

1.Step: Definition of elementary objects: largest information entities which have not to be differentiated further, relative to all design parameters.

2.Step: Definition of classes of objects: Dynamic aggregation of all elementary objects that have not to be distinguished further, relative to the design parameter "colour".

3.Step: Mapping parameter values onto classes of objects.

It is recommended for this type of problem not to use more than four colours. After having determinated the colour of the background (object class 1) the colours in step 3 for each "window" in the mask were

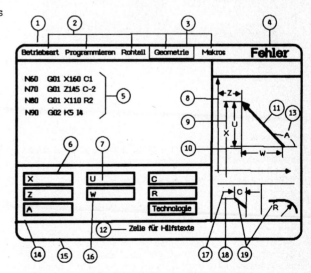

Figure 8: Object Structure of a CNC-Mask

chosen according to the actuality of information. Frames (1,14) and supporting graphic elements (10,18) etc. form the most static information. Dialog status information (2), part program (5), fields of the mask (16) etc. form the
third group. Highly topical information such as
actual input field (6), parameters to be entered
with their pertinent graphic presentation (11,
19), actual menue selection etc. are aggregated
in the fourth information class.

A suggestion for colour allocation on this basis
could be:

Object class 1: dark blue
Object class 2: bright blue
Object class 3: dark ocre
Object class 4: bright ocre

This design reflects the argument of coding semantical distance in the mask/menue system in an
adequate colour coding.

For future systems the organization of information as realised at present is too inflexible. A
full window system is momentarily under design.
Softwareergonomics (cf. /9/ for an overview of
the area) and computer science is rapidly going
beyond these ideas. On the horizon are emerging
more intelligent, adaptive man-computer interfaces /10/ /11/.

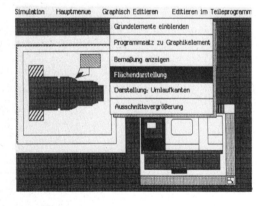

Figure 9: Organization of Information-
          Windowing

4. Advanced man-machine interface in the entire production area.

At the moment a broad empirical study is under
way where data on the state of introduction and
the quality of design of man-computer interfaces
for information technology in the entire production area is collected. Already now it can be
stated that in comparison to the office area the
softwareergonomic quality of the man-computer
interfaces is by far less developed and adapted
to the workers needs.

Bibliography

/1/ Bullinger,H.-J.; Lentes,H.P.: The Future of
Work. Prod. Res. 1982, Vol.20, No. 3, 259-296.

/2/ Work papers of the Puplications Committee
"Interactive Design", DIN NI AA D (man-machine
interaction)

/3/ Dzida,W.: Das IFIP-Modell für Benutzer-
schnittstellen. (The IFIP-model for user interfaces). Office Management 31 (1983), Special
issue for Workshop "Man-Machine Interaction".

/4/ Meier, H.: Workshop programming with CNC-
control with the example of the turning machine.
(Werkstattprogrammierung mit CNC-Steuerung am
Beispiel der Drehmaschine). Munich, Vienna:
Hanser, 1981.

/5/ Rolfes, J.: Beitrag zur Bestimmung des Pro-
grammieraufwands bei numerisch gesteuerten Dreh-
maschinen. (Paper on the dtermination of the
programming effort in numerically controlled
turning machines). University of Hannover, Faculty for Mechanical Engineering, Dissertation,
1979.

/6/ RKW: Wirtschaftliche und soziale Auswirkun-
gen des CNC-Werkzeugmaschinen-Einsatzes. (Econo-
mical and social consequences of the usage of
CNC-machine tools). Study of the Fraunhofer-
Institute for System Technique and Innovative
Research. Eschborn, 1981.

/7/ Oberhoff, H.: Beanspruchung der Arbeitsper-
sonen an hochtechnischen Arbeitsplätzen am Beispiel "Numerisch gesteuerter Werkzeugmaschinen".
(Stressing of workers at highly technical jobs
using the example of "numerically controlled machine tools"). Frankfurt/M.: Lang, 1976.

/8/ Diekmann, Th.; Klotz, U.: Veränderung der
Organisation des Arbeitsablaufs bei Werkzeugmaschinen durch den Einsatz von Micro-Computern.
(Alteration of the organization of task sequences of machine-tools with the use of micro-computers). Eggenstein-Leopoldshafen, 1980, BMFT-
Research Report; HA 80-050.

/9/ 83) Balzert,H. (ed.): Software-Ergonomie.
(Software Ergonomy). Stuttgart, Teubner, 1983.

/10/ Bullinger,H.-J.; Faehnrich,K.P.: Symbiotic
Man-Computer Interface and the User Agent Concept. Proc. of the first USA - Japan-Conference
on Human-Computer Interaction 1984 Honululu.

/11/ Faehnrich, K.P.; Ziegler, J.: Workstations
Using Direct Manipulation as Dialog Principle.
Aspects of Design, Application and Evaluation.
Proc. INTERACT 1984, London.

Human-Computer Interaction — INTERACT '84 / B. Shackel (ed.)
Elsevier Science Publishers B.V. (North-Holland)
© IFIP, 1985

GUIDELINES FOR USER PARTICIPATION IN THE SYSTEM DEVELOPMENT PROCESS

Bernard C. Glasson

School of Computing and Quantitative Studies
Western Australian Institute of Technology
Bentley, Western Australia 6102

Taking the need for effective user participation in computer-based information system
development as agreed, this paper argues that there are several user roles associated
with the system development process, each being required to participate to varying
degrees at different stages of system evolution, each having several parts to play in
the system development process, and each requiring detailed advice on how they might
best participate.   The paper then suggests and illustrates how a detailed task-based
set of guidelines for user participation relevant to each role could be derived from
an organisation's technical approach.

1.   INTRODUCTION

The need for user participation in the system
development process has long been recognised.
There are those like Lucas [7] who point to the
lack of effective user involvement in the system
development process as a contributing factor in
system failure.   There are others like Synnott
and Gruber [12] who put a different perspective
on the matter evidencing user involvement as
making a positive contribution to system success.   There are still others like Biggs, Birk
and Atkins [2] who warn that a lack of sufficient user interaction between the project team
and user management in organisation, planning,
scheduling, reporting, or review will result in
the creation of a system that belongs to the
project team, not the user.   Despite this apparent wide acceptance of the need for user participation in system development projects, there is
little evidence of serious attempts to define
what it is that System Developers would have the
User positively do in order to participate
effectively.   If we look at some of the more
serious surveys of the techniques available for
analysing and defining the information requirements of Users [13] [15] we find that even here,
where there should be no argument as to the need
for user involvement, the available techniques
are predominantly System Developer driven.   In a
wider study of successful system development
strategies McKeen [8] suggests changes to the
process of development to include, among other
things,

> "... implementing procedures to ensure
> meaningful and ongoing user particip-
> ation throughout the entire development
> cycle.   This can often be accomplished
> with parallel activities such as assign-
> ing users the responsibility of user
> training while the system designers
> attend to technical aspects such as
> programming ..."

While I have no argument with that, it is still
not enough.

What is needed is something more positive to
enable us to achieve this meaningful and ongoing
user participation.   I am not talking of the
superficial - "they should define their own
screens".   I am talking of a substantial model
of the system development process written from
the User perspective with which the User can
work.   That is, just as the System Developers
working on a particular project have a model for
managing their work efforts, De Marco [5] for an
instance or PRIDE/ASDM [9] for another, likewise, I would argue, the Users should have a
compatible user driven model with which to plan
and direct their work efforts - their participation.   Within the bounds of this paper I would
like to suggest and illustrate how such a model
might be constructed.

2.   COMPATIBLE MODELS

It might be convenient to have the one model for
user participation in system development projects - the one set of guidelines for user
participation in the system development process
if you prefer.   In practice, as evidenced by the
number of approaches used by System Developers,
this would appear to be impossible.   A recent
study of software development methodologies [14]
surveyed some 24 approaches.   Extensive and
sound as it was, many well known approaches (and
I am sure many more less well known) were not
represented in the survey which only serves to
illustrate the difficulty in identifying a
"standard" approach for System Developers.   Given
this diversity, I believe that it would be impossible to derive one "standard" set of guidelines for user participation in all situations.

What is possible is that the model for User
participation in one organisational situation
may be derived from that model used within that
same organisation by the System Developers. This
is not only possible but it is also desirable,
as it would ensure some compatibility between
the two models and therefore facilitate the coordination of User and System Developer efforts
towards a common goal.

The models of the system development process
used by System Developers in industry today are
more or less

a) founded on a preferred theory or approach to
solving system development problems (e.g. data-
oriented or process-oriented);

b) built around a particular interpretation of
that approach (e.g. within the "structured"
school there are several interpretations of
varying consequence which might be followed);
and

c) adapted to suit the particular organisational
environment.

An alternative is to acquire a packaged System
Development Methodology (e.g. SDM'70 [10] or
SPECTRUM [11]) and adapt that to suit the part-
icular organisational environment.

Whatever the origin or basis of the System Developers' model, on examination it will be found
to have underpinning it an explicit or implicit
task set.   That is a list of tasks that might
need to be performed by the System Developer
during some stage of target system evolution.
Allowing that the task set is complete and
correct it can be used as a basis for building
Users' models of the system development process
compatible with that followed by the organisation's System Developers.   The building of that
User model becomes essentially a three-step
process, as follows.

Step 1 - Define the several "User roles" or User
         actors who need to be involved in the
         system development process.

Step 2 - Define the several tasks that each User
         actor might need to perform during each
         stage of target system evolution.

Step 3 - Develop and define the appropriate
         procedures, methods, tools or techn-
         iques - be they manual or automated -
         that might be used in carrying out one
         or more of those tasks.

The discussion here will be confined to those
first two steps.   Until we understand and
define what we would have the Users do, there
is little point in trying to establish how
they might best carry out their tasks.

3.   USER ROLES

MIS writers [3] often refer to the Anthony's [1]
classification of planning and control activities into three categories: (1) strategic
planning, (2) management control, and (3)
operational control in defining levels of
decision-making within information systems and
decision support systems.   The Anthony classification is sometimes translated for MIS purposes into a decision-making pyramid showing
strategic decisions at the top, tactical decisions in the middle and operational decisions
at the bottom.   Thus we have three levels of
decision and three levels of decision-maker.
Taking the situation as simply as we can, then,
there could be said to be three User roles
associated with information systems in operation,
namely: executive strategist; manager tactician;
and operational supervisor.   Each would have
a different view of the information system in
operation consistent with their organisational
roles.   That being the case for the system in
operation, either now or in the future, it
follows then that appropriately representative
actors for each of these same three roles should
participate in the process of target system
evolution.   This role differentiation is important for two reasons.

First, because of their different perspectives,
there is a greater or lesser need for particular
User actors to participate in the different
stages of target system evolution.   Obviously,
for instance, the executive strategist would be
more concerned with the justification stage than
would the operational supervisor.   On the other
hand, once the development effort has been
justified and is under way a User actor, knowledgeable and representative of the operational
supervisors' view, and presumably that of the
workers he or she supervises, may well be sec-
onded to the system development team to fill the
role of User representative.

Second, having identified those stages of system
evolution in which a particular User actor ought
to participate, we can develop a set of tasks
that the actor might perform in order to participate effectively.

These User role/system evolution stage and User
role/task set relationships will be further
developed here.   However, in order to do that, it
is now necessary to introduce an illustrative
system development approach.

4.   EDP SYSTEM DEVELOPMENT GUIDELINES

EDP System Development Guidelines [6] describes
the system development process in terms of
those tasks that might need to be addressed by a
System Developer in any given system development
situation.   It is a life-cycle-based approach
best suited to commercial environments.   The
life-cycle model used represents the process of
system evolution in seven phases with each phase

Possible User Involvement / Life-cycle Phases	Executive Strate-gist	Manager Tacti-cian	Operat'l Super-visor
0. Project Justification	High	Med	Low
1. Background Study	Med	High	Med
2. System R'ments Determination	High	High	Low
3. System Design	Low	Med	High
4. System Specification	Low	Low	Med
5. Program Design & Construction	Low	Low	Low
6. System Implementation	Low	High	High
7. System Mainten-ance & Eval'n	Med	Med	Med
8. System Replacement	High	High	Low

Figure 1: A Possible User Role/System Evolution Stage Relationship

being broken down into tasks and each task being further broken down into sub-tasks. This model is consistent with, but not the same as, those used by many other approaches [2] [9] [10] [11] [14]. The approach has an underlying task set but, while a similar task set should be contained within other approaches to system development, there will be differences between this task set and others due to philosophical differences in approach and the reliance to the greater or lesser extent on particular procedures, methods, techniques or automated tools.

As an illustrative approach it has a number of advantages for our purposes here in that:

a) it is in the public domain;
b) it covers the full life-cycle;
c) it has a detailed task set (some 200 tasks) that covers both organisational and technical matters; and
d) it describes these tasks independent of technique.

Suffice to say for our purposes here that it is a representative and documented model of how a System Developer might participate in the process of target system evolution. We will use parts of it to illustrate how a similar model for User participation in that same evolu-

tionary process might be derived. Specifically we will use its life-cycle model to highlight differences in the degree of participation required of different User roles and then we will use extracts from its detailed task set to illustrate how similar User role oriented task sets could be derived to make better provision for ongoing and effective User participation.

5. USER ROLE/SYSTEM EVOLUTION STAGE RELATIONSHIP

As a first step in defining the required level of user participation we should attempt to identify the stages of system evolution that require a participative contribution from each of the three User roles. Figure 1 above illustrates how the results of a simple subjective test of "likely involvement" might be tabled. Even allowing for the looseness of the test two things are evident from the results.

First there is support for the view expressed earlier, that each User role needs to participate in the system development process to a greater or lesser extent dependent upon the stage of system evolution. This in turn indicates that we require different models of the development process for each, separate, User role.

Second, while the illustrative approach uses seven phases to describe the system's evolution process (denoted 1-7 in Figure 1), in taking a User view of that same process two new phases were identified (denoted 0 and 8 in Figure 1). Recognising these differences in perspective, and identifying the resultant changes that need to be made to the original System Developer model to derive an appropriate User model from it, is perhaps the most crucial step in the derivation approach being suggested here. These

1. Background Study
1.1 Project Objectives Determination
1.2 Organisational Environment Search or Summary
1.3 Establish the Organisation's Structure and Boundaries
1.4 Function Identification
1.5 Operation (Sub-Function) Definition
1.6 Compare Physical and Logical System Models
1.7 Prepare and Present the Project Definition Report

Figure 2: Phase 1 Tasks - A System Developer's View

differences in perspective become more apparent
if we take the analysis down a level.

6.   USER ROLE/TASK SET RELATIONSHIPS

At the next, lower, level of detail, we find
that the illustrative approach shows each phase
of system evolution broken down into a series of
possible system development tasks (e.g. Phase 1,
Background Study, consists of seven tasks as
shown in Figure 2). At this greater level of
detail the simple test of a user's "likely
involvement" can no longer be applied to the
System Developer's model as it stands. At this
level the tasks as described in the System
Developer's model need to be, at the very least,
re-phrased to reflect the User's view of each
task before we can attempt to establish a
relationship between a particular role and the
system development task that role should perform.   This is because the User actor has many
parts to play in the system development process
and the model needs now to be modified to reflect these several User viewpoints if it is to
serve any further useful purposes.   Figure 3
below highlights the problem by contrasting the
results of a "likely involvement" test carried
out in relation to one of the System Developer's
tasks before and after it had to be re-phrased
to reflect a User view.

Possible User Involvement Task 1.7	Executive Strate-gist	Manager Tacti-cian	Operat'l Super-visor
a) Sys. Developer Perspective: Prepare & Present Proj. Def'n Report	Nil	Low	Low
b) User Perspective: Receive & Review Project Def'n Report	Med	High	Med

Figure 3:   Test of Involvement from Two
            Perspectives

To avoid this problem one must consider the
several parts that any User role might be called
on to play during the system development process.

First the user could be simply a "bystander".
That is, the task concerned is a technical one
that, for the moment, calls for no participative
effort on behalf of the User role. For example,
during task 1.6, as shown in Figure 2, while the

System Developer is comparing the relative
efficiency of the existing (physical) system
model and a perceived ideal (logical) model,
there is little the User can contribute and nor
is there a related task for the User to perform.

Second, as an "authoriser" or controller of
system development effort the User may have
tasks to perform over and above those of the
System Developer. For example, in task 1.2 as
shown in Figure 2, the System Developer may well
wish to interview the information system's external "customers" or "suppliers".   This would
involve prior authorisation from the appropriate
User and, in order to give that authority, one
or more activities might need to occur.

Third, the User could act as a "facilitator".
That is in order to expedite the system development process the User could anticipate, or
request advice on, the System Developer's needs
(for information, facilities or whatever) and
take action to facilitate the System Developer's
performance of that task without the User actually directly participating. For example, in
task 1.3 in Figure 2, a User Manager, by giving
prior advice as to the project's purpose and
personally introducing the System Developer to
the staff concerned, will usually make the
System Developer's task of gathering background
data much easier. However the User manager does
not participate in the data gathering task
itself.

Fourth, the User will need on occasion to be a
"co-operative" partner working with the System
Developer on a common task. For example, task
1.1 in Figure 2, the task of defining the project initially, requires a great deal of interaction between Users and System Developers.

Fifth, the user has the additional role of
"reviewer". That is the System Developer
independently carries out a task and the User
reviews the outcome of that task.   For example,
task 1.7 in Figure 2 is a case in point as shown
in Figure 3. The System Developer produces and
presents the report, then the User receives and
reviews it.

Sixth, the User will be an "independent" actor
at times performing tasks that fall more within
his or her competence than that of the System
Developer (e.g. writing procedure manuals perhaps) or that might appear to be outside the
system development process itself but are a
necessary adjunct to it (e.g. staff recruitment,
negotiating for resources).

Allowing that the User role may be called on to
play one or more of these parts at one time or
another during the system development process,
the derivation of a system development model
for each User role should be carried out
systematically.

The Process of System Evolution	
A System Developer's View	A Possible User's View
N/A	0. Project Justification
1. Background Study	1. Project Definition & Authorisation
2. System R'ments Determination	2. New System R'ments & Constraint Def'n
3. System Design	3. Verification & Approval of Design Proposal
4. System Specification	4. Finalisation of Man/Machine Inter-faces & Human Work Efforts
5. Program Design & Construction	5. Monitor Programming Progress
6. System Implementation	6. Testing, Training Cutover & Accept'ce
7. System Maint'ce & Evaluation	7. System Operation & Review
N/A	8. System Replacement Investigation

Figure 4: The Process of System Evolution
         - Two Possible Views

7. DERIVING THE USER'S MODEL

The System Developer's model of system evolution expressed down to at least the task within phase level, and preferably the sub-task within task level, becomes the start point from which one derives a model of system evolution from the viewpoint of each identified User role in the organisation. The suggested procedure is to take that System Developer's detailed task set and - having regard to the particular viewpoint of the User role for which the model is being developed - to revise it, Phase by Phase, then Task by Task, and then Sub-Task by Sub-Task, by:

a) adding any prior "authorisation" activities;
b) adding any prior "facilitating" activities;
c) adding any prior or parallel "independent" activities;
d) re-phrasing any "co-operative" activity descriptions in terms relevant to the user viewpoint;
e) summarising and noting the "bystander" activities as such (while these technical tasks are not part of the User's task set it is well for the User to be aware of

the System Developer's parallel activity; this becomes essential if the particular User role encompasses project management); and

f) adding any post event "review" activities.

These then are the suggested mechanics for deriving a User model. Let us now speculate on what the task set for one of the User roles, namely the User manager, might contain if we continued the illustration.

8. AN ILLUSTRATIVE DERIVED USER MODEL

The User manager, that is the manager of that section of the organisation for which the new information system is being developed, is a key actor in the system development process. He or she has a two-fold responsibility. During development the User manager must ensure that the target system is developed within the agreed organisational constraints. Ultimately, however, and arguably more importantly, that User manager will be responsible for the information system in operation. A possible User manager view of system evolution, contrasted with that of the illustrative approach, is shown in Figure 4.

A System Developer's Model	A User Manager's Model
Phase 1 Background Study	Phase 1 Project Def'n & Authorisation
1.1 Project Objectives Determination	1.1 Information System Problem Definition
1.2 Org'n Environment Search or Summary	1.2 External Environ't Definition
1.3 Establish Org's Structure & Boundaries	1.3 Internal Environ't Definition
1.4 Function Identification	1.4 Review Developer's Def'n of Function
1.5 Operation (Sub-Function) Def'n	1.5 Verify Data Definition
1.6 Compare Physical & Logical System Models	1.6 Verify Physical & Logical System Model Comparisons
1.7 Prep. & Present Project Def'n Report	1.7 Receive and Review Project Def'n Report

Figure 5: Tasks Within a Phase - Two
         Possible Views

A further comparison between the illustrative approach for System Developers and the User manager model that might have been derived from it at the task within phase level (as shown in Figure 5) reveals that the two actors are working towards the same goal within their own sphere of organisational responsibility.

However, if we stopped here, even at this level of detail, it could be said that we only have a model of co-operation, that is to say a guideline as to how a User manager might best co-operate during the system development process. Co-operation is not enough; what is needed is participation. To ensure this participation at an active and practical level we need to take the User manager's model down one level further as is shown in Figure 6, that is down to the sub-task within task level.

System Developer's View

1.3   Establish the Organisation's Structure and Boundaries
1.3.1 Establish the Theoretical Organisation Structure
1.3.2 Establish the Actual Organisation Structure
1.3.3 Obtain Personal Details (name, title, duties)
1.3.4 Define Informational Outputs and Destination
1.3.5 Define Data Inputs and Source
1.3.6 Review Existing Data Dictionary
1.3.7 Determine Current Budgets and Resource Allocations

User Manager's View

1.3   Internal Environment Definition
1.3.1 Provide an Organisation Chart through the Personnel Function
1.3.2 Advise all Likely Affected Personnel of the Study and Set Aside Meeting Times as appropriate
1.3.3 Provide Duty Statements, Standard Procedures etc.
1.3.4 Advise System "Customers" & "Suppliers" of the Study and Arrange Meetings as appropriate
1.3.5 Review, with Operational Supervisors as appropriate, Analysts' view (Charts, Models) of the System Inputs/Outputs
1.3.6 Establish/Review Definitions of Key Information/Data Items
1.3.7 Define Present Information System Cost Elements and Rates if appropriate or Define New System Operational Budget

---

Figure 6: A Possible System Development Sub-Task - Two Views

The sub-tasks 1.3.1 - 1.3.7 shown under the User manager's view in Figure 6 represent tasks that a User manager might perform during the system development process. Given that these efforts were co-ordinated with those of the System Developer, I would contend that the User manager, in carrying out those tasks, would be effectively participating in the system development process.

9. GUIDELINES FOR PARTICIPATION

What I have attempted to do within the bounds of this paper is to suggest and illustrate how a set of guidelines for user participation in the system development process might be derived. The suggestion is that one starts with the system development approach or methodology used within the organisation by the system development staff. That approach should then be analysed and revised to provide alternative models for the several User roles that might need to participate in the system development process. This analysis should take into account that different User roles are called on to participate at different stages of target system evolution and that each User role has a number of parts to play in that evolutionary process such that there will not be a one-to-one relationship between the tasks of the System Developer and those of the particular User role. I believe that if organisations were to provide models along these lines in the form of guidelines for user participation in the system development process then the participation so many are seeking would be more readily attained.

REFERENCES

[1] Anthony, R.N. and Dearden, J., Management Control Systems Text and Cases (Richard D. Irwin, Inc. Homewood, Ill. Third Edition 1976).

[2] Biggs, C.L., Birks, E.G. and Atkins, W., Managing the Systems Development Process (Prentice-Hall Inc., Englewood-Cliffs N.J., 1980).

[3] Carlson, E.D., An Approach for Designing Decision Support Systems, Data Base (Winter 1979) 3-15.

[4] Boehm, B.W., Software engineering, IEEE Transactions on Computers, December (1976) 1226-1241.

[5] De Marco, T., Structured Analysis and System Specification (Prentice-Hall, Englewood-Cliffs N.J., 1979).

[6] Glasson, B.C., EDP System Development Guidelines (Butterworths, London, 1984).

[7] Lucas, H.C., Why Information Systems Fail (Columbia University Press, New York, 1975).

[8] McKeen, J.D., Successful development
     strategies for business application systems,
     MIS Quarterly/September 1983, 47-65.

[9] PRIDE-profitable information by design
     through phased planning and control, a
     proprietary product of M. Bryce and
     Associates, Inc., Cincinnati, USA, n.d..

[10] SDM'70, a proprietary product of Atlantic
     Software, Inc., Philadelphia, USA, n.d..

[11] SPECTRUM-1, a proprietary product of
     Toellner and Associates, Los Angeles, USA,
     n.d..

[12] Synnott, W.R. and Gruber, W.H., Information
     Resource Management (John Wiley & Sons
     Inc., New York, 1981).

[13] Taggart, W.M. and Tharp, M.O., A Survey of
     Information Requirements Analysis Techn-
     iques, Computing Surveys, Vol.9, No.4,
     (1977) 273-290.

[14] Wasserman, A.I., Characteristics of soft-
     ware development methodologies, in Olle,
     T.W., Sol, H.G. and Tully, C.J. (eds.)
     Information systems design methodologies:
     a feature analysis (North-Holland, Amster-
     dam, 1983).

[15] Yadav, S.B., Determining an organisation's
     information requirements: a state of the
     art survey, Data Base (Spring 1983) 3-20.

Human-Computer Interaction — INTERACT '84 / B. Shackel (ed.)
Elsevier Science Publishers B.V. (North-Holland)

597

EXPERIENCES ON USER PARTICIPATION IN THE DEVELOPMENT OF A
CONCEPTUAL SCHEMA BY USING A CONCEPT STRUCTURE INTERFACE

Hannu Kangassalo
University of Tampere, P.O. Box 607, SF-33101 Tampere 10, Finland

Pirjo Aalto
The Pohjola-Group, Lapinmäentie 1, SF-00300 Helsinki 30, Finland

Conceptual modeling of the universe of discourse (UoD) has been gaining increasing attention as an efficient method in the development of information systems. An important part of a modeling process is the collection of information from which the conceptual model will be built up. This information consists of concept definitions and structural descriptions concerning the UoD. In this paper we will describe methods and tools used for the development of a conceptual schema in a life insurance company. We will also describe experiences on user participation in conceptual modeling.
Two types of graphical notations were used: concept structure diagrams and conceptual schema diagrams. Finally we will describe a graphical workstation environment the development of which has been started on the basis of collected experiences.

1. INTRODUCTION

The development of a conceptual description, i.e. a conceptual schema of the universe of discourse has been recognized to be an important and inseparable part of the application development /12/. The purpose of the conceptual schema is to give a conceptual and implementation independent description of the meaning of data (i.e. a mapping between data and the UoD) stored in the data base and manipulated in the information system. At the same time a conceptual schema is also a theory of the UoD /8/.

In the development of a conceptual schema a problem arises from the fact that the best expertise of the UoD and user requirements is dispersed among large group of users who usually have no training in detailed requirement specification techniques. Therefore a methodology is needed which can be used to collect user's knowledge of the UoD in such a form that it can be used as a basis for the further development of the conceptual schema and the information system. The methodology must use only terms and notions which are oriented to the meaning of concepts and constructs used in the UoD. The methodology must also be such that users can themselves define their own concepts.

The purpose of this paper is to describe some experiences on user participation in conceptual modeling collected during the design of a new life insurance processing system in a large insurance company in Finland. The system was known to contain several hundreds of interrelated concepts and a lot of rules for handling different classes of exceptions. It was expected that users of the system would participate in the definition of concepts and rules used in the UoD. In fact, they were expected to make most of the definitions. However, from the previous experiments it was known that the task to develop written definitions of rather abstract things in a way which would be acceptable for various groups of people, may be extremely tedious and difficult task just for linguistic reasons.

Therefore, a graphical formalism for describing concept structures was used. It was required that the formalism should be rich enough to model in an understandable way as much as possible of abstract notions and constructs encountered in the life insurance system. The formalism should also make the detailed definition of concepts possible, not only show how they are applied to model the UoD. The formalism - called CONCEPT D /7/ - is based on the idea that the basic epistemological primitive of human knowledge is concept which can be described as an abstract object without any consideration on material instantiation of it. The basic epistemological relation is the relation if intensional containing which is based on the idea that a concept can be contained in the other concept. CONCEPT D will be shortly described in section 2.

First a series of experiments was made in order to test and develop the formalism to encompass different situations recognized in the UoD. After that the work for collecting concept definitions was started. More details of this work are given in section 3.

From concept definitions a definitional conceptual schema was developed. By the definitional conceptual schema (DCS) we mean a schema which contains detailed structural definitions of concepts and shows how these concepts have been applied to model the UoD. The notion of DCS will be described in section 4.

The experiences from the concept definition phase were collected after the work in order to find the deficiencies of the methodology. The most important findings are reported in section 5.

The methodology is being developed further and the development of a computerized graphical support system for conceptual modeling has been started.

2. CONCEPT D - A GRAPHICAL FORMALISM FOR REPRESENTING CONCEPT STRUCTURES

The fundamental notion on which the whole modeling methodology has been built is concept, which is regarded as a basic epistemological component of human knowledge. In the following a concept is defined to be an independently identifiable formal construct with an internal structure, and consisting of structured semantic information /2, 6, 7/. It can be said that a concept is a type of internal semantic structures /2, p.214- /, but it would be far too simplistic to regard a concept as an internal data model.

From the modeling point of view an essential aspect is that human knowledge is organized with aid of concepts and constructs made up of concepts. Concepts and constructs, recognized during the modeling process form a framework according to which the information acquired through observation processes is structured for further usage. Therefore the goal set for the development of CONCEPT D was to achieve as good as possible a structural correspondence with concepts and conceptual constructs used in human knowledge organization. Especially it was pursued to be as free as possible of all constraints and complexities imposed by the grammar of any language. The main goal was to be able to concentrate on concepts and their intensional and factual relationships in a natural and understandable way.

The working hypothesis used in this work is that the basic epistemological relation between concepts is the relation of intensional containing, and the methodology and notations used in conceptual modeling should be based on this relation. The relation of intensional containing is defined within the set of concepts and it holds between two concepts, A and B, if and only if concept A intensionally contains concept B /10/. A more intuitive explication can be given by saying that concept A contains intensionally concept B if the information forming concept A contains the information forming concept B. Please, note that we are talking about information required to recognize a phenomenon, not the way how the definition is constructed.

The relation of intensional containing has not been recognized in other approaches to conceptual modeling, see e.g. /1, 3, 4, 13/. It gives a possibility to develop all generally known modeling constructs in a systematic and consistent way, together with some novel modeling constructs /7/. The main constructs of a formalism based on these primitives are shortly described below.

In order to model the UoD a system of concepts must always be constructed. It consists of basic concepts and of derived concepts. A derived concept is a concept the properties of which have been derived from the properties of other concepts in a way described in the definition of that concept. A basic concept is a concept which can not be analyzed or defined using other concepts of the same conceptual system. In this context a definition of a concept is a graphical diagram which associates a new concept - that which is being defined - with the set of old, i.e.

already known, concepts in some specific way. The type of the structure of the definition together with some attached inscriptions specify how the properties of the defined concept are to be derived.

The description of a basic concept consists of the name of the concept together with references to semantical rules of the concept, to value set specification corresponding to that concept, and to recognition procedure which can be applied to recognize phenomena corresponding to that concept. The name of a basic concept is underlined with double lines to indicate the end the definition hierarchy.

In the definition of derived concepts, two types of definitions are recognized: intensional (or analytical) definitions and representational definitions. In intensional definition the internal structure of the defined concept is described. There are three main types of intensional definitions: aggregation, generalization and transformation. All these types have several subtypes /7/. In representational definition (if it is accepted as a proper definition at all) a concept is defined by specifying how the value representing it is derived from values representing defining concepts. In figure 1 some structural types of graphical concept definitions are shown.

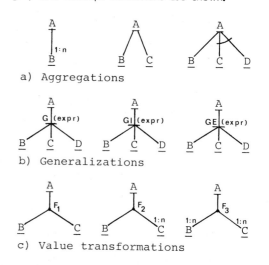

a) Aggregations

b) Generalizations

c) Value transformations

LEGEND: 1. A,B,C,.. concept names
2. A line represents intensional containing between concepts
3. F represents value transformation function
4. G,GI,GE are generalization types

Figure 1. Some structural types of concept definitions

3. COLLECTION OF CONCEPT DEFINITIONS

A concept structure is a construct which consists of the defined concept (definiendum) and of its definition hierarchy which derives the properties of the definiendum from the properties of basic concepts /5/. Any concepts relevant for the design of a conceptual schema and the content of a data base can be described as a concept structure by using the same notation, whether they be entities in the UoD, relationships in the UoD, data requirements or events. This is important for the collection of concept definitions from users because they can use only one notation to describe all kinds of concepts.

In our case it was known that there will be several hundred concepts, some of them on a rather high level of abstraction, some rather fuzzy and confusing ones, and only few concepts had a well written definition. From previous experiments it was also known that to try to achieve a written definition of all concepts and their relationships is an unrealistic task. The main reasons were that many users do not have a clear understanding of semantic and structural relationships between concepts, or of the relative positions of concepts in the definition hierarchies. It had also turned out that even the wording of definitions will cause problems, partly because of different opinions concerning the UoD, and partly because of different linguistic taste and style of persons. Therefore it was decided that it will be enough to get graphical definitions of concepts based on the relation of intensional containing together with the names of concepts.

The work covered the life insurance function which is one of the main functions of the company. A short (1 day) course on the goal of the work and on the graphical notation was given to users, who were expected to produce a graphical definition of most important concepts, down to a sufficient level of details. There were 10 persons involved. Also some written material on CONCEPT D was distributed. One person familiar with the notation and the UoD was allocated to give support to users in the use of the formalism, and to control and collect the results.

The work took several months. Usually several author - reader cycles between the user and the support person was required before a definition was satisfactory. In the beginning the relation of intensional containing caused some problems. Some users tended to think in process oriented terms related to flow of documents, rather than in structure oriented terms required to produce the definitions of concepts.

As a result 147 pages (in size A4 or A3) of graphical concept definitions were received. These definitions contained about 1400 concept names. From these, about 350-400 were basic concepts, all the others were derived concepts. The definitions contained a lot of conditions and structural constraints between concepts.

4. DEFINITIONAL CONCEPTUAL SCHEMA

On the basis of graphical concept definitions a definitional conceptual schema has been produced. A definitional conceptual schema (DCS) is a formal construct composed of concepts, intensional relationships between concepts, and of factual constrainst between concepts /9/. The set of concepts and intensional relationships between them specify the set of all possible worlds and their states recognizable with this set of concepts. However, usually this is too broad a view for practical purposes. Therefore more constraints dependent on the purpose of the modeling process, on the related UoD, and on the selected range of time will be needed to limit the number of possible worlds and their states modeled in the DCS. These constraints are called factual constraints. Thus a DCS does not only describe the entities and their attributes and relationships in the UoD, but it defines the whole system of concepts applied to describe the UoD. It contains more semantic information than conceptual schemata normally used to describe the content and behavior of a data base /12/. This property improves the understandability and applicability of the DCS as a tool for education and understanding the UoD and the content of a data base.

Structurally a DCS is a directed acyclic graph based on the relation of intensional containing. In this case the definition hierarchy has 22 levels. On the highest level there is only one concept - the life insurance function. Basic concepts are dispersed on different levels depending on the location of the lowest derived concept containing these basic concepts.

The graphical description of the DCS consists of nodes representing concepts and of arcs representing relationships between concepts. There are two types of arcs: arrows representing the relation of intensional containing, and dotted arcs representing factual constraints. On each arc additional inscriptions can be attached. These inscriptions specify cardinalities, conditionalities, alternatives, user views and time specifications.

The hierarchical structure of the manual version of the DCS has been implemented by using sheets of semi-transparent draftingfilm of 60x90 cm in size. Each sheet contains concepts and constraints on one level of the DCS. The sheets are stacked on each other in such a way that the highest level of the DCS is on top of the stack and the lower levels under it sequenced according to the number of the level. Because of the semitransparency of sheets, 2 to 3 lower levels can be seen through the sheet above them. Thus 3 to 4 levels of the DCS can be viewed at a time without being confused by the whole complexity of the DCS.

In its complete form a DCS is a theory of the UoD, describing the content and behavior of the UoD. However, in our case only those dynamic rules were taken into account which were explicitly stated in concept structures. Because of that simplification all the processes are not explicitly described although they could be added in a rather straightforward way.

As a by-product the relational data base schema and some process specifications can be derived from the DCS.

5. EXPERIENCES FROM THE DEVELOPMENT OF A LARGE DEFINITIONAL CONCEPTUAL SCHEMA

The user experiences from the construction of concept structures were collected for the evaluation of the methodology itself and for the estimation of the amount and type of work required if the methodology would be applied also in other areas in the company.

The experience shows that by using graphical concept definitions it is possible to develop with a reasonable effort detailed concept descriptions which are informative, understandable and in a very compact form. In many cases the corresponding verbal definition would have taken more space and been more difficult to read and to understand. In addition to that, in verbal definitions the wording is often likely to introduce additional problems.

In some cases the detailed description of concepts revealed that although the users are using these concepts in their own daily work, they may still have rather confused and fuzzy, even inconsistent knowledge about these concepts. Often they experienced the detailed analysis of their concepts as very useful, although not always too easy work. Quite often it took a lot of time to produce a consistent description of some complex concepts. However, in spite of the fact that errors were detected, the quality of resulting definitions was rather high.

A useful aspect of the methodology is that it does not require to classify phenomena of the UoD into entities, attributes, relationships, etc. All phenomena are simply described as structured concepts. In some other methodologies this classification is a source of integration problems between different views and it causes a lot of confusion among users.

A concept structure showing the intensional structure of the concept seems to be more useful for understanding of the behaviour of the UoD than a mere description of flow of documents and processes. Especially the detailed analysis and definition of complex bundles of constraints and exception rules contained in some concept definitions has been more clarifying than simple description of the effects of these rules on the handling of documents.

Although the construction of concept structures is not always simple, reading of them seems to be easy. The essential feature for understanding seems to be the use of the relation of intensional containing. Especially in the analysis of abstract high-level constructs, which often are very complex, concept structure diagrams have been of great help. Concept structures have also proven to be simple, efficient tools for communication between different groups of people.

Also the multilevel representation of a DCS has proven to be an efficient tool for describing complex conceptual constructs. The top-down view through several layers of the definition hierarchy gives a good overview of the DCS on the desired level of details. The layered structure made of semi-transparent sheets obscures the unnecessary lower level details which would make the schema extremely complex if they were all on a single level. However, it is easy to turn over some lower or higher levels, if needed.

The experiences described above were very clear but more research will be needed to give a scientific explanation of these findings. The number of people involved was too small and the phenomena observed too complicated to justify any detailed statistical analysis or far reaching conclusions. However, it seems to be clear that the definitional approach has some advantages over the procedural approach. Graphical concept definitions are useful tools for clarifying thinking and for communication. Also the multilevel DCS has proven its usefulness in conceptual modeling. These observations give good empirical support for the further work.

6. FURTHER DEVELOPMENT OF THE INTERFACE

For the interface described above a computerized tool is under development at the University of Tampere. The tool will be implemented on a 32-bit supermini with high resolution graphics. It consists of four interrelated components: concept editor, schema editor, concept base manager and integrator.

The concept editor can be used to construct and edit on the screen concept structures which are then transformed into internal representation and stored into the concept base. A user is using a 'mouse', menus, the keyboard and function keys for constructing concept structures. He can type in the name of a concept, show its location on the screen and press a function key. The function recognizes the name, stores it on the internal working area, and locates the name on the desired position on the screen. After having defined two or more concept names on the screen, the user can specify definition types and other relationships between concepts by using the menu and function keys. He can add new names, he can change the structure, or the names of concepts, etc. The original picture can be stored and returned back on the screen.

Very often a concept structure is much larger in size than what can be shown on the screen. Therefore it must be possible to scroll the diagram up or down, left or right, and manipulate all parts of the diagram without making any auxiliary operations.

The concept base manager is used to manipulate the concept base, i.e. a data base which contains the information contained in the definitonal conceptual schema together with additional information required for graphical representation of concept structures and the DCS. Information contained in concept structures and the DCS is normalized and stored in simple relations by using an ordinary data base management system. More than ten relations are needed to store information contained in a complex concept structure.

The integrator can be used to integrate a new concept structure into the DCS. During the integration it may happen that some conflicts between the DCS and the new concept structure are detected. To solve these conflicts interaction with the user may be required.

For the interaction two windows are opened on the screen: one showing a part of the DCS and the other showing a conflicting part of the new concept structure. The user can either modify his concept structure, insert a new view (i.e. his own concept structure) into the DCS, or require the DCS to be changed. After the integration process the new concept structure is included into the DCS.

The schema editor is a tool for inspection and modification of the DCS. The DCS or a part of it is shown on the screen from top to down through the levels. The levels are semitransparent in such a way that the highest level is most clearly visible whereas lower levels are the more obscured the lower they are. This feature creates an illusion of three-dimensionality which supports the understanding of the intensional structure of the DCS. The user can select any concept to be shown as the central object of interest (COI) on the highest level and concepts related to it by various factual constraints shown around it, and concepts intensionally contained into it to be shown 'behind' it, i.e. on the lower levels on the screen. He can also select the COI to be shown on some lower level on the screen and the concepts into which the COI is intensionally contained are shown in front of it.

The user will also have a possibility to edit the DCS. He can construct new concepts, relationships and constraints into the schema. A special feature which is currently in the specification phase is the set of concept operations which can be used to define new concepts in an algebraic manner. This set includes operations for intensional sum, intensional product, intensional difference, intensional negation and intensional division. First definitions of these operations have been presented in /6/ and /10/, but further research is still needed for handling various types of constraints occuring in concept definitions.

7. CONCLUSIONS

We have described the application of a graphical modeling formalism in a company in the development of the large definitional conceptual schema, which defines the concepts used in one function of the company and describes that function by using these concepts. Experiences collected after the work show that the definition of concepts may be a hard but rewarding task, even when the task is simplified by using a graphical language for the description of concept structures and the DCS. The resulting constructs are easy to read, understandable, and good tools for communication between people. On the basis of these experiences a project has been started to develop a software system which supports a graphical workstation for conceptual modeling, data base design and information system development.

Acknowledgement: We would like to express our thanks and appreciation to Mrs Sirkku Närevirta who worked as a control person, edited all the concept structures and helped us to collect user experiences.

REFERENCES:

1. Bubenko jr, J.A.: Information Modeling in the Context of System Development. In Lavington, S.H. (Ed.), Information Processing 80. North-Holland 1980.

2. Dretske, F.I.: Knowledge and the Flow of Information. Basil Blackwell Publisher, Oxford 1981.

3. Gustafsson, M.R., Karlsson, T., Bubenko jr, J.A.; A Declarative Approach to Conceptual Information Modeling. In /11/.

4. Hammer, M., McLeod, D.: Database Description with SDM: A Semantic Database Model. ACM Transactions on Database Systems, Vol. 6, No. 3, September 1981, Pages 351-386.

5. Kangassalo, H.: Phases and Intermediate Results of the Data Base Design Process. In Järvi, T. and Teuhola, J. (Eds.), Problems in Design and Application of Data Base Systems. University of Turku, Department of Mathematical Sciences/Computer Science, Report A27, December 1980.

6. Kangassalo, H.: On the Concept of Concept in a Conceptual Schema. In Kangassalo, H. (Ed.), The First Scandinavian Research Seminar on Information Modelling and Data Base Management. Acta Universitatis Tamperensis, Ser. B, Vol. 17, Tampere 1982.

7. Kangassalo, H.: Concept D - A Graphical Formalism for Representing Concept Structures. In Kangassalo, H. (Ed.), The Second Scandinavian Research Seminar on Information Modelling and Data Base Management. Acta Universitatis Tamperensis, Ser. B, Vol. 19, Tampere 1983.

8. Kangassalo, H.: Structuring Principles of Conceptual Schemas and Conceptual Models. In Bubenko jr, J.A. (Ed.), Information Modeling. Studentlitteratur, Lund 1983.

9. Kangassalo, H.: On Embedded Views in a Definitional Conceptual Schema. In Kangassalo, H. (Ed.), Third Scandinavian Research Seminar on Information Modelling and Data Base Management. (to appear)

10. Kauppi, R.: Einführung in die Theorie der Begriffssysteme. Acta Universitatis Tamperensis, Ser. A, Vol. 15. University of Tampere, Tampere 1967.

11. Olle, T.W., Sol, H.G., Verrijn-Stuart, A.A. (Eds.), Information Systems Design Methodologies: A Comparative Review. North-Holland, 1982.

12. van Griethuysen, J.J. (Ed.): Concepts and Terminology for the Conceptual Schema and the Information Base. ISO/TC97/SC5/WG3-report. 1982-03-15. Available from ANSI under publication number ISO/TC97/SC5-N695.

13. Verheijen, G.M.A. and van Bekkum, J.: NIAM: An Information Analysis Method. In /11/.

Human-Computer Interaction — INTERACT '84 / B. Shackel (ed.)
Elsevier Science Publishers B.V. (North-Holland)
© IFIP, 1985

FORMALIZING TASK DESCRIPTIONS
FOR COMMAND SPECIFICATION AND DOCUMENTATION

Paul Smolensky, Melissa L. Monty, Eileen Conway

Institute for Cognitive Science, C-015
University of California, San Diego,
La Jolla, California 92093

We consider the problem of formally describing computer tasks *not* in terms of procedures that will accomplish them but rather in terms of the input given and the output desired. A feasibility study in the domain of printing suggests that *task attributes* provide a powerful language for such descriptions. We describe the constraints such attributes must satisfy, and the procedure we used to design the printing attributes and test their usability. Applications to attribute-oriented interfaces and documentation are discussed. It is argued that task description is important for moving the center of human—machine interface design away from the machine and towards the user.

The goal of human—machine interface design is to maximize the effectiveness of a mapping between two worlds: the world of *tasks* users need to perform and the world of *tools* provided by the machine. Since, traditionally, designers have depended on users to adapt their task needs to the available tools, establishing a mapping that pays comparable attention to these two worlds would constitute significant progress in interface design. The advent of powerful computers means that tools can now adapt more to users' tasks. To take advantage of this, interface designers must deepen their understanding of the task world; this understanding is a prerequisite for making the design of human—machine systems less machine—centered and more user–centered.

Our sense of the term "task" must be distinguished from the sense it has acquired from "task analysis", a powerful tool for studying interfaces (Kieras & Polson, 1982; Bannon et al., 1983; Moran, 1983; Riley & O'Malley, 1984). Analyzing tasks has traditionally been taken to mean analyzing *the procedures used to perform tasks*. In our terminology, interface studies of this kind analyze the mapping between the *user's mental tools* and the *machine's tools* for performing tasks. By contrast, we are analyzing tasks in terms of transformations affected on objects *without considering the processes* ("tools") used to perform the transformation.

To develop a more formal understanding of the user's task world we are studying the limited domain of *printing tasks on a computer system*. This domain is rich and can be reasonably isolated from other computer tasks. Our investigation leads us to suggest that:

(a) tasks be described in a formal framework of *task attributes*;

(b) computer tools be redesigned using task attributes;

(c) documentation be redesigned using task attributes (even if attribute-oriented tools are not adopted).

In this paper, we first explain what is meant by task attributes, then discuss how we derived and tested our attributes for printing tasks and argue for the use of attributes in the design of interfaces and documentation. Our research is in its early stages; we are not describing a fully implemented system, but rather presenting an approach and reporting on some feasibility studies.

A Formal Framework for Task Description: Attributes

"Printing" refers to a large variety of tasks that differ in several minor and major respects. This diversity is reflected in the variety of hardware and software tools that have been developed for printing. Our UNIX computing environment, [1] for instance, has over 30 printing commands; each command can be invoked with several flags that each modify the command's result. Command lines in which the output of one program becomes the input of another are often required. Selecting the appropriate tools and creating the correct command line to take a source document file and produce the desired output is not a trivial matter. To isolate this piece of the user's responsibility, *we have assumed that the source document file has already been appropriately edited*; any necessary formatting macros are assumed to be included in the source file. We shall see that certain problems arise from this way of narrowing the scope of study, because printing in UNIX is not divided cleanly between the editing and post-editing phases when a task-based rather than tool-based viewpoint is adopted. [2] Incorporating editing of the source file will be an important and challenging extension of our approach.

Given a source document file, there are thus many different printing tasks that can be performed with it. The *attributes* of printing tasks are the dimensions along which these different tasks can be distinguished. An individual task is specified by a value (or in some cases, a set of values) for each attribute. The attributes [3] provide coordinates for the space of all printing tasks that can be carried out on a given computer system.

Initially we imagined that a half dozen attributes would suffice for printing. It quickly became apparent, however, that several times this many would be needed to specify tasks with sufficient precision. We now have 20 attributes, and have not yet fully covered the array of printing tasks. Several of these attributes are shown in Figure 1. The attribute names we have used are printed in boldface type; beneath each attribute, in italics, are its possible values, with hierarchical organization imposed in some cases.

Design of task attributes, like most such design problems, is at this stage more an art than a science; much iterative improvement is required. However, there are a number of properties that constrain the set of attributes.

(1)   Any printing task performable on the system must be describable using the values for the attributes.

(2)   Any two distinguishable printing tasks must have different values on at least one attribute.

(3)   Each attribute should measure a single conceptual dimension of the task.

(4)   Values must be definable with reference *only* to the input and output of the task; no reference to processes (software) is allowed.

(5)   Attributes and values must be comprehensible to users.

```
output
    hard copy
    soft copy
paper
    separated pages
        preprinted letterhead stationery
        plain lgp paper   ...
    continuous perforated pages
        11" x 14"   ...
printing method
    full character impact print (daisy wheel)
    electrostatic wet process print (laser printer)
    dot matrix impact print (decwriter)
    pen-scribed print (graphics plotter)
formatting
    none
    equations
    tables
    references
    text
        csl macros
        ms macros   ...
portion of file(s) printed
    all
    page(s) _____ through _____   ...
headers
    none
    date
    file name
    page number
    given in file   ...
columns
    none
    several files printed on each page,
    (each file in its own column)
    one file printed on a page, in _____ columns
  • • •
```

Figure 1. Examples of printing attributes (bold) and their values (italics).

Implementing Attributes: A Feasibility Study

Procedure for Determining Attributes

Finding a set of attributes and values that would meet all the above constraints required many developmental stages. We began by enumerating the printing commands available on our research-laboratory UNIX computer system. We then organized the various commands along a few obvious dimensions like hard/soft copy and formatted/unformatted text. We asked several users which factors tended to determine their choice of printing command. Some users demanded sufficient left margin to permit mounting in a loose-leaf notebook, others required that page breaks not artificially interrupt source program listings. At this point it became clear that the variety of contexts present in our lab and the variety of personal preferences required a long list of attributes for users to specify the important features of their printing tasks. This led to a list of many detailed properties that distinguish between the various printing programs.

To see what concepts seemed most important for experts in the printing domain, the method of *constructive interaction* was used (Miyake, 1982; O'Malley, Draper & Riley, 1984). Two experienced system users/developers were videotaped as they together tried to organize the printing commands in ways they thought were most useful. This refined somewhat but mostly confirmed our list of properties of printing programs.

To ensure that our attributes covered a representative variety of tasks, we recorded all uses of the printing commands for several weeks. User command-histories were also consulted for the printing tasks they contained. The printing-command lines were collected and used 1) to generate values for our list of printing attributes and 2) for checking whether the constraints cited above were satisfied. When command lines were encountered that could not be described, new attributes and values were added; when two different command lines (e.g. differing in only one flag) could not be distinguished in terms of their attribute values, again new attributes or values were added, or old ones refined.

Eventually we settled on a set of 20 attributes and corresponding values that seemed to meet constraints (1) through (4) above, in the restricted area of hard-copy printing. Most conceptual difficulties came from the fourth constraint of process-independent definitions. Time and time again we found ourselves wanting to define attribute values through the program or device that did the job rather than the job itself. We got most embroiled in printing details in the area of character size and spacing. The easiest dimensions along which to differentiate alternatives tended to vary across devices and programs, and it was challenging to find dimensions that worked in all cases. For instance, the point size of typeset print is most simply defined by the *height* of letters, while for the various print

sizes of our dot-matrix terminal, only the *width* of letters was variable. However it is *precisely because* it took effort for us to unify the ways of thinking about tasks across tools that we feel our attributes have something to offer in making coherent sense of the world of printing tasks.

The most serious difficulties arose from assuming that formatting macros were already present in the source document file. As mentioned earlier, in our UNIX system a clean distinction is not made between aspects of printed documents that are determined *within* the source document file and those that are determined *outside* the source file at the time of printing. The point size of type, for example, is usually determined by appropriate typesetting commands within the source file, but this can be overridden or supplied in the command line; page headings are sometimes determined explicitly by formatting commands in the source file but sometimes implicitly by the selection of a printing command that automatically creates a heading. As a result, a possible value for several of the attributes is *"determined within the source file"*. It would seem more elegant if a given attribute were either always determined within the source file or always determined outside the file, but that is not the case for our system.

Usability of Attributes

It remained to be seen whether criterion (5) was met: could users actually use our attributes for describing printing tasks? To assess this, we devised 7 hard-copy printing tasks that varied widely. Users familiar with our computer system to varying extents were shown a raw printout of the source document, and a hard copy that defined the "desired result". They were given a checklist with all possible values for all the attributes; their job was to check all the values that described the "desired result".

We concluded from this informal study that attributes provide a very useful mechanism for users to describe tasks. Users with an understanding of typesetting were able to use the attribute descriptions with no instruction; others quickly learned the meaning of the attributes when allowed to ask questions. Users did have considerable difficulty understanding the within/without source file distinction; some instruction here might have helped significantly. Like us, users had to think hardest about the attributes concerning character size and spacing; it is a level of detail that is rarely thought about with any comprehensiveness. However, when asked to address these matters and when given supporting documents to consult (with examples of different fonts, sizes, spacing, and so on), users did fairly well. They tended to be uncomfortable specifying attributes that do not consciously enter in their choice of printing commands. Several people made encouraging comments about the value of the approach, and most said they expanded their knowledge about the printing capabilities of our system.

A study was also done to explore which attributes users would want to specify when producing a document. Users were given a verbal description of a realistic task situation, a source file, and a sample of a hard copy suggesting what they *might* want to produce. They were given the attribute checklist and asked to indicate those values they wanted to specify. The usability of the attributes was comparable to that of the other study; in addition, users wanted to assign weights to various attributes, ignoring some altogether.

Extensibility of Attributes

It is important that the set of attributes and values be expandable to accommodate unforseen future task capabilities of evolving computer systems. This serves as a sixth constraint on the attributes, but one that is impossible to rigorously test. After the formulation of our attributes, the capability to make a hard copy of a bitmapped display screen was added to our system. This was a fairly good challenge to our attributes; for the first time one could print something that was not a file. However it was straightforward to change the attribute **source document file** to **source document**, adding the values *file:* name and *bitmapped screen*. We have yet to see any reason for doubting that attributes offer a language for describing tasks that is as easily expandable as any such language could be; in fact we suspect that the lack of explicit tool-dependence in the attributes enhances their ability to accommodate task expansion from new tools.

Applications of Attributes in System Design

Redesigning Printing Tools

Attributes provide a powerful set of primitives for precisely specifying the task a user wishes to perform. They can in principle be used as a new basis for issuing commands. In such an attribute-oriented computing environment, the user would simply specify values for relevant attributes, and the computer would perform the necessary actions.

An attribute-oriented environment would work something like this: the system designers would formulate a set of task attributes in the various task domains, e.g. printing. They would write a program that would take a collection of values for attributes, request values for necessary missing attributes, compute appropriate values for attributes the user didn't care to specify, and perform the task. Our experience with printing attributes leads us to feel that (at least in this domain) such a general tool is feasible. In addition to writing this printing program, the system designers would create a collection of printing—attribute prototypes. Each prototype would be a package of values for printing attributes that describes a frequently executed task, like formatting text and printing it on the laser printer, printing a file on the user's screen without interpreting formatting commands, etc. These attribute/value packages would be given names; the two examples just mentioned might be called *format* and *show*.

While *format* and *show* are ways of using the general printing tool, to new users they would be "printing commands". Documentation would state the values each attribute has for each "command". To go beyond one of the standard "commands", a user would be able to access the package of attribute values defining that "command", modify it, and save the modified package under a name that could then be used as a new "command".

Some combinations of values for our attributes are simply not possible to realize; the attributes are not truly independent in this sense. A facility to help users create feasible packages of attribute values could be based on a database of rules encoding the interdependence of feasible attribute values (e.g. "if output=soft-copy then paper=none"). Users would start by specifying values for the attributes most important to them, and as they did so the system would interactively guide them by spelling out the implications of their choices, soliciting further choices from feasible values for the remaining attributes.

Attributes can in fact be used not just for specifying commands, but also for accessing files; a proposal for a unified attribute-oriented interface is presented in Greenspan and Smolensky (1984).

Tool-Based Documentation

The attributes we have developed allow users to specify printing tasks within the existing capabilities of our laboratory computing system. Without redesigning the printing software in the manner described in the previous section, the knowledge about the printing task world contained in the attributes are extremely useful for *documenting* the existing printing tools (Kieras and Polson, 1982).

In O'Malley, et al. (1983), two types of documentation were found to be needed by users; we'll refer to them as *tool-based* and *task-based*. Tool-based documentation is designed for users who want information about a specific hardware or software tool, such as what the "m" flag for the *lprint* command does, or whether a daisy-wheel printer can move up and down half-lines. Task-based documentation is designed for users who have a task to perform and don't know what tools are needed or even whether the task can be done at all. The imbalance between respect paid to the tool- and task-worlds is nowhere more evident than in documentation, where task-based documentation is vastly under-represented relative to tool-based documentation. This is no surprise, for the people who design tools already have the knowledge required to write tool-based documentation; task-based documentation requires developing an understanding of the task world and a language for talking about it. Attributes provide such a language.

O'Malley, et al. (1983) found two distinct needs for tool-based documentation: *full explanation* and *quick reference*.

Full explanation. Full explanation encompasses the two forms of documentation usually called "tutorials" and "users manuals". Manuals are typically an alphabetical sequence of entries describing the tools available in the system; the descriptions typically assume the reader is familiar with the necessary concepts. These concepts are presumably explained in the tutorials.

Attributes are precisely-defined concepts that we suggest should be used in the full explanations of software and hardware tools comprising manuals. They offer a uniformity to tool descriptions that facilitates the user's task of assimilating the variety of tools offered by powerful systems. In addition, the uniform set of underlying concepts embodied in the attributes can be explained to users in a document analogous to a tutorial; this *attribute encyclopedia* will be discussed below.

Quick Reference. Attributes also enable concise but precise summaries of what commands achieve. Figure 2 shows a portion of the summary for one of our local printing commands, *lprint*. All printing commands can be summarized using the same set of attributes, and the precise meaning of the terms used can be found in the attribute encyclopedia. Task and tool characteristics are compar-

---

| lprint {*options*} {*files*} | | prints {files} on laser printer (lgp) in 8 point fixed-width type with pagination and header. Does not interpret formatting commands. |

* The {} brackets enclose items to be substituted for. Do not type the {}. *

attribute	default value	revised value . . . set by . . . option		
output	hard copy			
paper	plain laser paper			
printing method	electrostatic wet process (lgp)			
type font	stick font			
formatting	no macros interpreted			
portion of files printed	all	page {*n*} through end		+{*n*}
header	date, file name, page numbers	no header		-t
		{*word*} (no blanks)		-h {*word*}
		{*string*} (blanks ok)		-h "{*string*}"
direction of printing	standard	sideways on page, 2 columns		-l
columns	none	each {*file*} in its own column		-m
		each {*file*} printed in {*n*} columns		-{*n*}

Figure 2. Use of attributes to summarize the local command **lprint***.*

ably salient; in the corresponding summary developed for a quick-reference facility that did not use attributes (Bannon & O'Malley, 1984), tool characteristics like program flags are salient, while task characteristics are buried.

Task-based Documentation

Using attributes, documents can be written that describe precisely the tasks users can perform, leaving the tools that perform them in the background.

Kinds of output
  Soft copy
    Kinds of CRT screens
  Hard copy
    Kinds of paper
    Kinds of printing method
    Kinds of printers
Kinds of printed objects
  Graphics
  Text
Text printing
  Type fonts
  Character size
  Character spacing
  Line spacing
Text formatting
  Without software
  With software
    Equations
    Tables
    References
    Graphics
    Macro packages
• • •

Figure 3. Task—based documentation: portion of contents of printing attribute encyclopedia.

Attribute encyclopedia. Figure 3 shows a portion of the table of contents for the printing-attribute encyclopedia we are developing. Each entry of the encyclopedia explains one of the attributes and all the values it can assume. The entries are organized so that the document as a whole can be used as a tutorial on printing. The index to the encyclopedia directs users to the appropriate entry to learn about an attribute, value, or other term used synonymously or in connection with an attribute.

An attribute encyclopedia has several advantages over conventional tutorials and manuals. Unlike most manuals, it can be approached without prior knowledge about printing concepts. Unlike most tutorials, it goes into complete depth about the matters discussed. Like manuals, it consists of a number of separate entries that can be used independently for reference purposes. And like tutorials, it has some overall structure so that it can serve as an overview of the printing domain. The encyclopedia brings together all the information relevant to one aspect of a task, including information that in traditional, tool-oriented documentation, would be scattered across many documents. The information organized by attributes in Figure 3 is culled from many sundry traditional tool-based documents, a few of which are shown in Figure 4.

Talking to the Computer with your new Tektronix 4010 Computer Display Terminal

Hewlett Packard 7221A Graphics Plotter Operating and Programming Manual

Laser Graphics Printer LGP-1 Technical Manual

UNIX for Beginners

User's Manual for the UNIX System

Typesetting Mathematics - User's Guide

tbl - A Program to Format Tables

Newgraph Tutorial

Sample Text and User's Manual for the csl Macros Package

Typing Documents on the UNIX System Using the -ms Macros with troff and nroff
• • •

Figure 4. Tool—based documents.

The attribute encyclopedia is an excellent vehicle for expanding users' printing repertoire, because unfamiliar attributes would be clearly visible as would unfamiliar values for familiar attributes. In compiling the encyclopedia, the system documenters have already done the difficult work of pulling together the relevant pieces of myriad tool-based documents into a task-based structure. The encyclopedia is particularly valuable because the concepts and terms it presents are precisely those used in the other forms of documentation.

Task-to-tool Index. The attribute encyclopedia deals mostly with the task world, referring to hardware only to discuss certain attributes (e.g. printing method) and referring not at all to software. In fact the same encyclopedia could be used in the redesigned attribute-oriented environment described above. In the present system, there is need for an additional form of documentation, a *task-to-tool index* taking a user's specification of a task using attributes and pointing to the appropriate software tools. The task-to-tool index can be implemented at various levels of sophistication. Simplest would be an on-line or on-paper index in which users would look up values for individual attributes finding the names of all the programs capable of printing with that value for that attribute. The user or the computer would then try to find a single program, or a way of combining several programs, to achieve the entire package of attribute values. A somewhat more involved approach would rely on a large database of command lines, each with the task it performs completely described with attribute values. A user would give a set of attribute values, and the database would be searched to find command lines that matched as closely as possible. A more sophisticated on-line system would work interactively. As a user specified the desired values for attributes, the system would indicate which programs are possibilities, and guide subsequent choices by listing those values available with the possible programs.

For previously discussed types of documentation, we have argued that attributes offer improvements by giving a uniform language for describing tasks. Task-to-tool documentation would be an extremely valuable new form of documentation; it is simply impossible without the kind of language provided by attributes.

Conclusion

In the domain of hard-copy printing, our investigations suggest that a set of about 20 attributes suffice for specifying the tasks that can be performed in a fairly powerful research-laboratory computing environment. Users seem to find them useful ways of describing tasks. The attributes can be developed in a reasonable length of time. The attributes have potentially great utility for redesigning command specification, improving traditional forms of tool-based documentation, and permitting the development of powerful new kinds of task-based documentation.

Footnotes

This work is part of the research conducted by the Documentation Group of the Human Machine Interaction Project at the University of California, San Diego. Claire O'Malley made particularly important contributions to this work.

This research was conducted under Contract N00014-79-C-0323, NR 667-437 with the Personnel and Training Research Programs of the Office of Naval Research and a grant from the System Development Foundation.

1. UNIX is a trademark of Bell Laboratories. The comments in this paper refer to the 4.1a BSD version developed at the University of California, Berkeley.

2. For a general analysis of document formatting systems and a summary of UNIX document formatting, see Furuta, Scofield & Shaw (1982).

3. For conciseness, the term "attributes" will often refer to the set of all attributes and values.

References

[1] Bannon, L., Cypher, A., Greenspan, S., & Monty, M.L., Evaluation and analysis of users' activity organization, *Proc. CHI'83 Conference on Human Factors in Computing Systems* (Boston, December 1983).

[2] Bannon, L. & O'Malley, C., Problems in evaluation of human–computer interfaces: A case study, submitted to *Proc. of the First IFIPS Conference on Human–Computer Interaction* (London, September 1984).

[3] Furuta, R., Scofield, J., & Shaw, A., Document formatting systems: Survey, concepts, and issues, in Nievergelt, J., Coray, G., Nicoud, J.D., & Shaw, A.C. (eds.), *Document Preparation Systems* (North–Holland, Amsterdam, 1982).

[4] Greenspan, S. & Smolensky, P., DESCRIBE: Environments for specifying commands and retrieving information by elaboration, manuscript, Institute for Cognitive Science, University of California (San Diego, 1984).

[5] Kieras, D.E. & Polson, P.G., An approach to the formal analysis of user complexity, Project on user complexity of devices and systems, Working Paper no. 2, University of Arizona (1982).

[6] Miyake, N., Constructive interaction, Tech. Rep. No. 113, Center for Human Information Processing, University of California (San Diego, 1982).

[7] Moran, T.P., Getting into a system: External–internal task mapping analysis, *Proc. CHI'83 Conference on Human Factors in Computing Systems* (Boston, December 1983).

[8] O'Malley, C., Draper, S., & Riley, M., Constructive interaction: A method for studying user–computer–user interaction, submitted to *Proc. of the First IFIPS Conference on Human–Computer Interaction* (London, September 1984).

[9] O'Malley, C., Smolensky, L., Bannon, L., Conway, E., Graham, J., Sokolov, J., & Monty, M.L., A proposal for user-centered system documentation, *Proc. CHI'83 Conference on Human Factors in Computing Systems* (Boston, December 1983).

[10] Riley, M. & O'Malley, C., Planning nets: A framework for analyzing user-computer interactions, submitted to *Proc. of the First IFIPS Conference on Human–Computer Interaction* (London, September 1984).

Human-Computer Interaction — INTERACT '84 / B. Shackel (ed.)
Elsevier Science Publishers B.V. (North-Holland)
© IFIP, 1985

Developing Interactive Information Systems with the
User Software Engineering Methodology

Anthony I. Wasserman

Medical Information Science
University of California, San Francisco
San Francisco, CA 94143 USA

User Software Engineering is a methodology, supported by automated tools, for the systematic development of interactive information systems. The USE methodology gives particular attention to effective user involvement in the early stages of the software development process, concentrating on external design and the use of rapidly created and modified prototypes of the user interface. The key ideas and steps of the User Software Engineering (USE) methodology are described. The Unified Support Environment provides an integrated collection of tools to support the USE methodology.

1. SOFTWARE DEVELOPMENT METHODOLOGIES

Efforts to improve the quality of software systems and the process by which they are produced are at the heart of the field of *software engineering*. The key idea is to use a *software development methodology*, a systematic process for the creation of software. A methodology combines technical methods with management procedures for software development, and includes automated tools in a development support system for additional assistance [1, 2, 3].

The underlying philosophy is that use of a methodology can improve many aspects of the entire software development process, including a better fit to user requirements, fewer errors in the resulting system, better documentation throughout the entire process, and significantly reduced costs for system evolution.

Most methodologies give primary attention to the functions of the system being developed and the data upon which it operates. They follow a hierarchical decomposition of the problem, working from either a data-oriented or a function-oriented perspective. The user interface to the system is frequently considered only as an afterthought.

For interactive systems, though, these approaches may not work well, since user-oriented considerations must receive attention very early in the development process. Furthermore, user concerns and user preferences must have priority over some system-oriented considerations.

Accordingly, we created a methodology, named User Software Engineering (USE), that includes many user-oriented considerations in the framework of a software development methodology. User Software Engineering focuses on a particular type of interactive system, termed an interactive information system (IIS). An IIS may be characterized as providing conversational access to data, typically for persons who are not experts in computing.

Interactive information systems are used for applications such as airline reservations, bibliographic searching, medical record management, and banking. From a software perspective, an IIS may be seen as a human/computer dialogue, a database, and a set of transactions (operations, functions), where many of the transactions involve access to or modification of a database.

In the remainder of this paper, we outline first the goals of the USE methodology, and then present the steps of the methodology, giving emphasis to those aspects involving the design of the interactive interface to the IIS, and the tool support for the methodology.

2. GOALS OF THE USE METHODOLOGY

The User Software Engineering project was undertaken in 1975 with the intent of creating a methodology that would support the development of interactive information systems. Over that period, the USE methodology has evolved, along with many others that provide a diversity of approaches to building computer based systems [4, 5]. Different methods emphasize different aspects of the information system development process, e.g., database modeling or formal specification.

The development of the User Software Engineering methodology has been guided by seven goals for interactive information systems:

- **functionality** — The methodology should cover the entire development process, supporting creation of a working system that achieves a predefined set of requirements.

- **reliability** — The methodology should support the creation of reliable systems, so that users are not inconvenienced by system crashes, loss of data, or lack of availability.

- **usability** — The methodology should help the developer to assure, as early as possible, that the resulting system will be easy to learn and easy to use.

- **evolvability** — The methodology should encourage documentation and system structuring so that the resulting system is easily modifiable and able to accommodate changes in hardware operating environments and user needs.

- **user involvement** — The methodology should involve users *effectively* in the development process, particularly in its early stages.

- **automated support.** -- The methodology should be supported by automated tools that improve the productivity of software developers using the methodology; this requirement implies the availability of both a general set of automated aids and a methodology-specific set.

- **reusability** -- The methodology should be reusable for a large class of projects and the design products from a given application should be reusable on similar future projects.

The USE methodology, as with most other development methodologies, follows a well-defined set of phases beginning with analysis and terminating with a validated operational system. We now proceed to a description of the major steps of the USE methodology, and show how these seven goals have been addressed in the methodology.[1]

3. REQUIREMENTS ANALYSIS

This initial phase emphasizes activity and data modelling, along with identification of user characteristics. It is an *informal* process, intended to gain understanding of the problem domain, the context in which a system could be developed, and the nature of the expected usage of such a system.

In the past, we have successfully used several different techniques to aid in this process, including the A-graphs of ISAC and the dataflow diagrams of Structured Systems Analysis [6, 7]. More recently, we have approached this phase from a conceptual data modelling standpoint, identifying, again informally, objects and the operations (actions) performed upon them. Data modelling techniques such as the Semantic Hierarchy Model of Smith and Smith [8] and the Entity-Relationship model of Chen [9] have also worked successfully. We are evolving toward greater use of the data modelling (object-oriented) approach since it seems to provide a better transition to subsequent phases of the USE methodology.

Another important aspect of requirements analysis is understanding of user characteristics, so that the interface to the IIS can be properly designed. It is important to recognize the motivation and intended skill levels for the anticipated user population, to identify the needs for various types of output documents, e.g., hard copy vs. "soft" copy, and to see whether the IIS must support casual users as well as regular users. Other issues, such as discretionary use vs. mandatory use, and the need for alphanumeric input, are also taken into account at this stage.

Failure to understand the intended user community may lead to poor decisions concerning the user interface and the selection of information system functions. These errors will almost certainly lead to low user satisfaction and the need to make extensive (and expensive) modifications to the system.

4. EXTERNAL DESIGN

This phase involves the description of the various transactions or commands to be supported by the system, along with the user inputs and system outputs. At this stage, the model of system functions may still be incomplete, and no effort has been made to define these operations formally.

Rather than proceeding with further refinement of the system functions, following a traditional "top down" approach, the User Software Engineering methodology follows an "outside in" approach, in which the external interface to the system is defined.

There are two major reasons for this choice:

- It is easiest to work with the user community if the system is defined from the user perspective rather than from the system perspective.

- The "outside in" approach also serves the need of functional decomposition, since logical operations from the user viewpoint often map directly into transactions from the system standpoint.

We assume that the user will work at an alphanumeric terminal with a keyboard (teletypewriter-like or video display, depending on the previous phase). For many common IIS's, the obvious choices for a user interface are then command languages, multiple choice (menu selection screens), free text, or some combination of these. (Even many forms of non-keyboard input can be seen as equivalent to one of these.)

We then produce a preliminary design of the user interface. Our method for designing the dialogue was initially *ad hoc*, based on our own experience as summarized in a set of guidelines [10]. More recently, though, we have developed and are beginning to use metrics that help evaluate the properties of screen designs [11].

The user program dialogue is then specified with a set of USE transition diagrams. We began in 1977 using standard state transition diagrams for this purpose [12]. We associated an output message with each node (or state), and provided an arc (transition) for each distinguishable class of user input from a given state. An action could be associated with any transition. Others have followed a similar approach [13, 14, 15]. We found that state transition diagrams were a useful mechanism for modelling interactive systems. However, their basic form was inadequate for the range of user dialogues that one must model. For example, one could not distinguish between buffered and unbuffered input, truncate an input strings to fixed length, or terminate user input on some character other than a carriage return.

Even worse, the complexity of diagrams quickly became unmanageable for all but the smallest dialogues. We therefore introduced "subconversations" in a diagram as a useful structuring technique to manage the complexity of the diagrams. A subconversation is represented by a rectangle, and works in much the same way as a subprogram call in a programming language, suspending transitions in the current diagram and "executing" the called diagram, possibly repeating this process to an arbitrary depth.

In their basic form, transition diagrams are purely syntactic, having no memory and no ability to branch on the results of actions. Both of these restrictions are unrealistic when transition diagrams are used to model interactive information systems.

In an interactive dialogue, a user frequently provides input that is subsequently displayed or used as a parameter in some operation. Thus, one must be able to save a user input for additional processing. Variables are the standard means of doing this, so the transition diagrams were extended to allow alphanumeric and numeric variables, with optional constraints on string length and values.

Next, the sequence of a dialogue is often dependent on the results of actions. For example, if a user types in a name, an action may look up that name in a table. A different path must be followed if the name is found than if it is not found. Therefore, actions must be able to return values *and* it must be possible to branch in the diagram based on those returned values.

Finally, we included cursor and screen management symbols to be able to describe interactive dialogue on a full-screen display, not just on a line-oriented basis.

Thus, we have created an extended form of transition diagram notation to support this class of applications [16], and have found them to work well to specify both the user input(s) to the system and the resulting system actions and displays. We found transition diagrams to be preferable to BNF, particularly for users who must comprehend the description.

A small USE transition diagram, showing nodes, arcs, and subconversations (but not the messages associated with the nodes) is shown in Figure 1.

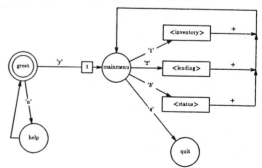

Figure 1 — A USE transition diagram

Of course, these input/output specifications are preliminary and are often changed considerably before the system is completed. As a result, one must separate the actual text of the user interface from the operations and from other aspects of the system, so that one may achieve "dialogue independence" in an IIS [17] in much the same way that one strives for data independence in using data abstractions and database management systems.

This separation of the dialogue specification from the operations allows several different dialogues to be specified for the same system. This approach facilitates the design of multilingual programs, of different interfaces for novices and experts, for low and high speed terminals, and for different styles of interaction, such as commands vs. menu selection.

5. PROTOTYPE OF THE HUMAN/COMPUTER INTERACTION

Following the initial design of the user/prototype dialogue, the transition diagrams are encoded in machine-processable form. This step may either be done automatically with a graphical Transition Diagram Editor [18] or manually. We have defined a dialogue specification language that supports direct encoding of the USE transition diagrams. Elements of this dialogue specification language include diagrams, nodes, arcs, messages, and variables. A small portion of such a specification is shown in Figure 2.

```
diagram library entry greet exit quit

node greet                    % first screen
        cs,r8, c_'Welcome to LIS'
        r+ 2,c_'(Library Information System)',
        r+ 4,c_'Do you need instructions (y/n)?'

node help
        cs,r3,'LIS is an interactive, menu-driven, system for',
        nl,'management of a small library.', nl,nl,
        'The system will prompt for all user input,',
        'and use of the system', nl,
        'should be straightforward and self-explanatory.', nl,
        'Good luck.'

node mainmenu
        cs,hm,'LIS',r10,c10,'Please choose subsystem:',r12,c15,
        '1) Book acquisition/removal',r+ 2,c15,
        '2) Book lending/return',r+ 2,c15,
        '3) Status inquiry',r+ 2,c15,'4) Quit',
        r+ 2,c10,'Your choice (1-4): '

node quit
        cs,r12,'Byebye....'

arc greet
        on 'n' to help
        on 'y' do 1 to mainmenu

arc help
        else to greet

arc mainmenu
        on '1' to <inventory>
        on '2' to <lending>
        on '3' to <status>
        on '4','q' to quit

arc <inventory> skip to mainmenu
arc <lending> skip to mainmenu
arc <status> skip to mainmenu
```

Figure 2 -- Portion of a USE dialogue specification

Node mainmenu in Figure 2 describes a display in terms of screen positioning primitives. It begins by clearing the screen (cs), going to the home position (hm), and then using absolute (r10) and relative (r+2) row and column movements to show where text should be placed on the screen. Figure 3 shows the screen layout that results from this specification.

LIS

Please choose subsystem:

    1) Book acquisition/removal

    2) Book lending/return

    3) Status inquiry

    4) Quit

Your choice (1-4):

Figure 3 -- Layout of the mainmenu node on a display

A Transition Diagram Interpreter (TDI), part of the RAPID/USE prototyping system [19, 20], then interprets the encoded diagrams, making it possible to allow a user to interact with a "mockup" of the user interface design.

This ability to "execute" the dialogue, even in the absence of actions, is of tremendous value in application of the methodology because it gives the user at the terminal a good understanding of the expected behavior of the IIS, and gives the developer a good understanding of the user's problems with the dialogue design. Since the dialogue specification is simply interpreted text, it is a very easy matter to edit the specification as changes are needed. Most cosmetic changes to the dialogue can be made in minutes rather than days, giving the user a sense of being an active participant in the design process.

Our initial approach, out of necessity, was to design and specify the dialogue using only transition diagrams. While this approach worked successfully, the use of TDI improves the entire development process substantially. Without the prototype of the dialogue, the user community had only a written description of the system under development. As a result, many changes to the dialogue and the functions were made after implementation, with all of the usual problems attendant to evolving systems.

Not only does the executable prototype of the interface give the user a better sense of the planned system, but it also allows objective evaluation of the interface and helps users to think more accurately about the necessary functions for the system.

The objective evaluation of the interface is made possible by the ability to keep session logs of the interaction. Two logs may be maintained: a raw input log and a transition log. The raw input log saves *every keystroke*, so that it may be serve as a scenario and be replayed later during system testing. Also, keystrokes are easily counted, giving a good measure of usability.

The transition log includes a record for each state transition. Each record includes a time stamp, the diagram name, the node name, any action called, and the user input. Analysis of this log permits analysis of task completion time, screen viewing times, user error patterns (if all error nodes have recognizable names), and frequency of action calls. A separate tool, rapsum, can do further analysis on the transition log, so that one can compute the percentage of nodes visited as a measure of test coverage.

RAPID/USE is designed and built specifically as part of the User Software Engineering methodology, and one can see that it supports many of the methodology's goals. It is extremely valuable in verifying and analyzing dialogue designs and therefore allows a satisfactory design to be achieved at a very early stage of the IIS development process. In many respects, this use of prototypes and the availability of RAPID/USE are the major contribution of the User Software Engineering methodology.

6. INFORMAL FUNCTIONAL SPECIFICATION

As noted, an IIS provides users with conversational access to data. Accordingly, a good specification method for such systems involves specifying the dialogue, the data base, and the operations performed by the system.

Operations in the IIS are defined during the requirements analysis phase and the creation of the USE transition diagrams. Similarly, data objects, and their interrelationships, are identified beginning with requirements analysis and entered into a data dictionary. The data dictionary contains names, descriptions, and constraints on the data objects.

The stage of informal specifications consolidates and reorganizes the information previously obtained, giving primary attention to clear definition of the operations. Each action defined in the state transition diagrams is described at this stage.

One approach to defining these operations is to use narrative text, since the actions are all relatively small. A second possibility, and our preference, is to use "structured text", such as that used in Structured Systems Analysis or Jackson System Design [21].

At this stage, we specifically avoid the use of a formal specification language, such as SPECIAL [22] or AXES [23], because such formal notations are not readily comprehensible to users and customers without formal computer science or mathematical training. This preference does not preclude formal specification methods, which may be done at a later stage, but rather states that an informal specification is necessary and useful whether or not a formal specification is eventually produced. Indeed, the analysis and review that goes into producing the informal specification is essential for a formal specification as well. We believe that an informal specification must precede a formal specification for this class of system, since the review of that specification by users as well as by developers yields a more accurate system definition (in terms of satisfying requirements), and thus reduces the need to modify a subsequently produced formal specification.

7. RELATIONAL DATABASE DESIGN

We next refine the data model developed earlier into a set of normalized relations. The transformation from an entity-relationship model or a semantic hierarchy model to relations is straightforward, and simply involves retaining separately the constraints that are lost in making the transformation.

The Troll/USE relational database management system is an important tool in the Unified Support Environment [24, 25]. Troll/USE is a compact system providing a relational algebra-like interface, including operations at the item, tuple, and relation level. Troll/USE works on a message passing basis, and has been used as the backend for numerous user interfaces.

Troll/USE supports specification and checking of data types for attributes of relations, including scalar types using enumerated values as in Pascal. A relational database definition for the library example is shown in Figure 4.

```
domain bookstat: scalar (onshelf, checkout, libloan, missing);
domain loantype: scalar (reference, overnight, seven_day, normal);
domain cardtype: scalar (normal, juvenile, libstaff);

relation book [key catalogid] of
        catalogid: string;
        title, authors, publisher: string;
        copyno: integer (1..1000);
        year: integer (1454..2000);
        chkoutstat: loantype;
        status: bookstat;
end;

relation staff [key empid] of
        empid: integer;
        name, dept: string;
end;

relation borrowers [key cardno] of
        cardno: integer (1..999999);
        name, address, telephone: string;
        expdate: string;
        privileges: cardtype;
end;

relation borrow [key cardno, catalogid, copyno] of
        cardno: integer (1..999999);
        catalogid: string;
        copyno: integer (1..1000);
        checkoutdate, duedate, returndate: string;
end;
```

Figure 4 — Normalized relations for library example
using Troll/USE data manipulation language

The description of the operations can be given more precisely, too, since the database is now defined as a set of relations. All operations that affect the database can be rewritten in a relational data manipulation language. We use the data manipulation language of Troll/USE for this purpose, but one could alternatively use a relational calculus language, such as SQL or QUEL [26, 27, 28].

Consider the library operations for displaying all of the books by a given author and for showing all of the books checked out by a borrower whose name is given. Each of these operations may be described as a Troll/USE procedure, involving a script of database operations that accept parameters. These two operations, bookbyauthor and chkouts, are shown in Figure 5.

If all of the operations are described in this way, we obtain not only a precise specification of the database, but also a precise and *executable* specification of the operations. These executable statements are then used in the creation of a functional prototype of the IIS.

```
operation bookbyauthor (authorname):

    ans1 := book where authors $ authorname;
    {ans1 is the set of books where the set of authors contains a
       string matching the given authorname}


operation chkouts (borrowername):

    {find borrower card number -- assume unique borrowername}
    $1 := borrowers[borrowername].cardno;
    {assigns number to Troll/USE variable $1}
    t2 (catalogid) := borrow where cardno = $1;
    {t2 gives the set of catalog numbers of borrowed books}
    ans2 := book.catalogid join t2.catalogid;
    {ans2 returns complete information on each book checked out}
```

Figure 5 -- Troll/USE scripts for library system operations

8. FUNCTIONAL PROTOTYPE

While the prototype of the dialogue alone is useful, particularly for identifying requirements and for obtaining usable interfaces to an IIS, such a prototype doesn't *do* anything. For example, it is then difficult to display the dialogue alternatives that may result from different values returned by an action. Similarly, it requires extra work to display sample results, since there is no real database and no actions. The dialogue prototype, as implemented with the TDI part of RAPID/USE, provides merely a "facade" for the system.

Thus, it is valuable to be able to implement some (or even all) of the actions specified for the system. The actions performed by an IIS may vary widely, from numerical computation to database management, and from language processing to application generation. Thus, the IIS developer may need access to any of several programming languages and, most important, to a database management system.

The Action Linker part of RAPID/USE serves this purpose. Routines may be written in C, Fortran 77, Pascal, or PLAIN [29,30]. The Troll/USE relational database management system is available through all of these languages, either directly (as in PLAIN), or through a set of function calls that manage the message passing between the program and the Troll/USE process.

The "main" program for the operations contains a routine named "actions" that accepts a single parameter, acnum, corresponding to an action number as given in the specification (and in the TDI input). This number is used as a parameter for a case statement in the actions routine. The developer may then write executable code for any of the actions. Builtin routines make it possible to use variables and values obtained in the TDI within actions, and to assign values to these variables in the actions.

RAPID/USE operates by linking together the TDI with the actions and with libraries that provide terminal and screen handling, access to the Troll/USE DBMS, and the action routines. With that combination, the developer may gradually implement actions, adding operations, error handling, online assistance, and other features as desired.

Because the action mechanism is completely general, one could build the *entire* IIS in this way. Indeed, for systems consisting almost entirely of dialogue and database manipulations, such an approach is quite easy. The RAPID/USE approach is also useful for use with programming languages having weak input/output management capabilities, since the dialogue specification can be handled with TDI and the actions can be implemented in the desired programming language.

Because the purpose of RAPID/USE is to facilitate the rapid implementation of prototype systems, it is not intended as a tool for the production of complex systems containing hundreds of action routines and/or variables (although it could be used for that purpose). Furthermore, it is not intended for the production of critical systems in which the security and correctness of the system must be verified (although this could also be done).

The technical reasons for these statements include the existence of globally accessible TDI variables, and the volume of data that must be communicated between TDI and the action routines for large systems. The volume can be reduced by performing input/output within the action routines, but such an implementation strategy decreases dialogue independence and complicates screen management.

Thus, RAPID/USE can be used very well to build small interactive systems, and is quite effective for modelling the user interface for larger systems, but becomes increasingly less attractive as a tool as the systems grow larger. In such a case, RAPID/USE can be used to build a prototype of the dialogue and a small number of actions to perform a subset of the system functions, but a well structured programming language should be used to build the production version. It is for this reason that RAPID/USE is described as a prototype construction tool rather than as a system construction tool.

9. FORMAL SPECIFICATION

Whether or not a functional prototype has been created, the previous steps provide sufficient information to produce a formal specification of system behavior. The transition diagrams give a formal definition of the input syntax, the output displays, and the possible sequences of state transitions, showing the points at which various operations are invoked. All that remains, then, is to give a formal specification of the behavior of the operations.

For this purpose, we follow the BASIS (Behavioral Approach to the Specification of Information Systems) method [31,32], which is an abstract model approach to specification, based on the ideas of Hoare, as refined for use in the Alphard programming language [33,34]. BASIS has five major steps: information analysis, semantic specification, verification of the design specification, implementation, and verification of the implementation. The first step, information analysis, includes the specification of the objects and transactions involved in the specification to be built. This information is derived from the requirements analysis phase (and can be done at that time).

The second step (semantic specification) includes the specification of the logical rules or properties (constraints) of the real world system. This information includes not only the operations of the system, but also the legal states of the data. If the data starts out in a legal or accurate state and only legal operations are applied, then the data will be guaranteed to have semantic integrity. (This specification can be verified as the next step.)

There are three main parts to a BASIS specification of semantic integrity: the image of the object, the invariant, and input and output constraints for each operation defined on each object. The image is a list of the attributes associated with the object along with constraints on the values of these attributes for instances of the object. The invariant is composed of the inter-attribute constraints, if any. This invariant can be replaced by placing such constraints in the input and output constraints for the operations. The operations are defined by the input and output constraints which characterize the effects of the operations, using Hoare's notations for preconditions and postconditions. The specification of the pre and post conditions is important for three reasons: (1) the checking of particular constraints is tied to particular operations, (2) the pre and post constraints for the operations act as a guide for the implementor, and (3) they are used to prove that the specification and implementation are correct.

Formal specifications are a valuable discipline and help to eliminate the ambiguity that is often present with informal specifications. Formal specifications are rarely requested by users, though, who normally prefer that the equivalent effort be given to development of the prototype or final system. Formal specifications may be difficult to write and are not easily understood. Furthermore, most users do not yet understand that they aid in the identification and removal of errors. Thus, they have little interest in the formal specifications of the operations.

We feel, though, that one must be *able* to formalize one's thinking (even if the process is not done on every system) and that the formal specification step is an essential part of the methodology. In addition, we believe that improvements in automated support for formal descriptions will encourage their use in the future.

10. SYSTEM DESIGN

From the approved specification, one can now follow a traditional life cycle approach beginning with architectural design of the system. Because the transition diagram modelling technique tends to support the decomposition of dialogues into subconversations, each of which represents a "transaction", it is quite easy to map the specification into a software architecture using the transaction model of Structured Design [35]. The operations defined in the USE transition diagrams perform well defined functions, so they can be mapped into modules for this purpose.

The detailed design is shown with a program design language, showing for each module the module interconnections (data passing plus calling structure), a brief statement of the module's function, and the high-level logic of the module. For many IIS's, much of this information, particularly the database manipulation, has already been developed.

Thus, the design phase creates two products: an architectural design and a detailed design in a program design language that define the structure and operations of the system in a manner suitable both for review, e.g., through structured walkthrough, and for implementation.

11. PRODUCTION IMPLEMENTATION

The program language PLAIN was designed as the application development language for the USE methodology. Although one could use other languages in conjunction with the methodology, PLAIN was conceived as a well-structured programming language that supported the application requirements of interactive information systems.

The design goals of PLAIN fall into two categories: those that support systematic programming practices, and those that support the creation of interactive programs. In practice, these goals meshed in the process of language design, but they can be separated when examining the design philosophy. The design goals for systematic programming include support for procedural and data abstraction, support for modularity, prevention of self-modifying programs, program verifiability, and program readability.

The design goals for supporting the construction of interactive programs include support for relational database definition and manipulation, support for strings and string-handling, facilities for exception-handling, a pattern specification and matching facility, and input/output features. With these features, PLAIN programs could be made resilient to user errors, could simplify user interaction with large databases, and could be made flexible in handling diverse forms of user input, all within the framework of a Pascal-like language.

Historically, the design of PLAIN, beginning in 1975, preceded development of the methodology, so that the concepts used in analysis and specification can be mapped directly into PLAIN constructs [36]. This compatibility supports transitions from specification through design to implementation, making PLAIN superior to other languages for use of the methodology.

Our experience in building systems in the absence of a PLAIN compiler led us to conclude, though, that one could follow the USE methodology and implement the system in another language. We have successfully used C, in conjunction with the C-to-Troll/USE library routines, for system implementation.

12. TESTING AND VERIFICATION

The USE methodology provides support both for testing and verification throughout the development process. Our goal has been to make it feasible to carry out systematic testing and/or verification for interactive information systems.

While testing can be done in traditional ways [37] for a program written in PLAIN or some other high level language, it is interesting to note that the USE methodology provides some assistance for this task. Of course, testing occurs throughout the development process, not just as code is written. Thus, a user session at the terminal during development of the dialogue serves to test the user interface design. Similarly, the use of a functional prototype, providing both the user dialogue and a set of operations, serves informally as a testing aid.

Verification may be done on the PLAIN program if one has produced the necessary formal specification. Verifying the correctness of the implementation includes proofs of the correctness of the representation of the objects and the implementations of the operations with respect to their pre and post constraints. This verification can be accomplished using standard methods.

PLAIN supports the verification process through the availability of assertions, which may be placed at the beginning and end of each module to check the pre and post conditions. In addition, assertions may be placed elsewhere within routines to handle the run-time checks.

13. CONCLUSION

The User Software Engineering methodology has evolved since the late 1970's and has been shown to be a practical method for the creation of interactive information systems. The availability of automated tools, including the Troll/USE relational database management system, the RAPID/USE prototyping system, and the PLAIN programming language, greatly improve developer productivity in the creation of interactive information systems.[2]

The USE methodology supports the goals of functionality, reliability, usability, user involvement, evolvability, reusability, and automated support by combining formal and informal methods for specification with extensive use of prototypes and a systematic software development process.

Current research and development on the User Software Engineering methodology is focused on extending the types of interactive media that can be supported by the specification method, on providing greater automated support for program generation, and on making the Unified Support Environment available on a large number of machines. All of these activities are intended to preserve the structure of the methodology while simplifying its use and reducing the effort needed to produce high quality interactive information systems.

---

[1]We intentionally omit discussion of the management and organizational issues associated with the use of the methodology, since these will differ from one organization to another, thereby providing a whole new dimension of variations on a methodology.

[2]The USE tools are implemented on the Unix^{TM} operating system. (Unix is a trademark of AT&T Bell Laboratories.) They are distributed by the University of California, San Francisco, by the Vrije Universiteit, Amsterdam, and by Interactive Development Environments, Inc., of San Francisco, which also provides support for the methodology and tools.

14. REFERENCES

[1] Wasserman, A.I., "Information System Development Methodology," *Journal of the American Society for Information Science* **31**(1) pp. 5-24 (1980).

[2] Wasserman, A.I., "Software Engineering Environments," in *Advances in Computers, vol. 22*, ed. M. Yovits,Academic Press, New York (1983),

[3] Porcella, M., Freeman, P., and Wasserman, A.I., "Ada Methodology Questionnaire Summary," *ACM Software Engineering Notes* **8**(1)(January, 1983).

[4] Olle, T.W., Sol, H.G., and (Eds.) Verrijn-Stuart, A.A., *Information System Design Methodologies: a Comparative Review*, North-Holland, Amsterdam (1982).

[5] Olle, T.W., Sol, H.G., and (Eds.), Tully, C.J., *Information System Design Methodologies: a Feature Analysis*, North Holland, Amsterdam (1983).

[6] Lundeberg, M., Goldkuhl, G., and Nilsson, A., *Information Systems Development -- a Systematic Approach*, Prentice-Hall, Englewood Cliffs, NJ (1981).

[7] Gane, C. and Sarson, T., *Structured Systems Analysis*, Prentice-Hall, Englewood Cliffs, NJ (1979).

[8] Smith, J.M. and Smith, D.C.P., "Conceptual Database Design," in *Tutorial: Software Design Techniques, 3rd edition*, ed. P. Freeman and A.I. Wasserman,IEEE Computer Society, Los Alamitos, CA (1980), pp. 333-356.

[9] Chen, P.P.-S., "The Entity-Relationship Model -- Toward a Unified View of Data," *Transactions on Database Systems* **1**(1) pp. 9-36 (March, 1976).

[10] Wasserman, A.I., "User Software Engineering and the Design of Interactive Systems," *Proc. 5th International Conference on Software Engineering*, pp. 387-393 (1981).

[11] Streveler, D. J. and Wasserman, A. I., "Quantitative Measures of the Spatial Properties of Screen Designs," *Proceedings: Interact '84 Conference*, North Holland, (1984).

[12] Wasserman, A.I. and Stinson, S.K., "A Specification Method for Interactive Information Systems," *Proc IEEE Computer Society Conference on Specification of Reliable Software*, pp. 68-79 (1979).

[13] Parnas, D.L., "On the User of Transition Diagrams in the Design of a User Interface for an Interactive Computer System," *Proc. 24th National ACM Conference*, pp. 379-385 (1969).

[14] Jacob, R.J.K., "Using Formal Specifications in the Design of a Human-Computer Interface," *Communications of the ACM* **26**(3) pp. 259-264 (March, 1983).

[15] Kieras, D. and Polson, P., "A Generalized Transition Network Representation for Interactive Systems," *Proc. CHI '83 Human Factors in Computing Systems*, pp. 103-106 (1983).

[16] Wasserman, A.I., *Extending State Transition Diagrams for the Specification of Human-Computer Interaction*, submitted for publication 1983.

[17] Roach, J., Hartson, H.R., Ehrich, R.W., Yunten, T., and Johnson, D.H., "DMS: a Comprehensive System for Managing Human-Computer Dialogue," *Proceedings: Human Factors in Computer Systems*, pp. 102-105 (March, 1982).

[18] Mills, C., "TDE -- an Editor for USE Transition Diagrams," M.S. Project Report, Computer Science Division, University of California, Berkeley (1984).

[19] Wasserman, A.I. and Shewmake, D.T., "Rapid Prototyping of Interactive Information Systems," *ACM Software Engineering Notes* **7**(5) pp. 171-180 (December, 1982).

[20] Wasserman, A.I. and Shewmake, D.T., "A RAPID/USE Tutorial," Laboratory of Medical Information Science, University of California, San Francisco (1983).

[21] Jackson, M., *System Development*, Prentice-Hall Int'l, London (1983).

[22] Roubine, O. and Robinson, L., "SPECIAL Reference Manual," Technical Report CSG-45, SRI International, Menlo Park, CA (1978).

[23] Hamilton, M. and Zeldin, S., "The Relationship between Design and Verification," *Journal of Systems and Software* **1**(1) pp. 29-56 (1979).

[24] Wasserman, A.I., "The Unified Support Environment: Support for the User Software Engineering Methodology," *Proceedings, IEEE Computer Society SoftFair Conference*, pp. 145-153 (July, 1983).

[25] Kersten, M.L. and Wasserman, A.I., "The Architecture of the PLAIN Data Base Handler," *Software -- Practice and Experience* **11**(2) pp. 175-186 (February, 1981).

[26] Date, C.J., *An Introduction to Database Systems, 3rd ed.*, Addison Wesley, Reading, MA (1982).

[27] Stonebraker, M.R. and Wong, E., "The Design and Implementation of INGRES," *Transactions on Database Systems* **1**(3)(September, 1976).

[28] Chamberlin, D.D. *et al.*, "SEQUEL2: A Unified Approach to Data Definition, Manipulation, and Control," *IBM Journal of Research and Development* **20**(6) pp. 560-575 (November, 1976).

[29] Wasserman, A.I., Riet, R.P. van de, and Kersten, M.L., "PLAIN: an Algorithmic Language for Interactive Information Systems," pp. 29-47 in *Algorithmic Languages*, ed. J.C. van Vliet, North-Holland, Amsterdam (1981).

[30] Wasserman, A.I., Sherertz, D.D., Kersten, M.L., Riet, R.P. van de, and Dippe, M.D., "Revised Report on the Programming Language PLAIN," *ACM SIGPLAN Notices* **16**(5) pp. 59-80 (May, 1981).

[31] Leveson, N.G., "Applying Behavioral Abstraction to Information System Design and Integrity," Ph.D. Dissertation, University of California, Los Angeles, 1980., (Available as Technical Report #47, Laboratory of Medical Information Science, University of California, San Francisco) (1980).

[32] Leveson, N.G., Wasserman, A.I., and Berry, D.M., "BASIS: a Behavioral Approach to the Specification of Information Systems," *Information Systems* **8**(1) pp. 15-23 (1983).

[33] Hoare, C.A.R., "Proof of Correctness of Data Representations," *Acta Informatica* **1**(3) pp. 271-281 (1972).

[34] M. Shaw (ed.), *ALPHARD: Form and Content*, Springer Verlag, New York (1981).

[35] Yourdon, E. and Constantine, L.L., *Structured Design*, Prentice-Hall, Englewood Cliffs, NJ (1979).

[36] Wasserman, A.I., "Specification and Implementations of Interactive Information Systems," *Proc. AFIPS 1984 NCC* **53**(1984). in press

[37] Adrion, W.R., Branstad, M., and Cherniavsky, M., "Validation and Verification of Computer Programs," *Computing Surveys* **14**(2) pp. 159-192 (June, 1982).

Human-Computer Interaction — INTERACT '84 / B. Shackel (ed.)
Elsevier Science Publishers B.V. (North-Holland)
© IFIP, 1985

AN APPROACH TO INFORMATION NEEDS ANALYSIS

Robert D. Galliers
School of Computing and Quantitative Studies
Western Australian Institute of Technology
Perth, Western Australia

> Information systems have value only if they contribute to improve the
> situation for people in the organization. They have no value of
> their own. It is therefore not enough that we study the contents of
> the information systems so that we can form an opinion about their
> values. We must instead study the activities that people perform
> in the organization and that somehow should be improved.
>
> Lundeberg et.al. [17, p.125]

Systems development methodologies tend to be approached either from the *human* or the
design aspects of the information system being developed. Regretably, more attention
has apparently been focussed on *design* in the past. Regretably, because much evidence
exists to suggest that the *human* considerations are of paramount importance.

What is perhaps of greater concern is that many of those methodologies which purport to
recognise the importance of the *human* considerations are misguided in their application
of technique within the methodology. The focus of many of the techniques tends to be
on the technical *design* of the existing system rather than on the information requirements of the human activity system which dictates the need for information. One could
go further; in certain instances, no technique for determining information needs is
provided at all.

This paper concentrates its attention on a means by which information needs can be
identified and compared with existing information provision, an approach which arises
from the *soft systems methodology* developed by Checkland [6,8]. It relates to the
very first steps to be taken prior to deciding on whether or not to proceed with an
information system development. It describes in some detail a methodology which has
been successfully applied in a range of actual studies with a view to identifying
information needs as a precursor to design, and it relates some of the views expressed
by those involved in the process. Further, it illustrates the way in which the
approach can be used in the strategic sense of setting out a coherent plan for
information systems development, organisation-wide, for a period of some years
ahead.

1.   THE NEED FOR INFORMATION NEEDS ANALYSIS

The significance of properly defining information
requirements prior to proceeding on to the design
phases of an information system development is
well documented. For example, Boehm [1,2,3]
graphically illustrates the relatively low cost
of correcting errors in the requirements stage
of system developments as compared to the
substantially increased costs involved in doing
so in the latter stages. This is illustrated in
Figure 1.

Wasserman et.al. [23] state that "a key assumption of modern software development practices
is that increased effort in the earlier stages
of development will result in a 'better'
system." Research, the results of which are

to be published in 1984, undertaken by the
author [9] concerned with identifying attitudes
of Western Australian managers towards
computerised information systems clearly
illustrates the view that senior management
believe a crucial factor contributing to the
successful implementation of a management
information system is the proper identification
of their information requirements in the first
instance.[1] This is very much in line with the
results of research undertaken by Taggart and
Tharp [22] and Carter et.al. [4] in the
United States.

_____

[1]   Respectively 34.5% and 52.4% of respondants
either strongly agreed or agreed with this
assertion, with only 9.5% disagreeing.

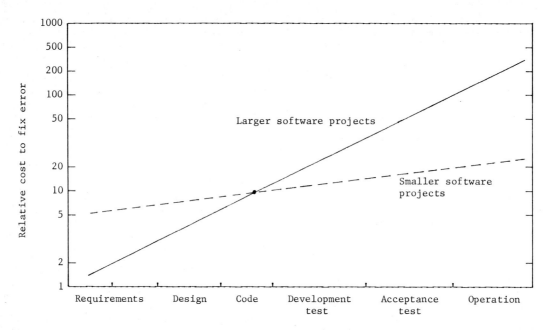

Phase in which error is detected and corrected

FIGURE 1: Increase in the cost of fixing or changing software
at various stages of the information system life-cycle

Source: Adapted from Boehm 1981 [3, p.40]

The absolute need to properly identify information requirements before embarking on an
information system development is therefore now
generally accepted. This was not always the case
however. As Yadav [25, p.3] explains in a paper
which draws attention to the gap between the
approaches adopted by designer/technicians and
those who stress the organisational environment
of information system developments:

> The development of design tools and
> techniques have not kept pace with
> the increasing complexity of the task
> of developing computer-based information
> systems for ... complex problem areas.
> In the early days of development of
> computer-based information systems
> the emphasis was on automating well
> defined repetitive tasks in an organ-
> isation. Each system essentially
> replicated and replaced a single
> organisational task. In a situation
> like this the development of a system
> was a relatively simple task. The
> analyst accomplished the task by
> observing and automating the organis-
> ational activities. Determining and
> specifying requirements was not
> considered to be a problem.

The point is sufficiently clear: thorough
information needs analysis is an absolute
requirement for successful information systems
development. However, when one reviews the
methodologies currently being proposed [10,12,20,
21], it would appear that the logical information
inputs and outputs to the new information system
to be developed are adequately identified in
only a third or so of the methodologies
presented [11]. Many identify the need for
information systems to be developed in line with
organisational objectives, but most fail to
show how this might be achieved. Reliance is
placed on an analysis of the current information
systems provision as compared with the
information actually needed - the latter is, by
some unidentified means, to be inferred from a
study of organisational goals. Further, emphasis
is placed on current operations rather than an
analysis of future requirements.

One of the more recent approaches - the I.S.A.C.
[17] approach - is a major improvement on
traditional methodologies in that it recognises,
through "change analysis" and "activity studies",
the need to ensure that, as Yadav puts it,
individual systems assist in "improving the
effectiveness of an organisation rather than
just the *efficiency* of individual operations"

[25, p.4, my italics] . The import of this is
that an analysis must focus on organisational
goals and associated measures of effectiveness
as a means of evaluating the appropriateness of
an organisation's existing information provision.

Criticisms can still be levelled at the I.S.A.C.
approach, however, especially from the viewpoint
of developing management information systems.
No differentiation is attempted between
operational activities and management activities
and therefore no differentiation is possible
between operational information and management
information.

A further criticism relates to the techniques
associated with change analysis. The analysis
is based on a listing of problems associated
with the existing system given by those
involved. The assumption is that stated
problems are accurate and that they are all
consistent one with another. In reality,
however, individuals will perceive problems in
a different light and a consistent view is often
difficult to find. In addition, the assumption
is that the group of people involved with a
particular operation within the organisation
understand the part this operation plays in
meeting organisational objectives. This is often
not the case and the change they wish to see
may very well be at variance with higher level
objectives. Little account is taken of this in
change analysis other than to describe the
objectives of *individual* activities [17, p. 112].

2. INFORMATION NEEDS ANALYSIS: AN ALTERNATIVE APPROACH

Yadav [25] also infers that the tools and
techniques available to analysts attempting
to define information needs may be outdated
since they tend to be more suited to the
computerisation of operational systems rather
than the support of management systems. From
this perspective, it is therefore no wonder
that the computing profession is seen to have
failed "to produce the goods" so far as
management information systems are concerned
[16]. What appears to be required is a technique
which places information in the context of
necessary activities, linked with organisational
plans/objectives, differentiates between management and operational activity, bears in mind the
different ways in which individuals might make
similar decisions (14) and their formal and informal information needs, but neither overempha
sises the existing organisational structure nor
places over-reliance on an examination of the
existing imformation system(s).

The approach advocated herein focuses on the
human activity system that dictates the need
for information. The approach is to build a
conceptual model - or picture - of what has to
be done in terms of management activity to
achieve objectives, to identify information

needs and outputs associated with each activity,
and to compare identified information needs
with the output of existing information systems.

By concentrating on what has to be done to meet
objectives - and the associated information
requirement - the analysis is not dominated by
organisational structure nor by the existing
means by which information is provided. The
intention is to provide a fresh analysis of
activity and information need. The approach
deliberately works from the top downwards,
increasing in detail but maintaining comprehensiveness. The objective is to arrive at a
coherent set of proposals for new or re-vamped
information systems that fit together and meet
needs within a framework agreed by both analyst
and user. Prototype systems can then be
implemented and then further developed/enhanced
by the user in the light of experience.

An argument central to this paper is that attention needs to be paid to the existing specific
system as a means of assisting in understanding
how the existing system contributes to the
attainment, or otherwise, of those organisational
objectives relevant to the study being undertaken.
The key to properly identifying information needs
is not, however, what happens now but what needs
to happen in order for current and future
organisational objectives to be met. The alternative information systems which enable and
support such required activity can then be
specified. A later comparison with the existing
situation can then identify deficiencies in
information provision.

Granted, a study of the current organisation
structure and its information systems is useful
in terms of gaining a sense of history, an
understanding of objectives and the means by
which they are achieved (including the quirks in
the current operation), together with an awareness of perceived problems. However, this should
be seen as useful background, not the basis for
determining future information system requirements.

The point is that attention should be focussed on
what activities should take place in order for
objectives to be met, rather than *how* these
activities are actually organised at present. As
Yadav points out [25, p.4], an information system
"providing support to an organisational unit
cannot be effective unless the organisational
unit itself is effective. The current organisational structure is not always in perfect
harmony with the functions it tries to perform."
Organisational boundaries and processes tend to
be accidents of time and are frequently out of
kilter with current and future organisational
objectives.

The implication is clear. Information requirements determination needs to be based on a
conceptual view of required activity, not on
current procedures.

Information systems, especially those in larger
organisations which have used computing technology
for some years, tend to be developed in response
to individual needs and circumstances appertaining at the time of their development. At any one
time, therefore, an organisation might have a
large number of information systems which have
grown over the years in an ad hoc or uncoordinated manner. Such systems tend not to correspond
particularly well to *overall* information
requirements.

Much has been written on the subject of the so-
called life cycle of an *individual* information
system. Less emphasis, until recently at any
rate, has been placed on the strategic issue
of developing coherent longer term plans for
information systems development organisation-
wide for a number of years ahead.

With the growing impact of computing throughout
all levels of activity in decision making (i.e.
from the operational right through to the
strategic) in modern-day organisations, such
longer term planning is becoming increasingly
crucial. This is a fact which has been noted by,
for example, Martin [18], Cash et.al. [5] and
Head [13], to name but a few. The approach
described in this paper has been used successfully in a large number of projects, either as a
means of formulating a strategic plan for
information systems development for a number of
years ahead, or as a means of specifying information requirements of an individual information
system in line with organisational objectives.

3. INFORMATION NEEDS ANALYSIS - THE APPROACH IN OUTLINE

The basic premise upon which this approach to
information needs analysis is founded is that
information is useful only insofar as it supports
the activities that have to be undertaken to meet
objectives and responsibilities. The approach
was originally developed by Wilson [24] and is
an extension of Checkland's *soft systems
methodology* [6,8].

Soft systems methodology arose following the
realisation that systems engineering is only
effective in situations where an objective can
be taken as given, with the system then being
engineered to achieve these stated objectives.
[6]. The implicit assumption in systems enginee-
ing "is that the problem which the systems
analyst faces can be expressed in the form:
How can we provide an efficient means to meet
the following objective ...?" [8, p.149].
However, most management problems - and management information system developments - occur
in situations where goals are often obscure
and over which there can often be disagreement.

In outline form, *soft systems methodology* can be
described by means of the diagram given in
Figure 2. The first two stages aim at building
as rich a picture as possible of the problem
situation, with the systems analyst collecting
as many perceptions of the problem as possible.
A central thought which would be borne in mind
during these stages would be that there is not a

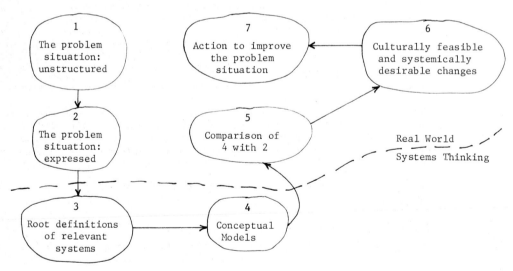

FIGURE 2: Soft Systems Methodology in Outline

Source: Adapted from Checkland 1981 [8, p.163]

single problem at all, but an nexus of inter-
related problems, perceived differently by the
different "actors" within the problem
situation. The second two stages aim at building
conceptual models of activity of systems
relevant to the problem situation. These should
take into account different "futures" for the
organisation, especially in studies concerned
with strategic planning. A comparison is then
made between models and the problem situation
with a view to initiating debate with the
"actors" involved to identify the means by
which improvements can be made.

Wilson [24] builds on this general problem
solving methodology and relates it to *information*
systems analysis by viewing each activity in
the conceptual model as a transformation process
with information inputs and outputs. The
information inputs (i.e. the information
required to enable the activities to take place)
can then be compared with existing information
provision (i.e. the outputs of existing
information systems). This comparison enables
gaps in information provision or unwanted/
duplicate system outputs to be identified. The
comparison forms the basis of discussions with
management concerning their information requirements and enables detailed information requirements to be identified. Proposals for information
system enhancements or totally new systems can
then be agreed upon.

Undertaking this kind of analysis also makes
it possible to gain an insight into the direction systems development should take through the
identification of areas of high potential for
system development and by highlighting areas of
development that should be progressed first.
By identifying priority areas, a work plan can
be drawn up and developments can be sequenced
according to greatest benefit or organisational
need, bearing in mind resource availability.

An example of this approach to information needs
analysis is given below. The illustration arises
from an action research project undertaken by
the author on behalf of the shipping function
within a major multi-national petroleum company.

4. INFORMATION NEEDS ANALYSIS - A CASE STUDY

The analysis commenced with a broad definition
of the activity system which most closely
mirrored the aims and associated activities of
the shipping function itself. This system was
called *The Cargo Shipping System* and was defined
as:

"A system which:
- is concerned with the marine transportation task within the company
- is accountable for its financial
  performance
- achieves a profit contribution through
  the deployment of a fleet of vessels
  either owned or chartered

- adjusts the shape and size of the
  fleet in line with identified business
  opportunities
- operates within the constraints of
  company policy and external
  legislation."

The definition implies four major groups of
activity, namely:
- scheduling the fleet (which was
  called the 'Run Fleet' system)
- trading (or 'Obtain Business')
- adjusting the shape and size of the
  fleet ('Maintain Cargo Capacity Balance')
  and
- 'Maintain Business Policy'.

In order to ensure that the above set of
activities is undertaken according to plan,
a fifth set of activities is also required,
namely:
- 'Monitor and Control Business
  Performance'.

The resultant high level conceptual model is
given in Figure 3.

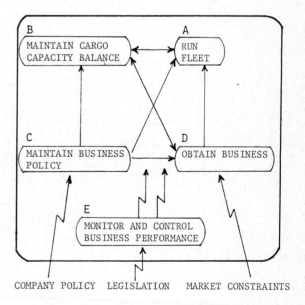

COMPANY POLICY LEGISLATION   MARKET CONSTRAINTS

FIGURE 3: The Cargo Shipping System in Outline

Clearly, however, this model is of insufficient
detail for analytical purposes. The next step
is therefore to provide this additional detail
and involves taking each set of activities
in turn and defining more precisely what each
is all about. Let us take the 'Run Fleet'
activities as an example. The Root Definition
for this set of activities was described as
follows:

"A System to meet orders to deliver bulk
cargoes for affiliates and third parties through
the economic, safe and timely day-to-day deployment of managed and chartered vessels in line
with company policy."

The Conceptual Model arising from this definition
is given in Figure 4.

By taking each set of activities in turn in like
manner the overall Conceptual Model for the
Cargo Shipping System was built up.

As part of the process of building the Conceptual
Model, it is crucial that those concerned are
consulted and are happy in the knowledge that
the model does correspond with their view of
what needs to happen in order to achieve agreed
objectives. Note that the model does not
necessarily mirror the activities which are
actually being undertaken. It does however mirror
those activities which are generally believed
to be necessary. Certain activities, believed to
be necessary, may not be undertaken particularly
well, either through oversight or because they

are not well supported information-wise. This
was the case in this particular study, especially
in the area of management activity.

It is also sometimes the case that the same
activity or activities are being undertaken in
different parts of the organisation. This, on
occasion, might have adverse effects on the
ability of the organisation to co-ordinate or
control such activity. In any event, agreement
should be reached that the activities which
go to make up the Conceptual Model are required
and that differences of opinion are settled at
this stage, prior to commencing the information
analysis phase.

Note also that, for the purposes of information
needs analysis, the model arises from a "primary
task" Root Definition [7] in that agreement is
sought as to what the human activity system is
attempting to achieve. If there are differing
views regarding objectives, it is likely that
no information system will meet all needs, since
no one activity system will meet the differing
objectives.

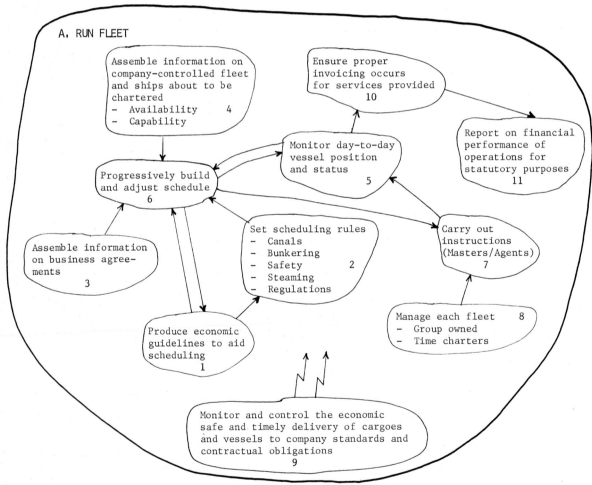

FIGURE 4:   The Run Fleet Sub-system of Activities

Management activities as distinct from operational activities[2] were identified by means of
the model depicted in Figure 5. As can be seen,
those activities concerned with policy making,
planning, assessing performance and deciding
on control action were viewed as management
activities, whereas those concerned with trading
(obtaining business), scheduling (running the
fleet) and the chartering aspects of maintaining
the appropriate fleet size and mix (maintaining
cargo capacity balance) were viewed as operational activities. Setting targets which correspond
to performance objectives is a necessary management task which enables actual performance to
be measured within a frame of reference.

The next step in the methodology was to identify
information needs associated with the necessary
activities. This was achieved by viewing each
activity as a transformation process, requiring
certain information and transforming this into
additional information. For example, the activity
concerned with monitoring the day-to-day
position and status of vessels (A5) requires
information on the actual location and status
of vessels as compared with the schedule (i.e.
the planned location and status), and produces
information which enables an assessment to be
made as regards the implications for further
scheduling decisions.

---

2   On the subject of the type of activity
    required to fulfill the goals of an
    organisation, Land et.al. [15] make the useful
    distinction between operational, problem
    avoidance/solving, co-ordination, control
    and development activities.

Having undertaken this analysis for each
activity, it is possible to summarise it in the
top half of a matrix of the type depicted in
Figure 6, which is a variation on the so-called
"Maltese Cross" developed by Wilson [24].

The information categories identified as being
required or produced by the conceptual activities form the x axis with the activities themselves
forming the top half of the y axis. Information
inputs (I) and outputs (O) are noted in the NW
and NE quadrants alongside the appropriate
activities. The top half of the matrix is
therefore a graphical representation of the
necessary flow of information from one activity
to another.

This can be compared with the actual availability
of information from existing systems by listing
these in the bottom half of the y axis. Where
possible, existing information categories are
used but it may be that additional information
categories need to be added to the x axis. Hopefully not, because this would tend to indicate
that either unnecessary information is being
produced or used by existing systems or that
required information had been omitted from the
earlier analysis!

The approach is now to identify apparent:
  - gaps in the information provision –
    which suggest the possible development
    of new or enhanced information systems
  - unnecessary information provision –
    which suggest the rationalisation of
    existing systems
  - duplication in output from or input to
    existing systems – which also suggest
    the rationalisation of existing
    systems.

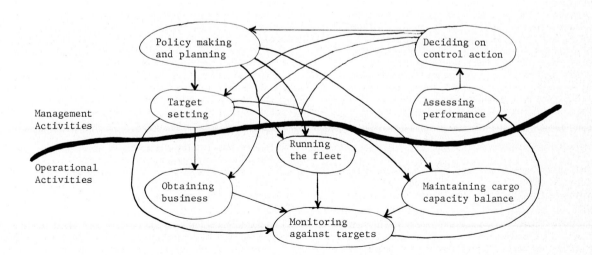

FIGURE 5: Overall Marine Management Activities Compared
with Operational Activities

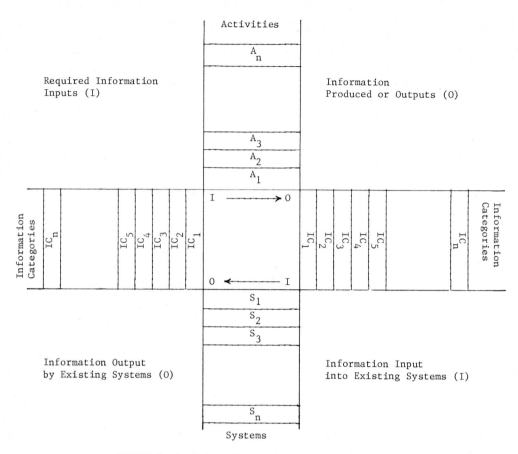

FIGURE 6: An Information - Activities - Systems
Matrix in Outline

Source: Adapted from Wilson 1981 [24, p.57]

In this particular study, a major information need appeared to be lacking in support of the trading activity (cf. the 'Obtain Business' sub-system). A decision support system was therefore proposed which would enable the traders to evaluate the financial results of past business obtained and thereby assist in deciding whether similar new business opportunities were worth pursuing or not.

5. REACTION TO THE APPROACH

In all those studies using this approach with which the author has been involved[3], the response of management has been most positive.

The active participation of those for whom resultant information systems are to be built is clearly crucial from an ownership viewpoint alone.[4] What is also particularly appreciated about the approach is that it is easy to follow, since it concentrates attention on objectives and their associated measures of performance on the one hand, and required activity and decision making on the other. Experience has shown that management appreciate the chance of discussing what they have to do as the focus of interviews rather than their perceived information requirement, particularly in the earlier stages of the study. Comments such as "For the first time, I've been able to think about how I fit into the organisation and how

---

[3] These include similar studies in the same group of companies from which the above case study is taken, local government agencies in England, State Government agencies and a Health Insurance Fund in Western Australia.

[4] Much useful work has been undertaken in the area of user participation in the information system development process by Mumford and her colleagues. See, for example, [19].

well our information systems meet my needs",
bear testament to the benefits of management
involvement in the process. Another perceived
benefit lies in the fact that, should organisational objectives change, the impact on
information needs can be identified by reworking
the analysis *for themselves*. The significance of
the activity analysis phase of the approach in
terms of identifying the need for reorganisation
or restructuring has not been lost on management
either.

The ability of the analysts to build into the
conceptual models different views or perspectives of the future also enables alternative
strategic plans for information systems
development to be proposed.

Two notes of caution need to be raised, however.
The first is concerned with reviewing the
conceptual model and asking for comments
as to its veracity. One runs the risk of
confusing the individual concerned if one simply
asks him or her to comment on the completed
model, in view of its likely complexity. By
concentrating on the major activities with
which he or she is principally concerned,
however, and gradually building up their inter-
relatedness with other activities, confusion
can be easily avoided.

The second problem relates to the time and
effort involved in manually building up the
matrices (cf. Figure 6) and relating the
significance of the gaps and duplications to
management.

Recent advances in computer graphics may play
a significant part in reducing the tedium of
drawing and redrawing both the models and the
matrices and in assisting in the communication
of the outcomes of the analysis to management.

5. CONCLUSION

An attempt has been made in this paper to
identify certain of the inadequacies of many of
the existing tools and techniques associated
with that aspect of systems development concerned
with information needs analysis, while at the
same time stressing the crucial significance of
the task.

The importance of examining the human activity
system which dictates the need for information
at the expense of detailed analysis of the
existing information provision has also been
stressed, as has the associated learning
process: for user as well as analyst.

The reactions of managers involved in the
process of building what, after all, are *their*
information systems has been positive and the
practical outcomes of the application of the
approach in a number of studies bears testament
to its usefulness, not only as a means of

identifying information needs but of developing
a coherent longer-term information systems
development plan organisation-wide.

6. REFERENCES

[1]   BOEHM, B.W., "Software Engineering".
IEEE Transactions, Computers, December
1976, pp. 1226-1241.

[2]   BOEHM, B.W., "Developing Small-Scale
Application Software Products: Some
Experimental Results", *Proceedings,
I.F.I.P. 8th World Computer Congress,*
October 1980, pp. 321-326.

[3]   BOEHM, B.W., *Software Engineering Economics*
(Englewood Cliffs, N.J.: Prentice-Hall,
1981).

[4]   CARTER, D.M., GIBSON, H.L. and RADEMACHER,
R.A., "A Study of Critical Factors in
Management Information Systems for the
U.S. Airforce", Colorado State University,
Fort Collins, March 1975; National
Technical Information Service AD-A-009-647/
9WA, NTIS, Springfield, Virginia.

[5]   CASH, J.I., McFARLAN, F.W. and McKENNY, J.L.
*Corporate Information Systems Management:
Text and Cases,* (Homewood, Illinois:
Richard D. Irwin Inc., 1983).

[6]   CHECKLAND, P.B., "Towards a Systems-Based
Methodology for Real-World Problem Solving",
Journal of Systems Engineering, Volume 3,
Number 2, 1972.

[7]   CHECKLAND, P.B. and WILSON, B., " 'Primary
Task' and 'Issue-Based' Root Definitions
in Systems Studies", *Journal of Applied
Systems Analysis*, Volume 7, 1980, pp. 51-54.

[8]   CHECKLAND, P.B., *Systems Thinking, Systems
Practice,* (London: Wiley, 1981).

[9]   GALLIERS, R.D. and LYONS, L.W., "Attitudes
of Western Australian Managers to
Computerised Information Systems", (in
press).

[10] GLASSON, B.C. and HODGSON, R., "I.F.I.P.
and Information System Design Methodologies",
Australian Computer Bulletin, Volume 7,
Number 3, April 1983, pp. 29-32.

[11] GLASSON. B.C. and HODGSON, R., "Information
System Design Methodologies: An Analysis
of Scope" (in press).

[12] GLASSON. B.C., "I.F.I.P. and Information
System Design Methodologies: An Update"
(in press).

[13] HEAD, R.V., *Strategic Planning for Information Systems*, Revised edition, (Wellesley, Massachusetts: Q.E.D. Information Sciences, 1982).

[14] KEEN, P.G.W. and MORTON, M.S.S., *Decision Support Systems: An Organisational Perspective*, (Reading, Massachusetts: Addison-Wesley, 1978).

[15] LAND, F., HAWGOOD, E. and MUMFORD, E., "Training the Systems Analyst for the 1980's: Four New Design Tools to Assist the Design Process", *Man-Machine Communications*, Volume 2, INFOTECH, State of the Art Report, 1979.

[16] LANKAU, W., "Decision Support Systems and the DP Crisis", *Australasian Computerworld*, September 24th, 1982, pp. 17-20.

[17] LUNDEBERG, M., GOLDKUHL, G. and NILSSON, A., *Information Systems Development: A Systematic Approach*, (Englewood Cliffs, New Jersey: Prentice-Hall, 1981).

[18] MARTIN, J., *Strategic Data-Planning Methodologies*, (Englewood Cliffs, New Jersey: Prentice-Hall, 1982).

[19] MUMFORD, E. and HENSHALL, D., *A Participative Approach to Computer Systems Design: A Case Study of the Introduction of a New Computer System*, (London: Associated Business Press, 1979).

[20] OLLE, T.W. and SOL, H.G., (eds), *Information Systems Design Methodologies: A Comparative Review*, I.F.I.P. TC8, Noordwijkerlout, The Netherlands, 10-14 May 1982, (Amsterdam: North-Holland, 1982).

[21] Olle, T.W., SOL, H.G. and TULLY, C.J. (eds) *Information Systems Design Methodologies*, I.F.I.P. WG 8.1, York, U.K., 5-7 July 1983, (Amsterdam: North-Holland, 1983).

[22] TAGGART, (Jr.), W.M. and THARP, M.O., "A Survey of Information Requirements Analysis Techniques", *Computing Surveys*, Volume 9, Number 4, December, 1977.

[23] WASSERMAN, A.I., FREEMAN, P. and PORCELLA, M., "Characteristics of Software Development Methodologies", in Olle et.al. (1983) *op.cit.*, pp. 37-62.

[24] WILSON, B., "The Maltese Cross - A Tool for Information Systems Analysis and Design", *Journal of Applied Systems Analysis*, Volume 7, 1980, pp. 55-65.

[25] YADAV, S.B., "Determining an Organisation's Information Requirements: A State of the Art Survey", *Data Base*, Volume 14, Number 3, Spring 1983.

Human-Computer Interaction — INTERACT '84 / B. Shackel (ed.)
Elsevier Science Publishers B.V. (North-Holland)
© IFIP, 1985

DIALOG SHELL DESIGN

Brian R. Gaines & Mildred L. G. Shaw

Department of Industrial Engineering
University of Toronto, Ontario, Canada M5S 1A4
&
Department of Computer Science, York University,
4700 Keele Street, Downsview, Ontario, Canada M3J 1P3

Many rules have been proposed for dialog engineering effective human-computer interfaces. The underlying technology has been changing rapidly with the introduction of windows, icons, and natural language. It is not clear how coherent, complete and consistent are the various systems of rules, and how applicable they are to the new technologies. A systematic model of human protocols is needed where the principles and technology dependencies are clearly expressed. There is a need also for such protocols to be made available as application-independent processes, dialog shells, that implement effective human protocols. This paper gives a systematic exposition of the principles of dialog engineering, shows how these structure effective human protocols in different dialog technologies, and how this leads to the design of dialog shells.

1. INTRODUCTION

Since the early days of interactive computer systems the need to design effective human-computer dialog has been recognized. In 1967 White [33] discussed the problems of on-line software, the use of different error messages for novice and expert users, and the advantage of HELP facilities. As experience grew various authors presented guidelines for the design of effective human-computer dialog: Hansen, 1971 [16]; Wasserman, 1973 [32]; Martin, 1973 [19]; Kennedy, 1974 [17]; Gaines and Facey, 1975 [11]; Pew and Rollins, 1975 [23]; Cheriton, 1976 [4]; Gilb and Weinberg, 1977 [15]; Gebhardt and Stellmacher, 1978 [14]; Turoff, Whitescarver and Hiltz, 1978 [31]; Kidd, 1982 [18]. Shneiderman [26] has collected many of these rules together, and Maguire [20] has analysed some of them systematically, noting contradictions and proposing their resolution.

The number of guidelines for dialog engineering has grown over the years. Ours [12] started as a set of 11 rules for **programming interactive dialog** in 1975 [11], growing to 15 in 1978 [8], 17 in 1981 [9], 22 as a **human protocol** in 1983 [25], and 30 **proverbs** in our 1984 book on the **Art of Computer Conversation** [13]. They were first formulated for interaction through low-speed, upper-case teleprinters, but generalized well to visual displays and dialog through menus and forms. They appear to generalize adequately to dialog through windows, icons and mice, and through restricted natural language. However, the proliferation of rules, the development of new technologies for HCI, the growing maturity of studies of human cognition, human-computer interaction and computer communication protocols, the need for standard dialog engineering tools, and the emergence of commercial products to satisfy that need, suggests that time is ripe for a new approach to dialog engineering.

What we might reasonably ask for at this stage in the development of human-computer interaction (HCI) is a set of **principles** that systematically **generates** rules for dialog engineering. The principles should be **grounded** in **system theory, computer science** and **cognitive psychology.** The principles should be **applicable** to the entire range of possible dialog **styles and technologies,** now and in the future. The principles should be **operational** so that they can be embedded in standard procedures, **dialog shells** widely available for all interactive systems.

There have been a number of developments that satisfy some of these objectives. Thimbleby [30] has explored a number of generative principles for dialog design such as **dialog determination.** Nelson [21] has proposed **virtuality** as an analytic principle, noting that we project to the user a virtual world from within the computer. In his development of Pygmalion, Smith [28] propounds the creation of visual worlds of virtual objects and this became the design principle of the Xerox Star [29]. Shneiderman [27] has subsumed a range of such recent developments in display-orientated systems as examples of **direct manipulation.** Each of these concepts gives a logic for HCI design that is supported psychologically and operationally, and hence satisfies some of the objectives expressed above.

This paper presents a first attempt to satisfy all the objectives and provide an overall framework for dialog design that contains such developments as particular instances of the application of general principles.

2. SOURCES OF INFORMATION ON HCI DESIGN

The design principles that we apply to human-
computer interaction are part of a larger
context of studies of applied psychology, human
and computer communication, and general
systemic principles. Although they may require
fresh validation in the context circumstances
of HCI, they have richer origins and support
than studies of HCI alone. This section
explores the wider context systematically.

2.1 Person-Computer Interaction

The basic situation of human-computer
interaction may be shown diagramatically as:

I. PERSON-COMPUTER INTERACTION

The primary analysis has to consider: the
nature of a person; the nature of a computer;
the interface from a person to a computer; the
interface from a computer to a person; and the
interaction between person and computer through
these interfaces.

2.2 System-System Interaction

However, there is also the possibility of
analysis through generalization, noting that
people and computers are both examples of
systems in general:

II. SYSTEM-SYSTEM INTERACTION
(Conversation Theory)

At an abstract level one notes that systems can
interact in many ways and that there are
constraints on the type of interaction that we
consider in HCI. In particular, we would
expect that at least one of the systems will be
goal-seeking and that the satisfaction of its
goals, and the cost in doing so, will give us a
basis for **evaluating** the interaction.

The goal of one system may be to transfer
information from the other through
communication, to predict the behavior of the
other through **modeling**, or to change the state
of the other through **control**.

Both systems may be goal-seeking in which case
considerations of **co-operation** and **competition**
arise. The goal of one system may be to aid
the other in, or to prevent it from,
communication, modeling or control.

It is also possible to consider goals relating
to the coupled systems that arise outside them
and may not be manifest to them. In this
context, we may wish to consider possible
interaction of one or both systems with an
environment:

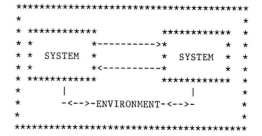

IIa. SYSTEM-SYSTEM & ENVIRONMENT INTERACTION

There are many system-theoretic principles that
have been developed for II and IIa which are
instantiated in the situation where one system
is a person and the other a computer. Wiener
[34] emphasized this is his development of
cybernetics as the study of "communication and
control in men and machines", and many
principles of communication theory and control
theory apply directly to HCI. For example,
Rule 9 (Appendix) that **the user should dominate
the computer** derives from a stability-theoretic
result in control theory, that two coupled
systems with similar time constants may
oscillate unstably around their intended
equilibrium state: the person modeling a
computer and adapting to it while the computer
is modeling the person and adapting to him is a
potential source of mutual instability.

The relationship between dialog rules and their
system-theoretic foundations is one of
dialectical tension. Concrete rules are needed
that can be applied within a range of contexts
without excessive development and inference.
However, when the context varies the rule may
become invalid, indeed the negation of a rule
may become valid instead. The system-theoretic
foundation for the rule is then essential in
order to enable the variant appropriate to the
new context to be derived. There are
situations where it is appropriate for the
computer to dominate the interaction, notably
ones where the person is not able to adapt, but
where the computer is able to do so to improve
the interaction. An example might be the
indexing of very large databases that a given
person accesses infrequently and does not learn
to navigate. The computer might then adapt its
portrayal of the indexing material to the
nature of the enquiry without ill-effects [35].

The theory of system-system interaction most
directly relevant to HCI is Pask's **conversation
theory** [22] which considers the problem of
systems validating mutual communication and of
observers comprehending its occurrence. Pask
gives systemic criteria for communication to

occur and has used these as a basis for
designing person-computer dialogs in education
through computer-based learning [22].
Conversation theory has been applied by Coombs
and Alty [5] to the design of expert systems,
by Shaw [24] to knowledge engineering, and by
Begg [1] to the analysis of HCI in CAD systems.
It provides basic systemic principles that may
be used in the context of specific situations
to generate rules of dialog design for
effective person-computer communication.

2.3 Computer-System Interaction

If one of the systems in II is taken to be a
computer then HCI can be seen to be analogous
to interfacing a computer to another system
such as a piece of equipment:

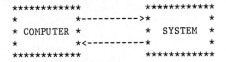

III. COMPUTER-SYSTEM INTERACTION
(Interfacing)

The design principles applicable to computer-
equipment interfaces are well known and carry
over to person-computer dialog. Problems arise
because the system to which the computer is to
be interfaced already exists and is not another
programmable computer. We may to take it as it
is and design an interface that copes with its
peculiarities. Rule 2 to use **the user's model**
derives from this, that the dialog engineer
should identify the existing interface and
attempt to emulate it rather than change it.
Problems also commonly arise through noise at
the interface and the designer attempts both to
provide a low-noise channel and to provide
error-detection and correction for unavoidable
noise. In HCI such noise may arise through
lack of clarity in information presentation
giving rise to perceptual errors in one
direction, mis-keying giving rise to errors in
the other direction, and so on. Rule 20 to
validate data on entry is a principle of
communication over a noisy channel.

2.4 Computer-Computer Interaction

When the systems on both sides are specifically
computers it is possible to define **protocols**
that it is reasonable to expect any
programmable digital system to be able to
implement, and dialog engineering rules may be
seen as defining a **human protocol** [25].

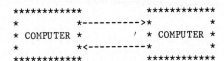

IV. COMPUTER-COMPUTER INTERACTION
(Networking)

The **Open System Interconnection** (OSI) ISO
standard [6] is particularly interesting
because it hierarchically structures computer-
computer protocols for networks in a way that
may have relevance for person-computer
protocols. The concept of an **open system** is
itself relevant because it expresses objectives
for computer networks that are equally
applicable to people using those networks. The
aim is to allow integrated systems to be formed
from multiple components not all from one
vendor and not all installed at the same time
[10]. The OSI concept is that the network is
open to all systems that conform in their
communications with certain well-defined
protocols. In human terms the protocols may be
seen as social norms for the behavior of
members of a club; anyone may join provide they
agree to conform to these norms.

The OSI standard is hierarchical defining a
number of layers, each with its own standard:

APPLICATION LAYER
PRESENTATION LAYER
SESSION LAYER
TRANSPORT LAYER
NETWORK LAYER
DATA-LINK LAYER
PHYSICAL LAYER

Each of these levels has an analogy in human
information processing and communication, e.g.
the physical layer corresponds to the audiovisual perceptual processes, and there is much
to be gained in applying the OSI concepts to
the human protocol.

2.5 Person-System Interaction

When one of the systems is specialized to be a
person we have the classic case of man-machine
interaction:

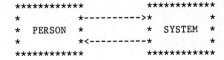

V. PERSON-SYSTEM INTERACTION
(Ergonomics)

Considerations of people interacting with
equipment has been treated as a branch of
applied psychology termed **ergonomics** that
arose, under the same pressures as computer
technology, out of World War II studies of
pilots, gunners and so on. There is a wealth
of results on general problems of human skills,
training, its transfer between different
learning situations, the effects of fatigue,
and so on, that is immediately applicable to
HCI. While interactive computers have been
used primarily as programming and data entry
systems these effects have not been major
considerations. However, as computer-based
interfaces become increasingly the norm for a
wide variety of human activities the classic
results of applied psychology and ergonomics

are becoming increasingly important. The novelty of the computer should not blind us to commonality with much earlier equipment. We do not have the time and effort to waste on rediscovering what is already known.

2.6 Person-Person Interaction

When both systems are people we have normal linguistic interaction from which the terms man-computer "conversation" and "dialog" have been generalized:

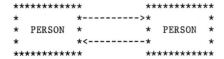

```
************        ************
*          *---------->*          *
*  PERSON  *          *  PERSON  *
*          *<----------*          *
************        ************
```

VI. PERSON-PERSON INTERACTION
(Linguistics)

Modern linguistic theory [2] has become increasingly concerned with the interaction between participants in a dialog, rather than a view of linguistic output as a predefined stream to be decoded. This provides a rich source of models for person-computer interaction, particularly as AI techniques take us closer to emulating people and their language behavior. There are also useful analogies of casual users in transactional analysis of the behavior of strangers meeting and **What do you say after you say hello?** [3].

Each of the five situations discussed provides a range of principles for interaction which are either directly applicable to HCI or, through analogies, have indirect application. One reason we have been able to develop effective interactive systems is that we can draw upon experience of these related situations. We can also use them more systematically to give foundations for dialog engineering.

3. DIALOG SHELLS

The considerations of Section 2 suggest that we consider a hierarchy of levels of dialog rule generation (Fig. 1): systemic principles; particular features of people and computers: consideration of their interaction: styles or technologies of interaction which lead to dialog shells; and particular applications.

The interaction level is interesting because it is where systemic, person and computer principles come together. For example, Rule 6 to **avoid acausality** has a system-theoretic foundation in that causal modeling systems generate meaningless models of systems with even slight acausalities. However, to apply this principle we have to know that people are causal modelers [7], and we would not regard the rule as significant unless we knew that time-sharing system generate apparently random delay distributions.

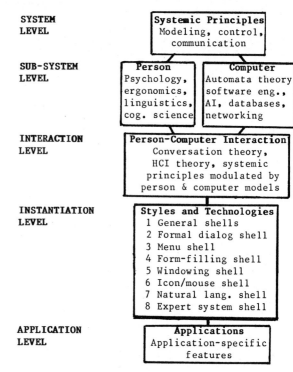

Fig. 1 Levels of dialog rule generation

At the instantiation level the rules are applied to instances of styles and technologies of interaction. To make this application-independent there has been a move to incorporate the rules in dialog shells that interface between the user and the computer system. The first general shells, such as IBM EXEC, originated from job control languages. We have given a shell [13] which incorporates the original formal dialog rules, and shells for form-filling transaction processing and menu-based systems are in widespread use. Several commercial companies have introduced window shells for the IBM PC and Apple Macintosh has a general icon/mouse shell. Intellect is a natural language shell for mainframes and Ask is one for micros. Expert system shells such as EMYCIN and AL/X are recent developments that incorporate significant new dialog techniques such as the uniform availability of **why** and **how** queries.

4. CONCLUSIONS

We are moving into a new era of HCI technology where well-designed dialog shells will provide uniform and consistent interfaces to a wide variety of applications. The systems of dialog engineering rules currently available can be generated systematically from basic principles that form a natural hierarchy. This paper has presented an initial framework for doing this which provides solid foundations for HCI engineering.

5. REFERENCES

[1] Begg, V., **Making computer aided design tools more useable: a study of a complex task shared by people and machines** (Kogan Page, London, 1984).

[2] Bennett, J., **Linguistic Behaviour** (Cambridge University Press, Cambridge, UK, 1976).

[3] Berne, E., **What Do You Do After You Say Hello?** (Andre Deutsch, London, 1974).

[4] Cheriton, D.R., Man-machine interface design for time-sharing systems, **Proceedings of the ACM National Conference** (1976) 362-380.

[5] Coombs, M. and Alty, J., Expert systems: an alternative paradigm, **International Journal of Man-Machine Studies, 20**(1) (1984).

[6] Day, J.D. and Zimmerman, H., The OSI reference model, **Proceedings IEEE, 71**(12) (1983) 1334-1340.

[7] Gaines, B.R., On the complexity of causal models, **IEEE Transactions on Systems, Man & Cybernetics, SMC-6**(1) (1976a) 56-59.

[8] Gaines, B.R., Programming interactive dialogue, **Pragmatic Programming and Sensible Software** (Online Conferences, Uxbridge, Middlesex, UK, 1978) 305-320.

[9] Gaines, B.R., The technology of interaction - dialogue programming rules, **International Journal of Man-Machine Studies, 14**(1) (1981) 133-150.

[10] Gaines, B.R., From word processing to image processing in office systems, **Proceedings of International Electrical, Electronics Conference and Exposition, IEEE 83CH1955-4** (1983) 622-625.

[11] Gaines, B.R. and Facey, P.V., Some experience in interactive system development and application, **Proceedings IEEE, 63** (1975) 155-169.

[12] Gaines, B.R. and Shaw, M.L.G., Dialog engineering, in Sime, M. and Coombs, M.J. (eds.), **Designing for Human-Computer Interaction** (Academic Press, London, 1983) 23-53.

[13] Gaines, B.R. and Shaw, M.L.G., **The Art of Computer Conversation: A New Medium for Communication** (Prentice Hall, New Jersey, 1984).

[14] Gebhardt, F. and Stellmacher, I., Design criteria for documentation retrieval languages, **Journal of the American Society for Information Science, 29**(4) (1978) 191-199.

[15] Gilb, T. and Weinberg, G.M., **Humanized Input** (Winthrop Publishers, Cambridge, Mass., USA, 1977).

[16] Hansen, W.J., User engineering principles for interactive systems, **Proceedings of the Fall Joint Computer Conference, 39** (AFIPS Press, New Jersey, 1971) 523-532.

[17] Kennedy, T.C.S., The design of interactive procedures for man-machine communication, **International Journal of Man-Machine Studies, 6** (1974) 309-334.

[18] Kidd, A., **Man-Machine Dialogue Design** (Martlesham Consultancy Services, BTRL, Ipswich, UK, 1982).

[19] Martin, J., **Design of Man-Computer Dialogues** (Prentice-Hall, New Jersey, 1973).

[20] Maguire, M., An evaluation of published recommendations on the design of man-computer dialogues, **International Journal of Man-Machine Studies, 16**(3) (1982) 237-261.

[21] Nelson, T., Interactive systems and the design of virtuality, **Creative Computing, 6**(11) (1980) 56-62.

[22] Pask, G., **Conversation, Cognition and Learning** (Elsevier, Amsterdam, 1975).

[23] Pew, R.W. and Rollins, A.M., Dialog specification procedure, **Report No.3129** (Bolt, Beranek & Newman, Cambridge, Massachusetts, 1975).

[24] Shaw, M.L.G., Knowledge engineering for expert systems, **Proceedings of INTERACT'84** (North-Holland, Amsterdam, 1984).

[25] Shaw, M.L.G. and Gaines, B.R., Does the human component in a network have a protocol?, **Proceedings of International Electrical, Electronics Conference and Exposition, IEEE 83CH1955-4** (1983) 546-549.

[26] Shneiderman, B., **Softare Psychology** (Winthrop, Cambridge, Massachusetts, 1980).

[27] Shneiderman, B., Direct manipulation: a step beyond programming languages, **Computer, 16**(8) (1983) 57-69.

[28] Smith, D.C., **Pygmalion** (Birkhauser, Basel, 1977).

[29] Smith, D.C., Irby, C., Kimball, R., Verplank, B. and Harslem, E., Designing the Star user interface, in Degano, P. and Sandewall, E. (eds.), **Integrated Interactive Computing Systems** (North-Holland, Amsterdam, 1983) 297-313.

[30] Thimbleby, H., Dialogue determination, **International Journal of Man-Machine Studies, 13**(3) (1980) 295-304.

[31] Turoff, M., Whitescarver, J. and Hiltz, S.R., The human machine interface in a computerized conferencing environment, **Proceedings of the IEE Conference on Interactive Systems, Man and Cybernetics** (1978) 145-157.

[32] Wasserman, T., The design of idiot-proof interactive systems, **Proceedings of the National Computer Conference, 42** (AFIPS Press, New Jersey, 1973) M34-M38.

[33] White, R.R., On-line software - the problems, in Gruenberger, F. (ed.), **The Transition to On-Line Computing** (Thompson, Washington, 1967) 15-26.

[34] Wiener, N., **Cybernetics** (MIT Press, Cambridge, Massachusetts, 1948).

[35] Witten, I.H., Greenberg, S. and Cleary, J., Personalizable directories: a case study in automatic user modelling, **Proceedings of Graphics Interface '83** (National Research Council of Canada, Ottawa, 1983) 183-189.

6. APPENDIX: DIALOG ENGINEERING RULES

6.1 General Principles

Rule 1 Introduce through experience: interactive systems need to be experienced before their operation can be discussed meaningfully. Get prospective users onto a terminal on a related, or model, system before discussing their preferred protocol for interaction with their own system.

Rule 2 Use the users' models: base the protocol on the users' models of their activities so that the interactive dialog is similar to a conversation between two users mutually accepting this model.

6.2 Continuing Design

Rule 3 Design never ceases: use the flexibility of the system through programming so as to close the adaptive loop between system and user through yourself as designer.

Rule 4 Log activities: use the network to maintain selective records of system and user activities and provide programs to analyse these in terms of, for example, errors, broken down by user and by dialog sequence.

6.3 Ease of Understanding

Rule 5 The User will Model the System: do not assume that the user is a passive static system to be controlled, modeled and directed by the computer. Evaluate the protocol in terms of its effect on an actively changing user who is attempting to comprehend the system.

Rule 6 Avoid acausality: make the activity of the system a clear consequence of the user's actions.

Rule 7 Consistency: ensure that all terminology and operational procedures are consistently applied throughout the protocol.

Rule 8 Uniformity: ensure that all terminology and operational procedures are uniformly available throughout the protocol.

Rule 9 User should dominate computer: either the computer or the user should dominate the interaction or there will be instability. If the computer is to dominate it must be programmed to, and have sufficient information to, model the user. If the user is to dominate then the computer system must be simple to understand. At the present state of the art the user should dominate the system.

6.4 Ease of Use

Rule 10 Parallel-sequential tradeoff: allow the user flexibility to make his responses holistically (in parallel) or serially (in sequence) according to his wishes.

Rule 11 Make the state of the dialog observable: give the user feedback as to the state of the dialog by making an immediate unambiguous response to any of his inputs which may cause the dialog to branch - the response should be sufficient to identify the type of activity taking place.

Rule 12 Provide a reset command: that cleanly aborts the current activity back to a convenient checkpoint. The user should be able at any stage in a transaction to abort it cleanly with a system command that takes him back to a well-defined checkpoint as if the transaction had never been initiated.

Rule 13 Provide a backtrack facility: that allows a user to return through the dialog sequence in reverse.

Rule 14 Provide default values: that are accepted by the user by   , for example, returning a null message.

Rule 15 Make corrections through re-entry: use the entry dialog with default field printouts from a record as a means of correcting the record.

6.5 Help Facilities

Rule 16 Query in context: distribute information and tutorial material appropriately throughout the protocol to be accessed by the user through a simple uniform mechanism, e.g. responding with a "?".

Rule 17 Query in depth: organize the response to queries so that the user accesses brief memory aids first at any point but has further access to more detailed explanations.

6.6 Training

Rule 18 User manuals should be based on actual user dialog: illustrate the use of the protocol by showing actual dialog sequences that achieve specific objectives. Illustrate the structure of the system through dialog sequences where queries are used to elicit information about the protocol.

Rule 19 Train through experience: get users interacting with an actual system as their initial training and introduce them to the system facilities such as query-in-depth.

6.7 Error Detection and Recovery

Rule 20 Validate data on entry: check syntax, and values against norms.

Rule 21 Be flexible in validation: beware of rejecting data or querying too much as being outside norms. Allow the user to over-ride the error checking where appropriate.

Rule 22 Have the user himself revalidate major updates: show the consequences of major actions clearly before acting upon them and ask for user confirmation.

DESIGN — GUIDELINES

Human-Computer Interaction — INTERACT '84 / B. Shackel (ed.)
Elsevier Science Publishers B.V. (North-Holland)
IFIP, 1985

THE USER INTERFACE TO COMPUTER-BASED INFORMATION SYSTEMS:
A SURVEY OF CURRENT SOFTWARE DESIGN PRACTICE

Sidney L. Smith and Jane N. Mosier

The MITRE Corporation
Bedford, Massachusetts 01730
USA

From a survey of 201 people concerned with information system design, estimates
for 83 systems indicate that on average 30-35 percent of operational software
is devoted to the user-system interface (USI). In the design of USI software,
survey responses indicate that improvements are needed in requirements
definition, design documentation, and design guidelines.

USI Software Design Survey

With widespread application of computer
technology there is increasing concern for
design of the user interface to on-line
computer-based information systems. Much of the
concern has been focused on conventional
ergonomic problems of equipment and workplace
design. But there is also growing concern for
the design of appropriate software, the computer
programs that control the logic of the
user-system interface (USI) and constitute a
significant portion of the USI design effort.

Atwood, Ramsey, Hooper and Kullas (1979) listed
61 core references and 478 other literature
citations in their comprehesive bibliography on
human factors in software development, and many
of the reports they cite pertain to user
interface design. One may question, however,
just how much attention is given to user
interface software in actual design practice.

To explore that question, for the past several
years, a questionnaire surveying design practice
for USI software has been distributed to
practitioners and other people interested in
this topic. That questionnaire covered various
aspects of USI design, including requirements
definition, design documentation, and design
guidelines. This paper summarizes the responses
of 201 people participating in the survey.[1]

Initial distribution of the questionnaire was at
the 1980 Annual Meeting of the Human Factors
Society, to attendees at a session on Designing

---

[1] A description of the survey in its early
stages, reporting 77 responses, was presented
at the 1981 Annual Meeting of the Human
Factors Society (Smith, 1981). Some wording
and examples from that initial report have
been preserved here.

Computers for People (Ramsey and Atwood, 1980;
Granda, 1980; Smith, 1980; Sidorsky and Parrish,
1980; Pew, Sidner and Vittal, 1980). Subsequent
distribution was to people requesting MITRE
reports on USI design.

As a consequence, most replies in this survey
are from United States respondents. Only 19
replies were received from other countries.
Thus one might qualify the survey responses as
reflecting primarily American design practice.
Perhaps the situation is better elsewhere.

The majority of respondents to this survey are
employed in commercial and industrial firms
(69%). Some respondents work in military or
other government settings (12%), and some are
affiliated with universities (16%).

In considering the results of this survey, we
should make some allowance for the professional
bias of these respondents. Most are involved in
human factors engineering, concerned with the
problems of designing complex systems for
efficient use, and keenly aware of any
deficiencies in system development that may lead
to non-optimal design. From this point of view,
it is not surprising that many are critical of
current USI design practices.

Investment in USI Software

All of the respondents answered some general
questions about the need for guidelines in USI
design. In 107 instances, respondents answered
more specific questions pertaining to the design
of some particular system with which they were
familiar. Different respondents, of course,
described different systems, which varied in
size and purpose, and which ranged in the stage
of design from early concept through actual
operation, evolution and redesign. Many of
these respondents, 70%, said that they were
involved in development of the system they
described.

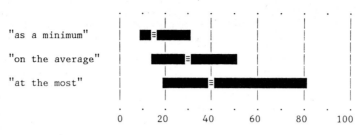

Figure 1. Median (≡) and quartile responses estimating the percent
of operational software devoted to implementing the user interface

Those people describing particular systems were
asked to estimate the percent of operational
software designed to implement the user
interface. This is a difficult question to
answer, both conceptually and practically, but
the aggregation of a great many estimates may
provide useful information nonetheless.
Respondents were asked to give minimum, average,
and maximum estimates for the type of system
they were describing.

There were 83 people who answered this question.
Their estimates are summarized in Figure 1,
which shows the medians and the interquartile
(25th to 75th percentile) ranges of survey
responses. Not shown in this figure are the
overall mean estimates for USI software
investment, which were calculated to be 21
percent "as a minimum", 35 percent "on the
average", and 47 percent "at the most".

Some systems place more emphasis on the user
interface than others, depending on their
purpose, and estimates of USI software "on the
average" for particular types of systems ranged
from 3 percent to 100 percent. However, either
the median estimate of 30 percent shown in
Figure 1, or the mean estimate of 35 percent
noted above, can probably be regarded as a
reasonable number for purposes of general
discussion.

Whatever the exact number may be, these
estimates suggest that the investment of time
and effort (and money) in USI software can
represent a sizable portion of the total system
software design effort. If human factors
specialists and ergonomists can devise effective
tools for designing USI software, they can
contribute significantly to the better design of
information systems.

Defining USI Requirements

It is often argued that system design will go
better if the designers are given more accurate
specifications of just what is required. For
the user interface, detailed task analysis and a
checklist of detailed functional capabilities
have been recommended as means to aid USI
requirements definition (Smith, 1982b).

In current design practice, are USI requirements
adequately covered in system specifications? In
the survey, 94 people answered this question.
Only 22% reported adequate coverage. Many more,
64%, judged that USI requirements were not
adequately defined. The rest were noncommittal.

For 15 of the systems described, there was
apparently no coverage of the USI in system
specifications. For 13 other systems, USI
specifications were too general: "Intent is
indicated, but detail and goals are lacking."
Even when specifications were detailed, they did
not always deal adequately with USI
requirements: "Requirements focus on discrete
functions the system will perform, not on user
(or task) needs." "No task analysis and
user/machine function allocation was ever done
and there was no description of the users."
"The operators' task was not defined before
software was designed."

Whether the specification of USI functional
requirements is missing, or incomplete, or not
specific enough, the result is to leave the
design of USI software up to the programmers,
who may not understand user needs. Several
respondents commented on this: "No specs ever
existed. This system was developed by
iteration, mostly in the heads of the
programmers, with limited advice from us." "How
the user thinks through the problem -- his/her
internal model of the process -- is poorly
understood by the programmer."

If bad design results from poor specifications, whose fault is it? When system developers do not specify what is needed, we cannot reasonably blame the programmers if they do not know how to create an effective USI design. When human factors specialists participate in system development, the fault may be ours for lacking the knowledge, the tools, and consequently the influence to fulfill our responsibilities. One respondent commented: "The requirement for design of interfaces is there, but human factors people rarely do it. Instead computer people generate the screens, write the code, and human factors is left to 'document' the rest." Other symptoms of inadequate participation by human factors specialists have been described in a recent report by Hammond, Jorgensen, MacLean, Barnard and Long (1983).

What can be done to improve the situation? Several respondents advocate early human factors involvement in system conceptualization, emphasizing the need for understanding users and their information handling tasks. Others believe that it is important to educate system analysts and designers in the importance of human factors expertise for definition of USI requirements.

Several respondents advocate user interface simulation and testing, including user evaluation of candidate USI designs as early as possible in system development. Prototype testing of proposed user interface designs has also been strongly recommended in a recent report by Gould and Lewis (1983). An extension of this approach is system development by incremental acquisition, where separate capabilities are implemented and tested in evolutionary stages. For such a system, requirements may be defined and redefined as a continuing process, based on operational experience.

When asked about specific aids for USI requirements definition, many respondents judged that a functional capabilities checklist of the sort proposed by Smith (1982b) could prove helpful. A number of respondents offered further comments, however, recommending that the checklist be used in conjunction with other techniques as part of a broader design methodology.

USI Design Documentation

74 people answered questions about documentation of USI design (and requirements) during system development. Of those respondents, 26% judged that documentation was adequate to support USI design. Significantly more, 51%, judged that USI design documentation was not adequate. The remainder were noncommittal in this regard.

Respondents provided page estimates of USI coverage in initial specifications for 47 systems. For seven of those systems, there was no documentation of the USI. Many respondents reported modest coverage of the USI, with several pages of specifications devoted to USI functional requirements, hardware and software design. A summary of estimated USI documentation devoted to each of those three topics is presented in Figure 2.

In commenting on inadequate documentation, several respondents cited a need for early USI documentation in system specifications, to provide more information about the user. Other respondents would incorporate more guidance in USI documentation, on specific topics ("population stereotypes for command language"), or more broadly ("a brief well-tailored guide with precise, germane examples with a set of basic standards"). Certainly that would seem desirable where general USI guidelines have been selectively tailored for a particular system design application.

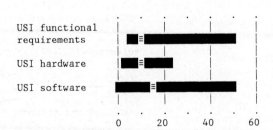

Estimated Pages of Documentation

Figure 2. Median (≡) and quartile responses estimating the pages of system specifications devoted to user interface design

Documentation should not be considered an end in itself. One respondent noted that maintaining effective day-to-day interaction among system designers is vitally important. From that viewpoint, documentation is just one means to help ensure effective design review and coordination. Presumably other tools might also prove of value for that purpose, perhaps including on-line computer aids to provide a current "library" of USI design for ready reference by individual designers. We still have much to learn about what forms of documentation will prove effective within a broader USI design methodology.

USI Design Guidelines

With regard to guidelines or standards for USI software design, 87 people answered questions on guidelines usage. Most of those respondents, 63%, reported that no guidelines were used. In 30 instances where the use of design guidelines was reported, most respondents described the establishment of ad hoc, system-specific guidelines based on published sources, as well as in-house system design experience.

Cited sources included the well known IBM report by Engel and Granda (1975). Also cited were more recent MITRE reports such as the recent report by Smith and Aucella (1983) or earlier versions of that report (e.g., Smith, 1982b). Some respondents referred to more conventional human engineering standards that give relatively little emphasis to USI software design, such as MIL-STD-1472C.

Several respondents cited in-house standards developed to fill a perceived need for USI design guidance. Although most in-house guidelines seem to have been developed for particular system design applications, some in-house guidelines have been stated and applied more generally. In-house guidelines are usually not available for general public review. A creditable exception are the guidelines developed for use at Lockheed by Brown, Brown, Burkleo, Mangelsdorf, Olsen and Perkins (1983), which are publicly available.

It would be interesting to know more about just how guidelines use used, by whom, and with what effect. The authors are presently designing a follow-up questionnaire to explore those questions. At present, published accounts of the results of guidelines application are still quite rare. However, an interesting example has been provided by Mosier (1983) on the use of guidelines for selection and evaluation of word processing systems. And Goodwin (1983) has described application of guidelines to menu design.

In the survey, when asked if guidelines could help USI software design for the described system, 83 people responded. Most of those

respondents, 80%, believe that guidelines would have facilitated USI software design for the particular system that they described. Only one person denied this proposition. Several others offered comments expressing reservations.

A number of different issues were raised. Guidelines may be too general, and lead designers to overlook task-specific issues. Guidelines may be too specific, perhaps focusing too closely on current technology. Guidelines may be wrong or misused. One potential advantage cited by many respondents is that guidelines can help direct attention to problem areas in user interface design.

Future Guidelines Development

In sum, this survey seems to confirm what many of us may have suspected, that there are several aspects of USI design methodology that need improvement. Some tools for improved requirements definition and documentation have been developed (e.g., Jacob, 1983; Smith, 1982a), and still others have been proposed (Kruesi, 1983). Much of the current activity in this field, however, involves the compilation and evaluation of design guidelines, i.e., an attempt to distill current human engineering wisdom into a form useful to software designers.

With some groups already moving toward the establishment of USI software design standards, and their critics arguing that such standards are obviously premature, this is a potentially controversial topic. Meanwhile, development of USI design guidelines continues apace, whether we like it or not. Recent work at MITRE has compiled 580 USI design guidelines covering six functional areas: data entry, data display, sequence control, user guidance, data transmission, and data protection (Smith and Aucella, 1983). Following critical review, that material has been revised and enlarged in a more current report that may be ordered from the present authors.

Improvement of USI design practice and the establishment of design guidelines is not, of course, the exclusive prerogative of any one group. Many organizations are moving toward the same objective, attempting to promote general improvement in USI design, or at least to establish design guidelines for in-house application. As an example in the United Kingdom, the Human Sciences and Advanced Technology Research Group at Loughborough has recently instituted a project to develop "man-machine interface" design guidelines for the Royal Navy (1983 HUSAT press release). We may expect other groups to undertake similar programs. The challenge for the future will be to develop USI design methodology and tools that will provide effective support to system designers.

References

Atwood, M. E., Ramsey, H. R., Hooper, J. N. and Kullas, D. A. Annotated bibliography on human factors in software development, Technical Report P-79-1. Alexandria, VA: US Army Research Institute, June 1979.

Brown, C. M., Brown, D. B., Burkleo, H. V., Mangelsdorf, J. E., Olsen, R. A. and Perkins, R. D. Human factors engineering standards for information processing systems, Report LMSC-D877141. Sunnyvale, CA: Lockheed Missiles and Space Company, 15 June 1983.

Engel, S. E. and Granda, R. E. Guidelines for man/display interfaces, Technical Report TR 00.2720. Poughkeepsie, NY: IBM Corporation, December 1975.

Goodwin, N. C. Designing a multipurpose menu driven user interface to computer based tools. In Proceedings of the 27th Annual Meeting. Santa Monica, CA: Human Factors Society, 1983, 816-820.

Gould, J. D. and Lewis, C. Designing for usability -- key principles and what designers think. In Proceedings of CHI'83 Human Factors in Computing Systems. New York, NY: Association for Computing Machinery, 1983, 50-53.

Granda, R. E. Man/Machine design guidelines for the use of screen display terminals. In Proceedings of the 24th Annual Meeting. Santa Monica, CA: Human Factors Society, 1980, 90-92.

Hammond, N., Jorgensen, A., MacLean, A., Barnard, P. and Long, J. Design practice and interface usability: Evidence from interviews with designers. In Proceedings of CHI'83 Human Factors in Computing Systems. New York, NY: Association for Computing Machinery, 1983, 40-44.

Jacob, R. J. K. Using formal specifications in the design of a human-computer interface. Communications of the ACM, 1983, 26(4), 259-264.

Kruesi, E. The human engineering task area. Computer, November 1983, 86-93.

MIL-STD-1472C. Military standard: Human engineering design criteria for military systems, equipment and facilities. Washington, DC: US Department of Defense, 2 May 1981.

Mosier, J. N. Development and validation of an aid in choosing word processor software, M.Sc. Thesis, Loughborough University of Technology, 1983.

Pew, R. W., Sidner, C. L. and Vittal, J. J. Man-machine interface design documentation: Representing the user's model of a system. In Proceedings of the 24th Annual Meeting. Santa Monica, CA: Human Factors Society, 1980, 103-107.

Ramsey, H. R. and Atwood, M. E. Man-computer interface design guidance: State of the art. In Proceedings of the 24th Annual Meeting. Santa Monica, CA: Human Factors Society, 1980, 85-89.

Sidorsky, R. C. and Parrish, R. N. Guidelines and criteria for human-computer interface design of battlefield automated systems. In Proceedings of the 24th Annual Meeting. Santa Monica, CA: Human Factors Society, 1980, 98-102.

Smith, S. L. Man-machine interface requirements definition: Task demands and functional capabilities. In Proceedings of the 24th Annual Meeting. Santa Monica, CA: Human Factors Society, 1980, 93-97.

Smith, S. L. Design guidelines for the user-system interface of on-line computer systems: A survey report. In Proceedings of the 25th Annual Meeting. Santa Monica, CA: Human Factors Society, 1981, 509-512.

Smith, S. L. Patterned prose for automatic specification generation. In Proceedings of Conference on Human Factors in Computer Systems. New York, NY: Association for Computing Machinery, 1982, 342-346. (a)

Smith, S. L. User-System Interface Design for Computer-Based Information Systems, Technical Report ESD-TR-82-132. Hanscom Air Force Base, MA: USAF Electronic Systems Division, April 1982. (b) (NTIS No. AD A115 853)

Smith, S. L. and Aucella, A. F. Design Guidelines for the User Interface to Computer-Based Information Systems, Technical Report ESD-TR-83-122. Hanscom Air Force Base, MA: USAF Electronic Systems Division, March 1983. (NTIS No. AD A127 345)

Human-Computer Interaction — INTERACT '84 / B. Shackel (ed.)
Elsevier Science Publishers B.V. (North-Holland)
© IFIP, 1985

DESIGNING INTERFACES FOR DIFFERENT TYPES OF USERS - EXPERIMENTAL CRITERIA

L A Macaulay Huddersfield Polytechnic and
M A Norman Heriot Watt University

The nature of the user interface should be adaptive to accommodate variations in user skill levels and cognitive style. The paper includes a brief review of current research on dialogue design, and describes aspects of an experiment carried out into the use of functional simplicity in dialogue design. The experimental session is described briefly and results based on keystroke timings are reported upon. Further findings from the experiments are reported upon elsewhere, including (16).

INTRODUCTION

The design of user interfaces has concentrated on the definition of a 'clean' interpretation of user and system interaction. The present approaches seem to assume that a single level of interaction can be designed and remain effective for all users of a particular system. It is suggested that the nature of the interface should be adaptive to accommodate variations in user skill levels and cognitive style. Further that the nature of the interaction will change over time.

A series of experiments have been embarked upon to establish the individual variations that will have to be accommodated in taking an adaptive approach to the construction of such interactive systems. The experiments are concerned with aspects of language and syntax and certain dialogue representations. The general aim of our research is to examine the form of the initial dialogues and language structures and to establish what are the important changes for users with very limited experience.

DIALOGUE DESIGN

Current research indicates a number of issues which should be considered in dialogue design (1), among these are: 1. Functional Simplicity: An important element of the interface language is its complexity, this is raised in a general sense by Du Boulay et al. (3) when referring to the acquisition of programming languages, and secondly by Cuff (4) in his study of casual users. For both casual users and inexperienced programmers "functional simplicity" is recommended, where the alternatives presented to the user are either limited or built up from a small number of primitive elements. Benbazat and Dexter (5) also consider language complexity, with high complexity referring to a large number of options available to the user at any one level in the computer system, and low complexity being represented by few response options available to the user at any one level but several levels are present. The total

number of response options may be the same, it is only their representation to the user that differs. 2. Command Complexity: One important assumption made by language complexity concerns the power of the commands in use. Functional Simplicity implies that commands have a restricted function i.e. they do one particular job. In contrast, commands may have several functions, depending on the use of options, flags or default conditions. The approach taken by Benbazat (5) is that complexity is increased by adding commands rather than by increasing the range of functions within the commands. 3. Response Flexibility: An issue raised by Miller and Thomas (6) is the degree of response choice given to the user in a dialogue, with either a fixed form of response or a flexible response allowed. Fitter (7) makes a similar distinction between the free responses of natural language systems and the constrained choice in system controlled dialogues. 4. Language Equivalence: This is derived from the theoretical separation of language and dialogue. In the literature cited above many of the dialogue examples contain different forms of stylised syntax for system and user e.g. the instructions may be in natural language but the user response is some form of abbreviation. The issue of equivalence and non-equivalence of syntax for system and for users requires further investigation. 5. Dialogue Control: Dialogue Control by either user or system is one important factor in dialogue structure (8,6,5). 6. Dialogue Format: There are certain obvious physical differences in screen layout for different dialogue representations. Menu selection, instruction response etc. (8,9,10). 7. Task and Control Dialogues: In many cases a man-machine dialogue isn't directed towards the interactive task due to confusion, errors and omissions by the user. Many dialogues contain some means of requesting help and have some error checking procedure built in. 8. Timing: The study of system response times has produced a number of conflicting findings. There is currently some debate over the most suitable structure for machine response times (13).

INITIAL EXPERIMENTATION

The main emphasis in our research work is the development of adaptive dialogues for naive users, particularly in a non-programming environment. We are interested in the development and change of command languages rather than the study of set formats. As a starting point for research on adaptive dialogues we have chosen the representation of a simple command language. However, few researchers have emphasised the global structures of command languages, instead most work has been concerned with the internal formats of commands. Benbazat and Dexter (5), describing the work of Carlisle on the layout of a command language, suggested that the complexity of a command language may be represented in two ways (i) the number of commands within the command language and (ii) the division of these commands into specific groups or levels. Thus complexity becomes not just the number of commands available to the user but the number of commands available at any one place in the dialogue.

For Benbazat and Dexter, high language complexity is when a large number of commands are available to the user at a single level, and low complexity when just a few commands are available at any one level but several levels are present. In the low complexity situation the command language is partitioned such that the user's choice of commands is limited and movement between levels is necessary for effective language usage.

In an earlier paper, Kennedy (15) noted that most command languages exist at one level and are what he terms linear structures. When each command is input by the user a series of actions are implemented in the system and then the system returns to the command level. Instead of directly addressing the complexity issue he has introduced the idea of "substructures" that may be attached to each command. A substructure is a set of prompts for the arguments required for any one command and may be considered as a loop in the dialogue where specific command details are entered. A key point for Barnard et al. is that even with a very simple system users are required to be aware of the number and format of arguments associated with each command. In such cases substructures would help by prompting for each argument as required.

Barnard et al. (14) provide some useful results indicating rules for organisation of 'introductory' command languages e.g. consistent argument first appears the best format for paired command arguments. Substructures have the advantage of (i) clearly presenting the argument format and (ii) allowing the system to check each argument as it is input. If an error is made with one argument specific prompts may be repeated and thus avoiding the situation of having to start the command again. In addition, complex argument structures consisting of more than two elements may be presented as sub-

structures, this allows the dialogue to depart from the paired argument structures. The use of substructures relegates the ordering of arguments to a more minor design issue. For naive users substructures are a way of introducing format structures and prompting for specific arguments in a combined move, and a way of helping the user achieve the correct formatting.

A primary objective of our research is to consider adaption processes within dialogues. Eventually, adaption will be directed by the 'monitor' built into the software at the interface. In the experimental situation, however, we have tasks carried out by users grouped together in blocks. Experimental changes were introduced between blocks to see the users adaption to enforced dialogue changes across blocks. Although dialogue changes occur at a set place they provide information on (i) the users capacity to accept this type of change after limited experience i.e. changes in performance, error rates etc. and (ii) what order of dialogue changes seem most appropriate to the user i.e. what should change first. (see conclusions).

In summary, therefore, the experiment on functional simplicity has three basic components: the complexity of the command language, use of linear structure or substructure commands and the changes between blocks of tasks.

The hypotheses for the experiment are described together with the results later in the paper.

THE EXPERIMENT

The experimental task:

It was felt to be important to give the experimental subjects a cognitive model of the tasks to be carried out. The subjects were told that a filing system contained information dealing with a set of companies and their industrial activities. That each company had its own file which could be accessed by reference number. Each company was composed of three sections (pages): the company details, the manufacturing details and the distribution details. The file is a summary in both written information and figures of the current status of the company.

For example page 1:

page 1.   COMPANY DETAILS,   ref. 6413

1. name of company: ---------- CROW WELDING CO
2. address: ------------------ CROW LANE
3.   ------------------ MILNSBRIDGE
4.   ------------------ HUDDERSFIELD
5. regional location: -------- WY
6. telephone: ---------------- 0274 654327
7. company status: ----------- C
8. industry code: ------------ 169
9. financial assistance: ----- NONE
10. b.s.o. reference: --------- 01 3289 6

The job of the experimental subject was to keep this information up-to-date by accepting requests for changes from "Head Office" and carrying them out on the company file. The number of company files remained constant and the Head Office instructions were directed towards particular files on the system. The experimental task was purely on-line, using screen and keyboard, with no attendant use of written information. The VDU screen was divided into two windows. The Head Office instructions for a particular company file appearing at the top of the screen and remaining there until the task was completed by the subject. The remainder of the screen scrolled upwards and contained the commands as entered by the subject, and system responses including display of pages. The screen was large enough to contain the Head Office instructions, to display one page of the company file and to include several commands and responses simultaneously.

For example:

Message from Head Office: Please amend Company File 6413; Page 1. The industry code should be changed from 169 to 482; and the regional location should read WY1921.

```
FETCH;6413;1          (page 'fetched' from
                       filing system)
DISPLAY;6413;1        (page 1 is displayed)
REPLACE;8;169;482
ADD;5;WY;1921
DISPLAY;6413;1        ('new' pl displayed)
SEND;6413;1           (page 'sent' back to
                       filing system)
FINISH                (task completed)
```

The commands available:

Linear structures:

```
File Handling:
  FETCH:<file no.>;<page no.>
  DISPLAY;<file no.>;<page no.>
  SEND;<file no.>;<page no.>
  FINISH

Editing:
  ADD;<line no.>;<string1>;<string2>
  DELETE;<line no.>;<string>
  REPLACE;<line no.>;<string1>;<string2>
  INSERT;<line no.>;<string>

Level 2 only:
  EDIT;<file no.>;<page no.>
  COMPLETE;<file no.>;<page no.>
```

Substructures:

Commands available were exactly as above except for the structure e.g.

```
user   : FETCH
system: which file:
user   : 6413
```

```
system: which page:
user   : 1

user   : ADD
system: on which line:
user   : 5
system: after:
user   : WY
system: what:
user   : 1921

user   : REPLACE
system: on which line:
user   : 8
system: what:
user   : 169
system: with:
user   : 482
```

The experiment is a mixed factorial design. The between subject factors are (i) dialogue complexity, where the command language consists of one or two levels (ii) the form of the command structure, with linear commands and substructures being used and (iii) block change, where changes occur between blocks.

The design structure is as follows:

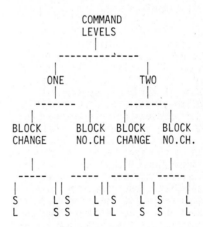

```
S  is Substructure
L  is Linear structure
```

The subjects:

The main thrust of our research programme is the development of adaptive dialogues for naive users. Our experimental subjects, therefore, needed to be naive users. In this experiment over 50 secretarial/general administrative staff were provided by Huddersfield Polytechnic's administration. The experiments took place mainly during Oct/Nov 1983.

The experimental session:

The subjects chosen had little or no experience of using an interactive computer terminal. Precise computing experience was determined by

means of a questionnaire. The organisation of
the experimental session was as follows:

(1) attitude/experience questionnaire
(2) typing test using terminals
(3) block1 -instructions
            -3 trial tasks
            -6 actual tasks
            -questionnaire
(4) tea and crumpets
(5) block2 -instructions
            -3 trial tasks
            -6 actual tasks
            -questionnaire
(6) GEFT(cognitive style) test.

Limitations of this paper:

A number of factors have arisen from the analysis
of this initial experiment. The purpose of this
paper, however, is to report upon the results
relevant to the three basic components of
functional simplicity i.e. the complexity of the
command language, use of linear structure or
substructure commands and the changes between
blocks of tasks. The results are given in the
order of the hypotheses. Only the sections of
the hypotheses relating to keystroke timings are
discussed here. The remainder of the results
will be reported elsewhere.

THE RESULTS

These results are based on timings recorded
during the experimental sessions. The first
hypothesis claims that: Naive users will show
better performance, in terms of keystroke
timings if the dialogue exhibits functional
simplicity, i.e. if substructures are used and
the commands are broken down into two levels...
Each subject carried out two blocks of experiments. A total time to complete each block was
calculated. A comparison of the mean times for
substructured blocks with linear structure
blocks for 24 subjects in each category, indicates at a 5% level of significance that blocks
of substructured tasks produce a better performance time for naive users than blocks of linear
tasks. There is no significant difference,
however, between command level 1 and command
level 2 apparent at this level of analysis. The
results from a two-sample T-Test are as follows:

	n	mean	stdev	se mean
SUB	24	1232	362	74
LIN	24	1507	604	123

95% confidence interval
TTest mu SUB = mu LIN (vs LT):
T=-1.91 P=0.032 DF=37.6

	n	mean	stdev	se mean
L1	24	1273	281	57
L2	24	1465	662	135

95% confidence interval:
TTest mu L1 = mu L2 (vs LT):
T=-1.31 P=0.10 DF=31.0

The second hypothesis states that: If the command
language is broken down into two levels there
will be an increase in 'think time' at the start
of the task when users change levels, reflecting
the cognitive separation of types of commands...
This hypothesis involves considerable discussion
of command groupings and detailed character
timings. This is beyond the scope of the
present paper.

A third hypothesis claims that: There will be a
reduction in keystroke times in the second block
due to user experience built up. User performance will be better for groups that have both
blocks containing substructures in comparison
with linear commands for both blocks... The
percentage improvement for each of the 48
subjects from block 1 to block 2 was calculated.

The average % improvement was as follows:

BLOCK1	BLOCK2	IMPROVEMENT
l1sub	l1lin	21%
l1lin	l1sub	52%
l1sub	l1sub	28%
l1lin	l1lin	35%
l2sub	l2lin	26%
l2lin	l2sub	45%
l2sub	l2sub	29%
l2lin	l2lin	44%

note: there are 6 subjects in each group
      l1 is command level1
      l2 is command level2

A positive improvement was shown for all subjects
(except one) from block 1 to block 2. The times
to complete both blocks was calculated for those
subjects who carried out no change blocks of
tasks. The average time to complete for linear
was 2141(level 1) and 2794(level 2) and for
substructure 1873(level 1) and 1958(level 2)
seconds. Thus user performance is better for
groups that have both blocks containing substructures in comparison with linear commands
for both blocks.

The fourth hypothesis claims: In the experimental
groups, the change between blocks should show
marked differences. Substructures followed by
linear commands will show less disturbance in
performance than if linear commands came first.
Substructures will facilitate later usage of
linear structures, but conversely linear commands
will show no positive effect on substructures...
The % improvements shown in the above table
indicate that Substructures followed by Linear
show a disturbance of 21% and 26% compared with
Linear followed by Substructures of 52% and 45%.
Thus there is less disturbance in performance in
a block change of substructure followed by

linear than linear followed by substructure.

CONCLUSIONS

The three aspects of functional simplicity included in the experimentation may be summarised as follows: (i) the complexity of the command language: no significant difference in timings across level 1 and level 2 commands were apparent at this level of analysis. The underlying reasons for the lack of difference is beyond the scope of this present paper. (ii) The use of linear and substructured commands: the naive users showed a better performance for substructured than for linear structured commands. (iii) changes between block: the results indicate that the subjects found linear structured commands more difficult as an initial structure than substructured commands (hyp1&4).

The conclusions, therefore, from timings recorded during the experimental session are that the notion of Functional Simplicity should also include Structural Simplicity and that for naive users substructured commands provide an advantageous starting point.

REFERENCES

(1) Internal Design Papers - Joint research report July 1983. MMI Research Groups Huddersfield Polytechnic and Heriot Watt University.

(2) Gaines, B.R., Infotech State of the Art Report: Man/Computer Communication, Vol.1, (Infotech Internation Ltd., England, 1979).

(3) Du Boulay, B., O'Shea, T., Monk, J., The black box inside the glass box: presenting concepts to novices, Int. Jrnl. Man-Machine Studies 14, 1981, 237-249.

(4) Cuff, R.M., On casual users, Int. Jrnl. Man-Machine Studies 12 (1980) 163-187.

(5) Benbazat, I., Dexter, A.S. and Masulis, P.S. An experimental study of the human/computer interface, Comm. A.C.M. 24 (1981) 752-762.

(6) Miller, L.A. and Thomas, J.C., Behavioural Issues in the use of Interactive Systems, Int. Jrnl. Man-Machine Studies 9 (1977) 509-536.

(7) Fitter, M., Towards more "natural" interactive systems, Int. Jrnl. Man-Machine Studies 11 (1979) 339-350.

(8) Martin, J., Design of Man-Computer Dialogues (Prentice-Hall, Englewood Cliffs, N.J., 1973).

(9) Kidd, A.L., Man-Machine Dialogue Design, (British Telecom Research Laboratories, April 1982).

(10) Robertson, G., McCracken, D. and Newell A., The ZOG approach to man-machine communication, Int. Jrnl. Man-Machine Studies 14 (1981) 461-488.

(11) Waterworth, J.A., Man-Machine speech "dialogue acts", Applied Ergonomics, 13 (1982) 203-207.

(12) Moran, T.P., the Command Language Grammar: a representation for the user interface of interactive computer systems, Int. Jrnl. Man-Machine Studies 15 (1981) 3-50.

(13) Maguire, M., An evaluation of published recommendations on the design of man-computer dialogues, Int. Jrnl. Man-Machine Studies 16 (1982) 237-261.

(14) Barnard, P.J., Hammond, N.V., Morton J. and Long, J.B., Consistency and compatibility in human-computer dialogue, Int. Jrnl. Man-Machine Studies 15 (1981) 87-134.

(15) Kennedy, T.C.S., The design of interactive procedures for man-machine communication, Int. Jrnl. Man-Machine Studies 6 (1974) 309-334.

(16) Norman, M.A., Macaulay, L.A., Keystroke level monitoring of man-machine interactions, First IFIP Conf. on Human-Computer Interaction, Sept. 1984.

This work is part of a S.E.R.C. funded research programme.

Human-Computer Interaction — INTERACT '84 / B. Shackel (ed.)
Elsevier Science Publishers B.V. (North-Holland)
IFIP, 1985

"HUMAN FACTORS GUIDELINES FOR THE DESIGN OF COMPUTER-BASED SYSTEMS"

Arthur Gardner, Tom Mayfield and Martin Maguire [1]

HUSAT Research Centre
University of Technology, 'The Elms', Elms Grove,
Loughborough, Leicestershire LE11 1RG

The HUSAT Research Centre has been awarded a four year contract by the U.K.
Ministry of Defence (Procurement Executive) to produce a new handbook of human factors
design guidelines and associated training for use by the Royal Navy and Industry.
The paper describes the project's aims and plans, reports progress and seeks to
stimulate discussion by presenting an outline of the handbook's proposed structure
and content.

1. INTRODUCTION

The HUSAT Research Centre has been awarded a
four year contract by the U.K. Ministry of
Defence (Procurement Executive) (MOD (PE)) to
produce a new handbook of human factors design
guidelines and associated training for use by
the Royal Navy and Industry.

The handbook will deal with human factors concepts and procedures for use throughout the
whole of the procurement process and will cover
both the design of operational systems and the
training simulators and part-task trainers which
will accompany them. The handbook will concentrate on total systems issues and man-software
interactions rather than physical ergonomics of
the interface or the workplace. It will be
written for human factors specialists, Project
Managers and end-user representatives.

As mentioned, the contract makes provision for
the design of training courses based upon the
knowledge, skills and attitudes advocated by the
guidelines. Two sorts of training are envisaged:
a short course to provide a general acquaintance
and a long course to teach a full specialism.
It is expected that this long course will be
modular to cater for students from a wide range
of backgrounds - mainly systems engineers, computer scientists and ergonomists/psychologists.

The project milestones reflect these twin aims:

'83 - '85
. draft new handbook and collect
expert reaction

. draft outline training specifications based on handbook

'85 - '87
. field trials of handbook, evaluate
and revise

. detailed specification of training
pilot courses, evaluate and revise

2. STRUCTURE AND CONTENT

The handbook has to be used as a training aid
and as a reference text. As such, it must provide some structured overview(s) to weld the concepts and procedures together and to help readers
navigate around the detail. Three structures
are being considered, at the moment, and these
will be described in the rest of this paper.

It will be seen that these 3 structures overlap.
This is not a disadvantage. The aim is to
provide many paths into the subject. These
structures serve to generate key words and
phrases for information retrieval. They are not
taxonomies of mutually exclusive categories.
Nor are they meant to be.

(a) Archetypal User Sub-system

The handbook is concerned with systems in the
special sense of combinations of humans and
machines (mainly computers) which are mutually
dependent upon each other for the attainment of
some goal(s).

A key concept, here, is the concept of a 'total
system' and the related concept of 'nested
systems'. Systems can almost always be encompassed into more total systems. There is no
limit to this nesting. For practical purposes,
therefore, the total system is taken to be the
next bigger unit to the one being designed. It
is essential that design teams take account of
the total system for which they are designing.
It is a matter of common experience that it is
all too easy to optimise sub-systems at the
expense of the total system performance.

That said, however, the main focus of the handbook will be the user sub-system and its
contacts with the external world (if any) and
other sub-systems (if any). Diagram 1 is the
top level description of the archetypal user
sub-system for the purposes of the handbook. It
is archetypal in that all user sub-systems can
be described in terms of these component

functions and their links to the external world
and/or other sub-systems.   The handbook will
illustrate the major variations.

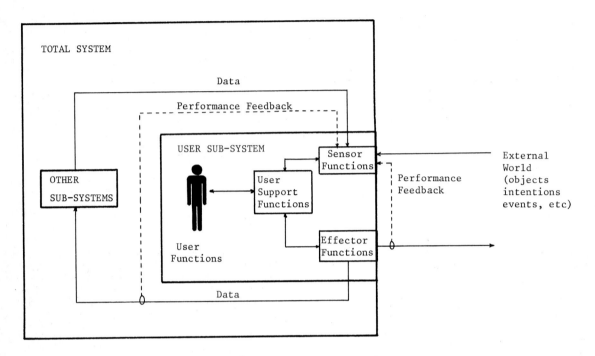

Diagram 1   Archetypal User sub-system

Diagram 1 does not suffice as a framework for all
human factors but it does have the merit of
emphasising that human factors are facets of
systems engineering and that the concern of the
human factors specialist is wider than a concern
merely with user interfaces and dialogues.

In particular, it helps to make clear that the
design team for the user sub-system has to be
alert to human factors in all of the following:

User sub-system

- User sub-system goals

- User characteristics

- User functions

- User/user support interactions
  (i.e. the user interface)

- User support functions

- User support adjuncts (e.g. manuals and
  stand alone training)

- Sensor functions

- User support/sensor interactions

- Effector functions

- User support/effector interactions

- Sensor interactions with the external
  world

- Effector interactions with the external
  world

- Sensor interactions with other sub-systems

- Effector interactions with other sub-
  systems

- Performance feedback from external world

- Performance feedback from other sub-
  systems

- User sub-system environment (including
  physical, social and legal)

Other sub-systems

- Other sub-systems' goals

- Characteristics and tasks of Superior,
  Peer and Subordinate sub-systems

Total Systems

- Total system's goals

- Input/Output with the external world

- Performance feedback from the external world

External World

- Objects, intentions, events etc. relevant to Total System

- Objects, intentions, events etc. relevant to user sub-system

- Objects, intentions, events etc. relevant to other sub-systems

(b) External and Internal Goals

A good system is one that meets all its goals. However, since there is rarely, if ever, only one goal for a system and since these goals are often incompatible it is a matter of subjective judgement as to how good is a good system. One aim of the handbook is to alert the design team to some human factors in the quality assessment they will have to make. No handbook can lay down absolute criteria of quality which will apply in all endeavours and circumstances. The handbook will offer a description of selected concepts and procedures which have found general approval amongst experienced users, managers and engineers. They are chosen to illustrate the range of possibilities and to stimulate thought about particular problems. The handbook is not a definitive statement on quality: it is intended to be a useful starting point.

External Goals

External goals are those that refer outside the sub-system in question. In the archetypal user sub-system (Diagram 1) external goals relate to the External World and to relationships with other sub-systems.

Of equal consideration are the goals of the design team. Their goals will include achieving the goals for the sub-system but, also, will include goals more personal to themselves.

Specifically the goals of the design team will include:

- Effective performance of the system being designed which includes such concepts as accuracy; speedy operation; and reaction to changing external circumstances.

- Acceptable cost which includes the concept of through-life-cost and hence, brings in costs associated with selection, training, maintenance and personnel turnover.

- Timeliness in the sense of product delivery dates.

- Quantity of systems produced

- Prestige of the system in the sense of esteem which it generates for those producing, purchasing and using it.

These goals, often, are mutually incompatible. For example, truly effective performance may be prestigious but too costly or impose too long a delay in delivery.

The impact of these pressures on the design team will reflect on the system being designed in the form of design compromises. For example, the system being designed will be judged not only from the point of view of effective performance (a user sub-system goal) but, also, from the point of view of it's ease of manufacture (a design team goal).

The handbook cannot say how to make such compromises. These are the responsibility of the design team exercising their judgement as best they can. The handbook will seek to make explicit some of the human factors involved. It is likely that the handbook will deal mainly with how to assess effective performance; say a little about through-life-costing and prestige; say nothing about timeliness and quantity.

Internal Goals

Internal goals refer to attributes internal to the system or sub-systems in question. They are secondary to the external goals in that they are formulated to facilitate achievement of the external goals. When made explicit in a system specification, these internal goals constitute a first prescription for designing the system in such a way that the external goals might be realised. Often they are not made explicit but are hidden in the user organisation's conventions or mores. Teasing out these internal goals is one of the most difficult tasks for the human factors practitioner.

The handbook will contain a description of the most common internal goals along with procedures for their assessment. Amongst these are:

User Characteristics

- Mental demand and variety

- User satisfaction

- Relationship of work to life outside work

- Health, safety and comfort

- Provision for learning and personal growth

User Tasks

- Simplicity

- Task centrality

- Processes compatible with goals

User Support

- Usability

- Power to facilitate rapid, decisive acts

- Integrate components and resolve conflict

- Time span of discretion

- Boundary management

- Balance the adaptive and steady-state mechanisms

- Transparency as to how components operate

- Cover for other components

- Multi-functional components to enhance further expansion

- Feedback to evaluate performance of components and sub-systems

- Computers to behave like tools (e.g. sympathetic, compliant and understandable)

The authors are currently involved in a survey of existing design handbooks, journals etc. It is likely that this search will generate a wealth of such attributes. The results of this survey will be reported in due course.

(c) The Procurement Cycle

Confusions arise in design teams when people assume they share a common view of the design process but, in fact, they do not. In practice, three views predominate and these are:

View 1 : procurement management orientated

View 2 : customer orientated

View 3 : technology orientated

These views reflect different intentions, activities and expectations within the design process. Often, as their names suggest, they are typified by different roles within the design team. Often, these roles are vested in different people (e.g. the project manager; the customer representatives; the computer engineers and software scientists) who, hence, find themselves in conflict.

The point to be made is that all three views are needed to achieve a successful product.

Conflict between them is inevitable but conflict is not necessarily harmful. Each view (or role) can act as a check on the others and help to keep the procurement process in balance.

Much of the frustration and mis-understanding that arises in design teams - and it is very common - arises because people fail to recognise the essential differences between their own view and those of other people.

The 'procurement management' view is that design starts with an assessment of operational requirements and progressively narrows down the possible solutions to achieve a working product at the right time and cost and in sufficient quantity. Provision is made for supporting the system implemented and subsequent modifications and improvements.

This view is pragmatic and compromise is accepted. It seeks to freeze options early and, therafter resists changes of direction.

The design process and the design team are formally organised into a series of roughly sequential activities, with overlaps, known as the 'procurement cycle'. This handbook will deal with major variations.

The 'customer view' is that design involves active analysis, synthesis and evaluation of all relevant factors (aims, current and future systems, constraints) in deciding on the right requirements and the right solutions. It is ideal seeking in the sense of optimising operational goals and emphasises the need to be adaptable and to keep options open. It emphasises the importance of re-evaluating one's ideas and reserves the right to change one's mind at the very last minute if need be.

The 'technical specialist' view is that design involves the active search for a practical solution to a stated aim (statement of requirements). It accepts the aims as given and seeks the best technical solution. It, too, is ideal seeking but in the sense that it is attracted by the ideal technology. New technology is seen as 'a good thing'. There is a tendency to prefer to modify the aims rather than to compromise the technology. Carried to extremes, this view runs the risk of over compartmentalisation such that the sub-systems are individually excellent but cannot be integrated. It is common to find each specialist over valuing its own contribution and under valuing that of others. This is as true of human factors engineers as it is of electronics engineers and computer scientists.

The three views are in conflict but must co-exist. Recognising their separate identities is a first step to achieving a co-ordinated design team. It is necessary also to recognise that they contribute differently to different facets of the overall design process. The free-ranging 'customer' role is most appropriate at the early and late stages of procurement. The 'technical specialist' role is most appropriate in the middle stages. The 'procurement management' view is essential throughout as, otherwise, nothing might be produced!

The handbook will advocate that the project manager must act as a facilitator to design by encouraging the right sort of contribution at the right time. As to what are the right contributions, the handbook will describe how to do the following:

Throughout the Procurement Cycle

- Management of the design team (incl. organisation)

Concept Study and Feasibility Study

- Brainstorming of requirements

- Personnel forecasting (incl. characteristics, supply and throughput of target users)

- Operational research (OR) into systems options (using analytic models; mathematical simulations; audits of current systems; mock-ups; and systems demonstrators).

- Market research of customers, users and competitors

- Assessment of human factors risks .

- Preparation of human factors research requirements

- Assessment of options

- Preparation of formal statement of user orientated requirements

Project Definition and Full Development and Build

- Devise design documentation procedures

- Functional and physical design of user tasks and user orientated components (hardware and software)

- System proving using pre-production prototype

- Design training (incl.courses, part-task trainers)

- Design user documentation (incl. commissioning procedures, operating instructions, maintenance manuals)

- Design personnel selection procedures

- Carry out training of 'first crew'

- Plan in-use support

- Plan system in-use audit

- Quality control of production

Implementation and Support and Audit

- User liaison

- Regular user training

- Troubleshooting

- Make corrections to user procedures, documentation, selection and training

- Suggest modifications and improvements.

3. CONCLUDING REMARKS

In the time available, this paper has tried to give a general insight into the plans for the handbook and to describe the content in terms of general structures and lists of topics. The next step is to flesh out these lists with details of specific concepts and procedures. Any suggestions as to what should be included would be gratefully received and duly acknowledged.

---

1 Work carried out under MOD Contract NSW 32A/1113. The opinions expressed are entirely those of the authors and in no way should be regarded as the official view of the Ministry of Defence (Procurement Executive) or of Loughborough University of Technology.

THE "IMPACT ANALYSIS TABLE" APPLIED TO HUMAN FACTORS DESIGN.

Tom Gilb

Independent Consultant, Iver Holtersvei 2, N-1410 Kolbotn, Norway

SUMMARY

The "Impact Analysis Table" is a tool for multiple viewpoint analysis of any system design idea.

It is used to estimate the impact of suggested design techniques on the target levels of multiple design objectives.

On a single table, multiple techniques, or groups of techniques can be evaluated against multiple objectives.

Using a series of tables, all suggested techniques can be evaluated against all design objectives.

The "Impact Analysis Table" was originally developed by this papers author in 1978 as a tool for use in the "Design by Objectives" (1) method for system analysis and design.

In principle, there is nothing more orginal or complex than ordinary cost estimation or budgetting. The originality stems from the fact that we try to estimate the impact of techniques on <u>all</u> specified measurable attributes (qualities and resources) of a system.

The estimates are normally made in terms of a percentage of the target level for a particular attribute. A 100% estimate means that we believe that the technique, if implemented properly, will allow us to achieve the target level of that attribute. A zero percent estimate means we believe there is no impact.

It is possible to estimate negative impacts, as well as impacts exceeding the target levels.

One percent (1%) is usually the smallest estimate. It is a rough but symbolic estimate. It indicates that there is some, but very little impact.

Estimates are usually rather rough and intuitive. But, they still speak a clearer language than mere words. Estimates can be backed up by more details on a separate estimation background sheet. Estimates can also be validated by peers using Fagan's Inspection method (1).

It is important to be aware that accurate estimation is not the primary objective of this method. We are mainly trying to find weak patches in our current design. These would be in the areas of objectives which have less than 100% total estimation. WE can then concentrate our attention on these weak objectives, designing more or better, until they are safe. It is not uncommon to insist on a <u>safety margin</u> of two ("200%") or more with this type of estimation.

There are several reasons why such estimation cannot be particularly accurate. They are mainly related to the fact that we use this tool in very early stages of design, where there is little detailed definition, and little control over implementation. For accurate estimates of complex design attributes,

I prefer to use early evolutionary
delivery steps of the system, to the real
environment (1). The limited objectives of
impact analysis are to give us some language
for overview of a complex set of design
ideas (techniques or solutions, I call them)
as compared with the design objectives target
levels - which are the only logical justification
for these design techniques.

I want the designer to take a greater professional responsibility for their design ideas,
by being asked to make estimates for all the
effects and side effects of each design idea
on all our critical design objectives.

HIERARCHICAL IMPACT TABLES

The tables can be applied at many levels of
analysis from total system overview (Fig.3)
to more detailed views of both objectives
and design techniques (Fig. 4 and 5.)
The ability to do this depends on a similar
initial hierarchical specification of the
design objectives (Fig. 1 and 2)

ADDING THE ESTIMATES TOGETHER

Since the estimates themselves are really
only a rough communications tool, we have
intentionally simplified the way we get
a "cumulative impact" estimate. We add the
detailed estimates arithmetically.
This is of course not completely realistic
for all kinds of reasons (synergistic and
"thrashing" or conflict effects). But anything else would be more complex than people are
willing to use, and would probably not serve
our limited purposes better (to spot
weak areas in design, early). There is of
course nothing in this method that prevents
people from making more accurate estimates
of cumulative effects. But, I would suggest
that it will be cheaper to measure realities.

UNCERTAINTY ESTIMATES

In many cases, though not in the case illustrated, we make uncertainty estimates.
For example 50 $\pm$ 20 - meaning we estimate
that the impact could be as low as 50-20 (30%)
or as high as 50+20 (70%), but we think 50% is
about right. We also cumulate these uncertainty
estimates algebraically, to give a total
uncertainty estimate. This is a healthy reminder
of the uncertainties caused by lack of knowledge
, by lack of detailed specification, and by
uncertainty about quality of implementation.

MAKING ESTIMATES

Estimates should be based on common sense
past experience and logic. They should be
acceptable to professional peers.
It is a useful test to let more than one
person make initial estimates, and ask why there
are different answers.

It would improve our software engineering
capability if we published more systematic
information on the multiple attributes of
techniques, as we have tried to do in
Humanized Input and Software Metrics.(2)&(3).

AUTOMATION OF THE IMPACT ANALYSIS TABLE

The table is suited to spread sheet analysis
techniques, and the impact of adding or
removing techniques can be analyzed dynamically.

We have also implemented it in a prototype
automated Design by Objectives system in UCSD
Apple PASCAL. (5). It is more integrated with
the other DBO tools there, than on a spread
sheet. For example the attribute specification
on the analysis table is directly derived
from the formal attribute (objectives) made
earlier in the DBO system specification. Also
the attributes of the techniques are brought in
from the software engineering handbook part
of the system.

```
----------------------------------------------------------------
   7 USABILITY
  .7.1 INPUT OUTPUT MEDIA INTEGRATEDNESS
measure = ease of using any (voice, graphics, text) with equal facility.
test= sample voice/text/graphics in & out handled by a novice "OK"(our demo)
worst (acceptable level) = 15 minutes.
plan  ( level of successful achievement) = 5 to 10 minutes
best ( state of the art limit ?)= one minute
now (present status of products) = not available at this meeting (18 Nov 82)
----------------
  .7.2 TRAINING NEED
measure = the node user training need
test = hours to solo capability ( no need for human assistance)
worst = less than one hour
plan = 6 minutes per application
best = approaching zero minutes (totally built in training and help).
see =  future detailed explsions by user tyep, see aslo objectives
        for demonstratability and installability which are related..
------------------
  .7.3  USER PRODUCTIVITY
measure = % time loss for user due to our systems obstruction
test = ratio of  ACTUALLY USED TASK TIME to IDEAL TASK TIME (no obstruction
worst= 1.5 to 1
plan=1.1 to 1
best 1 to 1
```

7. A D A P T A B I L I T Y

```
---------------
  .7.4 USER ERROR RATE
measure= their rate-of-correction to their own previous actions.
test = % of their previous actions changed, as measured by computer.
worst = less than 10%
PLAN = less than 3%
best = less than 1%
---------------------
  .7.5 USERS MINIMUM-QUALIFICATION LEVEL
measure = their ability in responding to their native language.(MINIMUM
test = our test , built into the system on-line.         REQ. )
worst =  90%* of responses correct in 15 minute test period.
PLAN = 80% correct responses  during 15 minute test.
best = we can teach our system to people who only get 40% correct in test.
note = we must plan to build a suitable simple dialogue test.
-----------------------
_.7.6  USER-LESS-NESS
measure = degree of system component ability to be unattended and remote
test = % of possible tasks which can be conducted in this mode  controlled.
worst =  50% ?
PLAN = approaching 100%
--------------------------
..7.7 COHERENTNESS
measure = perceived coherenttness as % of all products..
test = opinion survey.
worst = 95%
PLAN = approaching 100%
best = 100%
--------------------------
  .7.8 USER OPINION
measure = "positive feeling for product "
test = gallup of user sample about products they have used.
PLAN = 90% to 99%
now = ? 10% ??
```

FIG. 1 USABILITY QUANTIFIED

```
7.1 demonstratability
                    customer self-demonstratabiilty
                    our professional demonstr.7.1.2
7.2 installability
           customer    7.2.1
           professional on site  7.2.2
           professional ex works  7.2.3
7.3 interchangability
           replacability   7.3.1
           movability 7.3.2
           interface    7.3.3
7.4 upgradability
           node addability 7.4.1
           connection addability 7.4.2
           application addability 7.4.3
           subscriber addability 7.4.4
7.5 portability
           data portability 7.5.1
           logic portability 7.5.2
           command portability  7.5.3
           media portability 7.5.4
7.6 connectivity  ( see major  objective 2.)
```

FIG. 2 ANOTHER OBJECTIVE

```
example of actual definition
7.1.1 CUSTOMER SELF-DEMONSTRATABILITY
measure = ability of customer to solo self-demo any     product.
test = probability of successful completion of self-demo within 1 hour
worst acceptable case = 95% to 97%                  of arrival of it.
PLAN = approaching 99%
now = less than 5% of the line allows this now
```

THIS ESTIMATE WAS BUILT DIRECTLY ON DESIGNER INTUITION.
OBJECTIVES VS STRATEGIES ANALYSIS

infotecture; "softfaces"

FIG. 3

STRATEGIES (major design principles softfaces) OBJECTIVES top level	1. EXPERIENCE COLLECTION 9.Self-metric	2. USER SIMPLICITY + 3. VIRTUAL TERMINALS 6.PORTability 8.Self descrip.	ROBUSTNESS + STABILITY 10.Survival	7. Openendedness	FILE DESCRIPTOR ("FD")	Command + Mgr. Dialog Interface	SUM 100%=plan ±
0. profitability	5*	10	10	10	20	20	= 75%*
1. usability Plan= +10%better	30	30	30	20	20	40mo	=140%
2. connectivity	10	40	0	40	40	40	=170%
3. availability	30	20	30	10	20	20	=130%
4. integrity	10	10	20	5	20	-20(c) +10(mb)	=55% WEAK DESIGN MORE
5. performance	30	5	20	5	5	5	=70%
6. marketability >COMPETITORS	40	40	40	20	30	40	=%210
7. adaptability	30	30	10	50	30	30	=180%
8. dev. resources	20	30	30	0	30	30	=140%
9. mkt. cost&res.	0	0	0	0	0	0	= 0

ROBUSTNESS   OBJECTIVES VS STRATEGIES ANALYSIS
ANALYSIS

INFOTECTURE: "softfaces"

FIG. 4

strategies MS 4. ROBUSTNESS sub-objectives 1. USABILITY	4.1 AUTOMATIC CORRECTION 4.2 LOG 4.3Valid 4.4 CorCtl	4.5 SURVIVAL MODE 4.6Fail	4.7 REGRET	4.8 UNDO EASE	4.9 DEEP DIAGNOSIS	SUM 100%=plan
I/O MEDIA INTEGR (5-10 min. to use any)	5*	0	1	1	0	= 7%
TRAINING NEED (6 min./applic.)	20	10	1	1	5	=37%
USER PRODUCTIVITY (10% overhead)	20	20	1	1	-5	=38%
USER ERROR RATE (less than 3%)	1.	-10%	-10	-10	10	=-19%
USER QUALIFICATION (can give 80% correct responses)	5	0	2	2	5	=-14%
USER-LESS-NESS (ca. 100%)	10	30	0	0	5	=45%
COHERENTNESS (approach 100%)	5	5	1	1	0	=12%
USER OPINION (90% to 100%)	10	20	2	2	5	=39%

OBJECTIVES VS STRATEGIES ANALYSIS

"SIMPLICITY"
ANSIS INFOTECTURE: "softfaces"   FIG. 5

strategies 2. USER SIMPLICITY sub-objectives 1. USABILITY	MS 2.1 MINIMIZE WORK	MS 2.2 NATIVE TONGUE	MS 2.3 SELF TEACH	MS 2.4 NON ARBITRARINESS	MS 2.5 AUTO COMPLETION	OTHERS 2.6HD SUM 100%=plan	
I/O MEDIA INTEGR (5-10 min. to use any)	5 *	1	1	1	0	0	= 8% *
TRAINING NEED (6 min./applic.)	5	5	30	5	1	30	= 76%
USER PRODUCTIVITY (10% overhead)	20	5	10	5	1	20	= 61%
USER ERROR RATE (less than 3%)	10	10	10	5	1	5	41%
USER QUALIFICATION (can give 80% correct responses)	10	10	10	10	10	20	= 70%
USER-LESS-NESS (ca. 100%)	5	0	0	0	0	0	= 5%
COHERENTNESS (approach 100%)	5	6	5	5	5	10	= 35%
USER OPINION (90% to 100%)	20	30	30	20	10	30	=140%

THIS EXAMPLE SHOWS THE BUILDING UP OF AN ESTIMATE "BOTTOM UP"

REFERENCES

1. Gilb, T. Design by Objectives, North-Holland (1984 ?).

2. Gilb, T and Weinberg, G. M., Humanized Input, QED Publishers Inc. Wellesley Mass. USA 1984

3. Gilb, T. Software Metrics, Studentlitteratur, Lund, Sweden.

4. Gilb, T. Software Engineering Templates, (Manuscript)

5. Krzanik, L. and Gilb, T. Automated Design by Objectives. Available from UCSD Users Group Box 1148 La Jolla CA 92038 USA

OBJECTIVES VS STRATEGIES ANALYSIS

infotecture;   FIG. 6

STRATEGIES (major design principles softfaces) OBJECTIVES MS top level NIL	1. EXPERIENCE COLLECTION		
	2. USER SIMPLICITY	4. ROBUSTNESS	
	6.PORT-ability	STABIL-ITY	7.
	+ 9.Self-metric	8.Self-descrip.	10.Survival
0. profitability			
1. usability Plan= +10%better			
2. connectivity			

5→140% 60% *   -14→45% 25%

Human-Computer Interaction — INTERACT '84 / B. Shackel (ed.)
Elsevier Science Publishers B.V. (North-Holland)
© IFIP, 1985

GENERATIVE USER-ENGINEERING PRINCIPLES FOR USER INTERFACE DESIGN

Harold Thimbleby

Department of Computer Science
University of York
YORK, YO1 5DD, UK

Generative user-engineering principles are assertions about interactive system behaviour and have equivalent colloquial forms. Current work shows that they are a promising contribution to the design of acceptable user interfaces, because they effectively bridge the conceptual gap between designer and user. In colloquial form a generative user-engineering principle can be used to help clarify requirements in participative design, or to explicate documentation. In rigorous form, generative user-engineering principles provide a constructive higher order consistency on user interfaces.

1 INTRODUCTION

Currently, the best designed interactive systems are partly specified formally and partly developed through ad hoc accretion. Many such accretions are details for handling abnormal boundary conditions, which are usually afterthoughts to the formal specification. Despite 'user-engineering principles', no overall consistency emerges, and certainly no consistency which can be applied down to details. This is a disaster for the purposes of introducing an interactive system to new users, or for interactive systems which are intended for non-computer-expert use. This paper suggests that 'generative' principles should be employed as theorems over the system specification: this overcomes the bottom-up piece-meal approach of applying conventional user-engineering principles.

If, in addition, we require the user interface to be compatible with external requirements (and not merely internally consistent), the generative principles must be expressible in a form accessible to users. In a colloquial form a generative principle could be used in both requirements specification and in documentation. In one case, the principle would permit the user to contribute to higher-order requirements, and in the other case, even if the user has not participated in the system design, he could be given an unusually coherent view of it. The colloquial form must be judiciously chosen; in [1] the colloquial form is termed a 'metaphor' and excellent recommendations are given for their presentation.

We shall use the term 'generative user engineering principle' (abbreviated 'guep'), to distinguish a principle which has a colloquial form and can express constraints on the overt behaviour of a system. Necessarily a guep has to be compatible with human factors guidelines and this can be achieved weakly post hoc, because simply stating a system property makes a system easier to use. The longer term releases the basic term 'generative principle' to be used for specificational purposes where there may need be no human factors requirements at all.

Ideally, user interfaces may be designed by collaboration between user, ergonomist and computer scientist (using the three terms generally). However, each view has limitations which restrict communication and curtail the emergence of an overall design approach. This paper proposes using gueps as a 'thematic' requirement of the user interface behaviour expressible in colloquial task-oriented terms. With them, the user may have reasonable and well founded expectations; the ergonomist can check compatability of a system against them; and the computer scientist may rephrase them as theorems over the formal specification. In addition, gueps, as generative principles, impose a high degree of internal consistency.

The idea is not new, and appears to have been first used under the JOSS system, where gueps were termed 'rubrics'[2]. We could view the user model as an abstraction of required system behaviour, and under suitable definitions it could then be viewed as a guep.

1.1 Hypotheses

I am making a strong hypothesis that gueps exist and that they are useful for both designer and user. A weaker hypothesis is that only certain pre-evaluated forms of guep are properly effective, and therefore the approach is not applicable for novel user interfaces, where a set of suitable principles has not already been established. A still weaker hypothesis is that gueps have negligible effect on the user at the interface but are nonetheless useful in specification (as generative principles). Directions for research are discussed in §7.

2 GUEP VERSUS USER-ENGINEERING PRINCIPLE

User-engineering principles which are sufficiently constructive to be used in design are numerous and are highly task-specific[3]. In fact, many such principles appearing in the literature have been derived from very small experiments and it is dubious whether such hypotheses merit promotion to principles. It is unlikely that constructive principles can be generalised or used in combination reliably, certainly not without considerable design experience.

For example, it is not clear when a mouse outperforms key selection for selecting items from a known menu, though experiments suggest that unanticipated cursor positioning is faster using a mouse. Principles interact too strongly with user skill levels, task dimensions (frequency, openness), hardware (e.g. resolution, response times), psychosocial issues (e.g. consequences of user performance and error), and may even be in mutual conflict. Really, user-engineering principles, at this level, can be used no more constructively than as suggestions for particular design features.

A user-engineering principle is an informal requirements statement, which is yet too sophisticated for the user and can still be interpreted by the designer with considerable freedom. A typical user-engineering principle from [4] illustrates this: "User orientation must be maintained throughout a session. Information detailing the user's status should be displayed." However some principles operate at a higher level (e.g. be consistent, reduce modes) and could be formalised as requirements over the entire specification. These two particular principles happen to be relatively trivial in relation to a formal specification, but nonetheless are too sophisticated for computer-naive users.

Distinctively generative user-engineering principles meet four criteria: (i) they can be expressed formally (ii) they have a colloquial form (iii) in common with user-engineering principles (which can be instantiations of gueps), they embody certain ergonomic guidelines and (iv) they are constructive rather than descriptive.

3 EXAMPLES

3.1 Gueps for Concealed Information

Information in user interfaces may be concealed by a variety of means, usually with the intention of making the dialogue more rapid (e.g. because less needs to be said), catering for varying levels of user skill or for folding complex information into uncluttered forms.

Typical mechanisms for concealing information range from the straightforward absence of the information (as in default command operands), forms of abstraction (as in macros), to symbolic expressions (as in regular expressions). The purpose of the relevant guep is to express constraints on these kinds of mechanisms, and hence improve the chances of designing a consistent user interface (and, additionally, give the user an explicit key to the particular form of consistency). The distinction between gueps and user-engineering principles is now perhaps a little clearer: a plausible user-engineering principle might suggest that "defaultable operands should occupy a consistent position" but this is very specific; it has a limited domain (in this case certainly to linear command strings) and it is not at all clear that one can be used effectively in formal design, an area where human factors expertise is generally absent.

In comparison a plausible guep would be that (**a**) "only complete instances of syntactic categories may be abstracted (i.e. replaced by names, marks, abbreviations or stubs) or concealed (i.e. eliminated from the operand set altogether)". This might be supplemented by the following: (**b**) "information may be totally concealed locally, but there must be a convention to indicate this is occurring"; (**c**) "information concealing/revealing never occurs as a side-effect" (e.g. a search would not unfold data which contains the searched-for items so the user is left at the same level of abstraction); (**d**) "the body of an abstraction is consistently available as an operand"; (**e**) "the abstraction mechanism is conservative and invertible". In fact, these gueps might be part of a stronger set which implies the commutativity of the operations required to implement them.

For clarity we shall introduce the terminology: a **fold** is an instance of an abstraction or concealment and **folding** is the act of abstracting away or concealing information. Similarly, **unfolding** is the inverse act, of exposing the concealed information. If abstraction requires naming, unfolding is not normally considered to lose the name, nor the extent of the abstract's body — in other words unfolding is normally invertible.

The gueps above may be formalised in terms of the chosen formal specification method, thus their correct application may be established mechanically. As required by the user, a more colloquial expression of these gueps is that only entire objects are folded, one is always made aware of any folding, and objects must be folded by some direct act (this last point not only encourages faith in the predictable nature of the user-interface, but expresses the fact that the user is in control of the abstraction level of the interface and the skill level it consequentially requires).

Since these concepts may be unfamiliar, they are applied to two application areas:

3.1.1 Linear Command Languages

We may view a default as the user folding system-known information: however the system normally echoes the command which may remain displayed for some time, perhaps until it scrolls out of sight. In this case, the echoed form conceals information from the user about the history of the system's actions. Adhering to (**b**), the echoed form should minimally indicate that a default has been assumed. Adhering to (**e**), the user should be able to determine what default has been taken.

Macros are a very direct way of permitting the user control over abstraction. If we adhere to the suggested guep (**a**), the system should impose syntactic constraints on the bodies of macros. (Most macro interfaces fail to do this.)

3.1.2 Menu Based Systems

Single-level menus often grow to such size that the entire range of options cannot be displayed. Unfortunate systems exist which flaunt (**b**) and therefore surprise their users when they select non-displayed choices.

If rest of the menu is folded (for example, by providing an option 'others'), adherence to (**e**) suggests that a function must exist to return to the enclosing menu. Of course, if the menu is arranged as a tree, (**e**) suggests that this 'go back' function is uniformly available.

3.2 "What You See is What You Get"

The well worn maxim "what you see is what you get" is an ideal example. In simple English, this phrase specifies certain properties of a user interface which, with a little explanation, may be used for the user to develop hypotheses about system behaviour. The phrase may also be placed on a more formal base as follows [5]:

A display can be considered a function **content->view**, with **view** perhaps as **position->symbol** (= **pixel***). Operations on **content**s, such as edits are **content** transformations (**content->content**) with corresponding display transformations (**view->view**) to provide feedback on the outcome of the edits. The "what you see is what you get" simply requires the display function to be a morphism of the **contents** and **view** transformations. The user can then equally view commands acting on his data (**content**) or on what he can see displayed (**view**): this may be non-trivial to specify because in most applications the display function is a projection with no inverse, so some 'obvious' (easy to use) **view** transformations are complex **content** transformations. Indeed, most user interface problems stem from the non-uniform conventions for the display transformation: obscure quoting and meta conventions are introduced (cf §3.4). Consequently, a user interface which adheres to the "what you see" guep may well be more consistent and easier to use, but it is very likely to be much harder to implement.

It should be noted that the accepted interpretation of "what you see" by the computer-science community is different from the semantics presented above. Here, we have simply taken a workable phrase and shown how it might be utilised — after all, users who are presented with this guep need not know of its other (weaker) connotations. The non-standard semantics are explored in [6] and the usual interpretation is discussed further in §6.2.

3.3 "It Can Be Used With Your Eyes Shut"

Being able to use a system 'with your eyes shut' clearly implies a very predictable interface. But if the user really did shut his eyes, to be able to make effective use of the system, the interface would have to be mode free and indicate diagnostics in a non-visual mode (e.g. audibly) and rapidly, to be synchronised with the occurrence of the error, rather than at the end of a unit utterance in a dialogue. In a keyboarded application this requires per-character interaction and a postfix (or function key) command structure. Already we have quite definite technical constraints consistent with the view of the interface the user may have been encouraged to elaborate from exactly the same principle. See [7] for further discussion.

3.4 Gueps for Quoting Mechanisms

Any general purpose system will require quoting mechanisms. For example, a text editor must allow a user to issue commands and to enter text to a file which, for example, could document those commands. When the commands are entered as documentation, they should not be executed and therefore they have to be quoted, that is, interpreted in some non-command mode. In addition, a text editor would normally provide a command which allows the user to search for textual patterns: the patterns will use metacharacters which may be overloadings of textual characters. To search for a textual character which is overloaded requires the character to be quoted.

Perhaps quoting mechanisms most frequently arise where different input/output devices have different resolutions or character sets. Users are confused by the consequent overloading e.g. "^K" denoting 'control-shift-K', not 'up-arrow' 'K': the problem would not arise if there was a displayable form for 'control-shift-K' compatible with the keyboard legends. (In this particular case quoting is implicitly determined by context.)

Few systems impose any consistency over quoting mechanisms, and a number actually have misleading documentation in this respect†. This is probably because quoting is tedious to specify and usually slips past the formal specification. (A set theoretic approach is used in [8].) This often results in an unnecessary

---

† For example, **lex** [16] documentation asserts that \ followed by any character denotes itself. So * denotes a star, \\\\ a backslash, but \\n a newline! An alternative quoting mechanism provided by **lex** is to place literal text between quote marks. There is no simple relation between the two quoting mechanisms: "n" ‡ \\n, but "*" ≡ *. The latter mechanism cuts across the phrase structure (e.g. "ab"* ≡ "a"("b"*) where * is a postfix operator) and, indeed, is subordinate to certain operators (e.g. ["]" is ill-formed).

profusion of unrelated quoting mechanisms, some
of which cut across the phrase structure of the
interface.

A guep is needed which might express some of the
following constraints: there is one quoting
mechanism which is permanently available (e.g.
there is a dedicated `quote' key); quoted
composite objects become atomic; the quoting
mechanism superordinates all other functions.

4 CHARACTERISING GUEPS

Gueps will be most practical as a contribution
to design method, rather than as a contribution
to catalogues of acceptable interface
techniques. To this end we must recognise what
characterises gueps.

For the user, gueps explain in straight-forward
language higher-order properties of the user
interface which affect its `feel'. For example,
a guep may verbalise a perceptual-motor routine,
or a group of related routines (cf §5.1). Or
the principle might define a second level
grammar [9] or predicates over the formal
specification:- there are many possibilities and
until further research indicates a particularly
promising form it will be better to treat
`generative user-engineering principle' as a
generic term. For the designer, the principles
constrain the interface to avoid what has been
termed `interaction uncertainty' [10] or
`under-determination' [11] — as the user
interface is powerful enough to exhibit any
behaviour, the user has less confidence that it
will exhibit any particular behaviour.

Thus gueps constrain the machine and explain the
interface — in a manner which was not previously
accessible to the user, and once verbalised may
be used by the user constructively, probably
using an acquired or taught inference procedure.

5 THE CHARACTERISTICS OF SYSTEMS MOST
EFFECTIVELY DESCRIBED

Necessarily, gueps have an effective domain, and
it is constructive to characterise that property
of interactive systems which would make them
more suitable for applying gueps.

It seems clear that the purpose of a guep is
partly to make a property of the system `second
nature' (autonomic) to the user. This can only
occur when the user's reasoning can leave
symbolic processing and, instead, have rapid
feedback of progress and so on. In short, the
interface should be `manipulative'. The
condensed observations in the following section
are largely due to Ben Shneiderman, whose
excellent paper should be consulted[12]. Other
positive comments have been made about
manipulative interfaces in the literature, e.g.
[13].

5.1 Manipulative Interfaces

User interfaces which support direct
manipulation use a fixed and commensurate
representation for application objects (often a
`real world' view or reasonable icon). The
actions the user may perform affecting the
objects are atomic; consequently the user does
not have to reason about command composition to
achieve logically immediate goals. As all
atomic actions are rapid, they may be used
incrementally and reversibly.

An example of direct manipulation in an
interface is the use of four cursor control keys
(i.e. keys labelled `up', `down', `left' and
`right') instead of textual commands (such as
`move 23,47'), requiring numerical coordinates
or offsets. Manipulative interfaces provide
immediate feedback on each atomic action (e.g.
`per-character' interaction). On typing the key
labelled `up', the cursor would move up; whereas
with the command form, the cursor cannot be
moved until the multi-keystroke command `move
how much' is completed. To determine `how much'
cognitive processing (e.g. counting) is
required, in distinction to the (iterative)
perceptual-motor processing used with atomic
commands.

A manipulative interface supports layered
learning: a manipulative interface may be used
immediately by novices (probably after a hands-
on demonstration), and with growing experience
the user will be able to use it more and more
effectively without abandoning his initial
perceptions.

With manipulative systems, casual users can
retain essential concepts readily, yet expert
users can work rapidly. Users experience less
anxiety because the system is comprehensible,
because their actions are invertible. Since
objects have a fixed and commensurate
representation it is plain whether the users'
actions further their immediate goals. Indeed,
sophisticated diagnostics are rarely necessary.
Using a direct manipulation system is self-
motivating.

5.2 Self-Demonstrating Interfaces

If a system uses direct manipulation, it may be
demonstrated to the user by the system itself.
This is obviously easiest to do on a graphics
terminal using light pen or touch screen for
input (as a finger or light pen might be
displayed on the screen, demonstrating the
possible user actions explicitly). A self-
demonstration approach cannot be so direct using
a textual command system; and the prejudice that
`a system is not easy to use if it needs help'
presumably arises because non-manipulative,
non-self-demonstrable, systems are manifestly
harder to use.

5.3 Passive Interfaces

A user interface is passive if the manifest

action and object worlds are commensurate (for example, the commands and their operands must be mode-free); passivity requires an interface to be uniformly manipulative. A manipulative system is a candidate to be well described by a guep, but for the principle to be uniformly applicable, the user interface must in addition satisfy passivity[14].

Passivity is essentially a restraint on the system not to do too much in anticipation of the user (or worse, occasionally do too much): this anticipation may occur either during the system design or during a particular dialogue. Simply increasing passivity in the obvious way, by decreasing hidden activity, variation and complexity but keeping the dialogue style constant may be too restrictive — instead a different, more manipulative style should be chosen and passivity is thereby increased without loss of effectiveness.

6 A WARNING AGAINST PSEUDO-GENERATIVE PRINCIPLES

There is a class of principle which superficially meets the criteria for gueps. Two outstanding examples are (1) the 'desk-top model', that is, the interface should simulate a user's desk-top displaying appropriate icons mapping onto objects which might be found on office desk tops, such as calculators and spread sheets. And (2) the "what you see..." principle as conventionally interpreted.

6.1 The Desk-Top Model

It will expose the misconception in the desk-top view of man-machine interaction if you consider the horseless-carriage period at the beginning of this century. The initial approach to designing cars followed the obvious 'generative' principle of being compatible with the functional predecessor. This resulted in machines which were no doubt familiar and 'easy to use' but which pushed carriage technology to limits, e.g. in suspension, steering, coachwork and so on. The principle (not that it was ever espoused as such) led to the exposure of limitations in contemporary technology — far from constraining it. So far as I am aware the horseless-carriage period achieved no standardisation in the user interface, not even the development of the steering wheel. Similarly, the desk-top approach in office automation leads inevitably to display processing requirements (e.g. to scroll A4 text in real time in arbitrary direction) which are certainly an impetus to technological development but may not be a valid approach to designing a user interface per se.

6.2 What You See is What You Get

As conventionally interpreted, "what you see..." implies equivalent resolution for hardcopy and display devices (when there is usually an order of magnitude difference). It may also be taken to imply real-time formatting and screen updates. Again, the principle primarily encourages systems research rather than either an improved user interface or research towards one. See [6].

7 DIRECTIONS FOR RESEARCH

7.1 In Formal Specification

Gueps may be more defined in terms of formal requirements (e.g. as assertions about the specification). Whether algebraic (cf [15], which formalises such questions as, "Is it the case that pictures are not transparent or even translucent? I.e. if two pictures overlap does the bottom one have no effect on what one sees through the top one?") or constructive methods (such as VDM) are most suitable remains to be determined. Some of the gueps appear to require an explicit time metric and this is not satisfactorily modelled by any existing formal technique.

7.2 In User Interface Design Methodology

It is not clear how gueps may be used prescriptively in general, and a design methodology is wanting. For example, some gueps are very general and allow considerable choice over design.

7.3 In User Interface Evaluation

The gueps may alternatively be selected for their psychological effectiveness. Psychological experiments might establish whether gueps have any significant effect on end users — which is possible because the interface is better designed or because the users know more about the form of the design. Whether the effect, for example, is limited to accelerating the time to reach criterion; what gueps the users establish for themselves in the absence of explicit gueps; whether, conversely, semantic-free gueps have any effect.

These three research areas need to interact, to avoid unintelligible gueps which are helpful in design, or helpful gueps for users which are too vague for formal expression. It is also possible that there exist principles (i.e. certain forms of user-interface consistency) which are actually detrimental to usage, in which case the stronger hypothesis of §1.1 is falsified in an unhedged form.

8 SUMMARY

This paper has been an exploratory introduction to 'generative user-engineering principles', and has not been intended to be superficially rigorous when considerable effort is still required to find useful definitions. The intention has been to demonstrate the potential for higher-order guiding principles which may be used throughout design and help bridge the gap between designers and users.

Generative user-engineering principles are easily understood and used both by user and designer. They can be expressed in such terms that

- The user interface may be designed top-down, using gueps as guidelines to select appropriate low-level features.

- The user has a sound basis on which to construct an understanding of the system, even before using it.

- The user may generalise his knowledge reliably. The user is confident as to what <u>has</u> happened (e.g. after an error), and does not need debugging skills.

- The user is encouraged to use his skills fully. Gueps can help enhance the view that what the user does is <u>real</u> and not abstract. This is especially motivating.

- The designer can use gueps to meet clearly defined user expectations, often with specific techniques.

- A manipulative and passive style of interaction is encouraged.

Having once suggested a basis for the user model, the designer is under an obligation to ensure its coherent implementation through careful system design, which should maintain the model as understood by the user — this approach will entail evaluation and retrospective refinement.

I believe that generative principles, plus attention to detail, already provide a constructive approach to the top-down design of effective, acceptable, interactive systems. At the very least, even if a guep is ergonomically unsound, an interactive system explicitly designed around it will have more internal consistency and be more clearly documented than the average interactive system available today.

9 ACKNOWLEDGEMENTS

Michael Harrison, John Long, Ian Pyle, Andy Whitefield and others made major comments on earlier drafts of this paper for which I am very grateful.

10 REFERENCES

[1] Carroll J. M. & Thomas J. C., Metaphor and the Cognitive Representation of Computing Systems, IEEE Transactions on Systems, Man, and Cybernetics, **SMC-12**, 107-116 (1982)

[2] Baker C. L., JOSS: Rubrics, P-3560, RAND Corp. (1967).

[3] Smith S. L., User-System Interface Design for Computer-Based Information Systems, ESD-TR-82-132, MITRE Corp. (1982).

[4] Engel S. E. & Granada R. E., TR 00.2720, IBM Poughkeepsie Laboratory (1975)

[5] Harrison M. D. & Thimbleby H. W. Formalising User Requirements for a Display Editor, University of York, To appear.

[6] Thimbleby H. W., 'What you see is what you have got' – a user engineering principle for manipulative display? 70-84 in Balzert E. H. (ed) Software Ergonomie (Teubner, Stuttgart, 1983)

[7] Thimbleby H. W. Character Level Ambiguity: Consequences for User Interface Design, International Journal of Man-Machine Studies, **16**, 211-225 (1982)

[8] Sufrin B. Formal Specification of a Display Editor, PRG-21, Oxford University Computing Laboratory (1981)

[9] Green T. R. G & Payne S. J. Higer-Order Rules in the Perception of Grammars, Memo 544, MRC Social and Applied Psychology Unit, Sheffield University (1983)

[10] Hansen W. J., Doring R. & Whitlock L. R. Why an Examination was Slower On-line than on Paper, International Journal of Man-Machine Studies, **15**, 507-519 (1978)

[11] Thimbleby H. W. Dialogue Determination, International Journal of Man-Machine Studies, **13**, 295-304 (1980)

[12] Shneiderman B. Direct Manipulation: A Step Beyond Programming Languages, IEEE Computer, **16** 57-69 (1983)

[13] Brooks F. P. The Computer 'Scientist' as Toolsmith — Studies in Interactive Computer Graphics, in Gilchrist E. B. (ed) IFIP Conference Information Processing '77, Toronto, 625-634 (1977)

[14] Thimbleby H. W. Interactive Technology: The Role of Passivity, in Bensel C. K. (ed) Proceedings Human Factors Society, Boston, **23**, 80-84 (1979)

[15] Guttag J. & Horning J. J. Formal Specification as a Design Tool, in 7th ACM Symposium on POPL, Las Vegas (1980)

[16] Lesk M. E. Lex — A Lexical Analyser Generator, Computer Science Technical Report No. 32, Bell Laboratories, Murray Hill, New Jersey (1975)

Empirical Guidelines and a Model for Writing Computer Documentation

Darlene Clement

Institute of Human Learning
University of California, Berkeley
Berkeley, CA 94720

A model of the computer manual comprehension task is proposed in which four processes operate simultaneously: task-mapping of the structure of regular procedures onto the structure of computer commands, constructing a mental model of the computer system, inducing the command language grammar, and learning the structure of computer procedures. Findings from a study of five novices' comprehension problems with UNIX[1] documentation are analyzed in terms of these four processes. The model and the findings from the study yield general heuristics and specific recommendations for document developers.

1.0 INTRODUCTION

Discussions of how to make computer documentation comprehensible to novices have tended to emphasize superficial aspects of the problem, such as style, amount of jargon, or "good" sentence structure. However, the problem is fundamentally one of the cognitive processes involved in text comprehension, and the specific knowledge structures tapped by a technical text. This paper describes both an empirical study of novices' difficulties in understanding computer documentation, and a model derived from it which suggests guidelines for writing more effective documentation.

2.0 A STUDY AND A MODEL

An in-depth qualitative study was carried out in which 5 novices attempted to learn UNIX with only a manual to guide them. The subjects were asked to read a section of two locally produced tutorials in advance of meeting with the researcher. The tutorials covered file manipulation and text editing with a line-oriented editor called "Edit." During the meetings subjects used the computer to follow the instructions in the tutorial. The 5 sessions lasted two hours on average and were tape recorded, yielding approximately 10 hours of tape from each subject.

The model derived from the analysis of the data partitions the information contained in computer manuals into four classes, each with a corresponding comprehension task. **Functional** information describes the purpose of each command and triggers a **task-mapping** comprehension process. In this process, users map the new functional information given in the manual onto their tacit models of regular text-editing and general office procedures. Examples of such pre-existing models are the familiar procedures of cutting and pasting text in documents, creating new files, and typewriter editing. **Structural** information describes the underlying structures and processes of the computer system itself. A description of a device triggers a **model-building** process in which the reader attempts to construct a mental model of how the device functions, for example, how the editor buffer and disk (important entities which the user never sees) are related. **Command** information describes the way in which commands are issued. It triggers the **command learning** process in which users attempt to learn the syntax and semantics of the command language. **Procedural** information provides directions for navigating through the system, i.e., knowing which command to issue in which context. The corresponding **procedure learning** process entails recognizing these different program contexts, and learning the order in which commands must be issued.

Though each of these processes taps radically different knowledge structures, they are fundamentally the same: in each case it is necessary for the new information to connect with the reader's knowledge base. It is apparent from the problems novices had that the documentation they used had serious shortcomings in each of these areas. Examples of the problems the subjects had with each process will be described in turn.

2.1 TASK-MAPPING

The task-mapping process was initially described in [2] as a global process of mapping the structure of the regular editing task onto the corresponding computer version of the task. So, for example, the regular editing procedure of changing a word by crossing it out and writing another word above it, gets mapped to the text editor's substitute command. Recently, this process has been analyzed in more detail by Moran [5]. Moran states that the users' knowledge of editing procedures consists of at least eight editing functions (add, remove, change, transpose, move, copy, split, join) which operate on five text entities (character, word, sentence, line, paragraph). The 37 tasks that result from the combination of editing functions and text entities constitute the core knowledge the user possesses. This knowledge comprises the "external task space." The computer system also has entities and operations defined within it, but these may be very different from the ones the user knows. The entities and operations internal to the computer constitute the "internal task space." Moran gives the example of a system that defines only one entity (a character string) and only three editing operations. With this system users must learn to conflate the five separate text entities they are familiar with onto this one system entity, and the eight editing functions they are used to must be collapsed onto three: cut, paste, and insert. In other words, the task-mapping process requires that the user learn to carry out familiar tasks by means of unfamiliar functions which operate on unfamiliar entities.

The operation of this process was especially evident when subjects attempted to learn the UNIX **read** command. This command allows a file to be inserted into the file currently being revised, that is, it allows the user to cut and paste. How is it similar to conventional cutting and pasting? In both the computer version and the regular version of the cutting and pasting procedure, the point at which the new information is to be inserted must be located. Then the pasting action can be carried out: in the computer procedure the "read" command is issued; in the regular procedure the material is actually pasted in. There are two ways in which the procedures differ. First, in regular cutting and pasting the material pasted in typically no longer exists in its original location. In contrast, in the computer version of the task, the file pasted in still exists as a separate file. Second, in regular cutting and pasting usually only *part* of a remote document is spliced into the document under revision. In contrast, in computer cutting and pasting the *entire* remote file is pasted in, not just a section of it.

In the manual the command was described as follows:

Reading additional files (r)

The **read (r)** command allows you to add the contents of a file to the buffer at a specified location, essentially copying new lines between two existing lines. To use it, specify the line after which the new text will be placed, the **read (r)** command, and then the name of the file. If you have a file named "example", the command

　　:$r example
"example" 18 lines, 473 characters

reads the file "example" and adds it to the buffer after the last line. The current filename is not changed by the read command. [4] (p. 22)

In general, the subjects had difficulty understanding this paragraph. After they were told that it referred to cutting and pasting, further discussion revealed their attempts to map the structure of the regular procedure onto the computer procedure. Two subjects thought that the file pasted in disappears from its original location. Notice that this is what would be predicted from a model of regular editing. Another subject wondered if only part of the remote file is pasted in, or the whole file.

From a text comprehension standpoint this paragraph from the manual is reminiscent of passages used in text comprehension studies in the early 70's (e.g., [3]) where subjects were presented with texts that were incomprehensible without a title. Once a title was provided the texts were easily comprehended because *the title triggered the schema that the text was about.* Similarly, this text would have been easier for the subjects to assimilate had the cutting and pasting schema been activated at the outset, say, in the heading. This is a point that can be of use to document developers. Once the appropriate regular-editing schema is activated then the task-mapping process can be carried out more easily. The document developer can further facilitate the task-mapping process by explicitly comparing the similarities and differences between the regular editing procedure and the computer procedure. This is Heuristic 1 in table 1. Providing this information would reduce the amount of inferencing the reader would have to engage in, and would simultaneously answer the reader's questions.

2.2 MODEL BUILDING

Important components of the system were described in a glossary at the beginning of the manual (e.g., the executive program, the editor buffer, and the disk). Then various aspects of the system's functioning were explained as each command was introduced. For example, the manual explains that the editor program's **write** command causes a copy of the file in the editor buffer to be sent to the disk for storage. In short, the model of the system was distributed throughout the text. Though this method of presentation reduces the risk of information overload, the study revealed that novices have difficulty constructing a coherent model of the system when it is presented in a piecemeal fashion. For example, they confused both the buffer and the mail program with the executive program, and the buffer with the concept of a mode. One subject issued a command to the executive program to make a copy of an existing file. Afterwards, she asked if it was necessary to issue the editor program's **write** command in order to "save" the newly created file. The subject thought the editor buffer was involved here, since it is associated with the creation of files. Based on these examples, Heuristic 3 suggests that the device topology and important actions be presented (at a high level of abstraction) at the beginning of the manual so that novices can construct a coherent model of the system.

2.3 COMMAND LEARNING

The last two sections discussed problems users have mapping regular editing procedures onto computer editing procedures, and constructing a model of the computer system. The topic to be discussed in this section involves both of the preceding ones in addition to posing its own set of difficulties. Effective use of the command language requires: 1) knowing what command to issue (the mapping aspect), 2) knowing, at some level, how the system interprets the command (the system-model aspect), and 3) knowing *how* to issue the command (understanding the syntax and semantics of the command language). Non-programmers have difficulty deducing the syntax and semantics of the command language primarily because: 1) the syntax is complex, and 2) they have no familiarity with the entities referred to on the command line, viz., programs, files, and special symbols.

The data revealed many examples of the fuzzy notions novices have about command statements. One kind of error was to confuse program names with filenames. One subject asked if "people" in the command statement "cat people" is a filename or a command. Another subject typed "cat mail" which is incorrect because both **mail** and **cat** are pro-

grams. These errors, which subjects made after more than 5 hours using the system, are surprising because one would think that they would have noticed that program names always appear first on the command line, followed by nothing, or one or more files.

A second kind of error involved determining the placement of spaces on the command line. Subjects would look directly at command statements in the manual and ask if spaces were to be typed between the components. One subject asked why filenames cannot have embedded blanks. Together these questions reveal the subjects' inability to envision how the machine parses command lines. Despite the numerous examples of command statements in the manual, the subjects were unable to induce the grammar. Therefore, Heuristic 4 suggests that the grammar of the command language be made explicit.

2.4 PROCEDURE LEARNING

According to the Card, Moran, and Newell [1] model of the manuscript editing task, an expert's knowledge structure consists of goals, operators, methods, and selection rules. That is, experts have pre-stored information about the sequence of operations and alternative methods available for performing an editing task. It is this knowledge that the novice must acquire from the manual and from interactions with the system.

It is clear from the data that novices come to the procedure learning task with a rudimentary procedure schema containing slots for goals, steps, and methods. However, the process of filling these slots is not easy to do if the role of each piece of information is not clearly marked in the text. For example, one section of the tutorial described how to correct typographical errors with a line-oriented editor. To carry out this task the user must understand three things: 1) how the editor functions (the need to position it on the relevant line); 2) the sequence of steps necessary for carrying out the task; and 3) the various methods that can be used to carry out the task. The structure of the task is as follows:

Goal: Correct typographical error in text.

Step 1: Position editor on relevant line.

Method 1: Search for pattern on relevant line.

Method 2: Type number of relevant line.

Step 2: Issue substitute command.

This structure was not apparent in the manual as the following examples demonstrate. Two subjects assumed that the task had been completed, i.e., that the correction had been made, after performing only the first step in the procedure. This indicates that the two-step nature of the task was not evident. One subject read about the two methods for carrying out a step and assumed that each method was a necessary part of the sequence. This indicates that the various methods were not clearly marked as alternatives. After reading the two pages describing the procedure, one subject, after much thought, managed to induce the two-step structure of the task. Together these examples show how much inferencing the subjects were forced to do, and how difficult it was for them.

The research previously mentioned shows that the expert's knowledge is a finely articulated goal structure in which the steps and methods are clearly differentiated. The writer could facilitate the construction of this structure by simply making it explicit. If the goals, steps, and methods of the procedure were explicitly marked in the text, then the novice would be able to assimilate each piece of information, as it is read, to the appropriate slot in the schema. This is Heuristic 6. Like the suggestions put forth in the other sections, this suggestion also reduces the amount of inferencing the reader would have to do.

3.0 CONCLUSIONS

The model and the findings from the study give a general picture of the complex processes involved in comprehending a technical text. It was shown that the information contained in a computer manual taps four different kinds of knowledge which trigger four different comprehension tasks. In one respect, however, the tasks are the same: each one requires that a connection be established between the new information and the reader's knowledge base. The study revealed cases where these connections were weak, incorrect, or nonexistent.

Problems with the task-mapping process demonstrated the difficulty of understanding the relationship between the computer and non-computer ways of performing text-editing tasks. Non-programmers base their assumptions about the way computer commands function on their implicit model of office procedures. But while the task-mapping process was riddled by weak or incorrect connections between the new information and the reader's knowledge, the model building process was hampered because no connections were made at all. The subjects had sketchy and erroneous ideas of what the computer was like and how it worked, in part because they lacked knowledge of basic

computer concepts, and because the manual failed to present the information in a way that they could assimilate. Problems with the command-learning process revealed novices' inability to induce the grammar of the command language from the examples in the manual, which made no attempt to link the new information with the reader's knowledge. Possibly, English grammar might provide such a link. Finally, problems with the procedure learning process revealed consistent misinterpretations of sections of the manual which lacked an explicit goal-based organization. Since the structure of the text did not conform to reader's expectations, the information was assimilated to incorrect slots in their procedure schema.

The analysis of the schemata which novices bring to the text can aid in the task of *packaging* information to meet the reader's needs. The benefit of this approach is that it yields *psychologically-based* heuristics for document development which address the important conceptual aspects of comprehending computer documentation.

1UNIX is a trademark of Bell Laboratories.

REFERENCES

[1] Card, S. K., Moran, T. P., & Newell, A. Computer text-editing: An information-processing analysis of a routine cognitive skill, *Cognitive Psychology*, 12 (1980) 32-74.

[2] Clement, D. Comprehending Computer Documentation, Unpublished manuscript. (March, 1983).

[3] Dooling, D. J., & Lachman, R. Effects of comprehension on retention of prose, *Journal of Experimental Psychology*, 88 (1971) 216-222.

[4] *Edit: A Tutorial,* Documentation produced by the U.C. Berkeley Computer Center. (March, 1982).

[5] Moran, T. P. Getting into a System: External-Internal Task Mapping Analysis, *Proceedings of the Conference on Human-Computer Interaction* (Boston, MA. 1983).

Table 1		
Model-based Heuristics and Recommendations for Document Developers		
Task mapping	Heuristic 1: Compare steps and outcomes of regular procedures with computer procedures in order to anticipate reader's expectations and questions.	Recommendation 1: Make use of comparisons to regular text editing operations. Specifically, note the explicit differences and implicit parallels.
	Heuristic 2: Provide examples of common uses of each command.	Recommendation 2: Give examples of the regular tasks that a command performs.
Model building	Heuristic 3: Provide an overview at the beginning of the manual that describes the major components of the particular computer system.	Recommendation 3: Provide an overview of how each program functions.
		Recommendation 4: Use puzzles to help novices refine their mental models of the system.
Command learning	Heuristic 4: Make the structure of the command language explicit.	Recommendation 5: Exaggerate the spacing between components of example command lines in order to make the spacing obvious.
		Recommendation 6: Explain the syntax and semantics of the command language in terms of the knowledge people already possess.
Procedure learning	Heuristic 5: Make the relationship between program contexts clear.	Recommendation 7: Summarize typical procedural sequences within each program context.
		Recommendation 8: Indicate which commands must be issued in a fixed sequence.
	Heuristic 6: Use a goal-based organization to structure the text according to readers' expectations.	Recommendation 9: Use a step-by-step format organized in terms of goals, methods, subprocedures, etc.
		Recommendation 10: Provide overviews for manual sections and in them make explicit the goals of the section.
		Recommendation 11: Avoid the use of technical terms in headings.
		Recommendation 12: Make the interpretation of conditional statements clear.

EVALUATION — APPROACHES AND METHODS

Human-Computer Interaction — INTERACT '84 / B. Shackel (ed.)
Elsevier Science Publishers B.V. (North-Holland)
© IFIP, 1985

A HUMAN FACTORS EVALUATION OF THE IBM SHEFFIELD PRIMARY CARE SYSTEM

Mike Fitter, Garry Brownbridge, Bob Garber and Guy Herzmark

MRC/ESRC Social and Applied Psychology Unit,
The University
SHEFFIELD S10 2TN, UK

The IBM Sheffield Primary Care System was an experimental system developed by the IBM
UK Scientific Centre in co-operation with Sheffield University Medical School. It was
installed in two General Practices for a trial two year period and evaluated by the
Social and Applied Psychology Unit.

In this paper we report on our evaluation objectives and techniques which focus on the
'human factors' aspects of designing and implementing a complex and comprehensive
information system in an unfamiliar and relatively unstructured environment. We argue
that an effective way of learning from the project is to focus on difficulties that
arose and were experienced by users. We conclude that although certain specific
problems resulting from the design of the user interface did occur, these were relatively minor, and in this respect the system was well liked. The most significant
issues arose from the organisational impact and the mismatch between the system and
the user organisations ie the 'organisational interface'.

1   INTRODUCTION

'Human factors' research is concerned with understanding the requirements for the effective use
of information systems in a way that is acceptable and satisfying to users. This paper
contributes to this understanding by reporting
an evaluation of a complex and experimental
computer system installed in two user organisations which had no prior experience of computer
use. Users were highly satisfied with the 'user
interface', the keyboard and screen layout, and
the communication dialogue and structure were
agreed to be appropriate and designed to a high
standard. Yet by the end of the two year trial
period of installation one organisation was using
no more than half of the available facilities,
and the other had stopped using virtually all the
system. An effective way of learning from the
project, and from the experience of designers and
users is to focus on the difficulties that arose
and that led to substantially less than full use.
These lie in the area of the 'organisational
interface' rather than the user interface.

1.1   The evaluation objectives

In a collaborative three year project the IBM UK
Scientific Centre and the Sheffield University
Medical School developed the IBM Sheffield
Primary Care System (SPCS). This was installed
in two General Practices in the Sheffield area.
We undertook a human factors evaluation of the
system whose general aim, as stated in the
research agreement with IBM, was "... primarily
concerned with investigating the acceptability
and evaluating the usefulness and effect of the
IBM Sheffield Primary Care System within General
Practice, and particularly within the Practices

in which it is installed. The intention is to
determine those elements of the system which are
conducive to its use by doctors and other members
of the Practices' staff ... Factors which impair
use and inhibit the system's acceptability shall
be particularly scrutinised."

The users were 'computer naive' and worked in
relatively small and informal organisations not
used to formal management and information processing procedures. Thus the acceptability of
the system to users, and their ability to participate in the design and implementation process
were of particular interest. Of the two Practices
which participated in the project, one had 8,500
patients and four doctor partners (2 full time,
2 part time); the other was larger with 20,000
patients, six full time partners and operated
from two sites each with its own reception staff.
One of the partners in the larger Practice also
held a part-time appointment in the Medical
School and in this capacity took on role of
designer, working with IBM personnel in the
development of the system's requirements and
facilities.

1.2   The IBM Sheffield Primary Care System

In line with the project's objectives the SPCS
was a comprehensive multi-user information
system providing facilities for office and
consulting room use. It was implemented on an
IBM 370-3031 mainframe located in IBM's
Scientific Centre at Winchester, and was
connected to the Practices via British Telecom
high speed land lines. A total of 11 VDUs and
4 printers were installed in the offices and
consulting rooms at the three sites in Sheffield.

Although it was recognised that the use of a large mainframe system was not an economically viable means of implementing a General Practice information system, it suited the requirements for an experimental system. Software could be developed, assessed and revised remotely, and thus reduced the amount of time that IBM personnel would need to spend in the Practices some 200 miles away.

The SPCS was designed to provide facilities in four main categories:

1 Management facilities related to the general management of a Practice, eg maintenance of an age/sex register; production of Practice statistics such as morbidity; the control of financial claims information.

2 Reception facilities associated with the servicing of patients requests, eg repeat prescription requests; preparation of patient notes for each surgery; the booking of home visits.

3 Doctor facilities which enable the doctor to: eg review appointments in the current surgery; access patient records; enter encounter notes; medication, summary of medical history; follow a core protocol for hypertension.

4 Utilities to enable a wide range of questions to be asked of the data stored in the whole system.

The SPCS is described more fully elsewhere (1). An example of a screen used by receptionists for ordering repeat prescriptions is illustrated in Figure 1.

2 EVALUATION METHODS

As evaluators we took the role of 'active observers', which included the assessment of change over time by making 'before and after' observations (outcome evaluation), and observing the process of change as it occurred (process evaluation), and by feeding back our assessments to the participants during the project in a facilitating role.

The evaluation matched several of the criteria identified by Eason as desirable in an 'ideal' research strategy (2). The evaluation was a <u>longitudinal</u>, <u>field</u> investigation from a <u>socio-technical perspective</u> of a system design for <u>real use</u> by <u>ordinary users in their normal circumstances</u>. The design was <u>evolutionary</u> in that after a period of actual use it was to be redesigned in the light of feedback from users and evaluators.

2.1 Outcome evaluation

In order to meet the research objectives the research design required certain measures to be taken at three points in time:

- before the computer equipment was installed:

- at approximately 3 months after installation, whilst the practices were still learning to use the system;

- 12 months after installation by which time it was hoped routine use of the system would have been established.

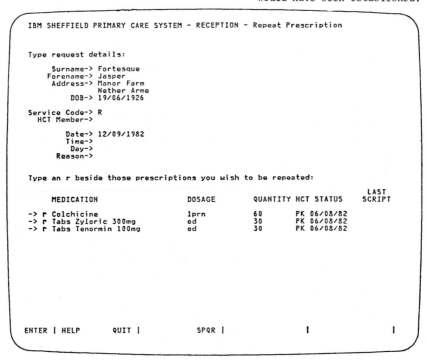

```
IBM SHEFFIELD PRIMARY CARE SYSTEM - RECEPTION - Repeat Prescription


 Type request details:

         Surname-> Fortesque
        Forename-> Jasper
         Address-> Manor Farm
                   Nether Arme
             DOB-> 19/06/1926

 Service Code-> R
   HCT Member->

            Date-> 12/09/1982
            Time->
             Day->
          Reason->


 Type an r beside those prescriptions you wish to be repeated:

                                                                    LAST
         MEDICATION              DOSAGE      QUANTITY HCT STATUS    SCRIPT

 -> r Colchicine                 1prn          60      PK 06/08/82
 -> r Tabs Zyloric 300mg         od            30      PK 06/08/82
 -> r Tabs Tenormin 100mg        od            30      PK 06/08/82






 ENTER | HELP      QUIT |         SPQR |            |              |
```

A variety of techniques were used to collect data; these included video recordings of consultations, activity sampling of reception work, structured interviews with users, patient questionnaires, and a record of computer use automatically logged by the SPCS.

These measures were designed to provide indication of:

- doctor behaviour during the consultation;
- receptionist behaviour, for example, patterns of work and activities that were to be computerised; and job perceptions and attitudes;
- patients' attitudes, perceptions of, and satisfaction with the doctor-patient relationship and the reception service.

2.2 Process evaluation

The structured interviews included questions to users and designers on their expectations and perceptions of change. We also spent several hours per month at each site talking to users and observing training, early use, and the routine operation of the Practices. In addition we attended many meetings, both within the Practices, and between users and designers.

2.3 Facilitator role

From our observations at each stage of the project we drew our own conclusions and made a number of recommendations, some of which were proposals for immediate action, and others were in the form of 'lessons learned' with a suggestion on how to tackle a problem 'next time'.

Recommendations were made on the subjects of:

* project communication
* training
* the need for pre-emptive action
* system redesign
* revision of project objectives

3 ACCEPTABILITY AND USER VIEWS

3.1 The doctors' views

The doctors used the SPCS for a trial period in their consulting rooms for recording diagnostic and treatment information. They also undertook a trial of a hypertension protocol through which the computer guided them in the management of patients undergoing treatment for chronic hypertension. They found the system relatively easy to learn to use and had few complaints about the design of the user interface. However all doctors ceased consulting room use prior to the end of the project. The principal reasons were:

(a) They found the system's response times less than satisfactory. Any delay, even of a few seconds, created difficulties for them within the severe time constraints imposed by 5 minute consultations.

(b) Some of the doctors felt the computer intruded on the consultation and chose to use it little or not at all while the patient was present.

(c) All but one of the doctors found the experience stressful, largely because they (correctly) perceived that use of the computer took longer than manual notes. Analysis of the video recordings revealed that almost twice as much time was spent on computer use than had previously been spent on note use (the pre-computer time averaging a little under 60 seconds per consultation).

(d) For a variety of reasons the doctors felt they could not abandon the keeping of manual records. Because of the overwhelming size of the task and the relatively short duration of the project only a small percentage of patients' records had been summarised and entered into the system. Thus a mixed mode of record keeping was unavoidable. On the occasions when some of the doctors did not write a manual note, for medico-legal reasons they felt it necessary to write on the notes 'comp' to indicate a computer record existed. Thus the workload of accessing manual notes from the filing system was not obviated. Finally the doctors did not sufficiently trust the reliability of the system to be able to rely on retrieving a computer record.

As a result of these factors, the computer increased the time pressure on the consultation. For some doctors this resulted in longer consultations, whilst for others they spent less time devoting their full attention to the patient. After a trial period varying between two weeks and ten months all the doctors ceased using the patient record functions because they did not perceive the benefits (improved record keeping) as outweighing the costs (the extra time taken, feeling stressed).

Interestingly an assessment of the patient questionnaires revealed that patients experienced no adverse effects from computer use by their doctor. Although their perception of doctor/patient rapport and of standard of treatment varied from doctor to doctor it was not influenced by whether or not the doctor was using a computer.

3.2 The receptionists' views

In the larger Practice, which operated from two
sites (P1 and P2), the receptionists' overall
satisfaction with the system was high and tended
to increase with experience. Thus towards the
end of the project all 13 reception staff were
either 'reasonably' or 'very' satisfied with the
computer's performance in general. In contrast
in the smaller Practice (P3) satisfaction with
the system was considerably lower and towards the
end of the project 5 out of 7 receptionists were
'not very' satisfied with the computer's
performance.

The low and decreasing satisfaction at P3 seemed
to stem from hardware problems that were specific
to P3, and from the organisation of reception work
which did not allow dedicated use by one person
for longer than half an hour or so (this is
discussed further below).

At all three sites the most criticised aspects of
the SPCS's performance were its reliability and
response times. IBM personnel worked hard to
improve response times and in the latter quarter
of the two-year trial they were down to an
average of about 3 seconds and all but one user
found them acceptable.

Reliability was more problematic. Difficulties
resulted mainly from hardware and the operating
system. Despite many attempts to improve reliability the answer to the question "What is the
worst thing about the computer?" revealed it to
be a continued concern for reception staff. IBM's
own assessment of availability revealed that the
system was available for between 90-95% of the
time in most weeks. A criterion was set that
the system should:

(a) fail no more than once a day;   and
(b) fail no more than for a 10 minute period

The criteria was achieved on between 60-80% of
days in an average week, but with the full
variation of 0 to 100% per week over the final
12 month period. IBM regarded this as reasonably good considering the remoteness of the
system and the experimental nature of the
project, and also compared favourably with what
might be expected of other systems. Nevertheless the users regarded it as poor, and it was
the main reason why they abandoned use of the
computer for booking home visits. This was
regarded as an especially crucial activity where
unreliability resulting in failure to retrieve
information could have particularly dire
consequences.

3.3 The machine/user interface

With the above exceptions the user interface was
generally speaking highly regarded during all
phases of the project. For example, receptionists
assessed user error messages, keyboard and screen
layout, and the system's hierarchical structure
as all 'reasonably' or 'very' satisfactory. The
one area in which they were critical was the work
station which was regarded as less than acceptable due to the cramped locations in which most
of the office terminals were placed. Little
extra space was available and special furniture
was generally not provided.

Notwithstanding these generally favourable views
it is instructive to note some particular
difficulties.

Although the tree structure was well liked it did
in some situations create inconvenience when a
receptionist wanted to move frequently between
two sub systems and had to move up and down in
hierarchies on each occasion. Interestingly this
had been designed as a security feature, with a
separate password required for each sub system.
Yet in practice because of the _actual_ operational
requirements of preparing repeat prescriptions
the arrangement was agreed to be impractical and
the designers agreed to insert a 'short-cut' as
part of an experienced user mode. This example
illustrates the consequences of designing a
facility around an 'ideal' rather than having a
sufficient appreciation of day-to-day practi-
calities.

Similarly, although receptionists liked the keyboard and screen layout there were some minor
difficulties. Because of the close proximity of
some frequently used keys ('ENTER-SHIFT' and
'RESET-ENTER') some receptionists reported mis-
hits were not uncommon. Also some confusion
arose because of different function keys (eg
ENTER and FIND) being used for similar functions
on different screens. Errors would have been
less likely had the same key been used on both
screens. Conversely, receptionists sometimes
used the function keys 'ENTER' when they
required 'QUIT' because to them the former key
'appeared' to have the same effect on the screen.
The difference needed to be made more visible to
the users because internally the effect was quite
different.

Apart from relatively minor difficulties with
the user interface in what was a complex system,
the design was extremely good from a human
factors point of view. The substantive difficulties that did arise were the perceived
unreliability of the system linked to 'organisational difficulties' and the integration of the
system into the day-to-day operations of the
Practices.

4   LEARNING TO USE THE SYSTEM

Training took place at each phase of the implementation and aimed to instruct all the receptionists and doctors in functions relevant to their work. Our assessment indicated that the training itself was carried out competently by IBM personnel giving individual or small group tuition on specific functions. Yet when asked after the first phase 12 out of 15 receptionists regarded training as less than adequate, and in the second phase so did 10 out of 17 receptionists. In fact when we later asked how they had learned to use the SPCS only one of these 17 thought that training had been an important factor.

At each phase the total amount of time available for training at each site was one or two days. However in the early stages the system was unreliable and became unavailable for substantial periods of time (several hours at a stretch), thus reducing the time available for training. In addition staff were liable to be called away from their training (which was taking place in the reception area) to help with some urgent task. This further reduced the time available for training, particularly in the smaller Practice (P3).

At the larger Practice (operating from two sites P1 and P2) two extra part-time staff (one with computing experience and the other a nurse) had been employed to take special responsibility for computer use. These 'key users' played a very significant role in that both regarded their initial training as adequate when supplemented by additional self tuition from the documentation provided. They had both the time and expertise to teach the other users (12 out of 13 stating this was their significant method of learning).

At the other Practice (P3) no specialist user role was created (though there was an overall increase in staff hours to cope with the extra work load of data capture) and thus receptionists were much more dependent on documentation and staff felt less adept in the use of the system.

The implementation phases would probably have been more effective if IBM personnel had been available on-site, for say a four week period, during the initial period of each phase. However this did not prove possible due to the pressure on resources and the distance between the IBM Scientific Centre and the Practices. The IBM documentation was little used, though the key users at the larger Practice developed their own material. This indicated initiative on their part, and appeared to be an effective step in the learning process.

The SPCS had a sophisticated interactive HELP facility, though little use was made of it. This seemed to be because the facility was not available during the initial training phase. For effective use the HELP facility would need to be included as an integral part of the training.

The Practices themselves needed to devote sufficient priority to the task of ensuring new users were not distracted by their normal duties. This would have been more likely had training taken place away from 'workface' operations and then later transferred into the normal working environment. The integration of the system into normal work procedures and the existing manual information systems needed more consideration by all parties concerned. Very little planning for this took place, problems being tackled piecemeal as they arose. IBM appear to have seen the integration as the Practices' task, and the Practices were not initially aware of its importance or the problems that might arise.

5   THE ORGANISATIONAL INTERFACE

Not all of the functions originally envisaged as part of the SPCS were fully implemented, and of those that were implemented, mainly because of the short term nature of the project, only some reached established use and replaced previous manual systems. The consulting room doctor functions, for example, despite an extended trial were never fully established and did not replace traditional note keeping methods. However, the doctors at the larger Practice established an 'Audit Group' which used data collected by the computer system to assess their own and colleagues' activities, particularly their prescribing patterns. This data derived from two functions which were introduced in the early stages of the implementation and were operated mainly by receptionists - those for patient registration and repeat prescriptions. In this section we consider one of these functions (repeat prescribing) which was well used and liked by staff at the larger Practice in order to illustrate the importance of the organisational interface for the successful use of computer systems in organisations such as are found in Primary Care. A fuller description of the human factors evaluation is provided elsewhere (3).

5.1 Repeat prescribing

Some patients (about 20%) receive prescriptions for medication without seeing their doctor. These are issued to patients who need the same medication over an extended period and once the course has been initiated by their doctor they can collect repeats from the receptionist which have been signed by the doctor. To improve the control over these prescriptions the computer system could be used to specify the number of occasions on which the prescription can be repeated without seeing the doctor again, and also the minimum and maximum interval between repeats, outside of which the patient is regarded as not complying with the necessary regime.

The SPCS was designed to print repeat prescriptions within this framework. The constraints determining whether a prescription should be issued were specified to the system. When a patient requested a repeat, receptionists had the facility to over-ride the constraints if they chose by 'forcing' a prescription to be printed. The data base established was also available to the doctors to review their prescribing behaviour and assess the operation of the repeat prescription system.

Although the repeat prescribing function became well established at the larger Practice (P1 and P2), it was not without its difficulties. In particular, a high level of 'forcing' was necessary over an extended period. On three two-week periods, spread over 9 months, we found that about 50% of prescriptions had at least one item of medication which was forced by receptionists. The reasons are outlined below:

1   The constraints, as initially set, were too inflexible. When the doctors became aware of this they began to change them, but with little overall effect on the level of forcing.

2   The doctors had the responsibility of ensuring that the system was informed of a re-authorisation. They were inconsistent in doing this, and thus not infrequently the computer information was out of date. Through the audit group the doctors received feedback on their behaviour and became aware of the problem that they were a weak link in the system. This was an important factor leading to the establishment of more systematic up-dating routines and a change in their behaviour.

3   Even when the system was up to date and the constraints set appropriately there could be a particular reason for over-riding them. Patients not infrequently had special requests, for example, wanting their medication early because they were going on holiday, which was regarded as legitimate by receptionists and doctors.

4   The system had been designed to increase the level of control over the issue of repeat prescriptions. However, in practice, the repeat prescribing procedure still required a substantial amount of discretion on the part of the receptionist. They needed to use their skill and expertise in 'knowing the patient', 'knowing the particular circumstance, drugs etc'. Thus the receptionists saw it as necessary and important to 'force' prescriptions frequently in order to maintain an effective service. When the receptionists were asked whether they felt more or less responsibility for the issue of repeat prescriptions with the computer system, 7 said there was no change, only 3 felt they had less, and one thought she had more.

Thus overall, what was intended as a 'safer' and more regulated procedure for repeat prescribing was in effect little different from the previous manual method because of the high level of forcing.

The doctors were responsible for issuing of repeat prescriptions and the design objective underlying the function had been to ensure that the doctor rather than the receptionist made the decision to issue a repeat. Yet the design did not achieve this objective - if anything the reverse occurred. The mechanism of constraints was not in itself adequate, particularly in view of the problems with updating. Thus receptionists were obliged to make a conscious and explicit decision whether or not to 'force' a prescription. Previously they had made such decisions through a more informal process involving use of the medical record. On most occasions when the constraints were not met receptionists did 'force' the prescriptions. During a short period when they did not force, doctors found they were seeing patients much more frequently than expected and some patients complained that they were being refused what they regarded as legitimate requests. This 'work to rule' by receptionists resulted in them being instructed to use their discretion to prevent such problems arising. (The doctor always makes the final decision in any case and takes responsibility by signing the prescription.)

A more effective way of achieving the objective that the doctor should make the decision would have been to design the function so that, provided the patient was registered as receiving the medication requested, the prescription should always be printed but with additional information on the recent history of medication supplied. This would enable the doctor to make an informed decision on whether or not to authorise the medication. The SPCS did provide a brief reason for 'forcing', for example 'too long' since the last issue, but without information on exactly how long it was the doctor could not make an informed decision on whether to over-ride the constraints. The doctor thus either had to examine the medical record or accept the receptionists 'decision'.

4.2 Organisational consequences

The process of introducing the computerised information system in itself changed the Practices' self-perceptions. The larger Practice was seen by its staff to have an orientation towards operational efficiency, and although the computer experience did not change this it did appear to lessen its interest in its own perceived weakness, that is, contact with the patients as expressed in terms of friendliness and accommodation to the patients and their needs. The Audit Group set up by this Practice to assess feedback from the computer was regarded as an important addition to Practice activity. The benefit from this use of a General Practice computer was the major justification for the Practice's decision to buy their own computer at the end of the IBM/SUMS project.

The other Practice was oriented more towards patient contact. This remained, but at the same time the Practice became more preoccupied with its perceived weakness, that is, operational efficiency. About the time this Practice decided to cease using the computer they created the position of Practice Manager - an alternative way of improving organisational effectiveness. Also this Practice set up a manual drug card system as part of its preparations for computerising repeat prescriptions. It retained this manual system after the termination of the project because it was perceived as more effective than the previous less structured method.

The computer acted therefore as a catalyst to the emergence of more structured organisational forms and methods of processing information. It could not create them of itself but made the participating Practices more aware of the organisational pre-requisites of effective computer use. At a meeting of the Audit Group in the larger Practice towards the end of the project the doctors observed that if nothing else the computer had enabled them to establish more effective manual systems. They also noted that the computer could probably have been used more effectively had they established these prior to its arrival. In fact they had shelved the improvement of their manual systems once they had decided to participate in the computer project.

5   CONCLUSIONS

In general the problems at both Practices were not predominantly 'technical', nor with 'human factors' in the narrow sense of machine/user interface design. They were with understanding in sufficient detail the day-to-day operation of the Practices. This lack of understanding applied to designers and also, in an important respect, to Practice staff themselves. Whereas there is little doubt that they knew their own job, they did not have a sufficiently coherent 'organisational' or 'systems' perspective. Without this understanding the consequences of integrating the system into the Practice operation was difficult to anticipate, and likely to produce unintended side effects.

At the end of the project both receptionists and doctors felt they now understood the requirements for a General Practice information system. Some they had already achieved, some facilities they now knew they did not want, and in other areas they knew what was required. Yet in retrospect they were aware that at the beginning, in the design phase, they had been computer naive and in no position to articulate their requirements and desired methods of working. Likewise the designers had little appreciation of the real nature of General Practice. At this stage designers and users had differing models of the organisation. By the end of the project these had tended to converge and reveal the requirements for a General Practice information system that matched the reality of General Practice. What was really needed was the means by which this convergence could take place as early as possible. This might perhaps have been facilitated by setting up more workshops involving designers and users to establish a common 'systems view' of the organisation.

Yet this approach would only achieve a system designed to meet the needs of the specific groups involved. However, there is a great variety of organisational forms and work procedures in General Practice. Virtually all Practices regard their organisation as unique. There is no guarantee therefore that the design of a particular General Practice Information System would be suitable for a wide variety of Practices - it probably would not.

Some progress has been made towards establishing the information handling requirements in General Practice and examining ways of effectively implementing systems in this environment. What is now required is a wider understanding of the diverse organisational forms in General Practice and their different requirements.

The case study reported here is however of wider relevance, and reflects the likely consequences of the introduction of any comprehensive computerised information system into a 'computer naive' and relatively unstructured environment such as may be found in many small service organisations.

6   ACKNOWLEDGEMENTS

Without the co-operation of the members of the two Practices participating in the project this evaluation would not have been possible. We value highly the way in which individuals gave their time and offered themselves for scrutiny. In particular we are grateful to Dr Alan Evans of Sheffield University Medical School with whom we have engaged in many useful discussions. We would also thank the IBM UK Scientific Centre which provided funding for the examination, and more particularly Peter Absolon and Geoff Kaye for their continued help and support.

7   REFERENCES

(1) Absolon, P.J., Denner, T.J. and Kaye, G., The IBM Sheffield Primary Care Computer Project - Introduction and Objectives. IBM Report UKSC108A (January 1983).

(2) Eason, K., Methodological issues in the study of human factors in teleinformatic systems. Behaviour and Information Technology, 2, (1983), 357-364.

(3) Garber, J.R., Brownbridge, G., Fitter, M.J. and Herzmark, G.S., Human factors evaluation of the IBM SPCS: Established use of the system. MRC/ESRC Social and Applied Psychology Unit, Memo No. 624, (October 1983).

Human-Computer Interaction — INTERACT '84 / B. Shackel (ed.)
Elsevier Science Publishers B.V. (North-Holland)
© IFIP, 1985

EVALUATION OF INTERACTIVE AUDIOVISUAL APPLICATIONS :
SOME RESULTS AND PERSPECTIVES

Francis KRETZ[1]
Head of Research Department ESA
CCETT
BP.59 35510 CESSON-SEVIGNE
FRANCE

News interactive media such as interactive audiovideography and videodisc lead to applications which combine audiovisual presentation and interactivity. Sound and audiovisual sequences much increase the creative capabilities of the media as compared to videotex. They tend to produce a "spectacle" attitude on the user who will also be asked through interactivity for an active motivation. More generally, results from the evaluation of four experimental applications will be presented, using a structured analysis schema to organize them.

INTRODUCTION :
AUDIOVISUAL INTERACTIVE SERVICES

The foreseen evolution of telematique services is certainly towards better representations of visual information, from the mosaic representation of graphics to 2D and furthermore 3D and photographic modes. Home computers and video games do evolve in such a way, also in some cases with elementary sound synthesis. Another approach has been started at CCETT by introducing realistic sound sequences with videotex, that is "audiovideotex" or interactive audiovideography (1,2). Parallely, laser videodiscs now allow to have access interactively to pictures and audiovisual sequences (3,4). Some arcade games already display these facilities.

This change in the representation modes of individual messages that are sent to the user is in fact a considerable modification of the medium. From dialogues using mostly textual information to dialogues conveying pictures, natural speech, music, movie sequences,..., the medium is evolving from, say, a rational informative one towards a more natural one allowing attraction, pleasure, aesthetics and better subjectivity. Some applications become merely feasible, others can be more fully developped : games, education, catalogues, encyclopedias, tourisme and culture, news, advertisements,.....

In the near future, switched networks with "medium" data capacity will become available : the digital telephony network at 64 kbit/s which will allow to multiplex sound (coded at some rate below 64 kbit/s) and videography using few kbit/s ; the data and telephony integrated networks (ISDN) at 144 kbit/s. Also,in France, cable TV networks are being developped using optical fibers with the video channels. This structure allow such networks to evolve in the future towards truly interactive wide-band networks, capable of audiovisual interactive services on a sizeable basis.

The network that is built in BIARRITZ already offers these facilities.

In a recent analysis (5), we have considered the field of applications for the interactive audiovisual services and suggested lines for the experimentation and development of such applications.

Before awaiting for the medium capacity data networks, audiovideography can be experimented using the usual telephony network with two lines per user or, for some applications where synchronism between sound and pages can be avoided, with one line and a share in time between sound and data. Another possibility is to use a speech and sound synthetizer in the terminal. But, in order to study the audiographic medium in its service aspects with the minimum of constraints, and allowing music or speech with enough quality and a variety of voice types and intonations, we didnot restrict ourselves to this two last system configurations.

Our objective of research being to analyse new media in terms of their potential applications, their advantages and constraints with respect to the creation and production of applications, the methodology of their evaluation,...., we started in 1981 by simulating audiovideographic applications using a two-track audio recorder (thus with no interactivity) and by studying the literature about the design of audiovisual messages. This convinced us with the high benefice of adding sound, a more cheerful medium, to videotex (1,2). Then we built an experimental audiovideographic data basis, now allowing to interactively present to an user sound sequences synchronously with videographic pages, the interaction device being an alphanumerical keyboard taken from a videotex terminal. In the meantime, we prepared a production of experimental applications.

In order to get realistic applications, we asked INA[2], a research centre in the field of audiovisual production and media in general, for a coproduction. After having asked few authors to write scripts, we selected three of them and INA organized with professionals the creation (pages and sound sequences, inter-action graph) of these applications. The different phases of the creation and realiza-tion process involve (6) to first write a precise script, to lay on the paper the inter-action graph (that is part of an interactive application script), to start a draft realiza-tion of pages and sound sequences, to edit them on a (noninteractive) video tape for checking their coherence and finally, to write the de-finite interaction graph and produce the defi-nite pages and sound sequences. This process ends with the software programming of the application.

Two applications were ready mid 1982, using the mosaic mode of videotex. One is a game "Bug Maldone" (approx. 100 pages and 20 mn of sound) where a detective, Bug, has to find a strangler in an evil repute town. After a sequence for the presentation of the game rules, the player has to help the detective in his task by inter-actively selecting informers who may or may not give partial informations, who may also bring Bug into a trap.... When enough informations have been gathered, Bug has to select the location where the strangler is. If he finds the good one, he has to be quick in pushing a given key to kill the strangler, otherwise.... The second one is "English Lessons", an inter-active educative application. After an intro-ductory series of tests, the learner chooses exercices of various levels and topics. The exercices usually present orally sentences or dialogues and ask for questions in form of queeze or by completing sentences with lacking words.... Both applications were evaluated end of 1982. The third audiovideographic applica-tion used the geometrical (teledrawing) mode of videotex. It is a game for children, "Coco le crocodile" (approx. 150 pages and 40 mn of sound). The child can interactively build a story by selecting step by step events that can occur to Coco and selecting an appropriate sound sequence on each selected visual sequences. At the end, he can have his complete stroy presen- ted. This application was ready march 1983 and evaluated in june.

On the field of interactive videodisc applica-tions, some experimental production has started in France, mainly by or at the initiative of IMEDIA, a group financed by CNET, the research center of PTT, and OCTET, a group connected to the ministry of Culture. At the moment, we have evaluated one of these applications[3], "A day in a circus". The user is welcomed by a circus presentator, Pat, to visit the circus facilities and attractions at his will. The device uses a touch sensitive screen for menu selections ("left", "right", "up", "down") and direct control of the videodisc ("fast forward", "stop", ...). It was ready and evaluated summer 1983.

The four applications were presented to a number of visitors at CCETT and IMEDIA or during several exhibitions. All were found to be very attractive. This is of course insuffi-cient to be indicative of a definitive interest in a realistic use. We thus needed to know more about the audiovisual interactive media. Quali-tative analytical evaluations were thus conduc-ted, as announced above.

EVALUATION METHODOLOGY FOR INTERACTIVE APPLICATIONS

The evaluation of interactive applications require to consider the methods that are used in various scientific disciplines and apply them to "user-service" dialogues (a more suitable expression than "man-machine dialo-gues" for our purpose). Those disciplines are psychophysics (earing, vision, touch), psycho-linguistics and more generally semiotics, cognitive psychology (memory, knowledge, learning,....) and psychosociology (attitudes, representations, projections, ...). Broadly speaking, this corresponds to the field of psychoergonomics. The methods for evaluating dialogues, whether in the case of repetitive usages in automated workstations or in the case of casual usages at home or at office, are not specific in terms of general procedures but they are at a finer level in terms of the analysis schema that underlines them. We will first summarize the various procedures that can be used (7) before presenting the type of methods we have used in the research.

Performance methods. They use some objecti-ve criterions in order to get direct quantita-tive measures. The main methods involve counting errors with a more or less fine clas-sification of error types, measuring the time spent for the whole dialogue or parts of it, the percentage of pages or dialogue steps ef-fectively passed through relative to the mini-mum that would have been necessary, etc.... More global indices can be derived from these kinds of indicators.

Subjective methods. They refer here to the use of evaluation scales for factors like un-derstanding, comfort of use, acceptability, annoyance, quality,... and more generally atti-tude scales (e.g. semantic differential scales) for factors like attraction, pleasantness,... The idea is to have some indirect quantitative measures corresponding to user reactions.

Observations. This is the usual method in the field of ergonomics. It consists in merely observing the usage of the application and the spontaneous reactions to it. It can be more or less formalized by using an observation pattern where only some of the user actions or reactions known to be significant are noted.

Interviews. Interviews following the use of the application are complementary to the previous procedures. Again they can be more or less formalized by using an interview pattern. An in-depth procedure can be used for a precise feedback on the design of an application : the test is recorded and consecutively played back step by step while asking the user to comment his actions and reactions.

Test conditions. Various parameters enter in this aspect. Tests can be performed in a laboratory environment or in the real situation of usage. The specific social status of the laboratory introduces some kind of bias but allows better control. To be representative of real usage, realistic test tasks must be used, avoiding "experimental abstractions". Test-tasks can be diversified depending on applications and objectives. From one side, free usage situations can be chosen or at the opposite, "closed" test tasks inducing a specific dialogue path through the application. By all means, they must be representative of the real or potential usage of the application and possibly more or less "critical" with respect of various aspects of the application. At last, the choice of the subjects sample raises a difficult problem. For quantitative tests, a sample representative of the users of the application is necessary but often the potential users are not precisely known and the usual sampling criterions as sex, age, location, profession, ... areindeed operational but questionnable : the experience of pocket calculators, video games, ..., or personality variables such as attitudes may be more determinative. For qualitative tests (with, say, a few tens of subjects), a "diversified" sample seems the best solution, with subjects naive with respect of the system and the application (7).

Method used in our study.

Our objectives were to get informations about the audiovisual interactive media, that are fundamental enough for some generalisations. Evaluation of the specific contents of each application was not aimed at, although it is a necessary intermediate (and biasing) stage. In this respect, global evaluation of the applications as well as quantitative measures were not appropriate. Analytical methods, at the opposite, were necessary to investigate all the numerous components of such applications. Qualitative methods were thus used, based on observations and interviews. This type of methods has been found the most efficient in terms of information gained over time spent for the tests and analyses, in our experience of the design and evaluation of the Electronic Directory application (8).

At the systems under study didnot enable a use

in real situation, tests were done in a laboratory-type environment (except a series of observations of "A day in a circus" during an exhibition : they proved to be less informative then the other tests). The task in the test was to use freely the system within a limit of time (e.g. 10 to 20 mn). Before this, a quick presentation of the system and of the objectives of the study were given. During the use of the system, passive observations were carried out by the experimenter. After it, an in-depth interview was passed. The main items were to give a description of the system as it is perceived, to comment its novelty and how it compares with other media, to relate the phases of the dialogue, to react on sound and visual messages, and finally to give feelings about the potential interest of such systems and their potential applications. In the case of "Coco le crocodile" (the game for children), the children had also access to a teledrawing pad before or after the test. In the case of "A day in a circus", subjects were also asked to draw the topography of the circus, in order to check for the spatial representation that was elaborated during the test.

The first two applications were tested with subjects who had a professional activity connected with media (TV, cinema, records, cartoons, newspaper, radio, ...) plus two teachers (the second application was an educative one) and two fanatics of videogames. The interviews were very rich but we found that such a sample may too much depart from a realistic one. The other applications were tested with 20 and 33 subjects, the samples being widely diversified, especially with respect to age and sex.

A STRUCTURED ANALYSIS SCHEME OF DIALOGUE COMPONENTS.

We define here the dialogue as the dynamical communication process (i.e. the exchange of significations) between an user and a service (or more strictly an application). An application results from the realization of a given service (more precisely an objective of service) with a given technical system. An interactive application is one which permits a dialogue between the user and the service. Various degrees of interactivity can be reached, such a degree combining at a first order approximation the rapidity of the system responses and the complexity of the space of actions offered to the user (5,6,9).

The components of a general dialogue are quite diversified, they are parameters describing various aspects of the applications : input interaction device, semantic analysis software, usage context, ..., that is from the physical level to the sociological and economical one. In order to apprehend user-service dialogues in their full complexity, we have gathered the components into five "communication levels"(7).

At each level, components belong to three classes : input parameters (user to service), output parameters (service to user) and processing parameters :

- the level DEVICE corresponds to the physical input and output interfaces, as apparent to the user. At the input, the interactive devices offer various facilities : input of characters, spatial selection (e.g. mouse, sensitive screen, ...), continuous control (e.g. joystick), vocal control. At the output, sound and visual messages are delivered by loudspeakers, TV or flat screens, ... Processings are transductions and pre- or post-signal processings.

- the level PRESENTATION describes the choices of presentation variables at the input (key-board setting, ...) or at the output (page lay-out, sound-page synchronisation,...) within the possibilities offered by the devices. Processings are coding and decoding schemes to transform input device signals into codes and inversely output codes into audio and video signals.

- the level LANGUAGE gathers parameters of individual message significations (syntax and semantics). At the input, these individual messages can be symbols, isolated characters, isolated words, groups of words, sentences, texts as well as graphical input messages. At the output, we find the textual language from words to instructions, texts,..... and the other languages that can be used : graphical, vocal and musical, pictorial, and more generally audiovisual in the case of "multi-media" applications. Processings are here linguistic ones (analysis-synthesis of expressions, spelling correction,....), speech, sound, graphical or video ones (analysis-synthesis).

- the level STRUCTURE corresponds to a higher order of communication by controlling input and output phases of the dialogues. It is described by a graph (state automaton) and by a "chronogram" which gathers the temporal parameters of the dialogue (either deterministic or random). This last aspect is important for multimedia applications where sound and video sequences induce a temporal structure as well as synchro nisation between the various information channels. Various types of structure can be used globally or locally in an application : linear structure, tree structure (strictly hierarchical or with some transversal and direct access paths), graph structure or even, in some future, unpredetermined structures where the structure itself is modified from the dialogue. It is often useful to distinguish the main structure from "substructures", one example of the latter being guidance procedures. At the opposite, speeding-up procedures can be superposed to the main structure. Both types of structures are useful to produce "variable speed dialogues " (7) which adapts in a more natural way to each user experience. Processings at this level are often simple, with no or very small memory of the past steps of the dialogue. They will nethertheless become more sophisticated in the future, and already educative applications or games do record scores obtained at given steps and use them to adapt the dialogue to the user.

- the level SERVICE, finally, incorporates such items as the objective of the application, its informational contents along with the context of usage (its location - at home, at the office, in public areas -, the type of users, their degree of experience,....). A useful criterion to classify the type of interactive applications (5,7) is their degree of personalisation, ranging from almost no personnalisation (access to date bases with all kinds of information, to catalogues,....) to some amount of it (education, games), further to transactions (booking, banking,....) and electronic mail.

Acting or reacting at these different levels of communication is ther USER. A parallel can be drawn between these levels and the type of user inner processes that are active during a dialogue. The two first levels mainly excite psychophysical and perceptive processes, the two others mainly psycholinguistic and psychocognitive processes and the last one psychosociological to psychoeconomical processes. Of course, depending of applications and users, the activity of these processes is more or less important and determinant. The levels we have chosen (7) slightly differ from those designed by T.P. Moran (10) which are : TASK, SEMANTICS, SYNTAW, INTERACTION, LAYOUT, DEVICE. Apart from the precise definition of each levels, we prefer to order them in a slightly different way, on the basis of a degree of abstraction and memory needed within the processings occurring at the various levels, both for the user and the system. With this respect, the level Structure becomes a conceptual one just below the level Service : at the former level, it is no more individual messages that are processed, or short-term memory that is active, but paths of the dialogue (before the current state) or longer-term memory for the user.

The dialogue itself is not a level in our analysis : it is the dynamical process which results from the communication (bidirectional exchange of significations) between the user and the application. It is described as paths in the structure, the structure itself being described as a graph. The dialogue can be looked at as an adaptation process, each level of communication introducing some loss from an ideal, so called "transparent", communication between user and application.

Of course, these levels are not at all independant and their dependancy has been proved (7) to come from both the system limitations (page capacity, reduced "intelligence",....) and the user limitations (perceptual, cognitive, socio-economical capacities). This non-independance leads to difficulties in the design as well as in the evaluation procedures. They need to be precisely analysed to get optimum results.

RESULTS FROM EVALUATIONS

The somewhat theoretical analysis that has been just described resulted (7) from our experience of design and evaluation of some videotex (8) and audiovideotex (2,6) applications. This structural analysis schema was designed to help both design and evaluation procedures by using a common language and analysis of dialogues components and of their interdependence. It will be used here to present the most signifi- cant results from the evaluations we conducted, that is, results which seem to allow some generalization.

AT LEVEL DEVICE : The keyboard was sometimes felt to be slow and to reduce sensuality as referred to the paper medium. At the opposite, the sensitive screen fascinated the users, but also raised few questions about its reliability and hygiene. The absence of sound on selection pictures in the videodisc application was cri- ticized (also in fastforward or backwards mo- des). This aspect has also implications at the Presentation and Language levels, but will not be recalled.

AT LEVEL PRESENTATION, the first results apply to the mosaic videographic presentation limi- tations. This mode has a poor resolution imply- ing schematization with sometimes a poor recog- nition performance. The second type of user re- actions relates to the slowness of the video- graphic display in both mosaic and geometric modes : a 1200 bit/s rate is used which is acceptable for pages with mostly texts but could be less acceptable for more complex pages with graphics. Although our graphists tried to overcome this limitation by changing only par- tially pages at certain steps (a sort of fade in/out ; or, for "Coco", a kind of animation), the slow progressive display disturbs both the perception of pictures in their globality and the perception of sound when presented simul- taneously. This asks for higher bitrates or for videodiscs. Otherwise, it an be noted that the response time of the systems were satisfying (time between a user action and the beginning of the related messages presentation).

AT LEVEL LANGUAGE, the presence of sound modifies drastically the videotex medium : sound is found attractive, warm, human. It better excites affectivity, desires, imagina- tion. Especially, the sound here doesnot seem to come from a machine (no synthetizer is used) and music is present. Also, sound in "English lessons" is clearly necessary. Apart from some understanding difficulties wuit some instruc- tions, symbols,....which have to be checked for

each applications, the potential richness of multimedia applications require to carefully design the combinations of text, picture, voice and sound messages. They have their specific perceptual properties. The sound channel is well fitted for instructions, redundant messa- ges (not a list of numerals) and atmosphere (music). Our applications imply to mix four types of messages : from the different possible combination, only text and voice raised some problems : a strict redundancy or opposition is to be avoided and thus they must be designed for complementarity and counterpoint (sequen- cial display). Synchronism between pictures and sounds come naturally in movie sequences. It can be achevied with videotex and sound, for example a gun shot and impact). For the balance between sound and visual channels, "Bug" and "Coco" correspond to two opposite realiza- tions : the former has more information in the sound channel, the inverse for the latter. In the case of "Coco", due to the author design choices, the selection phases are presented with vocal instructions and graphical sketches of well known movie actors (Chaplin, Marx Brothers,....) whereas phases which describe parts of the story use animated graphics with Coco and abstract music. The children were sometimes puzzled by these changes of style and reference.

AT LEVEL STRUCTURE, first, the introduction of sound or video sequences changes the temporal structures of the medium. This also tends to produce on the user a "spectacle" attitude (so called "passive" : we prefer "reactive"). At the end of a sequence, the application reaches an interaction phase asking the user for an action ; this breaks its preceding attitude. Thus, audiovisual interactivity must play with this alternation of reactive and active phases for the user. The applications we evaluated, except "English lessons" where sound sequences are shorter and the user better involved, were found in fact to be not much interactive. They offer mainly menu selections and their authors tried to show their talent in designing long attractive sound and visual sequences. One user reaction was to ask for the movie to go on automatically if he didnot answer to a menu. Users often asked to be able to play with the actors on the screen, to build their own story ("Coco" is such an application). The children were in fact often more attracted to play with the teledrawing pad which allows creation, than with "Coco", although they could here build a story. The other reactions at the level struc- ture relate to the lack of variations in the applications (when used repeatedly). Also, the lack of guidance or map showing the walk in the circus made hardly possible for users to build a realistic spatial representation of it.

AT LEVEL SERVICE, the applications we have con- sidered here were all found to be very attrac- tive when shown during visits or exhibitions. There was a striking difference in the results

of the evaluations, exceptfor "English lessons". This is an educative program and as such
it is usually found valuable. Here, interactivity is high and it allows to adapt to the user
capabilities. "A day in a circus" was found a
bit old-fashioned, it would have needed more
fun, motivation and interactivity. "Bug maldone" was hardly considered as a game, because
its rules were not clear enough and it requires
neither dexterity (except once where the user
must strike a given key quickly) or thinking.
"Coco" made use of some cultural references
(Marx Brothers, Marilyn,....) which could not
be appreciated fully by the children. The creation of the story was found at the end somehow
disappointing because oversimplified.

SOME CONCLUSIONS

It must be remembered that these applications
were experimental. Due to technical constraints, we could not evaluate them before they
were completed. For such new media, looking to
the storyboard doesnot tell enough. We respected the authors' creation and we thus got more
artist creations than communication applications (except for our educative program).
Although they are amply illustrative of the po-
tentialities of audiovisual interactive media,
they are not operational applications. Some
know-how do exist for telematique and for TV or
movie ; applying it to these new media require
some more experience. This can be helped by
evaluating the first applications as we did.
Furthermore, for newly going ones, a better
interaction between design and evaluation must
be achieved before completing a production.
This can be done though qualitative partial
evaluations of parts of the application. One
assistance for that will be to use high level
creation softwares which would enable directly
the authors to simulate partially his realiza-
tion and modify it easily at each step. We are
working on the design of such a language. Examples already exist for interactive education
programs and for tree-structure videotex ones.
But this is insufficient of course in itself to
choose real communication objectives and to
reach a good fit of them in the actual realiza-
tion. Some iterations will be needed in the
design process.

The evolution of the audiovisual interactive
media will be towards a better association of
the attractivity arising from the audiovisual
sequences and the motivation elicited from the
interaction phases. A solution for this is to
carefully prepare the user for the next interaction phase and offer him enough reflexion or
dexterity at these phases. By enlarging his
possibilities of action and shortening the duration between interactions, the degree of in-
taractivity will be increased in both its
semantic and temporal dimensions. Apart from
interpersonal applications where "social" interactivity is offered, joint interactive sound
and picture syntheses will allow the maximum

possibilities in some future. Before awaiting
for this, audiovideography and videodisc applications can be envisaged in their full development.

Footnotes.

1. This paper results from many discussions
with our colleagues from department ESA,
F. COLAITIS, B. MARQUET, P. SALLIO, and
with J. DE LEGGE (TMO Ouest) who run the
evaluations. They deeply deserve our acknowledgements.
2. The production of the audiovideographic,
"Bug Maldone", "English Lessons" and "Coco
le Crocodile" were conducted by C. BOUDAN
from INA in a close and efficient cooperation with CCETT.
3. The videodisc application "A day in a circus" realised with the help of IMEDIA is
due to A. LELU. The author likes to note
his cooperation in the evaluation stage
and analysis of the results.

References.

(1) F. COLAITIS, "L'adjonction d'un canal
sonore au videotex : l'audiovideotex",
L'Echo des Recherches, n°110, oct.1982,
pp 41-52.
(2) F. COLAITIS, "Introducing an audio channel
with videotex, audiovideotex", Xth HFT
(Human Factors in Telecom.) symposium,
Helsinki, june 1983, 6 pages.
(3) xxx, "Interactive videodiscs", BYTE, 7,
n°6, june 1982.
(4) M. MARCHAND, G. LAFARGE, "Premier catalogue des applications audiovisuelles inter-
actives", Bull.IDATE n°13, Oct.1983,
pp 346-406.
(5) F. KRETZ, F. COLAITIS, B. LORIG, "Banques
d'images", chap.10 of "Images pour le
câble" CNET-INA-Documentation Française,
juin 1983, pp 239-261.
(6) F. COLAITIS, J. DE LEGGE, "Audiovideogra-
phie et création de programmes audiovi-
suels interactifs", Bull.IDATE, n°13,
Avril 1983, pp 407-415.
(7) F. KRETZ, "Dialogue, service, interactivi-
té et leurs composants : aspects de conception et d'évaluation", Bull.IDATE,
n°11, Avril 1983, pp 77-103.
(8) M. BARDOUX, B. MARQUET, G. POULAIN, "On
the methodological aspects of the assessments of the French Electronic Directory
System", Xth HFT, Helsinki, june 1983, 19
pages.
(9) F. KRETZ, "Interactivity and videocommuni-
cation services", Xth HFT, Helsinki, june
1983, 4 pages.
(10)T.P.MORAN, "Introduction to the Command
Language Grammar", Xerox report SSL-78-3,
oct.1978.

Human-Computer Interaction — INTERACT '84 / B. Shackel (ed.)
Elsevier Science Publishers B.V. (North-Holland)
© IFIP, 1985

IT IS WHAT IT'S USED FOR - JOB PERCEPTION AND SYSTEM EVALUATION

Oleg de Bachtin

ELLEMTEL Utvecklings Aktiebolag
Älvsjö, Sweden

A study involving very experienced people representing two different professions
is presented. The data from this study indicates that such people regard the computer
systems as mere tools for their jobs. If the tools are in agreement with the mental
model a person has of her or his job, job satisfaction will increase. If not, the
tools are rejected.
Factors, commonly regarded as "good", like "ease of use" or "ease of learning", could
have a negative influence if they are perceived as a threat to ones professional role.
It is argued that developers of computer systems must consider the users mental job
models when building their systems. They should also use the knowledge from the field
of cognitive psychology in doing this.

1. INTRODUCTION

For many users of computer systems the terminal
used for communication with the computer represents the system. Much work has been done to
insure that the working site including the terminal is suitable from an ergonomic point of
view.(6) How to display data has also been refined during many years, and many standard
principles, like the use of menus have been
applied succesfully.(4)

We know fairly well how to display data, the
question is if we know what data to display.

Computer systems have evolved from data processing number-crunchers into information processors and today even into knowledge processors. Also it is now common to look at the man/
machine system as a whole. One illustration is
the naming of the IEE Manchester conference in
1982 'Man/Machine Systems'.(3) A further refinement recognizes the task itself as a main
component. The system to study is therefore a
task-user-computer system.(1)

The user is normally a human being. In the role
of operator she or he will be dependant on a
mental model of the computer aid used.(5) On
the higher level the way we humans think is
directly involved. As a consequence knowledge
from the science of cognitive psychology has to
be used, if one tries to understand and predict
the behaviour of task-user-computer systems.

As computers infiltrate our everyday working
life, their role as tools for the work to be
done, is getting more pronounced. Attitudes
towards computers change when one gets used to
them.(7) As people mature as computer users
they will accept these tools only if they are
conceived as an aid in the task to be performed.

This paper reports some data from a recent study, which indicates very strongly that the computer program must present its information in a
way that is in harmony with the users cognitive
view of her or his task. Indeed this seems a

critical factor that decides is the user will
accept a new system or not.

2. THE STUDY

The study involved two different groups of people working for the Swedish telephone administration. One group worked in sale offices and
the other group consisted of skilled technicians
responsible for the maintenance of SPC (Stored
Program Control) exchanges.

Both groups involved highly professional people.
The mean value of the time they had worked in
their respective capacity was 16 years for the
sales office people and 19 years for the technicians. It should be noted that their profession is to sell and to maintain. The use of
computer aids for their work was introduced
fairly late and those aids are still being improved today.

As part of their job both groups had to perform
the same task (from the technical point of view)
of making the final connection of subscribers
to the exchange.

In the experimental design the task was performed using a new "State of the Art" dialogue
on an alphanumeric display screen. This procedure was compared with the one they were used
to.

Afterwards they were asked to fill in a questionnaire involving 43 different questions. Half
of those concerned the new presentation form
itself. In the remainder the respondents were
asked to compare the new presentation with the
one they were used to.

Each person was also interviewed in order to
clarify the reasons behind the way she or he
answered.

Both groups rated the new presentation form
itself as better than the one they currently
used. The technician group was more enthusias-
tic that the sales people, who were more critical on some details of ergonomic nature in

the laboratory setup. Those differences were however not statistically significant.

But when they answered the type of questions which indicated how they liked the new way of performing the task, the sales group differed from the technical one.

When treating the data a very striking difference was found depending on what work category the respondent belonged to. The difference in response, when analysed according to ANOVA method, was significant on the 1% level or less, in 9 of 14 subquestions.

Figure 1 shows how the two groups judged the new dialogue from the point of using it, as compared with the dialogue they were using normally at their work. As can be seen the maintenance group found it easier to a larger degree than the sales people did. Of course one of the reasons could be that their usual dialogue was harder to use than the one the sales people had.

MAINTENANCE

SALES OFFICE

Figure 1 : New dialogue from the usage point of view.

One thing which is evident however is that "easier" is not the same as "better". On a significant level, the maintenance group as compared to the sales people, found the new dialogue :

- easier to learn
- easier to use
- helping them doing the task faster

In spite of these apparently positive judgements 50% of the people in the technical group answered a very firm NO on the question if they would like to change to the new procedure. The corresponding figure for the sales group was 0 %. In this group nearly 70% preferred the new method (while the rest needed more time to try

the system before they committed themselves).

It seems we have to face the fact that some commonly used indicators of the "goodness" of a system correlate negatively to the issue if it will be accepted by its assumed users.

What are the factors then which, in this study, were found to give a more valid indication of the users' overall reactions? In figure 2 you will find the responses concerning the question of user control.

MAINTENACE

SALES OFFICE

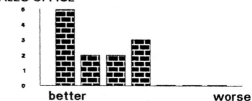

Figure 2 : The new dialogue from user control point of view.

The same striking difference in responses from the two groups, and correlating to the question of overall acceptance, appeared on the following issues :

- possibility of system control.
- how easy one could follow what the system did.
- ability to obtain information needed for the task.
- how efficient one performed the task.
- feeling of enjoyment in performing the task.
- degree of expertise needed for the task.

When studying the responses given during interviews, one can very clearly see that the reasons given for likes and dislikes are coupled to how the individual experiences what her or his work is.

The people from the sales offices no longer had to convert whatever the customer said to "computerese", but could inform the computer system in the same terms as was used with the customer.

The technicians on the other hand complained that "they did not know what happened". Their frame of reference was the exchange itself. Not the functions the exchange performed.

To illustrate the above, the following representative quotations are taken from the interview tapes (transcribed from Swedish by the author).

First from people in the sales office group :

> ".... we wish to sell what suits the customer"

> ".... we are able to be more service minded. The customer does not have to wait for his telephone"

> ".... and then you feel that you do the entire job yourself. It so much nicer to tell the customer that he will have his telephone when he gets home. This is what we have been waiting for"

Here one can see how they regard the dialogue in reference to their job of selling and having a satisfied customer.

> ".... one is less restrained. Because you can make notes in the order the customer tells what he wants"

> ".... a simple dialogue makes selling much more fun"

They liked the tool because it made this work easier.

> ".... that one could follow the customer all the way and have him connected. That was nice. So now I feel very satisfied with my job"

> ".... you are sort of responsible yourself that it is being done"

Last but not least they felt they had better control and larger responsibility, which enriched the job itself.

None of the sales people mentioned the work at the terminal to be part of their job. The job was to sell the products and to make the customer satisfied. The better one managed to do this the more feeling of satisfaction.

In the new dialogue tested there were three new functional facilities which the sales office people refered to. A note pad to write down what the customer wanted as he expressed it. That the names of various products were in plain language (as compared to the previous encoded form) and last but not least that they could complete the job up to the point of connecting the subscriber.

This last facility enabled the sales staff to activate the "whole system".

> ".... I see more of the system now. Now maybe I am learning more about it. And that, I think, creates a better self - confidence"

The quotations from comments made by the maintenance engineers shows that they regard their job to be something entirely different.

> ".... I suppose, what I am afraid of is that, when something goes wrong, one does not know what one is doing, where one is"

> ".... more and more you lose touch with machine and software, as you build more and more systems on top of each other, that handle everything. As a computer technician you feel that you must have a chance to correct errors. After all, that's my job"

> ".... sometimes one gets the feeling that it is too easy. Once I know how to use it I will no longer know what I am doing. What's happening behind"

Their job is to correct errors in the equipment. When the dialogue uses functional terms, what the equipment does as seen from a higher level, they feel that they lose control.

> ".... as a system technician one is a little afraid that one gets to far away from the system. That ones knowledge, ones system knowledge, will diminish"

> ".... to me this is negative. I like to learn more about the system all the time. I like to increase my knowledge. Here it goes backwards sort of"

> ".... it is an improvement, but on the expense of the individuals' way of thinking"

To have technical knowledge about the system is important to the engineers. They like to have tools that makes it possible for them to encrease this knowledge when performing the daily duties. When the conceptual level is upgraded, they are afraid of losing their detailed skills.

> ".... and if I sit here and just feed in lots of these things and don't know what happens to them in the computer, I feel it's uninteresting. And then I sort of feel that I don't do anything"

> ".... the feeling is that one does not know what one is doing. It's more robot like. You copy the paper you got, then it's finished. There is no satisfaction with what you are doing"

> ".... but for myself I really don't like to have it this way. I want to have more difficult things to do"

The job itself loses in quality - gets too easy.

These are not extreme quotations from the interviews. The above expresses what everyone in the maintenance group said in one way or the other.

One can see two main themes. The task one has to do is mainly to repair the system when something goes wrong. But the system, to the maintenance people, is the software and hardware units. To this kind of people it is important to relate what the system does to the way the system does it. Else one does not know "where one is".

The second theme has to do with job satisfaction.
For the maintenance people, the knowledge they
have acquired in order to perform their difficult
job, is part of their pride. They wish to refine
this knowledge all the time, they are afraid of
losing it, and perhaps still more afraid that
"progress" will result in that this knowledge no
longer will be needed. As a result the encreased
functionality is experienced as a threat to their
own professional role.

3.   CONCLUSION

Designers of computer systems must consider the
users viewpoint. If they do not, behavioural
problems may arise, causing the information system to fail.(2) That such reactions turn up is
supported also in this study. Some of the maintenance engineers stated that they would consider
quitting their jobs if the new dialogue was enforced on them. Because there is a high demand
on their kind of skill, this could lead to serious consequences for the organisation.

As is evident from this study, computer tools
have strong influence on job satisfaction. In a
positive way, as in the case of sales office
staff, or in a negative way as proven by the
reactions from the maintenance group.

This study also seems to indicate that professional people tend to regard computer terminals
simply as tools for their work. If these tools
are in discord with the mental model a person
has of her or his job, the tools will be rejected.

The reactions are psychological and based on
fundamental needs for control, achievement and
security. To explain, for instance, the sense of
losing control, expressed by the maintenance people, a cognitive psychologist could point out
the following :

> A professional skill involves a very large
> amount of knowledge stored in the individu-
> als' long term memory. It has taken years
> and years of learning and experience to
> achieve all this knowledge. But to reach
> various parts of this knowledge - to activate
> them - proper cues have to be given from the
> environment. The main error in the design
> tested (the psychologist would say), is that
> the dialogue used the wrong cues. The comm-
> unication process between the person and his
> tool broke down.

In order to achieve acceptable computer tools,
it is important to know what user reactions are
to be expected, already at an early stage of the
design phase. Knowledge from the field of psychology must therefore be used in the work of designing computer systems which involves humans (as
almost all systems do). Because it seems that
users regard computerised tools using a mental
model of their job, the humans cognitive skill
is used. The subfield of cognitive psychology
is therefore especially relevant. Even is much
more research has to be done here, there already
exist useful data as exemplified by (1).

REFERENCES

(1) Card,S.K.,Moran,T.P.,Newell,A., The Psycho-
    logy of Human-Computer Interaction, (Lawre-
    ce Erlbaum Ass, Publishers, Hillsdale,New
    Jersey,1983)
(2) Dagwell,R.,Weber,R.,System Designers' User
    Models - A Comparative Study and Methodolo-
    gical Critique,Communications of the ACM,
    Vol 26 Number 11 (1983), 987-997
(3) IEE, Man/Machine Systems,Conference Publi-
    cation 212,(Institution of Electrical Engi-
    neers, London and New York,1982)
(4) Martin,J.,Design of Man-Computer Dialogues
    (Prentice-Hall,Inc,.Englewood Cliffs,N.J.,
    1973)
(5) Rasmussen,J.,The Human as a Systems Compo-
    nent, in Smith,H.T. and Green,T.R.G (eds.),
    Human Interaction with Computers,(Academic
    Press,London,1980)
(6) Van Cott,H.P. and Kinkade,R.G. eds., Human
    Engineering Guide to Equipment Design,(U.S.
    Government Printing Office,Washington,D.C.,
    1972)
(7) Zetterberg,H.L.,End Users of Computer Pro-
    cessed Information in Working Life (in swedish),
    Arbetslivets slutanvändare av databehandlad
    information,(IBM Svenska AB,Stockholm,1979)

Human-Computer Interaction — INTERACT '84 / B. Shackel (ed.)
Elsevier Science Publishers B.V. (North-Holland)
© IFIP, 1985

Workstations Using Direct Manipulation as Interaction Mode -

Aspects of Design, Application and Evaluation

K.-P. Fähnrich, J. Ziegler

Fraunhofer-Institut für Arbeitswirtschaft und Organisation (IAO), Stuttgart, Germany

Some more recent developments of workstations have been using a new mode of man-computer interaction. As a term for this mode "Direct Manipulation" has been introduced in the literature. A characterization of direct manipulation is given on the basis of a suggested general man-computer interface model. The concept of "generic interaction modes " is introduced and discussed, where programming languages, direct manipulation and natural language are suggested to form generic interaction modes. Some work on the evaluation of an interface based on direct manipulation (Xerox STAR) is reported.

1. Introduction

Starting with systems like SMALLTALK /1/ during the last years a new generation of workstations (PERQ, STAR, SUN, LISA etc.) has appeared on the market which uses a new approach to the man-computer interface. For this new mode of interaction the term "direct manipulation" has been suggested /2/. In a simplified way it could be described as the interaction of the user with an information environment (which consists of the parallel display of dynamically changing "windows") using simple selection operations to point to objects in that information environment, certain "generic" operations applicable to these objects and the possibility to change a variety of inherent attributes of these objects.

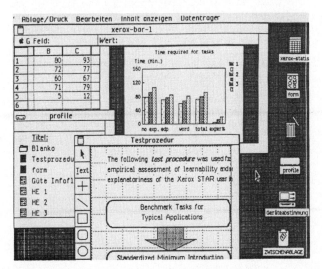

Figure 1: An example for an interface with direct manipulation (Apple LISA)

This kind of interface has been mainly intended by the designers for a class of users called "knowledge workers" or "professionals". Generally speaking, its main advantages lie in its high "self-explanatoriness" (in the sense of obviousness) and its "learnability".

The basic concept for the development of this mode of interaction can be considered as being contrary to programming or command language-oriented man-computer interfaces and as a substantial extension of the interaction through menus and forms.

2. Man-Computer Interfaces

The term "man-computer interface" is by no means sufficiently defined and elaborated. As a basis for discussion a reference model in the form of a layered model is presently being discussed by the European user group of the IFIP WG 6.5 /3/. This model can be extended as shown in Figure 2 and interpreted in the following way:

The model suggested tries to integrate ideas of the IFIP model, the general structure of the ISO reference model for open systems interconnection and formal interface descriptions as suggested e.g. in /4/.

o The organizational system represents nature, amount and structure of tasks jointly to be fulfilled by man and computer.
o In the communication process between man and computer four levels of common information structures (protocols in the sense of the ISO model) have to be established: the conceptual level, the semantic level, the syntactic level and the interaction level where the interaction level represents the physical link between man and computer.
o Successful communication depends on the degree of appropriateness of information representation on each of the interface's four le-

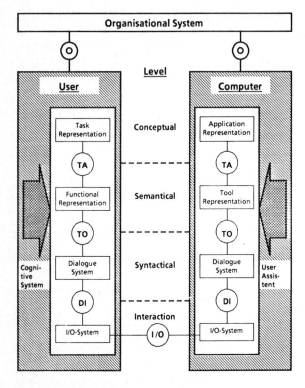

O : Organisational Interface   DI : Dialogue Interface

TA : Task Interface   IO : Input /Output Interface

TO : Tool Interface

Figure 2: A model of the man-computer interface

vels. On the side of the user the appro-priateness can be influenced by his cognitive system in a highly flexible manner limited however, by the capabilities and restrictions (individual characteristics, preknowledge, experience) of the user. On the side of the computer the adaption has to be achieved by the system design. There exist three approaches:

- Fixed layout of the computer-interface system matching specific task and user characteristics.
- Parameterised layout of the computer-interface system adaptable to different task and user characteristics by the user himself.
- Adaptive layout of the computer-interface system by adding a software system being capable of representing and/or collecting knowledge about task, user and interface characteristics and using this knowledge for adaptation.

The first approach has quite commonly been taken, in disregard of the quality of the results. Sometimes this approach has lead to inadequate

man-computer interfaces, sometimes it has produced rather efficient systems which of course are limited in in their scope of appliccation. The second approach mainly creates systems that - due to a higher amount of effort in the implementation - are more flexible. Recently first attempts have been made to work out concepts for the third approach /5/, /6/, /7/. The resulting construct often is called "user agent" or "user assistant", but is as yet widely removed from a general implementation.

All three approaches will benefit from an architectural design of the interface software according to the interface layers suggested in the architectural model as discussed above. The following section gives an idealized description for the software structure of such an interface.

The input/output interface (IO) is the physical link between the user and the computer. It accepts the physical input (keyboard input, voice input, pointing operations etc.) of the user. The associated I/O system of the computer transforms the input into a device-independent representation (dialogue interface DI) for the dialogue system. On the other hand the I/O system handles the dialogue system output and encodes it in a way appropriate for the physical output components (output of the text, graphics, voice, - in a manner which can be variously encoded and organized). For human factors, questions like the physical design of input/output components, the usage of different input/output modes, coding and organization of the information (e.g. window- systems) etc. are of relevance.

The dialogue system performs a syntactic analysis of the input and provides the tool representation with a specific representation of the input information which is independent of the dialogue technique. For human factors the range of the dialogue steps and the complexity of the syntax have to be considered. In the tool system different "generic" tools representing the available objects and functionality (semantic level) of the system are represented. For a given application representation its input information is built up by the tool representation at the task interface (TA).

When designing a man-computer interface the starting point should be the conceptual level. System standardization however, started on the interaction level.

3. Direct Manipulation

As started above some more recent developments of workstations have been using a new mode of interaction which SHNEIDERMAN /2/ has described by the following characteristics (cf. also /8/):

o Continuous representation of the object of interest.
o Physical actions or labelled button presses instead of complex syntax.
o Rapid incremental reversible operations whose impact on the object of interest is immediately visible.

Referring to the model of the user interface presented, direct manipulation could be provisionally defined by the following points:

(1) The interface has a fixed and restricted conceptual model which is designed for a specific application field. The possibility to interact through direct manipulation depends to a large extent on the adequacy of this concept to the task to be fulfilled by the user-computer system. Direct manipulation requires the application of metaphors (e.g. desk-top metaphor as used in the Xerox STAR System) which map the functionality of the system onto objects, relations among objects, and functions which provide a task-adequate (often almost real-world) context for the interaction. It is essential that the conceptual model can be made explicit to the user by displaying the actual context of interaction in a suitable manner.

(2) The semantics of the objects used in the conceptual model is composed of a generic (basic) part and a part specific to the instance of the generic object. The use of relatively few generic functions which can be applied universally to those objects completes this concept. Together with the conceptual model, these semantic characteristics describe the domain of "know-what" which is needed by the user and which is embedded in the design of the interface.

(3) The clear organization of the conceptual model with objects and functions is a prerequisite for the syntax of direct manipulation. Each action of the user is dealing with only one of these classes at a time. Commands of the user take the form of noun-verb. Thus the manipulative interaction consists of the sequence "selecting an object - invoking the function to be applied to this object" (including the specification of attributes). The system responds to each action of this sequence by an explicit feedback. Tasks are accomplished by combining these basic (reversible) steps in an incremental manner.

(4) At the physical interaction interface the output is organized in an information environment which consists of the parallel display of several hierarchically structured information areas (usually using window technique). This approach is contrary to the common, strictly sequential display of information. The screen must be capable of displaying textual and at least basic graphical objects. For the input, direct manipulation requires a pointing device (e.g. mouse), function keys on the keyboard and/or virtual keys on the screen. Points (3) and (4) describe the domain of "know-how" which is necessary for the interaction.

The most obvious aspect of direct manipulation is the visualisation of the conceptual model (more precisely that part of the model which is relevant in the actual context of interaction). Feedback is provided for each of the user´s elementary interaction steps. This feedback of the result of operations remains visible as long as the context of the interaction that has produced it is maintained. By these means the user is enabled to explore and to learn the functionality of the system. Many of the user´s recall operations are substituted by recognition operations.

The term direct manipulation is justified in so far as the characteristics of stepwise physical handwork with the immediate feedback of the result are simulated in the direct manipulation interface. It appears that direct manipulation represents a basic (or generic) mode of interaction whose characteristics can be discerned from the other interaction modes. In order to assess the advantages and shortcomings of direct manipulation (and its respective realizations) it is useful to discuss its role in a framework of basic interaction modes. This will be the aim of the following section.

4. Generic Interaction Modes

Recently the idea of "generic" interaction modes emerged /7/. As a hypothesis programming languages (PL), direct manipulation (DM) and natural language (NL) are regarded as generic interaction modes. According to the man-computer interface model suggested in chapter two the following overall characterization of the three techniques can be given:

o In the case of PL the user has to build up the application-oriented conceptual and mainly the semantic level. He has to adapt himself to a complex syntax but has the advantage of being able to introduce with the same language various conceptual and semantic models in a highly efficient way.

o In the case of DM a rather fixed conceptual model is built into the computer. On the semantic level generic objects and operations offer the semantic model to the user in a clustered way. The syntax is elementary, the interaction is rather natural.

o In NL systems man and computer jointly have

to establish and/or modify the underlying conceptual and semantic models. Communication mismatches on lower levels can be compensated by the rich common structure on the higher levels. The syntax is extremely complicated but familiar to the user.

In /9/ a set of evaluation criteria is given for the quality of man-computer interfaces. This set was derived from a questionnaire-based empirical study using factor analytical techniques to extract categories of the quality of user interfaces. Momentarily these categories discussed in the German DIN standardization body /10/. The following categories are suggested:

o Appropriateness for the task
o Self-explanatoriness
o Learnability
o Error tolerance
o Controllability
o Reliability

If one adds to these criteria the efficiency criterium steady state performance of expert users, one could hypothetically construct the following profiles of the so-called generic interaction modes.

Evaluation criterium	PL	DM	NL
Appropriateness for closed tasks	–	+	–
Appropriateness for open tasks	+	–	+
Self-explanatoriness learnability, error tolerance	–	+	+
steady state performance of expert users	+	–	–
Controlability, reliability	+	+	–
Adaptivity of Communication	–	–	+

Figure 3: Evaluation of generic interaction-modes

As a hypothesis, this framework for evaluation is constructed in a manner to achieve maximal differences between the interaction modes. From previous work and experience, there is some evidence for this classification. However, this is only intended to be a starting point for the empirical assessment of each of the hypothetical judgements. Currently, the marked fields in Figure 3 are studied empirically. Some initial results are reported in section 5.

For a more detailed analysis, the evaluation criteria have to discussed for each level of the man-computer interface and for certain classes of tasks and users. E.g. if programming tasks for high-skilled users are considered, PL is on the conceptual level adequate to the task and

user whereas NL seems not appropriate. The ranking of NL was made under the assumption that a very powerful (momentarily not existing) NL-system with a broad conceptual model will be invented. Especially the adaptability and the flexibility of the conceptual model can be expected to be a bottleneck for future system design.

It is an appealing task to try to integrate other interaction modes to this framework.

o Command languages (CL) and other classic "user-initiated" interaction modes are quite related to PL with a far more fixed conceptual and semantic model. The syntax is not as complex as in PL. The interaction is often efficient but rather unnatural for most user groups.
o Menue-/forms-systems (MF) which are more computer-initiated also have a rather fixed conceptual and semantic model, but in comparison to user-initiated interaction modes elementary syntactic and interaction concepts. This elementary way to interact with the computer is achieved at the price of an often rather inefficient and fixed interaction.
o Keyword techniques have some relation to NL without achieving the same degree of sophistication. Again the conceptual and semantic model is fixed (although sometimes prone to misinterpretation by the user). The syntax has some resemblance to NL but is very elementary.

Figure 4 summarizes these remarks:

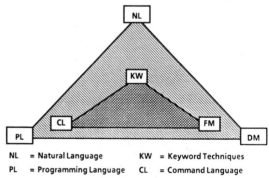

NL	= Natural Language	KW	= Keyword Techniques
PL	= Programming Language	CL	= Command Language
DM	= Direct Manipulation	FM	= Forms/Menue Techniques

Figure 4: Triangle of generic interaction modes with integration of some other modes

Within this framework the idea of man-computer interfaces which are adaptive to the task and the user can be discussed. A first step could be the development of "symbiotic" interfaces where a given task can be performed using different interaction modes. Eventually some aspects of the human's capability bto change the communication behaviour could be integrated in the computer. This leads to the concept of a "user agent or "user assistant". These ideas are discussed in more detail in /7/.

5. Empirical Evaluation

In order to establish empirical methods for the assessment of learnability and self-explanatoryness a prestudy was carried out. In the prestudy the XEROX STAR was used as a system with direct manipulation.

Several groups of persons were given three defined benchmark tasks with an increasing degree of difficulty. The test group for the prestudy consisted of 11 subjects (9 male, 2 female, age 21-30 years) with three different levels of EDP-specific skills (no experience, moderate experience in word processing, highly experienced programmers). None of them had previously used the STAR workstation. A control group of three expert users was employed in order to assess the range of performance and to obtain basic data about the execution of the task. The tasks were comprised of initially simple corrections of a text/graphics document (including operations like organizing documents on the desk top), more complex word-processing functions (including the usage of virtual keyboards) and finally the development of a more complex text/graphics document. The tasks contained only a relatively small amount of input where typing skills could influence the results. Furthermore the performance times were analysed only in relation to the periods needed by a control group of expert users.

The subjects (test persons) were given only a very short, standardized introduction to the system (about 10 minutes), explaining basic concepts of the interaction. However, they were allowed to ask the observing researcher for additional information at any time. By this approach it was intended to obtain information on the self-explanatoriness of the system.

The time required for each task, errors and the need for additional information were recorded by the session leader.

The aim of the prestudy was to observe the behaviour of users, who had no previuos knowledge about the STAR workstation, their need for additional information, the learning transfer effect between simple and more complex tasks and the occurrence of errors within the task context. The results were compared with a control group of expert users to determine the magnitude of learning effects to be expected.

In the prestudy the following aspects were not yet considered:

o time series characteristics of the learning process for identical tasks
o a detailed analysis of the components of the overall performance (e.g. components of the performance time)
o comparison of direct manipulation with other interaction modes

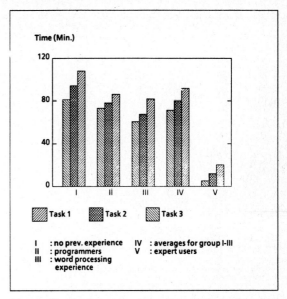

Figure 5: Performance time for tasks and user groups

The remarkable result is that the differences between STAR-experts and STAR-novices are by a factor of 4 higher than the differences within three the different STAR-novice user groups. This is all the more remarkable because the STAR novices varied from totally unexperienced users over medium experienced word-processing users to highly experienced EDP-users. This supports the hypothesis that direct manipulation gives a relatively high starting performance for novices. For the following considerations, the perfomance time for each task was standardized by the respective performance time of the expert control group in order to eliminate the differences in the performance time of each task.

According to the construction of the benchmark tasks their respective contents could be assumed to differ considerably. In the case of independent tasks the hypothesis for the central tendency of the observed standardized performance times would be that they are equal. This hypothesis could be rejected ($\alpha \leqslant 0.001$ with $\chi_r^2 = 130.1$ for the Friedman test).

Furthermore the standardized performance times show a clear learning effect (Figure 6). This can be explained by the possibility of knowledge transfer between the tasks. This supports the hypothesis of the high learnability of the interaction through direct manipulation.

The data on information demanded by the subjects and errors were interpreted on the basis of a task analysis for optimal (expert) execution. For each user the three tasks contained 129 elementary task steps (each elementary task step dealt with an object, the object's properties or with an operation). A total of 385 questions and

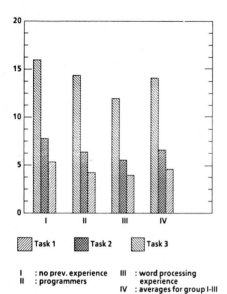

Task 1   Task 2   Task 3

I : no prev. experience   III : word processing
II : programmers   experience
                            IV : averages for group I-III

Figure 6: Ratio of performance times for
          subjects/control group

247 errors was observed for all subjects. The
handling of properties caused the biggest problems. There was a ratio of approximately 10 to
4 to 3 for events (questions and errors) related
to properties, operations and selection of objects. In comparison to optimal execution of the
respective task a question or error occurred for
almost every occurrence of a task step dealing
with properties. For the handling of properties,
questions were predominant to a high degree. For
operations an equal distribution of questions
and errors was observed whereas for selection
operations slightly more questions than errors
were observed. In a first attempt it was tried
to classify questions according to "know-what"
and "know-how" questions. According to this
rather unsharp classification know-how questions
were dominating, especially when using properties.

As another measure for the learnability of the
interface it was tied to cluster the events
(errors and questions). The ratio of events to
the number of event groups gives a measure how
often the user had problems with respect to the
same domain of functionality. Factors of approximately 6 - 5 - 3 were observed for the handling of properties, object selection and operations.

The problems observed concerning properties
could be interpreted by assuming that a lot of
the complexity of the interface is "hidden" in
the property structure.

As stated before this data and other observations not reported here mainly serve for the
construction of methods and hypotheses for the
next steps of empirical evaluation.

In a next step of empirical assessment learnability and self-explanatoriness will be further
operationalized. The results obtained in the
prestudy will be further validated and hypotheses developed from these results will be
tested.

After the establishment of methodology for
assessing the learnability and self-explanatoriness of interfaces with direct manipulation the
aim is to conduct a comparative evaluation of
direct manipulation and a second interaction
mode (command language) for a comparable task.
It is intended to use a type setting system with
a conventional command language interface for
comparison.

Literature:

/1/ Tessler, L.: The SMALLTALK environment.
BYTE, Aug. 1981, pp. 90 - 147.

/2/ Shneiderman, Ben: The Future of Interactive
Systems and the Emergence of Direct Manipula-
tion. Behaviour and Information Technology,
Vol.1, No.3, 1982, pp 237 - 256.

/3/ Williamson, H.: User Environment Model. Rep.
of the 1st Meeting of the European User Environment. Subgroup of IFIP, WG 6.5, 1981, pp. 6 - 7
ment Subgroup of IFIP, WG 6.5, 1981.

/4/ Moran, Th. P.: The Command Language Grammar:
A Representation for the User Interface of Interactive Computer Systems. Int. J. Man-Ma-
chine-Studies, 15, 1981, pp. 3 - 50.

/5/ Anderson, R.H. and Gillogly, J.J.: Rand Intelligent Terminal Agent (RITA): Design Philosophy. Rep. R - 1809- ARPA . RAND Corp., Santa Monica, Ca. 1976

/6/ Hayes, Ph.J.and Szekely, P.: Graceful Inter-
action Through the COUSIN Command Interface.
Carnegie-Mellon-University, Computer Science
Rep. CMU-CS-83-102, 1983.

/7/ Bullinger, H.-J.; Faehnrich, K.-P.: Symbio-
tic Man-Computer-Interface and the User Agent
Concept. Proc. of the 1st USA-Japan Conf. on
Human Computer-Interaction, Honolulu, 1984.

/8/ Smith, D.C. et al.: Designing the STAR user
interface. In: Degano, P. and Sandewall, E.
(Eds.): Integrated Interactive Computing Systems. North-Holland, Amsterdam 1983.

/9/ Dzida, W.; Herda, S.; Itzfeld, W. D.:
Factors of User-Perceived Quality of Interactive
Systems. Gesellschaft für Mathematik und Datenverarbeitung, Bonn, Institut für Software- Tech-
nologie (IST). Bericht Nr. 40 des IST der GMD,
1978.

/10/ DIN: DIN 66234, part 8, "Dialoggestaltung",
draft, 1984.

Human-Computer Interaction — INTERACT '84 / B. Shackel (ed.)
Elsevier Science Publishers B.V. (North-Holland)
© IFIP, 1985

RANDOMLY SAMPLED SELF-REPORT METHOD FOR COLLECTING FIELD DATA ON
HUMAN-COMPUTER INTERACTIONS

Paul D. Tynan, Ph.D.

IBM General Products Division
Human Factors Department, 76V/312
Tucson, Arizona 85744, U.S.A.

A variant of traditional work-sampling methods, the randomly sampled
self-report, has some advantages over other methods of collecting field data.
These advantages are especially important when studying information-processing
environments. Moreover, the method can improve collection of subjective data.
The history, application, and validity of the method is discussed.

1. INTRODUCTION

Human factors engineers need field data to
evaluate two important components of the utility
of computer systems. First, how productive is
the system for the customer, e.g., does the
system pay for itself? Second, how satisfied is
the customer with the user-system interface in
terms of ease of training, ease of use, quality
of the documentation, and susceptibility to
human error?

A variety of techniques are used to collect this
data. However, human factors engineers may use
techniques that are not optimally matched to
their investigations, because the best approach
may be too costly and time consuming.

A field-data-collecting method I call randomly
sampled self-report is well suited for
collecting several types of data in
information-processing environments. This paper
describes the application of this method, how
it compares with other methods, and its
validity.

2. RANDOMLY SAMPLED SELF-REPORT

The randomly sampled self-report is a variant of
work sampling, which is one of the basic tools
of Industrial Engineering (ref.1). The
participants of work-sampling studies are
observed at random intervals of time and their
activities at each instance are recorded. A
profile of the their activities can be created
if enough samples are collected. The randomly
sampled self-report is similar, except that
participants collect the data on themselves;
they are signaled to note their activity by some
external event that is not under their control.

Several such studies have already been done.
Carroll and Taylor (ref.2) flicked the overhead
lights of clerical workers and rang the
telephones of their managers to signal them to
note their activity. Robertsen (ref.3) placed
electronic devices on the desks of executives,
which signaled them with a beep to punch their
activity on data-processing cards.

I needed to make three enhancements to this
method to adapt it to the information-processing
industry:

- First, I had to make it portable because
  some of the participants (for instance,
  tape-drive operators) would be moving about
  a great deal.

- Second, I wanted to eliminate the record
  slips or cards used by other researchers, so
  that participants could record data more
  quickly and with less fumbling. I felt that
  this would make the system more acceptable
  in the hectic environments I wished to
  study.

- Third, I wanted to collect participants'
  ratings of the user-system interface, as
  well as their work activities.

I accomplished the first two objectives by
adapting a small hand-held computer to the task
(Radio Shack PC-1 Pocket Computer). I wrote a
program for it that generated random time
intervals, signaled the participants with a beep
to enter data, and collected and stored the data
for later collection. (This program is
available from the author upon request.) I
added a remote piezoelectric device that could
be worn like a police lapel microphone. This
allows participants to place the signal closer
to their ears when they are in noisy
environments. I also devised a holster for the
computer so that it could be worn on a belt.

3. PROCEDURE

I have found through experience that the
following procedure works well (for more details
see ref.4):

- First, I have to gain the cooperation of the
  participants by showing them that
  interfacing with the pocket computer will
  not be much of a burden to them. Typically,
  they spend only 5 to 10 seconds per report;
  reports are requested about 15 to 30 times
  per 8-hour work day. It is important to
  tell the participants that they will receive
  feedback on the results of the study.

- Next, I have to analyze the tasks of the subjects, and select a set of appropriate task codes and/or rating questions. Figure 1 shows a set of tasks used in a study of laser-printer operations. A key on the pocket computer was labeled with each task. Another type of coding scheme is illustrated in Figure 2. The combination of one word from each group describes participants' activities. In this case, the circled words represent the activity, "reading the help files while debugging a program." This type of scheme is more useful for complex jobs.

- I must try the coding scheme on a trial basis for several days or a week. The participants will probably suggest some improvements in the codes or ask for clarification. Also, this preliminary data gives me some idea of how many self-reports I will have to collect. See Allen (ref.5) for a formula for calculating this number.

- Finally, I need to collect the data and debrief the participants. Their qualitative statements about the study and about what was happening on the job will help when I interpret the data.

```
| PANEL | PAPER | MAINT |       |       |       |       |       |       |       |
|   Q   |   W   |   E   |   R   |   T   |   Y   |   U   |   I   |   O   |   P   |
| TERM  | OUTPU | NONP  |       |       |       |       |       |       |       |
|   A   |   S   |   D   |   F   |   G   |   H   |   J   |   K   |   L   |   =   |
|  CE   | ERROR |       |       |       |       |       |       |       |       |
|   Z   |   X   |   C   |   V   |   B   |   N   |   M   |  spc  |    ENTER      |

  - Interact with control panel (PANEL)
  - Monitor message terminal (TERM)
  - Consult customer engineer (CE)
  - Add paper (PAPER)
  - Remove output (OUTPU)
  - Error recovery (ERROR)
  - General maintenance (MAINT)
  - Nonprinter tasks (NONP)
```

Figure 1.   Laser Printer Tasks.   Keys of the pocket computer were labeled with the words in parentheses.

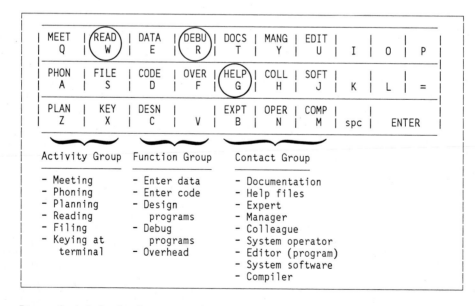

Figure 2. Labels for Programmer Activities

4. COMPARISON WITH OTHER METHODS

How does the method of randomly sampled self-reports compare with other methods of collecting field data? It is best to compare these methods in terms of the type of data collected.

4.1 Participants' Activities

The most straightforward way to find out what people are doing is to observe them. Detailed continuous observation provides a rich yield of information on the detailed structure of tasks, as well as on system activity, such as traffic and information flow. However, this method has some disadvantages, as follows:

- It can be very expensive. This method will occupy one or more human factors engineers for quite some time, and it is often difficult to free up a large block of time in the product-development environment.

- Coverage is difficult. I have found that the size of many data-processing centers makes it difficult to observe more than a small portion of their areas at a time. This also makes time-lapse photography difficult.

- Interpretation is difficult. Observing someone is not the same as knowing what they are doing and, more importantly, why they are doing it. You may observe programmers at a terminal, but you may not be able to tell if they are creating programs, debugging them, or just maintaining old ones; yet this may be the most important aspect of that situation.

An alternative to observing participants is to ask them to observe themselves by requiring them to keep a running log of what they do. They must note the start and stop times of each activity. However, this approach can only measure large global tasks, and relies too much on the patience and diligence of the participants.

On the other hand, you could just ask the participants how much time they think they spend doing different activities by interviewing them or giving them a questionnaire. Unfortunately, people are very poor at estimating these times accurately. Also, they are susceptible to subtle biases that they may not even be aware of (ref.6). For example, in the case of the programmers, I could ask them to estimate the amount of time they spend creating, debugging, and maintaining programs. Some may believe that the interviewer is expecting, and would like to hear, that a lot of their time is spent creating programs. This is likely to cause some of them to inflate their estimates of the amount of time spent in that activity. This is called the "interviewer effect." Or, they may believe that the better programmers spend more time creating

and less time maintaining programs. This would also increase their estimate of the time spent creating programs.

However, randomly sampled self-reports prevent participants from "wishful thinking"; they are only reporting one simple thing at a time: what they are doing at the time of the signal. And this information is tied to other variables, such as the people and equipment they are in contact with at the time.

4.2 Participants' Subjective Reports

Interviews seem better suited for collecting information on users' ratings of the human interface to the system. However, the same biases cited above may be even more disruptive in this situation. Participants' perceptions may be more colored by their initial and most-recent experiences with the interface than by the intervening ones.

It is much better to sample participants' opinions many times throughout their experience with the system. Each time they report their ratings, they are asked to confine it to their experience at that moment. By relieving them from the task of subjectively averaging over many experiences, (1) you eliminate distortions resulting from their imperfect memory; (2) multiple sampling provides a much more stable estimate of human behavior than does one report; and (3) you reduce the "interviewer effects," since the interviewer (in this case the pocket computer) is a neutral and consistent agent.

The resulting data base is much richer. You have tied their ratings to important variables in the environment, such as the specific part of the system they were interfacing with (i.e., documentation, help file, field personnel); what they were trying to do; the approximate time of day; the specific phase of their experience (orientation, training, novice, or proficient), and others.

As an example, assume you are studying the relationship between between video-display terminal (VDT) use and eyestrain. The best indicators of eyestrain are verbal reports of eye soreness, dryness, burning sensation, headache, nausea, and other distinct sensations (see ref.7). If you ask the participants of the study whether VDTs or paper-and-pencil tasks cause more eyestrain, they may have difficulty remembering which activity was more closely related in time with their discomfort. If they are uncertain about the facts of the matter, they may be strongly influenced by the status of the interviewer as a representative of a manufacturer, a labor union, a government agency, or an employer.

By contrast, during a self-report study, participants' verbal reports of eyestrain would be directly sampled, along with indications of whether they were working on a VDT or on a paper-and-pencil task. They could also enter the specific symptoms of eyestrain mentioned above, which may later provide clues about its causes. The data would also provide an estimate of how long they work at a task before the discomfort begins. Participants might still distort the data, but it would have to be much more deliberate on their part, and would be easier to detect during analysis.

4.3 Advantages of Using More Than One Method

The randomly sampled self-report is not the best method for collecting other types of data that you will need for fully describing an information-processing environment. You will need to directly observe the participants of your study to define and understand their tasks. Likewise, interviews are indispensable for determining the structure of an organization and the flow of information within it. Interviews also provide a wealth of information on the participants' background and the history of the situation or phenomenon you are investigating.

It would be a grave mistake not to do some preliminary investigation using interviews, questionnaires, and observations. And these methods should be used following the study; they could uncover low-frequency "critical incidents" that were missed by the random sampling.

5. THE VALIDITY OF THE RANDOMLY SAMPLED SELF-REPORT

How valid is this method? It is always difficult to assess the validity of field-study methods because you need a reliable and valid alternative source of data. For this reason, let us only consider the validity of methods that try and measure participants' past, present, or anticipated behavior.

Carroll and Taylor (ref.2) have matched data collected via the randomly sampled self-report with data collected via direct observation. About 2380 samples were collected with both methods on the same group of office workers at the same time. They measured the proportion of workers' time spent on each of 12 activities. The largest difference between the two sets of estimates was 3.3% for one of the tasks. The authors consider these differences to be tolerable.

It may be impossible to assess the validity of subjective data collected with the randomly sampled self-report when you collect data on unobservable events or behaviors. I can only repeat the advice given by Webb et al. (ref.8) to anyone collecting data that cannot be directly verified. They suggest collecting related information using quite different methods and determining whether or not these data sets support one another. For example, the investigator of eyestrain may observe how

frequently workers take their eyes off their work by stretching, taking breaks, and socializing. You would expect this measure to correlate with verbal reports of eyestrain.

5.1 Conclusion

The randomly sampled self-report method will provide better data than other methods under conditions that are common in information-processing environments. They can provide data on the "purpose" of participants' activities that may be difficult or impossible to collect by direct observation. Subjective data that is collected by this method will be more reliable, more valid, and easier to correlate with other variables. Finally, these advantages will be obtained at less cost to the investigator than direct observation.

6. REFERENCES

[1] Konz, S., Work Design (Grid Publishing, Columbus, Ohio, 1979) 145-167.

[2] Carroll, S. J., and Taylor, W. H., A Study of the Validity of a Self-Observational Central-Signaling Method of Work Sampling, Personnel Psychology 21 (1968) 359-364.

[3] Robertsen, J., Multidimensional Work Sampling at the Executive Level, Industrial Eng., (August 1980) 70-73.

[4] Tynan, P. D., An Improved Self-Logging Method for Studying Computer System Activities, in Proceedings of the Human Factors Society, (October 1983) 541-544.

[5] Allen, P., Multiple Activity Work Sample Needs X Samples, Industrial Eng., (December 1979) 20-21.

[6] Bouchard, T. J., Field Research Methods: Interviewing, Questionnaires, Participant Observation, Systematic Observation, Unobtrusive Measures, in Dunnette, M. D. (ed.), Handbook of Industrial and Organizational Psychology (John Wiley and Sons, New York, 1983).

[7] Birnbaum, R., Health Hazards of Visual Display Units with Particular Reference to Office Environments, NTIS PB82-120627 (1981).

[8] Webb, E. J., Campbell, D. T., Schwartz, R. D., and Sechrest, L., Unobtrusive Measures: Nonreactive Research in the Social Sciences (Rand McNally College Publishing Co., Chicago, 1966).

Human-Computer Interaction — INTERACT '84 / B. Shackel (ed.)
Elsevier Science Publishers B.V. (North-Holland)
© IFIP, 1985

USER ACCEPTANCE OF INFORMATION TECHNOLOGY THROUGH PROTOTYPING

Frances Clark, Peter Drake*, Marco Kapp and Peter Wong

Coopers & Lybrand Associates Ltd
* Xionics Limited

Prototyping is a method of complex systems design which is receiving more attention, as the tools and techniques which are now available have made the process more cost-effective.

This paper provides some theoretical perspectives on prototyping and suggests why a need for this approach exists. A working definition is proposed and an indication given of the types of situations where prototyping is most appropriate.

Next, two examples of successful prototyping are described, one in a military environment, the other in a commercial setting. Finally, some guidelines are offered, based on practical experience.

1. INTRODUCTION

Introducing technology into organisations and into society in general has a history which is, to say the least, stormy. Information technology has followed a similar course and set users and implementers alike wondering whether or not there is a more fruitful approach (even when the system can be cost-justified). The particular method of designing advanced systems which we are proposing to examine is called prototyping. The concept is well tried in engineering disciplines but has only recently become a possibility within the field of information systems design. A major reason has been that up till now, the 'tools' which are used were not widely available to make the process cost-effective. In short, designing a prototype could cost as much as designing the whole system. Before we describe prototyping and some examples, we will indicate the pressures that have brought about this change. These have been occurring in the market-place and have affected users, who have in turn 'reacted' by demanding changes in systems design.

2. INFORMATION TECHNOLOGY AND THE MARKET PLACE

The first pressure is towards packaged solutions. These have evolved from 'turnkey' designs required by users for tasks or processes which have been generally well defined and understood (eg stock control, accounts management and payroll) by users and subsequently system designers. The product is designed for general availability in a particular market segment and is "commodity-priced". The vendor expects a low entry cost to the market and a high volume of sales to yield adequate profit margins. The user has to accept that only limited modifications are possible outside the original design brief, although his perceived business needs might change.

Secondly, the need for equipment and software to operate more flexibly has meant that more functions are being integrated within systems and that the inter-working of heterogeneous systems is now possible. However, this still leaves the user to "tie everything together" to meet his needs, with the inevitable compromises.

Last, but not least, the rapid change in technology means that a product's market life is shortened, the development process has to be speeded up and the vendor has less desire and need to allocate precious resources to field maintenance and systems support. The user's reaction is to want to safeguard his investment in information technology, minimise the risks of failure and the need for costly update.

3. THEORETICAL PERSPECTIVES

3.1 Balancing the requirements in system development

These forces are imposing a need for a new method of systems design - something to balance the business need, the technological capability and the end users'(individuals and organisations) requirements. Over-emphasis on business and technology leads to user dissatisfaction, the "cog in the wheel" feeling or the inhuman face of technology. Over-compensation to meet user and technology 'friendliness' criteria, will not necessarily meet the business requirement. Lastly, the designer who places business and user needs before technology may find that the organisation will either not want to be changed by the potential of technology or be totally unrealistic and uncompromising about what its expectations are. How then do we tackle these problems of inbalance?

3.2 Two ends of a continumm: traditional
     systems design and prototyping

The 'prototyping' method is not necessarily
better than the traditional approach, nor is it
without problems.   However, it is more
appropriate in certain situations, as the
examples (from NATO and ICI) will show later in
this paper.   Martin (1) has detailed the main
differences of these two approaches on six
different dimensions and only a brief note will
be made of them at this point.   First, the
traditional approach starting with a
requirements analysis is a time-consuming and
formal operation and may generate application
backlogs.   The system specification document
may be lengthy and boring and may ultimately not
meet the user's needs.   The user when
accepting the specification, may not fully
realise the implications of what he is agreeing
and the system may be slow.   Documentation may
be tedious and time consuming and may not keep
up with the development process, as pressures
are created "to get things working".
Maintenance may also be slow.

In contrast, prototyping enables the users to
develop their own requirements (with or without
the aid of a systems analyst).   For example,
one of the most efficient ways of doing this, is
with a fourth generation language.   Prototyping
allows users to develop systems requirements in
a more stimulating and creative manner.   The
system specification may evolve in a more precise
and tested way and may even disappear, as the
system is continually modified.   The systems
specification becomes "what are we doing now"
and, as the user is thus continuously in touch
with the development of the system, the testing
is relatively speedy and error free.
Documentation becomes largely automatic and
'help' responses and interactive training on-line,
ensure that learning is continuous.

3.3 Why prototype?

Prototyping satisfies several requirements
generated by the business, technology and user
which are necessary to ensure a stable
equilibrium.   When meeting business
requirements, prototyping is relatively quick,
reduces the need for huge investments in systems
personnel and the potential costly failures in
design and implementation.   The result is that
the end user organisation will know very precisely
what its needs are and will, through direct
experience, know more than the vendor about his
products.   He will therefore be in a much
stronger negotiating position with the vendor in
ensuring that the equipment and services
required meet his requirements.

The techniques to be employed and their
assumptions can be subjected to early evaluation
and at low cost.   As complex systems can be
tackled in modular parts, they will not be
rendered totally obsolescent by rapidly changing

technology and allowances can be made for
flexibility, in case changes in business or user
requirements need to be made.

User requirements are more easily satisfied
through prototyping and motivational
advantages may be seen both at an individual
and organisational level.   The benefits of the
system may be demonstrated in a practical setting
to the organisation.   As the individual gains
confidence in the robustness of the tools, the
system can be tailored to individual needs
enabling the results of a person's efforts to be
quickly seen and evaluated.   The incremental
development more closely follows the human
thought process of idea generation, testing and
evaluation in an iterative loop.   This
contrasts with the linear progression of the
traditional approach, where the entirely
logical, systematic, grand design, unfolds
without any wrong turns, and whose totality
must be held in the human memory.   Through an
immersion and familiarity with the prototye
system, creativity can break through and lead
to new applications.   How then may we define
this process?

3.4 Definitions and descriptions

To encapsulate some of the above characteristics
we have chosen to employ the following
working definition of prototyping, based
on our experience:-

   "A means for end users to define, refine
   and re-define their own systems under
   their own control, within a systematic
   framework."

Let us examine more closely what the prototyping
process is.   First, one needs tools and
an 'enabling' organisational environment to
develop the prototype.   Tools range from the
simple to use (menu creator or key-stroke
procedure language) to the more complex fourth
generation language and electronic desk tools.
The tools may be conveniently classified,
for our purposes, as:-

(a) electronic desk tools (eg electronic mail
    and records management)
(b) database tools (eg retrieval techniques,
    such as query languages and report
    generators)
(c) communications tools (eg addressee list of
    services)
(d) procedural tools (eg building a set of test
    data)
(e) specialist packages (eg project management,
    modelling and expert systems)

Within the organisation, there must be an
understanding that the concept is experimental
and developmental.   The expectations must
be in harmony with this process as results
are constantly changing and the eventual full
scale system may be different from the prototype,
which itself might be discarded.   The key
decision makers at the highest levels must

support this culture and allocate time for end users to work in this way, with the result that performance and appraisal criteria may have to be changed. The use of the system will need to be controlled to ensure that results are not being achieved at random. The population of users should reflect the interconnection between jobs in terms of information inter-dependence, decision-making characteristics, and autonomy of action, which are just some of the important variables in job design. The readiness of the organisation to provide these conditions will therefore need to be carefully assessed.

As the end-users are so influential in the out-come of the design process, certain behavioural and attitudinal characteristics will need to be identified and harnessed. Take, for example, the need for a scientific attitude: to set up a hypothesis (or outline an idea), test it, systematically, observe the results and critically evaluate it. At the same time, the user must be emotionally detached enough to reject unworkable ideas, even though time and energy has been invested. However, a strong task orientation is necessary, as is a will to produce an adequate end result, rather than merely 'game playing' or searching for more interesting solutions when a practical one would suffice.

Defining and refining is a continuous process involving a constant monitoring and feedback of results. Knowledge of their own progress (and that of others) will increase individuals' motivation. As users are responsible for their results and the outcome is one which they have produced to enhance their own jobs, their commitment and ownership of the system increases. The fact that the systems design is under their control, enables their understanding to develop at a suitable pace.

However, the approach has its difficulties. Without a systematic framework within which to direct their creativity, user idiosyncrasies may come to dominate overall system design. User groups must therefore be "educated" not to be self-centred in their requirements. Where, then, can such systems be used?

3.5   Types of user

Organisations with complex activities or which are undergoing change will find prototyping valuable, as well as those which are attempting to introduce information technology into a totally new area. This is because such organisations are likely to be operating with a high degree of uncertainty. The result of introducing a new system into an uncertain organisational environment is therefore fraught with potential difficulty. This raises a second issue, that of needing to minimise or contain the risks associated with systems introduction: financial, political or commercial, to name but some.

Where these organisational uncertainties exist, they will be transmitted to different types of job holders (management, professional and clerical staff alike). If one system is to serve these end-users whose information needs may therefore be ill-defined or constantly changing, it has to be designed in a way that will allow its development to reflect the circumstances in which the user operates. To illustrate some of these points, we will describe two case studies of prototyping: one, in a military situation and the other in a commercial environment.

4.   PROTOTYPING IN A MILITARY HEADQUARTERS

4.1   Introduction

The case study here relates to a NATO Military Headquarters. However, the characteristics described may be equally valid for many top level managements in commercial and government organisations. Similar types of prototype systems have been trialed in the Cabinet Office (2) and the Alvey Directorate (3).

4.2   Background to the Prototype System

Command and Control Information Systems (C2) allow military chiefs of staff (or boards of directors) to take decisions in an effective and timely manner by enabling them to evaluate and respond to changing environments (4). In the NATO Headquarters, information is channelled from all echelons of the military hierarchy and evaluated on route by middle management for senior management decisions. Information in this context is relevant in both the raw data form and summarised versions. Many information sources that have complex interactions, may have been summarised using less than perfect assumptions and are difficult to quantify. Events and current status may be unpredictable, leading to new unforeseen situations.

Whilst the information received was unpredict-able, senior management had to provide decisions within deadlines, disseminate them, and manage the resulting actions. Because prototype systems aim to give users of the system more control, they can be used for this management role in preference to the traditional systems analysis approach. The prototype system referred to here operated from late 1977 to 1980, and the evaluation of the system formed the basis for subsequent NATO specifications for military C2 systems.

4.3   User Profiles

The users were military staff with no special aptitude for computing, aged between 20-50 years, and varying in seniority from a private to a four star general. Up to 150 users had access to the 25 terminals available within the system.

As any individual could be replaced at short notice and the prototype system had to support 15 different nationalities basic facilities had to be usable within half an hour's familiarisation.

However an important educational exercise was necessary for each group of users, as an aid to creating favourable attitudes and high motivation. This exercise involved describing the benefits and limitations of the particular prototype, and laid out guidelines of how to use the common tools available on the prototype system. Such a prototype system provided considerable flexibility for the users and devolved a greater responsibility on them for employing the tools correctly.

4.4 Tools Used

The tools available to the military personnel for adapting the system to their changing environment were as follows:-

(a) electronic desk tools provided each commander and his subordinates with word processing, electronic mail and graphics processing for manipulating their military situation displays and briefs. The word/ graphic processing packages handled colour, bit-map graphics and mixing of text and graphics. Graphics included free hand symbol positioning and colour hardcopy of text and graphics.

(b) database tools supported both a hierarchical structure and a relational model/data dictionary for in context retrieval. These tools allowed management to co-ordinate the various summaries and new data to provide rapid responses to certain decision making requirements.

(c) communications tools linked to other existing but specialised data processing equipment in an easy and timely manner, and allowed telex messages to be added.

(d) procedural tools enabled an interpretative language to be used to provide easy program and test data development.

4.5 Embryonic Growth of the Operational System

The initial prototype was supported on a single minicomputer, with basic tools used by the military to develop applications. This resulted in an iterative growth of the prototype system to 25 multi-functional workstations connected to a network of computers, closed circuit television system and communication facilities. Through this, a multitude of military-specific applications were developed, trialed in military exercises, evaluated and refined.

4.6 Benefits of the Prototype System

Whereas a traditional systems analysis approach,

taking approximately two years with expenditure in £M's, had failed, the prototype was established within three months, with a budget of £150,000. From the first three months, the system was of benefit to the military command. The level of benefit grew as the corporate memory, operational procedures, additional tools and better performance options were established.

The military staff expanded their computing and communications knowledge in line with the growth of the system. They felt they were in control, and were not being driven by a rigid set of statements of user requirements. Thus the operational system was accepted by all staff, meeting the formal and informal procedures upon which the organisation was based and was capable of being rapidly adapted to meet unpredictable events which arose from time to time.

4.7 Lessons Learnt

Prototype systems are highly successful if the management, information technology and specific tools are carefully co-ordinated in uncertain environments. Prototypes are particularly relevant for high grade users of corporate information systems. Office automation (OA) and its associated information tools are one type of prototyping system which suit many of the characteristics displayed in this case study.

5   PROTOTYPING IN A LARGE COMMERCIAL ENVIRONMENT

5.1 Introduction

Another area where prototyping can have rapid results is in bringing together several existing services into one integrated and unified system, to control complex activities. At ICI Mond Division a prototype system was installed based on the requirement that ICI had a need for a multi-functional terminal to meet all possible future access to different ICI computer systems.

5.2 Background to the Prototyping System

As in the first case, specifying in advance the statement of user requirements was extremely difficult because of the:-

(a) evolving requirements of other related ICI divisions

(b) need for rapid implementation

(c) difficulty of quantifying the existing manual procedures

(d) need to interwork with existing computer systems

(e) high volume and varied telephone usage

The prototype system was installed to overcome these difficulties by evolving a system which improved ICI Mond Division's co-ordination, communication and distribution of all quotations arising from overseas customers and agents. The prototype system was installed in 1981 and is continuing to be used in this role today.

5.3 User Profiles

Some 110 non-technical salesmen, office staff and managers each had a workstation connected to the prototype system. A database administrator was in charge of ensuring orderly use of the filing structures on the system. Any user with little computing knowledge could access the IBM, DEC, Xionics and Telex Systems by following a simple menu selection.

5.4 Tools Used

The results of the prototype system allowed ICI to adapt their telex messages into a form more meaningful to the ICI sales teams. ICI then experimentally developed access to customer and product information held on other remote and local computers by simple workstation menu selections. These were tailorable by individual groups of salesmen to meet market area needs.

Menu selections could be changed within half an hour by use of the Menu Builder and Keystroke Procedure Language (KPL). Users could cause their custom built menus to choose between alternative actions by defining the decision making process they themselves would have undertaken had they pressed the keys and inspected the screen. KPL can be "trained" to perform any sequence of actions a user would like to do and thereafter perform the sequence automatically using a single command. This sequence included calling several local applications (like CP/M packages) or controlling remote applications on other machines.

Other tools available to ICI were a powerful multi-level secure filing system. This was used to store and experiment with telexes, electronic mail, stock control figures and pricing/shipping information available on IBM and DEC mainframes. This database also provided a common base for all sales analysis on a daily basis.

5.5 Embryonic Growth of the System

Starting with a system of approximately 10 workstations it has now grown to 110 workstations. The storage capacity of the system has quadrupled and the number of connections to other computing systems tripled. ICI have developed many of their own procedures and "supertools" using the system. To date this has contributed to the saleman's acceptance of the system as a means of assessing all the corporate information pertinent to his job.

New IBM and DEC mainframes were installed and linked to the office system without having to change the salesmen's use of the system. The communications software package did this by automatically performing all network connections, IBM/DEC log ons, protocol conversion, monitoring, reservations and access rights.

5.6 Benefits of the Prototype System

Benefits of the ICI system are primarily financial and professional. Installing a prototype system, offering full office automation facilities, access to the telex network and IBM/DEC mainframes allows rapid improvements in sales executives' productivity. But more importantly it reduces ICI worldwide response time to a sales opportunity from 7-10 days to one day. One worthwhile contract thus obtained could pay for the complete prototype system.

5.7 Lessons Learned

This system is both an operational system and a prototype in that ICI continue to use the tools to build more embryonic information structures and new gateways on top of the existing system. ICI's ability to use the prototype system to develop new procedures and make more efficient use of the telex and telephone networks has clarified some of the firm's IT needs. Using this as a basis, ICI are now expanding OA to other divisions by extensive use of personal computers inter-connected by Network Office Systems.

6. GUIDELINES FOR PROTOTYPING

To summarise our conclusions, we offer some guidelines, which we believe are most characteristic of prototyping (as distinct from more traditional approaches to system design). However, there are many other guidelines which could apply to both approaches. The guidelines are drawn from our practical experience and we do not claim that they are exhaustive.

First, choose a suitable application area. Where there is uncertainty due to complex or ill defined activities or where the application for the technology is totally new, then the closely monitored evolutionary design of the prototyping approach will reduce the risks of failure. Clearly stating the assumptions and scope of the prototype system enables them to be tested and, with cost parameters defined, total costs can be extrapolated so that expenditure can be phased and controlled.

Secondly, tools should be practical and flexible, so that different types of user may employ them confidently. Easily understood tools will encourage self-teaching, while

clear and simple system messages will prevent
confusion in an already uncertain environment.
By ensuring that common and compatible tools
are used, the exchange of information is
forced to be more systematic and will yield a
more consistent and controlled set of results.
As the prototype may eventually be discarded,
tools must be financially affordable.

A third consideration is to ensure certain
attitudes are present in the organisation.
visible commitment from the top is critical
to ensure that the experimental nature of
the prototyping process is accepted and
understood in principle. Users'
expectations need to be assessed, so that their
tasks are seen to be achievable with the
existing tools.

Fourthly, the general requirements and skills
needed for prototyping should be analysed to
determine the degree of match with users'
abilities and to assess what type of education
and training programme may be appropriate.
Systematic yet flexible users are preferable,
as they will work with the tools in an
orderly and controlled way. Self-motivation
is a characteristic to be encouraged, since it
minimises the required level of supervision
and support, and develops personal
responsibility for system design.

Last but not least, the methodology should
provide a clear framework to guide and
schedule users' activities. The regular
monitoring of individuals to assess progress
and identify the most effective design methods
used is vital to success. Moreover, the
logging of the overall experience gained in
prototyping will help to avoid mistakes in
a full implementation and educate users in
the cyclical nature of the approach. Finally,
tracking the cultural impact of the prototype
is a 'must' for assessing the wider effects
of a fully developed system.

[1]   Martin J, Applications Development Without
       Programmers (Prentice-Hall) 1982.

[2]   Drake P, The Xionics system for the
       Cabinet Office Management and Trial
       (COMAT), DTI, Office Automation Pilot
       Evaluation Conference. EIU Informatics
       13-14 March 1984.

[3]   Drake P, Office Systems as the Interface
       to Corporate Information Systems,
       Comms 84 IEE conference 16-18 May 1984.

[4]   Drake P, Schmidt WHP, A Display System
       for High Level Decision Making. Electronic
       Display Conference 6-8 September 1979

Human-Computer Interaction — INTERACT '84 / B. Shackel (ed.)
Elsevier Science Publishers B.V. (North-Holland)
© IFIP, 1985

PROBLEMS IN EVALUATION OF HUMAN - COMPUTER INTERFACES:

A CASE STUDY

Liam Bannon and Claire O'Malley

Institute for Cognitive Science, C-015
University of California, San Diego,
La Jolla, California 92093

One of the most difficult aspects of interface design is evaluating new or changed features of an interface. In this paper we discuss methods of evaluation, their strengths and weaknesses, in the context of a program we developed to assist users in getting quick access to information contained in the UNIX[1] manual. We outline the problems encountered both in the design and the evaluation of this user interface.

A basic tenet held by our research group is that the design and evaluation components of software development should be treated as a whole and not isolated from one another — evaluation should be considered from the outset of the design and built into the development of the system. We have tried to adhere to this principle in conducting our research. However, the task is not as easy as it may seem at first. Our experience in designing, implementing, and testing a small program resulted in several practical problems which are the subject of this paper.

Description of the Study

The study which we describe is part of our research on the development and use of system documentation in the Human-Machine Interaction project at UCSD. (cf. O'Malley et al., 1983). We have been examining how people at our Institute use the existing online documentation by monitoring their use of the programs, and by soliciting online feedback from users as they sought information in the manual. We found that about 35% of the use made of the online reference manual [2] was for what we refer to as "quick reference": users needed to be able to verify the name of a program, or check on flags, options, and syntax, without having to scan through extraneous material. In an attempt to meet this need, we developed a prototype online Quick Reference facility that contained only the correct syntax of the command, a list of possible options, and a brief explanation. This prototype system had a limited database consisting of printing commands [3] which we felt would be both representative of the eventual system we had envisaged, and which would

be immediately useful to our user population.

We were interested in determining whether the new facility would meet the quick reference need that we had already identified. Because our earlier data had been collected from examining the use of existing facilities in our Institute, we decided to evaluate the proposed new program within this same context, and assess how users changed their use of the original online reference manual after we introduced our new facility. This meant that we had to accept much less control over the possible variables than in a traditional experimental study, but it was a more appropriate method of evaluation at this stage in the development of the facility, as we were concerned about whether users found it of practical use in their everyday activities. A more controlled study would be appropriate for the purposes of debugging the specific display design, after we had determined the usefulness of this type of facility.

To evaluate the usefulness of the new program we decided to compare the frequency of use of *pref* with the use of *man* before and after its implementation by means of system accounting data. However, we also wanted more detailed information than simple usage data, in order to determine whether or not there were any problems with the facility, and what improvements should be made to it. One way to obtain this kind of information is from users themselves, by eliciting comments after each use of the program. However, earlier studies showed that many of our users complained that the request for online feedback was obtrusive, and interfered with the tasks they were performing. Therefore, in designing the evaluation tools for our new facility we included in our quick reference program a simple menu facility to allow easy user feedback on the usefulness of the information provided.

However, despite the fact that we went to some lengths to ensure that our methods of evaluation were carefully designed and conducted, we still had difficulty in giving a complete account of our results. In the following sections, we document some of these problems and try to relate them to more general issues in evaluation.

Design Aims and Evaluation Methods

Our main design considerations were the need for quick scanning of the material on the screen, brevity and clarity of the information, relevance and lack of redundancy, and clarity of syntax. In working on the design, we were very conscious of the necessity to make tradeoffs, and of the very limited information that was available to make such decisions. Some of our design objectives, such as reducing ambiguity and jargon, are not affected by the mix of users, but there were several aspects of the design where the demands of brevity and clarity pushed for different solutions, depending on the user population envisaged. The intended users of our new program encompassed a wide range — students, administrative staff, research faculty and staff — with varying degrees of knowledge about the UNIX system. Producing an interface that would be acceptable to such a wide variety of users was a difficult task, and led to a somewhat uneasy compromise.

As we have already discussed, we had two methods for collecting information on the usefulness of our facility: information concerning frequency of use from the system accounting data, and online comments from users.

Online feedback. The online feedback was the most useful in *identifying common problems*, and it also served to suggest reasons for the patterns we found in the account data. The main drawback of this method was its intrusiveness on users, and we found that after a while users stopped providing comments. However, despite the potential annoyance to users, this method proved useful in identifying some of the problems encountered by our users.

System accounting information. The system accounting information, on the other hand, was useful in *identifying patterns of use*. It was espe-

cially useful in revealing the pattern which we characterize as "task-specific help", involving several successive calls to *man*, with different, but functionally related, arguments. However, there were some problems inherent in the use of the system accounting information. In investigating the frequency of use of the commands for which users were seeking help, it was difficult to determine exactly what users were doing, because the system accounting information also collects information on pre- and postprocessors called by the program, but not specified explicitly by the user. Distinguishing these data is difficult with the present system, since one has to use knowledge of the processors called, and timing information, to infer what was actually typed by the user. Thus the data had to be sifted "by hand" before any automated analysis could be conducted.

Given the problems outlined above, it seemed necessary to combine these two different means of collecting data: user comments indicated usage problems that were not obvious from examination of the system accounting information, while the latter data were more revealing of patterns of use. The more general point here is that the method of evaluation used should provide information on both the nature and range of problems, as well as their frequency of occurrence, and for this several methods of evaluation are required. On their own, these kinds of information provide only gross indications of problems, but in our case they did prove useful in identifying broad categories of help that users needed.

Results of Evaluation

System accounting information. One of our concerns in evaluating the system was whether our new program was more satisfactory than *man* for getting help on options and syntax. We reasoned that, if *pref* is useful, there should be some effect on the use of *man*. We had identified about 35% of the use of *man* with the need for quick reference, so we might expect about a 35% drop in *man* if that need was being fully served. We decided to compare the frequency of use of *man* for the period prior to implementing *pref*, with the use of *man* and *pref* following installation. [4] We did find a decrease in the use of *man* for *pref* users; however, there was also a decrease for those who did not use our facility. When we examined the frequency of use of the printing programs themselves we found a concomitant decrease, which could account for most of the overall decrease in the use of *man*. When we normalized the data to control for the decrease in use of printing commands, the difference in use of *man* between *pref* users and those who did not use *pref* was still large, so we can conclude that the use of *pref* had made a difference to the use of *man*.

Online feedback. The data described above gave us a general idea of the usefulness of *pref*, but we needed more detailed information. We had built into the design of the facility a means for obtaining this more detailed kind of evaluation which we felt would minimize disruption to users. Users were able to indicate their success or failure to obtain the information they wanted by a simple menu of commands (See Figure 1). In order to quit the program, the user types upper case **Q**(uit) if the facility is useful, and lower case **q**(uit) if it is not. [5] We also gave users the option of providing more detailed feedback, by typing **c**(omments), which puts them in the editor where they can type their comments and then return to the quick reference entry. Users are also able to get a more detailed explanation of the command from within the quick reference facility, by calling the regular online manual without having to quit the program, by using the command **m**(anual). They can also specify new arguments by using the "new" menu option. Users specify lower case **n**(ew) if the previous entry had been unhelpful, and upper case **N**(ew) if the previous entry had been helpful. Users can also get online help for the use of the facility, by typing **h**(elp).

We compared the use of upper and lower case quit commands, and found a significant difference in favour of the upper case (55%), indicating that users found the facility useful. We were concerned about whether or not users were simply perseverating by choosing to always type upper or lower case, so we examined the use of upper case N and lower case n, and found that there was no corresponding significant difference between these two, in fact there was a slight difference in the opposite direction. This ruled out simple case perseveration as an explanation of the result. We also considered the possibility that the use of *pref* and *man* might be for quite different sets of printing commands, which would therefore make a comparison between the two of rather limited usefulness. [6] However, when we correlated the use of the arguments to *pref* with the arguments to *man*, we found a significant positive correlation, indicating that the pattern was not appreciably different.

Another of the evaluation questions we had asked concerned what improvements could be made to the facility. The online feedback obtained from users provided useful suggestions about possible improvements: the comments indicated that they found the program a positive addition to existing facilities, and their suggestions were extremely helpful in further refining the facility at each design stage. For instance, the facility was changed to page rather than scroll after user comments indicated irritation with the scrolling.

Summary

In summary, our evaluation provided a number of measures that supported our hypothesis that a quick reference facility for system commands was needed. There was a drop in the use of the *man*

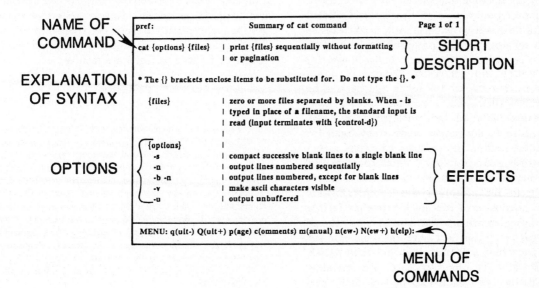

NAME OF COMMAND

SHORT DESCRIPTION

EXPLANATION OF SYNTAX

OPTIONS

EFFECTS

MENU OF COMMANDS

command for printing programs after *pref* was introduced, and online user evaluations of *pref* after each usage were, on balance, favorable. What of longer-term evaluation? When we examined the patterns of use which emerged over the period between initial implementation of the facility and after it had been in use for a few months, there was a reduction in use of the prototype system. Our methods of evaluation supplied no obvious reasons for this.

Conclusions

Some of the problems we encountered were due to the lack of control we had over the variables. Our study was not an experimental one in the tradition of laboratory studies, although we attempted to be as rigorous as possible in our data collection without intruding too much on our users. The main reason for choosing to test our system initially "in the field" was that we were concerned with the basic question of whether or not our program was serving its intended purpose in fulfilling a need which was not provided adequately by the existing documentation. The answer to this question could only be provided by studying the use of the system within the context of the existing facilities. Other questions concerning the details of the design, the format of the display, and so on, are more amenable to strictly controlled studies. However, we felt it important to test out our concept of the system before investing too heavily in details of a specific design.

We have discussed the importance of considering evaluation questions at the outset of the design. The need for iterative and piecemeal development, where prototypes are implemented and tested before the final version is developed, often leads to problems relating to the representability and scope of the system "pieces" that are initially chosen for implementation and evaluation. Testing of prototypes means that any modifications that have to be made cost less than with a complete version; however, the evaluation of the prototype system may not generalize to the proper context envisaged for the complete system. In our own case, one aspect of this problem of "modularity" which concerned us was whether or not the choice of domain in which to implement the prototype was a representative one. Our restriction of the quick reference facility to the printing commands was done for the sake of expediency, as we did not have the time nor the resources to build a database for the whole UNIX command set. The domain itself was certainly appropriate in that almost all of our users performed these tasks frequently, and often needed quick reference help. However, the database we implemented was still restricted in scope, and several users expressed dissatisfaction with the limited amount of information provided; users wanted information concerning programs which our prototype did not yet cover.

The reduction in use of our prototype over time is difficult to interpret. Some possible explanations include the following: some reduction in use of the facility is expected in the weeks following its introduction, as the novelty factor diminishes. Also, users may have forgotten about the facility, or they may have forgotten the name of the program — not an unlikely occurrence on a system with hundreds of commands. This latter problem is likely on our system because of the lack of support for accessing documentation (in general, the user needs to know the name of the program in order to access it.) Users may have memorized the relevant information in *pref*, thus reducing the need to actually call the facility.

Alternatively, rather than expending effort on trying to account for a slight reduction in usage of our new facility, perhaps we should consider a more basic question: what is an appropriate baseline level of use for such a facility? We had not really studied this issue prior to development, and we still do not have an answer to the question. The crucial issue about documentation facilities in general is not whether they are heavily used, but whether they satisfy the information needs of users on those occasions when they are used. (For example, our use of a dictionary may not be frequent, but can nevertheless be quite important.) This suggests that it may not be appropriate to rely on frequency of use information in the evaluation of the success or failure of a particular software facility.

Footnotes

This research was conducted under Contract N00014-79-C-0323, NR 667-437 with the Personnel and Training Research Programs of the Office of Naval Research. Work on Human-Computer Interaction was also supported by a grant from the System Development Foundation. This paper reports on a project carried out by the Structured Manual Group of the UCSD HumanMachine Interaction Project. Members involved in this project were: L. Bannon, E. Conway, J. Graham, M. Monty, C. O'Malley, P. Smolensky, and J. Sokolov. The programming was performed by D. Owen and P. Smolensky. Requests for reprints should be sent to the Institute for Cognitive Science C-015; University of California, San Diego; La Jolla, California, 92093, USA.

1. UNIX is a trademark of Bell Laboratories. The comments in this paper refer to the 4.1 BSD version developed at the University of California, Berkeley.

2. The UNIX online manual contains separate entries for each program, which is accessed by typing the command *man* with the program name as the argument. This produces several screenfuls of text in a standardized format, with the name of the program, a short synopsis, a longer description of the program and how to use it, examples, and some diagnostic information.

3. The prototype system that we developed was called *pref* for "printing reference".

4. One major problem was that *pref* was initially designed only to cater for the subset of commands to do with printing, so we had to select those calls to *man* that had the same arguments as those that *pref* covered, in order to do an accurate comparison.

5. The reason for using upper case to indicate success was to lessen the probability of response bias, since lower case is the normal form of a command, and it is easier to type.

6. The reasoning was that *pref* might just be supplementing specific inadequacies in some of the manual entries, as in some cases the information in the *pref* entries was more complete than that in *man*.

References

[1]   O'Malley, C., Smolensky, P., Bannon, L., Conway, E., Graham, J., Sokolov, J., & Monty, M. (1983, December). A Proposal for User Centered System Documentation. *Proceedings of the CHI 1983 Conference on Human Factors in Computing Systems* (pp. 282-285). Boston: ACM.

HUMAN ASPECTS OF OFFICE SYSTEMS - USER ACCEPTANCE RESEARCH RESULTS

Reinhard Helmreich

Siemens AG, Communications Group
PN PS 1, User Acceptance Laboratory
Hofmannstrasse 51, D - 8000 Munich 70

The vision that the "office of the future" conjures up is indeed an impressive sight: computer power at every office desk, within easy reach of every white-collar worker, electronic systems permitting worldwide communication by text, images and voice. But what real benefits can be expected from this new technology and how will they be exploited? Will the user be aware of the advantages technology has to offer? And how should advanced office systems be designed and organized if they are to gain acceptance?

OFFICE AUTOMATION - A NON-TECHNICAL APPROACH

Office automation (OA) must not be seen from the purely technological point of view, for often the benefits do not become obvious until implementation. The key issue here is user acceptance. In simple terms, this means that a new office system is unlikely to succeed if the people it is intended to serve are not consulted first.

Implementation of OA equipment must therefore be accompanied by a supporting program that takes a distinctly non-technical approach. The central here is acceptance, a concept which should be understood as the willingness of target users to apply technology to their jobs.

Here it is not only a question of the technical potential of OA, but also of the perceived benefits and ultimately of the role of the white-collar worker in an automated office environment. After all, technological innovations in the office sector are not introduced for the sake of technology alone, but to make innovations possible in the office environment as well.

This paper outlines several issues which have proved critical in the discussion on office automation. The theses put forward are less concerned with theoretical considerations than with practical experience gained from investigations into the use of modern technology in the office.

ACCEPTANCE - A SUBJECT FOR RESEARCH

The question of acceptance of new office technology has been the subject of research in the Federal Republic of Germany for several years now. Scientific institutions and manufacturers of OA equipment' have conducted large-scale field trials, some of them supported by the Federal Ministry for Research and Technology, and a large number of findings has been published. These deal with such issues as

- User requirements for OA functions and services

- User interaction with modern office equipment

- Experience relating to OA implementation, training, support and organizational adaptation

- Impact on persons and organizations

Three common factors have emerged from these surveys which play key roles in acceptance: the user, work organization and technology.

These three factors should not, of course, be viewed in isolation, as they closely interact in a complex relationship. To cite just one example: office work must be organized to suit users' qualifications if new technology is to be implemented. In other words, mere ergonomic improvements to equipment will be of little value if the work process is not properly structured.

MASTERING THE ACCEPTANCE PROBLEM

Scientific analysis is, however, only the first step towards mastering acceptance. The second step is to translate experience into strategies for action.

This definitely does not mean curing the symptoms after the illness has occurred, but developing a planning process so that resistance to change is largely avoided. This planning must be applied to all stages of technological innovation: design, development, implement and evaluation. The idea is to move away from acceptance research and towards acceptance planning.

DETECTING STRESS AND STRAIN

The traditional office, as yet unequipped with modern technology, is fondly depicted by the media as an intact world. Experience shows, however, that more complaints about the race against time, who-does-what disputes and stress are to be found in the office than anywhere else.

The obvious conclusion is that modern technology stands a good chance of being accepted if it can relieve what white-collar workers feel they suffer as stress and strain. The waste of effort, the inertia present in the office of today and the objectionable effects these have on staff must be pointed out.

A survey of these effects would go far beyond the scope of conventional text and communication analyses. It should be realized how much time is wasted on simply copying texts word for word. Evidence is also to be found of recurrent duplication of effort caused by exaggerated division of labor.

The aim of modern office technology must be first and foremost to reduce the wastage and weak points found in present-day office organization.

BOOSTING OFFICE PRODUCTIVITY

It has been estimated that the application of technology to manufacturing processes has accounted for a 1000 % growth in productivity over the past 80 years. In the office, by comparison, the growth in output over the same period is rated at a modest 50 %. Seen in this light, the office still has considerable scope for rationalization.

Statistics also show that in the Federal Republic of Germany, for example, over 50 % of employees will soon be working in offices. Up-to-the-minute data and an efficient information flow are of prime importance to white-collar workers. The office of today is no longer an unproductive appendage to manufacturing. In this sense, improvement of the instruments and quality of office work is a matter of priority.

The office is a factor of production. It contributes to the creation of wealth. An ergonomic analysis of the office is essential to implementation of OA in the future. This analysis must treat in depth both the processes taking place at the individual workstation and interaction between staff.

OA IS NOT THE "FULLY AUTOMATED OFFICE"

Thanks to electronic data processing, many of those office activities which are relatively structured and routine have now been automated. Beyond these, there is a wide range of office jobs which are characterized by varying, largely unstructured, information-intensive and communication-intensive activities. To a varying extent, activities like these can be found in any office job. This is true not only of support staff, but also of professionals and managers.

The design of modern office equipment will not, therefore, pursue automation as an end in itself. Instead, what is needed is a kind of "electronic toolbox" for independent, personalized use. A great deal of office work involves exercising judgment and does not lend itself to automation.

USER-ORIENTED SYSTEM DESIGN

What kind of technology is needed in the office? What requirements must be satisfied in terms of functions and services? An answer must be found to these questions if the service features of office systems are to be defined. But a few obstacles cannot be overlooked:

- Hardly any system designer can put his finger on those points of stress and strain in the office which might be relieved with OA.

- Few O&M scenarios or activity sampling studies have been able to shed light on what is actually happening in the office. Many activities seem practically incapable of structuring and tend to be shaped by the personality and style of the people during them.

- No theory of organizational interaction in the office exists from
  which specific requirements for the
  application of technology might be
  inferred.

- Prospective users, too, have little
  idea of the potential benefits of OA
  (at most they will be aware of the
  greater ease of correction offered by
  advanced text-handling tools).

In other words, neither a meticulous
pre-implementation O&M analysis of the
office as a system nor a survey of target users' felt needs will be sufficient
in itself to plot the right path for
implementation of OA. What is needed
is an iterative strategy offering the
user functions and options which he
then accepts or rejects, or which are
modified.

ERGONOMICS IS MORE THAN AN ADJUSTABLE
CHAIR

Ergonomics has traditionally concentrated on the physical aspects of work:
on humanizing equipment, such as chairs,
desks, keyboards and video screens, and
the general work environment. Ergonomic
findings form the basis of today's
design rules and standards.

But efforts must be stepped up in a new
sub-sector of ergonomics: software ergonomics. In the office context, this
means the design of the user interface
of a system. Catchwords such as "easy-
to-learn" or "user-friendly" indicate
what ought to be achieved. But to date
very few detailed design guidelines have
been formulated on how to reach these
goals.

Experience shows that a carefully designed system interface with easy-to-use
menus and prompts and easy-to-understand error messages is the key to userfriendliness. The user must be able to
stick to common-sense rules. He cannot
be expected to go into the fine points
of system architecture.

It is also important to define the
right proportion of help functions, as
the OA newcomer will obviously need
more assistance from the system than
the knowledgeable user. Office systems
must also offer a facility for cancel-
lation of entries already keyed in, as
if they had never been input. This gives
the user a chance to try things out.

WHAT THE USER VALUES MOST

In field trials with modern office
equipment, three features have emerged
which users rate very highly: availability, flexibility and data privacy.

Availability means that an office
system must be accessible at all times,
right from the user's normal workstation. Its capacity must be designed for
loads; the user cannot be expected to
put up with long waiting times inherent
in the system. Availability thus means
that the user should have not only his
own terminal, but also a stable, constantly running system.

Maximum flexibility of user options is
another indispensable feature. Every
user must be able to decide for himself
whether and how he wishes to take advantage of office technology. Here the
individual must be left considerable
latitude to accept or reject options,
for only he can judge which functions
are of real benefit to him.

Acceptance of an office system as an
instrument or tool for everyday work
primarily depends on the scope and
content of the job to be done. Job
structure is a decisive acceptance
factor. This does not mean, however,
that office work must be structured
before OA is implemented. The very fact
that the application potential is "open-
ended" gives the user ample scope for
controlled modification of his own
schedules and procedures. He must thus
be at liberty to arrange his files,
his appointments diary or his post
book as he sees fit. A technology that
forces users to turn everything upside
down has little chance of acceptance.

This also means that an office system
must be capable of continuous adapation
and enhancement. "Cast-iron" systems
which do not permit modifications even
to their current versions will remain
as unmanageable as ever.

The third feature which users prize is
data privacy. What one user does with
"his" office system is taboo for others.
An office system cannot become an integral part of office work until users
are convinced that their data is safe
from unauthorized access. This is a
further argument for the "private"
character of office systems.

IMPLEMENTATION AND TRAINING

Trials testing modern office systems
under everyday conditions have shown

again and again that implementation po-
lices and training of target users have
a profound impact on acceptance.

User involvement is vital to the success (or failure) of a new office
system. This means that the target
user must be informed about the new
technology long before implementation
and drawn into decision-making from
the outset. Implementation thus implies
a sincere desire to cooperate on the
part of users, planners and system designers.

There is much more to training than
learning to press the right button.
Most office systems can be operated
fairly smoothly after a few hours"
practice. But this is where the real
learning begins. What tasks can be performed with the system? What changes
are possible in personal work organization? For what tasks is the new technology unlikely to yield tangible benefits?

These are no longer questions of pressing the right button at the right time,
but center on the benefits which the
individual user can derive from the
technical system in doing his job. In
this phase users need motivation and
support, and considerable time and
effort must be expended on personal
guidance. Instructors must familiarize
themselves with the tasks and workstyles
of target users before suggesting how
they get the best out of the new system.
This phase of the learning process
lasts several weeks.

The group to which the user belongs
plays an important part. The behavior
of colleagues may motivate or discourage him. Our experience shows that the
users of an office system tend to share
their knowledge and pass on ideas. A
sense of group identity emerges.

During the learning phase, it is a
good idea just to let users play with
the new system now and then; they will
not be put off by initial setbacks and
will find familiarization that much
easier. Contrary to popular opinion,
the user's age is, we find, no obstacle
to learning and has no effect on acceptance.

QUALITATIVE COST-BENEFIT ANALYSIS

The decision to introduce an office
system will invariably be based on a
cost-benefit analysis. In the office
sector, however, a purely quantitative
assessment poses many problems. The

effects of modern office technology are
both quantitative and qualitative in
nature. Faster access to information,
improved document quality, improved communication facilities, etc. are difficult to simulate in the econometric
models of management science.

Decision-makers will be required in future to weigh up qualitative arguments
more and more. OA has a direct effect
on productivity in that it makes organizations more flexible and speeds up
their reactions. But buying technology
is simply not enough here; creating the
right background for OA is just as important. Introduction of advanced technologies in the office should therefore
be seen in the context of organizational adaptation.

As OA affects both the job satisfaction
of the individual and the working environment as a whole, it can do much
to humanize office work. The challenge
here is a dual one: office automation
must satisfy both human needs and economic necessities at the same time.

REFERENCES

(1) Helmreich, R., Acceptance Research
    Strategies in Computer Message
    Systems, in Uhlig, R.P. (ed). Com-
    puter Message Systems (North-
    Holland, Amsterdam, 1981)

(2) Helmreich, R., User Acceptance –
    the Key of Office Automation Suc-
    cess, data report 10 (1982) No. 1,
    4-7

(3) Helmreich, R. and Wimmer, K., Field
    Study with a Computer-Based Office
    System, Telecommunications Policy 6
    (1982) 136-142

Human-Computer Interaction — INTERACT '84 / B. Shackel (ed.)
Elsevier Science Publishers B.V. (North-Holland)
© IFIP, 1985

A COMPUTER-BASED TOOL FOR EVALUATING ALPHANUMERIC DISPLAYS

Thomas S. Tullis[1]

Burroughs Corporation
Mission Viejo, California
USA

A computer program has been developed to measure six characteristics
of alphanumeric displays: (1) the overall density of characters on the
display; (2) the local density of other characters near each character;
(3) the number of distinct groups of characters; (4) the average visual
angle subtended by those groups; (5) the number of distinct labels or
data items; (6) the average uncertainty of the positions of the items
on the display. A study of 520 CRT displays that varied on these measures was conducted. Multiple regressions indicated that search times to
locate items on the displays could be fit using these display measures
(R = .71), as could subjective ratings of ease of use (R = .90).

1. INTRODUCTION

The format of computer-generated alphanumeric displays clearly has a significant
impact on the user's ability to extract
information from the displays. For example, consider the CRT displays shown in
Figures 1 and 2, taken from a study evaluating alternative formats for results
from an automated telephone testing system (13). Figure 1 shows a "narrative"
format originally designed to convey the
test results to the user. Figure 2 shows
a "structured" format in which the display was redesigned using a variety of
techniques. An evaluation of these displays showed that, after practice, users
took an average of 8.3 sec to interpret
results in the "narrative" format, compared to 5.0 sec for the "structured"
format-- a 40% decrease.

The results of this study raise a general
question: What characteristics of alphanumeric display formats determine the
user's ability to extract information
from the displays? To answer that question, an extensive review of the literature on the design of formatted displays
was conducted. That literature can be
divided into two general categories:
guidelines and empirical studies. The
guidelines include highly specific lists
of rules for information display (e.g.,
(6, 9)), as well as more conceptual discussions of display design in general
(e.g., (7, 10)). The empirical studies
include numerous visual search studies
using simple arrays of characters or symbols (e.g., (1, 11)), as well as a variety of other studies using more complex
arrays of words or data (e.g., (4, 5)).

The purpose of the literature review was
to determine the basic characteristics

of display formats that either the guidelines or the empirical data suggest are
important determinants of the user's
ability to extract information from the
displays. These were limited to objectively defined characteristics related to
the display format. (The literature review and these display characteristics
are described in more detail in (12).)

As a result of the review, a computer
program was written in the "C" language
to measure six display characteristics
that the literature suggested are important:

1. Overall density- the number of
    characters displayed, expressed as
    a percentage of the total number
    of character spaces available.

2. Local density- the average percent-
    age of occupied character spaces in
    a 5-deg visual angle surrounding
    each character (essentially how
    "tightly packed" the display is).

3. Number of groups- the number of
    distinct groups of characters de-
    tected using a proximity cluster-
    ing technique adapted from (14).

4. Average size of groups- the aver-
    age visual angle subtended by the
    groups of characters.

5. Number of items- the number of in-
    dividual labels or data items on
    the display (closely related to
    overall density).

6. Item uncertainty- the average un-
    certainty, as defined in informa-
    tion theory, of the horizontal and
    vertical position of each item,

```
*******************************
*                             *
*     TIP GROUND      14 K     *
*                             *
*******************************


DC RESISTANCE     DC VOLTAGE      AC SIGNATURE

3500 K T-R                          9 K T-R
  14 K T-G        0 V T-G          14 K T-G
3500 K R-G        0 V R-G         629 K R-G

BALANCE                          CENTRAL OFFICE

  39 DB                          VALID LINE CKT
                                 DIAL TONE OK
```

Figure 2. Display of structured format from Tullis (1981)

```
11111111111111111111111111111
1                           1
1  222 222222      33 3     1
1                           1
11111111111111111111111111111

44 4444444444      55 5555555      66 666666666


7777 7 777         9 9 999          8 8 888
 77 7 777          9 9 999         88 8 888
7777 7 777                        888 8 888

:::::::                           :::::::: :::::::
<< <<                             ---- ----
                                  ---- ----
                                    --  --
```

Figure 4. Groups predicted for structured display from Tullis (1981)

```
TEST RESULTS    SUMMARY: GROUND

GROUND. FAULT T-G
3 TERMINAL DC RESISTANCE
  > 3500.00 K OHMS T-R
  =   14.21 K OHMS T-G
  > 3500.00 K OHMS R-G
3 TERMINAL DC VOLTAGE
  =    0.00 VOLTS T-G
  =    0.00 VOLTS R-G
VALID AC SIGNATURE
3 TERMINAL AC RESISTANCE
  =    8.82 K OHMS T-R
  =   14.17 K OHMS T-G
  =  628.52 K OHMS R-G
LONGITUDINAL BALANCE POOR
  =   39    DB
COULD NOT COUNT RINGERS DUE TO
  LOW RESISTANCE
VALID LINE CKT CONFIGURATION
CAN DRAW AND BREAK DIAL TONE
```

Figure 1. Display of narrative format from Tullis (1981)

```
1111 1111111    22222222 222222

3333333 33333 333
3 3333333 33 3333333333
3 3333333 3 3333 333
3   33333 3 3333 333
3 3333333 3 3333 333
3 3333333 33 3333333
3   3333 33333 333
    3333 3333 333
33333 33 333333333
3 3333333 33 3333333333
3   3333 3 3333 333
3   33333 3 3333 333
3   33333 3 3333 333
    333333 3 3333 333
333333333 333333 3333
3   33 33
3333333 333 33333 3333333 333 33
  333 33333333333
33333 3333 333 33333333333333333
333 3333 333 33333 3333 3333
```

Figure 3. Groups predicted for narrative display from Tullis (1981)

measured using techniques adapted from (2).

To illustrate the program, consider Table 1, which shows the results of these measures for the displays shown in Figures 1 and 2. In addition, Figures 3 and 4 show the specific groups of characters detected by the program.

2. METHOD

To determine which of these measures are associated with differences in display usability, an experiment was conducted using a wide variety of display formats. Specifically, 26 different formats for presenting listings of airline flights and 26 different formats for presenting listings of hotels were developed.

Ten clerical employees at Bell Laboratories participated in the study for about four hours each. The participants saw ten different examples of each format and answered a question about each display (e.g., "What is the coach fare from Denver to Newark?"). Thus, each participant saw 520 displays and associated questions. On each trial, the search time to locate the answer to the question was recorded.

The sequence of events for one trial was as follows. First, the question to be answered about the display was presented by itself. When the subject hit the space bar on the keyboard, the question disappeared and the display of airline or hotel listings appeared. The subject then searched for the answer to the question and hit the space bar again when it was found. The display then disappeared and the question reappeared, along with two multiple-choice answers. The subject then chose one of the two answers. Search time was defined as the time during which the display was actually presented.

After seeing the ten examples for one format, the subject was asked to rate how easy it was to use that format on a scale of 1 to 5, with 1 being "Very Easy to Use" and 5, "Very Difficult to Use."

3. RESULTS

The two main dependent measures in this study were search times and subjective ratings.

3.1 Search Time

Overall, the subjects answered 97.7% of the questions about the displays correctly, indicating that they were very accurate. A mean search time was calculated for each format based on the correct trials only. The simple correlations of the six display measures with mean search times are shown in Table 2.

Table 2
Simple Correlations of Six Measures
with Search Times and Subjective Ratings

	Search Time	Subjective Rating
Overall Density	.33	.63
Local Density	.39	.65
Number of Groups	-.06	-.16
Size of Groups	.56	.67
Number of Items	.34	.66
Item Uncertainty	.42	.75

Several multiple regressions using various subsets of the six display measures to predict search time were also conducted. The multiple regression using all six of the display measures resulted in a multiple R of .71, meaning that the regression accounted for 50% of the variance in search time. The results of this regression using all six measures are graphically depicted in Figure 5. Individual t tests on the regression coefficients showed that the coefficients for local density, number of groups, and size of groups were significant. The regression using only those three variables as predictors resulted in a multiple R of .66, and the regression using only the two grouping measures resulted in a multiple R of .65.

The results indicate that the number of

Table 1
Results of Applying Display Measures to Figures 1 and 2

	Overall Density	Local Density	Groups Number	Size	Number of Items	Item Uncertainty
Figure 1	17.9%	58.0%	3	13.3 deg	34	6.73 bits
Figure 2	10.8%	35.6%	13	5.2 deg	26	6.66 bits

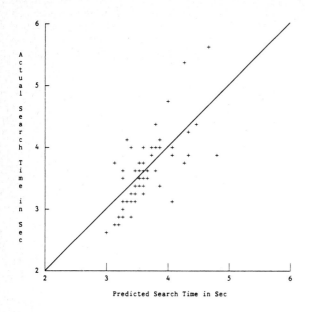

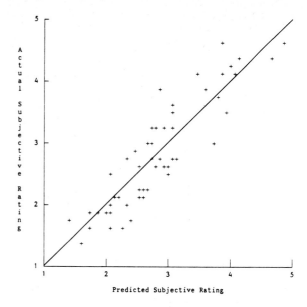

Figure 5. Results of multiple regression predicting search time from all six display measures (multiple $\underline{R}$ = .71)

Figure 6. Results of multiple regression predicting subjective rating from all six display measures (multiple $\underline{R}$ = .90)

groups of characters on the display and their average visual angle are the two most important predictors of search time. In essence, as either the number of groups or their size increases, the search time increases.

3.2 Subjective Ratings

A mean subjective rating on the 1 to 5 scale was calculated for each format based on the ratings that each of the ten subjects provided. Subjective ratings tended to be positively correlated with search times ($\underline{r}$ = .68), as one would expect.

The simple correlations of the six display measures with the mean subjective ratings are shown in Table 2. Most of the correlations were rather high, except for the correlation with number of groups.

The results of a multiple regression using all six display measures to predict subjective ratings are graphically illustrated in Figure 6. The regression resulted in a multiple $\underline{R}$ of .90, meaning that these six display measures accounted for 81% of the variance in rated ease of use. This is quite impressive, and indicates that the display measures are better at predicting subjective ratings than at predicting search times ($\underline{R}$ of .90 $\underline{vs}$ .71). In addition, individual $\underline{t}$

tests on the regression coefficients showed that all of the coefficients were significant, unlike the results for search time. This indicates that all six measures play a role in predicting subjective ratings.

4. CONCLUSIONS

The regression equations developed in this experiment have been validated in another experiment using a completely different set of displays. The correlations between predicted (a priori) and obtained values were quite high for both search times and subjective ratings ($\underline{r}$ = .80 for both). The equations have also been applied to search time data published in the literature: Dodson and Shields (5), Ringel and Hammer (8), and Callan, Curran, and Lane (3). The resulting correlations between predicted and actual search times were very high: .98, .79, and .91.

In conclusion, a computer-based tool for objectively evaluating the usability of a display has been developed and validated. It should be particularly useful to system designers who must choose between alternative designs for a user interface, but who do not have the time or resources to collect human performance data.

REFERENCES

1. Banks, W., and Prinzmetal, W. Config-
   urational effects in visual informa-
   processing. Perception & Psychophysics, 1976, 19, 361-367.

2. Bonsiepe, G. A method of quantifying
   order in typographic design. Journal
   of Typographic Research, 1968, 2,
   203-220.

3. Callan, J. R., Curran, L. E., and
   Lane, J. L. Visual search times for
   Navy tactical information displays
   (Report # NPRDC-TR-77-32). San Diego,
   CA: Navy Personnel Research and Devel-
   opment Center, 1977. (NTIS No. AD
   A040543)

4. Card, S. K. User perceptual mechanisms in the search of computer command menus. Proceedings: Human Factors in Computer Systems, Gaithersburg, MD, March 1982, 190-196.

5. Dodson, D. W., and Shields, N. L., Jr.
   Development of user guidelines for
   ECAS display design (Vol. 1) (Report
   No. NASA-CR-150877). Huntsville, AL:
   Essex Corp., 1978.

6. Engel, S. E., and Granda, R. E.
   Guidelines for man/display interfaces
   (Technical Report TR 00.2720).
   Poughkeepsie, NY: IBM, December 1975.

7. Peterson, D. E. Screen design guidelines. Small Systems World, February
   1979, pp. 19-21; 34-37.

8. Ringel, S., and Hammer, C. Information assimilation from alphanumeric
   displays: Amount and density of information presented (Technical Report
   TRN141). Washington, DC: US Army Personnel Research Office, 1964. (NTIS
   No. AD 601973)

9. Smith, S. L. User-system interface
   design for computer-based information
   systems (Technical Report ESD-TR-82-
   132). Bedford, MA: USAF Electronic
   Systems Division, 1982. (NTIS No.
   AD A115853)

10. Stewart, T. F. M. Displays and the
    software interface. Applied Ergonom-
    ics, 1976, 7.3, 137-146.

11. Treisman, A. Perceptual grouping and
    attention in visual search for fea-
    tures and for objects. Journal of
    Experimental Psychology: Human Per-
    ception and Performance, 1982, 8,
    194-214.

12. Tullis, T. S. The formatting of al-
    phanumeric displays: A review and
    analysis. Human Factors, 1983, 25,
    657-682.

13. Tullis, T. S. An evaluation of al-
    phanumeric, graphic, and color infor-
    mation displays. Human Factors,
    1981, 23, 541-550.

14. Zahn, C. T. Graph-theoretical meth-
    ods for detecting and describing
    Gestalt clusters. IEEE Transactions
    on Computers, 1971, C-20, 68-86.

FOOTNOTE

1. The research reported in this paper
   was conducted while the author was
   employed by AT&T Bell Laboratories,
   Whippany, New Jersey, USA.

Human-Computer Interaction — INTERACT '84 / B. Shackel (ed.)
Elsevier Science Publishers B.V. (North-Holland)
© IFIP, 1985

EVALUATING THE INTERFACE OF A DOCUMENT PROCESSOR:
A COMPARISON OF EXPERT JUDGEMENT AND USER OBSERVATION

N.Hammond(1), G.Hinton(2), P.Barnard(3), A.MacLean(3), J.Long(4) & A.Whitefield(4)

(1) Department of Psychology, University of York, UK
(2) Department of Computer Science, Carnegie-Mellon University, USA
(3) MRC Applied Psychology Unit, Cambridge, UK
(4) Ergonomics Unit, University College London, UK

Efforts to improve the usability of systems have resulted in the development of several techniques for interface evaluation. This paper explores evaluation through (1) assessment by Human Factors researchers and (2) analysis of user performance. Three pairs of researchers prepared reports on the interface of a document processor. Separately, five novice users were observed learning the system. The two evaluations generated overlapping but separable classes of information. User testing provided low-level information on procedural and conceptual difficulties, while experts provided a more integrated overview and hypotheses concerning the sources of problems.

1. INTRODUCTION

There is an increasing awareness of the need to improve the ease of use of interactive systems. Analytic approaches to design attempt to specify a formal representation of the user interface before the design is actually implemented (e.g., Moran, 1981), while more empirical approaches try to improve usability by means of successive design iterations (for details, see Carroll & Rosson, 1984). Although analytic methods undoubtedly form a sound basis for design, they are only a starting point, and design will continue to be an essentially empirical activity for some time to come. Until then, techniques for evaluating and refining prototype versions of systems will be of central importance. Appropriate evaluation and modification of prototypes within the design cycle can have marked effects on the efficiency with which the final product is used (Savage, Habinek & Barnhart, 1982), and, conversely, failure to run any evaluation can result in interface features, rectifiable at the design stage, which degrade performance unduly (Hammond et al., 1981). Nevertheless, just how the "ease-of-use" of an interactive system should be determined remains an open question, and a wide range of techniques is used in design. These include reliance on the designer's intuition and experience or on the advice of peers (Hammond et al., 1983a) as well as evaluations based on more formal "system walkthroughs" (Cooper et al., 1982) or on evidence from user performance (Mack et al., 1983). While an ideal means of interface evaluation would provide appropriate information in a speedy, valid and reliable fashion, any practical technique will involve compromises and tradeoffs. A greater understanding of the issues underlying these compromises and tradeoffs would allow more informed choices of evaluation method. This paper explores some of the issues in the use of system walkthroughs and user testing.

A commercially available document processor was evaluated by two methods: walkthroughs, conducted by six HF researchers (in three groups of two), and user evaluations, in which the performance of five novice users was analysed. The study was conducted both to collect usability information on the document processor and to compare the two evaluation methodologies, although only information relevant to the latter aim will be reported here. The study was designed to permit three classes of comparison: (i) amongst the three HF reports, (ii) amongst the performance analyses of the five users and (iii) between the HF evaluations and user performance. Classes (i) and (ii) reflect the internal consistency and reliability of the two methodologies, and class (iii) the validity of the walkthrough technique.

2. METHOD

2.1 The System

The study was conducted on a text-processing system used for the preparation of documents. The full system consisted of a cluster of display stations, a central controller and a high-quality printer. The system allows documents to be entered, edited and printed with full facilities for text formatting. Document storage and retrieval allows several levels of access to private and public files. Users are introduced to the system by means of an operator's course, a step-by-step manual divided into 36 lessons complete with many worked examples. The first ten lessons of this course, covering all the basic operating instructions, were the focus of the study.

2.2 Expert Evaluation

The six participants had all been actively engaged in HCI research for a number of years prior to the study, and five of the six had been involved in one or more previous evaluative studies of interactive systems (e.g., Hammond et

al., 1983b). Although none had had extensive
experience as HF consultants, for brevity we
will refer to them as "HF experts". The three
pairs of experts each spent one working day with
the system. Each saw the operator's course
prior to the session, but none had had any experience with the system itself. The objective
of the session was to work through the first ten
lessons of the course and to collect HF information relevant to (i) learning of the system by
novices, (ii) use of the system by more experienced users and (iii) potential modifications
of the system. After the session, each pair
produced a report consisting of (i) a corpus of
observations collected during the session, (ii)
a number of "points" based on the observations
and (iii) a general overview of HF aspects of
the system. To allow formal comparison at the
level of points, each pair coded the points on
standard forms. These required the specification of information about the point on: (i)
its nature, (ii) its underlying source (one or
more of the categories: system, manual, system-
manual interaction or task), (iii) its impact on
novice and expert performance, (iv) its psychological interest, (v) the nature of a possible
"fix" or change to the system or manual and (vi)
the difficulty of implementing the suggested
fix. In addition, the experts were required to
specify which observations (if any) were associated with each point. Two of the groups chose
to make use of a dictaphone to take notes during
the session, the other group making notes by
hand. Each individual alternated between the
roles of user and note-taker. The raw observations consisted of edited transcripts of the
session notes. There was no collaboration or
discussion between the pairs until all three reports had been completed.

2.3 User Performance

Five experienced typists were recruited from a
temporary agency to act as subjects. Their mean
age was 33 years and none had used a word processor before. Each used the system for one
working day, the aim being to complete as many
of the first ten lessons of the operator's
course as possible in the time available. Four
of the subjects completed the first nine lessons
and one only the first eight. Subjects were encouraged to think aloud as they used the system,
and assistance was given only either when the
subject was unable to proceed or when ample evidence of a particular problem had already been
demonstrated. A single observer recorded details of any difficulties encountered or
relevant comments made. Since the aims of this
part of the study were restricted to identifying
specific difficulties, we used a less labour-
intensive approach than we have used elsewhere
(Hammond et al., 1981; Hammond et al., 1983b).

3. RESULTS

3.1 Expert Evaluation

The three reports were compared at the levels of
observations, points and overviews. For reasons
of space, only details of the points are reported here. It is information at this
intermediate level that would form the basis of
detailed recommendations for a re-design of the
system. The analyses focus on the nature of the
agreement between the experts rather than on the
specific content of the reports. Accordingly,
suggested changes to the system will not be discussed here.

Agreement on Classification & Ratings. The
three pairs of experts recorded totals of 116,
105, and 102 separable observations, summarised
into 75, 65 and 47 points. The points were
classified (on occasions multiply) in terms of
their underlying source: system, manual, system-
manual interaction or task. The percentages of
points classified under each of these four categories were: pair 1 - 48%, 53%, 3%, 5%; pair 2 -
52%, 35%, 8%, 8%; pair 3 - 45%, 40%, 15%, 6%.
Each point was scored (on scales running from 0
to 4) for (a) its effect on novice performance
(mean ratings for the three pairs of 1.99, 2.55
& 1.68), (b) its effect on expert performance
(.52, 1.25 & .55) and (c) its psychological interest for HF researchers (1.80, 2.17 & 1.51).
Pair 2 rated points consistently higher on all
the scales. System-related points were thought
to disrupt performance more than manual-related
points for both novices (mean ratings of 2.14 vs
1.93, 2.82 vs 2.09 & 1.95 vs 1.32 for the three
pairs) and experts (.94 vs .13, 1.65 vs .78 &
1.00 vs .16). In all cases, the disruption on
novice performance was thought to be greater
than that on expert performance, and the novice-
expert difference was greater for manual-related
points than for system-related points (differences of 1.80 vs 1.20, 1.31 vs 1.17 & 1.16 vs
.95). This presumably reflects the greater
reliance by novices on ancillary information.
The three pairs also agreed that the psychological interest was somewhat greater for
system-related points than for manual-related
points (1.92 vs 1.75, 2.53 vs 1.70 & 1.52 vs
1.16). At this general level, then, we see substantial agreement between the three pairs.

Agreement on Content. Comparison between the
points was made by a single judge. Two points
were deemed to match if the judge considered
their meanings to be strongly overlapping and
either (i) their wordings were similar (e.g.,
"There is confusion between the contents of the
text to be typed and its status as an example"
and "Status of typed exercise content is unclear") or (ii) they were based on the same
underlying observations or (iii) no alternative
interpretation seemed plausible. In cases of
doubt, points were considered to differ. Comparison was made without seeing the associated
ratings. To simplify the analysis, each point

Table 1: Percentages of points from each pair judged to overlap with points from other pairs.

	Pair 1	2	3
No overlap	56	48	53
Overlap with:			
Pair 1 only	–	25	9
Pair 2 only	21	–	11
Pair 3 only	5	8	–
Both other pairs	17	20	28

could only be matched with a single point from each of the other pairs. When several specific points from one pair could be subsumed under a general point from another pair, only the most typical specific point was matched. Table 1 shows the percentages of overlapping points. About half the points from each pair overlapped with points from one or both of the other groups, the overlap being somewhat greater for pair 1 with pair 2 than for pairs 1 or 2 with pair 3. As a proportion of the maximum possible overlap (taking account of the different total numbers of points from each pair) the pairwise overlaps were: pairs 1 & 2, .45; pairs 1 & 3, .36; pairs 2 & 3, .38. Overlapping points were spread approximately equally across the main categories.

For all pairs, overlapping points were rated as having more influence on novice and expert performance as well as being of greater psychological interest, as shown in Table 2. However, the differences were statistically reliable only for novice performance in pair 1 ($t[73] = 2.02$, $p<.025$) and for expert performance ($t[63] = 2.52$, $p<.01$) and psychological interest ($t[63] = 1.68$, $p<.05$) in pair 2. There is thus modest support for the hypothesis that experts will tend to show the most agreement on points thought to have the greatest impact on performance.

Given this relationship, we would further expect some measure of agreement across the ratings for the overlapping points. Table 3 shows the correlations between the ratings for matched points. In terms of impact on performance, agreement was evident only between pairs 2 and 3; pair 1's ratings were quite unrelated to

Table 2: Mean ratings for overlapping (o/l) and non-overlapping (non-o/l) points for each pair.

	Novice Performance		Expert Performance		Psych. Interest	
	o/l	Non-o/l	o/l	Non-o/l	o/l	Non-o/l
Pair 1	2.21	1.81	0.55	0.50	1.97	1.67
Pair 2	2.68	2.42	1.50	0.97	2.68	2.42
Pair 3	1.86	1.52	0.64	0.48	1.73	1.32

Table 3: Correlations between the ratings for points shared between the three pairs.

	Correlations between pairs: 1 & 2	1 & 3	2 & 3
No of o/l points	29	17	18
Impact (Novice)	-0.015	0.145	0.441*
Impact (Expert)	0.121	0.010	0.412*
Psych. Interest	0.322*	0.426*	0.335+

Key: * $p<.05$; + $.05<p<.1$

those of pairs 2 and 3. However, all three pairs did show agreement on the level of psychological interest.

3.2 User Performance

The recorded notes from the sessions, consisting of a sequence of user difficulties, user comments and observer comments, were categorised by a stepwise procedure. First, the material was sorted into instances of specific difficulties (e.g. "could not find underscore key on keyboard"), general difficulties, events or user comments of ambiguous provenance ("you think, God, if I go wrong the thing will blow up") and general observer comments ("she is very pleased with HELP facility"). Only data from the first of these categories is considered here. Second, the specific difficulties were arranged in temporal sequence according to the page number in the operator's course. Third, difficulties encountered by each user in each subsection of the course were compared. Difficulties were judged to be the same or different on the basis of observed user behaviour rather than merely on the basis of the supposed underlying cause. Only evidence from the first eight lessons was considered, which all users completed. Fourth, the restriction of comparing observations only within the same subsection was lifted so as to identify similar problems occurring at different points in the course. A strict criterion was adopted, with matches only permitted when the contexts in which the difficulties occurred were similar.

Table 4: Percentage overlap of difficulties between users.

	User 1	2	3	4	5
No overlap	24	18	29	23	30
Overlap with:					
User 1	–	30	28	29	35
User 2	24	–	23	26	21
User 3	30	32	–	27	27
User 4	35	40	30	–	30
User 5	40	30	28	27	–
Total number of difficulties	63	50	69	77	71

Table 5: Extent of overlap of difficulties across the 5 users.

	No. of users showing difficulty				
	5	4	3	2	1
No. of instances	8	8	16	18	83
Mean no. of diff.	11.50	5.75	4.31	2.22	1
% of all diff.	27.9	13.9	20.9	12.1	25.2

This procedure resulted in a corpus of 330 difficulties, with about a quarter of these (83) remaining unmatched with difficulties from any other user. The overlapping observations resulted in a total of 50 difficulty categories; the pattern of overlap is shown in Table 4. It is evident that every user showed substantial overlap with every other user: in every case at least 20% of any one user's difficulties matched each of the other users' difficulties. Many of the difficulties were shared by more than two users; the extent of overlap is shown in Table 5. The mean numbers of difficulties in each overlap category exceed the sizes of overlap as one user could provide several instances of the same difficulty. This was increasingly the case as the size of the overlap category increased.

3.3 Expert Evaluation vs User Performance

Due to the complexity of the relationship between the evidence from the experts and that from the users, detailed comparisons on the basis of content are not presented here. For illustration, Table 6 shows (a) points shared by all three pairs of experts, and (b) difficulties shared by five or by four of the five users. The brief descriptions of the difficulties indicate their general nature; their actual categorisation was more specific.

4. DISCUSSION

In evaluating the interface of the system, three pairs of experts showed modest agreement on the points that they considered important determinants of user performance. The difficulties encountered by five novice users also overlapped. We will first consider the nature of the knowledge called upon by each of these two groups, and then discuss the ways in which the two classes of evidence might be compared.

To conduct the walkthrough successfully, the experts had to adopt a number of distinct roles. As novice users, they had to learn how to operate the system. Knowledge generated in this role is mostly manifested at the level of observations. In the dual roles of experienced users of systems and human factors psychologists they had to abstract the key usability issues and assess their impact. Finally, in the role of system designer, they had to suggest appropriate modifications to the system. From the session observations (not reported here), it is evident that, as users, the experts experienced diffi-

Table 6: Selected points and difficulties

(a) Points shared by all three pairs, with mean rating of impact on novice performance

P1 3.3 ENTER key has multiple functions
P2 3.3 Relations between "space" & "new line"
P3 2.7 Operation of SHIFT & SHFTLOCK keys
P4 2.7 Exercise text which describes system is confusing
P5 2.7 Manual conventions for giving instructions hard to follow
P6 2.7 Projected model for typing is unclear
P7 2.3 Distinction between Adjust & Non-Adjust modes is unclear
P8 2.0 Special symbols on screen cause uncertainty about output formatting
P9 2.0 Information in manual is poorly ordered
P10 2.0 Manual breaks its own conventions for instructions
P11 2.0 Structure of key labelling in relation to CODE key
P12 2.0 "Word delete" is from cursor to end of word, not whole word
P13 1.0 Inconsistencies between diagrams & text

(b) Difficulties, with frequency of occurrence
    (i) Shared by five users
D1 16 Getting to top of document
D2 16 Using the "clear" command
D3 15 Using the CODE key
D4 14 Using the "store" command
D5 10 Trying to use space bar to move cursor
D6   9 Confusion between screens & pages
D7   7 Difficulties with on/off knob on VDT
D8   5 Problems with "required space"
    (ii) Shared by four users
D9   8 Failures to follow manual conventions on instructions
D10 8 Finding special keys
D11 7 Use of "tab" in adjust mode
D12 5 Inserting and deleting spaces
D13 5 Parameters for "get" command
D14 5 Choice of names for files
D15 4 Moving to top or bottom of pages
D16 4 Navigation within HELP subsystem

culties similar both to each other and to our novices. The expert, however, should abstract information from these experiences which will be of use to those responsible for the re-design of the system. This information was embodied in the points and the overviews of the experts' reports. It is encouraging, therefore, that the three pairs showed some reliability at the level of points. Even with strict criteria for comparing points, at least one third of the points from each pair overlapped with each of the other pairs. These points were rated as more influential on performance and more interesting psychologically. However, the reliability was not sufficient for unanimity on the impact on performance. This may reflect both deficiencies of the matching method and the different approaches of the three pairs. While any one pair covered a wide range of points, each focussed on a number of recurring themes. Thus, pair 1 was concerned with the nature of the examples used in the course, pair 2 with aspects of keyboard use and pair 3 with inconsistencies between the course, the help information and the system. These different emphases are mirrored in different frameworks in the report overviews, and particular points are likely to be assessed within this context rather than in isolation. By tracing issues from raw observations, through the points to the final overview, it appears that the final content and structure of the reports depended not only on the experience and special interests of the teams, but also on the particular sets of difficulties encountered early in the session. The three HF reports can be regarded much as referees' reports of a journal paper: they each cover overlapping sets of issues from different viewpoints, and an "editorial" overview of all three gives a more complete picture than any single report.

Turning to the novices, the extent of overlap between the difficulties encountered by any two users lay between 20% and 40%. While this finding is again encouraging in that it indicates some inter-user reliability, it still implies that any one user will be a poor predictor of the difficulties encountered by another. This is despite the fact that activity was severely limited by the step-by-step nature of the course. Users' prior knowledge is likely to play a major part. Moreover, early problems experienced by users (or HF experts) can critically influence their burgeoning knowledge and subsequent performance (Hammond et al., 1983c). Different users may chance upon different initial difficulties. Nevertheless, there was a central core of problems which were encountered by all or nearly all of our users; indeed, some of these (e.g., D5, D6 & D12 in Table 6) have been noted as sources of difficulty with word processors in general. Our results, then, suggest that a relatively small sample of novice users can be used to discover both the set of frequently occurring difficulties and a wide range of the rarer difficulties. Of course the difficulties detected will depend critically on the tasks the users perform.

Comparison between the experts and users can be made at a number of levels. However, it would be a pointless exercise merely to demonstrate that HF experts encounter some of the same difficulties as novices. The experts should be able to inform the designer of those aspects of the interface which give rise to the most significant difficulties. It is therefore appropriate that many of the points listed in Table 6 should focus on system or manual features rather than on actual problems. The mapping of these onto user problems is to a large extent hypothetical; the formation of such hypotheses is the province of the HF expert. Direct comparison at the level of points is thus problematic, although many of the user difficulties can be viewed as exemplars of one or more of the expert "points". Comparison is further

limited by the fact that the user difficulties give little indication of their impact on performance. Thus, although difficulty D7 occurred with all users, it was of restricted scope, while the less frequent D12 might have far-reaching consequences. With the limited analysis possible in this paper, comparisons can only be made at a descriptive level.

The two forms of evaluation generate different classes of information. User testing provides low-level information on procedural and conceptual difficulties, with little or no overview. Interpretation is required to identify the sources of problems and to determine the effectiveness of interface changes. Expert walkthroughs provide a more integrated view together with hypotheses concerning the sources of difficulties. However, experts themselves are prone to various types of omission and bias.

5. REFERENCES

Carroll,J. & Rosson,M. (1984). Usability specifications as a tool in iterative development. In H.Hartson (ed.), Advances in Human-Computer Interaction. Ablex Publishing: Norwood NJ.

Cooper,R., Marston,P., Durrett,J. & Stimmel,T. (1982). A human-factors case study based on the IBM personal computer. Byte, 7, 56-72.

Hammond,N., Jorgensen,A., MacLean,A., Barnard,P. & Long,J. (1983a). Design practice and interface usability: Evidence from interviews with designers. In CHI '83: Human Factors in Computing Systems, Boston, December, 40-44.

Hammond,N., Long,J., Clark,I., Barnard,P. & Morton,J. (1981). Documenting human-computer mismatch in interactive systems. In Proceedings of the Ninth International Symposium on Human Factors in Telecommunication, Red Bank, NJ, September, 17-24.

Hammond,N., MacLean,A., Hinton,G., Long,J., Barnard,P. & Clark,I. (1983b). Novice use of an interactive graph-plotting system. Human Factors Report HF083, IBM (UK) Laboratories, Hursley Park.

Hammond,N., Morton,J., MacLean,A. & Barnard,P. (1983c). Fragments and signposts: Users' models of systems. In Proceedings of the 10th International Proceedings on Human Factors in Telecommunication, Helsinki, June, 81-88.

Mack,R., Lewis,C. & Carroll,J. (1983). Learning to use word processors: Problems and prospects. ACM Transactions on Office Information Systems, 1, 254-271.

Moran,T.P. (1981). The Command Language Grammar: a representation for the user interface of interactive computer systems. International Journal of Man-Machine Studies, 15, 3-50.

Savage,R., Habinek,J. & Barnhart,T. (1982). The design, simulation and evaluation of a menu driven user interface. Human Factors in Computer Systems, Gaithersburg, MD, March, 36-40.

Human-Computer Interaction — INTERACT '84 / B. Shackel (ed.)
Elsevier Science Publishers B.V. (North-Holland)
© IFIP, 1985

THE COGNITIVE REGULATION OF HUMAN ACTION AS A
GUIDELINE FOR EVALUATING THE MAN-COMPUTER DIALOGUE

Michael Paetau

Man-Machine-Communication Research Group of the
Institute for Applied Information Technology
Gesellschaft für Mathematik und Datenverarbeitung mbH Bonn
D-5205 St. Augustin, F.R.G.

Human Factors Research is changing. In the first phase systems designers defined and evaluated userfriendliness themselves, based on their own experiences and common sense. In the second phase computer scientists discussed the term "userfriendliness", as a recognized problem, and finally in the third phase human factor research is turning now to a more empirically oriented science. Due to the increasing problems with poorly designed interfaces, especially in application fields where users are non-computer-specialists, different institutions of computer science have started more empirical investigations about human-computer interaction. The Man-Machine Communication Research Group of GMD (Bonn) is engaged in controlled experiments. The GMD is presently building up a "Human-Computer Interaction Laboratory" in which selected elements of userfriendliness can be created in an rapid prototyping process and evaluated with social scientific methods. The general guideline of this research is the cognitive regulation of human action. On this theoretical basis we can derive the main criteria of software ergonomics and develop the stage for evaluating them.

1. Introduction

For some time human factors research has been undergoing a certain change. In B. SHNEIDERMAN's words: "Human factors research is turning from the argumentative discussions about the 'userfriendliness' of a system to a more scientific approach with objective and reliable results". Currently methods for the empirical evaluation of man-machine interfaces based on psychological and sociological theory are arising. This seems to announce the end of a period where the term 'userfriendliness' could be used without scruples and obligation as a convincing sales argument for nearly any technical innovation. Human factors research is developing into an empirical research approach that investigates not only the ergonomic adequacy of computer systems but also creates the human-science foundations of future system developments.

The first phase of human factors discussion was still heavily technology-centered. Software designers defined the human-computer interface in accordance with their experiences and functional ideas of the tasks to be accomplished by the potential users. Usually system designers evaluated userfriendliness themselves. But the problems increasingly occurring with poorly designed interfaces, especially in application fields where the users were non-computer-specialists, have led to more extensive empirical evaluations.

The second phase of human factors research was characterised by the discussion about 'userfriendliness'. What are userfriendly systems? Could we formulate general principles? System development should be based on more complex, not only functionalistic knowledge of the user. This required more information about behavioral patterns and user needs in a socio-technical context. Basic psycho-social understandings about human communicative behaviour had to be introduced into modelling as a basis for generalised design principles. Therefore, system development had to consider problem complexes that could not be mastered by the methods of computer science alone. Indications and methods of social science (e.g. those of cognitive psychology) began to increasingly invade computer science.

D. NORMAN commented on this evolution of computer science as follows: "We must aspire to more than responsiveness to the current need. The technology upon which the human-computer interface is built changes rapidly relative to the time with which psychological experimentation yields answers. If we do not take care, today's answers apply only to yesterday's concerns."

Emphatically Norman warned against beeing seduced by the sirens of technology. There is no doubt that there are existing meanwhile some very impressive techniques, thinking about them you could fall into enthusiasm. "High resolution screens, colour, three dimensions, mice, eye-movement detectors, voice-in, voice-out, touch-in, feelers-out; you name it, it will happen. Superficial pleasure, but not necessarily any lasting results. What general lessons will have been learned?" (CHI'83, p.2)

Currently we observe the beginning of the third phase of human factors research. By the cooperation of traditional computer science and social sciences, i.e. cognitive psychology and empirical social research, human factors research is developing into an empirical science that does not only attempt to create general principles for userfriendly systems, but that also evaluates them by empirical investigations.

Since the beginning of this year the GMD has established a research group aiming at empirical investigations in the field of man-machine communication. At the present this group is building up a technical environment enabling rapid prototyping of specific interface elements and their subsequent evaluation on the basis of social-science methods.

2. The Computer – a universal Tool?

In our investigations we have in mind the fundamental problems that arise from the claim that the computer should be available as an universal problem-solving tool. But this claim implies that the computer can be used simular to other tools as, for example, a hammer, a shovel, etc. There is however an important characteristic which distinguishes it from other tools. Its material condition alone does not allow any conclusions about its purpose, its operating facilities and its functioning as it is possible for other tools. The computer must first tell its purpose explicitly to the user by means of a human-computer dialogue. Therefore, the man-machine interface has to be designed in such a way that the user can get all the information he requires for using it. Necessary are not only information about the functionality of the specific application system but also beyond it, e.g. in cases of faults. A user is not able to understand faults and to avoid them in the future if he will not be informed explicitly about the characteristic and the reasons which lead to this fault.

The current efforts for improving man-machine

interface aim at adjusting it to the natural behavioural patterns of human communication. What does this actually mean? Which forms of help for explanation of a computer system are generally convenient? Which methods would overwhelm the user, and which would rob him of important control? What significance do on-line-tutorials, partial explanations of different states of system, or references for further explanations in user manuals have? How should we design structures and processes of human-computer dialogue to make it human-oriented, i.e. ergonomic?

3. The Cognitive Regulation of Action as an Approach to Evaluate Man-Machine Communication

Empirical research needs a theoretical basis. Without it it is not possible to decide which kind of data is relevant to collect for answering the above problems. In the German software ergonomic research an approach centered around the cognitive regulation of action has become dominant. If we follow this approach we have to see in the cognitive regulation of action the most important distinctive criterion of any work. This approach relies on the research results of MILLER/GALANTER/PRIBRAM and HACKER and is based on the following premises:

a) Any work is a task-oriented activity comparing actual actions with a mentally anticipated result and sequentially regulating these actions accordingly. In this context MILLER/GALANTER/PRIBRAM talk about "Test-Operate-Test-Exit Units (TOTE)".

b) These feed-back control operations (cognitive regulation of action) will only be successful if a human can develop an inner model of his work (a mental image of his environment and his own actions). According to HACKER inner models are "relatively stable memory representations acting

as indispensable task values in the comparison of task and actual values accompanying action guidance" (HACKER 1976, p. 25). The inner model acts as relatively stable invariant on whose basis the achieved actual state and the activity can be regulated.

c) The most essential characteristics of such inner models (memory representations) are
- representation of work results in the form of goals and sequences of subgoals;
- representation of execution conditions;
- representation of transformation steps between the actual state and the goal point (HACKER 1976, p. 27). For information processing that means, for example, anticipation and predication (goals, hypotheses, imaginary anticipation of consequences, imaginary anticipation of possible further measures) and modelling of actual facts. In this context the inner models serve for realising non-descriptive technological processes, being invisible to the user, for purposes of mental processing.

From these theoretical premises result a central – although not the unique – ergonomic criterion for all information processing work: The system must support the thinking and planning aspects of human work, avoiding conditions in which the user is overwhelmed with system details or prevented from developing plans by system constraints. It is very important that the form of the man-computer dialogue makes it possible to learn more and more about the technology by using the system. The dialogue should not be reduced to simple dialogue-steps. In this sense "ease of use" is not a criterion of software ergonomics. Principles of "ease of use" would determine the regulation of action on a low level and would lead to a "Partition of memory representation" (Volpert et al. 1983). Compared with this, it is a thesis generally accepted in industrial psychology that the development of adequate inner models is of great importance both to the efficiency and to the reduction of stress. These models are encouraged for building up the confidence of users, meaning that the human does not only operate the machine, but he learns to master it.

It may be possible that autonomous mastering of the technical requirements enables or even stimulates the human to train mental powers and to allow possible extensions of action competences (HACKER 1976, p. 31).

This demand, however, is always connected with a requirement to be met by the technical system: it should not prescribe only one kind of use and processing of information, but it should provide degrees of freedom allowing any person his/her own style of work (HACKER 1976, p. 30). In terms of industrial psychology that means: Beyond the mere increase of efficiency, man-machine communication has to allow the development of individual strategies for regulation actions in solving predefined problems.

Our investigations aim at a specific user group: the so-called "knowledge workers", who are working at the display sporadically and whose activity is a mixture of different tasks; only some of them to be accomplished via display, others, however, in another way (e.g. planning and decision making). Due to the infrequency of use in the interim a lot of gained knowledge will be forgotten. This kind of user has no prior knowledge and no special qualification in data processing. He expects from the computer system that the technical condition of its interface will again enable him every time he needs it to form a cognitive model of his "tool" (display) and the activities to be carried out by it.

4. Five Criteria of Software Ergonomics

In the Federal Republic of Germany the above principles have developed as the predominant theoretical framework for empirical research. On this basis and during recent discussions five central criteria derived: task adequate usability, self-descriptiveness, user-control, correspondence with user expectations and fault tolerance respectively fault transparency. The scientific community currently discusses the extent to which these criteria might be suitable as standard recommendations for computer industry (DIN-AA 1984). It is assumed that these are largely application-independent criteria that can be applied in a more or less modified form to any computer system. Currently these criteria are, however, still of a rather hypothetical character and, though being undoubtedly very evident, they require a careful empirical verification. The Man-Machine Communication Research Group of GMD will focus their investigations on them.

A human computer dialogue is of TASK-ADEQUATE USABILITY if it supports the handling of actual user tasks without burdening the user with extra work required by specific system characteristics.

A dialogue is SELF-DESCRIPTIVE if it is directly understandable or if the user can request comments on dialogue purpose and functioning during the dialogue itself. In the cases where the dialogue is not directly understandable, the system shall provide the user on request with information about the performance of system tools thus allowing the user to get an adequate mental representation of the system features suitable for his task accomplishment.

USER-CONTROL means that a user is able to influence the timing of the dialogue, its speed (including interruptions) and the order of the individual dialogue steps. This implies that he is not "driven" by the system, but that he can adjust the speed of the dialogue to his individual pace of work and he does not need to wait for system responses if he does not require them for dialogue continuation. If a user interrupts a dialogue he should be able to define "continue-points" which enable him to continue the dialogue whenever and where it suits his convenience and without extensive repreparations.

CORRESPONDENCE WITH USER EXPECTATIONS means that the dialogue behaviour of the system corresponds to those expectations of the user that are based on his experience with work processes (with computer support or without it).

FAULT TOLERANCE is a requirement that allows the user to achieve desired work results despite input errors. A fault is TRANSPARENT if a user will be extensively informed about the causes of the error in order to correct it. User input shall not lead to undefined states of system or breakdown. In some cases it might be reasonable to correct unambiguous errors automatically. The user must however be able to switch off the mechanism if required.

These recommendations for the design of computer interfaces are considered to be so general that they are applicable to any interface regardless of the specific application system. This is the preliminary result of the discussion about userfriendliness during the last years. It may be that some systems would allow these recommendations to be applied only in a modified form. The goal of the man-machine-communication laboratory of the GMD is to investigate the validity of these criteria, and modify or extend them according to the empirical results we obtain.

The empirical evaluation of these criteria requires however more than the mere availability of technical criteria. For determining the extent to which they correspond to human behavioural patterns and requirements, it is necessary to allow the observation of impacts on man at work. This dimensional framework alone is not yet suitable for investigating user satisfaction. First, these are principles that are evident and partly based on empirical investigations (DZIDA 1978), nevertheless they are of a rather hypothetical character though being of great significance as guidelines. As general guidelines they are important application-independent criteria, but the relative weightings of the different criteria may vary in different application systems. The extent to which these hypothetical assumptions about user requirements are actually the key aspects has to be empirically determined. This is one of the most important subjects of our research activities within the man-machine communication group.

REFERENCES

(1) CHI '83: Human Factors in Computing Systems, Conference Proceedings, Dec. 12-15, 1983, Boston

(2) DARLINGTON,J.; DZIDA,W. and HERDA,S.: The Role of Excursions in Interactive Systems. Int. J. of Man-Machine Studies (1983) 18,pp. 101-112

(3) DIN-AA-D (1984): Grundsätze der Dialoggestaltung. Redaktioneller Entwurf zur DIN 66.234,Teil 8 (20.1.1984)

(4) DZIDA,W.; HERDA,S. and ITZFELDT,W.D.: User Perceived Quality of Interactive Systems. IEEE-Transactions on Software Egineering. SE-4 (July 1978) pp. 270-276

(5) HACKER,W. (1978): Allgemeine Arbeits- und Ingenieurpsychologie. 2. Aufl. Bern: Huber

(6) HACKER,W. (1976): Psychische Regulation von Arbeitstätigkeiten. Berlin (DDR): Deutscher Verlag der Wissenschaften

(7) HACKER,W.; VOLPERT,W. and CRANACH,M. (Eds.) (1983): Cognitive and Motivational Aspects of Action. Amsterdam: Elsevier

(8) MILLER,G.A.; GALANTER,E. and PRIBRAM,K.H. (1960): Plans and the Structure of Behavior. New York: Holt, Rinehart and Winston

(9) VOLPERT,W. et al. (1983): Verfahren zur Ermittlung von Regulationserfordernissen in der Arbeitstätigkeit (VERA). Köln: TÜV-Rheinland

Human-Computer Interaction — INTERACT '84 / B. Shackel (ed.)
Elsevier Science Publishers B.V. (North-Holland)
© IFIP, 1985

ADAPTING A PSYCHOPHYSICAL METHOD TO MEASURE PERFORMANCE AND PREFERENCE TRADEOFFS IN HUMAN-COMPUTER INTERACTION

Jonathan Grudin
Wang Laboratories
Lowell, Mass., USA

Allan Maclean
MRC Applied Psychology Unit
Cambridge, England

ABSTRACT

An experimental methodology for contrasting certain design alternatives and quickly determining user preferences and performance tradeoffs is presented. It is shown how this experimental paradigm, used for psychophysical measurement, may be applied to the field of human-computer interaction. Where it can be applied, it promises a relatively quick determination of user preference and performance characteristics and tradeoffs on these measures with variation in parameters governing the user situation. Because the methodology is within-subject, it may also facilitate the study of individual differences.

INTRODUCTION

Often there are no optimal design features -- most features involve tradeoffs. The usefulness of a given feature may depend critically upon parameters that change within or across applications. (For a theoretical treatment of this issue, see Norman [1].)

However, the use of most standard experimental paradigms to determine the interacting influences of even a small number of variables may require a huge and often prohibitive investment of resources. A technique for collecting a large amount of data in as short a time as possible would obviously be highly desirable. This paper describes the adaptation to human-computer interaction of a technique designed to explore economically both performance and preference. The technique is in fact one of the oldest experimental paradigms in psychology -- psychophysical measurement.

Although the method has theoretical and pragmatic limitations (e.g., see Poulton [2]), it can potentially be used to investigate many situations where a tradeoff exists along a particular dimension. In a field quite distant from human-computer interaction, it is the method used by the optometrist when fitting lenses. The patient is asked to look through one lens, then through a second lens, and states his or her preference. The optometrist then varies one or both lenses along one or more dimensions and repeats the procedure, quickly homing in on the best fit.

This study is an illustration of how this method can be applied to the exploration of preference and performance tradeoffs in computer systems. We arbitrarily chose to examine two specific data entry methods for the purpose of illustrating the technique. We explored two procedural variations of the psychophysical method, our interest being more in that method than in analyzing data entry techniques. This is the first report of an experimental paradigm still under development, not a finished study of data entry alternatives.

THE DATA ENTRY TASK

On each trial a name appeared in the upper left of a VDU, and the subject was required to enter the code number associated with that name. The right side of the display consisted of an alphabetized directory of names and associated code numbers. Two different code entry methods were tried by each subject. (The procedures by which one method or the other was decided upon are described below.) One code entry method consisted of simply looking up the name in the directory, reading the associated number, and typing in that number using the keys above the top row of letters on the keyboard. Following the typing of the number the subject pressed the "ENTER" key. The second code entry method involved the use of an "option ring". When the subject pressed the space bar, the first name and associated number from the directory appeared in a small reverse-video window on the left side of the screen, below the target name. Each time the space bar was struck, the next name and code number from the directory appeared in the window. The subject thus used the space bar to step through the directory until the target name with its associated code number appeared in the window. Then the subject struck the ENTER key and the code number was entered, ending the trial.

In the code entry example in Figure 1, the code number is half entered. In the option ring example, the subject has begun stepping through the option ring.

A great many factors, ranging from the organization and layout of information on the screen (in the "directory") to performance incentives, could be varied within such a paradigm. In these studies, we varied two. One was the directory size, or the number of names through which the subject might have to search to find the target name and code number. The other was the length in digits of the code number that the subject had to enter.

```
Next Code Needed:   SAGGS                      CODE DIRECTORY

      Code Entry                  ANTCLISS   43        LEVITT    20
                                  BURGESS    18        NUTTING   80
  Type in Code Number             CHILDERS   58        SAGGS     90
  Then Press ENTER Key            DAVIDSON   42        THORPE    38
                                  FROY       17        UPSON     63
            9                     HUNT       21        WILSON    75
```

```
Next Code Needed:   RINALDI                    CODE DIRECTORY

                                  ABBOTT     298734   LARGE      921022
                                  BARNARD    510813   MARSHALL   781102
      NATHAN      295109          BREADMORE  549885   NATHAN     295109
                                  CASEY      816420   PALMER     610083
        Option Ring               COMINS     359071   RINALDI    891638
                                  DOYLE      309812   SCOTT      644201
  Bar    Advances Option Ring     FINLAY     100843   STEVENS    523551
  B      Backs Up Option Ring     GREEN      891119   TRACEY     646209
  ENTER  Select Current Option    HEDGE      287364   WHITEHEAD  784928
                                  JOHNSON    654291   WRIGHT     198617
```

Figure 1. Code entry display (top) and option ring
display. Underlined fields represent reverse video
fields.

We expected the setting of these parameters to influence both the entry method producing better performance and the entry method subjects would prefer. With a directory of many names and one-digit code numbers, subjects would presumably prefer to scan the directory visually for the name and enter the single digit. But where the directory had few names and the code numbers were long, the subject would presumably prefer to step through the option ring to the target name and hit the ENTER key, avoiding the need to remember and type in the several digit code number. What we sought was a methodology to tell us what the performance curves for the two entry methods would be, and thus where the cross-over point from one entry method to the other would occur. We also were interested to know which entry method a subject preferred for a given parameter setting, and whether the performance and preference cross-over points were identical.

EXPERIMENT ONE

The basic procedure was as follows: A given directory size and code length were established. The subject was asked to look at the directory and choose one or the other code entry method. A target name then appeared, and the subject had to enter the associated code number using the entry method just selected. Following the subject's completion of that task, the directory size and/or code number length were changed and the process repeated.

Because the subject selects the code entry method prior to each trial, this method produces considerably more preference data. However, there may not be data for a direct comparison of performance with the two entry methods for a given setting of directory size and code length. In addition, the subject's choices are not immediately preceded by experience with both entry methods. These latter concerns are addressed in Experiment Two. The large number of preference decisions does allow a relatively efficient discovery of the preference tradeoff points.

Method. Four subjects were run for a single two-hour session. Each subject had 5 blocks of 6 practice trials to acquaint them with the code entry methods. (Code lengths were 4,1,1,7,7; directory sizes were 16,4,36,4,36, respectively.) Then the procedure to be used in the experiment was introduced with a set of practice trials with code length 4. In this procedure, a code length was established for a set of trials. On the first trial, the directory size was 16. Prior to the identification of the target name, the subject chose the entry method by pressing the space bar (for option ring) or escape key (located adjacent to the row of numbers on the keyboard, for code entry). Then the target name appeared, and they entered the associated code number. Thus, their choice of entry method could reflect code length and directory size, but not the position of the target in the directory. The directory size was changed for the next trial, being incremented if the option ring was chosen and decremented if code entry was chosen. The step size began at 8. After three changes in preferred entry method, the step size was reduced to 4, and after six reversals it was reduced to 2. (If the new directory size would have fallen outside the range of 4 to 40, it was made to be the closer of the two values.) The set of trials terminated when one entry method had been selected 3 more times than the other or after nine trials, whichever came first.

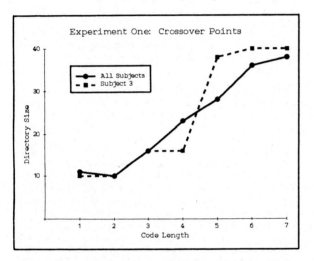

Figure 2. Tradeoff curve. Parameter space above solid line is code entry preference, below the line option ring is preferred.

Results. For each subject and each code length, the method identified the tradeoff point as being the final directory size. The subject typically homed in on the point, switching entry methods and thus reversing directory size growth when crossing it, until the requisite number of reversals. Of course, the floor of 4 and ceiling of 40 for directory size could prevent the tradeoff point from being reached, in which cases the subject reached the boundary and stayed there. Figure 2 presents performance data from Experiment One. For each code length, the tradeoff point represents the directory size for which the subjects on the average switched from using option ring (for the smaller sizes) to code entry (for the larger). Thus, the region above the solid line represents the parameter values for which code entry would be preferred, and the region below the line represents the parameter values for which subjects tended to prefer the option ring. The psychophysical method appeared to produce a clean determination of this tradeoff curve.

Of course, not all subjects adhere closely to the mean preference curve. Whatever their drawbacks, within-subject measures afford a look at individual differences, and the psychophysical method is designed for efficiency in this regard. The dashed line in Figure 2 represents the preference data of one subject. This subject preferred the code entry method for all but the smallest directory sizes through code length 4, but relied almost exclusively on the option ring for longer code numbers. Other subjects showed other patterns. The degree to which such preference differences might be based on differences in memory span, or motivation, or other factors requires further exploration. Some people may tend to prefer the more repetitive but less tiring route of leaning on the space bar in the option ring method, while others may respond to the challenge of trying to commit the longer code numbers to memory. In any case, exploration of such individual differences may require a method such as this to uncover the differences in the first place.

EXPERIMENT TWO

Experiment Two was essentially a procedural variant of Experiment One. The basic procedure was as follows: A given directory size and code length were established. Then, one of the two code entry methods was randomly selected. The subject was given four target names, one at a time, and asked to enter a code number for each using the specified code entry method. Then the subject used the other code entry method on four new targets. Finally, the subject chose the preferred code entry method to use on a final eight trials. Following those eight trials, the directory size and/or code number length were changed and the process repeated.

For each directory size - code number length pair examined, we recorded the following information: the time to complete four trials with each entry method, the subject's preference, the subject's accuracy rate, and the subject's time to complete the final eight trials. This procedure provided a very controlled comparison of performance data. It also insured that the subject had experience with both code entry methods immediately prior to choosing between them. Neither of these was obtained with the procedure of Experiment One. However, with 16 trials for each preference decision, it yielded less preference data than did the procedure of Experiment One, despite requiring longer participation by each subject.

Method. Four subjects were run. One was run in three sessions of one hour apiece and three were run in two sessions of two hours apiece. In each case, the first session was considered practice and not examined, leaving two hours of data for analysis. Three subjects were completely naive to the purpose of the experiment, and one (Subject 4) had some familiarity with it. (The design of this exploratory study was somewhat looser than that of Experiment One.)

In both practice and recorded sessions, subjects were given a block of trials with each of the code lengths from one to seven, pseudo-randomly ordered. An initial directory size was selected. Unlike in Experiment One, the initial directory size varied with the code length. The intention was to begin with a directory size distant from the hypothesized tradeoff point, in order to collect performance data across a wider range of parameter values. Step direction was tied to entry method choice as in Experiment One. Step functions were initially larger (as high as 16), decreasing by 4 with each second reversal to a minimum of 4. As in Experiment One, the directory size was kept between 4 and 40.

The code length for the block having been set and the initial directory size determined, one of the two entry methods was randomly chosen and the subject informed to use it for the subsequent four trials. A directory of names and numbers appeared. The four targets were randomly selected and presented with the constraint that their average distance from the beginning of the directory was half-way through. Then a new set of names and numbers (of the same code length and in a directory of the same size) appeared and the subject used the other entry method for four trials. Upon their completion, the subject was asked to choose the preferred method by typing "C" or "O". Then there were eight more trials on still a new directory of the same size and code length, using the chosen method (giving the subject a reason to choose carefully).

Following the completion of the eight trials, the directory size would be adjusted as described above and another set of 16 trials begun. Following a number of such 16-trial sets, the block would terminate and a new code length would be chosen.

We tried minor variations on the number of 16-trial sets prior to changing code lengths. The 3-session subject was given shorter sets and went through each code length twice, while the other subjects had longer sets and saw each code length for just one block (following the practice session).

Results. The tradeoff curve in Figure 3 was calculated in the same way as that of Figure 2 of Experiment One. The average of the two tradeoff determinations was used for the one subject (Subject 1) who had two blocks of real trials with each code length. The mean curve is very similar to that of the first experiment, each based on 4 subjects. Individual data for two subjects are shown, once again for the purpose of indicating the underlying individual differences captured by this method. Subject 1 shows a pattern similar to Subject 3 of the previous experiment, except that Subject 1 does not completely abandon code entry for larger directories with code length 5. Subject 2 however is unusually unperturbed by code length changes.

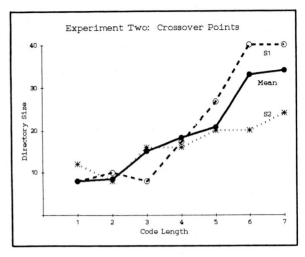

Figure 3. Tradeoff curve. Parameter space above solid line is code entry preference, below the line option ring is preferred.

This experiment allows us to determine whether performance (measured by completion time) matches preference. For the subjects studied, there may be a relatively close match when averaged, but there are clear individual exceptions. Subject 2, for example, is entering target numbers over twice as quickly with the option ring at code length 7, directory size 24 and code length 6, directory size 20, yet he consistently chose the code entry method for those parameter combinations, despite having just practiced with each. For code lengths 1–3, however, Subject 2 matches preference to performance. At the other end, Subject 4 (not shown) uses code entry for directory sizes of 4 with code lengths 1 and 2, despite performing more quickly with the option ring. These isolated examples indicate that the psychophysical method employed in this experiment offers one way to contrast performance and preference for certain tasks.

CONCLUSIONS

These exploratory studies indicate that the psychophysical method of threshold determination may be adapted in several ways to the exploration of certain human interface issues. First, though, we need more work on the adaptation of the method itself, and we must understand the limitations imposed by within-subject design and the repetitiveness of the task, which is artificial to most situations. However, the potential uses of the method are broad. By quickly mapping out the relationships among factors that may individually or collectively influence user preference and performance, it can produce results of both practical and theoretical significance. The method could be used to contrast specific alternative design options, prior to subsequent between–subject testing in the laboratory or in the field. It could balance our general reliance on performance measures with simultaneous measures of preference. The individual differences it uncovers could lead to investigations of their underlying cognitive and motivational structures. And the technique is also likely to be useful in evaluating and extending a model, such as that of Card, Moran, and Newell [3], when applied to parameters falling within the scope of the model.

ACKNOWLEDGEMENTS

The authors wish to thank Phil Barnard, Nick Hammond, and Richard Young for their contributions of ideas and criticisms.

REFERENCES

(1) Norman, D. A. Design principles for human-computer interfaces. In Proc. CHI '83 Human Factors in Computing Systems (ACM: New York, 1983) 1-10

(2) Poulton, E. C. Range effects in experiments on people. American Journal of Psychology 88 (1975) 3-32

(3) Card, S., Moran, T., & Newell, A., Applied information-processing psychology: the human-computer interface. (Erlbaum Associates, Hillsdale, N.J., 1983)

Human-Computer Interaction — INTERACT '84 / B. Shackel (ed.)
Elsevier Science Publishers B.V. (North-Holland)
© IFIP, 1985

THE ITERATIVE DEVELOPMENT OF USABLE COMPUTER INTERFACES

Kevin F. Bury

Human Factors Center
International Business Machines Corporation
San Jose, California

Of all the tools and techniques now available to aid in the design of usable computer interfaces, human-factors testing is by far the most comprehensive and reliable. For testing to be effective, however, it must be done early in the development process. This paper describes how user-interface prototypes can be used as vehicles for performing human-factors tests before actual product code exists. A specific type of test, namely iterative testing is described. An example will be given of how iterative testing with a prototype was used to evolve the usability of an interactive programming-language product. Lastly, this paper will discuss how other interface design tools can be used in conjunction with prototypes and iterative tests.

INTRODUCTION

Individuals directly involved in the development of software products often complain that many of the tools and techniques presented at user-interface design conferences are incomplete, too theoretical, and/or lack proper validation. It is, of course, necessary to constantly search for new and better design methodologies, and user-interface conferences are the proper forum for presenting new ideas. It is also important, however, to discuss and refine tools that already exist. The focus of this paper is human-factors testing. In the broadest definition of the term, human-factors testing includes everything from simple user walk-throughs all the way through elaborate multivariate experimental comparisons. This paper will challenge two common misconceptions about human-factors testing; first, that it must wait for the availability of product code, and second, that all human-factors tests are slow and cumbersome to perform.

EVOLUTION OF A USABLE PRODUCT

No one intentionally sets out to design a software product that will be difficult to use. The problem is that what makes perfect sense to the data processing professional designing the user interface may be perfectly confusing to the person for whom the product is designed. It is extremely difficult for the designers of any product to get into the shoes of the target user and anticipate what his or her needs and problems will be. The logical solution to this problem is, of course, to include representative target users in the development process. This is done by performing human-factors tests.

Releasing a product into the marketplace is a kind of human-factors test. Customers use the product, and feedback gets back to the product's designers concerning any usability problems encountered. An attempt is then made to improve the user interface for the next release (assuming, of course, that the first release wasn't so bad that the entire product was scrapped). This continues throughout the life of the product, and eventually, if the product survives, its user interface may evolve into something which is pretty good. Unfortunately, this process can take many years to complete. Alternatively, performing human-factors tests during development allows two things to occur. First, the evolutionary improvement of the user interface may be dramatically accelerated. Second, since this evolution has occurred before release of the product into the marketplace, the necessity of doing awkward (and costly) patchups on an existing product is eliminated.

PROTOTYPES

Obviously, the sooner testing begins the sooner results can start being applied to the design of the user interface. Unfortunately, complete operating code is often not available until near the announcement date of the product. By then, the design is so frozen that changes can be extremely difficult to make. Construction of a prototype allows testing to begin much sooner than would otherwise be possible (2,3). Problems with the user interface can thus be detected and corrected before any actual product code is written, thus avoiding much rewriting of code. If done correctly, prototypes are much easier to modify than real code. They are thus extremely useful as design tools (1,7). Designers can actually see how their ideas will look, and different alternatives can be easily explored. The prototype can be referred to when discussing the workings of the interface, and everyone can see how the interface will look and act, thus avoiding much confusion.

The completeness of a prototype depends on what the prototype will be used for. If the task is simply to explore different screen layouts, then no logic is required to control the screens, and the prototype falls on the left end of the following continuum.

| Screens alone | Screens with some logic | Complete interface |

However, if the designers wish to explore issues concerning the dynamic aspects of the user interface, then it is necessary to put at least some logic behind the screens. On the far right of the continuum are the "complete-interface prototypes" in which all features of the user interface are functional. Except for very simple interfaces, rarely are complete-interface prototypes constructed. Usually some subset of the user interface will be of primary concern, and it is this subset which is prototyped. In many cases functions will be faked; that is, made to look as though they function like the real product, when in fact they are only simulating the user interface to the product.

ITERATIVE TESTING

Iterative human-factors testing is a method of formalizing and controlling the evolutionary development of a user interface. The iterative design approach, particularly when it is used in conjunction with an interface prototype, is a comprehensive, efficient method of improving the usability of a user interface (4,5,8). Briefly stated, the procedure for iterative human-factors testing is as follows:

1. A group of representative target users are recruited and brought into a controlled laboratory setting. Users are given access to the user-interface prototype and to early drafts of training and reference documentation. A series of test problems are given which are typical of the kind of tasks it is anticipated users will be performing with the product once it is released.

2. While the users are working, their interactions with the computer are unobtrusively monitored.

3. Detailed analysis of user performance during the test sessions is conducted. This, combined with subjective information gathered from questionnaires, is used to uncover usability problems with the current version of the user interface.

4. Possible solutions are proposed and agreed on. The prototype and the documentation are then modified.

5. The process is repeated.

Typically when a user interface is first tested, a great many human-factors problems are discovered. Once the problems are known, pos-

sible solutions are proposed, and the interface is modified to reflect these solutions. Additional testing is then done to (1) determine if the solutions did, in fact, alleviate the problems uncovered in earlier tests, and (2) detect additional problems. This process is repeated with successively improved iterations of the interface until some criteria of acceptance is met.

REQUIREMENTS FOR ITERATIVE TESTING

Although the basic idea behind iterative testing is quite simple and intuitive, proper implementation of the test requires careful planning and preparation. What follows is list of basic requirements for any human-factors evaluation, including iterative tests:

1. Identify the target user. What kind of users will be using the product? What kind of educational background are they likely to have? What (if any) computer experience will they have? It is necessary to answer these questions so that the users brought in to test the product will match (as closely as possible) the ultimate users of the product.

2. Identify realistic tasks. Just as it is necessary to identify the kind of user who will be using the product, it is just as important to identify what kind of tasks users will be performing. Only then is it possible to generate realistic sample tasks for users to perform in the laboratory.

3. Provide a test vehicle. The effective analysis of usability requires that target users actually us the product or, as discussed earlier, a prototype of the user interface to the product.

4. Early drafts of training manuals. Since documentation (on-line and hard copy) is an integral component of most man-computer systems, it is essential that it be included in the testing process.

5. Data collection. Some means of monitoring user performance is needed. Approaches range from an observer sitting behind a one-way mirror with a notebook and a stopwatch all the way to highly automated event-monitoring data-collection systems (6).

Iterative testing is typically less formal than most experimental comparisons. The advantages of iterative testing are its realism, comprehensiveness, efficiency, and timeliness. Since there is no attempt to generalize the test results beyond the particular interface in question, and since no attempt is usually made to achieve statistically significant results, only a few subjects need be run through each iteration of the test.

Iterative testing closely approximates reality (about as close as can be achieved in a laboratory setting). It is therefore very effective in detecting the kinds of difficulties users will encounter with the product in the field. These difficulties often result from <u>unexpected</u> user behavior, something which is usually missed altogether in more rigidly controlled experiments. Note that iterative tests are not good at answering specific design questions (for example, "Is design alternative A better than design alternative B?"). For questions such as these, more controlled experimental comparisons are required.

AN EXAMPLE

IBM BASIC is an advanced-function BASIC-language product first announced for the IBM VM/SP-CMS operating system in November of 1982. IBM BASIC includes its own interactive environment for developing, debugging, and compiling BASIC programs. Many users of BASIC have little or no programming background. For this reason, it was particularly important to

```
list
90 option base 1
100 dim arr1(2,2), arr2(2,2), temp(2,2)
110 mat input arr1
120 mat input arr2
105 print "Input array number 1"
115 print "Input array number 2
                                 1
   1) BAS30139S ENDING QUOTE EXPECTED.
ch/2/2"/
auto
130 mat temp=(5)
140 mat arr1=arr1+temp
150 mat arr2=arr1-arr2
160 print "ARRAY1"
170 mat print arr1
180 print "ARRAY2
```

Screen alternative 1
(initial design)

```
* list
  90 option base 1
100 dim arr1(2,2), arr2(2,2), temp(2,2)
110 mat input arr1
   120 mat input arr2
* 105 print "Input array number 1"
* 115 print "Input array number 2
                                   1
  ###1) BAS30139S ENDING QUOTE EXPECTED.
* ch/2/2"/
  115 print "Input array number 2"
* auto
130 mat temp=(5)
140 mat arr1=arr1+temp
150 mat arr2=arr1-arr2
160 print "ARRAY1"
170 mat print arr1
180 print "ARRAY2
```

Screen alternative 2

```
  * list
90 option base 1
100 dim arr1(2,2), arr2(2,2), temp(2,2)
110 mat input arr1
120 mat input arr2
  * 105 print "Input array number 1"
  * 115 print "Input array number 2
                                     1
    ###1) BAS30139S ENDING QUOTE EXPECTED.
  * ch/2/2"/
115 print "Input array number 2"
  * auto
130 mat temp=(5)
140 mat arr1=arr1+temp
150 mat arr2=arr1-arr2
160 print "ARRAY1"
170 mat print arr1
180 print "ARRAY2
```

Screen alternative 3

```
  * list
90 option base 1
100 dim arr1(2,2), arr2(2,2), temp(2,2)
110 mat input arr1
120 mat input arr2
  * 105 print "Input array number 1"
  * 115 print "Input array number 2
                                     1
###1) BAS30139S ENDING QUOTE EXPECTED.
  * ch/2/2"/
115 print "Input array number 2"
  * auto
  * 130 mat temp=(5)
  * 140 mat arr1=arr1+temp
  * 150 mat arr2=arr1-arr2
  * 160 print "ARRAY1"
  * 170 mat print arr1
  * 180 print "ARRAY2
```

Screen alternative 4

Figure 1.   IBM BASIC screen-trace alternatives.

insure the overall usability of IBM BASIC. A prototype was thus constructed of the IBM BASIC user interface before coding of the actual product began. The prototype was intended to (1) serve as a design tool during specification of the IBM BASIC user interface, and (2) serve as a vehicle for a series of iterative human-factors tests of the product.

Exploring screen layout alternatives

The user interface to IBM BASIC was described in vague detail in the initial functional specification for the product. Before construction of the prototype began, screens without any logic behind them were used to explore different design alternatives. These screens were like slides, except that they actually appeared on the display screen. Because the screens were so simple to modify, various ideas could be easily explored, and design alternatives could be seen on the screen exactly as they would look in the actual product. Such things as location of the command line, type of error-message flag to be used, indentation of data on the screen, and command prompts were all manipulated on the screens. Decisions on these and other issues were then made either on the basis of available human-factors data, or on the consensus of those involved in the design of the product.

Figure 1 shows four different screen-trace alternatives. In each case, user input and system output begin at the bottom of the screen and scroll up (eventually off the top of the screen). Screen 1 shows the design as specified in the initial product functional specification. Screens 2 thru 4 are alternative screen traces which were considered. Screen 4 is the one that was eventually adopted. In Screen 4, all user input is indented one space and has an asterisk prompt in front of it. All system output is left-justified.

The IBM BASIC prototype

In order to evaluate the dynamic aspects of IBM BASIC, a limited prototype of the IBM BASIC environment was constructed using tools available under the IBM VM/CMS operating system. The prototype included a working editor capable of creating and modifying BASIC programs. Figure 2 contains a list of all IBM BASIC commands. The commands marked with asterisks are those which were included in the prototype. The commands included in the prototype were those that were to be taught in the IBM BASIC Programming Primer, and which a beginning user might be expected to need and use.

The prototype interfaced with VS BASIC (an earlier version of BASIC running on VM/CMS). This interface allowed for line-by-line syntax checking of program statements and for actual execution of BASIC programs. Aside from limitations in function, users of the prototype had no way of knowing they were not using the actual IBM BASIC product.

```
*AUTO            *FIND            *QUIT
 BREAK            GO              RENAME
*CHANGE           HELP           *RENUMBER
 COMPILE         *INITIALIZE     *RUN
 COPY            *LIST           *SAVE
*DELETE          *LOAD            STORE
 DROP             MERGE           SYSTEM
 EXTRACT          PURGE
 FETCH           *QUERY
```

Figure 2. IBM BASIC commands

Note: Commands flagged by asterisks were included in the prototype

The prototype was extremely useful as a design tool for exploring the dynamic aspects of IBM BASIC. Many questions arose during the construction of the prototype which were not addressed in the product functional specifications. Building of the prototype forced these decisions to be made early, before the product itself was built. Modifications to the prototype were made on a regular basis to reflect design changes in the product.

Iterative testing of IBM BASIC

To help insure the overall usability of IBM BASIC, a series of six iterative tests were performed. The first three were done using the IBM BASIC prototype as a test vehicle. The three subsequent tests were performed using early versions of the actual IBM BASIC product. Between seven and eight users were tested in each iteration. Users were college students with little or no data-processing experience. Users were told to read the IBM BASIC Programming Primer, following all instructions and performing all examples. Upon successful completion of the Primer, users were given, one at a time, five programming tasks to perform. The tasks ranged in complexity from writing a simple program to input two numbers, multiply them together, and print out the result (Prob 1), all the way to a relatively complicated statistical analysis application (Prob 5). Each user was tested for two days. Figure 3 summarizes the percentage of users in each iteration who completed the Primer and each of the five tasks. The six tests were spaced over a period of 14 months.

As can be seen in Figure 3, a substantial improvement in user performance was demonstrated over time. The reversal which occurred during Test 4 can be attributed to a new (unsuccessful) approach which was attempted in the Programming Primer.

Test Number

	1	2	3	4	5	6
Primer	0	0	100%	70%	100%	100%
Prob 1	-	-	75%	60%	85%	100%
Prob 2	-	-	75%	40%	70%	100%
Prob 3	-	-	75%	0	40%	75%
Prob 4	-	-	75%	-	40%	75%
Prob 5	-	-	0	-	30%	25%

**Figure 3. The percentage of users who success-
fully completed Primer exercises and
programming tasks in each of the 6
iterative tests.**

A UNIFIED APPROACH

While very effective at detecting problems
with a user interface, iterative testing, by itself,
provides no solutions to the problems uncovered.
These solutions have to come from somewhere
else. This isn't as bad as it sounds. In fact, in
the vast majority of cases, once the problems are
identified, the solutions become obvious. There
are, of course, times when this isn't the case.

Fortunately, iterative testing does not have to
operate in isolation. Other tools and techniques
are available which can assist in the development
of usable interfaces. Prototyping is a good example. Figure 4 shows a diagram of the iterative
process. The large arrow points to the juncture
at which the interface designer is aware of certain difficulties with the interface and is now

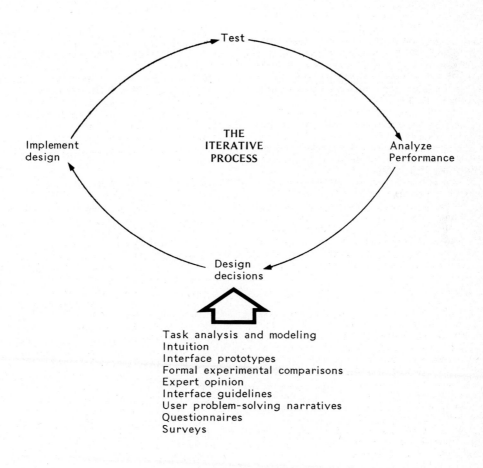

Figure 4.   The iterative process.

looking for possible solutions. Listed below the arrow are examples of some of the tools available in the user-interface design arsenal which can be helpful at this point. Note that the entry point to the design process is always at the bottom of the loop shown in Figure 4. Therefore, the tools listed actually come into use before the first iterative test. It is important that the design process not be allowed to progress too far before the first phase of testing begins.

Each of the tools shown in Figure 4 has its own strengths and weaknesses. While helpful in augmenting the use of iterative testing, it is important that iterative testing remain at the core of the interface development process. The yardstick provided by iterative testing provides a means of evaluating the effectiveness of each of the other tools in terms of the overall usability of the product.

REFERENCES

(1) Bewley, W. L., Roberts, T. L., Schroit, D., and Verplank, W. L. Human Factors Testing in the Design of Xerox's "Star" Office Workstation. Proceedings of the ACM/HFS Human Factors in Computer Systems Conference. Boston, MA: 1983.

(2) Bury, K. F., and Boyle J. M. An on-line experimental comparison of two simulated record selection languages. Proceedings of the Human Factors Society 26th Annual Meeting. Santa Monica, CA: 1982.

(3) Gould, J. D., Conti, J., and Hovanyecz, T. Composing letters with a simulated listening typewriter. Proceedings of the ACM/NBS Human Factors in Computer Systems Conference. Gaithersburg, MD: 1982.

(4) Gould, J. D., and Lewis, C. Designing for usability--Key principles and what designers think. Proceedings of the ACM/HFS Human Factors in Computer Systems Conference. Boston, MA: 1983.

(5) Mason, R. E. A., and Carey, T. T. Prototyping interactive information systems. Communications of the ACM, 1983, 26, 347-354.

(6) Neal, A. S. and Simons, R. M. Playback: A method for evaluating the usability of software and its documentation. Proceedings of the ACM/HFS Human Factors in Computing Systems Conference. Boston, MA: 1983.

(7) Smith, D. C., Irby, C., Kimball, R. and Verplank, B. Designing the Star User Interface BYTE, 1982, 7 (4), 242-282.

(8) Williams G. The Lisa Computer System. BYTE, 1983, 8 (2), 33-50.

LEARNING AND TRAINING

Human-Computer Interaction — INTERACT '84 / B. Shackel (ed.)
Elsevier Science Publishers B.V. (North-Holland)
IFIP, 1985

A USER-INTERFACE FOR TEACHING PIANO KEYBOARD TECHNIQUES

Martin Lamb and Veronica Buckley

Computer Systems Research Group
University of Toronto, Toronto
Ontario M5S 1A4, Canada

Those aspects of piano technique which can best be taught through computer-aided
instruction are identified. Two classes of programs to provide this instructional
aid are described. The first provides real-time visual feedback which analyses
rhythm and relative loudness. The second provides augmented visual and auditory feedback after the performance in which the computer functions as a 'magnifying glass' for
the ear, by revealing details crucial to the music, but which are difficult to perceive.
This then allows the pianist to analyse his own playing with respect to articulation,
ornamentation and rhythm, for example. Examples are presented in which the above aids
are used to improve the playing of students and professional pianists, as well as to
reveal a number of paradoxes contained in musical performances of the highest calibre.

Performance on a musical instrument is arguably
among the most complex of all human skills. To
the extent that it is a creative undertaking,
its subtlety remains largely beyond our understanding. In its technical aspects, however,
it has long been open to increasingly more
thorough investigation, giving rise to a variety
of technical 'aids' to performance. From the
finger-strengtheners (and finger-breakers) of
the nineteenth century to the sedate and harm-
less metronome so familiar to us today,
mechanical aids for the acquisition of technical
musical skills have undergone their own process
of natural selection until only the most effective remain. (Present-day mechanical aids are
summarised in Lamb, 1979). And it should come
as no surprise to witnesses of the computer
revolution of the past few years that new
technical aids have recently been developed,
not mechanical this time, but electronic. Owing
to the difficulty of inputting performed music
to a computer, the scope of these aids has to
date been very largely confined to piano technique, since an organ keyboard can fairly
easily be attached to a computer terminal
(cf. Fedorkow et al, 1980).

Four computer programs which have proved useful
in the analysis of a number of piano techniques
are a computerised music editor, a display
which highlights errors in polyrhythms, a display which highlights finger velocity, and a
system for the slowed-down playback of music
played on the computer's organ keyboard. These
four programs constitute a user interface for
teaching piano keyboard techniques, which is
summarised schematically in Figure 1. Much
more than just a music typewriter and a tape-
recorder, these aids enable pianists and piano
students to see and hear exactly what they have
played, or even what they are playing at the
very moment. In fact, the computer functions
as a kind of "magnifying glass" for the ear.

The music editor, called "MOD" for short,

displays on its screen, in modern 'isomorphic'
notation, musical examples played on the organ
keyboard (cf. Tucker et al, 1977). As it is
disarmingly accurate in revealing what has been
played, it is important that teachers regulate
carefully their students' use of MOD, so that
they may not be discouraged in their efforts.
No-one is perfect, after all, and even gifted
and experienced pianists, when using MOD, will
find their errors displayed, solid and unabash-
ed before their eyes (see Figure 2).

Indicating both pitch and duration of the notes
played, MOD is designed to display the articulation of a given passage. Any unevenness
in chords or in consecutive notes of equal
length will be immediately noticeable
(see Figure 3). It will be readily appreciated
that the aid is of particular value in revealing
the articulation of legato and staccato passages, trills, scales, and fast, reiterated
notes (see Figure 4). MOD also helps to identify the problems in smoothness so often
encountered in passages in octaves or where the
thumb is to pass under the hand (see Figure 5).

It should be pointed out that the user can
correct any inadvertent errors in the passage
played, once it is displayed on the screen, by
electronically 'pointing' to each one in turn
and playing simultaneously the correct note on
the organ keyboard. In this way, the teacher
can prepare "correct" examples for later scrutiny by the student, and even store examples of
performances by celebrated pianists for discussion. (Figure 6 illustrates such an example
in which technically inexact playing para-
doxically produces a more musically satisfying
result than pedantic exactitude.) Moreover,
MOD not only gives the student immediate
feedback about her playing, but can also store
examples of each exercise for later analysis
by teachers and researchers.

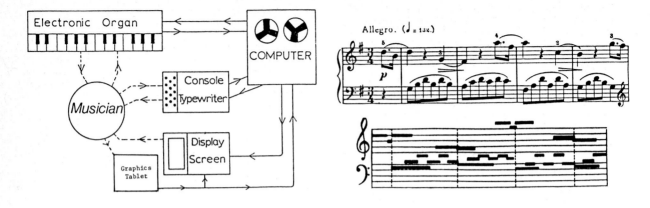

Figure 1. Layout of the computer system.

Figure 3. The Beginning of Mozart's Sonata in G, K.283. (Barlines have been added using computer programs.) The left-hand quavers are an example of an "Alberti Bass".

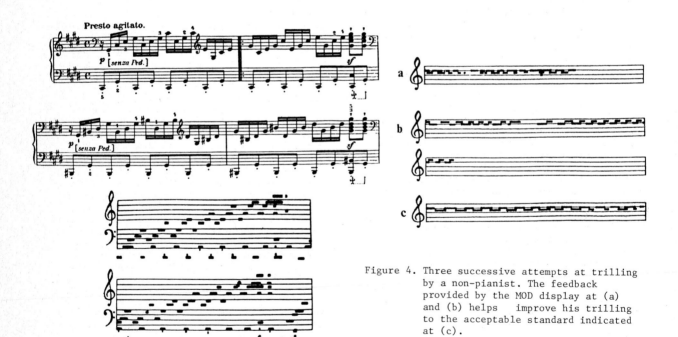

Figure 4. Three successive attempts at trilling by a non-pianist. The feedback provided by the MOD display at (a) and (b) helps improve his trilling to the acceptable standard indicated at (c).

Figure 2. The beginning of the last movement from the "Moonlight" Sonata. Irregularities in the playing are visible as 'blips' and overlapping notes.

The MOD display can be used with great benefit in conjunction with the feature, mentioned above, for the slowed-down playback of musical examples. This system far surpasses any tape recorder in that, being computerised, it can replay musical examples at differing speeds without distorting either pitch or sound quality. In this way it, too, functions as a kind of "magnifying glass" for the ear, whereby the finest details of rhythm and duration can easily be heard. Its particular advantage is that it can be used not only with MOD but with all the other computerised aids described below. Slowed-down playback could as well be used, of course, with non-computerised aids such as the metronome or video recorder, provided that the latter could be slowed down in synchrony.

A fascinating revelation occurred when a famous concert pianist played the triple trills from Beethoven's fourth piano concerto into the computer. Slowed-down playback revealed extraneous notes and irregularities, yet in that evening's concert the same passage sounded electrifying. Subsequent, pedantically accurate recording of these difficult trills in slow motion, then sped up on the computer to the proper speed, sounded like a sewing machine -- fast but unexciting. The irregularities (or "mistakes") seem to have added "spice" to the performance. Beethoven may have been aware of this bizarre phenomenon -- in the Archduke Trio, bar 190, his notation surprisingly suggests that the four simultaneous trills there need not be synchronized!

Let us consider the difficulty which a piano student faces when she comes to play a passage containing polyrhythms, that is, for example, four notes in the one hand against three in the other. This type of passage, of which there are many more complicated examples, presents a classic problem area in piano technique. Required to play simultaneously on and across the beat, the student confronts an evident difficulty in determining where each note should fall. Many hours of patient repetition are required, on the part of both teacher and student, in order to effect a successful execution of the passage in question.

In the diagram (see Figure 7), it can be seen that a given bar or part of a bar, represented by the box, has been twice divided: once into three even parts (as indicated by the three lines suspended from the top of the box) and again into two even parts (as indicated by the two lines mounted on the base). As the student plays the passage of three-against-two on the organ keyboard, each note is represented on the screen by an arrow, which indicates precisely the point in time at which that note was played. By observing the arrows in relation to the fixed lines, the student can pinpoint the inaccuracies in her rhythm, repeating the passage until it is exactly correct. By this means, the computer can help the young student

learn in minutes what would normally take hours.

The computer is not, of course, confined to examples of three-against-two, but can display divisions of a passage into up to seven parts in either hand! Moreover, it will be acknowledged that, as the young piano student advances, her sensitivity to rhythmical exactitude progresses accordingly. For this reason the computer can accept different levels of accuracy as correct, according to the degree of sensitivity which the user considers appropriate. To change the sensitivity, the student strokes an Allison slider - a computer input device (see Baecker, 1979) either while playing or during a rest.

The same sensitivity control can also be used in another of the computerised aids, designed to detect dynamic levels (levels of loudness and softness). Dynamic levels are notoriously subjective -- what does it mean to say, for instance, that a passage of music is very soft rather than simply soft? Objective decisions can be made, however, on the comparative dynamic levels of notes played consecutively or simultaneously.

Let us suppose that the passage played by the piano student is part of a fugue, so that one line is to be heard above the other. Programmed for this exercise, the computer will detect and display the comparative dynamic level of each note. (As the loudness of a note played on the piano -- or on the computer's organ keyboard -- depends on the speed with which the note is struck, the computer can also be said to detect the 'finger velocity' of each note). A note's loudness is represented beneath the music as a block appearing higher or lower on the screen according to its respective softness or loudness comparative to the other notes of the passage (see Figure 8). Examining the screen, the student can see whether or not she is allowing the melodic line of the passage to be heard predominantly. If not, she may repeat the exercise as often as she chooses, observing, it is hoped, her increasing accuracy in producing the necessary comparative dynamics. At the same time she may, if she wishes, hear the dynamics "magnified", that is, the soft notes softer and the loud notes louder (heard via sound synthesizer -- cf. Buxton et al, 1978). This exaggerates any unevenness in finger velocity, thereby bringing it to the student's attention. This magnification of dynamics can also take place in "real time", that is, while she plays.

As mentioned at the outset and as described above, musical examples are input to the computer by means of an attached electronic organ keyboard. It is of course recognised that in touch and tone such an organ is quite unlike a piano, and to this extent it may be protested that its use for piano students remains limited.

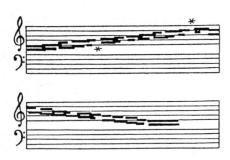

Figure 5. "MOD" display of C
chromatic scale in
minor thirds played
rapidly with the
right hand only.
Faulty changes in hand
position (at the places
marked*) are easily
recognized from the
undesirable breaks
in what should be a
smooth, unbroken
line. (In this
notation, black
notes are represented
by blocks whose
vertical position lie
midway between those
used in conventional
notation.)

Figure 6. The celebrated Waltz by A. Diabelli. An illusion is
revealed. The acciaccaturas (marked a) are
deliberately sustained to produce the effect of the
rhythm indicated by the composer. The pedantically
"correct" procedure (marked b) would not normally
have any overlap between the two notes involved.

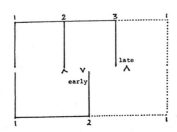

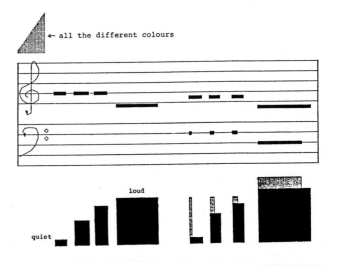

Figure 7. While playing a 3-against-
2 cross rhythm, the
student sees from the
positions of the arrows
that the 2nd note of the
group of 2 is being
played too soon, and the
3rd note of the group of
3 is being played too late.
(The words "early" and
"late" have been added to
the figure.)

Figure 8. The MOD notation for the start of the theme from
Beethoven's Fifth Symphony is displayed on the
colour screen, immediately after being played on
the computer's organ keyboard. The height of the
block beneath a note indicates its loudness. When
more than one note is played at once, the shorter
blocks (displayed here in solid black beneath the
music) are displayed in the foreground. Each note
and its block beneath have the same colour, coded
according to the key velocity. Above the clefs,
the colours are displayed in order of increasing
"loudness", as a memory aid.)

The designers of such keyboards, however, lay no claim to having achieved any more than an input device 'adequate' for the tasks at hand, a claim not excessive and evidently borne out in experiments with users. In one respect it is even possible to accord the much maligned electronic organ keyboard a higher position than its cousin, the piano. The electronic organ has no sustaining pedal -- no shadows beneath which the student can seek to conceal her heretofore clandestine non-legato playing. The organ turns a spotlight on the necessity for legato fingering -- a necessity which many students believe themselves to have avoided by mistaken use of the sustaining pedal.

It may well be argued, too, that a computer's capacity for detecting errors of rhythm or even of pitch is very much greater than that of the human ear, so that use of these aids to their fullest extent serves only to encourage a mechanical accuracy of execution inaccessible of appreciation by the human listener. Wasted effort! the cry goes up. We want music for our own enjoyment, not for the satisfaction of a blinking, demanding terminal. This is all without a doubt very true -- if an error is so subtle that, without a computer's detection, none of us could ever have known of its existence, why expend any energy at all in attempting to correct it? In fairness, however, it must be pointed out that certain errors, unnoticeable in themselves, can give rise to subsequent, obvious errors; a deliberate correction of the first may well entail an automatic correction of the second.

In one respect, however, the computer can justifiably be regarded as indispensable. It is a regrettable fact that human perceptual capabilities are limited (see Table 1). Our attention can be focussed on only a restricted number of stimuli at any given time, meaning simultaneously. We are further restricted in the number of stimuli which we can perceive within a given interval of time -- for most people, this is approximately ten per second. Classical music typically involves the perception of more than ten stimuli per second. For example, a pianist who performs all 1441 notes of Chopin's "Minute Waltz" in sixty seconds must play an average of 24 notes per second! Clearly, the rate of note output is higher than the 10 items per second limit set by (c) in Table 1. Thus, chunking - the uniting of several actions in a single will-impulse - must be taking place. Similarly, the person listening to the above performance must also be chunking - by uniting stimuli. This phenomenon is explained by Boynton (1961) who describes visual chunking as "temporal quantization of the visual input by the higher visual nervous system, so that the input is "packaged" into discrete time frames within which a purely temporal discrimination is not possible". The aspect of chunking that most inconveniences piano practice is the restriction that chunks cannot be analysed into their component parts,

in the central nervous system. Thus, when chunking takes place, it is possible to notice the existence of an error (i.e. that a "chunk" is wrong) without being able to identify the error itself exactly.

Practising slowly is of course one way of attending to more detail than usual. A teacher, too, can spend a good deal of time drawing attention to unperceived details. Successive replays of a tape recording also allow the performer to focus attention on previously ignored aspects of her playing. Musicians, however, are frequently prone to self-delusion in this respect -- too often, they hear only what they believe themselves to have played (Maazel, 1980).

The aural magnifying glass provided by the computer, however, reveals such details with disarming clarity. Its visual display reinforces this; what the eye has once seen, the ear may yet hear.

Those aspects of piano playing which can be learned with the aid of a computer are identified in Tables 2, 3, and 4. From these tables it can be seen that the computer is almost useless for sight-reading, moderately beneficial for interpretation, and invaluable with technical skills.

It may of course be objected that aids of the type described above in the long run serve only to encourage the student's dependence on the computer, at the same time diminishing her aural perception and consequently her musicianship. On the other hand, it may be claimed that, by recording examples for visual observation and by transforming them to enable their observation from differing perspectives, such aids develop the student's critical perception and, by extension, her musicianship. The middle road clearly lies in the sensible use of computerised aids. It must be emphasised that, never themselves intended to teach, they have been designed to assist teachers in those aspects of musical training which are tiresomely repetitive or mechanical. The teacher's time and energy can then be more profitably directed toward the more creative aspects of musical education, aspects beyond the understanding of any computer.

The computerised aid, like the metronome, like the practice clavier, is merely a tool for technical improvement. It enables us to move more quickly toward the real goals of instrumental training -- interpretative performance and the delight of music well played.

a. It is difficult to attend to more than one sensory source (e.g. eyes, ears) at a time.

b. The perception of relatively simple data is limited to about ten items per second.

c. The maximum rate of response is also limited to about ten items (or "chunks" - these are explained below) per second.

d. The maximum rate of repetitive movement is limited to about ten per second.

e. With a continuous task, error corrections are limited to two per second.

f. Hand and eye can track at up to five movements per second.

g. The reaction time for hand and foot movements lies between 140 and 180 milliseconds.

h. When responses are required for two successive stimuli, the second response has a longer than usual reaction time which decreases as the interval between the signals increases. This phenomenon occurs even when one signal is visual and the other auditory, and when the responses are in opposite hands. It also occurs when the subject expects the stimuli to occur in rapid succession.

Table 1. Human muscular and perceptual limitations which affect the rate of learning piano keyboard skills. (cf. Fitts and Posner, 1967; Craik, 1948; and Welford, 1952.)

MUSCULAR SKILLS FOR PIANISTS	SUITABLE FEEDBACK AIDS
(1) trills & other fast embellishments	MOD,SPB
(2) polyrhythms	PRA,SPB
(3) legato and staccato	MOD,tape
(4) velocity playing	SPB
(5) leaping	video
(6) dynamic contrasts	FV, tape
(7) production of different tone-colours	tape
(8) passing the thumb under	MOD, video
(9) octave-playing techniques	MOD,SPB,video
(10) rotation and pivoting	video
(11) rhythm precision	SPB,metronome
(12) crossing-over the hands	video
(13) fast, repeated notes	SPB,MOD,tape

Table 2. Some of the technical skills required by the advanced keyboard performer (cf. Bach, 1753). The computer can help detect faults that cannot easily be observed using non-computerised aids. (SPB = slowed-down playback, FV = finger velocity display, tape = tape recorder, video = videotape recorder, PRA = Polyrhythm analysis)

ELEMENTS OF MUSICAL INTERPRETATION	FACTORS INVOLVED	SUITABLE FEEDBACK AIDS: Computerized	Non-Computerized
Rhythm	timing	SPB,PRA	metronome,tape
Notes	pitch,duration	MOD,SPB	tape
Dynamics	loudness	FV	tape
Tempo	timing	PB	tape
Articulation	duration,loudness	MOD	tape
Pedalling	overall sound		tape, video
Tone	overall sound		tape
Accents	loudness	FV	tape
Phrasing	timing, loudness	SPB	tape
Rubato	timing	PB	tape
Ornamentation	pitch,duration	MOD,SPB	tape
Posture			video

Table 3. The elements of piano playing that are combined by the performer to form an "interpretation" of a piece of music. They should be chosen so as to be consistent with the musical style of the composition being performed. (cf. Bach, 1753; Kullak, 1893; and Scholes, 1950). (PB = playback by the computer programs).

SIGHT READING FUNDAMENTALS	APPROPRIATE FEEDBACK AIDS
(i) taking in entire chords and phrases at a glance	tachistoscope
(ii) good choice of fingering	video
(iii) independence of eyes and hands	video
(iv) immediate recognition of important features (e.g. the melody) and then bringing them out	tape,PB
(v) improvisation (where desperate)	tape,PB

Table 4. Aspects of piano playing involved in sight reading. The computerized aid seems of limited use here. (cf. Plaidy, 1853.)

REFERENCES

Bach, C.P.E. (1753) Essay on the True Art of
Playing Keyboard Instruments. Translated and
ed. by W.J. Mitchell: republished by Norton
and Co., New York (1949).

Baecker, R., Human-computer interactive systems:
A state of the art review. Proceedings of the
Second International Conference on Processing
of Visible Language, Niagara-on-the Lake,
Canada, 1979.

Buxton, W., Fogels, A., Fedorkow, G., Sasaki, L.
and Smith, K.C. An introduction to the SSSP
digital synthesizer. Computer Music Journal,
Vol. 2, no. 4, 1978: 28-38.

Boynton (1961) Some temporal factors in vision.
In Sensory Communication: ed. by W.A. Rosenblith.
Wiley, New York.

Craik (1948) Theory of the human operator in
control systems: 11. Man as an element in a
control system. British Journal of Psychology,
vol. 38: 142-148. Cited by Fitts and Posner
(1967).

Fedorkow, G., Buxton, W., Patel, S. and Smith,
K.C. An inexpensive clavier. Proceedings of
the Fourth International Conference on Computer
Music. Queen's College, New York, 1980.

Fitts, P.M. and Posner, M.I. (1967) Human
Performance. Prentice Hall International Inc.,
London.

Kullak, A. (1893) The Aesthetics of Pianoforte-
Playing. Translated by T. Baker and republished
by Da Capo Press, New York (1972).

Lamb, M.R. The Computer as a Musicianship
Teaching Aid. Ph.D. thesis (Electrical
Engineering), University of Canterbury,
Christchurch, New Zealand, 1979.

Maazel, L. Speech made to an international
youth orchestra, recorded in London, UK 1980.

Plaidy, L. (1853) Technical Studies.
Schirmer, New York.

Scholes, P.A. (1950) The Oxford Companion to
Music. Eighth edition. O.U.P., Oxford, U.K.

Tucker, W.H., Bates, R.H.T., Frykberg, S.D.,
Howarth, J.R., Kennedy, W.K., Lamb, M.R.,
and Vaughan,R.G. An Interactive Aid for
Musicians. International Journal of Man-
Machine Studies, vol. 9, no. 6, 1977: 635-651.

Welford, A.T. (1952) The psychological
refractory period and timing of high speed
performance: A review and a theory.
Brit. J. Psychol., vol. 43: 2-19.

Human-Computer Interaction — INTERACT '84 / B. Shackel (ed.)
Elsevier Science Publishers B.V. (North-Holland)
© IFIP, 1985

Preparing Hospital Staff for the changeover to Computerised Records

M.J. Barber, Senior Systems Analyst,
West Midlands Regional Health Authority.

J.W. Kempson, Medical Records Officer, Nuneaton Hospitals,
North Warwickshire Health Authority.

This paper describes the preparation, installation and implementation
of a computerised medical records system in the West Midlands Health
Region, with special reference to its introduction into the Nuneaton
Hospitals of North Warwickshire Health Authority. This computer system
is being run by hospital staff with no day-to-day assistance from
specialist computer personnel, with the central computer routine
operations being carried out by the hospital Medical Records Department.

INTRODUCTION.

Aim of West Midlands Regional Health Authority.

The aim of the West Midlands Regional
Health Authority was to produce a
Patient Services computer system which
would be able to be run entirely by the
local staff in the hospital where it is
sited, and be suitable for installation
in any of the twenty two Health
Districts in the West Midlands.

Main Objectives.

The main objectives for producing the
system were :-

1. To produce a system which would
    reliably identify patients so that
    their case notes can be located
    quickly.

2. To provide a system which would
    collect all patient administrative
    data and other information which has
    to be recorded by medical records
    staff.

3. To produce a system which was
    readily understood and
    straightforward to use.

4. To produce a system which would be
    able to be extended into Wards,
    Outpatient Clinics and other
    hospital areas using a common
    database and data handling methods.

5. To produce a system which needs
    minimum training to use, and whose
    operation does not require the
    attention of full time
    professionally trained operators.

BACKGROUND.

The West Midlands Region.

The West Midlands Health Region is the
largest in England, in population terms,
with 5.1 million inhabitants in an area
of 4,975 square miles (12,885 km^2). It
covers five counties of local
government: the West Midlands
Metropolitan County, Hereford-Worcester,
Shropshire, Staffordshire and
Warwickshire.

The West Midlands Regional Health
Authority (WMRHA) is responsible for the
strategic planning and monitoring of
Health Services on behalf of the
Secretary of State for Health & Social
Services. It also plays a key role in
the allocation of financial resources in
accordance with long-term priorities
designed to improve the quality of care
and ensure consistency of access to
services.

Following the re-organisation of the
National Health Service which came into
effect on April 1st, 1982, the
day-to-day running of Hospitals, Health
Centres, Clinics and other Community
Health services is carried out in the
West Midlands by 22 District Health
Authorities. North Warwickshire being
one of the 22.

History of Computerised Medical Records Services in West Midlands.

The Regional Standard Computer System
for Patient Services (R.S.S.) is the
outcome of an initiative by the Management
Services Division of the West Midlands
Regional Health Authority to make
computerised patient systems available

at a reasonable cost to all District
Health Authorities in the Region.

Its aim is to provide a standard set of
computer programs and associated
facilities operated on similar equipment
installed in each District. There had
been developed over a number of years
within the Region, several successful
computer systems mainly as an outcome of
the original Department of Health &
Social Services sponsored experimental
centres at Queen Elizabeth Medical
Centre, Birmingham, and the North
Staffordshire Royal Infirmary at
Stoke-on-Trent. These systems provided
a full range of patient administrative
and patient care facilities to the
individual districts where these
experimental projects were based. These
included master index, in-patient
administration, out-patient
administration, waiting list management,
laboratory reporting, nursing orders,
ward information, etc.

By competitive tender International
Computers Ltd.,(I.C.L.) were selected
as the manufacturer whose equipment was
to be used, primarily 2900 range
computers with Distributed Resource
System terminal equipment operating
under their Virtual Machine Environment
operating system. In order to encourage
D.H.A's to adopt the standard system the
W.M.R.H.A. provides, from central
funds, a 50% contribution to the main
items of equipment and certain
implementation costs. It also provides
through a regional implementation team
support and guidance in the setting up
and initial training in the use of the
system. The actual installation of the
system and technical support, after it
is installed and working, is provided by
a team of expert staff based at one of
the regional computer centres.
Maintenance and fault repair of the
equipment is through a contract between
the District and I.C.L.

It is the intention that Districts will
run their systems without employing any
specialist computer personnel, the
terminals being operated by the hospital
staff in the departments in which they
are situated. The central computer
routine operations are designed to be
kept to a minimum and carried out by
members of the Medical Records
Department. Each District also makes
someone from within their existing staff
resources the 'system manager' with the
responsibility for ensuring the smooth
day-to-day running of the system. It is
their job to make contact with the
support site as and when necessary and

to provide local assistance in solving
problems, organising maintenance, etc.

THE W.M.R.H.A. RSS COMPUTER SYSTEM.

Facilities for Hospital Use.

Most District General Hospitals provide
a twenty four hour, seven day per week
service throughout the year and to be of
real value any computer based system
must be sympathetic to this level of
service and be able to respond
accordingly. However, the period of
peak workload is generally Monday
through to Friday, 8.00 a.m. to 6.00
p.m., and the hardware and software
recommended for each individual District
reflects this pattern of work and demand
on the system.

Essentially the system consists of a
series of Video Terminals (VT's) sited
at specific locations within the
hospital which are linked via a
communications network to an ICL 2900
series main computer which holds a
common database.

There are two main categories of users.
The first includes a relatively small
number of clerical staff who, on
becoming proficient keyboard operators,
spend a high proportion of their working
day using the computer in medical
records areas of the hospital. The
second, and much larger group, includes
doctors, nurses and paramedical staff
who, in the course of their duties, may
require to retrieve information from or
make limited entries to, a patient's
record via a VT.

Confidentiality is at present effected
by controlling the range of computer
transactions available at each terminal
location. As the system is expanded to
cover a wider range of casual users,
each user will be given an individual
password which will determine the level
of access they are allowed, and their
identity, derived from their password,
is recorded with every entry they make.

The Patient Service Modules.

The central part of the system is a
Computer Managed Patient Master Index
and Health Care Register. This enables
the registration of patients' personal
details, their GP and any contact
details to be recorded. Immediately a
patient is registered on the Index or
any information is changed, the details
are immediately available at every
location where a computer terminal is

installed.

Although capable of operating on its own
as a free standing system, the Health
Care Register is designed as the core of
a total patient administration system,
other parts such as Inpatients,
Outpatients, and Waiting List
Administration systems can be added, as
outlined below, according to individual
D.H.A.'s requirements.

The Inpatient System provides an
administrative service for all patients
staying or due to stay in a Hospital.
Admission, discharge and patient
movement data is used to maintain an
up-to-date and instantly available
information service for Hospitals, thus
enabling empty beds to be located.

The Outpatient System provides complete
administrative control over clinic
appointment bookings and scheduling.
The system follows a patient through
from initial GP referral to discharge
and statistics production. Appointments
are made by the use of a computer
terminal, the system generates
confirmation letters as required.
Facilities exist to query an individual
patient's appointment or the booking
state of an outpatient clinic.
Appointments may be changed on an
individual basis or a clinic's
appointments may be collectively and
automatically rescheduled. Facilities
are also available to tidy up a clinic
in order to ensure that the appropriate
action is taken for all patients.

The Waiting List System provides a
comprehensive service for the
administration of lists of patients
waiting to be admitted to Hospital, from
patient registration through to
admission to the wards. The system is
governed by rules specified by
individual consultants such that the
management of each waiting list reflects
those requirements. In addition, the
system is supported by standard
functions which include priority
calculation of patients awaiting
selection, automatic statistics
production and the option of using
automatic letter generation.

System Software and Support.
A computer system for use by
non-computer specialist staff has, if it
is to succeed, to be 'user friendly'.
This is even more the case if those
staff have to carry out routine
operations functions for the main
computer equipment as well as use the
system. The equipment which District

Health Authorities in the West Midlands
purchase at the recommendations of the
Regional Health Authority is standard
ICL 2955 or 2946 hardware, with three
fixed discs, three exchangeable discs, a
tape drive, a line printer and an
operators console. To bridge the gap
between the VME2900 operating system and
the hospital staff, a series of
housekeeping and other routines have
been produced which take care of all
those functions needed to keep the
computer system running. These routines
cover such tasks as making security
copies of the database, initial set-up
of the operating regime, system journal
copies and other housekeeping functions.
All these routines are initiated by
typing in a command such as "RUNJOB
DUMPDATABASE" on the operator's console,
and from then on the routine asks for
discs or tapes to be loaded as required,
keeps records of what are the latest
versions of all files and advises the
medical records staff initiating the
command when the process is complete.
Gradually computer routines are being
developed so that most, if not all, of
these housekeeping functions can be run
on the VT's which are used throughout
the hospital. This means that these
jobs will be presented to the user in a
form similar to the medical records
modules they already use.

The medical records staff trained to
operate the machine are taught all
computer operations procedures, from
switching on the power at the main
supply and powering up the main central
hardware to the commands to reconfigur
the communications network, including
the phasing in and out of groups of
terminals and printers. These
procedures are all controlled by a few
major commands and each procedure is
written up in detail in an operations
manual, which those medical records
staff nominated to manage the computer,
are trained to use.

As the computer system installed in any
D.H.A. is only large enough for the
day-to-day work carried out
there, the computer configuration
purchased contains no facilities for
program development or software aids
such as compilers. All development work
and other support services are carried
out at one of the two development sites
mentioned above and any software
changes, new releases of software or
database corrections are carried out via
a dial-up telephone line between these
development sites and each hospital
district computer room. Any software
failures are initially dealt with over

the 'phone and via the dial-up line, and
only when this fails is a computer
officer called to visit the site to
assist the hospital staff there.
Hardware maintenance and fault repairs
are carried out by ICL but any call-out
of ICL engineers is co-ordinated by the
Operations Department of one of the two
Regional Computer Centres as some
failures of the system which the
hospital staff cannot cope with may give
ambigious indications as to whether the
cause is hardware, software or
misoperation.

North Warwickshire and Nuneaton Hospitals.

The Health Authority.

North Warwickshire Health Authority
encompasses Nuneaton and Bedworth
Borough Council and North Warwickshire
Borough Council. It currently serves a
population of 173,000 and covers both
Rural and Industrial areas. Health Care
in the District is divided into three
sections: Acute, Mental Handicap and
Community. The acute section consists
of George Eliot, Maternity, Manor and
Bramcote Hospitals known collectively as
the Nuneaton Hospitals.

The Medical Records Officer at the
George Eliot Hospital is
responsible for all Medical Records
services and staff within the Nuneaton
Hospitals. Medical Records procedures
are common to all three hospitals.
The main Medical Records Library and
previously the manual Master Index, are
situated at the George Eliot Hospital.
The work of the main department is
largely concerned with the
registration/retrieval of case notes and
their preparation for Outpatient
clinics, and then subsequently the
filing of case notes, pathology reports
and miniature X-Rays.

The Medical Records Officer has a
deputy who is responsible for the
day-to-day management of the Department,
and another assistant responsible for
statistical and information services,
and the day-to-day management of the
Patient Administration System computer.
There are 10 Higher Clerical Officers
(first line Supervisors) each responsible
for the work of a defined section of the
Medical Records Department and the staff
in that section.

Education and Orientation of Staff

The introduction of a computerised
Patient Administration System into a
Medical Records Department is a major
upheaval and has a tremendous impact on
the working lives of the staff in that
department. However, the staff in
Nuneaton coped very well, they liked the
computer, readily accepted its
introduction and during the
implementation period they were very
committed and hard-working. The
Regional computer team advised the
hospital to arrange visits and seminars
for the staff, but on looking back it
would now appear that the education of
the staff started two years before the
system went live, in October 1983.

A computer in the Medical Records
Department was first mentioned in the
Autumn of 1981 when plans were being
discussed for the new Medical Records
Department in the second building phase
of the new District General Hospital
(George Eliot site). The Medical
Records Officer's (MRO) knowledge of
computing was at least five years out of
date, so she started to update her
knowledge and to learn about R.S.S.
which at this time was just being
proposed. Some years earlier the MRO
had visited the patient administration
computer system at Stoke-on-Trent and
had been very impressed by it, so she
started to involve the Higher Clerical
Officers and explained to them the uses
of a computer in a Medical Records
Department.

During 1982 there were several visits
and courses which helped to extend the
staff's knowledge and understanding of
computers:

1.   January 1982 - The MRO took her
     Higher Clerical Officers to the
     WHICH COMPUTER show at the National
     Exhibition Centre. This was a very
     worthwhile visit as they saw what
     shapes and sizes computers come in
     and they started to use computer
     jargon.

2.   In the Spring of 1982 a Medical
     Records Officer user-group for the
     Regional Standard System was set up
     and the MRO was asked to serve on
     this Committee. This helped to fill
     some considerable gaps in her
     knowledge of patient administration
     systems and was also useful in
     keeping Nuneaton informed of what
     was happening at Regional level.

3. In September 1982 the Regional Health Authority held a one day seminar, a general introduction to computers, which the Higher Clerical Officers attended.

4. October 1982 - The MRO and two Higher Clerical Officers went on a one week course to learn Basic programming for B.B.C. micros. Although they will never write programs for the Regional Computer System, they do at least now appreciate the reasons for accuracy and detail when discussing systems.

5. December 1982 - The MRO and Higher Clerical Officers visited the computer system at the Queen Elizabeth Hospital in Birmingham.

The groundwork of staff education was achieved in 1982, for although the MRO and the Higher Clerical Officers were the lucky ones who went on courses and visits, as their knowledge and interest increased, so they passed it on to the staff.

During the early part of 1983 further visits were made to Stoke-on-Trent and various exhibitions, and now it was not only the Higher Clerical Officers but also some of the Clerks. The staff were involved as much as possible with the preparation for the first module. They were quite happy to have the O&M Officer from Management Services sit with them and record procedures. During the survey of the proposed terminal sites, the staff were involved in the selection of the actual position for the terminals. A tremendous amount of extra work was needed to prepare the manual index cards for transfer to magnetic tape, and although some temporary staff were employed, the permanent staff worked very hard. They came in early in the mornings, they stayed late, they worked weekends. Even the Ward Clerks and evening staff joined in, and a tremendous feeling of team spirit began to build up in the department.

In June 1983 a series of induction seminars were held for all disciplines of staff. The seminars included a history of the Regional Computer System, a video of the system at Stoke-on-Trent, an explanation of the modular approach of R.S.S. and the implementation timetable for North Warwickshire. A static display of photographs and printouts was mounted and the V.T. and printer equipment was on show. All Medical Records staff attended these seminars and in July the computer was delivered and installed.

As was remarked on at the beginning of this section, staff training began without it being realised, and on reflection this gradual process of education used in North Warwickshire is one certainly to be recommended. Seminars and training sessions alone can never replace the support and loyalty of a committed staff.

Conclusions.

In conclusion, it has been established in the West Midlands Health Region that quite large complex computer systems can be managed and run by non-computer staff with some technical and training support from a remote site and the management of such projects is well within the capacity of established Medical Records Departments

Acknowledgements.

The authors gratefully acknowledge the helpful comments of Mr. M.R. Carmichael, RSS Projects Co-ordinator; of the West Midlands Regional Health Authority and of Mr. John Tounsend, Unit Administrator, Nuneaton Hospitals.

They would like to acknowledge the support of Mr. S.W. Sargent, RSS Implementation Manager and the Medical Records staff of the George Eliot Hospital, Nuneaton.

Human-Computer Interaction — INTERACT '84 / B. Shackel (ed.)
Elsevier Science Publishers B.V. (North-Holland)
© IFIP, 1985

PROVIDING ONLINE ASSISTANCE TO INEXPERIENCED COMPUTER USERS

Robert C. Williges, Jay Elkerton, James A. Pittman,
and Andrew M. Cohill

Virginia Polytechnic Institute and State University
Blacksburg, Virginia USA

Inexperienced users of interactive computer systems often need online assistance to complete their task successfully. The results of several research studies are reviewed as a means of specifying the human-factors design considerations for online assistance. Alternatives such as automatic error detection, browsing and comparison of help facilities, and online expert aiding need to be considered. It was concluded that these features need to be incorporated into an adaptive interface tailored to the specific needs of the inexperienced user of the software interface.

1. INTRODUCTION

Online assistance can be an extremely important aid for inexperienced users of software systems who are using the computer system as a tool to perform certain tasks. For this class of users, the details, power, and flexibility of the computer are relatively unknown. Consequently, the novice often uses the computer system in an inefficient way, requires online assistance, or makes disastrous errors.

Several human factors issues need to be considered in determining both the form and nature of assistance to be provided to this class of users. The results of several behavioral research studies are summarized in this paper as a means of specifying human-computer interface design considerations for online assistance. Specifically, data from studies investigating methods of providing automatic error correction, controlling HELP information, and representing expertise are reviewed.

2. AUTOMATIC ERROR DETECTION

Large data entry systems are increasingly using computers both to enhance speed of entry and to reduce error detection and correction. Often data entry is the least reliable step in the process of maintaining these information systems. Consequently, it is important that errors be detected and corrected during the data entry process in order to reduce the large investment of effort required to make corrections at the central database.

Pittman and Williges [1] evaluated the efficacy of providing automated error detection and correction procedures for novice users as a means of reducing source data entry errors in computerized information systems. It was hypothesized that providing users with online error detection would improve performance when compared to no automated error detection. Likewise, it was assumed that error detection, rather than error correction, is the most important aid to provide users during data entry. Consequently, it was also hypothesized that online error detection would compare favorably with a fully automated system providing both error detection and correction.

2.1 Error Correction Procedures

Three error correction procedures were compared in a simulated personnel records task requiring novice users to make interactive source data entries using a simple query language. This simulation allowed for perfect detection and correction of any type if error, because it could match user inputs with the correct data to be entered. The three levels of the error correction procedure included the on-line error detection scheme and two control conditions. These three levels were:

(1) automated detection with enforced manual correction;
(2) totally automated error detection and correction (first control condition); and
(3) manual detection and correction (second control condition).

In the error detection system the computer reacted to an error by displaying the general error message "FORMAT ERROR", erasing the data, and awaiting the user's second attempt. Each user had to re-enter the data in the error field before continuing.

In the first control condition the computer facade changed the input data to correct any error. After correcting the error the new version of the data was displayed, with the message "FORMAT ERROR FIXED, IS THIS CORRECT?". The user had to answer "yes" or "no" before being allowed to continue. The user was allowed to proceed if the answer was "yes". If the answer was "no", the data were erased and the user had to enter them again.

In the second control condition the computer did not react to data entry errors. The data were accepted as entered, no message displayed, and the prompt returned to the command area so that the user might continue as usual.

2.2 Performance Evaluation

Essentially, the automatic conditions improved accuracy at the expense of reduced speed (p<.05). This effect is most prevalent in the automatic detection condition which required the users to retype each of the fields correctly. In this condition, users rated their accuracy the highest and achieved perfect final file accuracy, but required more attempts and more typing time to complete the task even though typing rates were faster during re-entry.

The major hypotheses of this study were concerned with the comparison of performance accuracy of the automatic error detection condition with the other two error correction conditions. These significant comparisons (p<.05) are shown in Figure 1 which summarizes initial and final mean accuracy of personnel records entered under the various error detection and correction procedures. When automated error correction and/or detection was provided, users were able to eliminate all the errors in the personnel records as compared to the control condition in which no automated assistance was provided. Additionally, automated error detection alone was sufficient to increase final file accuracy to 100%. Consequently, automated error correction procedures were not needed provided users were given assistance in detecting errors.

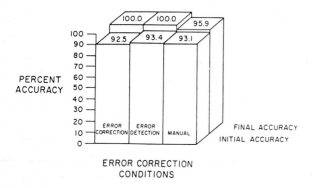

Figure 1 : Initial and final mean accuracy

2.3 Implications

Error detection, rather than error correction, appears to be a more important aid in eliminating data entry errors. The large size and high accuracy of this type of database may have something to do with the need for online assistance in detecting errors. The operator simply does not have the time for a careful study of each datum. Once it is known that a particular field contains an error, the operator will spend the time to locate and correct the error. It appears that the human operators can usually decide what to do very quickly once they are aware an error exists in the record. The results of this study suggest that merely providing aiding in the detection of source data entry errors may be sufficient to improve file accuracy.

3. ONLINE HELP

Novice users often require online assistance to aid them in using interactive systems. Cohill and Williges [2] evaluated nine procedures for initiating, presenting, and selecting HELP on interactive computer systems. Their primary concern was to determine what roles the novice user and the computer should perform in the retrieval of HELP information.

3.1 HELP Configurations

The nine conditions investigated included a control condition in which no HELP was available and eight experimental conditions formed by the factorial combination of initiation (user vs. computer), presentation (hard-copy manual vs. online), and selection (user vs. computer) of HELP information. Computer novice subjects learned a version of an experimental line editor. This editor was used to edit both text and data files using either a constrained or unconstrained set of editing commands. Various measures of time, accuracy, and commands used to complete the editing subtasks were recorded automatically.

3.2 Performance Analysis

Two general findings are evident from the data analysis as summarized in Table 1. First, providing any type of HELP information resulted in an improvement in operator performance when compared to the no HELP configuration. In addition, the time necessary to complete a task (in seconds), the errors per task, and the number of commands used were significantly larger (p<.05) when no HELP was provided as compared to the various HELP configurations.

The second general finding of this study is related to the relative comparisons among the various HELP configurations. Both the Initiation X Selection and the Selection X Presentation Mode interactions, as summarized in Table 2, demonstrate that user control rather than computer control of HELP is more beneficial to novice users of computer systems. User control of initiation and selection of HELP resulted in significantly less (p<.05) average time (in seconds) per task and reduced errors during text editing. Likewise, editing was completed faster and errors were reduced when the novice users selected the HELP and used hard-copy manuals.

TABLE 1. Comparison of Various HELP Configurations.

Conditions	Average Time Per Task	Average Error Per Task
Comparisons to Control Condition		
HELP	376.6	1.4
No HELP	679.1	5.0
Initiation X Selection Interaction		
User Initiated, User Selected	332.0	0.8
Other HELP Configurations	394.8	1.7
Selection X Presentation Mode Interaction		
User Selected, Hardcopy	330.5	0.9
Other HELP Configurations	392.0	1.6

3.3 Implications

The findings of this study suggest that user-initiated and user-selected hard-copy HELP yields the best performance with novice users. In this particular HELP configuration, the users spent most of their time browsing the HELP information and looking at a variety of information contained in the HELP file. All of the computer-initiated and selected configurations provided quite specific information, and perusing of other information was not possible. Additionally, during online presentation of HELP, the editing task was erased. When the HELP information was available through hard-copy manuals, the subjects could compare HELP presented in the manuals to the editing task presented on their terminal. Split-screen presentation of HELP may facilitate comparison in computerized HELP modes. A dialogue design consideration based on the results of this study would recommend that HELP information be constructed such that the user can browse and compare the various information files.

4. INTERACTIVE FILE SEARCH

Information retrieval of information from computer files is a complicated and time consuming task in many computer-based systems. In many situations, a computer user can only access a restricted subset of the large amount of stored information in the computer at any given moment. For example, the user is limited in the lines of text that can be presented on a terminal. Fortunately, a wide variety of automated retrieval procedures have been developed for manipulating electronically stored information through conventional interfaces.

4.1 File Search Assistance

A series of behavioral research studies were conducted to develop an empirically based procedure for capturing expertise, to compare novice and expert users in terms of file searching performance and strategies, and to evaluate the efficacy of providing expert aiding.

4.1.1 Information retrieval task. The information retrieval task used throughout these studies required subjects to search for information in a complex database containing hypothetical statistics on fighter aircraft, helicopters, and personnel. This task environment was implemented on a VAX 11/780 computer and contained a hierarchically structured, 703 line database file which consisted of table-oriented information. A performance metering file. was also embedded into the task environment software to provide online performance assessment.

4.1.2 Search procedures. Twelve search procedures were implemented and were designed to provide a wide variety of retrieval techniques. All search procedures were interfaced with a virtual keypad on the DEC VT100 terminal using a Carroll Technology touch entry device. The display also contained an input and message line, and a work area. These dedicated areas of the display were used by specific search procedures. A 7-line window based on the results of Elkerton, Williges, Pittman, and Roach [3] was used for the presentation of the database at the top of the display.

These dedicated areas on the display were used by specific search procedures. For example, the index procedure used the work area to display an index and the input line was used to echo a user's index selection. The input for some of the search procedures was done through a QWERTY keyboard. Each search procedure was activated by the touch entry keypad.

4.2 Expert Profile Methodology

A target profile methodology for representing expertise·was developed to define an automated file search assistant [4]. A target profile defines the selection of search procedures for a group of highly trained experts and is based on a polling procedure.

Conceptually, each expert is given a vector of 12 votes representing the 12 search procedures on a specific target. The votes of a group of experts are then summed to yield one profile for each target. This procedure guards against the bias introduced by a frequently used search procedure in that a repeated operation is counted only once in the polling.

4.2.1 Novice and expert performance. The expert profile methodology for empirically capturing expertise was evaluated by comparing the novice and expert search performance and target profiles. As expected, Elkerton and Williges [5] demonstrated large differences in the way novice and expert users performed the data retrieval task. The treatment means for total operations, number of different operations, total movement, total time, search time, planning time, between search time, and final detection time showed inferior performance for novice as compared to expert users (p<.01).

4.2.3 Novice and expert search strategies. Due to the potential bias of analyzing strategy differences with total operations, the selection of search procedures was examined using the polling procedure. Figure 2 presents the summed polls for novice and expert subjects on the 12 search procedures across all 80 targets investigated. Based upon the polling procedure, the search strategy of novice subjects consisted of several search procedures, the most frequent of which was scroll down. On the other hand, expert subjects used the node and search-and procedures most frequently. A chi-square analysis of the polls for the expert and novice subjects was highly significant $X^2(11)=433.75$, p<0.001, indicating different overall search strategies.

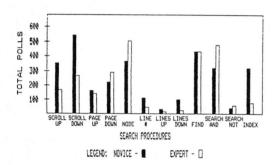

Figure 2 : Overall search strategies for expert and novice users

4.3 Evaluation of Expert Aiding

The final phase of this research was an initial evaluation of the efficacy of the providing online expert aiding using the expert profile methodology [6]. An overall evaluation of online assistance was made by comparing two online assistance groups to a group of experts and a control group of novice users who received no assistance. The two online assistance groups were defined in terms of the level of persuasiveness used in providing assistance. One group of novice users were forced to use the online assistance while another group of novices used an online assistance system which only suggested appropriate file search procedures.

4.3.1 Implementation of the online assistant. The expert assistant was closely related to the expert target profiles and was defined directly by the target profile methodology. Both the suggested and forced assistance conditions were manipulated through the touch entry keypad. If the suggestive assistant fired and provided advice, it would highlight keys on the keypad which were part of the expert strategy as determined by remedial flexibility. All other search procedures would remain active. When the forceful assistant fired, it would highlight appropriate expert search procedures and erase inappropriate search procedures from the keypad. In other words, from that point in a trial subjects could only use the expert search procedures. After providing advice, the assistant would not fire again on that trial. Also, both the suggested and forced conditions would cancel a search procedure if it was inappropriate. Of course, the suggested condition would allow subjects to select it again after the advice was given.

4.3.2 Search strategy. In order to analyze the search strategies with an ANOVA model, the polls were transformed into proportions for each subject. These proportions represented the relative number of polls for each subject on each of the 12 search procedures. A two-way ANOVA on the search procedure proportions revealed a significant user group by search procedure interaction, $F(33,660)=2.46$, p<0.0001. This interaction suggested that strategy differences existed between groups. Newman-Keuls procedures (p<.05) found that four search procedures were contributing to this interaction. These significant mean proportions for subject group and search procedures are presented in Figure 3.

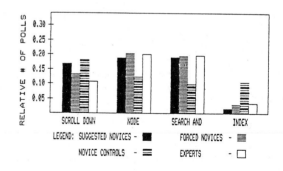

Figure 3 : Search procedures based on relative proportion of polls

The Newman-Keuls procedures also revealed several interesting contrasts between user groups. When using the novice controls as comparisons, the assisted novices increased the use of the node and search-and procedures, and decreased the use of the index procedure. On these search procedures, assisted novices were performing like experts. A similar, but more complicated trend existed in the use of the scroll down procedure for forced novices. These users decreased their use of scroll down to the expert's level, but not to the extent of introducing overall differences between novices. Thus, the use of the node, search-and, and index were dramatically changed with the introduction of the online file search assistant.

4.3.3 Diagnostic flexibility.

In addition to the overall evaluation of the efficacy of online assistance, the diagnostic flexibility of the assistance was evaluated by allowing 2, 3, 4, or 5 search procedures to be accepted by the file search assistant as appropriate search strategies. The flexibility of the diagnostic model influenced the total operations (as well as total time) on assisted trials. The plots of the means for total operations over the 4 levels of diagnostic flexibility are shown in Figure 4. Newman-Keuls analyses ($p<.05$) showed that the very lenient assistant with a diagnostic flexibility of 5 increased the number of operations on an assisted trial. Consequently, there is evidence to suggest that a very lenient assistant may not be effective on assisted trials, and flexibility should be reduced to 2 or 3 alternatives.

TOTAL OPERATIONS

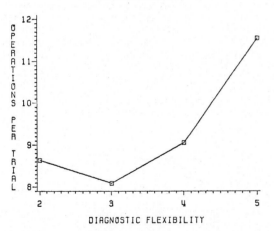

Figure 4 : Total operations across diagnostic flexibility on assisted trials

4.4 Implications

Results of the online HELP and the interactive file search research demonstrate the feasibility of developing empirically based design principles and assistance systems based upon a method of capturing empirically expert performance. The target profile methodology not only was sensitive to differences between novice and expert subjects in file search, but also was capable of being used to provide assistance to novice subjects. The file search assistant facilitated the development of expert search strategies by novice subjects and improved novice users' performance during

assisted, but unadvised, time periods. In terms of advice, however, the communication between the assistant and novice users was intrusive. To overcome this problem, the implementation of a suggestive assistant with a strict diagnostic model is recommended for future development.

5. CONCLUSIONS

Inexperienced users of software systems require various forms of online assistance. Alternatives such as automatic error detection, browsing and comparison of HELP facilities, and online expert aiding need to be considered. Ultimately, the goal should be the development of a truly adaptive interface that is tailored to the individual requirements and skill levels for the user. The principles and methods of online assistance for novice users investigated in these studies provide the initial step in developing such adaptive interfaces.

6. ACKNOWLEDGEMENTS

This paper is based, in part, on reserch supported by contracts from the Navy Personnel Research and Development Center and the Office of Naval Research.

7. REFERENCES

[1] Pittman, J.A., and Williges, R.C. Reduction of format errors in a personnel records task. Proceedings of the International Conference on Cybernetics and Society, IEEE, 1981, 33-37.

[2] Cohill, A.M., and Williges, R.C. Computer-augmented retrieval of HELP information for novice users. Proceedings of the 26th Annual Meeting of the Human Factors Society, 1982, 79-82.

[3] Elkerton, J., Williges, R.C., Pittman, J.A., and Roach, J.W. Strategies of interactive file searching. Proceedings of the Human Factors Society 26th Annual Meeting, 1982, 83-86.

[4] Elkerton, J. and Williges, R.C. Development of an adaptive assistant in a file search environment. Proceedings of the Artificial Intelligence Conference, Oakland University, 1983.

[5] Elkerton, J. and Williges, R.C. Evaluation of expertise in a file search environment. Proceedings of the Human Factors Society 27th Annual Meeting, 1983, 521-525.

[6] Elkerton, J. An experimental evaluation of an assistance system in an information retrieval environment, M.S. Thesis, Industrial Engineering and Operations Research, Virginia Tech, January 1985.

Human-Computer Interaction — INTERACT '84 / B. Shackel (ed.)
Elsevier Science Publishers B.V. (North-Holland)
© IFIP, 1985

Learning Pascal after BASIC

John D'Arcy

Department of Psychology
Queen's University of Belfast

This study compares the learning of Pascal by University students who either had previous training in BASIC with those who had no programming experience at all. Pascal program comprehension and modification tasks were used to see if those who had initially learned BASIC suffered the 'mental mutilation' suggested by computing and education experts. Data gathered during coursework show little evidence, given a well structured course, of the anticipated negative transfer of BASIC onto subsequent learning of Pascal.

1. INTRODUCTION

There is enormous pressure on educational institutions, from primary schools to universities, to provide education and training in the art or science of computer programming. Those involved in teaching programming are faced with choices ranging from expedient decisions about hardware to an almost philosophical choice of programming language to be taught. Du Boulay and O'Shea (1981) extensively review the literature on teaching programming to novices and conclude that while educators are presented with many such choices there is little or no empirical evidence to guide their decisions.

In theory, the choice of programming language is wide, with Logo, COMAL, Pascal, FORTH, and PROLOG often recommended as good languages for novices. In practice, one programming language –BASIC – has almost a monopoly, as by far the most widely used first language for beginners. Yet while BASIC is tremendously popular - in terms of widespread use - as a first programming language for training in schools and also with the vast self-trained armies of home computer users, it is almost universally disliked and vehemently criticized by both computer scientists and experienced educators.

BASIC is attacked on many fronts; as a programming language per se, for example:

"It is practically impossible to teach good programming to students who have had a prior exposure to BASIC: as potential programmers they are mentally mutilated beyond all hope of regeneration." (E.W. Dijkstra, SIGPLAN Notices, May 1982, page 14)

Opinions abound about what makes a good programming language for novices. Du Boulay, O'Shea and Monk (1981) quote 'simplicity' and 'visibility' as two important characteristics. They suggest that rules defining a language should be uniform, with few special cases to

remember, and without potential ambiguities. O'Shea and Self (1983) offer BASIC's use of the '=' symbol to perform a variety of functions, as an illustration of how BASIC is weak in this respect. A programming language should also provide constructs, for example procedures and choices for repetition and conditionals, to help the expression of problem solving strategies. O'Shea and Self (1983) suggest that BASIC's lack of such constructs encourages contortions which soon render a program incomprehensible. Taking such serious criticisms of BASIC together with it's widespread use it is surprising that virtually no empirical studies (as contrasted with expressions of opinion or anecdotal reports) of BASIC have been reported in the computing, educational or psychological literature. This seems even more surprising in comparison with the fairly extensive research carried out on other programming languages.

Thus Logo, although a relative newcomer in terms of widespread availability, has been the focus of a number of empirical studies. For example, Cannara (1976) looked at the difficulties children experience when learning Logo, while Austin (1976) carried out a similar type of study with student teachers. For Pascal Ripley and Druseikis (1978) studied the syntactic errors of two classes of graduate computer science students, while Pugh and Simpson (1979) carried out a less detailed study of students' errors. Experiences with COBOL have been observed by Litecky and Davis (1976), Al-Jarrah and Torsun (1979) and Youngs (1974). FORTRAN was the subject of studies by Knuth (1971) and Boies and Gould (1974).

BASIC's influence on the subsequent learning of other languages, especially more structured programming languages, is another source of criticism:

"We found that it took newly recruited graduates learning the high level structured language CORAL 66 twice as long to learn if

they had previously used BASIC or FORTRAN, than
if they had not learned programming before."
(C.J. Brady, Letter to Educational Computing,
May 1983, p 5)

Wexelblat (1981) collected opinions from educators about what they thought were good programming
languages for beginners, and also what features
they thought should be incorporated in a good
beginners language. He suggests:

"Few programmers who begin their programming life
with a language so limited as BASIC ever significantly extend their ability to make full use of
the data and program structuring capabilities of
higher level languages learned later."

This feeling that it is difficult to transfer
from unstructured BASIC to a more structured
language like Pascal is widely reported. In one
of the recent texts which aim to aid in the
transfer from BASIC to Pascal, Brown (1983)
suggests it is not just a case of learning new
syntax, but rather a case of learning how to
think again. The problem of transferring from
BASIC to other languages is an important one,
given the number of people who use BASIC. It is
a problem which clearly merits research, yet
again it is surprising to find that no empirical studies on the transfer of BASIC to any
other language are to be found in the literature. Indeed there are surprisingly few empirical studies of transfer between _any_ programming languages.

The present study uses program comprehension
and modification tasks, similar to those described by Shneiderman (1980), to see if students
who had previously learned to program in BASIC
did suffer the damage suggested by Dijkstra,
Wexelblat and others when they came to learn
Pascal.

The comprehension tasks aim to tap the subjects
understanding of a Pascal program. It is of
interest to see how students who have learned
BASIC cope with Pascal's less 'sign-posted'
notation. The modification task is designed to
test whether students initially trained in
BASIC utilize the more complicated constructs
available in Pascal. In particular, whether or
not they tend to use the more structured IF -
THEN - ELSE, instead of the 'jump - style' IF -
THEN.

2.METHOD

2.1 Subjects

Students were all enrolled in Queen's University, Belfast, Department of Computer Science,
second year course, 'Introduction to Computer
Programming' which teaches Pascal. From the 240

students enrolled on the course, eighty students were selected and agreed to participate in
the study. Forty of these had learned to program in an unstructured BASIC on the first year
Computer Science course at Queen's the previous
session. The other forty subjects who had never
programmed before, either at Queen's or elsewhere, came directly from school into second
year at university. The subjects who learned
BASIC will be referred to as the 'BASIC' Group,
and the other group will be known as the
'NOBASIC' Group.

Both groups of subjects were matched for sex
and A-level grades. There were 24 males and 16
females in the each group. On an A-level
'points' system (i.e. 5 points for an 'A' to 1
point for an 'E') the BASIC group had a range
of scores from 6 to 20 points, with a mean of
11.8 and s.d. of 3.05 while the NOBASIC group
had scores ranging from 6 to 23 points, with a
mean of 12.1 and s.d. of 3.28.

2.2 Teaching Environment

This 'core programming' course is taught by a
highly experienced lecturer who emphasises the
'top down / stepwise refinement' methodology in
a manner intended to minimise potential transfer problems. For example, GOTO statements are
avoided and the use of procedures is emphasised. The textbook for the course was Welsh
and Elder's (1982) 'Introduction to Pascal'.

2.3 Tasks

As the study had to be carried out within the
constraints of a formal academic course, the
programming tasks were administered so that
they would not interfere with the teaching of
the course, or increase the workload of students participating in the study. The tasks
were administered as tutorial or homework
questions.

2.3.1 Comprehension Tasks

Subjects were given programs in Pascal, and
asked to trace their execution given certain
data. For example in the first homework paper
the subjects were given the following programs
to trace. (Please note that line numbers are
not used in Pascal, they are only used in this
task as reference points for the trace.)

```
1     progam Powers ( input , output );
2
3        var
4           number , power , answer : integer;
5        begin
6        read ( number , power );
7        answer := 1 ;
8        while power > 0 do
9           begin
10          power := power -1;
11          answer := answer * number
12          end;
13       write ( answer )
14       end.
```

Students were asked to trace the execution of this program with the following data: 2 and 3

Fig (i)a Comprehension Example

```
1     program Divisor ( input , output );
2
3        var
4           first , second : integer;
5        begin
6        read ( first , second );
7        while first <> second do
8           if first > second
9           then first := first – second
10          else second := second – first;
11       write ( first )
12       end.
```

Students were asked to trace the execution of the program, when the input data was 49 and 70.

Fig (i)b Comprehension Example

Fig (i) Examples of programs to be traced by subjects

2.3.2 Modification Task

Subjects were given the following program, and were asked to modify it so that it would print out raw marks, average mark, and also a grade, where the grade is determined from the average mark as follows :   A (60 – 100)   B (40 – 59) C (0 – 39)

```
program Marks ( input, output );
   var
      english, maths, average, sum : integer;
   begin
   read ( maths, english );
   sum:= maths + english;
   average:= ( sum + 1 ) div 2;
   writeln ('AVERAGE : ', average :1)
   end.
```

fig (ii) Program used in modification task

3. RESULTS

3.1 Comprehension

Although the subjects were given a number of comprehension tasks, ranging from the ones shown in fig (i) to programs with procedures and variable parameters, it is only their performance on the programs shown in fig (i) that will be reported in this paper. Note that the two programs in fig (i) are quite similar, the main feature of both programs is the inclusion of a WHILE statement. In Pascal, if there is more than one statement in the body of the WHILE loop, then the body of the loop must be enclosed by BEGIN and END. If however, there is only one statement in the loop, then the BEGIN and END markers can be omitted.

All subject's traces were analysed for errors and the error paths recorded. In both programs the only error type recorded was the inclusion of the statements following the end of the WHILE loop within the WHILE loop. The results are shown in Tables 1a and 1b.

Table 1a. Results for program shown in fig (i)a.

	BASIC	NOBASIC
CORRECT	39 (97.5 %)	37 (100 %)
INCORRECT	1 (2.5 %)	0 (0 %)
Total	40	37

Table 1b. Results for program shown in fig (i)b.

	BASIC	NOBASIC
CORRECT	30 (75 %)	35 (94.6 %)
INCORRECT	10 (25 %)	2 (5.4 %)
Total	40	37

A Chi-Square test was carried out on this data, the Chi value (with Yeates correction) was 4.219 which was significant at the .05 level (p=.039).

3.2 Modification Task

Of most interest in this task, was the conditional structure employed by the subjects. It was anticipated, given the comments of Wexelblat and other writers, that subjects, who had learned BASIC, would not use the more structured IF-THEN-ELSE, rather that they would employ a number of IF-THEN's. The results are shown in Table 2.

Table 2. Results for modification of program in fig(ii)

	BASIC	NOBASIC
IF-THEN-ELSE	32 (86.5%)	19 (59.4%)
IF-THEN	5 (13.5%)	13 (40.6%)
Total	37	32

This data was subjected to a Chi-Square Test. A Chi value (with Yates's Correction) of 5.21 was found, this was significant at the .05 level (p = 0.022).

4. DISCUSSION

4.1 Comprehension Tasks

Performance on the program shown in fig(i)a was very similar for both groups. However, in the program in fig(i)b the BASIC group made significantly more errors than the NOBASIC group. All the errors recorded were of the same type, i.e. instead of recognising the WHILE loop to be

```
7          while first <> second do
8              if first > second
9              then first := first – second
10             else second := second – first;
```

subjects tended to include the remaining statements of the program in the WHILE loop also. Thus:

```
7          while first <> second do
8              if first > second
9              then first := first – second
10             else second := second – first;
11         write ( first )
12         end.
```

Subjects in the BASIC group seem to have been misled by the absence of BEGIN / END markers. They do not seem to recognise that the semi-colon at the end of line 10 signals the end of the WHILE statement. The indentation does not help overcome the omission of the markers either. Indeed it is suggested that subjects may have used the program terminating END as the END marker for the structure.

Sime and Green (1979) stress the importance of making the structure of the program clearly visible so that anyone reading it can successfully negotiate their way through the program. The types of signposts available in BASIC and Pascal are very different. In BASIC, the line numbers provide a very explicit signposting service, in Pascal however the programmer has to use less obvious cues. BEGINs and ENDs may signal the body of a particular structure, indentation and the 'fiddly' semi-colon also

play important roles in directing the programmer through the program. Thus the BASIC programmer has to learn new strategies, which give even more attention to the details of the text of the program. It is interesting to note that in subsequent program traces, the occurances of this type of error amongst the BASIC group, dropped to a level comparable with the NOBASIC group. This would indicate that this error of transfer is a very transient one.

4.2 Modification Task

The results from this task were completely opposite to what may have been expected. Wexelblat and others would lead one to believe that the BASIC group would not be as prone to use the more structured IF-THEN-ELSE form of the conditional. The data in Table 2 indicate that significantly more BASIC students utilized IF-THEN-ELSE. It is suggested that the reason for this difference is due to the BASIC groups' greater programming experience. They may have already written programs with a lot of IF-THENs, and have found that they lead to confusing and bugged programs. The responses from the NOBASIC Group tended to be too detailed, often they had three IF-THENs of the form:

If (average>39) and (average<60) then grade:='B'

4.3 General Discussion

The data suggest that those with prior BASIC experience have not suffered much apparent negative transfer in coming from BASIC to Pascal when compared to those learning their first programming via Pascal. Early problems with traces seemed to disappear quickly. They also showed no unwillingness to use so-called higher level features in their programs. There are several possible explanations for the findings.

First, the tasks used may have been too easy and thus not acted as discriminators. Certainly, by the third set of comprehension tasks, which featured procedures calling other procedures and procedures with local data, around 80% of both groups were getting the traces correct. Comprehension and modification tasks may also be poor instruments to measure 'programming'. Consequently, Pascal programs written by both groups have also been collected and their analysis may provide a better metric of the real relative programming proficiency of both groups of subjects.

A second reason for the failure to demonstrate negative transfer from BASIC may lie in the careful and deliberate structuring of the course to teach good programming technique rather than merely the syntax of Pascal. If so, it is significant to demonstrate that good teaching can mitigate against possible bad effects of a poor first programming language.

Thirdly, criticisms of BASIC as a beginners' language may be unwarranted. However, the data in this paper is limited by the types of task used, and cannot specifically be used to support such a notion. Moreover, this research gives no answer to the question of how much better would be a transfer group who had previously learned a supposedly good beginners language. More research is clearly needed on transfer between programming languages of all types.

5. References

Al-Jarrah, M.M. and Torsun, I.S. (1979). An empirical analysis of COBOL programs. **Software – Practice and Experience,** 9, 341-359.

Austin, H. (1976). Teaching teachers Logo. **A.I. Memo No.336.** Artificial Intelligence Laboratory, M.I.T., Cambridge, Massachusetts.

Boies, S.J. and Gould, J.D. (1974). Syntactic errors in computer programming. **Human Factors,** 16, 253-257.

Brown, P.J. (1982). **Pascal from BASIC.** London: Addison- Wesley.

Cannara, A.B. (1976). Experiments in teaching children computer programming. **Technical Report No. 271,** Institute for Mathematical Studies in Social Sciences, Stanford University.

Du Boulay, B. and O'Shea, T. (1981). Teaching Novices Programming, in Coombs, M.J. and Alty, J.L. (eds.). **Computing Skills and The User Interface.** London: Academic Press.

Du Boulay, J.B.H., O'Shea,T., and Monk, J. (1981). The Black Box inside the Glass Box : presenting computing concepts to novices. **International Journal of Man-Machine Studies,** 4, 237-249.

Knuth, D.E. (1971). An empirical study of FORTRAN programs. **Software – Practice and Experience,** 1, 105-133.

Litecky, C.R. and Davis, G.B. (1976). A study of errors, error proneness and error diagnosis in COBOL. **Communications of the A.C.M.,** 22, 335-340.

O'Shea,T. and Self,J. (1983). **Learning and Teaching with Computers.** Sussex: Harvester Press.

Pugh, J. and Simpson,D. (1979). Pascal Errors – empirical evidence. **Computer Bulletin,** 2, 26-28.

Ripley, G.D. and Druseikis, F.C. (1978). A statistical anaylsis of syntax errors. **Computer Languages,** 3, 227-240.

Shneiderman, B. (1980). **Software Psychology : Human Factors in Computer and Information Systems.** Cambridge, Massachusetts: Winthrop.

Sime, M.E. and Green, T.R.G. (1979). The structure and clarity of a program, **Memo 300, Social and Applied Psychology Unit,** University of Sheffield.

Welsh, J. and Elder, J. (1982). **Introduction to Pascal:**2nd Edition. London: Prentice – Hall International.

Wexelblat, R.L. (1979). The consequences of one's first programming language. **Software – Practice and Experience,** 7, 733-740.

Youngs, E.M. (1974). Human Errors in Programming. **International Journal of Man-Machine Studies,** 6, 361-376.

Acknowledgements

Considerable help and co-operation was given by Professor. F.J. Smith, Dr. H.C. Johnston and their colleagues in the Department of Computer Science, Queen's University, Belfast, and also by Mr. D.J. Hale of the Psychology Department.

Human-Computer Interaction — INTERACT '84 / B. Shackel (ed.)
Elsevier Science Publishers B.V. (North-Holland)
© IFIP, 1985

HOW NOVICES LEARN TO PROGRAM

Ann Jones, Institute of Educational Technology, Open University, England

This paper describes a study of the behaviour of novice programmers. A conceptual model is advocated as a framework for novices learning to program, du Boulay, O'Shea and Monk (1981), and this research is concerned with the detailed learning processes of novices learning with the provision of one such conceptual model. It presents some new results supported by protocol data of students learning SOLO, a data-base manipulation language designed especially for novices, (Eisenstadt, 1978). In particular this paper reports on learning about control statements and the hierarchical structuring of programming. The ultimate goal of this research is to improve instructiional materials for teaching at a distance and the paper concludes with some of the implications of this research for teaching novices to program.

1. WHAT DO WE ALREADY KNOW ABOUT NOVICE PROGRAMMERS AND THEIR NEEDS?

Although there is now a substantial body of research on the psychology of programming, we are only just beginning to learn about the nature of programming knowledge, and how programming skills are acquired. Studies on expert programmers suggest that programming can be viewed as collections of plans, - of stereotypical sequences: Soloway et al (1982) describe different kinds of looping plans and the different roles that variables play in each. It seems that experts have highly organised domain specific knowledge, - and studies of novices, especially comparative studies of novices and experts, (which are probably the most common), stress that novices have yet to acquire such conceptual chunks: they lack "tacit plan knowledge". (Soloway et al (1982), Ehrlich and Soloway, 1982). Kahney (1982) however found that the novices he studied did have quite developed recursion plans, but that these models were often inaccurate.

To understand how such a complex skill is learnt we need to find out how the knowledge involved in that skill can be structured: how the learner builds up a representation of it mentally, and the processes involved in forming the representation and interacting with it. We need to study the learning process in detail.

Taking a Piagetian stance we can argue that learning involves assimulating new information into existing structures: connecting that new information with older, organized knowledge. Programming knowledge however may be discontinuous from other knowledge: Sheil (1981) argues that programming skills are rather special and are radically different from the skills which most people already have. A particular problem for novices learning their first programming language, therefore, is the lack of an appropriate cognitive framework which will serve to relate new information

to existing knowledge. In the next section the provision of a conceptual model is advocated to provide such a framework.

2. THE NEED AND PROVISION OF CONCEPTUAL MODELS

Various researchers and educators advocate the provision of some form of conceptual model for novices learning complex tasks in computer domains (du Boulay et al (1981), Mayer (1981), Norman (1982). These approaches share a concern for presenting the workings of an abstract machine (representing the system which novices are to learn) by reference to mechanisms with which novices are familiar. The only framework which will be considered briefly here is that of du Boulay, O'Shea and Monk(1981). They argue that a major problem in teaching novices programming is describing the machine which the novice is learning to use at the right level of detail - as the novice usually does not know what the machine can be instructed to do (its range of behaviour)or how it manages to do it (the process of carrying out that behaviour). They suggest that one way of overcoming this problem is to base the teaching on the idea of a notional machine. This is an idealised model of the computer implied by the constructs of the programming language; that is, it is not related to the hardware but is language dependent: thus a BASIC notional machine is different from a LISP or PASCAL machine. They advocate two principles upon which to base the notional machine: conceptual simplicity and visibility.

Wherever possible methods should be provided for the learner to see certain of its workings in action, for instance the effects of commands. One way of doing this is by means of a commentary: a 'glass box' through which novices can see the workings of the machine. In the three systems they discuss

as examples, the commentary is provided in
different ways. One notional machine (for a
microcomputer), is essentially provided by the
machine itself - it is its own model and has been
designed so that its workings, at the appropriate level, are visible, (Open University,
1979). The other two notional machines are
for the programming languages SOLO (Eisenstadt,
1978)which is the language used in this
study and ELOGO (du Boulay and O'Shea, 1976).
In SOLO, some of the workings of the notional
machine are in the language itself, for
instance SOLO automatically shows the learner
the updated state of the database after an item
has been inserted or deleted, and others are
described in the mannual, sometimes by using
analogies. In using ELOGO novices progress
from using a turtle and button box where each
button stands for an instruction, to using a
teletype; but are still protected from parts
of the system which they don't need to know
about.

3. THE USER'S MENTAL MODEL

The work of du Boulay, O'Shea and Monk, (and
also Mayer (1981) is concerned with conceptual
models of the machine which are provided to
aid the learner. Another issue, however,
is the mental models which learners develop
and use in learning a domain: "The notion of
a user's "conceptual model" is a rather lazy
one but central to it is the assumption that
the user will adopt some more or less definite
representation or metaphor which guides his
actions and helps him to interpret the devices's
behaviour."

(Richard Young, 1981.) Young uses the term
conceptual model not to refer to the conceptual
model as I have discussed it but to refer to
what I shall call the user's mental model, to
make the distinction clear. Such mental
models have been the subject of research in
domains such as physics for some time (eg
Genter, 1982). In computing domains, however,
research in this area is much more recent,
although there is now a growing body of research
on learning to use text editors and word
processors, e.g. Bott's work (Bott, 1979) on
learning to use a text editor. It is how
learners can use the conceptual model of the
machine provided by the designer to form their
own mental models, and how accurate these
mental models are, which is one focus of this
study.

4. A STUDY OF BEGINNER PROGRAMMERS

I am investigating the mental models which
novices develop as they learn a language
called SOLO, designed by Marc Eisenstadt and
used by cognitive psychology students at the
Open University (Eisenstadt, 1978). Solo
provides an environment for students to
manipulate an assertional date base, as a tool
for learning about knowledge representation.
It is one of the examples cited by du Boulay,

O'Shea and Monk (op cit, 1981). It was
designed to be as easy as possible for
total novices to learn, by being restricted
to a small number of primitives, by incorporating many user aids (such as a spelling
corrector), and by presenting a carefully
thought out and consistent conceptual model.
Nevertheless learning to program in SOLO is
by no means trivial, and this study is the
beginning of an attempt to understand
precisely what the novice really thinks is
going on inside the machine i.e. his or her
mental model. In order to do this I have
focussed on what happens right at the start
of learning to program when the learner is
introduced, via a conceptual model, to the
constructs of the programming language. The
questions considered here are: Does the
conceptual model provide an adequate framework?
How does it map on to the user's developing
mental model, and vice versa? Which aspects
of the conceptual model are important? If
there are "gaps" in the framework provided
by the conceptual model, as, in a real world
there are bound to be, how does the learner
use what existing knowledge she has to work
out what's going on? Where does the conceptual
models break? Programming skill exists at many
different levels. This study is concerned
with the learner's knowledge of the effects
of the programming constructs, at the
appropriate level of detail. This is, the
learner does not need to know the internal
operations what happen when she types Print
or Note (a command for inserting a triple into
the data base) but she does need to know that
Note has an effect on the date base and that
Print does not. This is at a different and
lower level from that of programming schemas,
(e.g. Bonar et al, 1982). Such schemas involve
more of a problem solving activity, which will,
however, involve the dynamic application of
the 'knowledge' contained in the mental models
referred to here. At present, the study is
not concerned with the planning and coding of
programs of any complexity: the mental models
of the constructs, at this level, correspond
to the level of knowledge which Mayer and
Bayman (1982) are concerned with in their
work on BASIC transactions.

4.1 Methods and task

This paper reports on an analysis of 11 novice
students who were asked to think aloud as they
worked through the SOLO exercises and to
describe what they were thinking about as they
tried to solve the problem. This forms part
of a larger study involving other languages
including SOLO. In particular this paper
focusses on novices' behaviour in learning
about control statements; solving problems
using control statements and learning about
hierarchical structuring of programming.
Both verbalizations and the interactions on
the terminal screen were tape recorded using
Cyclops, a device developed as the University
enabling date and voice to be recorded

simultaneously. (Scanlon, in press)   The
experimenter remained in the room with the
subjects; to prompt them to think aloud and
to be 'on call' should the subject feel
totally stuck.   Clearly such a presence alters
the learning situation but it does not change
it more than the experimental paradigm - and,
if more obtrusive, is at, least capturing a
'natural' learning situation rather than
putting subjects into contrived experiments.
Issues surrounding the use of protocol data and
introspection are discussed at length elsewhere
(see for example Breuker, (1982). Here it
is sufficient to say that there is a role both
for in-depth protocol analysis and experimental
paradigms in this area: an in-depth study can
illuminate what is going on it the situation,
and can lead to models of the learner's
behaviour; once we have some models then
variables can be manipulated in the more
traditional experimental paradigm to uncover
various influences.

5.   PROTOCOL DATA

The protocol data presented here is discussed at
length in Jones (1984). This paper concentrates
on novices' behaviour in the following areas:
learning about SOLO's control statements CONTINUE
and EXIT; writing a short procedure using
control statement, and the hierarchical
structuring of programs. Protocoal segments
are labelled by a subject number (S1-S8) and
are also sometimes broken into numbered
segments.

5.1 Control statements: CONTINUE and EXIT

> look carefully at the difference ....
> Both are designed to "assess" someone's
> physical fitness by deciding whether to
> print FIT or UNFIT on the basis of certain
> known 'facts' (such as whether a person
> plays squash, rides bicycles, etc). The
> first procedure is a 'weak' assessment
> while the second one is 'strict' assess-
> ment, hence the names ... Notice how
> (they) differ in their usage of CONTINUE
> and EXIT.

FIGURE 1 Extract from SOLO manual on
sequency of programs.

Subjects were asked, in the SOLO manual, to
mentally execute two procedures, WEAKASSESS
and STRONGASSESS, (see fig. 1) and in
particular, to note the use of the control
statements, CONTINUE and EXIT, to which
they have just been introduced.

1. So it doesn't matter that Mary also
   rides bicycles as well and that she
   doesn't climb mountains, but is the
   actual procedure going to stop if she
   exits these?

2. I was just wondering if .. the exit just
   meant stopping on that line .. or going

to the next one but obviously it doesn't
because that's what continue means.

Figure 2 Extract from protocol of S1 talking
about control statements

At this point many of the novices were not clear
about the difference between the two control
statements and some have a mental model of the
machine as somehow keeping a watching brief.
Even when the procedure has exitted, there is
the notion that lines of code after the exit
are 'looked at' - just in case.

1. But then where it says Fred plays squash,
   which, if present, print fit exit, so
   would that exit not bother with those
   two checks as to whether he rides bicycles
   and climbs mountains?

2. I don't think it would only continue for
   the next check if the first was absent, so
   it would stop there.

Figure 3 Extract from protocol of S2
talking about control statements

The above extract also illustrates this to
some extent, although this subject's concern
was the 'redundancy' of the rest of the
information which the procedure was checking.
Another subject explained the use of CONTINUE
as follows:
   "CONTINUE is more or less to keep the
      machine on the boil, it keeps it going"
But she didn't know what was kept going.
Other students (including S1 did not
realise that it was not needed in the
CHECK statement, or why, and some had no
idea of when it should be used.

5.2 Programs using control statements

This section looks at the subjects' behaviour
on the first activity where they use control
statements, given in figure 4 below.

1. Define your own procedure called ASSESS,
   which prints out UNHEALTHY if someone
   (the node to which it is applied) either
   drinks whisky, on the one hand; or else
   if that person both smokes cigarettes
   and drinks beer.

2. Using the NOTE procedure, add some
   descriptions of your own to SOLO's data
   base, and try out your ASSESS procedure
   to get it working properly. You must
   decide for yourself how you are going to
   represent 'drinks whisky', etc., in the
   data base.

Figure 4 The ASSESS activity

In order to complete this activity, students
need to understand the logic of the problem;
work out a plan to achieve it and translate
that plan into SOLO statements. To do this

they need to understand what control statements
do and how to use them in different combinations.
Some of the novices had problems with all of
these stages. They could not work out the
logical form of the problem: "IF A OR ELSE B
AND C PRESENT, DO ...." - which should not be
surprising as we know this is difficult. Even
when they could work out what was needed they
still had problems trying to achieve this
logical structure using SOLO code: "I know
what I want to do out I can't see how to do
either or" (extract from protocol of S7). In
other words, they often could not work out how
to achieve the flow of control that they
wanted, using the CONTINUE and EXIT statements
which SOLO provides. The novices who were
most successful at this activity often used one
of the procedures they had already met, as a
model to work from.

> So what I did was to combine the weakassess
> and strictassess type programs here, so, ..
> here we've got line 10, if drinks whisky -
> if present print unhealthy and exit. If
> absent continue ... that's the weakassess
> model ...
>
> The next two take part of the strictassess
> type model, so somebody has to both smoke
> cigarettes and drink beer to be unhealthy,
> so, check smokes cigarettes.

Figure 5 Extract from S3 solving the
'Assess' problem

It was clear that S3 abstracted a schema from
the procedures given, which she used in
successfully completing this problem. S2 also
used the previous procedure as a model, but she
still has some problems with control statements
- fig 6 below.

> I was just thinking of the same procedure
> as the to assess, just to assess ...
>
> ... I am a bit confused because you want
> it to continue to check if he also drank
> beer as well but I'm not sure what the
> exit would mean, if he didn't actually.

Figure 5 Extract from S2 solving the
ASSESS problem

Other students were not able to easily abstract
such plans or program fragments and therefore
did not have access to them.

5.4 Hierarchical Sequencing of Programs

This is introduced in the text, immediately
after the Assess activity discussed above, in
the following way.

> Now suppose that instead of simply printing
> HOORAY at sub-step 2A, we had wanted to
> activate several different procedures, for
> example, the following three:

```
PRINT"I THINK"/X/"IS QUITE REMARKABLE"
PRING"I REALLY RESPECT" /X/
PRINT"HOORAY FOR" /X/
```

Since we are only permitted to activate one
procedure at any given step, what we must do
is decide what single overall thing we would
want to do at sub-step 2A which would encompass
all three of the above procedure - on other
words, we must try to group those three
procedures into one single new one. Let's
suppose that we decide that those three
procedures involve (roughly) an act of 'praise'
and so we decide to define a new procedure
called PRAISE.

How would you define this new procedure called
PRAISE?

Figure 6 Part of section on hierarchical
sequencing of program taken from the SOLO
manual

> Well it is possible what you try and
> activate it if line 2A is the relevant
> line ... maybe it's not legal, I have a
> feeling it's not legal.
>
> How would I define this procedure called
> praise? Could I insert at line 30, ...
> type in something like TO PRAISE and the
> definition .. no that's not legal, is it?
>
> Would we type out here separately a new
> procedure called praise?
>
> How I'm going to activate this praise
> procedure whilst in the middle of the
> judge, I don't know".

Figure 7 Extract from S1 on hierarchical
structuring of programs

From the beginning he can see only one possible
solution (which is the correct one) but believes
it cannot be the solution required as it would
be doing more than one 'single overall thing':
the problem is compounded because he is confused
about where the procedure is defined, and where
it is activated. He constantly refers back to
the question and reads it out

> I don't feel there's been any indication
> that once SOLO's been looking through
> this judge procedure that it's then able
> to sort of shoot down to line 3 and then
> suddenly go off and do an investigation
> of the praise procedure and then go back
> to judge.

Figure 8 Extract from S1 on hierarchical
sequencing of programs

One problem for S1, here is that he is relying
on the text to clarify what he believes to be
a problem. His first protocols indicate that
he can see only one possible solution - and this
is the right answer, - that he activates the
same procedure from within the judge procedure.

He find himself unable to carry this out however as it conflicts with his inaccurate mental model of what is required.He believes that to execute praise would be to have more than one "single overall thing" happen at sub-step 2A (because there are therefore 2 procedures). Furthermore he is confused about the definition and the activation of the procedure (Fig 7 .) Even after he has succeeded, his final comment (on this one) is given in fig 9 below.

> So it does work, so you can incorporate just another procedure just anyway - I thought it would require experimentation.
>
> I thought I'd read earlier that you couldn't ... since we are only permitted to activate one procedure at any given step ...
>
> Even if you're within another procedure it doesn't matter, ... is that what it's saying?

Figure 9 Extract from S1s protocol in hierarchical sequencing of programming

Like many of the other novices, S1, when he was unclear read and re-read the text scrutinizing it and comparing it to his own hypotheses about how the praise procedure must work.

5.5 Metaphors

One of the ways in which the conceptual model provides a familiar framework is by using analogies and metaphors to link the new with the familiar. For example the SOLO manual introduces SOLO's data-base by comparing it with a telephone directory. However students also produce their own 'spontaneous' metaphors from their previous experience.

> "To praise /X/".
> I think of it in relation to a word processor; that if I were doing a lot of letters I would do a letter and put an X in, Dear X, and each one I'd just put Fred, Mary.

Figure 10 Extract from S5 talking about procedures using parameters

In figure 10 above an extract is given of a protocol of a student who is learning about the idea of a procedure taking a parameter. She was commenting on the title line, "To Praise /X/" This metaphor of a word processor is very useful and appropriate in this context: which is the notion of a procedure taking a parameter. The learner is able to make sense of a new concept through its connection with prior knowledge. Although she had never used a word processor she held beliefs about the way they behaved, which seemed to be, for the most part, useful and accurate. However although the metaphor was helpful, in this context, for this learner, it also led her to have expectations about how the editor would behave for example that it would be able to delete single

words within a line of the procedure. This did not match the editor's actual behaviour - and yet these beliefs about its behaviour were persistent.

Here is a final example.

The two procedures in fig 11 below are presented in the mannual as the first examples of how a procedure can 'summarize' many tasks, - in this case to print three statements or to 'note' them, i.e., add them to the data base.

```
TO GRUMBLE
Print "I don't feel so good today"
Print "My feet are sore"
Print "Besides that, I have a headache"

To FOO
Note BAZ - GLUB - FOZ
Note BAZ - BIF - ZAP
```

Figure 11 TO GRUMBLE and TO FOO; two SOLO procedures, taken from SOLO manual.

> "I don't understand this; it says to grumble here. To grumble, to foo, they're still both verbs, right? I don't understand why that isn't the same format as that, I mean how can you apply those to a verb?
>
> I just thought if you wanted to do something it was a particular format; .. I don't see why it's got print here and note here, surely, if it's got one particular format applying to verbs why has it got print for one and note for another?

Figure 12 Extract from S6's protocol.

The protocol in fig 12 suggests that S6 is seeing the procedure literally as a verb. In the complete protocol it is apparent that the verb metaphor is constraining her understanding quite strongly. A procedure can be usefully thought as a verb, in some ways; however this subject believed that as such it behaved like a particular verb, e.g. grumble, and it has to have one particular format - and this was the SOLO primitive that it used, NOTE or PRINT so that it did one particular thing: NOTE, PRINT or whatever. Unlike a procedure, then, a verb is seen to be doing a particular job: to fit the metaphor, the notion of a procedure is constrained so that it is no longer a general function which can carry out a variety of tasks.

6. DISCUSSIONS AND CONCLUSIONS

In the absence of other information in a distance teaching situation novices are reliant on the programming environment to provide them with information - and clues - about what's going on. This information is provided through a conceptual model, and novices scrutinize any aspect of this that they can - the screen, the manual, error messages for confirmation of their own mental models -

of their hypotheses. Often it is the text that
is scrutinised - and although the SOLO manual is
very successful, novices do misinterpret the
text and often construct inaccurate mental
models, which for a while, at least, are
persistent. They experience different problems,
but what these problems have in common is that
they all arise from students very actively
interpreting the environment they are learning.
For example, subjects spontaneously use their
own metaphors to relate new information to
existing knowledge, and as we have seen, this
can lead to inappropriate expectations. It is
not clear yet whether such beliefs lead to long
lasting confusion: beginners' mental models
are likely to be unstable and will change; it is
also to be expected that misconceptions will be
held during the course of learning. What it
does indicate is that learners will not be
passive recipients of what we aim to teach, -
and I would argue that this is no bad thing!
This view of the very active learner is supported
by other research in similar domains, for example
Bott (1979) and Carroll and Mack (1982).

Caroll and Mack describe people learning to use
a word processor in the following ways: that
they "strike into the unknown, interpret on the
basis of little evidence, ... learn by generalizing interpretations, ... verify the hypotheses
they generate on the strength of single facts
...." The picture they paint could often apply
to SOLO learners too.

Clearly, teachers need to take time to try to
understand the models their students are using -
that is "where the student is"; but equally
clearly we need to understand more about how the
learner's mental models map on to, (or fail to
map on to) and interact with the conceptual
model provided.

One way of viewing beginner learners' problems
is to find out where the conceptual model
provided 'breaks' - i.e. where it won't or can't
accommodate the knowledge the learner brings
or generates. This is the next stage of this
research: the final objective is to have a
detailed understanding of the learning process
so that the teaching environment can make
learning a complex skill as easy as it can be.
This will entail building detailed computer
models of the learning behaviour. These
techniques are described by Scanlon (in press).

There are however some implications for how we
should teach these concepts in the meantime.
The data in this study indicates that many
novices are not able to easily abstract plans
from examples they are given, although the
most successful do (see figure 5). We cannot
presume that novices have schemas or plans for
how to go about solving problems and so we
should provide plenty of examples of similar
problems and make explicit in what ways the
problems are silimar, i.e. that they are
isomorphic or use a similar plan. Schoenfeld (1980)
has argued that algorithms should be explicitly

taught in maths problems solving and I would
argue that programming needs this too. The
various stages of problem solving a programming
problem (see Jones, 1981) need to be made
explicit and to be taught explicitly. Finally
we need to provide enough different ways for
learners with very different backgrounds and
experiences to be able to map new concepts
and ideas on to what they already know. This
should consist of a variety of conceptual
models so that the learner could choose from
alternative pathways through the material
the one that suits her best.

ACKNOWLEDGEMENTS

I would like to thank my supervisors Tim O'Shea
and Thomas Green for their help and support:
also to thank Tim for his comments on earlier
drafts of this paper.

I would also like to thank Tony Hasemer with
whom I shared running two experiments and many
hours of data collection.

References

[1] Adelson, B., Problem-solving and the development of abstract categories in programming languages. Memory and Cognition, 1981, 9, 422-433.

[2] Bonar, J., Ehrlich, K., Soloway, E., and Rubins, E., Collecting and analysing on-line protocols from novice programmers. Behaviour Research Methods and Instrumentation, 1982.

[3] Bott, R., A study of Complex Learning: Theories and Methods. University of California Centre of Human Information Processing report no. 82, 1979.

[4] Breuker, J., Availability of Knowledge. COWO - publicatie 81-JB, Amsterdam, 1981.

[5] Carroll, J. & Mack, R.L., Actively Learning to Use a Word Processor. Computer Science Dept., IBM Watson Research Laboratory, Yorktown. RC9482 Nol 41924, 1982.

[6] du Boulay, B., O'Shea, T., How to work the LOGO machine; a primer for ELOGO, Occasional paper No.4, 1976.

[7] du Boulay, B., O'Shea, T., Monk, J., The Black Box inside the Glass Box: presenting computer concepts to novices. International Journal of Man-Machine Studies, 1981, 14, 237-249.

[8] Ehrlich, K. & Soloway, E., An Empirical investigation of the tacit plan knowledge in programming. New Haven, Conn.: Tech. Report 82-236, Dept. of Computer Science, Yale University, 1982.

[9] Eisenstadt, M., SOLO: Units 3 & 4, D303 Cognitive Psychology, Open University,1978.

[10] Eisenstadt, M., Design features of a friendly software environment for novice programmers. Tech. Report No.3, Human Cognition Research Laboratory, Open University, 1982.

[11] Gentner, D., Are scientific analogies metaphors? In D. S. Miall (ed.) Metaphor, problems and perspectives, Harvester Press Ltd., Brighton, Sussex, 1982.

[12] Kahney, H., An in-depth study of the cognitive behaviour of novice programmers; Tech. Report No.5, Human Cognition Research Laboratory, Open University, 1982.

[13] Jones, A., How do novices learn programming? Computer Assisted Learning Research Group, Technical Report No.25, Open University, 1981.

[14] Jones, A., Learning to program: some protocol data. Computer Assisted Learning Research Group Technical Report No.41 Open University, 1984.

[15] Mayer, R.E., A psychology of learning BASIC, Commun. ACM 22, 1979, 589-594.

[16] Mayer, R.E., The psychology of how novices learn computer programming. Computing Surveys, 13, 1, March 1981.

[17] Mayer, R.E., and Bayman, P., Diagnosis of beginner programmers' misconceptions of BASIC programming statements, 1982, (unpublished report).

[18] Norman, D., Some observations on mental models. CHIP report No.112, Centre for Human Information Processing, University of California, San Diego, May, 1982.

[19] Open University, Microprocessors and Product Development. A course for Industry. Open University Press, Milton Keynes, 1978.

[20] Scanlon, E., Modelling students solving physics problems. In Jones, O'Shea and Scanlon (eds). The Computer Revolution in Education: New technologies for distance teaching. Harvester, Brighton, England (in press).

[21] Schoenfeld, A.H., Teaching problem-solving skills. American Mathematical Monthly, 1980, 87, 794-805.

[22] Sheil, B., Coping with Complexity, Proceedings of Houston Symposium 3, Information and Society, 1981.

[23] Soloway, E., Rubin, E., Woolf, B., Bonar, J., and Johnson, W.L., Meno 2: An AI based programming tutor. New Haven, Conn., Research Report No.258, Dept. of Computer Science, Yale University, 1982.

[24] Young, R., The machine inside the machine: users' models of pocket calculators, Int. Journal of Man-Machine Studies, 1981, 15, 51-85.

Human-Computer Interaction — INTERACT '84 / B. Shackel (ed.)
Elsevier Science Publishers B.V. (North-Holland)
© IFIP, 1985

SIMULATORS WHICH INVITE USERS INTO LEARNING CONVERSATIONS

Sheila Harri-Augstein and Laurie F. Thomas

Centre for the Study of Human Learning
Brunel University, Uxbridge, U.K.

The development of a range of new learning aids for complex computer-driven learning systems is described. An Air Intercept Control Skills Trainer is used to demonstrate the theory and technology of "Learning Conversations". This applies to the process of learning as well as to its content. The person-centred conversation paradigm of research accepts learners as active collaborators who are modelling, developing, reflecting upon and reviewing their learning skills. This requires freedom to structure activities, choose personal styles of execution and for evaluation of performance. The evidence reported demonstrates the emergence of a capacity for self-organised learning.

1. INTRODUCTION: The Need for a Conversational Methodology

A theory of learning must be concerned with how learners self-organise their own behaviour and experience to produce changes, which they themselves value. It requires techniques for making explicit the person's own constructions of the world, so that they may reflect upon them. The form given by George Kelly to his model of man as scientist has considerably influenced our approach (1). It is by its very nature content-free. It may be inhibited by any system of construction which would constitute "a person". The potency of Kelly's "construct system" is that it offers not only a theory but also the beginnings of an integral and systematic methodology. Together the theory and method contain an embryo of a new breed of aids for navigating the psyche. We have tried to develop this further into a more fully conversational technology. Our approach is concerned with developing aids which can represent personal experience and performance in ways which enable reflection, review and effective transformation of the quality of human learning. People can learn to distance themselves from the CONTENT of their own learning experiences and in achieving this, they are freed to explore and develop their learning competence. Conversational aids for talk-back are designed to achieve reconstruction of the learning events, which often cannot be fully experienced during the event itself.
The personal research process oscillates between structures of freedom, certainty and doubt. It depends on overcoming a universal tendency towards ultrastability and habitual content-bound modes of thought and feeling and behaviour (2).

2. On Constructing a Learning Conversation

In any effective Learning Conversation, control is passed back and forth among participants as they recognise the nature of what each has to contribute. But all participants are not equal.

Most conversations are asymmetric. In the early stages of the Learning Conversation the learners provide the evidence on which their collaborative research into the nature of their learning is based. The manager of the conversation guides and controls it. As the learners' awareness of their own processes increase the manager hands over control of the awareness raising activities to them. He or she then begins to encourage them to challenge their personal myths about their own learning capacity. The learners are encouraged to change the emphasis of their attention. The Learning Conversation moves into the next phase. They begin to explore how the learning can be improved. The manager encourages them to explore alternative models of their own processes and to develop and test in action, personally acceptable theories about how they can learn more effectively. Gradually the manager hands over control of this exploratory activity to the learners until eventually only the quality of the learners' personal investigation remains under the manager's review. The total conversation is phased to enable the learners to obtain insights which allow them to conduct more and more of the conversation for themselves. The ability to conduct most of a learning conversation with oneself is the essence of 'self-organisation'.

The process of a conversation can be distinguished and described separately from its content. The conditions for creative conversations require that an exchange is modulated through a shared understanding of how the conversation will be conducted and that this model of the process itself remain negotiable. Such conversation is rare. People may achieve such creative conversation within themselves. This is the core of self-organised learning. Our challenge has been to explore how a CAL system can facilitate this.

To be truly conversational, the technology of learning must allow relevance and viability to be assessed by the learner.

The criteria and referents used by the learner may be challenged and renegotiated but they cannot be ignored, denied or arbitrarily over-ridden by other perspectives without destroying the sources of self-confidence and self-sustaining growth. The Learning Conversation encourages and enables the growth of this capacity for self-organisation. Choice of specific techniques i.e. conversational learning aids to be recruited into the Learning Conversation depends upon the nature of the application. Learning Skills, learning situations and topics to be learned may all require special techniques for awareness-raising. The conversational learning aids used in conjunction with the AIC Skills Trainer (Footnote at end of Paper) represent some selected examples, here reported.

3. The Learning Aids Represented in the Skills Trainer

There are four categories of basic learning aids available to the user of the simulator. Together these are recruited to support Learning Conversations. These basic aids allow the learner and instructor to specify and file learning situations relating to the task and starting conditions for executing the task. Various forms of feedback are available during the run. Records of performance allow TALKBACK and experiential RECONSTRUCTION of the process of learning and records of expert performance can be used as demonstrations and as referents against which to evaluate learner performance. In details these facilities are categorised as follows:

i) Learning Tasks

The scenario and file facility offers an opportunity to define starting conditions and the type of intercept or safety conditions to be practised or both. It allows one learner to do a series of trials from the same situation or it allows learners to compare their performance against each other, and it allows one or more expert solutions to be generated and filed from the same starting conditions as the learner is faced with. It also offers the learners an opportunity for systematically developing their skills in initiating starting conditions, task definitions and learning purposes and to pose them learning experiences of increasing difficulty which systematically span the given range of experience.

ii) Feedback during the Run

Backtracks - normally the radar echo disappears after one or two sweeps but this facility retains the echoes tracing out the path of the aircraft. This provides a valuable aid to perceptual learning. Varitime - allows the learner to slow down or speed up the run to enhance awareness of performance in terms of judgement and timing. Arc - defines the weapon acquisition area within which the fighter must be guided to make a kill. Again this is a valuable aid to enhance perceptual training. Circles - provide a visual signal if a fighter gets dangerously near to stranger. Stop and Continue - together offer the learner an opportunity to pause and reflect during the run. During such a pause all the facilities under category three are available for assisting the learner to reflect on and review the learning process. In general all these run time facilities highlight the consequences of the learners' commands thus increasing their understanding of the system of causes and consequences embedded in the task.

iii) Records of Performance

The file allows the learners or instructor to store demonstration runs and allows the learners to replay ad take themselves back through their performance, reconstructing the experience and thus raising their awareness. This provides data for feedback in the process dialogue of the Learning Conversation. This talkback enables the learners to reconstruct the decision making which produced the performance and thus the strategy which they were using. Replay reruns the performance at whatever speed set by Varitime. Performances may be overlaid for comparisons. Thus the learners can compare themselves with the expert or with their own performances over a number of runs using the same scenario. Similarly peer learners can compare each others' performances. Print Picture coupled with the Stop facility allows the learners to photograph the screen at any point. Again this can be used as a valuable aid to perceptual learning. Trackdata provides a complete protocol of a run starting from the scenario conditions and recording the nature and time of every instruction to fighter, target or strangers. In addition it separates the instructions to each aircraft and prints a chronological record of the instructions to each record separately. By mapping Trackdata onto the Print Picture or by 'reading' the Print Picture, the trainees can learn to mentally connect the commands given to the visual representation. This offers a powerful tool for grouping commands into patterns . Thus, building up a perceptual language for visual representation.

iv) Expert-Performance

In addition to the records of expert performance provided by having an expert perform a run, the simulator is able to provide its own computer generated expert solutions. These are computed on the basis of a simple 3 turn mathematical optimalisation and can be shown via the Solve (immediate display), or Fly Yours and Fly Mine (real time displays) commands.

Expert performance and computer solutions offer

a tool for enhancing the Learning Conversation. They provide process measures of performance. By exhibiting the process by which expert results are achieved they offer a much richer opportunity for comparison and assessment.

4.   Becoming   an   Expert: The   Learning Conversation

Once learners are sufficiently familiar with the Skills Trainer they can begin to use it as a real aid to their own learning; the conversational procedures begin to encourage them to make this very process more explicit.(3)

The Personal Learning Task Analysis (P.L.T.A.) enable trainees to define and pursue their own learning purposes in relation to the task and to recognise these as separable from the instructors' or experts' definition of the task both in terms of the sequence in which a given sub-task should be learnt and of the instructor's own interpretation of the kinds of problems which the trainees are likely to experience.

This is an essential step in guiding the trainees to learn to take greater responsibility for their own learning .

4.1   Negotiating a Personal Learning Contract

The P.L.T.A. procedure encourages learners to: i) define their own purposes; ii) plan their strategy by which these may be achieved; iii) generate criteria by which they can judge the quality of their outcome; iv) review the whole learning process to discover how best to: -define their purposes more appropriately; -invent alternate strategies for optimalising the ways they achieve their self-chosen purposes; -generate more precise criteria for judging their outcomes.

They are thus enabled to control their learning in personally relevant significant and viable ways. As this Learning Conversation clarifies issues involved in negotiating and pursuing a Personal Learning Contract, the trainees are encouraged to identify how they will use the learning aids built into the machine to: i) define one or more scenarios best suited to their learning purposes; ii) to use feedback devices for reflective learning during the run; iii) to use records and playback devices in a self-debrief .

This phase of the Learning Conversation is also designed to enable learners to begin to see their learning within a time structure .

4.2   Taking Action in the P.L.T.A.

Having considered their plan of 'what' and 'how' they going to learn and then having put

this plan into action, the trainees attempt to monitor their learning as they are engaged in the self-defined exercise to do with one specific aspect of the task. It is here that the STOP facility available at any time during the RUN allows them to freeze this action, thus giving them space and time to reflect on their own processes, without interfering with the execution of the run. This reflective process allows them to reconstruct the immediate experience and so become conscious of what they are doing. The REPLAY facility in effect allows them to relive the same experience using their new insights to improve their performance. It is this opportunity to relive and personally observe this experience a number of times in a series of immediate 'mini self-debriefs' which encourages the development of a 'personal internal observer'. Eventually this observer is able to provide a meta-commentary on the primary process without interfering with it.

The STOP facility also focuses the learners' attention on the timing and structure of their skill as this plays out in their performance.

The P.L.T.A. procedure offers a heuristic for negotiating, identifying and carrying out Learning Contracts of different sizes or levels of complexity of learning activity. All the perceptually enhancing learning aids are available during each pause and also at sequences of pauses and at the end of a RUN. The learners can begin to see a continuously developing hierarchy of sub-contracts - contracts and superordinate contracts, during the process of learning. (Fig.1). PRINT PICTURES taken during a series of pauses in a run, not only provide a visual feedback about each sub-contract, but they also build up into a sequential record of the process by which the whole contract was achieved.

At the end of ACTION or RUN phase of the Personal Learning Contract, the conversational procedures encourage the learners to reconstruct the whole learning experience to reflect on it. All the learning aids available during the STOP facility are also available on completion giving the learner an opportunity to relive, observe and reflect upon the structures of their behaviour and experience the learning process over a longer time span.

Trainees have very underdeveloped capacity to remember the precise nature and sequence of events and to reconstruct sensitively and accurately the experience associated with these events. The RECORDS of performance, i.e. FILES, REPLAYS, PRINT PICTURE AND PRINT TRACK DATA provide an objective referent against which events can be recalled more accurately and the experience more validly reconstructed.

The P.L.T.A. technique is designed to progressively lead the learners into an ever

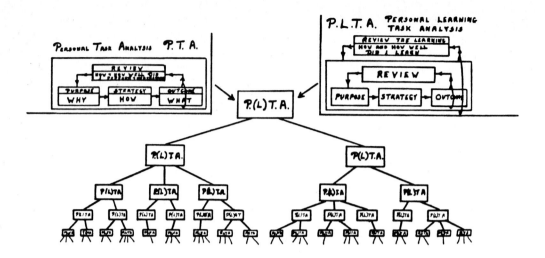

Fig.1   The Hierarchial Structure of P.L.T.A. and The Structure of Each Mode in the Hierarchy.

increasing awareness of their own learning processes. This is achieved by negotiating and carrying out learning contracts within which sub-contracts are increasingly well articulated. The learners are also aided to gradually recognise the part that the prespecified learning contract plays in their longer term learning activities.

As shall be seen later from the results of these conversational studies this process of representing learning within a hierarchy of learning contracts each of which has its own PSOR Structure allows learners at any level of achievement and competence to get to grips with their performance at just that level that conscious attention can make the greatest personal impact. This challenges existing understanding and skill in the task so that they can thrust forwards towards creating new levels of competence. The conversational learning aids which form part of the P.L.T.A. as well as the basic learning aids already addressed by the Skills Trainer are designed to achieve this awareness and self-organisation of learning.

5.   THE CONVERSATIONAL RESULTS

5.1 Case 1. A Naive Learner

Initially Jack had great difficulty in identifying and defining his own learning purposes and he tended to be rather haphzard and random in his activities. Using the P.L.T.A. procedures in conjunction with the aids addressed by the machine, he began to formulate clearer and more relevant purposes.

After the third session Jack began to formulate contracts with much shorter time spans and more precise purposes. The execution of these

yielded results which he was encouraged to explore with the REPLAY and PRINT PICTURE facilities. From this he began to define the task in a much clearer and more realistic way which in turn gave him the criteria for generating his next purpose. As he learnt to control the movement of the aircraft around the screen he began to attempt intercepts, but with very little success. He intensified his P.L.T.A. activities and began to explore the idea of strategy in greater detail and to define exactly how he planned what he was going to do. This led him to realise that he had no clear idea of what an intercept was in terms of the instructions which could be given to the fighter to control its position relative to the target. To explore this intensively he worked on the dynamic grid facility. The autopilot aid demonstrated the difference between an A1, A2, A3, and A4 intercepts, which intrigued him and he began to seriously try out his skill in completing 90 degree intercepts. In fairly rapidly moving from being wildly out in both displacement and the point at which he started his final turn he rapidly came to achieve three good intercepts consecutively. However as soon as he changed the direction of the target, this newly acquired skill disintegrated.

For the first time he became animated and started to really try to explore the dynamic relationships between direction and position of the target and positioning of the fighter to make the final turn. In his self-debrief he revealed that for the first time he could control his own learning and it became clear that   he had experienced a perceptual reorganisation of the task. Whilst originally he had been seeing the target and fighter in terms of their absolute positions on the screen (which explains why a change in the direction of the target led to a disintegration of the skill), he soon came to see fighter and

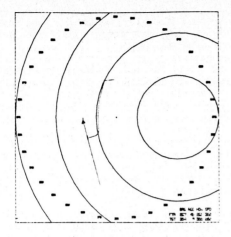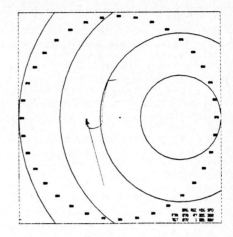

Figs. 2 & 3 Exploring the Dynamic Geometry of a 90 Degree Intercept

target in a <u>pattern relative to each other</u> .
He realised that this pattern persists
irrespective of their absolute positions.
Having identified this pattern for himself he
was able to set himself a series of learning
contracts which enabled him to explore and
consolidate his understanding of the dynamic
geometry of a 90 degree intercept, Figs. 2 & 3
illustrate this.

This was a turning point in Jack's learning.
He was able to put his two new skills together
in a series of successful intercepts. He went
back to the grids and learned the dynamic
geometry of the A1 (180 degree), A3 (120
degree) and A4 (150 degree) intercept types and
did a series of intercept sorties in which he
specified both <u>type</u> of intercept and <u>where</u>
this would take place.

5.2   Case Study 2. Skilled Practitioners: Two
Officers with Falklands Experience.

Towards the end of the first day they were
familiar enough with the Skills Trainer to be
setting up their own scenarios and carrying out
their own sorties. They also formulated their
first Personal Learning Contract, although this
was defined and achieved entirely in
<u>task-bound</u> terms. On the second day they
quickly developed a routine of creating their
own Personal Learning Contracts and working
these out with the Skills Trainer, gradually
familiarising themselves with the learning aids
although at this stage these were again seen
entirely as <u>task aids</u> . On the third day they
set up a whole series of Falklands scenarios
and began to exchange experience by <u>both</u> in
turn trying out the same task from the same
scenario. Towards the end of this day they
began for the first time to formulate learning
purposes which, while still completely in terms
of the task, were specifically related in
improving their tactics rather than executing
complete and perfect sorties. This was the
first sign that they were beginning to

understand the difference between a <u>Task</u>
<u>contract</u> (P.T.A.) <u>and</u> <u>a</u> <u>Learning</u> <u>contract</u>
<u>(P.L.T.A.)</u>. On the fourth day both officers
explored quite personal issues of skill. They
worked privately. They made extensive use of
<u>all</u> learning aids. They reported going
through a very anxious period whilst their
usually high level of calm and skill appeared
to have deserted them. They were enabled to
work their way through this and expressed
considerable satisfaction at the insight they
had gained into the emotional dynamics behind
their tactics. On the last day the officers
developed a whole series of detailed
suggestions for how the skills trainer could be
modified and elaborated for use as a learning
aid at sea.

This in depth conversational study with two
experienced fighter controllers highlighted the
potential of the Skills Trainer as a <u>practise</u>
and <u>planning</u> device for <u>the</u> <u>expert</u> . It also
proved to be an effective conversational
vehicle for enabling two skilled controllers to
converse and exchange experience <u>operationally</u>
with a depth and precision they could not
achieve verbally. They would be unlikely to
find a real (operational or training) situation
where such conversation could take place.

Again the study showed the need for methods of
generating effective Learning Conversations if
the potential of the Skills Trainer as a
learning aid is to be exploited.
<u>It took Paul and James three intensive days to</u>
<u>recognise the difference between task bound and</u>
<u>task free learning contracts i.e. between task</u>
<u>practise and self-organised learning activities.</u>

Their assessment was that a computer aided
learning device such as the Skills Trainer, in
a form more fully addressing the practise of
Learning Conversations as embodied by the
P.L.T.A. procedures could make a significant
contribution to improving the quality of
learning "on the job" at sea.

5.3 Case Study of Three Officer Trainees.

Each trainee used the Skills Trainer intensively with at least some of its Learning Aids. They worked together on it in their own private study time and they helped each other to solve specific learning difficulties. Each trainee used the STOP and CONTINUE facility to create 'mental space' to think, reflect and re-plan. Each used VARITIME, largely to quickly locate the critical event, which demanded some reflection. Each tried the COMPUTER SOLUTIONS but found these on the whole unhelpful. Each had used the PRINT PICTURE sequences as aids for their P.L.T.A. activities.

Their major learning experiences included: i) I moved from the tunnel vision to more global, but I still have a long way to go. ii) One can't pidgeon-hole purposes, I need to integrate these into a plan of action. iii) Stop in order to Reflect enables advances to be made in different directions. iv) Very useful to have to write down personal responses or/and explain to someone else. v) I learnt to diagnose my own problems and to set specific tasks relating to these, and to set up appropriate scenarios. - Up to now my instructor diagnosed problems for me, and these I feel are not always right for me. vi) I learnt to become more aware of the whole picture, to identify a wider range of variables in the whole task. vii) I learnt to imagine patterns on the screen and to understand the PROCESS of pattern contruction. viii) I realised the need to plan ahead, so as to achieve specific intercepts, particularly with Bravos and Charlies 4's. ix) I learnt to improve planning of a whole SORTIE and to achieve most of my aims or to flexibly adapt these according to changing circumstances. x) I learnt to use the P.L.T.A. Heuristic for getting to know 'more about me as a learner' and I learnt how to achieve greater awareness of my own learning style.

One outstanding finding in this case study was the ease and enthusiasm with which all the trainees carried out their personal experiments, once they had understood the task involved and how they could use the machine as a learning device.

It has not been possible to build specific formal evaluation measures into the study, but some findings are useful indicators of effectiveness. The instructor who was responsible for the whole training course during this study informally rank ordered the trainees at the beginning. One was border-line in terms of predictions of final success. In rank ordering them towards the end, this trainee was ranked as <u>first</u> and very likely to succeed. Interestingly, this trainee had spent most time on the Skills Trainer and had used its learning aids intensively and set himself many learning contracts through the

P.L.T.A. activities. A consistent feature within his learning contracts was that of 'pattern making' and 'anticipation exercises'.

In comparison with other trainees on earlier courses, who had also worked on the Skills Trainer, but without the conversational P.L.T.A. procedures the trainees could debrief <u>themselves</u> much more fluently and the quality of these events were significantly better both in terms of <u>process and in terms of task performance</u>. In all three case studies it became clear that in the absence of the P.L.T.A. procedures the Skills Trainer was used largely as a Practise and not as a Learning Device.

In learning a task a person is building up a model of the operating situation in his head and is gradually developing an understanding of 'what goes with what', i.e. of the causal relationships in the system. This model of the causes and consequences develops usually in an unconscious and unreviewed way, but is very complex and subtle, being a system of detailed perceptual motor relationships underlying the learner's ability to anticipate and control the situation. The learning aids addressed by the machine and the conversational P.L.T.A. aids opened up a new level of understanding about individual processes of learning.

These conversational results substantiate our functional framework for Self-Organised Learning. They have implications for developing a taxonomy of CAL-based conversational learning aids. (Table 1). These can be recruited to form a "Learning Shell" for a computer based system.

TABLE 1. Aids to Self-Organised Learning
(i.e. The Learning Conversation)

KEY - x Aids addressed by the Skills Trainer
       ◊ Aids addressed by the P.L.T.A. Procedures

A. Aids to Learning the Task; Task Focused Conversational Learning Aids

x	1. Aids that Enhance Feedback about Task Performance.
◊	2. Aids for Eliciting and Representing Personal Knowledge about the Task.
◊	3. Aids for Task Definition, i.e. Topic and Purpose.
x	4. Aids for Building a Bank of Records of Performance.
x◊	5. Aids for Comparison of Performances.
◊	6. Aids for Identifying Criteria of Success.
◊	7. Aids for Reflecting on Performance.
◊	8. Aids for Reflecting on knowledge and Experience.
◊	9. Aids for Challenging Personal Myths about the Task.
◊	10. Aids for Comparison of Learner's Knowledge with Learner's Performance.

B. Aids to Enhance the Capacity to Learn; Learning Focused Conversational Aids

◊	1. Conversational Machine Familiarisation Procedures.
◊	2. The Learning Conversation - Phase 1.
	2(i) The Personal Learning Contract and the Personal Learning Task Analysis Procedure (P.L.T.A.).
	2(ii) The Double Debrief (i.e. the task debrief and the learning debrief (P.S.O.R. Procedures).
	3. The Learning Conversation - Phase 2
	3(i) Review of P.L.T.A. Contracts.
	4. The Needs and Relevance Conversation.
	4(i) Pegasus and other Reflective Repertory Grid Technology.
	5. The Learning-to-Learn Conversation.
	5(i) Talkback of Behavioural Records and Personally Elicited Models of Experience.

6.   Awareness and the Learning Conversation

In looking at the process by which someone
learns a task it is possible to identify three
stages in moving from the unconscious doing of
the task (i.e. the task robot) to fully
self-organised learning. i) In the first
stage of learning the person does the task by
dogged practise and repetition with an often
implicit tactic of 'trial and error', they
acquire some level of competence. Many years
of such practise leads to the
skilled technician . But he is totally content
or task-bound. ii) In the second stage of
learning the person stands back, observes and
reflects upon the implications of their
practise. Thus, raising the blind trial and
error method into a more rational and coherent
approach to the process of doing the task.
But, at this stage in the development of
learning the task is still the total focus of
attention.
Awareness is concentrated on observing the
process of doing the task and using the results
these observations to systematically experiment
and improve one's performance. iii) At the
third stage of learning, the focus of attention
shifts. At certain intervals in acting out
stages 1 and 2 the person stands back one a
further step, to take stock not only of how one
is doing the task,

but also to reflect upon the process of
learning itself   It   is   this
second phase of awareness   which   is   the
crucial trigger to total   self-organisation
in learnng. It is this which proved so
difficult (or impossible) for some of the
subjects of our study, without the aid of the
Personal Tutorial Learning Conversations. In
stage one there is no awareness of process
and therefore no possibility of conversation
about learning the task. Many of our subjects
found that being lead into systematic
observations of themselves doing the task
(stage 2) was a significant insight. This
allowed them to change learning a task from a
ritualistic, determined and sustained use of
practise with occasional haphazard insights,
into systematic learning activity. The proper
use of the learning aids in the Skills Trainer
provided a mechanism for articulating these
systematic insights. We term this the content
-focused or task -focused conversation. A
Learning process - focused conversation arises
in moving from stage 2 to stage 3 where the
process of learning is the new content or
'task' focus for the conversation. Fig.4
illustrates these stages.

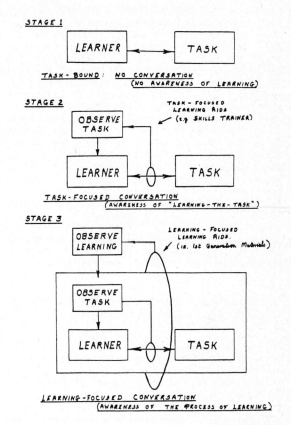

Fig.4   Three   Stages   Towards   Self-Organised
Learning

Thus the Task Debriefs used in many
conventional RN Skills Training courses can be
seen as falling into stages 1 and 2. What is
missing is the construction of a
Learning Debrief which can elevate the
conversation into Stage 3. This is the essence
of what we call the Learning Conversation. The
Personal Task Analysis procedure (P.T.A.) can
be used for systematising the conversations
about learning the task (stage 2) whereas the
Personel Learning Task Analysis (P.L.T.A.) is
the procedure for facilitating the whole
Learning Conversation (stage 3).

7.   Towards a Conversational CAL-Simulator

As has been seen, the mere existence of the
learning aids built into
the machine does not ensure that they will be us
ed either effectively or at all. Learners
need sufficient understanding of their own

processes to be able to recruit the learning aids into their personal learning processes. This is what Self-Organised Learners can do. The trainee who sets out to become a Self-Organised Learner is developing an entirely different cognitive model of the task and of himself as a learner. He uses the learning aids in the machine for reflection upon how he performs the task (i.e. stage 2 task-focused conversation) and tests out within a Self Debrief of the task, whether he has performed well, according to the agreed standards of performance. When available he also compares his achievements against peers or/and a number of different experts performances on the task, to evaluate his own skills. This learner can relate the trainer diagnosis of his performance to his own diagnoses. But the skilled Self-Organised Learner can do more than this. He can define learning in relation to his own previous performances and develop precise criteria of his own for the ways in which he is learning the task. He is in a position to ask himself not only whether the task can be done better but also can he learn in a better way .

The Self-Organised Learner is able to conduct two phases of awareness-raising conversations. At one phase (i.e. stage 2, Fig.4) the task itself is the primary focus of attention, everything acquires meaning in terms of whether the Skills Trainer and its aids assist in performing the task well. At the other phase (i.e. stage 3, Fig.4) the process of acquisition of skill, knowledge, attitude, etc. is the focus of attention. Everything acquires meaning in terms of whether the Skills Trainer and its aids offer greater awareness of the personal processes of learning, and thus greater self-control of these.

The cognitive modelling capacity and hence the learning capacity of those trainees who learn to use the CAL device for reflective learning in both phases 1 and 2 modes develop their own sophisticated internal feedback generating mechanisms about their experiences, and relate these to external feedback or 'knowledge of results' obtained about their own behaviour or performance. These then are the flexible, adaptive learners who have the potential to develop into the real experts in training others to develop equally high standards of expertise.

The conversational methods used in the case studies, revealed the processes of human behaviour and experience at work on 'real' tasks. The raw results appeared at first sight to be episodic and enrepeatable but once an appropriate conversational model is used to systematise and organise them they immediately became coherent.

The P.L.T.A. conversational procedures were designed as stepping stones towards such a model which the learner can come to use to explain and thus predict and control his own learning processes.

8.   Towards   Specifications   for   an 'Intelligent',   fully   Conversational Computer-Aided-Learning Simulator.

Our basic argument is that a conversational CAL simulator must address the following issues: i) the representation of behaviour or performance must be complemented by a facility for addressing representations of knowledge and experience . ii) The performance records must be capable of hierarchical analysis, e.g. in a form analogous to the Print Picture/Print T Data syntax discussed in the Case Studies. Timing and other indications of display-control discontinuities can be used to parse the performance. iii) The model of performance analysis and the representational forms of task knowledge and experience must be compatible one with the other, allowing a matching between how a person performs the task and how they consciously understand what they do. iv) One or more records of expert knowledge and performance serves as a referent against which the knowledge and performance of the learner may be evaluated and an analysis of this comparison can be used to identify a tutoring strategy by which the learner can be led step by step into the experts' expertise. v) The idea of a Personal Learning contract allows the learner freedom to define the task in their own way, and to identify their own methods and understanding of how the task may be done. vi)   The Personal Learning Contract also allows the learner to reflect on the personal process of learning.   It is this which transforms the capacity   to   learn. This involves the need for a second level of representation in the CAL device, shown as Stage 3 in Fig. 4 where the P.L.T.A. embodies both performance and knowledge representations of the activity of learning, addressed separately from the process of doing the task.   vii)   Finally, within the Learning Conversation, the learner is helped to become aware of the process of managing Self-Organised Learning so that they learn to take this over for themselves and become more fully self-organised. Fig.4 and 5 illustrate this.

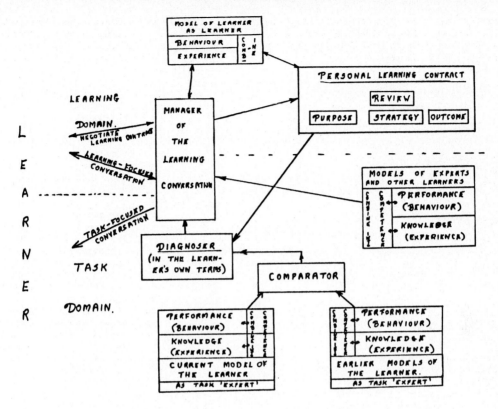

Fig.5 Outline of Computer-Aided Learning, Based on Learning Conversations

In education and training the development of computer-aided learning systems has enormous potential for promoting self-organised learning. A wide range of tasks and skills from Appraisal, Recruitment, Management Skills, Quality Control, Training of Trainers, Course Design and Evaluation, Reading and Communication Skills, Decision Making, Skilled Performance of Highly Complex Tasks and Creativity can all be systemised within a technology for Reflective Learning. Individual groups and whole organisations can be so enabled to function as effective learning systems.

Footnote: The Air Intercept Control Skills Trainer was developed at the Applied Psychology Unit of the Admiralty Marine Technology Establishment in 1980. SCICON Int. Ltd. were the programming contractors and the Centre for the Study of Human Learning acted as consultants on Task Analysis and Learning Aids.

REFERENCES:

1. Kelly, G.A., The Psychology of Personal Constructs. (Vols. 1 and 2, Norton, New York, 1955)

2. Thomas, L.F. and Harri-Augstein, E.S., The Self-Organised Learner as Personal Scientist: a Conversational Technology for Reflecting on Behaviour and Experience. Adams-Webber, J. and Mancuso, J.C. (eds.) Applications of Personel Construct Theory (Academic Press, Canada 1983)

3. Thomas, L.F. and Harri-Augstein, E.S., The Self-Organised Learner and Computer Aided Learning Systems: An Exploratory Study with the AIC Skills Trainer, FINAL REPORT for the AMTE, Applied Psychology Unit. Contract No. 2066/020, Centre for the Study of Human Learning, Brunel University, Uxbridge, U.K.

4. Thomas, L.F. and Harri Augstein, E.S., The Self-Organised Learner - A Conversational Science (Routledge and Kegan Paul, London 1984)

5. Thomas, L.F. The CSHL Reflective Learning Software, Centre for the Study of Human Learning, Brunel University, Uxbridge, U.K.

Human-Computer Interaction — INTERACT '84 / B. Shackel (ed.)
Elsevier Science Publishers B.V. (North-Holland)
© IFIP, 1985

THE USE OF A COLOUR GRAPHICS DISPLAY AND TOUCH SCREEN TO HELP NAIVE
USERS UNDERSTAND AND CONTROL A MULTI-FUNCTION COMPUTER SYSTEM

D.E. Penna

Philips Research Laboratories,
Redhill, Surrey, England

The work described in this paper is aimed at the production of computer based systems
which are understandable and controllable by computer-naive people. All options open
to the user are displayed diagrammatically on a colour graphics display and a pointing
device such as a touch screen or graphics tablet used for selection. A tree structure
of selection frames is used with short cuts to frequently used items at the lower
levels. The control technique is designed to give a good idea of context and eliminate
some common types of user error.
This paper describes the design considerations and application of this control
technique.

1. INTRODUCTION

This paper describes work aimed at the
production of a relatively complex computer-
based system which is understandable and
controllable by computer-naive people. It
displays a pictorial representation of the
options available to the user on a colour
graphics screen so that a device such as
a touch screen or graphics tablet can be used
to select from them.

This contrasts with the approach used in most
traditional computer systems whereby the user
types commands to a system using a keyboard and
sees responses on a monochrome character based
display. In such systems the occasional or
untrained user may have difficulty remembering
commands. It may be difficult to remember
which command format belongs with which
computer. We have attempted to avoid these
problems by using a graphics display based
control technique which does not require the
use of a keyboard for system control.

This paper indicates the considerations which
led to the design of this control technique and
describes how it has been applied to some of the
applications implemented in the system. This
work has been carried out in the context of
future electronic equipment in the home but the
type of control technique described could be of
benefit in many application areas.

2. THE CONTROL TECHNIQUE

Computer based systems are increasingly using
graphics displays and some are using the display to help with the user dialogue (1,2,3,4,5).
We have followed this trend, displaying a dia-
grammatic representation of the options available to the user. Fig.1 shows the initial
frame. Each option is represented by a
coloured and labelled 'selection area'.

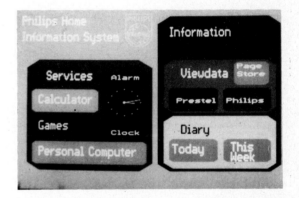

Fig. 1

Selection areas have a distinctive shape (a
rectangle with the corners trimmed) so that it
is always clear which items on the screen are
selectable. The initial work used a touch
screen so that the user simply had to touch the
required item on the screen. Later systems
have used devices such as graphics tablets
controlling a cursor on the screen. Many
selection areas lead directly to the required
item but others cause a new set of selection
areas to be displayed giving a more detailed
view of a set of options. This is illustrated
in Fig.1 where selection of the 'Information'
area will cause the information options to be
shown in more detail (Fig.2). In some cases
selection areas are shown within other areas
allowing some of the more likely selections at
the lower levels to be accessed without going
through an intermediate level. Again Fig.1
contains examples such as the area marked
'Today' which causes today's diary to be
displayed without the user having first to
select 'Information' and then 'Diary'. Apart
from the obvious advantage of direct selection

of the users likely requirements this form of
display gives the user an overview of the
contents of the system. The front page (Fig.1)
shows some of the items under the 'Information'
entry in a structured manner.

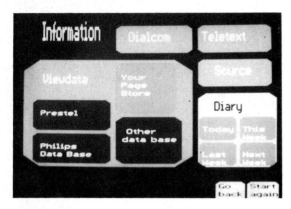

Fig. 2

2.1 Context

This overview is one of the ways in which we
attempt to give the user a good idea of context.
We have found in the past that some information
systems, while superficially easy to use, can
confuse the user because of the complexity of
structure. Some viewdata systems can cause
difficulty because the structure of the data
is very complex with many cross-links in the
tree structure of pages. The user is often
uncertain how the current page was reached or
where it is in the overall structure. We
believe this context information to be important
and have tried to make the structure of the
system as clear as possible to the user. The
'overview' provided by the nested selection
areas is intended to give advance warning of
the items to be expected at the lower levels
and we attempt to reinforce the sense of context by the use of colour. Whenever a selection
is made, the background colour of the new frame
will usually be similar to the colour of the
selection area. This implies that each application area will tend to have a characteristic
colour or set of colours. Because of the
nested selection area structure of frames such
as the initial frame (Fig.1), applications will
tend to be grouped together by colour. For
example the information area is dark green and
items inside the 'Information' area have been
given colours in the yellow/green range. There
is a limit to the extent to which this can be
done since the number of distinguishable colours
that can tastefully be used on the screen at a
time is limited. The problem of colour choice
is made much easier if, as in the equipment
described, there is a hardware colour look up
table allowing choice of colour to a very fine
resolution instead of the choice of primaries
and complementaries found in many systems.

All frames (except the initial one) have two
standard areas at the bottom right. 'Start
again' takes the user back to the initial frame
(Fig.1) while 'Go back' moves back up the tree
of selections one step at a time retracing the
route taken to reach the current state. These
allow the user to backtrack within an application, start working with a new application package or simply recover from an erroneous selection.

The system offers several application packages
and it is anticipated that the user will want to
move easily between them. In order to allow
this the context of each application is preserved whenever the user leaves it and restored
on return. Suppose the user temporarily leaves
the calculator in order to consult the diary.
On return to the calculator the screen will be
restored to its previous state and calculations
can carry on as if there had not been an
interruption.

2.2 Error avoidance

It is a common complaint about computer systems
that they are too fussy about details of spelling and syntax and irritate users by continually
'telling them off' with error messages which
seem often not be helpful. Also it has been
suggested that it is important that first reactions to a computer system are correct. The
user will rapidly form a model of they system
behaviour and incorrect models can take a long
time to be abandoned (6). This is likely to be
particularly serious for the casual or
occasional user.

A design aim of the system described has been to
make the operation of the system and the options
available very clear to avoid these difficulties.
Since all choices are displayed on the screen
the user is not left in any doubt about whether
a particular command or option is appropriate.
Also choices which are erroneous are simply not
displayed. If the telephone line is in use
then selection areas which invite the user to
use it for another service are switched off.
Another example occurs in the diary at a point
where the user is invited to select a day of
the month. If the month is September then no
area is displayed for the 31st of the month so
the user cannot make the error of selecting a
non-existent day. There are of course no
spelling or syntax errors in these types of
selection.

It is the authors experience that packages like
the diary written for conventional keyboard
based systems have a high proportion of code
designed for validating user input and producing error messages. The entire system described in this paper has only two error messages
apart from those resulting from the user writing programs in BASIC. These are 'Overflow'
and 'Division by zero' in the calculator.

This type of control technique eliminates some, though not of course all, classes of user error.

2.3 Response times

Good response times are important. It is vital that something must happen immediately a selection is made or the user will be uncertain whether the selection action has been registered and may attempt to repeat the action. The design rule is that something should start to happen on the screen immediately as far as the user is concerned although the completion of the action may take a noticeable amount of time. Where a new frame is to be displayed the screen is cleared to the new background colour within ≈ 100 mS. There is no perceivable delay between the touch screen selection and the start of the screen action. Where 'soft' keys are displayed on the screen the keys are flashed to confirm a selection.

Once the initial selection confirmation has taken place the rule is that the remaining part of the screen update should happen rapidly unless there is some user perceived reason for a delay, such as a telephone connection. Complete screen images are typically built up in 0.5 - 1 seconds.

3. APPLICATIONS IMPLEMENTED IN THE SYSTEM

As suggested by Fig.1 there are a number of applications implemented in the system. Following sections will describe some of them. The diary and calculator illustrate the way in which the basic control technique has been applied. The viewdata access application shows the system adapting to the control of an external data base to a limited extent and the viewdata page store shows an attempt to use pictorial representations to help locate items stored in a computer data base.

3.1 The diary

The diary illustrates the basic control technique well. Fig.3 is displayed if the diary area in Fig.1 or Fig.2 is selected. As usual the options which are considered more likely (like 'Today' or 'Next week') are provided as simple selections.

Selecting 'September' causes Fig.4 to be displayed. Here a day or week can be selected. Also there are areas allowing the user to step forward or backward a month. There is no need to read a manual to discover these options. Note that there is no selection area displayed for the 31st of the month so the user cannot select this non-existent day.

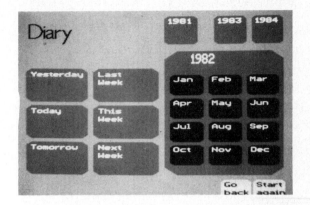

Fig. 3

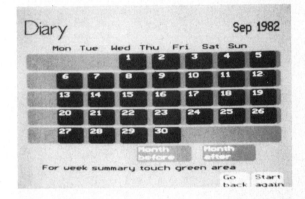

Fig. 4

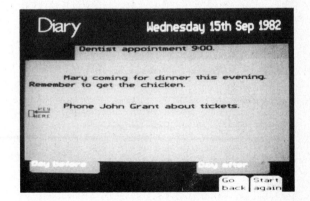

Fig. 5

The selection of a day causes a frame such as Fig.5 to be displayed containing the diary entries for that day. The cursor (the box marked 'key here') is positioned after the last entry but can be moved to any other point simply by touching the screen. Text is then entered on the keyboard. It is stored

permanently as soon as it is entered. It would
be possible to use a 'soft' keyboard displayed
on the screen for text entry but this has two
disadvantages. Firstly it occupies a large
part of the screen area and secondly it is not
as easy to use as a conventional keyboard
because of its orientation and lack of tactile
response. Soft keyboards can be used for the
entry of small amounts of text but we prefer a
normal keyboard. The keyboard is better for
text entry, and the touch screen (or other
pointing device) for system control.

3.2   The calculator

Fig.6 shows the calculator. This is a four
function calculator with the keyboard on the
screen. In order to provide user feedback each
key is flashed to white for a short period when
selected. The last few steps of the calculation
are displayed giving some of the advantages of a
printing calculator. If the user sees a mistake
in this 'history' the 'Forget last calculation'
area can be used to step back past the incorrect
part of the calculation so that it can be repeated correctly.

Fig. 6

3.3   Data base access

The system can access a number of external data
sources including viewdata, broadcast teletext
and the British Telecom electronic mail service
Telecom Gold. In most cases the user has to
revert to use of the keyboard to control these
external services because that is what the
service has been designed to expect.

In the case of access to a Philips experimental
viewdata service however the system knows enough
about the external service to be able to interpret its structure and allow the user to control
it using touch screen selections in the usual
way. Since routing pages in this data base
have a fixed format it is possible to detect
where the selection options are on the screen
and draw hollow selection boxes around them
(Fig.7). The user can then make selections by
touching these boxes. If the user touches the

'Leisure' entry the terminal sends '3' to the
viewdata computer. This seems a more natural
means of selection than requiring the user to
read the number alongside the required entry
and then find it on a keypad. In most cases it
is not possible to interpret the external
service structure in this way.

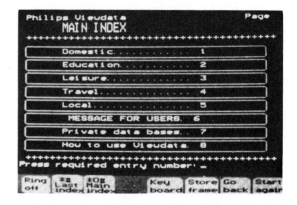

Fig. 7

3.3   The viewdata page store

The area marked 'Store frame' at the bottom of
Fig.7 allows the user to store the currently
displayed page in a local store of viewdata
pages. The process that follows is designed
to gather information about the page which will
help the user to find it again later. The
intention is to provide several ways of finding
the required page in the same way that, when we
are looking for a document on a desk we use
several cues (position, colour and shape as well
as title). (7).

The user is first requested to key a short name
for the page. During this process the page
being stored is faded down and a full alphanumeric keyboard displayed over it. This soft
keyboard or the normal hard keyboard can be
used. Once the name has been given the key-
baord is removed and the user specifies which
'category' the page should be put in. When the
system is empty there is only one category
called 'Other' but the user can define new
categories up to a maximum of eight. The page
is then stored together with information such
as the time and date of storage, name, category
and a miniature pictorial representation of the
page. These reduced size pages are formed by
representing each character position in the page
by one dot of the appropriate colour. The page
is not of course readable in this reduced form
but can give an impression of its overall layout
and colouring.

When the user requires to retrieve a page the
options offered for selection include 'Last
page stored' and 'Last page viewed' as the most
likely choices. If the required page is not one
of these then a list of pages can be displayed

(Fig.8). This list shows the page names and miniature pictures. The category of each page is represented by the colour of the lines and text associated with the entry. A one dimensional roller device is used to scroll the list when it is too big to fit on the screen. If the page category is known then the list can be filtered so that it only shows pages of that category.

Fig. 8

The user can find the page easily if it was the last one stored or retrieved or if the name is remembered. Knowledge of the category helps considerably as does memory of the overall layout and colouring of the page. An uncompleted part of the system would allow a page to be retrieved given its approximate date and time of storage.

CONCLUSION

I have described a technique for the control of computer based systems which gives a pictorial representation of the options available. This technique gives the user a clear idea of the structure of the system and the options available. It is structured to avoid certain classes of user error. We see techniques similar to those described here being applicable to the control of many types of computer based system.

REFERENCES

[1] Teitelman, W., A display oriented programmer's assistant, International Journal of Man-Machine Studies, Vol. 11 (1979) 157-187.

[2] Lipkie, D.E. Evans, R.E. Newlin, J.K. and Weissman, R.L., Star Graphics: An object-oriented implementation, SIGGRAPH '82 proceedings (1982) 115-124.

[3] Engel, F.L. Andriessen, J.J. and Schmitz, H.J.R., WHAT, WHERE and WHENCE: Means for Improving Electronic Data Access, Int. Jrnl. of Man-Machine Studies (to be published).

[4] Donelson, W.C., Spatial management of information, SIGGRAPH '78 Proceedings, August 23-25, 1978.

[5] Herot, C.F., A Prototype Spatial Data Management System, SIGGRAPH '80 Proceedings, (1980) 63-70.

[6] Gaines, B.R. and Facey, P.V., Some experience in system development and application, Proc. IEEE, Vol. 63 (1975) 894-911.

[7] Feiner, S. Nagy, S. van Dam, A., An integrated system for creating and presenting complex computer-based documents, SIGGRAPH '81 Proceedings, (1981) 63-70.

AIDS FOR THE DISABLED

Human-Computer Interaction — INTERACT '84 / B. Shackel (ed.)
Elsevier Science Publishers B.V. (North-Holland)
© IFIP, 1985

VIDEOTEX FOR THE BLIND: DESIGN AND EVALUATION OF BRAILLE AND SYNTHETIC SPEECH TERMINALS

R.W. King, N. Cope[*], and O.R. Omotayo[+]

Department of Electronics and Information Engineering, University of Southampton, U.K.
* now with Ferranti Computer Systems Ltd., Bracknell, U.K.
+ now with Department of Electrical Engineering, The University, Ibadan, Nigeria.

Videotex and similar computer based information services cannot be used directly by blind people without special non-visual terminals. We describe the design of such terminals with dynamic Braille and synthetic speech output. The interface has two main processes - reformatting of the Videotex source pages into linearised text - and translation of this text into contracted Braille and synthetic speech. The controls for the displays are also important for overcoming some of the deficiencies of the two processes. Subjective tests are described which show that, on average, Braille is approximately twice as slow to use as normal visual access, whereas speech is approximately four times slower than visual access to Videotex.

1. INTRODUCTION

Interaction between humans and information technology systems is dominated by the visual medium. Blind people are, in consequence, denied direct access to computer systems and the information held within them unless special non-visual terminals are made available. The development of 'dynamic' or 'soft' Braille terminals in which a single row of re-addressable Braille cells is used to display the output has allowed their blind users to interact directly with computer systems. The dynamic Braille display and associated keyboard form a direct equivalent to the conventional visual display terminal. Dynamic Braille displays are used outside the context of computer access for the output for material such as that contained in a diary, address directory, and notebook [1]. The reading speed which may be attained by the users of these displays approaches that of reading conventional embossed Braille (up to 150 words per minute). In the work described in this paper, a dynamic Braille display is used as one non-visual output for Videotex systems.

Hearing, arguably more natural than vision for many types of language based information input is the major input medium for blind people. Indeed many of them, either through other disability or age have insufficient tactile sensitivity for Braille. The development of low-cost synthetic speech has opened up opportunities of access to computer systems that were inconceivable even a decade ago. Nevertheless, the provision of cheap synthesis and the proliferation of business and home computers does not necessarily mean that blind people can benefit immediately and increase successfully their direct access to information technology systems.

Speech synthesis development [2] has focussed largely on the problems of generating speech of a sufficiently natural quality and intelligibility to satisfy any particular need. Many applications require only a restricted vocabulary for which a 'copy synthesis' technique may be adopted. This is based upon efficient storage and processing of recorded human speech and is of higher quality and intelligibility per unit cost than 'synthesis by rule' methods adopted in applications requiring unlimited vocabulary. The present application requires a cheap speech synthesis approach which can operate in near real-time and with unlimited vocabulary. We discuss how such synthesisers despite their unnatural speech quality may be incorporated succesfully in a Videotex interface.

Our prime motivation is to determine the effectiveness of dynamic Braille and cheap synthetic speech in interfaces for Videotex. Videotex has a 'page orientated' data structure and a very simple user dialogue based on a 10 numeral,*, # key pad. Its users are assumed to be naïve as far as computers are concerned.

That is not to imply that the work described here is irrelevant to blind computer users and the design of non-visual terminals for computers. Blind people will be able to benefit from developments in information technology systems generally as suitable effective interfaces are provided. Our design conception is one in which the output device - the Braille display or speech synthesiser - can be used at the core of a general information facility and be interfaced to computers, storage media and specialised sources as required. This study of interfacing to Videotex is, in this context, a case study of the requirements of one particular type of information source.

Good interface design requires understanding of user requirements. As sighted designers it is all too easy to make invalid assumptions about the needs of blind users and devise inappropriate design solutions. In the present work this has been avoided, at least to some extent, by involving a blind potential user at various stages in the design process. The conclusions presented here are based on experiments with a group of blind and partially sighted subjects.

2. DESIGN CONSTRAINTS AND PROCEDURE

We chose to use existing both tactile and
synthetic speech output devices. Our concern,
therefore, is with providing suitable interface
hardware and software between the Videotex
source and the output devices. In the following
we describe the constraints imposed by the
displays and by the Videotex source, and propose
a three stage procedure which has particular
merits for evaluation.

2.1 Output Devices

Dynamic Braille and synthetic speech are
essentially 'linear' output media. The Braille
displays which are now commercially available
consist of a number of Braille cells, typically
20-48, arranged in a single row.   Data is
presented to the display under user control, and
read by touch and the display is then refreshed
with the next data required.   In the present
work a display of 48 cells was available. The
tactile quality of displays of this type is very
good, but the overall ease of use depends
significantly on the controls which the user has
to scan text and set and use 'tabs' and page
markers. The controls depend to some extent on
the source material.

The essential difference between the Braille
display and the synthetic speech output described below is the extra degree of control
which may be exercised by the Braille reader. A
row of Braille remains displayed until no longer
needed.   Furthermore, the display may be used
for either basic (Grade I) or contracted (Grade
II) Braille, as described in Section 4.1.

The linear and ephemeral qualities of speech are
obvious. Natural though speech is for information gathering tasks, it tends to be used as an
adjunct to visual text.   It appears at the
outset, therefore, that synthetic speech is not
likely to be ideal as an output for computer
based information systems such as Videotex,
quite irrespective of the synthetic speech
quality itself. To some extent the shortcomings
can be overcome by giving the user appropriate
controls over the utterance.

The synthesisers used here are electronic vocal
tract models of the formant type with phoneme
input. The translation of text into suitable
phoneme codes is part of our interface, and is
performed at a word translation level. Thus no
prosodic features - stress, pitch and rhythm
-are included in the synthesised utterance. This
lack of prosody leads to the rather unnatural
characteristic of word based speech synthesis,
and some loss of intelligibility.

2.2 Videotex

We seek to design non-visual interfaces which
require no modification to existing Videotex

terminals, thereby allowing our interface to be
simply added-on. The layout and content of
Videotex material must be considered in detail.
The displayed characters are either alphanumeric
(ASCII) or graphical (3×2 matrix) and form pages
of 24 rows of 40 characters per row. A number
of layout features can be identified as having
significance for the present work [3]. These
are continuous text, alphabetic graphics,
pictorial graphics, multiple columns, tables and
indexes of list or sentence forms. Most pages
contain two or more layout features. It was
decided that graphical characters, wherever they
appear, could not be translated into either
Braille or speech. The other forms of layout
need to be reproduced in a suitable linear
fashion as described in Section 3.

The final aspect of Videotex which demands
attention is the interactive page facility.
These pages used typically for ordering or
booking services, are of considerable practical
value, no less for blind than sighted people.
The user is prompted to supply a suitable keypad
response to a specific question.   A visual
cursor is used to identify the question. The
non-visual terminals therefore incorporate a
facility to allow responses of this type via the
normal keypad

2.3 Design Procedure

The above considerations allow the interface
design to be divided into three distinct
stages:-
reformatting:- to convert the page layout into a
                   suitable   form   for   linear
                   display
   translation:- to convert the reformatted text
                   into suitable Braille or phoneme
                   codes
        output:- to present the material to the
                   user in dynamic Braille or
                   synthetic speech and provide
                   suitable user controls.

One of the advantages of this division is that
it allows design and evaluation of the reformatting and translation stages to be performed
independently of the overall system evaluation.
Thus the limitations of the reformatter will not
be confused with the intelligibility of the
speech synthesiser,   when judging a user's
response to the whole system.

The interface design and evaluation have been
conducted around a microcomputer development
system.   The ultimate intention is to incorporate the required hardware and software in
suitable units together with the Braille display
or synthetic speech devices.

3. REFORMATTING AND ITS EVALUATION

The reformatting process is required to identify
the page layout features listed above and then
present the textual material to the translation

stage in a suitable order. The identification task is a straightforward pattern recognition one which is aided by the use of colours in the normal display. The colour background and character display codes are processed in the reformatting stage to give a rough 'blocking' of the layout components. This blocking may be tidied up by infilling incomplete boundaries and removing small blocks. Graphics blocks are removed at this stage. The second stage of the process is to examine the character content of each block in turn and classify it as continuous text, multiple column or tabular. This is done by scanning the rows and columns of characters for spaces and numerals. This process itself can permit further blocking within, say, a multiple column layout. The blocks are finally assigned a type marker and order marker. The latter is based on a left-to-right, top-to-bottom scan.

Figure 1(a) shows a typical page containing a title formed from graphics characters and a multiple column format. The automatically reformatted version in Figure 1(b) shows the removal of the title and the resolution of the two columns into a single line of text, and a list index. The *B*, *U*, *P* markers show where the formatter has inserted end of block, line and page markers.

(a) original page

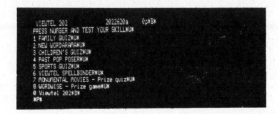

(b) reformatted page displayed on a VDU

Figure 1   An example of the reformatting process

In order to assess the effectiveness of the reformatting procedure a sample of 200 pages of British Telecom's Prestel service was processed. The resulting layouts were examined carefully, and the reformatting performance was categorised as:-

perfect - correct reformatting and block/line marking
imaged - page effectively unformatted-line markers only
mixed - some perfect, some imaged blocks
disordered - incorrect reformatting, ambiguous result.

Table 1 shows the results for four types of page. The sample sizes reflect approximately the relative proportions of those types of page in the Prestel service.

Page Type	Index	Text	Tables	Multiple Column
Sample size	100	60	20	20
Perfect	80%	80%	100%	60%
Imaged	19%	10%	--	15%
Mixed	1%	10%	--	--
Disordered	--	--	--	25%

Table 1 Reformatter Evaluation

The reformatter thus works constructively on most pages - it may fail to do a perfect job on occasions but it is only the 25% of 10% of the pages where it introduces disorder. For these cases it is desirable to allow a blind user to have recourse to the unformatted source page. The tables are left unchanged from their original form.

4.   TRANSLATION STAGES AND THEIR EVALUATION

In this section we describe briefly the translation of the reformatted text into both Braille and phonemes suitable for driving speech synthesis and discuss the evaluation of translation quality.

4.1   Braille Translation

The six dots of the Braille cell form a six-bit character code. Braille incorporates a number of 'shift' symbols to indicate capitals and numerals. To reduce the quantity of Braille a number of contractions are adopted in Grade II Braille. The formal rules for these contractions are quite complex [4] being syllabic, syntactic and semantic. Most Braille readers progress to the contracted form, and there is, therefore, a very strong impetus to incorporate the contractions in any dynamic Braille interface. Many

automatic Braille contraction procedures are now
used in systems for the production of embossed
Braille [5] but their use in dynamic terminals
is less common.

The translation provided here is a compromise
between accuracy, speed and memory requirement.
All standard contraction rules are stored,
together with a dictionary of the most common
words in contracted form. The algorithm
attempts to minimise contracted word length, a
process which can lead to 'illegal' contractions
for long and relatively uncommon words. At the
time of writing we have examined the transla-
tion/contraction accuracy for the 4000 most
common words in English. 98% of these are
contracted correctly while most of the remaining
2% are described by a Braille reader as incorrect but readable. In order to reduce the
disturbance of miscontraction our display allows
recourse to Grade I output at any time. The
Braille readers who evaluated the system
regarded this practice as acceptable, it being
one which is possible only with a dynamic
output. The translation algorithm and dictionary occupies 8 kbytes of memory and operates
faster than the output is transferred to the
Braille display itself.

4.2 Translation to Phonemes

The synthetic speech conversion system contains
a two stage translation process. The first stage
is a text-to-IPA (International Phonetic
Alphabet) translator while the second stage maps
the IPA codes into the appropriate codes to
drive the particular synthesiser device being
used. The text-to-IPA rules are based on those
of Elovitz [6] and are arranged in a data
structure such that a character and its surrounding sub-strings may be matched rapidly to
the appropriate IPA string, which is inserted
into a buffer. When this buffer contains the
phonemes for the required speech segment, such
as a sentence or line of text, the phoneme codes
are converted into the form for the synthesiser.

Synthesiser quality and intelligibility depends
on the accuracy of the text-to-speech rules as
well as the intrinsic nature of the synthesiser
model. A number of experiments with blind and
sighted subjects has been conducted to gauge
synthesiser intelligibility. Details of the
intelligibility measures and their use will be
published in due course. One aspect of interest
is learning time. It took on average 40 minutes
to improve the initial 50% word accuracy score
to 95% for both blind and sighted groups.

The text-to-IPA rules have been developed to
provide accurate phonemes for the 7500 most
common English words. The translation of names,
which tend to occur frequently in Videotex
systems, is often rather poor. The text-
to-speech rules occupy about 40 kbytes of memory
and operate in less than one second for a 20
word speech segment.

5. OUTPUT STAGES AND OVERALL EVALUATION

The user of a non-visual Videotex terminal has
to have suitable means of moving the linear
dynamic Braille or utterance 'window' around the
reformatted Videotex page. The control functions are discussed in Section 5.4, in the
light of the experiments.

5.1 Braille Display Length

Of considerable importance is the optimum
Braille display length, as the cost of such
displays is largely dependent upon the number of
cells in the row. In order to determine whether
an optimum length could be found, an experiment
was conducted with 8 Braille readers, reading
purely textual material using uncontracted
Braille. Although the absolute speed ranged
widely, corresponding to the individual's basic
Braille reading speed, it was found that more
than 3 words or about 20 cells does not significantly increase Braille reading speed.
Figure 2 shows the result of this experiment.
The absolute reading speeds attained are about
half the values given by the individual
for his normal Braille speed. The loss is due
partly to having to activate the refresh and
wait for the row to be set up with new Braille,
and also to using uncontracted Braille.

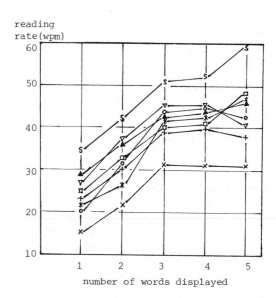

Figure 2 Reading rate for 8 Braille readers
against words displayed.

5.2 Videotex Evaluation Experiments

Rather than use a set of pages selected from a 'live' Videotex service, most of the overall evaluation was performed on a graded set of pages created for the purpose. The pages were stored on a limited access basis on Prestel. The following tests explored the use of the principal page types:

1.   Single index page
2.   Use of two levels of index page
3.   Use of three levels of index page
4.   Reformatted multiple column page
5.   Unformatted multiple column page
6.   Time-table page
7.   Interactive page
8.   Free-run on Prestel.

Each test required the subject to determine a particular piece of information. For example, the time-table was used to find the departure time of a train required at a given destination before a specified time. The free-run on Prestel was used to determine a foreign currency exchange rate.

Four groups of subjects participated:-

    SV: 4 sighted users of visual Videotex
    SS: 9 sighted users of synthetic speech
    BS: 8 blind users of synthetic speech
    BB: 8 blind users of Braille

The subjects answered a short questionnaire on various aspects of the system.

5.3 Results

Two measures of performance are of interest. The first is accuracy, or success in finding the required information, the second is the time taken to complete each task.

(a) Accuracy
The four groups performed equally well, and perfectly, in tests 1,2,3,4,6, and 7. In test 5, using the unformatted page the groups scored as follows
SV: 90%; SS:50%; BS:50%; BB:30%
These results confirm the need for reformatting.

(b) Times taken on tasks 1-7
The times vary quite markedly between the groups, and between the tasks as shown in Figure 3. As anticipated, the synthetic speech terminal was the most time consuming to use. On average the time taken to access Videotex via Braille is 2 times that of visual access, while synthetic speech access is 4 times slower.

(c) The free-run experiment on Prestel.
This experiment revealed the complexity of the searching task on a Videotex system, and the difficulty of using a linear output media. Although the blind subjects were able to attain the required information with similar time

ratios as found in the previous tasks, times of up to 35 minutes in the synthetic speech case lead one to question the viability of such a system for routine, everyday use. The problem is that of memorising on-route indexing information. The use of keyword searching would be a major advantage.

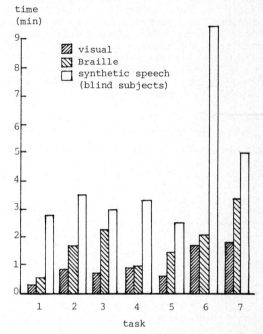

Figure 3 Average times for three groups of subjects to execute tasks 1-7.

5.4 Display Control

One of the aims was to determine how the controls for the synthetic speech and Braille displays should be provided.

The Braille display controls must allow easy movement of the display window up and down, thereby effecting simple reading of tabular formats. In addition, the tab marker allows rapid recall of a particular row, such as the table headings. This has been effected by the inclusion of a standard 7-key Braille input keyboard. Additional controls move the display window to left and right, rewrite the window and move the window to the page top and bottom. Grade I/II selection and reformat/source keys complete the controls. A proposed layout is shown in Fig. 4.

For the synthesiser it is necessary to provide controls to reduce the utterance down to phrase, word and spell levels from the root sentence or line modes. This helps the user to overcome some of the limitations of the poor speech quality, and pace the speech output. Repeat, previous utterance, top and bottom of page controls are similar to those for the Braille display. Further investigation is needed to determine the value of more sophisticated control to aid scanning of tables etc.

6. CONCLUSIONS

This detailed study of non-visual output for Videotex has shown that both dynamic Braille and synthetic speech are technically viable and potentially useful for blind people. The access times, compared with normal visual access, are large, but not necessarily prohibitive, and the standard of presentation of the Videotex material after reformatting and translation is sufficient for Videotex material to be accessed accurately. The blind subjects found the prototype systems stimulating - 'when will they be available?' - was a typical question asked at the end of the experiments.

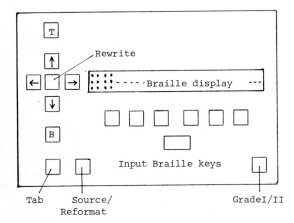

Figure 4   Proposed layout for Braille display controls. Continuous use of the → key reads through the whole page.

For both Braille and synthetic speech output imperfections in translation may be compensated by provision of suitable control functions, such as recourse to Grade I Braille and word spelling. Similarly an imperfect and practical reformatter is greatly aided by the facility to translate and present the source pages unformatted, but with graphics removed.

These displays can form the core of non-visual terminal for blind people. We envisage a means to interface, via suitable software, other source material for which different formatting, for example, would be suitable.

The synthetic speech output is less satisfactory than Braille. For the large number of blind people who are unable to read Braille, synthetic speech is viable, and with improving quality, will become more so. Speech output is also potentially cheaper than dynamic Braille. For sighted users, however, synthetic speech output for such systems is of dubious benefit and should only be proposed where no visual output is available.

7. ACKNOWLEDGEMENTS

The authors wish to acknowledge the financial support of the SERC, British Telecom and Clark and Smith Ltd and thank Mr. Brian Payne and all the blind and sighted subjects who participated in the experiments.

8. REFERENCES.

[1] Dalrymple, G.F., Braille Computer Terminals, Computer Decisions, U.S.A., 3, (Oct. 1976) pp42-4.

[2] I.H. Witten, Principles of Computer Speech, Academic Press (1983).

[3] Cope, N. and King, R.W., Conversion of Teletext and Viewdata into Braille, Proceedings of the Man-Machine Systems Conference, IEE Conf. Pub. No. 212, (1982), pp.196-200.

[4] Standard English Braille, Royal National Institute for the Blind, London (1971).

[5] Croisdale, C.W., Kamp, H., and Werner. H., (eds), Computerised Braille Production, Springer-Verlag (1983).

[6] Elovitz, H.S., et.al., Letter to Sound Rules for the Automatic Translation of English Text to Phonetics, IEEE Trans. ASSP, 24, 6, pp446-459.

Human-Computer Interaction — INTERACT '84 / B. Shackel (ed.)
Elsevier Science Publishers B.V. (North-Holland)
© IFIP, 1985

CAN DEAF CHILDREN INTERACT WITH COMPUTERS? EVIDENCE FROM SPEECH ACQUISITION TRAINING

E. Gulian, F. Fallside & P. Hinds.

Department of Psychology, University of Warwick
and Department of Engineering, University of Cambridge
United Kingdom

The paper discusses the ways in which deaf children learn to use computer-based systems in order to gain control over their articulators and produce intelligible speech. Two systems are presented which analyse and display features of speech. The stages of the children's interaction with the systems and their use of the available feedback are described.

During the last decade the use of computers as instructional and prosthetic aids for a variety of learning deficits and handicaps has dramatically increased (Levitt, 1973; Lundman, 1978; Steward et al. 1976; Peterson et al. 1979).

In a not uncharacteristic fashion all reported results indicated an improvement in the particular behaviour aided in this way. However, only limited information conducive to the understanding of why and how this improvement came about is presently available. This is not surprising since in general the man-computer interaction is still little understood.

The question we are addressing in this paper is the following: can congenitally deaf children relate meaningfully to computer-generated information and use it to achieve intelligible speech? And, if the answer is positive, what are the mechanisms enabling them to do so? Of course, we cannot but touch upon this issue, since perhaps naively, we assumed a priori, that this was the case.

The following discussion is a by-product of three investigations on speech learning by deaf children using computer-generated information and feedback which have been carried out over a period of five years at Cambridge University, Engineering Department. The first study dealt with teaching vowel articulation and the next two with teaching frication and the voicing distinction.

THE COMPUTER-BASED AIDS

Two purpose-built microprocessors were developed for these studies. The first, the Computer Vowel Trainer (CVT) used linear prediction to estimate and display the shape of the vocal tract and showed its idiosyncratic modifications during distinct vowel utterances (Brooks et al 1981). A typical display is presented in Figure 1. It shows the form of the vocal tract from the glottis (on the left) to the lips (on the right) when articulating the vowel /a/. There are two area traces in the display, the target trace (dotted line) and the moving

attempt trace, the current segment of speech analysed by the CVT (unbroken line). As the attempt gets closer to the correct sound, the moving trace assumes a shape that is closer to the target and hence the user receives visual feedback to indicate whether the attempt is correct or not. The speed of analysis is pseudo-real time and this allows the user to home in on the target during an attempt. Moreover, when a certain match between target and attempt is reached the display "freezes". This is a difficulty criterion, which can be preset from levels 1 to 5 corresponding to a poor - excellent attempt. This level is shown by the upper ball to the left of the display, the lower ball shows instantaneously how near the attempt is to the target.

The second microprocessor - the Fricative and Timing Aid (FTA) - displays visual information and gives feedback regarding frication, vowel length and voice onset time (VOT). The FTA uses analogue processing to classify the signal from a microphone as silence, voiced or unvoiced sound and these decisions are passed to digital circuitry which stores them and generates a corresponding display on a domestic TV set. Voicing is shown as white, unvoiced/fricative/affricate sounds as chequered pattern and silence/stops as black.

Figure 2 shows the contrast between word final /k/ and /g/ in the words "lock" and "log". Note the longer vowel duration in "log" (492 msec) compared with that in "lock" (277 msec). Figure 3 shows the contrast between word final fricative sh and affricate ch as in wash/watch. Note the black part of the trace in "watch" which denotes the stop feature of the final affricate.

The display shows traces which evolve with time from left to right as the sound/word is uttered. By providing two traces - one a target generated by the teacher the other the subject's attempt, the FTA allows the user to perceive and correct errors made in speech (Gulian et al 1984 a,b).

THE USERS

These were congenitally deaf children attending partially hearing units attached to primary and secondary schools in Cambridgeshire.
Children in the CVT and Voicing Distinction
Groups aged 4-17 years were profoundly deaf
(90dB mean hearing loss in the better ear and
useful hearing only up to only 2KHz) with very
poor speech ability (an average of 12 out of
68 points on the Edinburgh Articulation Test).
Children in the Fricative Group aged 9-17 years
were severely hearing-impaired (65dB mean
hearing loss in the better ear and useful
hearing up to 6KHz) and poor speech ability (26
out of 68 points on the Edinburgh Articulation
Test)..

The auditory characteristics of the CVT and
Voicing Distinction Groups indicate that these
children were unable; a) to perceive the second formant frequency of vowels, which is a
major cue for defining vowel quality and discriminate between vowels; b) to discriminate
between voiced and unvoiced consonants with
the same place and manner of articulation such
as in the pairs /p/ - /b/, /t/ - /d/ and /k/ -
/g/ (the only difference between these being
that /b/, /d/ and /g/ are voiced, i.e. that
the vocal cords vibrate when they are produced).

At the beginning of the training programme,
analyses of the children's speech production
showed that they had neither the awareness nor
the ability to produce intelligible speech
i.e. to realize qualitatively different vowels
and to voice or devoice the phonemes according
to the rules of English.

The auditory characteristic of the children in
the Fricative Group indicated that they could
not hear high frequency sounds such as fricatives and affricates (for example sh, f, v, s,
ch). Examination of their speech ability showed that they did not use fricatives, or when
they did they produced them indiscriminately,
usually one phoneme covering for all.

THE INTERACTION

What emerges markedly when looking at the two
terms of the interaction is the mismatch between
on the one hand the totally unsophisticated
users and on the other hand, the highly complex
and abstract displayed information they were
supposed to understand, interpret and act upon.
Indeed, the deaf children were to a great extent
unaware of their ability to produce speech, let
alone of their ability to match complex visual

Figure 1: The Computer Vowel Trainer: microprocessor and display

patterns by using vocal commands. The children therefore had to perform an extremely difficult task and their interaction with the computers followed a distinctly complex pattern,
consisting of a number of stages.

Firstly, in what we consider to be the *information processing stage* they had to: attend to
the display; analyse the visual pattern; relate
it to a picture-card/word/written letter; dis-

criminate among features, when several were
present - for instance in the word "wash", between the vowel (white trace) and the fricative
(chequered pattern); contrast features, as between the fricative *sh* and the affricate *ch* (in
wa*sh* - wat*ch*), the difference being represented
by the blackband preceding the chequered pattern in the latter case; or contrast features
of different displays, in the case of the CVT
groups, when differences between targets were

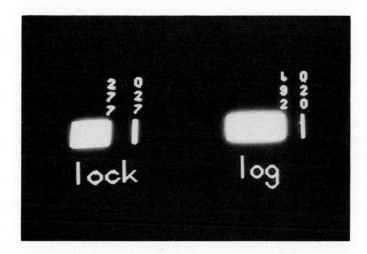

Figure 2: The contrast between voiced /g/ and unvoiced /k/ stop consonants
as cued by the preceding vowel length

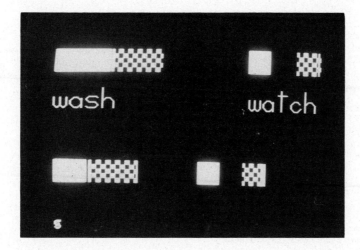

Figure 3: The contrast between fricative /sh/ and affricate /ch/ consonants

sometime very small - for example between the
vowels /a/ as in bαd, and /e/ as in bed; syn-
thesize information, i.e. combine various features important to the production of a particular word, such as voicing, vowel duration and
VOT represented in the display by various lengths of the black and white traces on the FTA;
or vowel quality and voice loudness expressed
by a certain pattern configuration on the CVT.

The information-processing stage was followed
by and partly overlapped with the *action/learn-
ing stage*. At this stage, the children began
to discover the relationship between a visually
displayed temporal pattern and the corresponding articulatory pattern and to translate the
visual information into motor commands to their
articulators, i.e. into speech. This was a relatively fast process as shown by the rather
small number of trials necessary to achieve
substantial improvement in speech intelligibility, compared with the infinitely larger number
of trials by hearing children during their
speech acquisition stage. To exemplify: children in the Fricative Group, during the 6 months
of training had an average of 88 sessions, in
which they practised on average 325 words with
fricatives in initial and final position, with
about 10 trials per word. By the end of this
training period, the intelligibility of their
speech (words and phrases containing fricatives)
had increased from about 15% to over 40% and
remained at that level after a two-month no-
practice period. Interestingly enough, during
this stage, irrespective of age the children
also quickly learned the mechanics of bringing
about the targets, i.e. they acquired the skill
of actually manipulating the controls/keys of
the micro-processor.

During this stage, the children progressed from
trial and error tactics to a systematic recognition of, and increasingly closer matching of
the patterns. After only two or three sessions
the interaction became swift, natural, with the
children themselves pointing to their errors
and trying to correct them. This does not mean
that the control over the articulators had been
achieved, and as a result, the production of
speech had become easy, spontaneous and correct.
It only suggests that a three way association
between articulatory targets, the related visual feature(s) on the display and the articulatory movements to match the target had emerged and that its consolidation was under way.
As a result, cognitive/motor schemata were
formed which acted as framework for further
interactions. These schemata also allowed for
abstraction of rules regarding the type of interaction required and selection of appropriate
commands according to the various salient features of the display. This was more the case
for the Fricative and Voicing Group, since the
targets were characterized by a high degree of
generality. For example, the same chequered
pattern appeared for all fricatives, and all
affricates were represented by the same chequered pattern but preceded by a black trace.

Or, as in the case of VOT, the clue was the delay in onset of voicing represented by the length of the initial black trace - very short (up
to 25 msec) for voiced stops /b,d,g/ and long
(up to 100 msec) for voiceless stops /p,t,k/.
The children had to apply the rule, i.e. make a
phonological decision and specify the response
commands according to contextual cues.

The third stage in the interaction was the *use
of the available feedback* or knowledge of results (KR). The KR was immediate, objective
and in analogous form to the target information
(augmented in the CVT by the levels of difficulty). This meant that the children had to
process this information, too, evaluate its con-
gruity with the target and act upon it.

The KR involved, therefore, continuous and active interaction with the computer by eliciting
comparison of the cognitive-motor schemata already formed for a class of sounds with the
actually realised articulatory configurations.
The result was a reduction in incongruity between target and attempts in further trials.

There were, however, differences in the type of
interaction between users and computers depending on the characteristics of the display and,
in particular, the format of the feedback. The
CVT gave graded as well as global KR, by displaying the level of difficulty achieved as well
as "freezing" the schematic pictorial representation of the vocal tract during production of
a particular vowel. Children could use, therefore, a variety of sources for processing this
information and evaluating their own perfor-
ance. The final "verdict" from the CVT indicated clearly not only whether there was a discrepancy between goal and realization, but made
it possible to locate the locus of the error
(whether at the level of the glottis, of the
lips, tongue position). In this sense feedback
was direct and no further elaboration was required.

This was also shown by the way children discrim-
inated between the necessary feedback and the
redundant KR, optionally represented in the
display by a teddy bear which smiled or frowned
according to whether the attempt was correct or
incorrect. After only a few sessions of practice, the children stopped looking at the teddy
bear and shifted their attention to that part
of the display which gave them direct feedback
about their performance.

The FTA, on the other hand, provided different,
and reduced feedback opportunities: neither intermediary steps (such as the non-freezing -
freezing displays of the vocal tract) nor grading or successful attempts were available. KR
was global and rested on the comparison of the
target and attempt displays.

Evaluation of similarities and discrepancies
between these was more difficult in that it implied fine judgements of the lengths of white/

black traces and the presence or absence of
chequered patterns. Users, therefore, had to
process more deeply the feedback made available
and, to a certain extent make inferences about
the correctness of their performance.

CONCLUSION

We have considered here a special kind of user-
computer interaction. The emphasis lay not on
learning the input commands or those necessary
to obtain information from the computer, but on
learning to control one's own articulators to
match the targets and, implicitly to produce
speech. Following an initial analysis of the
task/display the children were able to elaborate a schema acting as a framework for further
interaction.

In spite of the multiple features of the display, due to the consistency of the targets and
consequently of the commands required to match
them it was possible to store these in long-
term memory as independent units or schemata
which could be retrieved in the absence of relevant visual information. The response to the
question "can deaf children interact with
computers?" is, therefore positive: yes, they
do and in this way they can learn to produce intelligible speech.

REFERENCES

(1) Brooks S., Fallside, F., Gulian, E., &
     Hinds, P. Teaching vowel articulation
     with the Computer Vowel Trainer. *British
     Jrnl Audiology*, 15, (1981) 151-163.

(2) Gulian, E., Fallside, F., Hinds, P. &
     Keiller, C. Acquisition of frication by
     severely hearing-impaired children.
     British Jrnl Audiology, 17, (1983) 219-231.

(3) Gulian, E., Hinds, P., Fallside, F. &
     Keiller, C. Acquisition of the voicing
     distinction by profoundly hearing-impaired
     children. *British Jrnl Audiology*, 17,
     (1983) 233-244.

(4) Levitt, H. Speech processing aids for the
     deaf: an overview. I.E.E.E. Trans. Audio·
     Electroacoustics, 21 (1973) 269-273.

(5) Lundman, M. (ed) Technical aids for the
     speech-impaired. ICTA Information Centre
     (Stockholm 1978).

(6) Steward, L.E., Larking, W.D. and Houde,
     R.H. A real-time spectrograph with impli-
     cations for speech training of the deaf.
     I.E.E.E. Internat Conf. on Acoustics,
     Speech and Signal Processing,
     (Philadelphia, 1976).

(7) Peterson, B., Galbraith, G., Miller, C.,
     Butkiss, D., Borthwick, S. and Lennan, R.
     Teaching language communication skills to
     deaf children by means of CAI. Proceed
     of Ass. Computer Based Instructional
     Systems. (San Diego, 1979).

Human-Computer Interaction — INTERACT '84 / B. Shackel (ed.)
Elsevier Science Publishers B.V. (North-Holland)
© IFIP, 1985

PREDICTION AND ADAPTION IN A COMMUNICATION AID FOR THE DISABLED

J. A. Pickering, J. L. Arnott, J. G. Wolff+ and A. L. Swiffin,

The Department of Electrical Engineering and Electronics
and +the Department of Psychology,
The University of Dundee,
Dundee,
Scotland, UK.

Many physically disabled persons suffer communication impairment as part of
their handicap. It is possible to improve their effective communication rate in
any language task, such as typing, by exploiting the redundancy of natural
language. Many systems which do this are often equipped with fixed knowledge
bases determined by 'a priori' statistical data about the language. This paper
describes a system which exploits language redundancy in an adaptive, predictive
aid for the disabled that has been specifically designed to be moduar and thus
have general purpose applications.

Introduction

Written language is, from an informational
viewpoint, a very redundant coding method.
For those who are able-bodied this is not
something that causes inconvenience. Most
of us write and type using this code without
much effort. However a person with a motor
handicap becomes very conscious of the
redundancy in the code. Many such people,
such as Cerebral Palsy sufferers, have no
trouble in deciding what they wish to say or
write but then have to communicate it
through a 'channel' whose information
capacity is severely constrained. Thus it
is vital for such people to make the most of
the residual channel capacity.

A number of microcomputer based aids for
communication have been developed that
enable text to be created by those who are
so physically handicapped that they cannot
use a standard keyboard (1,2,3,4,5,6,7).
These systems commonly use one or more
switch type sensors, placed where the user
can exercise the best control over them, in
combination with a scanning letter/function
matrix. Some more recent communication aids
take account of n-gram letter combination
statistics in order to heighten the speed of
letter selection (2,3,4). Further
improvements can be achieved if the lists
produced by the aid extend to probable words
rather than just the next letter or so
(5,6,7).

These communication aids have been limited
in application for two main reasons.
Firstly, they have been developed
specifically for a particular type of
microcomputer and in a manner that prohibits
easy porting between machines. Secondly,
the design of the aid is centred around a
particular degree of handicap and is not
suited for use by the more able person who

may prefer to use a standard type keyboard.
This paper describes a word predictive
communication aid which has been designed to
be modular and thus general purpose. The
philosophy behind the design approach was to
decouple the predictor interface from (a)
the application with which it may be used
and (b) the peculiarities of the user
interface. The predictor itself
automatically adapts to the user's
vocabulary though the user may adjust the
word lists explicitly in a simple and
streamlined fashion.

Outline system description

For able bodied computer users the typical
interface to a program is the character
stream generated by the terminal keyboard.
Thus the type of interface is constrained to
the extent that an aid that facilitates use
of an unadapted program by the disabled must
emulate the character stream that a keyboard
produces(8). Thus the predictive aid's
output interface to the program is, from a
functional point of view, a keyboard
emulator.

The interface with which the user directly
interacts has to be tailored to his/her
particular physical needs. Since this part
is individual to the user it should be
isolated to facilitate adaption and change.
In order to achieve this an intermediate
interface must be identified by which many
differing types of tailored input module may
be attached to the predictor.

The central part of the predictor system is
called the Predictive, Adaptive, Lexicon
based interface (PAL). The major feature of
PAL is its ability to predict the word or
phrase which the user requires. These
predictions are derived from

(a) the characters that the user has just input and
(b) historical information about the user's vocabulary.

The characters are input by the user by the means offered by the input interface module, which may be a standard or adapted computer style keyboard or a scanning matrix system. In order to make use of a prediction the input interface must offer the facility of communicating to PAL the selection of a prediction, as distinct from another character. Thus the nature of the interface between PAL and the input module becomes evident. Effectively it must behave like an enhanced keyboard which can transmit the normal character set and also special information directed only at PAL. Figure 1 shows the resultant scheme with PAL as the central component in the input chain.

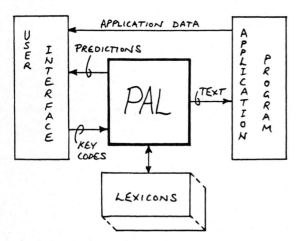

Figure 1. Block diagram of an application incorporating PAL.

The word lists and historical information about the user's vocabulary are held in lexicons. Several lexicons may be maintained so that PAL may be able to respond easily to differing contexts. One lexicon might be used for letter writing, another for technical writing and another for composing shopping lists and so on. PAL both manages the use of these lexicons and enables them to be updated. Generation of new lexicons and explicit updating of lexicons is done using a lexicon editor which forms part of the PAL module.

The modular construction of an input system based around PAL facilitates a variety of possible implementations. Each module may be built as a separate process in a multi-processing environment with inter-process communication via character channels. A more attractive approach is to use a microprocessor for each module with

physical hardware interfaces between them. As the character stream into most computers is implemented using serial data communications, this provides a simple connection that enables the disabled user to gain access to the same wide range of software that is available to able bodied computer users.

Prototype system description

The PAL scheme was tested using a prototype system in which all the modules, including an application task, were bound into a single program. A block diagram of the prototype is shown in Figure 2. The logical properties of the interfaces were preserved in the implementation by using the procedure parameter passing mechanism. The program chosen for prototype testing was a rudimentary text editor suited for the composition of pieces of text. The arrangement was made suitable for disabled users who can use a standard computer keyboard so that trials could be performed. In the trials the user could usefully compose pieces of text using the prototype PAL system and make the remaining minor adjustments with an existing, easy to use screen editor to produce a finished result.

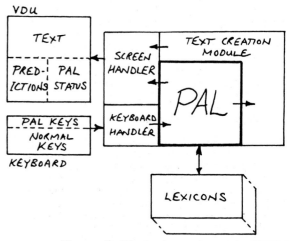

Figure 2. Block diagram of the prototype PAL system.

The user's input from the keyboard can be classified into three types:

(a) ordinary letters, numbers or symbols which are forwarded to the text creation program and are used as the basis for generating suitable predictions,

(b) selections from the prediction list which cause PAL to make the prediction, usually comprising a sequence of several letters, to the text creation program,

(c) PAL commands which affect the operation of the PAL module only and are not forwarded to the text creation program.

The task of the keyboard handler is to convert from whatever codes the keyboard happens to use into the standard code understood by PAL for these classes of input. It also performs a single letter 'shift' function needed by those disabled users who cannot press two keys simultaneously.

The predictions that PAL produces need to be displayed along with the information from the text creation program. The data from these two sources are combined by the VDU screen manager and displayed in dedicated zones on the screen.

The lexicon manager of PAL enables the user to select the appropriate lexicon for the task he wishes to perform. This is then used by the predictor functions within PAL for deriving lists of predictions according its content in conjunction with the current word prefix being entered by the user. Each lexicon contains word lists and usage statistics derived from previous sessions. The form of the lexicon was developed by one of the authors in connection with studies on language acquisition and is a tree-like data structure whose nodes are word prefixes and whose leaves are words.

The prototype system software was written in PASCAL, for portability, and implemented on a UNIX-like Z80 based microcomputer system which offers emulation of the popular CP/M operating system.

Prototype system operation

The operation of the system from the user's view point proceeds as follows. PAL initially asks the user whether text creation is required or whether a lexicon is to be edited. If text is to be created then a lexicon is chosen from those available and is loaded into the computer system memory from a backing store file. Once loaded, PAL immediately attempts to predict words that the user may want. These predictions are the most common words found in the lexicon which was loaded and are always displayed when PAL detects the start of a new word. The predictions are shown in the prediction display area for the user to examine. If the desired word is seen then the user identifies the word by pressing the appropriate prediction list key (a 'function' key in the prototype). If the prediction list does not contain the required word the user continues to type the word in the usual way. PAL continues to produce predictions based on the word prefix which has been entered together with past usage information so that the predictions

given are always the ones the user is most likely to want. If the user sees the required word appear in the list then a further single key press will cause the remainder of the word and the following space to be sent to the text creation program.

If the user deletes letters PAL correctly responds by re-analysing the remaining prefix and presenting the appropriate predictions in the usual way. An 'undo' facility is also available to easily correct mistakenly chosen predictions. When in use for ordinary text PAL continues to help the user by performing automatic capitalisation and spacing after sentence-ending punctuation and punctuation mark placing.

In between text creation sessions PAL offers the facility to update any of the existing lexicons or create new ones. This function is performed by the lexicon editor which enables editing in two modes:

(a) From existing texts. This method is used to refine lexicons automatically so that they adapt to the user's patterns of vocabulary. A file containing text, created with or without the aid of PAL, is specified and then the PAL editor reads it and updates the lexicon, incorporating new words and updating the word usage information of words already existing in the lexicon.

(b) Interactive. This method is useful if the user wishes to tailor a lexicon for a text creation session. For example, prior to writing a letter, some names such as 'Smith' and 'Paul' could be added to the lexicon. Also redundant or mis-spelled words can be explicitly removed from the lexicon. The manner in which the edit is performed is almost the same as that during the text creation sessions. The user specifies a prefix long enough to obtain the target word in the prediction list and one further keystroke deletes it from the lexicon. Words and symbol sequences that the file based update mode does not recognise, such as a telephone number, can also be added using this mode.

Once the user has edited the lexicon then it is returned to the set of available lexicons ready for further use in a text creation session.

Prediction presentation

The predictions list must be able to be easily and quickly assessed by the user. The length of the list is physically constrained (a) by the screen size and (b) by the number of prediction selection keys available. The latter figure has to be balanced against the user's alternative of searching for the next character on the keyboard. The list could be presented in a variety of different ways which will affect the amount of cognitive effort required in its assessment:

(a) present whole words with matching prefixes or just the remaining affixes,

(b) present the list in alphabetic order or rank order of probability.

In order to exploit the user's powerful word recognition capabilities fully, the list should comprise whole words. Also studies by Card (9) have shown that alphabetic order of presentation is always superior even when the user becomes familiar with some of the lists. The terminal used for the prototype system limited the maximum number of predictions to 10 and so up to 10 of the most likely predictions are presented as whole words, alphabetically ordered.

Changing the user interface

In order to test the modular concept, for which PAL was designed as a central component, a scanning matrix type disabled user interface was built. A VDU was used with similar dedicated zones for the display of the application program data and the prediction list but with an extra area for the letter matrix. The input device was a 'suck/blow' tube controlling a scanning cursor moving over an 8x8 symbol matrix. The content and ordering of the matrix was similar to that used on the Possum systems since the system would be field trialled with an existing Possum user(1). The prediction list area was adjacent to the matrix and the cursor could be made to jump directly to the list and start to scan it by blowing on the suck/blow tube whereas a suck on the tube would cause the cursor to scan the symbol matrix. The resulting text would appear in the application program area on the screen.

The interface between the suck/blow interface and PAL was implemented using UNIX-like 'pipes' (character channels) with each being run as a separate process. The prototype software already described was used, the only modification was the substitution of the keyboard and screen handlers.

Evaluation of the system

The purpose of PAL is to achieve a net saving of effort in communicating a given text sequence to a program. If the text were to be created using a conventional keyboard then the effort would be in proportion to the number of letters in the text. The tasks that an unskilled keyboard user would perform for inputting each letter would be (a) selection of the character and

(b) confirming that the correct character had been selected. For a PAL based system, however, extra tasks are involved that increase the amount of cognitive effort involved in creating the text sequence. Before many of the selection operations the task of assessing the prediction list content has to be performed. Provided that the effort and time spent in the physical selection task dominates, which it does for a disabled user, this extra overhead can be absorbed very easily. Thus a good indication of the value of a PAL based system is the reduction in selection operations necessary to create a text sequence. This rather physical measure of the effectiveness of PAL in the prototype system is the 'keysaving' and may be expressed as a percentage. This figure is the difference between the number of characters in the created text file and the number of keystrokes used to produce them divided by the number that would have been necessary without PAL.

Use of the prototype system both by the implementors and with disabled persons together with simulations have shown the keysavings to be better than 30%. The figure is very dependent on how well the lexicon is matched to material being input. For instance for an artificial and very verbose language, such as the programming language COBOL, the keysaving can be as high as 65%. An advantage of the PAL system, important for users who have poor selection accuracy and thus a high error rate, is that predictions carry with them an associated keysaving because the remaining affix is forwarded to the application correctly. The keysaving figure may be validly applied to the scanning matrix scheme as well since the symbol matrix is static and because the physical effort is dominant.

Comments made by disabled users were that the physical effort saving was very worthwhile and particularly so for weak users. However the effort in its use is composite and a tradeoff is being made between physical effort and the cognitive effort in assessing the prediction list. In order to reduce the total effort the cognitive element must also be reduced as well. If such systems are used by more able persons then the balance of effort turns cognitive and the importance of reducing it is heightened. The methods of presentation of the prediction lists is key to the reduction in the assessment effort and this has been partially addressed in the prototype system described. For frequently used words the selection pattern can very quickly be learned so that the user avoids the need to examine the prediction list. However the PAL system is adaptive and, because the list is always alphabetically ordered, the adaption to new usage information may lead to these popular words being displaced from the position in the list that the user has learned. Even if the lists are presented in probability order the problem still exists though the displacement is less 'random'. Methods of gently alerting the user to the process of lexicon adaption as it occurs are being researched at present.

Conclusions

An aid for the disabled that enables the communication of textual material in a more effort efficient manner has been described. The system is adaptive, which enables the system effectiveness to improve through extended use, though the very process of adaption presents its own man-machine problems. The system is implemented in a manner that facilitates porting and its use in a variety of different situations. The user interface can be tailored to the needs of the individual user with very little impact on the central predictor component. Also, since the output of the system is logically indistinguishable from the output of a standard computer keyboard, it can be used as the input method to existing computer programs.

Acknowledgements

The authors gratefully acknowledge the financial assistance of the Spastics Society and the assistance given by the Scottish Council for Spastics.

References

[1] Possum Controls Ltd., Product information, 63 Mandeville Road, Aylesbury, Buckinghamshire, UK.

[2] Tufts-New England Medical Center, Product information, 171 Harrison Avenue, Boston, MA 02111, USA.

[3] Thomas, A., The Quicktic Communicator, Proc. Int. Conf. on Rehabilitation Eng., Toronto, Canada. (1980).

[4] Morasso, P., Sandini, G., Suetta, G., et al., LOGOS: A microprocessor based device as a writing aid for the motor handicapped, Med. and Biol. Eng. and Computing, 16, p309-315. (1978).

[5] Odor, J. P., Personal communication, (1983).

[6] Poon, P., MACApple product information, Dept. Electronic and Electrical Eng., Kings College, Strand, London, UK. (1983).

[7] Heckathorne, C. W., Childress, D. S., Applying anticipatory text selection in a writing aid for people with severe motor impairement, IEEE Micro. (June 1983) 17-23.

[8] Vanderheiden, G. C., Kelso, D. P., Dual and Nested Computer Approach to Vocational and Educational Computer Systems, Proc. 5th Ann. Conf. on Rehabilitation Engineering, Houston, Texas. (1982) 46.

[9] Card, S. K., User perceptual mechanisms in the search of computer command menus, Proc. Conf. Human Factors in Computer Systems, Gaithersburg, MD, USA. (March 1982) 190-196.

[10] Battison, M. J., A modular microprocessor-based interface for the disabled, M. Sc. Thesis, School of Bioengineering, University of Dundee. (December 1983)

ORGANISATION AND SOCIAL ISSUES

Human-Computer Interaction — INTERACT '84 / B. Shackel (ed.)
Elsevier Science Publishers B.V. (North-Holland)
© IFIP, 1985

CONCEPTUAL DATA MODELING AS AN OBSTACLE FOR ORGANIZATIONAL DECENTRALIZATION

Clas-Olof Kall

Human-Infological Research Group (HUMOR)
Department of Information Processing
Chalmers University of Technology
S-412 96 Göteborg, Sweden

During the last decade a very large number of more or less different modeling approaches to conceptual data modeling have been presented. These research efforts seem to be based on a technological research tradition. Theories concerning use of conceptual data modeling approaches and of information systems by human actors in an organizational context are usually not considered. However, the conceptual data modeling strategy is not "neutral" in regard to organizational and behavioural aspects. In this paper one of the most characteristic features of conceptual data modeling, the integration of local views is analyzed by using a theory on information systems based on social sciences denoted the language action theory.

1. INTRODUCTION

Conceptual data modeling is a data base oriented and dominating strategy in the area of information system development and research. A characteristic feature of this strategy is the integration of different local views (information needs of different user groups) into one consistent global conceptual model.[1] Design methodologies (datamodels) such as The Relational Model (6), The Entity-Relationship Model (5), The Diam Model (15), The Ansi/x3/Sparc DBMS framework (17), The ISO framework (10) and many more constitutes this kind of strategy.

The integration of local views into one consistent global conceptual model is analyzed by using the language action theory on information systems and the concept of information system quality suggested by this theory. The conceptual data modeling strategy is not "neutral" to organizational and behavioural aspects. Human interpretation and understanding of data and prerequisites for data and information to support human actions in organizations, especially in decentralized organizations, are discussed.

The language action theory is based on humanistic traditions in social science especially communication action theory, hermeuneutics and sociology of knowledge. Information systems are considered as social linguistic systems technically implemented. (9) An information system is considered to comprise a formal professional language. To specify an information system means to transform and develop professional languages (natural languages) in use into a formal professional language.

2. AN ANALYSIS OF INTEGRATION IN CONCEPTUAL DATA MODELING

2.1 The integration process outlined

All local views (information needs and rules for information processing) of different user groups are integrated into one Global Conceptual Model (GCM). Local views must be consistent otherwise these cannot be integrated into one GCM. All generalizations, abstractions, assumptions about the reality and terms used to refer to these phenomena must be consistent in all local views. A GCM must be internally consistent and in an accurately way reflect each of the original local views. (19) The problem of inconsistencies are solved by reformulation of local views. (2, 13).

A GCM seems to encompass all data in an organization considered suitable for formalization and data processing. Limitations of how many views and how great the inconsistencies can be between local views, are not treated by the CDM strategy. All views of an organization consistent or not are considered possible to integrate and shall be integrated. All applications (local views) of an organization are included in a GCM. (17) Each application is a part of the organization organized to accomplish a specific subgoal. There will be many local views and a single GCM. (8) All our views, assumptions and rules about the reality are specified in a GCM. (3) A community view of data shall be established, so that a wide variety of users can interact with a GCM. (7) The design of a GCM can be both very large and complex. (16)

The problem of integrating local views is not well understood. (14) Some kind of integration policy have been suggested to guide the reformulation of inconsistent views. (14) E g "all local views in the salesdepartment are to be prefered over views in prod dept at all times".

A GCM acts as a basis for an efficient physical design and implementation. (2) The information system in use will include several consistent local views. Each user group use their local view. Local views in use are more or less equivalent to original views defined before the process of integration was performed.

2.2 Purpose and quality of information systems

The CDM strategy aims to establish an efficient technical control of all data suitable for formalization and data processing in an organization. (9) The quality of an information system is dependent on this criteria. To integrate all local views (all data) is a necessary condition to get a high degree of technical control. E g this means there will only be one information system to maintain and data occuring in more than one local view is defined and represented by other data at only one place and at only one time. The concept of economy of scale is favoured in a couple of ways.

In the language action theory on information systems this technical interest or criteria is subsumed a practical interest[2]. The purpose of an information system is to inform some people, as support to their performance of organizational tasks. The quality of an information system in use is dependent on the intersubjective understanding among users of a formal professional language that comprises an information system and how well the system (language) is adjusted to the tasks of human actors. (9) This quality criteria focus upon some important issues. If users do not understand the meaning of a formal professional language comprising an information system e g generalizations, abstractions, terms etc, the quality will be low. The quality will also be low in situations where users can interpret the formal professional language in an adequate way, but where the information (knowledge) obtained is not adjusted to the tasks performed by users. The quality concept of the language action theory is based on the theory of language game. In this theory, the use of data (a professional language) is always related to a specific organizational task and a specific type of understanding (frame of reference). (1,18) These three factors form a dialectical unit. Hence, that humans in different organizational units of an organization performing different kinds of tasks also use and develop different kinds of professional languages with corresponding frame of references.

There exists in organizations strictly local data or parts of professional languages that are local. (12) This kind of data cannot and should not be shared because this data is meaningless outside a limited local community (e g a specific work station or an organizational unit). Nobody outside this unit is interested in this kind of data, because this data is only needed and adjusted to the performance of internal tasks by humans inside this organizational unit. This data can only be interpreted in an adequate way by human actors inside this specific unit holding an adequate frame of reference (preknowledge). This kind of local data used in one unit will certainly be inconsistent to various degrees with local

data used in other units, e g the same data refers to different phenomena (generalizations, abstractions etc) in different units. Expressed in terms of conceptual data modeling, this implies that the same data in local views have different meanings to different user groups. That inconsistencies exist can easily be defended from the ontological belief that there exist no objectively given reality. The reality (including professional languages in use) is a socially constructed reality with more or less intersubjectively shared meanings among people. Further, this belief lies behind the theory of language game that people develop and use different professional languages and different terms of references depending on what kinds of organizational tasks they perform. Professional languages cannot only consist of local data. To coordinate actions and tasks performed by different units call for communication. This means that professional languages have some parts in common. These parts have the same meaning to (some) actors in different units. To design and use an information system for coordination, means that only some parts (not everything) of only some views must be integrated (intersubjectively shared).

2.3 The quality of an IS in use based on a GCM

Integration presupposes that all local views are analyzed and defined by use of the same kind of data model. (16) There is no right or wrong modeling approach in an absolute sense. (2) In the range of 100 data models have been presented. (4) This gives reason to suppose that some data models are more suitable than others in different situations (e g depending on tasks, professional languages and frame of references). The use of one kind of data model to define all views, can of course affect the quality of an information system in use.

However, given a set of local views all defined by the same kind of data model and various degrees of inconsistencies between these views the process of integration into one GCM shall be performed. It seems reasonable to put forward that the more local views defined and the more of inconsistencies between these views there are the greater the difference will be between reformulated views comprising a GCM and the corresponding original local views defined. The result of the process of integration will be a GCM including reformulated views. May be all original local views have been reformulated more or less or only one of the original local views have not been changed. However, as indicated by Navathe & Gadgil, this process of integration is not well understood. (14) Probably, it will be possible to design in accordance to the consistency criteria a GCM comprising views that not reflects any of the original local views in an adequate way. Regardless of how great differences there will be between original views and corresponding reformulated views in the GCM (the information system in use) there prevails an obvious risk of a low quality of the information system. The generalizations, abstractions, assumptions, rules etc and the terms used to refer to this kind of phenomena have more or less been changed.

Reformulated views in use will comprise a formal professional language,technical implemented, not tied to the frame of references held by user groups and to the organizational tasks of these groups and to their professional languages. Analytically two situations can be distinguised. In the case of other terms (data) are used to refer to the same generalizations, abstractions etc as in original views users can probably learn to use these terms because these terms refer to generalizations, abstractions etc prevailing in user´s frame of references and tied to professional languages in use and organizational tasks. The quality of an information system will not be affected as a consequence of reformulation and integration if users can learn and accept other terms (data).

In the case of terms (data) refereing to other generalizations, abstractions etc the situation becomes much more problematic. The terms refer to generalizations,abstractions etc not familiar to user groups and not familiar with the user´s conception of the social constructed reality. The terms refer to a social constructed reality established in the process of reformulation and integration. The quality of an information system in use will be very low. This situation will probably call for unlearning and fundamental changes in the frame of references held by user groups. If user groups are able to unlearn one social constructed reality and learn a new one (change their frame of references) in such a way that terms make sense to them, they can obtain information and knowledge. This information or knowledge will not be adjusted to user´s performance of tasks. The quality will still be low.

To change local views in an information system in use, e g as a result of organizational development can result in new inconsistencies that must be identified and solved. Maybe many local views in use must be reformulated once again. Probably, there will be a risk to only accept changes in local views consistent with views in use.

The quality of an information system in use will be depending on differences between original local views defined and corresponding reformulated views in use. Great differences will result in a low quality.

3. EVALUATION IN RELATION TO ORGANIZATIONAL DECENTRALIZATION

3.1 On the concept of decentralization

In a decentralized organization the authority to make decisions is spread down in the organization hierarchy. There are many actors ("user groups") or "selfsteering" units that make their own tasks and make their own decisions of how these tasks shall be performed. Many organizational members act as decision makers performing different tasks and interact with different environments. Such actors (decison-makers), groups or organizational units use and develop different frame of references (e g decision styles and competences) and different professional (natural) languages in regard to and tied to their different tasks. Some parts of frame of references and professional languages must be intersubjectively shared among (some) actors in different units in order to coordinate different tasks.

3.2 The performance of the integration process and consequences

The integration process presupposes that all local views are defined by using the same data model. (16) If there is no consensus of which data model to be used, a choice must be made among available alternative data models. This means that not all local units or user groups can make a choice of their own on which data model to be used to define their local view. Probably, such choices are never intended to exist among user groups. Such choices are determined by a special function (staff) usually denoted "The Enterprise Administrator". (17)

However, the integration of inconsistent local views means that some, many, all or all except one local view (prefered view) must be reformulated. This means that user groups cannot determine or define their own local view in such a way as they want and change their local view in use based upon their own will. The authority to decide which views that should be reformulated if consensus among user groups cannot be achieved is located to the special function mentioned above. The way this process must be carried out when inconsistencies exist does not harmonize with decentralization.

In a decentralized organization it is reasonable to expect much more inconsistencies between different local views (organizational units) compared to a centralized organization. This means that many views must be reformulated and the differences between these views and corresponding original views defined will be great. An information system in use (reformulated views in use) will not be tied to frame of references held by user groups, professional languages in use and organizational tasks of user groups. According to the quality concept of the language action theory, the quality of a information system in use will be low.

The conceptual data modeling strategy does not permit dispersed authority in decentralized organizations to encompas control over information and information processes. Managers or decision makers of (local) units have authority to make decisions and to take responsibility of their own decisions and actions, but they cannot determine based upon their own judgements and investigations, what kind of information they have to use. The conceptual data modeling strategy seems to restrict the dispersion of authority in decentralized organizations on a very important area in such organizations, the control of information. If managers or decision makers (user groups) cannot control the information support of their units, they probably will refuse to make their own decisions and to take responsibility of these decisions, because they cannot make decisions without suitable information.

4. SUMMARY

The quality concept of the language action theory has been applied to the integration process of the conceptual data modeling strategy by an analysis of the integration process. The analysis shows that the integration of all data of all local views in an organization into one global conceptual model (one total information system) will lead to a low quality of an information system in use, especially in decentralized organizations. Advocates of the conceptual data modeling strategy seem not to be aware of that:i) Local data exist in organizations. ii) Data are not information but can be information by interpreting human actors holding adequate frame of references. iii) The reality is a socially constructed reality, not objectively given, which means that actors perceive and constitute the reality in different ways. iiii) Professional languages and frame of references are tied to organizational tasks.
The global conceptual model (conceptual schema) or the so called conceptual level was introduced by the conceptual data modeling strategy as a mean to allow data independence, which means e g that a global conceptual model can be unchanged if the physical representation is changed and new local views can be defined without changes in the physical representation. (17) The conceptual data modeling strategy seems also to presuppose an other kind of data independency that data are independent of human actors (user groups), their actions, tasks and professional (natural) languages.

Integration of only some common parts of only some views, seems to be necessary if an information system will be used to coordinate actions of different user groups (units). Reformulation and integration of inconsistent views must otherwise be avoided to gain a high degree of information system quality. This means many local unintegrated information systems.

FOOTNOTES:

1) This kind of models are also denoted conceptual schema, data models, informations models or infological models. (2)

2) See Habermas about the theory of different knowledge interests. (11)

REFERENCES:

(1) Apel, K-O., Analytic philosophy of language and the geisteswissenschaften (D. Reidel Publishing Company, Dordrecht, Holland, 1967).

(2) Bubenko, J., Validity and verification aspects of information modeling, Proc Third international conference on very large data bases (Tokyo, 1977).

(3) Bubenko, J., Information modeling in the context of system development, in Lavington, S. (ed), Information Processing 80 (North-Holland, Amsterdam, 1980).

(4) Bubenko, J., Information and data modeling: State of the art and research directions, Syslab report No 20, University of Stockholm (April 1983)

(5) Chen, P.P-S., The entity-relationship model - towards an unified view of data, ACM Transactions on data base systems Vol 1 No 1 (1976) 9-36.

(6) Codd, E.F., A relational model of data for large shared data banks, CACM Vol 13 (1970) 377-387.

(7) Codd, E.F., Recent investigations in relational data base systems, IFIP 74 Proc (North-Holland, Amsterdam, 1974).

(8) Date, C.J., An introduction to data base systems, (Addison-Wesley, 1982).

(9) Goldkuhl,G. and Lyytinen,K., A language action view of information systems, in Bemelmas, T.(ed), Beyond productivity: Information systems development for organizational effectiveness (North-Holland, Amsterdam, 1984).

(10) van Griethuysen, J.J.,(ed) Concepts and terminology for the conceptual schema and the information base, ISO/TC97/SC5 N695 (American National Standards Institute, 1982).

(11) Habermas, J., Knowledge and human interest (Heinemann, London, 1972).

(12) Langefors,B., Integrated versus decentralized information resource management, Dept of Information processing, Chalmers University of Technology and University of Göteborg (1983).

(13) Lindencrona-Ohlin,E., A study on conceptual data modeling, Ph D Thesis, Dept of Information processing, Chalmers University of Technology and Univ of Göteborg (1979).

(14) Navathe, S.B. and Gadgil, S.G., A methodology for view integration in logical data base design, Proc Eigth international conference on very large data bases (Mexico City, 1982).

(15) Senko, M., Conceptual schemas, abstract data structures,enterprise descriptions, in Morlet, A. and Ribbens, G. (eds), International computing conference (North-Holland, Amsterdam, 1977).

(16) Smith, D.C.P. and Smith, J.M., Conceptual data base design, Info tech state of art report on data design (1980).

(17) Tsichritzis, D and Klug, A., (eds), The Ansi/x3/Sparc DBMS framework: Report of the study group on data base management systems, Information Systems Vol 3 (1978).

(18) Wittgenstein, L., Philosophical investigations (Basil Blackwell & Mott, Oxford,1958).

(19) Yao, S.B.; Navathe, S.B. and Weldon, J-L., An integrated approach to logical data base design, Proc NYU Symp on data base design (May 1978).

Human-Computer Interaction — INTERACT '84 / B. Shackel (ed.)
Elsevier Science Publishers B.V. (North-Holland)
© IFIP, 1985

THE LEGITIMACY OF INFORMATION SYSTEMS DEVELOPMENT - A NEED FOR CHANGE ANALYSIS

Göran Goldkuhl and Annie Röstlinger

Human-infological Research Group (HUMOR)
Department of Information Processing
Chalmers University of Technology
S-412 96 Göteborg, Sweden

The decision on whether to develop computerized information systems or not must be made in a rational and transparent way. This kind of decision process is called change analysis. If a computerization decision is taken without a proper change analysis, then such a change action is not organizationally legitimate. A methodology for change analysis is presented consisting of problem analysis , goal analysis, change requirement analysis, change action determination and activity analysis. Some applications of and experiences from method use are noticed.

1. INFORMATIONS SYSTEM DEVELOPMENT - LEGITIMATE CHANGE ACTIONS?

The decision on information system development is not an unproblematic one. The decision whether to computerize some parts of the enterprise's work or not, can be made with different degrees of rationality. The development of computerized information information systems (CIS) can be seen as an attempt to resolve some organizational goals. To make this decision on computerization rational, these different problems and goals must be made explicit. There can be other ways of resolving certain organizational problems than by computerization. Before one starts a CIS development process, a decision process must be accomplished.

CIS development is one type of human action. Is such an action (in a specific situation) organizationally legitimate? Are there clear reasons and motives for performing this kind of action? To legitimate a human action, one must explain and justify it (4, 10). However, many times CIS development efforts seem to start from rather vague ideas and needs. The decisions on CIS development are often made rather implicitly. The decisions are thereby not rationally legitimated. Vague ideas on CIS solutions to organizational problems are unfortunately often taken for granted and not problemized.

There is a need for a separate stage or area before CIS development, where this kind of decision is developed and made. Work in this area can lead to a decision to develop computerized information systems. But it can also lead to other types of change actions. This is an initial stage general for many types of organizational problems and changes. We call this area change analysis (CA).

Is change analysis important for information systems science and practice? We claim that it is

very important. A systems designer that develops a CIS without considering the reasons for this CIS investment is becoming a "mere technician". He can develop a CIS that is solving the wrong problem; just aiming at symptons. He is then (not totally, but) partly responsible for this kind of CIS failure. A systems designer, as a morally responsible agent, cannot take vague CIS-solutions to ill-stated organizational problems for granted. If nobody else does it, he must force a problemization of this kind of solution. He must require a rational legitimacy of this CIS development decision. From the view point of a systems designer: change analysis is an investigation of the motives, conditions and postulates for specific CIS developments. This will lead to a rational (i e well-grounded) decision whether to develop CIS or not.

A change analysis process must involve identification, formulation and diagnosis of problems, reconstruction and analysis of goals and values, and creation and evaluation of change requirements and change actions.

To have a legitimate decision on CIS development the different problems, goals, change requirements and anticipated consequences (of the changes) must be well described. These form together a basis for the legitimacy of the specific change action. A prerequisite for a rational decision of this kind is that the structure of problems and goals etc (i e the decision motives and postulates) is visible. The decision process must be transparent.

Let us continue to describe different factors for making the decision process rational and thereby the decision result legitimate. The legitimation should not be solution biased. In this case we have a back-wards legitimation. A change analysis process perhaps starts from some solution ideas. If we are only searching for favourable factors (problems,consequences,etc) that justi-

fy these solutions, then we are performing a solution biased legitimation. Instead we must put
our solution ideas into brackets and only let
them govern the delimitation of our problem area.
We must then search for and identify problems in
a "presuppositionless" manner. The problem analysis should be as comprehensive as possible. We
must take a critical stance against solution ideas in order to distinguish between good and bad
ideas. This can only be made if we are open-mind-
ed towards the fragility of our own ideas.

The decision developed through a change analysis
should be characterized as a <u>reflected action</u>.
A proper change analysis should avoid the two extremes: Verbalism (reflection without action) and
activism (action without reflection).(6) Verbalism is in this context fact-collections and
surveys leading to no other result than pre-study reports. No succeeding action is taken. Many
people reacting to this kind of nonaction, instead take an "activism" position: "Here we do
not make a lot of investigations. We are result
oriented. We act". This kind of action without
enough reflection usually has different consequences as e g curing symptoms, solving the wrong
problems, getting unpleasent surprises, repeating
old mistakes.

A proper change analysis is a synthesis between
these extremes. A change analysis involves a rational investigation leading to well-grounded decisions and actions.

When we are talking about rationality in change
analysis, we do not take a rationalistic position. We reject a mechanistic stepwise procedure
optimizing between well-known quantified obtec-
tives[1]. Instead we propose a decision development manifested as a reconstructed rationality[2].

2. CHANGE ANALYSIS - A METHODOLOGY

There do not exist many methods for change analysis or corresponding area[3]. Some methods do
not have a clear distinction between the analysis and decision on CIS development and the succeeding CIS development process. We present below, in an introductory way, a methodology for
change analysis. This methodology has been developed in the Human-Infological research group
(HUMOR).

2.1 Some principles

The main purpose of this methodology is to support
- a development of deep problem understanding
- a reconstruction and critical development
  of goals/values
- a creative development of change ideas
- a critical assessment of proposed change
  actions
in order to reach a rational and transparent decision development process. The method should
support a stepwise elicitation and refinement

of problems, goals, etc, with a continuous development of understanding of the CA-participants. (8, 14) The method should support an authentic communication and constructive cooperation between different participants with the
purpose of arriving at an intersubjectivity on
problems, goals and changes.

We have so far elaborated what can be called an
ideal change analysis situation. One must notice
that such a situation is hard to establish even
if there exists a proper method as a support and
other facilitating conditions. We have, however,
found it important to outline this kind of ideal
situation, since it,in some sense, should be anticipated in every conscious CA-situation[4].

As an initial stage in organizational development CA is a fuzzy area. CA must be pre-struc-
tured in a general way, in order to increase the
probability that the analysis acts taken mean a
real progress of the CA work. A method gives
guidelines to manage this fuzzy area in a more
conscious way.

One must, however, have a paper balance between
structured and unstructured work. Initially we
are working with vague and ill-stated problems.
We cannot have too much structure and formalism
in this early problem formulation phase. The method must be sensitive to the essential character of a continuous process of problem elicitation and refinement. Some guidelines are possible for the creation of change ideas, but this
process can, of course, not be reduced to a simple derivation of solutions from stated problems
and goals.

A CA-method must be possible to use in many different situations. Therefore, this kind of method
must be contingency oriented. It should be possible to adapt to different situations with respect to problem types, activity areas, scope,
complexity and analysis resources. The method
should be possible to use with different time-
spans of the CA work; from a couple of hours
discussion on problems and changes to a large
"formal" pre-study of half a year or even more.
It should be contingent to various degrees of
experience and competence of the participants.
Following this contingency principle, we must
avoid a "cook-book-method" with a strictly sequential procedure. Instead the method should
be more like a "tool-kit" with analysis areas
and tasks which can be combined in different
ways.

In order to enchance participation and involv-
ment of different interest parties ("user groups"
the method must be simple to learn and use. The
CA work supported by the method, should in a natural way include the production of meaningful
documentation. Analysis,communication and documentation should be an integrated process. The
result of the CA process should be proper objectives and delimitations for the succeeding work,
which might be (but does not need to be) CIS development.

2.2 Methodological structure

The change analysis methodology, developed in the HUMOR group, consists of the analysis areas: Problem analysis, goal analysis, activity analysis, change requirement analysis and change action determination. (9, 8, 14) Each analysis area consists of a number of tasks. Within every analysis area the work focuses on some specific questions and on some specific knowledge acquisition. A proper CA-work means often a number of iterations between the different analysis areas and tasks. Some final order between the different analysis areas and tasks can therefore not be given. It is not even desrable to give a final order as the free order is a question of the possibility to utilize the contingency approach. However, we can still give a main structure of the relations between the different analysis areas (fig 1).

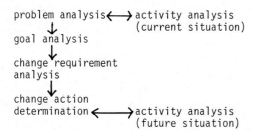

Figure 1. Principal relations between different analysis areas.

The work during the problem analysis starts from the different problematic situations in the organization. The activity analysis is aimed at supporting the problem comprehension by analysis of different aspects of the activity in the organization. During the goal analysis one clarifies the goals in order to understand the problems and to be aware of the desirable situations in the organization. After acquiring knowledge of the problems and the goals, one can evaluate the problematic situations and state the need for changes ; this is worked out during the change requirement analysis. Different change actions can then be generated during the change action determination. By the activity analysis one tries to predict the effects/consequences of the different change actions in the organization.

The CA-work is supposed to be documented during the CA-process. This documentation can be used as a visible representation of motives and postulates enhancing a transparent and rational decision process. The work with the documentation during the CA is supported by documentation techniques and rules.

Below a brief description of each analysis area and the tasks follows:

Problem analysis means a stepwise elicitation

and refinement of problem conceptions and the connections between different problem situations. (14) In the intial phase of the CA-work, it is important to make a delimitation of the problem area. This first delimitation is often based upon intuitive conceptions of problems that are supposed to be important. Although, an explicit delimitation of the problem area is important, in order to clarify the expectations of the CA-work and in order to get an early stage involvement of appropriate CA-participants. The work with the identification and formulation of problems is based on situations, which are comprehended as problematic in some sense by some people. It is often necessary to discuss and reformulate the initial problem conceptions in order to get less complex and more comprehensible problem statements. This process also supports a deeper and common problem understanding among the CA-participants. If the result of the identification and formulation process is a lot of quite different statements, it is convenient to make a partitioning of the problem area and the problems into relevant sub problem areas. This partitioning also makes it possible to consider a further delimitation of the problem area for the continued CA-work. In order to get an understanding of the factors, which influence the different problem situations, it is important to perform an analysis of problem relations. The problem relations express in what way the different problems are connected. The connections can be regarded as problem causes vs problemeffects.

The work during the problem analysis is often based upon implicit comprehension of different goals/values. In order to get a transparent and reliable evaluation of problems and a determination of change requirements and actions it is important to clarify the goals which are related to the problem area. The goals/values express partly why a situation is comprehended as a problematic situation and partly the desirable situation one is trying to reach by performing some kind of change action. The work during the goal analysis focuses on making relevant goals explicit. This process means a reconstruction of existing goals/values and a development of new relevant goals/values. Existing goals and values are reconstructed and made explicit during the identification of goals. Identified goals can be of different types e g policies, activity goals, activity rules. The goals can be institutionalized and legitimated to various degrees. They can exist as official and documented objectives or only implicit. A critical analysis of e g adaption to reality, relevance and conflicts is performed during goal evaluation. In order to support the critical analysis, it can be fruitful to analyse and express the relation between different goals. This process can result in e g changed values of the goals, reformulation and specification of goals, development of new goals and making the goals more official. Goals which are relevant for the further CA-work are then settled during the goal determination.

Change requirement analysis means a relating of problems to corresponding goals and an evaluation of problems in order to determine the current need for changes. The change requirement expresses the problematic situations, which should be changed, but not how the problematic situation shall be changed for getting satisfaction at the settled goals. The problems are evaluated through a consideration of the problem connections and the relations to relevant goals. Each problem can be classified as either there is a need for changing the situation or there is not a need for changes. If the judgement indicates that there is no need for changing the situation this can depend on: The goals are changed, the problem is not so important/relevant or the earlier problematic situation is already changed during the CA-work. Analysis of power and opportunities is a preparation for the creative work with different change ideas. The work during this task is focusing on positive resources within and outside the organization. The change requirements can be formulated from evaluated problems and the knowledge of power and opportunities.

The work during the analysis area change action determination focus on different possible ways of changing in order to abtain more unproblematic situations in the organization. One and the same change requirement can be provided in several ways. And the intention is to choose the combination of change actions, which can be estimated as the best change/solution for the organization. Creation of change actions is performed for every change requirement. One requirement /problem can call for several change actions and one change action can change/solve several problems/requirements. In order to investigate different possibilities for changes, a creation of alternative change actions is very urgent. The change actions are evaluated in order to estimate the effects/consequences of the change actions in the organization. The evaluation is done both from an economic and noneconomic point of view. Different prerequisites and obstacles for a successful accomplishment of the change actions are identified. The choice of change actions is then based on the holistic evaluation. The choice is a proposal which expresses the combination of change actions, which are estimated to improve the initial problematic situations. The choice also expresses important and critical factors of the judgement.

The activity analysis is intended to, mainly, support the work during the problem analysis and the change action determination. The purpose is to aid a deeper understanding of problems and change actions. The activity analysis means studies of different aspects of the activity in the organization in relation to the problems or the change actions. Different tasks can be performed as analysis of activity structure, activity relating, analysis of work operations, analysis of work responsibility and analysis of activity principles. The direction and the proportion of

the activity analysis are completely depending on the need of a deeper knowledge and understanding of problems and change actions.

The result from the different tasks is continuously recorded in different types of document/descriptions,(9) eg the problem relations are documented in Problem-graphs, the goal relations in Goal-graphs the activity relation in Activity-graphs (8, 11) and the consequences of the change actions in Effect-documents.

3.   USE AND TEST OF THE METHODOLOGY

The value of a method lies in the results arrived at using the method. The inquiry problem is how to study and gain experiences from method use. Different test situations can be distinguished.(15) One can have a laboratory setting, where different parts and aspects of the method can be studied. In such a setting it is possible to use both made up cases and real cases (done once again). It is also possible to study the method in a real-life setting.

What does it mean to study the quality of a method? A method is a prescription for human action. (7) It is not an aid for a physical instrumental action. It is an aid for action aiming at development of understanding. (12) A method should improve problem solving, knowledge development, communication and social interaction. As investigators, our knowledge interest (12) must be of praxis character (6) aiming at social meanings of action and understanding. Our method studies cannot be governed by a technical knowledge interest aiming at getting control over parts of nature, in order to manipulate it. A method (in the area of change analysis) is not a physical tool, and we are not studying how well a tool fits to a physical environment. We should not use a test situation strictly imitating natural science laboratory experiments. Instead we should use an inquiry situation, which permits closeness to investigated phenomena and with possibilities to see meaning relationships rather then causal relationships. It must be possible to reconstruct flaws and effectiveness of the method. We must arrange for interpretation and reconstruction.

The arguments above points at mainly using real life cases for method tests. This has been done in our research. We have studied the method in use in some real change analysis projects. Scientifically we have used a multi-methodological approach with a combination of different empirical observation methods as participant observation, interviewing and document collecting. (15)

The method has been used in different kinds of change analysis applications. Some of them are listed below:
- Changes in an accounting system due to orga-
  nizational decentralization (airline company)

- Administration and distribution of large paper rolls (paper producing company).
- Regional development of transportation and container management (several industries and transportation companies).

Some important experiences from method use are:

- Problem analysis (with problem graphs) is very powerful to reach an understanding of different problematic situations.
- The role of the analyst is very important for getting the participants ("users") to take an active part in the CA-work.
- People are usually not accustomed to participate in a presuppositionless problem analysis. It takes time to escape from a solution oriented work.
- The methodology must be implemented in a CA-situation well integrated with adequate forms of cooperation.
- The descriptions of problems, goals and change requirements form a good basis and frame for a creative development of change proposals.

FOOTNOTES:

1) Confer critique in (5, 13)

2) This follows critical social theory (10, 12)

3) Bemelmans and Eloranta (3) motivate the importance of this area. They make a survey of different methods but notice the low amount of methods.Cf also (1).

4) Confer Habermas´argumentation (10, 12) that aspects of ideal communication are anticipated in normal communication and discourse.

REFERENCES:

(1) Argelo, S.M., Pitfalls in automation projects, in (2) (1984).

(2) Bemelmans, T., Beyond productivity: Information systems development for organizational effectiveness, North-Holland, Amsterdam (Ed, 1984).

(3) Bemelmans, T. and Eloranta, E, On systelogical design of information systems in (2), (1984).

(4) Berger, P.L. and Luckmann, T., The social construction of reality, Doubleday & Co, Garden City, N.Y. (1967).

(5) Ciborra, C.V., Management information systems: A contractual view in (2) (1984).

(6) Freire, D., Pedagogy of the oppressed, Herder and Herder, New York (1970).

(7) Goldkuhl, G., Human-infological research - framework and strategy, IFIP 8.2 work group meeting 'Frameworks,methods,tools and procedures for user-oriented information systems design, Copenhagen, 1982.

(8) Goldkuhl, G. and Lyytinen, K., Information systems specification as rule reconstruction. in (2).Minneapolis, Aug 22-24, 1983.

(9) Goldkuhl, G. and Röstlinger, A., Förändringsanalys enligt SIM - från problem till förändringsåtgärder, HUMOR, Chalmers Univ of Technology, Göteborg (in Swedish) (1983).

(10) Habermas, J., Communication and the evolution of society, Heinemann, Londond (1979).

(11) Lundeberg, M., Goldkuhl, G., Nilsson, A., Information systems development - a systematic approach, Prentice-Hall, Englewood Cliffs, (1981).

(12) McCarthy, T., The critical theory of Jürgen Habermas, MIT Press, Cambridge, Mass (1978).

(13) Mintzberg, H., Beyond implementation. An analysis of the resistance to policy analysis. IFORS Conference, Toronto, (1978).

(14) Röstlinger, A., Problem analysis - a methodological outline, in Goldkuhl,G,.Kall,C-O., (Eds, 1982) Report from the fifth Scandinavian Research Seminar on Systemeering,Dept of Information Processing, Chalmers Univ of Technology, Göteborg (1982).

(15) Röstlinger, A. and Selldén, J., How to perform an empirical study on a change analysis method, 6th Scandinavian Research Seminar on Systemeering, Univ of Bergen (1983).

Human-Computer Interaction — INTERACT '84 / B. Shackel (ed.)
Elsevier Science Publishers B.V. (North-Holland)
IFIP, 1985

MICROCOMPUTER INSTALLATIONS IN "COMPUTER-UNTOUCHED" ENVIRONMENTS

László Tolnai

Mihály Csákó

MIKROORG Systems House
Budapest

SZÁMALK Computer Application Co.
Budapest

Just as all over the world, in a rather short time microcomputers have become very popular in Hungary too. Popularity has especially grown in consequence of the fact that several Hungarian companies because of their limited active capital, could not afford to make use of the services of big computer centres.

One of the most considerable public service companies joining the "microcomputerization wave" is the group of Property Management Companies dealing with state-owned properties. About 750 thousand flats, 23 per cent of the whole national dwelling stock, are in state ownership in Hungary; about a quarter of the citizens live in state-owned flats. 470 thousand of these properties can be found in the capital, Budapest, thus the biggest property management organization in the country is here. The structure of the Budapest organization contains 15 District Property Managements /DPM/; each of them controls about 6 to 12 Local Property Managements /LPM/ with 2000-4000 properties in a local area. This organization is in charge of the operation and maintenance of these properties, plans, arranges, and sponsors the renewal of the flats, providing appropriate lodging conditions for the tenants.

The data of all properties are recorded by a central computer but this old system is rather out of date and complic-

ated. LPMs keep a card indexing system with the data of the properties managed; in case of data changes LPM employees update the card file and at the same time fill in a data form. These update forms are monthly collected and sent to the central computer operated by a public computer service called FÜTI. Here the National Property Data Base will be updated with the data of the update forms.

The new system under development will leave the main information channels unaltered but data recording and management will be performed by a hierarchy of computers. In the first period each LPM will be equipped with a microcomputer; so they can store and update the local property data. Changes will be forwarded to the central computer off-line, on a magnetic disk. The final aim is to create a network — through several development stages — in which the central computer /FÜTI/ is on the top of the hierarchy, connected on-line via minis at the medium level /DPMs/ to the bottom level micros /LPMs/.

The first version of the system was prepared to TAP-34, the second one to PROPER-8 microcomputers; both are Hungarian-made professional micros suitable for operation as intelligent terminals. Data files stored on floppy disks are made up of 512 bytes long records; one record contains more than 300 data of one property. In recent times tests are

being done with high capacity Winchester
disks as replacements to the multivolume
floppy files, and with compact tape
units as data archives.

The structured program system is written
in standard PASCAL. In the course of
programming the most difficult problem
was the effective handling of the vast
mass of data; this difficulty will disappear in a later stage when minicomp-
uters with high storage capacity will
enter the system. For the time being the
micros and the software are installed at
the Local Property Managements, one by
one. In order to develop application
programs, prepare the data files, provide the LPMs with microcomputers, and
train the personnel FÜTI established a
subsidiary company under the name MIKRO-
ORG.

The education of the employees who will
operate the micro systems is rather insufficient in view of the requirements
of the job. After primary school most of
them attended some sort of courses /e.g.
typing/ or gained a general secondary
school certificate /often in evening
classes/ or became trained in a trade a
long way from property management /e.g.
dressmaker/. Employees with business or
secretary training can seldom be found
among them.

The level of education and the way they
came into possession of it refer to a
specific subcultural background characterized by the following features:
- Almost all of the employees are females
  born in the provinces.
- A remarkable number of them came from
  families of divorced parents and the
  rate of divorced among them is higher
  than the national average.

- Partly due to the facts mentioned, almost all of them faced the serious
  problem of finding dwelling; working
  for a LPM was perhaps the only way to
  solve this problem.

This composition of the personnel is a
result of another fact too: DPMs and
LPMs cannot offer competitive salaries
and work conditions, that is, they cannot employ labour force with higher education and social level.

Knowing these factors, there was no
wonder that - after the first information
- the employees had not any positive
ideas of the changes the computerization
in their work would mean. Only an optim-
istic expectation was revealed in their
vague opinions: "The computer will certainly make easier our work." The lack of
concrete conception can be simply explained: they have never seen a computer,
or only on television.

It is noteworthy that those having a
business school certificate expressed
their expectations in more detailed
terms. Their hopes were:
        - to write less,
        - to calculate less,
        - to keep fewer things in mind,
        - data can be found immediately.

In spite of their curiosity and hopes,
these positive attitudes, only the
younger ones said that they would glad-
ly operate the computer. Older employees
- and the age means here lower education
as well - expected they would use the
computer only in temporary need.

Under such circumstances the software
to be developed was to comply with the
following requirements:

- application with a minimum of keyboard usage;
- function selection with extended menu system;
- detailed textual instructions to be displayed when programs require the operator's intervention or decision;
- but for a sequence of operator receipts data files should be unaccessible to avoid unintentional damage;
- the computer is to accomplish automatically as many operations as possible.

The training of the would-be operators was an extremely important part of the venture: their educational level was always to be kept in mind. On the other hand, their positive attitude helped a lot in surmonting the difficulties. Their training was very detailed, it comprised not only the most important information on the system and its application but gave an outline of the process of development, the problems and their solutions too.

The length of the training course was 27 hours in 3-hour units discussing the following topics:

1. General information on computers and data processing techniques.
2. Information on the hardware to be used.
3. Structure and processes of the Property Management System.
4. Updating the data files.
5. Use of inquiry modules.
6. Use of reporting modules.
7. Recording and processing data of other /than flat/ properties.
8. Tasks in the interim period of changing from card files to the computer-aided work.

More than half of the training period was spent practically training with the computers.

In the course of training we often used some "tricks of temptation", e.g. by means of common analogies we explained the most frequent words of the "computer slang" and then consistently used them. Thus, we practically raised the LPM employees out of the "laymen" and purposfully developed a kind of "pride of trade" in their mind. The feeling of "being initiated" proved to be very stimulating though it required excess efforts as well.

Despite all the careful preparations and very many efforts, our expectations have only been partly realized. Almost at the beginning of the project LPMs showed some opposition, due to two reasons:

/1/ workload on the employees increased, because of the training courses they often left their desks with work undone;

/2/ directors in the LPMs found that there were a lot of other tasks more important to computerize and the system to be installed would not help their work as much as they would have required.

The opposition of the bosses in the LPMs made the courses drag on and caused a change in the attitude of the employees too. They understood that computerization would not reduce their work significantly, on the contrary, in the interim period they would be expected to work with both the old card file and the microcomputer system at the same time. The change in the mood of the employees comprised also the sociologist: they

considered him as one of the programming experts.

Our examination carried out with soft
interview technique and observation revealed strong coherence of the socio-
cultural, sociopsychological, and organizational factors. The reaction of the
organization proved to be a crucial
factor concerning the success of the
project. And yet a most important condition remained unaltered: directors at
the DPMs consider the work very significant and provide full support.
Tensions in the other two factors of
human side have eased: software will
include programs required by the LPM
directors so their opposition is not
really strong any more and the attitude
of the employees has also improved.

Human-Computer Interaction – INTERACT '84 / B. Shackel (ed.)
Elsevier Science Publishers B.V. (North-Holland)
IFIP, 1985

TRAINING FOR SUBJECTION OR PARTICIPATION

Niels Bjørn-Andersen

Information Systems Research Group
Copenhagen School of Economics and Business Administration
10, Julius Thomsens Plads
DK-1925 Copenhagen V, Denmark

The work role is undergoing substantial changes when new microelectronic systems are introduced in the office and the factory. Based on a recent study of changes in work role in eight Danish companies, the training offered for this future work role is discussed.

Most training programs made available in these and other companies for users are oriented towards making the user appreciate and operate the systems. In other words, subjection to the system.

However, alternative training programs could be designed in order to allow the users to participate in the design, i.e. to evaluate equipment and to maintain, modify and even design new systems. This is illustrated in a project within local government, which turned out to be very successful for the organization. The training program and some of the methods used are described and discussed.

1. INTRODUCTION

Introduction of new technology has always been accompanied by predictions and analyses of the extent to which workers will experience a dequalification or a requalification and, following from that, the educational requirements necessary to work with the new technology. Silbermann concluded in 1966 that "New technology is exerting far less impact than has been assumed on the kinds of work men do and the amount of education and skill they need to do it." However, 17 years have passed since the citation from Silbermann appeared and the R & D investments in that period are almost of the same magnitude as all R & D (1) investments from the industrial revolution until 1966.

Many observers see the introduction of microelectronics as causing major changes in the work role and indeed in our whole life as reflected in concepts as "Second Industrial Revolution" or "Third Wave" (2).

In the middle of the sea fog from the third wave, there is an obvious interest in assessing whether Silbermann's original thesis still holds true or whether major changes will take place in relation to an increased use of microelectronics. This issue has primarily been discussed in relation to the concepts of requalification or dequalification of the work force.

The requalification hypothesis is often supported by manufacturers and management and may be expressed by the words of Drucker (3): "... Little doubt that automation means a tremendous upgrading of the labour force in terms of skills, employment, standard of living and opportunity." Some support for this hypothesis is found in a number of studies in the office as well as on the shop floor (4, 5).

On the other hand there is also convincing support for the hypothesis of dequalification. Bright formulates a hierarchy of 18 levels of automation from a work situation without any tools to completely automated machinery, and he argues that workers will experience an increase in work qualifications when moving from hand tools to different types of machinery but that the demands on their qualifications will drop to an even lower level when they move towards the automated factory (6). Even though one might argue that work in offices has not yet reached the turning point when dequalification sets in, many reports on the impact of microelectronics point to jobs being dequalified (7, 8, 9, 10).

Our conclusion from these seemingly very contradictory evaluations in the literature of the impact of technology on qualification structures can be summarized in the following points:

1. We have yet to see the tremendous increase in skill requirements predicted by many optimists.

2. Microelectronics is an abstract technology which has very few deterministic features in itself. It also has no value unless, somewhere down the line, it results in the fulfillment of some human needs. Accordingly we shall see very different impacts on qualification structures depending on the type of application and on the strategic choice of systems characteristics.

3. If microelectronics is applied in order to meet fairly narrow efficiency objectives, this will normally result in

   - a high level of automation

- a systems design aiming at the use of
  the cheapest labour (normally the
  lowest skilled)

- a systems design aiming at a high
  degree of substitution between workers

In order to get a better understanding of the
role of education/training in the innovation
processes related to the introduction of new
technology, a three-country empirical study
was launched by the European Centre for the
Development of Vocational Traninng (CEDEFOP).
The total results are reported elsewhere (11).
Below some wider implications are discussed,
especially related to future work role and educational requirements as a prerequisite for
change.

2. CHANGING WORK ROLE

The increased use of microelectronics and production equipment based on microelectronis will
gradually change the work role from manual work
to more intellectual work. Tasks will be carried
out (semi-)automatically as more and more information is processed in the machine (12). Man is
left with the challenging task of designing the
machine and with the routine task of monitoring
it. The extent to which that has taken place in
eight Danish companies is briefly summarized
below.

2.1 Employment

The application of microelectronics in the eight
companies studied has been for process innovations and not for product innovations. This
means that microelectronics has been used primarily to increase the efficiency in the production of products and services, i e to produce the same product with reduced consumption
of material, energy, and labour. One striking
example is from the food sector where a new-
built highly automated factory can produce the
same amount of goods with only 40 per cent of
the work force necessary in a conventional plant.
In the other companies there had been little or
no reductions in staff accompanying the introduction of the new system. In all cases, however, the new system meant that existing staff
was able to produce more goods/services than
before.

In general it is assumed that jobs lost in direct operations are gained in the maintenance
field. That was not supported in our study. We
found for example within the office equipment
sector that product innovations were very much
oriented towards simplifying the maintenance
task to just plugging in a new microprocessor.
Cooley (13) similarly describes how the new UK
telephone exchanges "X-25" are provided with
self-diagnostic error facilities reducing the
need for skilled maintenance personnel. This
supports hypotheses to the effect that

"In the past, substituting equipment for
human skill has increased the number of

maintenance personnel, but this will no
longer be true. Microelectronics is intended
to cut the number of maintenance workers and
to reduce their power." (14)

In spite of the short period of our study, we
find support for the hypothesis that companies
use the great potential of microelectronics
first and foremost for improving their overall
effectiveness through making their organisation
more efficient through cutting costs. This could
of course be due to the economic recession. Perhaps the main focus of most innovations will
change in an economic boom. However, taking into
consideration the nature of the microelectronic
technology we would expect that the main applications also in the future would be in the area
of process innovations (substituting human
labour) rather than product innovations (creating more jobs through the creation of "new
products").

2.2 Job function

It is generally assumed that in the long run
there will be a change in the job functions
leading from executing to monitoring, i e from
manually or tool assisted tasks to a supervisory task of controlling that something is
carried out more or less automatically. In all
of the studies the change brought about by the
introduction of the (new) microelectronically-
based system was a small step in that direction.
Except in one case, the change was moderate
and affected only parts of the tasks of the employee. This will gradually lead to new demands
being made on the employees. Vieum summarizes
the "new" qualifications of the operators mentioned in literature:

- attention (15)
- alertness (16)
- interpret information quickly (16)
- responsibility (17, 18)
- knowledge about process (19)
- ability to assessment and choice making
  (20)
- concentration (18)
- analytical ability (21, 22)

These abilities, however, are of a fairly general nature and in our relatively brief study
it was not possible to assess the extent to
which these qualifications would be necessary
or the extent to which these were more in demand
than before. What we did find, however, was
that the education/training necessary to carry
out the tasks of operating the new system were
very limited. In almost all cases, the operators
were able to work with the new pieces of equipment after a couple of days. In our opinion,
this goes to show that the demands were restricted to some very simple instructions on how
to operate the new piece of machinery. The upgrading of skills of the operators which the
training seems to indicate is only a transi-
tional phenomenon which should be seen in the
more long-term historical tendency towards

deskilling. Accordingly we may cautiously conclude that, if anything, the new technology is easier and less demanding to operate than the old one and that any upgrading of jobs must be sought in maintenance, programming, and design functions.

2.3 Specialization

The division of labour has been a predominant feature in the Western society and is one of the cornerstones in raising the material prosperity. But at the same time, division of labour carries its costs in the form of narrowly defined, deskilled jobs creating alienation. New technology plays a major role in defining the level of specialisation, and many studies of the impact of new technology have concentrated on identifying the degree to which the level of specialization has changed. Some studies of impact of technology on the shop floor point in the direction of specialization (9, 13, 17) and the same tendency is found in studies of office technology (23).

The present study in eight companies does not support these findings. In the offices, we found a clear division of labour between the operators (clerks) and the designers of the system (programmers). But contrary to earlier studies the tasks of the operators had generally been enlarged, i e the operator was carrying out more different tasks than before. The reason was twofold. Firstly the system took away some of the routine tasks (automated e g typing) leaving the operator more time for other things. Secondly, so much information and so much standardization had been incorporated into the system that an operator almost without any training could sit down and carry out tasks which previously required more extensive training, decision competence etc. Job enlargement has occurred as many small tasks are simplified and easier to handle. The microprocessor system guides the operator through series of pre-programmed instructions.

On the shop floor the tendency to specialize seems larger. Three distinct clusters of functions emerged in our study:

  - operator functions (unskilled jobs where the main tasks consist in mounting objects on the CNC machine, in starting the flow production, in carrying out monitoring and control functions, and in calling somebody when deviations from norms occur)
  - maintenance functions (skilled jobs, servicing the machines and carrying out minor repairs according to, to a large extent, predescribed procedures)
  - programming and repair functions (technicians/engineers who can repair, program, and modify the equipment)

In the companies studied we found a polarization between these three groups of functions, a ten-

dency which is supported in other empirical studies reported by the European Trade Union Institute (24) and Braverman (8) who concludes that

> "The mass of workers have nothing to gain from the fact that a decline in their command of the labour process is more than compensated for by the increasing demand on the part of managers and engineers."

In our opinion the specialization and polarization is a result of a strategic choice rather than an expression of technological determinism. Several job design projects have been launched in the Scandinavian countries proving that it is possible to enlarge and enrich jobs on CNC machines and in office equipment with modern office technology.

2. Own control

Almost all interviewees said that they now had a better overview of the production and the work process. The information system had made the work process more transparent and they were better able to trace missing orders, to discover malfunctions, to make a new print-out etc. This is also supported in other studies (25).

This does not mean that the individuals feel capable of correcting the faults, or explaining why something has gone wrong. The reason is that the level of understanding has not increased. Almost in all cases did the operators and others complain that the education provided was not adequate and that their level of understanding of what was happening had decreased. Almost all microprocessor-based systems were perceived as very complex and the operators were not aware of the consequences of not following the prescribed procedures. In one office system we were told by the operator that there were three keys on the terminal that she was not allowed to touch. She was not told what would happen if whe did - and she had not ventured to try!

In the shop floor situations the lack of understanding meant that operators in general could not make the error diagnosis themselves let alone carry out the repair. Experts/technicians had to be called in.

3. TRAINING PROVIDED

In all of the eight companies studied, some training was provided in order for the staff to handle the new technology. For the operators it varied between a few hours and a couple of days with the exception of the company where a completely new factory was built. In this case the training took approx. 40 days as the employees also had to be introduced to the company at large.

The training provided was not always perceived as adequate but a distinction has to be made between short and long-term needs. In three of the eight companies the training was perceived

as inadequate in the short run, e g in a company
where only half of the operators were sent on a
course and then told to teach the rest of the
group when they came home. It is quite obvious
why this was perceived as inadequate even for
operating the present system in the short run.

In the long run employees in most of the companies found that the training provided did not
meet their needs. The objectives of the training
exercises were restricted to general awareness/
information material on a very superficial level
and some detailed instructions on how to operate
the machine or the system. This was satisfactory
for carrying out the pre-programmed tasks but
did not provide a sound basis for handling unstructured situations nor did it provide a
platform for modifications of the system to suit
future needs.

The long-term implications of this are devasta-
ting. Staff is getting the right to participate
in the decisions about the acquisitions of new
technology but they are not given the training
background for participating in these decisions.

In relation to the innovation decisions on new
technology one might define a skill hierarchy
going from the lowest level of accepting a new
system to the highest level of actually designing it:

- appreciate the system	low
- operate the system	
- observe malfunctions	
- start and stop procedures	
- regular service	educational level
- simple maintenance	
- diagnose faults	
- repair	
- program, make modifications	
- design new system	high

As indicated, the educational requirements get
higher as we move down the list. All the training programmes in the companies visited were
oriented towards training for the first three
to four levels while different types of experts
were relied upon to handle the latter tasks.
This is obviously related to the specialization
and polarization registered in the companies
where the staff saw the systems as black boxes.

Furthermore, in none of the companies, training
was provided which would enable the staff to
evaluate the consequences for the work organization of the new system. To meet that demand,
which is included in the technology agreements,
training will have to be intensified as well as
broadened in scope to take the human/organiza-
tional aspects into account in the design process. Staff will then be able to play an active
role in evaluating, controlling and exploiting
the new technological developments (9, 26).

When training is only oriented towards making
staff appreciate/operate the new technology, it
hampers the long-run flexibility of the organization because the organization will go from its

unfrozen stage created in relation to the new
system to another frozen stage. A few years
later, when another system is to be introduced,
the organization must unfreeze again with all
the efforts and risks entailed. While a very
limited training seems sufficient for "getting
the production rolling", it does not provide
a platform for change. Only a training aiming
at mastering the technology in a democratic
form gives the organization the capability to
innovate.

Training will thus serve a dual purpose: the
purpose of performing the day-to-day operation
of the technology where the aim would be in the
direction of job-enlargement and job-enrichment
and the democratic purpose of enabling staff to
participate in the design/development of new
types/versions of systems. Such a training
should focus on understanding (verstehen), i e
the ability to formulate problems, to plan, to
program, to take into account complex issues,
etc. Furthermore, it should take place in a
pedagogical form based on open communication,
co-operation, group work and cross-disciplinary
problem solving.

4.   TRAINING PROGRAM FOR PARTICIPATION

As an alternative to the fairly poor technically oriented training programs provided in the
eight companies investigated, I present below
elements in a participation strategy for the
introduction of computer systems and office
automation within local government.

Our research unit was called upon to give advice
to five small municipalities as to how they
should solve their computing task in the future.
More specifically we were asked whether they
should acquire a minicomputer jointly or
separately. Our reply was that although we
could provide this kind of advice based on the
current and foreseeable technological development, we would rather assist these municipalities by providing them with the training necessary for carrying out a socio-technical analysis
by themselves.

A full account of the project is given elsewhere (26), and I shall only provide a brief
account of the training program offered and the
tools for carrying out organizational analysis.

4.1 Initial training program

In order to enable the participants to carry
out analysis and specifications of requirements
of a new information system and its organizational environment, it is necessary to provide
employees and other participants with some education (see also (27)). This education focuses
on analysis tools and methodologies for working
and incorporating these tools.

The program for the three-day course is shown
in figure 1. As to the content, it is worth
noting that technological issues make up a

COURSE IN ADMINISTRATIVE PLANNING AND SYSTEMS DEVELOPMENT
(illustrated by the course program actually used in five municipalities)

Objective

The objective of the course is to provide the participants with an increased knowledge of planning and analysis techniques and the possibilities and constraints of the developments in information technology. On termination of the course, the participants should be able to carry out requirements specification of new information systems using experts as consultants.

PROGRAM -1st Day

Introduction to the course
- presentation and discussion of the program

The development of information technology in general
- hardware and software developments
- functions of information technology
- facts and fiction of actual possibilities

Typical systems relevant to the user situation
- systems development strategies within the public sector
- types of systems within municipal management

Municipal experience hitherto with mini-computers
- field of application
- consequences
- plans for further development
- strategies pursued by systems suppliers

Group work 1: Framing of questions to Computer Service Bureau regarding development plans etc.

Presentation by Computer Service Bureau
- strategies, products, service to municipalities

Plenary discussion of these development plans etc.

PROGRAM - 2nd Day

The consequences of computer systems
- the impact of computer systems on jobs and organizations

Group work 2: Discussion of the consequences of existing computer systems on the participants' own jobs within the municipal administration

Plenary discussion of consequences already perceived

Job analysis - job design
- methods of analysing the job situation (see fig. 2)

Group work 3: Analysis of present job situations desirable characteristics of future job situations

Plenary discussion of desirable job content characteristics

PROGRAM - 3rd Day

Systems work, requirements specifications
- phases, methods and tools (wall-graph method)

Project work in general
- principles
- practical approaches and empirical results
- user participation in systems work

Plans for future activities
- summary of municipal analyses and joint meetings so far
- types of tasks to be attached
- the future role of the consultants (only on call)

Group work 4: Proposals for plans of activities (objective, definition, organization of work, methods applied, time and resource plan), defined by participants

Plenary discussion of plans of activities

Figure 1.

rather small part and that we spend more time on issues like organizational consequences of information systems and on organizational analysis relative to requirements specification.

However, a socio-technical strategy with a high degree of user particiaption will not work unless there is a certain level of consensus on values between management and employees and between the different employee groups. Many employees are afraid of the technological development and resist change. They are even afraid that the socio-technical design strategy with a high degree of user participation is

just another way of deceiving the employees.
Accordingly, discussions on values of management and change agents must be taken during a
course like this.

Furthermore we want the employees to critically
evaluate proposals from vendors, something
which demands self-consciousness - the feeling
that "we are able to carry out the analysis ourselves". It is thus mandatory to make sure that
participants in the course get this feeling of
self-reliance.

The objectives of the three-day course are best
achieved if the course is held outside of the
work place with overnight accomodation facilities. This provides extra time for informal
discussions and contributes towards making this
course a kind of organizational development
exercise.

Similar training programs have been carried
out in a number of organizations including
The Copenhagen Business School as a supplement
to the technical programs offered by vendors.

The evaluation of the training program has been
very positive on the participant as well as on
the municipal level. Approximately half of the
employees felt that they themselves and the
municipality in general have an improved
ability to evaluate the utilization of existing
systems, to evaluate new proposals and to plan
and implement new systems.

On the municipal level, three activities were
started after the project had been terminated.
The first was to organize seminars on word processing in order to provide knowledge and discuss the implementation of word-processing
systems. These seminars were organized by the
word-processing working group itself on the
basis of the experience gained in the project.

The second main activity was the establishment
of a seven-person joint computing steering
committee for the five municipalities. This
committee was given very high status with three
politicians, two municipal executive officers,
one section head, and a trade union shop
steward as members.

The third activity was to establish a computing
group in each of the five municipalities
which could coordinate activities on data processing and office automation. These groups reported to the joint steering committee.

The total results of the project can be summarized in the following points:

- organizational and social issues are
  evaluated alongside with the economic
  ones, when new information systems are
  planned,

- there is a very high degree of consensus
  on new systems based on more qualified
  discussions among employees,

- implementation of new systems is much
  easier than before,

- there is now a development organization
  capable of handling almost any technical
  change,

- the general strategy for requirements
  analysis has been pursued since, and
  everybody seems happy with it.

4.2 Framework for organizational requirement specification

One of the important elements in the three-day
course was the method for specifying organizational requirements.

Previously, one of the main difficulties has
been a lack of an adequate language for talking
about the organizational environment of a system.

This need was perceived by, among others, the
Swedish Datadelegation, a Government committee,
which commissioned me to outline such a framework. The result was published recently (28).
The main idea is simple. Based on a very large
survey of studies of the impact of information
systems on organizations, we have identified
the 14 dimensions of a job which are potentially changed when a new information system is
introduced (see figure 2).

To give an example: One such dimension is
"degree of specialization". A particular task
like telephone sales may be handled by many
employees, each taking care of only one sub-
task (e.g. receipt of order, check whether
goods are in stock, check solidity of customer,
settle accounts, etc.). Alternatively one employee may perform the full task from receiving
the order to following up on the customer's
payment.

For each of the 14 dimensions we have given an
example, as far as possible from real-life
application, as to what constitutes the two
ends of the dimension. When working with the
specification of organizational requirements
of a particular application, the design group
is then recommended to use this list as a check
list and specify where, on each dimension, their
future system ideally should be. Preferably,
they should illustrate it by giving a concrete
description of e.g. the degree of specialization which will be preferable. This forms the
basis for the specification of systems characteristics.

5. CONCLUSION

It has been illustrated how the work role is
changing as a result of the introduction of
information systems.

To a very large extent these changes are not
planned for and happen by accident.

Companies which have experienced these problems are looking to socio-technical design
strategies with a high degree of user participation.

However, participation is little more than
hostage-taking, if the users are not given
a training over and above the technical
training traditionally offered by systems
vendors. This training is first and foremost
oriented towards appreciation and operation of
the system.

More elaborate training programs are called
for in order that users may be trained to
understand, evaluate and even design systems.
The content of such a program is suggested and
one of the key tools for organizational requirement specification is described.

It is my firm belief that only training
programs of the above-mentioned type with a
large element of organizational development
will provide a platform for change in the
future.

FRAMEWORK FOR SPECIFICATION OF ORGANIZATIONAL REQUIREMENTS

A. Job content

Strongly specialized job	Varied, enlarged job
Polarized division of work	No division of work
Structured pre-programmed work	Methods and sequence of subtask is free
Norm or rule-oriented behaviour	Consequence-oriented behaviour

B. Autonomy and control

Monitoring of work performance	No monitoring of performance
Much stress	No stress
No influence on own job	Total self-control
No influence on company issues	Large influence on company issues

C. Social relations

No job security	Total job security
No possibility of self-actualization	Great possibility of self-actualization
Working alone all day	All work done in contact with others
Alienated	Well integrated

D. Personal development

| No training demands | Many training demands |
| No personal development | High rate of personal development |

Figure 2.

REFERENCES:

(1) Silberman, Ch.E., The Myths of Automation (New YorK, 1966).

(2) Toffler, A., The Third Wave (William Collins Sons, USA, 1980).

(3) Veium, K., Ny teknologi og kvalifikationer - hva vet vi? (Institut for Industriell Miljøforskning, Trondheim, 1980).

(4) Edwards, S., The Urgency of Education (New Scientist, June 8, 1978, p.656-657).

(5) Jessup, G., Techology as if People Mattered (Paper presented at ILO symposium "New Trends in the Optimisation of the Working Environment", May 1978).

(6) Bright, J.R., Automation and Management, Division of Research (Graduate School of Business Administration, Harvard University, 1958).

(7) Albons, B., E. Gunnarsson & I. Söderberg, På vinst och förlust, rapport om datorisering i USA (Stockholm, 1981).

(8) Braverman, H., Labor and Monopoly Capital: The Degradation of Work in the Twentieth Century (Monthly Review Press, Chicago, 1964).

(9) DUE, Klubarbejde og edb (DUE report no. 4, Århus, 1981).

(10) Sandberg, Å. (ed.), Computers Dividing Man and Work (Arbetslivscentrum, Stockholm, 1979).

(11) McDerment, W.G. (ed.), Microelectronics and Informatics Technology and Their Training Implications in Firms (CEDEFOP, Berlin, 1983).

(12) Galjaard, J.H., A Technologybased Nation (Science and Technology Policy Research Group, Interuniversity Institute of Management, Delft, 1981).

(13) Cooley, M., Architecht or Bee (CAITS, Slough, 1980)

(14) CSE Microelectronics Group, Microelectronics, Capitalist Technology and the Working Class (London, 1980).

(15) Faunce, W.A., Problems of an Industrial Society (McGraw-Hill, New York, 1968).

(16) Davis, L.E., The Effects of Automation on Job Design (Industrial Relations, vol. 2, Oct. 1962, p. 53-71).

(17) Blauner, R., Alienation and Freedom: The Factory Worker and his Industry (University of Chicago Press, Chicago, 1964).

(18) Fine, S.A., The Nature of Automated Jobs and their Educational Requirements (McLean, Virgina, 1964).

(19) Slocum, J.W. & H.P. Sims, A Typology for Integrating Technology, Organization, and Job Design (Human Relation, vol. 33, 1980, p. 193-212).

(20) Friedman, G., Industrial Society. The Emergence of Human Consequences of Automation (Illinois, 1955).

(21) Walker, Ch.R., Life in the Automated Factory (Harvard Business Review, vol. 36, 1958, p. 111-119).

(22) Crossman, E.R., Automation and Skill (Dept. of Scientific and Industrial Research, HMSO, London, 1960).

(23) Bjørn-Andersen, N., B. Hedberg, D. Mercer, E. Mumford & A. Solé, The Impact of Systems Change in Organisations (Sijthoff & Noordhoff, Alphen aan den Rijn, 1979).

(24) European Trade Union Institute, The Impact of Microelectronics on Employment in Western Europe in the 1980s (Brussels, 1979).

(25) Bjørn-Andersen, N., K. Eason & D. Robey, The Challenges of Information Systems to Management (Samfundslitteratur, Copenhagen, 1984).

(26) Bjørn-Andersen, N. & T. Skousen, A Strategy for User Control of Systems Development - Illustrated by a Local Government Case (IFA, Copenhagen Business School, Copenhagen, 1981).

(27) Mumford, E. & Henshall, D., A Participative Approach to Computer-Systems Design (Business Allied Press, London, 1979).

(28) Arnberg, B. & Bjørn-Andersen, N., Computerization and Work (Datadelegationen, 1983).

Human-Computer Interaction — INTERACT '84 / B. Shackel (ed.)
Elsevier Science Publishers B.V. (North-Holland)
© IFIP, 1985

WORK ORGANISATION IMPLICATIONS OF WORD PROCESSING

S.M. Pomfrett, C.W. Olphert and K.D. Eason

The HUSAT Research Group,
Department of Human Sciences
Loughborough University of Technology.

This paper describes a study which aimed a) to classify the forms of work organisation used for word processing and b) to evaluate responses of job holders and organisations towards the different forms. The paper concludes that the picture of the use of word processing is a complex one with more and more pluralistic forms of work organisation being employed. There does not appear to be a strong relationship between the form of work organisation and the job satisfaction of operators or the satisfaction of authors with the service they receive. Organisations which adopted a mixture of forms of working tended to be more satisfied with their word processing than those which used only 'small group' working arrangements; these in turn were more satisfied than organisations which used only word processing 'pools'.

1. INTRODUCTION

This paper describes a two year study which was funded by the Social Science Research Council.

Much has been said and written about the 'office of the future' and many predictions have been made about the implications of the rapidly changing new technology on office work. Word processing is the element of the 'office of the future' which has been most readily taken on board by organisations across the land.

Despite the abundance of speculative articles, both serious and 'pop', little seems to be known about what is actually happening as a result of using word processors and what effect the technology is having on the jobs of those involved.

Previous research (1) found that word processing was being used in different ways and that each way had advantages and disadvantages. The research pointed towards a range of forms of work organisation which might exist along an integration/differentiation continuum.

INTEGRATION
1) One man operation; author as typist
2) One author to one operator
3) Group of authors to one operator
4) Centralised system with the operators performing all word processing for the group of authors
5) Centralised system with task specialisation, e.g. printing, editing, checking etc.

DIFFERENTIATION

Figure 1 : Possible variations of forms of work organisation for word processing

The study described here uses and extends the idea of using such a continuum.

2. OBJECTIVES OF THE STUDY

This study had the aims of discovering a) what forms of work organisation are presently used for word processing, b) why the specific form of work organisation used was chosen and c) what effects different forms of work organisation have on word processor users (including authors) and on the organisations themselves.

More formally, the research set out to test the following primary hypotheses:

- that the more differentiated the form of work organisation the more negative the attitudes of the job holders(i.e. both authors and operators)

- that the more differentiated forms of work organisation result from design processes that do not include the active and effective participation of users.

3. METHODOLOGY

In order to test these hypotheses the work was split into two stages:

Phase I : The classification of forms of work organisation

Phase II : The evaluation of responses to forms of work organisation

The methodology used in each stage will be described separately.

3.1   The Classification of Forms of Work Organisation

Over the period of approximately one year (Summer 1982 – Summer 1983) a questionnaire was sent to over 200 organisations in the UK known to use word processing. A letter was sent with the questionnaire which explained the project and invited participation. A total of

92 completed questionnaires were returned from
a wide variety of organisations.

The questionnaire was divided into 6 sections :
- technical description of the system
- the organisation served by the word
  processor
- the work of the system
- work organisation
- system development (to date)
- future development

Organisations taking part in phase I were also
asked if they would like to participate in the
second stage.

The Unit of Analysis

It was not appropriate to use an entire
organisation as the unit of investigation.
Likewise at the other end of the scale to focus
on a single word processing system or installation would not have been useful. Instead, the
focus was on the community of users served by
a word processing system or systems for a
specific application. This was called an
'organisational unit'. The concept was still
difficult to use as the borders of an 'organisational unit' were sometimes fuzzy but it has
been a useful unit to use nonetheless.

Sampling

In order to be able to generalise any findings,
it was desirable to include different sizes and
types of organisational unit in the   phase I
survey. It was not possible for practical
reasons to control the sample tightly but
partial control was achieved by sending out
questionnaires in batches over time rather than
in one mailshot.

In phase II the available choice of sample was
limited to those organisational units willing
to take part. Endeavours were made to include
units from the major categories of work
organisation and also to include a range of
sizes of unit. It was ensured that some public
organisations were involved.

3.2   The Evaluation of Responses to Forms of
         Work Organisation

In the second stage, initially three word
processing applications were chosen as pilot
sites where the measures developed were tested
and refined. Then 17 more sites out of those
willing to participate were chosen as a sample
of the types of work organisation found in
stage 1.

Staff at each site were interviewed using
structured and semi-structured interviews as
described below.

An Evaluation by Authors

A sample of the users of the word processing
service were interviewed employing an adapted
version of instruments developed and used
previously by the authors of this paper. In
this way, the authors of material for word

processing evaluated 'task match' (the extent
to which the service meets task needs in terms of
accuracy, speed etc) and 'ease of use' (the
acceptability of the effort required of the user
to employ the service).

The authors also gave an assessment of their
involvement in the design/development process
and attitudes towards other forms of work
organisation were investigated.

The Job Satisfaction of Operators

Structured interviews were used to establish
areas of job satisfaction and disatisfaction
of a sample of operators. Part of the interview
emphasised work directly related to word
processing and part focussed on the job in
general. (The latter was based on the Requisite
Task Attribute Index of Turner and Lawrence.)
The operators were also interviewed with regard
to the design/development process and their
involvement in it.

('Author-operators' were interviewed as both
authors and operators using a special interview
structure.)

An Evaluation by Management/Designers

In order to obtain a more complete picture,
the evaluations of operators and authors were
complemented by semi-structured interviews
with the management and /or someone responsible
for the purchase and development of the
installation. The evaluation in this case was
in terms of organisational effectiveness.

4.   FINDINGS

4.1 Classification of Forms of Work Organisation

The different forms of work organisation which
were identified in this study are described
below.

Author-operator

This is where the originator or manipulator of
the text to be processed actually operates
the equipment himself.

One to One Relationship Between Author and Operator

In this situation, one operator works with the
system on behalf of one specific author. The
operator may perform other functions apart
from word processing. More than one working
'pair' may exist in the organisational unit.

Small Work Groups

One or two (occasionally more than two)
operators process work for a small group of
authors who usually work in a team or department
and have similar or associated functions. Each
operator may be called upon to work for a number
(if not all) of the authors and does not have
an exclusive relationship with just one. A
number of such small groups may exist within
one organisational unit. Again operators may

also perform other secretarial/clerical/admin-
istration tasks.

Pools
This is where a number of operators serve a
large number of authors. The boundary between
a large 'small group' and a small 'pool' may be
difficult to distinguish. Apart from size, it is
usually the case that the authors are not closely
associated in pool arrangements and that the
pool itself becomes an organisational entity,
e.g. a department or section. A small group is
likely to remain a part of an organisational
entity. Once more, it is possible that operators
perform other tasks apart from word processing.

A few complex variations were identified involving for example task specialisation within a
pool, e.g. some operators woul type in first
drafts while others dealt with amendments.

Out of the 92 responses received in this study,
64 organisational units (70%) said that they
used one of the forms of work organisation
outlined above. The remaining 30% however,
used 2 or more different forms.

Number of Organisational Units	Forms of Work Organisation
32	Small groups
31	Pools
15	* Mixtures with small groups
11	* Mixtures with pools
2	Mixture of author-operator and one to one relationships
1	One to one relationships

Figure 2 : Frequency of forms of work
organisation

* The two major categories with mixtures
require further explanation.

The cases which used mixtures with pools
employed a pool or pools and at least one other
more integrated form of work organisation. This
could include small groups. The cases which
used mixtures with small groups employed a small
group or groups and at least one other more
integrated form. These mixtures did not use
pools.

4.2 Other Findings from the Survey
The survey conducted in Phase 1 revealed many
other interesting findings, some of which are
outlined below.

Predictably, there was a relationship between
form of work organisationand size of organisational unit. The pools are found more frequently in large organisational units than are
the small groups and small groups are found
more in small organisational units. The trend
is the same although not as strong for the 2
main types of mixture.

More organisational units introduced word
processing in order to improve turnround time
or achieve greater flexiblity than to
reduce staff or other costs.

Benefit	% of organisational units expecting benefits
Improved turnaround	86
Greater flexiblity	75
Better use of staff	67
Services to authors	54
Reduced manning	49
Other(indirect) costs	15

Figure 3 : Expected benefits

In the majority of cases, the expected benefits
were acheived. Those units which had expected
improved turnaround, greater flexiblity and
improved services to authors were more likely
to acheive the benefits sought than were those
seeking the other improvements.

The trend in work organisation seems to be
towards small groups or the mixtures of work
organisation.

Form of work organisation	% of units not anticipating change
Small groups	18
Pools	8
Small group mixtures	28
Pool mixtures	18

Figure 4 : Organisational units not anticipating
change

The results suggest that organisational units
with pools are least satisfied with the
status quo. 20% of organisational units with
mixtures were planning organisational change
compared with 34% of units with small groups
and 44% of units with pools.

The majority of units with pools who were
anticipating organisational change saw the
change being towards a situation with pools
and other forms of working.

For the organisational units with small groups,
the majority could see a change to pool
mixtures or small group mixtures.

For both these sets, a move towards more
author-operation was also envisaged.

4.3 Relationship of work organisation to job
     holders' satisfaction

The first hypothesis explored in Phase II of
the study was that the form of work organisation
adopted would have an effect on the level of
satisfaction of job holders.   In particular,
the literature on job design and job satisfaction
implies that the more integrated forms of work
organisation might give rise to higher job
satisfaction than the more differentiated forms.

The sample of 20 field sites did not include any
examples of the extremely differentiated form
shown in Figure 1 (i.e. one in which there was
centralisation with task specialisation), and
only one case of the most integrated form (i.e.
author as operator).   The sample was divided
as follows:

Work Organisation	No. of Sites
Small Groups	7
Mixed (Small Group & Pool)	3
Mixed (Small Group & Other)	3
Pool	6
Other	1

Figure 5: Types of Work Organisation
          in Phase II Field Sites

Analysis of the results showed only a minor
trend for operators and authors to be less
satisfied where word processing was organised in
pools than in the other forms encountered.
There appear to be other, more important factors
than work organisation alone which affect the
satisfaction of job holders with word processing.

4.4 Other factors influencing job satisfaction

If job satisfaction is not directly influenced
by the form of work organisation, then what
factors do seem to be important?   There appear
to be different factors influencing the satisfaction of authors and operators, as well as
the satisfaction of the organisation itself with
the effectiveness of word processing.   Some of
these factors will be discussed for each of the
groups concerned.

4.4.1 Author satisfaction

Perhaps the critical factor for author satisfaction is the closeness of the author-operator
relationship. In all sites where word processing
was organised in small groups, authors' expressed
satisfaction with the word processing service
was high or fairly high. By contrast, in the
sites with pools only, author satisfaction varied
between very high and very low, even at the same
site.   Low ratings appeared to be due in many
cases to a perceived mismatch between authors'
needs and expectations of the service and the
facilities they thought were available from the

word processing service.   This perceived mismatch persisted when there was a lack of
communication of authors' needs to the word
processor operators or the supervisor.

However, whilst this communication gap did
cause problems, few problems seemed to occur
for authors when word processing and typing
services were fully integrated, with allocation
of work to one process or the other being done
by their secretary or a supervisor.   Several
authors commented that they did not need to know
what happened to their work, they were merely
concerned with the end result - especially
the quality, accuracy and speed of turnaround
time of the work.

A long turnaround time is, in fact, one source
of frustration for authors which is more likely
to occur when work is processed in a pool.
Authors often attribute delays to poor scheduling of work in the pool, but it is equally often
due to poor indications of priority given by
them.   All authors tend to say that their work
should have high priority, but when the work is
sent to a pool someone has to take a decision
about which of many "high priority" pieces of
work should be dealt with first.

Long turnaround time may not be a problem for
authors whose word processing work is handled
by a small group, but a particular problem in
these cases can occur if secretaries have to
be away from their normal workstations for long
periods of time to operate the word processor.

Training is an important issue when any form of
new office technology is introduced, but contrary to the findings of another recently-
published research study (2), there was no
evidence from authors in this survey of a strong
desire for more author training.   Although
many acknowledged that word processing was
probably not exploited to its full potential,
most felt that better operator training was
more important than training for themselves.
This finding is supported by the fact that more
than half of the operators who participated in
this survey said that their training on word
processors had only been "adequate" or worse.

Operator training is one area where the form
of work organisation has an effect, since it
can have a bearing on the frequency and variety
of opportunities which they have to put their
training into practice.   In a small group
situation (i.e. with operators in a traditional
secretarial role), the workload may not be
high enough for operators to become very familiar with different facilities.   In one case,
for example, operators only used the word processor once a month to produce a particular
document.   In pools, on the other hand, word
processor usage is normally migh higher and
operators may be under pressure to produce
large volumes of certain types of documents,
without having the opportunity to experiment
and practice with different facilities.

Authors could help this situation by ensuring that operators have some time to "play" with facilities on the word processor without the pressure of having to complete a real task.

4.4.2 Operator satisfaction

The reasons why operators are satisfied, or not, with word processing are different to those expressed by authors. To begin with, there was a universally high level of operator satisfaction with word processing in general. The majority of operators felt that, although working with word processing had often increased the volume of work which they handled, it had also improved the quality and variety of their work and their control over it. None of the operators interviewed would have wished to revert to their previous working methods, and several said they would like to do even more work with word processors.

Work organisation factors do not, in fact, seem to be critical for operators' satisfaction unless there is a change in a negative direction. Working in a pool is seen by many operators as having a slightly lower status than working in a more traditional secretarial relationship, and therefore a move from an integrated form of working to a more differentiated one could cause problems (at any time - regardless of the introduction of word processing). Having said this, however, the trend in the companies surveyed in Phase II was in the reverse direction, and since some of the operators working in pools expressed a wish to undertake tasks of a more secretarial type as well as their typing/inputting tasks, this is likely to be an acceptable trend from the point of view of operator satisfaction.

One of the companies surveyed had actually set up a small pool for word processing in a department which had previously been used to small group working. This had been a success both in terms of providing good author service, and increasing the variety of work (and consequently the satisfaction) of operators. However, this change had been brought about with the full consultation and co-operation of everyone concerned, and given the preceding comments, would not necessarily be acceptable in other situations.

Many sources of operator dissatisfaction seem to be related to working in a pool, although only a few operators working in very large pools actually said they disliked working in a pool. One fairly frequent cause of difficulties, and one which has been highlighted in other studies (3), is the quality of supervision. Not all the pools in the sample had supervisors, and in those that did the role was sometimes informally assigned to or assumed by the senior operator. In such cases, there were usually few problems with supervision, but in other cases where word processor operators worked alongside typists in pools headed by a traditional typing supervisor, the operators felt that these supervisors did not fully understand the problems of their particular job or provide adequate back-up when problems occurred with their equipment or work.

Operators in pools tended to experience fewer opportunities for learning or progress in their jobs than those in a more traditional secretarial role, and as previously mentioned, many said they would like to do more secretarial-type work than high levels of copy typing, although they did not necessarily want to move away from working in pools or with word processors.

Generally, those operators with supervisory responsibility experienced slightly higher levels of job satisfaction (reflected by higher ratings of variety, autonomy and greater opportunities for learning) than other operators.

In one or two companies with small group working, a word processing co-ordinator or administrator post had been created for one of the senior secretaries, and the holders of these posts also tended to be slightly more satisfied with some aspects of their work than their colleagues.

In a few cases, secretaries experienced some de-skilling of their jobs because of the use of word processors. This happened, for example, in one situation where only one or two secretaries became the focal point for word processing work and advice to their colleagues, and they both felt they spent more time doing word processing and associated tasks than they had previously spent typing, with a consequent reduction in variety and job satisfaction.

It is clear that the factors affecting operators' satisfaction are complex and interdependent. However, whilst operator satisfaction is not directly related to work organisation issues alone, this does not mean that they do not matter. Perhaps the most significant finding from this survey of operators was that they often found compensatory factors in their work which counteracted the negative aspects caused by word processing. It is important for managers to realise therefore that just because operators stay in their jobs and do not complain about these issues, there is nothing wrong; the operators may only be staying because of these compensatory factors, such as a pleasant working group.

4.4.3 Organisational satisfaction

There was a relationship between organisational satisfaction and the form of work organisation which they had adopted. Generally speaking, those organisations which had adopted a mixture of forms of working (e.g. typically a pool and one or more of the integrated forms such as author-operator or small groups) tended to be more satisfied with word processing than those which had small group forms alone; these, in turn, were more satisfied with word processing than those organisations which only had pools.

This, combined with the fact that organisational satisfaction is closely related to the
level of author satisfaction, would seem to
indicate that a flexible approach, combining
the advantages of both pool and small group
working, is most adaptable to authors' needs
and consequently the most satisfactory to the
organisation.   Many of the organisations with
pools in the sample seem to have recognised
this, and stated that they were planning to
move towards mixed forms of work organisation.

Finally, levels of organisational satisfaction
depend to some extent upon the organisation's
initial reasons for choosing to install word
processors.   When word processing was put
in with the aims of improved presentation of
documents, time saving or better handling of
specific documents, these aims were more likely
to be achieved than when word processors were
installed to achieve increased productivity,
staff savings or improved service to authors.

4.5 Relationship between work organisation and participation in the design process

The second major hypothesis to be investigated
was that the more differentiated forms of work
organisation would result from design processes
that did not include the active and effective
participation of users.   That is to say that,
where users have some say in the design and
selection of the system and the forms of work
organisation which are chosen, they are likely
to prefer the integrated forms rather than the
differentiated forms.

This hypothesis was not supported by the findings
which highlighted a generally low level of user
involvement in the design and selection of word
processing systems.   There was no indication
that either of the 'pure' forms (i.e. where only
one kind of work organisation existed in one
organisational unit) were influenced by user
involvement – some operators and authors had
opted for a pool organisation when given a choice
and sometimes a small group situation was imposed
on users.   However, where users had been involved to some extent, there was a slight trend
towards choosing a mixture of both centralised
and decentralised forms of working.

This suggests again that perh   what users want
is flexibility in their word processing service,
with a pool to cope with high volumes of typing
and small groups to provide those authors who
need it with a more personalised service.

An interesting finding was that authors and
operators tended to contribute in quite different ways to the selection of word processors.
Operators tended to have more involvement in the
process than authors, although often it was one
senior secretary or a supervisor, representing
all the other operators, who was involved.
Many managers felt that it was important to
involve operators, since they were actually going

to be using the equipment on a regular basis,
and they also felt that operators had expertise
to contribute in deciding what features would
be necessary or desirable on the system to be
purchased.   However, one comment frequently
made by operators was that, as many of them had
not used word processors before, they did not
feel able to contribute anything useful to the
selection process.   Since operators' expertise
may well be valuable to organisations in selecting a system which is appropriate to their
requirements (and therefore more likely to be
fully used), it would be worthwhile trying to
overcome this lack of knowledge by allowing
operators to see and compare a number of different systems before making a choice.

Authors, on the other hand, tended to be less
involved in the actual selection of equipment,
and when they were involved in the implementation
of word processing, it was more often in deciding
on potential areas of application for word processing in their departments.   Many authors
commented that they did not have time to get
involved in the selection process (even if they
would have liked to), and therefore left it to
the person responsible for making the decision.

It is clear, then, that even where there was
user involvement in the selection process, it
did not usually take the form of deciding on the
form of work organisation to be adopted.   In
the majority of cases in this study, the introduction of word processing was not accompanied
by a change in the form of work organisation,
and word processors were put into existing pools
or small secretarial groups.   Since most participants in the survey were apparently happy with
the way their work was organised, there was no
perceived need to change things because of word
processing.   (The original hypothesis may still
be valid, but it would need to be investigated
in the context of why that particular form of
work organisation had been chosen originally,
before the introduction of word processing.)

5. CONCLUSIONS

What conclusions can be drawn from this study
about the consequences of organising word processing work in a particular way?

Firstly, many organisational units do not use
one 'pure' form of work organisation. They use
a mixture of two or more.   It is those organisations which use these mixed forms that appear to
be most satisfied with word processing: the
results of both phases come to this same conclusion.

Many predictions have suggested that it is the
extremes of the work organisation integration/
differentiation continuum (see Figure 1) which
will predominate when word processing installations become widespread. (That is, where the
author operates the equipment himself, or where
there is a pool with division of functions.)

Our findings, however, show that so far at least, there is little evidence of this revolution taking place.   There is also little evidence of a revolution in terms of staff numbers.

It appears to be the case that word processing in itself does not dictate a change in work organisation; indeed, in many cases there is no change, at least to begin with.   What the introduction of the technology does do, however, is to create the potential for change; it allows the opportunity for reappraisal.

Instead of a revolution in the offices then, the picture seems to be definitely one of evolution with the use of word processors gradually changing a) as the technology changes and b) as organisations learn.

Although it is possible to say that this evolution is taking place, it is more difficult to say that it is planned evolution, that is that organisations have a policy of using an evolutionary approach to the development and use of new technology.   Few organisations had such a strategy.   Many did not have a definite and coherent idea at the outset of of which facilities they required from a system, nor how useful the system was likely

to be.   Many companies therefore adopted an iterative approach, buying a few machines from one manufacturer and using them almost as 'pilot' systems.   If they proved satisfactory, they might buy more; if unsatisfactory, they might try a different make.   This can be a satisfactory way for the organisation to learn precisely what its word processing needs are; on the other hand, a proliferation of many different types of system can have disadvantages in terms of, e.g. operator training and support, and flexibility to transfer work between different types of equipment.

Having said this, companies who expect an evolution in their working procedures to result from the introduction of word processors are much more likely to achieve their aims than those who expect a revolution which will produce cost and staff savings.

Organisational satisfaction with word processors is related to the satisfaction of authors, and this is one reason why a mixture of forms of work organisation - whether of a pool and small groups or a combination of small groups and other small-group forms, seems to be the most satisfactory arrangement for many organisations. It has the advantage of providing a flexible service to match the needs of individual authors or groups of authors.

Another important factor for author satisfaction, and consequently for the organisation, is the locus of control over the word processing service. Authors are happy to delegate control over their work if they are confident that the best decision will be taken about how their work should be

handled.   However, if there is a barrier to communication between the authors and operators (whether through the 'filter' of a supervisor, or by organisational or geographical distance), they are less likely to achieve a satisfactory match between the service and their needs.

Finally, this study has principally been an attempt to describe the situation which exists in organisations with respect to word processing at this time, and to compare this with some of the predictions which have been made about the effects and consequences of word processors.

The implications of this study suggest that, if anything, a mixture of forms is likely to be the most satisfactory way of organising work for all concerned.   Because of the complex nature of the interacting variables, however, it is not possible to say that this will be the most appropriate in every case.

6.   REFERENCES

1.   Simpson, A., Eason K.D., Damodaran L. (1980)   'Job Design and Training in Word Processor Applications' HUSAT Subscription Report No. 2, Loughborough University.

2.   The Manpower Services Commission Training Division, (1982)   Set of four booklets in the series 'MSC Text Processing: The Implications of New Technology for Managers, Operators, Supervisors and Text Authors'.

3.   Klinger, N. (1980) 'Changing Styles in Secretarial Support' (Texaco Limited). In: 'Word Processing: Current Practices and Future Developments'. On-line Publications Ltd.

Human-Computer Interaction — INTERACT '84 / B. Shackel (ed.)
Elsevier Science Publishers B.V. (North-Holland)
© IFIP, 1985

IMPLEMENTING COMPUTER-BASED INFORMATION SYSTEMS IN ORGANISATIONS: ISSUES AND STRATEGIES

R. Hirschheim, F. Land and S. Smithson

London School of Economics
Houghton Street
London WC2A 2AE

The history of computer-based information system implementation in organisations
points to the fact that implementation is not a simple nor straightforward process.
It is very much based on human beliefs, emotions, perceptions, and the like. It has
to be treated with care and effective strategies. This paper explores the nature of
implementation - how people react to change and why - as well as how the reactions
are often manifested in terms of computer-implementation. A consequentialist perspective is advocated as one way to help understand the basis for such reactions.

INTRODUCTION

Of the four main phases of the systems life
cycle: analysis, design, programming and implementation, the first three have enjoyed a great
deal of attention; c.f. Jackson (1983), De
Marco (1978), Weinberg (1980), Gane and Sarson
(1979). The last phase, implementation, has,
until recently, received considerably less. It
has been regarded as little more than the
delivery of a carefully constructed product to
a client. Implementation was thought to include
data collection and entry, system testing, the
preparation of documentation and staff training
(Davis 1974, Bingham and Davies 1978): necessary
but uncontroversial operations. The actual cut-
over of a new system signalled the end of the
project. Implementation then was thought to be
uncomplicated and warranting little research
effort.

However, in the 1970s it was realised that many
systems that looked good on paper, whose designs
were technically elegant and whose programming
faultless, were failing to meet expectations.
Some were being used, but ineffectively, while
others swiftly fell into disuse c.f. Schmitt
and Kozar (1978) , Conrath and du Roure (1978),
and Markus (1981). Lucas (1975) noted that many,
perhaps a majority of, systems had been failures
in one way or another, due to their inappropriate
implementation. The area known as implementation research developed to study these phenomena.

IMPLEMENTATION STRATEGIES

Interest in research on implementation has
surged over the past years giving rise to a
number of conferences on the subject as well as
numerous published papers in the journals. The
results of implementation research have been a
proliferation of platitudes based on user
involvement, evolutionary change, information
analysis, change agents, and the like, c.f.
Bostrom and Heinen (1977), Ginzberg (1978,1979),
Lucas (1981), and Feeney and Sladek (1977).
Consequently, many of the proposed solutions
are somewhat superficial and/or obvious. See,
for example, Alter (1980) who presents a list of
implementation strategies based on four central
points: (1) divide the project into manageable

pieces, (2) keep the solution simple, (3) develop
a satisfactory support base, and (4) meet user
needs and institutionalize the system, which he
asserts should be applied when confronted with
various 'risk factors' such as nonexistent or
unwilling users, inability to specify purpose
or usage patterns, and loss or lack of support.

This list of strategies however seems to be a
motley collection of methodological alternatives
(e.g. prototyping), obvious essentials for any
project (e.g. obtain management support) and
rather dubious advice (e.g. be simple). Also,
what are listed as strategies would be better
termed tactical measures to deal with immediate
problems, i.e. the risk factors. This tactical
approach is developed further by Keen (1981) but,
warns Markus (1983), "no tactics are useful in
every situation".

In discussing strategies one should perhaps consider the introduction of computer-based information systems (CBIS) as a subset of the general
problem of implementing change in organisations.
Organisations are social systems and a successful implementation implies the acceptance of the
new system by the members of the organisation
(Child 1977). Given they are made up of
different interest groups, each with their own,
often conflicting, norms, interests and objectives (Crozier 1964, Dalton 1959) such acceptance
is not easily effected nor understood, as
political power within organisations is distributed, inequitably, amongst these groups. This
is the view held by the so-called 'pluralist'.

Chin and Benne (1976) identify three types of
strategies for change:

1) Rational-Empirical (e.g. operational research)

This approach assumes that men are rational and
will follow their self-interest and the problem
is merely a case of presenting people with the
necessary information. This has been the traditional stance of the DP community and ignores
the pluralist perspective.

2) Normative-Reeducative (e.g. human relations)

This approach recognizes the existence of

apparently irrational norms which govern the
acceptance or rejection of proposals for change.
Thus instead of 'factual' information, what is
seen to be needed are ways of changing people's
attitudes and norms.

3) Power-Coercive (e.g. collective bargaining)

Recognising the power dimension within organisations, a strategy should highlight:

a) Negotiation between groups, with the
   implicit use of sanctions should
   negotiations fail,
b) the degree of legitimacy and authority
   attached to the proposals for change.

Adopting a pluralist perspective leads one to
favour a power-coercive model at a strategic
level, whilst recognizing the benefits of the
normative-reeducative stance in tactical deal-
ings with individuals.

Implementation strategies such as those proposed
by Alter (1980) are therefore too simplistic
because:

1) It is not clear who is selecting the
strategy(s): the individual analyst, project
manager, DP manager or the system sponsor. The
individual should be the 'leader' of the forces
for change: the high-level 'fixer' of Bardach
(1977). The forces for change are a coalition
of interest groups, plus some isolated
individuals, who anticipate some benefit to
themselves or the organisation, as they perceive
it, through the adoption of the new system. The
coalition would normally include the DP department plus other beneficiaries, which would vary
according to the particular application, but may
often include, for example, management accounting. The coalition may fall together spontaneously or else be set up by the 'fixer'.

2) Risk factors are not banana-skins that appear
by chance but are largely symptoms of underlying causes such as: technical and design
problems, resistance to change, uncertainty and
lack of user involvement. The first area is
beyond the scope of this paper but the other
three areas are closely inter-related: for
example, resistance to change (discussed below)
may be caused partly by uncertainty on the part
of the potential users as to how the new system
will affect them, which in turn may be
exacerbated by the lack of user involvement
(Land 1982). Uncertainty may be felt by the
developers regarding how the new system will
perform, its impact on the organisation and the
extent of resistance to change.

A danger in selecting a strategy is that the
perception of the problem by the 'fixer' may be
rooted in the visible results of the existing
system. The implementation and operation of
the new system may dramatically change the
nature of the problem; like old admirals it
is very easy to prepare to fight the last war
rather than the next. Thus it is extremely
important that any strategy successfully handles
the consequences of system implementation.

These consequences are social in nature and hence
not simply predicted.

COUNTER-IMPLEMENTATION

One of the consequences that may be predicted
is some form of counter-implementation measures
from the forces that oppose change; these
measures are covert and/or overt attempts by
groups or individuals to sabotage (or make
ineffectual) the implementation strategies being
used. Bardach (1977) categorizes counter-
implementation strategies into 3 types.

1. diverting resources - stalling the systems
   project or depleting it through lack of
   resources.

2. deflecting goals - making the system's goals
   seem ambiguous and/or unrealistic.

3. dissipating energies - diverting attention
   away from the system to alternative
   approaches.

These are by no means the only ways in which a
person or group can employ counter-implementation strategies. Keen (1981) saw less overt
techniques which could be used, almost passive
resistance in nature.

1. 'lay low' - the less encouragement or help,
   the greater the chance of failures.

2. 'rely on inertia' - inaction often causes
   the implementation process to stall or fail.

3. 'keep the project complex, hard to coordinate and vaguely defined' - very similar
   to the second point on Bardach's list above.

4. 'minimize the implementers legitimacy and
   influence' - the less favourably system
   implementers are viewed, the less influence
   they will be able to command.

5. 'exploit their lack of inside knowledge' -
   use the lack of exposure to the organisations
   politics to put the system implementers at
   a disadvantage.

As in the case of implementation strategies and
risk factors, the recognition of counter-
implementation as an organisational phenomenon
is noteworthy but, in order to counter it
effectively it is necessary to understand its
causes. Counter-implementation is a particular
manifestation of resistance to change, a closer
examination of which is given below.

RESISTANCE TO CHANGE

This may be defined as an adverse reaction to a
proposed change that may either manifest itself
fairly quickly in counter-implementation moves
or may remain latent only to surface much later
during the operations of the system. Alternatively it may wither away unnoticed.

One problem in discussing resistance to change
is the loaded nature of the terminology. The
word 'implementation' has connotations of
legitimacy and an unarguable matter-of-factness.
It is easy to think of change as being
synonymous with progress with the implicit

assumption that the change is beneficial.
'Resistance' conjures up visions of unlawful
acts with the added implication that, in the
long term, the stance is hopeless and resistance
will crumble in time. Needless to say, change
is not always beneficial in which case, any
resistance should be encouraged. Even beneficial
changes may encounter resistance that has been
legitimised through the norms of the groups
concerned and accepted as such by the remainder
of the organisation.

The basic causes of resistance to change are
many and varied; in any particular case they
usually occur as a tangle of different threads,
from which it is difficult to isolate individual
elements. Moreover, it is the interaction of
the elements that produces the particular
instance of resistance, so that the isolation
of component elements may be of limited value.
The notion of interaction is developed by Markus
(1983) who proposes that resistance is caused by
"the interaction of specific system design
features with aspects of the organisation
context".

These organisational elements emerge from three
different, but closely related, dimensions:
the psychological, social, and structural, a
selection of which are given below:

1) Psychological (Watson 1966)
   Natural complacency
   Habit
   Fear of the unknown
   Fear of being unable to cope or of
     redundancy
   Insecurity

2) Social (Child 1977, John 1973)
   Group norms
   Perceived history of past changes that
     were mismanaged
   Fear of loss of authority or status
   New system seen as something 'foreign'
   Disruption of existing social network

3) Structural (Burns & Stalker 1961,
             Flanders 1964)
   Misfit with existing organisational
     structure
   Mechanistic/bureaucratic organisation
   Multiple unionism

As well as being, at times, functional for the
organisation resistance may be:

a) Rational; the people concerned may unavoidably suffer the loss of jobs or status,
b) Healthy; representing a belief on the part
   of the workforce in continuity and loyalty
   to the organisation's (old) methods.

Resistance to change is not a simple black and
white acceptance or rejection of a proposed
change. Mumford and Banks (1967) found that the
factors affecting attitudes to change, and thus
the strength of feeling, could be grouped under
four headings: (i) variables within the
individual, (ii) variables in the situation,
(iii) variables in the change strategies adopted

and (iv) the objective consequences of the
change. In some cases resistance crumbles almost
immediately, in others, e.g. the Times/Sunday
Times dispute of 1978/79, the strength is
demonstrated by the length and intensity of the
dispute. It also follows that counter-
implementation varies according to the weapons
in the armoury of a particular group or individual.

Resistance may lie dormant throughout the
implementation phase, only to emerge when the
system is operational in low productivity, low
effectiveness, high labour turnover, disputes,
absenteeism, psychological withdrawal and
aggression.

This resistance during operation can be found at
all levels in the organisation:

a) Manual workers indulging in outright sabotage
   of new machinery (Dickson, Simmons,and
   Anderson 1974),

b) White-collar workers using the computer as a
   scapegoat for every difficulty encountered,
   inputting incorrect data (Alter 1980) and
   maintaining alternative sets of manual records
   (Markus 1983),

c) Management failure to use, or give credence
   to, the output produced by a new information
   system (Schmidt and Kozer 1978).

Furthermore the aim of the objectors may not be
a straightforward rejection of a computerised
system; it is perhaps just as likely that
groups would support a new system, but not the
one proposed. They may be seeking major changes
or changes that, to the DP department, are
relatively minor.

Above all, resistance to change should be seen
as something inherently normal, "a universal
phenomenon" (Child 1977, p195), and not an act
of God sent to plague a particular project. A
change of any substance will be advantageous to
some groups within the organisation and dis-
advantageous to others. An often quoted para-
phrase of a passage from Machiavelli (The Prince
1514) reads:

> "There is nothing more difficult to plan,
> more doubtful of success, nor more dangerous
> to manage than the creation of a new system.
> For the initiator has the enmity of all who
> would profit by the preservation of the old
> system and merely lukewarm defenders in those
> who would gain by the new one."

The introduction of a new information system
represents both a threat and a challenge to
individuals and interest groups. The threat is
one of disruption to the existing modus operandi
and a potential attack on the groups' interests.
The challenge is to improve or defend those
interests in the redistribution of resources
occasioned by the arrival of the new system.
These resources include departmental budgets,
equipment, staff and territory and the related
individual's authority, status, salary and span
of control. In addition, Keen (1981) emphasises

the importance of data as a political resource and the implications of changes in its ownership and control caused by the implementation of a new system (see also Pettigrew 1973, Bariff and Galbraith 1978).

Resistance to change then is a complex phenomenon whose particular causes and manifestations vary considerably between cases. In order to predict these organisational and social consequences of a proposed change one must somehow 'get inside' the people concerned and try to experience their conflicting loyalties, fears and social norms.

COUNTER-COUNTER-IMPLEMENTATION STRATEGIES

When counter-implementation measures are encountered during an implementation they command a response from the forces for change; both Bardach (1977) and Keen (1981) prescribe certain counter-counter-implementation strategies/ tactics. Bardach recognizing the bargaining nature of the situation, suggests that the DP department should:

  a) Use their monopoly of technical knowledge for bargaining purposes,
  b) Co-opt likely opposition early on in the project,
  c) Provide clear incentives for agreement,
  d) Create a bandwagon effect.

Keen recommends:

" a) Make sure that you have a contract for change,
  b) Seek out resistance and treat it as a signal to be responded to,
  c) Rely on face-to-face contracts,
  d) Become an insider and work hard to build personal credibility,
  e) Co-opt users early. "

Whilst recognizing the value of Keen's tactical approach, there are problems with some individual tactics:

1) Between having no contract at all and having a clear, detailed contract, agreed by all parties affected by the change, there is a large grey area of ambiguity. It is suggested that many implementations lie within this area and achieving that clear contract is likely to be as difficult as achieving the change itself.

2) When seeking out resistance there is a danger of probing too deeply and cultivating the seeds of resistance where they might not otherwise have taken root or else bringing to the surface resistance that would have harmlessly withered away (Johns 1973).

3) Whilst the personal credibility of the front-line forces for change is a powerful resource (Pettigrew 1974) the advice to become an insider seems not only to be a shallow confidence trick destined to be uncovered by the group to be infiltrated but also a tactic that is hardly calculated to inspire credibility. The individual analyst is a representative of the DP department with certain corresponding norms, objectives, etc. and although he can legitimately

represent the 'human face' of that department he will not be accepted as a fully-fledged member of a group opposed to that change.

One must, as in the previous sections, guard against superficial solutions. A detailed analysis of the situation is essential before embarking on counter-counter-implementation moves. In the Ford strike of 1969/70 it was assumed that resistance was due to lack of information. Management responded by writing to each worker individually explaining the changes, the individuals realized just how bad the package was and resistance increased (Benyon 1973).

Counter-counter-implementation should be seen in its organisational context; organisations are dynamic social systems that are ever-changing. Change, no matter how large or small or how fiercely resisted, like resistance itself, is normal (Lupton 1965). For even the most inflexible bureaucratic organisation to survive there must be mechanisms for dealing with change, e.g. sub-committees, collective bargaining, particular bureaucratic rules, managerial authority. These mechanisms, which may be inadequate, confer a degree of legitimacy on the change proposal and act as a bargaining table; it is up to the forces for change, in the first instance, to utilise these political channels to further their cause. This would include accepted 'dirty tricks', e.g. agenda-setting (Pfeffer 1981). If however the 'fixer' steps outside these channels, there is an acute danger that the project will be derailed on the grounds that procedural norms have been broken.

Thus it follows that the weaponry available for counter-counter-implementation is dependent upon:

a) the relative political power of the forces for change,
b) The ability and willingness to use that power in the case in question,
c) the efficacy of the legitimate change mechanisms within the organisation.

The political nature of organisational change demands the attention of those involved in the change process, as politics has been shown to be a key ingredient in implementation. Markus (1983) advocates a thorough analysis of the organisational context prior to the technical systems analysis.

RECOMMENDATIONS AND CONCLUSIONS

This paper has argued that computer-based information system implementation is not a simplistic operation, i.e. the delivery of a constructed product to a client. Nor is it something that systems developers can ignore or shift the responsibility to someone else. Implementation, with all its intrinsic, behavioural ramifications, has to be dealt with in some meaningful fashion. But this is far from easy. The difficulty stems from the fact that any organisational intervention (such as CBIS introduction) has human consequences: some real, some imagined. Because of the dynamic and pluralist nature of the organisation different people will have different perceptions of what the consequences are: some perceive one subset of consequences, others a different subset. Thus, it is not clear what kind of implementation strategy to adopt because CBIS consequences are not easily determined. Counter-implementation and counter-counter-implementation **are** manifestations of consequences and means to deal with them but their situation-dependent nature provides little general guidance on how to predict consequences.

The consequentialist perspective as advocated by Klein and Hirschheim (1983) and the use of a hermeneutic-interpretive method holds some promise for consequence prediction. It attempts to predict the consequences of an organisational intervention through the use of a well-tested and proven technique - role playing. The military refer to it as 'the manoevre' and have used it happily for centuries. The technique relies on individuals' innate ability to predict how others will react to some stimulus; a teacher can normally guess how his colleagues would respond to some student request; and so on. The notion can be extended to other environments by having one group putting itself in the shoes of another. Role playing, if done properly, can provide tremendous insights such that consequence determination and prediction become viable propositions, which in turn would lead to more appropriate implementation strategies.

REFERENCES

(1) Alter S.L., _Decision Support Systems;_ _Current Practice and Continuing Challanges,_ Addison Wesley, 1980.

(2) Bardach, E., _The Implementation Game,_ MIT Press, 1977.

(3) Bariff, M. and Galbraith, J., "Intra-organisational Power Considerations for Designing Information Systems", _Accounting, Organisations and Society,_ Vol.3, No.1, 1978.

(4) Beynon, H., _Working for Ford,_ Penguin, 1973.

(5) Bingham, J. and Davies, G., _A Handbook of Systems Analysis,_ 2nd ed., Macmillan, 1978.

(6) Bostrom, R. and Heinen, S., "MIS Problems and Failures: A Socio-Technical Perspective", Part I and II, _MIS Quarterly,_ Sept. and December 1977.

(7) Burns, T. and Stalker, G.M., _The Management of Innovation,_ Tavistock, 1961.

(8) Child, J., _Organisation - A Guide to Problems and Practice,_ Harper & Row, 1977.

(9) Chin, R. & Benne, K.D., "General Strategies for Effecting Changes in Human Systems", in Bennis, W.G., Benne, K.D., Chin, R. and Corey, K.E. (eds.), _The Planning of Change,_ 3rd edn., Holt Rinehart & Winston, 1976.

(10) Conrath, D. and du Roure, G., "Organisational Implications of Comprehensive Communication-Information Systems: Some Conjectures", working-paper, Aix-en-Provence, France, Institute d'Administration des Enterprises Centre d'Etude et de Recherche sur les Organisations et la Gestion, 1978.

(11) Crozier, M., _The Bureaucratic Phenomenon,_ Tavistock, 1964.

(12) Dalton, M., _Men Who Manage,_ Wiley, 1959.

(13) Davis, G., _Management Information Systems,_ McGraw-Hill, 1974.

(14) De Marco, T., _Structured Analysis and Systems Specifications,_ Yourdon Press, 1978.

(15) Dickson, G., Simmons, J., and Anderson, J., "Behavioural Reactions to the Introduction of a Management Information System at the U.S. Post Office: Some Empirical Observations" in D. Sanders (ed.), _Computers and Management,_ 2nd ed., McGraw-Hill, 1974.

(16) Feeney, W. and Sladek, F., "The Systems Analyst as a Change Agent", _Datamation,_ November, 1977.

(17) Flanders, A., _The Fawley Productivity Agreements,_ Faber, 1964.

(18) Gane, C. and Sarson, T., _Structured Systems Analysis: Tools and Techniques,_ Prentice-Hall, 1979.

(19) Ginzberg, M., "Steps Toward more Effective Implementation of MS and MIS, _Interfaces,_ Vol.8, No.3, May, 1978.

(20) Ginzberg, M., "A Study of the Implementation Process", _TIMS Studies in Management Science,_ Vol.13, 1979.

(21) Jackson, M., _System Development,_ Prentice-Hall, 1983.

(22) Johns, E.A., _The Sociology of Organisational Change,_ Pergamon, 1973.

(23) Keen, P., "Information Systems and Organisational Change", _Communications of the ACM,_ Vol.24, No.1, Jan. 1981.

(24) Klein, H. and Hirschheim, R., "Issues and Approaches to Appraising Technological Change in the Office: A Consequentialist Perspective", _Office: Technology & People,_ Vol.2, No.1, 1983.

(25) Land, F.F.,"Adapting to Changing User
     Requirements", Information & Management,
     No.5, 1982.

(26) Lucas, H., Why Information Systems Fail,
     Columbia University Press, 1975.

(27) Lucas, H., Implementation: The Key to
     Successful Information Systems, Columbia
     University Press, 1981.

(28) Lupton, T.,"The Practical Analysis of
     Change in Organisations", Journal of
     Management Studies, May, 1965.

(29) Markus, M.L., "Implementation Politics -
     Top Management Support and User Involve-
     ment", Systems, Objectives, Solutions,
     1981.

(30) Markus, M.L.,"Power, Politics, and MIS
     Implementation", Communications of the
     ACM, Vol.26, No.6, 1983.

(31) Mumford, E. & Banks, O., The Computer
     and the Clerk, Routledge, Kegan Paul, 1967.

(32) Pettigrew, A., The Politics of Organis-
     ational Decision Making, Tavistock, 1973.

(33) Pettigrew, A.,"The Influence Process
     between Specialists and Executives",
     Personnel Review, Vol.3, No.1, 1974.

(34) Pfeffer, J., Power in Organisations,
     Pitman, 1981.

(35) Schmitt, J. and Kozar, K., "Management's
     Role in Information System Development
     Failures: A Case Study", MIS Quarterly,
     June, 1978.

(36) Watson, G.,"Resistance to Change", in
     Watson, G.(ed.), Concepts for Social Change,
     Cooperative Project for Educational Develop-
     ment Series, Vol.1, National Training
     Laboratories, Washington, 1966.

(37) Weinberg, G., Structured Systems Analysis,
     Prentice-Hall, 1980.

BEHAVIOURAL ISSUES IN THE SYSTEM DEVELOPMENT CYCLE

Human-Computer Interaction — INTERACT '84 / B. Shackel (ed.)
Elsevier Science Publishers B.V. (North-Holland)
© IFIP, 1985

BEHAVIORAL ISSUES IN THE SYSTEM DEVELOPMENT CYCLE

John L. Bennett, Session Organizer

IBM Research Laboratory
San Jose, California 95193

INTRODUCTION

The development of computer software is increasingly directed toward the consumer market. As a result, we see a new emphasis placed on managing behavioral issues during development. The first U.S. conference on "Human Factors in Computer Systems" (Gaithersburg; March, 1982) served as a forum for discussing practical user interface issues. However, several people from industry were troubled by what appeared to be a fragmented approach to human factors design issues. They knew that achieving an easy-to-learn and easy-to-use system requires sensitive management throughout the development cycle.

These four theme sessions at INTERACT 84 offer an opportunity to observe how human factors expertise (professional and amateur) is used to good effect in industry, in academic advanced technology groups, and in work under government agency contracts. Such projects often span several years and require the contributions of many people who have widely differing backgrounds and attitudes. Successful system development requires that explicit steps be taken to provide continuity.

THE PLAN OF THE THEME SESSIONS

Last September we distributed a "Prospectus" outlining activities in the phases of the development cycle. This was intended to aid authors in organizing experiences from a variety of environments.

1. Requirements
   Establishing meaningful, measurable, testable targets for performance needed to support users; statements of system goals.

2. Design of the System
   Drawing on technology to shape the system concepts; developing the conceptual model to be understood by the user; establishing the role of user-oriented metaphors.

3. Development
   Managing technology and resources so that behavioral issues relating to user needs are addressed throughout the process.

4. Evaluation of the System
   User advocates give feedback to designers during development through use of prototypes, during system assurance, and during field use as input for design of new releases.

5. Selling the System
   Helping persons (management or individuals) who may buy the system see potential power and benefits from use.

6. Installation and Training
   Matching a general system capability to the particular requirements of the environment; helping the user to cope with complexity during learning and use.

The directions to authors pointed out that the theme papers were meant to supplement, not replace, the kind of scientific papers reporting the results of controlled experiments. In fact, several groups reference earlier published work from their projects. The sessions are intended to emphasize, particularly for students and professors in formal university programs, a sense of what it is like to do human factors work in a system-building environment.

OBSERVATIONS ON THE SPECIFIC PAPERS

Session 1

Bennett reviews current developments that are leading to a user interface "architecture". By architecture he means an abstraction from the concrete details of a particular design to identify structures and concepts that appear in many user interface designs. This work in progress is seen as necessary to support user transfer of habits developed during interaction with one system to a peer or successor system. The "Basic Interaction Techniques" listed by Woodmanse (see below) represent one such set of abstractions for which specific developer tools have been provided to achieve a level of standardization among applications in one particular environment.

Woodmanse tells us what needs to be done to manage the development of a user interface to software for a small computer to be used by professionals in an office. We see the kind of controls needed as a product requiring a "consistent, intuitive, and streamlined interface" evolves from design by a close-knit small team to development by groups containing dozens of application implementers. The constraints of existing hardware, budgeted costs, and tight schedules force compromises. Marketing people constantly point out the tangible and intangible cost of even a week's delay in sending the product to software stores. The lessons learned and recommendations are echoed in Boyle et al.

Boyle, Ogden, Uhlir, and Wilson take us behind the scenes in development of an IBM software product. They show how the diverse team worked to simplify user learning and operation of a product to be used in an environment where "the way the function was presented was (as) important as the amount of function provided." They describe the series of studies intended to answer specific design questions on error messages, command formats, and report generation controls. Itera-

tive tests tracked query formulation, display panels, and evolving function. One of the recommendations for "next time" is to get involved with
customers through joint study contracts. See Akscyn and McCracken (below) for one kind of significant user group involvement.

Session 2

Shafer presents a series of vignettes to illustrate various aspects of the development cycle in
government sponsored work. It might be surprising that "selling the system" would appear as an
activity important to a Human Factors group working with the military. However, these large
systems require several years to design and
build, and military tours of duty are generally
shorter. New contract administrators need to be
"resold" as they arrive on board. Another vig-
nette addresses techniques used for system
installation and for training to meet the needs
of military personnel. These may be adaptable to
the commercial world.

Kloster and Tischer outline the kind of development process used for large military and govern-
mental systems such as air traffic control. In
these cases completing the requirements process
itself becomes a major subcontracted project.
While the full technologies (e.g., Interaction
Technique Diagrams, System Specification Language) may not be needed in commercial projects,
the concepts may have a useful transfer to industry. The authors explicitly assume that a system
can be (successfully) decomposed into machine
function and human information-processing tasks.
The challenge is to avoid losing sight of the individual (undecomposed, whole) operator at the
terminal as the design is subdivided.

Phillips and Tischer describe the Operations Concept, one part of the overall methodology outlined by Kloster and Tischer. A "User Team"
serves as an important check on the realism of
the assumptions made during the decomposition
process. It must be a challenge for the User Team
to keep a focus on the operators' job in spite of
the need to "divide and conquer" to get the enormous design and implementation job done. Note
the comments of Woodmanse and of Boyle et al on
how hard it is for even experienced people to
gain a "feel" for the dynamics of a system when it
is only described on paper. It will be interesting to hear how well the User Team, professional
air traffic controllers but not experienced in
system design, can envision projected system operation from the Composition Graph and the Task
Description Language representations. It would
also be interesting to compare the experiences of
this User Team with the experiences of the ZOG
user team (see Akscyn and McCracken below.)

Session 3

Akscyn and McCracken encapsulate in 13 recommendations their thoughts about their experience in
taking a system directly from a Computer Science
laboratory to operational use on a U. S. Navy
aircraft carrier. The recommendations to "Devise
effective strategies for users to employ prototypes" and "Treat the users as part of the
development team" relate to observations made in
many of the papers in these theme sessions. Others also observe the difficulty of maintaining an
effective perspective on actual user requirements

when designing a system to be used for a broad
range of tasks by a a broad range of people.

Yoder, McCracken, and Akscyn give more detail on
one aspect of their work in developing the ZOG
computer-aided management system for the ship.
Of interest is the instrumentation to serve both
the diagnostic needs of the purchasers of the
service (the ship management) and the maintainers
of the service (the computer science design and
development team). They suggest that the problem
of arriving at an overall view of system operation requires skills much like those of an
archeologist. The detailed data collected
through typical instrumentation was accessed
through the system itself. This served as a basis for human induction about how well the system
was performing so that it could be tuned to better serve user needs.

Gruenfelder and Whitten argue that prototyping in
order to validate designs empirically will always
be needed. Even though we can learn from generic
research (i.e., some results can be validly abstracted from the particular experimental situation where they were obtained), situation-
specific circumstances can reverse predicted behavior. Their online telephone-routing example
suggested to them cases where guidelines and experimental results reported in the literature are
not always applicable within a particular design.
People who interpret research results must always
ask the question, "Under what conditions do the
results hold?"

Session 4

As these theme sessions took form, it became
clear that many issues are best illustrated
through anecdotal experiences suitable for a panel session. For example, some phases of the development cycle are not addressed by the papers.
While advertisements make claims for "user
friendly" software, no one from the human factors
community has offered a paper indicating how such
claims are validated. On another point, some references cite the important role that tools used
by the developer play in shaping the user interface, but no one is yet reporting on the human
factors contribution to the establishment of such
tools.

Thus, the closing panel will be an opportunity to
discuss how well theme papers (and others at the
INTERACT Conference) represent the state of the
art in addressing behavioral issues during system
development. The panel can comment on experience
across systems indicating what remains to be done
and can outline current critical problems.

ACKNOWLEDGEMENTS

T. Moran and J. Thomas, members of the International Program Committee for INTERACT 84, took on
additional duties to work with prospective authors and to review contributions. R. Bernotat,
R. Pew, T. Stewart, and R. Yates also served as a
special subcommittee to oversee progress. And
special thanks to all the authors who worked ov-
ertime to develop papers.

Human-Computer Interaction — INTERACT '84 / B. Shackel (ed.)
Elsevier Science Publishers B.V. (North-Holland)
© IFIP, 1985

THE CONCEPT OF ARCHITECTURE APPLIED TO USER INTERFACES IN INTERACTIVE COMPUTER SYSTEMS

John L. Bennett

IBM Research Laboratory
San Jose, California

Work is emerging that will influence the evolution of the interfaces presented to users of computer systems. A central question is: "What abstractions from current specific systems are needed to support transfer of productive user habits as people adapt to new hardware and software technology?" An orderly evolution requires that users recognize similarity of control functions (e.g., select an object) even though the details of object presentation and of the way the user invokes the function are clearly different in different products. Managing such an evolution requires that we understand what must be held in common across products. Details of work in industry are proprietary; this brief paper outlines some of the problems that are being solved to make the concept of a "user interface architecture" become a reality.

1. INTRODUCTION

Users of interactive systems become accustomed to a style of operation as they work (e.g. the touch typist relies on a particular keyboard layout, the text creator relies on familiar editing commands). Because of added function (e.g., graphics manipulation offered in a text application) and new devices (e.g., selection via a mouse), users may be asked to change currently-productive interaction habits as they move to new products.

Attention to the specific processes used by people during interaction has often been secondary to continued technical innovation in function. As a result, users are occasionally bewildered and dismayed by the different procedures they must follow. Applications sometimes differ arbitrarily in what people perceive should be similar processes (e.g., text editing.)

People do not resist change in interaction patterns where those changes permit them to stop doing what they did not want to do in the first place. For example, people were quite willing to change radically (without complaint) the procedure they used in starting an automobile when the the electric starter replaced the hand crank. Similarly, people do not object when an operating system provides automatic file management so that they no longer need to control the details of disk space. However, the expert typist objects vigorously when changes in layout of a keyboard prevent the use of touch-typing skills acquired over several years of practice.

Development of a "user interface architecture" (UIA) presumes that we can identify structural elements important to users and then manage the evolution of the user interface (both hardware and software) so that users can carry over productive habits to new systems. The problem of a "UIA" is to identify which features of current interactive systems are important to current users. In addition, the computer industry (through personal computers) is offering function to people who have never before interacted with computers. Here the issue is to identify those aspects of user interfaces that such new users find "hard to learn".

Thus, central problems are 1) which concrete details of a user interface are "incidental" and need not be held invariant and 2) which structural relationships are "crucial" for users and must be preserved as we add new function and as we design new user-effective processes made possible by new technology.

Of course, motivated people can always learn and adapt. The issue is how to identify and control those design features that will require retraining experienced users and will cause problems in training new users.

In this paper I explore how the concept of architecture is beginning to be applied to user interfaces. We open by suggesting the relation of "architecture" to familiar concepts. We then suggest how "architects" are drawing on cognitive science, computer science, and current product technology as they develop concepts needed for a "UIA". The final section suggests what will be required to manage the evolution of such a "UIA" -- to maintain a workable balance between architectural abstractions and concrete design details of products.

2. WHAT IS AN "ARCHITECTURE"?

Many companies in the computer industry are now planning for a controlled evolution in their products by providing a frame of reference and a set of rules for guiding trade-offs during product development. VisiCorp (1) and Apple (2) appear to have work in progress. Goldberg (3) mentioned IBM plans for an "end user architecture" to guide the development of workstation software. Rutkowski (4) suggests that an evolution toward "architectural stabilization" is needed if computers are to be easy-to-use. The details of work in industry are currently proprietary; the fragments appearing in the press indicate developments we may expect.

The concept of "architecture" is most familiar in connection with the description of buildings. An architecture is an abstraction from the detail of any one building in order to define a style. We speak of a "federal" or "gothic" architectural

style, and we expect to see distinctive features
such as windows and arches, where they appear in
a building, to be constructed in a particular arrangement and proportion. The development of an
architecture can also lead to standard building-
blocks, conventional designs for office buildings
such as modules (four foot increments), plumbing,
and light fixtures. These conventional details
allow the architect to create a building of distinctive appearance and usefulness from a catalog
of relatively standard parts.

Though we may not have thought of it as such, we
are also familiar with an "architecture" in the
controls of the automobile. Drivers of cars
around the world rely on the car turning right
when the steering wheel is turned clockwise.
Note that this convention is abstracted from such
concrete details as the diameter of the steering
wheel, the number of spokes it has, the size of
the rim, and the details of how the internal
steering mechanism accomplishes the result. The
architecture of other standard controls specifies
the relative placement of the clutch, brake, and
accelerator pedals (though not their exact size
or length of travel). Some important controls
are not in a standard place or not operated in a
standard way (e.g., horn, windshield wipers,
lights). Safety authorities are concerned about
the delay that the driver of a rented car may experience in operating these controls in an
emergency. The operation of still other controls
(e.g. radio, hood latch) are less important and
are typically designed in accord with styling and
cost considerations.

The concept of computer "architecture", as distinguished from design, was described by Brooks
(5). He wrote of "the underlying conceptual constructs that define the complete and detailed
specification of the user interface". In his example, the user manual for the IBM/360 family of
computers specified the order code for the machines, and designers of different models were
free to make trade-offs affecting internal details. For example, data in different models
could be transferred in blocks 8 bits or 32 bits
wide to improve speed without affecting the interface seen by the programmer. The focus in
this use of the term "architecture" was on hiding
internal design decisions from the programmer if
they did not affect the semantics of the order
code.

The emergence of personal computing as a consumer
industry prompts us to consider how the concept
of architecture suggested by Brooks might be
adapted. Can it be combined with our experience
of architecture in buildings and of "architecture" in the controls of automobiles and then applied to making those computer controls that are
exposed to the user be easy to learn and easy to
use?

Development of a "UIA" shares many problems with
the development of any architecture. If we establish "standards" too closely tied to current
designs, it may be difficult to take full advantage of new technology. If structural principles
are too general, designers of specific products
will not be guided effectively, and productive
user habits will not transfer. Thus, one problem
is to capture all (and only) those distinctions
which make a difference in user learning,
throughput, error rate, and attitude about use.

Carroll (6) points out an important distinction
between "architectural presentation" and "architectural form". "Presentation" refers to the details of specific applications as seen by the
user working at a specific workstation. "Form"
refers to how "portions of a system's function
are interrelated in typical user scenarios, but
not how each piece of function is represented to
the user ...." Carroll cites "contextual dependence" as a typical issue in form architecture --
whether commands are constrained to a particular
context (e.g., only the commands explicitly presented in a menu on the screen can be invoked) or
whether the user has relative freedom to request
any command in any context. For example, in a
working environment with low contextual dependency, direct commands, in addition to those
explicitly presented in a menu, may be requested
by the knowledgeable user who can recall them
from personal memory and explicitly invoke them.

Carroll suggests that the distinction between
presentation and form in architecture has important implications for the direction of research.
He suspects that principles can be developed for
form, but that presentation details are likely to
be influenced more by:
• user characteristics (e.g. frequent dedicated
  use, occasional use),
• available technology (e.g. high-resolution col-
  or displays attached to fast, large processors;
  inexpensive low-resolution monochrome displays
  with slow response to user requests), and
• application requirements (e.g., computer-aided
  design, office text processing).
Thus, matters of architectural form may be amenable to research, but details of architectural
presentation may need to be handled case by case
through prototyping and user testing.

At this stage it is not clear how successful we
will be in developing "form architectures". Progress will require iterative refinement in any
event. The immense variety of tasks that can be
supported by computer function, the well-known
individual differences observed in users as they
do tasks, and the wide variety of technology
(hardware and software) available will all make
the establishment of appropriate distinctions and
abstractions a continuing challenge. We will
need to draw on work from a variety of sources.

3. SOURCES OF EXPERIENCE FOR "UIA" DEVELOPMENT

The user interface can be thought of as a "surface" between user and computer. The development
of any one "UIA" will require abstractions for
representing both important properties of the user and fundamental constructs from computing. In
addition, we will need to abstract from current
designs, separating the specific implementation
techniques from the general processes being supported.

3.1 Cognitive Science -- Representing the User

A body of ergonomic knowledge is becoming available to help the designer respond to user physiological capability (e.g., 7). We assume this
will serve as a base for design of physical
equipment.

The cognitive capability of a user is a central
element in the development of architectural con-

cepts. Ramsey and Grimes (8) point out the need
for new work in understanding human information
processing capabilities to support designers as
they choose abstractions. The results of classical experiments in comparing performance when
people use two specific designs for a specific
task does not transfer well to different applications or to new technology. By moving to higher
levels of abstraction (termed "features", "factors", and "calculational models"), the results
of human factors and experimental psychology work
can assist designers to see needed structure.

Card (9) shows how human information processing
theory can be applied to represent the user. He
describes a calculational model in terms of perceptual, cognitive, and motor processors, working
and long term memories, and principles of operation. The model is simple and practical enough
to be used in some design calculations. The discussion of pointing devices and their use in
common workstation tasks is a move toward abstraction from the details of any particular
device. The model helps us focus on the physical
and cognitive limits of the human user -- the information processing rate of the user's hand-eye
coordination mechanism. Thus, while the particulars of a specific design might lead to minor
variations in performance, the model sets criteria to guide engineering trade-offs.

Ramsey and Grimes (8) also survey ways in which
users acquire a model of the computer system.
Designers find it useful to construct "conceptual
models" representing those features of the system
that they anticipate must be understood by the
user. Analogy and metaphor may be helpful in
transferring the conceptual model to a person who
is forming a "mental model" through use of the
system.

A growing body of literature (10), documenting
human performance in a variety of interactive situations, is becoming available to the architect.
However, we are a long way from relating this to
"design equations" in the same way that electrical engineers rely on Ohm's Law.

3.2 Computer Science -- Program Abstractions

Computer scientists and mathematicians have examined programming languages to identify and organize the distinctions intended by such words as
"object", "type", and "operation". The purpose
has been to make programs written in these new
languages easier to develop and to use. One result of this work in the domain of computer
science is the design of carefully crafted "object" languages (e.g., 11).

Non-programmers do not usually think of the "procedures" they use as "programs", a series of "operations" on "objects" along with decision points
needed to achieve useful results. We may bridge
from the domain of computer science (aids for
formal programming) to the domain of a "UIA" as
we define:
a) the distinctions to be made for users (e.g.,
   application objects such as memos, project
   charts, inbaskets; actions such as modify,
   copy, send) and
b) an interaction structure which users need to
   express actions to the computer.
In addition to representing job-related objects,
already meaningful to individual users from their

work experience, a "UIA" must also define computer-related objects (e.g. print queues, network
nodes) which users may need to understand during
interaction. These architectural elements are
closely related to the idea of a "user's model of
the system" (8, 12).

In one experimental system under development
(13), the designers make use of such concepts as
they outline the mechanisms needed to generate
system response messages to error conditions.
Personalized Abstract Machines (AM), tailored to
the objects, actions, and terminology of an application, are built from a Basic Abstract
Machine (BAM). Unnecessary information about the
underlying system structure, both physical and
logical, is hidden from the user. The paper suggests the computer science constructs needed to
map from computer-oriented detail at lower levels
to the user-oriented language familiar to a person working within an application environment.
Unnecessary information about the underlying system structure is hidden from the user. The
authors acknowledge, "We have no well-defined
criterion for determining whether a message can
be understood by the receiver." This makes clear
a needed link to cognitive science models and human factors testing.

Earlier computer science work (e.g., 12) was directed to development of specific designs, but
the methods of task analysis, of identifying user
objects and actions, and of synthesizing system
objects and actions will be useful in "UIA" work.

3.3 Analyzing Current Designs

Interaction techniques used in current products
provide concrete instances for architectural
analysis. The architect reviews the "objects"
presented to a user and the "actions" the user
can take on these objects during interaction.
For example, a movable pointer (often called a
cursor) shown on the screen might be positioned
through user interaction with step keys, by fin-
ger-pointing on a touch-sensitive screen, by
mouse movement, or by voice command. The architect distinguishes "selection" as the abstraction; the particular device used in an implementation serves as the means to accomplish that
action.

The architect works in the domain of abstractions
from specific designs in order to identify elements of form important to users. Rutkowski (4)
points out that the establishment of architectures allows "the design effort and creativity
... previously engaged in the random creation of
architectures (to be) geared toward the refinement of design elements that comprise the
stabilized architecture." Gilb (14) suggests
that eventually the design elements may be collected into a "catalog of techniques", sample
design decisions that can be employed by other
designers.

4. MANAGING THE EVOLUTION OF A "UIA"

We now turn to work which must be done to manage
the evolution of a "UIA" itself. We have touched
on various disciplines and abstraction skills
that will be needed. A "UIA" will be documented
on paper (1, 2) but will also need to be represented in prototypical implementations. The
continuing problem, requiring iteration, will be

to establish practical bounds between abstractions and particular designs.

Because products are the focus of the system development cycle, we mention the constraints in
this process in Figure 1. The development of a
product begins at a specific time in order to
achieve a marketable result in accord with a
schedule. Specific FUNCTION (e.g. services needed to create, save, retrieve, modify, print, and
send letters electronically) is mapped to specific TECHNOLOGY. The product is typically targeted
for an intended USER COMMUNITY, and the designers
may tailor procedures and choose terminology so
that these users are supported in their current
way of carrying out their work (PRODUCT HISTORY).
And, of course, the COST of development affects
the price of the product. The product manager is
conscious of trade-offs among design decisions
that may affect the SCHEDULEd release. If a
"UIA" exists, then it serves as another guiding
constraint.

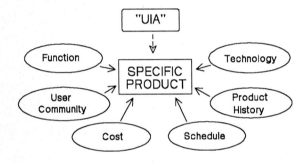

Figure 1. Factors affecting development of a
  specific product

In Figure 2 we show schematically a separation
between a "UIA" in the top box and the specific
design of specific products. In contrast with
the developers of a specific product, architects
seek to define a general structure abstracted
from the detail of specific products and yet relevant to the design of many products. The
purpose of a "UIA" is to identify the fundamentals needed to guide product developers so that
users may:
a) move among contemporary products used in their
   workplaces,
b) move to new releases of a current product, and
c) migrate to new products as they appear.
With specified, limited training, users familiar
with the function should be able to apply their
accustomed practices as they move among members
in the product "family" (the analog of becoming
familiar with the controls of a rental car in the
agency parking lot.)

In addition, those maintaining a "UIA" must work
closely with developers to keep it responsive to
technical developments and relevant to new
trade-offs that must be made by developers.
Maintainers must also understand evolving user
capabilities and needs in order to keep the "UIA"
a "living" and vital source of guidance.

Figure 3 lists categories we might expect to see
described in an architectural document. The user

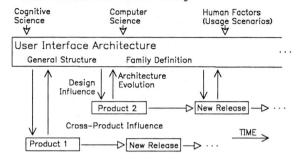

Figure 2. The establishment of a "UIA" presumes
  setting workable bounds between specific products and newly abstracted architectural concepts. Architecture must influence specific
  design, and architecture must evolve as a result of particular product-development and
  marketing experience.

will need to control the arrangement of "windows"
on the screen and the activities represented in
the windows. The content of windows serves as
cues for (and with menus, as a basis for) user actions -- represented as commands and as series of
commands packaged into procedures. Protocols for
feedback must be outlined. Operator assistance
can include immediate specific aid (HELP) or tutorial sequences. Concepts and controls exposed
to the user for managing data, system resources,
and special equipment must be specified -- at an
"architectural form" level.

Conventional representations for user objects
(e.g., mail boxes, calendars) also appear in products, but the appropriate abstractions for these
is especially controversial.

Considerable work has been done on screen format
guidelines (e.g., 15), and an example (Figure 4)
highlights the problem of separating presentation
details from "architectural form". Some proprietary guidelines, available to product developers
within companies, have prescribed concrete de-

Workstation Management
  Screen Layout
  Activity Control
Dialog Management
  Window Content
  User Actions
    Commands
    Procedures
  Feedback and Error Handling
    Messages
  Operator Assistance
  Help
  Interactive Training
Management of Stored Data
System Management
Device-Related Services
  (Printer, Facsimile, Telephone)

Figure 3. Typical distinctions that will be made
  in a user interface architecture.

tails, including window content, for products. But guidelines often do not identify fundamentals and often do not separate conventional presentation practices from essential form. An architectural approach abstracts to a rectangular window, and the product designer makes decisions about relative placement within this window. This allows attention to conventions (e.g. place instructions centered near the top) responding to the fact that readers are accustomed to scan top to bottom, left to right. At the same time it leaves freedom for trade-offs in a particular implementation.

Figure 4 shows the form of a simplified menu screen. A presentation issue would be whether the menu item identifiers should be shown as letters from the alphabet, numbers, or as fields to be filled in by the user during the selection process. Another design issue, relating both to form and to presentation, is the feedback that should be given to the user during the selection process.

Architecture developers may find it useful to treat "UIA" concepts, the implementations serving as model prototypes, and the working documentation as if they were, taken together, a "product". That is, a "UIA" must itself be validated for effectiveness. Many of the customary "product assurance" techniques found in product development processes can be applied. Human factors testing can use interaction scenarios to help validate the architectural concepts for ease of learning and use (Figure 2). The "UIA" as a "product" can have its scope and content refined through a series of "releases". An approach to "managing" development against measurable, testable objectives is outlined in Bennett (16).

4.1 Human Factors Experimentation

Experimental work, informal and product-specific (17) or formal and more general (18), is important in discovering what architectural abstractions and concrete product details are needed for transfer of user habits. How do different presentation details affect user performance? What is an appropriate level of abstraction for the concept of menus? How do we define the "architectural form" necessary to support a successful evolution in user experience and new technology?

Figure 5 shows two particular instances of how a menu "architectural form" might be made concrete in products. Readers may see that the function of a menu is the same whether the list is displayed vertically or horizontally. We need to

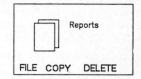

a) vertical format   b) horizontal format

Figure 5. Two examples of menus that might be found in products.

test in practice what percentage of users under what conditions are able to recognize the similarity and incorporate that understanding into their use of the system with a minimum of "think" time and a minimum of errors.

Developers of a "UIA" focus on the basic elements and principles for interaction. However, the architecture may well provide specific rules for specific technologies where human factors experiments and user experience suggest that one specific style of interaction serves users well.

Finally, implementation tools form an important means for putting architectural concepts into design practice. Carlson (19) pointed out the value of "standard details" in software tools "to make it easier for the developer to follow than not to follow conventions." We are now seeing this featured in products such as the Apple Macintosh (20): "... the toolbox saves development time and ... memory space, ... a positive incentive for doing it our way." "(It) provides a flexible structure capable of evolving as we learn how to improve the user interface."

5. SUMMARY

We have taken a short glance at problems which must be solved if a "UIA" is to become a reality. We have outlined some "UIA" developments we may expect, and we have sketched how progress in cognitive science and computer science might be fruitfully incorporated into the work. Human Factors experimentation will be important for validation of this empirical and iterative endeavor.

ACKNOWLEDGEMENTS

I have benefited from working with many colleagues over several years. H. Gladney has been especially generous in sharing his understanding of the computer science concepts needed as a foundation for a "UIA". C. Hauser and S. Zilles have been a helpful source of ideas and perceptive responses to my questions. P. Reisner and J. Karat have helped keep me alert to important work in human factors and experimental psychology. And I am indebted to colleagues R. Berry, J. McInroy, and T. Ruiz who bring a pragmatic development viewpoint to leaven what might be otherwise philosophical discussions.

Top Instruction

ID	ITEM	DESCRIPTION
Id1	label1	text for 1
Id2	label2	text for 2
id3	label3	text for 3

Bottom Instruction

Form Purpose: User chooses ...

Presentation Detail: Layout ...

Interaction Protocol: For pick, select, error recovery ...

Figure 4. A simplified abstract concept of a menu screen established to meet user requirements for transfer of habits.

REFERENCES

1. Lemmons, P., A guided tour of VisiOn; BYTE, June 1983, pp. 256-277.

2. Morgan, C., An interview with Wayne Rosing, Bruce Daniels, and Larry Tesler; BYTE, February 1983, pp. 90-114.

3. Goldberg, V., Unpublished keynote address, V. Goldberg, President, Communications Products Division, IBM, to 56th GUIDE Meeting, Chicago, May 18, 1983.

4. Rutkowski, C., An introduction to the human applications standard computer interface; BYTE, October 1982, pp. 291-310, November 1982, pp. 379-390.

5. Brooks, F. P. Jr., The Mythical Man-Month (Addison-Wesley, Reading MA, 1975).

6. Carroll, J., Presentation and form in user-interface architecture; BYTE, December 1983, pp. 113-122.

7. Woodson, W. E., Human Factors Design Handbook (McGraw-Hill, New York, 1981).

8. Ramsey, R., and Grimes, J., Human factors in interactive computer dialog, in Williams, M. (ed.), Annual Review of Information Science and Technology, Vol. 18 (Knowledge Industry Publications, Inc., White Plains, NY, 1983).

9. Card, S., Human limits and the VDT computer interface, in Bennett, Case, Sandelin, Smith (eds.), Visual Display Terminals: Usability Issues and Health Concerns (Prentice-Hall, Englewood Cliffs, NJ, 1984).

10. Association for Computing Machinery, Human Factors in Computing Systems; (ACM CHI 83 Proceedings, 11 West 42nd St, New York, NY 1983).

11. Goldberg, A. and Robson, D., SMALLTALK-80: The Language and its Implementation (Addison-Wesley, Reading MA, 1983).

12. Newman W., and Sproul, R., Principles of Interactive Computer Graphics, Second Edition, Chapter 28 (McGraw-Hill, New York, 1979).

13. Efe, K., Miller, C., and Hopper, K., The Kiwinet-Nicola approach: response generation in a user friendly interface, IEEE Computer, September 1983, pp. 66-78.

14. Gilb, T. Design by Objectives, Unpublished book manuscript, 1981.

15. Smith, S. and Aucella, A., Design Guidelines for the User Interface to Computer-Based Information Systems, ESD-TR-83-122, MITRE Corporation, Bedford MA (March 1983).

16. Bennett, J. L., Managing to meet usability requirements, in Bennett, Case, Sandelin, Smith (eds.), Visual Display Terminals: Usability Issues and Health Concerns (Prentice-Hall, Englewood Cliffs, NJ, 1984).

17. Tesler, L., Enlisting user help in software design, ACM SIGCHI Bulletin, January 1983, Vol 14, 3, pp. 5-9.

18. McDonald, J. and Karat, J., personal communication; paper to appear, 1984.

19. Carlson, E., Developing the user interface for decision support systems; in Bennett, J. (ed.), Building Decision Support Systems (Addison-Wesley, Reading MA, 1983).

20. Williams, G., The Apple Macintosh computer; Interface; BYTE, February 1984, pp. 30-54.

Human-Computer Interaction — INTERACT '84 / B. Shackel (ed.)
Elsevier Science Publishers B.V. (North-Holland)
© IFIP, 1985

The Visi On™ Experience – From Concept to Marketplace

George H. Woodmansee

VisiCorp
San Jose, California U.S.A.

The Visi On™ system[1,2] is a personal computer software operating environment for business oriented application programs. It was developed to increase the effectiveness of personal computers in the office by providing an easy to learn, use, and remember problem solving tool for office professionals. This paper describes its development from the perspective of interface engineering in a small market driven company where competitive time pressures substantially shape the development process.

1. THE PROJECT

1.1 Overview

Work began on Visi On in early 1981. From a modest beginning involving only a handful of people, the project grew over three years to include the efforts of many. When it shipped in late 1983, total costs had exceeded ten million dollars, total size exceed 350,000 source lines of code, and over 70 software development, publications, marketing and sales people had left their mark on the product.

During its three year development, the project passed through four major stages: specification, prototyping, analysis and respecification, and implementation.

The first two stages occupied roughly the first half of the project and dealt primarily with the Visi On operating environment rather than with the applications. This work was accomplished through informal interactions among a small, highly focused, tightly knit team.

During the latter half of the project, four applications (a spreadsheet, business graphics package, data base, and a word processor) were designed and implemented. The former two were shipped with the initial Visi On release. Applications development required that application specialists, people from the core Visi On system, marketing, and publications all work together. Results were accomplished through more formal and complex interactions necessitated by the ever increasing number of participants.

1.2 The Starting Point

Visi On began as a fairly general product concept targeted at the office market. As the first major step on the road to a concrete product, three questions had to be answered in detail: What, exactly, was the product to do? Who was to use it? and What constraints would shape its design and development?

What would it do?

The core of the Visi On system was viewed as an easy to learn and use problem solving aid which would integrate individual applications. This led to three initial requirements:

* Provide a consistent, intuitive, and streamlined interface across all applications to facilitate learning and use.

* Enable a number of applications to run and interact concurrently under user control.

* Provide convenient transfer of information between applications under user control.

Who would use it?

Visi On is intended for office professionals. While a detailed characterization of this diverse group is beyond the scope of this paper several important characteristics should be mentioned.

Most importantly, the office professional is a discretionary user, usually having alternative means of getting the job done and thus the option of not using the system. This person must find system interaction a beneficial, enjoyable, and nonconfronting experience.

The office professional is an occasional user who probably spends the majority of time interacting with people rather than with machines. He is not computer fluent and would probably find unacceptable a system steeped in jargon or requiring time consuming manual reading or training.

What constraints would affect its design?

A number of constraints shaped the final product. Among the most significant were: the nature of the software market for personal computers, competitive time pressure requiring rapid development, and the requirement to

operate on off-the-shalf, popular, relatively
inexpensive hardware.

These factors, together with the limited testing
resources available, precluded an extensive
external testing program during the early and
mid stages of the project. Most of the early
testing was informal and performed with VisiCorp
employees as users. Many of the significant
interface design ideas for the applications
were, of necessity, "solved on paper" and the
design was frozen without benefit of detailed
prototyping.

VisiCorp was not in the hardware business.
Visi On was a software solution to the requirements subject to the constraints imposed by the
host hardware. Initially, the product was
intended for a generic high performance third-
generation personal computer. This was defined
as one having a 16 bit CPU, 256K of primary
memory, a bit mapped display, one floppy disk
and a Winchester disk with at least a 5 MB
capacity. High display bandwidth was a critical
requirement for rapid re-display of changed data
during interaction with the user. Although the
intended host was "high performance", the
designers often found that they were working at
the outer edge of the machine's capabilities.

1.3 The Designer's Conceptual Model

Introduction

Much of our early thinking about human-computer
interaction was influenced by work done at
Xerox PARC/OSD (3,4). Several alternatives
were considered in detail. The initial Visi On
design attempted to combine the best interface
technologies known to us at the time with the
unique requirements of the office professional
market and the limitations imposed by the host
hardware. This led to a prototype of the core
system and an initial design specification.

During this period, the small design team agreed
among themselves on the same design philosophy.
However, we knew that as the project grew and
diversified, if the end product was to present
a consistent and effective interface, some
mechanism would be required to transfer this
design philosophy to new members of the development team. We needed a designer's conceptual
model of the system which, once assimilated,
would guide designers to make consistently good
design choices. This was especially important
when, at 4 a.m. in the morning, they discovered
the inevitable gaps in the design specification.

The designer's conceptual model began as a list
of fourteen overlapping, loosely defined
principles and ultimately was expressed in an
internal, proprietary, 60 page document titled
"The Designer's Guide to Well Behaved Products".
This document culminated several months of
effort in refining and extending the original
principles, and continued to grow even late in

the project. It familiarized new project
members with our intended user and extensively
discussed the overall effect we were attempting
to achieve and the methods for achieving that
effect.

The fourteen principles are:

- Guidedness
- Single/Multiple Activation
- Display Inertia
- System Information Access
- Progressive Disclosure
- User Feedback
- Cognitive Load
- Consistency
- Operation Optimization
- Product Structuring
- Selection/Entry
- What You See Is What You Get
- Novice/Expert
- Least Astonishment

They formalize the intuitions, common wisdom,
and ideas present in the literature which seemed
to be valuable to the members of the original
design team.

Putting these principles on paper helped in two
areas. The initial designers were sensitized
to critical interface issues, and each statement provided a framework for thinking about the
design problem. The principles were a start at
instilling a design philosophy in software
developers who would soon appear on the scene.

User Feedback provides a typical example of
these principles:

User Feedback

Immediate feedback for immediate operations
should be provided. Processing feedback to
reassure the user that processing is occurring
for extended operations should also be provided. The nature of the processing feedback
should be dependent upon the direction and
context of the processing. Based on the
human factors literature, the feedback should
be clear as to whether the processing will
take less than 3 seconds, from 3 to 15
seconds, or greater than 15 seconds.

User feedback may be used to illustrate how the
principles were developed, interpreted and
applied.

As stated, it has a relatively limited scope
and requires further specification and extension.
Analysis of the ideas behind user feedback led
us to the conclusion that it was part of the
more general problem of helping the user to
feel and be in control. This line of thought
eventually led to a number of interface
"solutions" which were then described in "The
Designer's Guide to Well Behaved Products".

They include:

- uniform commands
- basic interaction techniques (the same thing is always done the same way)
- a single method of initiating actions
- visually and behaviorally reinforced contexts
- engendering a feeling of familiarity through the use of physical metaphors
- what you see is what you get (WYSIWYG)
- direct manipulation

Basic interaction techniques (BITs) are particularly noteworthy and are discussed further in section 2.2 below.

Predictable behavior was probably one of the most important ideas underlying feeling in control. The intended user was people-oriented, not machine-oriented. He had no idea what was going on behind the screen. Had the machine heard him? Was it doing the right thing? Should he abandon it and use more familiar, tried, and true methods?

The interface had to capture the user's trust by helping him to feel in control at all times. This requirement led to a reactive interface philosophy in which the system waited for the user to initiate an action, let him know what it needed to complete the action, told him what was happening as the action was performed, and then signaled completion of the action or stated why the action couldn't be performed. This behavior was formalized in the "user interaction model" illustrated in figure 1.

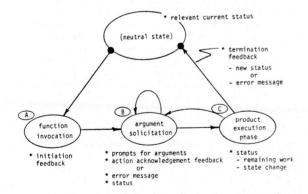

figure 1

2. REDUCTION TO PRACTICE

2.1 Introduction

The core Visi On system interface is based on a desk top metaphor similar to that found in the Xerox® Star (3). The screen displays over-lapping rectangular areas, called windows, in which applications run and display results. These are akin to pieces of paper on the user's desk.

All application windows have the same spatial layout, including a menu line which provides application-dependent courses of action. At the bottom of the screen is a fixed, application-independent menu for controlling the desk top. This menu allows the user to move and change the size of the windows, set windows aside, transfer data between applications, solicit help, and open other windows which provide application specific-options.

The core system interface and several demon-stration applications were prototyped early in the project. Informal testing with VisiCorp staff and limited external testing with repre-sentative users was performed. While the utility of the initial test results was limited because no production applications were avail-able, the need for a small number of changes was indicated. Appropriate parts of the proto-type were accordingly modified and reevaluated. The interface developed smoothly.

Application interfaces, on the other hand, were a real organizational and educational challenge. While the core system team was small and in reasonable accord, the applications involved a steadily increasing number of people with diverse backgrounds and their own ideas on what constituted a good interface. These ideas were not limited to software developers. Almost everyone had an opinion - "I'm not an artist but I know what I like". Forging a cohesive team whose members didn't think in terms of "we" versus "they" was a major undertaking. Keeping everyone headed in the same direction was initially a problem.

2.2 Application Interface Development

A number of techniques were used to promote uniformity. In addition to the designer's guide already mentioned, we held weekly inte-gration meetings which dealt with interface issues relevant to all applications, and periodic interface design reviews for individual applications. These reviews were primarily paper design evaluations with some accompany-ing blackboard scenario simulation. The sup-porting interface mockups were static and only told part of the story.

A small number of people were utilized as inter-face technique resources and participants in interface "gedanken" experiments. In this capacity they functioned more as advisors and

teachers than as legislators. When differences
of opinion arose, as was inevitable, they were
solved in one of several ways: an appeal was
made to supporting results in the literature if
they existed (rarely), an appeal was made to
the designers guide (usually requiring interpretation), one faction attempted to convince
the other faction of the correctness of their
position through appeals to logic or interpretation of market data (sparse), or a central
authority simply made a decision. Later in the
project, differences of opinion were resolved,
by necessity, on the basis of their projected
effect on the schedule.

Where mechanisms for standardizing aspects of
the interface were possible, they were put into
place. A small group of technical writers were
initially given responsibility for producing
error messages, prompts and help frames in
accord with their interpretation of the
designer's guide. This required close coordination among the writers, software developers,
and interface resource people.

Another method of standardization involved
designing a set of fifteen basic interaction
techniques (BITs) which the application
designers were required to use when performing
specified interactions with the user. They
are:

- prompting the user
- invoking actions via an application's
  command menu
- choosing from multiple choices
- line edited input
- unedited keystroke input
- mouse input
- list input
- form input
- option sheet interaction
- multi-media input (mouse, keyboard, ...)
- confirmation
- delay feedback (machine is busy)
- error message presentation
- sound response

BITs help the user to feel in control as discussed in section 1.3, by guaranteeing that the
same things are always done in the same way.
In all cases the BITs supply a standard method
of interaction. They encapsulate all user-
machine activity necessary to carry out a
specific task, including providing selection
feedback and error messages.

The Development Process

An application's development proceeded as
follows:

The designers produced a product specification and mockup (clarification of the
specification) based on the known product
requirements, user characteristics, hardware constraints and designer's conceptual

model. The specification was reviewed,
modified and approved.

As the product developed, the uniformity
techniques mentioned above were applied.
Evolving application interfaces were monitored periodically by interface techniques
resource people and marketing.

Once the software was reasonably complete and
stable, its interface was evaluated. The
earliest testing involved VisiCorp employees
as subjects, followed somewhat later by external subjects. Relatively late in the development cycle, tests with cooperative corporate
customers willing to sign a confidentiality
agreement was performed. Finally, some pre-
shipment user feedback was obtained during
several weeks of extensive dealer demonstrations and training.

3. LESSONS LEARNED

3.1 Introduction

The Visi On operating system made heavy use of
prototyping early in its development cycle.
Thus there were relatively few interface surprises. In contrast, the application interfaces were developed using a paper based evaluation approach.

As described above, the paper-based approach
involved evaluation and approval of interfaces
based primarily on their paper specifications.
These evaluations were augmented by scenario
walk through and mockups, but these ultimately
required the reviewer to visualize something
that didn't exist based on an inevitably
incomplete description.

Because a reasonably complete working interface
became available relatively late in the development cycle, the process was somewhat open
loop. The risk that there would be late problems which only heroic efforts could correct
was very real.

3.2 A Paper Based Methodology is Fine But ...

The paper-based design specification is necessary and has several things to recommend it.
Most importantly, it provides a record of
design decisions and their rationale. Of
somewhat lesser importance, it can be widely
disseminated and read, or carried about and
studied at leisure in almost any location.
But as a method of evaluating an interface, it
is sadly deficient.

There are just too many important details for
it to be really complete or to work effectively.
The design gaps, which always appear under time
pressure, produce a vacuum which the software
engineer obligingly fills with a personalized
design which is exactly what he would want if
he were a representative user - but he isn't.

Paper specifications, even if they were complete would not tell the story. They fail to portray the dynamics and synergy of the interface and are consequently imperfect mechanisms, at best, for review. The reviewer tends to use the specification to simulate the interface in his head. To do so, he must interpret liberally. This process is tedious, not enjoyable, and leads to incomplete reviewing. Further, the interpretation inherent in the simulation process leads to nasty surprises - "But that's not how I thought it worked!"

The solution to these problems is extensive early rapid prototyping and testing. This is discussed briefly under conclusions below.

3.3 Product Evaluation Context

Another trap is over reacting to interface test results obtained out of context. One gets quite different results if the subject is asked to "just play with the system" and perform a set of artificial mini-tasks, or to perform useful and familiar work. Mini-tasks are useful for studying specific interface problem areas, but they may give results which are at odds with tests performed within a problem solving context. An example is comparing function activation times via mouse-pick and keystroke without regard to context.

3.4 The Novice/Expert Design Point

We began with the goal of accommodating a totally naive user, an expert, or a user anywhere in between. We were able to produce sample interface designs for certain tasks which appeared to be so guided that almost any user who could understand english could correctly perform the task. This was accomplished by breaking the task into many primitive subtasks and liberally supplying prompts.

These designs were reminiscent of some mainframe interfaces which used teletypes. They did not make reasonable use of the output bandwidth of the system and were excruciatingly painful for anyone other than a novice. The Visi On interface philosophy was essentially visual, rather than symbolic. To accommodate both the truly novice user and the expert, and still properly utilize the display bandwidth, we would require two essentially different interfaces. We eventually biased the interface in favor of the more experienced user. A totally naive user has to acquire a certain amount of knowledge before he can solo. The requirement is not great, but neither is it zero.

3.5 Conclusions

The reality of compressed schedules in a competitive market, the frequent dearth of published human factors material relevent to our work, and the inadequacies of paper evaluation methodologies all underscore the need for rapid prototyping tools applied as a formal part of the early design process.

A prototype implemented early, refined and tested may serve as the nucleus of the interface design specification supporting the conventional paper functional specification. The prototype would provide an unambiguous review mechanism, provide a concrete gauge for measuring the production software, and could be evaluated early enough in the development cycle to allow end user reactions to substantially influence the final product.

References

(1) Woodmansee, G. H.
Visi On's Interface Design
BYTE, July, 1983; Volume 8 Number 7
(Pages 166-182)

(2) Lemmons, P.
A Guided Tour of Visi On
BYTE, June 1983; Volume 8 Number 6
(Pages 256-278)

(3) Smith, D.C.; Harslem, E.; Irby, C.;
Kimball, R.
The Star User Interface: An Overview
Proc. of National Computer Conference;
1982
June 7-10; Houston
(Pages 515-528)

(4) Goldberg, A. et al.
Smalltalk
BYTE, August, 1981; Volume 6, Number 8
Smalltalk Theme Issue

Human-Computer Interaction — INTERACT '84 / B. Shackel (ed.)
Elsevier Science Publishers B.V. (North-Holland)
© IFIP, 1985

QMF USABILITY: HOW IT REALLY HAPPENED

James Boyle, William Ogden, Steven Uhlir, and Patricia Wilson

International Business Machines Corporation
Santa Teresa Development Laboratory
San Jose, California, USA.

QMF is a query and report generator product that can easily be used by non-programmers. An easy to use human interface was a primary design goal, and this paper describes how this goal was met by a combination of techniques. First, and probably foremost, the design team consisted of a group of software engineers, quality assurance specialists, and human factors engineers whose design effort was focused on the required information and actions that users would need in order to complete their tasks. Next, there was a commitment to obtain empirical input to the early design process by testing representative subjects using early prototypes. Controlled tests were very useful, especially when they came early in the development cycle and were broadly focused. These proved to be more useful than pre-planned, formal, paper evaluations. In general, iterative testing was always useful and should be a part of every interface design effort.

INTRODUCTION

Query Management Facility (QMF) is a query and report generator product designed to be used by people with little or no programming background. This paper describes the way the user interface of QMF was developed and tested, and also describes some of the challenges associated with the application of human factors within the constraints of a commercial program product development cycle.

QMF provides a full screen interactive interface to the relational database products SQL/Data Systems and Data Base 2. It allows a user to specify a query in either an English-like syntax using Structured Query Language (SQL) [1], or a pictorial representation of the desired result using Query By Example (QBE) [2]. Report formatting is controlled through the use of a fill-in-the-blanks technique. By remembering the objects the user is currently dealing with, and allowing the user to move between these objects by using single keystrokes, QMF encourages the iterative development of reports. Also, an extensive set of on-line help information is available at any time to assist a user who is having difficulties.

A QMF user deals with a small number of different types of objects and a set of commands which operate on these objects. The most frequently used QMF objects are: the QUERY, the FORM, and the REPORT. The QUERY is used to select information from the data base; the FORM is used to control the formatting of the data; and the REPORT is the data selected by the QUERY formatted according to the instructions in the FORM. The most frequently used commands are: DISPLAY, RUN, and SAVE. DISPLAY is used to view an object; RUN retrieves the data requested by a QUERY; and SAVE makes a permanent copy of a QMF object. A user who knows only these objects and commands can make effective use of QMF.

At any time in a QMF session a user has access to a current set of objects consisting of the most recently used object of each type. Any of the current objects can be displayed by typing a single keystroke. This QUERY/FORM/REPORT and DISPLAY/RUN/SAVE model provides an environment which is well suited to the iterative development of a desired REPORT.

For example, a user might begin a QMF session with only a rough idea of the REPORT which is desired. The user might begin by composing a simple QUERY to "peek" at the data which is available, or by tailoring a QUERY which had been saved earlier. Figure 1 shows a simple example of an SQL QUERY and a QBE QUERY. The results of the QUERY are displayed as a REPORT with default formatting. If the result does not satisfy the user, he can return to the current QUERY, modify it, and RUN it again to see the new result. This iterative process can be continued until the user is satisfied with the information the QUERY retrieves.

Once the user has composed a QUERY which appears to satisfy the information needed, the presentation can be tailored by DISPLAYing the current FORM object. Figure 1 also shows an example FORM. The user modifies the FORM and returns to the REPORT to see the way the information looks in its new presentation. This iterative process can be continued until the user is satisfied with the format. If, while modifying the FORM, the user decides the QUERY needs modification, he can simply return to the QUERY to modify it and RUN it again.

THE FOUNDATION

Because the intended QMF user is a person with little or no programming training, it was recognized from the beginning that the focus of the development process should be on simplifying the amount and kind of information that a user would need to learn and use the product. Therefore,

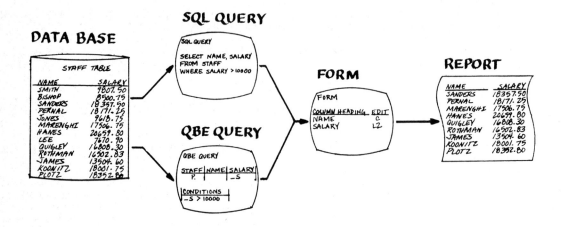

Figure 1. The QMF Model

the way the function was presented was equally, if not more, important than the amount of function QMF provided. This focus was maintained throughout the development process.

Initially the team consisted of a small number of software designers. In time the team grew to include human factors engineers and quality assurance specialists. This team generated a set of core assumptions for the product. They included: using an IBM 3270 type terminal in a full-screen mode to communicate with the user; making a clear distinction between the functions the user could ask the system to perform (the commands) and the things the user could ask the system to operate on (the objects); having a small number of different types of objects and a relatively small set of commands which operated uniformly on all of the objects.

The core assumptions resulted partly from marketing requirements and partly from the judgment of the developers. All of these assumptions were selected to make QMF easy to use. They were based on the human factors folk lore which the team was aware of rather than on results from formal studies. Some customers of similar products were surveyed, but this information tended to be specific to a product, was difficult to generalize, and ultimately did not turn out to be very useful.

Part of the success of the early stage could be attributed to the fact that the design group thought in terms of what tasks users might perform, what experience users might already have, and what would be easy for users to do. It was this focus and sensitivity which led to the basic QMF model. When it came to designing the details of the human interface, however, it was felt that more than sensitivity and commitment to ease of use was needed to ensure that the design decisions actually supported user tasks. Since there were (and are) no complete theories for designing the user interface of a product, a prototype was planned as the vehicle for testing

the design decisions as they were made. Thus, there was a commitment to have people use the proposed design alternatives in order to allow an assessment of ease of use based on empirical evidence rather than the analytical guesswork upon which many human interface designs are based.

To obtain empirical input to the design process, potential users must have something to interact with. Several things need to occur before such prototypes can be built. First the layout of the proposed screens that would be seen by the users were specified on paper. Next the transitions between the proposed screens were specified so each user action could be mapped into a specific system action. Thus an informal "paper simulation" technique was used by the design group early in the specifications of the external interface.

The use of paper simulations as a lead-in to prototype testing was a valuable way of obtaining feedback earlier than was possible from prototype testing alone. However, when paper simulations were used formally, as an end in themselves, the results sometimes turned out to be misleading. What is lacking in paper simulation techniques is the dynamics of the interaction. A realistic task context cannot be maintained as each screen and function is evaluated for ease of use. As a result, potential users will not respond in the same way as they will when interacting with a dynamic simulation. Therefore, the focus of the usability testing was on observing the user of the proposed design in situations which simulated the dynamics of actual QMF use as closely as possible.

As work proceeded on a prototype, many small-scale tests were performed using the functional parts of the prototype as they became available. However, it became clear that the established schedules did not allow enough time to build a fully functional prototype, test it, and then build the final product. As a result, work on the prototype was stopped and the development effort concentrated on the final product. But the team was faithful to the commitment to developing a usable product, and the parts of the prototype that were built were used effectively.

TESTING THE HUMAN INTERFACE.

Most of the tests which were conducted on QMF could be classified as "observational" tests and were carried out quite informally. This is in contrast to conducting tests that are intended to determine how well the product converges on predetermined usability criteria. Although a formal usability plan was considered, it turned out to be impossible to predict the areas which needed the most attention until some testing had been performed. Thus, the usability work which was needed could not be specifically planned.

Much of the testing was simply the use of the early prototypes by members of the design team who would incorporate their experience back into the design. Some of the tests, however, were considered formal because they used potential users as subjects who were typically recruited from a group of upper-division and graduate-level business students. We will focus our discussion on these more formal tests which were of two basic types:

- Controlled studies focusing on particular issues using simulation techniques to control particular aspects of the proposed interface.

- Iterative testing of the interface and documentation.

A number of examples will be discussed which fit into these two basic categories.

Controlled studies.

These studies were directed at determining answers to specific design questions. In order to be useful, these tests had to be both timely and non-trivial. In other words, the results of these tests had to be available soon enough to have an impact on the design; and further, the question that the test investigated had to be appropriate in the context of the constraints operating on the design.

Command vs form fill-in. One specific problem concerned the selection of a method for changing the format specification for a QMF report. Two basic methods were considered, a command method and a full-screen form method. A prototype was used to compare user performance and preference when learning and using both methods. The prototype was constructed so that subjects could make changes to the format of a displayed report either by typing a linear command while viewing the report or by displaying and entering information into a fill-in-the-blanks form specification screen. Twelve subjects were given several tasks requiring changes to be made to the report format while learning each method. After learning each method, they were allowed to use the method of their choice. The results of

this test showed that while the performance advantage for the form fill-in method was small, subjects chose to use this method rather than the command method. Details of this test have been reported in [3]. This was an important test in that it confirmed a preliminary decision to provide the form method.

Error message/message HELP evaluations. Users will make errors using the best of designs. Therefore, a well-designed interface will provide users with information that will help them recover from error situations. QMF provides one-line error messages when an error is first detected and users have an option of receiving more error message help information, on-line, by pressing a function key. Providing accurate and understandable information to enable users to correct their errors is a key feature of QMF. Initially, an Error Message Review Board was formed to evaluate proposed messages. This was a panel established to review QMF's end-user messages for usability, consistency, and effectiveness, and to make appropriate improvements. Unfortunately, members of the panel attempted to conduct the review by examining the text of the messages in a document, not by actually exercising the product and forcing the messages in context. This board met several times before being abandoned. Again, it was determined that paper reviews of error messages did not capture enough of the dynamics of error situations to contribute to the production of quality messages.

Therefore, a controlled study was directed at improving the quality of the error messages and help information generated by QMF. A message testing technique described by [4] was used to present practiced QMF subjects with hypothetical QMF error situations. To test the effectiveness of the error messages, subjects were asked to correct the error without and then with the QMF error message help associated with the situation. Subjects could then rate the quality of the message and suggest new error messages. Messages that were rated poorly or did not lead to improved error correction performance were rewritten and retested.

Ninety-five different messages and HELP panels were evaluated in an iterative evaluation that consisted of three parts. On the first pass, the product developers were tested in a pilot study. As a result of this test, approximately 25% of the messages were rewritten. It is worth noting that the software developers, with their understanding of precisely what diagnostic information is available for a particular error condition, were able to improve message content once they were able to view the error condition from the end user's perspective. Probably the testing of developers (something not initially considered) was one of the most productive aspects of this exercise. Next, there were two iterations of testing done on the 95 test cases using 14 subjects who were representative of the QMF user population. As a result of this testing, additional changes were made to the message text and more particularly to the content of the HELP panels. During the formal test phase, 18 messages were changed and 37 HELP panels were modified.

The message evaluation resulted in substantive changes in the information that users have when attempting to correct their errors. Therefore this test was both timely and non-trivial.

Format preference test. A preference test was conducted to evaluate the kind of graphics that might be used for the cross-column headings on the QMF formatted report. Sixteen people were asked to choose the graphic they thought was most appealing from 44 different combinations. As expected, someone liked almost every choice, although everyone agreed that one was particularly un-aesthetic. Surveys of aesthetic preferences often produce results similar to these. They do not allow designers to select a "best" alternative but they can alert them to alternatives that are going to be met with significant dislike.

Format code test. This was a paper-and-pencil test to compare a set of codes used on the Form Panel to define the format for numeric data (e.g., with or without leading zeros, with or without thousands separator). A set of codes that was meaningfully associated with the format (e.g., the digit "0" (zero) to indicate that leading zeros were desired, the character "," (comma) to indicate that a thousands separator was desired) was compared to the originally proposed set of codes which had been selected more arbitrarily. The comparison was made by having 12 test subjects learn both code sets and then perform formatting tasks.

The results showed that test subjects did significantly better with the more meaningful set of codes than with the original set. These results verified what would have been expected given research findings of human learning and memory [5]. However, the test did not consider a number of significant characteristics of the QMF environment. One of the things that was overlooked was that some people prefer to use a period (rather than the comma) as the thousands separator. Others prefer to use a blank. A user can instruct QMF to use any of these characters (a comma, a period, or a blank) as the thousands separator. If the user chooses a period or a blank as a thousands separator, a format code of a comma would be a poor way of indicating that a thousands separator was desired. Another thing which was overlooked was the possibility of future expansion of the number of format options. It was clear that meaningful format codes would be difficult to generate for each new instance. Thus, the meaningful codes that were tested and shown to provide a more usable set in the context of the test were abandoned in favor of the original set which provided more flexibility.

The outcome of simple tests like this needed to be interpreted in the context of the current product and possible future enhancements. We do not as yet have formal methods for conducting the type of trade-off study this situation requires [6]. By interpreting the results of simple tests in this way, what seemed at face value to be a poor choice became the best alternative in the long run.

Iterative tests

These tests were designed to simulate as much of the human interface as practical with the goal of finding out as much as possible about the usability of QMF. The questions were therefore very general, and the results were analyzed informally. Of major concern was determining where and why subjects had problems using the prototypes and early code. These tests are presented in chronological order.

Function prototype test. An early prototype test evaluated use of the QBE query format, the distinction between active and saved objects, Command/PF Key compatibility, and the mechanics of query formulation using the graphic query form.

Problems found with the graphic query form were in the areas of cursor positioning, table skeleton manipulation, use of the Condition Box, LIKE syntax, and Output Tables. PF Keys for command entry were found to be used effectively and preferred. The action/object concept, when specifically described and demonstrated, was understood.

This was one of the first "formal" human factors evaluations of the human interface.

Market review board. This was a several-day session with IBM customer-support specialists who were knowledgeable about customer needs and capabilities. The product was explained in detail and they were given a chance to try out what was currently working as well as to critique the then-current teaching approach. Much valuable input was obtained from this somewhat informal "usability walk through" about how customers would learn, view, and use QMF. This walk through would have been even more valuable had it been conducted earlier in the design cycle.

QMF panel prototype test. This test was conducted early in the development cycle when some of the original thinking about what QMF should look like was being done. One of the things that prompted this test was the first draft of a "QMF Introductory User's Guide" that was intended to give first-time users a product overview and instruction for using QMF at the terminal.

An initial goal of the "Guide" was to get the user doing something constructive at the terminal within five minutes. While it was found that in general this could be accomplished, the more important goal of having the user understand the product after finishing the book was not met. In addition, several serious product design problems were found, most notably: (a) the presentation of a Prompt panel when an QMF command error was detected was found by test subjects to be completely misleading, (b) the HELP facility was very difficult to use, (c) cryptic Table and Column names in the sample data base were frequently misspelled during query writing.

The identification of these problems led to the following changes. The goals of the "Introductory User's Guide," as well as the general tone and approach of the book, were completely changed.

HELP was simplified to a two-level hierarchy, and the content of the panels was simplified. The method of accessing the Prompt Panels was changed. The sample data base tables and column names were given full word names. All of these changes resulted in better user performance and satisfaction in later tests.

Final full-function test. This was a usability evaluation of the entire product that was conducted late in the development cycle using completed product code and copies of near-final drafts of the user documentation. One of the major purposes of this evaluation was to take a comprehensive look at usability in an extended test situation. It was also viewed as a way to verify the overall usability of the many changes made as a result of earlier human factors testing on individual parts of the product.

This test phase was very important in the usability development cycle in that it provided valuable information about how the product would function in its entirety and how it would be perceived by users who were permitted to approach the test problems without restrictions.

The test was successful in that there were few surprises or problems that had not been encountered in earlier prototype testing. The value was in getting an opportunity to look at comprehensive use of QMF. One particularly useful step in this test was a group debriefing of test subjects that occurred after formal testing was completed which gave the design team a chance to receive input from the subjects about their experiences with QMF and about what they "wished" they could have done with QMF. This provided good input for future releases.

WHAT WE WOULD HAVE LIKED TO DO BETTER.

In retrospect, the development process had "too much reliance on rational analysis and not enough empirical testing" [7]. This was in part due to the standard development process that calls for the completion of a functional specification and associated design documentation to various levels of detail at certain prescribed times during the development cycle. Various proposals in the form of draft specifications were iteratively reviewed by the project team in order to meet the required process deadlines. When the implementation stage of the cycle began, the publications department took the specification as input for producing the required user publications. While certain aspects of this procedure were good, the balance needs to swing toward less specification and internal review in the beginning and more building of prototypes/simulators and associated draft user publications in order to develop the user interface.

During the life cycle of a product, there is constant contention between the needs of the marketplace and the cost of the associated development. Product content and schedules are put in place after an analysis of these factors. Frequently, trade-offs will be made. For example, a particular aspect of the product will be redesigned to be more usable in light of the competition or a particular function will be left out due to cost. A particularly frustrating aspect of this process is to encounter a problem which has no obvious solution, which requires a sustained design effort to think through the current and future implications, and which will cause a certain amount of "breakage" to the existing product. The solution often must wait for inclusion into the next release of the product. We feel the answer to this dilemma lies in the more flexible development process alluded to earlier with early verification and testing of the product and publications.

Due to the constraints involved in developing a program product within IBM, there was little direct involvement with actual customer end users during the early design and development stages of QMF. The team was able to compensate somewhat for this critical lack of involvement by visiting customers who were using the QBF and System R precursor products, and by working with the marketing divisions who had direct contact with our potential future customers. These contacts and the work documented by the IBM Research Division on the precursor products gave us some perspective on the issues we were struggling with, but they were a poor substitute for having end users participate as members of the project team.

Perhaps a better approach would have been to establish joint study contracts with potential QMF customers with the intention of having their users directly involved in design iterations as full-fledged members of the project team.

Our future plans include obtaining as much feedback as possible through participation in conferences and various user groups. In addition, customers who gain some experience with the first release of the product should be in a position to influence any future direction of the product in a very positive way. We hope to be able to consult with these users concerning the current product content and to enlist their aid in exercising and critiquing prototype enhancements to the product. However, even with an available product, IBM must take care to avoid disclosing planned enhancements prior to the official announcement.

SUMMARY

The cornerstone of the QMF development project was ease of use. During the product development cycle, the attention of the product development team was focused on the needs of the QMF user.

The design process began by understanding the kinds of tasks a user of QMF would want to perform. Next, we had to consider the user's needs, capabilities, and limitations. Product design goals, considered in terms of both task and user descriptions, thus formed the basis for the initial design of QMF externals.

Basic QMF end-user tasks include learning about the product, writing queries, and producing formatted reports. In support of these tasks, the user interface to QMF can be described in terms of four elements: the query languages, QMF commands and panels, user manuals, and messages. Since each of these elements influence the ease with which a user will learn and use QMF, we had to know as early in the development cycle as possible whether the initial design choices would meet the needs of prospective users. This was accomplished by iteratively testing each part of the interface. This testing was done under controlled laboratory conditions using representative users as test subjects.

Several human factors evaluations were performed on each of the QMF user interface elements throughout the development process. The techniques used to understand user interaction with the product and to confirm design direction included: iterative testing, prototyping of interface alternatives, stand-alone error message evaluations, group meetings between test users and developers, and further testing. This was a dynamic process in which results of usability evaluations were used to influence QMF design. Finally, all the interface elements were assembled and an all-inclusive user/product evaluation was run, again using people who were like the target QMF user.

There is no magic formula to guide the usability aspects of design. Neither is there any guarantee that development, assurance, or human factors professionals have intuitive answers or facts at their fingertips that will insure product usability. Seeking out expert opinions and keeping the user in mind during design are helpful approaches, but only when these are done in conjunction with controlled observations of product use by typical users can we begin to appreciate the end user's perspective. Keeping this perspective has been the QMF development team's approach to designing a usable interface.

REFERENCES

1. Chamberlin, D.D., Astrahan, M.M., Eswaran, K.P., Griffiths, P.P., Lorie, R.A. Mehl, J.W., Reisner, P. and Wade, B.W., "SEQUEL 2: A unified approach to data definition, manipulation, and control," IBM Journal of Research and Development, Nov. 1976, 20, 556-575.

2. Zloof, M.M., "Query-by-example: A data base language," IBM Systems Journal, 1977, 16, 324-343.

3. Ogden, W.C., and Boyle J.M., "Evaluating human-computer dialog styles: Command vs. form fill-in for report modification." Proceedings of the Annual Meeting of the Human Factors Society, Seattle WA., 1982.

4. Isa, B.S., Boyle J.M., Neal A.S., and Simons R.M., "A methodology for objectively evaluating error messages." Proceeding of the CHI 1983 conference on Human Factors in computer systems. Boston, December, 1983.

5. Hintzman, D.L., The Psychology of Learning and Memory, W.H. Freeman and Company, San Francisco, 1978.

6. Norman, D.A., "Design principles for human-computer interfaces," Proceeding of the CHI 1983 conference on Human Factors in Computer systems. Boston, December, 1983.

7. Gould, J.D., and Lewis, C., "Designing for usability: Key principles and what designers think." Proceeding of the CHI 1983 conference on Human Factors in Computer systems. Boston, December, 1983.

Human-Computer Interaction — INTERACT '84 / B. Shackel (ed.)
Elsevier Science Publishers B.V. (North-Holland)
© IFIP, 1985

HUMAN FACTORS ROLES IN MILITARY SYSTEMS

John B. Shafer

IBM Federal Systems Division - Owego, NY

A series of vignettes are used to illustrate various Human Factors roles in the life-cycle of military systems. As programs progress through requirements, design, development, evaluation, selling, installation and training; the Human Factors roles flex and change to meet project demands. The successful human interface design, produced on schedule within budget constraints is the result of a great deal of creativity and resourcefulness.

INTRODUCTION

While development programs for defense systems in general follow a functional sequence similar to that in industry, each specific project presents its own individual challenge. Typically, military programs step through a series of formal development phase reviews which provide the Department of Defense a management technique for guiding and monitoring development progress. Government and military systems, because of their unique objectives and requirements, offer a variety of human-system interactions requiring creative yet practical solutions. It would be fascinating to trace the Human Factors challenges of a single program through all of its development phases, however, some of the interesting details of many of these programs are classified. Also, new and captivating programs that advance the state of the art, have yet to progress through all of the development phases. Thus, it seemed more appropriate to use a series of vignettes to illustrate the Human Factors role during various stages of development of military and government systems.

REQUIREMENTS

IBM Owego Human Factors was awarded a contract to design a very reliable human interface for a military computerized transmitting/receiving system.

We are all familiar with unique and unusual designs that have actually invited human error. Consider, however, that even if the design reflects good Human Factors principles, there still exists some probability for human error. Some researchers have investigated the problem of quantifying human reliability as it relates to various tasks. Munger, Smith and Payne (1) published a table of human reliabilities associated with elemental tasks (Data Store) to aid others in estimating human reliability. Meister has published a review of the literature on human reliability since 1970, (2) with partic-

ular attention to theoretical and quantitative models and the data bases that support them. The necessity for highly accurate transmissions precipitated a very high accuracy requirement for human input. The task was to enter latitude, longitude, time, and other codes for appropriate communications. Under certain circumstances, a small error could send an aircraft into the wrong airspace. Analytical calculations of human error probability required certain assumptions with respect to input keying error. Data collected by the author were germane to achieving a solution but also presented two practical concerns: 1) the data were considered company sensitive, preventing public dissemination as supporting evidence, and 2) since it was internal company generated data, it could be considered biased. After some searching, "Data Store" came to the rescue providing a list of human reliability estimates for input keying. Applying this human error probability to task and reliability analyses, it was reluctantly determined that standard operating procedures would not meet the low-error probability requirement.

Preliminary attempts to solve the problems considered reducing procedural steps or providing some sort of mental or mechanical aids. As one trial solution was rejected after another for various practical reasons, brute force gave way to creative insight.

The solution to meeting the requirement turned out to be typically military- have a second person double check the first person! Historically it reminds one of keypunch verification. The fact that the error rate requirement was so stringent raised a practical test and evaluation issue of verifying that the design solution actually met the requirements. While a test of many thousand operations could reveal unacceptably high error rates, success would not indicate that the error rate was below the required "one-in-a-million." In practice the requirement was untestable. This was solved by analytically determining the potential human reliability in the following manner.

Assume:

-   Two people are independently required to
    enter the same character string of length
    L.

-   An auto comparator can detect all errors
    except for matching substitution errors.

-   Each character has an equal probability of
    substitution error.

Let: Se   =   The probability of a
                 substitution error

        N   =   The number of characters
                 available

        L   =   The length of the character
                 string

The probability of a matching error is

$$\frac{(Se)^2}{N}$$

The probability of not encountering a matching
error is

$$1 - \frac{(Se)^2}{N}$$

The probability of not obtaining a matching
error on a string of length L (assuming
independence) is

$$\left[1 - \frac{(Se)^2}{N} \right]^L$$

The probability of at least one matching error
in a string of length L is

$$\left[1 - \left[1 - \frac{(Se)^2}{N} \right] \right]^L$$

Since L and N were known requirements then it
can be seen that the acceptable credibility of
the probability of a substitution error (Se)
became crucial to the analytical argument.

It has been said that when the Human Factors
interface is well designed, it goes unnoticed.
Personal communication with the field-test
engineer indicated that procedures to operate
the control panel flowed very naturally and
testing concentrated on getting the job done
without any particular notice of the man-machine
interaction. As expected from the mathematical
analysis, no human errors were recorded during
Test and Evaluation.

DESIGN

Advances in technology often present challenges
to the Human Factors Engineer because there is

scant information relating to the human interfaces of new technology.

The advanced helicopter programs represent a
dramatic evolution from present traditional
cockpit instrumentation to technology for the
'80s and '90s respectively. Functions that are
presently allocated to electromechanical
instruments are being allocated to CRT
displays. Cockpits reflecting the traditional
standard design will have a "T" cluster of
instruments (see Figure 1) with the attitude
indicator at the top of the "T," the airspeed
to the left, the altitude to the right and the
horizontal situation indicator (HSI) below.
These instruments are placed in the "T" to
minimize eye travel when viewing the instrument
panel. The functions of the instruments are to
give the pilot information about his position
in the air relative to the earth. Other
sensors and instruments provide additional
information relative to navigation, threats,
terrain, communication, and tactics. The pilot
provides the first level of integration to fly
the aircraft, perform tactics, avoid threats
and coordinate operations.

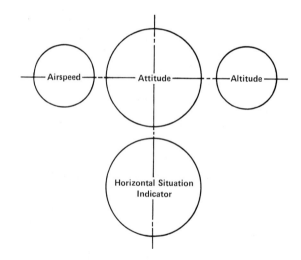

Figure 1. Standard "T" cluster

As the mission objectives of helicopters become
more complex, then the information required by
the pilot increases both in volume and complexity. Space available on the instrument
panel during this evolution has decreased and
become a critical constraint for trade-offs
between space and required information. These
requirements and constraints have led to recommending the use of multipurpose displays for
the presentation of flying information, sensor
information and tactics. Often the standard
"T" cluster has remained on the instrument
panel as back up (see Figure 2).

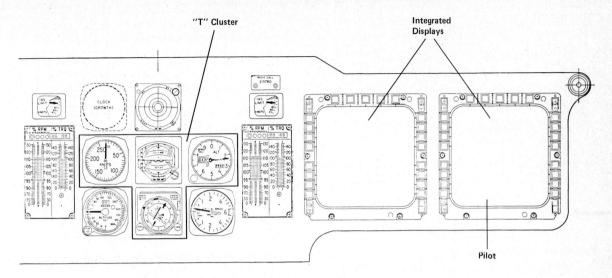

Figure 2. Advanced helo instrument panel, right side

The Human Factors role now advances from trading off the constraints of space to designing a compatible software interface. Formats must be uncluttered and meaningful, response time very quick, and the total interface absolutely consistent. If the computer is to take over the flying functions and free the pilot to make other decisions then the system interface must be consistent, reliable and friendly enough to gain the pilot's confidence. If the flight is in bad weather in the dead of night, and the computer is expected to keep the pilot safely aloft, it requires a great deal of creative effort to build that kind of confidence into the human interface of the system. Imagine trusting the driving of your car to a computer under the same conditions!

The evolution of advanced integrated data bus architectures along with intelligent systems, plus advances in storage and computing power have opened the door for a number of creative possibilities. The key to taking advantage of opportunities new technologies offer is to understand the basic functions and objectives of the system independent of equipment of software. For example, if we are aware that the basic objective of low level flight is to hide from radar detection while also avoiding the next hill or tree, one can conceive a number of technical alternatives to accomplishing that mission objective. The challenge for Human Factors as development progresses is to verify through progressive evaluations that the design achieves the fine balance of compatibility and gains the confidence required.

Thus, functions that were accomplished by the combinations of traditional instruments and pilot judgement, will in the future be allocated to CRT displays and smart software. The pilot will become more of an executive manager and the computer will take on the role of a copilot. The role of Human Factors efforts must concentrate on keeping the pilot's information manageable to avoid cognitive overload and in the advanced helicopters, provide appropriate operational designs to reduce prolonged operator stress.

DEVELOPMENT

There is a large complex Anti-Submarine Warfare (ASW) system in which a ship sends a helicopter out to detect submarines that may be attacking the fleet. The first challenge in the development role faced by Human Factors was to generate a comprehensive, top-down structured functional flow which identified the complex mission-oriented functional relationships. Functional flows have been a practice of Human Factors for many years usually done to determine development requirements and often reflecting authors individual formats. Recently some authors have attempted to bring some standardization to structured analyses (3) (4) (5).

Figure 3 illustrates schematically the technique of decomposing flows in a top-down structured analysis. The top level flow is usually mission oriented, encompassing all the mission objectives at a gross level. Each block of these flows is successively decomposed to lower level flows and the fourth level of decomposition of the flows identifies the human interfaces within the system. These flows continue decomposing for three more levels to reach the level of "button-pushing" procedures.

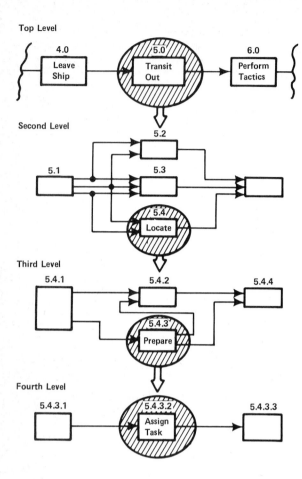

Figure 3. Technique for decomposing flows

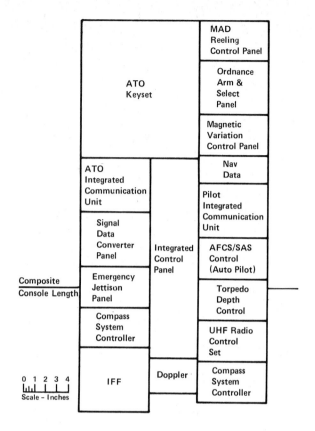

Figure 4. First center console configuration

The identification of human interfaces in the
ASW system led Human Factors to the challenge of
meeting mission objectives by blending together
existing, off-the-shelf, equipment and new
technology into each operator interface both for
the shipboard subsystem and helicopter subsystem. The following indicates the nature of
successfully meeting the challenge of evolving
an acceptable design for the center console of
the helicopter. First there was a determination
of the space available and what existing and new
equipment was required to fit into that space
(Figure 4). It can be seen, from the composite
console line, that there was more equipment than
space, a common phenomenon in cockpit design.
Eventually, after many interactions of design,
eliminating redundancies and combining
functions, a console design meeting mission
requirements was achieved. Part of the design
solution was to lengthen the center console
requiring the pilot to reach further. The Human
Factors team was required to assess the
trade-offs and determine how the development
solution was to meet overall requirements. This
process continued for the helo instrument panel
and shipboard systems as well.

Many other like decisions were made by the
development team to achieve a total systems
design. The IBM team was able to produce ahead
of schedule, within budget, the best ASW system
the US Navy has ever tested.

EVALUATION

Human Factors evaluations of some form are done
at every stage of system development. As
development progresses evaluations draw closer
to the final operating environment but require
resourcefulness to implement. In the early
conceptual phases full-scale cardboard mockups
are constructed to understand work flow in
three dimensions. Human Factors built two
different full-scale cardboard helicopters for
the ASW program to evaluate competing designs
(figure 5). As a project moves into development, mockups become better defined evolving to
wood and metal. They become "electrified"
emulating or simulating proposed functions.
During advanced helo development an IBM Personal
Computer was used to generate interactive
display formats in the cockpit mockup used for
evaluation. The evaluation continues to evolve
in phase with the development program as "Hot
Benches" become active simulators used for
structured testing. When the first system is
built it is field tested under operational and
maintenance conditions by real users.

Figure 5. Cockpit mockup

For the Navy this first field test is usually a technical evaluation (TECHEVAL) to demonstrate hardware and software feasibility. For the ASW system TECHEVAL was performed at sea. The U.S. Navy at sea does not offer controlled laboratory conditions. The challenge for the Human Factors evaluator is to collect data on human interface activity without disturbing the military operations or technical objectives. Collecting data at sea under real world operating conditions can be an exhilarating experience all by itself but to gather human interface data unobtrusively presents unique challenges. To view other console displays in parallel or to hear various selectable sets of conversations, requires special or unique rigging of the operating equipment by Navy technicians.

While highly motivated to achieve a successful technical test, the Navy technicians often needed some "extra" incentive to perform special tasks for contractor personnel. Contractor technicians were exchanging favors with Navy technicians by helping to fix the ships radar or communications gear, but these repair skills are typically not part of the Human Factors skill profile. It was soon discovered that insignia pens issued by IBM to contractor personnel were high value items with Navy technicians. Thus, even though data were collected with stubbier pencils, it was collected on a much broader range of events.

Field evaluation usually requires comprehensive flexible planning and then on-site resourcefulness to implement.

SELLING THE SYSTEM

IBM was requested to demonstrate incremental productivity in an experimental Post Office using recently installed advanced mail sorting equipment. The experimental mail sorting system represented a case where psychological aspects of the human interface and job environment had equal or greater importance in the productivity achieved than the equipment or software internal interfaces. Achieving the required system productivity was directly dependent upon operator performance at a code desk.

After careful analytical study of the operator interface, Human Factors determined that performance feedback would provide the most fruitful results in motivating a productivity increase. The computer interfacing with the code desk was programmed to record operator coding rates. At first, a team motivation approach was applied by posting the average rate for the whole group each day. The team approach proved to be painfully ineffective with no improvement in performance. A second approach provided private individual feedback in a report-card like form with unnamed individual rates posted on the bulletin board. Individual competitiveness sprung forth with low performers struggling not to be last and high performers scrambling to be first. The average rate of individual productivity increased 29 percent.

Another aspect of selling the system is the question, "To whom? The buyer or the user?". Clearly it must be sold to both. Traditionally, admirals and generals buy systems, but the actual users are lower-ranked individuals who may be willing to try new technology. Also, buyers and users change over the long life of a large military program. New buyers are often interested in improving design and changing the course of a system's development. While these may be worthy goals they usually increase costs and delay delivery. The challenge to the Human Factors engineer is to keep a convincing audit trail that justifies the existing design position to the new buyer. What "sold" to the initial buyer may not always "sell" to the latest buyer. The ASW system was overseen by a series of Naval Officers as tours of duty shifted over a period of 9 years before the first production model appeared. A clean audit trail of design decisions provided a clear picture which prevented arbitrary changes making the system less usable.

INSTALLATION AND TRAINING

Human Factors is often required to establish training requirements and to support the production of training materials. The challenge presented by large military systems is the enormous size of the training program. As the ASW system functional flows and Mission Tasks Analyses were being generated, it became obvious from the number of human interfaces that requirements for training would overwhelm existing internal capacity. Staff for seven operator positions had to be trained as well as a host of maintainers for hundreds of equipment items. Human Factors and the Mission Task Analyses played a key role in defining objectives and structuring an Instructional Systems Development Approach (ISD) (5). ISD is a systematic method for implementing a large complex training program.

Government and industry have focused significant attention on the systematic use of behavioral data for the design and evaluation of instructional programs for complex skill training. These systematic methods have been developed from an approach first identified by Miller (6). Over the years, refinement through experience and research and development efforts have changed the applied techniques, but the fundamental approach remains the same. That approach seeks to accurately and completely identify the specific behavioral skills expected to be demonstrated by graduates of the training program. These expectations are matched against the actual skills of new students. The differences between current and desired skill define the training objectives, and subsequently courses, media, equipment, instructors and facilities of the contemplated training program.

As a result of the intensive, focused, ASW system training development effort, courses and manuals were smoothly integrated into the Navy training structure. Pilots, operators and maintainers now acquire new skills on complex sophisticated simulators at various sites across the United States. A high level of funding (hundreds of millions) and years of creative effort produced a very successful training program.

SUMMARY

The practice of Human Factors in military systems may differ in design objectives, size and complexity, but the basic application of Human Factors Engineering principles are similar. There is a strong reliance on creative efforts to apply existing knowledge to future applications. Design of human-system interfaces often go beyond the limits of existing research data. The billions of dollars and immense human resources invested in military projects rely heavily on systematic approaches to protect investment risks. The vignettes have illustrated that Human Factors plays a crucial role in protecting those investments.

References:

(1) De Marco, T. Structured Analysis and System Specification (Yourdan Press, 1978).

(2) Dickover, M. A concept for a structured system description and analysis methodology (Softech 2123-1, Waltham, Mass 1980).

(3) Gane, C. and Sarson, T., Structured Systems Analysis (Prentice-Hall Inc., Englewood Cliffs, N.J. 1977).

(4) Johnson, S.L., Buckenmaier, C.C. and Sugarman, R.C. Instructional system design for air crew training (Proceedings of the Eighteenth Annual Meeting of the Human Factors Society, 1974).

(5) Meister, David, Human reliability, Human Factors Review, (1984).

(6) Miller, R.B. A method for determining human engineering design requirements for training equipment. WADC Technical Report TR53-135 (1953).

(7) Munger, S.J., Smith, R.W. and Payne, D. An index of electronic equipment operability (American Institute for Research, 1962).

Human-Computer Interaction — INTERACT '84 / B. Shackel (ed.)
Elsevier Science Publishers B.V. (North-Holland)
© IFIP, 1985

MAN-MACHINE INTERFACE DESIGN PROCESS

Gregory V. Kloster and Kristine Tischer

Computer Technology Associates, Inc.
5670 S. Syracuse Circle, Suite 200
Englewood, Colorado 80111

Many systems are built by selecting computers and displays, developing software, and only then retrofitting the human, his procedures, idiosyncracies and experiences into the design. Such retrofits are done almost as an afterthought resulting in systems in which the Man-Machine Interface (MMI) is re-engineered within the constraints of a fixed hardware system. To mitigate the risks associated with these approaches, a structured process is being used which focuses on an interdisciplinary and user-involved approach to better engineer the MMI. This approach presumes that man is a starting point in the design process.

1.0 INTRODUCTION

The system designer seeks to "optimize" the design of the human-computer subsystem and "maximize" human performance. This is achieved when the human element is balanced with the other system elements (hardware and software), to achieve cost effective, operationally reliable, and maintainable system design solutions. The system designer maximizes human performance by solving the end-users' information needs and by providing them with ergonomic display qualities appropriate for task demands to minimize errors and maximize motivation and productivity.

In recent years, a body of knowledge, technology, and experience on how to better design the MMI has emerged. Present methods of MMI design often depend more upon individual judgement than on systematic application of knowledge. Specifications may include only general statements that the system must be "easy-to-use". In the absence of more effective guidance, both the design and implementation of the MMI has become the responsibility of software development personnel often unfamiliar with operational requirements, human performance requirements, and techniques for enhancing human motivation and productivity.

MMI design is best practiced by specialists experienced in the human engineering of interactive systems. But such experts are not always available, and they certainly cannot guide every step of MMI design. We need to capture expert judgement and experiences (derived from the new emerging research in decision-aiding, expert systems, human factors, etc.) in the form of explicit procedures and guidelines.

Present human engineering standards are oriented toward improving the design of hardware. Other areas of MMI technology, such as software are not addressed. This paper summarizes an interdisciplinary and structured approach to engineering the MMI.

2.0 ORIGINS AND STATUS OF THIS MMI DESIGN METHODOLOGY

The MMI Design Process methodology, started in 1978, consists of 6 major steps. Each of these steps (shown in Figure 1) is organized into specific designer tasks. This process has been documented in a design guidebook [1] which is still undergoing revision as the methodology is applied to various projects. The methodology is now being applied to the engineering of the U.S. Federal Aviation Administration's (FAA) Advanced Automation System (AAS) Air Traffic Controller MMI. See reference [2] and other reports in a series.

Since 1978 accomplishments include the development of an MMI Test Bed and dialogue design language called FLAIR [3, 4]. The MMI Test Bed is a powerful tool which supports Steps 2, 3 and 5 of the MMI Design Process. Other specific analysis and design tools include composition graph formalisms [5], specification languages, and Task Description Languages (TDL) [2].

Further work needs to be done to refine techniques for performing Step 6 — "Measure/Evaluate Human Performance and Ergonomic Quality" of the methodology. Metrics (e.g., language robustness and extensibility) for assessing ergonomic quality require additional refinement and experimental use [6].

3.0 STEPS IN THE MMI DESIGN PROCESS

Each of the 6 steps in this Process corresponds to a critical phase in system development. Also each step results in design information (i.e., decisions, assumptions, or decompositions) used in a subsequent step.

Figure 1 — "MMI Design Process" depicts the MMI as it evolves from operational requirements to human task requirements to design requirements. Operational requirements, MMI functions, and automation decisions are derived from a decomposition process in Step 1. These results are used in the development of a system level specification. Step 2 decomposes the human activities identified in Step 1 and produces the "Operations Concept". This provides the foundation for early MMI prototyping (Step 5) and evaluation (Step 6) which is necessary to validate the operations concept. Step 3 uses the operations concept to define MMI subsystem functional and performance requirements. These results are then used to define the overall system design. Step 4 formalizes these aforementioned requirements into functional specifications for MMI software and user workstations.

Step 5 uses the operations concept to develop early hands-on MMI prototypes which serve to validate or change user concepts. Step 5 is also performed in support of Step 3 to help define and validate the conceptual model of user interaction (i.e., the description of what the system looks like to the user in terms of command language input and information coding/presentation techniques). Step 6 is done iteratively with Steps 4 and 5 to evaluate and improve the ergonomic quality of the system from the user's standpoint.

In Step 1 we describe the functional and performance characteristics of the MMI subsystem. Three outputs are:

a. Assumptions about the level of automation which determine the definition of man versus machine tasks. These tradeoffs include determinations of which tasks are best performed by users versus computers and software.

b. Top-level functional and performance requirements for the MMI subsystem and human information processing activities.

In Step 1 we examine the system environment (e.g., events, black-box inputs/outputs, etc.) to decompose system functions. For each function, levels of automation are determined by evaluating alternative schemes which allocate functionality to either the machine or man-machine pair. Once each function has been partitioned, it can be explicitly allocated to the MMI subsystem. Thus, an "interface" is synthesized to facilitate information transfer between human and machine-performed functions.

Step 2 (essentially a task analysis) defines *"what the human's role (in terms of tasks) should be in the MMI subsystem".* We found that Step 2 states the role of the human in terms understandable to the user, behavioral scientist, and engineer.

Designer tasks in Step 2 are:

a. Specify events (associated with timelines) which trigger human response. (Human response must be defined in terms of performance criteria such as accuracy and timeliness.)

b. Decompose and analyze human activities (man-machine pairs derived in Step 2) into information processing tasks.

c. Specify the organization and crew/team influences

on task performance.

d. Specify the training, machine aiding, and supervision necessary to maximize human performance and minimize fatigue and stress.

e. Begin task workload assessment.

f. Specify the required skill levels (position descriptions) and environmental requirements for the user workstation.

g. Allocate tasks to positions and define user dialogue definitions for each position.

The results of the above are documented in the Operations Concept for the MMI. The use of a dialogue definition language (DDL) is key to the execution of Steps 3 and 5. The DDL describes a decomposed sequence of information processing tasks. Each task in a sequence is characterized by a description of the logical displays required, one or more types of input/display interactions, specific operator decisions or actions, and inferences drawn from the interaction. The DDL conveys each task's *"Semantic"* meaning to the designer. [The designer captures in one place tasks as envisioned and understood by the user and the knowledge required to further decompose the "machine portion" of the MMI.]

In Step 3 we translate the DDL into the functional requirements of the MMI. *This step begins the process of defining what the system "should be like" to the end-user.*

Designer tasks in Step 3:

a. Translate the DDL tables into task elements (called task transactions) which document interaction techniques [7], frequency of task execution, and number of displayed objects involved in task evaluation. The result is a set of *policies* which guide the decomposition of tasks into subtasks

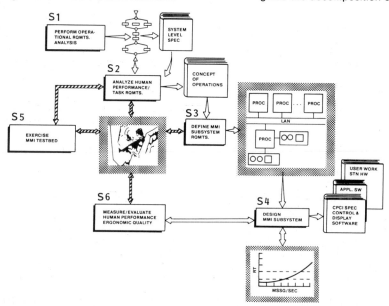

Figure 1. MMI Design Process

(using Interaction Technique Diagrams [7]. These policies are stated as guidelines and directives to the designer or human engineer responsible for decomposing subtasks. A policy might direct the designer to decompose tasks for reasons of user performance, efficiency (fewest number of keystrokes), training, ease-of-use, etc. This, in essence, represents a top-down subtask analysis.

b. Develop a conceptual model of user interaction which defines user display objects, static and dynamic relations between those objects, and user operations on those objects. Such a model might take the form of a command language versus a menu-show-by-example where either approach would have a marked impact on the requirements for the user interface language.

c. Use the subtask analysis and conceptual model, to identify and decompose the next level-of-detail functional capabilities within the MMI subsystem. Those typically are functions which comprise the user interface language, user applications, and display management.

d. Allocate these capabilities to hardware and software elements based on considerations of technology, performance, reliability and cost. This allocation results in a more detailed interface design which supports the partitioning of the MMI into user workstation and software elements. Resource Management is added to manage the concurrent/time sensitive performance attributes of the allocation. A failure mode effects analysis is performed and the allocation is augmented to include a function which handles MMI error detection/recovery [5].

e. Decompose all "MMI software" oriented functions to define inputs, outputs, and performance indices.

f. Identify user workstation characteristics such as resolution, brightness, intensity, character size and quality. Also identify performance requirements for interaction devices.

g. Derive the display bandwidth, size, capacity, and response time capabilities that influence the design of the overall computer system architecture and the user workstation.

h. Use the logical displays identified in the DDL to derive the requirements for the user data base(s) and the data base management system.

The analytical results from this step are requirements statements, trade studies, composition graphs, and Task Description Language. This results in a requirements baseline (including an allocation of functional requirements to user workstations and MMI software elements) prior to a "final" determination of the system architecture. Products of this step are reviewed (early in the system life cycle) at the system design review.

In Step 4 we translate the conceptual model of user interaction into semantic and syntactical level design [6]. We also formalize the Step 2 decompositions into functional hardware and software specifications. The designer tasks are:

a. Design semantic and syntactic levels of the user interface language by specifying the logical components of the user-computer dialogue, identifying user command operations and assigning performance criteria for response time and accuracy to each component in the user interface language (semantic design). Definition of input/display formats, command language syntax, and user feedback messages is covered by syntactic design.

b. Design or select the display management software which best matches the capabilities of the user workstation.

c. Design the user workstation.

d. Design applications software.

e. Estimate size and response time of the MMI applications, user interface language, display management software and device dependent software. These should be mapped to transactions of user tasks that are associated with execution frequencies. Engineering analysis and modeling can be used to determine impact of the design on the overall system architecture as well as size and timing requirements for the software functions.

f. Develop a set of specifications for each element which makes up the MMI subsystem. These specifications "formalize" and further decompose the requirements identified in Step 3.

Step 4 occurs prior to the preliminary design review and it is the concluding step in the MMI Design Process. Traditional and contemporary software and hardware engineering methods and standards lead to development, integration, and test of the MMI subsystem. In addition, Step 4 sets the stage for detailed design of the User Interface Management System (UIMS). The UIMS describes the user interface language and display management functions. The UIMS preserves the conceptual model of user interaction and offers language extensibility for new user functions as well as application program independence from changing display device technology.

Step 5 and Step 6 do not necessarily occur later than all the steps previously described. An MMI Test Bed is employed by the designer to allow end-users to exercise dialogue design concepts in a physical prototype layout of the user workstation. This test bed provides prototyping languages which can be used to construct user simulations and displays for interaction by end-users.

The use of MMI Test Bed prototypes allows:

a. User to assess and make a qualitive evaluation of performance and interaction with the "envisioned" dialogues.

b. Validation by the users of the operations concept for his critical functions.

c. Evaluation by the users of the operations concept for his critical functions.

d. Recognition of dialogue or workstation changes needed to improve user performance.

For early prototyping, Step 5 uses the DDL tables contained in the operations concept. This enables the designer to develop alternative conceptual models of user interaction in support of Step 3 and to redefine the model given feedback from the end-user. For example, the designer may want to evaluate alternative models of user interaction including command language models versus menu-shown-by-example models versus object-oriented icon selection models. The test bed also allows measurement of user performance.

Step 6 is carried out in conjunction with Steps 4, and 5. Step 6 is first applied in early prototyping to make mid-course corrections to the operations concept. Step 6 provides the means for the user to judge MMI design quality and for the designer of the system to measure and evaluate the human's performance as the system is being designed. Usually the behavioral scientist or human engineer conducts this step with the designer. Their tasks are to:

a. Plan human performance experimentation and evaluations to be conducted using the test bed or the actual system. Instrument the test to collect human performance data; design the experiments needed to assure validity or utility of results.

b. Measure and evaluate human performance to ascertain appropriateness of design concepts, and later system operational effectiveness.

c. Expand the task and subtask analysis (performed in Steps 2 and 3) to incorporate the modeling and estimation of user workload. Early measurements can be provided by using the MMI test bed. Assessments can be incorporated by the designer when doing Steps 3 and 4. Later measurements of human performance (during test and operational phases) can be used to validate and update task workload models.

d. Evaluate the MMI design for ergonomic quality. Use of metrics (e.g., efficiency, completeness, naturalness, robustness, feedback, responsiveness, etc. [6]) are critical to assessing user workstation and MMI software design quality.

e. Develop test requirements for human engineering evaluation of the MMI during test of the system.

An essential part of the methodology is the formation of a User Team including current and future users of the system. Ideally, this team should be formed during the systems requirements analysis and remain intact throughout system design and development. This team can assist the system designers and engineers in developing an acceptable final product. In point of fact, the FAA has chartered such a user team to work with the Advanced Automation Program Office (and CTA, Inc.) in the formulation of the Operations Concept, MMI subsystem requirements, and draft workstation requirements. This user team will continue with the program through all phases of development. This user team has reviewed the products of the first 3 steps in this methodology.

4.0 ASSUMPTIONS AND UNDERLYING FORMALISMS TO THE METHODOLOGY

Figure 2 describes the MMI Design Process and the flow of the various decompositions from functional representations, through task analysis, to requirements definition to preliminary design of the MMI subsystem. Table 1 describes the tools and techniques which support the execution of Steps 1 through 6 in the methodology.

Fundamental to MMI Design Process is the assumption that a system may be decomposed into machine functions and human information processing tasks using rigorous axiom-based decomposition formalism [5, 8]. We assume a function or task may be described in a strictly mathematical sense as a rule which, when applied to an input set, transforms it into an output set. A system function must include in this rule, applicable system parameters (e.g., air traffic separation rules), performance indices, and completion criteria for the transform. (See Figure 3, Composition Graph Formalisms for further details.) In the case of task decomposition, system parameters denote global knowledge needed by the user in carrying out tasks, and performance indices denote criteria for assessing user task behavior. These formalisms enable the designer to represent all attributes of a system (both human and machine). Note in Table 1 that all levels of these composition graphs must be represented in either specification terminology or structured english e.g. TDL, STDL.

5.0 CONCLUSIONS AND SUMMARY

CTA's effort with the FAA focuses on applying Steps 1, 2, 3, and eventually 6 of the MMI Design Process as previously described. Steps 4 and 5 will be performed by two Prime Contractors responsible for AAS design and development. The CTA team is composed of system engineers, cognitive psychologists, human factor engineers, display system engineers, and software engineers. All members have been essential to the successful application of this methodology. This interdisciplinary team and the user team involvement in this process represent an FAA commitment to quality and operational acceptance of the end-product. We recognize that additional work is needed in "packaging" this methodology and developing the underlying structure of supporting tools, techniques, and guidelines.

In summary, the challenge to the designer for this decade and into the 1990's is to bring computer and interactive display capabilities — usefully and simply — to people (in the case of air traffic control, even to the point of making these "new" methods and techniques seem more reliable and effective than the old). The eventual goal of this methodology is to express the knowledge of the behavioral scientist, the human engineer and the user in a form useful to system designers.

ACKNOWLEDGEMENTS

The authors thank Mr. Valerio R. Hunt, Director, FAA Advanced Automation Program, and Dr. Andres Zellweger, Division Manager, Systems Engineering for their support, vision, and risk-taking in allowing CTA, Inc. to apply this methodology. Efforts by Messrs. Delbert Weathers, Rod Bourne, Larry Fortier, and Ralph Cooper of the United States Federal Aviation Administration to facilitate and guide this process are also greatly appreciated. The review comments of Dr. John Bennett are also appreciated. Finally special thanks go to Mr. Mack Alford of TRW for helping to bring a technical discipline to this methodology and Mr. John J. Rosati for support in MMI Design Guidebook development.

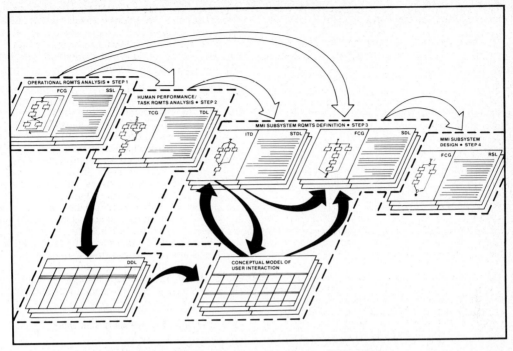

Figure 2. MMI Design Process Decomposition Flow

STEP	TECHNIQUES	RECOMMENDED TOOLS
1. PERFORM OPERATIONAL REQUIREMENTS ANALYSIS	• Functional Decomposition	• Function Composition Graphs (FCG) with system specification language (SSL)
	• Static Analysis to determine completeness of data flows, state transitions, control flows, event traceability.	• System Rqmts. Engineering Methodology (SYSREM) [2] • Data Dictionaries
2. ANALYZE HUMAN PERFORMANCE/ TASK REQUIREMENTS	• Task Analysis/Task Decomposition	• Task Composition Graph (TCG) plus Task Description Language (TDL)
	• Task Attribute analysis to determine machine aids, information rqmts., human performance assessments.	• Data base which supports traceability of tasks to task attribute characterizations.
	• Dialogue Definition	• Dialogue Definition Language (DDL)
3. DEFINE MMI SUBSYSTEM REQUIREMENTS	• Interaction Technique Analysis	• Interaction Technique Diagrams (ITD) [4] plus Subtask Description Language (STDL)
	• Subtask Analysis	• Data base which supports user model description
4. DESIGN MMI SUBSYSTEM	• User Interface Language Analysis • Functional Decomposition	• Requirements Statement Language (RSL) àla SREM/REVS [2]
5. EXERCISE MMI TESTBED	• Dialogue Generation/Rapid Prototyping	• FLAIR [4], MMI Testbeds
	• Conceptual Model of User Interaction Analysis	• FLAIR [4], DDL
	• Assessment of User Interaction with prototype	• MMI Testbed Human Performance Measurement
6. MEASURE/ EVALUATE HUMAN PERFORMANCE AND ERGONOMIC QUALITY	• Task Workload Assessment/Modeling using task time or difficulty measures	• TCG, TDL, ITD and STDL • Prototype evaluation tools to measure user performance in MMI Test bed
	• Qualitative evaluation of designs, using Ergonomic Quality Metrics	• RSL plus static analysis/metric evaluation tools
	• Operational Evaluation of human performance	• Tools which monitor system responsiveness and human performance during training and operational use.

Table 1. Tools and Techniques Applicable to Methodology

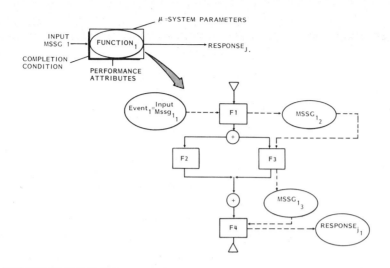

Figure 3. Composition Graph Formalisms

FUNDAMENTAL CONCEPTS

THE DEFINITION OF DECOMPOSITION TAKES PLACE IN THREE STEPS. FIRST, SEQUENCES FUNCTIONS ARE DEFINED IN TERMS OF COMPOSITION GRAPHS. THESE ARE DIRECTED GRAPHS IN WHICH NODES ARE FUNCTIONS, AND EDGES REPRESENT TIME PRECEDENCE RELATIONSHIPS (THE DOTTED LINES REPRESENT INPUT/OUTPUT RELATIONSHIPS BETWEEN FUNCTIONS.) SIMILARLY, SEQUENCES OF INPUTS AND OUTPUTS ARE REPRESENTED AS SCHEMA. THESE ARE DIRECTED GRAPHS WITH ATOMS (GENERIC UNIT OF INPUT/OUTPUT) AND EDGES REPRESENTING POSSIBLE PRECEDENCE. SUCH GRAPHS HAVE SPECIAL NODES TO INDICATE CONCURRENCY, ITERATION, AND REPLICATION OVER AN INDEX SET. THE SECOND STEP IS TO DEFINE A FUNCTION COMPOSITION BY SYNTHESIZING THE COMPOSITION GRAPH AND ITS REFERENCED FUNCTIONS INTO THE CHARACTERISTICS OF A SYSTEM FUNCTION. THIS IS DONE BY COLLECTING THE OVERALL INPUTS AND OUTPUT SEQUENCES, TRANFORMATION, COMPLETION CRITERIA, AND PERFORMANCE INDICES.

FINALLY, DECOMPOSTITION IS DEFINED AS A RELATIONSHIP BETWEEN AN ORIGINAL FUNCTION AND A FUNCTION COMPOSITION IF FOUR CRITERIA ARE SATISFIED:

1) INPUT SEQUENCES AND OUTPUT SEQUENCES MUST BE PRESERVED WHERE DEFINED, ALTHOUGH THE FUNCTION COMPOSITION INPUTS AND OUTPUTS MAY ADD MORE DETAIL.

2) ANY INVARIANTS OF THE FUNCTION TRANSFORMATIONS MUST BE PRESERVED.

3) THE COMPLETION CRITERIA MUST MATCH, IN PARTICULAR THE NUMBER AND TYPE OF EXITS.

4) THE PERFORMANCE INDEX OF THE FUNCTION MUST BE COMPUTABLE FROM THOSE OF THE SUBFUNCTIONS OF THE FUNCTION COMPOSITION.

THIS DEFINITION IS TRANSITIVE (i.e., THE DECOMPOSITION OF A DECOMPOSITION IS A LEGAL DECOMPOSITION OF THE ORIGINAL FUNCTION). MOREOVER, THIS DEFINITION OF DECOMPOSITION INCORPORATES HIERARCHICAL CONTROL THEORY, GENERALIZED STATE SPACE THEORY, CONURRENT FUNCTIONS, AND A VERSION OF THE MICHAEL JACKSON DESIGN METHOD AS SPECIAL CASES.

REFERENCES

[1] Kloster, G.V. and Rosati, J.J., Draft and Guidelines for the Development of the MMI Guidebook, TRW, Redondo Beach, California, (TRW Independent Research and Development Report Number 81006201), 1981.

[2] Kloster, G.V., Phillips, M.D., Tischer, K., Ammerman, H.A., Jones, G.W., Operations Concept for AAS Man-Machine Interface, Technical Report prepared for FAA Contract Number DTFA01-83-Y-10554, CDRL A002. Computer Technology Associates, Inc., Denver, Colorado, 1984.

[3] Wong, P.C.S., MMI: The Man-Machine Interface, QUEST Technology at TRW Electronics and Defense Sector, Winter 82/83, Volume 6, Number 1.

[4] Wong, P.C.S. and Reid, E.R., FLAIR — User Interface Dialogue Design Tool, Computer Graphics, Volume 16, Number 3, July 1982, ACM reprint ACM-0-89791-076-1/82/007/0087.

[5] Alford, M.W., Smith, T.C., and Smith D.L., Formal Decomposition Applied to Axiomatic Requirements Engineering, Final Report prepared for Ballistic Missile Defense Advanced Technology Center, Contract Number DASG60-78-C-C0158. TRW DSSG, December 1979.

[6] Foley, J.D., Van Dam, A., Fundaments of Interactive Computer Graphics. The System Programming Series, Addison Wesley, Copyright 1982.

[7] Foley, J.D., Wallace, V.H., and Chan, P., The Human Factors of Graphic Interaction, Washington, D.C.: The George Washington University. GWU-IIST-81-3. January 1981.

[8] Alford, M.W. and Burns, I.F., Axiomatic Requirements Engineering, Volume I, Final Report prepared for Ballistic Missile Defense Advanced Technology Center, Contract Number DASG60-78-C-015, TRW DSSG, September 1978.

Human-Computer Interaction — INTERACT '84 / B. Shackel (ed.)
Elsevier Science Publishers B.V. (North-Holland)
© IFIP, 1985

OPERATIONS CONCEPT FORMULATION FOR NEXT GENERATION AIR TRAFFIC CONTROL SYSTEMS

Mark D. Phillips and Kristine Tischer

Computer Technology Associates
5670 S. Syracuse Circle, Suite 200
Englewood, CO 80111

in association with
Valerio R. Hunt and Andres Zellweger
United States Federal Aviation Administration,
Department of Transportation

A comprehensive requirements derivation and validation methodology was used to define the user-system interface for a proposed upgrade to the United States Air Traffic Control (ATC) System. This paper focuses on one step in the overall methodology — the formulation of the Operations Concept for this system. The analyses were performed to provide functional descriptions of what the system would look like to the end user — the air traffic controller. Cognitive and perceptual aspects of displays, viewability criteria, implicit information coding and presentation and interaction techniques are documented. As such, the Operations Concept formally records the allocation of functions between controllers and machines.

1.0 INTRODUCTION

Advances in computer hardware and software have enabled significant enhancements to many command and control systems. Air traffic control systems have been evolving in concert with these developments. A new ATC system, incorporating significant advanced automation capabilities, is currently under development in the United States. The Operations Concept [1] tracks the evolution of this system and defines the future role of the air traffic controller.

In large command and control systems, "operations concepts" are usually expressed as high level descriptions of how a system will interact with other external systems and how the system will operate internally. The Operations Concept development described here assumes that the user (in this case the air traffic controller) is the starting point in requirements formulation, and ultimately, the design. The Operations Concept therefore, consistently analyzes system requirements from the *user's* viewpoint. The basis for development of this "user's view" of the system is the incorporation of a forward looking task analysis, which becomes refined throughout system design, development and test phases.

Early in this requirements analysis, a team comprising a cross section of current and future system users was formed to aid in the derivation and validation of the Operations Concept. This User Team (UT), remains involved through all phases of system design, development, test and operational deployment. This user review process is iterative, provides the basis for mutual understanding between system engineers and the user community, and should help ensure the acceptability of the final product by air traffic controllers.

The UT serves as the "voice of the controllers". They examine user-system interface requirements as they are derived. They provide clarification of ATC procedures, and ultimately, either "sign-off" or disallow requirements.

Requirements validated by the UT are documented in the Operations Concept and serve as metrics to assess various design prototypes as they are produced.

2.0 OBJECTIVES

The new ATC system is being developed to ensure the safe, orderly and expeditious flow of air traffic throughout the United States up to and beyond the year 2000. The documentation of controller information processing tasks, dialogue, and task performance criteria will ultimately determine the functional, physical and performance characteristics of the controller workstation. The goal of the Operations Concept is to foster an optimum implementation of the controller-machine interface. Controller concurrence is fundamental to these analyses, and has been provided through the user review process.

The primary objective of the Operations Concept is to decompose controller tasks to the level of detail such that the controller's job is described in terms of:

   a. sequences of tasks which the controller performs when responding to a given ATC event;

   b. a high-level outline of the dialogue between the controller and his/her workstation;

   c. interactions with other controllers, pilots, and supervisory personnel; and

   d. information needed by the controller to successfully execute tasks accurately and in a timely fashion.

This primary objective enables the system designers to understand the controller's job and to use Operations Concept task descriptions as a basis for workstation hardware and software design. This objective also enables the UT to verify and validate the documentation and to understand the impact of proposed changes to controller tasks, dialogue definitions, and interaction techniques.

A secondary objective is to characterize controller tasks in terms of:

    a. human capacity and workload;

    b. machine aids required to maximize controller performance; and

    c. required controller training, experience and skill development.

This secondary objective enables human resource management personnel to recognize necessary changes in controller training and skills acquisition policy.

2.1 Assumptions

The Operations Concept model assumes air traffic controller activities are primarily event sensitive. Through the identification and clustering of air traffic events, we derive the top level activity structure for the Controller. These activities can then be decomposed, according to formal rules of decomposition [2,3] to arrive at specific event stimuli, and the requisite response in the form of controller information processing tasks. Information processing tasks are thus initiated by an event stimulus and invoke an observable response. Controller task performance is influenced by global system parameters, i.e., knowledge of ATC procedures, handbooks, and memoranda of agreements. Different types of tasks result in behaviors which are either measured by human performance indices, such as how accurate or timely a controller performs a given task, or subjective estimates of expected behavior. The rules of decomposition require that each task achieve a closure condition: either transition to another task in an information processing sequence or a task closure such as completion of aircraft maneuver, acceptance of control, or completion of a message entry (see Figure 1).

Controller tasks define the required sequence of interactions between man and machine. An example of a task is: "Request restricted airspace probe." The event stimulus (as shown in Figure 1) is a message input via visual display or voice. Response to this stimulus requires controller integration of global system parameters (e.g., separation standards, geography, route structures, current sectorization) and controller action (e.g., initiate flight plan conflict probe). This response is related to the completion of a task and the time and effort (mental load) required to achieve some completion criteria.

The set of events for the current ATC system has been defined and validated by the UT. We assume that the current classes of operational ATC events will be equally applicable when the new system becomes fully operational. In other words, the modes of controller-machine interaction will markedly differ in the new system, but the event domain will be largely the same as in today's system. ATC events will continue to result from interactions between aircraft, airports, airspace, weather and the operational environment.

3.0 METHODS

3.1 Scenario Development

The ATC system level operational requirements [3] provide the functional baseline from which this analysis proceeds. Operational requirements are translated into a set of scenarios which both define the ATC event domain and the relationship between ATC operations and the external environment.

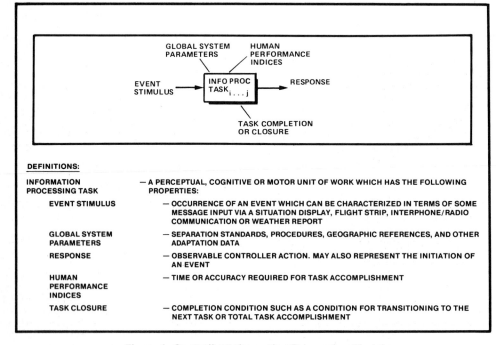

Figure 1: Controller Information Processing Model

An event is a distinct occurrence which the controller perceives and responds to in some specific way. To identify tasks, the controller may be modeled as an event sensitive multi-tasking information processor. The advantage of using this model as an analysis tool is that, if a comprehensive list of events which the controller observes is documented, along with a similarly extensive list of tasks, one may achieve a degree of accuracy in describing the controller's work. The disadvantage in modeling the controller as an information processor, whose response to events is to perform tasks, is that the dynamic operational complexity of the controller's job necessitates a highly interactive analysis model, which is difficult to apply. One event may trigger another event before an appropriate controller response occurs. In addition, it may not be appropriate for the controller to take action immediately. A mental response is difficult to document until an overt action is taken. Therefore, in viewing the controller as an individual who processes information in response to discrete events, we do not have an entirely accurate picture of the controller's overall job. We do, however, obtain a sufficiently accurate and useful model for understanding user-system interface requirements.

3.2 Controller Information Processing Task Analysis

The identification and decomposition of controller information processing tasks follows from the scenario development and event definitions. The top-level set of Controller activities is directed toward meeting the ATC goal of separation standards and procedures. The meeting of these goals by the controller assures the safe, orderly and expeditious flow of air traffic in today's system, and remains as the *raison d'etre* of the future ATC system.

Activities represent the top-level functions performed by the controller-machine pair. The term "controller-machine pair" is used in this context to denote the actions a controller performs at his/her workstation in response to an event or a series of events. The activities are therefore the results of either external events, the coordination among controllers on a sector team, or coordination among adjacent sectors.

3.3 Composition Graphs for Information Processing Tasks

Given the top-level set of controller activities, one can perform a logical decomposition into subactivities and finally, tasks. The decomposition must preserve consistency, completeness, and transitivity of event stimuli and controller output responses. Composition graphs show the multiprocessing nature of the controller's job. Figure 2 illustrates composition graph symbols which define sequential, concurrent, iterative, and decision making (path selection) flow of sub-activities.

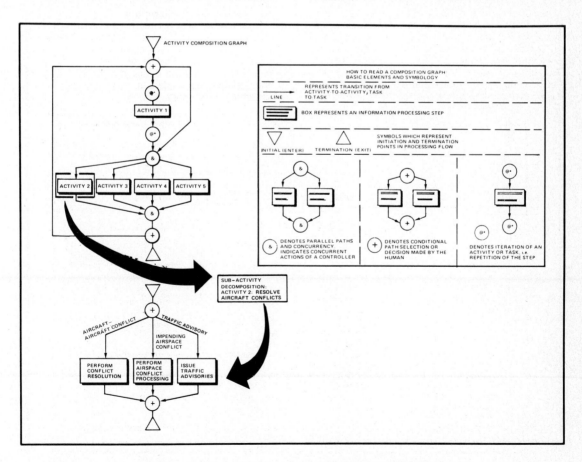

Figure 2: Example of Controller Activity Decomposition

A composition graph of tasks reflects linkages among the tasks, not a hierarchical arrangement that implies the "level" of the task. The first task is not an "overall task" to be accomplished by performance of the tasks that follow on the graph. Nor is a composition graph a flow chart in the usual sense, though a sense of task sequencing is inherent in the graphic portrayal.

Tasks define what must be accomplished by the Controller. Low level procedures or precise steps which detail how a task is performed on a given set of equipment are not presented. Rather, the intent is to reflect what is done without unnecessarily implying a particular design (e.g., object vs. command-oriented dialogue) or display equipment selection.

3.4 Task Description Language (TDL)

The resultant graphical task decomposition is then translated into a tailored version of structured English called Task Description Language (TDL). The TDL ensures logical consistency in the graphical task decomposition and communicates the task structure both to controllers and to engineering personnel. The TDL provides essentially the same information as the composition graphs, but presents it in a way which forces an analysis of the logical connections among the tasks. This is done by first standardizing the task statement in terms of a set of well-defined, mutually exclusive verbs, objects, and qualifiers to ensure

consistent use of terminology. A set of logical constructs is then applied to organize the tasks. The use of TDL in conjunction with the graphs serves as a validation tool which ensures that the task analysis is both internally consistent and complete. Figure 3 shows the relationship between composition graphs and TDL.

3.5 Characterization of Controller Information Processing Tasks

The subsequent analytic steps [5] presented in the Operations Concept rely on the task decomposition. The level of detail represented in the composition graphs and TDL allows for characterizations of tasks based upon information inputs and controller output requirements. Tasks are characterized in terms of both ATC complexity factors and sector type (e.g., low altitude arrival, high altitude en route). ATC complexity factors include coordination, traffic density, traffic orientation, traffic separation, sequencing and time responsiveness.

This initial characterization is used later for operator workload assessments and to test the crew/team organization model. Cognitive and perceptual task attributes are used to derive machine aiding requirements such as display highlighting or alarms. Another series of task characterizations provides the basis for determining controller skill level requirements and developmental training requirements per task.

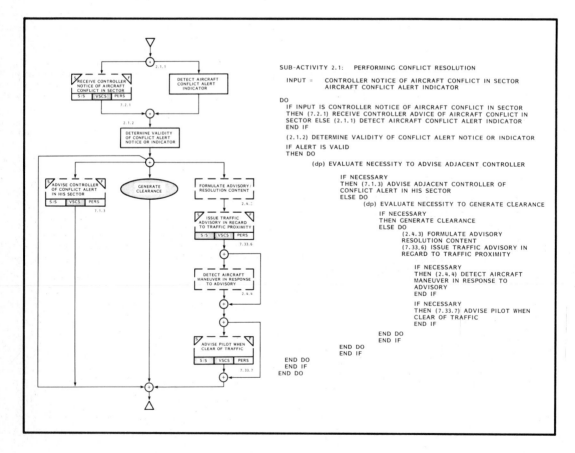

Figure 3: Relationship Between Composition Graphs and TDL

3.6 Controller Dialogue Definition

The dialogue between the controller and the display console is termed the Dialogue Description Language (DDL). The DDL requires a multi-step development process for each Controller information processing task which has been identified. The DDL aids in the conceptualization of the model of user interaction, display information requirements, and development of logical interaction techniques at the task level. The first step in developing the DDL is to analyze each of the tasks with respect to the following components:

- Task Type
  - Entry
  - Receipt
  - Analytical
  - Verbal Coordination

- Logical Display
  - Aggregates of related data (e.g., situation display data) documented in the System Level Specification [4] and needed for task performance.

- Characteristic Action Type
  - Application and device independent methods of controller input to the workstation (e.g. select, position, text entry) [6].

- Display Content
  - Information directly viewed or manipulated in the course of task accomplishment (e.g., runway list).

By characterizing each task in terms of these four components, information presentation and coding and interaction techniques may be added to the task statement.

The enhanced task statements impart semantic meaning to the tasks and serve as unequivocal requirements statements. The final step in DDL development involves the documentation of inferences the controller would make as a result of task performance. These inferences serve both as a validation tool for the individual DDL statements and as inputs for training program development.

The construction of the DDL establishes the link between the event-sensitive controller information processing tasks (shown in composition graph and TDL form) and the input and display requirements of the controller-system interface. The Operations Concept, therefore, ensures that ATC controller-system interface requirements are in all cases directly derived from and traceable to controller task requirements. An example of the DDL is presented in Figure 4.

4.0 CONCLUSION

This paper describes a set of analyses which were used to decompose controller activities into sequences of tasks which are performed in response to ATC events. The information network which defines interactions with other controllers, pilots, supervisory and metering/flow personnel, along with the conceptual dialogue between the controller and the workstation are an integral part of Operations Concept development. In specifying this information, the Operations Concept provides the foundation for development of console hardware, software and associated design documentation.

Implementation of the ATC system improvements described in the Operations Concept will constitute a first step in changing the controller's role in the ATC system. The current model of the controller as an "event sensitive, multi-tasking, interruptible, information processor" begins to evolve more towards a model of the controller as a dynamic programming processor with the advent of significant automated air traffic planning tools. In short, the controller will place greater emphasis on strategic planning rather than to solely rely on tactical execution to maintain separation of aircraft. The controller's role as a system manager will grow because selective application of traffic

Task Statement	Task Type	Logical Display	Characteristic Action Type	Display Content	Enhanced Task Statement	Controller Inference
Observe range/bearing between aircraft.	Entry/ Receipt.	Situation.	Select & text entry.	Range/ bearing list.	Observe range/bearing between selected aircraft on the Situation Display obtained by identifying/ selecting the desired aircraft and invoking the range/bearing function.	Utilize range/bearing information to determine multiple aircraft relationships.
Observe air-space intrusion by a non-controlled object.	Receipt.	Situation.	N/A	Target(s).	Observe appearance on Situation Display of any target reflecting intrusion into controlled airspace by non-controlled object(s).	Detect/monitor non-controlled objects which could become hazard to controlled aircraft.
Compose/ enter reminder note of airspace intrusion.	Entry.	Situation.	Text entry & select.	Note field, limited data block, or a full data block.	Compose/enter reminder note and/ or track i.d. associated with target on Situation Display to annotate non-controlled intruding object.	N/A
Flight-follow an observed non-controlled object.	Receipt/ Analytical.	Situation.	Text entry & select.	Note field, limited data block, or a full data block.	Flight-follow (continually monitor the movements/behavior of) a non-controlled object on the Situation Display to determine possibility of a hazardous situation.	Monitor behavior of unpredictable, non-controlled object for possible impact on controlled aircraft.

Figure 4: Example of Controller DDL.

management tools and machine aids will be under the controller's discretion.

The Operations Concept provides explicit documentation of the role of the controller in the future air traffic control system. Through UT involvement, this document forges an understanding between system developers and the user community of what the ATC system should look like to the controller. This understanding, established prior to user-system interface design, provides the essential first step toward ultimate controller acceptance of this critical system.

ACKNOWLEDGEMENTS

The technical approach described in this paper reflects the pioneering work of Mr. Gregory V. Kloster. Our thanks also to Mr. Ralph Cooper, Mr. Delbert Weathers and Mr. Rod Bourne of the United States Federal Aviation Administration for their technical guidance. The review comments of Dr. John Bennett are also appreciated.

REFERENCES

[1]   Kloster, G.V., Phillips, M.D., Tischer, K, Ammerman, H.A., Jones, G.W., Operations Concept for the Advanced Automation System Man-Machine Interface., Technical Report prepared for FAA contract number DTFA01-83-Y-10554, CDRL A002. Computer Technology Associates, Inc., Denver, Colorado, 1984.

[2]   Alford, M.W. and Burns, I.F., Axiomatic Requirements Engineering, Volume I. Final Report prepared for Ballistic Missile Defense Advanced Technology Center, Contract No. DASG60-78-C-0015. TRW DSSG, September 1978.

[3]   Alford, M.W., Smith, T.C. and Smith, D.L., Formal Decomposition Applied to Axiomatic Requirements Engineering. Final Report prepared for Ballistic Missile Defense Advanced Technology Center, Contract No. DASG60-78-C0158. TRW DSSG, December 1979.

[4]   Federal Aviation Administration Advanced Automation System-System Level Specification. FAA-ER-130-005D. April 1983.

[5]   Kloster, G.V., and Rosati, J.J., Draft and Guidelines for the Development of the MMI Design Guidebook. Redondo Beach, CA: TRW Independent Research and Development Report Number 80116210, 1981.

[6]   Foley, J.D., Wallace, V.H., and Chan P., The Human Factors of Graphic Interaction. Washington, DC: The George Washington University. GWU-IIST-81-3. January 1981.

Human-Computer Interaction — INTERACT '84 / B. Shackel (ed.)
Elsevier Science Publishers B.V. (North-Holland)
© IFIP, 1985

ZOG and the USS CARL VINSON: Lessons in System Development

Robert M. Akscyn and Donald L. McCracken

Computer Science Department
Carnegie-Mellon University
Pittsburgh, PA. 15213

This paper contains recommendations for developing computer systems for other organizations using emerging technologies. These recommendations are based on our experience developing a computer-assisted management system for the USS CARL VINSON, a nuclear-powered aircraft carrier, during the past four years. We recommend that such projects be conducted in a highly cooperative manner between the users' organization and the developers' organization over a planned period not longer than 18 months, obtaining feedback via a series of instrumented prototypes that are exercised by both users and developers for actual tasks.

Introduction

Since 1975, the ZOG Project at Carnegie-Mellon University has been studying problems of human-computer communication. This research has proceeded empirically via the development of a general-purpose interface system called ZOG--a system that combines features normally associated with operating systems, databases, and editors. ZOG provides rapid response (less than one second) to user selections for browsing in a large, network-structured database in which the nodes are formatted, display-oriented chunks. These nodes, called "frames", have a structure general enough to support a variety of applications such as those listed in the example ZOG frame shown below. In addition, any item in a frame can be used to activate a process. A more detailed description of ZOG can be found in [1] and [3].

```
Application areas supported by ZOG          ZogProject27

To develop ZOG as a total environment for users, we have
used ZOG to support the following applications areas:

  1. Project management

  2. Document development and management

  3. Training

  4. Issue analysis

  5. Software development and management

  6. On-line help

  7. Electronic communication (mail, bulletin boards, etc.)

edit help back next prev top goto old zog xchg print jump
```

Figure 1: An Example ZOG Frame

In February of 1980, we were visited by Captain Richard Martin, who had recently been assigned to shepherd the USS CARL VINSON through its final construction and serve as the ship's commander for its first operational cruise. He was investigating ZOG's potential for information management on board the VINSON, a task he foresaw as being monumental. At the time, we were looking for a real-world application to drive the further development of ZOG, and we agreed to work with the VINSON to develop a ZOG-based management system. Between then and February 1983, we jointly developed a distributed version of ZOG that runs on a network of 28 powerful personal computers (PERQs).This system supports a number of management applications, including an expert system that assists decision-making for the launch and recovery of the ship's aircraft. A description of the ZOG/VINSON project is contained in [2].

On a higher plane, this project was an experiment in what might be called "direct technology transfer", in that it bypassed the traditional procurement mechanisms for placing such systems in operational military environments. For us the experience was a rich one, and we believe that some of the lessons we learned may be applicable to developing computer systems in other contexts. In this paper we have tried to encapsulate a number of these lessons in the form of recommendations. We believe they are most relevant to researchers-turned-project-managers who are trying to exploit emerging technologies and develop systems for operational use. Table 1 gives a preview of the recommendations.

R1: Let the requirements evolve over time

R2: Develop a broad, multi-level model of the system

R3: Make progress on multiple levels in parallel

R4: Devise effective strategies for users to employ prototypes

R5: Treat the users as part of the development team

R6: Build a system the users' organization can support

R7: Insist that the developers use the system being developed

R8: Collect performance data by instrumenting the system

R9: Don't start on a shoestring

R10: Don't try to do too much (or too little)

R11: Use scripts of user-level behavior for automatic testing

R12: Keep a running log of the most recent user actions

R13: Give documentors a central role in the project

Table 1: Recommendations for managing development

Recommendations based on experience

This section contains our recommendations for managing the computer system development process, based on our four years of experience with the ZOG/VINSON project. In the following section we will cover some recommendations based on hindsight, i.e., ones that we did not follow this time but would be inclined to follow in future projects.

R1: Let the requirements evolve over time

Our view of how system requirements should be specified contrasts sharply with conventional system development procedures. Traditionally, complete functional specifications for a system are written in the initial phase of its development. To our way of thinking, this strategy is not applicable to projects that are based on rapidly emerging technologies (e.g., distributed software). In such projects, requirements should not be too detailed or rigid at the beginning since it is impossible to accurately determine them at that time. This is so for several reasons.

First of all, the various technological components may not mature soon enough to permit them to be exploited. Researchers are somewhat prone to setting their sights too high in development projects--offering to deliver results which, in some cases, require solving genuine research problems. Some of the development may depend on systems (e.g., an operating system) being developed by other groups whose goals could diverge from yours at any time. Consequently, it is prudent to seek explicit commitment for support from these other groups. Even so, since such commitments do not reduce

the technological risks involved, backup solutions should be planned for all the subsystems that are based on emerging technology (including the subsystems under your control). Our project contained an excellent illustration of this point. We had planned from the beginning to use an advanced network operating system being developed by another group at Carnegie-Mellon, but this group was not responsive to the urgent deadlines contained in our project. As a result, we were finally forced to switch to a less capable, but working, operating system at the eleventh hour -- an extremely disruptive move.

A second reason to develop the specifications over time is that users will discover new functions (and abandon old ones) as their appreciation of the technology's potential matures. This understanding takes time for the developers as well, since initially they are not well informed about the nature of work in the users' organization.

Finally, we believe that adopting such a development paradigm has important ramifications for the future of the system. Rather than viewing the system as an entity which gets "completed", the developers and the users begin to view the system in more evolutionary terms--i.e., that a crucial feature is its ability to adapt to the needs of the users even after the developers are no longer involved.

Obviously we are speaking of a tradeoff here, not a categorical imperative, but the basic point still remains: a specification document can become a security blanket to which the developers cling, rather than cope with the rich opportunities that progressively reveal themselves.

R2: Develop a broad, multi-level model of the system

We believe there is a substantial payoff in developing a broad conceptual model of the system. By providing the individual developers with a view of the total system, it helps them make design decisions with global tradeoffs in mind. It also provides them with a framework for discussing their results with others. In addition, it provides a structure for documenting not just the design of the system, but the tradeoffs made as it is developed.

We believe that this model should have a *multi-level* structure, for a number of reasons. First, computer systems in general have this structure. Consequently, a strong correspondence with the technological levels of computer systems promotes incorporating future advances in those technologies. The model we developed for our own work had seven levels:

hardware (PERQs), operating system (POS), language (Pascal), software (ZOG), applications (management), content (ZOG frames), and maintenance (including training and continued development). This framework is discussed in [2].

A second reason for a multi-level structure is that users learn more readily if shielded from some of the system's complexity. A system in which each level makes minimal assumptions about other levels reduces the need for users (and developers) to know the details about those levels.

However, there is a serious danger that developers of lower levels will become too isolated from the needs of higher levels--a problem compounded by the fact that experience with the higher levels lags behind experience with the lower levels. The crux of the problem is that the design of the lower levels implicitly constrains the capabilities of the higher levels, yet it is the higher levels which are the "value producing" parts of the system. We feel there must be a conscious effort on the part of the developers to make the lower levels of the system serve the higher levels--otherwise the system the users see will not truly exploit the technology.

R3: Make progress on multiple levels in parallel

In our view, there is only one good way for the needs of the higher levels of the system to take shape so that they can guide the development of the lower levels: progress must occur on the various levels in parallel. To accomplish this, the development of the system must proceed iteratively by implementing a series of functioning prototypes, so that the developers of higher levels have a platform to work upon.

However, parallel development creates a number of decision problems with which the managers of the development process must cope. One such problem is deciding when to stop development of the current version for a given level and move on to the next. These transitions, which generally occur from the bottom up, can involve fairly radical changes such as moving to a new machine or language -- making the subsequent transfer of higher levels relatively problematic. In our case, we created five major versions of the system (see the list below), necessitating four major transitions for the developers. All versions except the last one were "throwaways". We believe this shows that we were willing to pay very high costs to gain the benefits of parallel progress.

Jan 81	Decided to create a temporary environment to develop application software on the old VAX version of ZOG, rather than waiting for the PERQ version.
Nov 81	Decided to build an interim standalone version of ZOG on the PERQ, using the existing operating system (POS).
Apr 82	Decided to build an interim ZOG on an early version of the new operating system, in order to make progress with the ZOG network server software.
Sep 82	Converted interim ZOG to a later (but still inadequate) version of the new operating system (with significant changes from the early version of Apr 82).
Nov 82	Made major decision to abandon new operating system and revert back to the POS operating system. (Required a major effort to reimplement many components of the system -- especially the network servers).

We were never able to plan well for these transitions, but rather had to make the decisions dynamically, often on quite short notice. The problems of transition are compounded when the next version of the lower levels is not yet ready for higher levels to move aboard (perhaps because the leap is too large!), but yet the current version has problems that are severely constraining progress at the higher levels. This leads to a "schizophrenic" style of development, in which developers of lower levels must also work on "obsolete" versions for the good of the project (much to their consternation).

R4: Devise effective strategies for users to employ prototypes

In order to receive meaningful feedback from actual users, we recommend providing the users' organization, as early as possible, a prototype that can be used to perform actual tasks.

There are some natural tendencies to postpone or avoid installing prototypes in the users' organization. Users will resist adopting a system that is partially formed and has lots of problems, while developers will want to tinker endlessly with the system before exposing it to the real world. However, gaining experience via a series of prototypes helps users develop a feel for the technology. In addition to generating many suggestions for design change, this understanding will enable the users to see for themselves how their current practices could be modified to better utilize the technology (you won't be able to see it for them). Developers, on the other hand, typically underestimate the contribution that users can make; users are often more creative than the developers!

R5: Treat the users as part of the development team

We believe that the users should be treated as part of the development team--after all, they are the only ones who can really know what is needed. This does not imply abdicating technical leadership, but it does mean accepting the users as equal partners. In other words, the relationship should be a peer relationship, like a marriage should be, with neither side trying to dominate the other. Although placing the users in the design loop makes iterative design more difficult, the potential benefit is that both sides accept responsibility for the success of the system. In our case, much of the high-level design of the system was done in joint sessions with officers from the ship. We also assimilated into our development group several Navy officers who were stationed with us for extended periods of time. These officers became valuable members of our team -- the project could not have been completed without them.

R6: Build a system the users' organization can support

We believe that the users' organization should be capable of supporting the system at the end of the project. This is especially important when the system is not a product supported by a commercial organization. However, the users' organization may be unaccustomed to this point of view and therefore be reluctant to assume responsibility for continued maintenance. Part of the problem seems to be that many people view software as a form of perpetual motion--they expect that once it is set in motion (developed), it will run forever without any additional input of energy (maintenance). Others believe that maintenance is a relatively inexpensive activity and can be performed by people without much experience. Our view, on the other hand, is that proper maintenance is quite difficult and finding programmers with the right "service orientation" is a real organizational challenge.

The issue of ongoing maintenance is such an important one that we recommend it be resolved in the initial project negotiations. If the users' organization is unwilling to commit "upfront" the appropriate resources to establish its own support group (one which will ultimately take over full responsibility for the system), the development group may not wish to participate in the project. The developers, of course, must share the task of grooming such a support group, and must be willing to provide the support themselves until the new support group is fully ready to take over.

R7: Insist that the developers use the system being developed

In our project, we made every attempt to use ourselves the same system we were developing for the users' organization. (This would not be possible for all development projects, but for us it was quite feasible due to the generality of the tools we were creating). Making ourselves guinea pigs was often an inconvenience, but we persevered because we were getting double mileage out of our time: we were getting our work done (though not as efficiently as we might have liked) and exercising the system at the same time. This exercising was remarkably good for turning up problems with the system -- problems that we otherwise might not have become aware of until the real users had tripped across them. Problems also tended to get fixed more rapidly, since they were holding up our *own* progress. A valuable side effect of using ZOG for our project work was the development of additional capabilities; for example, facilities for documentation and software management.

R8: Collect performance data by instrumenting the system

In addition to the anecdotal feedback from users and developer-users, there are other, more systematic, methods for obtaining data on the performance of the system. These methods are a valuable supplement to traditional feedback collection mechanisms because their precision can pinpoint problems that would otherwise be missed.

Based on our previous experience with mainframe versions of ZOG, we embedded within the system a number of data collection mechanisms for measuring the behavior of both the user and the system. A description of some of the mechanisms we developed and the rationale behind them is contained in [4].

For example, in our operating system, a software bug that causes the program to crash (a "runtime error") triggers a listing of the stack of procedure calls at the point of the error. Like a radiologist's x-ray, this listing can be very informative about the problem. We designed the system so that these listings would be automatically included in the performance data collected by the system. In addition, we sensitized early users to the potential value of these listings and encouraged them to record what behavior they were engaged in at the time of the error, since this information provided the appropriate context in which to interpret the listing.

R9: Don't start on a shoestring

There are a number of important issues about resources that arise in projects based on emerging technology. You must clearly acknowledge that such projects require an enormous investment in time. If the developers are not prepared to spend a significant amount of time learning about the users' organization, or if the users' organization is not prepared to make available the time for meaningful cooperation, we would recommend against the project. Consequently, you should expect that the project will last at least 18 months; not much can happen in less time.

However, there is a flip side to this problem: taking too long. When the project goes beyond 3 years, you're no longer managing a project, you're running a business. Organizational factors such as personnel turnover and burnout can begin to dominate the project.

R10: Don't try to do too much (or too little)

There is a fine line to walk between trying to do too much versus missing golden opportunities that arise along the way. However, the greatest danger lies with trying to do too much, since the result is that nothing gets done well. Since it is such a common mistake to set goals that are too ambitious, we forced ourselves at the beginning of the project to narrow our objectives to something we could carry off with a reasonably high probability. In retrospect, it is fortunate that we did this, because we were then able to take on two additional tasks that presented themselves as irresistible opportunities along the way. One of these additions (the expert system for aiding launch and recovery of aircraft) became more important in many people's minds than our original management applications. Even so, the situation was a mixed blessing, since it is painfully apparent to us that our effort was spread so thin that all of the applications suffered to some extent.

Recommendations based on hindsight

Of course, not all of our recommendations are based on things we did right. In this section, we include recommendations that we would implement in future projects because our experience proved them to be valuable by their omission. (We have selected only several of the more interesting ones; the brevity of the list does not imply that we made very few mistakes in managing the project.)

R11: Use scripts of user-level behavior for automatic testing

It is very time-consuming to test a new version of a system that has enormous richness. We believe that many of the problems detected by users after the release of a version could be detected much further upstream by exercising the system under the control of scripts that simulate a user's behavior. Part of the difficulty of validating complex man-machine systems arises from the fact that many problems are not just functions of single user behavior, but also interactions of multiple users that arise probabilistically.

R12: Keep a running log of the most recent user actions

When an unrecoverable error occurs, users do not reliably recall their actions which led up to the problem. Rather than counting on users to document their behavior and forward it with the appropriate error listing to the developers, we believe it would be much more effective to have this context information collected automatically and stored with the other information about the error.

R13: Give documentors a central role in the project

Since the documentors have to work with an image of the system from the users' perspective, they are able to see problems with the system to which the programmers are blind. We found the documentation of the system to be a useful measure of the quality of the system design: unnecessary complexities in the system became apparent through the attempts to document them for the users. We recommend that the documentor be respected as a valuable source of feedback for the design process.

Another important function of documentors should be to maintain central control over messages the system displays to users. Messages should be centralized in one location-- preferably a data file rather than a program file for ease of modification. We allowed individual programmers to author messages, and were surprised in retrospect to see how inconsistent they were. When programmers control the messages, documentors often end up having to write a whole paragraph in the user's guide to explain a confusing message, when a comprehensible message would have done the job alone.

Summary

We believe that the development process for computer systems utilizing emerging technologies must preserve considerably more flexibility than suggested by more traditional development strategies. This need must be recognized by all participants in such projects. Goals are likely to change significantly over the life of the project as the understanding of the technology and the users' needs matures. Therefore, we recommend that such projects be conducted in a highly cooperative manner between the users' organization and the developers' organization over a planned period not longer than 18 months, obtaining feedback via a series of instrumented prototypes that are exercised by both users and developers for actual tasks.

Acknowledgements

We wish to acknowledge the contributions of many people over the years. Those who have been involved with ZOG at CMU: Allen Newell, George Robertson, Kamila Robertson, Elise Yoder, Sandy Esch, Patty Nazarek, Angela Gugliotta, Marilyn Mantei, Kamesh Ramakrishna, Roy Taylor, Mark Fox, and Andy Palay. Those officers from the USS CARL VINSON who worked with us at CMU: Mark Frost, Paul Fischbeck, Hal Powell, Russ Shoop, and Rich Anderson. Captain Richard Martin, Captain Tom Mercer, Cdr Ted Kral and other officers and crew of the USS CARL VINSON. And finally, Marvin Denicoff from the Office of Naval Research, our original ZOG research sponsor.

This work was supported by the Office of Naval Research under contract N00014-76-0874. It was also partially supported by the Defense Advanced Research Projects Agency (DOD), ARPA Order No. 3597, monitored by the Air Force Avionics Laboratory under contract F33615-78-C-1551. The views and conclusions contained in this document are those of the authors and should not be interpreted as representing the official policies, either expressed or implied, of the Office of Naval Research, the Defense Advanced Research Projects Agency, or the U.S. Government.

References

[1] McCracken, D. and Akscyn, R., Experience with the ZOG human-computer interface system, to appear in the International Journal of Man-Machine Studies (July 1984).

[2] Newell, A., McCracken, D., Robertson, G. and Akscyn, R., ZOG and the USS CARL VINSON, Computer Science Research Review, Carnegie-Mellon University (1981) 95-118.

[3] Robertson, G., McCracken, D. and Newell, A., The ZOG approach to man-machine communication, International Journal of Man-Machine Studies, 14 (1981) 461-488.

[4] Yoder, E., McCracken, D. and Akscyn, R., Instrumenting a human-computer interface for development and evaluation, in the proceedings of Interact '84.

Human-Computer Interaction — INTERACT '84 / B. Shackel (ed.)
Elsevier Science Publishers B.V. (North-Holland)
© IFIP, 1985

Instrumenting a Human-Computer Interface
For Development and Evaluation

Elise Yoder, Donald McCracken, and Robert Akscyn

Carnegie-Mellon University
Pittsburgh, PA, USA

The ZOG human-computer interface has been instrumented to collect data about the system's performance and the users' behavior. We explain which data are collected and how they are recorded. We then suggest that analyzing the instrumentation data is akin to archaeology, because one must infer behavior patterns from low-level data "artifacts". Finally, we provide some guidelines for instrumentation design.

1. Introduction

Throughout the life cycle of a computer system, various people need information about how that system is performing and how it is being used:

- The system developers need to know what problems and inefficiencies are plaguing the system so that they can improve the design and implementation.
- Managers who are introducing the system into their organization need to know how people feel about the system and how it is affecting their job performance and social environment.
- System evaluators are typically concerned with job performance, too, but they may also be evaluating the system's potential for use at other sites or in other applications.
- Researchers studying human-computer interaction need detailed information about the users' interaction with the system.

One method of finding out how the system is being used is to instrument the computer system itself. The data collected by such system instrumentation can supplement data collected by more traditional methods such as direct observation, questionnaires, and controlled experiments.

Instrumenting the system (sometimes referred to as "automatic monitoring") has several significant advantages over more traditional methods. By letting the computer do the work, data may be collected systematically from each user, and at many points in time. Humans without computer assistance must usually resort to monitoring a sample of users at a limited number of times. Also, measurements made by the computer can be more precise than if performed by humans.

On the other hand, there are drawbacks to collecting data automatically. Often it is hard to determine ahead of time which aspects of a situation will prove interesting, or which

measures will provide answers for the interesting questions. The result may be the collection of a relatively large amount of low-level data. When the computer is used to collect such data, the sheer amount of data may be overwhelming. Processing the data is also problematic, because it is difficult to relate low-level information (for instance, about keystrokes and error rates) to "higher-level" user behavior patterns and categories. In other words, objective measures are only approximations of certain behaviors and therefore may be distorted. [3]

This paper describes our experience instrumenting a human-computer interface called ZOG, developed at Carnegie-Mellon University (CMU). Section 2 provides background about ZOG and its application on board an aircraft carrier. In Section 3 we describe the instrumentation which was developed for that application and illustrate how it may be used to answer questions about ZOG. Finally, in Section 4 we offer several guidelines for the design of instrumentation.

In this paper, "instrumentation" refers to system software that automatically collects data for system design and evaluation. The data itself we call the "statistics"; these are descriptive statistics (and simple frequency counts) on the behavior of the user and of the system. It should be noted that all of the automatically-collected data is objective; while it is certainly possible to collect subjective data using the computer (employing, for instance, short event-triggered questionnaires), such data were not gathered by the ZOG instrumentation. For an overview of the uses of computer instrumentation, see [5].

2. ZOG and the ZOG/VINSON system

In 1980, the ZOG Project at CMU and the Commanding Officer of the USS CARL VINSON agreed to jointly develop a computer-aided management system for the VINSON. The system was to be based on the concepts of ZOG, a human-computer interface developed at CMU. The following sections describe the ZOG interface and the ZOG-based computer system used on the aircraft carrier.

2.1. ZOG

ZOG is a general-purpose human-computer interface which has been under development at the CMU Computer Science Department since 1975 [2] [6]. It is based primarily on the five concepts described in the example ZOG frame shown in Figure 2-1. This frame contains four types of components: a unique identifier in the upper right corner, a title, local selections (which contain text and may link to other frames), and global selections, which are available on the bottom line of every frame.

```
┌─────────────────────────────────────────────────────────┐
│ Concepts on which ZOG is based                    Basic3 │
│                                                          │
│  1. Menu selection: Most ZOG frames contain a menu of    │
│       selections which are made using mouse or keyboard. │
│                                                          │
│  2. Active selections: Selections can also activate      │
│       programs.                                          │
│                                                          │
│  3. Large database: ZOG is capable of handling hundreds  │
│       of thousands of frames.                            │
│                                                          │
│  4. Rapid response: After the user makes a selection,    │
│       ZOG displays another frame in less than 1 second.  │
│                                                          │
│  5. Modifiable frames: Frames may be created and edited  │
│       by users.                                          │
│                                                          │
│ edit help back next prev top goto old zog xchg print jump│
└─────────────────────────────────────────────────────────┘
```

Figure 2-1: Sample ZOG frame

Frames are grouped into subnets. Subnets usually take the form of a hierarchy (tree) of frames. For example, all the ship's tasks composing the major task "Getting Underway" might be contained in a subnet called "GUWay". The subnets are combined into one database. In the distributed version of ZOG, every user can access any frame in the entire database, regardless of physical location.

2.2. The ZOG/VINSON system

The USS CARL VINSON represents a complex management problem because of its size and the number of personnel: it is 1100 feet long, and holds 100 aircraft and 5700 people. Approximately 4 percent of the people are officers, who perform the middle- and upper-level management of the ship; the officers are the ZOG/VINSON system's intended users.

Onboard the VINSON, 28 PERQ personal computers run ZOG in a distributed mode linked by a 10 MHz Ethernet local-area network. The ship's PERQs currently contain over 60,000 ZOG frames. Over 40 application programs operate on these ZOG frames [1] [4]. The system is designed to support the following ship's functions:

- Representing management information--about tasks and task assignments--in networks of ZOG frames. Frames in this database may be used to produce schedules for management activities. Organized by activity (e.g. refueling) or by person (e.g. Executive Officer), the schedules are available in hardcopy or on-line in ZOG frames.

- Training in weapons- and aircraft-elevator operation and maintenance (done from ZOG frames that control a videodisk player).

- Interface to AirPlan--a rule-based artificial intelligence expert system which aids in aircraft launch and recovery.

3. The ZOG/VINSON instrumentation

The following sections describe the instrumentation that was developed for the ZOG system on board the USS CARL VINSON. The parties involved in the instrumentation development were the system developers at CMU and the ZOG/VINSON evaluators from the Naval Personnel Research and Development Center (NPRDC) in San Diego, California.

3.1. Questions to be answered

The instrumentation was designed to answer certain questions about the ZOG/VINSON system. The system developers were especially interested in these questions:

- Which errors do users commonly make?
- When does the system malfunction?
- What is the average system response time (the time to display a frame) for local and remote frame accesses?
- To what extent are the subsystems/features (e.g. editors, programs) exercised by the users?

The evaluators focused on these questions:

- Is the system being used for the target application (ship's management) functions? for additional functions?
- Is total system use (measured in number and length of uses) growing?

3.2. What statistics are recorded (and when)

Several types of statistics are recorded during each ZOG session (the time between a user's logging in and logging off). "Snapshot" statistics are recorded at the session's beginning and every 20 minutes thereafter until the session's end. These statistics, which are a small proportion of the total statistics, give very general information about the state of the system at the time of recording (for instance, the amount of time that has

Snapshot Frames

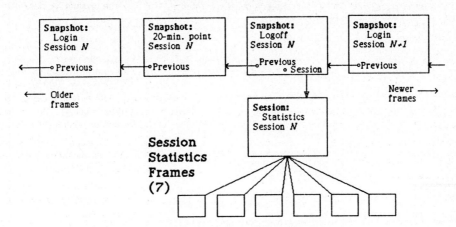

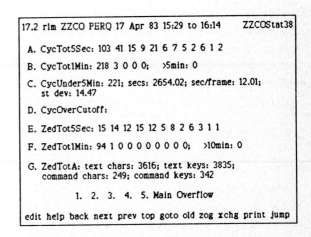

Figure 3-1: Types of statistics frames

elapsed in the current session). When the user logs off, the main "session" statistics are recorded (and displayed to the user) in addition to the final snapshot. The session statistics contain detailed information about the user's and the system's behavior during that session.

Another form of statistics is recorded on program executions within ZOG. Whenever the user activates a program inside ZOG, a record of that activation is made. For instance, if the user runs a program to create a management schedule, the program name is recorded along with the arguments to the program (for example, that it was a 6-day schedule for the Air Strike Department).

3.3. How statistics are recorded

In an earlier version of ZOG, statistics were stored in a huge text file--a file which often grew so large that text editors could no longer read it. The sheer mass of the statistics seemed to deter people from browsing through and analyzing the statistics. Therefore, the designers decided to record the ZOG/VINSON statistics in linked ZOG frames (collected in a separate subnet on each PERQ).

Figure 3-1 shows, in schematic form, the types of statistics frames and their interconnections. Not shown are the statistics frames for program executions; they are copies of the actual frames used to input arguments, saved in a chain in the same way as the snapshot statistics frames. An example session statistics frame is presented in Figure 3-2.

3.4. What information is recorded

As you can see from the frame in Figure 3-2, information is recorded in considerable detail. This frame contains several identification fields in the top line. It also provides the following data about ZOG cycles (a cycle is the interval

between one keystroke and the next when outside the editor-- essentially, the time spent at a single frame):

- CycTot5Sec: Number of cycle durations in each 5-second interval (from 0-60 seconds)
- CycTot1Min: Number of cycle durations in each 1-minute interval (from 1-5 minutes)
- CycUnder5Min: For cycle durations under 5 minutes: Total number, total seconds, average length, standard deviation of length
- CycOverCutoff: List of cycle durations above cutoff (5 minutes)

The table in Figure 3-3 summarizes the statistics which are collected for each ZOG session. For a given ZOG feature or capability, the types of data collected about that feature are listed, along with the primary reasons for their collection.

```
17.2 rlm ZZCO PERQ 17 Apr 83 15:29 to 16:14        ZZCOStat38

A. CycTot5Sec: 103 41 15 9 21 6 7 5 2 6 1 2

B. CycTot1Min: 218 3 0 0 0;   >5min: 0

C. CycUnder5Min: 221; secs: 2654.02; sec/frame: 12.01;
   st dev: 14.47

D. CycOverCutoff:

E. ZedTot5Sec: 15 14 12 15 12 5 8 2 6 3 1 1

F. ZedTot1Min: 94 1 0 0 0 0 0 0 0 0;   >10min: 0

G. ZedTotA: text chars: 3616; text keys: 3835;
   command chars: 249; command keys: 342

         1.  2.  3.  4.  5. Main Overflow

edit help back next prev top goto old zog xchg print jump
```

Figure 3-2: Sample session statistics frame

ZOG feature	What is recorded	Analysis/use
ZOG selection cycles	Cycle duration distributions as in Section 3.4	Pattern of user behavior (e.g. rapid browsing)
Frame editor (ZED)	No. of text, command and error chars ZED session duration distributions	Extent ZED use ZED interface redesign Keystroke-level analysis of ZED use
Editor for slots on program input frames (SLED)	No. of text, command and error chars SLED session duration distributions No. of slots edited by slot type	Extent SLED use Extent use of different slot types
Mouse	No. of mouse uses for selections, slot editing, ZED functions such as repositioning, errors	Extent and nature of mouse use Error rate
ZOG selections, actions, and commands	No. of selections outside editor No. of actions invoked, created, deleted by action type No. of each particular global selection	Extent and nature of action language use Global selection set redesign
Frames created and deleted	List of every frame created List of every frame deleted	Extent ZOG/ZED use Rate of database growth
Subnets accessed, created, deleted, edited	List for each operation: subnet name, no. of operations, (if access) total access time	Determine function Extent use by function Extent ZOG use Pattern of accesses (e.g. localized vs. wide-spread)
Programs run	List in order run: program name, run time for that invocation	Determine function Extent use by function
System response	Three response time distributions: Disk: frames accessed on local disk Net: frames accessed on remote disks Action: accesses involving actions	Speed of frame access (especially local vs. remote)
Ethernet traffic	No. of Ethernet requests, incoming or outgoing, for each type (e.g. frame read) and for each remote machine No. of message errors by type (e.g. timeout)	Extent network use Network soft/hardware reliability Pattern of remote accesses by request type (e.g. ratio of reads to writes) and by identity of remote machines

Figure 3-3: Summary of ZOG session statistics

3.5. Analysis of the statistics

One way to analyze the statistics is to aggregate them by different categories: user, machine, time period. This aggregation is necessary when comparing the use patterns of different ship's departments or different phases of the ship's cruise. However, another sort of analysis requires inferring from the low-level data some higher-order behavior patterns. We have not yet completed either type of analysis, so this section will deal with the process of analysis and not the results.

Interpreter as archaeologist. Interpreting the statistics is like going on an archaeological dig. The interpreter might, at first blush, seem more comparable to an anthropologist, who observes a culture and draws conclusions about its activities.

But the statistics interpreter does not observe the culture (the ZOG users on board the VINSON) first-hand. Instead, he sorts through the artifacts left by that culture, trying to reconstruct a picture of its activities. These artifacts (data) consist of fragments, as described in Section 3.4: numbers of keystrokes, lists of frames accessed, etc. His task is to construct profiles of user behavior and characterize user interaction patterns by piecing these fragments together into a coherent image.

Fortunately, the ZOG/VINSON developers who were analyzing the statistics were luckier than their bones-and-pottery-shards counterparts. First, the culture they were studying still existed and could be revisited for clarification and further data collection. Secondly, the developers were able to predetermine which artifacts would be "left behind" by the culture; in other words, they were able to design instrumentation for the ZOG/VINSON system.

Inferring functions. One analysis task requiring inference from the statistical data was determining which functions were being performed in ZOG. A function is a broad type of task. There are <u>external functions</u> which contribute directly to the ship's operations (e.g. creating a weekly management plan), and <u>internal functions</u> which are necessary to use the ZOG system (e.g. learning to use the ZOG editor) [3]. The ZOG/VINSON evaluators were chiefly concerned with the system's effectiveness: did it help people do their jobs? Therefore the evaluators needed information about which external ship's functions were being performed using ZOG. The system developers were especially interested in information about the internal functions.

The challenge for both groups was to determine which function was being performed at any given time during a ZOG session; only then could the "low-level" information be categorized by functions. But the determining of functions was complicated by the general-purpose nature of the tools in ZOG. (For instance, navigation through ZOG frames can be done to browse through frames, reach particular information, or move within located information. The ZOG editor is used for all text-editing in frames, regardless of the text's content.) Here is where the archaeologist's process of inferring activity from data artifacts came in. Determining the function required synthesizing several pieces of information.

For example, here is how the developer/archaeologist might infer that a particular function is being performed during a given session. The function in question is creating a new task subnet with reference to an existing task subnet. One useful "artifact" is the subnets-accessed information. This shows the majority of time being spent in a subnet named "Dock", with brief forays into a subnet called "LandTasks". The forays suggest that the latter subnet (presumably containing task information) is being used for reference. The frames-created and subnets-edited information corroborate this by showing that many frames are being edited in the "Dock" subnet, but none in "LandTasks". Taken together, these bits of information are probably enough to conclude that the user is creating a subnet of management tasks for docking the ship. If a program that creates management plans from task subnets is run during the session, and if the saved program input frame indicates that the program was run on "Dock", the function determination is confirmed.

4. Some guidelines for instrumentation design

Based on our experience with instrumenting the ZOG/VINSON system, we offer the following guidelines for instrumentation design.

Iteratively develop the statistics over time. We found instrumentation to be like many other pieces of software: hard to design, hard to program, and hard to debug. It is difficult to anticipate all possible behavioral acts and system states--especially if the system is complex and multifunctional--and to form partitions from them. Until you exercise the instrumented system by using it for "real" tasks you won't know if the instrumentation is accurate or if it addresses your questions about the system and its use. We found it advantageous to use the CMU development group as the initial test site for the instrumentation.

Have all the instrumentation programming done by one person. Since the pieces of instrumentation code are highly interdependent, it is advisable to have one person do all the programming. For the ZOG/VINSON system, one instrumentation programmer worked with the programmers of the various subsystems to ensure an adequate understanding of those subsystems.

Record intermediate statistics which summarize session in progress. It is a good idea to periodically record summaries of the session in progress so that some data about the session will exist even if it is aborted due to system malfunction. Our snapshot statistics were intended to serve this purpose, but not enough of their information contributed to the cumulative picture of the session.

Devise a method for validating the instrumentation. A good way to validate the instrumentation is to embed in the system a "session playback" capability. This involves capturing all the user inputs (with their relative timing) and being able to play back the input stream, thus recreating the entire session. You can then replicate the same set of actions in order to verify the instrumentation. Even if an input stream cannot be exactly recorded, it is worthwhile to design scripts that can be "walked through" manually using a watch; these scripts should test all the subareas covered by the instrumentation.

Expect to devote much effort to post-processing the data. The analysis tools should be developed before data collection is started. The process of building the analysis tools yields lessons for redesign of the instrumentation.

Provide easy access to the statistics. Statistics will probably be more useful if they can be easily accessed and browsed through. When browsing, people can form an impression of what is contained in the statistics; they may notice unexpectedly interesting phenomena; and they can scan for a particular item across many sessions without gearing up a large processing effort.

Acknowledgements

We wish to acknowledge the contributions of many people over the years. Those who have been involved with ZOG at CMU: Allen Newell, George Robertson, Kamila Robertson, Sandy Esch, Patty Nazarek, Angela Gugliotta, Marilyn Mantei, Kamesh Ramakrishna, Roy Taylor, Mark Fox, and Andy Palay. Those officers from the USS CARL VINSON who worked with us at CMU: Mark Frost, Paul Fischbeck, Hal Powell, Russ Shoop, and Rich Anderson. Captain Richard Martin, Captain Tom Mercer, and other officers and crew of the USS CARL VINSON. And finally, Marvin Denicoff from the Office of Naval Research, our original ZOG research sponsor. We would especially like to acknowledge Allen Newell and Kamila Robertson for their contributions to the ZOG/VINSON instrumentation.

The ZOG/VINSON work was supported by the Office of Naval Research under contract N00014-76-0874. It was also partially supported by the Defense Advanced Research Projects Agency (DOD), ARPA Order No. 3597, monitored by the Air Force Avionics Laboratory under contract F33615-78-C-1551.

References

[1] Akscyn, R. and McCracken, D., ZOG and the USS CARL VINSON: Lessons in System Development, Proceedings of Interact '84, IFIP conference on human-computer interaction.

[2] McCracken, D. and Akscyn, R., Experience with the ZOG Human-Computer Interface System, to appear in the International Journal of Man-Machine Studies (July 1984).

[3] Newell, A., Evaluation of the ZOG CARL VINSON System, project memo, Computer Science Department, Carnegie-Mellon University (1983).

[4] Newell, A., McCracken, D., Robertson, G. and Akscyn, R., ZOG and the USS CARL VINSON, Computer Science Research Review, Carnegie-Mellon University (1980-81) 95-118.

[5] Penniman, W. and Dominick, W., Monitoring and Evaluation of On-line Information System Usage, Information Processing and Management 16 (1980) 17-35.

[6] Robertson, G., McCracken, D. and Newell, A., The ZOG Approach to Man-Machine Communication, International Journal of Man-Machine Studies 14 (1981) 115-123.

Human-Computer Interaction — INTERACT '84 / B. Shackel (ed.)
Elsevier Science Publishers B.V. (North-Holland)
© IFIP, 1985

AUGMENTING GENERIC RESEARCH WITH PROTOTYPE EVALUATION

EXPERIENCE IN APPLYING GENERIC RESEARCH TO SPECIFIC PRODUCTS

Thomas M. Gruenenfelder and William B. Whitten II

AT&T Bell Laboratories

Holmdel, NJ 07733 U.S.A.

Generic research in the area of human-computer interaction is aimed towards discovering general principles of user interface design that can be applied to a wide variety of specific interfaces. In this paper, we point out some important limitations of generic research that make some results difficult to apply to specific designs. The most important limitation is the insensitivity of generic research to the context of a full design. We suggest guidelines for the designer to use when evaluating the applicability of generic research. Finally, we discuss new approaches to generic research that may help overcome these limitations.

Much of the current human factors research in the area of human-computer interaction falls into a category that we call generic research. Generic research is directed at uncovering general design principles that have broad applicability across many different specific applications. Examples of questions that might be addressed in generic research include: What is the optimal number of choices to put on a single menu (e.g., Miller, 1981; Snowberry, Parkinson, & Sisson, 1983)? What is the optimal method of selecting items from a menu or display (e.g., Whitfield, Ball, & Bird, 1983)? What names for a command are good and what names are bad (e.g., Black & Moran, 1982)? Generic research can be contrasted with prototype testing, where the designer of a user interface builds a prototype of the interface that is complete enough to evaluate any number of specific design choices within the context of that complete interface (cf. Reitman, Whitten, & Gruenenfelder, 1982).

This paper discusses some of the problems that may be encountered by designers who rely primarily upon generic research. We begin by illustrating some of the limitations of generic research, based on examples from our own work. Next, we discuss ways a designer can cope with these limitations. Finally, we discuss directions that generic research might take to become more useful to the designers.

Limitations of Generic Research

Our examples come from our work done on a system that allowed users to enter into a database and update complex decision trees. Our own responsibility was to design the user interface to this system. An important design constraint was that the tree was to be entered, viewed, and updated on standard and inexpensive alphanumeric terminals--graphic display devices were ruled out. In order to illustrate the problem, Figure 1 shows a sample decision tree that describes the dialing plan for a large corporation's private network. A potential user of the system would be a telecommunications manager responsible for entering and updating such a dialing plan. The nodes in the tree correspond to different categories of calls, and the branches to instances of those categories. Each branch also points to the next appropriate node in the sequence.

Figure 2 shows the basic screen display we developed for entering and viewing the decision tree. The top portion of the screen is used to display context information. The bottom portion displays a menu of the commands available to the user. The central portion is used for entry and display of the tree. This portion is divided into four columns. In each column, a node name can be displayed at the top with its branches listed underneath. The second column can show the node that is connected to the topmost branch of the node displayed in the first column. Similarly, nodes and branches can be displayed in the third and fourth columns. Details about the interface can be found in Reitman, Whitten, and Gruenenfelder (1982) and Reitman, Whitten, Gruenenfelder, and Sorce (1983). We will present enough details in this paper to illustrate our interpretation of the relation between generic research and the results of our prototype testing.

Our first example pertains to the need to move the locus of display and control from one node's column to another. Certain commands, such as Up, Down, Add Branch, etc., apply to one node at a time. This node, which we call the "active node", is indicated by highlighting. We provided two commands to move the highlighting from one node to another. One command allows the user to move the "active" status from the currently active node to the next node in the sequence; the other command allows the user to make the previous node in the tree the active node. What should these commands be named?

Initially, we named them Right and Left. Superficially, at least, these names are consistent with command-naming guidelines. They are not overly general (Barnard, Hammond, MacLean, & Morton, 1982), and they use congruent

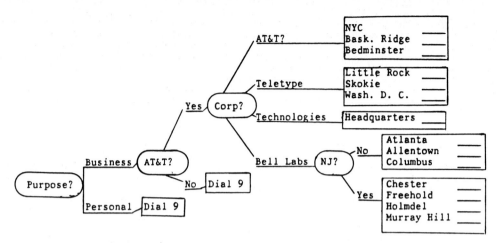

Figure 1: Decision tree to be represented on interface.

or coordinate terms (Carroll, 1980; Black & Moran, 1982). Nevertheless, during prototype evaluation, users frequently used one command when they intended the other. We believe that the reason for much of this confusion can be seen if we consider the case where the active node is in the rightmost column and the user wishes to make the next node active. To do so, the user should say "Right." But because the to-be-active node is not part of the current display, the system must shift each node on the display one column to the left, to make room for it, causing the leftmost node to disappear from the display. Apparently, the left-shift of the nodes interferes with issuing a command named "Right." We were able to correct this problem by re-naming the commands "Next" and "Back."

As a second example, consider how a user moves a branch under the active node into the top position. The user needs to do this for two reasons. First, it is not always possible to display all of the branches of a node on the screen simultaneously. Second, in this particular design, the next-displayed node is pointed to by the top displayed branch of the current column. Consequently, the user must have a mechanism to control what branch is in the top position.

Two commands, Up and Down, allow the user to order the branches underneath a node. The question is, what happens when the user invokes "Up." Consider the third node (WHICH CORP?) in Figure 2. Does "Up" change the display to AT&T, Teletype, Technologies, Bell Labs or is the order of the list Technologies, Bell Labs, AT&T, Teletype? (Note that the branches are not designed as a simple list, but as a wheel or circular list.) The more general question is whether the command "Up" moves the data up under a window or moves a window up over the data. Bury, Boyle, Evey, and Neal (1982) asked this more general question and found that users prefer and perform better with a model of the window moving over the data rather than the data scrolling under the window. Yet in our prototype, which was developed before the results of Bury et al. appeared, we implemented the nonpreferred mode--the data scrolling under the window, which changes the display to AT&T, Teletype,...--and found no user performance problems.

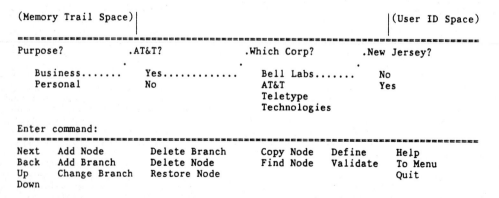

Figure 2: Interface displaying portions of the decision tree.

There are several possible reasons why we found no difficulties with the nonpreferred mode of scrolling. One possibility is that we conceptualize the data as being on a wheel (much like an odometer) rather than as being a simple list. Another is that there are four windows on the display--each node has its own window--and it may be easier to think of the windows as fixed and the data as moving when there are multiple windows.

Our examples do not show that the cited research is incorrect (we believe it to be correct), but that it does not always apply in the full context of a design. Conclusions based on research of a generic nature must always be appended with some sort of qualifier, such as "under the experimental condition studied." But what does "under the experimental conditions" mean? How can we tell, a priori, which of the many experimental conditions that we did not explicitly manipulate could have affected the results? Our position is that, a priori, we cannot tell. We must always prototype the design and conduct a thorough human factors' evaluation of the design. Even a design based on solid, well documented design guidelines can fail when each of those guidelines is operating in the particular context of a complete system.

We would like to discuss one last example showing the limitations of generic human factors research. Suppose a user wishes to build a new decision tree using the interface in Figure 2. In one approach, the user calls up a screen with the large central workspace blank, and enters the root node and its branches in the first column. When the user indicates that all branches for the first node have been entered, the system draws a pointer, consisting of periods, from the top displayed branch of the first node to the node entry row of the second column, highlights the node entry row of the second column, and prompts the user to enter the next node. In our prototype evaluation we found that users frequently were not sure which first-column branch was attached to the second-column node. This problem disappeared when we highlighted the top displayed branch of the first column as well as the node entry row in the second column.

The point of this example is that we are not sure that any generic design guideline could have told us how to design this part of the interface correctly on the first try. In addition, we are not certain that our solution has much to offer as a generic design guideline. Many design questions are not generic in nature, but are specific to a particular interface. Such questions may not be answerable by referring to design principles, but workable answers may be found through prototype evaluation.

We should comment that we were successful in having all the aforementioned design changes incorporated into the system. There are several reasons for our success. First, the design of the user interface was the responsibility primarily of a human factors team rather than of an implementation team. For this approach to work, of course, the human factors team must

have a clear view concerning which design aspects are critical from a human factors perspective, and what features can be implemented within the scheduled time (cf. Thomas, 1982). Second, our prototype effort was conducted well in advance of the requirements deadline. Third, our recommendations for change were based on data, not intuition. These points are not new, but our experience does show that when these conditions are fulfilled, human factors considerations can affect the design.

To summarize this section, there are two primary limitations to generic research. The first is that the results frequently do not apply within the context of a particular design. Second, many critical design questions are simply not questions that are likely to be addressed through generic research.

A Logical Argument on the Limitations of Generic Research

The previous section provided examples of some limitations of generic research where prototyping work was necessary to decide design questions. There is also a theoretical, abstract argument showing the limitations of generic research. Generic research is typically directed at uncovering the principles that apply to a particular cognitive, perceptual, or motor subsystem. Only rarely do questions address how different subsystems interact. Laboratory researchers investigate subsystems operating in relative isolation, in an effort to determine the laws and principles that apply to those subsystems. This general model of research has been highly successful in a number of sciences. User performance and satisfaction with a user interface, however, are a function of a complex interaction of many different subsystems. Further, the particular mix of subsystems will differ from one interface to another, from one context to another, from one situation to another. The laws and principles that describe the operation of a subsystem in a laboratory environment may not describe how that subsystem will interact with the mix of subsystems involved in a particular interface. Prototype evaluation is typically necessary to see how the interactions among the subsystems of a design in a particular context actually affect user performance.

Guidelines for the Designer

Faced with these limitations, how is a designer to evaluate the applicability of a particular research result to a particular design? The obvious answer is to prototype the design and perform a human factors evaluation of the design. Unfortunately, time constraints sometimes prohibit prototype evaluation and never allow testing of every design decision in the context of a complete prototype.

Nevertheless, there are ways a designer can evaluate the applicability of general design principles to a particular design. The wider the variety of designs in which controlled research has shown a particular principle to hold, the more confident a designer can be that the results will apply to a new design.

Similarly, confidence is increased when the variable of interest (e.g., a scrolling technique) is shown not to interact with a variety of other variables. To the extent that interactions occur, prototype evaluation of that design component is warranted. Confidence in the applicability of the result decreases to the extent that interactions do occur. For example, if the commands that control scrolling are shown to be best for a number of conditions--for displays with single windows, for displays with multiple but independent windows, for displays with multiple but dependent windows, and for displays mixing windows with fixed, unmovable areas of the screen--then our confidence increases that the result will apply to a new design.

A second important consideration is the extent to which the rationale of a result is given. Why is one set of command names better than another? If a clear answer to that question can be found, then the designer is in a good position to judge the applicability of the research to a new design. If the rational is not addressed, the designer cannot make that judgment, and prototype evaluation becomes necessary.

Guidelines for the Researcher

A question complementary to the one concerning how designers can best use generic research concerns how researchers can make their work more useful to the designers. First, it is imperative that we investigate plausible explanations for our observed phenomena. It is not sufficient to report a result without also investigating why that result, and not some other result, occurred.

Second, we must investigate the limitations of our results. We noted earlier that the results of studies may not be generalizable beyond the particular conditions of the experiment in which they were found, and that it is often quite difficult to determine when the results of an experiment can be generalized. Thus, once we find a result, we must follow through to investigate the conditions under which that result holds, and the conditions under which it does not hold. In addition, we must document the trade-offs in our guidelines. Our studies need to address questions of how to weigh different conditions in particular designs.

Thirdly, we need a program of research directed at developing a theory of context. When and why do particular subsystems of the complex human organism become more and less important (cf. Card, Moran, & Newell, 1983)? How do the subsystems of the cognitive, perceptual, and motor systems interact with each other? What aspects of a full design context need to be considered, and what aspects do not need to be considered? Although we see a definite need for research directed at these questions, we admit that it is difficult to suggest how such research should proceed.

Fourth, we need to conduct large parametric studies, using many levels of many different variables. For example, to determine the optimal number of choices to place on a menu, it is not sufficient to manipulate just the breadth and depth of the menu hierarchy. A partial list of other variables that must also be varied includes the organization of menu alternatives (e.g., Snowberry et al., 1983), display formats (e.g., Apperly & Spence, 1983), display devices, the mechanism and devices for selecting alternatives, the response time and its variability to a selection, the memory load placed on the user from sources other than the menu, the length and clarity of the alternatives, the similarity of the alternatives to each other, and the extent to which the alternatives fit into a hierarchical structure. Such studies are extremely time-consuming to conduct, but they provide detailed answers to complex questions. They allow the researcher to see the boundary conditions of a result, and they let the designer focus on the conditions of most importance to his or her specific design.

Summary

There are two important limitations to design guidelines based on generic research. First, it is difficult to determine if a particular result will hold within the context of a particular design. Second, many crucial design decisions do not lend themselves to resolution through generic research. Faced with such difficulties, we have suggested ways designers can judge the applicability of research to their designs. Finally, we have considered how researchers could tailor their studies to the needs of the designers. The most important of these suggestions was to conduct large parametric studies that investigate the interactions among a number of variables.

References

[1] Apperley, M. D., & Spence, R. Hierarchical dialogue structures in interactive computer systems. *Software--Practice and Experience*, 1983, 13, 777-790.

[2] Barnard, P., Hammond, N., MacLean, A., & Morton, J. Learning and remembering interactive commands. *Proceedings of Human Factors in Computer Systems*, Gaithersburg, MD, 1982.

[3] Black, J., & Moran, T. Learning and remembering command names. *Proceedings of Human Factors in Computer Systems*, Gaithersburg, MD, 1982.

[4] Bury, K., Boyle, J., Evey, R. J., & Neal, A. Windowing vs. scrolling on a visual display terminal. *Proceedings of Human Factors in Computer Systems*, Gaithersburg, MD, 1982.

[5] Card, S. K., Moran, T. P., & Newell, A. *The psychology of human-computer interaction.* Hillsdale, NJ: Lawrence Erlbaum Associates, 1983.

[6] Carroll, J. M. Learning, using, and designing command paradigms. *IBM Research Report RC 8141*, 1980.

[7] Miller, D. P. The depth-breadth tradeoff in hierarchical computer menus. <u>Proceedings of the 25th Annual Meeting of the Human Factors Society</u>, 1981, 296-299.

[8] Reitman, J. S., Whitten, W. B. II, & Gruenenfelder, T. M. A general user interface for creating and displaying tree structures, hierarchies, decision trees and nested menus. <u>New York University Symposium on User Interfaces</u>, New York, 1982.

[9] Reitman, J. S., Whitten, W. B. II, Gruenenfelder, T. M., & Sorce, J. A. Design and evaluation of computer interfaces. <u>Tenth International Symposium on Human Factors in Telecommunications</u>, Helsinki, Finland, 1983.

[10] Snowberry, K., Parkinson, S. R., & Sisson N. Computer display menus. <u>Ergonomics</u>, 1983, <u>26</u>, 699-712.

[11] Thomas, J. C. How to ensure usable products. <u>New York University Symposium on User Interfaces</u>, New York, 1982.

[12] Whitfield, D., Ball, R. G., & Bird, J. M. Some comparisons of on-display and off-display touch input devices for interaction with computer generated displays. <u>Ergonomics</u>, 1983, <u>26</u>, 1033-1053.

Human-Computer Interaction — INTERACT '84 / B. Shackel (ed.)
Elsevier Science Publishers B.V. (North-Holland)
© IFIP, 1985

USAGE ISSUES IN ELECTRONIC MAIL, CONFERENCE AND JOURNAL SYSTEMS

Introduction to the Theme of 4 Sessions

B Shackel

Electronic communication networks enable people to send and receive information, opinions and ideas by media other than paper and the spoken word.   Various methods have been developing slowly since the first use of telex and teletypewriter dialogue during the Berlin crisis in 1948.   However, it is only since the mid-1970's that significant practical usage of electronic communication has developed in commerce and industry.   Even today, there are only a few public-access electronic mail services and conferencing systems, and just one or two experimental electronic journal systems.   For an overview of progress with these systems see Connell & Galbraith (1982), Hiltz & Turoff (1978) and Johannsen et al (1979), and Shackel (1982).

The development of such systems and services has been slower than expected, and part of the reason is to be found in difficulties with human factors.   Such systems for widespread public usage must obviously be extremely simple to learn and use.   Hence, this co-ordinated theme of four sessions will concentrate not upon the technical details of systems but upon the functionality and especially the usability needs in the future.

The first session is especially planned to give a general introduction for an audience assumed not to be very familiar with these systems.   An overview will be presented of the purpose and operation of electronic mail, conferencing and journal systems.   The similarities and differences between electronic systems and the current familiar postal mail, face-to-face conferences and traditional paper journals will be explained.   The key features of several current experimental systems will be briefly described.

The second and the third sessions will concentrate upon user experience, usage results, and the human factors problems and issues of present and future systems.

In the fourth session, a panel, consisting of some of the principle authors, will discuss the inter-relations between the usage aspects of these systems.   There are some differences of opinion about the most appropriate ways to provide mail,

conferencing and journal facilities.   Some consider that the same form of electronic system can support all types of communication use, whereas others consider that systems need to be tailored specifically to the particular type and format of communication involved.   The panel will discuss this and similar questions and will review the needs for research on usage issues for the systems.

It is believed that successful development of these communication systems will require not only technological development and good human factors research, but also well-founded and perceptive development of international standards.   Only in this way will compatible systems be achieved worldwide, which both provide a good range of facilities and are also easy to use.   It is hoped that perhaps this theme may lead to the development of some ´Pre-Standardisation Activity´, such as a working group to draft recommendations for standards with some special emphasis upon human usability needs.

References

Connell S & Galbraith I A 1982 The Electronic Mail Handbook. London, Kogan Page; London, Century Publishing; New York, Knowledge Industry Publications.

Hiltz S R and Turoff M 1978   The Network Nation : Human Communication via Computer.   Reading, MA: Addison-Wesley.

Johansen R, Vallee J and Spangler K 1979 Electronic Meetings : Technical Alternatives and Social Choices.   Reading, MA: Addison-Wesley.

Shackel B 1982   The BLEND system — programme for the study of some ´Electronic Journals´. The Computer Journal, 25.2, 161-168; Ergonomics, 25.4, 269-284.

Human-Computer Interaction — INTERACT '84 / B. Shackel (ed.)
Elsevier Science Publishers B.V. (North-Holland)
© IFIP, 1985

Survey of computer-based message systems

Jacob Palme

QZ computer center
Box 27322, S-102 54 Stockholm, Sweden

This paper provides a survey of computer-based mail and conference systems. The paper discusses systems for both individually addressed mail and group addressing through conferences and distribution lists. Various methods of structuring the text data base in existing systems is discussed and the networks of interconnected systems (ARPANET, CSNET, BITNET, USENET, JNT-MAIL, EURNET, MAILNET etc.) are described. The emerging standards for the interconnection of message systems are described.

The beginning: Electronic mail

As soon as people who previously met at the card reader got their own computer terminals, so that they could sit in their own room and use the terminal to communicate with the computer, a need for communication between all those people sitting at their different terminals arose. Often, the people at the terminals were spread in different places, even different cities, making communication through other means than the computer difficult. Thus, electronic mail was first born.

A typical simple electronic mail system has a set of messages sent to each user, often simply a set of files, one file for each message, stored in an area of the file system for incoming mail to this user. When someone writes a message to one or more other users, a copy of the file with the message is made for each recipient and stored in his area for incoming mail.

When a user reads his mail, one message at a time is displayed, and the user can choose whether to delete the message when read, keep it so that it will be shown again the next time s/he reads messages, or copy it to some other personal file.

To make message writing simpler, some information in the message was filled in fully or partly automatically by the system. This could include calendar date and time, author name, and a list of other recipients of the same message. Thus, a delivered message will consist of two parts, a header and a body.

Distribution lists

To understand what happened after that, and why, note the effect of the fact that you read much faster than you write, first pointed out by Murray Turoff (see Turoff 1978).

The figure below compares the time efficiency of computer message communication versus face-to-face meetings with 12 participants:

Message system: Long writing time but short reading time:

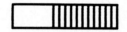

Writing   Reading
3.6 min.   11 times 0.47 = 5.2 minutes.
Total time 3.6 + 5.2 = 8.8 minutes.

Face-to-face meeting: Shorter speaking time but longer listening time:

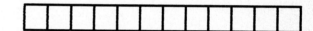

Speaking and listening:
12 times 1.7 = 20.4 minutes.

The figure is based on statistics on use of the COM computer conference system.

The figure shows that the total time of communicating certain information to a group of 12 people is much less with computerized written communication than with spoken communication. This is not only caused by the difference between writing and reading time. Important is also that with written communication, each reader decides how much time to spend on each message. You can read an important message carefully, and skip fast across a less important message or a message saying things you already know.

In a face-to-face meeting, a common occurrence is that some person is saying certain things, and some other people would much prefer him to stop talking. He may be saying something they have already heard, or something of little value to them.

On the other hand, the same statement by the same person may be very important and valuable to other participants in the same meeting who have not heard it before.

Another side of the same coin is that a people will often not say, or be allowed to say, what they want because of lack of time or consideration for those who have heard it before. This can often mean that things which should have been said are left unsaid.

It is a well-known fact, that face-to-face meetings with more than about five or seven participants meet with psychological problems. These problems will not occur in a good computer message system until the group size becomes much larger, perhaps fifty or a hundred participants.

Thus, computer messaging is especially advantageous when communication with many other people. This soon led to the addition, in computer message systems, of a facility called "distribution list". This is a facility for sending a message to a group of people by just inputting the name of the list instead of inputting the names of all the individual members of the list.

And experience shows that a very large percentage of messages are sent via distribution lists. In the COM system, for example, which supports conferences (a kind of distribution lists) and individually addressed mail equally well, more than 90 % of all messages read are sent via conferences.

Information overload

If all messages were sent from one person to one other person, information overload would very seldom occur, since the time to write a message is so much larger than the time to read that people would spend most of their time writing, and only a little time reading.

With the advent of distribution lists, however, it becomes as easy to send a message to ten or a hundred or even more people than to send it to only one person. And the fact that computer mail systems make it so easy, through distribution lists, to send the same message to very many people, is the main cause of the information overload problem.

When message systems grow larger, or get connected via networks, the audience you can reach with a message gets larger, the distribution lists get longer, and the information overload problems get worse.

Electronic publishing

One should here note that mail systems with distribution lists are conceptually close to electronic publishing. Electronic publishing is also the distribution of a text document to many people, just as distribution lists.

We thus have a spectrum of different systems for electronic dissemination of text:

- Individually addressed electronic mail.
- Distribution lists.
- Computer conferences or bulletin boards.
- Electronic publishing.
- Archiving and retrieval systems.

Videotex systems are also a special way of handling similar things.

Since there is no sharp limit between these different functions, and since the same text item may during its life e.g. first be an electronic mail to an editor, and later be a paper in an electronic journal, future systems will probably be required to support well all the alternatives in the table above.

To avoid information overload, a system must give the recipients of messages better ability to choose what they want to read and not to read.

This is achieved by putting a structure on the set of messages, so that already when you connect to a system, the messages are ordered to allow you to choose what to read.

A common such structure is the computer conference. When you connect to a typical computer conference system, you may get a list of what you have not read in the different conferences, such as is shown below:

You have 5 unseen letters
2 unseen entries in GILT meeting
13 unseen entries in Supercomputers
5 unseen entries in English language
6 unseen entries in Conference announcements
19 unseen entries in Speakers corner
19 unseen entries in User presentations
1 unseen entries in Fifth generation project
18 unseen entries in Packet-switched networks
11 unseen entries in Microcomputers
5 unseen entries in TeX inter-network list
1 unseen entries in KERMIT experience
34 unseen entries in TOPS-10/20 SIG

You have 134 unseen entries

Every message which was sent to the user via a computer conference (distribution list, bulletin board) is also delivered to him as an entry in that conference. The user normally will read one conference at a time. The users decide themselves in which order to read the conferences, and they can save some conferences to read at a later time. If they get too much information, they can also withdraw completely from conferences they are not interested in, or skip part of the discussion in that conference but still stay as a member.

For every user who is a member of a conference, a conference system keeps a counter of how far this user has read in the list of messages in this conference. The user is shown only new messages when connecting to the system. Users can however review old messages if they wish to do so.

The figure below shows the main principles of the news control facility in a computer conference system. In the figure, Peter Jonsen is a member of the first and second conference, and Mary Smith is a member of the second and third conference. There is a pointer in the data base for each person and each conference of which this person is a member. This pointer shows how far that person has read. Thus, users can enter the system at different times, and the system can show each user what is new to that user.

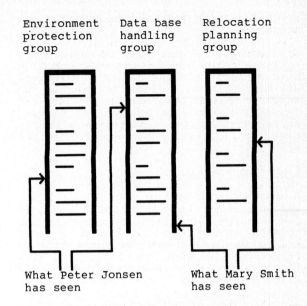

Environment protection group   Data base handling group   Relocation planning group

What Peter Jonsen has seen   What Mary Smith has seen

Other structuring facilities

Experience with computer conferencing shows that there is a need for structuring of the message data base on a more detailed level than that provided by conferences.

Subconferences

Some systems provide an explicit mechanism for splitting up a conference into subconferences. One example of this is the "topics" facility first introduced into the EIES computer conference system and later used in the PARTICIPATE conference system.

In topics, every new subject taken up in a conference becomes a new subconference, and each participant in the main conference is given the option of joining or not joining the subconference.

The topics structure is a very powerful tool for controlling information overflow. In fact, it is so powerful that it can completely kill all activity in a conference by splitting up the participants into too many subgroups with too few participants in each subgroup.

In EIES, you can choose whether to use the topics facility or not for a conference.

Keywords

Another structuring facility is the use of keywords. Authors are asked to give messages keywords, and readers can instruct the system to only show messages with certain keywords. A disadvantage with this is that the reader will sometimes get a rather fragmented picture of what is happening, with one message here and one message there.

One should here note that the concept of conference the way it is implemented in some systems, and the concept of keyword are very similar. Giving a message the two keywords "Pascal programming language" and "human-computer interaction", or linking the message to two conferences with the same name, are really two ways of doing the same things.

Links between entries

A common structure in many systems are various links between items. Thus, in COM/PortaCOM, users are encouraged by the command structure to link entries into tree structures of entries commenting on each other. In EIES, there is a facility for defining a "walk through path" as a chain of messages in the system.

Special kinds of conferences

Write-protected and selection conferences (containing selected items from other conferences), and abstracts of discussions written by some participants for those who do not wish to take part in the whole conference, are also common facilities.

Shelves and folders

Some designs of office automation systems structure documents into shelves and folders. The idea is that since these are common ways of structuring non-electronic messages, they will be easy to use and understand. I am however not convinced that the best way to design a computerized document handling system is to try to closely mirror the non-electronic world. Computers have different properties than non-electronic document handling, for example the ability to handle references and links between documents, and to store one and the same document in many places without actually copying the text of the document, and a good system should exploit these properties of a computer.

However, the best solution might be to use a computer-oriented structure internally, but show this to novice users in a simplied way using concepts like shelves and folders in the beginning, until they become accustomed to the more advanced structures which the computer actually can offer.

Simultaneous conferences

A simultaneous conference is a computer conference in which all participants are sitting at the same time at their terminals connected to the system. With a non-simultaneous conference, the news control facility in the system allows a conference to go on (usually over many days) even though every member only joins now and them and not all at the same time.

Experience has shown that computer conference systems are seldom used for simultaneous conferences, even if the software supports this mode of operation. The advantages of non-simultaneous conferences (better control of your time) seem to outweigh the advantages of simultaneous conferences (faster interaction).

Conference systems versus networks

Computer mail and conference systems actually grew in two different communities. One of them was the computer conference system community. They typically developed large, data base oriented systems with lots of structuring facilities, which were used stand-alone and not interconnected.

The EMISARI system, designed by Murray Turoff in 1971, and the PLANET-FORUM system (on DEC-10/20 computers) designed by Jacques Vallee at the Institute of the Future at about the same time, were the first of these systems. Later, Murray Turoff moved to the the New Jersey Institute of Technology where he designed the EIES system on Perkin-Elmer computers and Jacques Vallee founded a new company called Infomedia Corp., which today markets a conference system called NOTE-PAD. The CONFER system runs under the MTS operating system for IBM-type computers. Well-known is also the german KOMEX system, developed by the GMD in Darmstadt for Siemens computers. The COM system was developed by the Swedish Defense Research Institute for DEC-10/20 computers. Porta-COM is a version of COM which runs under a multitude of different computer models and operating systems. COM and PortaCOM are today marketed by the QZ computer centre in Stockholm.

The other community was the network mail community which grew around the ARPANET. This computer network links many universities and research laboratories in the United States. Beginning with simple file transfer systems, the mail systems on the individual computers in the network began to exchange mail items. This has grown into networks of hundreds of linked computers and using large distribution lists in ways very similar to the conferences in the computer conference systems.

The network mail community has grown in a more haphazard manner, and do not provide the same coherent structure as a well-designed computer conference system. Usually, the facilities for structuring and reducing information overload is much less powerful than in conferencing systems.

On the other hand, the facility of joing together hundreds of computers at different places is a strong advantage of the network mail community.

I therefore believe that a joining of the best ideas from the two communities would generate better ideas for the future. This has not happened until very recently, when the MAILNET network started by EDUCOM has finally succeeded in getting COM and EIES connected into the electronic mail networks in 1983.

Mail networks today

ARPANET still lives strongly, and has been split into two networks, MILNET for military applications and INTERNET for non-military applications.

CSNET joins computer science computers in the United States and works closely together with ARPANET.

BITNET started with IBM computers, but today also joins many non-IBM-type computers. A European continuation of BITNET called EARNET is under development supported by IBM.

USENET is a network of UNIX computers all around the world.

JNT-MAIL is a british network.

MAILNET is a network of university computing centers, mostly in the United States.

Several gateways, some official and some unofficial, link the above networks so that in most cases a message can be sent between any two computers in the networks if you know the right way to route the message.

An interesting difference is in the way these networks are funded. Some networks are funded by central funds, or by a fixed participation fee, independent of how many messages you send. Other networks charge a fee per message. This causes some problems with gateways, since the systems funded centrally or by fixed fees have no way of handling charges for messages sent to networks which charge for each individual message.

Interconnection standards

In order to connect mail systems on different computers, a standard for the interaction between the systems and for message formatting is needed.

The oldest such standard was that used by ARPANET. CSNET, BITNET, USENET, MAILNET and JNT-MAIL and many other networks use slightly modified versions of the ARPANET standards. The standard was from the beginning not centrally developed, rather it grew gradually and was only later encoded on paper.

A big problem with the ARPANET mail standards is that the description in the standards documents do not agree with actual usage. This means that those who develop an interface, following the standards document, will soon find that this interface will not work very well. There are a number of more-or-less unwritten rules, both restrictions and extensions to the standard, which you have to obey.

The only standards in widespread use today (1984) are those deriving from the ARPANET standards.

The latest versions of the ARPANET standards are described in the documents RFC821 (interaction between mail systems), RFC822 (message formatting) and RFC819 (addressing).

There is an american Federal Information Processing Standard FIPS 98 for formatting messages when sent between message systems.

The CCITT is developing a new standard, which will probably be ready in 1984.

The COST-11-bis project, jointly funded by nine European Countries, has developed a standard called GILT.

Here is a summary of the functions provided by the different standards:

Function	ARPA	CCITT	GILT
The sending of a message on the initiative of the sender.	Yes	Yes	Yes
The sending of a message on the initiative of the receiver.	No	No	Yes
Finding out where a certain mailbox resides.	Yes	Yes	Yes
Use of relaying in the normal distribution of a message.	Yes	Yes	No
Receipt and non-delivery notification.	No	Yes	Yes
Distribution lists, computerized bulletin boards and conferences.	No	No	Yes
Searching and retrieval in a message data base.	No	No	Yes

General note: Many of the functions described above are provided locally by some systems even though there is no support in the standard for them. For example, there are many distribution lists sent via the ARPANET standards, but the lack of support for this in the standards causes some problems. The lack of a standard for receipt and nondelivery notification in the ARPANET standard is also a cause of difficulty.

References

Only an abbreviated list of references is given here. For further references, see the book "computer-mediated communication systems" referenced below, which has a very complete list of references in the area.

The network nation - Human Communication via Computer, by S.R. Hiltz and M. Turoff, Addison-Wesley 1978.

Experience with the use of the COM computerized conferencing system, by Jacob Palme, FOA report C 10166E, 1981.

Simple Mail Transfer Protocol (RFC821), by Jonathan B. Postel, Information Sciences Institute, University of Southern California, 1982.

The Domain Naming Convention for Internet User Applications (RFC819), by Zaq-Sing Su and Jon Postel, 1982.

Standard for the Format of Arpa Internet Text Messages (RFC822), by David H. Crocker, University of Delaware, 1982.

Computer-Mediated Communication Systems, Status and Evaluation, by Elaine B. Kerr and Starr Roxanne Hiltz, Academic Press 1982.

Computer Conferencing is More than Electronic Mail, by Jacob Palme, EUTECO - European Teleinformatics Conference, North-Holland 1983.

COM Teleconferencing system - Advanced manual, by Jacob Palme and Eva Albertson, September 1983.

Introducing the Electronic Mailbox, by P. A. Wilson, National Computer Centre Publications, England, 1983.

You Have 134 Unread Mail! Do You Want To Read Them Now? by Jacob Palme, IFIP WG 6.5 Conference on Computer Message Services, Nottingham, England, 1984, edited by H.T. Smith, North-Holland 1984.

Human-Computer Interaction — INTERACT '84 / B. Shackel (ed.)
Elsevier Science Publishers B.V. (North-Holland)
© IFIP, 1985

The Computer Conferencing System KOMEX

Uta Pankoke-Babatz
Gesellschaft für Mathematik und Datenverarbeitung
St. Augustin Germany

It was in 1979 that an initial configuration of the computer conferencing system KOMEX developed in the GMD was presented to a broader public at the Hannover Trade Fair. Since the beginning of 1982 KOMEX has been installed on a GMD computer network and has been used by GMD members as an in-house communication tool.

The KOMEX Facilities

KOMEX is programmed in PASCAL and is implemented under operating system BS2000 on SIEMENS computers of series 7000. The system consists of two components: the user agent and the mail agent. (This is in accordance with the CCITT architecture model for message handling systems.)

The User Agent

Each user agent handles the private archives of a specific user. These archives cannot be accessed by any other user. Only the mail agent is able to take messages from the archives for transport purposes or to enter them into the archives.

The user agent supports the following activities:

- creating and handling texts;
- mailing and distributing texts as messages;
- generating and handling references between messages;
- archiving and retrieving messages automatically;
- filing;
- receiving messages.

The above functions are presented to the user in form of services (information service, address administration service, received mail service, text editing service, filing service). KOMEX distinguishes between texts, documents and messages. Texts are local objects being edited. Upon first mailing they become 'global' and are provided with a document identifier that is unique throughout the system and that will be used in any future mailing operation. Thus, it is possible to produce a reference between a new document and a preceding one upon replying. Furthermore, upon text modification the system will automatically generate a new document identifier and also a reference (revision of) to the original text.

The user agent generates and supports these references so that the user can make the system to display the names of the persons to whom a specific document was mailed, the replies already received and any reference if the messages and documents referred are available in the user's archives.

A message consists of an envelope showing addressee, sender etc. and a document or a complete previously mailed message. This 'encapsulation' of messages allows to provide a message with its history.

All incoming or outgoing messages and documents are automatically archived in the private archives of the user. Furthermore, the user can explicitly file messages according to his own criteria (file catalogue). Any message can be retrieved by means of selection criteria (date of creation, sender, recipient, author etc.).

Directory

Furthermore, the user agent allows the inspection of the directory of KOMEX members and the entry of local distribution lists, so-called conferences.

Each user can send messages to any addressee registered in the directory. On the one hand, addressees are the KOMEX members entered by the system manager, on the other, each user can enter so-called 'conferences' into the directory. By means of these 'conferences' that are above all public distribution lists with different access authorities (read/write permissions, open, closed, joinable, secret) each user can model simple organisational contexts (projects, services, conferences).

The Mail Agent

The mail agent secures the distribution and delivery of messages in store and forwarding technique via the whole network. Messages to conferences are copied and delivered in accordance with the distribution list.

Usually messages are delivered by transmitting them to the archives of the recipient. In case of recipients, entered in the directory as passive KOMEX members, the mail agent can also print the messages on a central printer. These automatically printed messages will then be delivered to the recipients by messenger. Thus, the group of people to be reached via KOMEX can be extended considerably.

The various mail agents can be connected. In the GMD such a network is currently installed, it consists of three mail agents securing communication between the headquarters at Birlinghoven and the GMD location Darmstadt.

User Guidance

KOMEX can be used by means of format display terminals of SIEMENS type 8160 or 9750 or by any other terminal in the so-called line or page mode. KOMEX handling in form mode (menu technique) is very easy even for non-experts on data processing or for occasional users. For experienced users the system provides greater flexibility by jump facilities and command concatenation. Line by line input is also possible in form mode. Line mode also enables terminals to access the user agent via switched lines, thus allowing GMD members being on missions at distant places to inspect their received mail lists via external access and, furthermore, the connection of external persons to KOMEX. A user can specify the desired mode and the desired language (english or german) upon each session.

References

Santo,H. Babatz,R., Bogen,M., Pankoke-Babatz,U., Theidig,G., Computer Conference System KOMEX V 4.1 User Manual (Arbeitspapiere der GMD Nr.71, 1983)

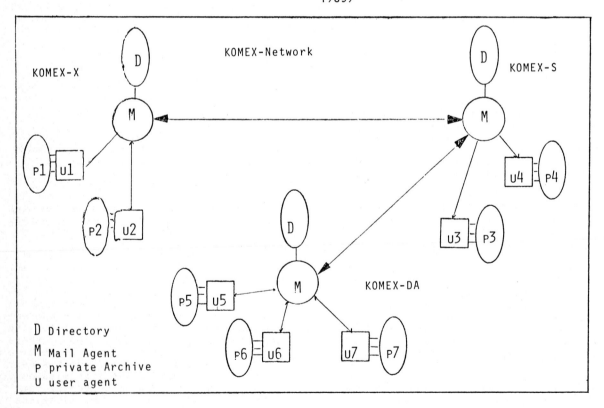

Human-Computer Interaction — INTERACT '84 / B. Shackel (ed.)
Elsevier Science Publishers B.V. (North-Holland)
© IFIP, 1985

COM/PortaCOM conference system
Design goals and principles

Jacob Palme

QZ computer center
Box 27322, S-102 54 Stockholm, Sweden

The COM/PortaCOM computer conference system has been designed to be both easy to use for the novice user and powerful for the experienced user at the same time. This goal is achieved by having a powerful general-purpose basic data base structure, and by providing a user interface where the novice can understand the data base structure based on a simple model in the beginning, and then enhance this model with more experience with the system. The command structure combines menu-s and commands to suit both novice users and experienced users with the same user interface.

The COM and PortaCOM[TM] computer mail and conference systems are functionally very similar, but COM runs on DEC-10/20 computers, and PortaCOM runs today on Univac 1100 and Norsk Data Nord 100 computers and will be available on IBM, Control Data, Siemens, Burroughs and Digital Vax/11 computers.

Subconferences = comment trees

To start a new conference in COM/PortaCOM takes less than five minutes, but experience still shows that users are reluctant to start new conferences to the degree which is really neccessary to create a good subconference structure. Because of this, the users need not give any explicit command to start a subconference. Instead, COM/PortaCOM has a command structure which encourages users to write new entries as comments on previous entries, with an explicit link in the data base between the commenting and the commented entry. The set of all entries linked together by such comment links will implicitly be a subconference, which thus also could be called a "comment tree".

Simple and general purpose structure

COM/PORTA COM DATA BASE

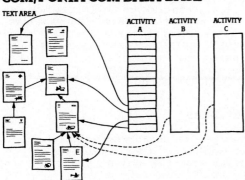

This figure shows the data base structure of COM/PortaCOM, with links between messages and activities containing lists of links to messages.

A message can belong to one or more ordered sets of messages. Such a set can for example be the letters to or from a certain person, or the messages in a conference. We use the word activitity for such a set of messages. An activity also has a name and a list of users who are members of the activity, and a sequential list of references to messages. One message can be entered into several activities. Only one copy of the text is stored, with references from the activities to the message text.

Every user has a personal mailbox, which is an activity containing letters to and from this user. A user can also create additional personal activities and sort messages by entering references to them in one such personal activity. A computer conference is an activity with several users as members.

Example: A certain message may be entered into the three activities "Joan Smith", "COM experience" and "PortaCOM development". This message is then available to "Joan Smith" as a letter and to all members of the conferences "COM experience" and "PortaCOM development" as a conference entry. When someone writes a comment to the message, the comment is normally sent to the same receivers so that all who read the original message also receive the comment.

Example I: Electronic publishing

A new item is first sent by the author to an activity for incoming manuscripts. This is a closed activity, in which one or more of the editors can read. They look at the paper, and establish a new link from it to the personal mailbox of one or more referees. The comments by the referees are entered into a special activity for such comments, together with a reference link in the data base, connecting the comment to the original entry. The editor decides to accept the paper (possibly after revision by its author) and then establishes a link between the paper and the activity for published papers, e.g. the electronic journal itself. The journal is writeprotected, so that only the editors can link items to it.

Example II: System development

A conference is opened for users of a certain software system. In this conference, a user suggests an improvement to the system. Some other users comment on this improvement. The system designers will then discuss how to implement this improvement in a closed conference for those responsible for development of the system. Even though their discussion is in a separate conference, it can still be linked to the original discussion, since commentary links in COM/PortaCOM can cross conference boundaries. When the change has been implemented, a comment is entered into the user conference again, commenting on the original proposal and informing the users that now it has been implemented.

Example III: Selecting messages

Someone who reads in large public conferences can select messages of special interest to him/herself or someone else and link them to special selection conferences, or as personal mail to someone who would otherwise not read them.

Novice users need not see the advanced structure:

To a novice user, COM/PortaCOM is a system for handling letters and conference entries. The fact that both letters and conference entries are handled by the general-purpose activity concept need not be understood by novice users.

Menu- and command-driven dialogue

A menu-driven user interface is easy to use for novice users. The users are presented with alternatives and tell the computer what they want to do by choosing one of the alternatives. Experienced users can skip the menus when they know the commands.

To make COM/PortaCOM suitable to all classes of users, the systems use a combination of menus and commands in its user interface. Example:

What do you want to do? (Read) next notice, Quit, Comment (on entry), (Send a) letter (to), Personal (answer), Other. -

When you get such a menu, you can type a command chosen from the menu, e.g.:

- next notice

However, you need not choose from the menu only. Any valid command is accepted. The menu is just a guide-line from the system to the user. Experienced users can ask the system not to show the menus at all.

The menu choices are intentionally not numbered, since we want you to learn the commands, not learn the numbers of menu choices. In this way, the system helps you to learn more about the system. To answer with command names is just as easy as to answer with numbers, since, as long as it is not ambiguous, every command can be shortened, for example "next notice" to "n n".

If you give an ambiguous command, the system will simply type out the alternatives and let you input the command again.

Names of activities (users and conferences) can be abbreviated in the same way.

In order to make COM/PortaCOM easier to use for inexperienced users, the system tries to anticipate user needs. Thus, the system does not use fixed menus. Instead, the main menu is composed individually for each user on the basis of what the system knows about that user.

For example, if you have just read a message (and might thus want to "comment" on this message) and if you have more unseen messages in the same activity (and might thus want to read the "next notice" in the activity), the menu might be:

What do you want to do? (Read) next notice, Quit, Comment (on entry), (Send a) letter (to), Personal (answer), Other. -

The first menu alternative is the most commonly used alternative. If you just reply to a menu question by hitting the RETURN key, this is interpreted as the first menu alternative. By having successively as first menu item "next letter", "next conference", "next notice", "next conference etc, a user can scan all unread notices, one at a time, by just pushing the RETURN key between each read notice.

We have tried to design COM/PortaCOM so that any command can be given at almost any time. Also, an action is easy to interrupt by simply not answering the subquestions.

Other facilities

There are also facilities for information retrieval, statistics collection on usage, and for sending and receiving messages via the international academic mail networks (MAILNET, BITNET, CSNET, JNT-MAIL etc.), including the establishment of parallel conferences betweeen COM systems on different computer sites.

References

This paper is an abbreviation of a longer paper with the same title, which can be obtained from the author. The longer paper contains further references.

Human-Computer Interaction — INTERACT '84 / B. Shackel (ed.)
Elsevier Science Publishers B.V. (North-Holland)
© IFIP, 1985

Software Infrastructure for the BLEND "electronic journal" experiment

W.P. Dodd, T.I. Maude,
Centre for Computing & Computer Science, Universiy of Birmingham
and

D.J. Pullinger, B. Shackel
Department of Human Sciences, University of Technology, Loughborough

The rational is discussed for the initial selection of software to support the BLEND electronic journal project; the preferred solution was the NOTEPAD computer teleconferencing system. The mapping of a journal format onto the NOTEPAD information structure is considered, as are a number of experimental extensions to NOTEPAD to provide additional facilities for the journal editors and referees.

1. THE AIMS OF THE BLEND PROJECT

BLEND (the Birmingham and Loughborough Electronic Network Development) is an experimental system supported by the Research & Development Department of the British Library (B.L.R.D.D.) as one of the projects in its programme to study the relevance and potential usage of new technology in the world of libraries and related information systems. The initial and principal aim if the project is to develop and gain experience of an "Electronic Journal" and Information Network in order to assess the cost, efficiency and subjective impact of such a system; the further aim is to explore and evaluate alternative forms of user communication through the system. The background and plans for the experiment are provided by Shackel (1982-a), while the initial findings are presented by Pullinger and others (1982), Shackel (1982-b), Shackel and others (1983), and Pullinger and others (1984). The purpose of the present paper is to describe the software system for the electronic journal and discuss the differences between BLEND and computer conference and electronic mail systems.

Communications between people involved in any scientific or learned discipline takes place at a number of levels from the informal to the highly structured, represented by the learned journal and, although the BLEND study is aimed at the latter, we have attempted to produce an electronic information exchange system which will provide many levels of interaction.

We were also concerned to make an early start of research into electronic journal systems from the users' viewpoint, so in order to save 3 to 5 years of development and cost, and to gain information other than intuitive to act as a firm base for future development, it was decided to start with the nearest possible software suite and to enhance that if possible. A review of the available software led to a choice of computer teleconferencing as a basis for experimentation on electronic journals for a number of reasons including :- the journal is only one part of the communication fabric of a scientific community; the software needs to be flexible enough to permit development of different types of "journal" as yet, perhaps unenvisaged. Separate surveys by Shackel and Kirstein (Chairman of the B.L.R.D.D. "New Technology" Committee) suggested "NOTEPAD" (a proprietary product of the Infomedia corporation of San Bruno, California) rather than the EIES system used in an earlier experiment of electronic journals (Sheridan and others, 1981). One key factor identified in both surveys was the evaluation that NOTEPAD is easier for naive users than is EIES, and this was subsequently substantiated by the Sheridan report.

NOTEPAD was developed from the FORUM and PLANET conferencing systems mentioned in a previous paper (Palme, 1984); it has a well- researched design and the further advantage, for our purposes, of a separate usage data collection facility so that users' behaviour can be studied.

2. THE NOTEPAD TELECONFERENCING SYSTEM

Any conferencing software is designed to mirror and extend the face-to-face conference or committee meeting onto the computer. In NOTEPAD this mapping is performed in a well-structured and controlled manner. For example, a conference may have a small, closed membership such as a committee, or it may be open to everyone as in a general meeting and conversation in the bar. These meetings are called "activities" in NOTEPAD, and they may have either an "assigned" or an "open" membership, with discussion in any one activity being kept distinct from all others (although messages can be transferred from one activity to another just as papers can be passed between committees in the face-to-face situation).

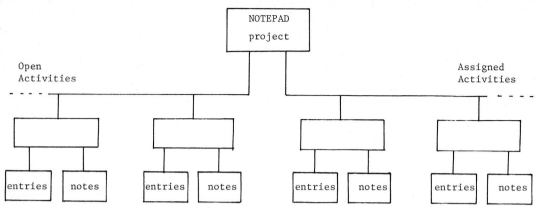

Figure 1   Information structure in NOTEPAD

This discussion can be either public ("entries" in NOTEPAD terminology), or private between pairs of participants ("notes"), and all text is retained in the activity so that it may be re-read using a variety of search mechanisms. Past entries can therefore be regarded as the official record of the conference activity and cannot normally be altered, although special editorial privileges can be given to individuals by the "conference administrator". The conference administrator is the only person who can set up new activities (on requests from the participants), and remove activities no longer required; while within each activity there is an activity "organiser" whose primary function is to add and remove members in the assigned activities.

Within a conference there may be any number of open and assigned activities, usually each set up around a particular topic or for a special purpose and the membership lists for these activities will normally be overlapping. A possible image of the structure of information in NOTEPAD is given in Figure 1. Various NOTEPAD conferences (or "projects") can be set up, but they are all autonomous, each being reserved for members of a particular group. Normally each group would have a different log-in procedure which would give access to its particular project.

3. EXTENSIONS TO NOTEPAD

The purpose of NOTEPAD is to mirror conferences whereas in BLEND we wished to map printed journals as well as providing a general meeting facility. This necessitated extending the mapping of the NOTEPAD structure, and we chose the con figuration shown in Figure 2, where distinct functions in the journal system are mapped onto separate conferences. This required a different log-in procedure for each functional use, however our

original conjecture was that the conference participants would normally be interested in only one function at a time.

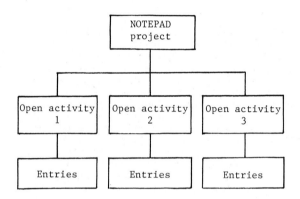

Figure 2   Public information structure
in NOTEPAD

For reasons discussed in Pullinger (1984) this proved not to be the case, and an early extension in BLEND was to allow users to change from one NOTEPAD conference to another without having to leave the system and go through another log-in (and dial-up) procedure. As each conference has to be run in a separate directory, this extension has to change directories in order to change conferences, and it also has to provide a certain amount of protection in that some conferences (eg Referee) have a restricted membership. The extension software controls the movement between conference directories, using the standard directory protection mechanism to control access, and then invokes NOTEPAD as a sub-process. On exit from NOTEPAD the user is returned to the superior process, and is allowed to access other conferences, either directly or via password control. The users

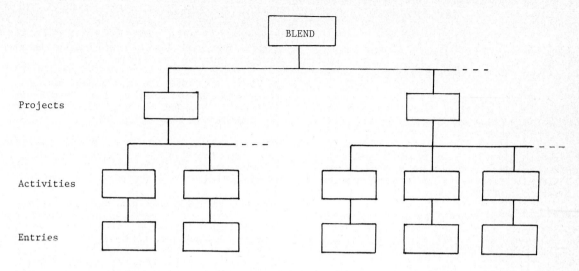

Figure 3 Public information structure of the BLEND system

need to know nothing of directories and sub-processes; to them it appears only as an extra layer (Figure 3) in the information structure.

The above extension was undertaken by the BLEND team, however there have been a number of modifications to NOTEPAD itself carried out by Infomedia at the suggestion of the BLEND team. For example, one result of the extended structure was that participants were less certain of where they were in the structure (what activity in which conference), so an early modification was a simple query facility to obtain this information. However the primary modification concerned the mapping of journal articles onto the NOTEPAD information structure.

In a computer conference the public entries are normally fairly short in length and not necessarily related to each other except in some loose manner. However a journal article is usually at least a few pages of typescript and, moreover, the reader may wish to read the article in a non-serial manner. For example, reading the abstract and conclusions prior to deciding whether to read the entire article, and even then moving to and fro between the body of the article and the list of references. This suggested that we could not map an article onto a single entry since NOTEPAD does not provide facilities for moving around within one entry. Instead we decided to map each article onto an activity with an "issue" of the electronic journal mapped onto a conference. Using this method we could readily obtain the "index" to the journal since NOTEPAD provides a list of all available activities on accessing a conference. We then decided to map each paragraph of the article onto one NOTEPAD entry, instructing authors

to limit their paragraphs to 24 lines of 80 characteres - a typical VDU screen. Our initial release of NOTEPAD allowed access these paragraphs by entry number (either individually or serially through a list of entry numbers) or by a single keyword, however at our suggestion Infomedia provided additional facilities for moving forwards or backwards in the entry list and redisplaying the current entry.

This was as far as we were able to go within NOTEPAD, however we were still short of our objective of providing aids for the journal refereeing and editorial processes. A particular need was for some facility whereby the referee could anotate the article within the computer information structure, and additional facilities for reading the article based on the contents rather than the order of presentation. Fortunately NOTEPAD provides a mechanism for running external processes from within the NOTEPAD command structure, and we made use to this to provide another layer of software for reading, refereeing and browsing (Maude & Pullinger, 1983). This facility is not completely integrated into the NOTEPAD information structure and it has been necessary to duplicate some of the text files, however it has provided an excellent mechanism for experimentation on alternative approaches to these important journal production functions, and this is the purpose of the BLEND project.

4. REFERENCES

Maude, T.I., Dodd, W.P., Pullinger, D.J., Shackel, B. (1982), The BLEND electronic journal system. I.U.C.C. Bulletin Vol. 5(1), p22.

Maude, T.I., Pullinger, D.J., Software for reading, refereeing and browsing in the BLEND system. Computer Jrnl. (to be published).

Palme, J. (1984), An overview of electronic mail and computer conferencing systems. Proc. 1st I.F.I.P. Conference on Human-Computer Interaction, (INTERACT '84).

Pullinger, D.J., (1984), Enhancing NOTEPAD Teleconferencing in the BLEND 'Electronic Journal'. Behaviour & Information Technology 3(1), pp13-23.

Pullinger, D.J., Shackel B., Dodd, W.P., Maude, T.I., (1982), Questions answered relating to the BLEND electronic journal experimental programme. A.L.P.S.P. Bulletin, June 1982, p11.

Pullinger, D.J., Shackel, B., Dodd, W.P., Maude, T.I., (1984), Experience with the BLEND system. Proc. 1st I.F.I.P. Conference on Human-Computer Interaction, (INTERACT '84).

Shackel, B. (1982-a), The BLEND system - programme for the study of some 'electronic journals'. Computer Journal, Vol. 25(2), p161; and Ergonomics, Vol. 25(4), p269.

Shackel, B. (1982-b), Plans and initial progress with BLEND - an electronic network communication experiment. Int. J. of Man-machine Studies, Vol. 17, p225.

Shackel, B., Pullinger D.J., Maude, T.I., Dodd, W.P. (1983), The BLEND-LINC project on 'electronic journals' after two years. Computer Journal Vol. 26(3), p247.

Sheridan, T., Senders, J., Moray, N., Stoklosa, J., Guillaume, J., Makepeace, D. (1981) Experimentation with a multi-disciplinary teleconference and electronic journal on mental workload. Unpublished report to the National Science Foundation (division of Science Information Access Improvement).

Human-Computer Interaction — INTERACT '84 / B. Shackel (ed.)
Elsevier Science Publishers B.V. (North-Holland)
© IFIP, 1985

Experience with the COM computer conference system

Jacob Palme

QZ computer center
Box 27322, S-102 54 Stockholm, Sweden

The main emphasis of the results of this study of the experience with the COM computer conference system is that computer conferencing is not mainly a replacement for neither face-to-face meetings, letters or telephone calls. Rather, it is a new communication medium, providing new modes of human interaction which to a large extent were not possible without this new medium.

COM is a computer conferencing and electronic mail system used by thousands of users at many different computer installations.

Messages in COM can either be sent as letters, where the sender gives the names of all the people who are to receive the letter, or as conference entries, where the sender gives the name of the conferences to which the entry is sent. All members of a computer conference can read all entries in the conference and usually also write their own entries into the conference.

This is a short summary of a longer report "Experience with the use of the COM Computerized Conferencing System", reporting on the experience with COM usage mainly at the original site in Stockholm. The longer report can be ordered from the QZ computer center, Box 27 322, 102 54 Stockholm, Sweden.

Letters or conference entries

	Letters	Conferences	All
Mean no. of readers	1.9	32.9	14.1
Percentage of no. of written messages	61 %	39 %	100 %
Percentage of no. of read messages	8 %	92 %	100 %
Percentage of user time spent writing	23 %	17 %	40 %
reading	8 %	51 %	60 %
total time spent	32 %	69 %	100 %

Conclusion: There is a large difference between letters and conference entries.

Although 61 % of all messages written in COM are letters, the letters represent only 8 % of all messages read in COM and only 32 % of the total user time is spent on letter communication.

Time spent in COM

An average user connects to the COM system twice every working day or ten times a week. Each session lasts 10 minutes, so COM is used about 100 minutes/week or about 4 % of the working time. During one such week, an average user reads 131 messages and writes 6 messages.

Conclusion: COM does not dominate the time usage of its users, but quite a lot of communication is done during the 20 minutes a day spent using COM.

When is COM used and from where?

62 % of the COM usage is done during office hours (monday-friday between 08:00 and 17:00 hours). 38 % of the COM usage is done outside office hours. 9 % of the COM usage is done from terminals at home, 91 % from terminals at the place of work. The high percentage of COM usage outside office hours shows the advantage of a medium which can be used at any time when the user wants, and where everyone does not have to collect at the same place and time.

Speed of the medium.

The median time from the writing of a letter to the time it is read is 5.5 hours and the median length of a discussion on a particular subject in COM is 23 hours. This can be compared with a face-to-face meeting, where the mean time before the next meeting is usually one or two weeks. So COM is a very fast medium in spite of the fact that all participants do not meet at the same place and time.

Which people use COM?

<u>Percentage of persons who are bosses in different groups</u>

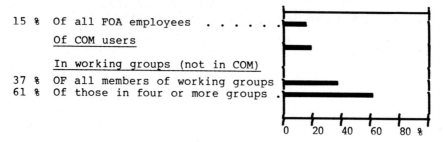

15 %   Of all FOA employees . . . .

     <u>Of COM users</u>

     <u>In working groups (not in COM)</u>

37 %   Of all members of working groups
61 %   Of those in four or more groups .

<u>Percentage of people above 40 years of age in different groups</u>

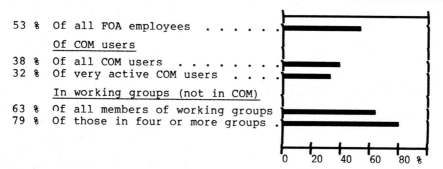

53 %   Of all FOA employees . . . . . .

     <u>Of COM users</u>

38 %   Of all COM users . . . .
32 %   Of very active COM users . . . .

     <u>In working groups (not in COM)</u>

63 %   Of all members of working groups
79 %   Of those in four or more groups .

<u>Percentage of people with university education in different groups</u>

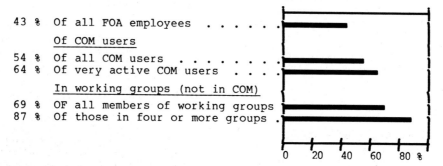

43 %   Of all FOA employees . . . . . .

     <u>Of COM users</u>

54 %   Of all COM users . . . .
64 %   Of very active COM users . . . .

     <u>In working groups (not in COM)</u>

69 %   Of all members of working groups
87 %   Of those in four or more groups .

<u>Conclusion</u>: COM has increased the possibility to communicate in groups of people at organizational distance. This increase in communication is largest for young people who are not bosses and to some extent for people without university education.

Organizational distance between users

This table shows how much of the communication in COM during a test week in 1980 went between people who are close or distant within the FOA organization which at that time was the main user of COM.

	Letters	Conferences	All
Within one FOA main department	46 %	18 %	21 %
Between FOA main departments	14 %	29 %	28 %
Between people in and outside FOA	31 %	40 %	39 %
Both reader and writer outside FOA	9 %	13 %	13 %
Total	100 %	100 %	100 %

Conclusion: Letter communication, where you have to know the name of the person you are sending the letter to, tends to favour communication between people who are organizationally close. Conference communication on the other hand makes communication possible between people who are organizationally distant from each other.

This is interesting because sociologist have found (Allen 1977) that organizations with more contacts at large organizational distances tend to produce better results. They are more willing to accept new ideas and less prone to get stuck with non-optimal patterns of work. Computer conferencing favours such contacts over large distances much more than computer mail.

Does COM replace other media?

The communication done through COM would otherwise have been done in the following ways:

Replaces	Percentages of written messages	read messages	time in COM
Letters, handwritten notes, circulars	7 %	4 %	6 %
Telephone calls	23 %	8 %	14 %
Different kinds of face-to-face meetings	17 %	11 %	13 %
New communication which would not have occured without COM	50 %	75 %	65 %
Other media	3 %	2 %	2 %
Total	100 %	100 %	100 %

Conclusion: Most use of COM is not a replacement for other communication media. Instead, COM represents new communication which would not have been feasible without COM. COM has thus not only or mainly meant the transfer of communication to a new medium. COM has meant a change in whom people communicate with, probably also in what they communicate with these people about. People perform their work and solve their problems i a different way using COM. A new kind of community of people is created which did not exist before.

The time spent using COM would otherwise have been spent in the following ways:

23.2 %	Telephoning
12.1 %	Letters, circulars, messages
10.9 %	Computer programming, research, technical development
9.3 %	Leisure, sleep, eating, hobbies, family, friends, exercise
8.0 %	Books, papers and journals
7.5 %	Dead time
5.4 %	"Other work" (not specified)
5.4 %	Committee and conference meetings
4.8 %	Television and radio
4.7 %	Nothing
3.7 %	Face-to-face talks
1.8 %	Breaks, small talk
1.4 %	"Don't know"
1.4 %	Planning
0.4 %	Travel
100.0 %	Total

Conclusion: Note that although this kind of system is usually called "Computer conference system" or "Electronic mail system" only 5 % replaces conferences and 12 % replaces mail. Instead, COM also replaces a number of other activities. Notable is telephone with 23 %, mass media 13 % and non-work 9 %. Note also that only about 10-15 % of the time using COM would otherwise have been spent in face-to-face meetings. The fears that these kind of media will stop people from meeting face-to-face thus do not seem founded in reality.

References

Managing the Flow of Technology, by J Allen, MIT Press 1977.

The Network Nation: Human Communication via Computer. By Roxanne Hiltz and Murray Turoff. Addison-Wesley Publishers 1978.

Face-to-face vs. Computerized Conferences: A Controlled Experiment, by S.R. Hiltz, K. Johnson, C. Aronovitch and M. Turoff, NJIT 1980.

Experience with the use of the COM Computerized Conferencing System, by Jacob Palme, FOA 1 report C 10166E, 1981.

Human-Computer Interaction — INTERACT '84 / B. Shackel (ed.)
Elsevier Science Publishers B.V. (North-Holland)
© IFIP, 1985

Results from Evaluation Studies with the Computer Conferencing System KOMEX

Uta Pankoke-Babatz

Gesellschaft für Mathematik und Datenverarbeitung
St. Augustin, Germany

Abstract:
- technical and organisational facts that influence acceptance of CBMS
- appropriate long term training procedure with KOMEX
- results from the evaluation study
- main user groups and main tasks performed with KOMEX

Introduction:

The distributed computer conferencing system KOMEX was developed at the GMD. Since 1980 we have gained experiences of how user react to this system. We developed an introduction procedure for this type of systems which was explored when introducing KOMEX as inhouse CBMS in the GMD.

We investigated user reaction to this by an evaluation study performed by an external institution (BIFOA). The changing of user reaction within approximately one year of practical use of KOMEX was evaluated by questionnaires. More feedback from user's point of view was gained by group discussions and personal talks with people by the user services staff.

All this gives evidence for what purposes people (managers, administrators, knowledgeworkers) use the system, how the system fits in the organisational environment, and how the system is accepted etc..

1. Acceptance of CBMS

CBMS are systems that support interpersonal communication via computer. Therefore, they are no single user systems but systems whose benefit will only appear if several communication partners use them. Communication is an activity that is carried out more or less frequently by persons of any profession. It is an integral part of office activities. Communication is a process that consists not only of the pure exchange of individual, isolated informations, but communication is also depending on contexts, i.e. depending on the persons involved (organisational context) and on the information exchanged previously (subject context).

Computer-based message systems offer the advantage that exchanged messages are recorded and can be processed by computers. Furthermore, communication is an every days activity and should at any time be feasible at the desk as it is the case with the telephone (availability, access, security).

1.1 Technical Requirements

CBMS should try to consider these facts and to provide appropriate technical support:

- simple use (even for non-experts on data processing) and permanent availability of the system at the working place;
- text editing and processing functions (for creating information);
- reference generation and management for pieces of information (replies, revisions, references ...);
- filing and retrieval of information;
- mailing, distributing and receiving information.

Moreover, a CBMS should be attractive for as many different groups as possible to secure a maximum number of communication partners using the system, i.e. a maximum number of persons you are able to contact by means of the system. The CBMS should therefore provide local user stations of different functional scope, for example, sophisticated word processing functions for typists and access to data base systems etc. for managers; that means, workstations should allow individual configuration.

1.2 Organisational Requirements

CBMS should also provide tools of organisational support. These should however not be restricted to the specific working place, but they should be

available at "central places" where they
constitute the so-called "common
knowledge" of several users.

The major part of communication,
especially in technical and management
areas, is however not performed in
strictly regulated form but is rather
"unregulated" and "spontaneous". Even in
these cases, however, there are also
"hidden" regulations that are realised
in traditional media by natural habits
and that vary according to medium (telephone, letter, conversation, meeting).

The use of a CBMS for new tasks or by
new users must be preceeded by the definition of organisational regulations.
These regulations should be modelled by
means of available CBMS components
considering the formerly existing organisational environment. This constitutes
more or less a division of labour betwe-
en computer-based and human-based organisations, i.e. everything that is not
supported by the CBMS has to be solved
by agreement and coordination as
previously. In the worst case the CBMS
will only be the transport medium, and
any organisational information will also
be distributed as messages to be processed by the recipient (copying,
filing, forwarding etc.).

Organisational regulations, however, have to be modifiable at any time, as
everyday work shows, and they have to be
easily adjustable to new work processes,
new tasks, new staff members etc. The
acceptance of the CBMS will however be
considerably reduced if technical
support of organisational regulations
allows also improved control of the
persons involved and if it restricts
their individual freedom. the decision
functions of each individual user should
not be affected. The CBMS should support
the coordination of communication, but
it should not perform any control function.

Classical CBMS support the organisation
of communication by so-called computer
conferences (EIES, COM) or public
distribution lists (KOMEX). For these
conferences and distribution lists to be
managed centrally the users can define
rights of access and use. These are the
basic elements that can be used for
modelling simple organisational processes. Further complex elements will
surely be developed in the future. These
should however be also components
allowing the modelling of different
organisational structures.

2. Implementation Procedure with KOMEX

The development of rules of utilisation
is of great importance to the introduction of a new communication medium, i.e.
in the initial phase existing rules
should be integrated into the new medium. In practice, this is however not
such simple since the new users have not
yet gathered any experience with using
the new medium and the
developers/vendors do not know the
specific communication habits of the new
users. Our experiences in the first
field trial (1980/81) with KOMEX have
shown that we expect too much from the
users if they are to define themselves
organisational regulations for handling
KOMEX in the initial phase. Furthermore,
this uses to lead to considerable
acceptance problems.

In our GMD-wide experimental use of
KOMEX (1982) we therefore initially
tried to provide new users as early and
as quickly as possible with experience
by extensive training thus supporting
the organisational integration of the
new medium.

Any GMD staff member could participate
in this experiment that was announced
very early for enabling interested
persons to familiarise with the specific
problems and for reducing thus excessive
expectations or fears.

2.1 Training Procedure

About 100 people participated
simultaneously in the experiment. About
60 people began simultaneously and
participated in the training, 20 among
them had not yet gained any experience
with handling data processing systems.

Training consisted of a two hours'
presentation of the system, its basic
functions, their handling etc. and also
included indications to organisational
problems.

During the three weeks following the
training we daily distributed tasks
concerning the various system functions.
These tasks should help the participants
to familiarise with the system. On request the tasks could also be solved
with the immediate personal advice of
the KOMEX team. This facility was
however used only by DP newcomers for a
duration of about 1 hour each.

It was the primary aim of training to accustom all participants to the daily use of the system and to secure the daily receipt of messages. Training itself was an example for the use of organisational support by KOMEX (conferences).

After the training period the participants were able to define themselves how to organise tasks to be handled by KOMEX. However, they can still get assistance and advices by the user services staff.

2.2 Evaluation Study

Two months after the start of the experiment two questionnaire inquiries were conducted among those participants who had become regular KOMEX users (at least one session per week). About 40 users replied on both questionnaires. Eight months after the start of the experiment representatives of all active KOMEX users participated in group discussions. These inquiries were conducted by an external institution (BIFOA). Furthermore, automatically collected technical utilisation statistics (measurements) and results of personal advisory conversations with KOMEX user services staff extending over the whole period are available for evaluation.

We received the most interesting suggestions and results by personal advisory conversations and by group discussions. This is mainly to be explained by the fact that a new technology uses to produce unexpected results and that the individually percepted advantages and disadavantages are very different so that it is very difficult to include them in predefined questionnaires. The evaluation of the questionnaire and measurement data may confirm or disprove individual statements. Altogether, the various data collection methods produce a rather nice picture of user estimations about the system.

From the very outset the management was strongly represented in the experiment, i.e. all members of the board of directors and their secretaries actively participated, and all heads of institutes or departments were either active users or they could be reached via the system. Therefore, managers are overrepresented in the inquiries. The opinions of scientific or administrative staff members, however, are represented by the inquiries to a restricted extent only since at the date of inquiry only some of these groups participated in the experiment. Furthermore, the number of returned questionnaires was rather small in this area. However, the recent heavy increase of KOMEX members coming from these groups seems to confirm system acceptance subsequently.

3. Results of Evaluation

The KOMEX users in the GMD come primarily from the following three areas:

- management (head of institutes and departments, board of directors);
- research area;
- administration.

From the very outset the managers had been most interested in KOMEX. Among the about 100 initial KOMEX users 10 % belonged to that group. These managers mainly use KOMEX personally and type their messages themselves. Only longer texts are delegated to the secretaries for typing. For securing cooperation between secretary and manager copies of all messages sent to the manager are automatically presented to the secretary though the manager processes the messages himself.

From the administrative area those people have become KOMEX members who are in intensive contacts with managers. Since KOMEX does not yet support strictly regulated form-oriented procedures, a further extension of KOMEX use is not to be expected at present.

From the research area mainly the people working on office communication were interested in the KOMEX use. Beyond that KOMEX is an important tool for communicating with external divisions, i.e. to date with the GMD people in Darmstadt and in the future also with those in Berlin and Karlsruhe. The inquiries confirm a considerable improvement of the contacts between Darmstadt and the headquarters at Birlinghoven. In the meantime most people from the research area who have such 'supralocal' contacts have become KOMEX users.

The people from the research areas have most intensive communication with their project colleagues who mostly use to sit in nearby rooms so that they can be contacted by face to face talks. This is also confirmed by technical measurement data. Between Birlinghoven and Darmstadt about two to three times as many messages are interchanged as within Darmstadt.

3.1 Results of Inquiries

The inquiries have shown that the opinions about the medium considerably changed between the first and the second inquiry. In the first inquiry conducted about 2 months after start of use the opinions varied from sceptical to euphorical. The second inquiry after half a year of usage, however, showed a more realistic evaluation, less euphorical, but altogether more positive. This confirms that a realistic evaluation can only be expected after a use of about at least six months.

We think that the most important statement of the KOMEX users is that they feel better informed than previously.

The respondents mentioned the following advantages:

- broader distribution of information;
- distribution of additional information (e.g. marginal notes or hints);
- quicker message processing;
- more frequent and quicker message answering;
- no disturbance or interruption as in telephone communication and therefore greater predisposition to transmit information;
- messages can be processed individually at the most convenient time;
- simultaneous attendance required, messages can be processed at any terminal for mailing to any other terminal (e.g. even if being on a mission);
- messages are formulated more spontaneously and personally than any other written information;
- less copying and mailing effort.

3.2 Results of Technical Measurements

The available technical measurement data extend to the present day and comprise all KOMEX users. In the past six months about 2300 messages were mailed, about 3500 messages were received and about 2500 sessions were performed per month. Since messages that are mailed to a conference are copied, the amount of messages received is greater than that of messages mailed. The use clearly varies during vacations and holidays.

The last months of 1983 show a clear increase of figures concerning use and members (from about 200 in July 1983 to about 350 members in December 1983). On the one hand, this is to be explained by the internal reorganisation of GMD which

had the effect that remotely located groups were combined to organisational units. On the other hand, since the beginning of July KOMEX can be used by any video terminal via public networks (line interface). This enables external cooperation partners of GMD to use KOMEX. Of course, this fact has led to an increase of the number of KOMEX members, and new members use also to increase the attractiveness of the system for further users.

The expansion within the GMD did not produce any acceptance problems on the side of 'newcomers' though these were not provided with such an effective and extensive training. They were quite 'naturally' integrated by those members who recommended them to use KOMEX. In this case, habits and experiences could be immediately transferred.

4. Conclusion

The experimental use produced many suggestions for further system functions. Some of them have already been implemented in the meantime thus improving acceptance. The user suggestions clearly indicate the requirement for further organisational support by the system. In addition the users demand for:

- more individual support (improved word processing, filing, integration of graphics functions etc.) though these requirements greatly vary according to the specific working place;
- increase of the number of reachable members, i.e. getting at all GMD members via the system and integration into a public network to support communication with external people.

Today KOMEX is an as natural communication medium in the GMD as the telephone, for example, and obviously nobody could imagine to do without it.

References

Holt,A.W., Cashman,P.M., Designing Systems to Support Cooperative Activity: An Example from Software Maintenance Management, IEEE Compsac (1981)

Kerr,E.B., Hiltz,ST.R., Computer-Mediated Communication Systems -Status and Evaluation-, (Academic Press, New York London, 1982)

Ohlson,M., The Impact of Office Automation on the Organisation: Some Implications for Research and Practice, CACM Nov. (1982), pp.838

Panko,R., Sprague, R.H., Toward a new Framework for Office Support, ACM (1982)

Palme,J., Experience with the use of the COM computerized Conferencing System, (FOA, Rapport 1981)

Human-Computer Interaction — INTERACT '84 / B. Shackel (ed.)
Elsevier Science Publishers B.V. (North-Holland)
© IFIP, 1985

USER SURVEYS IN THE BLEND-LINC 'ELECTRONIC JOURNAL' PROJECT

Pullinger, D.J., Shackel, B.   Dept. of Human Sciences,
                                Loughborough University of Technology,
                                U.K.

Dodd, W.P., Maude, T.I.   Centre for Computing and Computer Studies,
                                University of Birmingham, U.K.

This paper describes two telephone surveys of users in the 4 year experimental programme on electronic communication organised jointly by two Universities as the
Birmingham and Loughborough Electronic Network Development (BLEND). Several
communities of users are being studied; herein is described the first community of
initially about 50 scientists (the Loughborough Information Network Community –
LINC). Considerable problems have been experienced with the hardware available to
LINC members, with communications equipment, with modifying and developing software
to obtain an acceptable operating system, and with various unexpected bureaucratic
and organisational difficulties. Nevertheless, more than 50 papers are in the
system and successful teleconferences have been held.

INTRODUCTION

Electronic communication networks enable people
to exchange information, views and ideas by
means other than paper and the spoken word.
Material to be exchanged is entered into a computer store by a variety of means, and is
accessed on-line through local terminals. These
networks are relatively new and in the United
Kingdom little explored from the user's viewpoint. Research is needed to establish their
potential and to assess the problems and costs
of using them for different purposes.

As a result, approval was given, by the British
Library Research & Development Department, to a
proposal to establish an experimental programme
in electronic network communication. Birmingham
University is providing and developing the hardware and software facilities, and Loughborough
University is developing the documentation,
training and the information community; thus we
are organising the Birmingham and Loughborough
Electronic Network Development (BLEND). Using
the host computer at Birmingham University, a
community of initially about 50 scientists (the
Loughborough Information Network Community –
LINC) is connected through the public telephone
system to study various types of electronic
journals and to explore other possible types of
communication through this form of network.

The BLEND System therefore starts with the aim
of experiencing and studying the problems of
setting up an information community and establishing an experimental electronic journal. The
concept of the electronic journal is one which
involves using a computer to aid the normal
procedures whereby an article is written,
refereed, accepted and published. With the help
of suitable software an author may enter a text
into a system, and the editor, referees, and
ultimately the readers, as well as himself, can
have access to the text at their computer ter-

minals. The procedures involved are somewhat
similar to those already developed by various
studies in the area of computer conferencing
(cf. Hiltz & Turoff, 1978; Johansen, Vallee &
Spangler, 1979).

PROGRAMME PLANS

Aims

The initial plans placed the principal emphasis
upon a refereed papers journal. While that
remains the starting point, the proposal for the
project recommended exploring various other possible uses of electronic communication networks,
and this widening of the scope was approved. As
a result, the aims of the BLEND system programme
are to explore and evaluate the usage of an
electronic communication network as an aid to
writing, submitting and refereeing papers, and
also as a medium for other types of scientific
and technical communication. (For more details
of the programme plans, and for previous BLEND
reports, see Shackel 1982 a,b and Shackel et al.
1983).

To further these aims it was planned, from the
start of the programme from mid-1980, that
several different communities, with different
types of work and subject contents, should be
brought on to the BLEND system during its
operating life. Two such communities are
already using BLEND, and others are under
development.

The remainder of this paper will summarise the
plans and progress during the first three years
of the first community (the Loughborough
Information Network Community – LINC).

The LINC Procedures

The subject of interest in the LINC programme is

Computer Human Factors, and the members of LINC are all studying or involved with this topic. Approximately 40 members receive funds to cover telephone connection time equivalent to one hour per week at afternoon charge rates (which allows about 3 1/2 hours per week if all connection is in the evenings or at weekends). They have undertaken to submit one longer paper and one shorter 'dispatch' in each year of the programme.

The hardware and software facilities to support the programme are provided at Birmingham University. The large DEC20 computer there is accessed via the public telephone network or via other networks or services (e.g. PSS in Britain, TRANSPAC in France, DatexP in Germany, etc.). The operation for BLEND is based upon a computer conferencing software suite — NOTEPAD (from Infomedia Corporation, California). This is resident within a 'shell' system which further simplifies the operation for users (Maude et al, 1983).

At first the procedures for submitting and refereeing papers was very similar to traditional practice, while members became accustomed to the technology and its procedures. After members were familiar with the technology, formal experiments were instituted with alternative refereeing and other procedures to explore and exploit the capabilities of the electronic medium.

From the beginning it was planned to provide alternative means of entering papers, alternative procedures for refereeing papers, etc. Therefore, from the start three methods for entering papers have been provided:

1. author or secretary directly on-line;
2. typical typescript (with corrections) sent to Loughborough for entry via secretary and word-processor;
3. perfect typed manuscript sent to Birmingham for entry via OCR machine.

Types of Journal to be explored

Types of communication between scientists can range from the very informal chit-chat over coffee, through discussion and questions at conferences, to the very formal refereed papers journal (see Table 1). It was planned that as many of these as possible should be explored during the LINC programme.

Other aspects include co-operative writing and access to the journals by 'Readers Only'. Of course, the plan was to be implemented in stages; the programme started with 1, 2, 3, 7, 8, and others are being introduced in due time.

BACKGROUND AND AIMS

The LINC community started full trials on the BLEND system on January 15th 1981. Naturally, not all LINC members had obtained the necessary equipment for full participation by this date, but must members gradually received the terminals and modems.

Over the five month period from January to May 1981, computer usage statistics showed that approximately one third of the LINC community had logged in regularly (though with different frequencies), a second third had logged in regularly until Easter and hardly at all subsequently, and, finally, the remaining third had never entered the BLEND system.

Various facts were known that might be contributory to an emerging pattern of decreasing usage in the second third of users, for example, that the DEC computer at the University of Birmingham was down 15% of the time from April to May 1981; another example was that many LINC members had experienced long delays in obtaining modem equipment etc; the University Grants Committee cuts demanded both financial and discussion time sacrifices.

In order to establish how the LINC participants expressed their feelings about the system, the Project Team members at Loughborough University of Technology instigated the idea of a survey whose general aims were:

1. To establish the perceived reactions of the LINC community to the BLEND system, in particular to note what gave the community the most concern about their participation.

2. To discover any problems with which the Project Management Team might help, in particular to linking hardware and software to facilitate communication.

Various survey techniques were considered, including written questionnaires sent through the postal system, questionnaires sent via the computer based message system in BLEND, tele-

===

TABLE 1   Types of Communication and 'Journal' Planned for LINC Programme

1.	Chit-chat	Informal
2.	Work Messages	:
3.	LINC News — network & related information in a monthly newsletter	:
4.	Enquiry-answer system between experts	:
5.	Bulletin — project and work progress reports	:
6.	Annotated Abstracts Journal	:
7.	Discussion and Questions on Papers	:
8.	Poster Papers Journal	:
9.	Refereed Papers Journal	Formal

===

phone interviews and face-to-face interviews.
Factors that influenced these considerations
included the relative cost, the number of LINC
members that would probably be contacted successfully by each technique, the availability of
members' and the researcher's time.

In order to cover both those who had never and
those who regularly logged into the BLEND system
it was decided to hold a telephone survey. This
survey presented structured questions while
allowing free responses which were subsequently
analysed.

1981 AND 1983 SURVEYS

Two such surveys were carried out in June 1981
and November 1983, i.e. after 6 and 35 months of
use respectively. The same questions were asked
in the same order, excepting the addition of a
question on the content found on the BLEND
system in the latter survey. The general
response to being called by phone was very
positive and all members seemed prepared to give
up time to answer questions and express views
openly. In particular there was a general
pervading opinion that research undertaken on
and with BLEND was worthwhile and needed
increasing.

The two surveys form part of a large programme
of research into users' reactions to the introduction of the availability of an electronic
network system into their working lives. Figure
1 gives an overview of the way in which these
contribute to the research programme.

THE INTERVIEW

There were very similar experiences in both
surveys in the results of attempting to reach
people by phone. In 1981, 130 calls were made,
14 of which reached the person required on the
first attempt and 36 of which were successful in
the end. In 1983, 101 calls were made, 6 of
which reached the person required at the first
attempt and 32 of which were successful in the
end (see Figure 2).

An analysis of the area in which LINC members
spent most time talking, as noted during the
interview, revealed that access to the BLEND
system and suitable equipment, how the software
should be changed, and how to create a more
active community of users, were the main
concerns.

ACCESS TO EQUIPMENT

There were many problems of access to equipment
and via these various pieces of hardware and
network services to the software on the computer
at the University of Birmingham.

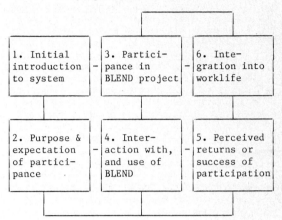

FIGURE 1: The components of the evaluation
programme of the LINC Community

Evaluation:

Initial intro- duction and interviews 1980-1981	BLEND usage data; LINC experiences; 6-month phone survey; 35-month phone survey;	1984 inter- views for longitudinal study usage data analysis

time: --------------->----------->------------->

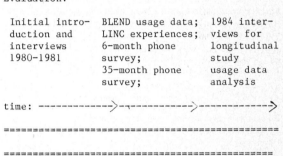

FIGURE 2: Telephone calls made to reach
LINC members

Year	1981	1983
Number of calls	130	101
First time success	14	6
Final success	36	32
Number of people trying to be reached	59	66

Many organisational, bureaucratic, social or
psychological problems were revealed by the 1981
survey, and subsequent experience, to add to the
present technological limitations. Some of
these are listed to illustrate the diversity of
difficulties which beset the introduction of a
radically new system into existing situations.

1. Delays up to 5 months in installing lines
   and modems by British Telecom.
2. Bureaucratic and 'political' resistance to
   installing less noisy direct telephone lines
   instead of going through the campus or
   institution switchboard, because they are
   not under control nor monitored by the
   organisation.

3. Existing equipment, e.g. mainframe or local
   network, not able to be used to connect to
   an outside computer.
4. Therefore, existing familiar procedures
   (e.g. familiar editor, network commands or
   local mainframe command language) not able
   to be used, with consequent 'unlearning and
   new learning' penalty to use BLEND on DEC20.
5. Bureaucratic and 'political' resistance to a
   terminal being in a LINC member's room (e.g.
   this might unbalance status relationships,
   or the terminal must be seen as 'owned' by
   the institution and not by the individual).
6. Dislike or avoidance by users of the conflict situation when others are found to be
   using a shared terminal or modem or external
   telephone line.
7. Time constraints upon the use of equipment
   at the user's end, and upon the use of the
   Birmingham DEC20 computer during term time
   (10-12 and 2-4 weekdays) because of teaching
   class workloads.

The attitudes inside institutions towards
'ownership' and control of new technology may be
expected to change as the general attitudes in
society change. The technology will improve
considerably; indeed all the facilities which we
at present speculate to be needed do exist somewhere already, but of course at a price.

The members of the LINC community who were
surveyed made 53 suggestions in total as to the
changes they would like to see made. Of these
16 related to the ease of accessing the DEC
computer:

    Get autodialler and auto login device 9
    Get 1200 baud model 4
    Make sure DEC is always operative 3

That one quarter of those surveyed expressed a
hindrance caused by the dialling and log-in
procedure in free responses, illustrates that
users (despite admitting the need for, and
requiring, security) wish to walk to a terminal
and after one or two key presses access a useful
and usable part of the system.

Other suggestions included facilities that would
like to be seen on the system, altering the
software to fit the users' way of working better
and eliminations of the small inconsistencies
and confusions.

The main suggested alteration relates to the
structuring of the software. At the time of the
survey it was a 2-level hierarchical tree structure and this was considered to be akin to an
imposed filing structure. Further questioning
revealed that a major difficulty was maintaining
an updateable overview of the contents in
relation to where one was.

To summarise, there were problems in -

knowing where one is
knowing where one can go to
knowing what there is to see
knowing what-there-is-to-see involves
knowing whether one has seen everything
knowing where one saw something.

The 1981 survey revealed that for satisfactory
use, a ring of five factors should be in operation and that no single item should have so
much cost to the user so as to prevent usage.
This is presented in Figure 3 with every comment
being made by at least one person interviewed.

==

FIGURE 3: Factors for Satisfactory Use

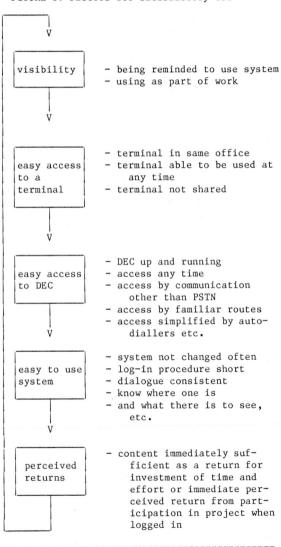

visibility
- being reminded to use system
- using as part of work

easy access
to a
terminal
- terminal in same office
- terminal able to be used at
  any time
- terminal not shared

easy access
to DEC
- DEC up and running
- access any time
- access by communication
  other than PSTN
- access by familiar routes
- access simplified by auto-
  diallers etc.

easy to use
system
- system not changed often
- log-in procedure short
- dialogue consistent
- know where one is
- and what there is to see,
  etc.

perceived
returns
- content immediately sufficient as a return for
  investment of time and
  effort or immediate perceived return from participation in project when
  logged in

==

COMMUNICATING MICROCOMPUTERS

In 1982 a new British product appeared on the market which was the first microcomputer to contain an integral 1200/75 baud modem (approved for use with the British Telecom phone system) and have automatic dialling and log in to a host computer, while allowing sending of prepared (word-processed) text files. Thirteen such TORCH microcomputers were purchased for LINC members to use and they reported that access had been "dramatically" altered by their availability. Like those who had arranged terminal equipment and good telecommunication access in their offices, members being interviewed in the 1983 survey reported a change in their patterns of use from occasional long sessions to short daily sessions with a commensurate degree of increased satisfaction in use. Not all, it is to be noted, prefer this change with one interviewee reporting he preferred long sessions out of his office in another building, where he would not be interrupted by phones or secretaries.

This change in general usage has led to an increase of activity in the following areas on the BLEND system:

a) Chit-chat and general remarks
b) Discussion about issues in Computer Human Factors, for example about how we will design terminals for reading and writing in the future.
c) A release of many scientific papers by some LINC members.
d) The introduction of a Software Reviews Journal.

It was found that nearly all the active users had more than one way of accessing the system, sometimes three different pieces of equipment or routes. This allowed a continuity of interaction and communication when, for one of the many reasons that occur, one access procedure is not operational.

CHANGES TO THE SOFTWARE

The interviewer analysed all the suggested changes, many of which were able to be partially implemented in conjunction with the designers, Infomedia, Palo Alto, California (see Pullinger 1984 for a description of enhancing this computer conferencing suite for the BLEND system). Between June 1981 and November 1983 there were two enhancements of the BLEND system, with the result that in the later survey 10% said that they were entirely satisfied with the software and a further 6% approvingly noted the vast improvement and attributed this to genuine changes rather than just getting used to the 'nasties'! There was no request for a satisfaction rating but only suggestions for improvement, so these remarks are quite voluntary.

There were, however, still a large number of suggestions for improvements, the majority of which had to do with two areas: handling messages and manipulation of the display of text. Both point to one aspect of the design of the system which we might summarise as "We want more - we want less".

There were many LINC members who commented on the 'overwhelming' number of messages and new information that appeared on the BLEND system, particularly if they had not had the opportunity to log in for a week or two. At the same time (and sometimes by the same people) there was an expression of there not being enough material on the system. It seems that we have here the focal point of the difficulties with designing a system which allows all levels of communication from short messages to papers. Expressed in another way, we have the problems associated with designing an integrated store of messages and information which is considerably more archival in nature than only an electronic mail system but 'active' compared to an archived datebase for information retrieval.

There are no solutions yet to this problem, but it is hoped that the work done in the BLEND system and other electronic mail and computer conferencing systems will lead to a more integrated service which will help users communicate with each other at all the required levels, including electronic journals.

CONCLUSION

Both phone surveys achieved their stated purposes and revealed problems that remain with the technology used in accessing the BLEND system and with the software itself. The surveys caught 'snapshots' of the usage, attitudes and feelings of the LINC members interviewed and will be incorporated into the 4 year longitudinal studies of interviews and usage as recorded by the computer system. The former survey led to a reassessment of the ways in which LINC members might be helped, in particular by the loan of suitable communicating microcomputers and in design of the software.

Many difficulties have been experienced by users, for example with organisations, telecommunications and software systems, in trying to incorporate use of the BLEND system into their established working routines; nevertheless BLEND has been developed as planned and anticipated in conjunction with LINC. More than 50 papers have been submitted by LINC members, 25 to the Poster and more than 25 to the Refereed Papers Journal. This progress could reasonably be compared with the time schedule for the start of any new journal. These papers and the willing participation of the LINC community continue to support the breadth of experimentation originally envisaged for this programme.

REFERENCES

Hiltz, S. & Turoff, M., The Network Nation –
    human communication via computer (Addison-
    Wesley, Reading, Mass., 1978).

Johansen, R., Vallee, J. & Spangler, K., Elec-
    tronic Meetings: technical alternatives
    and social choices (Addison-Wesley,
    Reading, Mass., 1979).

Maude, T.I., Dodd, W.P., Pullinger, D.J. &
    Shackel, B. (1983) The BLEND electronic
    journal system, Paper to the Inter Univer-
    sity Committee on Computers 1982 Col-
    loquium, I.U.C.C. Bulletin 5(1) 22–26.

Pullinger, D.J. (1984) Enhancing NOTEPAD Tele-
    conferencing for the BLEND 'Electronic
    Journal', Behaviour and Information Tech-
    nology 3(1) 13–23.

Shackel, B., (1982a) The BLEND System – pro-
    gramme for the study of some 'Electronic
    Journals', The Computer Journal 25(2) 161–
    168; Ergonomics 25(4) 269–284; and the
    Journal of the American Society for Infor-
    mation Science 34(1) 22–30.

Shackel, B., (1982b) Plans and initial progress
    with BLEND – an electronic network communi-
    cation experiment, International Journal of
    Man-Machine Studies 17, 225–233.

Shackel, B., Pullinger, D.J., Maude, T.I. &
    Dodd, W.P. (1983) The BLEND-LINC project on
    'Electronic Journals' after two years,
    ASLIB Proceedings 35(2) 77–91, and The
    Computer Journal 26(3), 247–252.

Human-Computer Interaction — INTERACT '84 / B. Shackel (ed.)
Elsevier Science Publishers B.V. (North-Holland)
© IFIP, 1985

Structures for Group Working in Mailbox Systems

Paul Wilson

Office Systems Division, National Computing Centre
Oxford Road, Manchester, M1 7ED, UK.

Basic electronic mailbox facilities allow individuals to send and receive messages.
However, for more formal work (eg running meetings or projects) structured facilities
are required. This paper provides a generic categorisation of mailbox structures and
identifies those currently being used in 5 categories of mailbox group working
applications. The structures used in a group working experiment on the BLEND system are
critically described, and recommendations for further work in this area are made.

1   Introduction

Many organisations are trying out a new
breed of communications - MAILBOX SYSTEMS -
which do not require the caller and recipient to
be present at the same time. Instead a message
can be sent to the mailbox of the recipient who
can access it at the time and place of his
convenience.

Although most contemporary mailbox systems
are text based, voice mailbox systems (often
referred to as Voice Message Systems) are becoming available. These can do most of the things
that a text system can (ie. messages can be
pended, answered, filed etc), and are likely to
be popular as they can be accessed by an ordinary telephone handset. Image mailbox systems (in
which you would see a recorded picture of the
sender speaking a message) are still too costly
and I know of no existing systems. However, all
types of mailbox systems have the same basic
features so, as the technologies of voice, image
and text converge, so mailbox systems will handle the range of text, voice and image messages.

2   Basic mailbox facilities

All mailbox systems have basic facilities
which can be categorised as follows (1):
Message preparation: eg. word processing;
message annotation prior to forwarding/filing.
Sending messages: eg. multiple addressing;
distribution lists; message priorities.
Receiving messages: eg. mailbox scanning; new
message notification; replying; forwarding.
Security/reliability: eg. passwords; encryption;
inhibiting hard copy; message loss protection.
Message filing and retrieval: eg. message
classification; retrieval facilities; archiving.
Message logging: accounting/management reports.

Such basic facilities provide good informal
communications in the same way as the telephone
does. Most contemporary systems are of this type
and used mainly for informal communications
between people separated by geographical distance and/or time zone differences (2). This saves
time, reduces interruptions and improves commu-

nications. However such benefits are intangible,
difficult to measure and often make no directly
apparent impact on profitability.

3   Mailbox Structures

Alternatively, mailbox communication can be
STRUCTURED to undertake specific tasks. Mailbox
structuring is equivalent to the order that we
impose in face-to-face communication; eg
meetings often have a Chairman, an agenda, procedures for conducting the meeting and minutes
are produced. However, whereas face-to-face
structures largely rely on the compliance of the
individual and the memorising or recording of
the communication that has taken place, mailbox
structures can be easily controlled and no communication is lost or forgotten. Consequently
Mailbox structures have far greater scope and
constitute a powerful new form of communication.
Moreover their use for specific applications can
produce tangible, directly apparent, benefits.

Structuring does not reduce the need for
basic mailbox facilities, but is added onto them
to provide extra tools for specific applications. Hiltz and Turoff have described structuring as tailoring the computer mediated communication process around the particular group and
the application (3). Structuring has also been
termed 'Groupware' by Johnson and Lenz (4).

The concept of mailbox structuring was not
widely understood in the UK at the time of
writing. This is hardly surprising since people
are largely influenced by the products they have
seen or are using, and most products on the UK
market provided only basic mailbox facilities: I
suspect the position is no different in the rest
of the world. Despite this however, enough progress has been made in various organisations -
mainly in the USA - to be able to get a picture
of the range of possible structures. They seem
to fall into three major categories (2):
- Structures for organising the information
- Structures for getting things done
- Structures for controlling who does what

3.1 Ways of implementing structures

Since mailbox communication is performed via computers, any structures needed can be programmed in (eg chairman to receive copies of all messages). This is SOFTWARE STRUCTURING. It is advantageous since such rules will be imposed and policed impartially by the system; but it has the drawback of being rigid and inflexible.

MANAGEMENT STRUCTURING, on the other hand, involves the application and policing of rules by users. As in face-to-face communication, it relies on the committment to the rules by users and their ability to perform those roles the rules demand of them. However management structures have the advantage of flexibility and require no software to be written or changed.

Both Software and Management structures can be used in one application: it may often be good to have a combination of rigid policing and a degree of flexibility. Each approach, and a combination of the two, should always be considered when designing application structures.

Structures themselves can be selected by other structures. Hiltz and Turoff describe one example in which user contributions are restricted if their contributions to date exceed a certain percentage of the contributions made by the whole group (3). This can be thought of as a hierarchy of structures - the upper level structure controlling which of the lower level structures to apply. Little is known about what such higher levels of structures might consist of, nor how useful they might be.

3.2 Types of Structures

3.2.1 Organising the information generated

These structures are summarised in Fig 1.

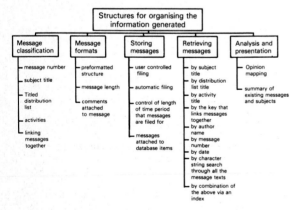

Figure 1 Structures for organising information.

Message classification: message linking allows browsing through message chains; 'activities' allow specific topics to be discussed in isolation - users must log into an activity to send or receive mail on the particular topic.
Message formats: message length limitation can aid efficiency; attaching comments to a message can be an alternative to message linking.
Message storage: automatic filing, by which the system stores all messages, is a feature of

'activities'. Messages attached to database items can contain qualifying information which is presented upon access of the data concerned.
Retrieving messages: Any standard techniques for retrieving information could be used here.
Analysis and presentation of message content: Opinion mapping refers to the potential capability of a computer to scan the contents of messages and to place the facts and opinions they contain in the context of the facts and opinions contained in other messages.

3.2.2 Structures for getting things done

These structures are summarised in Fig 2.

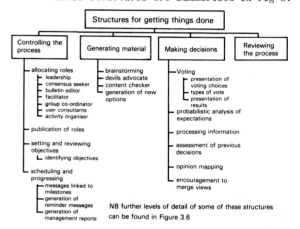

Figure 2 Structures for getting things done

Controlling the process: A facilitator looks out for signs of the discussion flagging and takes steps to regenerate interest (5). Messages linked to project milestones allows all discussion about a project phase to be reviewed together.
Generating material: Brainstorming is a formalised technique for generating and evaluating ideas and producing solutions to problems. The devils advocate approach injects ideas contrary to accepted opinion in order to stimulate thinking. A content checker identifies emotionally charged terms and indicates to the sender what effects they might have on the recipient (5).
Making decisions: An example of Probabalistic Analasis of expectations is Robert Bittlestone's Metaconferencing system which analyses voting patterns to inform users of who else is most in agreement or disagreement with their views in general or on particular votes (6). Processing of information in a message could take place, for instance, in a preformatted message in which data has been input.
Reviewing the process: These structures provide facilities for reviewing a current piece of work or project, or for the assessment of a completed project to ensure that the lessons learned are recorded for use in subsequent projects.

3.2.3 Structures for controlling who does what

These structures are summarised in Fig 3.
Control of the communication flows: Pen names enable people to play different roles, whilst anonymity seems to avoid embarrassment (3). A

'read only' member of an activity is the equivalent of being an observer at a meeting.
Control over the creation of mailbox communities:
A data base of user interests/profiles is held in messages in an activity and accessed by keyword. Activities can be 'open' (to all), 'closed' (except to selected users) or 'restricted' (open to some but closed to others).

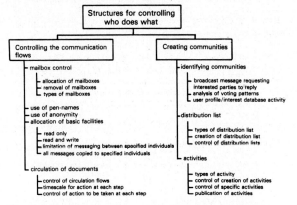

Fig 3   Structures for controlling who does what.

4   Applications for mailbox systems

The purpose of using mailbox structures is to enable mailbox systems to be applied to specific communication tasks and to solve specific communication problems. Only limited knowledge is currently available of the applications that are feasible and of the associated structures that are needed. However, current useage indicates the following categories of application: Controlling branches; Transaction processing; Distributing information; Educational activities; Communicating with suppliers and customers; Bringing like-minded people together; Buying and selling; Booking and control of facilities; Planning and progressing; Joint working arrangements; Meetings; Project teams and working parties; Managing people. The final five of these all have some relevance for Group Working and are described in more detail below:

4.1   Planning and Progressing

Mailbox systems can control the achievement of targets eg in projects with several people responsible for various goals, informal communication relating to progress can be attached to specific milestones and be easily reviewed. The system can also check on timescales and issue reminder messages accordingly (4).

4.2   Joint working arrangements

Mailbox systems can be used by co-authors to create documents. They can also provide communication facilities between people who work closely together, eg managers and secretarys or people who are sharing the same job (2).

4.3   Meetings:

Much meeting time is spent dealing with routine, non-immediate matters. These can be more effectively dealt with via a mailbox system

eg a weekly Branch Managers meeting might be held only once every two months if augmented by a structured mailbox system. Meetings in a mailbox system give individuals a greater chance to contribute, and to think about suggestions and opinions. Suitable structuring can ensure better controlled meetings which emerge with clear decisions within a specified time scale. Actions can also be automatically progressed (7)(8).

4.4   Project teams and working parties:

In organisations that use mailbox systems extensively, geographical and hierarchical constraints are removed and cross company, cross location, project teams emerge. In such an environment the best personnel can be chosen for projects since no relocation is needed and management can be kept informed of their staff's activities. In effect this is Matrix Management by which individuals can have more than one boss and sets of responsibilities (8)(9)(10).

4.5   Managing people:

Mailbox systems can enable managers to talk more often to their staff, and to be kept informed of conversations among their staff by being included on a messages distribution list. Planning and progressing structures can be used for managing the work of individuals.

5   Structures for group working applications

An inspection of the generic structures in section 3 indicates that most could have relevance for mailbox group working. To establish what structures are being used a survey was done of existing or proposed mailbox useage (11). Those identified, grouped within the appropriate generic structure categories, are shown in Figure 4.

The results indicate that few mailbox structures have been tried out and developed, and that probably relatively little group working is being undertaken on mailbox systems.

However, the potential for mailbox group working is enormous. Project working is common in the Engineering industry, in Research & Development and in Computer Systems Development. Working Parties are a common mechanism for getting things done in Government, National Bodies, Standardisation bodies and Clubs and Societies. Committees and regular meetings are also a common feature in most organisations. For many of these most of the communication could probably be achieved more efficiently, and to the greater convenience of participants, through a suitably structured mailbox system. The potential impact is vast: for meetings alone there must be tens of thousands occurring worldwide EACH DAY.

Potential there may be, but is it really feasible to conduct group working over mailbox systems? Research at the New Jersey Institute of Technology indicates that mailbox group working can be an effective replacement for at least some face-to-face meetings. From an experiment in which 16 groups were given two group decision making tasks, with the chief dependant variable being mode of communication (mailbox or face-to-face), Hiltz concluded that "Quality of decision is likely to be just as good. If the group wants consensus, a computer based conference can be structured to make this a probable outcome"(12).

However, laboratory feasibility is one thing - feasibility in a day to day working office is another.To test the latter, a group of 5 people within the BLEND system (13) organised themselves, discussed ideas, took decisions on work to be done and wrote 2 conference papers (14,15) entirely through the network. The structures explored in this work are described below.

6   Structures employed in the BLEND Group Working Experiment

6.1 Structures for organising the information

The group was limited in this respect by the NOTEPAD software on which the BLEND system runs. NOTEPAD messages can be of two types; ENTRIES (which are displayed to all) or NOTES (which can be sent to one person only): a distribution list facility is not available. This did not seem to hinder the group working process (perhaps because there were only 5 people in the group), though it may have restricted discussion on parallel topics (as reported in (15)). However it is not known whether more parallel discussion would have assisted the group working process.

The NOTEPAD software requires that all communication takes place within a hierarchy of 'electronic spaces'. At the upper level are 'Projects'. At the lower level, within each

Project, are 'Activities'. Messages can only be sent or read within a specific activity. This structure assisted the group working process by experience within BLEND has shown that in activities with a broad topic range it is difficult to pursue subjects to a satisfactory conclusion and that the deluge of such a variety of information gives the impression of information overload. For this reason the group split their work into a general discussion activity, a planning activity, a series of activities for writing specific sections of the paper they were producing, and an activity for integrating and formatting completed parts of the paper. This arrangement did enable work to be done and results to be achieved, though some activities still suffered from a wide diversity of topics. Therefore it is possible that a facility to define even lower levels of activity within the Project/Activity hierarchy might be useful. Facilities for graphically representing what Projects and Activities exist, and their relationships, would be a useful adjunct to Project/Activity structures.

NOTEPAD messages have a line of Header information which includes author and date/time of creation, but does not include a 'subject' field - and this was recognised by the group as a shortcoming (15). NOTEPAD also lacks a facility to reply to messages (by which the mailbox system automatically generates the header and distribution list from the message being replied to). It is possible that provision of the com-

Planning and progressing
Organise info...Message formats....Preformatted message structure for reporting progress.
Get things done...Control process..All project-related messages attached to appropriate milestones.
　　　　　　　　　...Reminder message generated when date of action message exceeded.
　　　　...Making decisions...Diaries can be searched to set up meetings requested in messages.
Joint working arrangements
Organise info...Classification.....For joint authorship each message in an activity can be a section
　　　　　　　　　of text. An activity can also be used by a manager/secretary team.
　　　...Message formats....Facility for joint workers to add comments to messsages.
　　　...Storing messages...All versions of text being jointly authored are automatically filed
Meetings
Get things done...Control process..Election of chairman for a meeting.
　　　　　　　　...Consensus seeker can be appointed by meeting chairman.
　　　　　　　　...Facilitator uses intervention tools when the debate deteriorates.
　　　　　　　　...Agenda items put forward by individuals.
　　　　　　　　...Agenda items accepted/rejected as mailbox or face-to-face topics.
　　　　　　　　...Reminder messages generated in meetings to ensure that agenda items
　　　　　　　　are discussed and that action items are reported back on.
　...Generate material..A content checker identifies emotionally charged-terms etc
　　　　　　　　...New options could be inserted into a meeting discussion.
　...Making decisions...Message content analysis identifies options with most consensus.
　　　　　　　　...Mapping of the views of attendees at meetings for comparison.
　　　　　　　　...Metaconference encourages participants to produce 'foci of concern'
Who does what..Create communities..Distribution lists can be used to assemble and run ad-hoc meetings.
Project teams and working parties
Organise info...Classification.....Use of activity to discuss text being prepared in a separate file.
Get things done...Control process..Chairman decides how often to send hard copy of mailbox proceedings
　　　　　　　　to those members who have no access to the mailbox system.
　...Generate material..One person generates a document, para by para, in a file, making
　　　　　　　　changes according to discussion in activity by team members.
Managing people
Organise info...Classification.....A manager links all messages between himself and one of his staff.

Figure 4 Results of a survey of appropriate structures for mailbox group working applications.

bined facilities of Subject Header, Reply
helping to concentrate communication on a topic
and keep it all in one place. Previous
feature and Distribution Lists could significantly affect the Group Working process.

All messages are automatically filed in
NOTEPAD and there are extensive facilities for
retrieving them including by number, date,
author, recipient and keyword search through all
the text of specified messages. However problems
were still encountered in establishing the history of a topic or finding specific information.
A facility for summarising what had gone before
would have been invaluable. This could be
achieved by the system collecting and presenting
a list of message numbers, subject headings and
their frequency (though, in the long term, automated summarising of the text of messages might
be possible). An alternative or complementary
approach would be to provide individuals with
the ability to create their own message files (a
feature ommitted from NOTEPAD). I would have
liked an indexing facility, available to me
wherever I was in the system, which enabled me
to record the Project and Activity a message was
in, its number, a title and any keywords I
wished to specify. With such a facility individuals could record details of messages important
to them and search their own index when subsequently wanting to find those messages.

6.2 Structures for getting things done

Five different formal Roles are built-into
the NOTEPAD system: for each Project an Administrator must be specified whose responsibilities
include assigning an Organiser to each Activity
that is set up. An Organiser is empowered to
join or leave people from Activities, to disallow public or private communication, to delete
or restore Entries or Notes and to erase the
activity itself. Ordinary members of an Activity
are referred to as Contributors, while a special
class of Contributors, called Editors, are able
to replace existing Entries (16).

Despite participants of the Group Working
experiment having to take on these roles because
the system required it of them, in fact they did
not play a significant part in the Group Working
process. On the contraray the Group found it
necessary to create a number of other roles
(described below) for themselves. To assess what
functions these roles performed, the Entries in
the main Discussion activity and the Planning
activity were analysed. The results, indicated
by an *, are shown below for each role created
(the numbers in brackets after a stated function, eg (4,8), refer to the number of messages
on that topic sent in, first, the general discussion activity (total No of messages = 317
between 3rd May and 19th December and, second,
in the Planning activity (total No of messages =
262 between 1st July and 23rd December)

Project Organiser
*Setting objectives (2,8)
 - defining objectives
 - defining responsibilities for roles
*Obtaining and allocating resources (4,2)

 - identifying who is prepared to work
 - allocating work tasks
 - ensuring that role stand-ins are arranged
 - finding new members
*Scheduling and progressing (3,4)
 - sending reminders of impending deadlines
 - suggesting that rescheduling is required
*Defining procedures (7,5)
 - identifying need for roles and structures
 - identifying how to do the work
*Controlling the work flow (3,5)
 - encouraging members to contribute
 - keeping the discussion on the subject
*Decision making (1,6)
 - encouragement to reach a decision
 - announcement of decisions based on discussion
*Reviewing current status (2,4)
 - Summarising what work has been done so far
 - identification of outstanding tasks
*Organising the information generated (3,-)
 - definition of activity titles
 - storage of files
 - control of hard copy distribution
*Announcement of significant events (5,8)
 - informing group of Planning Team decision
 - notification of people taking up roles
 - introducing new people

Timescale watcher
*Drawing up/revising schedules (2,5)
*Assessment of current position (12,6)
 - verbal assessment of tasks done/left (6,4)
 - formal status chart (6,2)
*Notification of impending deadlines (4,-)

Verbal assessments were typically given
from halfway through a phase and expressed
increasing urgency as the deadlines approached.
The formal Status Chart was issued in the main
Discussion activity at intervals of roughly 1 or
2 weeks. It was not issued in the final 2 months
of the experiment because most of the work was
taking place in the activities set up to write
and produce the paper. An incomplete example of
the status chart is shown in Figure 5.

```
(305)  Maude (Tim)  31-Oct-83  8:17 AM
Week beginning (Monday)
====---------============---------============---------
Aug Aug Aug Aug Aug Sep Sep Sep Sep Oct Oct Oct
 1   8  15  22  30   5  12  19  26   3  10  17
====---------============---------============---------
Planned phases
 1   2   2   2   2   2   2   3   4   4   5   5
Replanned phases
 1   2   2   2   2   2   2   3   3   3   4   4
Actual phases
 1   2   2   2   2   2   2   3   3   3   4   4
```

Figure 5 Timescale Status Chart (incomplete)

The Timescale Watcher played a key role in
ensuring that results were achieved. Publication
of the Status report enabled Group members to
see what had been achieved, where the work was
up to and what had yet to be done. The verbal
assessments and deadline notifications generated
a sense of purpose and urgency. Many structures

could be devised to assist the Timescale Watcher
in his work eg the system could prompt the
Timescale Watcher to update the Status Chart on
a regular basis - perhaps a day or two before
the system automatically published the updated
Chart. Alternatively the Status Chart could be
placed on permanent view in a corner of the
screen and/or automatically displayed to users
as they log in. The system could aid the
scheduling process by automatically generating
schedules based on information given it about
individual task timescales.

Absence Co-ordinator
*Getting information re future absences (-,4)
*Presenting info re future absences (-,4)

The absence information was published in a
'Notification of absence' chart, shown in Fig 6.

```
(86) Marshall (Chris) 17-Aug-83  2:09 PM
--------------------------------------------------
Notification of absence from this activity
--------------------------------------------------
******NAME******      ******PERIOD OF ABSENCE******
Marshall (Chris)      22nd Aug-----30th Aug
                      14th, 15th, 16th Sept.
Maude (Tim)           1 week sometime in Sept.
Wilson (Paul)         Present------End of Aug.
Tagg (Stephen)        29 Aug---3 Sept(50% probable)
                      1 week in Sept (to be confirmed)
```

Figure 6 'Notification of absence' chart

It is important to establish absence information when working to deadlines in mailbox
systems because the lack of immediacy of the
medium, while allowing individuals to choose
when they wish to communicate, can also result
in several days being lost before it is realised
that someone is missing. Absence information
could be efficiently collected by the system
requesting it each time a user logged off.
Absence notification reports could then be automatically generated by the system and displayed
in the same way as the Timescale Status Chart.

Planning Team
Following an initial 2 month period of open
discussion, the Project Organiser decided that,
if tangible results were to be achieved, it
would be necessary to know who would be prepared
to do the work, and to establish clear goals and
schedules. Consequently he used the systems
voting facility (using the free text response
option) to ask those people who would be willing
to work to identify themselves. These people
were then made members of the Planning Team
which did its work in a newly formed 'Planning
and Control' activity. After 1 months work the
Planning Team produced a report which identified
overall goals and a 5 phase schedule; this was
published in the main discussion activity.

The following functions were carried out by
the Planning Team over the experimental period:
*Setting objectives
*Long term planning
*Reviewing current status
*Allocating resources

*Defining procedures
Many aspects of the Planning Team's work
could have been augmented by appropriate structures eg from the first day of operation the
system could have prompted the Team to produce a
statement of the overall project objectives, and
subsequently for a breakdown of this goal into
phases with objectives, sub-tasks and timescales. Using a form filling approach this information could have been input to the system as it
was decided and the system itself could have
maintained and updated appropriate records
thereby overcoming a major problem experienced
during the experiment - that of updating completed records. Another difficulty encountered
was in providing easy access to completed
reports, schedules, text etc. One possible solution to this problem is to provide a permanent
menu of official documents in a corner of the
screen and allow users to access them from anywhere in the system.

Phase Directors
Phase Directors, appointed by the Project
Organiser for Phases 2-5, were responsible for
ensuring that the phase objectives (eg Raise
knowledge level to common level; Determine high
level structure of paper; Write paper) were met.
First, in conjunction with other Group Members,
they identified sub-tasks and schedules. Then,
injecting leadership as required, and working in
conjunction with the Timescale Watcher, they
ensured that sub-tasks were completed and, finally, produced a short end of phase report of the
results. Analysis of the messages indicates that
Phase Directors carried out the functions below:
*Setting objectives
 - defining goals
 - responding to requests for direction
 - identification of tasks
*Decision making
 - announcement of decisions based on discussion
 - compilation of end of Phase report
*Scheduling
 - Suggesting changed schedules
 - emphasising urgency
*Announcement of significant events
*Obtaining and allocating resources

Software structures to prompt Phase Directors to establish sub-tasks and schedules and to
write reports would have been helpful. Form
filling, maintainance, updating and presentation
structures such as those proposed for Timescale
Watching, Absence Co-ordination and Planning
would also be useful to Phase Directors.

Writing Teams and section writers
The joint production of a complex document
by several people is a difficult affair at the
best of times. It was achieved successfully in
this experiment by allocating responsibility for
particular sections of the document to Writing
Teams consisting of 1 Section Writer (who was
responsible for actually writing the text) and 2
others. Different sections were assembled together into the final paper in a separate Activity
to which all members of the Group belonged. Many
difficulties were encountered in the writing

phase including: cluttering up the message store
with long Entries of draft text; inability to
comment on long sections of text until the whole
of the message had been displayed; not knowing
the locations of the latest drafts of the text;
setting and applying format standards; proofreading; having to read whole sections of redrafted
text because one didn't know what had been
changed. Appropriate structuring could make
dramatic inroads into these problems.

Moving on from Role structures, the generation of ideas during the experiment proved to be
no problem, but, as described in (15), lack of
suitable structures for pursuing and evaluating
ideas meant that some were not made full use of.
One solution to this problem is simply to embody
formal Brainstorming methodology (17) into mailbox structures.

Before starting the experiment I anticipated that NOTEPAD's voting facilities would be
an important feature of the group working process. However, in the two activities analysed,
it was used only 3 times. This may have been due
in part to a lack of experience in putting the
facility to good use, and partly to the working
culture developed by the group. However it may
also be that the delay in getting feedback from
a vote (because people might not log in for some
time after the vote is initiated, and because
only the person initiating the vote can find out
who has voted and publish the results) made it a
less attractive facility. One way of improving
this would be to provide a constant summary of
outstanding votes, and numbers who had voted, in
a corner of the screen.

As is often, sadly, the case in business
life, the group did not review the project after
it had been completed, and so did not formally
establish if all objectives had been met satisfactorily or if any extra work was required. Nor
did it record, for the benefit of future
projects, the lessons that had been learned both
about the work that had been done and the
methods used to do it. Such a review process
could easily be built into a set of structures
(in effect a final Phase) such that the system
could prompt group members for replies to a
checklist of questions, and build the answers
into a short report.

6.3 Structures for controlling who does what

Few structures for controlling the
communication were used: NOTEPAD's
facility to restrict Note sending between
individuals was not used - it would
have interered with the work by resulting in
more Entries for all Group members to have to
read. Two Observers were allocated (members with
the ability to read Entries but not to send
them) and one of them, I know, found it
interesting to watch the work develop.

The creation of communities by using the
vote facility has been described in the section
dealing with the creation of the Planning Team.
The use of distribution lists and activities to
identify and keep together communities of
interest has been discussed in section 6.1.

7   Conclusions

7.1 Little mailbox group working is being
undertaken at present and few structures have
yet been developed for the purpose.

7.2 Group working over mailbox systems can be
effective and, with suitable structures,
promises very high levels of efficiency.

7.3 Outside of a small community of researchers
there is little appreciation that all kinds of
Group Working can be undertaken satisfactorily
over mailbox systems, and that it's potential
impact on efficiency and effectiveness is vast.

7.4 Identifying the need for specific structures by drawing conclusions based on the use of
inappropriate systems and existing ways of working, is likely to be less productive than
undertaking a functional analysis of the application concerned and specifying structures to
meet the functional requirements identified.

7.5 It is possible that many people concerned
with mailbox systems design do not appreciate
that mailbox structures need to be added onto a
comprehensive set of basic mailbox facilities if
applications such as mailbox Group Working are
to be successfull.

7.6 Mailbox group working would probably
benefit a great deal from a multi-window/multi-
tasking capability, a graphics facility (such as
that enabled by a mouse device), voice
annotation and an object oriented approach to
command input.

7.7 Defining structures for mailbox group
working is, in many ways, akin to building 'best
practice' into a computer system. Of course the
issue of what is 'best practice' is always open
to question, and, in any case, different
individuals and groups may prefer to utilise
different approaches. Hence two important
principles that should be followed when defining
mailbox structures are:
a) Structures should guide and prompt, not
force.
b) The system should allow users to turn structures on or off, to modify them or, ideally, to
define them.

8   Recommendations

8.1 Functional analyses of specific group
working applications (eg Committee Meetings,
Working Parties) should be done and a complete
and interlocking set of mailbox structures
specified and developed to meet the functional
requirements identified.

8.2 More non-laboratory, practical, group
working exeriments should be carried out to
establish how differences in individuals,
management styles, group cultures, group
numbers, task types and working environments
affect the mailbox group working process.

8.3 Mailbox group working experiments should be carried out utilising systems capable of multi-windowing/multi tasking, free format graphics input, voice annotation and the object oriented approach.

8.4 The full range of basic mailbox facilities should be identified, described, and published in a single volume.

8.5 The mailbox structure classification in section 3 should be updated to reflect the knowledge gained in the BLEND group working experiment.

References

(1) WELCH J A, WILSON P A, "Electronic Mail Systems - A Practical Evaluation Guide", NCC Publications, 1981.

(2) WILSON P A, "Introducing the electronic mailbox", NCC Publications, 1983.

(3) HILTZ S R, TUROFF M, "The Network Nation" Addison-Wesley Publishing Company, 1978.

(4) TUROFF M, "Management issues in Human Communication via computer" In 'Emerging Office Systems' edited by Landau R, Bair H J, Siegman H J, Ablex Publishing Corporation, 1982.

(5) KOCHEN M, 'On-line Communities for conflict management', in Human Systems Management, Vol 3 No 2, June 1982.

(6) BITTLESTONE R G A, "The 1982 Operational Research Society Metaconference", Company document issued by Metapraxis Ltd, 26 Barham Road, London SW20 OET, July 1983.

(7) SHARP I P, PERKINS F J, "The impact of effective person-to-person telecoms on established management structures", In the proceedings of the 'Business Telecoms Conference', September 1981.

(8) Turoff M, Hiltz S R, "Exploring the future of Human Communication via computer', Computer Compacts Vol 1 No 2, April 1983.

(9) Wickstrom N, "College scholarships post big benefits with Telemail", Edunet News No 24 in EDUCOM Vol 17 No 2/Summer 1982.

(10) Ferson L M, "ISA stepping up communications over EIES', Edunet News No 25 in EDUCOM Vol 17 No 3/Fall 1982.

(11) WILSON P A, "Applications and structures for mailbox systems", in State of the Art Report 11:8iii 'The Wired Society', Pergamon Infotech Limited, 1983.

(12) HILTZ S R, "Experiments and experiences with computerized conferencing", In 'Emerging Office Systems' edited by Landau R, Bair H J, Siegman H J, Ablex Publishing Corporation, 1982.

(13) SHACKEL B, PULLINGER D J, MAUDE T I, DODD W P, "The BLEND-LINC Project on 'Electronic Journals' after two years", In The Computer Journal Vol 26 No 3, 1983.

(14) WILSON P A, MAUDE T I, MARSHALL C J, HEATON N O, "The active mailbox - your on-line secretary", Proceedings of the IFIP 6.5 working conference on 'Computer-based message services', Nottingham, North-Holland Publications, 1984.

(15) MAUDE T I, HEATON N O, GILBERT G N, WILSON P A, MARSHALL C J, "An experiment in Group Working on Mailbox Systems", Proceedings of the IFIP INTERACT 84 conference, London, North-Holland Publications, 1984.

(16) PULLINGER D J, "BLEND Users Guide", British Library Research & Development Department, Electronic Journal Programme, 1980-1983.

(17) RICKARDS T, "Problem solving through creative analysis", British Institute of Management:Gower Press.

Human-Computer Interaction — INTERACT '84 / B. Shackel (ed.)
Elsevier Science Publishers B.V. (North-Holland)
© IFIP, 1985

959

An Experiment in Group Working on Mailbox Systems

T I Maude, N O Heaton, G N Gilbert, P A Wilson and C J Marshall.

Tim Maude,Centre for Computing & Computer Science,University of Birmingham,B15 2TT,UK.
Nigel Heaton/Chris Marshall,GEC Hirst Research Centre,East Lane,Wembley HA9 7PP,UK.
Nigel Gilbert,University of Surrey,Guildford,GU2 5XH,UK.
Paul Wilson,Office Systems Division,National Computing Centre,Oxford Rd,Manchester,UK.

A computer conference on the subject of electronic mailbox systems was held over the
BLEND system in 1983. After nine months the ideas generated had been developed,
written up and submitted to an international meeting as a paper, entirely by means of
the computer conferencing system. The work that was done to prepare that paper, the
roles and structures adopted and the patterns of communication between the mailbox
members are described. Comparisons between mailbox and face to face group working are
made, and some of the strengths and weaknesses of mailbox group working are identified.
The paper, which has itself been written using the BLEND mailbox system, concludes that
mailbox systems can be used successfully by groups of otherwise unrelated people to
produce work jointly and within a previously defined timescale.

1   Background

This paper describes the experiences and
results of an experiment carried out on the
Birmingham and Loughborough Electronic Network
Development (BLEND). BLEND is an experimental
electronic journal system supported by the
Research and Development Department of the
British Library (a full description of the
system is given in Shackel (1)).   During 1983 a
paper was written using the BLEND system and
submitted to an IFIP conference (Wilson et al.
(2)). This paper was prepared entirely on-line
with no recourse to any other form of
interaction eg. face-to-face meetings,
conventional mail.

The experiences which the authors gained,
plus a complete record of all the transactions
which occurred (3) in the discussion and
preparation phases of the original paper form a
unique record of the development of group
working on remote systems. This paper describes
these changing practices and examines, compares
and contrasts them with 'face-to-face' group
working.

2   Method

2.1 Development Path

This section traces the machinations of the
teleconference from its inception in May to the
production of a completed paper in December.

In May the declared aim of the
teleconference was: "To identify appropriate
mailbox structures to meet those communication
needs of scientists which are currently met by
scientific journals". By December the same
teleconference contained an announcement that:
"'The Active Mailbox - your on-line Secretary'
has now been completed"

This reflected the radical change in ideas
and direction which occurred during the course
of the teleconference. In the early stages of
the teleconference it had a clear aim and strong

direction (as shown by the large number of
messages from the eventual project organiser).

It was this project organiser who initiated
the idea of producing a paper. Whilst previous
teleconferences had followed an almost randomly
determined path (with no real guidance), this one
was developing to fulfil a fixed aim. The
discussion stage of the teleconference involved
several users over an extended period of time.
However this model (which had become a standard
procedure for a BLEND teleconference) was not
suitable for the on-line production of a paper.

In order to produce a paper, individuals
had to be persuaded to write small sections based on
assimilating the ideas of the group and
translating them into concise, meaningful, text.
The manner in which this was done was via the
creation of a series of 'activities' to which
only a small number of people had access. These
activities emerged in two stages. The first
activity was created in July and was concerned
with planning the teleconference; the other six
were created at the start of November and were
concerned with the writing and production of the
final paper (see 2.2.4).

Problems occurred when the planning activity
started covering areas which the discussion
activity should have covered eg. Junk Mail.

Individual contributors waxed and waned
throughout the teleconference, two of the four
final authors were not involved in the discussion
until the creation of the planning activity.
Only 4 of the 12 contributors to the
teleconference became authors of the final paper;
a fifth was to be an author but was forced to
retire; the rest stopped participating for no
apparent reason.

The need to meet deadlines forced the pace,
and casual users appear to have been discouraged
from contributing. By the time the final stages
of the paper had been reached (as signified by
the creation of the writing activities) the
active participants in the teleconference had
been reduced to five. A survey conducted in

October showed that of the twelve contributors
to the teleconference five had input less than 3
messages, two accounted for more than 60% of all
the messages and only four (the eventual
authors) had produced more than 10 messages.

2.2 Structure and Organisation
2.2.1 Roles
Roles were taken on by individuals and
groups within the team. These roles and their
responsibilities were as follows:
Project organiser: Ensure appointment of people
to fill roles; provide suitable structures to
facilitate the work; undertake administrative
tasks; direct the project.
Timescale watcher: Monitor project schedule;
take steps to avoid overruns; inform
participants of schedule status.
Absence co-ordinator: Establish when
participants were scheduled to be absent from
the project; inform participants of same.
Phase directors: Establish objectives for
phase; take steps to achieve objectives; provide
leadership as appropriate.
Writing team: Comment on section writer's
drafts; approve drafts of section.
Section writer: Within the framework of the
writing team to write successive drafts of the
section.
Planning team: Plan the structure of the
project; oversee the whole project.

2.2.2 Generation of ideas
A community using the BLEND system
participated in a computer teleconference on the
subject of 'Mail and Conference systems needs'.
The ideas generated over a period of about three
months were used as the basis for the subsequent
work. The project organiser provided strong
leadership during this period, directing the
discussion towards points that would help
achieve the stated aims of the project.

2.2.3 Setting Objectives
The aims of the project were set by the
project organiser at the beginning. After the
ideas generation stage the planning group split
the project up into five distinct phases, each
having a general aim which was contained in the
title. The specific objectives of the phases
were identified by the phase directors, presented
to group members and agreed by them.

2.2.4 Writing
The high level structure of the paper and
the procedure for writing was discussed by the
authors. The main sections were then allocated
two people each, and these, together with the
project organiser, were the writing team for that
section. The section writer wrote the
successive drafts and submitted them to the
writing team for approval. To keep this work
separate from the other writing teams, separate
activities were used. Once the section was
agreed by the team the completed text was passed
to other group members in a separate activity
reserved for that purpose. The project
organiser was in every writing team and so could

ensure no accidental duplication or omission of
material.

2.2.5 Scheduling
After the ideas generation stage the planning
team instituted five phases. They were:

1. Discussion of planning group report.
2. Raise knowledge level to common level.
3. Determine high level structure of paper.
4. Decide on writing procedure.
5. Write paper.

Each had a set timescale and ran
sequentially. These phases provided milestones
which were used to monitor progress. The
timescale watcher produced regular reports on
what stage the group was at and messages of
urgency when it appeared that there was a
possibility of not reaching the milestones on
time.

3   Analysis of the interaction

3.1 Stages in development
Bales (4) developed a category system for
analysing interaction in face-to-face decision
making groups and showed that the predominant
type of activity shifts as the group progresses
towards a decision (5). If the overall activity
is divided into three equal periods, acts
involving the provision of information to other
members of the group decrease in frequency
steadily from the initial to the final period,
while the rate at which suggestions are given to
the group increases. Reactions, both positive
and negative, to other members' ideas and
suggestions increase in rate from the initial to
the final period. Bales suggested that in the
first period members are primarily collecting
information, in the second they are evaluating
it and in the third, they are pressing for a
consensus with a concomitant increase in support
for the opinions of some members and a rejection
of the opinions of others.

Parallels can be drawn between these
stages and the mailbox group activity. An
opening period of collecting information, a
middle period of evaluating ideas, and a final
period of writing that required establishment of
consensus, can be distinguished. Each of these
periods lasted approximately three months. The
first period centred round a general discussion
of mailbox systems, clarification of
terminology, and reports on existing
international standards. There was also concern
with defining objectives and setting out a
timetable for further work. This period was
characterised by a high number of participants -
11; a high level of information provision in the
messages; and a generally low level of positive
or negative reactions to others' messages.

During the second period the concept of an
'active mailbox' was developed and the structure
for the paper evolved. The four authors
contributed most of the messages, which were
much shorter and more informal. They contained

a much higher rate of positive reactions (and some negative reactions), and a very much higher rate of suggestions than in the first period. Almost all the messages contained some direct reaction to immediately preceding entries, for example:

(142) I think Paul and Nigel are right (sic) about the idea of a summary...

During the third period, the paper was written. The interaction during this period does not closely resemble that predicted by Bales, probably because of the nature of the group's task: writing and editing a number of blocks of text. Most messages consisted of either large blocks of text - the draft sections - or long lists of detailed comments on the drafts.

3.2 Creating and enforcing structures

In contrast with face-to-face groups, in which membership can be assumed from physical co-presence, the only signs of membership in mailbox working are the messages participants contribute. Failure to send regular messages can lead other members to the inference that participation has lapsed. Thus there is pressure on committed members to contribute some message, no matter how trivial, on each occasion of accessing the system to demonstrate their continued presence.

The mechanisms for eliciting contributions from reluctant members appeared to be much weaker than those available to face-to-face groups. Continued participation may have been assisted by the definition of a structure of 'phases', each with a planned duration and objective. After three months, a 'timewatcher' was appointed to attempt to enforce the planned timetable. A week later, a suggestion to appoint a 'phase director' to oversee the work in each phase and to summarise its achievements was also approved. The members filling these roles injected short warning messages into the interaction as the end of each phase drew near, and these seemed to create both a sense of urgency, and a feeling of achievement as each phase was completed.

Once the phases had been established and agreed, the phase directors were able to appeal to the agreed phase objectives to rule certain topics brought up by participants as out of order. For example, the following occurs in the middle of phase 3:

(178) PHASE 4
This next phase will discuss in what order we write the material, can we leave that discussion until then please.

and a message in phase 4 that re-introduces a phase 3 issue begins

(220) Sorry to continue with this hoary chestnut...

Thus the participants had constructed a

structure for their interaction, had evolved a set of roles to superintend that structure, and had then oriented to the structure. Similar construction of normative structures and differentiation of roles is reported in many studies of small groups engaged in face-to-face interaction (6), (7).

3.3 Developing norms of interaction

Norms of interaction developed quickly, and without conscious design by participants. Message titling illustrates the way that interaction norms developed. From the beginning, Wilson always started his messages with a short, underlined title, for example:

(17) The Mailbox Concept

Only one of the 18 messages from Wilson in the sequence (50) to (100) did not begin with this type of heading. Only one other contributor used this style; others either did not use headings at all, or less commonly, did not underline the heading. Gradually, however, the underlined heading convention was more widely adopted and eventually became a group norm. By the end of the interaction, the norm was always followed except for some messages that contained draft blocks of text, and a series of 'quickfire' messages between two participants who were using the system simultaneously to conduct a 'conversation'.

No member specified that underlined headings were to be used; it seems that over the course of time participants began to feel that this was the correct way to write messages. A mailbox 'social skill' had developed. Another norm which evolved in a similar way was that of referring to previous messages by the numbers provided by the system. This was rare at first, but soon became accepted practice. That groups form norms and then conform to them is of course a finding well known to psychologists, from the pioneering studies of Sherif (8).

3.4 Interaction Problems

A lack of consistency at the user interface affected the efficiency of the interaction. For example:

(1) Can we please not refer to activities by their number anymore. This is because the numbers will be different for everyone.

Sometimes the system failed to provide adequate feedback to members:

(205) I'm not sure my response to Paul's questions has got through. There is a problem with the voting process. Are you receiving me Paul?

Lack of system feedback is only one side of the coin:

(127) This is the same question he asked in his first entry and to which I have replied. There

is no acknowldgement that anyone has had any idea. A real viscious circle!

This member's complaint arose from a perceived lack of feedback from other participants. Users felt that the system itself ought to assist in providing such feedback, and should provide facilities to summarise, store, locate and easily retrieve selected previous messages, rather than forcing people to rely on their memories:

(122) ...it is very difficult to keep up with the discussion in this conference because it is largely impractical to store a lot of the generated information anywhere but in your memory.

Thus interaction was hindered by a lack of consistency at the user interface, by lack of appropriate feedback, and by inadequate facilities to summarise and retrieve earlier messages.

3.5 Comments analysis

Comments made by members, inter alia, provide an interesting insight into the advantages, disadvantages and possibilities for mailbox systems. Some comments indicate nicely the differences between mailbox and face-to-face working.

(135) One of the advantages of mailbox systems is that you cannot see your colleagues accusing stares and you don't have to duck any angry swipes aimed at you.

(201) Glad you enjoyed all the excitement and sweat eventually Chris - even if it was only at a later date (this is a peculiarity of mailbox systems isn't it? - you too can experience it all even if it happened weeks ago!).

Humour helped to establish a familiar frame of reference. For example:

(185) Title Suggestion.
- "Active and Passive Mailboxes"
- "Active Mailboxes - your on-line secretary"
- "Mailboxes and Sex" (this should get people to read it even if it is not very accurate!)

Finally, some comments indicated that mailbox working is prone to some of the same difficulties as more conventional group activities:

(193) What a day this has been on the system. Proofreading was a drag. There are many lessons to be learnt; things can't be left until the last day in a mailbox system.

3.6 Message Analysis

It was expected that messages would be related in a complex tree structure, with several topics being pursued in parallel. In fact, it was found that, as in face-to-face conversation, messages tended to relate sequentially to each other until another topic

intruded. Analysis of the content of, and relationship between, messages indicated that they fall into three types (see Figure 1).

Primary: mainstream discussion
             (70% of all messages)
Serial (unbranched) dialogue structure
Messages 30-70 words long (mean 45)

Secondary: unrelated discussion
               (25% of all messages)
Parallel to mainstream (unbranched)
Messages 30-75 words long, mean 50
Terminated by initiator or organiser

Tertiary: 'throw away' remarks
             (5% of all messages)
Single messages
Messages 10-90 words long, mean 40

Figure 1. Types of Message

About 80% of the Secondary discussion (on topics unrelated to the mainstream) was terminated by the organiser in order to steer the discussion back into the Primary mainstream. Secondary discussion proliferated when members were seeking direction or light relief but soon died or was terminated. This suggests that in a mailbox system the interaction can be constrained and focused successfully because digressions can be easily ignored by other group members. The system appears to help members to 'stick to the point' and thereby achieve a predetermined goal.

Further evidence for this finding comes from analysis of message chains, ie. sequences of messages on a common topic stemming from an initiating message, and ending with the start of a new chain on a different topic. Chains may be temporarily interrupted by a message on a different topic, but then resume. The median chain length was 4 messages. Chains consisting of more than 10 messages were rare. About 50 of the chains survived two interrupts, but few continued after four interrupts. Many of the interrupts may have been caused by members with new ideas to communicate. Since the system only allowed messages to be added to the end of the accumulating mail, such new ideas had to interrupt any existing chain. The difficulties this caused may have parallels with those noted by Schutz (9) in face-to-face groups in which ideas are mooted without any note being taken of them.

Because discussion of topics in parallel was rare, and chains survived few interrupts, ideas were quickly buried by further messages on new topics, and retrieval and reassessment involved backtracking up a long serial dialogue structure.

4   Conclusions

4.1 Mailbox group working appears to follow a patern of development similar to that identified by Bales for face-to-face group working ie. a 3 stage process involving the collection of information, evaluating the information collected and, finally, pressing for a consensus.

4.2 There is pressure on individuals participating in mailbox group working to contribute some message no matter how trivial, each time they log into the system, to maintain a presence.

4.3 Mechanisms for eliciting contributions from reluctant members appear to be much weaker than those available in face-to-face groups.

4.4 Mailbox groups appear to establish norms, and then conform to them, in much the same way that face-to-face groups do.

4.5 There is a need to establish facilities for summarising information contained in a series of messages in order to be able to comprehend all the information that is available and to make effective use of it when it is required.

4.6 A mailbox system is particularly suited to ensuring that participants 'stick to the point' and focus on predetermined goals.

4.7 A mailbox system which places all new messages at the end of an accumulating list of messages tends to restrict the pursuance of new ideas to a full and thorough assessment.

4.8 A mailbox system provides a satisfactory medium through which a working group of previously unconnected individuals can develop a common understanding and produce useful outputs to a given time schedule.

5   Recommendations

5.1 That the experiment reported in this paper be replicated to identify whether any of the results were obtained because of the characteristics of individual participants rather than because of characteristics of the mailbox group working environment.

5.2 That a further analysis of the messages sent during the experiment be made to see what other conclusions may be drawn.

5.3 That more sophisticated versions of the structures identified in this paper, and alternative structures, are developed and made available to mailbox group working teams as an assortment of ready packaged tools.

5.4 That appropriate means of summarising and synthesising the information from many messages be researched and developed.

References

(1) Shackel B. "The BLEND System - Programme for the Study of some Electronic Journals" Ergonomics 25(4), 269-284, 1982.

(2) Wilson P A, Maude T I, Marshall C J & Heaton N O "The Active Mailbox - your on-line Secretary, IFIP conference on computer-based message services, Nottingham University, 1984.

(3) BLEND mailbox conference 1983, The BLEND system, Project: News, mailbox conference activities May 1983 - December 1983. (University of Birmingham DEC 2060 disc structure RS).

(4) Bales R F, Interaction Process Analysis (Reading, Mass.: Addison-Wesley, 1950).

(5) Bales R F, "How people interact in conferences", Scientific American, Vol. 192(3), 1955, pp. 31-35.

(6) Whyte W F, Street Corner Society (Chicago: University of Chicago Press, 1943).

(7) Bales R F, "Task roles and social roles in problem solving groups", in E E Maccoby, T M Newcomb and E L Hartley (eds.) Readings in social psychology (3rd ed.) (New York: Holt, 1958), pp 437-447.

(8) Sherif A M, The psychology of social norms (New York: Harper, 1936).

(9) Schutz W C, "What makes groups productive", Human Relations, vol. 8, 1955, pp 429-465.

Acknowledgements

Rosemary Moorhouse, for the preparation and production of the camera-ready copy of this paper.

Human-Computer Interaction — INTERACT '84 / B. Shackel (ed.)
Elsevier Science Publishers B.V. (North-Holland)
© IFIP, 1985

METHODOLOGICAL PROBLEMS OF HUMAN FACTORS RESEARCH
IN LONG-TERMED CBMS FIELD-TRIALS

Michael Pieper

Research Group for Man-Machine-Communication
Institute for Applied Information Technology
Gesellschaft für Mathematik und Datenverarbeitung (GMD)
POB 1240, D-5205 St. Augustin, F.R.G.

With special purpose to reveal changes of habitual communication to be caused by introducing Computer-Based-Message-Systems (CBMS), sociologists of GMD's 'Impact Research Group' evaluated a field-trial with the Computer Conferencing System KOMEX. KOMEX was developed by GMD's former 'Institute for Planning and Decision Support Systems'. The trial involved as pilot-users five subgroups working at different locations on different aspects of a common scientific project, founded by the 'German National Science Foundation (DFG)'. Evaluating changes of habitual communication induced by CBMS-technology required a quasi-experimental research-design. According to technical and non technical preconditions for communication within the field setting, different methodological approaches were used to control different aspects of user-behaviour before and after the introduction of KOMEX. All of these methods centered upon an approach to content-analyse all 356 messages distributed via KOMEX during the field-trial. The paper will discuss the practical problems arising from applying these methodologies with regard to the *validity*, *reliability* and *representativity* of generalized results. Finally, it shall be questionized whether the requirements of the quasi-experimental research design could be met, and in how far the methodological approaches have been appropriate to answer the analytical question outlined above.

1. INTRODUCTION
Computer Conferencing with KOMEX: An Exemplified Approach to Evaluate Behavioural Consequences of Computer-mediated Communication

In December 1981 the first practical test of the computer conferencing system KOMEX was terminated. The test had extended over a period of almost 18 months. A group of social scientists distributed over five different universities in the Federal Republic of Germany participated in the field-trial as pilot users. Within this trial the scientists carried out a long-termed research project supported by the 'German National Science Foundation (DFG)'.

The pilot users expected from KOMEX to support inter-group discussions of research-problems and to enhance thus scientific contacts among the decentralised subgroups of the project network. This expectation agreed with the original idea of 'computer conferencing', i.e. to structure, by means of computer-based communication media, the discussion processes in decentralised, remote problem solving or planning groups in a way to allow a more competent and finally more consensus-oriented discussion of complex problems that cannot be solved by formalisms.

Therefore, the KOMEX field-trial should above all reveal changes of habitual communication among the pilot users to be expected by the introduction of KOMEX. Results of US investigations that are mainly based on experimental small-group research indicate an increased variety of opinions and a restricted ability to reach consensus in computer

conferences (cf. HILTZ, 1978, p.109). The KOMEX field trial allowed to analyse related issues in the problem solving behaviour of the pilot users under more practice-oriented conditions of use. Our main interest was directed towards analysing technology-induced changes in the communicative behaviour of system users.

2. RESEARCH DESIGN
Experimental Research in Field-Settings

Since we intended an analysis of these changes as practice-oriented as possible, we chose a research design differentiating the so-called 'field-experiment' from the overall design of a so-called 'field-study'. In empirical social research the term 'field investigation' is used in contrast to so-called laboratory experiments if the behaviour of individuals is analysed from the conditions of their natural environment, e.g. their working environment. The differentiation of the mentioned research designs originates from FRENCH (cf. FRENCH 1953): In *field-experiments* the researcher modifies specific environmental components in order to explain causally possibly resulting changes in the behavioural patterns of individuals by the (modified) components of their environment. In a *field-study* the researcher selects certain individuals and describes the correlation of specific behavioural characteristics assuming constant field or environmental conditions. Concerning the KOMEX field-experiments this meant
...

i) to manipulate the conditions of communication in the field-setting by introducing KOMEX as an additional device for communication in a specific stage of investigation;

ii) to maintain optimum constancy or control of the other exogenous factors defining the working environment of the pilot users.

Especially in comparing the two fields states before and after introduction of technology, the very control of exogenous factors defining the working environment involved considerable methodological difficulties of data-collection. First, the following comments on the pertinent methods of data-collection shall illustrate these difficulties. In a concluding discussion concerning the 'reliability' and 'validity' of our findings, we shall then focus on certain restrictions of our methodological approach.

3. METHODOLOGY
Mixed-Methods of Data Collection

For achieving our general research goals, we had to analyse communication in the field states before and after the introduction of KOMEX as extensively as possible. We had to assume that communication within the field of investigation was carried out in most different ways or via most different channels of communication:

- verbally, via telephone;
- verbally and visually, on workshops and conferences;
- written, by conventional mail or electronic mail via KOMEX.

These different communication facilities required different methods of data-collection to gain as many indications on the communication pattern within the field-setting as possible.

3.1 Problems of Objective Observation

In verbal or verbal-visual communication we could hardly rely on any written documents when performing communication analyses. Empirical data could only be collected by means of adequate observation methods.

'Participatory Observation' by an own observer, delegated temporarily to workshops and conference meetings of the pilot users, was a quite efficient method to be kept informed about experiences in system application and ongoing working-activities of the pilot users. At least rough control of the most essential exogenous factors of communication in the field of investigation was thus secured. Furthermore, participatory contacts were used for informing the pilot users about paralleling Human Factors Research and planned or already completed system modifications.

Communicative circumstances originating from current work requirements in the decentralised, remote pilot user subgroups were more difficult to control. In these cases we had to resort to self-observation methods, i.e. the corresponding facts had to be recorded by the pilot users themselves. For this

purpose one member of each of the five subgroups was assigned the function of a rapporteur. In intervals of two weeks at the beginning and one month in the later course of the field-trial this rapporteur had to deliver brief reports on changes or invariable tendencies in workload, manpower and actual task accomplishment of his own subgroup. These brief reports had to be set up according to a questionnaire containing specific questions directed towards the recognition goals pursued by the field-trial. Indications concerning telephone communication within the project network could be obtained from short memos, similar to the semi-standardised notepad questionaires usually used in offices for taking a note of a telephone call not reaching the person it was intended for. We agreed with the pilot users to equip each telephone in their working environment with one or two of this notepads. The pilot users were asked to take a note of each telephone conversation conducted within the project network. For allowing reliability checks these notes had to be taken both by the caller and the person called. The data should be laid down as immediately as possible after the conversation and only in exceptional cases these memos should be filled in later on from memory.

We had to assume that mainly the self-observation methods outlined above would involve some additional work for the pilot users. Especially, in periods of heavy workload the recording requirements were, of course, considered to be of low priority. Therefore, the brief reports delivered by the various subgroups were often relatively undifferentiated updates of previous reports. Since even extended report periods could not induce more substantial information to be obtained from these reports, we had to resort to interviewing the pilot users according to predifined interview guidelines in order to control the communicative circumstances in the field of investigation. These interviews were carried out regularly. Also in self-recording of telephone communication systematic biases could not be excluded since some pilot users, especially the project responsibles, frequently worked at home where they did not use the corresponding notepad questionaires.

Nevertheless, we should not overestimate the indicative value of self-observation methods, especially with respect to the intended comparison of the field states before and after the introduction of KOMEX. The explorative value of the indications obtained from these methods, however, was of great importance for deducing descriptive categories in order to content analyse written records and documents.

3.2 Use of Documents and Records

Apart from the observation and interview methods aiming at the control of exogenous communication factors and the description of verbal and verbal-visual communication we had to develop above all a method allowing to content-analyse written communication.

For the sake of comparison both an adequate analysis of folder filed paper and pencil communication and an analysis of all documents distributed electronically via KOMEX should be carried out. According to our general research purposes, first of all we had to develop a basic description scheme allowing an as comprehensive and selective as possible description of communicated messages, documents and records. In a second step, the categories of the description scheme were quantified according to numerical codes, in order to analyse coded data by means of the SPSS ('Statistical Package of the Social Sciences') application programme.

Content of communication, *Kind* of communication and communicative *manner* resp. *Style* of communication were the main dimensions underlying our content-analytical description scheme. To date, Human Factors Research in the CBMS field has scarcely focussed upon empirical indications concerning content, kind and style of interpersonal communication. Maybe these dimensions have been regarded to imply too many peculiarities as to be able to ascribe and observe generalisable attributes. In that sense, 'content of communication' was most difficult to classify in a valid and comparable way, because it was determined by the peculiarities of the tasks of each of the five subgroups. Nevertheless, although beeing rather peculiar, all subgroup-tasks aimed at the common scientific purpose of the whole project network. From that point of view task-oriented content of communication could be classified by the degree of immediacy in which this general objective was met. We distinguished between five degrees of immediacy:

- *instructive* and *private* communication effected by task-oriented communication (e.g. questions concerning system's handling and getting to know each other)
- *avocational* or *secondary* tasks (e.g. announcements of conventionally mailed information)
- *administrative* tasks (e.g. procurement, accountancy etc.)
- tasks *accompanying* accomplishment of general scientific purpose (e.g. inormation about official journeys and conferences)
- tasks *closely related* to the generation of scientific results (e.g. writing research reports)

Analysing the messages distributed via KOMEX we found out that 'kind of communication' could exhaustively be described by five different categories of goal-oriented interpersonal behaviour, deduced from basic theories of organisational problem-solving:

- *task-definition* (i.e. discussing resp. deciding what to do)
- *task-coordination* (i.e arranging what to do in which order)
- *task-documentation* (i.e. informing about the state-of-the-art of of task-accomplishment)
- *task-evaluation* (i.e. discussing the quality of task accomplishment) and...
- *task-support* (e.g. time scheduling for working-groups)
  ...as an additional category attached to the distribution of general-interest information for task accomplishment.

'Style of communication' resp. 'communicative manner' was operationalised according to the 12 categories of the famous procedure for 'Interaction Process Analysis' developed by R.F. Bales (cf. BALES 1950, p. 258).

HILTZ has already succeeded in using this originally observational method for analysing communication processes in some small-group experiments aiming at comparing conventional negotiations and computer conferences (cf. HILTZ/TUROFF 1978, p. 104). For the content-analytical application of the BALES scheme, four socio-emotional categories, which are only observable, had to be excluded. Additionally the other categories had slightly to be modified according to certain peculiarities of the field-setting. Finally we obtained a category scheme divided into 10 variables which differentiated between certain types of information-delivering and information-requesting:

- 'communicating *agreement*' or '*disagreement*' with respect to certain information received from others;
- 'making *suggestions*' to induce others to accomplish certain tasks or 'requesting *suggestions*' whether and how to accomplish tasks;
- 'delivering personal *opinions*' or 'requesting personal *opinions*', i.e. exchanging poorly-founded value judgements on certain facts being typical of the task to be accomplished;
- 'delivering scientific *arguments*' or 'requesting scientific *arguments*', i.e. exchanging well-founded conclusions, deduced from the task to be accomplished;
- 'delivering *hints*' or 'requesting *hints*', i.e. exchanging neutral task-oriented directions.

An important part of 'style of communication' is 'communicative manner'. Certain aspects of 'communicative manner' that immediately refer to the addressee of a message can be derived from the composition style of addresses and salutations. The most important prerequisite for operationalising these aspects is a basic syntactic structure allowing to map on it most different kinds of addresses and salutations. This enabled us to compare the various phrases. From the lack or the existence of specific basic syntax components we could deduce content-analytical conclusions about communicative manner.

Other, rather text-oriented than addressee-oriented attributes of 'communicative manner' could be represented by four further variables describing 'text style'. For this purpose we determined whether a text...

- mainly consisted of incomplete sentences (telegram style);
- contained a remarkably great number of substantivised verbs;
- contained remarkably many abbreviations;
- contained colloquial phrases.

As already mentioned, the content-analytical method outlined above should be applied not only to texts transmitted by KOMEX. For comparative purposes, it should also be extended to documents and records transmitted by conventional mail. Especially the analyses of 'communicative manner' would only reveal significant results if performed within such a comparison. In the course of the field trial, however, it became evident that paper and pencil communication was mainly carried out by the subgroups' senior consultants and not by assistant researchers. However, since mostly working at home, senior consultants hardly participated in the KOMEX field trial. Therefore, paper and pencil communication was hardly accessible for content-analytical purposes.

3.3 Data Collection by Interviewing

Though being confronted with the mentioned prpoblems of data collection in applying content-analytical and observational methods, we did not intend to give up the goal of analysing technology-induced changes in the communication behaviour of the pilot users and to favour instead a mere description of the communication processes performed via KOMEX. For this reason we used additional interview methods in order to consider the exogenous causes of change in habitual communication adequately. Based on certain data on system utilisation collected by a so called MONITOR program running in parallel when using KOMEX, we asked questions concerning usability problems, task-oriented frequency of use and planned project activities being relevant to communication.

At the end of the field trial we additionally interviewed those pilot users who used KOMEX most intensively in order to get a feeling about the reliability and validity of the conclusions derived from content-analysis. These conclusions conmcerning possible or actual changes of habitual communication should be confronted with the experiences of pilot users itself. For organisational reasons these interviews had partly to be carried out as individual, partly as group interviews. Partly we had even to rely on telephone interviews. In all these cases, however, we followed the principle of a guideline-oriented, narrative interview technique. Beginning with more general questions we asked more and more specific questions thus directing the answers of the pilot users towards our recognition interests. The conversation was recorded on tape. Written records were sent to the pilot users who authorised them after making small corrections and additional remarks.

In the past relatively unstandardised open interview methods were above all used in so called action-research approaches, e.g. approaces of participative system design. Originally, these methods have been developed as reaction to the critical comments on data collection methods which, like the quantifiable content-analysis, pretend to collect objective data in the restricted sense of natural sciences. In reality, however, these methods are based on relatively uncontrollable interpretations of reality by the scientists. This even applies to the selection of the variables to be investigated. In case of the KOMEX field-trial, this methodological criticism was considered by trying to counterbalance conclusions of Human Factors Scientists investigating technology utilisation with the experiences of pilot-users applying this technology by means of concluding interviews.

4. RESULTS
Analytical Problems of Validity, Reliability and Representativity

Compared with conventional communication hardly any changes in volume and structure of communication occured when using KOMEX within the field-setting. However, we obtained some quite interesting results from content-analysing all 356 messages, documents and records which had been generated and distributed via KOMEX.

For example, the research categories 'content', 'kind' and 'style of communication' helped to find indications concerning the extent of KOMEX use for discussing scientific problems within the project network. The more immediate communication focusses upon 'tasks closely related to the generation of scientific results', so the underlying assumption, the more complex and contradictory are the problems to be solved for task accomplishment.

Indeed, a considerable amount of KOMEX communication referred to problems arising from scientific task accomplishment of the pilot-users. These problems, however, were only articulated by simple indications and statements, they were never discussed argumentatively in the form of interpersonal negotiations. Referring to these findings, the example of two subgroups working most closely together within the project network was particularly distinctive. In that case communication arising from 'scientific task-accomplishment' outweighed KOMEX communication directed towards 'administrative' and 'secondary' tasks by 54%. However, BALES' Interaction Process Analysis proved that only about 2% of that communication focussed upon scientific problem-solving by expressing 'agreement', 'disagreement', 'suggestions' or 'opinions' referring to scientific arguments of others.

Interviewing the pilot users revealed that mainly difficulties of conversational context reconstruction, i.e. difficulties in reconstructing argumentative references among different points of view, prevented the pilot users from using the KOMEX system for corresponding problem-solving discussions. The disclosure of argumentative agreements and disagreements was much easier in conventional face-to-face communication.

The significance of these findings can generally be determined by two criteria of goodness which have to be met by the data and hence the data collection methods: 'validity' and 'reliability'. Most generally 'validity' refers to the degree of compatibility of a measure with the empirical characteristics it is supposed to measure. 'Reliability' means independence of a result from the measuring process, i.e. reproducibility of the result under identical measuring conditions.

Like any content-analytical approach the method for analysing the documents and records distributed via KOMEX involves problems of validity because of the interpretive degrees of freedom in assigning content-analytical attributes. If the encoder cannot gain insight into the contextual and situational origins of a message, his interpretation of its connotative significance has to rely on more or less subjective judgements. Even a description of assignable attributes as exclusive and exhaustive as possible is still insufficient to minimize speculative liberties. At least in cases in which connotative significance is particularly difficult to deduce, conmtent-analytical attribute assignment by the text author himself would be the one and only solution. However, for organisational reasons this is often impossible. In case of the KOMEX field trial we followed the already mentioned double-strategy to solve this methodological problem.

- The content-analytical approach of task-oriented attribute assignment has largely been deduced from observational control of exogenous communicative circumstances in the field-setting.
- Assumptions deduced from corresponding attribute assignments have finally been validated by the pilot users themselves in applying so called narrative interview techniques.

The claim of 'reliability' is finally also a rather idealistic criterion for the significance of findings from empirical social research. Just in view of continuously changing environmental circumstances in practice-oriented field trials, it is impossible to secure reproducibility of results under identical measuring conditions. Indeed, corresponding reliability measures are mostly founded on the statistical correlation of splitted data-sets from *one and the same* sample. In our context, reliability should rather be discussed by focussing upon the comparability of results obtained from similar observations. This will raise the question to what extent the findings are indeed comparable or in how far differences belonging to the fact that the research designs are only similar but not identical have to be taken into consideration.

Another criterion for the significance of findings from empirical Human Factors Research is their 'representativity'. In empirical sociology, measures of representativity are normally obtained from inference-statistical procedures of sample comparison, indicating the probability with which the sample findings represent a universe, which cannot be surveyed completely for reasons of research-economy. Since such a procedure would require an accordingly large sample and since only a small part of the pilot users used KOMEX intensively, a representativity check by inference statistical methods would have been completely inadmissible. Moreover, the prototypical system-design of KOMEX proved to be rather instable and required some changes during the field-trial. From that problems of system acceptance arised, which inevitably biased the representativity of our results.

Therefore, the KOMEX field trial is to be understood as a case study whose findings do not claim any representativity. However, against the background of sufficiently validated methods of data-collection the findings that are comparable with results of similar investigations can by no means be regarded as being accidental.

5. CONCLUSION
System Acceptance as a Crucial Precondition for Ambitious Impact Research

The initial expectation to improve the problem-solving ability of decentralised, remote planning or project groups by means of computer conferencing systems can only be satisfied if adequate tools for a computer-supported reconstruction of problem-oriented reasoning are available. Against the background of similar experiences gained by the use of comparable computer conferencing systems this opinion has in the meantime obviously been confirmed by important representatives of the scientific community (cf. JOHANSEN et al. 1979, p. 131; HILTZ 1981, p. 750).

Nevertheless, the representativity of such a conclusion about the current *gap between intention and reality of Computer Conferencing* (cf. PIEPER 1982) can be confirmed by an adaequte evaluation methodology only if system acceptance is to be guaranteed. However, Human Factors Research engaged in improving usability and thus enhancing acceptance of CBMS technology ist often impaired by the so called 'volunteer user bias': "A limited number of field trials with volunteer users but without control groups may be useful for system evolution guidelines; but they generate spurious reports of effectiveness and satisfaction. Among the reasons this is so are: 1) volunteers have a vested interest in the system in which they have invested their time, and 2) volunteers are likely to have been predisposed towards use of the system (in the process of becoming volunteers)"(HILTZ 1982, p.89).

The KOMEX field-trial revealed a special lack of system usability for group decision-making. In that sense, the pilot users involved formed a real control group which generated unpleasant but nevertheless remarkable results. It is *that* kind of Human Factors Research which challenges improvements in CBMS design and which is "likely to develop a science rather than an art form in this new field of endeavor" (HILTZ 1982, p.89).

REFERENCESS

BALES, R. F. (1950):'Interaction Process Analysis: A method for the Study of Small Groups', Reading (Mass.)

FRENCH, J. R. P. (1953):'Experiments in Field-Settings', in: FESTINGER/KATZ (eds.): Research Methods in the Behavioral Sciences, New York

HILTZ, S. R. and M. TUROFF (1978):'The Network Nation. Human Communication via Computers', Reading (Mass.)

HILTZ, S. R.(1981):'The Evolution of User Behavior in a Computerized Conferencing System', in: Communications (ACM), Vol.24, No.11

HILTZ, S.R.(1982):'Computer Support for Group versus Individual Decisions', in: IEEE Trans. on Com., No.1 (Jan.)

PIEPER, M. (1982):'Computer Conferencing and Human Interaction', in: M. B. WILLIAMS (ed.): Pathways to the Information Society, Amsterdam-New York-Oxford (pp. 653-657)

Human-Computer Interaction — INTERACT '84 / B. Shackel (ed.)
Elsevier Science Publishers B.V. (North-Holland)
© IFIP, 1985

DESIGN CRITERIA FOR THE ELECTRONIC JOURNAL

John W. Senders

University of Toronto & University of Maine-Orono

An electronic journal (EJ) must meet the needs and satisfy the expectations of the readers if it is to succeed. Some reasonable criteria for an EJ are derived from consideration of the qualities of a paper journal (PJ). None of the requirements can be shown to be impossible to achieve or to be very much beyond today's state of the art.

I. INTRODUCTION

Although a variety of techniques has been used from the earliest days of telegraph to transmit alphanumeric information, the application to the handling of large volumes of scientific and tech nical communication has arisen as a possibility only in relatively recent times. Certainly in the early days it would have been possible to transmit complete manuscripts from one scientist to another in the form of Morse Code. Few readers would have had the skill, or if the skill, the patience to make the translation. Similarly, the teletype permits large documents to be sent from one place to another swiftly but usually only under time pressure which makes it reasonable to absorb the cost. For most ordinary scientific and technical communication-communication between a producing scientist and a using scientist- the costs in time and money associated with such transmission have made it unfeasible.

When in the early 1960's it became possible to imagine the storage of large volumes of text in digital form, it also became possible to conceive of a digital computer and a system of data handling lines as a complete substitution for the more traditional way of disseminating scientific and technical information. Early experiments done under the direction of J.C.R.Licklider at Bolt,Beranek and Newman in 1961 and 1962 showed that a number of the functions which deal with whole texts could be performed entirely on a computer without the necessity of reduction to hard copy.(I) Unfortunately the available memory was relatively small and the amount of text that could be stored was limited to a few demonstration manuscripts.

The rapid increase in size and speed and decrease in cost of memories and large storage systems, and the proliferation of computers in the scientific and technical community suggest a publication system can now be set up which is entirely in digital form and is never reduced to hard copy except at the will or whim of the reader.

A paper journal (PJ) has three basic components: an editorial processing center; a search and retrieval system; and a dissemination system. The last is usually a printer-binder which delivers to a post-office. The first two of these parts have already been extensively computerized. The third constitutes what has been called the Electric Journal (EJ). A successful EJ must have acceptance by its readers for it to be successful; acceptance, in turn, requires that the EJ be not less good than the PJ it may replace. The design criteria of a good EJ must use the PJ as a point of departure.

2. CHARACTERISTICS OF THE PJ

An issue of a PJ (Human Factors for example) is about 175 by 250 mm and 10 mm thick. This is a comfortable size which can be held in one hand and,since it weighs about 300 grams, can be so held for a long time without great discomfort.

The print is black on white and provides a high level of contrast. This facilitates reading in less than optimal lighting and minimizes the fatigue induced by strain.

The local memory is excellent. No power is required either to maintain the material nor, much of the time, to read it.

There are two pages facing in a PJ. These make it easier to compare tables and graphs (although this feature is not often taken advantage of). The fact that two pages are simultaneously available makes it easy (at least half the time) to refer back without having to change anything except the line of regard.

The local store pf an issue of a PJ is impressively large. Human Factors typically contains in an issue 100 pages of 45 lines of 70 characters each. This is a total per issue of 315,000 characters. If there are 26 alphabetic symbols, in two sizes and two fonts,we have 104 different characters. We must add the 10 numeric symbols, and a generous allowance for mathematical and special symbols and punctuation marks and obtain slightly less than 256 different characters or

8 bits per character. The memory equivalent of an issue is therefore about 315,000 8 bit words.

A PJ has a table of contents which is usually on the face of the cover and is therefore easily located and referred to. The table also facilitates browsing and serendipitous discovery.

An issue of Human Factors is rugged. It can be dropped from any height; it can serve as a rest for a hot coffee pot and keep the table from being scorched. It can have coffee spilled on it with no penalty except for the telltale stain.

One can bend down the corner of a page or many pages and find them easily again with the finger tips.

One cannot change the scale of a graph nor extract a table corresponding to the points on a plot of data. Nor can one direct the PJ to plot the data in a table, or to produce a composite plot of two or more tables.

One cannot direct the issue to search itself for instances of a word or phrase.

The PJ is inert. What is done is done by the reader on scratch pads of one sort or another. Yet this inert device is a remarkably handy way of doing things and has survived with few changes for some hundreds of years.

3. CHARACTERISTICS OF THE EJ

An EJ must be able to do all or nearly all that a PJ can do, and to add some functions that the PJ cannot do.

Within the last 6 months as of this writing new (if somewhat expensive) personal computers which have modems built in have become available in a very small package. The GRID, weighing at **4.5** kgs. , and the GAVILAN at 4.0 kgs., are examples of such devices. They occupy about .1 sq.meter of surface and are about 10 cm. thick. Both have modems and communication software. The GRID with 256KB RAM will store 125 single space pages of text.

The page size displayed is smaller than that of a PJ. The GRID shows 25 lines of 80 caracters. The GAVILAN screen is wider and shorter. This latter screen is probably too small to serve as a substitute for a conventional journal page.

The weights are too large for convenient use anywhere except on a supporting surface. Thus much of the convenient portability of the PJ is absent. The GRID can store up to three complete issues of Human Factors (with the 512KRAM as an option. It also has 384KB non-volatile memory which would be madatory for use as a local EJ. Whether this is available for permanent storage of text material is not clear from the descriptions.

A table of contents is easy enough to provide in an EJ; and to arrange to call it up with a single button push is trivial.

The ruggedness of the PJ is not matchable in a presently available terminal unless some of the military requirements have engendered such a one in recent times. One can imagine that it would be possible to make a well encapsulated package which would withstand the casual use given to a copy of a PJ. The cost would probably be very large and prohibitive for users in the scientific community except for those on very rich grants indeed. In no case is it likely that even a well engineered EJ could be used to stand a hot coffee pot on. This is not a serious drawback whereas the ability to withstand having hot coffee spilled on it would be very important.

Keeping one's place in an EJ might be rather difficult to emulate. The bending down of a page is more than just a marking. It presents spatial information which enables the reader to recall what was there which was to be remembered.

The facing pages on the PJ are the result of the fact that all the pages simultaneously exist in human legible form and can be bound in that format. The EJ has no convenient way to replicate the appearance of the PJ except by use of a very wide screen. In this case the resolution requirements become a problem. The smallest detail in an issue of Human Factors is the fullstop at about .2 mm diameter. The page contains, therefore the equivalent of about 875×1250 pixels or approximately 10^6 in all. Such screens are not presently available in the convenient size of a PJ although there is no fundamental obstacle to their construction.

We are left with the impression that weight and fragility are the major difficulties to be overcome by the designers of local EJ formats. Cost must be reduced, but if the last 20 years of experience in the computer industry continues, one has but to wait a while for all of the obstacles to vanish.

An EJ can do much that the PJ cannot do. If some of these capabilities are offerred, readers may find it convenient to tolerate many of the present shortcomings of the hypothetical EJ-

Software, either local or central or preferably both, must be provided to change the scales on data plots; to present plots and graphs in various forms of data presented in the form of tables in the published "paper" ; to combine the data from one paper with those from another and present the result in a new plot. In short the EJ should be able to do everything that was demonstrated in 1962 and much more as well.

A reader should be able to store a graet quantity of text for portable use and to avoid tying up communication lines, or be able to work on line with the power of a central computer to perform statistical analyses of published data and to fit other models or whatever comes to the mind of the reader.

The local formats must be capable of high speed acquisition of text from the central store in order to avoid interference with other communications needs.

They must also be capable of performing various word-processing functions and of transmitting textual material back to the central computer. Thus the reader will be able to be an author as well and to submit material directly to the editorial center as a new "paper" or as a comment on an old one.

4. CONCLUSIONS

The natural evolution of computers and computer-associated devices will bring about the necessary development of suitable devices for the local format of an acceptable, perhaps a highly desirable, EJ. It is merely a matter of time.

The EJ must be able to give what the PJ gives, or very nearly so. In compensation for what is lost, it must offer possibilities which are inconceivable with a PJ.(unless someone is able to "print" on paper a computer, its memory and in human readable form; and endow it with variable type.)

Most presently available personal computers and terminal devices are patently unsuitable for use as the local format of an EJ. It would be unfortunate if the advent of the EJ were further delayed by reader rejection of the experimental systems of today, and a consequent slowing of the effort to achieve the necessary formats to obtain reader acceptance.

5. REFERENCES

1. Library of the 21st. Century Project; under the auspices of the Council for Library Resources ; Bolt,Beranek & Newman, Cambridge, MA 1962

Note: The information about the GRID and the GAVILAN computers was obtained from advertisements, March, 1984 Things may have changed since then!

AUTHOR INDEX

AUTHOR INDEX

CONTENTS INDEX

CONTENTS INDEX